Frommer's

Hawaii 2004

POSTCARDS FROM

Helicopter tours are a memorable way to survey the lush landscapes of Kauai, as you swoop over towering waterfalls, emerald valleys, and the majestic cliffs of the rugged and inaccessible Na Pali Coast. See chapter 9. © Douglas Peebles Photography.

Waikiki boasts Hawaii's best nightlife, with beachfront bars, traditional Hawaiian music, hula, jazz, blues, dance clubs, and a thriving performing arts scene. See chapter 4.
© Cliff Hollenbeck Photography.

"The
Lonely
Planet"

The scenic Pali Trail starts just 6 miles from downtown Honolulu. See chapter 4. © Len Kaufman Photography.

Horseback riding at Kualoa Ranch on Oahu's windward side. See chapter 4.
© Catherine Karnow Photography.

A visit to the USS Arizona Memorial at Pearl Harbor is one of Hawaii's most moving experiences. See chapter 4. © Douglas Peebles Photography.

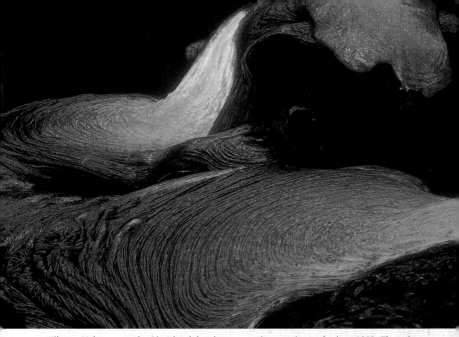

Kilauea Volcano, on the Big Island, has been erupting continuously since 1983. Though sometimes the volcano is quiet and visibility is limited to giant plumes of steam, you may get lucky and find yourself treated to the unforgettable sight of fiery lava pouring into the sea. One of the best ways to guarantee yourself a good view is to take a helicopter tour (below). See chapter 5. Photo above: © G. Brad Lewis / Photo Resource Hawaii; photo below: © Jay Freis / The Image Bank.

A totem in Haleiwa, Oahu's Surf City. See chapter 4. © Len Kaufman Photography.

Hawaii is a great place for a wedding. More than 20,000 marriages are performed in the islands annually, many in picturesque locations like this simple church on Kauai. See chapter 2 for details on requirements and local wedding planners. © Catherine Karnow Photography.

Oahu's North Shore is the place to see daredevil surfers in action. Some of the world's largest waves rise up between November and January. See chapter 4. © *Inner Light / The Image Bank.*

From December through April, humpback whales come to winter in the warm waters of the Pacific. Maui is a particularly great place to spot these gentle giants. See chapter 6. © *Michael S. Nolan / Douglas Peebles Photography.*

Though the crowded beach-party scene on the sands of Waikiki originally put Oahu on the tourist map, the island boasts many gorgeous, secluded beaches less than two hours from the high-rises of Waikiki. See chapter 4. © Douglas Peebles Photography.

Frommer's

Hawaii

2004

by Jeanette Foster

Here's what the critics say about Frommer's:

"Amazingly easy to use. Very portable, very complete."

—Booklist

"Detailed, accurate, and easy-to-read information for all price ranges."
—Glamour Magazine

"Hotel information is close to encyclopedic."

—Des Moines Sunday Register

"Frommer's Guides have a way of giving you a real feel for a place."
—Knight Ridder Newspapers

WILEY

Wiley Publishing, Inc.

About the Author

A resident of the Big Island, **Jeanette Foster** has skied the slopes of Mauna Kea—during a Fourth of July ski meet, no less—and gone scuba diving with manta rays off the Kona Coast. A prolific writer widely published in travel, sports, and adventure magazines, she's also a contributing editor to *Hawaii* magazine and the editor of *Zagat's Survey to Hawaii's Top Restaurants*. In addition to this guide, Jeanette is the author of *Frommer's Maui, Frommer's Hawaii from $80 a Day,* and *Frommer's Honolulu, Waikiki & Oahu.*

Published by:

Wiley Publishing, Inc.

111 River St.
Hoboken, NJ 07030

ISBN 0-7645-3707-5
ISSN 1090-3180

Editor: Christine Ryan
Production Editor: M. Faunette Johnston
Cartographer: Roberta Stockwell
Photo Editor: Richard Fox
Production by Wiley Indianapolis Composition Services

For information on our other products and services or to obtain technical support, please contact our Customer Care Department within the U.S. at 800-762-2974, outside the U.S. at 317-572-3993 or fax 317-572-4002.

Wiley also publishes its books in a variety of electronic formats. Some content that appears in print may not be available in electronic formats.

Manufactured in the United States of America

5 4 3 2 1

Frommer's

Hawaii

2004

by Jeanette Foster

Here's what the critics say about Frommer's:

"Amazingly easy to use. Very portable, very complete."

—*Booklist*

"Detailed, accurate, and easy-to-read information for all price ranges."
—*Glamour Magazine*

"Hotel information is close to encyclopedic."

—*Des Moines Sunday Register*

"Frommer's Guides have a way of giving you a real feel for a place."
—*Knight Ridder Newspapers*

WILEY

Wiley Publishing, Inc.

About the Author

A resident of the Big Island, **Jeanette Foster** has skied the slopes of Mauna Kea—during a Fourth of July ski meet, no less—and gone scuba diving with manta rays off the Kona Coast. A prolific writer widely published in travel, sports, and adventure magazines, she's also a contributing editor to *Hawaii* magazine and the editor of *Zagat's Survey to Hawaii's Top Restaurants*. In addition to this guide, Jeanette is the author of *Frommer's Maui, Frommer's Hawaii from $80 a Day,* and *Frommer's Honolulu, Waikiki & Oahu.*

Published by:

Wiley Publishing, Inc.

111 River St.
Hoboken, NJ 07030

ISBN 0-7645-3707-5
ISSN 1090-3180

Editor: Christine Ryan
Production Editor: M. Faunette Johnston
Cartographer: Roberta Stockwell
Photo Editor: Richard Fox
Production by Wiley Indianapolis Composition Services

For information on our other products and services or to obtain technical support, please contact our Customer Care Department within the U.S. at 800-762-2974, outside the U.S. at 317-572-3993 or fax 317-572-4002.

Wiley also publishes its books in a variety of electronic formats. Some content that appears in print may not be available in electronic formats.

Manufactured in the United States of America

5 4 3 2 1

Contents

9 Kauai, the Garden Isle   529

Appendix: Hawaii in Depth   614

Index   634

List of Maps

An Invitation to the Reader

In researching this book, we discovered many wonderful places—hotels, restaurants, shops, and more. We're sure you'll find others. Please tell us about them, so we can share the information with your fellow travelers in upcoming editions. If you were disappointed with a recommendation, we'd love to know that, too. Please write to:

Frommer's Hawaii 2004
Wiley Publishing, Inc. • 111 River St. • Hoboken, NJ 07030

An Additional Note

Please be advised that travel information is subject to change at any time—and this is especially true of prices. We therefore suggest that you write or call ahead for confirmation when making your travel plans. The authors, editors, and publisher cannot be held responsible for the experiences of readers while traveling. Your safety is important to us, however, so we encourage you to stay alert and be aware of your surroundings. Keep a close eye on cameras, purses, and wallets, all favorite targets of thieves and pickpockets.

Other Great Guides for Your Trip:

Frommer's Hawaii from $80 a Day
Frommer's Maui
Frommer's Honolulu, Waikiki & Oahu
Frommer's Portable Big Island
Frommer's Portable Maui
The Unofficial Guide to Hawaii
Hawaii For Dummies

Frommer's Star Ratings, Icons & Abbreviations

Every hotel, restaurant, and attraction listing in this guide has been ranked for quality, value, service, amenities, and special features using a **star-rating system.** In country, state, and regional guides, we also rate towns and regions to help you narrow down your choices and budget your time accordingly. Hotels and restaurants are rated on a scale of zero (recommended) to three stars (exceptional). Attractions, shopping, nightlife, towns, and regions are rated according to the following scale: zero stars (recommended), one star (highly recommended), two stars (very highly recommended), and three stars (must-see).

In addition to the star-rating system, we also use **seven feature icons** that point you to the great deals, in-the-know advice, and unique experiences that separate travelers from tourists. Throughout the book, look for:

Finds	Special finds—those places only insiders know about
Fun Fact	Fun facts—details that make travelers more informed and their trips more fun
Kids	Best bets for kids, and advice for the whole family
Moments	Special moments—those experiences that memories are made of
Overrated	Places or experiences not worth your time or money
Tips	Insider tips—great ways to save time and money
Value	Great values—where to get the best deals

The following **abbreviations** are used for credit cards:

AE	American Express	DISC	Discover	V	Visa
DC	Diners Club	MC	MasterCard		

Frommers.com

Now that you have the guidebook to a great trip, visit our website at **www.frommers.com** for travel information on more than 3,000 destinations. With features updated regularly, we give you instant access to the most current trip-planning information available. At Frommers.com, you'll also find the best prices on airfares, accommodations, and car rentals—and you can even book travel online through our travel booking partners. At Frommers.com, you'll also find the following:

- Online updates to our most popular guidebooks
- Vacation sweepstakes and contest giveaways
- Newsletter highlighting the hottest travel trends
- Online travel message boards with featured travel discussions

What's New in Hawaii

The minute you step off the plane, the incredible dramatic beauty of Hawaii—the deep sapphire ocean, the vivid blue sky, the verdant green valley—would be enough for anyone to make the journey to these floating isles of paradise. But the 50th state is constantly improving on what Mother Nature (or as we say in Hawaii, Pele, the volcano goddess) originally built.

Hawaii is a lot easier to get to these days with more direct flights from the mainland than ever. Lots of new attractions have blossomed in the past year—everything from improved old favorites to brand new excursions under the sea, over the sea and even on dry land. New eateries have opened, new nightlife jaunts now beckon, and even a new hotel is coming to the Big Island in 2004.

If you have ever dreamed of coming to Hawaii, now is the time.

PLANNING YOUR TRIP Getting to Hawaii has never been easier—**Aloha Airlines** (© **800/367-5250** or 808/484-1111; www.alohaairlines. com) now offers direct service from Honolulu to Oakland and Burbank, California, Vancouver, Canada and Las Vegas, Nevada; plus direct flights from Oakland to Kona, Lihue and Maui.

A new website to help you plan your vacation to the islands is **www. hawaii.com**. The step-by-step planner includes information about travel deals, lodging, transportation, booking activities, tours, attractions, maps, and exchange rates. Also included are local events, cultural activities and news, plus the latest on the weather, surf conditions and Hawaii's history.

OAHU Attractions The **Waikiki Aquarium** (p. 192) has spent $500,000 and nine months to create the South Pacific Marine Life Communities gallery, which features more than 145 species from the south and western Pacific. The 5,000-gallon saltwater aquarium (15 ft. long and 6 ft. high) has such wonderful attractions as a 25-year old, 167-pound clam, an archerfish that spits water to catch bugs, a yard-wide sea anemone, and jellyfish so clear you can see what they've eaten for lunch.

Another marine attraction is the new $13 million **Marine Education Center,** in **Hanauma Bay** (p. 160), which recently opened with informational exhibits and a 7-minute video orienting visitors to this Marine Life Sanctuary. The 10,000-square-foot center includes a training room, gift shop, public restrooms, and a snack bar. Hanauma Bay is Oahu's most popular snorkeling spot, consisting of a volcanic crater with a broken sea wall; its small, curved, 2,000-foot gold-sand beach is packed elbow-to-elbow with people year-round. The bay's shallow shoreline water and abundant marine life are the main attractions, but this good-looking beach is also popular for sunbathing and people-watching.

If you'd rather stay on dry land, you can visit the **Hawaii State Art Museum** (p. 194), which just opened in downtown Honolulu, in the original

Royal Hawaiian Hotel built in 1872 during the reign of King Kamehameha V (250 South Hotel St, at Richards St; ℂ 808/586-0900). All of the 360 works currently displayed were created by artists who live in Hawaii. The pieces were all purchased by the state thanks to a 1967 law mandating that 1% of the cost of state buildings be used to acquire works of art. Nearly 4 decades later, the state has amassed some 5,000 pieces. The current exhibit depicts Hawaii and its history, culture, and ideals through a variety of mediums.

BIG ISLAND Accommodations As we went to press, Starwood Hotels and Resorts announced a $40 million renovation of the old Kona Surf Hotel in Keauhou, to be renamed the Sheraton Keauhou Bay Resort, opening in 2004. The vision for the new resort, which closed in 1999, is to "bring back the Hawaii of yesteryear" by showcasing the historical characteristics of the area. Also in the plans are a multi-level fantasy pool, a network of bike/jogging paths throughout the resort area, the only rock-climbing wall on the Big Island, and unique historical activities such as traditional Hawaiian sports and classes in Hawaiian martial arts.

Activities Torpedo Tours (ℂ 808-938-0405;www.torpedotours.com) offers snorkelers and divers an easier, faster way to explore Kona's underwater world. The battery-operated, lightweight, maneuverable submersible propels the diver or snorkeler through the water at 2 knots (the pace of a freestyle sprint) and can be stopped abruptly to hover over anything interesting you may spot in the water. Operating out of Honokohau Harbor, on a 32-foot custom dive boat, the tours start at $59 for snorkel tours and $129 for scuba diving tours.

All Terrain Vehicle Outfitters (ℂ 888/ATV-7288 or 808/889-6000; www.outfittershawaii.com) features "native Hawaiian" guides leading a variety of tours off the beaten path and into remote rainforests and along secluded beaches on motorized off-road vehicles. The tours on ATVs range from a historic tour of Kohala's sea cliffs and secluded beaches, a 90-minute experience costing $90; to a 15-mile adventure into Hawaii's tropical rainforests, stopping at waterfalls ($159 for 2½ hr.); to an all-day 30-mile adventure, which includes lunch ($250 for 5½ hr.). Children under 16 or those who would prefer to be chauffeured can ride along in a special "scenery machine."

You can also tour the Big Island by yourself, with a local resident as your guide. Steve Slater, long-time Big Island resident, has produced the **Big Island Audio Tour** (e-mail: kipuka@ hilo.net or call ℂ 808/934-7817 to order). His CD has 36 tracks of information essential for any newcomer to the Big Island including driving laws; safety considerations; Hawaiian word pronunciation; and excellent directions to well-known and not so well-known sites like off-the-beaten-path beaches, where to collect fruit, and various side trips. Several tracks talk about the geography, geology, culture, and history of the Big Island, and other tracks identify Hawaiian flora and fauna. The CD comes with a full color map, with keyed numbers corresponding to the tracks, and 36 color photos of the island you can view on a computer.

MAUI Activities If the local cuisine is a little too attractive and the local brew a bit too tempting, you now can work off any extra pounds at the Hyatt Regency Maui Resort's "**Beach Boot Camp**" (ℂ 808/661-1234). Every Wednesday, Friday, and Saturday at 8 am you can participate in a high-impact workout on the beach, with stretching and cardio exercises (sprints in the sand, lunges through the water and abdominal crunches along a hill). Classes are $5 for hotel guests and $7 for non-hotel guests.

Kaanapali's **Whalers Village Museum** (p. 442) has refurbished its theater. Free movies are shown daily from 9:30am to 10pm in the newly renovated theater (padded chairs, new surround-sound and a 50-inch screen). Popular films shown recently included: *Onboard the Morgan* (depicting the life of 19th century whalers), *Red Turtle Rising* (Hawaiian folklore on turtles), and *Hawaiian Humpback: Pacific Voyager* (which follows the whales from Alaska to Hawaii).

If you are wondering what to do with the kids, take them to **Maui Menehune Golf,** 32-A Lono Ave., Kahului (© **808/877-5599**), which recently opened a miniature golf course in the heart of central Maui, across the street from Sears and the Kaahumanu Shopping Center. It's open Monday to Friday from 3 to 7pm and Saturday to Sunday from 10am to 11pm; admission ranges from $5 to $7 for clubs and balls and a flat $3 rate on Wednesday and Friday.

After Dark   Go to a wedding next time you are on Maui, no gift necessary. The Hyatt Regency Maui is the site of the off-Broadway play, *Tony n' Tina's Wedding.* The 2-hour musical comedy allows the audience to attend the wedding and then follow the cast to the reception and dinner (you really get to eat). After dinner there's the traditional toast and dancing. All the while you are watching a play that involves two Italian families coming together for their children's (Tony and Tina) wedding, along with the pregnant maid of honor, a drunken priest and a host of other characters. Tickets are $75; call © **808/667-4727** for more information.

MOLOKAI   Activities   The **Kaluakoi Golf Course** (p. 494), which closed along with the Kalaukoi Hotel in 2000, has now reopened. The first 9 holes went online with $150,000 in repairs to the irrigation system and work on the fairways, tees and greens. The back 9 holes, scheduled for completion in 2004, will cost $6 million more for development of a new water supply.

KAUAI   Activities   This is every parent's dream: a place to take kids on rainy days (hey, it's so much fun, the kids will beg to come back even on sunny days). The **Kauai Children's Discovery Museum** (p. 582), located in Kapaa (© **808/823-8222;** www.kcdm.org), arose out of a grass-roots community effort to have a fun place where kids could learn about science, culture, arts, technology, and nature. In addition to the exhibits, which range from playing with Hawaiian musical instruments to participating in virtual reality television to hiding out in a "magic tree house" and reading a book (there's even a baby area for kids 4 and under), there also are Keiki Camps (Children Camps), where you can leave the kids all day.

Don't miss the recently opened **Na Aina Kai Botanical Gardens** (p. 604), an incredible, magical garden on some 240 acres, sprinkled with some 70 life-size or larger bronze statues, hidden off the beaten path of the North Shore. This is the place for avid gardeners as well as people who think they don't like botanical gardens. The fairy-tale creativity that has gone into these grounds will make the gardens one of your fondest memories of Kauai.

1

The Best of Hawaii

There's no place on earth quite like this handful of sun-drenched, mid-Pacific islands. The Hawaii of South Seas literature and Hollywood films really does exist. Here you'll find palm-fringed blue lagoons, lush rain forests, hidden gardens, cascading waterfalls, wild rivers running through rugged canyons, and volcanoes soaring 2 miles into the sky. And oh, those beaches—gold, red, black, and even green sands caressed by an endless surf. The possibilities for adventure—and relaxation—are endless. Each of the six main islands is separate, distinct, and infinitely complex. There's far too much to see and do on any 2-week vacation, which is why so many people return to the Aloha State year after year.

Unfortunately, even paradise has its share of stifling crowds and tourist schlock. If you're not careful, your trip to Hawaii could turn into a nightmare of tourist traps selling shells from the Philippines, hokey faux culture like cellophane-skirted hula dancers, overpriced exotic drinks, and a 4-hour time-share lecture before you get on that "free" sailing trip. That's where this guide comes in. As Hawaii residents, we can tell the extraordinary from the merely ordinary. We're here to steer you away from the crowded, the overrated, and the overpriced—and toward the best Hawaii has to offer. No matter what your budget, this guide will help ensure that every dollar is well spent.

1 The Best Beaches

- **Lanikai Beach** (Oahu): Too gorgeous to be real, this stretch along the Windward Coast is one of Hawaii's postcard-perfect beaches—a mile of golden sand as soft as powdered sugar bordering translucent turquoise waters. The year-round calm waters are excellent for swimming, snorkeling, and kayaking. To complete the picture are two tiny offshore islands that function not only as scenic backdrops but also as bird sanctuaries. See p. 161.
- **Hapuna Beach** (Big Island): This ½-mile-long crescent regularly wins kudos in the world's top travel magazines as the most beautiful beach in Hawaii—some consider it one of the most beautiful beaches in the world. One look

and you'll see why: Perfect cream-colored sand slopes down to crystal-clear waters that are great for swimming, snorkeling, and body-surfing in summer; come winter, waves thunder in like stampeding wild horses. The facilities for picnicking and camping are top-notch, and there's plenty of parking. See p. 286.
- **Kapalua Beach** (Maui): On an island with many great beaches, Kapalua takes the prize. This golden crescent with swaying palms is protected from strong winds and currents by two outstretched lava-rock promontories. Its calm waters are perfect for snorkeling, swimming, and kayaking. The beach borders the Kapalua Bay Hotel, but it's long

The Hawaiian Islands

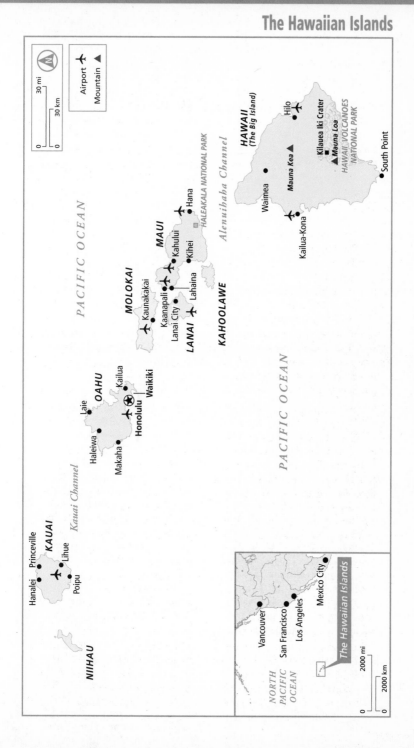

Airport ✈
Mountain ▲

0   30 mi
0   30 km

PACIFIC OCEAN

NIIHAU

KAUAI
Hanalei Princeville
Lihue
Poipu

Kauai Channel

OAHU
Kailua
Laie
Waikiki
Haleiwa
Honolulu
Makaha

MOLOKAI
Kaunakakai

MAUI
Kahului
Kaanapali Kihei
Lanai City Lahaina
Hana

LANAI

KAHOOLAWE

HALEAKALA NATIONAL PARK

Alenuihaha Channel

HAWAII
(The Big Island)
Hilo
Waimea
Mauna Kea ▲
Kilauea Iki Crater
▲ Mauna Loa
Kailua-Kona
South Point
HAWAII VOLCANOES
NATIONAL PARK

PACIFIC OCEAN

NORTH
PACIFIC
OCEAN

Vancouver
San Francisco
Los Angeles
Mexico City

The Hawaiian Islands

0   2000 mi
0   2000 km

enough for everyone to enjoy. Facilities include showers, restrooms, and lifeguards. See p. 413.

- **Papohaku Beach** (Molokai): One of Hawaii's longest beaches, these gold sands stretch on for some 3 miles and are about as wide as a football field. Offshore, the ocean churns mightily in winter, but the waves die down in summer, making the calm waters inviting for swimming, picnics, beach walks, and sunset watching. See p. 487.

- **Hulopoe Beach** (Lanai): This golden, palm-fringed beach off the south coast of Lanai gently slopes down to the azure waters of a Marine Life Conservation District, where clouds of tropical fish flourish and spinner dolphins come to play. A tide pool in the lava rocks defines one side of the

bay, while the other is lorded over by the Manele Bay Hotel, which sits prominently on the hill above. Offshore, you'll find good swimming, snorkeling, and diving; onshore, there's a full complement of beach facilities, from restrooms to camping areas. See p. 516.

- **Haena Beach** (Kauai): Backed by verdant cliffs, this curvaceous North Shore beach has starred as Paradise in many a movie. It's easy to see why Hollywood loves Haena Beach, with its grainy golden sand and translucent turquoise waters. Summer months bring calm waters for swimming and snorkeling, while winter brings mighty waves for surfers. There are plenty of facilities on hand, including picnic tables, restrooms, and showers. See p. 576.

2 The Best Island Experiences

- **Hitting the Beach:** A beach is a beach is a beach, right? Not in Hawaii. With 132 islets, shoals, and reefs and a general coastline of 750 miles, Hawaii has beaches in all different shapes, sizes, and colors, including black. The variety on the six major islands is astonishing; you could go to a different beach every day for years and still not see them all. For the best of a spectacular bunch, see "The Best Beaches," above.

- **Taking the Plunge:** Don mask, fin, and snorkel and explore the magical world beneath the surface, where you'll find exotic corals and kaleidoscopic clouds of tropical fish; a sea turtle may even come over to check you out. Can't swim? That's no excuse—take one of the many submarine tours offered by Atlantis **Submarines** (✆ **800/548-6262;** www.go-atlantis.com) on Oahu, the Big Island, and Maui. See chapters 4, 5, and 6.

- **Meeting Local Folks:** If you go to Hawaii and see only people like the ones back home, you might as well not have come. Extend yourself—leave your hotel, go out and meet the locals, and learn about Hawaii and its people. Just smile and say "Owzit?"—which means "How is it?" ("It's good," is the usual response)—and you'll usually make a new friend. Hawaii is remarkably cosmopolitan; every ethnic group in the world seems to be represented here. There's a huge diversity of food, culture, language, and customs.

- **Feeling History Come Alive at Pearl Harbor** (Oahu): The United States could turn its back on World War II no longer after December 7, 1941, when Japanese warplanes bombed Pearl Harbor. Standing on the deck of the USS *Arizona* Memorial (✆ **808/ 422-0561;** www.nps.gov/usar)—the eternal tomb for the 1,177 sailors and Marines trapped below when the battleship sank in just 9 minutes—is a moving experience you'll never forget. Also in Pearl Harbor, you can visit the USS *Missouri* Memorial; World War II came to an end on the deck of this 58,000-ton battleship with the signing of the Japanese surrender on September 2, 1945. See p. 188 and 189, respectively.

- **Watching for Whales:** If you happen to be in Hawaii during humpback-whale season (roughly December to April), don't miss the opportunity to see these gentle giants. A host of boats—from small inflatables to high-tech, high-speed sailing catamarans—offer a range of whale-watching cruises on every island. One of our favorites is along the Big Island's Kona Coast, where **Capt. Dan McSweeney's Year-Round Whale-Watching Adventures** (© **808/322-0028;** www.ilovewhales.com) takes you right to the whales year-round (pilot, sperm, false killer, melon-headed, pygmy killer, and beaked whales call Hawaii home even when humpbacks aren't in residence). A whale researcher for more than 25 years, Capt. Dan frequently drops an underwater microphone or video camera into the depths so you can listen to whale songs and maybe actually see what's going on. See p. 288.

- **Creeping Up to the Ooze** (Big Island): Kilauea volcano has been adding land to the Big Island continuously since 1983. If conditions are right, you can walk up to the red-hot lava and see it ooze along, or you can stand at the shoreline and watch with awe as 2,000°F molten fire pours into the ocean. You can also take to the air in a helicopter and see the Volcano Goddess's work from above. See "Hawaii Volcanoes National Park" under "Seeing the Sights," in chapter 5.

- **Going Big-Game Fishing off the Kona Coast** (Big Island): Don't pass up the opportunity to try your luck in the sportfishing capital of the world, where 1,000-pound marlin are taken from the seas just about every month of the year. Not looking to set a world record? Kona's charter-boat captains specialize in conservation and will be glad to tag and release any fish you angle, letting it go so someone else can have the fun of fighting a big-game fish tomorrow. See "Sportfishing: The Hunt for Granders" under "Watersports," in chapter 5.

- **Greeting the Rising Sun from atop Haleakala** (Maui): Bundle up in warm clothing, fill a thermos full of hot java, and drive up to the summit to watch the sky turn from inky black to muted charcoal as a small sliver of orange light forms on the horizon. There's something about standing at 10,000 feet, breathing in the rarefied air, and watching the first rays of sun streak across the sky. This is a mystical experience of the first magnitude. See "House of the Sun: Haleakala National Park" under "Seeing the Sights," in chapter 6.

- **Riding a Mule to Kalaupapa** (Molokai): If you have only a day to spend on Molokai, spend it on a mule. The trek from "topside" Molokai to Kalaupapa National Historic Park (Father Damien's world-famous leper colony) with **Molokai Mule Ride** (© **800/ 567-7550;** www.muleride.com) is a once-in-a-lifetime adventure. The cliffs are taller than 300-story skyscrapers—but Buzzy Sproat's surefooted mules go up and down the narrow 2.9-mile trail daily, rain or shine, and have never lost a rider or a mount on the 26 switchbacks. Even if you can't afford to mule or helicopter in, don't pass up the opportunity to see this hauntingly beautiful peninsula. It takes nothing more than a pair of hiking boots, a permit (available at the trailhead), and some grit to hike down the trail. The views are breathtaking: You'll see the world's highest sea cliffs and waterfalls plunging thousands of feet into the ocean. See "The Legacy of Father Damien: Kalaupapa National Historic Park" under "Seeing the Sights," in chapter 7.

- **Taking a Day Trip to Lanai** (Maui): If you'd like to visit Lanai but have only a day to spare, consider taking a day trip. **Trilogy** (② **800/874-2666** or 808/661-4743; www.sailtrilogy.com) offers an all-day sailing, snorkeling, and whale-watching adventure. Trilogy is the only outfitter with rights to Hulupoe Beach, and the trip includes a minivan tour of the little isle (pop. 3,500). See p. 421. You can also take **Expedition's Lahaina/Lanai Passenger Ferry** (② **808/661-3756;** www.go-lanai.com) from Maui to Lanai, then rent a four-wheel-drive vehicle from **Dollar Rent-A-Car** (② **800/588-7808**) for a day of backcountry exploring and beach fun. See p. 422.

- **Soaring Over the Na Pali Coast** (Kauai): This is the only way to see the spectacular, surreal beauty of Kauai. Your helicopter will dip low over razor-thin cliffs, fluttering past sparkling waterfalls and swooping down into the canyons and valleys of the fabled Na Pali Coast. The only problem is that there's too much beauty to absorb, and it all goes by in a rush. See "Helicopter Rides over Waimea Canyon & the Na Pali Coast" under "Seeing the Sights," in chapter 9.

3 The Best of Natural Hawaii

- **Volcanoes:** The entire island chain is made of volcanoes; don't miss the opportunity to see one. On Oahu, the entire family can hike to the top of the ancient volcano, world-famous **Diamond Head** (see "Diamond Head Crater" under "Nature Hikes," in chapter 4). At the other end of the spectrum is fire-breathing Kilauea at **Hawaii Volcanoes National Park,** on the Big Island, where you can get an up-close-and-personal experience with the red-hot lava ooze (see "Hawaii Volcanoes National Park" under "Seeing the Sights," in chapter 5). On Maui, **Haleakala National Park** provides a bird's-eye view into a long-dormant volcanic crater (see "House of the Sun: Haleakala National Park" under "Seeing the Sights," in chapter 6).

- **Waterfalls:** Rushing waterfalls thundering downward into sparkling freshwater pools are some of Hawaii's most beautiful natural wonders. If you're on the Big Island, stop by **Rainbow Falls** (p. 323), in Hilo, or the spectacular 442-foot **Akaka Falls** (p. 318), just outside the city. On Maui, the Road to Hana offers numerous viewing opportunities; at the end of the drive, you'll find **Oheo Gulch** (also known as the Seven Sacred Pools), with some of the most dramatic and accessible waterfalls on the islands (see "Tropical Haleakala: Oheo Gulch at Kipahulu" under "Seeing the Sights," in chapter 6). Kauai is loaded with waterfalls, especially along the North Shore and in the Wailua area, where you'll find 40-foot **Opaekaa Falls,** probably the best-looking drive-up waterfall on Kauai (see "Wailua River State Park" under "Seeing the Sights," in chapter 9). With scenic mountain peaks in the background and a restored Hawaiian village on the nearby river banks, the Opaekaa Falls are what the tourist-bureau folks call an eye-popping photo op.

- **Gardens:** The islands are redolent with the sweet scent of flowers. For a glimpse of the full breadth and beauty of Hawaii's spectacular range of tropical flora, we suggest spending an afternoon at a lush garden. On Oahu, amid the high-rises of downtown Honolulu, the leafy oasis of **Foster Botanical Garden** (p. 191) showcases 24 native Hawaiian trees and the last stand of several rare trees, including an East African whose white flowers bloom only at night. On the Big Island, **Liliuokalani Gardens** (p. 320), the largest formal Japanese garden this side of Tokyo, resembles a postcard from Asia, with bonsai, carp ponds, pagodas, and even a moon gate bridge. At Maui's **Kula Botanical Garden** (p. 449), you can take a leisurely self-guided stroll through more than 700 native and exotic plants, including orchids, proteas, and bromeliads. On lush Kauai, **Na Aina Kai Botanical Gardens** (p. 604) on some 240 acres, is sprinkled with some 70 life-size (some larger than life size) whimsical bronze statues, hidden off the beaten path of the North Shore.

- **Marine Life Conservation Areas:** Nine underwater parks are spread across Hawaii, most notably **Waikiki Beach** (p. 157) and **Hanauma Bay** (p. 160), on Oahu; the Big Island's **Kealakekua Bay** (p. 290); **Molokini,** just off the coast of Maui (see "Watersports," in chapter 6); and Lanai's **Manele and Hulopoe bays** (see "Beaches," in chapter 8). Be sure to bring snorkel gear to at least one of these wonderful places during your vacation here.

- **Garden of the Gods** (Lanai): Out on Lanai's North Shore lies the ultimate rock garden: a rugged, barren, beautiful place full of rocks strewn by volcanic forces and shaped by the elements into a variety of shapes and colors—brilliant reds, oranges, ochers, and yellows. Scientists use phrases such as "ongoing posterosional event" or "plain and simple bad-lands" to describe the desolate, windswept place. The ancient Hawaiians, however, considered the Garden of the Gods to be an entirely supernatural phenomenon. Natural badlands or mystical garden? Take a four-wheel-drive trip out here and decide for yourself. See p. 523.

- **The Grand Canyon of the Pacific—Waimea Canyon** (Kauai): This valley, known for its reddish lava beds, reminds everyone who sees it of Arizona's Grand Canyon. Kauai's version is bursting with ever-changing color, just like its namesake, but it's smaller—only a mile wide, 3,567 feet deep, and 12 miles long. All this grandeur was caused by a massive earthquake that sent all the streams flowing into a single river, which then carved this picturesque canyon. You can stop by the road and look at it, hike down into it, or swoop through it by helicopter. See p. 596.

4 The Best of Underwater Hawaii

- **Hanauma Bay** (Oahu): It can get crowded, but for clear, warm, calm waters, an abundance of fish that are so friendly they'll swim right up to your face mask, a beautiful setting, and easy access, there's no place like Hanauma Bay. Just wade in waist-deep and look down to see more than 50 species of reef and inshore fish. Snorkelers hug the safe, shallow inner bay—it's like swimming in an outdoor aquarium. Serious divers shoot "the slot," a passage through the reef, to enter Witch's Brew, a turbulent cove. See p. 160.

- **Kahaluu Beach** (Big Island): The calm, shallow waters of Kahaluu are perfect for beginning snorkelers or those who are unsure of their swimming abilities and want the comfort of being able to stand up at any time. The sunlight through the shallow waters casts a dazzling spotlight on the colorful sea life and coral formations. If you listen closely, you can actually hear the parrot fish feeding. See p. 283.

- **Kealakekua Bay** (Big Island): Mile-wide Kealakekua Bay, at the foot of massive U-shaped sea cliffs, is rich with marine life, snorkelers, and history. A white obelisk marks the spot where, in 1778, the great British navigator Capt. James Cook, who charted most of the Pacific, was killed by Hawaiians. The bay itself is a marine sanctuary that teems with schools of polychromatic tropical fish. See p. 290.

- **Molokini** (Maui): The islet of Molokini is shaped like a crescent moon that fell from the sky. Its shallow concave side serves as a sheltering backstop against sea currents for tiny tropical fish; its opposite side is a deep-water cliff inhabited by spiny lobsters, moray eels, and white-tipped sharks. Neophyte snorkelers should report to the concave side, experienced scuba divers the other. The clear water and abundant marine life make this islet off the Makena Coast one of Hawaii's most popular dive spots, so expect crowds. See "Watersports," in chapter 6.

- **Kee Beach** (Kauai): Where the road ends on the North Shore, you'll find a dandy little reddish-gold–sand beach almost too beautiful to be real. It borders a reef-protected cove at the foot of fluted volcanic cliffs. Swimming and snorkeling are safe inside the reef, where long-nosed butterfly fish flitter about and schools of *taape* (bluestripe snapper) swarm over the coral. See p. 577.

5 The Best Golf Courses

- **Mauna Kea's Beach and Hapuna Courses** (Big Island; ℂ **808/882-5400** for Beach Course, or ℂ **808/882-3000** for Hapuna Course): The Mauna Kea Golf Course (p. 300), located out on the Kohala Coast, is everyone's old favorite. One of the first fields of play to be carved out of the black lava, the dramatic, always-challenging, par-72, 18-hole championship course is still one of Hawaii's top three. The new Arnold Palmer/Ed Seay–designed Hapuna Golf Course (p. 299) rests in the rolling foothills above Hapuna Beach Prince Hotel and provides a memorable links-style golf experience along with one of the best views of this unusual coast. See chapter 5.

- **Mauna Lani Frances I'i Brown Championship Courses** (Big Island; ℂ **808/885-6655**): Mauna Lani's two resort courses, North and South, feature a combination of oceanfront and interior lava-lined holes; both offer wonderful scenery accompanied by strategic, championship-level golf. See p. 300.

- **Kapalua Resort Courses** (Maui; ℂ **808/669-8044**): Kapalua is probably the best nationally known golf resort in Hawaii, thanks to the PGA Kapalua Mercedes Championship, played here each January. The Bay and Village courses are vintage Arnold Palmer designs, while the new Plantation Course is a strong Ben Crenshaw/Bill Coore design. See p. 434.
- **Wailea Courses** (Maui; ℂ **808/875-7450**): On Maui's sun-baked South Shore stands Wailea Resort, *the* hot spot for golf in the islands. Three resort courses complement a string of beachfront hotels: The Blue Course is an Arthur Jack Snyder design, while Robert Trent Jones Jr. is the mastermind behind the Emerald and Gold courses. All three boast outstanding views of the Pacific and the mid-Hawaiian Islands. See p. 435.
- **The Lanai Courses** (Lanai; ℂ **808/565-GOLF**): For quality and seclusion, nothing in Hawaii can touch Lanai's two resort offerings. The **Experience at Koele** (p. 521), designed by Ted Robinson and Greg Norman, and the **Challenge at Manele** (p. 521), a wonderful Jack Nicklaus effort with ocean views from every hole, both rate among Hawaii's best courses.
- **Poipu Bay Golf Course** (Kauai; ℂ **808/742-8711**): On Kauai's flat, dry South Shore is a 210-acre, links-style course, designed by Robert Trent Jones Jr. The course, which hosts the PGA Tour's Grand Slam of Golf, is not only scenically spectacular but also a lot of fun to play. A flock of native Hawaiian nene geese frequents the course's lakes, and you can often see whales, monk seals, and green sea turtles along the shore. See p. 591.
- **Princeville Golf Club** (Kauai; ℂ **800/826-1105**): Here you'll find 45 of the best tropical holes of golf in the world, all the work of Robert Trent Jones Jr. They range along green bluffs below sharp mountain peaks and offer stunning views in every direction. One of the top three courses in Hawaii, the 18-hole Prince provides a round of golf few ever forget; it winds along 390 acres of scenic table land bisected by tropical jungles, waterfalls, streams, and ravines. See p. 591.

6 The Best Ways to Immerse Yourself in Hawaiian Culture

- **Experiencing the Hula:** For a real, authentic hula experience on Oahu, check out the **Bishop Museum** (p. 183), which has excellent performances on weekdays, or head to the Halekulani's **House Without a Key** (p. 163) at sunset to watch the enchanting Kanoelehua Miller dance beautiful hula under a century-old kiawe tree. The first week after Easter brings Hawaii's biggest and most prestigious hula extravaganza, the **Merrie Monarch Hula Festival** (p. 346), at Hilo on the Big Island; tickets sell out by January 30, so reserve early. In May, there's the **Molokai Ka Hula Piko** (p. 492), at Molokai's Papohaku Beach Park, a wonderful day-long festival that celebrates the hula on the island where it was born.
- **Watching the Ancient Hawaiian Sport of Canoe Paddling** (Oahu): From February to September, on weekday evenings and weekend days, hundreds of canoe paddlers gather at Ala Wai Canal and practice the Hawaiian sport of canoe paddling. Find a comfortable spot at Ala Wai Park, next to the canal, and watch this ancient sport come to life. See chapter 4.

- **Attending a Hawaiian-Language Church Service** (Oahu): **Kawaiahao Church** (© **808/522-1333**) is the Westminster Abbey of Hawaii. The vestibule is lined with portraits of the Hawaiian monarchy, many of whom were crowned in this very building. The coral church is a perfect setting in which to experience an all-Hawaiian service, held every Sunday at 10:30am, complete with Hawaiian song. Admission is free; let your conscience be your guide as to a donation. See p. 163.

- **Buying a Lei in Chinatown** (Oahu): There's actually a host of cultural sights and experiences to be had in Honolulu's Chinatown. Wander through this several-square-block area with its jumble of exotic shops offering herbs, Chinese groceries, and acupuncture services. Before you leave, be sure to check out the lei sellers on Maunakea Street (near North Hotel Street), where Hawaii's finest leis go for as little as $2.50. If you'd like a little guidance, you can follow our walking tour on p. 196.

- **Listening to Old Fashioned "Talk Story" with Hawaiian Song and Dance** (Big Island): Once a month, under a full moon, **"Twilight at Kalahuipua'a,"** a celebration of the Hawaiian culture that includes story-telling, singing, and dancing, takes place oceanside at Mauna Lani Bay Resort (© **808/885-6622**). It hearkens back to another time in Hawaii, when family and neighbors would gather on back porches to sing, dance and "talk story." See the box "Old-Style Hawaiian Entertainment," in chapter 5.

- **Visiting Ancient Hawaii's Most Sacred Temple** (Big Island): On the Kohala Coast, where King Kamehameha the Great was born,

stands Hawaii's oldest, largest, and most sacred religious site: the 1,500-year-old Mookini Heiau, used by kings to pray and offer human sacrifices. This massive three-story stone temple, dedicated to Ku, the Hawaiian god of war, was erected in A.D. 480. It's said that each stone was passed from hand to hand from Pololu Valley, 14 miles away, by 18,000 men who worked from sunset to sunrise. Go in late afternoon, when the setting sun strikes the lava-rock walls and creates a primal mood. See p. 312.

- **Hunting for Petroglyphs** (Big Island): Archaeologists are still uncertain exactly what these ancient rock carvings—the majority of which are found in the 233-acre Puako Petroglyph Archaeological District, near Mauna Lani Resort on the Kohala Coast—mean. The best time to hunt for these intricate depictions of ancient life is either early in the morning or late afternoon, when the angle of the sun lets you see the forms clearly. See "Kohala Coast Petroglyphs" under "Seeing the Sites," in chapter 5.

- **Exploring Puuhonua O Honaunau National Historical Park** (Big Island): This sacred site on the South Kona Coast was once a place of refuge and a revered place of rejuvenation. You can walk the same consecrated grounds where priests once conducted holy ceremonies and glimpse the ancient way of life in pre-contact Hawaii in the re-created 180-acre village. See p. 290.

- **Visiting the Most Hawaiian Isle:** A time capsule of old Hawaii, Molokai allows you to experience real Hawaiian life in its most unsullied form. The island's people have woven the cultural values of ancient times into modern life.

The Welcoming Lei

There's nothing like a lei. The stunning tropical beauty of the delicate garland, the deliciously sweet fragrance of the blossoms, the sensual way the flowers curl softly around your neck. There's no doubt about it: Getting lei'd in Hawaii is a sensuous experience.

Leis are much more than just a decorative necklace of flowers; they're also one of the nicest ways to say hello, good-bye, congratulations, I salute you, my sympathies are with you, or I love you. The custom of giving leis can be traced back to Hawaii's very roots; according to chants, the first lei was given by Hiiaka, the sister of the volcano goddess Pele, who presented Pele with a lei of lehua blossoms on a beach in Puna.

During ancient times, leis given to *alii* (high-ranking chiefs) were accompanied by a bow, since it was *kapu* (forbidden) for a commoner to raise his arms higher than the king's head. The presentation of a kiss with a lei didn't come about until World War II; it's generally attributed to an entertainer who kissed an officer on a dare and then quickly presented him with her lei, saying it was an old Hawaiian custom. It wasn't then, but it sure caught on fast.

Lei-making is a tropical art form. All leis are fashioned by hand in a variety of traditional patterns; some are sewn with hundreds of tiny blooms or shells, or bits of ferns and leaves. Some are twisted, some braided, some strung; all are presented with love. Every island has its own special flower lei—the lei of the land, so to speak. On Oahu, the choice is *ilima*, a small orange flower. Big Islanders prefer the *lehua*, a large, delicate red puff. On Maui, it's the *lokelani*, a small rose; on Kauai, it's the *mokihana*, a fragrant green vine and berry; on Molokai, it's the *kukui*, the white blossom of a candlenut tree; and on Lanai, it's the *kaunaoa*, a bright yellow moss. Residents of Niihau use the island's abundant seashells to make leis that were once prized by royalty and are now worth a small fortune.

Leis are available at all of the islands' airports. Other places to get wonderful, inexpensive leis are the half-dozen lei shops on **Maunakea Street** in Honolulu's Chinatown, and **Greene Acres Leis** (② **808/329-2399**), off Kaimiminani Drive in the Kona Palisades subdivision, across from the Kona International Airport on the Big Island. If you plan ahead, you can also arrange to have a lei-greeter meet you and your travel party as you deplane. Reliable companies that can greet you at Honolulu International Airport on Oahu, Kahului Airport on Maui, Kona Airport on the Big Island, and Lihue Airport on Kauai are **Greeters of Hawaii** (② **800/366-8559** or 808/836-0161, or 808/836-3246) and **Aloha Lei Greeters** (② **800/367-5255** or 808/951-9990).

Leis are the perfect symbol for the islands: They're given in the moment and their fragrance and beauty are enjoyed in the moment, but when they fade, their spirit of aloha lives on. Welcome to Hawaii!

In addition to this rich community, you'll find the magnificent natural wonders it so cherishes: Hawaii's highest waterfall, its greatest collection of fish ponds, and the world's tallest sea cliffs, as well as sand dunes, coral reefs, rain forests, and gloriously empty beaches. The island is pretty much the same Molokai of generations ago. See chapter 7.

7 The Best Luxury Hotels & Resorts

- **Halekulani** (Oahu; ℂ **800/ 367-2343;** www.halekulani.com): When price is no object, this is really the only place to stay. An oasis of calm amid the buzz, this beach hotel is the finest Waikiki has to offer (heck, we think it's the finest in the state). Even if you don't stay here, pop by for a sunset mai tai to hear Sonny Kamehele sing the old hapa-haole tunes of the 1930s and 1940s while a lovely hula dancer sways to the music. See p. 108.
- **Kahala Mandarin Oriental Hawaii** (Oahu; ℂ **800/367- 2525;** www.mandarinoriental. com): This palatial oceanside resort has the grace and elegance of a softer, gentler time, when all of Hawaii moved at a more leisurely pace. Its old Hawaii spirit is accented with pan-Asian touches and all the conveniences you could wish for, including a fabulously secluded beach. And the location, 10 minutes from Waikiki in the quiet residential community of Kahala, rounds out the get-away-from-it-all vibe and keeps everything close at hand at the same time. See p. 124.
- **Kona Village Resort** (Big Island; ℂ **800/367-5290;** www.kona village.com): This is the best place in Hawaii if you want to stay in a vintage Polynesian village–style resort. The sublimely peaceful, eclectic Polynesian village, with thatched huts and various styles of Pacific architecture clustered by the big blue ocean, stands on 82 coastal acres of palms and tropical flowers. The authenticity and isolation of this oasis revive wounded

urban souls, who swing in hammocks, splash like children in the bay, actually smile when spoken to, and move slowly with the calm and grace that come from great leisure. Why anyone ever leaves is a wonder. See p. 240.
- **Four Seasons Resort Hualalai at Historic Kaupulehu** (Big Island; ℂ **888/340-5662;** www.four seasons.com): Private pools, unimpeded ocean views, excellent food, and a new 18-hole championship golf course—what more could any mortal want? This new low-impact, high-ticket hideaway under the dormant Hualalai volcano ups the ante with its residential resort of two-story bungalows clustered around five seaside swimming pools on a black lagoon. See p. 240.
- **Ritz-Carlton Kapalua** (Maui; ℂ **800/262-8440;** www.ritz carlton.com): For location, style, and hospitality, this is perhaps the best Ritz anywhere. The breezy grand hotel stands on the coast below the picturesque West Maui Mountains, overlooking the Pacific and Molokai across the channel. The natural setting, on an old coastal pineapple plantation, is the picture of tranquillity. The service is legendary, the golf courses daunting, and the nearby beaches perfect for snorkeling, diving, and simply relaxing. See p. 372.
- **Four Seasons Resort Maui at Wailea** (Maui; ℂ **800/334- MAUI;** www.fshr.com): This is the ultimate beach hotel for latter-day royals, with excellent cuisine, spacious rooms, gracious service,

and Wailea Beach, one of Maui's best gold-sand strips, out the front door. Every guest room has at least a partial ocean view from a private lanai. The luxury suites, as big as some Honolulu condos, are full of marble and deluxe appointments. See p. 379.

- **Fairmont Kea Lani Maui** (Maui; ℂ **800/659-4100;** www.kealani. com); This is the place to get your money's worth; for the price of a hotel room you get an entire suite—plus a few extras. Each unit in this all-suite luxury hotel has a kitchenette, a living room with entertainment center and sofa bed (great if you have the kids in tow), a marble wet bar, an oversize marble bathroom with separate shower big enough for a party, a spacious bedroom, and a large lanai that overlooks the pools, lawns, and white-sand beach. See p. 379.

- **Hyatt Regency Kauai Resort & Spa** (Kauai; ℂ **800/55-HYATT;** www.kauai-hyatt.com): This Art Deco beach hotel recalls Hawaii in the 1920s—before the crash— when gentlemen in blue blazers and ladies in summer frocks came to the islands to learn to surf and play the ukulele. The hotel's architecture and location, on the sunny side of Kauai, make this the island's best hotel. The beach is a bit too rough for swimming, but the saltwater swimming pool is the biggest on the island. An old-fashioned reading room by the sea houses club chairs, billiards, and a bar well stocked with cognac and port. Golf, horseback riding, and the shops of Koloa, a boutiqued plantation town, are nearby diversions. See p. 539.

- **Princeville Resort Kauai** (Kauai; ℂ **800/826-4400;** www. princeville.com): This palace of green marble and sparkling chandeliers recalls Hawaii's monarchy period of the 19th century. It's set in one of the most remarkable locations in the world, on a cliff between the crystal-blue waters of Hanalei Bay and steepled mountains; you arrive on the ninth floor and go down to the beach. Opulent rooms with magnificent views and all the activities of Princeville and Hanalei make this one of Hawaii's finest resorts. See p. 551.

8 The Best Moderately Priced Accommodations

- **Doubletree Alana Waikiki** (Oahu; ℂ **800/222-TREE;** www. alana-doubletree.com): This hotel, located within walking distance of Waikiki Beach, offers beautiful, comfortable rooms and the kind of prompt service that you usually get only at twice the price (rack rates here start at $199). Downstairs is the excellent cuisine of Chef Phillip Padovani in Padovani's Restaurant and Wine Bar. See p. 106.

- **Santa's by the Sea** (Oahu; ℂ **800/ 262-9912;** www.bestbnb.com): Setting, price ($135 a night), and style make this a great choice if you plan to see Oahu's North Shore. Santa's is one of the few North Shore B&Bs right on the beach—and not just any beach, but the famous Banzai Pipeline. You can go from your bed to the sand in less than 30 seconds—it's the perfect spot to watch the sun rise over the Pacific. The impeccable one-bedroom units feature finely crafted woodwork and bay windows. See p. 128.

- **Holualoa Inn** (Big Island; ℂ **800/ 392-1812;** www.konaweb.com/ HINN): The quiet, secluded setting of this B&B—40 pastoral acres just off the main drag of the artsy village of Holualoa, on the slopes at 1,350 feet above Kailua-Kona—provides stunning panoramic views of the entire coast. This contemporary 7,000-square-foot Hawaiian home built of golden woods has six private suites (starting at $175) and window-walls that roll back to embrace the gardens and views. Cows graze on the bucolic pastures below the garden Jacuzzi and pool, and the coffee plantation on the property is the source of the morning brew. See p. 245.

- **Kona Tiki Hotel** (Big Island; ✆ **808/329-1425**): Right on the ocean, away from the hustle and bustle of downtown Kailua-Kona, is one of the hottest budget deals in Hawaii: tastefully decorated rooms with private lanais overlooking the ocean, starting at just $59 a night! Although it's called a hotel, this small, family-run operation is more like a large B&B, with plenty of friendly conversation around the pool at the morning continental breakfast buffet. See p. 244.

- **Waipio Wayside B&B Inn** (Big Island; ✆ **800/833-8849**; www.waipiowayside.com): Jackie Horne renovated this 1938 Hamakua sugar supervisor's home—nestled among fruit trees and surrounded with sweet-smelling ginger, fragile orchids, and blooming birds of paradise—and transformed it into a gracious B&B. Just minutes from the Waipio Valley Lookout and Honokaa village, this comfy five-bedroom house abounds with thoughtful touches, such as a help-yourself tea-and-cookies bar with 26 different kinds of tea. Jackie's friendly hospitality and excellent gourmet breakfasts really round out the experience. Rooms start at $95 for two. See p. 254.

- **Old Wailuku Inn at Ulupono** (Maui; ✆ **800/305-4899**): This 1924 former plantation manager's home, lovingly restored, offers a genuine old Hawaii experience. The theme is Hawaii of the 1920s and '30s, with decor, design, and landscaping to match. The spacious rooms are gorgeously outfitted with exotic ohia-wood floors, high ceilings, and traditional Hawaiian quilts. A full gourmet breakfast is served on the enclosed back lanai or, if you prefer, delivered to your room. The inn is located in the old historic area of Wailuku, about 10 to 15 minutes to the beach. Once you settle in, you may not want to leave—with rooms starting at $120 for a double, you can afford to stay a while. See p. 358.

- **Paniolo Hale** (Molokai; ✆ **800/367-2984**; www.paniolohaleresort.com): This is far and away Molokai's most charming lodging, and probably its best value. The two-story, old Hawaii, ranch-house design is airy and homey, with oak floors and walls of folding-glass doors that open to huge screened verandas. The whole place overlooks the Kaluakoi Golf Course, a green barrier that separates these condos (which start at $95 for two) from the rest of Kaluakoi Resort. See p. 478.

- **Dunbar Beachfront Cottages** (Molokai; ✆ **800/673-0520**; www.molokai-beachfront-cottages.com): Each of these green-and-white plantation-style cottages sits on its own secluded beach—you'll feel like you're on your own private island. Impeccable decor, a magical setting, and reasonable rates ($140 for two) make these cottages a must-stay. See p. 482.

- **Hotel Lanai** (Lanai; ✆ **800/795-7211**; www.hotellanai.com): Lanai's only budget lodging is a simple, down-home, plantation-era relic that has recently been Laura Ashley–ized. The Hotel Lanai is homey, funky, and fun—and, best of all, a real bargain (starting at $105 for two) compared to its ritzy neighbors. See p. 512.

- **Aloha Sunrise Inn/Aloha Sunset Inn** (Kauai; ✆ **888/828-1008**; www.kauaisunrise.com): Hidden on the North Shore, these two unique cottages are nestled on a quiet 7-acre farm. They come fully furnished with all the great videos you've been meaning to watch and an excellent CD library. They're close enough to activities, restaurants, and shopping, yet isolated enough to feel the peace and quiet of old Hawaii. Priced at $125 to $130. See p. 552.

9 The Best Places to Stay with the Kids

- **Royal Kuhio** (Oahu; ✆ **800/ 367-5205**; e-mail: pmchi@gte. net): Families, this is one of the best deals in Waikiki. Just 2 blocks from world-famous Waikiki Beach, this high-rise condo features apartments with full kitchens, separate bedrooms, living areas with TVs, and private lanais—all for as little as $110. Lots of on-site extras, ranging from a pool to volleyball and basketball courts and a putting green, round out the family-friendly appeal. *Tip:* Ask for a corner unit—they're the nicest. See p. 116.

- **J. W. Marriott Ihilani Resort & Spa in the Ko Olina Resort** (Oahu; ✆ **800/626-4446**; www. ihilani.com): This resort on Oahu's virgin leeward coast is a haven of relaxation and tropical fun for travelers of all ages. The year-round Keiki Beachcomber Club offers a wide variety of outdoor adventures and indoor learning activities, from kite-flying and tide-pool exploration to Hawaiian cultural activities like lei-making and hula dancing. The resort is so intent on pleasing the entire family that the kids even have their own clubhouse, with a Computer Learning Center (complete with CD-ROMs, SEGA Genesis, and Super Nintendo), a 125-gallon fish tank, an evening lounge for teen parties, and much more. See p. 129.

- **Kona Village Resort** (Big Island; ✆ **800/367-5290**; www.kona village.com): This is a parent's dream: custom-designed programs to entertain your kids, from tots to teenagers, from dawn to well after dusk, all at no charge. There's even a dinner seating for children, so Mom and Dad can enjoy an intimate dinner for two later in the evening. See p. 240.

- **Guest House at Volcano** (Big Island; ✆ **808/967-7775**; www. volcanoguesthouse.com): If you're planning to visit Hawaii Volcanoes National Park, here's the place to bring the family. A mother herself, Bonnie Gooddell has completely childproofed her house and installed a basketball hoop in the driveway; her truckload of toys will keep the kids happy for hours. You can make yourself right at home in Bonnie's freestanding two-story guest cottage, which comes outfitted with everything down to extra wool socks for cold nights. And at $75 for two plus $10 for each of the kids, it's easy on the family budget. See p. 257.

- **Four Seasons Resort Maui at Wailea** (Maui; ✆ **800/334- MAUI**; www.fshr.com): The most kid-friendly hotel on Maui not only offers a complimentary kids' program year-round and an every-day activities center (daily 9am–5pm), but also makes the children feel welcome with extras such as complimentary milk and cookies on their first day and children's menus at all resort restaurants and even from room service. See p. 379.

- **Koa Resort** (Maui; ✆ **800/ 541-3060;** www.bellomaui.com): These spacious, privately-owned one-, two-, and three-bedroom units just across the street from the ocean start at just $85. They come fully equipped with everything you'll need, including plenty of room for your family to stretch out and get comfortable. Extras like a swimming pool, a hot tub, two tennis courts, and an 18-hole putting green make this an extra good value. See p. 374.

- **Ke Nani Kai Resort** (Molokai; ✆ **800/535-0085;** www.marc resorts.com): This place is great for families, who will appreciate the space and quiet. These large apartments are set up for full-time living with real kitchens, washer/ dryers, VCRs, attractive furnishings, and breezy lanais. Spend your time at the huge pool, the volleyball court, the tennis courts,

or the beach—just a brief walk away. See p. 478.

- **Hyatt Regency Kauai Resort & Spa** (Kauai; ✆ **800/55-HYATT;** www.kauai-hyatt.com): In addition to the Camp Hyatt program (for kids ages 3–12), it's the collection of swimming pools—freshwater and salt, with slides, waterfalls, and secret lagoons—that makes this oceanfront Hyatt a real kids' paradise. During the summer months and the holiday season, there's Rock Hyatt, an activity room for teens to gather in and play electronic games. Summertime also boasts Family Fun Theatre Nights, when the whole family can enjoy a showing of one of the more than 400 movies filmed on Kauai. See p. 539.

- **Kauai Coconut Beach Resort** (Kauai; ✆ **800/22-ALOHA;** www.kcb.com): This Coconut Coast resort has an excellent deal for families: Not only do kids 17 and under stay free, but those 11 and younger also eat free when dining with a grown-up. The resort is situated on 10½ acres fronting Waipouli Beach, right next door to the Coconut Marketplace, so kids have plenty of room to play. See p. 548.

10 The Best Resort Spas

- **Ihilani Spa at the J.W. Marriott Ihilani Resort & Spa** (Oahu; ✆ **800/626-4446;** www.ihilani. com): An oasis by the sea, this freestanding 35,000-square-foot facility is dedicated to the traditional spa definition of "health by water." This modern, multistoried spa, filled with floor-to-ceiling glass looking out on green tropical plants, combines Hawaiian products with traditional therapies to produce some of the best water treatments in the state. You'll also find a fitness center, tennis courts,

and a bevy of aerobic and stretching classes. See p. 129.

- **Na Ho'ola Spa in the Hyatt Regency Waikiki** (Oahu; ✆ **800/ 233-1234;** www.hyattwaikiki. com): Waikiki's first spa, just opened in 2000, is an airy, modern 10,000-square-foot facility with a small fitness center, a sauna, Vichy showers, and a relaxation area. The 19 treatment rooms are twice the usual size, with plenty of room to accommodate couples massage. See p. 118.

- **Hualalai Sports Club & Spa at Four Seasons Resort Hualalali** (Big Island; ℂ **888/340-5662;** www.fourseasons.com): It's easy to see why some 6,000 *Condé Nast* readers voted this 13,000-square-foot facility their favorite resort spa. Five of its 16 treatment rooms are thatched huts (with bamboo privacy screens) nestled into a tropical garden. This is the place to come to be pampered. The fitness facilities, classes, and adventure activities are all excellent, but the attentive service and dreamy facilities are what you will remember long after your vacation. See p. 335.

- **Kohala Spa at the Hilton Waikoloa Village** (Big Island; ℂ **800/HILTONS;** www.hilton waikoloavillage.com): The Big Island's oldest (since 1989) and largest (25,000 sq. ft.) spa has something for everyone, including 33 treatment rooms, 50 classes, and a variety of sports ranging from racquetball to indoor rock climbing. Spend the day luxuriating in the lava whirlpool, steam room, and sauna before or after your treatment. See p. 252.

- **Mauna Lani Spa** (Big Island; ℂ **800/845-9905;** www.orchid-maunalani.com): The Mauna Lani Resort has opened a one-of-a-kind spa, which not only utilizes traditional treatment centers in a relaxing indoor atmosphere but also nine stand-alone Hawaiian thatched huts (totaling some 15,000 sq. ft. in size) with cutting-edge, Hawaiian-influenced treatments. One of the most unique new treatments is the lava sauna, an outdoor, open-air sauna using black lava rocks and warm, black sand as a natural sauna. No other spa in the state has this unusual treatment, which incorporates

mud clay, cooling water, and soothing lotion. See p. 250.

- **The Health Centre at the Four Seasons Resort Maui** (Maui; ℂ **800/334-MAUI;** www.fshr.com): Imagine the sounds of the waves rolling on Wailea Beach as you are soothingly massaged in the privacy of your cabana, tucked into the beachside foliage. This is the place to be absolutely spoiled. Yes, there's an excellent workout area and tons of great classes, but their specialty is hedonistic indulgence. See p. 379.

- **Spa Grande at the Grand Wailea Resort** (Maui; ℂ **800/888-6100;** www.grandwailea.com): This is Hawaii's biggest spa, at 50,000 square feet, with 40 treatment rooms. The spa incorporates the best of the old world (romantic ceiling murals, larger-than-life Roman-style sculptures, mammoth Greek columns, huge European tubs); the finest Eastern traditions (a full Japanese-style traditional bath and various exotic treatments from India); and the lure of the islands (tropical foliage, ancient Hawaiian treatments and island products). This spa has everything from a top fitness center to a menu of classes and is constantly on the cutting edge of the latest trends. See p. 381.

- **Spa Moana at the Hyatt Regency Maui** (Maui; ℂ **800/233-1234;** www.maui.hyatt.com) You cannot match the location—this is Hawaii's only oceanfront spa. The 9,000-square-foot spa houses 11 relaxing treatment rooms and features a full-service fitness center, plus a relaxation lounge, a romantic couple's treatment room, and a salon/retail shop. See p. 363.

- **Spa Kea Lani at the Fairmont Kea Lani Maui** (Maui; ℂ **800/ 569-4100;** www.kealani.com): This intimate, Art Deco boutique

C Pampering in Paradise

Hawaii's spas have raised the art of the relaxation and healing to a new level. The traditional Greco-Roman–style spas, with lots of marble and big tubs in closed rooms, have evolved into airy, open facilities that embrace the tropics. Spa goers in Hawaii are looking for a sense of place, seeped in the culture. They want to hear the sound of the ocean, smell the salt air, and feel the caress of the warm breeze. They want to experience Hawaiian products and traditional treatments they can get only in the islands.

The spas of Hawaii, once nearly exclusively patronized by women, are now attracting more male clients. There are special massages for children and pregnant women, and some spas have created programs to nurture and relax brides on their big day.

Today's spas offer a wide diversity of treatments. There is no longer plain, ordinary massage, but Hawaiian lomilomi, Swedish, aromatherapy (with sweet-smelling oils), craniosacral (massaging the head), shiatsu (no oil, just deep thumb pressure on acupuncture points), Thai (another oilless massage involving stretching), and hot stone (with heated, and sometimes cold, rocks). There are even side-by-side massages for couples. The truly decadent might even try a duo massage—not one, but *two* massage therapists working on you at once.

Massages are just the beginning. Body treatments, for the entire body or for just the face, involve a variety of herbal wraps, masks, or scrubs using a range of ingredients from seaweed to salt to mud, with or without accompanying aromatherapy, lights, and music.

After you have been rubbed and scrubbed, most spas offer an array of water treatments—a sort of hydromassage in a tub with jets and an assortment of colored crystals, oils, and scents.

Those are just the traditional treatments. Most spas also offer a range of alternative health care like acupuncture and chiropractic, and more exotic treatments like ayurvedic and siddha from India or reiki from Japan. Many places offer specialized, cutting-edge treatments, like the Grand Wailea Resort's full-spectrum color-light therapy pod (based on NASA's work with astronauts).

Once your body has been pampered, spas also offer a range of fitness facilities (weight-training equipment, raquetball, tennis, golf) and classes (yoga, aerobics, step, spinning, stretch, tai chi, kickboxing, aquacize). Several even offer adventure fitness packages (from bicycling to snorkeling). For the nonadventurous, most spas have salons, dedicated to hair and nail care and makeup.

If all this sounds a bit overwhelming, not to worry, all the spas in Hawaii have individual consultants who will help design you an appropriate treatment program to fit your individual needs.

Of course, all this pampering doesn't come cheap. Massages are generally $95 to $150 for 50 minutes and $145 to $200 for 80 minutes; body treatments are in the $120 to $195 range; and alternative health-care treatments can be has high as $150 to $220. But you may think it's worth the expense to banish your tension and stress.

spa (just a little over 5,000 sq. ft., with 9 treatment rooms), which opened in 1999, is the place for personal and private attention. The fitness center next door is open 24 hours (a rarity in Hawaii resorts) with a personal trainer on duty some 14 hours a day. See p. 379.

- **ANARA Spa at the Hyatt Regency Kauai** (Kauai; ℭ **800/ 323-3589;** www.kauai-hyatt.com): This is the place to come to get rid of stress and to be soothed and pampered in a Hawaiian atmosphere, where the spirit of aloha reigns. An elegant 25,000-square-foot spa, ANARA (A New Age Restorative Approach) focuses on Hawaiian culture and healing, with some 16 treatment rooms, a lap pool, fitness facilities, lava rock showers that open to the tropical air, outdoor whirlpools, a 24-head Swiss shower, Turkish steam rooms, Finnish saunas, and botanical soaking tubs. See p. 540.

- **Princeville Health Club & Spa, Princeville Resort** (Kauai; ℭ **808/826-5030**): This spa offers good value. Not only are the treatments a full 60 minutes (versus the standard 50 min. in most spas), but prices are also quite a bit lower (hour-long massages and body treatments start at just $85, half of what many spas charge). Just a short 7-minute drive (via the free resort shuttle) from the Princeville Hotel, this 10,000-square-foot boutique spa has amenities like a 25m heated lap pool, outdoor whirlpool, sauna, steam room, five treatment rooms (plus massage cabanas poolside at the hotel), exercise classes, a weight room, a cardio room, and even babysitting services. See p. 551.

11 The Best Dining, Hawaii Style

- **Tropical Fruit: Mangosteen,** the queen of fruit in Indonesia, is the sensation at the Hilo Farmers Market on the Big Island. Mangosteen's elegant purple skin and soft, white, floral-flavored flesh (like litchi, but more custardlike than translucent) make this fruit a sure winner. It joins the ranks of rambutan, durian, sapote, sapodilla, and other exotic Asian newcomers. These fruits are not generally available in supermarkets yet, but they will occasionally appear in Honolulu's Chinatown and at neighbor-island green markets. The mango is always a much-anticipated feature of late spring and summer. **Hayden mangoes** are universally loved for their plump, juicy flesh and brilliant skins. **White Piries,** with their resinous flavor and fine, fiberless flesh, are even better; this rare and ambrosial variety can be found in Honolulu's Chinatown or at roadside fruit stands in rural Oahu. Watch for the **Rapoza,** a new species of large, sweet, fiberless mango, introduced to Hawaii several years ago. Papaya lovers, take note: **Kahuku papayas**—firm, fleshy, dark orange, and so juicy they sometimes squirt—are the ones to watch for on menus and in markets; check out the roadside stands in Kahuku on Oahu, and at supermarkets. **Sunrise papayas** from Kapoho and Kauai are also top-notch. White, acid-free, extra sweet, and grown on Kauai and the Big Island, **Sugarloaf pineapples** are the new rage. Hilo is the town for **litchis** (also known as lychees) in summer, but Honolulu's Chinatown markets carry them, too. Decidedly Hawaiian are **Ka'u oranges,** grown in the volcanic soil of the southern Big Island and available in supermarkets and health-food stores. Don't be fooled by their brown, ugly skin—they're juicy, thin-skinned, and sweet as honey.

- **Noodles:** Ramen, udon, saimin, pho, pasta, chow mein—Hawaii is the epicenter of ethnic noodle stands and houses, with many recommendable and inexpensive choices. **Jimbo's Restaurant** (Oahu; ✆ **808/947-2211**), a neighborhood staple, is tops for freshly made udon with generous toppings and a homemade broth (p. 151). On the neighbor islands, noodle-mania prevails at **Hamura's Saimin Stand** (Kauai; ✆ **808/245-3271**), where saimin and teriyaki sticks have replaced hamburgers and pizza as the late-night, comfort-food tradition (p. 558). **Nori's Saimin & Snacks** (Big Island; ✆ **808/935-9133**) is charming Hilo's secret for consummate saimin of every stripe (p. 281). And, of course, **Oodles of Noodles** (Big Island; ✆ **808/329-9222**) remains the epitome of noodle heaven (p. 265).

- **Plate Lunches:** For seasoned plate lunchers who favor the traditional "two scoop rice" lunches weighted with carbohydrates and hefty meats, **Zippy's** (21 locations throughout Oahu; call ✆ 808/973-0880 for the one nearest you) is a household word. Other favorite plate-lunch spots on Oahu include **Kaka'ako Kitchen** (✆ 808/596-7488), Ward Centre (p. 143), serving dinner at indoor and outdoor tables; **I ♥ Country Cafe** (✆ 808/596-8108; p. 143); and **Yama's Fish Market** (✆ 808/941-9994), where the chocolate/macadamia nut cookies and chocolate biscotti have legions of fans (p. 215). On Maui, **Pauwela Cafe** (✆ 808/575-9242) serves gourmet feasts from a tiny kitchen, including the best smoked turkey

sandwich in the world (p. 412), while **Aloha Mixed Plate** (✆ 808/661-3322) lets you nosh on fabulous shoyu chicken at ocean's edge—and with a mai tai, too (p. 397). On Kauai, **Pono Market** (✆ 808/822-4581; p. 557), **Fish Express** (✆ 808/245-9918; p. 556), and **Koloa Fish Market** (✆ 808/742-6199; p. 556) are at the top of the plate-lunch pyramid.

- **Shave Ice:** Like surfing, shave ice is synonymous with Haleiwa, the North Shore Oahu town where **Matsumoto Shave Ice** (✆ 808/637-4827; p. 209) and neighboring **Aoki's** (no phone; p. 224) serve mounds of icy treats to long lines of thirsty takers. This tasty and refreshing cultural phenomenon is even better over ice cream and adzuki beans.

- **Other Mighty Morsels:** Poi biscotti from the **Poi Company,** available at supermarkets and gourmet outlets such as Hawaii Regional Cuisine Marketplace (in Liberty House Ala Moana), is a new taste treat, the consummate accompaniment to another island phenomenon, Kona coffee. Coffee growers of highest esteem (all based on the Big Island, of course), include: **Rooster Farms** (✆ 808/328-9173), which sells and ships only organic coffees; **Bong Brothers** (✆ 808/328-9289); **Kona Blue Sky Coffee** (✆ 808/322-1700); **Langenstein Farm** (✆ 808/328-8356); and **Holualoa Kona Coffee Company** (✆ 800/334-0348). See the box "Kona Coffee Craze!," on p. 266.

The buttery, chocolate-dipped shortbread cookies of **Big Island Candies** (Big Island; ✆ 808/935-8890) are worth every calorie and every dollar (p. 343). If you're going through Waimea, don't miss **Cook's Discoveries** (Big Island;

(C) 808/885-3633), where superlatives never end—the best cookies, preserves, vinegars, poi, and many other marvelous taste treats, as well as Hawaiian gift items (p. 338). From Kauai, Hanapepe town's venerable **Taro Ko chips** ((C) 808/335-5586 for the factory) are the crunchy snack neighbor islanders drive long miles to find, then cart home in hand-carried bundles (p. 609). Finally, whether it's takeout stuffed oysters, grilled vegetables, caviar, or designer olive oil you're after, Honolulu's **Strawberry Connection of Hawaii** ((C) 808/521-9777) will reward your search; it's paradise for foodies, chefs, aspiring chefs, and those in pursuit of the best in Hawaii food products.

12 The Best Restaurants

• **Alan Wong's Restaurant** (Oahu; (C) **808/949-2526**): Master strokes at this shrine of Hawaii Regional Cuisine include warm California rolls made with salmon roe, wasabi, and Kona lobster instead of rice; luau lumpia with butterfish and kalua pig; and gingercrusted fresh onaga. Opihi shooters and day-boat scallops in season are a must, and grilled lamb chops are a perennial special. The menu changes daily, but the flavors never lose their sizzle. See p. 150.

• **Chef Mavro Restaurant** (Oahu; (C) 808/944-4714): Honolulu is abuzz over the wine pairings and elegant cuisine of (James Beard award-winner) George Mavrothalassitis, the culinary wizard from Provence who turned La Mer (at the Halekulani) and Seasons (at the Four Seasons Resort Wailea) into temples of fine dining. He brought his award-winning signature dishes with him and continues to prove his ingenuity with dazzling a la carte and prix-fixe ($48–$85) menus. See p. 148.

• **Hoku** (Oahu; (C) **808/739-8780**): Elegant without being stuffy, and creative without being overwrought, the fine-dining room of the Kahala Mandarin offers elegant lunches and dinners, and one of Oahu's best Sunday brunches. This is fusion that really works—European finesse with an island touch. The ocean view, open kitchen, and astonishing bamboo floor are stellar features. Reflecting the restaurant's crosscultural influences, the kitchen is equipped with a *kiawe* grill; an Indian tandoori oven; and Szechuan woks. See p. 153.

• **La Mer** (Oahu; (C) **808/923-2311**): This romantic, elegant dining room at Waikiki's Halekulani is the only AAA Five-Diamond restaurant in the state. The second-floor, open-sided room, with views of Diamond Head and the sound of trade winds rustling the nearby coconut fronds, is the epitome of fine dining. Michelin-award–winning chef Yves Garnier melds classical French influences with fresh island ingredients. It's pricey but worth it. Men are required to wear jackets (they have a selection if you didn't pack one). See p. 129.

• **Padovani's Restaurant & Wine Bar** (Oahu; (C) **808/946-3456**): Chef Philippe Padovani's elegant, innovative style is highlighted in everything from the endive salad to the pan-fried moi at this two-tiered restaurant. Downstairs is a swank dining room with Bernaudaud china and Frette linens; upstairs is an informal Wine Bar with excellent single-malt Scotches, wines by the glass, and a much more casual, but equally sublime, menu. See p. 134.

- **Roy's Restaurant** (Oahu; ✆ **808/396-7697**): Good food still reigns at this busy, noisy flagship Hawaii Kai dining room with the trademark open kitchen. Roy Yamaguchi's deft way with local ingredients, nostalgic ethnic preparations, and fresh fish makes his menu, which changes daily, a novel experience every time. See p. 154.

- **Keei Cafe** (Big Island; ✆ **808/328-8451**). The darling of South Kona is still going strong. Formerly a fish market, Keei Cafe is about as far as you can get from the famous dining rooms of the Kohala resorts, but the food is "so much more ono" as we say in Hawaii, people gladly drive the long distance to eat here. This is Hawaii's version of a bistro, with a friendly, casual ambience, great food, and affordable prices. See p. 268.

- **Merriman's** (Big Island; (✆ **808/885-6822**): Chef Peter Merriman, one of the founders of Hawaii Regional Cuisine, displays his creativity at this Waimea eatery, a premier Hawaii attraction. Dishes include his signature wok-charred ahi, kung pao shrimp, or lamb from nearby Kahua Ranch. His famous platters of seafood and meats are among the many reasons this is still the best, and busiest, dining spot in Waimea. See p. 273.

- **Gerard's** (Maui; ✆ **808/661-8939**): The charm of Gerard's—soft lighting, Edith Piaf on the sound system, excellent service—is matched by a menu of uncompromising standards. A frequent winner of the *Wine Spectator* Award of Excellence, Gerard's offers French cuisine with the chef's own island touches. Housed in an old Victorian house (ask for a table on the lanai outside), Gerard's dreamy, romantic atmosphere and innovative cuisine will linger in your memory. See p. 394.

- **Haliimaile General Store** (Maui; ✆ **808/572-2666**): Bev Gannon, one of the 12 original Hawaii Regional Cuisine chefs, is still going strong at her foodie haven in the pineapple fields. You'll dine at tables set on old wood floors under high ceilings, in a peach-colored room emblazoned with works by local artists. Gannon's Texas roots shine through in her food, a blend of eclectic American with ethnic touches that puts an innovative spin on Hawaii Regional Cuisine. See p. 407.

- **Nick's Fishmarket Maui** (Maui; ✆ **808/879-7224**): This classic seafood restaurant sticks to the tried and true (i.e. *not* an overwrought menu) but stays innovative with excellent ingredients and a high degree of professionalism in service and preparation. The blackened mahimahi has been a Nick's signature for eons, and why not—it's wonderful. The ambience is spectacular: overlooking the ocean with the aroma of sweet-smelling flowers wafting through. A fantasy setting on the south Maui shoreline makes for a romantic evening. See p. 405.

- **Henry Clay's Rotisserie** (Lanai; ✆ **808/565-7211**): Henry Clay Richardson, a New Orleans native, has made some welcome changes to Lanai's dining landscape with his rustic inn in the middle of Lanai City. It's very popular and always full. Maybe that's because it's the only option on Lanai that occupies the vast gap between deli-diner and upscale-luxe. The menu focuses on French-country fare, gourmet pizzas, and crispy salads in a quaint, country-inn atmosphere. See p. 514.

- **A Pacific Cafe Kauai** (Kauai; ℃ **808/822-0013**): The first restaurant Jean-Marie Josselin opened in his burgeoning culinary empire is still the reigning fave. The signature items (tiger-eye sushi, garlic-crisped mahimahi) are staples. Foodies agree: It's the way he uses Kauai produce and seafood that gives this dining room the edge. See p. 564.

- **The Beach House** (Kauai; ℃ **808/742-1424**): This beachfront magnet in Lawai was formerly owned by Jean-Marie Josselin, who sold it to smart Maui restaurateurs who knew a good thing when they saw it. Subscribing to the if-it-ain't-broke-don't-fix-it philosophy, the new owners left the staff and operation intact. There has been a major cosmetic overhaul, the food is as good as ever, and Beach House remains the south shore's premier spot for sunset drinks, appetizers, and dinner—a treat for all the senses. See p. 559.

- **Dondero's** (Kauai; ℃ **808/742-1234**): If you are looking for a romantic dinner either under the stars overlooking the ocean or tucked away in an intimate table surrounded by inlaid marble floors, ornate imported floor tiles, and Franciscan murals, this is your best bet. You get all this atmosphere plus the best Italian cuisine on the island, served with efficiency. It's hard to have a bad experience here. Dinners are pricey and worth every penny. See p. 560.

- **La Cascata** (Kauai; ℃ **808/826-9644**): The North Shore's special-occasion restaurant is sumptuous—a Sicilian spree in Eden. Try to get here before dark, so you can enjoy the views of Bali Hai, the persimmon-colored sunset, and the waterfalls of Waialeale, all an integral part of the feast. Click your heels on the terra-cotta floors, take in the trompe l'oeil vines, train your eyes through the concertina windows, and pretend you're being served on a terrazzo in Sicily. See p. 568.

13 The Best Shops & Galleries

- **The Contemporary Museum and Honolulu Academy of Arts** (Oahu): These two architectural and cultural wonders, legacies of the same *kamaaina* (old-timer) family, house peerless collections in garden settings. For Asian, American, and European masters, go to the Academy; for a look at some of America's most significant art since 1940 (and the prettiest forest drive in Honolulu), TCM is the only game in town. For those who want to buy as well as browse, both museums have stellar shops: The **Academy Shop** (℃ **808/523-8703**) features ethnic and contemporary gift items representing the arts-and-crafts traditions of the world, from basketry and beadwork to ikats and saris. At the **Contemporary Museum Gift Shop** (℃ **808/523-3447**), everything is art: The avant-garde jewelry, stationery, books, and gift items are brilliant, spirited, and functional. See the box "Oahu's Vibrant Art Scene," in chapter 4.

- **Avanti Fashion** (Oahu; ℃ **808/926-6886** and two other Waikiki locations): Avanti aloha shirts and sportswear, in authentic prints from the 1930s and 1940s reproduced on silk, elevate tropical garb from high kick to high chic. Casual, comfortable, easy-care, and light as a cloud, the silks look vintage but cost a fraction of collectibles' prices. These nostalgic treasures are available at many stores statewide, but the best bets are at the three Avanti retail stores in Waikiki. See p. 211.

- **Native Books & Beautiful Things** (Oahu; ✆ **808/596-8885**): Hawaii is the content and the context in this shop of books, crafts, and gift items made by island artists. Musical instruments, calabashes, jewelry, leis, fabrics, clothing, home accessories, jams and jellies—they're all high quality and made in Hawaii. See p. 219.

- **Nohea Gallery** (Oahu; ✆ **808/596-0074** and three other locations): Works by some of the finest artists and craftsmen of Hawaii can be found here. From handcrafted fine jewelry to hair accessories, paintings, hand-blown glass, ceramics, and stunning curly koa furniture, the works are top-drawer. See p. 219.

- **Silver Moon Emporium** (Oahu; ✆ **808/637-7710**): It just keeps getting better at this sleek and chic magnet that's drawing adventurous fashionistas to Haleiwa. Bevies of fans from California, New York, France, and Japan, not to mention Hilo and Honolulu, have left this boutique with hats, handbags, sandals, jewelry, party dresses, beachwear, and the perfect sarong skirt for the perfect backyard luau. See p. 224.

- **Dragon Mama** (Big Island; ✆ **808/934-9081**): All-natural, mostly organic comforters, cushions, futons, fabrics, antique kimono and obi, as well as designer teas and incense, make Dragon Mama the dreamiest of stops in Hilo. The bolts of lavish silks are the most sumptuous you'll find in the islands. See p. 342.

- **Hula Heaven** (Big Island; ✆ **808/329-7885**): You'll turn giddy at Hula Heaven, *the* spot for collectors of Hawaiiana—like aloha shirts, hula-girl lamps, vintage ukuleles, one-of-a-kind 1940s textiles, and Don Blanding dinnerware. It's a celebration of nostalgia. See p. 331.

- **Sig Zane Designs** (Big Island; ✆ **808/935-7077**): Sig Zane never runs out of ideas, inspiration, and energy for his culturally meaningful and visually striking Hawaiian wear. Whether it's a Sig Zane shirt, muumuu, pareu, T-shirt, house slippers, or bedspread, it's uniquely identifiable and imbued with the spirit of Hawaii—like bringing the rain forest into your home. See p. 343.

- **Volcano Art Center** (Big Island; ✆ **808/967-8222**): We love the creaky wooden floors, the smoky scent in the air, the rolling mists, and the art. Thriving in an 1877 building, the art center offers art education, programs and performances, and wondrous works in all media, featuring the most prominent artists on the island. See p. 344.

- **Hui No'eau Visual Arts Center** (Maui; ✆ **808/572-6560**): Upcountry in Makawao, this 1917 Mediterranean manse on a 9-acre estate is part gallery, part exhibition space, and part gift shop, classrooms, and demonstration center—and every inch is a paean to beauty. See p. 464.

- **Hana Coast Gallery** (Maui; ✆ **808/248-8636**): The long and winding road to Hana leads to the Hotel Hana-Maui, where the works in the Hana Coast Gallery reflect a deep commitment to Hawaii's cultural art. Native Hawaiian artists and master craftspeople have a presence and integrity here unlike any other gallery in the islands. See p. 467.

- **Ola's** (Kauai, ✆ **808/826-6937**): Fine crafts from across the country find their way to this temple of good taste: lamps, vases, blown glass, drum sticks, jewelry, hard-to-find books, and the peerless paintings of award-winning artist Doug Britt. See p. 612.
- **Bambulei** (Kauai; ✆ **808/823-8641**): Celebrate the charm and style of 1930s to 1940s collectibles in this treasure trove at the edge of the cane field. Fabulous one-of-a-kind vintage finds—Mandarin dresses with hand-sewn sequins, 1940s "pake muumuus" in mint condition, Peking lacquerware, Bakelite jewelry—fill this jewel of a boutique, owned by two women with a passion for the past. See p. 610.
- **Kong Lung** (Kauai; ✆ **808/828-1822**): You'll be surprised by what you find inside this 1922 stone building: a showcase of design, style, and quality items, from dinnerware, books, jewelry, and clothing to the finest sake and tea sets on the island. Throw in a lacquer bowl or two, a pair of beaded sandals, and a silk dress from the women's section, and the party's on at "Gump's of the Pacific." See p. 611.
- **Robert Hamada's Studio** (Kauai; ✆ **808/822-3229**): Wood turner Robert Hamada makes works of art for wood purists: museum-quality bowls and large sculptural shapes in kou, milo, kauila, camphor, mango, and native woods he logs himself. He works in his studio at the foot of the Sleeping Giant, quietly producing luminous pieces with unique textures and grains. His skill, his lathe, and his more than 60 years of experience put him in a class of his own. See p. 610.
- **Yellowfish Trading Company** (Kauai; ✆ **808/826-1227**): Surprise yourself at Yellowfish Trading Company, where vintage bark cloth and that one-of-a-kind 1940s rattan sofa are among owner Gritt Benton's short-lived pleasures. The collectibles—1940s vases, '50s lunch boxes, '30s lampshades, antique silk piano shawls—move quickly. See p. 612.

14 The Best Spots for Sunset Cocktails

- **Duke's Canoe Club,** at the Outrigger Waikiki (Oahu; ✆ **808/922-2268**): It's crowded in the evening, but who can resist Hawaiian music with Waikiki sand still on your feet? Come in from the beach or the street—it's always a party at Duke's. Entertainment here is tops, reaching a crescendo at sunset. See "Hawaiian Music" under "Oahu After Dark," in chapter 4.
- **House Without a Key,** at the Halekulani (Oahu; ✆ **808/923-2311**): Oahu's quintessential sunset oasis, located outdoors on the ocean, offers a view of Diamond Head, great hula and steel-guitar music, and the best mai tais on the island—all under a century-old kiawe tree. Even jaded locals are unable to resist the lure. See "Bars" under "Oahu After Dark," in chapter 4.
- **Mai Tai Bar,** at the Royal Hawaiian Hotel (Oahu; ✆ **808/923-7311**): This bar without walls is perched a few feet from the sand, with views of the South Shore and the Waianae Mountains. Surfers and paddlers ride the waves while Diamond Head acquires a golden sunset halo. This is one of the most pleasing views of Waikiki Beach; sip a mighty mai tai while Carmen and Keith Haugen serenade you. See "Bars" under "Oahu After Dark," in chapter 4.

- **Sunset Lanai Lounge,** at the New Otani Kaimana Beach Hotel (Oahu; ✆ **808/923-1555**): The hau tree here shaded Robert Louis Stevenson as he wrote poems to Princess Kaiulani; today, it frames the ocean view from the Sunset Lanai Lounge, next to the Hau Tree Lanai restaurant. This lounge is the favorite watering hole of Diamond Head–area beachgoers, who love Sans Souci beach, the ocean view, the mai tais, and the live music during weekend sunset hours. See p. 121.

- **Jameson's by the Sea** (Oahu; ✆ **808/637-6272**): The mai tais here are dubbed the best in surf city, and the view, though not perfect, doesn't hurt either. Across the street from the harbor, this open-air roadside oasis is a happy stop for North Shore wave-watchers and sunset-savvy sightseers. See p. 156.

- **Huggo's on the Rocks** (Big Island; ✆ **808/329-1493**): Here's a thatched-bar fantasy that's *really* on the rocks. This mound of thatch, rock, and grassy-sandy ground right next to Huggo's restaurant is a sunset lover's nirvana. Sip a tropical drink while reclining on a chaise and nosh on island-style appetizers while the ocean laps at your feet. See p. 264.

- **Beach Tree Bar and Grill,** at the Four Seasons Resort Hualalai (Big Island; ✆ **808/325-8000**): The bar on the beach seats only a handful, but the restaurant will accept the overflow. This is the finest sunset perch in North Kona, with consummate people-watching, waterbirds strutting by, tasty drinks, and the gorgeous ocean. The open-air restaurant, with Hawaiian music and hula dancing at sunset, also serves excellent fare. See p. 262.

- **Kimo's** (Maui; ✆ **808/661-4811**): An oceanfront dining room and deck, upstairs dining, and happy-hour drinks draw a fun-loving Lahaina crowd. Nibble on sashimi or nachos and take in the views of Lanai and Molokai from this West Maui institution. See p. 397.

- **Hula Grill** (Maui; ✆ **808/667-6636**): Sit outdoors at the Barefoot Bar, order drinks and macadamia nut/crab wontons, and marvel at the wonders of West Maui, where the sun sets slowly and Lanai looks like a giant whale offshore. It's simply magical. See p. 399.

15 The Best Hawaii Websites

- **Hawaii Visitors & Convention Bureau** (www.gohawaii.com): This site provides an excellent, all-around guide to activities, tours, lodging, and events, plus a huge section on weddings and honeymoons. But keep in mind that only members of the HVCB are listed.

- **Planet Hawaii** (www.planet-hawaii.com): Click on "Island" for an island-by-island guide to activities, lodging, shopping, culture, the surf report, weather, and more. Mostly, you'll find short listings with links to companies' own websites. Click on "Hawaiian Eye" for live images from around the islands.

- **Internet Hawaii Radio** (www.hotspots.hawaii.com): A great way to get into the mood, this eclectic site features great Hawaiian music, with opportunities to order a CD or cassette. You can also purchase a respectable assortment of Hawaiian historical and cultural books.

- **Visit Oahu (www.visit-oahu. com)**: This site provides an extensive guide to activities, dining, lodging, parks, shopping, and more from the Oahu chapter of the Hawaii Visitors and Convention Bureau.
- **Big Island Home Page (www.big island.com)**: Though not the most beautifully designed site, it does include lots of listings for dining, lodging, and activities, most with links to more information and images.
- **Maui Island Currents (www. islandcurrents.com)**: Specializing in arts and culture, Island Currents gives the most detailed lowdown on current exhibitions and performance art. Gallery listings are organized by town, while in-depth articles highlight local artists. Consult restaurant reviews from the *Maui News* "Best of Maui" poll for suggestions and prices.
- **Maui Net (www.maui.net)**: The clients of this Internet service provider are featured in this extensive directory of links to accommodations, activities, and shopping. The Activity Desk has links to golf, hiking, airborne activities, and ocean adventures, such as scuba and snorkeling. These links lead to outfitters' sites, where you can learn more and set up excursions before you arrive.
- **Molokai: The Most Hawaiian Island (www.molokai-hawaii. com)**: This is a very complete site for activities, events, nightlife, accommodations, and family vacations. Enjoy the landscape by viewing a virtual photo tour, get driving times between various points, and learn about local history.
- **Kauai: Island of Discovery (www.kauai-hawaii.com)**: Extensive listings cover activities, events, recreation, attractions, beaches, and much more. The Vacation Directory includes information on golf, fishing, and island tours; some listings include e-mail addresses and links to websites. You'll also find a clickable map of the island with listings organized by region.
- **The Hawaiian Language Website (http://hawaiianlanguage. com)**: This fabulous site not only has easy lessons on learning the Hawaiian language but also a great cultural calendar, links to other Hawaiiana websites, a section on the hula, and lyrics (and translations) to Hawaiian songs.

2

Planning Your Trip to Hawaii

Hawaii has so many places to explore, things to do, sights to see—it can be bewildering to plan your trip with so much vying for your attention. Where to start? That's where we come in. In the pages that follow, we've compiled everything you need to know to plan your ideal trip to Hawaii.

The first thing to do: Decide where you want to go. You may stare at a map of Hawaii, looking at the six major islands—Oahu, the Big Island of Hawaii, Maui, Molokai, Lanai, and Kauai—and wonder how to choose. Each island is distinct from the others and has its own personality, which we've tried to capture in the chapters that follow. Read through each chapter (especially each chapter introduction) to see which islands fit the profile and offer the activities that you're looking for.

We strongly recommend that you **limit your island-hopping to one island per week.** If you decide to go to more than one in a week, be warned: You could spend much of your precious vacation time in airports, waiting to board flights and for your luggage to arrive, and checking in and out of hotels. Not much fun!

Our second tip is to **fly directly to the island of your choice;** doing so can save you a 2-hour layover in Honolulu and another plane ride. Oahu, the Big Island, Maui, and Kauai now all receive direct flights from the mainland; if you're heading to Molokai or Lanai, you'll have the easiest connections if you fly into Honolulu.

So let's get on with the process of planning your trip. We fully believe that searching out the best deals and planning your dream vacation to Hawaii should be half the fun.

1 Visitor Information

For information about traveling in Hawaii, contact the **Hawaii Visitors and Convention Bureau (HVCB),** Suite 801, Waikiki Business Plaza, 2270 Kalakaua Ave., Honolulu, HI 96815 (© **800/GO-HAWAII** or 808/ 923-1811; www.gohawaii.com). The bureau publishes the helpful *Accommodations and Car Rental Guide* and supplies free brochures, maps, and the *Islands of Aloha* magazine, the official HVCB magazine. If you want information about working and living in Hawaii, contact the **Chamber of Commerce of Hawaii,** 1132 Bishop St., Suite 402, Honolulu, HI 96813 (© **808/545-4300**).

INFORMATION ON HAWAII'S PARKS

Hawaii has several national parks and historic sites—four on the Big Island, one each on Maui, Oahu, and Molokai. The following offices can supply you with hiking and camping information:

- On the **Big Island:** Hawaii Volcanoes **National Park,** P.O. Box 52, Hawaii National Park, HI 96718 (© **808/985-6000;** www. nps.gov/havo); **Puuhonua o Honaunau National Historical Park,** P.O. Box 129, Honaunau,

HI 96726 (© **808/328-2326;** www.nps.gov/puho); **Puukohola Heiau National Historic Site,** P.O. Box 44340, Kawaihae, HI 96743 (© **808/882-7218;** www. nps.gov/puhe); and **Kaloko-Honokohau National Historical Park,** 72–4786 Kanalani St., Kailua-Kona, HI 96740 (© **808/ 329-6881;** www.nps.gov/kaho).

- On **Maui: Haleakala National Park,** P.O. Box 369, Makawao, HI 96768 (© **808/572-9306;** www.nps.gov/hale).
- On **Molokai: Kalaupapa National Historical Park,** P.O. Box 2222, Kalaupapa, HI 96742 (© **808/ 567-6802;** www.nps.gov/kala).
- On **Oahu: USS** *Arizona* **Memorial at Pearl Harbor,** (© **808/422- 0561;** www.nps.gov/usar).

To find out more about Hawaii's state parks, contact the **Hawaii State Department of Land and Natural Resources,** 1151 Punchbowl St., no. 130, Honolulu, HI 96813 (© **808/ 587-0300;** www.hawaii.gov). The office can provide you with information on hiking and camping at the parks and will send you free topographic trail maps.

HAWAII ON THE WEB

Listed below are some of the most useful sites.

- **Hawaii Visitors & Convention Bureau:** www.gohawaii.com
- **Hawaii State Vacation Planner:** www.hshawaii.com
- **Planet Hawaii:** www.planet-hawaii.com
- **Oahu Visitors Bureau:** www.visit-oahu.com
- Big Island's **Kona-Kohala Resort Association:** www.kkra.org
- **Big Island Visitors Bureau:** www.bigisland.org
- **Maui Visitors Bureau:** www.visit maui.com
- **Maui information:** www.maui.net
- **Maui's Kaanapali Beach Resort Association:** www.maui.net/~kbra
- **Molokai information:** www.molokai-hawaii.com
- **Kauai Visitors Bureau:** www.kauaivisitorsbureau.org
- Kauai's **Poipu Beach Resort Association:** www.poipu-beach.org
- **Weather information:** http://lumahai.soest.hawaii.edu/index.html or www.weather.com or www.cnn.com/WEATHER

2 Money

ATMS

Hawaii pioneered the use of automated-teller machines (ATMs) more than 2 decades ago, and now they're everywhere. You'll find them at most banks, in supermarkets, at Long's Drugs, at Honolulu International Airport, and in some resorts and shopping centers, such as Ala Moana Center and Aloha Tower Market Place on Oahu, and Whalers Village in Kaanapali, Maui.

To find the ATM location nearest you, call © **800/424-7787** for the **Cirrus** network or © **800/843-7587** for the **PLUS** system. You can also

locate Cirrus ATMs on the Web at **www.mastercard.com/cardholder services/atm** and PLUS ATMs at **www.visa.com/atms**.

The U.S. dollar is the coin of the realm in Hawaii, but you can easily exchange most major foreign currencies (see "Money," in chapter 3).

TRAVELER'S CHECKS

Traveler's checks are something of an anachronism from the days before the ATM made cash accessible at any time. Traveler's checks used to be the only sound alternative to traveling with dangerously large amounts of cash. They were as reliable as currency, but, unlike cash, could be replaced if lost or stolen.

These days, traveler's checks are less necessary because most cities have 24-hour ATMs that allow you to withdraw small amounts of cash as needed. However, keep in mind that you will likely be charged an ATM withdrawal fee if the bank is not your own, so if you're withdrawing money every day, you might be better off with traveler's checks—provided that you don't mind showing identification every time you want to cash one.

You can get traveler's checks at almost any bank. **American Express** charges a service fee ranging from 1% to 4%. You can also get American Express traveler's checks over the phone by calling ⓒ **800/221-7282;** Amex gold and platinum cardholders who use this number are exempt from the service fee. AAA members can obtain checks without a fee at most AAA offices.

Visa offers traveler's checks at Citibank locations nationwide, as well as at several other banks. The service charge ranges between 1.5% and 2%. Call ⓒ **800/732-1322** for information. **MasterCard** also offers traveler's checks. Call ⓒ **800/223-9920** for a location near you.

If you choose to carry traveler's checks, be sure to keep a record of their serial numbers separate from your checks in the event that they are stolen or lost. You'll get a refund faster if you know the numbers.

CREDIT CARDS

Credit cards are a safe way to carry money. They provide a convenient record of all your expenses and generally offer good exchange rates. You can also withdraw cash advances from your credit cards at banks or ATMs, provided you know your PIN. If you've forgotten yours or didn't even know you had one, call the number on the back of your credit card and ask the bank to send it to you. It usually takes 5 to 7 business days, though some banks will provide the number over the phone if you tell them your mother's maiden name or some other personal information.

3 When to Go

Most visitors don't come to Hawaii when the weather's best in the islands; rather, they come when it's at its worst everywhere else. Thus, the **high season**—when prices are up and resorts are often booked to capacity—is generally from mid-December through March or mid-April. The last 2 weeks of December in particular are the prime time for travel to Hawaii. If you're planning a holiday trip, make your reservations as early as possible, expect crowds, and prepare to pay top dollar for accommodations, car rentals, and airfare.

The **off season,** when the best bargain rates are available and the islands are less crowded, is spring (from mid-Apr to mid-June) and fall (from Sept to mid-Dec)—a paradox, since these are the best seasons to be in Hawaii, in terms of reliably great weather. If you're looking to save money, or if you just want to avoid the crowds, this is the time to visit. Hotel rates and airfares tend to be significantly lower; good packages and special deals are often available.

Note: If you plan to come to Hawaii between the last week in April and mid-May, be sure you book your accommodations, interisland air reservations, and car rentals in advance. In Japan, the last week of April is called **Golden Week,** because three Japanese holidays take place one after the other. Waikiki is especially busy with Japanese tourists during this time, but the neighbor islands also see dramatic increases.

> **Tips** Travel Tip
>
> Your best bets for total year-round sun are **Waikiki Beach** and the **Ko Olina** (southwest) coast of Oahu, the Big Island's **Kona–Kohala Coast,** the south (**Kihei–Wailea**) and west (**Lahaina–Kapalua**) Maui coasts, and **Poipu Beach** and the southwest coast of Kauai.

Due to the large number of families traveling in **summer** (June through August), you won't get the fantastic bargains of spring and fall. However, you'll still do much better on packages, airfare, and accommodations than you will in the winter months.

CLIMATE

Since Hawaii lies at the edge of the tropical zone, it technically has only two seasons, both of them warm. There's a dry season that corresponds to **summer,** and a rainy season in **winter** from November to March. It rains every day somewhere in the islands any time of the year, but the rainy season sometimes brings gray weather that can spoil your tanning opportunities. Fortunately, it seldom rains in one spot for more than 3 days straight.

The **year-round temperature** usually varies no more than 15°. At the beach, the average daytime high in summer is 85°F (29°C), while the average daytime high in winter is 78°F (26°C); nighttime lows are usually about 10° cooler. But how warm it is on any given day really depends on *where* you are on the island.

Each island has a leeward side (the side sheltered from the wind) and a windward side (the side that gets the wind's full force). The **leeward** sides (the west and south) are usually hot and dry, while the **windward** sides (east and north) are generally cooler and moist. When you want arid, sunbaked, desertlike weather, go leeward. When you want lush, sometimes wet, junglelike weather, go windward.

Hawaii is also full of **microclimates,** thanks to its interior valleys, coastal plains, and mountain peaks. Kauai's Mount Waialeale is the wettest spot on earth, yet Waimea Canyon, just a few miles away, is almost a desert. On the Big Island, Hilo is the wettest city in the nation, with 180 inches of rainfall a year, while at Puako, only 60 miles away, it rains less than 6 inches a year. If you travel into the mountains, the climate can change from summer to winter in a matter of hours because it's cooler the higher you go. So, if the weather doesn't suit you, just go to the other side of the island—or head into the hills.

On rare occasions, the weather can be disastrous, as when Hurricane Iniki crushed Kauai in September 1992 with 225 mph winds. Tsunamis, huge tidal waves caused by far-off earthquakes, have swept Hilo and the south shore of Oahu. But those are extreme exceptions. Mostly, one day follows another here in glorious, sunny procession, each quite like the other.

HOLIDAYS

When Hawaii observes holidays (especially those over a long weekend), travel between the islands increases, interisland airline seats are fully booked, rental cars are at a premium, and hotels and restaurants are busier.

Federal, state, and county government offices are closed on all federal holidays: January 1 (New Year's Day), the third Monday in January (Martin Luther King Jr. Day), the third Monday in February (Presidents' Day, Washington's Birthday), the last Monday in May (Memorial Day), July 4th (Independence Day), the first Monday in September (Labor Day), the second Monday in October (Columbus Day), November 11 (Veteran's Day), the fourth Thursday in November (Thanksgiving Day), and December 25 (Christmas).

State and county offices are also closed on local holidays, including Prince Kuhio Day (March 26), honoring the birthday of Hawaii's first delegate to the U.S. Congress; King Kamehameha Day (June 11), a statewide holiday commemorating Kamehameha the Great, who united the islands and ruled from 1795 to 1819; and Admissions Day (the 3rd Fri in Aug), which honors the admittance of Hawaii as the 50th state on August 21, 1959.

Other special days celebrated in Hawaii by many people but which involve no closing of federal, state, and county offices are the Chinese New Year (which can fall in Jan or Feb; in 2004, it's Jan 22), Girls' Day (Mar 3), Buddha's Birthday (Apr 8), Father Damien's Day (Apr 15), Boys' Day (May 5), Samoan Flag Day (in Aug), Aloha Festivals (in Sept and Oct), and Pearl Harbor Day (Dec 7).

HAWAII CALENDAR OF EVENTS

Please note that, as with any schedule of upcoming events, the following information is subject to change; always confirm the details before you plan your trip around an event. For a complete and up-to-date list of events throughout the islands, check out **www.calendar.gohawaii.com**.

January

Morey World Bodyboarding Championship, Banzai Pipeline, North Shore, Oahu. Competition is determined by the best wave selection and maneuvers on the wave. Call © **808/396-2326.** Early January.

PGA Kapalua Mercedes Championship, Kapalua Resort, Maui. Top PGA golfers compete for $1 million.

Call © **808/669-2440; www.kapaluamaui.com**. January 5–11, 2004.

Sony Open, Waialae Country Club, Oahu. A $1.2-million PGA golf event featuring the top men in golf. Call © **808/734-2151; www.sonyopenhawaii.com**. January 12–18, 2004.

MasterCard Championship, Jack Nicklaus Signature Course, Four Seasons Resort Hualalai, Kona, Big Island. Formerly known as the Tournament of Champions, this is the season-opening competition for golfers who have won a Senior PGA Tour event. Call © **800/417-2770** or 808/325-8000; www.pgatour. com. January 19–25, 2004.

Chinese New Year, Maui. Lahaina town rolls out the red carpet for this important event with a traditional lion dance at the historic Wo Hing Temple on Front Street, accompanied by fireworks, food booths, and a host of activities. Call © **888/310-1117** or 808/667-9175. Also on Market Street in Wailuku, call © **808/270-7414.** On Oahu, a big celebration takes place in Chinatown; call © **808/533-3181** for details. January 22, 2004, starts the year of the monkey.

Narcissus Festival, Honolulu, Oahu. Taking place around the Chinese New Year, this cultural festival includes a queen pageant, cooking demonstrations, and a cultural fair. Call © **808/533-3181** for details.

Ka Molokai Makahiki, Kaunakakai Town Baseball Park, Mitchell Pauole Center, Kaunakakai, Molokai. Makahiki, a traditional time of peace in ancient Hawaii, is re-created with performances by Hawaiian music groups and hula halau, ancient Hawaiian games, a sporting competition, and

Hawaiian crafts and food. It's a wonderful chance to experience the Hawaii of yesteryear. Call ✆ **800/800-6367** or 808/553-3876, www.molokai-hawaii.com. Late January.

Ala Wai Challenge, Ala Wai Park, Waikiki, Oahu. This all-day event features ancient Hawaiian games, like *ulu maika* (bowling a round stone through pegs), *oo ihe* (spear-throwing at an upright target), *huki kaula* (tug of war), and a quarter-mile outrigger canoe race. It's also a great place to hear Hawaiian music. Call ✆ **808/923-1802.** Last weekend in January.

Senior Skins Tournament, Gold Course, Wailea Golf Courses, Maui. Longtime golfing greats participate in this four-man tournament for $600,000 in prize money. Call ✆ **800/332-1614; www.seniorskinswailea.com.** January 31, 2004.

Hula Bowl Football All-Star Classic, War Memorial Stadium, Maui. An annual all-star football classic featuring America's top college players. Call ✆ **808/871-4141; www.hulabowlmaui.com**; ticket orders are processed beginning April 1 for the next year's game, January 31, 2004.

February

NFL Pro Bowl, Aloha Stadium, Honolulu, Oahu. The National Football League's best pro players square off in this annual gridiron all-star game. Call ✆ **808/486-9300; www.nfl.com**.

Waimea Town Celebration, Waimea, Kauai. This annual party on Kauai's west side celebrates the Hawaiian and multiethnic history of the town where Captain Cook first landed. This is the island's biggest 2-day event, drawing some 10,000 people. Top Hawaiian entertainers, sporting events, rodeo,

and lots of food are on tap during the weekend celebration. Call ✆ **808/245-3971.**

Sand Castle Building Contest, Kailua Beach Park, Oahu. Students from the University of Hawaii School of Architecture compete against professional architects to see who can build the best, most unusual, and most outrageous sand sculpture. Call ✆ **808/956-7225.**

Punahou School Carnival, Punahou School, Honolulu. This event has everything you can imagine in a school carnival, from high-speed rides to homemade jellies. All proceeds go to scholarship funds for Hawaii's most prestigious high school. Call ✆ **808/944-5753.**

The Great Aloha Run, Oahu. Thousands run 8¼ miles from Aloha Tower to Aloha Stadium. Call ✆ **808/528-7388.** Presidents' Day (3rd Mon in Feb).

Buffalo's Big Board Classic, Makaha Beach, Oahu. This contest involves traditional Hawaiian surfing, long boarding, and canoe-surfing. Call ✆ **808/951-7877.** Depending on the surf, it can be held in February or March.

Whalefest Week, Maui. This event celebrates Maui's best-known winter visitors, the humpback whales. Activities include seminars, art exhibits, sailing, snorkeling and diving tours, and numerous events for children. Call ✆ **808/667-9175** or 808/879-8860, www.calendarmaui.com. February or March.

March

Run to the Sun, Paia to Haleakala, Maui. The world's top ultra-marathoners make the journey from sea level to the top of 10,000 foot Haleakala in 37 miles. Call ✆ **808/573-7584** or 808/741-2726 or www.virr.com.

East Maui Taro Festival, Hana, Maui. Taro, a Hawaiian staple food, is celebrated through music, hula, arts, crafts, and, of course, food. Call ℂ **808/248-8972;** www.taro festival.org.

Hawaii Challenge International Sportkite Championship, Kapiolani Park, Oahu. The longest-running sportkite competition in the world attracts top kite pilots from around the globe. Call ℂ **808/ 735-9059.** First weekend in March.

Annual St. Patrick's Day Parade, Waikiki (Fort DeRussy to Kapiolani Park), Oahu. Bagpipers, bands, clowns, and marching groups parade through the heart of Waikiki, with lots of Irish celebrating all day. Call ℂ **808/524-0722.** March 17.

Kona Brewer's Festival, King Kamehameha's Kona Beach Hotel Luau Grounds, Kailua-Kona, Big Island. This annual event features microbreweries from around the world, with beer tastings, food, and entertainment. Call ℂ **808/334-1133.** Second Saturday in March.

Prince Kuhio Celebrations, all islands. Various festivals throughout the state celebrate the birth of Jonah Kuhio Kalanianaole, who was born on March 26, 1871, and elected to Congress in 1902. Kauai, his birthplace, stages a huge celebration in Lihue; call ℂ **808/826-9272** for details. Molokai also hosts a daylong celebration; call ℂ **808/ 553-5215** to learn more.

April

Buddha Day, Lahaina Jodo Mission, Lahaina, Maui. Each year, this historic mission holds a flower festival pageant honoring the birth of Buddha. Call ℂ **808/661-4303.** First Saturday in April.

Annual Ritz-Carlton Kapalua Celebration of the Arts, Ritz-Carlton Kapalua, Maui. Contemporary and traditional artists give free hands-on lessons. Call ℂ **808/669-6200.** The 4-day festival begins the Thursday before Easter.

Annual Easter Sunrise Service, National Cemetery of the Pacific, Punchbowl Crater, Honolulu, Oahu. For a century, people have gathered at this famous cemetery for Easter sunrise services. Call ℂ **808/566-1430.**

Merrie Monarch Hula Festival, Hilo, Big Island. Hawaii's biggest hula festival features 3 nights of modern (*auana*) and ancient (*kahiko*) dance competition in honor of King David Kalakaua, the "Merrie Monarch" who revived the dance. Tickets sell out by January 30, so reserve early. Call ℂ **808/ 935-9168.** The week after Easter.

David Malo Day, Lahainaluna High School, Lahaina, Maui. This day-long event with hula and other Hawaiian cultural celebrations commemorates Hawaii's famous scholar and ends with a luau. Mid-April. Call ℂ **808/662-4000.**

Honolulu International Bed Race Festival, Honolulu, Oahu. This popular fund-raiser event allows visitors a small taste of Honolulu, with food booths sponsored by local restaurants, live entertainment, a *keiki* (children's) carnival with games and rides, and a race through the streets of Honolulu with runners pushing beds to raise money for local charities. Call ℂ **808/696-2424.** Mid-April.

Ulupalakua Thing! Maui County Agricultural Trade Show and Sampling, Ulupalakua Ranch and Tedeschi Winery, Ulupalakua, Maui. The name may be long and cumbersome, but this event is hot, hot, hot. It features local product exhibits, food booths, and live entertainment. Call ℂ **808/875-0457.** Last Saturday in April.

May

Outrigger Canoe Season, all islands. From May to September, nearly every weekend, canoe paddlers across the state participate in outrigger canoe races. Call © **808/ 261-6615,** or go to www.y2kanu. com for this year's schedule of events.

Annual Lei Day Celebrations, various locations on all islands. May Day is Lei Day in Hawaii, celebrated with lei-making contests, pageantry, arts and crafts, and the real highlight, a Brothers Cazimero concert at the Waikiki Shell. Call © **808/924-8934** or 808/524-0722 for Oahu events (© 808/ 597-1888 for the Brothers Cazimero show); © **808/886-1655** for Big Island events; © **808/879-1922** for Maui events; and © **808/ 245-6931** for Kauai events. May 1.

World Fire-Knife Dance Championships and Samoan Festival, Polynesian Cultural Center, Laie, Oahu. Junior and adult fire-knife dancers from around the world converge on the center for one of the most amazing performances you'll ever see. Authentic Samoan food and cultural festivities round out the fun. Call © **808/293-3333;** www.polynesianculturalcenter.com. Mid-May.

In Celebration of Canoes, West Maui. Celebration of the Pacific islands' seafaring heritage. Events include canoe paddling and sailing regattas, a luau feast, cultural arts demonstrations, canoe-building exhibits, and music. Call © **888/ 310-1117;** www.calendarmaui.com. Mid- to late May.

Molokai Ka Hula Piko, Papohaku Beach Park, Kaluakoi, Molokai. This daylong celebration of the hula takes place on the island where it was born. It features performances by hula schools, musicians, and singers from across Hawaii as well as local food and Hawaiian crafts, including quilting, woodworking, feather work, and deerhorn scrimshaw. Call © **800/800-6367** or 808/553-3876; www. molokai-hawaii.com. Third Saturday in May.

Memorial Day, National Memorial Cemetery of the Pacific, Punchbowl, Honolulu, Oahu. The armed forces hold a ceremony recognizing those who died for their country, beginning at 9am. Call © **808/ 532-3720.**

June

Hawaiian Slack-Key Guitar Festival, Maui Arts and Cultural Center, Kahului, Maui. Great music performed by the best musicians in Hawaii. It's 5 hours long and absolutely free. Call © **808/239-4336** or e-mail kahokuproductions@ yahoo.com.

King Kamehameha Celebration, all islands. It's a state holiday with a massive floral parade, *hoolaulea* (party), and much more. Call © **808/586-0333** for Oahu events, © **808/329-1603** for Big Island events, © **808/667-9175** for Maui events, © **808/553-3876** for Molokai events, and © **808/245-3971** for Kauai events, or visit www.state.hi.us/dags/kkcc. First weekend in June.

Maui Film Festival, Wailea Resort, Maui. Five days and nights of screenings of premieres and special films, along with traditional Hawaiian storytelling, chants, hula and contemporary music. Call © **808/ 579-9996; www.mauifilmfestival. com.** June 16–20, 2004.

King Kamehameha Hula Competition, Neal Blaisdell Center, Honolulu, Oahu. This is one of the top hula competitions in the world, with dancers from as far away as Japan. Call © **808/586-0333;**

www.state.hi.us/dags/kkcc. Third weekend in June.

Taste of Honolulu, Civic Center Grounds, Honolulu, Oahu. Hawaii's premier outdoor food festival features tastings from 30 restaurants, as well as entertainment, beer and wine tastings, cooking demos, a gourmet marketplace, and children's activities. Call ☏ **808/536-1015; www. easterseals.org**. End of June.

July

Parker Ranch Rodeo, Waimea, Big Island. This is a hot rodeo competition in the heart of cowboy country. Call ☏ **808/885-7311** or go to www.rodeohawaii.com.

Hawaiian Slack-Key Guitar Festival, King Kamehameha's Kona Beach Hotel, Kona, Big Island. The best of Hawaii's folk music (slack-key guitar) performed by the best musicians in Hawaii. It's 5 hours long and absolutely free. Call ☏ **808/239-4336** or e-mail kahokuproductions@yahoo.com.

Makawao Parade and Rodeo, Makawao, Maui. The annual parade and rodeo event have been taking place in this upcountry cowboy town for generations. Call ☏ **800/525-Maui** or 808/244-3530.

Hoolaulea O Ke Kai-A Molokai Sea Fest, Kaunakakai, Molokai. Canoe races, windsurfing competition, Hawaiian music, and food are offered at this daylong celebration of the sea. Call ☏ **800/800-6367,** 800/553-0404 (interisland), or 808/553-3876; www.molokai-hawaii.com.

Kapalua Wine and Food Festival, Kapalua, Maui. Famous wine and food experts and oenophiles gather at the Ritz-Carlton and Kapalua Bay hotels for formal tastings, panel discussions, and samplings of new releases. Call ☏ **800/KAPALUA;** www.kapaluaresort.com.

Fourth of July Fireworks, Desiderio and Sills Field, Schofield Barracks, Oahu. A free daylong celebration, with entertainment, food, and games, ends with a spectacular fireworks show. Call ☏ **808/656-0110.**

Turtle Independence Day, Mauna Lani Resort and Bungalows, Kohala Coast, Big Island. Scores of endangered green sea turtles, which have been raised in captivity, race down to the sea each year when they're released from the historic fish ponds at Mauna Lani. Call ☏ **808/ 885-6677; www.maunalani.com**. July 4.

Great Waikoloa Food, Wine & Music Festival, Hilton Waikoloa Village, Big Island. One of the Big Island's best food and wine festivals features Hawaii's top chefs (and a few mainland chefs) showing off their culinary talents, wines from around the world, and an excellent jazz concert with fireworks. Not to be missed. Call ☏ **808/886-1234;** www.hiltonwaikoloavillage.com. Weekend closest to July 4th.

Hawaii International Jazz Festival, Sheraton Waikiki, Honolulu, Oahu. This festival includes evening concerts and daily jam sessions plus scholarship giveaways, the University of Southern California jazz band, and many popular jazz and blues artists. Call ☏ **808/ 941-9974.** Mid-July.

Prince Lot Hula Festival, Moanalua Gardens, Honolulu, Oahu. Authentic ancient and modern hula, as well as demonstrations and arts and crafts are some of the things you'll encounter at this festival. It's a good alternative to April's much better known (and much more crowded) Merrie Monarch Hula Festival. Call ☏ **808/839-5334.** Third Sunday in July.

Ukulele Festival, Kapiolani Park Bandstand, Waikiki, Oahu. This free concert has some 600 kids (ages 4–92) strumming the ukulele. Hawaii's top musicians all pitch in. Call ✆ **808/732-3739** or check out www.ukulele-roysakuma.com. Last Sunday in July.

Crater Rim Run and Marathon, Hawaii Volcanoes National Park, Big Island. Some 1,000 runners from around the globe line up to compete in 5-, 10- and 26.2-mile races over uneven lava terrain, up the walls of volcanic craters, and through lush rain forests. Call ✆ **808/967-8222.** Late July.

August

Queen Liliuokalani Keiki Hula Competition, Neal Blaisdell Center, Honolulu, Oahu. More than 500 *keiki* (children) representing 22 *halau* (hula schools) from the islands compete in this dance fest. The event is broadcast a week later on KITV-TV. Call ✆ **808/521-6905.** Early August or last weekend in July.

Hawaii State Farm Fair, Aloha Stadium, Honolulu, Oahu. The annual state fair is a great one: It features displays of Hawaii agricultural products (including orchids), educational and cultural exhibits, entertainment, and local-style food. Call ✆ **808/531-3531.** Early August.

Annual Hawaiian International Billfish Tournament, Kailua-Kona, Big Island. One of the world's most prestigious billfish tournaments, the HIBT attracts teams from around the globe. Call ✆ **808/329-7371; www.kona billfish.com**. August 7–14, 2004.

Puukohola Heiau National Historic Site Anniversary Celebration, Kawaihae, Big Island. This is a weekend of Hawaiian crafts, workshops, and games. Call ✆ **808/882-7218.** Mid-August.

Admissions Day, all islands. Hawaii became the 50th state on August 21, 1959. The state takes a holiday (all state-related facilities are closed) on the third Friday in August.

Style Hawaiian Slack-Key Guitar Festival, Sheraton Waikiki, Oahu. The best of Hawaii's folk music (slack-key guitar) performed by the best musicians in Hawaii. It's 5 hours long and absolutely free. Call ✆ **808/239-4336** or e-mail kahoku productions@yahoo.com. Third Sunday in August.

September

Aloha Festivals, various locations statewide. Parades and other events celebrate Hawaiian culture and friendliness throughout the state. Call ✆ **800/852-7690,** 808/545-1771, or 808/885-8086, or visit www.alohafestivals.com for a schedule of events.

Great Molokai Mule Drag and Hoolaulea, Kaunakakai, Molokai. As part of the Aloha Festivals celebration on Molokai, local residents honor the importance of the mule with a mule race (which is sometimes a mule-dragging contest) down the main street of Kaunakakai. Call ✆ **800/800-6367** or 808/553-3876; www.molokai-hawaii.com.

Sam Choy Poke Recipe Contest, Hapuna Beach Prince Hotel and Mauna Kea Beach Resort, Kohala Coast, Big Island. Top chefs from across Hawaii and the U.S. mainland, as well as local amateurs, compete in making this Hawaiian delicacy, *poke* (pronounced po-*kay*): chopped raw fish mixed with seaweed and spices. Here's your chance to sample poke at its best. Call ✆ **808/885-8086.**

Long Distance Outrigger Canoe Races, Kailua Pier to Honaunau and back, Big Island. Some 2,500 paddlers from all over Hawaii, the U.S. mainland, Canada, and the Pacific vie in the world's longest canoe event. Call © 808/329-7787. Labor Day weekend.

A Taste of Lahaina, Lahaina Civic Center, Maui. Some 30,000 people show up to sample 40 signature entrees of Maui's premier chefs during this weekend festival, which includes cooking demonstrations, wine tastings, and live entertainment. The event begins Friday night with Maui Chefs Present, a dinner/cocktail party featuring about a dozen of Maui's best chefs. Call © 888/310-1117 or e-mail action@maui.net. Second weekend in September.

Maui Marathon, Kahului to Kaanapali, Maui. Runners line up at the Maui Mall before daybreak and head off for Kaanapali. Call © 808/871-6441; www.maui marathon.com. Sunday in mid-September.

October

Emalani Festival, Kokee State Park, Kauai. This festival honors Her Majesty Queen Emma, an inveterate gardener and Hawaii's first environmental queen, who made a forest trek to Kokee with 100 friends in 1871. Call © 808/245-3971.

Aloha Classic World Wavesailing Championship, Hookipa Beach, Maui. The top windsurfers in the world gather for this final event in the Pro Boardsailing World Tour. If you're on Maui, don't miss it—it's spectacular to watch. Call © 808/575-9151.

Hamakua Music Festival, Hamakua, Big Island. This event features a surprisingly eclectic mix of well-known musicians, ranging from blues and jazz to rock-and-roll, Hawaiian, and even classical.

Call © 808/775-3378. Early October.

Maui County Fair, War Memorial Complex, Wailuku, Maui. The oldest county fair in Hawaii features a parade, amusement rides, live entertainment, and exhibits. Call © 800/525-MAUI or 808/244-3530. First weekend in October.

Molokai Hoe, Molokai to Oahu. The course of this men's 40-mile outrigger contest runs across the channel from Molokai to finish at Fort DeRussy Beach in Waikiki. Call © 808/261-6615; www.molokai-hawaii.com. Mid-October.

Ironman Triathlon World Championship, Kailua-Kona, Big Island. Some 1,500-plus world-class athletes run a full marathon, swim 2.4 miles, and bike 112 miles on the Kona-Kohala Coast of the Big Island. Spectators can watch the action along the route for free. The best place to see the 7am start is along the seawall on Alii Drive, facing Kailua Bay; arrive before 5:30am to get a seat. The best place to see the bike-and-run portion is along Alii Drive (which will be closed to traffic; park on a side street and walk down). To watch the finishers come in, line up along Alii Drive from Holualoa Street to the finish at Palani Road/Alii Drive; the first finisher can come as early as 2:30pm, and the course closes at midnight. Call © 808/329-0063; **www.ironmanlive.com**. October 16, 2004.

Halloween in Lahaina, Maui. There's Carnival in Rio, Mardi Gras in New Orleans, and Halloween in Lahaina. Come to this giant costume party (some 20,000 people show up) on the streets of Lahaina; Front Street is closed off for the festivities. Call © 808/667-9175. October 31.

November

Hawaiian Slack-Key Guitar Festival, Kauai Marriott Resort, Lihue, Kauai. The best of Hawaii's folk music (slack-key guitar) performed by the best musicians in Hawaii. It's 5 hours long and absolutely free. Call ✆ **808/239-4336** or e-mail kahokuproductions@yahoo.com.

Annual Kona Coffee Cultural Festival, Kailua-Kona, Big Island. Celebrate the coffee harvest with a bean-picking contest, lei contests, song and dance, and the Miss Kona Coffee pageant. Call ✆ **808/326-7820** or go to www.konacoffee.com for this year's schedule.

Big Island Festival, Kona-Kohala coast, Hawaii. This is one of the state's largest festivals on the largest island. It lasts 5 days and nights celebrating the Big Island's cultural diversity with lots of foodie events, excellent Hawaiian music, golf and sport activities, spa extravaganzas, agricultural products, and exhibits and cultural activities. Call ✆ **808/326-7820** or visit www.bigisland festival.com. Early November.

Hawaii International Film Festival, various locations throughout the state. This cinema festival with a cross-cultural spin features filmmakers from Asia, the Pacific Islands, and the United States. Call ✆ **808/528-FILM,** or visit www. hiff.org. First 2 weeks in November.

MasterCard PGA Grand Slam, Poipu Bay Resort Golf Course, Kauai. Top golfers compete for $1 million in prize money. Call ✆ **800/ PGA-TCKT** or 888/744-0888; www.pga.com. Last weekend in November.

Triple Crown of Surfing, North Shore, Oahu. The world's top professional surfers compete in events for more than $1 million in prize money. Call ✆ **808/638-7266** or visit www.triplecrownofsurfing.com.

Hawaii Pro, November 12–22, 2004; World Cup of Surfing, November 23–December 7, 2004; and Pipeline Masters, December 8–20, 2004.

December

Festival of Trees, Honolulu, Oahu. This downtown display of one-of-a-kind decorated trees, wreaths, and decorations benefits Queen's Medical Center. The lighting takes place the first or second week of the month. Call ✆ **808/547-4371.**

Old-Fashioned Holiday Celebration, Lahaina, Maui. This day of Christmas carolers, Santa Claus, live music and entertainment, a crafts fair, Christmas baked goods, and activities for children takes place in the Banyan Tree Park on Front Street. Call ✆ **888/310-1117** or e-mail action@maui.net. Second Saturday in December.

Festival of Lights, all islands. On Oahu, the mayor throws the switch to light up the 40-foot-tall Norfolk pine and other trees in front of Honolulu Hale, while on Maui, marching bands, floats, and Santa roll down Lahaina's Front Street in an annual parade. Molokai celebrates with a host of activities in Kaunakakai; on Kauai, the lighting ceremony takes place in front of the former county building on Rice Street, Lihue. Call ✆ **808/547-4397** on Oahu; **808/667-9175** on Maui; **808/567-6361** on Molokai; and **808/828-0014** on Kauai. Early December.

Honolulu Marathon, Honolulu, Oahu. This is one of the largest marathons in the world, with more than 30,000 competitors. Call ✆ **808/734-7200** or go to www. honolulumarathon.org. December 13, 2004.

Aloha Bowl, Aloha Stadium, Honolulu, Oahu. A Pac-10 team plays a

Big 12 team in this nationally televised collegiate football classic. Call ℂ **808/545-7171** or go to www.alohagames.com. Christmas Day.

Rainbow Classic, University of Hawaii, Manoa Valley, Oahu. Eight of the best NCAA basketball teams compete at the Special Events Arena. Call ℂ **808/956-6501.** The week after Christmas.

First Night, Maui Arts and Cultural Center, Maui, and Kailua-Kona, Big Island. Hawaii's largest festival of arts and entertainment takes place on two different islands. For 12 hours, musicians, dancers, actors, jugglers, magicians, and mimes perform. Afterwards, fireworks bring in the New Year. Alcohol-free. Call ℂ **808/326-7820** on the Big Island, or ℂ **808/242-7469** on Maui. December 31.

First Light 2003, Maui Arts and Cultural Center, Maui. Major films are screened at this festival (the 2002 festival included *Adaptation, Chicago, Frida, Gangs of New York, The Good Girl,* and *The Hours,* among others). Not to be missed. Call ℂ **808/579-9996,** or visit www.mauifilmfestival.com. Late December to early January.

4 Insurance

Check your existing insurance policies and credit-card coverage before you buy travel insurance. You may already be covered for lost luggage, cancelled tickets or medical expenses. The cost of travel insurance varies widely, depending on the cost and length of your trip, your age, health, and the type of trip you're taking.

TRIP-CANCELLATION INSURANCE Trip-cancellation insurance helps you get your money back if you have to back out of a trip, if you have to go home early, or if your travel supplier goes bankrupt. Allowed reasons for cancellation can range from sickness to natural disasters to the State Department declaring your destination unsafe for travel. (Insurers usually won't cover vague fears, though, as many travelers discovered who tried to cancel their trips in October 2001 because they were wary of flying.) In this unstable world, trip-cancellation insurance is a good buy if you're getting tickets well in advance—who knows what the state of the world, or of your airline, will be in 9 months? Insurance policy details vary, so read the fine print—and especially make sure that your airline or cruise line is on the list of carriers covered in case of bankruptcy. For information, contact one of the following insurers: **Access America** (ℂ 800/284-8300; www.accessamerica.com); **Travel Guard International** (ℂ 800/826-1300; www.travelguard.com); **Travel Insured International** (ℂ 800/243-3174; www.travelinsured.com); and **Travelex Insurance Services** (ℂ 800/228-9792; www.travelex-insurance.com).

MEDICAL INSURANCE Most health insurance policies cover you if you get sick away from home—but check, particularly if you're insured by an HMO. If you require additional medical insurance, try **MEDEX International** (ℂ **800/527-0218** or 410/453-6300; www.medexassist.com) or **Travel Assistance International** (ℂ **800/821-2828;** www.travelassistance.com; for general information on services, call the company's Worldwide Assistance Services, Inc., at ℂ **800/777-8710**).

LOST-LUGGAGE INSURANCE On domestic flights, checked baggage is covered up to $2,500 per ticketed passenger. On international flights (including U.S. portions of international trips), baggage is limited to approximately $9.07 per pound, up to approximately $635 per checked bag.

If you plan to check items more valuable than the standard liability, see if your valuables are covered by your homeowner's policy. You may also get baggage insurance as part of your comprehensive travel-insurance package or buy Travel Guard's "BagTrak" product. Don't buy insurance at the airport, as it's usually overpriced. Be sure to take any valuables or irreplaceable items with you in your carry-on luggage, as many valuables (including books, money and electronics) aren't covered by airline policies.

If your luggage is lost, immediately file a lost-luggage claim at the airport, detailing the luggage contents. For most airlines, you must report delayed, damaged, or lost baggage within 4 hours of arrival. The airlines are required to deliver luggage, once found, directly to your house or destination free of charge.

5 Health & Safety

ON LAND

Like any tropical climate, Hawaii is home to lots of bugs. Most of them won't harm you. However, three insects—mosquitoes, centipedes, and scorpions—do sting, and may cause anything from mild annoyance to severe swelling and pain.

MOSQUITOES   These pesky insects are not native to Hawaii but arrived as larvae stowed away in water barrels on the ship *Wellington* in 1826, when it anchored in Lahaina. There's not a whole lot you can do about them, except to apply commercial repellent, burn mosquito punk or citronella candles, and use ointments (which you can pick up at any drugstore) after you've been stung to ease the itching and swelling.

CENTIPEDES   These segmented insects with a jillion legs come in two varieties: 6- to 8-inch-long brown ones and 2- to 3-inch-long blue guys. Both can really pack a wallop with their sting. Centipedes are generally found in damp, wet places, such as under wood piles or compost heaps; wearing closed-toe shoes can help prevent stings if you happen to accidentally unearth one. If you're stung, the reaction can range from something similar to a mild bee sting to severe pain; apply ice at once to prevent swelling. See a doctor if you experience extreme pain, swelling, nausea, or any other severe reaction.

SCORPIONS   Rarely seen, scorpions are found in arid, warm regions; their stings can be serious. Campers in dry areas should always check their boots before putting them on, and shake out sleeping bags and bed rolls. Symptoms of a scorpion sting include shortness of breath, hives, swelling, and nausea. In the unlikely event that you're stung, apply diluted household ammonia and cold compresses to the area of the sting and seek medical help immediately.

(*Tips*   **A Few Words of Warning about Crime**

Although Hawaii is generally a safe tourist destination, visitors have been crime victims, so stay alert. The most common crime against tourists is rental-car break-ins. Never leave any valuables in your car, not even in your trunk: Thieves can be in and out of your trunk faster than you can open it with your own keys. Be especially leery of high-risk areas, such as beaches, resorts, scenic lookouts, and other visitor attractions. Also, never carry large amounts of cash in Waikiki and other tourist zones. Stay in well-lighted areas after dark.

HIKING SAFETY

In addition to taking the appropriate precautions regarding Hawaii's bug population, hikers should always let someone know where they're heading, when they're going, and when they plan to return; too many hikers get lost in Hawaii because they don't let others know their basic plans.

Always check weather conditions with the **National Weather Service** (© **808/973-4381** on Oahu; see individual island chapters for local weather information) before you go. Hike with a pal, never alone. Wear hiking boots, a sun hat, clothes to protect you from the sun and from getting scratches, and high-SPF sunscreen on all exposed areas of skin. Take water. Stay on the trail. Watch your step. It's easy to slip off precipitous trails and into steep canyons. Incapacitated hikers are often plucked to safety by fire and rescue squads, who must use helicopters to gain access to remote sites. Many experienced hikers and boaters today pack a cellphone in case of emergency; just dial © **911.**

VOG

The volcanic haze dubbed *vog* is caused by gases released when molten lava-from the continuous eruption of Kilauea volcano on the Big Island-pours into the ocean. This hazy air, which looks like urban smog, limits viewing from scenic vistas and wreaks havoc on photographers trying to get clear panoramic shots. Some people claim that long-term exposure has even caused bronchial ailments, but it's highly unlikely to cause you any harm in the course of your visit.

There actually is a vog season in Hawaii: the fall and winter months, when the trade winds that blow the fumes out to sea die down. The vog is felt not only on the Big Island but also as far away as Maui and Oahu.

One more word of caution: If you're pregnant or have heart or breathing problems, you might want to think twice about visiting the Big Island's Hawaii Volcanoes National Park. You're cautioned to avoid exposure to the sulfuric fumes that are ever-present in and around the park's calderas.

OCEAN SAFETY

Because most people coming to Hawaii are unfamiliar with the ocean environment, they're often unaware of the natural hazards it holds. With just a few precautions, your ocean experience can be a safe and happy one. An excellent book is *All Stings Considered: First Aid and Medical Treatment of Hawaii's Marine Injuries* (University of Hawaii Press, 1997) by Craig Thomas and Susan Scott.

Note that sharks are not a big problem in Hawaii; in fact, they appear so infrequently that locals look forward to seeing them. Since records have been kept, starting in 1779, there have been only about 100 shark attacks in Hawaii, of which 40% have been fatal. Most attacks occurred after someone fell into the ocean from the shore or from a boat; in these cases, the sharks probably attacked after the person was dead. But general rules for avoiding sharks are: Don't swim at sunrise, sunset, or where the water is murky due to stream runoff—sharks may mistake you for one of their usual meals. And don't swim where there are bloody fish in the water, as sharks become aggressive around blood.

SEASICKNESS The waters in Hawaii can range from calm as glass (off the Kona Coast on the Big Island) to downright frightening (in storm conditions), and they usually fall somewhere in between. In general, expect rougher conditions in winter than in summer. Some 90% of the population tends toward seasickness. If you've never been out on a boat, or if you've been seasick in the past, you might want to heed the following suggestions:

Tips   Don't Get Burned: Smart Tanning Tips

Hawaii's Caucasian population has the highest incidence of malignant melanoma (deadly skin cancer) in the world. And nobody is completely safe from the sun's harmful rays: All skin types and races can burn. Dr. Craig Thomas, author of *All Stings Considered*, tells us that "the risk of melanoma is even worse with intermittent sun exposure than it is with long-term exposure; the worst thing you can do is to go to the tropics once a year for 10 years and get burned." To ensure that your vacation won't be ruined by a painful sunburn (especially in your first few days in the islands), here are some helpful tips.

- **Wear a strong sunscreen at all times.** Use a sunscreen with a sun-protection factor (SPF) of 15 or higher; people with a light complexion should use 30. Apply it liberally, 1 tablespoon per limb is recommended, and reapply every 2 hours.
- **Wrinkle prevention:** Wrinkles, sagging skin, and other signs of premature aging can be caused by Ultraviolet A (UVA) rays. For years, sunscreens concentrated on blocking out just Ultraviolet B (UVB) rays. The best protection from UVA rays is zinc oxide (the white goo that lifeguards wear on their noses), but other ingredients also provide protection. Read the label, and get another brand if your sunscreen doesn't contain one of the following: zinc oxide, benzophenone, oxybenzone, sulisobenzone, titanium dioxide, or avobenzone (also known as Parsol 1789).
- **Wear a hat and sunglasses.** The hat should have a brim all the way around, to cover not only your face but also the sensitive back of your neck. Make sure your sunglasses have UV filters.
- **Protect children from the sun.** Infants under 6 months should not be in the sun at all. Older babies need zinc oxide to protect their fragile skin, and all children should be slathered with sunscreen frequently.
- **If you start to turn red, get out of the sun.** Contrary to popular belief, you don't have to turn red to tan; if your skin is red, it's burned, and that's serious. The best remedy for a sunburn is to get out of the sun immediately and stay out of the sun until all the redness is gone. Aloe vera (straight from the plant or from a commercial preparation), cool compresses, cold baths, and anesthetic benzocaine also help with the pain of sunburn.

- The day before you go out on the boat, avoid alcohol, caffeine, citrus and other acidic juices, and greasy, spicy, or hard-to-digest foods.
- Get a good night's sleep the night before.
- Take or use whatever seasickness prevention works best for you—medication, an acupressure wristband, gingerroot tea or capsules, or any combination. But do it **before you board;** once you set sail, it's generally too late.
- While you're on the boat, stay as low and as near the center of the boat as possible. Avoid the fumes (especially if it's a diesel boat); stay out in the fresh air and watch the horizon. Do not read.

• If you start to feel queasy, drink clear fluids like water, and eat something bland, such as a soda cracker.

STINGS The most commons stings in Hawaii come from jellyfish, particularly Portuguese man-of-war and box jellyfish. Since the poisons they inject are very different, you need to treat each sting differently.

A bluish-purple floating bubble with a long tail, the **Portuguese man-of-war** causes some 6,500 stings a year on Oahu alone. These stings, although painful and a nuisance, are rarely harmful; fewer than 1 in 1,000 requires medical treatment. The best prevention is to watch for these floating bubbles as you snorkel (look for the hanging tentacles below the surface). Get out of the water if anyone near you spots these jellyfish.

Reactions to stings range from mild burning and reddening to severe welts and blisters. *All Stings Considered* recommends the following treatment: First, pick off any visible tentacles with a gloved hand, a stick, or anything handy; then rinse the sting with salt- or freshwater, and apply ice to prevent swelling and to help control pain. Hawaii folklore advises using vinegar, meat tenderizer, baking soda, papain, or alcohol, or even urinating on the wound. Studies have shown that these remedies may actually cause further damage. Most Portuguese man-of-war stings will disappear by themselves within 15 to 20 minutes if you do nothing at all to treat them. Still, be sure to see a doctor if pain persists or a rash or other symptoms develop.

Transparent, square-shaped **box jellyfish** are nearly impossible to see in the water. Fortunately, they seem to follow a monthly cycle: 8 to 10 days after the full moon, they appear in the waters on the leeward side of each island and hang around for about 3 days. Also, they seem to sting more in the morning hours, when they're on or near the surface. The best prevention is to get out of the water.

The stings can cause anything from no visible marks to red, hivelike welts, blisters, and pain (a burning sensation) lasting from 10 minutes to 8 hours. *All Stings Considered* recommends the following treatment: First, pour regular household vinegar on the sting; this may not relieve the pain, but it will stop additional burning. Do not rub the area. Pick off any vinegar-soaked tentacles with a stick. For pain, apply an ice pack. Seek additional medical treatment if you experience shortness of breath, weakness, palpitations, muscle cramps, or any other severe symptoms. Again, ignore any folk remedies. Most box jellyfish stings disappear by themselves without any treatment.

PUNCTURES Most sea-related punctures come from stepping on or brushing against the needlelike spines of sea urchins (known locally as *wana*). Be careful when you're in the water; don't put your foot down (even if you have booties or fins on) if you can't clearly see the bottom. Waves can push you into *wana* in a surge zone in shallow water. The spines can even puncture a wet suit.

A sea-urchin puncture can result in burning, aching, swelling, and discoloration (black or purple) around the area where the spines entered your skin. The best thing to do is to pull any protruding spines out. The body will absorb the spines within 24 hours to 3 weeks, or the remainder of the spines will work themselves out. Again, contrary to popular wisdom, do not urinate or pour vinegar on the embedded spines—this will not help.

CUTS All cuts obtained in the marine environment must be taken seriously, because the high level of bacteria present in the water can quickly cause the cut to become infected. The most common cuts are from coral. Contrary to popular belief, coral cannot grow inside your body. Bacteria, however, can. The best way to prevent cuts is to wear a wet suit, gloves, and reef shoes. Never, under any circumstances, should you touch a coral head; not only can you get cut, but you can also damage a living organism that took decades to grow.

The symptoms of a coral cut can range from a slight scratch to severe welts and blisters. *All Stings Considered* recommends gently pulling the edges of the skin open and removing any embedded coral or grains of sand with tweezers. Next, scrub the cut well with fresh water. Never use ocean water to clean a cut. If you're bleeding, press a clean cloth against the wound until it stops. If the bleeding continues, or the edges of the injury are jagged or gaping, seek medical treatment.

WHAT TO DO IF YOU GET SICK AWAY FROM HOME

In most cases, your existing health plan will provide the coverage you need. But double-check; you may want to buy **travel medical insurance** instead. (See the section on insurance, earlier.) Bring your insurance ID card with you when you travel.

If you suffer from a chronic illness, consult your doctor before your departure. For conditions like epilepsy, diabetes, or heart problems, wear a **Medic Alert Identification Tag** (© 800/825-3785; www.medicalert.org), which will immediately alert doctors to your condition and give them access to your records through Medic Alert's 24-hour hotline.

Pack **prescription medications** in your carry-on luggage, and carry prescription medications in their original containers, with pharmacy labels—otherwise they won't make it through airport security. Also bring along copies of your prescriptions in case you lose your pills or run out. Don't forget an extra pair of contact lenses or prescription glasses.

Contact the **International Association for Medical Assistance to Travelers (IAMAT)** (© 716/754-4883 or 416/652-0137; www.iamat.org) for tips on travel and health concerns in the countries you're visiting, and lists of local, English-speaking doctors. The United States **Centers for Disease Control and Prevention** (© 800/311-3435; www.cdc.gov) provides up-to-date information on necessary vaccines and health hazards by region or country. If you get sick, consider asking your hotel concierge to recommend a local doctor—even his or her own. You can also try the emergency room at a local hospital; many have walk-in clinics for emergency cases that are not life-threatening. You may not get immediate attention, but you won't pay the high price of an emergency room visit.

6 What to Pack

Hawaii is very informal. Shorts, T-shirts, and tennis shoes will get you by at most restaurants and attractions; a casual dress or a polo shirt and khakis are fine even in the most expensive places. Dinner jackets for men are required only in some of the fine dining rooms of a very few ultra-exclusive resorts, such as the Halekulani on Oahu, the Big Island's Mauna Kea Beach Hotel, and the Lodge at Koele on Lanai—and they'll cordially provide you with a jacket if you don't bring your own. Aloha wear is acceptable everywhere, so you may want to plan on buying an aloha shirt or a *muumuu* (a Hawaiian-style dress) while you're in the islands.

So bring T-shirts, shorts, long pants, a couple of bathing suits, a long-sleeve cover-up (to throw on at the beach when you've had enough sun for the day), tennis shoes, rubber water shoes or flip-flops, and hiking boots and good socks, if you plan on hiking.

The tropical sun poses the greatest threat to anyone who ventures into the great outdoors, so be sure to bring **sun protection:** a good pair of sunglasses, strong sunscreen, a light hat (like a baseball cap or a sun visor), and a canteen or water bottle if you'll be hiking—you'll easily dehydrate in the tropical heat, so figure on carrying 2 liters of water per day on any hike. Campers should bring water-purification tablets or devices. Also see "Health & Safety," earlier in this chapter.

You won't have to stuff your suitcase with 2 weeks' worth of shorts and T-shirts. Almost all of Hawaii's hotels and resorts—even the high-end ones—have **laundry facilities.** If your accommodation doesn't have a washer and dryer or laundry service, there will likely be a Laundromat nearby. The only exception to this is Hana on Maui; this tiny town has no launderette, so check with the place where you're staying beforehand.

One last thing: **It really can get cold in Hawaii.** If you plan to see the sunrise from the top of Maui's Haleakala Crater, venture into the Big Island's Hawaii Volcanoes National Park, or spend time in Kokee State Park on Kauai, bring a warm jacket; 40°F (4°C) upcountry temperatures, even in summer when it's 80°F (27°C) at the beach, are not uncommon. It's always a good idea to bring at least a windbreaker, a sweater, or a light jacket. And be sure to toss some **rain gear** into your suitcase if you'll be in Hawaii from November to March.

7 The Active Vacation Planner

If all you want is a fabulous beach and a perfectly mixed mai tai, then Hawaii has what you're looking for. But the islands' wealth of natural wonders is equally hard to resist; the year-round tropical climate and spectacular scenery tend to inspire almost everyone to get outside and explore.

If you don't have your own snorkel gear or other watersports equipment or if you just don't feel like packing it, don't fret: Everything you'll need is available for rent in the islands. We discuss all kinds of places to rent or buy gear in the island chapters that follow.

SETTING OUT ON YOUR OWN VERSUS USING AN OUTFITTER

There are two ways to go: Plan all the details before you leave and either rent gear or schlepp your stuff 2,500 miles across the Pacific, or go with an outfitter or a guide and let someone else worry about the details.

Experienced outdoors enthusiasts may head to coastal campgrounds or even trek to the 13,796-foot-high summit of Mauna Loa on their own. But in Hawaii, it's often preferable to go with a local guide who is familiar with the conditions at both sea level and summit peaks, knows the land and its flora and fauna in detail, and has all the gear you'll need. It's also good to go with a guide if time is an issue, or if you have specialized interests. If you really want to see native birds, for instance, an experienced guide will take you directly to the best areas for sightings. And many forests and valleys in the interior of the islands are either on private property or in wilderness preserves accessible only on guided tours. The downside? If you go with a guide, plan on spending at least $100 a day per person. We've recommended the best local outfitters and tour-guide operators on each island in the chapters that follow.

But if you have the time, already own the gear, and love doing the research and planning, try exploring on your own. Each island chapter discusses the best spots to set out on your

Outdoor Etiquette

Act locally, think globally, and carry out what you carry in. Find a trash container for all your litter (including cigarette butts; it's *very* bad form to throw them out of your car window or to use the beach as an ashtray). Observe *kapu* (taboo) and NO TRESPASSING signs. Don't climb on ancient Hawaiian *heiau* (temple) walls or carry home rocks, all of which belong to the Hawaiian volcano goddess Pele. Some say it's just a silly superstition, but each year, the national and state park services get boxes of lava rocks in the mail that have been sent back to Hawaii by visitors who've experienced unusually bad luck.

own, from the top offshore snorkel and dive spots to great daylong hikes, as well as the federal, state, and county agencies that can help you with hikes on public property; we also list references for spotting birds, plants, and sea life. We recommend that you always use the resources available to inquire about weather, trail, or surf conditions, water availability, and other conditions before you take off on your adventure.

For hikers, a great alternative to hiring a private guide is taking a guided hike offered by the **Nature Conservancy of Hawaii,** 1116 Smith St., no. 210, Honolulu, HI 96817 (© **808/537-4508** on Oahu, **808/572-7849** on Maui, **808/553-5236** on Molokai; www.tnc.org/hawaii), or the **Hawaii Chapter of the Sierra Club,** P.O. Box 2577, Honolulu, HI 96803 (© **808/538-6616** on Oahu; www.hi.sierraclub.org). Both organizations offer guided hikes in preserves and special areas during the year, as well as day- to week-long work trips to restore habitats and trails and to root out invasive plants. It might not sound like a dream vacation to everyone, but it's a chance to see the "real" Hawaii—including wilderness areas that are ordinarily off-limits.

All Nature Conservancy hikes and work trips are free (donations are appreciated). However, you must reserve a spot for yourself, and a deposit is required for guided hikes to ensure that you'll show up; your deposit is refunded once you do. The hikes are generally offered once a month on Maui, Molokai, and Lanai, and twice a month on Oahu. For all islands, call the Oahu office for reservations. Write for a schedule of guided hikes and other programs.

The Sierra Club offers weekly hikes on Oahu and Maui. Hikes are led by certified Sierra Club volunteers and are classified as easy, moderate, or strenuous. These half-day or all-day affairs cost $1 for Sierra Club members and $3 for nonmembers (bring exact change). For a copy of the club newsletter, which lists all outings and trail-repair work, send $2 to the address above.

Local ecotourism opportunities are also discussed in each island chapter. For more information, contact the **Hawaii Ecotourism Association** (© **877/300-7058;** www.hawaii ecotourism.org).

USING ACTIVITIES DESKS TO BOOK YOUR ISLAND FUN

If you're unsure of which activity or which outfitter or guide is the right one for you and your family, you might want to consider booking through a discount activities center or activities desk. Not only will they save you money, but good activities centers should also be able to help you find, say, the snorkel cruise that's right for you, or the luau that's most suitable for both you *and* the kids.

Remember, however, that it's in the activities agent's best interest to sign you up with outfitters from which they earn the most commission. Some agents have no qualms about booking you into any activity if it means an extra buck for them. If an agent tries to push a particular outfitter or activity too hard, be skeptical. Conversely, they'll try to steer you away from outfitters who don't offer big commissions. For example, Trilogy, the company that offers Maui's most popular snorkel cruises to Lanai (and the only one with rights to land at Lanai's Hulupoe Beach), offers only minimum commissions to agents and does not allow agents to offer any discounts at all. As a result, most activities desks will automatically try to steer you away from Trilogy.

Another important word of warning: Stay away from activities centers that offer discounts as fronts for time-share sales presentations. Using a free or discounted snorkel cruise or luau tickets as bait, they'll suck you into a 90-minute presentation-and try to get you to buy into a Hawaii time-share in the process. Not only will they try to sell you a big white elephant you never wanted in the first place, but since their business is time-shares, not activities, they also won't be as interested, or as knowledgeable, about which activities might be right for you. These shady deals seem to be particularly rampant on Maui. Just do yourself a favor and avoid them altogether.

Our favorite islandwide discount clearinghouse is the **Activity Warehouse** (✆ 800/343-2987; www.travel hawaii.com), which offers discounts of up to 50% on all kinds of activities (although most discounts are in the 10%–20% range), with lots of operators to choose from. The company has offices on **Kauai** (✆ 808/822-4000), the **Big Island** (✆ 808/334-1155), and **Maui** (✆ 808/875-4050) in

Kihei, 808/661-1970 in Lahaina). All in all, we've found Activity Warehouse to be helpful and not too hard-sell. While the company does represent time-shares, we've never once had anyone pitch us. The Maui and Kauai locations also function as branches of **Rental Warehouse,** offering discount rentals of all kinds of equipment, from snorkel sets and beach chairs to golf clubs and kayaks.

There are also a number of very reliable local activities centers on each of the neighbor islands. On Maui, your best bet is **Tom Barefoot's Cash-back Tours** (✆ 888/222-3601; www. tombarefoot.com), 834 Front St., Lahaina (✆ 808/661-8889). Tom offers a 10% discount on all tours, activities, and adventures if you pay using cash, a personal check, or traveler's checks. If you use a credit card, you'll get a 7% discount.

On the Big Island, check out the **Activity Connection,** Bougainvillea Plaza Ste. 102, 75-5656 Kuakini Hwy., Kailua-Kona (✆ 800/459-7156 or 808/329-1038; www.beach activityguide.com); it offers up to 15% off on various island activities.

On Kauai, call **Chris The Fun Lady,** 4–746 Kuhio Hwy., Kapaa (✆ 800/353-4020 or 808/822-7759; www.christhefunlady.com). Chris doesn't offer discounts, but she's great for one-stop shopping.

Finally, you can book activities yourself and get the commission by booking via the Internet. Most activities offer from 10% to 25% off their prices if you book over the net. Check the net first and save a bundle.

OUTDOOR ACTIVITIES A TO Z

Here's a brief rundown of the many outdoor activities available in Hawaii. For our recommendations on the best places to go, the best shops for renting equipment, and the best outfitters to use, see the individual island chapters later in this book.

BIRDING   Many of Hawaii's tropical birds are found nowhere else on earth. There are curved-bill honeycreepers, black-winged red birds, and the rare o'o, whose yellow feathers Hawaiians once plucked to make royal capes. When you go birding, take along *A Field Guide to the Birds of Hawaii and the Tropical Pacific,* by H. Douglas Pratt, Phillip L. Bruner, and Delwyn G. Berett (Princeton University Press, 1987). If you go bird watching with a local guide, you'll usually be provided with a good pair of binoculars; you can also rent them from **Activity Warehouse** (see above) and at other gear-rental locations throughout the islands.

Kauai and Molokai, in particular, are great places to go birding. On Kauai, large colonies of seabirds nest at Kilauea National Wildlife Refuge and along the Na Pali Coast. The lush rain forest of Molokai's Kamakou Preserve is home to the Molokai thrush and Molokai creeper, which live only on this 30-mile-long island. For details, see "Birding," in chapters 5 and 9, as well as the discussion of the Kamakou Preserve under "Seeing the Sights," in chapter 7.

BOATING   Almost every type of nautical experience is available in the islands. You can go to sea on old-fashioned Polynesian outrigger canoes, high-tech kayaks, fast-moving catamarans, inflatable rubber Zodiac boats, smooth-moving SWATH vessels that promise not to make you seasick, gaff-rigged schooners, America's Cup racing sloops, submarines, and even an interisland cruise ship. You'll find details on all these seafaring experiences in the individual island chapters.

No matter which vessel and type you choose, be sure to see the Hawaiian islands from offshore if you can afford it. It's easy to combine multiple activities into one cruise: Lots of snorkel boats double as sightseeing cruises and, in winter, whale-watching cruises. The main harbors for visitor activities are Kewalo Basin, Oahu; Honokohau, Kailua-Kona, and Kawaihae on the Big Island; Lahaina and Maaalea, Maui; Nawiliwili and Port Allen, Kauai; and Kaunakakai, Molokai.

BODY BOARDING (BOOGIE BOARDING) & BODYSURFING
Bodysurfing—riding the waves without a board, becoming one with the rolling water—is a way of life in Hawaii. Some bodysurfers just rely on their outstretched hands (or hands at their sides) to ride the waves; others use hand boards (flat, paddlelike gloves). For additional maneuverability, try a Boogie Board or body board (also known as belly boards or *paipo* boards). These 3-foot-long vehicles, which support the upper part of your body, are easy to carry and very maneuverable in the water. Both bodysurfing and body boarding require a pair of open-heeled swim fins to help propel you through the water. Both kinds of wave riding are very popular in the islands, as the equipment is inexpensive and easy to carry, and both sports can be practiced in the small, gentle waves. See the individual island chapters for details on where to rent boards and where to go.

CAMPING   Hawaii's year-round balmy climate makes camping a breeze. However, tropical campers should always be ready for rain, especially in Hawaii's winter wet season, but even in the dry summer season as well. And remember that mosquitoes are abundant when the air is still; bring a good mosquito repellent. If you're heading to the top of Hawaii's volcanoes, you'll need a down mummy bag. If you plan to camp on the beach, bring mosquito net and a rain poncho. Always be prepared to deal with contaminated water (purify it by boiling, filtration, or using iodine tablets) and the tropical sun (protect yourself with sunscreen, a hat, and a long-sleeved shirt). Also be sure to check out

"Health & Safety," earlier in this chapter, for hiking and camping tips.

But in general, camping is ideal in the islands. There are many established campgrounds at beach parks, including Kauai's Anini Beach, Oahu's Malaekahana Beach, Maui's Waianapanapa Beach, and the Big Island's Hapuna Beach. Campgrounds are also located in the interior at Maui's Haleakala National Park and the Big Island's Hawaii Volcanoes National Park, as well as at Kalalau Beach on Kauai's Na Pali Coast and in the cool uplands of Kokee State Park. See "Beaches" and "Hiking & Camping," in the individual island chapters for the best places to camp. For details on who to contact for regulations and information on camping in any of Hawaii's national or state parks, see section 1 of this chapter, "Visitor Information."

Hawaiian Trail and Mountain Club, P.O. Box 2238, Honolulu, HI 96804, offers an information packet on hiking and camping throughout the islands. Send $2 and a legal-size, self-addressed, stamped envelope for information. Another good source is the *Hiking/Camping Information Packet,* available from **Hawaii Geographic Maps and Books,** 49 S. Hotel St., Honolulu, HI 96813 (© **800/538-3950** or 808/538-3952), for $7. The **University of Hawaii Press,** 2840 Kolowalo St., Honolulu, HI 96822 (© **888/847-7737;** www.uhpress.hawaii.edu), has an excellent selection of hiking, backpacking, and bird-watching guides.

GOLF Nowhere else on earth can you tee off to whale spouts, putt under rainbows, and play around a live volcano. Hawaii has some of the world's top-rated golf courses. But be forewarned: Each course features hellish natural hazards, like razor-sharp lava, gusty trade winds, an occasional wild pig, and the tropical heat. And greens fees tend to be very expensive. Still, golfers flock here from around the world and love every minute of it. See the individual island chapters for coverage of the best resort courses worth splurging on (with details, where applicable, on money-saving twilight rates), as well as the best budget and municipal courses.

A few tips on golfing in Hawaii: There's generally wind—10 to 30 mph is not unusual between 10am and 2pm—so you may have to play two to three clubs up or down to compensate. Bring extra balls: The rough is thick, water hazards are everywhere, and the wind wreaks havoc with your game. On the greens, your putt will *always* break toward the ocean. Hit deeper and more aggressively in the sand, because the type of sand used on most Hawaii courses is firmer and more compact than usual (lighter sand would blow away in the constant wind). And bring a camera—you'll kick yourself if you don't capture those spectacular views.

See our coverage in each island chapter, and see also "The Best Golf Courses," in chapter 1.

HIKING Hiking in Hawaii is a breathtaking experience. The islands have hundreds of miles of trails, many of which reward you with a hidden beach, a private waterfall, an Eden-like valley, or simply an unforgettable

---

Tips **Travel Tip**

When planning sunset activities, be aware that Hawaii, like other places close to the equator, has a very short (5–10 min.) twilight period after the sun sets. After that, it's dark. If you hike out to watch the sunset, be sure you can make it back quickly, or take a flashlight.

(*Value* **Fun for Less: Don't Leave Home Without a Gold Card**

Almost any activity you can think of, from submarine rides to Polynesian luaus, can be purchased at a discount by using the **Activities and Attractions Assocation of Hawaii Gold Card,** 355 Hukilike St., no. 202, Kahului, HI 96732 (© **800/398-9698** or 808/871-7947; fax 808/877-3104; www.hawaiifun.org). The Gold Card, accepted by members on Oahu, the Big Island, Maui, Molokai, Lanai, and Kauai, offers a discount of 10% to 25% off activities and meals for up to four people; it's good for a year from the purchase date and costs $30.

Your Gold Card can lower the regular $149 price of a helicopter ride to only $119.20, saving you almost $120 for a group of four. And there are hundreds of other activities to choose from: dinner cruises, horseback riding, watersports, and more—plus savings on rental cars, restaurants, and golf.

Contact Activities and Attractions to purchase your card; you then contact the outfitter, restaurant, rental-car agency, or other proprietor directly, supply your card number, and receive the discount.

---

view. However, rock climbers are, sadly, out of luck: Most of Hawaii's volcanic cliffs are too steep and too brittle to scale.

Hawaiian Trail and Mountain Club, P.O. Box 2238, Honolulu, HI 96804, offers an information packet on hiking and camping in Hawaii; to receive a copy, send $2 and a legal-size, self-addressed, stamped envelope. **Hawaii Geographic Maps and Books,** 49 S. Hotel St., Honolulu, HI 96813 (© **800/538-3950** or 808/ 538-3952), offers a *Hiking/Camping Information Packet* for $7. Also note that the **Hawaii State Department of Land and Natural Resources,** 1151 Punchbowl St., no. 131, Honolulu, HI 96809 (© **808/587-0300;** www. hawaii.gov), will send you free topographical trail maps.

The **Nature Conservancy of Hawaii** (© **808/537-4508** on Oahu, **808/572-7849** on Maui, **808/553-5236** on Molokai; www.tnc.org/ hawaii) and the **Hawaii Chapter of the Sierra Club,** P.O. Box 2577,

Honolulu, HI 96803 (© **808/538-6616**) both offer guided hikes in preserves and special areas during the year. Also see the individual island chapters for complete details on the best hikes for all ability levels.

Before you set out on the trail, see "Health & Safety," earlier in this chapter, for tips on hiking safety, as well as "What to Pack," earlier in this chapter.

HORSEBACK RIDING One of the best ways to see Hawaii is on horseback; almost all the islands offer riding opportunities for just about every age and level of experience. You can ride into Maui's Haleakala Crater, along Kauai's Mahaulepu Beach, through Oahu's remote windward valleys on Kualoa Ranch, or you can gallop across the wide-open spaces of the Big Island's Parker Ranch, one of the largest privately-owned ranches in the United States. See the individual island chapters for details. Be sure to bring a pair of jeans and closed-toed shoes to wear on your ride.

KAYAKING Hawaii is one of the world's most popular destinations for ocean kayaking. Beginners can paddle across a tropical lagoon to two uninhabited islets off Lanikai Beach on Oahu, while more experienced kayakers can take on Kauai's awesome Na Pali Coast. In summer, experts take advantage of the usually flat conditions on the North Shore of Molokai, where the sea cliffs are the steepest on earth and the remote valleys can be reached only by sea. See "Watersports," in chapters 5 through 9 for local outfitters and tour guides.

SCUBA DIVING Some people come to the islands solely to take the plunge into the tropical Pacific and explore the underwater world. Hawaii is one of the world's top 10 dive destinations, according to *Rodale's Scuba Diving Magazine.* Here you can see the great variety of tropical marine life (more than 100 endemic species found nowhere else on the planet), explore sea caves, and swim with sea turtles and monk seals in clear, tropical water. If you're not certified, try to take classes before you come to Hawaii so you don't waste time learning and can dive right in.

If you dive, **go early in the morning.** Trade winds often rough up the seas in the afternoon, especially on Maui, so most operators schedule early-morning dives that end at noon. To organize a dive on your own, order the *Dive Hawaii Guide,* which describes sites on the various Hawaiian Islands, by sending $2 to **UH/ SGES,** Attention: Dive Guide, 2525 Correa Rd., HIG 237, Honolulu, HI 96822.

Tip: It's usually worth the extra bucks to go with a good dive operator. Check "Scuba Diving" in the island chapters; we've listed the operators that'll give you the most for your money.

SNORKELING Snorkeling is one of Hawaii's main attractions, and almost anyone can do it. All you need is a mask, a snorkel, fins, and some basic swimming skills. In many places, all you have to do is wade into the water and look down at the magical underwater world.

If you've never snorkeled before, most resorts and excursion boats offer snorkeling equipment and lessons. You don't really need lessons, however; it's plenty easy to figure out for yourself,

---

Tips Snorkel Bob's

If you're planning on visiting several islands and would like to rent snorkel gear on one island and keep it with you for your whole trip, try **Snorkel Bob's** (www.snorkelbob.com), which lets you rent snorkels, masks, fins, Boogie Boards, life jackets, and wet suits on any one island and return them on another. The basic set of snorkel gear is $3.50 a day, or $9 a week—a very good deal. The best gear is $6.50 a day, or $29 a week; if you're nearsighted and need a prescription mask, it's $9 a day, or $39 a week.

You can find Snorkel Bob's on **Oahu** at 702 Kapahulu Ave. (at Date Street), Honolulu (© 808/735-7944); on **Maui** at 1217 Front St., in Lahaina (© 808/661-4421), at Napili Village, 5425-C Lower Honapiilani Hwy., Napili (© 808/669-9603), and in South Maui at Kamole Beach Center, 2411 S. Kihei Rd., Kihei (© 808/879-7449); on the **Big Island** at 75–5831 Kahakai St. (off Alii Drive, next to Huggo's and the Royal Kona Resort), in Kailua-Kona (© 808/329-0770); and on **Kauai** at 4–734 Kuhio Hwy. (just north of Coconut Plantation Marketplace), in Kapaa (© 808/823-9433), and in Koloa at 3236 Poipu Rd., near Poipu Beach (© 808/742-2206).

especially once you're at the beach, where everybody around you will be doing it. If you don't have your own gear, you can rent it from dozens of dive shops and activity booths, discussed in the individual island chapters that follow.

While everyone heads for Oahu's Hanauma Bay—the perfect spot for first-timers—other favorite snorkel spots include Kee Beach on Kauai, Kahaluu Beach on the Big Island, Hulopoe Bay on Lanai, and Kapalua Bay on Maui. Although snorkeling is excellent on all the islands, the Big Island, with its recent lava formations and abrupt drop-offs, offers some particularly spectacular opportunities. Some of the best snorkel spots in the islands—notably, the Big Island's Kealakekua Bay and Molokini Crater just off Maui—are accessible only by boat; for tips on the islands' top snorkel boats, see "Watersports," in chapters 5, 6, 7, and 9.

Some snorkel tips: Always snorkel with a buddy. Look up every once in a while to see where you are and if there's any boat traffic. Don't touch anything; not only can you damage coral, but camouflaged fish and shells with poisonous spines may surprise you. Always check with a dive shop, lifeguards, or others on the beach about the area in which you plan to snorkel and ask if there are any dangerous conditions you should know about.

SPORTFISHING   Big-game fishing at its best is found off the Big Island of Hawaii at **Kailua-Kona,** where the deep blue waters offshore yield trophy marlin year-round. You can also try for spearfish, swordfish, various tuna, mahimahi (dorado), rainbow runners, wahoo, barracuda, trevallies, bonefish, and various bottom fish like snappers and groupers. Each island offers deep-sea boat charters for good-eating fish like tuna, wahoo, and mahimahi. Visiting anglers currently need no license.

Charter fishing boats range widely both in size—from small 24-foot open skiffs to luxurious 50-foot-plus yachts-and in price—from about $100 per person to "share" a boat with other anglers for a half-day to $900 a day to book an entire luxury sportfishing yacht on an exclusive basis. Shop around. Prices vary according to the boat, the crowd, and the captain. See the individual island chapters for details. Also, many boat captains tag and release marlin, or keep the fish for themselves (sorry, that's Hawaii style). If you want to eat your mahimahi for dinner or have your marlin mounted, tell the captain before you go.

Money-saving tip: Try contacting the charter boat captain directly and bargaining. Many charter captains pay a 20% to 30% commission to charter-booking agencies and may be willing to give you a discount if you book directly.

SURFING   The ancient Hawaiian practice of *hee nalu* (wave sliding) is probably the sport most people picture when they think of Hawaii. Believe it or not, you too can do some wave sliding—just sign up at any one of the numerous surfing schools located throughout the islands; see "Surfing," in chapters 5, 6, 8, and 9. On world-famous Waikiki Beach, just head over to one of the surf stands that line the sand; these guys say they can get anybody up and standing on a board. If you're already a big kahuna in surfing, check the same chapters for the best deals on rental equipment and the best places to hang ten.

TENNIS   Tennis is a popular sport in the islands. Each island chapter lists details on free municipal courts as well as the best deals on private courts. The etiquette at the free county courts is to play only 45 minutes if someone is waiting.

WHALE-WATCHING   Every winter, pods of Pacific humpback whales

Not So Close! They Hardly Know You

In the excitement of seeing a whale or a school of dolphins, don't forget that they're protected under the Marine Mammals Protection Act. You must stay at least 100 yards (the length of a football field) away from all whales, dolphins, and other marine mammals. This applies to swimmers, kayakers, and windsurfers. And yes, visitors have been prosecuted for swimming with dolphins! If you have any questions, call the **National Marine Fisheries Service** (© 808/541-2727) or the **Hawaiian Islands Humpback Whale National Marine Sanctuary** (© 800/831-4888).

make the 3,000-mile swim from the chilly waters of Alaska to bask in Hawaii's summery shallows, fluking, spy hopping, spouting, breaching, and having an all-around swell time. About 1,500 to 3,000 humpback whales appear in Hawaiian waters each year.

Humpbacks are one of the world's oldest, most impressive inhabitants. Adults grow to be about 45 feet long and weigh a hefty 40 tons. Humpbacks are officially an endangered species; in 1992, the waters around Maui, Molokai, and Lanai were designated a Humpback Whale National Marine Sanctuary. Despite the world's newfound ecological awareness, humpbacks and their habitats and food resources are still under threat from whalers and pollution.

The season's first whale is usually spotted in November, but the best time to see humpback whales in Hawaii is between **January and April**, from any island. Just look out to sea. Each island also offers a variety of whale-watching cruises, which will bring you up close and personal with the mammoth mammals; see the individual island chapters for details.

Money-saving tip: Book a snorkeling cruise during the winter whale-watching months. The captain of the boat will often take you through the best local whale-watching areas on the way, and you'll get two activities for the price of one. It's well worth the money.

WINDSURFING Maui is Hawaii's top windsurfing destination. World-class windsurfers head for Hookipa Beach, where the wind roars through Maui's isthmus and creates some of the best windsurfing conditions in the world. Funky Paia, a derelict sugar town saved from extinction by surfers, is now the world capital of big-wave board sailing. And along Maui's Hana Highway, there are lookouts where you can watch the pros flip off the lip of 10-foot waves and gain hang time in the air.

Others, especially beginners, set their sails for Oahu's Kailua Bay or Kauai's Anini Beach, where gentle onshore breezes make learning this sport a snap. See the individual island chapters for outfitters and local instructors.

8 Getting Married in the Islands

Hawaii is a great place for a wedding. The islands exude romance and natural beauty, and after the ceremony, you're already on your honeymoon. And the members of your wedding party will most likely be delighted, since you've given them the perfect excuse for their own island vacation.

More than 20,000 marriages are performed annually on the islands, mostly on Oahu; nearly half are for couples from somewhere else. The booming wedding business has spawned more than 70 companies that can help you organize a long-distance event and stage an unforgettable wedding, Hawaiian style or your style. However, you can also plan your own island wedding, even from afar, and not spend a fortune doing it.

THE PAPERWORK

The state of Hawaii has some very minimal procedures for obtaining a marriage license. The first thing you should do is contact the **Honolulu Marriage License Office,** State Department of Health Building, 1250 Punchbowl St., Honolulu, HI 96813 (© **808/586-4545;** www.state.hi.us/doh/records/vr_marri.html), which is open Monday through Friday from 8am to 4pm. The office will mail you the brochure *Getting Married* and direct you to the marriage-licensing agent closest to where you'll be staying in Hawaii.

Once in Hawaii, the prospective bride and groom must go together to the marriage-licensing agent to get the license, which costs $60 and is good for 30 days. Both parties must be 15 years of age or older (couples 15–17 years old must have proof of age, written consent of both parents, and written approval of the judge of the family court) and not more closely related than first cousins. That's it.

Gay couples cannot marry in Hawaii. After a protracted legal battle, and much discussion in the state legislature, in late 1999, the Hawaii Supreme Court ruled that the state will not issue marriage licenses to same-sex couples.

PLANNING THE WEDDING

DOING IT YOURSELF   The marriage-licensing agents, who range from employees of the governor's satellite office in Kona to private individuals, are usually friendly, helpful people who can steer you to a nondenominational minister or marriage performer who's licensed by the state of Hawaii. These marriage performers are great sources of information for budget weddings. They usually know wonderful places to have the ceremony for free or for a nominal fee. For the names and address of marriage-licensing agents on Hawaii (Big Island) call © **808/974-6008;** on Kauai, © **808/241-3498;** on Maui, © **808/984-8210;** on Molokai, © **808/553-3663;** and on Lanai, © **808/565-6411.**

If you don't want to use a wedding planner (see below), but you do want to make arrangements before you arrive in Hawaii, our best advice is to get a copy of the daily newspapers on the island where you want to have the wedding. People willing and qualified to conduct weddings advertise in the classifieds. They're great sources of information, as they know the best places to have the ceremony and can recommend caterers, florists, and everything else you'll need. If you want to have your wedding on the Kona/Waimea side of the Big Island, get *West Hawaii Today,* P.O. Box 789, Kailua-Kona, HI 96745 (© 808/329-9311; www.westhawaiitoday.com); for the Hilo/Puna side, try the *Hawaii Tribune Herald,* P.O. Box 767, Hilo, HI 96720 (© 808/935-6621; www.hilohawaiitribune.com). On Maui, get the *Maui News,* P.O. Box 550, Wailuku, HI 96793 (© 808/244-3981; www.mauinews.com). On Kauai, try the *Garden Island,* 3137 Kuhio Hwy., Lihue, HI 96766 (© 808/245-3681; www.kauaiworld.com). And on Oahu, check out the *Honolulu Advertiser,* P.O. Box 3110, Honolulu, HI 96802 (© 808/525-8000; www.honoluluadvertiser.com); the *Honolulu Star Bulletin,* 7 Waterfront Plaza, Suite 500, Honolulu, HI 96813 (© 808/529-4700; www.honolulustarbulletin.com); and *MidWeek,* 45–525 Luluku Rd., Kaneohe, HI 96744 (© 808/235-5881; www.midweek.com).

USING A WEDDING PLANNER
Wedding planners—many of whom are marriage-licensing agents as well—can arrange everything for you, from a small, private, outdoor affair to a full-blown formal ceremony in a tropical setting. They charge anywhere from $225 to a small fortune—it all depends on what you want. On the Big Island, contact **Paradise Weddings Hawaii** (© **800/428-5844** or 808/883-9067; http://planet-hawaii.com/weddings/); on Maui, contact **A Wedding Made in Paradise** (© **800/453-3440** or 808/879-3444; www.

wedinparadise.com); on Kauai, try **Coconut Coast Weddings & Honeymoons** (© **800/585-5595** or 808/826-5557; www.kauaiwedding.com); on Oahu, contact **Aloha Wedding Planners** (© **800/288-8309** or 808/943-2711; www.alohaweddingplanners.com), which offers wedding services on the other islands as well. The Hawaii Visitors and Convention Bureau (see section 1 of this chapter) can provide contact information for other wedding coordinators, and many of the big resorts have their own coordinators on staff.

9 Specialized Travel Resources

FOR TRAVELERS WITH DISABILITIES

Travelers with disabilities are made to feel very welcome in Hawaii. There are more than 2,000 ramped curbs in Oahu alone, hotels are usually equipped with wheelchair-accessible rooms, and tour companies provide many special services. The **Hawaii Center for Independent Living,** 414 Kauwili St., Suite 102, Honolulu, HI 96817 (© **808/522-5400;** fax 808/586-8129; cpdppp@aloha.net), can provide information and send you a copy of the *Aloha Guide to Accessibility* ($15).

Many travel agencies offer customized tours and itineraries for travelers with disabilities. **Flying Wheels Travel** (© **507/451-5005;** www.flyingwheelstravel.com) offers escorted tours and cruises that emphasize sports and private tours in minivans with lifts. **Rumpleduck Travel** (© **877/401-7736** or 310-850-5340) brings a personal touch to designing itineraries and specializes in trips to the U.K., Hawaii and Las Vegas. **Accessible Journeys** (© **800/846-4537** or 610/521-0339; www.disabilitytravel.com) caters specifically to slow walkers and wheelchair travelers and their families and friends.

Organizations that offer assistance to travelers with disabilities include the **Moss Rehab Hospital** (www.mossresourcenet.org), which provides a library of accessible-travel resources online; the **Society for Accessible Travel and Hospitality** (© **212/447-7284;** www.sath.org; annual membership fees: $45 adults, $30 seniors and students), which offers a wealth of travel resources for all types of disabilities and informed recommendations on destinations, access guides, travel agents, tour operators, vehicle rentals, and companion services.

For more information specifically targeted to travelers with disabilities, the community website **iCan** (www.icanonline.net/channels/travel/index.cfm) has destination guides and several regular columns on accessible travel. Also check out the quarterly magazine **Emerging Horizons** ($14.95 per year, $19.95 outside the U.S.; www.emerginghorizons.com); **Twin Peaks Press** (© **360/694-2462;** http://disabilitybookshop.virtualave.net/blist84.htm), offering travel-related books for travelers with special needs; and *Open World Magazine,* published by the Society for Accessible Travel and Hospitality (see above;

subscription: $18 per year, $35 outside the U.S.).

More resources on the Web include **Access-Able Travel Source** (www.access-able.com), which provides information, and **Accessible Vans of America** (www.accessiblevans.com), which offers details on renting a van in Hawaii.

For more details on wheelchair transportation and tours around the islands, see "Getting Around," in the island chapters.

For travelers with disabilities who wish to do their own driving, hand-controlled cars can be rented from **Avis** (© 800/331-1212) and **Hertz** (© 800/654-3131). The number of hand-controlled cars in Hawaii is limited, so be sure to book at least a week in advance. For wheelchair-accessible vans, contact **Accessible Vans of Hawaii** (© 800/303-3750 or 808/879-5521; fax 808/879-0640), which has vans on Oahu, Kauai, Maui, and the Big Island. Hawaii recognizes other states' windshield placards indicating that the driver of the car is disabled, so be sure to bring yours with you.

Vision-impaired travelers who use a Seeing Eye dog can now come to Hawaii without the hassle of quarantine. A recent court decision ruled that visitors with Seeing Eye dogs need only to present documentation that the dog has had rabies shots and is a trained Seeing Eye dog. For more information, contact the **Animal Quarantine Facility** (© 808/483-7171; www.hawaii.gov). The **American Foundation for the Blind** (© 800/232-5463; www.afb.org), also provides information on traveling with Seeing Eye dogs.

FOR GAY & LESBIAN TRAVELERS

Hawaii is known for its acceptance of all groups. The number of gay- or lesbian-specific accommodations on the islands is limited, but most properties welcome gays and lesbians like any other travelers.

The best guide for gay and lesbian visitors is the *Rainbow Handbook Hawaii,* available for $19.95 (© 800/260-5528; www.rainbowhandbook.com).

The Center, mailing address: P.O. Box 22718, Honolulu, 96823 or 2424 S. Beretania St., between Isenberg and University, Honolulu (© 808/951-7000; fax 808/951-7001; thecenter hawaii.org), open Monday through Friday from 10am to 6pm and on Saturday from noon to 4pm, is a referral center for nearly every kind of gay-related service you can think of, including the latest happenings on Oahu. Check out their community newspaper, *Outlook,* published quarterly on local issues in the gay community in the islands.

To get a sense of the local gay and lesbian community on the island of Maui, contact **Out in Maui** (© 808/244-4566), which publishes a monthly newspaper on issues and events for Maui's gay, lesbian, bisexual, and transgender community.

For information on Kauai's gay community and related events, contact the **Gay/Lesbian/Bisexual/Transgender Audio Bulletin Board** (© 808/823-6248).

On the Big Island check out the website for **Out in Hawaii,** www.out inhawaii.com, for information on vacation ideas on the Big Island.

The International Gay & Lesbian Travel Association (IGLTA) (© 800/448-8550 or 954/776-2626; www.iglta.org) is the trade association for the gay and lesbian travel industry, and offers an online directory of gay- and lesbian-friendly travel businesses; go to their website and click on "Members."

Many agencies offer tours and travel itineraries specifically for gay and lesbian travelers. **Above and Beyond Tours** (© 800/397-2681;

www.abovebeyondtours.com) is the exclusive gay and lesbian tour operator for United Airlines. **Now, Voyager** (© **800/255-6951;** www.nowvoyager. com) is a well-known San Francisco–based gay-owned and operated travel service. **Olivia Cruises & Resorts** (© **800/631-6277** or 510/655-0364; www.olivia.com) charters entire resorts and ships for exclusive lesbian vacations and offers smaller group experiences for both gay and lesbian travelers. **Pacific Ocean Holidays** (© **800/735-6600** or 808/923-2400; www.gayhawaii.com), offers vacation packages that feature gay-owned and gay-friendly lodgings. The company also publishes the *Pocket Guide to Hawaii: A Guide for Gay Visitors & Kamaaina.* Send $5 for a copy (mail order only), or access the online version on the website.

The following travel guides are available at most travel bookstores and gay and lesbian bookstores, or you can order them from **Giovanni's Room** bookstore, 1145 Pine St., Philadelphia, PA 19107 (© **215/923-2960;** www.giovannisroom.com): *Out and About* (© **800/929-2268** or 415-644-8044; www.outandabout.com), which offers guidebooks and a newsletter 10 times a year packed with solid information on the global gay and lesbian scene; *Spartacus International Gay Guide* and *Odysseus,* both good, annual English-language guidebooks focused on gay men; the *Damron* guides, with separate, annual books for gay men and lesbians; and *Gay Travel A to Z: The World of Gay & Lesbian Travel Options at Your Fingertips* by Marianne Ferrari (Ferrari Publications; Box 35575, Phoenix, AZ 85069), a very good gay and lesbian guidebook series.

FOR SENIORS

Discounts for seniors are available at almost all of Hawaii's major attractions, and occasionally at hotels and restaurants. The Outrigger hotel chain, for instance, offers travelers ages 50 and older a 20% discount off regular published rates—and an additional 5% off for members of AARP. Always ask when making hotel reservations or buying tickets. And always carry identification with proof of your age—it can really pay off.

Mention the fact that you're a senior citizen when you make your travel reservations. Although all of the major U.S. airlines except America West have cancelled their senior discount and coupon book programs, many hotels still offer discounts for seniors. In most cities, people over the age of 60 qualify for reduced admission to theaters, museums, and other attractions, as well as discounted fares on public transportation.

Members of **AARP** (formerly known as the American Association of Retired Persons), 601 E St. NW, Washington, DC 20049 (© **800/ 424-3410** or 202/434-2277; www. aarp.org), get discounts on hotels, airfares, and car rentals. AARP offers members a wide range of benefits, including *AARP: The Magazine* and a monthly newsletter. Anyone over 50 can join.

If you're 62 or older and plan to visit Hawaii's national parks, you can save sightseeing dollars by picking up a **Golden Age Passport** from any national park, recreation area, or monument. This lifetime pass has a one-time fee of $10 and provides free admission to all the parks in the system, plus a 50% savings on camping and recreation fees. You can pick one up at any park entrance; be sure to have proof of your age with you. For more information, go to www.nps. gov/fees_passes.htm or call © **888/ 467-2757.**

Many reliable agencies and organizations target the 50-plus market. **Elderhostel** (© **877/426-8056;** www.elderhostel.org) arranges study programs for those aged 55 and over (and a spouse or companion of any age) in the U.S. and in more than 80 countries around the world. Most courses last 5 to 7 days in the U.S. (2–4 weeks abroad), and many include airfare, accommodations in university dormitories or modest inns, meals, and tuition. **ElderTreks** (© **800/741-7956;** www.eldertreks. com) offers small-group tours to off-the-beaten-path or adventure-travel locations, restricted to travelers 50 and older.

Recommended publications offering travel resources and discounts for seniors include: the quarterly magazine *Travel 50 & Beyond* (www.travel50andbeyond.com); *Travel Unlimited: Uncommon Adventures for the Mature Traveler* (Avalon); *101 Tips for Mature Travelers,* available from Grand Circle Travel (© **800/221-2610** or 617/350-7500; www.gct.com); *The 50+ Traveler's Guidebook* (St. Martin's Press); and *Unbelievably Good Deals and Great Adventures That You Absolutely Can't Get Unless You're Over 50* (McGraw Hill).

FOR FAMILIES

Hawaii is paradise for children: beaches to run on, water to splash in, and unusual sights to see. Be sure to check out the boxes in each island chapter for kid-friendly places to stay and family activities.

The larger hotels and resorts offer supervised programs for children and can refer you to qualified babysitters. By state law, hotels can accept only children ages 5 to 12 in supervised activities programs, but they often accommodate younger children by simply hiring babysitters to watch over

them. You can also contact **People Attentive to Children (PATCH),** which can refer you to babysitters who have taken a training course on child care. On Oahu, call © **808/839-1988;** on the Big Island, call © **808/329-7101;** on Maui, call © **808/242-9232;** on Kauai, call © **808/246-0622;** or visit www.patch-hi.org.

Baby's Away (www.babysaway.com) rents cribs, strollers, high chairs, playpens, infant seats, and the like on Maui (© **800/ 942-9030** or 808/875-9030), the Big Island (© **800/996-9030** or 808/987-9236), and Oahu (© **800/496-6386** or 808/222-6041). The staff will deliver whatever you need to wherever you're staying and pick it up when you're done.

Familyhostel (© **800/733-9753;** www.learn.unh.edu/familyhostel) takes the whole family, including kids ages 8 to 15, on moderately priced domestic and international learning vacations. Lectures, field trips, and sightseeing are guided by a team of academics.

You can find good family-oriented vacation advice on the Internet from sites like the **Family Travel Network** (www.familytravelnetwork.com); **Traveling Internationally with Your Kids** (www.travelwithyourkids.com), a comprehensive site offering sound advice for long-distance and international travel with children; and **Family Travel Files** (www.thefamilytravelfiles.com), which offers an online magazine and a directory of off-the-beaten-path tours and tour operators for families.

The book *How to Take Great Trips with Your Kids* (The Harvard Common Press) is full of good general advice that can apply to travel anywhere.

10 Planning Your Trip Online

SURFING FOR AIRFARES

The "big three" online travel agencies, **Expedia.com, Travelocity.com,** and

Orbitz.com sell most of the air tickets bought on the Internet. (Canadian travelers should try expedia.ca and

Travelocity.ca; U.K. residents can go for expedia.co.uk and opodo.co.uk.) Each has different business deals with the airlines and may offer different fares on the same flights, so it's wise to shop around. Expedia and Travelocity will also send you **e-mail notification** when a cheap fare becomes available to your favorite destination. Of the smaller travel agency websites, **Side-Step** (www.sidestep.com) has gotten the best reviews from Frommer's authors. It's a browser add-on that purports to "search 140 sites at once," but in reality only beats competitors' fares as often as other sites do.

Also remember to check **airline websites.** You can often shave a few bucks from a fare by booking directly through the airline and avoiding a travel agency's transaction fee. But you'll get these discounts only by **booking online:** Most airlines now offer online-only fares that even their phone agents know nothing about. For the websites of airlines that fly to and from your destination, go to "Getting There & Getting Around," below.

Great **last-minute deals** are available through free weekly e-mail services provided directly by the airlines. Most of these are announced on Tuesday or Wednesday and must be purchased online. Most are only valid for travel that weekend, but some can be booked weeks or months in advance. Sign up for weekly e-mail alerts at airline websites or check mega-sites that compile comprehensive lists of last-minute specials, such as **Smarter Living** (smarterliving.com). For last-minute trips, **site59.com** in the U.S. and **lastminute.com** in Europe often have better deals than the major-label sites.

If you're willing to give up some control over your flight details, use an **opaque fare service** like **Priceline** (www.priceline.com; www.priceline.co.uk for Europeans) or **Hotwire** (www.hotwire.com). Both offer rock-bottom prices in exchange for travel on a "mystery airline" at a mysterious time of day, often with a mysterious change of planes en route. The mystery airlines are all major, well-known carriers—and the possibility of being sent from Philadelphia to Chicago via Tampa is remote; the airlines' routing computers have gotten a lot better than they used to be. But your chances of getting a 6am or 11pm flight are pretty high. Hotwire tells you flight prices before you buy; Priceline usually has better deals than Hotwire, but you have to play their "name our price" game. If you're new at this, the helpful folks at **BiddingForTravel** (www.biddingfortravel.com) do a good job of demystifying Priceline's prices. Priceline and Hotwire are great for flights within North America and between the U.S. and Europe.

For information on surfing for package deals, see "Money-Saving Package Deals," later in this chapter. And for much more about airfares and savvy air-travel tips and advice, pick up a copy of *Frommer's Fly Safe, Fly Smart* (Wiley Publishing).

SURFING FOR HOTELS

Shopping online for hotels is much easier in the U.S., Canada, and certain parts of Europe than it is in the rest of the world. Of the "big three" sites, **Expedia** may be the best choice, thanks to its long list of special deals. **Travelocity** runs a close second. Hotel specialist sites **hotels.com** and **hotel discounts.com** are also reliable. An excellent free program, **TravelAxe** (www.travelaxe.net), can help you search multiple hotel sites at once, even ones you may never have heard of.

Priceline and Hotwire are even better for hotels than for airfares; with both, you're allowed to pick the neighborhood and quality level of your hotel before offering up your money. Priceline's hotel product even covers Europe and Asia, though it's much better at getting five-star lodging for three-star prices than at finding anything at the bottom of the scale. *Note:* Hotwire overrates its hotels by one star—what Hotwire calls a four-star is a three-star anywhere else.

SURFING FOR RENTAL CARS

For booking rental cars online, the best deals are usually found at rental-car company websites, although all the major online travel agencies also offer rental-car reservations services. Priceline and Hotwire work well for rental cars, too; the only "mystery" is which major rental company you get, and for most travelers the difference between Hertz, Avis, and Budget is negligible.

11 The 21st-Century Traveler

INTERNET ACCESS AWAY FROM HOME

Travelers have any number of ways to check their e-mail and access the Internet on the road. Of course, using your own laptop—or even a PDA or electronic organizer with a modem—gives you the most flexibility. But even if you don't have a computer, you can still access your e-mail and even your office computer from cybercafes.

WITHOUT YOUR OWN COMPUTER

It's hard nowadays to find a city that *doesn't* have a few cybercafes. Although there's no definitive directory for cybercafes—these are independent businesses, after all—three places to start looking are at **www.cybercaptive.com**, **www.netcafeguide.com**, and **www.cybercafe.com**.

Aside from formal cybercafes, most **public libraries** across the world offer Internet access free or for a small charge. **Hotel business centers** generally provide access, but most charge exorbitant rates.

Most major airports now have **Internet kiosks** scattered throughout their gates. These kiosks, which you'll also see in shopping malls, hotel lobbies, and tourist information offices around the world, give you basic web access for a per-minute fee that's usually higher than cybercafe prices. The kiosks' clunkiness and high price means they should be avoided whenever possible.

To retrieve your e-mail, ask your **Internet Service Provider (ISP)** if it has a Web-based interface tied to your existing e-mail account. If your ISP doesn't have such an interface, you can use the free **mail2web** service (www.mail2web.com) to view (but not reply to) your home e-mail. For more flexibility, you may want to open a free, Web-based e-mail account with **Yahoo! Mail** (mail.yahoo.com). (Microsoft's Hotmail is another popular option, but Hotmail has severe spam problems.) Your home ISP may be able to forward your e-mail to the Web-based account automatically.

If you need to access files on your office computer, look into a service called **GoToMyPC** (www.gotomypc.com). The service provides a web-based interface for you to access and manipulate a distant PC from anywhere—even a cybercafe—provided your "target" PC is on and has an always-on connection to the Internet (such as with a cable modem). The service offers top-quality security, but if you're worried about hackers, use your own laptop rather than a cybercafe to access the GoToMyPC system.

WITH YOUR OWN COMPUTER

Major Internet Service Providers (ISP) have **local access numbers** around the world, allowing you to go online by simply placing a local call. Check your ISP's website or call its toll-free number and ask how you can use your current account away from home, and how much it will cost.

If you're traveling outside the reach of your ISP, the **iPass** network has dial-up numbers in most of the world. You'll have to sign up with an iPass provider, who will then tell you how to set up your computer for your destination(s). For a list of iPass providers, go to www.ipass.com and click on "Individuals." One solid provider is **i2roam** (www.i2roam.com; © **866/811-6209** or 920/235-0475).

Wherever you go, bring a **connection kit** of the right power and phone adapters, a spare phone cord, and a spare Ethernet network cable.

Most business-class hotels throughout the world offer dataports for laptop modems, and a few thousand hotels in the U.S. and Europe now offer high-speed Internet access using an Ethernet network cable. You'll have to bring your own cables either way, so **call your hotel in advance** to find out what the options are.

Many business-class hotels in the U.S. also offer a form of computer-free Web browsing through the room TV set. We've successfully checked web-based email accounts on these systems.

If you have an 802.11b/**Wi-fi** card for your computer, several commercial companies have made wireless service available in airports, hotel lobbies, and coffee shops, primarily in the U.S. **T-Mobile Hotspot** (www.t-mobile.com/hotspot) serves up wireless connections at more than 1,000 Starbucks coffee shops nationwide. **Boingo** (www.boingo.com) and **Wayport** (www.wayport.com) have set up networks in airports and high-class hotel lobbies. iPass providers (see above) also give you access to a few hundred wireless hotel lobby setups. Best of all, you don't need to be staying at the Four Seasons to use the hotel's network; just set yourself up on a nice couch in the lobby. Unfortunately, the companies' pricing policies are byzantine, with a variety of monthly, per-connection, and per-minute plans.

Community-minded individuals have also set up **free wireless networks** in major cities around the U.S., Europe, and Australia. These networks are spotty, but you get what you (don't) pay for. Each network has a home page explaining how to set up your computer for their particular system; start your explorations at

www.personaltelco.net/index.cgi/Wire
lessCommunities.

USING A CELLPHONE

Just because your cellphone works at
home doesn't mean it'll work elsewhere in the country (thanks to our
nation's fragmented cellphone system). It's a good bet that your phone
will work in major cities. But take a
look at your wireless company's coverage map on its website before heading
out—T-Mobile, Sprint, and Nextel
are particularly weak in rural areas. If
you need to stay in touch at a destination where you know your phone
won't work, **rent** a phone that does
from **InTouch USA** (© **800/872-
7626;** www.intouchglobal.com) or a
rental car location, but beware that
you'll pay $1 a minute or more for air-
time.

If you're venturing deep into
national parks, you may want to consider renting a **satellite phone** (satphones), which are different from
cellphones in that they connect to
satellites rather than ground-based
towers. A satphone is more costly than
a cellphone but works where there's no
cellular signal and no towers. Unfortunately, you'll pay at least $2 per
minute to use the phone, and it only
works where you can see the horizon

(i.e., usually not indoors). In North
America, you can rent Iridium satellite
phones from **RoadPost** (www.road
post.com; © **888/290-1606** or 905/
272-5665). InTouch USA (see above)
offers a wider range of satphones but
at higher rates. As of this writing, satphones were amazingly expensive to
buy, so renting is your best option.

If you're not from the U.S., you'll
be appalled at the poor reach of our
**GSM (Global System for Mobiles)
wireless network,** which is used by
much of the rest of the world (see
below). Your phone will probably
work in most major U.S. cities; it definitely won't work in many rural areas.
(To see where GSM phones work in
the U.S., check out www.t-mobile.
com/coverage/national_popup.asp)
And you may or may not be able to
send SMS (text messaging) home—
something Americans tend not to do
anyway, for various cultural and tech-
nological reasons. (International
budget travelers like to send text messages home because it's much cheaper
than making international calls.)
Assume nothing—call your wireless
provider and get the full scoop. In a
worst-case scenario, you can always
rent a phone; InTouch USA delivers
to hotels.

12 Getting There & Getting Around

For additional advice on travel within
each island, see "Getting Around,"
in the individual island chapters that
follow.

ARRIVING IN THE ISLANDS

Most major U.S. and many international carriers fly to Honolulu International Airport. Some also offer
direct flights to Kailua-Kona, on the
Big Island; Kahului, Maui; and Lihue,
Kauai.

United Airlines (© **800/225-5825;**
www.ual.com) offers the most frequent
service from the U.S. mainland, flying

not only to Honolulu, but also offering
nonstop flights from Los Angeles and
San Francisco to the Big Island, Maui,
and Kauai. **Aloha Airlines** (© **800/
367-5250** or 808/484-1111; www.
alohaairlines.com) has direct flights
from Oakland to Maui, Kona, and
Honolulu, and from Orange County,
CA, to Honolulu and Maui. Aloha also
offers connecting flights from Las Vegas
to Oakland and Orange County.
American Airlines (© **800/433-
7300;** www.americanair.com) offers
flights from Dallas, Chicago, San Francisco, San Jose, Los Angeles and St.

Louis to Honolulu, plus several direct flights to Maui and Kona. **Continental Airlines** (© 800/231-0856; www.continental.com) offers the only daily non-stop from the New York area (Newark) to Honolulu. **Delta Air Lines** (© 800/221-1212; www.delta.com) flies non-stop from the West Coast to both Honolulu and Maui. **Hawaiian Airlines** (© 800/367-5320; www.hawaiianair.com) offers nonstop flights to Honolulu from several West Coast cities (including new service from San Diego), plus nonstop flights from Los Angeles to Maui. **Northwest Airlines** (© 800/225-2525; www.nwa.com) has a daily nonstop from Detroit to Honolulu.

For information on airlines serving Hawaii from places other than the U.S. mainland, see chapter 3. For details on navigating Hawaii's airports, see each island chapter.

AGRICULTURAL SCREENING AT THE AIRPORTS

At Honolulu International and the neighbor-island airports, baggage and passengers bound for the mainland must be screened by agricultural officials before boarding. The process is usually quick and easy. Officials will confiscate fresh avocados, bananas, mangoes, and many other kinds of local produce in the name of fruit-fly control. Pineapples, coconuts, and papayas inspected and certified for export, boxed flowers, leis without seeds, and processed foods (macadamia nuts, coffee, jams, dried fruit, and the like) will pass. Call federal or state agricultural officials before leaving for the airport if you're not sure about your trophy.

INTERISLAND FLIGHTS

Don't expect to jump a ferry between any of the Hawaiian islands; today, everyone island-hops by plane. In the past year, due to the September 11, 2001 terrorist attacks, and the not-so-bright economic picture for the airline industry in Hawaii, the two interisland carriers have cut way, way, way back on the number of interisland flights. Gone are the days when you could catch a flight every 30 or 40 minutes. The number of flights is fewer and you have to book in advance. The airlines warn you to show up at least 90 minutes before your flight and believe me, with all the recent inspections (bag inspections, security inspections, etc.) you will need all 90 minutes to catch your flight. For details on making interisland connections at Honolulu International Airport, see section 1 of chapter 4.

Aloha Airlines (© 800/367-5250 or 808/484-1111; www.alohaairlines.com) is the state's largest provider of interisland air transport service. It offers daily flights throughout Hawaii, using an all-jet fleet of Boeing 737 aircraft. Aloha's sibling company, **Island Air** (© 800/323-3345 or 808/484-2222), serves Hawaii's small interisland airports on Maui, Molokai, and Lanai.

Hawaiian Airlines (© 800/367-5320 or 808/835-3700; www.hawaiianair.com), Hawaii's first interisland airline, has carried more than 100 million passengers to and around the state.

CAR RENTALS

Hawaii has some of the lowest car-rental rates in the country. (An exception is the island of Lanai, where they're very expensive.) The average, nondiscounted, unlimited-mileage rate for a 1-day rental for an intermediate-size car in Honolulu was $44 in 2002; that's the lowest rate in the country, compared with the national average of $55 a day. To rent a car in Hawaii, you must be at least 25 years of age and have a valid driver's license and credit card.

At Honolulu International Airport and most neighbor-island airports,

C Traveling Interisland Post-9/11

Jumping on an interisland flight is not as quick and easy as it was before September 11, 2001. Due to increased security, be sure to check in at least 90 minutes before an interisland flight and 2 hours before a flight to the mainland.

Be prepared to stand in line. The first line you will stand in for interisland travel is the ticket line. Once you make your way to the counter, be prepared to show a photo I.D. (driver's license is best), and keep your I.D. out, as you will have to show it at several other check points.

After you have your ticket, you will then get in another line to have your luggage screened. **DO NOT LOCK YOUR LUGGAGE,** as baggage screeners may have to open your luggage if they see anything out of the norm. We suggest that you go to a hardware store and get plastic tie locks (like minihandcuffs). If the baggage screeners need to open your luggage, they will just cut the plastic and replace it with their own "certified" inspected plastic tie locks. This way when you pick up your bag it should either have your plastic ties or the "certified" ties from security. If your lock is missing and there is no "certified" lock replacing it, someone has gotten into your bag—report it to the airline at once.

Once you and your luggage are checked in (only 1 carry-on is allowed; this is STRICTLY enforced), proceed to the security area to get you into the airport gates.

Here you have to again show your photo ID and your ticket. If you have a laptop, remove it from its carrying case to go through the x-ray scanning device.

You may be asked to remove your shoes and/or to have your carry-on luggage hand inspected. If you are wearing boots or other shoes with a metal shaft in them, save yourself some time and send them through the x-ray machine yourself along with your carry-on. Otherwise you'll set off the metal detector and have to undergo a search.

At the gate area, you will once again go through another inspection (have photo ID and tickets ready) before your board the airplane. Random checks will pull some passengers out of the boarding line, and you and your carry-on will be searched again.

These various lines and checkpoints add up quickly to the full 90 minutes.

you'll find most major rental-car agencies, including **Alamo** (© 800/327-9633; www.goalamo.com), **Avis** (© 800/321-3712; www.avis.com), **Budget** (© 800/935-6878; www.budgetrentacar.com), **Dollar** (© 800/800-4000; www.dollarcar.com), **Enterprise** (© 800/325-8007; www.enterprise.com), **Hertz** (© 800/654-3011; www.hertz.com), **National** (© 800/227-7368; www.nationalcar.com), and **Thrifty** (© 800/367-2277; www.thrifty.com). It's almost always cheaper to rent a car at the airport than in Waikiki or through your hotel (unless there's one already included in your package deal).

A Cruise Through the Islands

If you're looking for a taste of several islands in a single week, consider taking a cruise with **Norwegian Cruise Line** (© **800/327-7030;** www.ncl. com) the only cruise line that operates year-round in the Hawaiian islands.

Norwegian Cruise Line's 91,000 ton, 2,240-passenger ship, *Norwegian Star*, leaves every Sunday from Honolulu and makes stops on The Big Island, Maui, Kauai, and Fanning Island in the Republic of Kiribati, before returning to Honolulu the following Sunday. Prices start at $659 per person, based on double occupancy in a budget cabin and go way up for the nicer staterooms and suites, but deals are often available through travel agents.

The disadvantage of a cruise is that you won't be able to see any of the islands in depth or at leisure; the advantage is that you can spend your days exploring the island where the ship is docked and your nights aboard ship sailing to the next port of call.

Rental cars are usually at a premium on Kauai, Molokai, and Lanai and may be sold out on the neighbor islands on holiday weekends, so be sure to book well ahead.

INSURANCE   Hawaii is a no-fault state, which means that if you don't have collision-damage insurance, you are required to pay for all damages before you leave the state, whether or not the accident was your fault. Your personal car insurance may provide rental-car coverage; read your policy or call your insurer before you leave home. Bring your insurance identification card if you decline the optional insurance, which usually costs from $12 to $20 a day. Obtain the name of your company's local claim representative before you go. Some credit-card companies also provide collision-damage insurance for their customers; check with yours before you rent.

DRIVING RULES   Hawaiian state law mandates that all car passengers must wear a **seat belt,** and all infants must be strapped into car seats. The fine is enforced with vigilance, so buckle up—you'll pay a $50 fine if you don't. **Pedestrians** always have the right of way, even if they're not in the crosswalk. You can turn **right on red** from the right lane after a full and complete stop, unless there's a sign forbidding you to do so.

ROAD MAPS   The best and most detailed road maps are published by *This Week Magazine,* a free visitor publication available on Oahu, the Big Island, Maui, and Kauai. For island maps, check out the University of Hawaii Press maps. Updated periodically, they include a detailed network of island roads, large-scale insets of towns, historical and contemporary points of interest, parks, beaches, and hiking trails. They cost about $3 each or about $15 for a complete set. If you can't find them in a bookstore near you, contact **University of Hawaii Press,** 2840 Kolowalu St., Honolulu, HI 96822 (© **888/847-7737;** www. uhpress.hawaii.edu). For topographic and other maps of the islands, go to the **Hawaii Geographic Society,** 49 S. Hotel St., Honolulu, or contact P.O. Box 1698, Honolulu, HI 96806 (© **800/538-3950** or 808/538-3952).

13 Tips on Accommodations

Hawaii offers all kinds of accommodations, from simple rooms in restored plantation homes and quaint cottages on the beach to luxurious oceanview condo units and opulent suites in beachfront resorts. Each type has its pluses and minuses, so before you book, make sure you know what you're getting into.

TYPES OF ACCOMMODATIONS

HOTELS In Hawaii, "hotel" can indicate a wide range of options, from few or no on-site amenities to enough extras to qualify as a miniresort. Generally, a hotel offers daily maid service and has a restaurant, on-site laundry facilities, a pool, and a sundries/convenience–type shop (rather than the shopping arcades that most resorts have these days). Top hotels also have activities desks, concierge and valet service, room service (though it may be limited), business centers, airport shuttles, bars and/or lounges, and perhaps a few more shops.

The advantages of staying in a hotel are privacy and convenience; the disadvantage is generally noise (either thin walls between rooms or loud music from a lobby lounge late into the night). Hotels are often a short walk from the beach rather than right on the beachfront (although there are exceptions).

RESORTS In Hawaii, a resort offers everything a hotel does—and more. You can expect such extras as direct beach access, with beach cabanas and lounge chairs; pools (often more than one) and a Jacuzzi; a spa and fitness center; restaurants, bars, and lounges; a 24-hour front desk; concierge, valet, and bellhop services; room service (often around the clock); an activities desk; tennis and golf (some of the world's best courses are at Hawaii resorts); ocean activities; a business center; kids' programs; and more.

The advantages of a resort are that you have everything you could possibly want in the way of services and things to do; the disadvantage is that the price generally reflects this. And don't be misled by a name—just because a place is called "ABC Resort" doesn't mean it actually *is* a resort. Make sure you're getting what you pay for.

CONDOS The roominess and convenience of a condo—which is usually a fully equipped, multiple-bedroom apartment—makes this a great choice for families. Condominium properties in Hawaii generally consist of several apartments set in either a single high-rise or a cluster of low-rise units. Condos usually have amenities such as some maid service (ranging from daily to weekly; it may or may not be included in your rate, so be sure to ask), a pool, laundry facilities (either in your unit or in a central location), and an on-site front desk or a live-in property manager. Condos vary in

---

Nickel-and-Dime Charges at High-Priced Hotels

Several upscale resorts in Hawaii have begun a practice that we find distasteful, dishonest, and downright discouraging: charging a so-called "resort fee." This daily fee is added on to your bill (and can range from $10–$15 a day), for such "complimentary" items as a daily newspaper, local phone calls, use of the fitness facilities, and the like. Amenities that the resort has been happily providing its guests for years are now tacked on to your bill under the guise of a "fee." In most cases you do not have an option to decline the resort fee—in other words, this is a sneaky way to further increase the prices without telling you. We are very opposed to this practice and urge you to voice your complaints to the resort management. Otherwise, what'll be next—a charge for using the tiny bars of soap or miniature shampoo bottles?

price according to size, location, and amenities. Many of them are on or near the beach, and they tend to be clustered in resort areas. While there are some very high-end condos, most are quite affordable, especially if you're traveling in a group that's large enough to require more than one bedroom.

The advantages of a condo are privacy, space, and conveniences—which usually include a full kitchen, a washer and dryer, a private phone, and more. The downsides are the standard lack of an on-site restaurant and the density of the units (versus the privacy of a single-unit vacation rental).

BED-AND-BREAKFASTS   Hawaii has a wide range of places that call themselves B&Bs: everything from a traditional B&B—several bedrooms (which may or may not share a bathroom) in a home, with breakfast served in the morning—to what is essentially a vacation rental on an owner's property that comes with fixings for you to make your own breakfast. Make sure that the B&B you're booking matches your own mental picture. Would you prefer conversation around a big dining-room table as you eat a hearty breakfast or just a muffin and juice to enjoy in your own private place? Note that laundry facilities and private phones are not always available. We've reviewed lots of wonderful B&Bs in the island chapters that follow. If you have to share a bathroom, we've spelled it out in the listings; otherwise, you can assume that you will have your own.

The advantages of a traditional B&B are its individual style and congenial atmosphere. Bed-and-breakfasts are great places to meet other visitors to Hawaii, and the host is generally happy to act as your own private concierge, giving you tips on where to go and what to do. In addition, they're usually an affordable way to go (though fancier ones can run $150 or more). The disadvantages are lack of privacy, usually a set time for breakfast, few amenities, generally no maid service, and the fact that you'll have to share the quarters beyond your bedroom with others. Also, B&B owners

---

ⓒ What If Your Dream Hotel Becomes a Nightmare?

To avoid any unpleasant surprises, find out when you make your reservation exactly what the accommodation is offering you: cost, minimum stay, included amenities. Ask if there's any penalty for leaving early. Discuss with the property or booking agency what the cancellation policy is if the accommodation fails to meet your expectations—and get this policy in writing.

When you arrive, if you're not satisfied with your room, notify the front desk or booking agency immediately. Approach the management in a calm, reasonable manner, and suggest a solution (like moving to another unit). Be willing to compromise. Do not leave; if you do, you may not get your deposit back.

If all else fails, when you get home, write to any association the accommodation may be a member of (the Hawaii Visitors and Convention Bureau, a resort association, or an island association). Describe your complaint and why the issue was not resolved to your satisfaction. And be sure to let us know if you have a problem with a place we recommend in this book!

usually require a minimum stay of 2 or 3 nights, and it's often a drive to the beach.

VACATION RENTALS This is another great choice for families and for long-term stays. "Vacation rental" usually means that there will be no one on the property where you're staying. The actual accommodation can range from an apartment in a condominium building to a two-room cottage on the beach to an entire fully equipped house. Generally, vacation rentals allow you to settle in and make yourself at home for a while. They have kitchen facilities (which can be either a complete kitchen or just a kitchenette with microwave, refrigerator, burners, and coffeemaker), on-site laundry facilities, and phone; some also come outfitted with such extras as a TV, VCR, and stereo.

The advantages of a vacation rental are complete privacy, your own kitchen (which can save you money on meals), and lots of conveniences. The disadvantages are a lack of an on-site property manager and generally no maid service; often, a minimum stay is required (sometimes as much as a week). If you book a vacation rental, be sure that you have a 24-hour contact to call if the toilet won't flush or you can't figure out how to turn on the air-conditioning.

BARGAINING ON PRICES

Rates can sometimes be bargained down, but it depends on the place. In general, each type of accommodation allows a different amount of latitude in bargaining on their rack (published) rates.

The best bargaining can be had at **hotels** and **resorts.** Both regularly pay travel agents a commission of as much as 30%; if business is slow, some places may give you the benefit of at least part of this commission if you book directly instead of going through an agent. Most hotels and resorts also have *kamaaina* (local) rates for islanders, which they may extend to visitors during slow periods. It never hurts to ask about discounted or local rates; a host of special rates are available for the military, seniors, members of the travel industry, families, corporate travelers, and long-term stays. Also ask about **package deals,** which might include a car rental or free breakfast for the same price as a room by itself. Hotels and resorts offer packages for everyone: golfers, tennis players, families, honeymooners, and more (see "Money-Saving Package Deals," below). We've found that it's worth the extra few cents to make a local call to the hotel; sometimes the local reservations person knows about package deals that the toll-free operators are unaware of. If all else fails, try to get the hotel or resort to upgrade you to a better room for the same price as a budget room, or waive the parking fee or extra fees for children. Persistence and polite inquiries can pay off.

It's harder to bargain at **bed-and-breakfasts.** You may be able to negotiate down the minimum stay or get a discount if you're staying a week or longer. But generally, a B&B owner has only a few rooms and has already priced the property at a competitive rate; expect to pay what's asked.

You have somewhat more leeway to negotiate at **vacation rentals** and **condos.** In addition to asking for a discount on a multi-night stay, also ask if they can throw in a rental car to sweeten the deal; believe it or not, they often will.

USING A BOOKING AGENCY VERSUS DOING IT YOURSELF

If you don't have the time to call several places yourself to bargain for prices and to make sure they offer the amenities you'd like, you might consider a booking agency. The time an agency spends on your behalf may be well worth any fees you'll have to pay.

Tips B&B Etiquette

In Hawaii, it is traditional and customary to remove your shoes before entering anyone's home. The same is true for most bed-and-breakfast facilities. Most hosts post signs or will politely ask you to remove your shoes before entering the B&B. Not only does this keep the B&B clean, but you'll be amazed how relaxed you feel walking around barefoot. If this custom is unpleasant to you, a B&B may not be for you. Consider a condo or hotel, where no one will be particular about your shoes.

Hotels, resorts, condos, and vacation rentals generally allow smoking in the guest rooms (most also have nonsmoking rooms available), but the majority of bed-and-breakfast units forbid smoking in the rooms. If this matters to you, be sure to check the policy of your accommodation before you book.

The top reservations service in the state is **Hawaii's Best Bed & Breakfasts** (© **800/262-9912** or 808/985-7488; fax 808/967-8610; www.bestbnb.com). This service charges $15 to book the first two locations and $5 for each additional location. The owners personally select the traditional homestays, cottages, and inns, based on each one's hospitality, distinctive charm, and attention to detail. They also book vacation rentals, hotels, and resorts.

Other great statewide booking agents are **Bed & Breakfast Hawaii** (© **800/733-1632** or 808/822-7771; fax 808/822-2723; www.bandb-hawaii.

com), offering a range of accommodations from vacation homes to B&Bs, starting at $75 a night; and **Ann and Bob Babson** (© **800/824-6409** or 808/874-1166; fax 808/879-7906; www.mauibnb.com), who can steer you in the right direction for both accommodations and car rentals.

For vacation rentals, contact **Hawaii Beachfront Vacation Homes** (© **808/247-3637;** fax 808/235-2644). **Hawaii Condo Exchange** (© **800/442-0404;** http://hawaiicondoexchange.com) acts as a consolidator for condo and vacation-rental properties.

14 Money-Saving Package Deals

More often than not, the most cost-effective way to travel to Hawaii is by booking an all-inclusive travel package that includes some combination of airfare, accommodations, rental car, meals, airport and baggage transfers, and sightseeing. The best place to start looking for a package deal is in the travel section of your local Sunday newspaper. Also check the ads in the back of such national travel magazines as *Travel Holiday, National Geographic Traveler,* and *Arthur Frommer's Budget Travel.* **Liberty Travel** (© **888/271-1584;** www.libertytravel.com), one of

the biggest packagers in the Northeast, usually boasts a full-page ad in the Sunday papers. **American Express Travel** (© **800/AXP-6898;** www.americanexpress.com/travel) can also book you a well-priced Hawaiian vacation.

Some packagers specialize in Hawaiian vacations. **Pleasant Holidays** (© **800/2-HAWAII** or 800/242-9244; www.pleasantholidays.com) is by far the biggest and most comprehensive packager to Hawaii; it offers an extensive, high-quality collection of 50 condos and hotels in every price range. **Travelzoo** (www.travelzoo.com) often has package deals to Hawaii as well.

Other reliable packagers include the airlines themselves, which often package their flights together with accommodations. **United Vacations** (© 800/328-6877; www.unitedvacations.com) is the most comprehensive airline packager to Hawaii, offering great air-inclusive and land-only deals on a surprisingly wide selection of accommodations throughout the islands. Other airlines offering good-value packages to the islands are **American Airlines Vacations** (© 800/321-2121; www.aa.com), **Continental Airlines Vacations** (© 800/634-5555 or 800/301-3800; www.coolvacations.com), and **Delta Dream Vacations** (© 800/872-7786; www.deltavacations.com). If you're traveling to the islands from Canada, ask your travel agent about package deals through **Air Canada Vacations** (© 800/776-3000; www.aircanada.ca).

GREAT PACKAGE DEALS AT HAWAII'S TOP HOTEL CHAINS

For years, the name **Outrigger** has been synonymous with excellent, affordable accommodations that all have consistently clean and well-appointed rooms. In 1999, the Outrigger chain divided its properties into two categories: the 15 moderately priced "Ohana" (Hawaiian for family) Hotels in Waikiki (and one in Maui), offering quality accommodations (with air-conditioning, in-room safe,

TV, refrigerator, and coffeemaker) from $109 to $139; and more upscale "Outrigger" resorts and condominiums on Oahu, Maui, Kauai, and the Big Island. The **Ohana Hotels** (© 800/462-6262; www.ohanahotels.com) offer a range of affordable package deals, while the **Outrigger** properties (© 800/OUTRIGGER; www.outrigger.com) also offer discounts for multinight stays, family plans, cut rates for seniors, and even packages for golfers and lovers.

The **Aston** chain (© 800/92-ASTON; www.aston-hotels.com), which celebrated 50 years in Hawaii in 1998, has some 37 hotels, condominiums, and resort properties scattered throughout the islands. They range dramatically in price and style, from the luxurious Whaler on Kaanapali Beach, Maui to the more budget Aston Coconut Plaza Hotel in Waikiki. Aston offers package deals galore including family packages; discounted senior rates; car, golf, and shopping packages; and multinight deals. The wonderful Island Hopper deal allows you to travel from island to island and get 25% off on 7 nights or more at Aston properties.

Marc Resorts Hawaii (© 800/535-0085; fax 800/633-5085; www.marcresorts.com) has 18 properties on every island but Lanai, ranging from the Embassy Vacation Resort Kaanapali on Maui, to Molokai Shores, an affordable condominium property. It offers packages for seniors, multinight stays, honeymooners, and golfers, as

---

⌐ Tips A Package-Buying Tip

For one-stop shopping on the Web, go to **www.vacationpackager.com**, a search engine that can link you up with many different package-tour operations; be sure to look under both "Hawaii" and "Hawaiian Islands." Or, point your browser to **www.2travel.com/2where/america/hawaii/index.html**, which takes you directly to a page with links to all of the big-name companies offering package tours to Hawaii.

well as corporate discounts and car-rental deals.

Castle Resorts and Hotels (© **800/ 367-5004;** fax 800/477-2329; www. castle-group.com) has 14 condominiums and hotels on every island except Lanai, ranging from the budget Hotel Molokai to the mid-range Hawaiian Monarch Hotel in Waikiki. Package deals that range from a free car rental to a free night's stay are available.

FAST FACTS: **The Hawaiian Islands**

AAA Hawaii's only American Automobile Association (AAA) office is at 1270 Ala Moana Blvd., Honolulu (© **808/593-2221**). Some car-rental agencies now provide auto club–type services, so you should inquire about their availability when you rent your car.

American Express For 24-hour traveler's check refunds and purchase information, call © **800/221-7282**. For local offices, see "Fast Facts" sections in the individual island chapters.

Area Code All the Hawaiian Islands are in the **808** area code. Note that if you're calling one island from another, you'll have to dial 1-808 first, and you'll be billed at long-distance rates (which can be more expensive than calling the mainland).

Business Hours Most offices are open Monday through Friday from 8am to 5pm. The morning commute usually runs from 6 to 8am, while the evening rush is from 4 to 6pm. Bank hours are Monday through Thursday from 8:30am to 3pm and Friday from 8:30am to 6pm; some banks are open on Saturday as well. Shopping centers are open Monday through Friday from 10am to 9pm, Saturday 10am to 5:30pm, and Sunday from noon to 5 or 6 pm.

Emergencies Dial © **911** for police, fire, or ambulance.

Legal Aid Contact the **Legal Aid Society of Hawaii**, 1108 Nuuanu Ave., Honolulu (© **808/536-4302**).

Liquor Laws The legal drinking age in Hawaii is 21. Bars are allowed to stay open daily until 2am; places with cabaret licenses are able to keep the booze flowing until 4am. Grocery and convenience stores are allowed to sell beer, wine, and liquor 7 days a week.

Newspapers The *Honolulu Advertiser* and the *Honolulu Star Bulletin* are circulated statewide. Other weekly newspapers on Oahu include the *Honolulu Weekly* and *Pacific Business News.* Neighbor-island newspapers are published daily on Maui (*Maui News*), Kauai (*Garden Island* and *Kauai Times*), and the Big Island (*West Hawaii Today* and *Hawaii Tribune Herald*); Molokai has two weeklies.

Smoking It's against the law to smoke in public buildings, including airports, grocery stores, retail shops, movie theaters, banks, and all government buildings and facilities. Hotels have nonsmoking rooms available, restaurants have nonsmoking sections, and car-rental agencies have smoke-free cars. Most bed-and-breakfasts prohibit smoking indoors.

Taxes Hawaii's sales tax is 4%. The hotel-occupancy tax is 7.25%, and hoteliers are allowed by the state to tack on an additional 0.1666% excise tax. Thus, expect taxes of about 11.42% to be added to your hotel bill.

Time Zone Hawaii is 2 hours behind Pacific standard time and 5 hours behind eastern standard time. In other words, when it's noon in Hawaii, it's 2pm in California and 5pm in New York during standard time on the mainland. There's no daylight saving time here, so when daylight saving time is in effect on the mainland, Hawaii is 3 hours behind the West Coast and 6 hours behind the East Coast; in summer, when it's noon in Hawaii, it's 3pm in California and 6pm in New York.

Hawaii is east of the International Date Line, putting it in the same day as the U.S. mainland and Canada, and a day behind Australia, New Zealand, and Asia.

3

For International Visitors

The pervasiveness of American culture around the world may make the United States feel like familiar territory to foreign visitors, but leaving your own country for the States—especially the unique island state of Hawaii—still requires some additional planning.

1 Preparing for Your Trip

ENTRY REQUIREMENTS

Check at any U.S. embassy or consulate for current information and requirements. You can also obtain a visa application and other information online at the **U.S. State Department**'s website, at **www.travel.state.gov**. Click on "Visas for Foreign Citizens" for the latest entry requirements, while "Foreign Consular Offices" and "Links to Foreign Embassies" will provide you with contact information for U.S. embassies and consulates worldwide.

VISAS The U.S. State Department has a **Visa Waiver Program** that allows citizens of certain countries to enter the United States without a visa for stays of up to 90 days. At press time, this visa waiver program applied to citizens of Andorra, Australia, Austria, Belgium, Brunei, Denmark, Finland, France, Germany, Iceland, Ireland, Italy, Japan, Liechtenstein, Luxembourg, Monaco, the Netherlands, New Zealand, Norway, Portugal, San Marino, Singapore, Slovenia, Spain, Sweden, Switzerland, the United Kingdom, and Uruguay. Citizens of these countries need only a valid "machine readable" passport; proof of financial security; and a round-trip air or cruise ticket in their possession upon arrival. Further information is available from any U.S. embassy or consulate. Canadian citizens may enter the United States without visas; they need only proof of residence.

Citizens of all other countries must have: (1) a valid passport that expires at least 6 months later than the scheduled end of their visit to the United States, and (2) a tourist visa, which may be obtained from any U.S. consulate.

To obtain a visa, you must submit a completed application form (either in person or by mail) with two 1½-inch-square photos and a US$100 fee, and must demonstrate binding ties to a residence abroad. Since the September 11, 2001 terrorist attacks, the State Department now subjects visa applications to a greater degree of scrutiny than in the past. Expect delays, the days of 24-hour turn around are gone. The only estimate that the State Department will make is their recommendations to "build in apply time before planned travel date." *Note:* It may take even longer to get a visa during the summer rush from June through August. If you cannot go in person, contact the nearest U.S. embassy or consulate for directions on applying by mail. Your travel agent or airline office may also be able to provide you with visa applications and instructions. The U.S. consulate or embassy that issues your visa will determine if you will be issued a multiple- or single-entry visa and any restrictions regarding the length of your stay.

British subjects can obtain up-to-date passport and visa information by calling the **U.S. Embassy Visa Information Line** (✆ **0891/200-290**) or the **London Passport Office** (✆ **0990/210-410** for recorded information) or they can find the visa information on the U.S. Embassy Great Britain website at www.passport. gov.uk.

Irish citizens can obtain up-to-date passport and visa information through the **Embassy of USA Dublin,** 42 Elgin Rd., Dublin 4, Ireland (✆ **353/ 1-668-8777**) or by checking the visa page on the website at www.us embassy.ie.

Australian citizens can obtain up-to-date passport and visa information by calling the **U.S. Embassy Canberra,** Moonah Place, Yarralumla, ACT 2600 (✆ **02/6214-5600**) or check the website's visa page at www. usis-australia.gov/consular/niv.html.

Citizens of **New Zealand** can obtain up-to-date passport and visa information by calling the **U.S. Embassy New Zealand,** 29 Fitzherbert Terr., Thorndon, Wellington, New Zealand; ✆ **644/472-2068** or get the information directly from the website at http://usembassy.org.nz.

Foreign driver's licenses are recognized in Hawaii, although you may want to get an international driver's license if your home license is not written in English.

MEDICAL REQUIREMENTS

Unless you're arriving from an area known to be suffering from an epidemic (particularly cholera or yellow fever), inoculations or vaccinations are not required for entry into the United States. If you have a medical condition that requires **syringe-administered medications,** carry a valid signed prescription from your physician—the Federal Aviation Administration (FAA) no longer allows airline passengers to pack syringes in their carry-on baggage without documented proof of medical need. If you have a disease that requires treatment with **narcotics,** you should also carry documented proof with you—smuggling narcotics aboard a plane is a serious offense that carries severe penalties in the U.S.

For **HIV-positive visitors,** requirements for entering the United States are somewhat vague and change frequently. According to the latest publication of *HIV and Immigrants: A Manual for AIDS Service Providers*, the Immigration and Naturalization Service (INS) doesn't require a medical exam for entry into the United States, but INS officials may stop individuals because they look sick or because they are carrying AIDS/HIV medicine.

If an HIV-positive noncitizen applies for a non-immigrant visa, the question on the application regarding communicable diseases is tricky no matter which way it's answered. If the applicant checks "no," INS may deny the visa on the grounds that the applicant committed fraud. If the applicant checks "yes" or if INS suspects the person is HIV-positive, it will deny the visa unless the applicant asks for a special waiver for visitors. This waiver is for people visiting the United States for a short time, to attend a conference, for instance, to visit close relatives, or to receive medical treatment. It can be a confusing situation. For further up-to-the-minute information, contact the Centers for Disease Control's **National Center for HIV** (✆ **404/332-4559;** www.hivatis.org) or the **Gay Men's Health Crisis** (✆ **212/367-1000;** www.gmhc.org).

CUSTOMS
WHAT YOU CAN BRING IN

Every visitor more than 21 years of age may bring in, free of duty, the following: (1) 1 liter of wine or hard liquor; (2) 200 cigarettes, 100 cigars (but not from Cuba), or 3 pounds of smoking tobacco; and (3) $100 worth of gifts.

These exemptions are offered to travelers who spend at least 72 hours in the United States and who have not claimed them within the preceding 6 months. It is altogether forbidden to bring into the country foodstuffs (particularly fruit, cooked meats, and canned goods) and plants (vegetables, seeds, tropical plants, and the like). Foreign tourists may bring in or take out up to $10,000 in U.S. or foreign currency with no formalities; larger sums must be declared to U.S. Customs on entering or leaving, which includes filing form CM 4790. For more specific information regarding U.S. Customs, contact your nearest U.S. embassy or consulate, or the **U.S. Customs** office (*☎* **202/927-1770** or www.customs.ustreas.gov).

WHAT YOU CAN TAKE HOME

U.K. citizens returning from a non-EU country have a Customs allowance of: 200 cigarettes; 50 cigars; 250g of smoking tobacco; 2 liters of still table wine; 1 liter of spirits or strong liqueurs (over 22% volume); 2 liters of fortified wine, sparkling wine or other liqueurs; 60cc (ml) perfume; 250cc (ml) of toilet water; and £145 worth of all other goods, including gifts and souvenirs. People under 17 cannot have the tobacco or alcohol allowance. For more information, contact HM Customs & Excise at *☎* **0845/010-9000** (from outside the U.K., 020/8929-0152), or consult their website at www.hmce.gov.uk.

For a clear summary of **Canadian** rules, request the booklet *I Declare*, issued by the **Canada Customs and Revenue Agency** (*☎* **800/461-9999** in Canada, or 204/983-3500; www.ccra-adrc.gc.ca). Canada allows its citizens a C$750 exemption, and you're allowed to bring back duty-free one carton of cigarettes, 1 can of tobacco, 40 imperial ounces of liquor, and 50 cigars (if you're bringing tobacco or alcohol products back, you must meet local age restrictions). In addition, you're allowed to mail gifts to Canada valued at less than C$60 a day, provided they're unsolicited and don't contain alcohol or tobacco (write on the package "Unsolicited gift, under $60 value"). All valuables should be declared on the Y-38 form before departure from Canada, including serial numbers of valuables you already own, such as expensive foreign cameras. *Note:* The $750 exemption can only be used once a year and only after an absence of 7 days.

The duty-free allowance in **Australia** is A$400 or, for those under 18, A$200. Citizens age 18 and over can bring in 250 cigarettes or 250 grams of loose tobacco, and 1,125 milliliters of alcohol. If you're returning with valuables you already own, such as foreign-made cameras, you should file form B263. A helpful brochure available from Australian consulates or Customs offices is *Know Before You Go*. For more information, call the **Australian Customs Service** at *☎* **1300/363-263,** or log on to www.customs.gov.au.

The duty-free allowance for **New Zealand** is NZ$700. Citizens over 17 can bring in 200 cigarettes, 50 cigars, or 250 grams of tobacco (or a mixture of all 3 if their combined weight doesn't exceed 250g); plus 4.5 liters of wine and beer, or 1.125 liters of liquor. New Zealand currency does not carry import or export restrictions. Fill out a certificate of export, listing the valuables you are taking out of the country; that way, you can bring them back without paying duty. Most questions are answered in a free pamphlet available at New Zealand consulates and Customs offices: *New Zealand Customs Guide for Travellers, Notice no. 4*. For more information, contact **New Zealand Customs,** The Customhouse, 17–21 Whitmore St., Box 2218, Wellington (*☎* **0800/428-786** or 04/473-6099; www.customs.govt.nz).

INSURANCE

Although it's not required of travelers, health insurance is highly recommended. Unlike many European countries, the United States does not usually offer free or low-cost medical care to its citizens or visitors. Doctors and hospitals are expensive, and in most cases will require advance payment or proof of coverage before they render their services. Policies can cover everything from the loss or theft of your baggage and trip cancellation to the guarantee of bail in case you're arrested. Good policies will also cover the costs of an accident, repatriation, or death. See "Insurance," in chapter 2 for more information. Packages such as **Europ Assistance's "Worldwide Healthcare Plan"** are sold by European automobile clubs and travel agencies at attractive rates. **Worldwide Assistance Services, Inc.** (© 800/821-2828; www.worldwideassistance.com) is the agent for Europ Assistance in the United States.

Though lack of health insurance may prevent you from being admitted to a hospital in nonemergencies, don't worry about being left on a street corner to die: the American way is to fix you now and bill the living daylights out of you later.

INSURANCE FOR BRITISH TRAVELERS
Most big travel agents offer their own insurance and will probably try to sell you their package when you book a holiday. Think before you sign. **Britain's Consumers' Association** recommends that you insist on seeing the policy and reading the fine print before buying travel insurance. **The Association of British Insurers** (© 020/7600-3333; www.abi.org.uk) gives advice by phone and publishes *Holiday Insurance,* a free guide to policy provisions and prices. You might also shop around for better deals: Try **Columbus Direct** (© 020/7375-0011; www.columbusdirect.net).

INSURANCE FOR CANADIAN TRAVELERS
Canadians should check with their provincial health plan offices or call **Health Canada** (© 613/957-2991; www.hc-sc.gc.ca) to find out the extent of their coverage and what documentation and receipts they must take home in case they are treated in the United States.

MONEY

CURRENCY The U.S. monetary system is very simple: The most common **bills** are the $1 (colloquially, a "buck"), $5, $10, and $20 denominations. There are also $2 bills (seldom encountered), $50 bills, and $100 bills (the last two are usually not welcome as payment for small purchases). All the paper money was recently redesigned, making the famous faces adorning them disproportionately large. The old-style bills are still legal tender.

There are seven denominations of coins: 1¢ (1 cent, or a penny); 5¢ (5 cents, or a nickel); 10¢ (10 cents, or a dime); 25¢ (25 cents, or a quarter); 50¢ (50 cents, or a half dollar); the new gold "Sacagawea" coin worth $1; and, prized by collectors, the rare, older silver dollar.

EXCHANGING CURRENCY Exchanging foreign currency for U.S. dollars is usually painless in Oahu. Generally, the best rates of exchange are available through major banks, most of which exchange foreign currency. In Waikiki, go to **A-1 Foreign Exchange,** which has offices in the Royal Hawaiian Shopping Center, 2301 Kalakaua Ave., and in the Hyatt Regency Waikiki Tower, 2424 Kalakaua Ave. (© **808/922-3327**), or **Pacific Money Exchange,** 339 Royal Hawaiian Ave. (© **808/924-9318**). There also are currency services at **Honolulu International Airport.** Most of the major hotels offer currency-exchange services, but generally the rate of exchange is not as good as what you'll get at a bank.

On the other islands, it's not so easy. None of the other airports have currency-exchange facilities. You'll need to either go to a bank (call first to see if currency exchange is available) or use your hotel.

TRAVELER'S CHECKS Though traveler's checks are widely accepted at most hotels, restaurants, and large stores, *make sure that they're denominated in U.S. dollars,* as foreign-currency checks are often difficult to exchange. The three traveler's checks that are most widely recognized—and least likely to be denied—are **Visa, American Express,** and **Thomas Cook/MasterCard.** Be sure to record the numbers of the checks, and keep that information separately in case they get lost or stolen. Most businesses are pretty good about taking traveler's checks, but you're better off cashing them in at a bank (in small amounts, of course) and paying in cash. *Remember:* You'll need identification, such as a driver's license or passport, to change a traveler's check. It's generally easier to use ATMs than to bother with traveler's checks.

CREDIT CARDS Credit cards are widely used in Hawaii. You can save yourself trouble by using plastic rather than cash or traveler's checks in most hotels, restaurants, retail stores, and a growing number of food and liquor stores. You must have a credit card to rent a car in Hawaii.

SAFETY

GENERAL SAFETY Although tourist areas are generally safe, visitors should always stay alert, even in laid-back Hawaii (and especially in Waikiki). It's wise to ask the island tourist office if you're in doubt about which neighborhoods are safe. Avoid deserted areas, especially at night. Don't go into any city park at night unless there's an event that attracts crowds—for example, the Waikiki Shell concerts in Kapiolani Park. Generally speaking, you can feel safe in areas where there are many people and open establishments.

Avoid carrying valuables with you on the street, and don't display expensive cameras or electronic equipment. Hold onto your pocketbook, and place your billfold in an inside pocket. In theaters, restaurants, and other public places, keep your possessions in sight.

Recently, there has been a series of purse-snatching incidents in Oahu. Thieves in slow-moving cars or on foot have snatched handbags from female pedestrians (in some instances, dragging women who refuse to let go of their pocketbooks down the street). The Honolulu police department advises women to carry their purses on the shoulder away from the street or, better yet, to wear the strap across the chest instead of on one shoulder. Women with clutch bags should hold them close to their chest.

Remember also that hotels are open to the public and that, in a large hotel, security may not be able to screen everyone entering. Always lock your room door—don't assume that once inside your hotel, you're automatically safe.

DRIVING SAFETY Safety while driving is particularly important. Ask your rental agency about personal safety, or request a brochure of traveler safety tips when you pick up your car. Get written directions or a map with the route marked in red showing you how to get to your destination.

Recently, crime has involved more burglary of tourist rental cars in hotel parking structures and at beach parking lots. Park in well-lighted and well-traveled areas if possible. Never leave any packages or valuables visible in the car. If someone attempts to rob you or steal your car, do not try to resist the thief or carjacker—report the incident to the police department immediately.

For more information on driving rules and getting around by car in Hawaii, see "Getting There & Getting Around," in chapter 2.

2 Getting to & Around the United States

Airlines serving Hawaii from places other than the U.S. mainland include **Air Canada** (✆ 800/776-3000; www.aircanada.ca); **Air New Zealand** (✆ 0800/737-000 in Auckland, 643/379-5200 in Christchurch, 800/926-7255 in the U.S.; www.airnewzealand.com), which runs 40 flights per week between Auckland and Hawaii; **Qantas** (✆ 008/177-767 in Australia, 800/227-4500 in the U.S.; www.qantas.com.au), which flies between Sydney and Honolulu daily (plus additional flights 4 days a week); **Japan Air Lines** (✆ 03/5489-1111 in Tokyo, 800/525-3663 in the U.S.; www.japanair.com); **All Nippon Airways (ANA)** (✆ 03/5489-1212 in Tokyo, 800/235-9262 in the U.S.; www.fly-ana.com); **China Airlines** (✆ 02/715-1212 in Taipei, 800/227-5118 in the U.S.; www.china-airlines.com); **Air Pacific,** serving Fiji, Australia, New Zealand, and the South Pacific (✆ 800/227-4446; www.airpacific.com); **Korean Airlines** (✆ 02/656-2000 in Seoul, 800/223-1155 on the East Coast, 800/421-8200 on the West Coast, 800/438-5000 from Hawaii; www.koreanair.com); and **Philippine Airlines** (✆ 631/816-6691 in Manila, 800/435-9725 in the U.S.; www.philippineair.com).

Operated by the European Travel Network, **www.discount-tickets.com** is a great online source for regular and discounted airfares to destinations around the world. You can also use this site to compare rates and book accommodations, car rentals, and tours. Click on "Special Offers" for the latest package deals. Students should also try **Campus Travel** (✆ **0870/240-1010** in England, 0131/668-3303 in Scotland; www.usitcampus.com).

If you're traveling in the United States beyond Hawaii, some large American airlines—such as **American, Delta, Northwest, TWA,** and **United**—offer travelers on transatlantic or transpacific flights special discount tickets under the name **Visit USA,** allowing travel between any U.S. destinations at reduced rates. These tickets must be purchased before you leave your foreign point of departure. This system is the best, easiest, and fastest way to see the United States at low cost. You should obtain information well in advance from your travel agent or the office of the airline concerned, since the conditions attached to these discount tickets can change without advance notice.

Visitors arriving by air should cultivate patience and resignation before setting foot on U.S. soil. Getting through immigration control may take as long as 2 hours on some days, especially summer weekends. Add the time it takes to clear Customs, and you'll see that you should make a very generous allowance for delay in planning connections between international and domestic flights—an average of 2 to 3 hours at least.

For further information about travel to Hawaii, see "Getting There & Getting Around," in chapter 2.

ⓒ *FAST FACTS:* **For International Travelers**

Automobile Organizations Auto clubs will supply maps, suggested routes, guidebooks, accident and bail-bond insurance, and emergency road service. The major auto club in the United States, with 955 offices nationwide, is the **American Automobile Association** (AAA; often called

"Triple A"). Members of some foreign auto clubs have reciprocal arrangements with the AAA and enjoy its services at no charge. If you belong to an auto club, inquire about AAA reciprocity before you leave. The AAA can also provide you with an **International Driving Permit** validating your foreign license. You may be able to join the AAA even if you are not a member of a reciprocal club. To inquire, call © **800/736-2886** or visit www.aaa.com.

Oahu's local AAA office is at 1270 Ala Moana Blvd., Honolulu (© **808/593-2221**). Some car-rental agencies now provide automobile club–type services, so inquire about their availability when you rent your car.

Automobile Rentals To rent a car in the United States, you need a valid driver's license, a passport, and a major credit card. The minimum age is usually 25, but some companies will rent to younger people and add a surcharge. It's a good idea to buy maximum insurance coverage unless you're positive your own auto or credit-card insurance is sufficient. Rates vary, so it pays to call around.

Business Hours See "Fast Facts: The Hawaiian Islands," in chapter 2.

Climate See "When to Go," in chapter 2.

Electricity Hawaii, like the U.S. mainland and Canada, uses 110–120 volts (60 cycles), compared to the 220–240 volts (50 cycles) used in most of Europe and in other areas of the world, including Australia and New Zealand. Small appliances of non-American manufacture, such as hair dryers or shavers, will require a plug adapter with two flat, parallel pins; larger ones will require a 100-volt transformer.

Embassies & Consulates All embassies are in Washington, D.C. Some countries have consulates generally in major U.S. cities, and most have a mission to the United Nations in New York City. If your country isn't listed below, call for directory information in Washington, D.C. (© **202/555-1212**), or point your Web browser to **www.embassy.org/embassies** for the location and phone number of your national embassy.

The embassy of **Australia** is at 1601 Massachusetts Ave. NW, Washington, D.C. 20036 (© **202/797-3000**; www.austemb.org). There is also an Australian consulate in Hawaii at 1000 Bishop St., Penthouse Suite, Honolulu, HI 96813 (© 808/524-5050).

The embassy of **Canada** is at 501 Pennsylvania Ave. NW, Washington, D.C. 20001 (© **202/682-1740**; www.canadianembassy.org). Canadian consulates are also at 1251 Avenue of the Americas, New York, NY 10020 (© 212/596-1628), and at 550 South Hope St., 9th floor, Los Angeles, CA 90071 (© 213/346-2700).

The embassy of **Japan** is at 2520 Massachusetts Ave. NW, Washington, D.C. 20008 (© **202/238-6700**; www.embjapan.org). The consulate general of Japan is located at 1742 Nuuanu Ave., Honolulu, HI 96817 (© 808/543-3111).

The embassy of **New Zealand** is at 37 Observatory Circle NW, Washington, D.C. 20008 (© **202/328-4800**; www.nzemb.org). The only New Zealand consulate in the United States is at 780 Third Ave., New York, NY 10017 (© 202/328-4800).

The embassy of the **Republic of Ireland** is at 2234 Massachusetts Ave. NW, Washington, D.C. 20008 (© **202/462-3939**; www.irelandemb.org).

There's a consulate office in San Francisco at 44 Montgomery St., Suite 3830, San Francisco, CA 94104 (© 415/392-4214).

The embassy of the **United Kingdom** is at 3100 Massachusetts Ave. NW, Washington, D.C. 20008 (© **202/588-6640**; www.fco.gov.uk/directory). British consulates are at 845 Third Ave., New York, NY 10022 (© 212/745-0200), and 11766 Wilshire Blvd., Suite 400, Los Angeles, CA 90025 (© 310/477-3322).

Emergencies Call © **911** to report a fire, call the police, or get an ambulance.

Gasoline (Petrol) One U.S. gallon equals 3.8 liters, while 1.2 U.S. gallons equal 1 Imperial gallon. You'll notice there are several grades (and price levels) of gasoline available at most gas stations. You'll also notice that their names change from company to company. The ones with the highest octane are the most expensive, but most rental cars take the least expensive "regular" gas, with an octane rating of 87.

Holidays See "When to Go," in chapter 2.

Legal Aid The ordinary tourist will probably never become involved with the American legal system. If you're pulled over for a minor infraction (for example, driving faster than the speed limit), never attempt to pay the fine directly to a police officer; you may wind up arrested on the much more serious charge of attempted bribery. Pay fines by mail or directly into the hands of the clerk of the court. If accused of a more serious offense, it's wise to say and do nothing before consulting a lawyer (under the U.S. Constitution, you have the rights both to remain silent and to consult an attorney). Under U.S. law, an arrested person is allowed one telephone call to a party of his or her choice; call your embassy or consulate.

Mail Mailboxes, which are generally found at intersections, are blue with a blue-and-white eagle logo and carry the inscription U.S. POSTAL SERVICE. If your mail is addressed to a U.S. destination, don't forget to add the five-figure postal code, or ZIP code, after the two-letter abbreviation of the state to which the mail is addressed. The abbreviation for Hawaii is HI.

At press time, domestic postage rates were 23¢ for a postcard and 37¢ for a letter. For international mail, a first-class letter of up to 1 ounce costs 80¢ (60¢ to Canada and Mexico); a first-class postcard costs 70¢ (50¢ to Canada and Mexico); and a preprinted postal aerogramme costs 70¢. Point your Web browser to **www.usps.com** for complete U.S. postal information, or call © **800/275-8777** for information on the nearest post office. Most branches are open Monday through Friday from 8am to 5 or 6pm, and Saturday from 9am to noon or 3pm.

Taxes The United States has no VAT (value-added tax) or other indirect taxes at a national level. Every state, and every city in it, has the right to levy its own local tax on all purchases, including hotel and restaurant checks, airline tickets, and so on. In Hawaii, sales tax is 4%; there's also a 7.25% hotel-room tax and a small excise tax, so the total tax on your hotel bill will be 11.42%.

Telephone & Fax The telephone system in the United States is run by private corporations, so rates, particularly for long-distance service and operator-assisted calls, can vary widely—especially on calls made from public telephones. Local calls—that is, calls to other locations on the island you're on—made from public phones in Hawaii cost 50¢.

Generally, hotel surcharges on long-distance and local calls are astronomical. You are usually better off using a **public pay telephone,** which you will find clearly marked in most public buildings and private establishments as well as on the street. Many convenience stores and newsstands sell **prepaid calling cards** in denominations up to $50.

Most **long-distance** and **international calls** can be dialed directly from any phone. **For calls within the United States and to Canada,** dial 1 followed by the area code and the seven-digit number. **For other international calls,** dial 011 followed by the country code, city code, and the telephone number of the person you are calling. Some country and city codes are as follows: **Australia** 61, Melbourne 3, Sydney 2; **Ireland** 353, Dublin 1; **New Zealand** 64, Auckland 9, Wellington 4; **United Kingdom** 44, Belfast 232, Birmingham 21, Glasgow 41, London 71 or 81.

If you're calling the **United States from another country,** the country code is 01.

In Hawaii, interisland phone calls are considered long-distance and are often as costly as calling the U.S. mainland. The international country code for Hawaii is 1, just as it is for the rest of the United States and Canada.

For **reversed-charge** or **collect calls,** and for **person-to-person calls,** dial 0 (zero, not the letter "O"), followed by the area code and number you want; an operator will then come on the line, and you should specify that you are calling collect, person-to-person, or both. If your operator-assisted call is international, ask for the overseas operator.

Note that all phone numbers with the area code 800, 888, 866, and 877 are toll-free. However, calls to numbers in area codes 700 and 900 (chat lines, "dating" services, and so on) can be very expensive—usually a charge of 95¢ to $3 or more per minute.

For **local directory assistance** ("information"), dial 411. For **long-distance information,** dial 1, then the appropriate area code and 555-1212; for **directory assistance for another island,** dial 1, then 808, then 555-1212.

Fax facilities are widely available and can be found in most hotels and many other establishments. Try **Mail Boxes, Etc.** or **Kinko's** (check the local Yellow Pages) or any photocopying shop.

Telephone Directories There are two kinds of telephone directories in the United States. The general directory, the so-called White Pages, lists private and business subscribers in alphabetical order. The inside front cover lists the emergency numbers for police, fire, and ambulance, along with other vital numbers. The first few pages are devoted to community-service numbers, including a guide to long-distance and international calling, complete with country codes and area codes.

The second directory, printed on yellow paper (hence its name, Yellow Pages), lists all local services, businesses, and industries by type of activity, with an index at the front. The listings cover not only such obvious items as automobile repairs and drugstores (pharmacies), but also restaurants by type of cuisine and geographical location, bookstores by special subject and/or language, places of worship by religious denomination, and other information that the visitor might not otherwise readily find. The Yellow Pages also include detailed maps, postal ZIP codes, and a calendar of events.

Time Zone Hawaii is 2 hours behind Pacific standard time and 5 hours behind eastern standard time. In other words, when it's noon in Hawaii, it's 2pm in California and 5pm in New York during standard time on the mainland. There's no daylight saving time here, so when daylight saving time is in effect on the mainland, Hawaii is 3 hours behind the West Coast and 6 hours behind the East Coast; in summer, when it's noon in Hawaii, it's 3pm in California and 6pm in New York.

Hawaii is east of the International Date Line, putting it in the same day as the U.S. mainland and Canada, and a day behind Australia, New Zealand, and Asia.

Tipping It's part of the American way of life to tip. Many service employees receive little direct salary and must depend on tips for their income. The following are some general rules:

In **hotels,** tip bellhops at least $1 per piece of luggage ($2–$3 if you have a lot of luggage), and tip the housekeeping staff $1 per person, per day. Tip the doorman or concierge only if he or she has provided you with some specific service (for example, calling a cab for you or obtaining difficult-to-get theater tickets). Tip the valet-parking attendant $1 to $2 every time you get your car.

In **restaurants, bars,** and **nightclubs,** tip service staff 15% to 20% of the check, tip bartenders 10% to 15%, and tip valet-parking attendants $1 to $2 per vehicle. Tip the doorman only if he or she has provided you with some specific service (such as calling a cab for you). Tipping is not expected in cafeterias and fast-food restaurants.

Tip **cab drivers** 15% of the fare.

As for **other service personnel,** tip skycaps at airports at least $1 per piece ($2–$3 if you have a lot of luggage), and tip hairdressers and barbers 15% to 20%. Tipping ushers at theaters is not expected.

Toilets Foreign visitors often complain that public toilets are hard to find in most U.S. cities. True, there are none on the streets, but visitors can usually find one in a bar, fast-food outlet, restaurant, hotel, museum, or department store—and it will probably be clean. (The cleanliness of toilets at service stations, parks, and beaches is more open to question.) Note, however, a growing practice in some restaurants and bars of displaying a notice that toilets are for the use of patrons only. You can ignore this sign or, better yet, avoid arguments by paying for a cup of coffee or soft drink, which will qualify you as a patron.

4

Oahu, the Gathering Place

A wise Hawaiian *kahuna* once told me that the islands are like children—each is special yet different, and each is to be loved for its individual qualities. One thing's for sure: You'll never find another island like Oahu, the commercial and population center of Hawaii.

Honolulu offers a fast-paced urban setting, with Hawaii's hottest nightlife, its best shopping, and a huge array of restaurants. Yet at the same time, the North Shore and the Windward side of the island present a different face: miles of white-sand beaches and a slower, country way of life. If just the thought of rush-hour traffic, freeways, high-rise towers, and having to pay for parking makes your back molars hurt, then either head for the North Shore or take the next plane out to a quieter neighbor island.

It's astounding to spend hours flying across the barren blue of the Pacific and then suddenly see below the whites and pastels of Honolulu, the most remote big city on earth, a 26-mile-long metropolis of some 865,000 souls living in the middle of nowhere. Once on its streets, you'll find bright city lights, excellent restaurants, nightclubs, world-class shopping, a vibrant arts scene, and grand old hotels.

Nine out of 10 visitors to Hawaii—some 5 million people a year—stop on Oahu, and most of them end up along the canyonlike streets of Waikiki, Honolulu's well-known hotel district and its most densely populated neighborhood. Some days, it seems like the entire world is sunning itself on Waikiki's famous beach. Beyond Waikiki, Honolulu is clean and easy to enjoy. The city is coming of age for the 21st century: The old port town opened a new convention center in 1998 and is reshaping its waterfront, altering its skyline, opening new world-class hotels, and all the while trying to preserve its historic roots and revive its Polynesian heritage.

Out in the country, Oahu can be as down-home as a slack-key guitar. This is where you'll find a big blue sky, perfect waves, empty beaches, rainbows and waterfalls, sweet tropical flowers, and fiery Pacific sunsets. In fact, nowhere else within 60 minutes of a major American city can you snorkel in a crystal-clear lagoon, climb an old volcano, surf monster waves, kayak to a desert isle, picnic on a sandbar, soar in a glider over tide pools, skin dive over a sunken airplane, bicycle through a rain forest, golf a championship course, or sail into the setting sun.

And in terms of weather, no other Hawaiian island has it as fine as Oahu. The Big Island is hotter, Kauai is wetter, Maui has more wind, Molokai and Lanai are drier. But Oahu enjoys a kind of perpetual late spring, with light trade winds and 82°F (28°C) days almost year-round. In fact, the climate is supposed to be the best on the planet. Once you have that, the rest is easy.

1 Orientation

ARRIVING

Honolulu is your gateway to the Hawaiian islands; even though more and more transpacific flights are going directly to the neighbor islands these days, chances are still good that you'll touch down on Oahu first. **Honolulu International Airport** sits on the south shore of Oahu, west of downtown Honolulu and Waikiki near Pearl Harbor. Many major American and international carriers fly to Honolulu from the mainland; see "Getting There & Getting Around," in chapter 2, for a list of carriers and their toll-free numbers.

LANDING AT HONOLULU INTERNATIONAL AIRPORT

The airport at Honolulu is probably the most cosmopolitan spot in the Pacific, with passengers from every corner of the globe. Although the airport is large and constantly expanding, the layout is quite simple and easy to grasp. You can walk or take the **Wiki-Wiki Bus,** a free airport shuttle, from your arrival gate to the main terminal and baggage claim, on the ground level. After collecting your bags, unless you're getting on an interisland flight immediately, you'll exit to the palm-lined street, where uniformed attendants can either flag down a taxi or direct you to **TheBus** (for transportation information, see below). For Waikiki shuttles and rental-car vans, cross the street to the center island and wait at the designated stop.

Passengers connecting to neighbor-island flights take the Wiki-Wiki shuttle or walk to the large interisland terminal serving Aloha and Hawaiian airlines or the more distant commuter terminal, which serves the smaller Island Air. (For details on interisland flights, see "Getting There & Getting Around," in chapter 2.)

GETTING TO & FROM THE AIRPORT

BY RENTAL CAR   All major rental companies have cars available at the airport (see "Car Rentals" under "Getting There & Getting Around," in chapter 2). Rental-agency vans will pick you up curbside at the center island outside baggage claim and take you to their off-site lot.

BY TAXI   Taxis are abundant at the airport; an attendant will be happy to flag one down for you. Taxi fare is about $18 from Honolulu International to downtown Honolulu, about $25 to $30 to Waikiki. If you need to call a taxi, see "Getting Around," later in this chapter, for a list of cab companies.

BY AIRPORT SHUTTLE   Shuttle vans operate 24 hours a day every day of the year between the airport and all 350 hotels and condos in Waikiki. The

---

Tips **Airport Tip**

When departing the islands or making interisland connections, allow yourself extra time to catch your flight. Like most major airports, Honolulu sprawls over a huge area—you won't want to have to sprint across it in the tropical heat. The Wiki-Wiki Bus links the various terminals and connects distant gates with baggage areas, but it's not automated and therefore only somewhat more *wiki-wiki* (fast) than walking. Allow time to fit the relaxed island-style schedule.

Here's your first sightseeing tip: As you make your descent into Honolulu International, you can see Pearl Harbor from the left side of the airplane.

Oahu

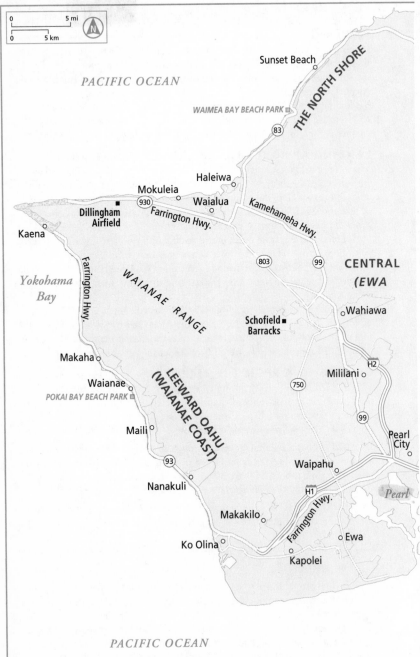

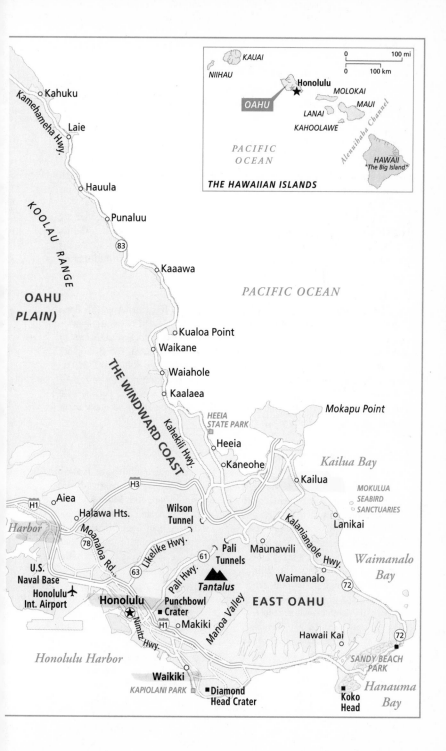

cheapest shuttle service is **The Shuttle** (©866/900-5005 or 808/955-1156), with 24-hour service in air-conditioned vans for just $6 from the airport to Waikiki ($10 round-trip). You'll find the shuttle at street level outside baggage claim. You can board with two pieces of luggage and a carry-on at no extra charge. Backpacks are okay. Tips are welcome. For advance purchase of group or family tickets, call the number above.

BY BUS   TheBus nos. 19 and 20 (Waikiki Beach and Hotels) run from the airport to downtown Honolulu and Waikiki. The first bus from Waikiki to the airport leaves at 4:50am Monday through Friday and 5:25am Saturday and Sunday; the last bus departs the airport for Waikiki at 11:45pm Monday through Friday, 11:25pm Saturday and Sunday. There are two bus stops on the main terminal's upper level; a third is on the second level of the interisland terminal. You can board TheBus with a carry-on or small suitcase, as long as it fits under the seat and doesn't disrupt other passengers; otherwise, you'll have to take a shuttle or taxi. The approximate travel time to Waikiki is an hour. The one-way fare is $1.50 for adults and 50¢ for students, exact change only. For more information on TheBus, see "Getting Around," later in this chapter.

VISITOR INFORMATION

The **Hawaii Visitors and Convention Bureau,** 2270 Kalakaua Ave., 7th floor, Honolulu, HI 96815 (© 800/GO-HAWAII or 808/923-1811; www.gohawaii. com), supplies free brochures, maps, accommodations guides, and *Islands of Aloha,* the official HVCB magazine. The **Oahu Visitors Bureau,** 735 Bishop St., Suite 1872, Honolulu, HI 96813 (© 877/525-OAHU or 808/524-0722; fax 808/521-1620; www.visit-oahu.com), distributes a free travel planner and map.

A number of free publications, such as *This Week Oahu,* are packed with money-saving coupons and good regional maps; look for them on racks at the airport and around town.

THE ISLAND IN BRIEF

Honolulu

Hawaii's largest city looks like any other big metropolitan center with tall buildings. In fact, some cynics refer to it as "Los Angeles West." But within Honolulu's boundaries, you'll find rain forests, deep canyons, valleys and waterfalls, a nearly mile-high mountain range, coral reefs, and gold-sand beaches. The city proper—where most of Honolulu's 850,000 residents live—is approximately 12 miles wide and 26 miles long, running east-west roughly between Diamond Head and Pearl Harbor. Within the city are seven hills laced by seven streams that run to Mamala Bay.

Surrounding the central area is a plethora of neighborhoods, ranging from the quiet suburbs of **Hawaii Kai** to *kamaaina* (native-born) neighborhoods like **Manoa.** These areas are generally quieter and more residential than Waikiki, but they're still within minutes of beaches, shopping, and all the activities Oahu has to offer.

WAIKIKI ★★★   Some say that Waikiki is past its prime—that everybody goes to Maui now. If it has fallen out of favor, you couldn't prove it by us. Waikiki is the very incarnation of Yogi Berra's comment about Toots Shor's famous New York restaurant: "Nobody goes there anymore. It's too crowded."

When King Kalakaua played in Waikiki, it was "a hamlet of plain cottages . . . its excitements caused by the activity of insect tribes and the occasional fall of a coconut." The Merrie Monarch, who gave his name to Waikiki's main street, would love the scene today. Some 5 million tourists visit Oahu every year, and 9 out of 10 of them stay in Waikiki. This urban beach is where all the action is; it's backed by 175 high-rise hotels with more than 33,000 guest rooms and hundreds of bars and restaurants, all in a 1½-square-mile beach zone. Waikiki means honeymooners and sun seekers, bikinis and bare buns, a round-the-clock beach party every day of the year—and it's all because of a thin crescent of sand that was shipped over from Molokai. Staying in Waikiki puts you in the heart of it all, but also be aware that this is an on-the-go place with traffic noise 24 hours a day and its share of crime—and it's almost always crowded.

ALA MOANA ★/★ A great beach as well as a famous shopping mall, Ala Moana is the retail and transportation heart of Honolulu, a place where you can both shop and suntan in one afternoon. All bus routes lead to the open-air **Ala Moana Shopping Center,** across the street from **Ala Moana Beach Park.** This 50-acre, 200-shop behemoth attracts 56 million customers a year (people fly up from Tahiti just to buy their Christmas gifts here). Every European designer from Armani to Vuitton is represented in Honolulu's answer to Beverly Hills's Rodeo Drive. For our purposes, the neighborhood called "Ala Moana" extends along Ala Moana Boulevard from Waikiki in the direction of Diamond Head to downtown Honolulu in the Ewa direction (west), and includes the **Ward Centre** and **Ward Warehouse** complexes as well as **Restaurant Row.**

DOWNTOWN ★★ A tiny cluster of high-rises west of Waikiki, downtown Honolulu is the financial, business, and government center of Hawaii. On the waterfront stands the iconic 1926 Aloha Tower, now the centerpiece of a harbor-front shopping and restaurant complex known as the **Aloha Tower Marketplace.** The whole history of Honolulu can be seen in just a few short blocks: Street vendors sell papayas from trucks on skyscraper-lined concrete canyons; joggers and BMWs rush by a lacy palace where U.S. Marines overthrew Hawaii's last queen and stole her kingdom; burly bus drivers sport fragrant white ginger flowers on their dashboards; Methodist churches look like Asian temples; and businessmen wear aloha shirts to billion-dollar meetings.

On the edge of downtown, **Chinatown Historic District** ★★★ is the oldest Chinatown in America and still one of Honolulu's liveliest neighborhoods, a nonstop pageant of people, sights, sounds, smells, and tastes—not all Chinese, now that Southeast Asians, including many Vietnamese, share the old storefronts. Go on Saturday morning, when everyone shops here for fresh goods such as gingerroot, fern fronds, and hogs' heads.

Among the historic buildings and Pan-Pacific corporate headquarters are a few hotels, mainly geared toward business travelers. Most visitors prefer the sun and excitement of Waikiki or choose a quieter neighborhood outside the city.

MANOA VALLEY ★ First inhabited by white settlers, the Manoa Valley above Waikiki still has vintage *kamaaina* (native-born) homes, one of Hawaii's premier botanical gardens in the Lyon Arboretum, the ever-gushing Manoa Falls, and the 320-acre campus of the University

Honolulu Neighborhoods in Brief

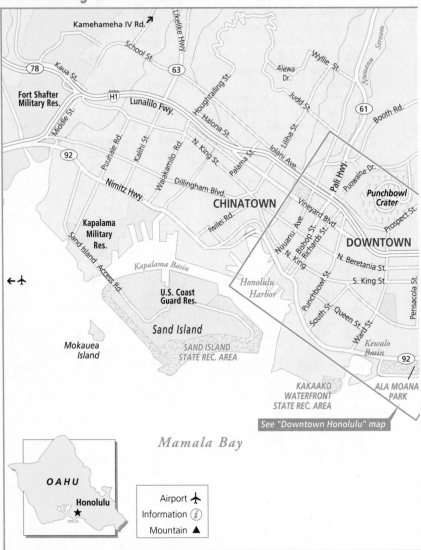

of Hawaii, where 50,000 students hit the books when they're not on the beach.

TO THE EAST: KAHALA Except for the estates of millionaires and the luxurious Kahala Mandarin Oriental Hotel (home of Hoku's, an outstanding beachfront restaurant), there's not much out this way that's of interest to visitors.

East Oahu

Beyond Kahala lies East Honolulu and suburban bedroom communities like Aina Haina, Niu Valley, and Hawaii Kai, among others, all linked by the Kalanianaole Highway and loaded with homes, condos, fast-food joints, and shopping malls. It looks like Southern California on a good day. There are only

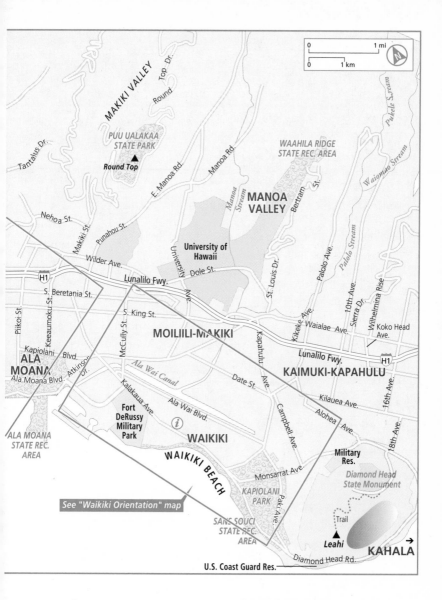

a few reasons to come here: to have dinner at **Roy's,** the original and still-outstanding Hawaii Regional Cuisine restaurant, in Hawaii Kai; to snorkel at **Hanauma Bay** or watch daredevil surfers at **Sandy Beach;** or just to enjoy the natural splendor of the lovely coastline, which might include a hike to **Makapuu Lighthouse.**

The Windward Coast

The windward side is the opposite side of the island from Waikiki. On this coast, trade winds blow cooling breezes over gorgeous beaches; rain squalls inspire lush, tropical vegetation; and miles of subdivisions dot the landscape. Bed-and-breakfasts, ranging from oceanfront estates to tiny cottages on quiet residential

Waikiki Orientation

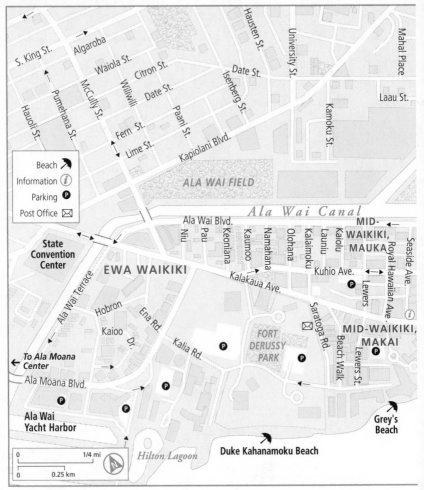

streets, are everywhere. Vacations here are spent enjoying ocean activities and exploring the surrounding areas. Waikiki is just a 15-minute drive away.

KAILUA ✦ The biggest little beach town in Hawaii, Kailua sits at the foot of the sheer green Koolau Mountains, on a great bay with two of Hawaii's best beaches. The town itself is a funky low-rise cluster of timeworn shops and homes. Kailua has become the B&B capital of Hawaii; it's an affordable alternative

to Waikiki, with rooms and vacation rentals starting at $60 a day. With the prevailing trade winds whipping up a cooling breeze, Kailua attracts windsurfers from around the world.

KANEOHE ✦ Helter-skelter suburbia sprawls around the edges of Kaneohe, one of the most scenic bays in the Pacific. A handful of B&Bs dots its edge. After you clear the trafficky maze of town, Oahu returns to its more natural state. This great bay beckons you to get

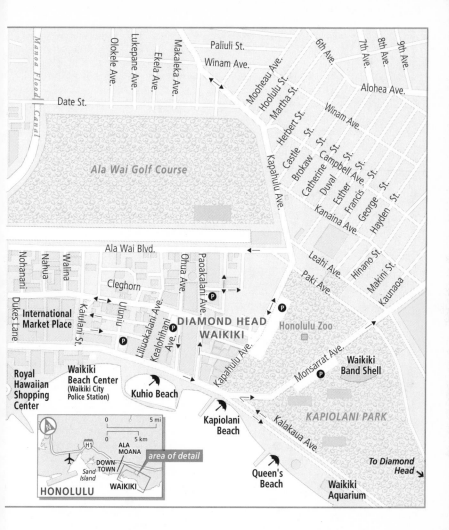

out on the water; you can depart from Heeia Boat Harbor on snorkel or fishing charters and visit Ahu a Laka a, the sandbar that appears and disappears in the middle of the bay. From here, you'll have a panoramic view of the Koolau Range.

KUALOA/LAIE ★★ The upper northeast shore is one of Oahu's most sacred places, an early Hawaiian landing spot where kings dipped their sails, cliffs hold ancient burial sites, and ghosts still march in the night. Sheer cliffs stab the reef-fringed seacoast, while old fish ponds are tucked along the two-lane coast road that winds past empty gold-sand beaches around beautiful Kahana Bay. Thousands "explore" the South Pacific at the **Polynesian Cultural Center,** in Laie, a Mormon settlement with its own Tabernacle Choir of sweet Samoan harmony.

The North Shore ★★★

Here's the Hawaii of Hollywood—giant waves, surfers galore, tropical

Downtown Honolulu

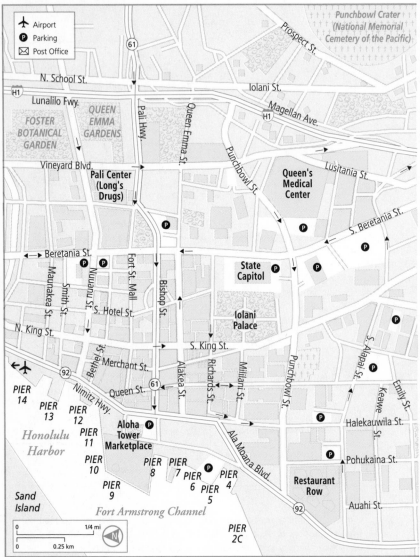

jungles, waterfalls, and mysterious Hawaiian temples. If you're looking for a quieter vacation, closer to nature, and filled with swimming, snorkeling, diving, surfing, or just plain hanging out on some of the world's most beautiful beaches, the North Shore is your place. The artsy little beach town of **Haleiwa** ✶✶

and the surrounding shoreline seem a world away from Waikiki. The North Shore boasts good restaurants, shopping, and cultural activities—but here they come with the quiet of country living. Bed-and-breakfasts are the most common accommodations, but there's one first-class hotel and some vacation

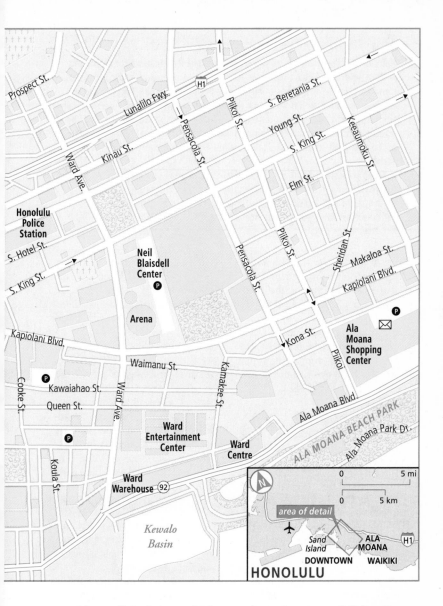

rentals as well. Be forewarned: It's a long trip—nearly an hour's drive—to Honolulu and Waikiki, and it's about twice as rainy on the North Shore as in Honolulu.

Central Oahu: The Ewa Plain

Flanked by the Koolau and Waianae mountain ranges, the hot, sun-baked Ewa Plain runs up and down the center of Oahu. Once covered with sandalwood forests (hacked down for the China trade) and later the sugarcane and pineapple backbone of Hawaii, Ewa today sports a new crop: suburban houses stretching to the sea. But let your eye wander west to the Waianae Range and Mount Kaala, at 4,020

Tips Finding Your Way Around, Oahu Style

Mainlanders sometimes find the directions given by locals a bit confusing. Seldom will you hear the terms east, west, north, and south; instead, islanders refer to directions as either **makai** (ma-*kae*), meaning toward the sea, or **mauka** (*mow*-kah), toward the mountains. In Honolulu, people use **Diamond Head** as a direction meaning to the east (in the direction of the world-famous crater called Diamond Head), and **Ewa** as a direction meaning to the west (toward the town called Ewa, on the other side of Pearl Harbor).

So, if you ask a local for directions, this is what you're likely to hear: "Drive 2 blocks makai (toward the sea), then turn Diamond Head (east) at the stoplight. Go 1 block, and turn mauka (toward the mountains). It's on the Ewa (western) side of the street."

---

feet the highest summit on Oahu; up there in the misty rain forest, native birds thrive in the hummocky bog. In 1914, the U.S. Army pitched a tent camp on the plain; author James Jones would later call **Schofield Barracks** "the most beautiful army post in the world." Hollywood filmed Jones's *From Here to Eternity* here.

**Leeward Oahu:
The Waianae Coast**

The west coast of Oahu is a hot and dry place of dramatic beauty: white-sand beaches bordering the deep blue ocean, steep verdant green cliffs, and miles of Mother Nature's wildness. Except for the luxurious J. W. Marriott Ihilani Resort and Spa in the Ko Olina Resort and the Makaha Golf Course, you'll find virtually no tourist services out here. The funky west coast villages of Nanakuli, Waianae, and Makaha are the last stands of native Hawaiians. This side of Oahu is seldom visited, except by surfers bound for **Yokohama Bay** and those coming to see needle-nose **Kaena Point** (the island's westernmost outpost), which has a coastal wilderness park.

2 Getting Around

BY CAR Oahu residents own 600,000 registered vehicles, but they have only 1,500 miles of mostly two-lane roads to use. That's 400 cars for every mile, a fact that becomes abundantly clear during morning and evening rush hours. You can avoid the gridlock by driving between 9am and 3pm or after 6pm.

All the major car-rental firms have agencies on Oahu, at the airport and in Waikiki. For a complete list, as well as tips on insurance and driving rules, see "Car Rentals" under "Getting There & Getting Around," in chapter 2.

BY BUS One of the best deals anywhere, **TheBus** will take you around the whole island for $1.50. In fact, every day more than 260,000 people use the system's 68 lines and 4,000 bus stops. TheBus goes almost everywhere almost all the time. The most popular route is **no. 8,** which arrives every 10 minutes or so to shuttle people between Waikiki and Ala Moana Center (the ride takes 15–20 min.); the **no. 19** (Airport/Hickam), **no. 20** (Airport/Halawa Gate), **no. 47** (Waipahu), and **no. 58** (Waikiki/Ala Moana) also cover the same stretch. Waikiki service begins daily at 5am and runs until midnight; most buses run about every 15 minutes during the day and every 30 minutes in the evening.

The Circle Island–North Shore route is no. 52 (Wahiawa/Circle Island); the Circle Island–South Shore route is no. 55 (Kaneohe/Circle Island). Both routes leave Ala Moana Shopping Center every 30 minutes and take about 4½ hours to circle the island. Be aware that at Turtle Bay Resort, just outside of Kahuku, the 52 becomes the 55 and returns to Honolulu via the coast, and the 55 becomes the 52 and returns to Honolulu on the inland route. (Translation: You have to get off and switch buses to complete your island tour.) If you want to go to one specific area, you may be able to take an express bus (i.e., 54 to Pearl City; 46 to Kailua-Kaneohe; and 57 and 58 to Sea Life Park).

You can buy a **Visitors Pass** for $15 at any ABC store in Waikiki (ABC stores are everywhere). It's good for unlimited rides for 4 days.

For more information on routes and schedules, call **TheBus** (© 808/848-5555,** or 808/296-1818 for recorded information) or check out **www.thebus. org**, which provides timetables and maps for all routes, plus directions to many local attractions and a list of upcoming events. Taking TheBus is often easier than parking your car.

BY TROLLEY   It's fun to ride the 34-seat, open-air, motorized **Waikiki Trolley** (© 800/824-8804 or 808/593-2822; www.waikikitrolley.com), which looks like a San Francisco cable car (see "Orientation Tours," later in this chapter). The trolley loops around Waikiki and downtown Honolulu, stopping every 40 minutes at 12 key places: Hilton Hawaiian Village, Iolani Palace, Wo Fat's in Chinatown, the State Capitol, King Kamehameha's Statue, the Mission House Museum, the Aloha Tower, the Honolulu Academy of Arts, the Hawaii Maritime Museum, Ward Centre, Fisherman's Wharf, and Restaurant Row. The driver provides commentary along the way. Stops on the new 2-hour fully narrated Ocean Coast Line (the blue line) of the southeast side of Oahu include Sea Life Park, Diamond Head, and Waikki Beach. A 1-day trolley pass—which costs $20 for adults, $14 for kids age 12 to 18, or $10 for children under 12—allows you to jump off all day long (8:30am–11:35pm). Four-day passes cost $45 for adults, $31 for kids age 12 to 18, and $15 for children under 12.

BY TAXI   Oahu's major cab companies offer islandwide, 24-hour, radio-dispatched service, with multilingual drivers and air-conditioned cars, limos, vans, and vehicles equipped with wheelchair lifts (there's a $5 charge for wheelchairs). Fares are standard for all taxi firms; from the airport, expect to pay about $25 to $30 (plus tip) to Waikiki, about $18 to downtown, about $40 to $45 to Kailua, about $40 to $45 to Hawaii Kai, and about $85 to $95 to the North Shore. For a flat fee of $18, **Star Taxi** ★ (© 800/671-2999 or 808/942-STAR) will take up to five passengers from the airport to Waikiki (with no extra charges for baggage); however, you must book in advance. After you have arrived and before you pick up your luggage, re-call Star to make sure that they will be outside waiting for you when your luggage arrives.

For a metered cab, try **Aloha State Cab** (© 808/847-3566), **Charley's Taxi & Tours** (© 808/531-1333), **City Taxi** (© 808/524-2121), **Royal Taxi & Tour** (© 808/944-5513), **Sida Taxi & Tours** (© 808/836-0011), or **TheCab** (© 808/422-2222). **Coast Taxi** (© 808/261-3755) serves Windward Oahu, and **Hawaii Kai Hui/Koko Head Taxi** (© 808/396-6633) serves east Honolulu/southeast Oahu.

WHEELCHAIR TRANSPORTATION   Handicabs of the Pacific (© 808/524-3866), offers wheelchair taxi services and tours in air-conditioned vehicles that are specially equipped with ramps and wheelchair lockdowns. Handicabs

TheBus

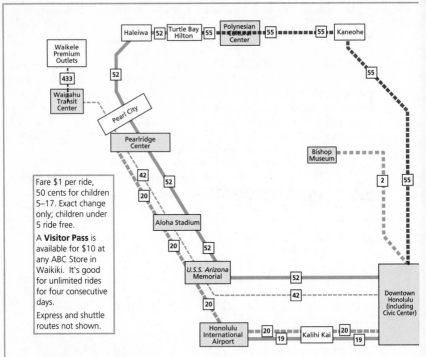

Common Bus Routes:

Ala Moana Shopping Center: Take bus #19 & #20 AIRPORT. Return via #19 WAIKIKI, or cross Ala Moana Blvd. for #20.

Bishop Museum: Take #2 SCHOOL STREET. Get off at Kapalama St., cross School St., walk down Bernice St. Return to School St. and take #2 WAIKIKI.

Byodo-In Temple: Take bus #2 to Hotel-Alakea St. (TRF) to #55 KANEOHE-KAHALUU. Get off at Valley of the Temple cemetery. Also #19 and #20 AIRPORT to King-Alakea St., (TRF) on Alakea St. to #55 KANEOHE-KAHALUU.

Circle Island: Take a bus to ALA MOANA CENTER (TRF) to #52 WAHIAWA CIRCLE ISLAND or #55 KANEOHE CIRCLE ISLAND. This is a 4-hour bus ride.

Chinatown or Downtown: Take any #2 bus going out of Waikiki to Hotel St. Return, take #2 WAIKIKI on Hotel St., or #19 or #20 on King St.

The Contemporary Museum & Punchbowl (National Cemetery of the Pacific): Take #2 bus (TRF) at Alapai St. to #15 MAKIKI-PACIFIC HGTS. Return, take #15 and get off at King St., area (TRF) #2 WAIKIKI.

Diamond Head Crater: Take #22 HAWAII KAI-SEA LIFE PARK to the crater. Take a flashlight. Return to the same area and take #22 WAIKIKI.

Dole Plantation: Take bus to ALA MOANA CENTER (TRF) to #52 WAHIAWA CIRCLE ISLAND.

Foster Botanic Gardens: Take #2 bus to Hotel-Riviera St. Walk to Vineyard Blvd. Return to Hotel St. Take #2 WAIKIKI, or take #4 NUUANU and get off at Nuuanu-Vineyard. Cross Nuuanu Ave. and walk one block to the gardens.

Aloha Tower Marketplace & Hawaii Maritime Center: Take #19-#20 AIRPORT and get off at Alakea–Ala Moana. Cross the street to the Aloha Tower.

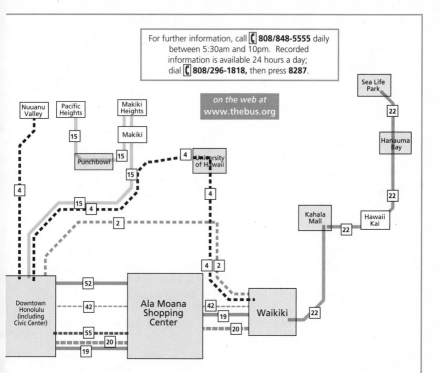

For further information, call ☏ **808/848-5555** daily between 5:30am and 10pm. Recorded information is available 24 hours a day; dial ☏ **808/296-1818,** then press **8287**.

on the web at
www.thebus.org

Honolulu Zoo: Take any bus on Kuhio Ave. going DIAMOND HEAD direction to Kapahulu Ave.

Iolani Palace (also **State Capitol, Honolulu Hale, Kawaihao Church, Mission Houses, Queen's Hospital, King Kamehameha Statue, State Judiciary Bldg.**) Take any #2 bus and get off at Punchbowl and Beretania St. Walk to King St. Return #2 WAIKIKI on King St.

Kahala Mall: Take #22 HAWAII KAI–SEA LIFE PARK to Kilauea Ave. Return, #22 WAIKIKI.

Pearl Harbor (*Arizona* **Memorial):** Take #20 AIRPORT. Get off across from Memorial, or take a bus to ALA MOANA CENTER (TRF) to #52.

Polynesian Cultural Center: Take a bus to ALA MOANA CENTER (TRF) to #55 KANEOHE CIRCLE ISLAND. Bus ride takes 2 hours one-way.

Queen Emma's Summer Home: Take #4 NUUANU, or board a bus to ALA MOANA CENTER (TRF) to #55 KANEOHE.

Sea Life Park: Take #22 HAWAII KAI-SEA LIFE PARK. #22 will stop at Hanauma Bay en route to the park.

University of Hawaii: Take #4 NUUANU. The bus will go to the University en route to Nuuanu.

Waimea Valley & Adventure Park: Take a bus to ALA MOANA CENTER (TRF) to #52 WAHIAWA CIRCLE ISLAND or #55 KANEOHE CIRCLE ISLAND.

Waikele Premium Outlets: Take bus #42 from Waikiki to Wapahu Transit Center, then bus #433 to Waikele.

offers a range of taxi services (airport pickup to Waikiki hotels is $40 one-way, transportation within Waikiki is $20 one-way) as well as complete tours (including a Honolulu city tour, a Circle the Island tour, a Pearl Harbor cruise and tour, and a sunset dinner sail and tour).

FAST FACTS: Oahu

American Express The Honolulu office is at 1440 Kapiolani Blvd., Suite 104 ((C) **808/946-7741**), and is open Monday through Friday from 8am to 5pm. There's also an office at **Hilton Hawaiian Village,** 2005 Kalia Rd. ((C) **808/947-2607** or 808/951-0644), and one at the **Hyatt Regency Waikiki,** 2424 Kalakaua Ave. ((C) **808/926-5441**); both offer financial services daily from 8am to 8pm.

Dentists If you need dental attention on Oahu, contact the **Hawaii Dental Association** ((C) **808/593-2135**).

Doctors **Straub Doctors on Call,** 2222 Kalakaua Ave., at Lewers Street, Honolulu ((C) **808/971-6000**), can dispatch a van if you need help getting to the main clinic or to any of their additional clinics at the Royal Hawaiian Hotel, Hyatt Regency Waikiki, Hawaiian Regent Hotel, Hilton Hawaiian Village, Kahala Mandarin Oriental, and Ihilani Resort and Spa.

Emergencies Call (C) **911** for police, fire, and ambulance. The **Poison Control Center** is at 1319 Punahou St. ((C) **808/941-4411**).

Hospitals Hospitals offering 24-hour emergency care include **Queens Medical Center,** 1301 Punchbowl St. ((C) **808/538-9011**); **Kuakini Medical Center,** 347 Kuakini St. ((C) **808/536-2236**); **Straub Clinic and Hospital,** 888 S. King St. ((C) **808/522-4000**); **Moanalua Medical Center,** 3288 Moanalua Rd. ((C) **808/834-5333**); **Kapiolani Medical Center for Women and Children,** 1319 Punahou St. ((C) **808/973-8511**); and **Kapiolani Medical Center** at Pali Momi, 98–1079 Moanalua Rd. ((C) **808/486-6000**). Central Oahu has **Wahiawa General Hospital,** 128 Lehua St. ((C) **808/621-8411**). On the windward side is **Castle Medical Center,** 640 Ulukahiki St., Kailua ((C) **808/263-5500**).

Internet Access If your hotel doesn't have Web access, head to **Web Site Story Café,** 2555 Cartwright Rd. (in the Hotel Waikiki), Waikiki ((C) **808/922-1677**). It's open daily from 7am to 11pm (but closed on holidays) and serves drinks.

Newspapers The *Honolulu Advertiser* and *Honolulu Star-Bulletin* are Oahu's daily papers. *Pacific Business News* and *Honolulu Weekly* are weekly papers. *Honolulu Weekly,* available free at restaurants, clubs, shops, and newspaper racks around Oahu, is the best source for what's going on around town.

Post Office To find the location nearest you, call (C) **800/275-8777**. The downtown location is in the old U.S. Post Office, Customs, and Court House Building (referred to as the "old Federal Building") at 335 Merchant St., across from Iolani Palace and next to the Kamehameha Statue (bus: 2). Other branch offices include the Waikiki Post Office, 330 Saratoga Ave. (Diamond Head side of Fort DeRussy; bus: 19 or 20), and in the Ala Moana Shopping Center (bus: 8, 19, or 20).

Safety Recently, there has been a series of purse-snatching incidents in Oahu. Thieves in slow-moving cars or on foot have snatched handbags from female pedestrians (in some instances, dragging women who refuse to let go of their pocketbooks down the street). The Honolulu police department advises women to carry their purses on the shoulder away from the street or, better yet, to wear the strap across the chest instead of on one shoulder. Women with clutch bags should hold them close to their chest.

Weather For National Weather Service recorded forecasts for Honolulu, call ✆ **808/973-4380;** for elsewhere on the island, call ✆ **808/973-4381.** For marine reports, call ✆ **808/973-4382.** For surf reports, call ✆ **808/973-4383.**

3 Where to Stay

Before you reach for the phone to book a place to stay, consider when you'll be visiting. The high season, when hotels are full and rates are at their highest, is mid-December to March. The secondary high season, when rates are high but rooms are somewhat easier to come by, is June to September. The low seasons—when you can expect fewer tourists and better deals—are April to June and September to mid-December. (For more on Hawaii's travel seasons, see "When to Go," in chapter 2.) No matter when you travel, you can often get the best rate at many of Waikiki's hotels by booking a package; for details, see "Money-Saving Package Deals," in chapter 2.

See "The Island in Brief," earlier in this chapter, for a description of each neighborhood. It can help you decide where you'd like to base yourself.

Remember that **hotel and room taxes** of 11.42% will be added to your bill. And don't forget about parking charges—in Waikiki, they can add up quickly.

BED-AND-BREAKFASTS For a more intimate experience, try staying in a B&B. Accommodations on Oahu calling themselves bed-and-breakfasts vary from a room in a house (sometimes with a shared bathroom) to a vacation rental in a private cottage. Breakfast can be anything from coffee, pastries, and fruit to a home-cooked gourmet meal with just-caught fresh fish. Due to space limitations, we can include only a handful of Oahu's best B&Bs below; for a wider selection, check out *Frommer's Honolulu, Waikiki & Oahu* or call one of the statewide booking agencies recommended in "Tips on Accommodations," in chapter 2.

AIRPORT HOTELS If you have a late-night flight, a long layover between flights, a delayed flight, or a long period of time between your noon check-out and your flight, consider the services of the hotel choices near the airport (certainly not a place to spend your Hawaiian vacation but a good overnight resting place): **Best Western—The Plaza Hotel,** 3253 N. Nimitz Hwy., Honolulu (✆ **800/800-4683** or 808/836-0661; www.bestwestern.com), where rooms go from $97 to $136; and the **Honolulu Airport Hotel** (✆ **800/800-3477** or 808/836-0661; www.honoluluairporthotel.com), with rooms from $125. Both offer free airport shuttle service.

WAIKIKI
EWA WAIKIKI

All the hotels listed below are located from the ocean to Kalakaua Ave., and between Ala Wai Terrace in the Ewa direction (or western side of Waikiki) and

Waikiki Accommodations

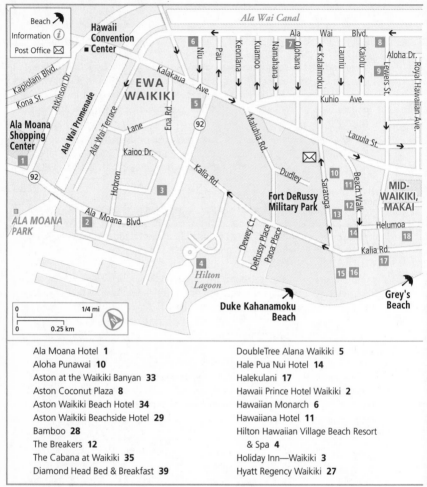

Ala Moana Hotel **1**
Aloha Punawai **10**
Aston at the Waikiki Banyan **33**
Aston Coconut Plaza **8**
Aston Waikiki Beach Hotel **34**
Aston Waikiki Beachside Hotel **29**
Bamboo **28**
The Breakers **12**
The Cabana at Waikiki **35**
Diamond Head Bed & Breakfast **39**

DoubleTree Alana Waikiki **5**
Hale Pua Nui Hotel **14**
Halekulani **17**
Hawaii Prince Hotel Waikiki **2**
Hawaiian Monarch **6**
Hawaiiana Hotel **11**
Hilton Hawaiian Village Beach Resort
  & Spa **4**
Holiday Inn—Waikiki **3**
Hyatt Regency Waikiki **27**

Olohana Street and Fort DeRussy Park in the Diamond Head direction (or eastern side of Waikiki).

Very Expensive

Hawaii Prince Hotel Waikiki ★★ For a vacation with a view and the feel of a palace, stay in this striking $150-million modern structure (actually, twin 33-story high-tech towers). The high-ceilinged lobby is a mass of pink Italian marble with English slate accents; a grand piano sits in the midst of the raised seating area, where high tea is served every afternoon. A glass-encased elevator with views of all of Honolulu whisks you up to your room. All bedrooms face the Ala Wai Yacht Harbor, with floor-to-ceiling sliding-glass windows that let you enjoy the view (sorry, no lanais). All of the comfortably appointed rooms are basically the same, but the higher the floor, the higher the price.

Following Japanese standards, the level of service is impeccable; no detail is ignored, and no request is too small. The location is perfect for shopping—Ala

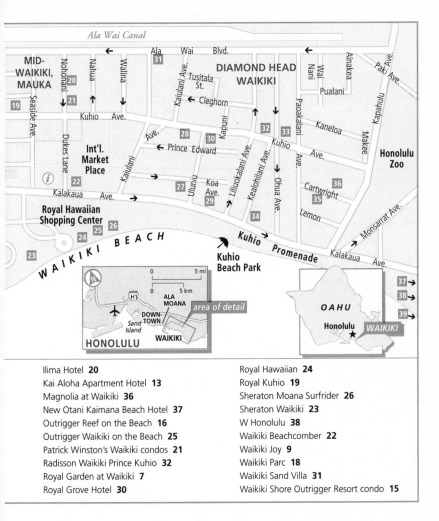

Ilima Hotel **20**

Kai Aloha Apartment Hotel **13**

Magnolia at Waikiki **36**

New Otani Kaimana Beach Hotel **37**

Outrigger Reef on the Beach **16**

Outrigger Waikiki on the Beach **25**

Patrick Winston's Waikiki condos **21**

Radisson Waikiki Prince Kuhio **32**

Royal Garden at Waikiki **7**

Royal Grove Hotel **30**

Royal Hawaiian **24**

Royal Kuhio **19**

Sheraton Moana Surfrider **26**

Sheraton Waikiki **23**

W Honolulu **38**

Waikiki Beachcomber **22**

Waikiki Joy **9**

Waikiki Parc **18**

Waikiki Sand Villa **31**

Waikiki Shore Outrigger Resort condo **15**

Moana Center is a 10-minute walk away—and Waikiki's beaches are just a 5-minute walk away (both are also accessible via the hotel's own shuttle bus).

100 Holomoana St. (just across Ala Wai Canal Bridge, on the ocean side of Ala Moana Blvd.), Honolulu, HI 96815. ⓒ **800/321-OAHU** or 808/965-1111. Fax 808/946-0811. www.princeresortshawaii.com. 521 units. $310–$450 double; from $550 suite. Extra person $40; children 17 and under stay free using existing bedding. Online packages include room and a car from $199. AE, DC, MC, V. Valet parking $14, self-parking $10. Bus: 19 or 20. **Amenities:** 2 excellent restaurants (Japanese, Hawaii Regional Cuisine and a terrific buffet at a great price—see Prince Court review on p. 135); outdoor bar; outdoor pool; 27-hole golf club a half-hour drive away in Ewa Beach (reached by hotel shuttle); small but newly renovated fitness room; Jacuzzi; concierge; car-rental desk; business center; room service (6am–midnight); babysitting; coin-op washer/dryers; laundry service; dry cleaning; executive-level rooms. *In room:* A/C, TV, dataport, fridge, coffeemaker, hair dryer, iron, safe.

Hilton Hawaiian Village Beach Resort & Spa ★★ *(Kids)* Sprawling over 20 acres, this is Waikiki's biggest resort—a minicity unto itself, so big it even has its own post office. You'll find tropical gardens dotted with exotic wildlife (flamingos, peacocks, and even tropical penguins), award-winning restaurants (like the Golden Dragon, p. 133), 100 different shops, a secluded lagoon, two minigolf courses, and a gorgeous stretch of Waikiki Beach. This is a great place to stay with the kids.

There's a wide choice of accommodations. Rooms, which range from simply lovely to ultradeluxe, are housed in five towers: Rainbow, Tapa, Diamond Head, Alii, and the recently closed for renovation Kalia (mold was discovered in 2002 and extensive renovations were still going on when we went to press). Despite the hotel's mega-Vegas-size, this division into towers, each with its own restaurants and shopping, cuts down on the chaotic, impersonal feeling that might have resulted. Still, this is the place for a lively, activity-packed vacation; those seeking a more intimate experience might want to look elsewhere.

All rooms are large and beautifully furnished; if you can afford it, we highly recommend the ones in the Alii Tower, located right on the ocean. Guests in these 348 amenity-laden rooms and suites get the royal treatment, including in-room registration, an exclusive health club and pool, and the full attention of a multilingual staff. Each room has no fewer than three phones (one of which is PC-compatible) and even a mini-TV on the bathroom vanity. But if you choose a room in one of the more affordable towers, you'll still be happy.

In 2001, the new Kalia Tower opened, along with two new spas: **Holistica Hawaii** 🌟🌟 (a wellness center with high-tech body scanning equipment) and **Mandara Spa** 🌟🌟 (a state-of-the-art fitness center and traditional body-treatment spa). Also new at the Hilton is Waikiki's first full-service, 24-hour hotel business center, located on the ground floor of the Diamond Head tower.

Even if you don't stay here, stop by the **Bishop Museum at Kalia** 🌟🌟🌟, a sort of mini-version of the main museum, focusing on Hawaiian culture and the history of Waikiki in a very visitor-friendly format. You can easily take in the entire collection in a couple of hours.

2005 Kalia Rd. (at Ala Moana Blvd.), Honolulu, HI 96815. ✆ **800-HILTONS** or 808/949-4321. Fax 808/947-7898. www.hawaiianvillage.hilton.com. 2,998 units. $380–$510 double; from $455 suite. Package deals start as low as $189. Extra person $45; children 18 and under stay free in parent's room. AE, DISC, MC, V. Valet parking $15, self-parking $11. Bus: 19 or 20. **Amenities:** 18 restaurants; 6 bars; 3 outdoor pools; 2 minigolf courses; fitness center with free classes and high-tech equipment; brand-new superplush Mandara Spa; watersports equipment rentals; year-round children's program (one of Waikiki's best); game room; concierge; activity desk; car-rental desk; Waikiki's only 24-hr. business center; huge shopping arcade; salon; room service (6am–midnight); in-room massage; babysitting; coin-op washer/dryers; same-day laundry service; dry cleaning; concierge-level rooms. *In room:* A/C, TV, dataport, fridge, coffeemaker, hair dryer, iron, safe.

Expensive

DoubleTree Alana Waikiki 🌟   This boutique hotel is a welcome oasis of beauty, comfort, and prompt service. It's an intimate choice, offering the amenities of a much larger, more luxurious hotel at more affordable prices. The guest rooms are comfortable and homey; some of the rooms can be small but make good use of the space and offer all the amenities you'd expect from a more expensive hotel. Many guests are business travelers who expect top-drawer service—and the Alana Waikiki delivers. The staff is attentive to detail and willing to go to any lengths to make you happy. Waikiki Beach is a 10-minute walk away and the Convention Center is about a 7 minute walk.

1956 Ala Moana Blvd. (on the Ewa side, near Kalakaua Ave.), Honolulu, HI 96815. ✆ **800/222-TREE** or 808/941-7275. Fax 808/949-0996. www.alana-doubletree.com. 313 units. $199–$219 double; from $250 suite. Extra person $30; children under 18 stay free in parent's room. AE, DC, DISC, MC, V. Valet parking $10. Bus: 19 or 20. **Amenities:** An excellent restaurant (Padovani's, p. 134); bar; outdoor heated pool; small fitness center with sauna and massage services; concierge; activity desk; car-rental desk; well-equipped business center;

room service (7am–9pm); in-room massage; babysitting; laundry service; dry cleaning. *In room:* A/C, TV, data-port, fridge, coffeemaker, hair dryer, iron, safe.

Moderate

Holiday Inn—Waikiki   Just 2 blocks from the beach, 2 blocks from Ala Moana Shopping Center, and a 7-minute walk from the Convention Center, this Holiday Inn has a great location and offers this chain's usual amenities for prices that are quite reasonable (for Waikiki, anyway). All rooms, which have a modern Japanese look, come with either a king or two double beds. The property sits back from the street, so noise is at a minimum. The staff is unbelievably friendly.

1830 Ala Moana Blvd. (between Hobron Lane and Kalia Rd.), Honolulu, HI 96815. © **888/992-4545** or 808/955-1111. Fax 808/947-1799. www.holiday-inn-waikiki.com. 199 units. $140–$180 double. Extra person $15; children 19 and under stay free in parent's room using existing bedding. AE, DC, DISC, MC, V. Parking $6. Bus: 19 or 20. **Amenities:** Restaurant; outdoor pool; small fitness room; activity desk; limited room service; coin-op washer/dryers; laundry service; dry cleaning; executive level rooms. *In room:* A/C, TV, dataport, fridge, coffeemaker, hair dryer, iron, safe.

Royal Garden at Waikiki ★ *Finds*   For people looking for a quieter stay, this elegant boutique hotel, tucked away on a tree-lined side street, offers a lobby filled with European marble and chandeliers in addition to the plush guest rooms, which feature a pantry kitchenette, marble bathroom, lanai, lots of closet space, and views. The beach is a few blocks away, but at these prices, it's worth the hike.

440 Olohana St. (between Kuhio Ave. and Ala Wai Blvd.), Honolulu, HI 96815. © **800/367-5666** or 808/943-0202. Fax 808/946-8777. www.royalgardens.com. 220 units. $150–$250 double; $325–$425 1-bedroom double; $500–$1000 2-bedroom (sleeps up to 4). Packages galore. Extra person $25; children under 12 stay free in parent's room. AE, DC, DISC, MC, V. Parking $8. Bus: 19 or 20. **Amenities:** 2 restaurants; 2 freshwater outdoor pools (one with cascading waterfall); small fitness room; 2 Jacuzzis; 2 saunas; concierge; small business center; babysitting; coin-op washer/dryers; laundry service; dry cleaning; complimentary shuttle service to Honolulu shopping centers. *In room:* A/C, TV, dataport, kitchenette, fridge, coffeemaker, hair dryer, iron, safe.

Inexpensive

Hawaiian Monarch   Part hotel and part condo, this high-rise is just across the street from the Ala Wai Canal, within walking distance of the Hawaii Convention Center. It offers tropically decorated but very tiny budget rooms (the bathrooms are so small you have to close the door to sit on the toilet). However, this is one of the more affordable places to stay in Waikiki near the convention center. If you want more complete kitchen facilities, go for one of the suites, which have kitchenettes with a hot plate/oven and toaster. The cheapest doubles have either two twin beds or a queen; fans of king beds will have to pay a bit more for a deluxe room. The location allows easy access in and out of Waikiki by car, and the beach is just a 10- to 15-minute walk away. There's a huge sun deck (the largest in Waikiki, they claim) with a pool on the sixth floor if you don't want to schlepp to the sands. Request a room facing the Ala Wai Canal for the best view.

444 Niu St. at Ala Wai Blvd.), Honolulu, HI 96815. © **800/367-5004** or 808/922-9700. Fax 808/922-2421. www.castleresorts.com. 439 units. High season $119–$129 double, $139–$149 double studio suite with kitchenette; low season $109–$119 double, $129–$139 double studio suite with kitchenette. Extra person $15; children under 18 stay free in parent's room using existing bedding. Internet specials start at $69. AE, DC, DISC, MC, V. Parking $6. Bus: 2 or 13. **Amenities:** Restaurant/sports bar; outdoor pool; coin-op washer/dryers. *In room:* A/C, TV, kitchenette, fridge, coffeemaker, hair dryer, safe.

MID-WAIKIKI, MAKAI

All the hotels listed below are between Kalakaua Avenue and the ocean, and between Fort DeRussy in the Ewa (west) direction and Kaiulani Street in the Diamond Head (east) direction.

Very Expensive

Halekulani ★★★ *Kids*   Here's the ultimate heavenly Hawaii vacation. Halekulani translates as "House Befitting Heaven"—an apt description of this luxury resort, selected the number-one hotel in the world by *Gourmet* magazine. It's spread over 5 acres of prime Waikiki beachfront in five buildings that are connected by open courtyards and lush, tropical gardens. Upon arrival, you're immediately greeted and escorted to your room, where registration is handled in comfort and privacy.

There are so many things that set this luxury hotel apart from the others, the most important being the rooms: About 90% face the ocean, and they're big (averaging 620 sq. ft.), each with a separate sitting area and a large, furnished lanai. Each bathroom features a deep-soaking tub, a separate glassed-in shower, and a marble basin. Recent renovations to this luxury property include total refurbishment of the rooms, new entertainment center with DVD player, a bed-side control panel, wireless Internet service, and a new spa.

Other perks include complimentary tickets to any or all of the following: Ihi-lani Palace, Bishop Museum, Contemporary Art Museum, Honolulu Academy of Art, and the Honolulu Symphony (about $100 per person worth of art and culture). The hotel's restaurants are outstanding (see the reviews of La Mer and Orchids on p. 129 and 134, respectively), and the **House Without a Key** ★★ is surely one of the world's most romantic spots for sunset cocktails, light meals, and entertainment. You can't find a better location on Waikiki Beach or a more luxurious hotel.

2199 Kalia Rd. (at the ocean end of Lewers St.), Honolulu, HI 96815. ✆ **800/367-2343** or 808/923-2311. Fax 808/926-8004. www.halekulani.com. 456 units. $325–$520 double; from $750 suite. Extra person $125; 1 child under 17 stays free in parent's room using existing bedding; maximum 3 people per room. AE, DC, MC, V. Parking $10. Bus: 19 or 20. **Amenities:** 4 superb restaurants; 2 bars; gorgeous outdoor pool; recently opened spa; watersports equipment rentals; bike rentals; children's program during the summer and at Christmas; concierge; activity desk; complete business center; top-drawer shops; salon; 24-hr. room service; in-room massage; babysitting; same-day laundry and dry cleaning. *In room:* A/C, TV/VCR, dataport, minibar, hair dryer, iron, safe.

Royal Hawaiian ★★   This flamingo-pink oasis, hidden away among bloom-ing gardens within the concrete jungle of Waikiki, is a symbol of luxury. Built by Matson steamship lines and inspired by popular silent-screen star Rudolph Valentino (*The Sheik*), the Spanish-Moorish "Pink Palace" opened in 1927 on the same spot where Queen Kaahumanu had her summer palace—on one of the best stretches of Waikiki Beach.

Entry into the hotel is past the lush gardens, with their spectacular banyan tree, into the black terrazzo-marble lobby, which features handwoven pink car-pets and giant floral arrangements. My heart was won over by the rooms in the Historic Wing, which contain carved wooden doors, four-poster canopy beds, flowered wallpaper, and period furniture. Historic touches abound, including Hawaiian craft displays (Hawaiian quilts, leis, weaving, and more) by local artists every Monday, Wednesday, and Friday. Another plus: 24-hour medical services on property.

One of Waikiki's best spas, **Abhasa** ★★, (✆ **808/922-8200;** www.abhasa. com) is located on property. This contemporary spa, spread out over 7,000 square feet, concentrates on natural, organic treatments in a soothing atmosphere (the smell of eucalyptus wafts through the air) with everything from the latest aroma-therapy thalassotherpie (which translates into soaking in a sweet-smelling hot bath) to shiatsu massages. Their specialty is a cold-laser, anti-aging treatment that promises to give you a refreshed, revitalized face in just 30 minutes.

In the culinary department, the Surf Room is known for its elaborate seafood buffets; the casual Beach Club features an oceanfront patio that's a great place to start your day. The Royal Hawaiian luau is done in grand style on Monday nights. The hotel's **Mai Tai Bar** ✦✦ is one of the most popular places in Waikiki for its namesake drink, which supposedly originated here.

2259 Kalakaua Ave. (at Royal Hawaiian Ave., on the ocean side of the Royal Hawaiian Shopping Center), Honolulu, HI 96815. ⓒ 800/325-3535 or 808/923-7311. Fax 808/924-7098. www.sheraton.com. 527 units. $380–$605 double; from $850 suite. Extra person $80. Ask about Sheraton's Escape package rates, with rates starting at $287. AE, MC, V. Valet parking $15, self-parking at Sheraton Waikiki $10. Bus: 19 or 20. **Amenities:** 2 restaurants; landmark bar; good-size outdoor pool; preferential tee times at Makaha Resort and Golf Club (about 1 hr. away); nearby fitness room (next door at the Sheraton Waikiki); excellent full-service spa (Abhasa), one of Waikiki's best; watersports equipment rentals; bike rentals; excellent year-round children's program ($30 a day, $20 for half-day); game room; multilingual concierge desk; activity desk; car-rental desk; business center; elegant shopping arcade; 24-hr. room service; in-room massage; babysitting; 24-hr. laundry service and dry cleaning (except Sun). *In room:* A/C, TV, dataport, fridge, hair dryer, iron, safe.

Sheraton Waikiki ✦ *Kids*   Occupying two 30-story towers, this is by far the biggest of the four Sheratons on the beach. The lobby is immense and filled with shops, travel desks, and people. Not surprisingly, this hotel hosts numerous conventions; if you're not comfortable with crowds and conventioneers, book elsewhere. However, size has its advantages: The Sheraton has everything from a fabulous kids' program to historical walks and cooking demonstrations for Mom and Dad. Plus, you can "play and charge" at Waikiki's other Sheraton hotels.

It's hard to get a bad room here. A whopping 1,200 units have some sort of ocean view, and 650 rooms overlook Diamond Head. Accommodations are spacious, with big lanais to take in those magnificent views. For the budget-conscious, the Sheraton Manor Hotel occupies a separate adjacent wing and offers all the services and beachfront of the main hotel. The views aren't the best, the rooms are small (2 people, max) and modestly appointed (no lanai), but the price is hard to beat.

2255 Kalakaua Ave. (at Royal Hawaiian Ave., on the ocean side of the Royal Hawaiian Shopping Center and west of the Royal Hawaiian), Honolulu, HI 96815. ⓒ 800/325-3535 or 808/922-4422. Fax 808/923-8785. www.sheraton.com. 1,852 units. $115 Sheraton Manor Annex double; $290–$570 Waikiki double; from $865 suite. Extra person $50; children under 18 stay free in parent's room. Ask about Escape rates, which could save you as much as 32%. AE, DC, DISC, MC, V. Valet parking $15, self-parking $10. Bus: 19 or 20. **Amenities:** 4 restaurants; 3 bars; nightclub; 2 large outdoor pools, including one of the biggest and sunniest along the Waikiki beachfront; access to Makaha Golf Club's golf and tennis facilities (about 1 hr. away); fitness center; watersports equipment rentals; bike rentals; children's program with activities ranging from catamaran sailing to nightly movies; game room; concierge; activity desk; car-rental desk; business center; shopping arcade; room service (6am–midnight); in-room massage; babysitting; coin-op washer/dryers; same-day laundry service and dry cleaning (except holidays). *In room:* A/C, TV, dataport, kitchenette, minibar, fridge, coffeemaker, hair dryer, iron, safe.

Expensive

Outrigger Waikiki on the Beach ✦ *Kids*   The same value and quality that we've come to expect in every Outrigger hotel are definitely in evidence here, only multiplied by a factor of 10. Even the standard rooms in this 16-story oceanfront hotel are large and comfortable. In 2003 the Outrigger poured some $14.3 million into the guest rooms, upgrading the furniture and sprucing up the bathrooms with new granite vanity tops, ceramic floor tiles, and new lighted make-up mirrors. The prime beachfront location and loads of facilities help make this one of the chain's most attractive properties. The guest rooms all have huge closets, roomy bathrooms, and plenty of amenities, plus a spacious lanai; the price is entirely dependent on the view.

A Room for Everyone in Waikiki: The Outrigger & Ohana Hotels Dynasty

Among the largest hotel chains in Waikiki, Outrigger and Ohana Hotels offer excellent accommodations across the board. The Outrigger chain used to include both the budget-priced Ohana Hotels and the current Outrigger resort properties, but the chain has now divided its properties into two brands.

The Outrigger properties are more resort-oriented, with amenities like concierge service, children's programs, and a variety of restaurants and shops. You'll be comfortable at any of their outposts: **Outrigger Waikiki on the Beach** (see complete review, above), **Outrigger Reef on the Beach** (rooms from $220), and **Waikiki Shore Outrigger Resort Condo** (condominiums from $245).

There are lots of package deals available for these properties. You may be able to get a free rental car when you book at nondiscounted rack rates, the 6th night free when you book at rack rates, bed-and-breakfast rates, island-hopper rates that allow you to save 20% if you stay at an Outrigger on another island, family plans (children 17 and under stay free in parent's room using existing bedding), 20% off for seniors (25% off for AARP members), and even deals for golfers. To ask about current offerings and make reservations at any of these or other Outrigger properties throughout the islands, contact **Outrigger** (© **800/OUTRIGGER** or 808/942-7722; www.outrigger.com).

The 13 budget and moderately priced Ohana Hotels offer dependable, clean, well-appointed rooms—great deals for more frugal travelers. The chain's price structure is based entirely on location, room size, and amenities: Rooms go from $129, $149, or $189, and they also offer plenty of deals, including rooms from $69, a free night's stay after your fifth night, room and car packages, and bed-and-breakfast rates; for information, contact **Ohana Hotels** (© **800/462-6262**; www.ohana hotels.com).

2335 Kalakaua Ave. (on the ocean, between the Royal Hawaiian Shopping Center and the Sheraton Moana Surfrider), Honolulu, HI 96815. © **800/OUTRIGGER** or 808/923-0711. Fax 800/622-4852. www.outrigger. com. 530 units. $275–$450 double; from $600 suite. 20% discount for seniors 50 and over, 25% discount for AARP members; free rental car when booking at rack rates; ask about other package deals. Extra person $30; children 17 and under stay free in parent's room using existing bedding. AE, DC, DISC, MC, V. Parking $10. Bus: 19 or 20. **Amenities:** 5 restaurants (including one on the beach, serving great island-style seafood and steaks; see the review of Duke's Canoe Club on p. 136); 3 bars; showroom with nightly entertainment; giant outdoor pool; fitness center; Jacuzzi; watersports equipment rentals; year-round children's program; concierge; activity desk; car-rental desk; business center; large shopping arcade; salon; limited room service (7am–2pm and 5–9:45pm); babysitting; coin-op washer/dryers; laundry service; dry cleaning; concierge-level rooms. *In room:* A/C, TV, dataport, some kitchenettes, fridge, coffeemaker, hair dryer, iron, safe.

Sheraton Moana Surfrider ⭐⭐   Step back in time at Waikiki's first hotel, which dates from 1901 and is listed on the National Register of Historic Places. Considered an innovation in the travel industry, the Moana featured a private bathroom and a telephone in each guest room—an unheard-of luxury at the turn of the 20th century. Yesteryear lives on at this grand hotel: Entry is through the original colonial porte cochere, past the highly polished front porch dotted with rocking chairs, and into the perfectly restored lobby with detailed millwork and intricate plasterwork. The female employees even wear traditional Victorian-era muumuus. The aloha spirit that pervades this classy and charming place is infectious.

The hotel consists of three wings: the original (and totally restored) Banyan Wing, the Diamond Wing, and the Tower Wing. It's hard to get a bad room here; most have ocean views, and all come with pampering amenities like bedside controls and plush robes. But we're especially taken with the Banyan Wing rooms: What they lack in size (they're on the smallish side and don't have lanais), they make up for in style; even the fixtures in the smallish bathrooms are modern-day replicas of 19th-century hardware. You get the feel for Old Hawaii here, with daily activities like Hawaiian arts and crafts such as coconut-palm weaving and Hawaiian quilting; be sure to visit the Historical Room, where a variety of memorabilia is on display.

One of the best reasons to stay here is the hotel's prime stretch of beach, with lifeguard, beach chairs, towels, and any other service you desire. The Beach Bar and a poolside snack bar are located in the oceanfront courtyard that's centered around a 100-year-old banyan tree, where there's live music in the evenings.

2365 Kalakaua Ave. (ocean side of the street, across from Kaiulani St.), Honolulu, HI 96815. ✆ **800/ 325-3535** or 808/922-3111. Fax 808/923-0308. www.moana-surfrider.com. 793 units. $270–$575 double; from $1025 suite. Extra person and roll-away bed $50; children under 18 stay free in parent's room using existing bedding. Ask about special package rates, which could save you as much as 32%. AE, DC, MC, V. Valet parking $15, self-parking at sister property $10. Bus: 19 or 20. **Amenities:** 5 restaurants; 2 bars; outdoor pool; nearby fitness room (about a 2-min. walk down the beach at the Sheraton Waikiki); watersports equipment rentals; children's program (featuring both onsite activities and excursions to the Honolulu Zoo and the Waikiki Aquarium); nearby game room (a stroll down the beach at the Sheraton Waikiki); concierge; activity desk; car-rental desk; nearby business center (a few min. away at the Royal Hawaiian); very upscale shopping arcade; salon; room service; massage; babysitting; coin-op washer/dryers; same-day laundry service and dry cleaning. *In room:* A/C, TV, dataport, fridge, coffeemaker, hair dryer, iron, safe.

Waikiki Parc ⋆ Terrifically located just 100 yards from the beach, this hotel is for people who want a taste of the Halekulani's elegance, grace, and style but at a more reasonable price. It's tucked just behind the Halekulani and is owned and operated by the same company. The compact, beautifully appointed rooms all have lanais with ocean, mountain, or city views; ceramic-tile floors with plush carpeting; and conversation areas with a writing desk and rattan couch and chair. Nice extras include adjustable floor-to-ceiling shutters for those who want to sleep in.

The Parc features the same level of service that has made the Halekulani famous and offers two excellent restaurants. On a recent visit, we asked room service for a few items that were not on the menu—not only did they happily comply, but the manager also checked back later to make sure we got what we wanted.

2233 Helumoa Rd. (at Lewers St.), Honolulu, HI 96815. ✆ **800/422-0450** or 808/921-7272. Fax 808/923-1336. www.waikikiparchotel.com. 298 units. $225–$320 double. Extra person $50; children 14 and under stay free in parent's room. Ask about room/car, bed-and-breakfast, and family packages. AE, DC, MC, V. Self-or valet parking $15. Bus: 19 or 20. **Amenities:** 2 restaurants (fine buffet restaurant, Kyoto-style Japanese restaurant); concierge; activity desk; business center; limited room service; babysitting; coin-op washer/dryers; same-day laundry and dry cleaning. *In room:* A/C, TV, dataport (in some rooms), fridge, hair dryer, safe.

Inexpensive

Aloha Punawai *(Value)* Here's one of Waikiki's best-kept secrets: a low-profile, family-operated (since 1959) apartment hotel just 2 blocks from the beach and within walking distance of most Waikiki attractions. The Aloha Punawai offers

---

Tips   **Family-Friendly Hotels**

Hilton Hawaiian Village (p. 105)   The Rainbow Express is Hilton's year-round daily program of activities for children ages 5 to 12. The program costs $50 for a full day, including lunch and an excursion, or $25 for a half day (a half day without excursion and lunch is $22). It offers a wide range of educational and fun activities: Hawaiian arts and crafts, nature walks, wildlife feedings, shell hunting, fishing, and much more. Everything about this hotel is kid-friendly, from the wildlife parading about the grounds to the submarine dives offered just out front. In three of the resort's restaurants, kids ages 4 to 11 eat free.

Halekulani (p. 108)   Between early June and mid-August and during Christmastime, the Halekulani, possibly our favorite hotel in the islands, has a wonderful supervised program for children ages 5 to 12, called the Keiki Lani (Heavenly Child) Club, available Monday to Friday, 8:30am to 4pm. The $25 fee includes goodies like a complimentary backpack with matching water bottle, plus lunch and admission to activities (the second child in the same family is only $15). Daily programs include crafts, games, sightseeing, and excursions (to Sea Life Park, Bishop Museum, the Waikiki Aquarium, or the Honolulu Zoo).

Outrigger/Ohana Hotels (p. 110)   Kids staying at any Outrigger or Ohana Hotel in Waikiki can enjoy a special activities program with a surfing theme. Located at the **Outrigger Reef**, the Cowabunga Kids Club offers daily programs for children ages 5 to 13. The half-day ($35) and full-day ($55 including lunch, snack, and Cowabunga T-shirt) programs include games, arts and crafts, beach walks, shoreline fishing, and excursions around Waikiki. Professional counselors are in charge, but parents can join in if they wish (adult rates are $45 for full day, $30 for half). For those parents who want to go off on their own, they can choose to have the option of taking a free pager while their children are enrolled in the program. Transportation to the Outrigger Reef is provided from other hotels in the chain. Reservations are necessary; call © 808/923-3111.

Sheraton Waikiki Hotel (p. 109)   The Keiki Aloha Program offers year-round activities for children ages 5 to 12 ($30 for a full day, $20 for a half day), from 9am to 9pm, and includes a supervised lunch ($6.50) and dinner ($12). Activities include boogie boarding, flying a kite, sailing on a catamaran, watching nightly movies, and more.

Royal Kuhio (p. 116)   If you have active kids, this is the place for you. The seventh-floor recreation area has volleyball courts, billiards, basketball courts, shuffleboard, an exercise room, and even a putting green. Located just across the street from the International Market

---

some of the lowest prices in Waikiki; if you stay a week, prices drop even more. And the location is great, just across the street from Fort DeRussy Park and 2 blocks to Grey's Beach—the same great beach facing the luxury Halekulani and Sheraton Waikiki hotels. The apartments contain a mishmash of furniture and come with full kitchens and lanais. Don't expect the Ritz (or any interior

Place and two blocks from the beach, the Royal Kuhio features one-bedroom apartments with sofa sleepers and full kitchens. You're allowed up to four people per unit at the regular rate and can have five for an extra charge of $15 for a roll-away or crib.

Ilima Hotel (p. 116)   This hotel was designed with families in mind. The units are large, and all have full-size kitchens. Although there's no formal children's program, you'll find free HBO, the Disney Channel, and Super Nintendo video games in each room, and the coin-operated laundry is a big help to mom and dad. The beach and the International Market Place are both only a short walk away, and TheBus stops just outside. Very popular with neighbor-island families.

Kahala Mandarin Oriental Hawaii (p. 124)   The Keiki Club is the year-round activities program for kids ages 5 to 12. Your youngsters will have a blast dancing the hula, making leis, designing sand sculptures, putting on puppet shows, learning to strum a ukulele, making shell art and fish prints, listening to Hawaiian folk tales and legends, playing Hawaiian games, and more. The cost is $50 for a full day (including lunch), $35 for a half day.

Laie Inn (p. 127)   There's no charge for kids under 18 to stay with you at this two-story, plantation-style North Shore hotel. Within walking distance of the Polynesian Cultural Center, the Rodeway is set up for families, with features like free continental breakfast, a pool, and laundry. A terrific white-sand beach is just across the street.

J. W. Marriott Ihilani Resort & Spa (p. 129)   The Keiki Beachcomber Club, for children ages 5 to 12 (4-year-olds are admitted at the discretion of the program coordinator), is available daily in the winter (Dec 15–Feb 15) and Monday, Wednesday, Friday and Saturday from mid-February to May 31. Activities (9am–3pm) include kite-flying, tide-pool exploration, snorkeling, golf, tennis, swimming, aerobics, and international games like les boules (similar to bocce ball), Indian kickball, and tinikling (a bamboo dance from the Philippines). Hawaiian cultural activities include lei-making, hula dancing, and so many other activities that you're unlikely to even see the kids until you're ready to get on the plane to go home. The cost is $55 per child, which includes all activities, lunch, and a T-shirt; half day rate is $35 with lunch and $30 without.

Sheffield House (p. 126)   Many B&Bs aren't very child friendly, but Sheffield House is an exception. The owners have three kids of their own so they're sensitive to traveling families' needs and have lots of gear on hand.

decoration, for that matter)—just sparkling clean accommodations in a great location. Towels and linens are provided. The phone wiring has been installed and is ready for service; you have to pay for hookup.

305 Saratoga Rd. (across from Fort DeRussy and the Waikiki Post Office, between Kalia Rd. and Kalakaua Ave.), Honolulu, HI 96815. (C) **808/923-5211.** Fax 808/622-4688. www.alternative-hawaii.com/alohapunawai/.

19 units (studios have shower only). $85–$95 studio double; $95–$125 1-bedroom double (sleeps up to 5). Extra person $10. Discounts for weeklong (or longer) stays. MC, V. Parking $7. Bus: 19 or 20. **Amenities:** Coin-op washer/dryers. *In room:* A/C, TV, kitchen, fridge, coffeemaker.

The Breakers ★ *Value*   The Breakers is full of old-fashioned Hawaiian aloha—and it's only steps from the sands of Waikiki. This two-story hotel has a friendly staff and a loyal following. Its six buildings are set around a pool and a tropical garden blooming with brilliant red and yellow hibiscus; wooden jalousies and shoji doors further the tropical ambience. Each of the tastefully decorated, slightly oversize rooms comes with a lanai and a kitchenette. Every Wednesday and Friday, you're invited to a formal Japanese tea ceremony from 10am to noon. One of the best things about the Breakers is the location, just a 2-minute walk to numerous restaurants, shopping, and Waikiki beach.

250 Beach Walk (between Kalakaua Ave. and Kalia Rd.), Honolulu, HI 96815. ℂ **800/426-0494** or 808/923-3181. Fax 808/923-7174. www.breakers-hawaii.com. 64 units (shower only). $94–$100 double; $135 garden studio double. Extra person $8. AE, DC, MC, V. Limited free parking, $6–$8 across the street. Bus: 19 or 20. **Amenities:** Restaurant (poolside bar and grill for lunch); outdoor pool; babysitting; coin-op washer/dryers; dry cleaning. *In room:* A/C, TV, kitchenette, fridge, coffeemaker, iron available, safe.

Hale Pua Nui Hotel   Don't expect the modern look of a budget Ohana Hotel. The 1950s motel-style Hale Pua Nui offers clean, older, budget units at 1970s prices. A step above a hostel, the large studios have seen better days—the furniture's worn, and the carpet is showing its age—but the bargain rates make up for the lack of luxury. Each unit contains two single beds, a small table, and a kitchenette. The Beach Walk location puts you just 1½ blocks from the beach, 1½ blocks from a bus stop, and within walking distance of restaurants, nightclubs, and other Waikiki activities. The property is safe for single woman travelers, and the owners are so friendly you'll feel like you're visiting a relative.

228 Beach Walk Ave. (across from Helumoa St.), Honolulu, HI 96815. ℂ **808/923-9693.** Fax 808/923-9678. 22 units (shower only). $57 double. Extra person $5. 3-night minimum. MC, V. Parking $5. Bus: 19 or 20. *In room:* A/C, TV, kitchenette, fridge, coffeemaker, iron, safe.

Hawaiiana Hotel ★ *Finds*   The hotel's slogan—"The spirit of old Hawaii"— says it all. The lush tropical flowers and carved tiki at the entrance on tiny Beach Walk set the tone for this intimate low-rise hotel. From the moment you arrive, you'll be embraced by the aloha spirit: At check-in, you're given a pineapple, and every morning, complimentary Kona coffee and tropical juice are served poolside. All the concrete, hollow-tiled guest rooms feature kitchenettes, two beds (a double and a single or a queen plus a sofa bed), and a view of the gardens and two swimming pools. Hawaiian entertainment is featured every week. The hotel is about a block from the beach and within walking distance of Waikiki shopping and nightlife.

260 Beach Walk (near Kalakaua Ave.), Honolulu, HI 96815. ℂ **800/367-5122** or 808/923-3811. Fax 808/926-5728. www.hawaiianahotelatwaikiki.com. 95 units (some with shower only). $95–$105 double; $165–$195 deluxe studio with kitchenette; $135 1-bedroom with kitchenette (sleeps up to 4). Extra person $10. AE, DC, DISC, MC, V. Parking $8. Bus: 19 or 20. **Amenities:** 2 good-size outdoor pools; coin-op washer/dryers. *In room:* A/C, TV, kitchenette, fridge, coffeemaker, iron, safe.

Kai Aloha Apartment Hotel *Value*   If you want to experience what Waikiki was like 40 years ago, stay here. This small apartment hotel just a block from the beach is reminiscent of the low-key hotels that used to line the blocks of Waikiki in the good old days. It offers one-bedroom apartments and studios, all furnished in modest rattan and colorful island prints. Each of the one-bedroom units has a bedroom with either a queen bed or two twins, a living room with a couch and two additional twins (Hawaiian houses of 40 years ago all had extra beds in the living room, called *punee,* for guests to sleep on), a full kitchen, plus a dining table, and even voice mail. These rooms are even large enough to accommodate a roll-away bed for a fifth person. Glass jalousies take advantage of the cooling trade winds, but there's also air-conditioning for the very hot days. The studios have two twin beds, a kitchenette, a balcony, a Plexiglas roof in the bathroom (the forerunner of the skylight), and a screen door for ventilation. The units aren't exactly designer showrooms, but they do have a homey, comfortable feel and provide daily maid service. You're sure to forgive the lack of aesthetics when you're presented with the bill. A large deck on the second floor is a great place to sip early morning coffee or watch the sun sink into the Pacific.

235 Saratoga Rd. (across from Fort DeRussy and Waikiki Post Office, between Kalakaua Ave. and Kalia Rd.), Honolulu, HI 96815. © **808/923-6723.** Fax 808/922-7592. www.its.caltech.edu/~tpkmc/kaialoha/KaiAloha. htm. 18 units. $65–$70 studio double; $76–$80 1-bedroom double; $85–$95 1-bedroom for 3; $95–$105 1-bedroom for 4; $110–$115 1-bedroom for 5. Extra person $15. 3-night minimum. AE, DC, MC, V. Parking $7. Bus: 19 or 20. **Amenities:** Coin-op washer/dryers. *In room:* A/C, TV, kitchenette, fridge, coffeemaker.

MID-WAIKIKI, MAUKA

These mid-Waikiki hotels, on the mountainside of Kalakaua Avenue, are a little farther away from the beach than those listed above. All are between Kalakaua Avenue and Ala Wai Canal, and between Niu Street in the Ewa direction and Kaiulani Street in the Diamond Head direction.

Expensive

Waikiki Beachcomber   A room/car package makes this stylish Waikiki hotel a real deal. One of its main pluses is the great location—a block from Waikiki Beach, across the street from the upscale Royal Hawaiian Shopping Center, and next door to bargain shopping at the International Market Place. The rooms feature Berber carpets, TV armoires, contemporary furniture, handheld showers, convenient hot pots for making coffee or tea, and voice mail. Yet another reason to stay at this conveniently located hotel is that it hosts *The Magic of Polynesia,* a show with illusionist John Hirokana and the king of Hawaiian entertainment, Don Ho, a Hawaii legend for more than 40 years.

2300 Kalakaua Ave. (at Duke's Lane), Honolulu, HI 96815. © **800/622-4646** or 808/922-4646. Fax 808/926-9973. www.waikikibeachcomber.com. 495 units (shower only). $220–$270 double; from $380 suite. Extra person $25. Internet rates from $99. Room/car packages from $129. AE, DC, MC, V. Parking $8. Bus: 19 or 20. **Amenities:** Restaurant (poolside coffee shop); Hawaiian entertainment show; outdoor pool; children's program from July–Aug; activity desk; car-rental desk; small shopping arcade; limited room service (6am–11am); coin-op washer/dryers; laundry service; dry cleaning. *In room:* A/C, TV, fridge, coffeemaker, hair dryer, iron on request, safe.

Moderate/Inexpensive

Aston Coconut Plaza (★ (Value   This small hotel is an island of integrity in a sea of tourist schlock. Calling itself a "studio apartment boutique hotel," the Coconut Plaza offers perks that are rare in Waikiki, such as free continental breakfast and the kind of personalized service that only a small hotel can provide. The recently renovated property has a tropical-plantation feel, with big, airy, island-style rooms, terra-cotta tile, and lots of greenery. The bedrooms have been redone in rattan and earth tones; all have private lanais, ceramic-tile bathrooms, and daily maid service. The units with kitchenettes are especially good deals. Most rooms have views of the Ala Wai Canal and the mountains (if you prefer quiet, ask for a city-view room). Ala Wai Golf Course is just across the canal, and the beach is 4 blocks away.

450 Lewers St. (at Ala Wai Blvd.), Honolulu, HI 96815. ⓒ 800/92-ASTON or 808/923-8828. Fax 808/922-8785. www.aston-hotels.com. 80 units. $90–$100 double; $110–$195 suite with kitchenette. Rates include continental breakfast. Extra person $12. AE, DC, MC, V. Parking $9. Bus: 19 or 20. **Amenities:** Tiny outdoor pool with sun deck; activity desk; coin-op washer/dryers. *In room:* A/C, TV, kitchenette, fridge, coffeemaker, hair dryer, iron, safe.

Ilima Hotel ⭐ *Kids*   The Teruya brothers, former owners of Hawaii's Times Supermarket, wanted to offer comfortable accommodations that Hawaii residents could afford, and they've succeeded. One of Hawaii's small, well-located condo-style hotels, the 17-story, pale pink Ilima (named for the native orange flower used in royal leis) offers value for your money. Rooms are huge, the location (near the International Market Place and the Royal Hawaiian Shopping Center, 2 blocks to Waikiki Beach) is great, and prices are low. A tasteful koa-wood lobby lined with works by Hawaiian artists greets you upon arrival. Perks include free local phone calls (a nice plus), and a full kitchen in every unit; in addition, all the couches fold out into beds, making this a particularly good deal for families. The one-bedroom units now have a Jacuzzi tub to soak in. There are three sun decks, a dry sauna, and truly nice people staffing the front desk to help you enjoy your vacation. The only caveat: no ocean views.

445 Nohonani St. (near Ala Wai Blvd.), Honolulu, HI 96815. ⓒ 800/801-9366 or 808/923-1877. Fax 888/864-5462. www.ilima.com. 99 units. $129–$175 double; $159–$209 1-bedroom (rate for 4); $230–$270 2-bedroom (rate for 4, sleeps up to 6); $355–$375 3-bedroom (rate for 6, sleeps up to 8). Extra person $10. Discounts available for seniors and business travelers. AE, DC, DISC, MC, V. Limited free parking, $8 across the street. Bus: 19 or 20. **Amenities:** Outdoor pool with sauna; exercise room; Jacuzzi in 1-bedroom units; tour desk; coin-op washer/dryers. *In room:* A/C, TV, kitchen, fridge, coffeemaker, hair dryer, iron, safe, free local phone calls.

Patrick Winston's Waikiki Condos ⭐ *Finds*   Looking for a condo priced to fit a tight budget, with a hefty dose of old-fashioned aloha thrown in? Try Patrick Winston's rentals, located on a quiet side street. When this five-story condominium hotel was built in 1981, Winston bought one unit; he has since acquired 24 more, spent hundreds of thousands of dollars on refurbishment, and put his spacious suites on the market at frugal prices. Staying here is like having a personal concierge; Winston has lots of terrific tips on where to eat, where to shop, and how to get the most for your money, and he can book any activity you want.

Four types of units are available: standard/budget rooms, one-bedroom suites, ground-floor junior business suites, and one two-bedroom unit. All have sofa beds, separate bedrooms, lanais with breakfast table and chairs, ceiling fans, and full kitchens; most have a washer and dryer. All are individually decorated. Eight units are "standard budget," which means the carpet has not been replaced or the walls need repainting but are otherwise a terrific deal for those looking for a condominium unit at a penny-pincher price. Waikiki Beach is just a 10- to 15-minute walk away, shopping is a ½-block away, and restaurants are within a 5- to 10-minute walk.

Hawaiian King Building, 417 Nohonani St., Suite 409 (between Kuhio Ave. and Ala Wai Blvd.), Honolulu, HI 96815. ⓒ 800/545-1948 or 808/924-3332. Fax 808/922-3894. www.winstonswaikikicondos.com. 24 units (shower only). $75–$95 double budget units; $95–$125 double; $115–$135 2-bedroom unit. Extra person $10. 4-night minimum. Ask for the Frommer's reader's discount. AE, DC, DISC, MC, V. Parking $7. Bus: 19 or 20. **Amenities:** Bar; small outdoor pool surrounded by a tropical courtyard; babysitting; coin-op washer/dryer. *In room:* A/C, TV, dataport, kitchen, fridge, coffeemaker, hair dryer, iron, washer/dryer (in most units).

Royal Kuhio ⭐ *Kids*   Families, take note: This is one of the best deals in Waikiki. All the units in this high-rise condo are privately owned, and some are owner-occupied. Several companies handle apartments here, but Paradise Management offers some of the best deals. Each of its units has a full kitchen, separate bedrooms, and a living area with a lanai. Because the units are individually owned, they're all decorated and furnished uniquely. It's 2 blocks from Waikiki Beach and within walking distance of everything else of interest. And this is one of the few places in Waikiki where parking is free. *Tips:* Ask for a corner unit (they're the nicest); if you plan to go in February, be sure to book a year in advance (it's the condo's busiest month).

2240 Kuhio Ave. (between Royal Hawaiian Ave. and Seaside Ave.), c/o Paradise Mgmt., 50 S. Beretania St., Suite C207, Honolulu, HI 96813. ✆ 800/367-5205 or 808/538-7145. Fax 808/533-4621. pmchi@gte.net. 389 units. $110–$145 apt for 4. Extra person $15. AE, MC, V. Free parking. Bus: 19 or 20. **Amenities:** Small fitness room; sauna; game room; coin-op washer/dryers; volleyball; billiards; basketball court; shuffleboard; putting green. *In room:* A/C, TV, dataport, kitchen, fridge, coffeemaker, iron.

Waikiki Joy ✪   Tucked away, down a narrow path on a side street, this hidden jewel offers not only outstanding personal service but also a Bose entertainment system and a Jacuzzi in every room! Complimentary continental breakfast is included in the price. The Italian marble–accented open-air lobby and the tropical veranda set the scene for the beautifully decorated guest rooms, each with a marble entry, tropical island decor, and a lanai wide enough for you to sit and enjoy the views. Another plus: All the rooms are soundproof. The suites are even more luxurious: Club suites have either a king bed or two doubles, a fridge, a microwave, a coffeemaker, and a wet bar, while executive suites come with two double beds and a kitchen with microwave and full fridge; the executive king suites add a separate living room and bedroom. Every unit comes with voice mail, as well as fax and modem hookups. There are, however, a couple of downsides: The beach is 4 or 5 blocks away (a 10- to 15-min. walk), and although there's a sandwich/coffee shop on-site, the food's nothing to brag about.

320 Lewers St. (between Kuhio and Kalakaua aves.), Honolulu, HI 96815. ✆ 800/92-ASTON or 808/923-2300. Fax 808/924-4010. www.aston-hotels.com. 94 units. $125–$185 double; $180–$205 club suite; $220–$245 junior suite with kitchen (sleeps up to 4); $270–$295 1-bedroom executive suite with kitchen (up to 4). Rates include continental breakfast. Extra person $20. Ask about the Island Hopper rates (25% off if you stay 7 or more consecutive nights with Aston). AE, DC, DISC, MC, V. Valet parking $10. Bus: 19 or 20. **Amenities:** Restaurant; bar (karaoke); miniscule outdoor pool with dry sauna; concierge; activity desk; coin-op washer/dryers; laundry service; dry cleaning. *In room:* A/C, TV, dataport, kitchenette (full kitchen in suites), fridge, coffeemaker, hair dryer, iron, safe.

DIAMOND HEAD WAIKIKI

You'll find all these hotels between Ala Wai Boulevard and the ocean, and between Kaiulani Street (1 block east of the International Market Place) and world-famous Diamond Head itself.

Very Expensive

Hyatt Regency Waikiki ✪   This is one of Waikiki's biggest hotels, a $100 million project sporting two 40-story towers and covering nearly an entire city block, just across the street from the Diamond Head end of Waikiki Beach. Some may love the location, but others will find this behemoth too big and impersonal—you can get lost just trying to find the registration desk. The second-floor lobby is huge, decorated in koa and wrapped around an atrium that rises *40 floors* from the ground level. It's filled with the squawks of parrots, tumbling waterfalls, and traffic noise from busy Kalakaua Avenue outside.

The guest rooms are spacious and luxuriously furnished. But please, when room rates start at $265 a night, do they have to charge you an extra $3.25 per package of coffee for the "free coffeemaker" in your room? (Not only that, but

Take a Healthy Vacation: Have Your Next Medical Checkup in Waikiki

Souvenirs from your next vacation to Waikiki could include more than pictures of the sunset: How about photos of your colon? Holistica Hawaii Health Center, Hawaii's only high tech, preventative medical facility, offers a way for you to find out a total picture (literally, in CD format, even) of your "inner" self.

Set in the tropical resort atmosphere of the Hilton Hawaiian Village Beach Resort and Spa, the Holistica center looks and operates more like a high-class spa in a luxury resort than a medically-oriented well-ness center. Clients are attracted to this spacious facility not only for the complete physical and health assessment but also for the Electron Beam Tomography scanner, which offers a safe, rapid, and non-inva-sive way to detect heart disease, lung cancer, aneurysm, stroke, osteo-porosis, colorectal disorders, cancerous abnormalities, and other diseases—all without even taking your clothes off.

This $2 million EBT scanner is considered the "gold standard" in detection. The doctors at Holistica can cite case histories where the scanner revealed potential problems that 10 years down the road could have been fatal, but thanks to early detection, the clients had time to change high-risk behaviors and to reverse the harmful effects.

In addition to the scan, the center offers ultrasound testing, genomic testing, lab work, and medical/nutritional consulting. They have 2- and 7-day programs, which include comprehensive medical testing and evaluation, fitness and nutritional consulting (with cook-ing classes and lifestyle workshops), spa treatments (at the 3-level Mandara Spa, just next door), personal training, physical therapy, and a comprehensive follow-up program.

For more information, call ⓒ **808/951-6546,** or visit www.holistica. com.

if you want to empty your minibar to use it as a fridge, the cost is $7!) The deluxe oceanview rooms overlooking Waikiki Beach are fabulous but can be noisy (traffic on Kalakaua is constant). For a few dollars more (well, actually more than a few dollars), you can upgrade to the Regency Club floors, where the rooms are nicer (and the coffee is free); you'll also be entitled to an expedited check-in and entry to a private rooftop sun deck and Jacuzzi and the Regency Club, which has concierge service all day and serves complimentary continental breakfast and afternoon pupu.

Just opened in April 2001 is a 10,000-square-foot, two-story, luxury spa, with all the massage services, body treatments, and facials you can imagine.

2424 Kalakaua Ave. (at Kaiulani St., across the street from the beach), Honolulu, HI 96815. ⓒ **800/233-1234** or 808/923-1234. Fax 808/923-7839. www.hyattwaikiki.com. 1,230 units. $265–$410 double; $410–$485 Regency Club double; from $800 suite. Extra person $35 ($50 Regency Club); children under 19 stay free in parent's room using existing bedding. AE, DC, DISC, MC, V. Valet parking $14; self-parking $10. Bus: 19 or 20. **Amenities:** 7 restaurants (see Ciao Mein review on p. 136); 4 bars (including a very elegant pool-side bar); outdoor pool with a view of Waikiki; fitness room; brand-new elegant spa; Jacuzzi; children's pro-gram (Fri–Sat year-round and daily in summer); game room; concierge; activity desk; car-rental desk; business

Booked aisle seat.

Reserved room with a view.

With a queen – no, make that a king-size bed.

With Travelocity, you can book your flights and hotels together, so you can get even better deals than if you booked them separately. You'll save time and money without compromising the quality of your trip. Choose your airline seat, search for alternate airports, pick your hotel room type, even choose the neighborhood you'd like to stay in

Travelocity

Visit www.travelocity.com or call 1-888 TRAVELOCITY

center; large shopping arcade; salon; room service (6am–11pm); in-room massage; babysitting; coin-op washer/dryers; same-day laundry service and dry cleaning; concierge-level rooms. *In room:* A/C, TV, dataport, kitchenette (in some units), minibar, coffeemaker (with expensive coffee!), hair dryer, iron, safe.

W Honolulu ★★★ It's expensive but worth every penny to be totally pampered in a low-key, elegantly casual hotel that caters to the business traveler but takes excellent care of vacationers, too. The W Honolulu can be summed up in a nutshell by the button on your room phone that says "whatever/whenever." That's what we call service! If you're craving peace and quiet away from the crowds of Waikiki but want to be close enough (about a 15-min. walk) to shops and restaurants, this is a perfect location. Formerly part of the Colony Surf (the adjacent, beachside condominium), this newly renovated hotel became part of the upscale W chain in 1999. You'll feel like you've entered a luxurious private world here: The hotel lobby looks like an elegant living room, and check-in occurs in the privacy of the guest rooms, which are decorated with handmade teak furniture from Bali. In addition to the large balconies with great views of Diamond Head, there are numerous excellent touches: from Hawaiian music CDs to dual-line cordless phones, plush robes, top-drawer bathroom amenities, twice-daily maid service (great to have clean towels when you return from the beach), and various business equipment available on request.

Although the W is not on the beach, guests still have access to the small, private beach in front of the Colony Surf (great swimming here), about a 30-second walk away; Kapiolani Park is across the street, and the Waikiki Aquarium is just a few steps away.

2885 Kalakaua Ave. (on the ocean side between the Waikiki Aquarium and Outrigger Canoe Club), Honolulu, HI 96815. © **877/W-HOTELS** or 808/922-1700. Fax 808/923-2249. 48 units. $400–$825 double. Extra person $65. Children under 18 stay free in parent's room. AE, DC, DISC, MC, V. Valet parking $15. Bus: 19 or 20. **Amenities:** Outstanding restaurant (Diamond Head Grill, p. 132); elegant bar (entertainment nightly); outstanding concierge service; 24-hr. room service; in-room massage; babysitting; coin-op washer/dryers; laundry service; dry cleaning. *In room:* A/C, TV, dataport, minibar, coffeemaker, hair dryer, iron, safe.

Expensive

Aston Waikiki Beachside Hotel ★ This luxury boutique hotel is right across the street from Waikiki Beach. There's a feeling of elegance and charm throughout this intimate place: You step off busy Kalakaua Avenue into a marble-filled lobby with classical music wafting in the background, sprays of flowers everywhere, and a soothing Italian fountain. The staff is attentive to every detail (including twice-daily maid service). The bedrooms are very, very tiny, but they're tastefully decorated with artwork and antiques (including hand-painted Oriental screens and 18th-century furnishings). There's no on-site restaurant, but there is a complimentary continental breakfast daily in the lobby. On Saturday and Sunday afternoons, a three-course tea service (with different teas, sandwiches, desserts, and more), served on antique china, is presented in the lobby and courtyard.

2452 Kalakaua Ave. (between Uluniu and Liliuokalani aves.), Honolulu, HI 96815. © **800/922-7866** or 808/931-2100. Fax 808/931-2129. www.aston-hotels.com. 79 units. $195–$350 double; $270–$405 junior suite. Rates include continental breakfast. No more than 2 adults per room. Some discounts for seniors over 50. Island Hopper rates give you 25% off if you stay 7 or more consecutive nights with Aston. AE, DC, DISC, MC, V. Parking $9.50 at nearby hotel. Bus: 19 or 20. **Amenities:** Concierge; same-day laundry service and dry cleaning. *In room:* A/C, TV, dataport, fridge, hair dryer, iron, safe.

Radisson Waikiki Prince Kuhio Formerly the Outrigger's Prince Kuhio, this 37-floor hotel, located just 3 blocks from the beach and a couple of blocks from the zoo, offers pleasantly appointed, mid-size rooms furnished in tropical decor, with a lanai and the all-important black-out drapes so you can sleep in. All of the rooms are the same; the floor and the view determine the price (from the 18th floor and up, the mountain views overlooking the Ala Wai Canal are spectacular and not as pricey as the oceanview rooms).

2500 Kuhio Ave. (Liliuokalani Ave.), Honolulu, HI 96815. (© 800/333-3333 or 808/922-0811. Fax 808/9231-5507. www.radisson.com/waikiki. 620 units. $225–$275 double; $295–$325 Kuhio Club floor double; from $525 suite for 4. Extra person $30. AE, DC, DISC, MC, V. Parking $9. Bus: 19 or 20. **Amenities:** 2 restaurants; bar; outdoor pool; small fitness room; Jacuzzi; concierge; activity desk; small business center; shopping arcade; limited room service; babysitting; coin-op washer/dryers; laundry service; dry cleaning; concierge-level rooms. *In room:* A/C, TV, dataport, kitchenette, fridge, coffeemaker, hair dryer, iron, safe.

Moderate

Aston at the Waikiki Banyan   The one-bedrooms here combine the homey comforts of a condo apartment with the amenities of a hotel. You'll get daily maid service, bellhop service, the assistance of the front desk, and much more, including an enormous sixth-floor recreation deck with a panoramic mountain view, complete with sauna, barbecue areas, snack bar, and children's play area— a great boon for families. Your introduction to this complex is through the open-air lobby with impressive lacquer artwork, hand carved and painted in Hong Kong. All units have a fully equipped full-size kitchen, a breakfast bar that opens to a comfortably furnished living room (with sofa bed), and a separate bedroom with two double beds or a king. The one we stayed in had an old-fashioned air-conditioner in the wall, but it did the job. Each apartment opens onto a fairly good-size lanai with chairs and a small table; there's a partial ocean view, with some buildings blocking the way.

201 Ohua Ave. (on mountain side, at Kuhio Ave.), Honolulu, HI 96815. (© 800/922-7866 or 808/922-0555. Fax 808/922-8785. www.aston-hotels.com. 307 1-bedroom apts. $175–$255 for up to 5. Some discounts for seniors over 50. Island Hopper rates give you 25% off if you stay 7 or more consecutive nights with Aston. AE, DC, DISC, MC, V. Parking $5. Bus: 19 or 20. **Amenities:** Huge outdoor pool; free tennis courts; coin-op washer/dryers. *In room:* A/C, TV, dataport, kitchen, fridge, coffeemaker, hair dryer, iron, safe.

Aston Waikiki Beach Hotel   After a $30 million renovation on a very old and tired hotel, Aston opened this kitschy 717-room (85% with ocean views) property in late 2002. The location could not be better—directly across the street from the beach. The rooms couldn't be smaller. The theme is Hawaiian nostalgia with a "contemporary island feel." But what you really have is a former budget hotel that has been repainted (garish colors—screaming yellow or red), and a few decorating oddies that do not work. For example, the closets have beaded curtains (instead of doors) of a hula dancer who dances when the wind blows through. Sounds great, but it's not practical; every time you go into your closet you have to fight with the beads. We stayed here just a month after the opening and already the beaded curtain was falling apart. In the bathroom, another impractical idea is the arched shower curtain for a rectangle bath tub. Every time you take a shower, the semi-circle shower curtain lets all the water run on the floor. One of the good ideas is the "Breakfast on the Beach" deal where you get a free breakfast, which you can pack up in an insulated carrying bag and walk across the street to eat. This is a full, hot breakfast too, with several food stations offering everything from burritos (veggie, ham or cheese), pastries, fruit, and cereals to a Japanese breakfast of miso, rice, and fish. If you can get a hot deal on the Internet ($104 was the going rate when we stayed here), it's worth it. But if you have to pay rack rates, you can do better.

2570 Kalakaua Ave. (at Paoakalani St.), Honolulu, HI 96815. (© 800/922-7866 or 808/922-2511. Fax 808/923-3656. www.aston-hotels.com. 717 units. $150–$387 double; $400 suite double. Some discounts for seniors over 50. Island Hopper rates give you 25% off if you stay 7 or more consecutive nights with Aston. AE, DC, DISC, MC, V. Parking $5. Bus: 19 or 20. **Amenities:** Restaurant/bar (Tiki's Grill, p. 137); outdoor pool; activity desk; coin-op washer/dryers; dry cleaning. *In room:* A/C, TV, dataport, fridge, coffeemaker, hair dryer, iron, safe.

New Otani Kaimana Beach Hotel ★ *Finds*   This is one of Waikiki's best-kept secrets: a boutique hotel nestled right on a lovely stretch of beach at the foot of Diamond Head, with Kapiolani Park just across the street. Robert Louis Stevenson's description of Sans Souci, the beach fronting the hotel, still holds true: "If anyone desires lovely scenery, pure air, clear sea water, good food, and heavenly sunsets, I recommend him cordially to the Sans Souci." The Waikiki-side guest rooms are tiny but tastefully decorated in pale pastels; they open onto large lanais with ocean and park views. A good budget buy is the park-view studio with kitchen, for just $160 to $180. You can stock up with provisions from the on-site Mini-Mart, open until 11pm.

Because the hotel overlooks Kapiolani Park, guests have easy access to activities such as golf, tennis, jogging, and bicycling; kayaking and snorkeling are available at the beach. The hotel also arranges for visitors to climb to the top of Diamond Head. The airy lobby opens onto the alfresco Hau Tree Lanai restaurant, a delightfully romantic beachfront restaurant, set under the same banyan tree that sheltered Robert Louis Stevenson a century ago (p. 133). The Miyako Restaurant offers gourmet Japanese dining with an ocean view. The beachfront **Sunset Lanai Lounge** ★ is great for cocktails and has live Hawaii music at lunch on Friday.

2863 Kalakaua Ave. (ocean side of the street just Diamond Head of the Waikiki Aquarium, across from Kapiolani Park), Honolulu, HI 96815. ⓒ **800/356-8264** or 808/923-1555. Fax 808/922-9404. www.kaimana.com. 124 units. $140–$345 double; from $210 suites. Extra person $25; children 12 and under stay free in parent's room using existing bedding. AE, DC, DISC, MC, V. Valet parking $12. Bus: 2 or 14. **Amenities:** 2 restaurants; beachfront bar; fitness room; watersports equipment rentals; concierge; activity desk; small shopping arcade; salon; limited room service (7am–8:45pm); in-room massage; babysitting; coin-op washer/dryers; laundry service; dry cleaning. *In room:* A/C, TV/VCR, dataport, some kitchenette, minibar (on request), fridge, coffeemaker (on request), hair dryer, iron (on request), safe.

Inexpensive

Bamboo ★ *Value*   If you are looking for a boutique hotel set apart from the hustle and bustle of the beach, this 90-room renovated property a block from Waikiki Beach is for you. Formerly a very neglected budget hotel, Bamboo has been transformed into a contemporary "hip" hotel, decorated with an Asian flair. The rooms are stylish and functional with modern furniture, marble bathrooms, and kitchenettes or kitchens. It's a good location (behind the Hyatt Regency), within walking distance to numerous restaurants and shopping, the Honolulu Zoo, and just 3 minutes to the beach. Since it is small, the staff gives guests personalized attention. When booking be sure to reserve a parking space, as the parking lot has a limited number of spaces.

2425 Kuhio Ave (Kaiulani Ave.), Honolulu, HI 96815. ⓒ **800/367-5004** or 808/922-7777. Fax 808/922-9473. www.aquabamboo.com. 90 units. $145 double; $165 studio double; $185–$265 1-bedroom for 4. Extra person $17. Check out Internet rates, which begin at $85 for a hotel room and go up to $159 for a 1-bedroom suite. Parking $5. Bus: 19 or 20. **Amenities:** Outdoor pool; Jacuzzi; sauna; concierge; laundry service; dry cleaning. *In room:* A/C, TV, dataport, kitchenette or kitchen, fridge, coffeemaker, hair dryer, iron, safe.

The Cabana at Waikiki   Located on a quiet street in Waikiki, this boutique hotel caters to a clientele of gay men and features exquisitely decorated rooms. Each has a queen bed and pullout sofa bed, entertainment center with VCR and CD player, lanai, and well-equipped kitchenette. A free continental breakfast is served every morning. Free Internet access is available in the lobby. A giant, eight-person spa also is on the property. The Cabana is within walking distance of gay nightclubs and the gay scene at Queen's Surf Beach.

2551 Cartwright Rd. (between Paoakalani and Kapahulu aves.), Honolulu, HI 96815. (℃) **877/902-2121** or 808/926-5555. Fax 808/926-5566. www.cabana-waikiki.com. 15 units. $115–$135 double; $175 Dec. 20–Jan. 7. Rates include continental breakfast. Extra person $15. AE, DC, DISC, MC, V. Parking $7. Bus: 19 or 20. **Amenities:** Complimentary access to a nearby (about a 15-min. walk) fitness complex; Jacuzzi; concierge; coin-op washer/dryers. *In room:* A/C, TV, dataport, kitchenette, fridge, coffeemaker, hair dryer, iron, safe.

Diamond Head Bed & Breakfast ⭐ *(Finds* Hostess Joanne and her longtime housekeeper, Sumiko, offer a quiet, relaxing place to stay on the far side of Kapiolani Park, away from the hustle and bustle of Waikiki. Staying here is like venturing back 50 years to a time when *kamaaina* (native-born) families built huge houses with airy rooms opening onto big lanais and tropical gardens. The house is filled with family heirlooms and Joanne's artwork. One of the two rooms features the beyond-king-size carved koa bed that once belonged to Princess Ruth, a member of Hawaii's royal family. You'll feel like royalty sleeping in it.

Noela Dr. (at Paki Ave., off Diamond Head Rd.), Honolulu. c/o Hawaii's Best Bed & Breakfasts, P.O. Box 758, Volcano, HI 96785. (℃) **800/262-9912** or 808/985-7488. Fax 808/967-8610. www.bestbnb.com. 2 units. $115 double. Rates include large breakfast. Extra person $30. 2-night minimum. No credit cards. Free parking. Bus: 2. *In room:* TV, fridge, hair dryer.

Magnolia at Waikiki ⭐ *(Finds* Hidden in the high-rise jungle of Waikiki is this two-story oasis that evokes the Waikiki of yesteryear. You enter through a wooden gate into a garden with a burbling fountain to one- and two-bedroom units (ask for number 2—our favorite) with all the comforts of home: a huge living area with a TV and VCR, a CD player, soft, comfy furniture, complete kitchen, separate dining area, firm beds and outside sitting areas. Extras include free local phone calls, free newspaper, free parking (a rarity in Waikiki), a big Jacuzzi tub and on-site laundry facilities. It's just a short walk to the beach and to Kapiolani Park, with easy access in and out of Waikiki.

2566 Cartwright Rd. (Kapahulu Ave.), Honolulu. c/o Hawaii's Best Bed & Breakfasts, P.O. Box 758, Volcano, HI 96785. (℃) **800/262-9912** or 808/985-7488. Fax 808/967-8610. www.bestbnb.com. 7 units. $150 double. Extra person $15. No credit cards. Free parking. Bus: 19 or 20. **Amenities:** Jacuzzi; coin-op washer/dryers. *In room:* A/C, TV/VCR, kitchen, fridge, answering machine.

Royal Grove Hotel ⭐ *(Value* This is a great bargain for frugal travelers. You can't miss the Royal Grove—it's bright pink. Among Waikiki's canyons of corporate-owned high-rises, it's also a rarity in another way: The Royal Grove is a small, family-owned hotel. What you get here is old-fashioned aloha in cozy accommodations along the lines of Motel 6—basic and clean. For years, *Frommer's* readers have written about the aloha spirit of the Fong family; they love the potluck dinners and get-togethers the Fongs have organized so their guests can get to know one another. And you can't do better for the price—this has to be *the* bargain of Waikiki. For $44.50 (about the same price a couple would pay to stay in a private room at the hostel in Waikiki), you get a clean room in the older Mauka Wing, with a double bed or two twins, plus a kitchenette with refrigerator and stove. We suggest that you spend a few dollars more and go for an air-conditioned room ($60) to help drown out the street noise. Even the most expensive unit, a one-bedroom suite with three beds, a kitchenette, and a lanai, at $125, is half the price of similar accommodations elsewhere. At these rates, you won't mind that maid service is only twice a week.

The hotel is built around a courtyard pool, and the beach is just a 3-minute walk away. All of Waikiki's attractions are within walking distance. *Tip:* If you book 7 nights or more from April to November, you'll get a discount on the already low rates.

151 Uluniu Ave. (between Prince Edward and Kuhio aves.), Honolulu, HI 96815. ✆ **808/923-7691**. Fax 808/922-7508. www.royalgrovehotel.com. 85 units. $45 double (no A/C); $60 standard double; $75 standard 1-bedroom; $125–$150 deluxe condo double. Extra person $10. AE, DISC, DC, MC, V. Parking nearby $6. Bus: 19 or 20. **Amenities:** Pool; activity desk; coin-op washer/dryers. *In room:* A/C, TV, kitchen, fridge.

Waikiki Sand Villa   Budget travelers, take note: This very affordable hotel is located on the quieter side of Waikiki, across the street from the Ala Wai Canal. The 10-story tower has medium-size rooms, most with a double bed plus a single bed (convenient for families) and a lanai with great views of the green mountains. The adjacent 3-story building features studio apartments with kitchenettes (refrigerator, stove, and microwave). Another plus for families is the Nintendo system in every room (available for $7.95 an hr.). For guests arriving early or catching a late flight there's a hospitality room (complete with shower) for late checkout and a luggage-storage area.

2375 Ala Wai Blvd. (entrance on Kanekapolei Ave.), Honolulu, HI 96815. ✆ **800/247-1903** or 808/922-4744. Fax 808/923-2541. www.waikiki-hotel.com. 232 units. $109–$139 double; $162–$310 studio with kitchenette. Check the Internet—specials start as low as $65. Rates include continental breakfast, served poolside every morning. Extra person $15; children under 12 stay free in parent's room using existing bedding. AE, DC, DISC, MC, V. Parking $7.30. Bus: 19 or 20. **Amenities:** 70-ft. outdoor pool, which has its own island in the middle and an adjoining whirlpool spa; activity desk; coin-op washer/dryers; laundry service; dry cleaning. *In room:* A/C, TV w/ Nintendo, dataport (with free Internet access), some kitchenette, some fridge, some coffeemaker, safe.

HONOLULU BEYOND WAIKIKI
ALA MOANA
Ala Moana Hotel   This hotel's 1,152 rooms on 36 floors make it feel like a metropolis. Its proximity to Waikiki, the downtown financial and business district, the new convention center, and Hawaii's largest mall, Ala Moana Shopping Center, makes it a popular spot for out-of-state visitors and locals alike. Lots of Asian tourists choose the Ala Moana Hotel, probably because the management does an excellent job of providing a multilingual staff and translators. Guests mainly are people attending a convention at the Convention Center, a short 2-minute walk away, or shoppers, mostly from neighboring islands (especially in Dec). The rooms vary in size according to price: The cheaper rooms are small, but all come with two double beds and all the amenities you'll need to make your stay comfortable. The views of Waikiki and Honolulu from the upper floors are spectacular.

410 Atkinson Dr. (at Kona St., next to Ala Moana Center), Honolulu, HI 96814. ✆ **800/367-6025** or 808/955-4811. Fax 808/944-6839. www.alamoanahotel.com. 1,152 units. $125–$215 double; from $250 suite. Check the Internet for specials as low as $99. Extra person $25; children under 18 stay free in parent's room. AE, DC, DISC, MC, V. Valet parking $12, self-parking $9. Bus: 19 or 20. **Amenities:** 5 restaurants (from coffee shop to exquisite Japanese food); 2 bars (plus a Polynesian show); large outdoor pool; small fitness room; game room; concierge; activity desk; business center; shopping arcade; salon; limited room service (6:30am–10:30 pm); coin-op washer/dryers; laundry service; dry cleaning. *In room:* A/C, TV, dataport, fridge, coffeemaker, hair dryer, iron, safe.

Pagoda Hotel   This is where local residents from neighbor islands stay when they come to Honolulu. Close to shopping and downtown, the Pagoda has been serving Hawaii's island community for decades. This modest hotel has very plain (motel-ish) rooms: clean and utilitarian with no extra frills. For a quieter room, ask for the mountain view, where you'll be away from the street noise. There's easy access to Waikiki via TheBus—the nearest stop is just a ½ block away. Ask about rental car packages. Studios and one- and two-bedroom units have kitchenettes.

1525 Rycroft St. (between Keeaumoku and Kaheka sts.), Honolulu, HI 96814. (C) **800/367-6060** or 808/ 923-4511. Fax 808/922-8061. www.pagodahotel.com. 361 units. $130–$140 double; $140 1-bedroom double (sleeps up to 4); $190 1-bedroom deluxe double (sleeps up to 6); $200 2-bedroom double (sleeps up to 5); $230 suite. Extra person $15; free cribs available. Ask about free breakfast packages (from $92) and excellent car/room deals (from $92). AE, DC, DISC, MC, V. Parking $3. Bus: 5 or 6. **Amenities:** Restaurant; bar; 2 outdoor pools; activity desk; salon; babysitting; coin-op washer/dryers; laundry service; dry cleaning. *In room:* A/C, TV, dataport, kitchenette (some units), fridge, coffeemaker, hair dryer, iron, safe.

DOWNTOWN

Aston at the Executive Centre Hotel ⭐   Located in the heart of downtown, this is the perfect hotel for the business traveler. Not only is it close to the business and financial center of Honolulu, but the staff also goes out of its way to meet every need. The hotel occupies the top 10 floors of a 40-story multiuse, glass-walled tower. Every room is a spacious suite, with three phones (with voice mail), a whirlpool bath, and unobstructed views of the city, the mountains, and Honolulu Harbor. Executive suites add a full kitchen, washer/dryer, and VCR. All guests awaken to the local newspaper outside their doors. Free local phone calls make this place a huge plus for business travelers.

1088 Bishop St. (at S. Hotel St.), Honolulu, HI 96813. (C) **800/92-ASTON** or 808/539-3000. Fax 808/922-8785. www.aston-hotels.com. 114 suites. $190–$200 suite; $240–$270 executive suite. Rates include complimentary daily continental breakfast and free daily paper. Extra person $18; children under 17 stay free in parent's room. AE, DC, DISC, MC, V. Parking $10. Bus: 1, 2, 3, 9, or 12. **Amenities:** Restaurant (American cuisine); outdoor pool; 24-hr. fitness center with free weights and aerobic equipment; in-room whirlpool bath; concierge; a staffed business center; shopping arcade; coin-op washer/dryers; laundry service; dry cleaning. *In room:* A/C, TV, dataport, kitchenette, fridge, coffeemaker, hair dryer, iron, safe, some washer/dryers.

MANOA VALLEY

Manoa Valley Inn ⭐ *(Finds)*   It's completely off the tourist trail and far from the beach, but that doesn't stop travelers from heading to this historic 1915 Carpenter Gothic home, on a quiet residential street near the University of Hawaii. This eight-room Manoa landmark—it's on the National Register of Historic Places— offers a glimpse into the lifestyles of the rich and famous of early Honolulu.

Those who find resorts impersonal will find the eclectically furnished inn refreshing. Each room has its own unique decor, and each has been named for a prominent figure in Hawaii's history. The John Guild Suite, for instance, has a turn-of-the-20th-century parlor with antiques and old-fashioned rose wallpaper; the adjoining bedroom contains a king-size koa bed, while the bathroom features an old-style tub as well as a separate modern shower. The three top-floor rooms share a full bathroom; the others have private bathrooms. A genteel ambience pervades the entire place. Guests regularly gather in the parlor to listen to the Victrola or play the nickelodeon. There's also a billiards room with an antique billiards table, a piano in the living room, and croquet set up in the backyard.

2001 Vancouver Dr. (at University Ave.), Honolulu, HI 96822. (C) **808/947-6019.** Fax 808/946-6168. www. aloha.net/~wery/index. 10 units (3 with shared bathroom). $99–$120 double with shared bathroom; $140–$190 double with private bathroom (shower only); $150 cottage double; $165 carriage house for 4. Rates include continental breakfast. Inquire about packages. AE, DC, MC, V. Free parking. Bus: 4 or 6. Children 8 and older preferred. **Amenities:** In-room massage; laundry service. *In room:* A/C, TV, dataport, safe.

TO THE EAST: KAHALA

Kahala Mandarin Oriental Hawaii ⭐⭐⭐ *(Kids)*   Since 1964, when Conrad Hilton first opened it as a place to relax far from the crowds of Waikiki, the Kahala has always been rated one of Hawaii's premier hotels. A veritable who's who of celebrities have stayed here, including several U.S. presidents. This grande dame of hotels has now reached a new level. It retains the traditional feeling of an earlier time in Hawaii but accents it with exotic Asian touches. The result is a resort hotel for the 21st century coupled with the grace and elegance of a softer, gentler time. And the location offers a similarly wonderful compromise. Situated in one of Oahu's most prestigious residential areas, the Kahala offers the peace and serenity of a neighbor-island vacation, but with the conveniences of Waikiki just a 10-minute drive away. The lush, tropical grounds include an 800-foot crescent-shaped beach and a 26,000-square-foot lagoon (home to 2 bottle-nosed dolphins, sea turtles, and tropical fish).

All guest rooms feature 19th-century mahogany reproductions, teak parquet floors with hand-loomed Tibetan rugs, overstuffed chairs, canopy beds covered with soft throw pillows, and works by local artists adorning the grass-cloth–covered walls. Views from the floor-to-ceiling sliding-glass doors are of the ocean, Diamond Head, and Koko Head. In-room amenities include two-line phones, 27-inch TV, large bathrooms with vintage fixtures, a freestanding glass shower, a large soaking tub, "his" and "her" dressing areas, plush bathrobes and slippers, and an illuminated makeup mirror.

Other extras that make this property outstanding: Hawaiian cultural programs, shuttle service to Waikiki and major shopping centers, free scuba lessons in the pool, and daily dolphin-education talks by a trainer from Sea Life Park.

5000 Kahala Ave. (next to the Waialae Country Club), Honolulu, HI 96816. (✆ **800/367-2525** or 808/739-8888. Fax 808/739-8800. www.mandarinoriental.com. 371 units. $295–$690 double; from $565 suite. Extra person $140; children 17 and under stay free in parent's room. AE, DC, DISC, MC, V. Parking $12. **Amenities:** 4 restaurants (see the Hoku's review on p. 153); bar; large outdoor pool; nearby golf course; tennis courts; great fitness center with steam rooms, Jacuzzis, and dry sauna; watersports equipment rentals; bike rentals; children's program; game room; concierge; activity desk; car-rental desk; multilingual business center; shopping arcade; salon; 24-hr. room service; in-room massage; babysitting; laundry service; dry cleaning. *In room:* A/C, TV, dataport, minibar, hair dryer, iron, safe.

THE WINDWARD COAST

Windward coast accommodations are located on the "Eastern Oahu & the Windward Coast" map on p. 201.

KAILUA

Pat O'Malley of **Pat's Kailua Beach Properties,** 204 S. Kalaheo Ave., Kailua, HI 96734 (✆ **808/261-1653** or 808/262-4128; fax 808/261-0893; www.10k vacationrentals.com/pats), books a wide range of houses and cottages on or near Kailua Beach. Rates start at $70 a day for a studio cottage near the beach and go up to $425 per day for a multimillion-dollar home right on the sand with room to sleep eight. All units are fully furnished, with everything from cooking utensils to telephone and TV, even washer/dryers.

Ingrid's ⍟ Ingrid has impeccable taste. Decorated in modern Japanese style, her cute one-bedroom apartment is straight out of a magazine. The pristine white walls and cabinets are accented with such dramatic touches as black tile counters, black-and-white shoji doors, and a black Oriental screen behind a king-size bed dressed in white quilts and red, red, red throw pillows. The tiled bathroom is done in complementary gray and has a luxurious soaking tub. The kitchenette has everything—microwave, refrigerator, cooking utensils, and even a dishwasher. A huge tiled deck extends out from the apartment, while a small alcove off the bedroom can house a third person or serve as a reading nook. Fresh flowers are everywhere. The apartment is located upstairs, past the Japanese garden and through a private entrance.

Pauku St. (across from Enchanted Lakes School), Kailua. c/o Hawaii's Best Bed & Breakfasts, P.O. Box 758, Volcano, HI 96785. (✆ **800/262-9912** or 808/985-7488. Fax 808/967-8610. www.bestbnb.com. 1 apt. $135 double. Rates include continental breakfast. Extra person $25. 4-night minimum. No credit cards. Free parking. Bus: 52, 55, or 56. *In room:* A/C, TV, kitchenette, fridge, coffeemaker, hair dryer, iron.

Lanikai Bed & Breakfast ★ *Finds* This old-time bed-and-breakfast, a *kamaaina* (native) home that reflects the Hawaii of yesteryear, is now into its second generation. For years, Mahina and Homer Maxey ran this large, comfortable, island-style residence; today, their son, Rick, and his wife, Nini, are the hosts. The recently renovated 1,000-square-foot upstairs apartment, which easily accommodates four, is decorated in old Hawaii bungalow style. There's a king-size bed in one bedroom, twin beds in the other bedroom, a large living/dining room, a big bathroom, a kitchenette, and all the modern conveniences—VCR, cordless phone with answering machine—plus oversize windows to let you enjoy wonderful views. Or, you can follow the ginger- and ti-lined path to a 540-square-foot honeymooner's delight, a quaint studio with a huge patio outside and queen-size bed and sitting area with VCR, cordless phone, answering machine, and recently remodeled full-size kitchen inside. The units are stocked with breakfast fixings (bagels, juice, fruit, coffee, tea) and all the beach equipment you'll need (towels, mats, chairs, coolers, water jugs). Picture-perfect white-sand Lanikai Beach access is across the street, bus routes are close by, and a 2½-mile biking–walking loop is just outside.

1277 Mokulua Dr. (between Onekea and Aala Dr. in Lanikai), Kailua, HI 96734. © **800/258-7895** or 808/261-1059. Fax 808/262-2181. www.lanikaibb.com. 2 units. $125 studio double; $150 apt double. Rates include breakfast items in fridge. Extra person $25. 5-night minimum. MC, V. Free parking. Bus: 52, 55, or 56. **Amenities:** Washer/dryer. *In room:* TV, dataport, kitchenette or kitchen, fridge, coffeemaker, iron, hair dryer.

Sheffield House *Kids* Unlike many other B&Bs, Sheffield House welcomes children. The owners, Paul Sheffield and his wife, Rachel, have three kids, so things like a portable baby bed are no problem. There are two units here, a one-bedroom and a studio (which is fully wheelchair-accessible), each with a private entry (through elaborately landscaped tropical gardens), with full kitchen. The two units can be combined and rented as two-bedroom/two-bathroom accommodations.

131 Kuulei Rd. (at Kalaheo Dr.), Kailua, HI 96734. © and fax **808/262-0721.** 2 units. $65 double studio (shower only); $85 double apt. (some lower rates depending on the season). Rates include first day's continental breakfast. Extra person $10. 3-night minimum. AE, DISC, MC, V. Free parking. Bus: 56 or 57. *In room:* TV, kitchen, fridge, coffeemaker.

KANEOHE

Alii Bluffs Windward Bed & Breakfast Located on a quiet residential street just 15 minutes from the beach, this traditional B&B is filled with antiques and collectibles as well as the owners' original art. The guest wing has two rooms, one with a double bed and adjacent bathroom, the other with two extralong twins and a bathroom across the hall. The yard blooms with tropical plants, and the view of Kaneohe Bay from the pool area is breathtaking. Lots of extras make this B&B stand out from the crowd: daily maid service, a large breakfast served on the poolside lanai, afternoon tea, and sewing kits in the bathroom—they'll even lend you anything you need for the beach.

46–251 Ikiiki St. (off Kamehameha Hwy.), Kaneohe, HI 96744. © **800/235-1151** or 808/235-1124. Fax 808/236-4877. www.hawaiiscene.com/aliibluffs. 2 units. $60–$75 double. Rates include continental breakfast. 2-night minimum. MC, V. Free parking. Bus: 55 or 65. Children must be 16 or older. **Amenities:** Outdoor pool. *In room:* Hair dryer, no phone.

Schrader's Windward Country Inn Despite the name, the ambience here is more motel than resort, but Schrader's offers a good alternative for families.

The property is nestled in a tranquil, tropical setting on Kaneohe Bay, only a 30-minute drive from Waikiki. The complex is made up of cottage-style motels and a collection of older homes. Cottages contain either a kitchenette with refrigerator and microwave or a full kitchen. There's also a picnic area with barbecue grills. Prices are based on the views; depending on how much you're willing to pay, you can look out over a Kahuluu fish pond, the Koolau Mountains, or Kaneohe Bay. Lots of watersports are available at an additional cost; don't miss the complimentary 2-hour boat cruise with snorkeling and kayaking. Evening activities include Hawaiian music night and karaoke night, both with free *pupu* (Hawaii-style appetizers). *Tip:* When booking, ask for a unit with a lanai; that way, you'll end up with at least a partial view of the bay.

47–039 Lihikai Dr. (off Kamehameha Hwy.), Kaneohe, HI 96744. (*C*) 800/735-5711 or 808/239-5711. Fax 808/239-6658. www.hawaiiscene.com/schrader. 20 units. $60–$125 1-bedroom double; $110–$190 2-bedroom for 4; $200–$320 3-bedroom for 6; $400–$450 4-bedroom for 8. Low-season rates are 30% less. Rates include continental breakfast. Additional person $7.50. 2-night minimum. AE, DC, DISC, MC, V. Free parking. Bus: 52, 55, or 56. **Amenities:** Outdoor pool; watersports equipment rentals. *In room:* TV, kitchenette, fridge, coffeemaker.

THE NORTH SHORE

The North Shore doesn't have many accommodations or an abundance of tourist facilities—some say that is its charm. **Team Real Estate,** 66–250 Kamehameha Hwy., Suite D–103, Haleiwa, HI 96712 (*C* **800/982-8602** or 808/637-3507; fax 808/637-8881; www.teamrealestate.com), manages vacation rentals on the North Shore. Its units range from affordable cottages to condos to oceanfront homes, at rates ranging from $43 a night for a one-bedroom apartment to $930 for a three-bedroom oceanfront luxury home. A minimum stay of 1 week is required for some properties, but shorter stays are available as well.

North Shore accommodations are located on the "Oahu's North Shore" map on p. 210.

Laie Inn *Kids* This two-story, plantation-style hotel is a small, intimate property within walking distance of the Polynesian Cultural Center, Brigham Young University Hawaii, and the Mormon Temple. The rooms are standard, with two double beds, microwave on request, and full bathroom. Access to a secluded white-sand beach is just across the street. Other amenities include a sun deck, barbecues with free charcoal, and free local calls.

55–109 Laniloa St. (off Kamehameha Hwy., near the Polynesian Cultural Center), Laie, HI 96762. (*C*) 800/526-4562 or 808/293-9282. Fax 808/293-8115. www.laieinn.com. 49 units. $84–$99 double. Extra person $10. Children under 18 stay free in parent's room. AE, DISC, MC, V. Free parking. Bus: 52 or 55. **Amenities:** Restaurant; outdoor pool; activity desk; coin-op washer/dryers. *In room:* A/C, TV, fridge.

Ke Iki Beach Bungalows This collection of rustic studio, one-, and two-bedroom duplex cottages has a divine location. It's snuggled on a large lot with its own 200-foot stretch of white-sand beach between two legendary surf spots: Waimea Bay and Banzai Pipeline. The winter waves are rough stuff; we regular folks can only venture in to swim in the flat summer seas. But there's a large lava reef nearby with tide pools to explore and, on the other side, Shark's Cove, a relatively protected snorkeling area. Nearby are tennis courts and a jogging path. Ke Iki is not for everyone, though. The furnishings are modest, though clean and comfortable; kitchens, barbecues, and hammocks provide some of the comforts of home. The one-bedrooms have one or two single beds in the living room, a double in the separate bedroom, and a full kitchen. *Note:* The units are now under new ownership and have been remodeled with new paint and new

furniture from Bali, and the oceanfront units now have TVs and phones. *Tip:*
Stay on the beach side, where the views are well worth the extra bucks.

59–579 Ke Iki Rd. (off Kamehameha Hwy.), Haleiwa, HI 96712. ✆ **866/638-8229** or 808/638-8829. Fax 808/
637-6100. www.keikibeachbungalows.com. 10 units. $65 studio double; $90 1-bedroom double; $140–$200
2-bedroom double; plus a one-time cleaning fee ranging from $45 for studio to $85 for 2-bedroom units.
Extra person no charge. AE, MC, V. Free parking. Bus: 52. **Amenities:** Complimentary watersports equipment
and bicycles; in-room massage; coin-op washer/dryers. *In room:* TV, kitchen, fridge, coffeemaker.

Santa's by the Sea ★ *Finds*

This certainly must be where Santa Claus comes
to vacation: St. Nick knows a bargain when he sees it. The location, price, and
style make this a must-stay if you plan to see the North Shore. It's one of the few
North Shore B&Bs right on the beach—and not just any beach, but the famous
Banzai Pipeline. You can go from your bed to the sand in less than 30 seconds
to watch the sun rise over the Pacific. Hosts Gary and Cyndie renovated this
vacation hideaway into an impeccable one-bedroom unit with finely crafted
woodwork, bay windows, and a collection of unique Santa figurines and one-of-
a-kind Christmas items. It may sound schlocky, but somehow it gives the apartment a country charm. Honeymooners, take note: There's lots of privacy here.
The unit has its own entrance; a living room with VCR and stereo; and a full
kitchen with everything a cook could need. Fruit, cereal, bread, coffee, tea, and
juice are provided on the first morning to get you started.

Ke Waena Rd. (off Kamehameha Hwy.), Haleiwa. c/o Hawaii's Best Bed & Breakfasts, P.O. Box 758, Volcano,
HI 96785. ✆ **800/262-9912** or 808/985-7488. Fax 808/967-8610. www.bestbnb.com. 1 apt (shower only).
$135–$150 double. Rates includes breakfast items in refrigerator. Extra person $15. 2-night minimum. No
credit cards. Free parking. Bus: 52 or 55. **Amenities:** Washer/dryer. *In room:* A/C (in bedroom), TV/VCR,
kitchen, fridge, coffeemaker, hair dryer.

Turtle Bay Resort ★★

This property has recently undergone a management
change (for years it was a Hilton) and just completed a $35 million dollar massive
renovation. When the resort was built 30 years ago, there was hope that it would
become a "gaming operation" (i.e. Las Vegas–type gambling). That never materi-
alized, but the dark interior, closed to the awe-inspiring view remained. With the
renovations, the lobby is now open and airy with floor to ceiling windows to the
dramatic ocean shoreline view. The resort is spectacular: an hour's drive from
Waikiki, but eons away in its country feeling. Sitting on 808 acres, this place is
loaded with activities and 5 miles of shoreline with secluded white-sand coves. It's
located on Kalaeokaunu Point ("point of the altar"), where ancient Hawaiians
built a small altar to the fish gods. The altar's remains are now at the Bishop
Museum, but it's easy to see why the Hawaiians considered this holy ground.

All the rooms have ocean views and balconies. The renovated rooms feature
marble floors and counter tops in the bathroom, good reading lamps over the
beds, and comfy bedding. The 42 separate beach cottages have been renovated
(hardwood floors, poster beds with feather comforters, even a personalized butler)
and have their own check in and private concierge (like a hotel within a hotel).

The biggest change is the new zen-like spa with six treatment rooms, a meditation waiting area, an outdoor workout area, plus complete fitness center and
a private elevator to the rooms on the second floor, reserved for guests getting
spa treatments.

P.O. Box 187 (Kuilima Dr., off Kamehameha Hwy. [Hwy. 83]), Kahuku, HI 96731. ✆ **800/203-3650** or 808/
293-8811. Fax 808/293-9147. www.turtlebayresort.com. 485 units. $295–$400 double; $550–$700 cottages;
from $500 suite. Extra person $45; children under 18 stay free in parent's room. Daily resort fee of $12.
AE, DC, DISC, MC, V. Valet parking $12. Bus: 52 or 55. **Amenities:** 4 restaurants; 2 bars (live entertainment
Thurs–Sat at the Bay Club Lounge, plus a poolside bar for sunset cocktails); 2 outdoor heated pools (with 55-
ft. water slide); 36 holes of golf; 10 Plexipave tennis courts; just-opened spa with complete fitness center;

3 Jacuzzi; watersports equipment rentals; concierge; activity desk; business center; shopping arcade; salon; room service; babysitting; coin-op washer/dryers; laundry service; dry cleaning. *In room:* A/C, TV, fridge, coffeemaker, hair dryer, iron.

LEEWARD OAHU: THE WAIANAE COAST

J. W. Marriott Ihilani Resort & Spa at Ko Olina Resort ★★★ *Kids*   When the 640-acre Ko Olina Resort community opened, some 17 miles and 25 minutes west of Honolulu Airport (and worlds away from the tourist scene of Waikiki), critics wondered who would want to stay so far from the city. Lots of people, it turns out. Ihilani ("heavenly splendor") is nestled in a quiet location between the Pacific Ocean and the first of four man-made beach lagoons. Featuring a luxury spa and fitness center, plus tennis and one of Hawaii's premier golf courses, it's a haven of relaxation and well-being. The spa alone is reason enough to come here. Treatments include thalassic treatments, Swiss showers, Vichy showers, Roman pools, and various kinds of massages. You can even have a fitness and relaxation program custom-designed.

Marriott took over management of the resort in late 1999. It's hard to get a bad room in the 15-story building—some 85% of the units enjoy lagoon or ocean views. Accommodations are luxuriously appointed and spacious (680 sq. ft.) and come with huge lanais outfitted with very comfortable, cushioned teak furniture. There's even a state-of-the-art comfort-control-system panel to operate the ceiling fans, air-conditioning, lights, and so on. Luxurious marble bathrooms have deep soaking tubs, separate glass-enclosed showers, yukata robes, and many more amenities. Other extras include daily newspaper, transportation to Waikiki and Ala Moana Shopping Center, a 3-mile coastal fitness trail, and a stretch of four white-sand beaches for ocean activities.

The Ihilani's children's program puts all others to shame, offering year-round outdoor adventures and indoor learning activities for toddlers and teens alike. There's a Computer Learning Center, a 125-gallon fish tank, an evening lounge for teen-themed parties, and more.

92–1001 Olani St., Kapolei, HI 96707. © **800/626-4446** or 808/679-0079. Fax 808/679-0080. www.ihilani. com. 387 units. $354–$549 double; from $800 suite. Extra person $50; children under 18 stay free in parent's room using existing bedding. Ask about Paradise-Plus package rates, which include a free car or daily breakfast for 2 starting at $269. AE, DC, MC, V. Parking $9. No bus service. Take H-1 west toward Pearl City/Ewa Beach; stay on H-1 until it becomes Hwy. 93 (Farrington Hwy.); look for the exit sign for Ihilani Resort; exit road is Alinui Dr., which goes into the Ko Olina Resort; turn right on Olani Place. **Amenities:** 3 restaurants; 2 bars (with nightly entertainment); 2 huge outdoor pools; championship 18-hole Ko Olina Golf Course, designed by Ted Robinson; tennis club with pro shop; world-class spa; watersports equipment rentals; excellent children's program; game room; concierge; activity desk; business center; shopping arcade; salon; 24-hr. room service; in-room massage; babysitting; same-day laundry service and dry cleaning. *In room:* A/C, TV, dataport, minibar, hair dryer, iron, safe.

4 Where to Dine

WAIKIKI
VERY EXPENSIVE

La Mer ★★★ NEOCLASSIC FRENCH   This is the splurge restaurant of Hawaii, the oceanfront bastion of haute cuisine where two of the state's finest chefs (George Mavrothalassitis and Philippe Padovani, each with his own eponymous restaurant now) quietly redefined fine dining in Hawaii. La Mer is romantic, elegant, and expensive; dress up not to be seen but to match the ambience and food (jackets or long-sleeved shirts required for men). It's the only AAA Five-Diamond restaurant in the state, with a second-floor, open-sided room with views of Diamond Head and the sound of trade winds rustling the nearby

Waikiki Dining

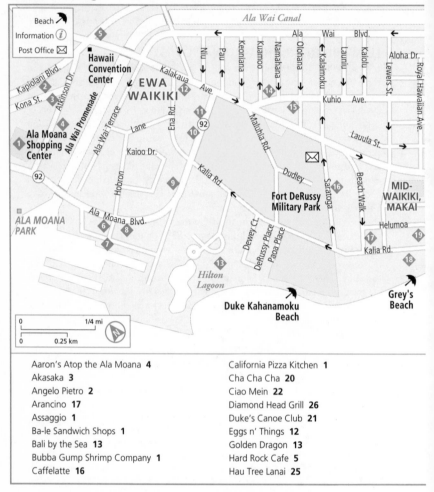

Aaron's Atop the Ala Moana **4**	California Pizza Kitchen **1**
Akasaka **3**	Cha Cha Cha **20**
Angelo Pietro **2**	Ciao Mein **22**
Arancino **17**	Diamond Head Grill **26**
Assaggio **1**	Duke's Canoe Club **21**
Ba-le Sandwich Shops **1**	Eggs n' Things **12**
Bali by the Sea **13**	Golden Dragon **13**
Bubba Gump Shrimp Company **1**	Hard Rock Cafe **5**
Caffelatte **16**	Hau Tree Lanai **25**

coconut fronds. Michelin-award–winning chef Yves Garnier melds classical French influences with fresh island ingredients: elegant soups with saffron, chanterelles, and savory fresh fish filets; *moano* (a delicate goatfish) in strudel with basil and niçoise olives; ruby snapper, skin crisped, in exotic sauces hinting of truffle and herbs. The wine list, desserts, and service—formal without being stiff—complete the dining experience.

In the Halekulani, 2199 Kalia Rd. ☏ **808/923-2311**. Reservations recommended. Long-sleeve collared dress shirts for men; jackets provided if necessary. Main courses $36–$45; 9-course prix fixe $115, with wine pairings $145. AE, DC, MC, V. Daily 6–10pm.

Michel's ★★ FRENCH/HAWAII REGIONAL   The room on the sand at Sans Souci Beach has windows that open to the ocean air. One side opens to the sunset, torches on the breakwater, and a hula moon above the palm fronds; the entire Waikiki skyline is visible to the leeward side. All tables have an ocean view, and dining here is less stiff and more welcoming than in bygone years. Jackets

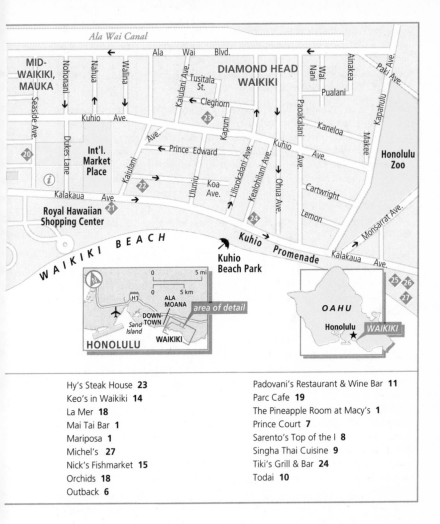

Hy's Steak House **23**
Keo's in Waikiki **14**
La Mer **18**
Mai Tai Bar **1**
Mariposa **1**
Michel's **27**
Nick's Fishmarket **15**
Orchids **18**
Outback **6**

Padovani's Restaurant & Wine Bar **11**
Parc Cafe **19**
The Pineapple Room at Macy's **1**
Prince Court **7**
Sarento's Top of the I **8**
Singha Thai Cuisine **9**
Tiki's Grill & Bar **24**
Todai **10**

are no longer required for men, and the live music (slack-key and classical guitar with a vocalist Thurs–Sat, and strolling musicians on Sun) attracts sunset- and music-lovers, too. Chef Hardy Kintscher has added his touch to the classics (onion soup, steak tartare, chateaubriand, bouillabaisse) and prepares fresh seafood, vegetarian creations, and rack of lamb with restraint and creativity.

In the Colony Surf Hotel, 2895 Kalakaua Ave. ✆ 808/923-6552. Reservations recommended. No shorts or beach wear. Main courses $26–$39. AE, DC, DISC, MC, V. Sun–Thurs 5:30–9:30pm; Fri–Sat 5:30–10pm.

EXPENSIVE

Bali by the Sea ★★ CONTINENTAL/PACIFIC RIM This is another memorable oceanfront dining room—pale and full of light, with a white grand piano at the entrance and sweeping views of the ocean (ask for a table by the window). The menu merges island cooking styles and ingredients with the chef's Alsatian roots: an excellent herb-infused rack of lamb coated with orange hoisin glaze; sake-steamed Kona lobster; and fresh seafood in sauces hinting of plum wine, kaffir lime, black bean, ginger, and lemongrass. Save room for dessert—a replica of Diamond Head (the one you see out the window) created with chocolate truffles.

In the Hilton Hawaiian Village, 2005 Kalia Rd. 🕿 808/941-2254. Reservations recommended. Main courses $26–$45. AE, DC, DISC, MC, V. Mon–Sat 6–9:30pm.

Caffelatte 🌟 NORTHERN ITALIAN   Chef/owner Laura Proserpio makes everything from scratch and to order; you won't catch her near a microwave oven. As a result, you won't find a better bruschetta, pasta carbonara, marinara, or risotto in Waikiki. The menu is built on uncompromising basics such as generations-old recipes and long hours of simmering soups and sauces. The prix fixe dinner consists of appetizer or salad, soup (usually fish, lentil, or vegetable, and always good), and entree, which could be a porcini risotto, homemade ravioli, or any of several veal selections.

339 Saratoga Rd. 🕿 808/924-1414. Reservations recommended. Prix fixe $35. MC, V. Wed–Mon 6:30–10pm.

Diamond Head Grill 🌟🌟 HAWAII REGIONAL   Talk about buzz. From judges and fashionistas to politicos and the boy next door, they're all here, either dining in the sleek and stylish dining room or being seen at the "bar with the bed," the serpentine DHG Bar that is the social nexus of Friday-night Honolulu. But it's not all flash at this dining room of W Honolulu.

Executive chef Todd Constantino offers noteworthy fare that highlights the flavors and ingredients of Hawaii teamed with a "chop house" menu of prime dry-aged beef, corn-fed and flown in from the Midwest. The filet mignon and New York strip steak are rubbed with sea salt, organic fresh herbs, and roasted garlic and prepared with homemade Worcestershire; or you can choose oak-aged soy sauce or a demi-glace of roasted shallots. The fresh fish comes grilled, sautéed, steamed, or wok-fried. Among DHG's staples are opakapaka with Kahuku corn and truffled clam broth and guava-mustard rack of lamb. The room features burnished copper columns, large windows overlooking Kapiolani Park and Diamond Head, a private dining room for the "Chef's Table" of up to 10 people, and the notorious DHG Bar, where there really is a bed and the drinks are as stylish as the crowd. There's live jazz entertainment nightly (p. 229).

In the W Honolulu, 2885 Kalakaua Ave. 🕿 808/922-3734. Reservations recommended. Main courses $7–$14 breakfast; $18–$34 dinner. AE, DC, DISC, MC, V. Daily 7–10:30am and 6–10pm; Bistro menu nightly 10–11:30pm; live entertainment daily 8:30pm–midnight.

Room Service from 3 Dozen Restaurants

You are no longer limited by the room service menu in your hotel room, **Room Service in Paradise** (🕿 808/941-DINE; www.rsiponline.com), delivers almost a dozen different cuisines (from American/Pacific rim to Italian to sandwiches and burgers) from 36 restaurants to your hotel room. All you do is select a restaurant and order what you want (see their online menu or pick up one of their magazines in various Waikiki locations), and they deliver. You are charged for the food, a $4 delivery charge in Waikiki ($4–$8 in outlying areas), and a tip for the driver. Best of all, you can pay with your credit card. Both lunch and dinner are available; you can even call in advance, and they'll deliver whenever you want.

Golden Dragon ✦✦ CHINESE   For a second, you might think you've been transported to one of Hong Kong's finest Chinese restaurants—until you notice you can see Waikiki Beach from the outdoor terrace. This is where local residents go if they want to celebrate a special occasion or just enjoy the finest Chinese cooking in Hawaii. Chef Steve Chiang has an extraordinary light touch, turning well-known Chinese cuisine into a rare exotic treat. Several items from the Golden Dragon's original chef, Dai Hoy Chiang, remain on the menu (like the lobster tail stir-fry with curry sauce served with haupia—a coconut pudding). Chiang's own creations include beggar's chicken (wrapped in lotus leaves, covered with clay, baked, and then broken open at your table), which you must order 24 hours in advance. For a real treat, get the 9-course "lotus dinner," which showcases the restaurant's finest dishes.

In the Hilton Hawaiian Village Beach Resort & Spa, 2005 Kalia Rd. ℂ **808/946-5336.** Reservations recommended. Main courses $11–$32; prix fixe dinners $30–$48. AE, DC, DISC, MC, V. Daily 6–9pm.

Hau Tree Lanai ✦ PACIFIC RIM   Informal and delightful, this Honolulu institution scores higher on ambience than on food. The outdoor setting and earnest menu make it a popular informal dining spot; an ancient hau tree provides shade and charm for diners. A diverse parade of beachgoers at Sans Souci Beach (called "Dig Me Beach" for its eye-candy sunbathers) is part of the scenery. Breakfast here is a must: choices include salmon Florentine, served with a fresh-baked scone; poi pancakes; Belgian waffles; eggs Benedict; and the Hawaiian platter of miniature poi pancakes, eggs, and a medley of island sausages. Lunchtime offerings include house-cured Atlantic salmon and an assortment of burgers, sandwiches, salads, and fresh-fish and pasta specialties. Dinner selections are more ambitious and less reliable: fresh moonfish, red snapper, opakapaka, ahi, and chef's specials, in preparations ranging from plain grilled to stuffed and over-the-top rich.

In the New Otani Kaimana Beach Hotel, 2863 Kalakaua Ave. ℂ **808/921-7066.** Reservations recommended. Main courses $19–$33. AE, DC, DISC, MC, V. Mon–Sat 7–11am, 11:30am–2pm, and 5:30–9pm; Sun 7–11:30am, noon–2pm, and 5:30–9pm. Late lunch in the open-air bar, daily 2–4pm.

Hy's Steak House ✦ AMERICAN   This is as good as it gets in steakhouses. Think dark, clubby, lots of leather, good Scotch, and filet mignon. This is a great choice for steak lovers with hefty pocketbooks or for those who have tired of Hawaii Regional Cuisine. Hy's has demonstrated admirable staying power in the cult of the low fat, still scoring high among carnivores while offering ample alternatives, such as a grilled vegetable platter and excellent salads prepared tableside (spinach and Caesar are textbook perfect). "The Only" is its classic best, a kiawe-grilled New York strip steak served with a mysterious signature sauce. Garlic lovers swear by the Garlic Steak Diane, a richly endowed ribeye with sliced mushrooms.

2440 Kuhio Ave. ℂ **808/922-5555.** Reservations recommended. Main courses $18–$59 or market price. AE, DC, DISC, MC, V. Mon–Fri 6–10pm; Sat–Sun 5:30–10pm.

Nick's Fishmarket ✦ SEAFOOD   With its extensive fish and lobster specialties, Nick's is the restaurant for seafood lovers with upscale tastes. It's a bit of a time warp (extravagant '80s) and the atmosphere is unremarkable, but you will find first-rate seafood and professional service from crisp, formally-clad servers. Come here for the classics: bouillabaisse, Alaskan crab legs, lobster tail (prepared 6 different ways), and fresh fish in a medley of preparations. Meat lovers can order veal, rack of lamb, chicken, New York steak, or filet mignon; appetizers range from Beluga caviar and escargots to ahi and salmon tartare, oysters Rockefeller, and blackened sashimi. The kids' menu appeals to families, the pasta and risotto to less-formal tastes. The Kalakaua Room has a window for people-watching, but we prefer the intimacy of the banquettes on the opposite side of the room. Live entertainment and dancing in the lounge attract the after-dinner crowd (p. 229).

In the Waikiki Gateway Hotel, 2070 Kalakaua Ave. (✆) **808/955-6333.** Reservations recommended. Main courses $21–market price. AE, DC, DISC, MC, V. Sun–Thurs 5:30–10pm; Fri–Sat 5:30–11pm. Late-night entertainment Thurs–Sat 9:30pm–1:30am.

Orchids ★★ INTERNATIONAL SEAFOOD   Orchids highlights fresh local produce and seafood in elegant presentations and in a fantasy setting with consummate service. It's an extraordinary setting, and the food is good to excellent. Blinding white linens and a view of Diamond Head from the open oceanfront dining room will start you off with a smile. (The parade of oiled bodies traversing the seawall is part of the entertainment.) At lunch, the seafood and vegetable curries, though pricey, are winners, and the steamed ehu (short-tail red snapper) is an Orchids signature. For dinner, onaga (ruby snapper) is steamed with ginger, Chinese parsley, shiitake mushrooms, and soy sauce, then drizzled with hot sesame oil—delightful. Delicately textured pink snapper (opakapaka) is sautéed and presented with wasabi mashed potatoes and wasabi cream, another pleaser with Asian undertones. There are lamb, chicken, and beef entrees as well, and the desserts, especially the chocolate brioche pudding and haupia lemongrass brûlée, are extraordinary. **Sunday brunch** ★★★, with its outstanding selection of dishes, is one of the best in Hawaii.

In the Halekulani, 2199 Kalia Rd. (✆) **808/923-2311.** Reservations recommended. Dinner main courses $25–$35. AE, DC, MC, V. Daily 7:30–11am and 6–10pm; Mon–Sat 11:30am–2pm; Sun brunch 9:30am–2:30pm.

Padovani's Restaurant & Wine Bar ★★★ FRENCH/MEDITERRANEAN Expect excellent fare, Frette linens, Riedel stemware, romantic lighting, and highly polished service and presentation. It won't be inexpensive, and don't wear jeans. There's an extravagant wine list to complement the culinary inspirations of chef Philippe Padovani. He has worked at Halekulani's La Mer, the erstwhile Ritz-Carlton Mauna Lani, and the Manele Bay Hotel, so of course his own swank dining room (and fantasy kitchen) would be top-drawer, with food and service that overcome a windowless room with not-so-soaring ceilings. A bamboo floor (à la Hoku's in the Kahala Mandarin), custom-made 1930s-style lamps, Bernardaud china, and a 16-bottle Cruvinet (which keeps wines fresh for by-the-glass orders) are other impressive features of this Waikiki winner.

The menu is pure Padovani: *ogo* (seaweed) bread, the best clam chowder in town, a panfried veal chop with sun-dried tomatoes and chervil sauce, grilled John Dory with fresh asparagus and tomatoes, and a wildly popular risotto of Dungeness crab and asparagus. The menu changes regularly, but count on the sautéed portobello mushrooms with polenta or the herbed endive salad with toasted almonds and Roquefort—superb.

Upstairs is a relaxing wine bar (more than 50 wines by the glass and an extensive single malt selection) with casual dining (a la carte menu selections ranging from excellent appetizers to sandwiches and salads to gourmet cheeses and desserts) in an after-hour dinner-club atmosphere.

In the Doubletree Alana Waikiki Hotel, 1956 Ala Moana Blvd. (✆) **808/946-3456.** www.padovani-e-gourmet. com. Reservations recommended. Dinner main courses $24–$44; prix fixe $36, $48, $98. AE, DC, DISC, MC, V. Restaurant: Mon–Sat 7–10am, 11:30am–4:30pm, and 6–9:30pm; Sun 7–10am and 11:30am–4:30pm. Wine bar: Sun–Thurs 4:30–11:30pm, Fri–Sat 4:30pm–12:30am.

Sunday Brunch at the Waikiki Block Party

Waikiki, the state's main visitor destination, continues to re-invent itself. The latest attraction is monthly Sunday brunches. On the second Sunday of each month, the city closes down all traffic on Kalakaua Avenue, from Kaiulani to Liliuokalani Avenues, from 9:30am to 1:30pm and has a giant block party.

Astroturf is rolled out into the street and tables, chairs, and bright tropical umbrellas are set up. The hotels and restaurants of Waikiki send their chefs out on the sidewalks where you can purchase everything from just-made pastries to finger-licking ribs. Entertainment ranges from a 60-member chorus to a hula troop of children. For information to reconfirm the dates (occasionally, the dates do change), call ℂ 808/523-2489.

If you are staying in Waikiki, you can just wander out to the party, but if you are coming from another part of the island, parking can be a problem. We suggest either parking on the streets around the Honolulu Zoo and Kapiolani Park, where a shuttle will run you down to the brunch, or for $1 you can park at the Royal Hawaiian Shopping Center or the Waikiki Trade Center.

Prince Court ✦ CONTEMPORARY ISLAND CUISINE   Floor-to-ceiling windows, sunny views of the harbor, and top-notch buffets are Prince Court's attractions, especially at lunch, when locals and visitors line up at the international buffet. Chef Goran Streng, formerly of Mauna Kea Beach Hotel's Batik room, keeps the menu fresh and the dining room busy. The harbor view is particularly pleasing at sunset or on Friday nights when fireworks light up the sky. Wednesday and Thursday, diners can sample the shellfish appetizer bar with a half entree (a bargain at $35 for both) from the varied a la carte menu, which features fresh island seafood, Hawaii Regional specialties (like melt-in-your-mouth ahi carpaccio), and excellent grilled and roasted meats. Desserts, too, are legendary, especially the custard-drenched bread pudding and the macadamia nut flan.

In the Hawaii Prince Hotel Waikiki, 100 Holomoana St. ℂ 808/944-4494. Reservations recommended. Main courses $18–$28; breakfast buffet $19; weekend brunch $26; luncheon buffet $21; shellfish appetizer bar $35; dinner buffets $38–$39. AE, DC, MC, V. Daily 6–10:30am; Mon–Fri 11:30am–2pm; Sat–Sun brunch 11:15am–1pm; Mon–Thurs 6–9:30pm; Fri–Sun 5:30–9:30pm.

Sarento's Top of the I ✦ ITALIAN   The ride up in the glass elevator at this special-occasion Italian restaurant is an event in itself, but Sarento's is not all show. Diners rave about the romantic view of the city, the stellar Greek salad (a trademark of this restaurant chain, whose president is Aaron Placourakis), the Opakapaka Portofino (with asparagus, in a lemon-dill-butter sauce), and the Seafood Fra Diavolo in marinara sauce. Things can be buttery here, so leave your inhibitions at the door. The pasta selections include lobster ravioli and the simple (and divine) capellini pomodoro. Veal lovers come for the osso buco with saffron risotto and the veal saltimbocca, served with a special touch: shiitake mushrooms.

In the Renaissance Ilikai Waikiki hotel, 1777 Ala Moana Blvd. ℂ 808/955-5559. Reservations recommended. Main courses $16–$32. AE, DC, MC, V. Sun–Thurs 5:30–9pm; Fri–Sat 5:30–9:30pm.

MODERATE

Arancino ITALIAN   When jaded Honolulu residents venture into Waikiki for dinner, it had better be good. Arancino is worth the hunt. Here's what you'll find: a cheerful cafe of Monet-yellow walls and tile floors, respectable pastas, wonderful pizzas, fabulous red-pepper salsa and rock-salt focaccia, we-try-harder service, and reasonable prices. The risotto changes daily. Don't miss the Gorgonzola-asparagus pizza if it's on the menu. The line on the sidewalk to get in is worth the wait.

255 Beach Walk. ℂ 808/923-5557. Main courses $8–$16. AE, DC, DISC, MC, V. Daily 11:30am–2:30pm and 5–10pm.

Ciao Mein ITALIAN/CHINESE   Risotto with chopsticks, fried rice with a fork—such is the cross-cultural way of Ciao Mein, a dozen years old and still going strong. The large, pleasant dining room, efficient service, surprisingly good Chinese food (especially for a hotel restaurant), and award-winning menu items have made this a haven for noodle lovers. The honey-walnut shrimp, with snap peas and honey-glazed walnuts, is a hit. The angel hair pasta with spicy ginger-garlic shrimp is a big seller, and few who have tasted Ciao Mein's tiramisu will forget its creamy, ambrosial kick. The antipasto is Italian, the seafood fun (as in chow fun) is a form of lasagna, and the Chinese roast duck is cannelloni "collision cuisine." Choose from six different pastas and six sauces.

In the Hyatt Regency Waikiki, 2424 Kalakaua Ave. ℂ 808/923-2426. www.ciaomein.com. Reservations recommended. Main courses $16–$35; prix fixe $29–$75. AE, DC, DISC, MC, V. Daily 6–10pm.

Duke's Canoe Club ★ *Value* STEAK/SEAFOOD   Hip, busy, and oceanfront, this is what dining in Waikiki should be. There's hardly a time when the open-air dining room isn't filled with good Hawaiian music. It's crowded at sunset, though. Just because Duke's is popular among singles, don't dismiss it as a pickup bar—its ambience is stellar. Named after fabled surfer Duke Kahanamoku, this casual, upbeat hot spot buzzes with diners and Hawaiian-music lovers throughout the day. Lunch and the Barefoot Bar menu include pizza, sandwiches, burgers, salads, and appetizers such as mac-nut and crab wontons and the ever-popular grilled chicken quesadillas. Dinner fare is steak and seafood, with decent marks for the fresh catch, prepared in your choice of five styles. There's live entertainment nightly from 4pm to midnight, with no cover.

In the Outrigger Waikiki on the Beach, 2335 Kalakaua Ave. ℂ 808/922-2268. www.hulapie.com. Reservations recommended for dinner. Main courses $10–$20; breakfast buffet $10. AE, DC, MC, V. Daily 7am–midnight.

Keo's in Waikiki ★ THAI   With freshly spiced and spirited dishes and familiar menu of Thai delights, Keo's arrived in Waikiki with a splashy tropical ambience and a menu that islanders and visitors love. Owner Keo Sananikone grows his own herbs, fruits, and vegetables without pesticides on his North Shore farm. Satay shrimp, basil-infused eggplant with tofu, evil jungle prince (shrimp, chicken, or vegetables in a basil-coconut-chile sauce), Thai garlic shrimp with mushrooms, pad Thai noodles, and the ever-delectable panang, green, and yellow curries are among his abiding delights. The menu includes a heat rating for spiciness, a plus for the delicate palate.

2028 Kuhio Ave. ℂ 808/951-9355. www.keosthaicuisine.com. Reservations recommended. Main courses $10–$14; prix fixe $30 per person. AE, DC, DISC, MC, V. Daily 7:30am–2pm; Sun–Thurs 5–10:30pm; Fri–Sat 5–11pm.

Parc Cafe ★ GOURMET BUFFETS   As the saying goes, Wow! Laulau! The Halekulani's sister hotel has redefined the buffet and made it—surprise!—a culinary attraction. Breakfast, sushi lunch, noodles, Hawaiian, and seafood/prime rib are among the buffet themes featured throughout the week. The Hawaiian buffet is great for visitors—it gives them a taste of real, down-home Hawaiian food with an elegance that is nonthreatening. It's multicultural too, so you have roast duck and Portuguese bean soup among the Hawaiian staples of laulau, beef stew, chicken long rice, kalua pig, squid luau, and the pièce de résistance, Kauai (or sometimes, Molokai) taro au gratin, a brilliant treatment of the Hawaiian corn that is too often misunderstood. Hawaii lunch buffet is $17 and dinner is $19. Chafing dishes notwithstanding, this is gourmet fare, using fresh, fine ingredients. A carving station serves up rotisserie duck and prime rib, and the seafood soup is reliably good.

In the Waikiki Parc Hotel, 2233 Helumoa Rd. © 808/931-6643. www.waikikiparchotel.com. Reservations recommended. Breakfast, lunch, and dinner buffets $13–$26. AE, DC, DISC, MC, V. Daily 5:30–10am; Sun sushi brunch 11am–2pm; Mon–Tues, Thurs, and Sat noodle buffet 11am–2:30pm; Wed and Fri Hawaiian buffet 11:30am–2pm; dinner buffet 5:30–9:30pm (Prime rib on Mon–Tues and Thurs; Hawaiian on Wed; seafood/prime rib Fri–Sun).

Singha Thai Cuisine THAI   The Royal Thai dancers arch their graceful fingers nightly in classical Thai dance on the small center stage, but you may be too busy tucking into your Thai chile fresh fish or blackened ahi summer rolls to notice. Imaginative combination dinners and the use of local organic ingredients are among the special touches of this Thai-Hawaiian fusion restaurant. Complete dinners for two to five cover many tastes and are an ideal way for the uninitiated to sample this cuisine, as well as the elements of Hawaii Regional Cuisine that have had considerable influence on the chef. Some highlights of a diverse menu: local fresh catch with Thai chile and light black-bean sauce; red, green, yellow, and vegetarian curries; ginseng chicken soup; and many seafood dishes. Such extensive use of fresh fish (mahimahi, ono, ahi, opakapaka, onaga, and uku) in traditional Thai preparations is unusual for a Thai restaurant. The entertainment and indoor-outdoor dining add to this first-class experience.

1910 Ala Moana Blvd. (at the Ala Moana end of Waikiki). © 808/941-2898. Reservations recommended. Main courses $12–$31. AE, DC, DISC, MC, V. Daily 4–11pm.

Tiki's Grill & Bar AMERICAN/PACIFIC RIM   When the newly renovated Aston Waikiki Beach Hotel opened in 2002, the surprise was not the renovations but the great food coming from the kitchen of Chef Fred DeAngelo (formerly of Palomino fame). Located on the second floor (pool level) of the hotel and overlooking Waikiki Beach (get an outside table on the lanai at sunset), this casual eatery is decorated in palm wood flooring with fish nets hanging from the ceiling and lava rock walls. A 30-foot volcano is the show piece in the bar (where you can snack on pupus). DeAngelo's cuisine is good ole American, with his particular touch of Pacific rim, apparent in all his fish dishes. His signature dish is king salmon ($16), glazed with lemongrass beurre blanc. Also high on the list is the mahimahi ($16) grilled with a spicy seafood salsa. Save room for pastry chef Ron Villoria's chocolate bread pudding and outstanding lilikoi cheesecake with basil syrup served in a white chocolate cylinder. Check out the live Hawaiian music in the bar every night.

Aston Waikiki Beach Hotel, 2570 Kalakaua Ave. (at Paoakalani St.). © 808/923-TIKI. Lunch entrees $8–$17, dinner main courses $11–$37. AE, DC, DISC, MC, V. Daily 10:30am–midnight.

INEXPENSIVE

Cha Cha Cha MEXICAN/CARIBBEAN   Its heroic margaritas, cheap happy-hour beer, pupu, excellent homemade chips, and all-around lovable menu make this a Waikiki treasure. From the beans to the salsa to the gilled Jamaican chicken, there's nothing wimpy about the flavors here. The lime, coconut, and Caribbean spices make Cha Cha Cha more than plain ol' Mex, adding zing to the blackened mahimahi and fresh fish burritos, the jerk chicken breast, and the grilled veggies in a spinach tortilla. Tacos, tamales, quesadillas, soups, enchiladas, chimichangas, and a host of spicy pork, chicken, and fish ensembles are real pleasers. Ask about the specials because they're likely to be wonderful. Blackened swordfish, curried fresh grilled vegetables, and homemade desserts (including a creamy toasted coconut custard you won't want to miss) are some of the highlights. Its location, across from two of Waikiki's three movie theaters, makes it a choice spot for pre- and after-theater dining.

342 Seaside Ave. ✆ **808/923-7797.** Complete dinners $7–$13. MC, V. Daily 11:30am–1am; happy hour 4–6pm and 9–11pm.

Eggs n' Things ⋆⋆ BREAKFAST   Like the mythical Phoenix, this breakfast-only eatery was resurrected within a year of the Christmas 2001 fire. This popular place is famous not only for its great food but also for its all-night hours (drop in at 3am and check out the clientele scarfing down the humongous breakfasts). Go when you are hungry; you'll find the fluffiest omelets (which come with pancakes, potatoes and toast), melt-in-your-mouth waffles (piled high with fruit and whipped cream), and hot coffee constantly being poured into your cup. Prices are surprisingly reasonable, making this place worth standing in line for.

1911-B Kalakaua Ave. (at Ala Moana Blvd.). ✆ **808/949-0820.** Breakfast entrees in the $8–$12 range. No cards. Daily 11pm–2pm.

HONOLULU BEYOND WAIKIKI
ALA MOANA & KAKAAKO
Expensive

Aaron's Atop the Ala Moana ⋆ AMERICAN/CONTINENTAL/ SEAFOOD   Take the express elevator to the 36th floor, where the circular dining room reveals the city in its mountain-to-sea splendor. This may be the best view from a Honolulu restaurant that isn't on the beach. Tables line the sweeping windows while intimate banquettes curve around the interior. A private dining room next to the wine cellar serves parties of up to 10. Aaron's offers beluga caviar, its famous black-and-blue ahi (sliced asymmetrically and seared in Cajun spices), and seafood entrees such as the famous Opakapaka Gabriella, with lemon butter and capers. This is rich continental fare with some lively local touches and some heavy sauces. Among the excellent salads, the Greek Maui Wowie—chopped tomatoes, bay shrimp, avocado, Maui onions, feta cheese, lettuce—is tops.

Ala Moana Hotel, 410 Atkinson Dr. ✆ **808/955-4466.** www.tri-star-restaurants.com. Reservations recommended. Main courses $22–$43. AE, DC, DISC, MC, V. Sun–Thurs 5:30–10:30pm; Fri-Sat 5:30–11:30pm; live music Sun–Thurs until 1am, Fri–Sat until 3am.

Mariposa ⋆⋆ PACIFIC RIM/SOUTHWESTERN   Once you get past the gourmet food department of the new Neiman Marcus, you'll be in Mariposa, a popular lunch spot in town (along with OnJin's Café, another fave). High ceilings for indoor diners, plus tables on the deck with views of Ala Moana Park and its Art Deco bridges, add up to a pleasing ambience, with or without the shopping. You'll find cordial service, nearly 4 dozen reasonably priced wines by the glass, and a menu of Pacific and American (called "heritage cuisine") specialties that include everything from opakapaka with a three-pepper vinaigrette to an excellent seared salmon salad. Chef Doug Lum's mashed potatoes and steamed Manila clams are legendary, and the Hamakua Meyer lemon tart is a force of nature. But the lunchtime favorite is invariably the starter of chicken broth—like the towering, eggy popover with poha (cape gooseberry) butter, it's the perfect welcome.

In Neiman Marcus, Ala Moana Center, 1450 Ala Moana Blvd. © 808/951-3420. Reservations recommended. Lunch main courses $10–$20; dinner main courses $19–$35. AE, DC, MC, V. Sun–Thurs 11am–9pm; Fri-Sat 11am–10pm.

The Pineapple Room at Macy's ★★ HAWAII REGIONAL   Yes it's in a department store, but the chef is Alan Wong, a culinary icon. The food is terrific, particularly anything with fresh island fish (like the ahi "meat" loaf) to kalua pig (like the kalua pig BLT). Wong conjures culinary masterpieces that will probably leave you wanting to come back and try breakfast, lunch, and dinner, just to see what he will present. The room features an open kitchen with a lava-rock wall and abundant natural light, but these are details in a room where food is king. The menu changes regularly, but keep an eye out for the ginger scallion shrimp scampi, nori-wrapped tempura salmon, and superb gazpacho made of yellow and red Waimea tomatoes.

Macy's, 1450 Ala Moana Blvd. © 808/945-8881. www.alanwongs.com. Reservations recommended for lunch and dinner. Main courses $10–$17 lunch, prix fixe lunch $17–$20; $20–$29 dinner, sampling dinner $49. AE, DC, DISC, MC, V. Mon–Fri 11am–8:30pm; Sat 8am–8:30pm; Sun 9am–3pm.

Sushi Sasabune ★★ *Finds* SUSHI   This elegant sushi restaurant, tucked away amongst indescript shops along a very busy street, is one of the marvels of the edible world. Don't miss the chirashi/fish bowl, a neat rectangular box with warm rice, several types of tuna and white fish, marinated octopus, and other slices of sashimi. If you wish to order from the regular menu, by all means grab a table. But if you sit at the sushi bar, you must submit to the Japanese version of the Seinfeld Soup Nazi, otherwise known as omakase. You obey the chef, eat what's served, and God help you if you drop a grain of rice or dip something in wasabi without permission. The payoff is that whatever you eat is freshly shipped in that day and often exotic. Whether it's salmon from Nova Scotia, sea urchin from Japan, halibut from Boston, Louisiana blue crab, or farmed oyster from Washington, chef Seiji Kumagawa's sushi comes with a strict protocol: Dip only with permission, and then with restraint. This is an extraordinary experience for sushi aficionados—a journey into new tastes, textures, and sensations. It's expensive but well worth it.

1419 S. King St. © 808/947-3800. Reservations recommended. Sushi $4–$7; sashimi $3–$15. AE, DC, DISC, MC, V. Mon–Fri noon–2pm; Mon–Sat 5:30–10pm.

Moderate

Akasaka ★ JAPANESE/SUSHI BAR   Akasaka is difficult to find, and once you do find it you enter through a back door, but this cozy, busy, casual, and occasionally smoky restaurant wins high marks for sushi, sizzling tofu and scallops, miso-clam soup, and the overall quality of its cuisine. Highlights include the zesty spicy tuna hand-roll (temaki), scallop roll with flying-fish roe, hamachi, and soft-shell crab in season. Lunch and dinner specials help ease the bite of the bill, and ordering noodles or other less expensive a la carte items can also reduce the cost considerably. Don't expect geshi girls, or even friendly service—the staff is efficient but not necessarily accommodating.

1646B Kona St. © 808/942-4466. Reservations recommended. Main courses $10–$25. AE, DC, DISC, MC, V. Mon–Sat 11am–2:30pm and 5pm–2am; Sun 5pm–midnight.

Assaggio ★ ITALIAN   This wildly popular chain, until recently the toast of suburban Oahu (see p. 155 for the Kailua location), moved into Ala Moana

Honolulu Dining Beyond Waikiki

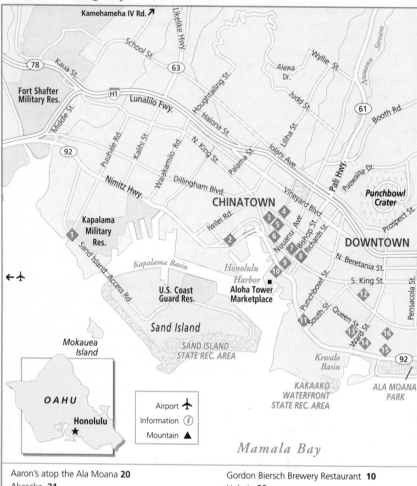

Aaron's atop the Ala Moana **20**
Akasaka **21**
Alan Wong's Restaurant **26**
Angelo Pietro **22**
Assaggio **19**
C & C Pasta **36**
Cafe Laufer **34**
Chai's Island Bistro **10**
Che Pasta **8**
Chef Mavro Restaurant **27**
Chiang Mai Thai Cuisine **28**
Contemporary Museum Cafe **40**
Dixie Grill **13**
Don Ho's Island Grill **10**
Duc's Bistro **5**
Genki Sushi **32**

Gordon Biersch Brewery Restaurant **10**
Hoku's **39**
I ♥ Country Cafe **19**
Indigo Eurasian Cuisine **7**
Jimbo's Restaurant **25**
Kaka'ako Kitchen **14**
Kincaid's Fish, Chop, and Steakhouse **14**
Kua Aina **15**
L'Uraku **18**
La Mariana **1**
Legend Seafood Restaurant **4**
Little Village Noodle House **6**
Maple Garden **29**
Mariposa **19**
Ninniku-Ya Garlic Restaurant **33**
Ocean Club **11**

Olive Tree Cafe **39**
OnJin's Café **16**
Palomino **9**
Panda Cuisine **23**
The Pineapple Room at Macy's **19**
Roy's Restaurant **37**
Ruth's Chris Steak House **11**
Sam Choy's Breakfast, Lunch, Crab
    & Big Aloha Brewery **2**

Sam Choy's Diamond Head Restaurant **38**
Sansei Seafood Restaurant and Sushi Bar **11**
Side Street Inn **17**
Sushi King **31**
Sushi Sasabune **24**
3660 On the Rise **35**
To Chau **3**
Willows **30**
Yanagi Sushi **12**

Center to a roar of approval and immediate success. Townies can now enjoy Assaggio's extensive, high-quality Italian offerings—at good prices. The lighter lunch menu features pasta dishes and house specialties (shrimp scampi, rigatoni alla ricotta) at prices around $10 and less. At dinner, a panoply of pastas and specialties streams out of the kitchen: at least nine chicken entrees, pasta dishes ranging from mushroom and clam to linguine primavera, and eight veal choices. One of Assaggio's best features is its prodigious seafood selection: shrimp, scallops, mussels, calamari, and fresh fish in many preparations, ranging from plain garlic and olive oil to spicy tomato and wine sauces. Assaggio's excellent service paired with entrees priced under $20 deserves our applause.

In the Ala Moana Center, 1450 Ala Moana Blvd. (© **808/942-3446.** Reservations recommended. Main courses $9–$15 lunch, $11–$21 dinner. AE, DC, DISC, MC, V. Daily 11am–3pm; Sun–Thurs 4:30–9:30pm; Fri–Sat 4:30–10pm.

Kincaid's Fish, Chop, and Steakhouse ✦ SEAFOOD/STEAKS   Kincaid's
is always winning surveys for one thing or another—best place for a business lunch, best seafood restaurant—because it pleases wide-ranging tastes and pocketbooks. Brisk service, a harbor view, and an extensive seafood menu keep the large dining room full. Fresh-fish sandwiches; seafood chowders and French onion soups; kiawe-grilled and herb-buttered salmon; fresh mahimahi with keylime butter; and garlic prawns are among the extensive choices. We love the devil-may-care Dungeness crab and artichoke sandwich—open-faced, rich, and fabulous. You might want to save room for the true-blue key lime pie. Kincaid's is also a popular happy-hour rendezvous, with inexpensive beer and appetizers and live entertainment from 8:30 to 11:30 Friday and Saturday nights.

In the Ward Warehouse, 1050 Ala Moana Blvd. (© **808/591-2005.** Reservations recommended. Lunch $9–$15; dinner main courses $13–$50. AE, DC, DISC, MC, V. Daily 11am–10pm (open later for pupu).

L'Uraku ★★ (Value) EURO-JAPANESE   L'Uraku's pleasant, light-filled dining
room and expanded fusion menu make it a great spot for lunch or dinner. It's not overly fussy but still has the right touch of elegance for dining in style without breaking the bank. Chef Hiroshi Fukui, born in Japan and raised in Hawaii, was trained in the formal Japanese culinary tradition called *kaiseki;* he combines this training with fresh island ingredients and European cooking styles. Dishes such as seared scallops, garlic steak, and superb misoyaki butterfish are among the many stellar offerings. The $15 "Weekender lunch" is an unbelievable value: crab cake or shrimp, salad, and a choice of entree such as fresh salmon, almond-crusted fresh snapper, or the succulent misoyaki butterfish. Vegetarians should find comfort and pleasure in the Vegetarian's Dream, a medley of grilled tomatoes, eggplant, portobello mushrooms, and seasonal vegetables with a lively tofu sauce. L'Uraku is a find that has only gotten better with the years.

1341 Kapiolani Blvd. (© **808/955-0552.** Reservations recommended. Main courses $9–$18 lunch, $16–$28 dinner; $34 prix fixe. AE, DC, MC, V. Daily 11am–1:45pm and 5:30–9:45pm

OnJin's Café ★★ (Value) FRENCH/ASIAN   OnJin's could appear in both
"moderate" and "inexpensive" categories because it's fabulously inexpensive for lunch (gourmet fare at plate-lunch prices) and, although more expensive for dinner, is still a noteworthy value. OnJin Kim is a brilliant chef (formerly of the erstwhile Bagwell's in the Hyatt Regency and her own former Hanatei) who serves excellent fare at excellent prices. Expect long lines at lunch, a more relaxed mood at dinner, pleasant service, and an indoor-outdoor ambience in a rapidly developing part of Kakaako. (A movie multiplex recently sprung up nearby.) At lunch, you order and pay at the counter, but your superbly prepared snapper

with lemon caper beurre blanc or salmon misoyaki arrives on a real plate—for under $7.50. Specials (beef bourguignonne, seafood jambalaya) change daily. For dinner, there's charred ahi with seven Japanese spices and a selection of entrees remarkable not only for their friendly prices but also for the sophisticated execution that is OnJin's signature. Whether it's soft-shell crab lightly fried in almond flour or the top-of-the-line bouillabaisse (an OnJin signature), you'll know you've arrived in OnJin heaven.

401 Kamakee St. ℂ **808/589-1666.** Reservations not accepted for lunch. Lunch main courses and specials $5.50–$7.50; dinner main courses $18–$22. AE, DISC, MC, V. Mon–Fri 11am–2pm; Tues–Sat 5–9pm.

Inexpensive

Angelo Pietro PIZZA/SPAGHETTI   Two motifs go over well here: the create-your-own pasta and the quirky take on Italian food that could come only from Japan. At this Italian-Japanese pasta house, you can order raw potato salad with any of four dressings—shoyu, ginger, ume (plum), and sesame-miso—and chase it with more than 4 dozen spaghetti choices, with sauces and toppings ranging from several types each of mushroom, shrimp, chicken, spinach, and sausage to squid ink and eggplant. Pescatore, carbonara (with asparagus!), pickled mustard cabbage with sausage, codfish eggs—everything is grist for the spaghetti mill at the hands of Angelo Pietro. Garlic lovers adore the crisp garlic chips that are heaped atop some of the selections.

1585 Kapiolani Blvd. ℂ **808/941-0555.** Reservations accepted for groups of 6 or more. Main courses $7–$14. AE, DC, DISC, MC, V. Sun–Thurs 11am–10pm; Fri–Sat 11am–11pm.

Dixie Grill AMERICAN   Popcorn, video games, a TV bar, and a lusty, noisy atmosphere—that's Dixie Grill, the busiest (and perhaps noisiest) spot on Ward Avenue. You can't miss it—just look for the fire-engine red walls and turquoise painted fence. You can sit outside on wooden tables (with a view of Sports Authority), or indoors in a high-decibel, quirky atmosphere much loved by families with kids. The all-American menu features barbecued ribs, burgers, shrimp, salads, sandwiches, and a "mess o' crabs." Watch for the "Screamin' Mai Tai" specials.

404 Ward Ave. ℂ **808/596-8359.** Reservations accepted for groups of 8 or more. Sandwiches and entrees $6–$20. AE, DC, DISC, MC, V. Sun–Thurs 11am–10pm; Fri–Sat 11am–11pm.

I ❤ Country Cafe INTERNATIONAL   Give yourself time to peruse the lengthy list of specials posted on the menu board, as well as the prodigious printed menu. Stand in line at the counter, place your order and pay, and find a Formica-topped table; or wait about 10 minutes for your takeout order to appear on a Styrofoam plate heaped with salad and other accompaniments. The mind-boggling selection includes nine types of cheese steaks (including vegetarian tofu), Cajun meat loaf, Thai curries, various stir-fries, shoyu chicken, vegetarian or eggplant lasagna, chicken Dijon, Cajun-style ahi, and other choices spanning many cultures and tastes. Take a good look at the diners, and you'll see that the menu appeals equally to bodybuilders and hedonists.

In Ala Moana Plaza, 451 Piikoi St. ℂ **808/596-8108.** Main courses $5–$8.75. AE, DC, DISC, MC, V. Mon–Thurs 10am–9pm; Fri 10am–9:30pm; Sat 8am–9:30pm; Sun 8am–9pm.

Kaka'ako Kitchen ★★ Finds GOURMET PLATE LUNCHES   This popular industrial-style plate-lunch haven is busier than ever since it moved to the trendy Ward Centre in March 2000, with an expanded concept that includes dinner and breakfast service. You'll get excellent home-style cooking (it's owned by Chef Russell Siu, of 3660 on the Rise) served on Styrofoam plates, in a warehouse ambience, at budget prices. The menu, which changes every 3 to 4 months, includes a seared ahi sandwich with tobiko (flying-fish roe) aioli; the signature charbroiled ahi steak; sandwiches; beef stew; five-spice shoyu chicken; the very popular meat loaf; and other multiethnic entrees.

In the Ward Centre, 1200 Ala Moana Blvd. ✆ 808/596-7488. Breakfast $5–$8; lunch and dinner main courses $7–$13. AE, DC, MC, V. Mon–Thurs 7am–9pm; Fri–Sat 7am–10pm; Sun 7am–5pm.

Kua Aina ⭐ *Value* AMERICAN   The ultimate sandwich shop, for years a North Shore fixture, expanded to the Ward Centre area (near Borders and Starbucks), and the result is dizzying. Phone in your order if you can. During lunch and dinner hours, people wait patiently in long lines for the famous burgers and sandwiches: the beef burgers with heroic toppings; mahimahi with ortega and cheese (a legend); grilled eggplant and peppers; roast turkey; tuna and avocado; roast beef and avocado; and about a dozen other selections on Kaiser roll or multigrain wheat or rye breads. The sandwiches and fries are excellent, and the outdoor section with tables, thank God, has grown—but there still may be a wait during lunch hour. The takeout business is brisk.

In Ward Village, 1116 Auahi St. ✆ 808/591-9133. Sandwiches $3.50–$5.70. No credit cards. Mon-Sat 10:30am–9pm; Sun 10:30am–8pm.

Panda Cuisine ⭐ DIM SUM/SEAFOOD/HONG-KONG STYLE CHINESE   This is dim sum heaven, not only for the selection, but for the late-night dim sum service, a rare thing for what is a morning and lunchtime tradition in Hong Kong. Panda's dim sum selection—spinach-scallop, chive, taro, shrimp dumplings, pork hash, and some 50-plus others—is a real pleaser. (*Tip:* the spinach-scallop and taro puff varieties are a cut above.) The reckless can spring for the live Maine lobster and Dungeness crab in season, or the king clam and steamed fresh fish, but the steaming bamboo carts yielding toothsome surprises are hard to resist. Noodles and sizzling platters are good accompaniments to the dim sum.

641 Keeaumoku St. ✆ 808/947-1688. Main courses $8–$29. AE, MC, V. Mon–Sat 10:30am–2:30pm and 5pm–2am; Sun 5–10pm.

Side Street Inn ⭐ *Finds* LOCAL   After their own fancy kitchens have closed, some of Honolulu's top chefs head to this smoky bar with TV sets on the walls and a back room with a dart board and Miller Lite and Budweiser neon lights. Very camp. The terrific food is a surprise; this small side street near Ala Moana Center is noted more for its seedy bars than for pesto-crusted ahi and gourmet Nalo greens. But hey—the grinds (that's local slang for eats) are fabulous, with no pretensions and a spirited local feeling. The barbecued baby back ribs in lilikoi sauce are tender, flavorful, and a steal at $11, and you can find 10- to 16-ounce steaks, charbroiled or on sizzling platters, for $14 to $15. Our faves are the blackened ahi, pesto-crusted ahi, fresh steamed manila clams (tender, in a wine-garlic broth), shrimp scampi, and escargots. By the end of the meal, your clothes may smell like smoke—but chances are, you'll return.

1225 Hopaka St. ✆ 808/591-0253. Reservations accepted. Main courses $7–$16. AE, DC, DISC, MC, V. Mon-Fri 10:30am–1:30pm; daily 4pm–1am.

ALOHA TOWER MARKETPLACE

Chai's Island Bistro ⭐ PACIFIC RIM/ASIAN   We give Chai's high marks for food but have less enthusiasm for service and ambience, especially at dinner, when the overamped music can detract from the dining experience. Also, the dinner entree prices have risen significantly. But the food is generally of high quality and creativity. The 200-seat restaurant has high ceilings, a good location (though not on the waterfront), indoor-outdoor seating, and a discreetly placed (not in-your-face) open kitchen. The appetizer sampler for two appears on a boat-size platter—a feast of ahi katsu with yellow curry sauce and wasabi; crisp duck lumpia, tasty and greaseless; macadamia-nut–crusted tiger prawns; and Alaskan king crab cakes. This is an appetizer that could be an entree, or a starter for two, and is my favorite item on the menu. The fusion dishes include steamed, fresh, Chinese-style onaga, and an ample selection of vegetarian dishes. A caveat: The nightly entertainment (usually live music) tends to be excruciatingly loud.

Aloha Tower Marketplace, 1 Aloha Tower Dr. ℂ **808/585-0011.** Reservations recommended. Main courses $12–$20 lunch, $29–$46 dinner. AE, DC, MC, V. Mon–Fri 11am–10pm; Sat–Sun 4–10pm.

✓ **Don Ho's Island Grill** HAWAIIAN/CONTEMPORARY ISLAND Don Ho's Island Grill's shrine to Don Ho is a mix of nostalgic interior elements: koa paneling, thatched roof, split-bamboo ceilings, old pictures of Ho with celebrities, faux palm trees, and open sides looking out onto the harbor. It's kitschy and charming, down to the vinyl pareu-printed tablecloths and the flower behind the server's ear. Don Ho's has become one of the significant late-night musical venues of Honolulu, packing in sold-out crowds for special concerts by local musical icons like Amy Gilliom and Willie K.

Aloha Tower Marketplace, 1 Aloha Tower Dr. ℂ **808/528-0807.** Reservations recommended. Main courses $11–$26. AE, DC, DISC, MC, V. Daily 10am–10pm; nightclub (days vary) open until 2am.

Gordon Biersch Brewery Restaurant NEW AMERICAN/PACIFIC RIM German-style lagers brewed on the premises would be enough of a draw, but the food is also a lure at Gordon Biersch, one of Honolulu's liveliest after-work hangouts. Fresh Pacific and Island seafood highlights the eclectic menu. The lanai bar and the brewery bar—open until 1am—are the brightest spots in the marketplace, teeming with downtown types who nosh on pot stickers, grilled steaks, baby back ribs, chicken pizza, garlic fries, and any number of American classics with deft cross-cultural touches. Extensive renovations in 1999 created a stage area for live music, a popular weekend feature.

Aloha Tower Marketplace, 1 Aloha Tower Dr. ℂ **808/599-4877.** Reservations recommended. Main courses $8–$20. AE, DC, DISC, MC, V. Sun–Thurs 10am–10pm; Fri–Sat 10am–10:30pm; daily late-night menu to 11:30pm.

DOWNTOWN

Downtowners love the informal walk-in cafes lining one side of attractive **Bishop Square,** at 1001 Bishop St. (at King Street), in the middle of the business district, where free entertainment is offered every Friday during lunch hour. The popular **Che Pasta** is a stalwart here, chic enough for business meetings and not too formal (or expensive) for a spontaneous rendezvous over pasta and minestrone. Some places in Bishop Square open for breakfast and lunch, others just for lunch, but most close when business offices empty.

Note: Keep in mind that **Restaurant Row** (Ala Moana Blvd., between Punchbowl and South St.), which features several hot new establishments, offers free validated parking in the evening.

Duc's Bistro ★ *Finds* FRENCH/VIETNAMESE Surrounded by lei stands and marked by a cheery neon sign, this cozy 80-seater stands out at the mauka end of Maunakea in Chinatown. Narrow and quietly elegant, the restaurant has three components: the front room with windows looking out to Maunakea Street, the windowless back room, and the tiny bar. It has an edgy chic more like Manhattan than Honolulu, and the food is beautifully prepared and presented.

Sauces for the meats hint of Grand Marnier (duck supreme), Bordeaux (lamb Raymond Oliver), VSOP cognac (steak aux poivre), Pernod (prawns and oysters), and fresh herbs and vegetables. From the seafood spring rolls with shrimp, taro, and mushrooms, to the Meal in a Bowl (rice noodles heaped with fresh herbs and julienned vegetables, topped with lime dressing—excellent!), creative touches abound. There's live jazz nightly except Thursday, when Hawaiian music takes over and surprise vocalists and hula dancers are known to join in the fun.

1188 Maunakea St., Chinatown. (C) **808/531-6325.** Reservations recommended. Main dishes $10–$16 lunch, $13–$28 dinner. AE, MC, V. Mon–Fri 11:30am–1:30pm; daily 5–10pm; bar open later.

Indigo Eurasian Cuisine ★★ EURASIAN   Hardwood floors, red brick, wicker, high ceilings, and an overall feeling of Indochine luxury give Indigo a stylish edge. You can dine indoors or in a garden setting on menu offerings such as pot stickers, Buddhist bao buns, savory brochettes, tandoori chicken breast, vegetable tarts, Asian-style noodles and dumplings, lilikoi-glazed baby back ribs, and cleverly named offerings from East and West. Chef Glenn Chu is popular, but many claim that Indigo is more style than flavor. We disagree—this is a great restaurant. The adjoining Green Room is packed and smoky.

1121 Nuuanu Ave. (C) **808/521-2900.** Reservations recommended. Lunch $6–$16; dinner main dishes $16–$26. DC, DISC, MC, V. Tues–Fri 11:30am–2pm; Tues–Sat 6–9:30pm; martini time in the Green Room Tues–Fri 5–6:30pm.

Legend Seafood Restaurant ★ DIM SUM/SEAFOOD   It's like dining in Hong Kong here, with a Chinese-speaking clientele poring over Chinese newspapers and the clatter of chopsticks punctuating conversations. Excellent dim sum comes in bamboo steamers that beckon seductively from carts. Although dining here is a form of assertiveness training (you must wave madly to catch the server's eye and then point to what you want), the system doesn't deter fans from returning. Among our favorites: deep-fried taro puffs and prawn dumplings, shrimp dim sum, vegetable dumplings, and the open-faced seafood with shiitake, scallops, and a tofu product called *aburage*. Dim sum is served only at lunch, but dinnertime seafood dishes comfort sufficiently. Not a very elegant restaurant, but the food is serious and great.

In the Chinese Cultural Plaza, 100 N. Beretania St. (C) **808/532-1868.** Reservations recommended. Most items under $15. AE, DC, MC, V. Mon–Fri 10:30am–2pm and 5:30–10pm; Sat–Sun 8am–2pm and 5:30–10pm.

Little Village Noodle House CHINESE   Ignore the decor: no, not the usual lack of decor that Chinese restaurants affect, the interior design here reminds me of a French bistro with overhanging roof like you are eating on the back porch of a small place in Provence. No matter, the food here is "simple and healthy" (their motto) and authentic Chinese (Northern, Canton and Hong Kong style). Our picks are the Shanghai noodles with stir-friend veggies, the walnut shrimp, and the butterfish in black bean sauce. The menu is eclectic and offers some interesting selection you don't often see. The service is not only friendly (a rarity in Chinatown), but the wait help are quite knowledgeable about the dishes. Yes, there is takeout, but even more unique (for Chinatown) they have parking in the back!

1113 Smith St. (C) **808/545-3008.** Most items under $10. AE, DISC, MC, V. Sun–Thur 10:30am–10:30pm; Fri–Sat 10:am–midnight.

Ocean Club ★ SEAFOOD   Ocean Club could be listed as a restaurant or a nightclub. This sleek, chic magnet has redefined happy hour with its extended hours of slashed prices, excellent appetizer-only seafood menu, and ultracool ambience for the 30 and under set. Galvanized steel counters, mahogany bars lined with shoyu bottles, linoleum tile floors, and oddly attractive pillars resembling *pahu* (Hawaiian drums) make for a wonderfully eclectic mix. Add DJs spinning hip-hop, and you get the picture. The menu of appetizers lives up to its "ultimate cocktail hour" claim, especially from 4:30 to 8pm nightly, when great seafood is slashed to half-price and the upbeat mood starts spiraling. A happy-hour sampling: toothsome dips of spinach, artichoke or crab, served with tortilla chips, salsa, and sour cream; ahi tacos and sashimi for a pittance; and standards such as buffalo wings and fried calamari.

On Restaurant Row, 500 Ala Moana Blvd. © **808/526-9888.** www.oceanclubonline.com. No T-shirts or beachwear allowed. Minimum age 23. All items $5–$9 ($2.45–$5 before 8 pm). AE, DISC, MC, V. Tues–Thurs 4:30pm–2am; Fri 4:30pm–3am; Sat 6pm–3am.

Palomino ★★ AMERICAN REGIONAL   Palomino offers splendid harbor views, interesting architecture, conscientious service, and excellent food. It is more Chicago than Hawaii but proffers dishes that will likely bring you back (especially since it is within walking distance from Hawaii Theatre). Don't miss the wild mushroom salad and cedar-plank roasted salmon. The pizzas (one with caramelized onion and spinach), roasted garlic, shrimp in grape leaves, and kiawe-grilled fish get high marks, as does the devastating dessert called Caffè Affogato (white-chocolate ice cream, espresso, and whipped cream).

In the Harbor Court Building, 66 Queen St., mezzanine. © **808/528-2400.** Reservations recommended. Main dishes $7–$27. AE, DC, DISC, MC, V. Mon–Fri 11:15am–2:30pm; Sun–Thurs 5–10pm; Fri–Sat 5–11pm; late-night bar menu Mon–Fri till 11pm; Fri–Sat till 12:30am.

Sansei Seafood Restaurant and Sushi Bar ★★ SUSHI/ASIAN-PACIFIC RIM   Perpetual award-winner D. K. Kodama, who built Kapalua's Sansei into one of Maui's most popular eateries, has become something of a local legend with his exuberant brand of sushi and fusion cooking. Although some of the flavors (sweet Thai chile sauce with cilantro, for example) may be too fussy for sushi purists, there are ample choices for a full range of palates. On the extensive menu appear Sansei's trademark, award-winning Asian rock shrimp cake and Sansei special sushi (crab, cilantro, cucumber, and avocado with a sweet chile sauce), as well as Spam musubi (help!) and miso scallops. In the traditional selections you can choose from a wide range of selections, from very fresh yellowtail sushi to Japanese miso eggplant. Kodama has added karaoke and late-night programs beginning at 10pm.

On Restaurant Row, 500 Ala Moana Blvd. © **808/536-6286.** www.sanseihawaii.com. Reservations recommended. Main courses $11 (appetizer size) to $38. AE, DISC, MC, V. Daily 5–10pm; Tues–Sat 10pm–2am; lunch Mon–Fri 11am–2pm; local DJ Thurs–Sat 10pm–2am.

To Chau ★★ (Value) VIETNAMESE PHO   The two stars are strictly for the pho, which many think is the best in a city studded with pho houses. Ambience is nil; you'll have to stand in a line that normally numbers 13 to 15 hopefuls, and service can be brusque. But that is all part of the charm of this no-nonsense Formica-style pho house, located in Chinatown, in a stone building along a river and marked, without fail, by a queue of Asian diners who bespeak authority regarding what is and is not the real Vietnamese beef and noodle soup. This is. The anticipation is heightened by the view of diners relishing their steaming, long-awaited orders, visible through the windows as you wait your turn on the sidewalk. There are shrimp and spring rolls and chicken and pork chop plates, but I've never seen anyone order anything but pho. And what a soup this is! The broth is clear, hearty, and marvelously flavored with hints of cinnamon and spice. You can order it with several choices of steak, and it comes with a heaping platter of fresh bean sprouts, basil, hot green peppers, and an Asian green called boke (bo-kay). It's worth the wait, and so inexpensive.

1007 River St., Chinatown. ⓒ 808/533-4549. Reservations not accepted. Pho $3.85–$5.20. No credit cards. Daily 8am–2:30pm (or until they run out of food).

Yanagi Sushi ⭐ JAPANESE   We love the late-night hours, the sushi bar, and the extensive choices of combination lunches and dinners. But we also love the a la carte Japanese menu, which covers everything from *chazuke* (a comfort food of rice with tea, salmon, seaweed, and other condiments) to shabu-shabu and other steaming earthenware-pot dishes. Complete dinners come with choices of sashimi, shrimp tempura, broiled salmon, New York steak, and many other possibilities. You can dine here affordably or extravagantly, on $6 noodles or a $30 lobster nabe (cooked in a single pot of seasoned broth). Consistently crisp tempura and fine spicy ahi hand-rolled sushi also make Yanagi worth remembering.

762 Kapiolani Blvd. ⓒ **808/597-1525.** Reservations recommended. Main courses $8–$33; complete dinners $12–$18. AE, DC, DISC, MC, V. Daily 11am–2pm; Mon–Sat 5:30pm–2am; Sun 5:30–10pm.

KALIHI/SAND ISLAND

La Mariana AMERICAN   Just try to find a spot more evocative or nostalgic than this South Seas oasis at lagoon's edge in the bowels of industrial Honolulu, with carved tikis, glass balls suspended in fishing nets, shell chandeliers, and old tables made from koa trees. In the back section, the entire ceiling is made of tree limbs. This unique, nearly 50-year-old restaurant is popular for lunch, sunset appetizers, and impromptu Friday- and Saturday-night sing-alongs at the piano bar, where a colorful crowd (including some Don Ho look-alikes) gathers to sing Hawaiian classics like a 1950s high school Glee Club. It is delightful. The seared Cajun-style ahi is your best bet as an appetizer or entree; La Mariana is more about spirit and ambience than food.

50 Sand Island Rd. ⓒ 808/848-2800. Reservations recommended, especially on weekends. Main courses $6–$12 lunch, $10–$22 dinner. AE, MC, V. Daily 11am–3pm, pupu 3–5pm; Mon 5–8pm; Tues, Thurs and Sun 5–9pm; Fri–Sat 5–10pm. Turn makai (toward the ocean) on Sand Island Rd. from Nimitz Hwy.; immediately after the first stoplight on Sand Island, take a right and drive toward the ocean; it's not far from the airport.

Sam Choy's Breakfast, Lunch, Crab & Big Aloha Brewery ISLAND CUISINE/SEAFOOD   This is a happy, carefree eatery—elegance and cholesterol be damned. Chef/restaurateur Sam Choy's crab house features great fun and gigantic meals (a Choy trademark). Imagine dining in an all-wood sampan (the centerpiece of the 11,000-sq.-ft. restaurant) and washing your hands in an oversize wok in the center of the room. A 2,000-gallon live-crab tank lines the open kitchen with an assortment of crabs in season: Kona, Maryland, Samoan, Dungeness, and Florida stone crabs. Clam chowder, seafood gumbos, oysters from the oyster bar, and assorted poke are also offered at dinner, which, in Choy fashion, comes complete with soup, salad, and entree. Children's menus are an attractive feature for families. Several varieties of "Big Aloha Beer," brewed onsite, go well with the crab and poke.

580 Nimitz Hwy., Iwilei. ⓒ **808/545-7979.** www.samchoy.com. Reservations recommended for lunch and dinner. Main courses $5–$10 breakfast, $6–$27 lunch, $19–$35 dinner. AE, DC, DISC, MC, V. Sun–Thurs 6:30am–9:30pm; Fri–Sat 6:30am–10pm. Located in the Iwilei industrial area near Honolulu Harbor, across the street from Gentry Pacific Center

MANOA VALLEY/MOILIILI/MAKIKI
Very Expensive

Chef Mavro Restaurant ⭐⭐⭐ PROVENÇAL/HAWAII REGIONAL Chef/owner George Mavrothalassitis, a native of Provence, has fans all over the

Local Chains & Familiar Names

Todai, 1910 Ala Moana Blvd. (© **808/947-1000**), a string of Japanese seafood buffet restaurants with locations ranging from Dallas to Portland to Beverly Center, is packing 'em in at the gateway to Waikiki with bountiful tables of sushi (40 kinds), hot seafood entrees (tempura, calamari, fresh fish, gyoza, king crab legs, teppanyaki), and delectable desserts. There's not much ambience, but no one cares; the food is terrific, the selection impressive, and the operation as smooth as the green tea cheesecake.

Ala Moana Center's third floor is a mecca for dining and schmoozing. The open-air **Mai Tai Bar** is a popular watering hole. Next door are the boisterous **Bubba Gump Shrimp Company** (© **808/949-4867**) and the **California Pizza Kitchen** (© **808/941-7715**), which also maintains branches in Kahala Mall, 4211 Waialae Ave. (© **808/737-9446**), and Pearlridge, 98-1005 Moanalua Road (© **808/487-7741**).

L&L Drive-Inn remains a plate-lunch bonanza islandwide, with 45 locations in Hawaii (36 on Oahu alone). **Zippy's Restaurants** ★—at last count 21 of them on Oahu—is the maestro of quick meals, with a surprisingly good selection of fresh seafood, saimin, chili, and local fare, plus the wholesome new low-fat, vegetarian "Shintani Cuisine," sold in selected branches and deli counters. Every restaurant offers a daily Shintani special, and at several locations (Kahala, Vineyard, Pearlridge, Kapolei, Waipio) you can order cold Shintani items in 2-pound portions to take home and heat up.

It's hard to spend more than $7 for the French and Vietnamese specials at the **Ba-le Sandwich Shops:** pho, croissants as good as the espresso, and wonderful taro/tapioca desserts. Among Ba-le's 20 locations are those at Ala Moana Center (© **808/944-4752**) and 333 Ward Ave. (© **808/591-0935**). A Ba-le location at Manoa Marketplace, 2855 E. Manoa Rd. (© **808/988-1407**), serves a terrific selection of Thai dishes in an enlarged dining area, making it as much a restaurant as a place for takeout food. For smoothies, head to **Jamba Juice,** with seven locations at last count, from Kahala Mall to Ward Village, Kapahulu, Pearlridge, Kailua, and the new DFS Galleria on Kalakaua Ave. (© **808/926-4944**). The ubiquitous **Boston's North End Pizza Bakery** chain claims an enthusiastic following with its reasonable prices and generous toppings. Boston's can be found in Kaimuki, Kailua, Kaneohe, Pearlridge, and Makakilo.

For Italian food, the American chain **Buca di Beppo** (© **808/591-0880**) is in the Ward Entertainment Center, 1030 Auahi. Heaping plates of Italian food, enough to feed a very hungry family, make this place quite popular, along with the reasonable prices. Reservations are a must.

In Waikiki, the local **Hard Rock Cafe** is at 1837 Kapiolani Blvd. (© **808/955-7383**), while at the Ala Moana end of Waikiki, **Outback Steakhouse,** 1765 Ala Moana Blvd (© **808/951-6274**), serves great steaks and is always full. In downtown's Restaurant Row, beef eaters can also chow down at **Ruth's Chris Steak House,** 500 Ala Moana Blvd. (© **808/599-3860**).

world who have admired his creativity since his days at Halekulani's La Mer and Seasons at the Four Seasons Resort Wailea. His restaurant is the only independently operated AAA Four-Diamond restaurant in Hawaii, located in a conveniently accessible, non-touristy neighborhood in McCully where you can order prix fixe or a la carte, with or without wine pairings. And they are dazzling pairings. To his list of signature items (filet of moi with crisp scales, sautéed mushrooms, and saffron coulis; award-winning onaga baked in Hawaiian-salt crust), he's added new favorites: Keahole lobster in an Asian broth; a Hawaiian/Marseilles bouillabaisse; and you-can-cut-it-with-a-fork filet of beef tenderloin crusted with red wine confit onion. Hints of Tahitian vanilla, lemongrass, ogo, rosemary, and Madras curry add exotic flavors to the French-inspired cooking and fresh island ingredients. The desserts are extraordinary, especially the All-American apple tart with Hawaiian vanilla yogurt ice cream. The split-level room is quietly cordial, and the menu changes monthly to highlight seasonal ingredients.

1969 S. King St. ℭ 808/944-4714. Reservations recommended. Main courses $27–$38; prix fixe $48–$85. AE, DC, DISC, MC, V. Tues-Sun 6–9:30pm.

Expensive

Alan Wong's Restaurant ★★★ HAWAII REGIONAL CUISINE Alan Wong is one of Hawaii's most popular chefs, and it's definitely worth the sometimes long waits at this bustling eatery. Worshipful foodies come from all over the state, drawn by the food—which is brilliant—and a menu that is irresistible. The 90-seat room has a glassed-in terrace and open kitchen. Sensitive lighting and curly koa wall panels accent an unobtrusively pleasing environment—casual, but not too. The menu's cutting-edge offerings sizzle with the Asian flavors of lemongrass, sweet-and-sour, garlic, and wasabi, deftly melded with the fresh seafood and produce of the islands. The California roll is a triumph, made with salmon roe, wasabi, and Kona lobster instead of rice, and served warm. We love the opihi shooters, day-boat scallops, and fresh-fish preparations. But don't get attached to any one item; the menu changes daily.

1857 S. King St., 3rd floor. ℭ 808/949-2526. www.alanwongs.com. Reservations recommended. Main courses $26–$38; chef's tasting menu $65. AE, DC, MC, V. Daily 5–10pm.

Moderate

Contemporary Museum Cafe ★ *Finds* HEALTHFUL GOURMET The surroundings are an integral part of the dining experience at this tiny lunchtime cafe, part of an art museum nestled on the slopes of Tantalus amid carefully cultivated Asian gardens, with a breathtaking view of Diamond Head and priceless contemporary artwork displayed indoors and out. The menu is limited to sandwiches, soups, salads, and appetizers, but you won't leave disappointed: They're the perfect lunchtime fare, especially in this environment. Try the grilled vegetable bruschetta, Gorgonzola-walnut spread, tofu burger, black-bean pita wrap, or fresh-fish specials, then crown your meal with flourless chocolate cake. If Noreen Lam's fresh-baked chocolate chip cookies are hiding in the kitchen, snatch 'em.

In The Contemporary Museum, 2411 Makiki Heights Dr. ℭ 808/523-3362. www.tcmhi.org. Reservations recommended. Main courses $8–$10. AE, MC, V. Tues–Sat 11:30am–2:30pm; Sun noon–2:30pm.

Maple Garden SZECHUAN It hums like a top and rarely disappoints. Maple Garden is known for its garlic eggplant, Peking duck, and Chinaman's Hat, a version of mu shu pork, available in a vegetarian version as well. The crisp green beans are out of this world. Other hits: braised scallops with Chinese mushrooms, sautéed spinach, and prawns in chile sauce. There are ample vegetarian selections and dozens of seafood entrees—everything from sea cucumbers and braised salmon to lobster with black-bean sauce. An ever-expanding visual feast adorns the dining-room walls, covered with noted artist John Young's original drawings, sketches, and murals. The staff is unbelievably friendly, and service is top notch.

909 Isenberg St. ⓒ **808/941-6641.** Main courses $5–$23 (most $8–$9). AE, DISC, MC, V. Daily 11am–2pm and 5:30–10pm.

Sushi King *Value* JAPANESE   This is a top value for lovers of Japanese food. Brusque service can't deter the throngs that arrive for the excellent lunch specials. It's tricky to find, located in a small minimall (look for University Flower Shop). Don't pass up the jumbo platters that come with soup, pickles, California roll sushi, and your choice of chicken teriyaki, beef teriyaki, shrimp and vegetable tempura, or calamari and vegetable tempura, all at arrestingly low prices. Other combination lunches offer generous choices that include sashimi, tempura, butterfish, fried oysters, and noodles hot and cold. Early bird specials are offered daily from 5:30 to 6:30pm.

2700 S. King St. ⓒ **808/947-2836.** Reservations recommended. Lunch $7–$10; dinner main courses $12–$25. AE, DC, DISC, MC, V. Wed–Mon 11:30am–2pm and 5:30pm–2am; Tues 5:30–10pm.

Willows LOCAL   Food is not the headliner here; the ambience is. Willows will never re-achieve the charm and nostalgia of its early kamaaina days, but it has been beautifully restored, and the food is more than adequate, with some of the Hawaiian dishes (laulau, lomi salmon, poke) quite good. There just aren't many places in Hawaii anymore with this kind of tropical setting. Shoes click on hardwood floors in rooms surrounded by lush foliage and fountains fed by the natural springs of the area. The dining rooms are open-air, with private umbrella tables scattered about. While the restaurant is buffet only, the upstairs dining room, called Top of the Willows, offers sit-down service and a pricier a la carte menu.

817 Hausten St. ⓒ **808/952-9200.** Reservations recommended. Lunch buffet $15; dinner buffet $25; Sat lunch buffet $18; Sun brunch $25; upstairs a la carte main dishes $12–$20. AE, DC, DISC, MC, V. Mon–Fri 11am–2pm, 5:30–9pm; Sat–Sun 10am–2 pm, 5-9pm. No parking in the neighborhood, valet parking $3.

Inexpensive

Chiang Mai Thai Cuisine THAI   Chiang Mai made sticky rice famous in Honolulu, serving it in bamboo steamers with fish and exotic curries that have retained a following. Menu items include toothsome red, green, and yellow curries; the signature Cornish game hen in lemongrass and spices; and a garlic-infused green papaya salad marinated in tamarind sauce. Spicy shrimp soup, eggplant with basil and tofu, and the vegetarian green curry are favorites.

2239 S. King St. ⓒ **808/941-1151.** Reservations recommended for dinner. Main courses $8–$14. AE, DC, DISC, MC, V. Mon–Fri 11am–2pm; daily 5:30–10pm.

Jimbo's Restaurant ★ *Value* JAPANESE   Jimbo's is the quintessential neighborhood restaurant—small, a line of regulars outside, fantastic house-made noodles and broths, everything good and affordable. A must for any noodle lover, Jimbo's serves homemade udon in a flawless broth with a subtly smoky flavor, then tops the works with shrimp tempura, chicken, eggs, vegetables, seaweed, roasted mochi, and a variety of accompaniments of your choice. Cold noodles (the Tanuki salad is wonderful!), stir-fried noodles, donburi rice dishes with assorted toppings, and combination dinners are other delights. The earthenware pot of noodles, with shiitake mushrooms, vegetables, and udon, plus a platter of tempura on the side, is the top-of-the-line combo. But our fave is the *nabeyaki* (an earthenware pot of udon with tempura on top). Owner Jimbo Motojima, a perfectionist, uses only the finest ingredients from Japan.

1936 S. King St. ℂ 808/947-2211. Reservations not accepted. Main courses $5–$11. MC, V. Daily 11am–2:50pm; Sun–Thurs 5–9:50pm; Fri–Sat 5–10:30pm.

KAIMUKI/KAPAHULU
Expensive

Ninniku-Ya Garlic Restaurant EURO-ASIAN   This is a great garlic restaurant, a paean to the stinking rose. Ninniku-Ya is located in a cozy old home, with tables in a split-level dining room and outdoors under venerable trees. The menu titillates with many garlic surprises and specials. Seasonal specialties (winter pumpkin in garlic potatoes, opah in winter, beet-colored sauces for Valentine's Day) are fine but not necessary, as the staples are quite wonderful. The three-mushroom pasta is sublime, the hot-stone filet mignon tender and tasty, and the garlic rice a meal in itself. Every garlic lover should experience the garlic toast and the roasted garlic with blue cheese. Everything contains garlic, even the house-made garlic gelato, but it doesn't overpower. Yes, that's garlic gelato—and it gets high marks from us. Look for the festive fairy lights lining the building.

3196 Waialae Ave. ℂ 808/735-0784. Reservations recommended. Main dishes $12–$28. DC, DISC, MC, V. Tues–Sun 5:30–9:30pm.

Sam Choy's Diamond Head Restaurant ★ HAWAII REGIONAL   You'll know you're in the right place if you see a parade of exiting diners clutching their Styrofoam bundles, for leftovers are de rigueur at any Sam Choy operation. The servings here are gargantuan, verging on off-putting. Choy has won over a sizable chunk of Hawaii's dining population with his noisy, informal, and gourmet-cum-local style of cooking. Now his kitchen is also the set for his cooking show. The master of poke, Choy serves several of the best versions to be had, and the best way to try them is in the $13 poke sampler (which could even include a tofu poke). We recommended the fried Brie wontons, the seafood laulau, and seared ahi. All dinners include soup and a salad.

449 Kapahulu Ave. ℂ 808/732-8645. www.samchoy.com. Reservations required. Main courses $21–$35; prix fixe $40; Sun brunch buffet $25 adults, $15 children. AE, DC, DISC, MC, V. Mon–Thurs 5:30–9pm; Fri–Sun 5–9:30pm; Sun brunch 9:30am–2pm.

3660 On the Rise ★★ EURO-ISLAND   Since the *Wine Spectator* gave this restaurant its "Award of Excellence" this place has been packed, and with good reason. In his 200-seat restaurant, chef Russell Siu adds an Asian or local touch to the basics: rack of lamb with macadamia nuts, filets of catfish in ponzu sauce, and seared ahi salad with grilled shiitake mushrooms, a local favorite. The ahi katsu, wrapped in nori and fried medium-rare, is a main attraction in the appetizer department, and for dessert, Lisa Siu's warm chocolate cake is one of many raves.

3660 Waialae Ave. ℂ 808/737-1177. Reservations suggested. www.3660.com. Main courses $18–$32; prix fixe $37. AE, DC, DISC, MC, V. Tues–Thurs and Sun 5:30–9pm; Fri–Sat 5:30–10pm.

Moderate

C & C Pasta ★★ *Finds* ITALIAN   Once primarily a takeout place (the deli case is still there), and now Honolulu's best Italian eatery (still with great sauces and homemade pasta to go), this tiny neighborhood gem really sizzles. Dress casual for this neighborhood eatery, relax to the opera playing in the background, but be sure to make a reservation because there's always a line for dinner. Oenophiles gather regularly to uncork their best bottles of red, while an eclectic crowd of pasta lovers tucks into toe-tingling feasts: a *sublime* mushroom risotto with truffle butter, excellent bruschetta and raviolis, and my perpetual favorites, linguine with clams and spaghetti puttanesca. Other excellent choices include the lasagna (meat and vegetarian) or penne with roasted eggplant. If that's not enough, try one of the specials on the blackboard, like the linguine I had recently that was generously flavored with spinach and roasted garlic. Owner Carla Magziar recently added pizza to the menu (with garlic, Gorgonzola, and other such tasty toppings) and a heroic salad of mixed greens, Gorgonzola, hazelnuts, roasted onions and peppers, with fig balsamic dressing. The quality is tops at C & C, the atmosphere is casual, and even the pickiest palates should find something to rave about. *Tip:* If the bread pudding or tiramisu are on the menu, they're a must-have. And if you're in a rush, there's always a pot of puttanesca sauce simmering, and it's great to go. Although service can lag when it's busy, the food is hard to beat.

3605 Waialae Ave. © 808/732-5999. Reservations required for dinner. Main courses $14–$20. MC, V. Mon–Sat 11am–3pm; Sun–Thurs 5–9pm; Fri–Sat 5pm–10pm.

Genki Sushi ⭐ SUSHI   Take your place in line for a seat at one of the U-shaped counters. Conveyor belts parade by with freshly made sushi, usually two pieces per color-coded plate, priced inexpensively. The possibilities are dizzying: spicy tuna topped with scallions, ahi, scallops with mayonnaise, Canadian roll (like California roll, except with salmon), sea urchin, flavored octopus, sweet shrimp, surf clam, corn, tuna salad, and so on. Genki starts with a Japanese culinary tradition and takes liberties with it, so don't be a purist. By the end of the meal, the piled-high plates are tallied up by color, and presto, your bill appears. Combination platters are available for takeout.

900 Kapahulu Ave. © 808/735-8889. A la carte sushi from $1.20 for two pieces; combination platters $7–$39. AE, DC, DISC, MC, V. Daily 11am–3pm; Sun-Thurs 5–9pm; Fri–Sat 5–10pm; takeout available daily 11am–9pm.

Inexpensive

Cafe Laufer ⭐ BAKERY/SANDWICH SHOP   This small, cheerful cafe features frilly decor and sublime pastries—from apple scones and linzer tortes to fruit flan, decadent chocolate mousse, and carrot cake—to accompany the latte and espresso. Fans drop in for simple soups and deli sandwiches on fresh-baked breads; biscotti during coffee break; or a hearty loaf of seven-grain, rye, pumpernickel, or French. The place is a solid hit for lunch; the small but satisfying menu includes soup-salad-sandwich specials for a song, a fabulous spinach salad with dried cranberries and Gorgonzola, and gourmet greens with mango-infused, honey-mustard dressing. The orange-seared shrimp salad and the Chinese chicken salad are hits for the light eater, and the smoked Atlantic salmon with fresh pumpernickel bread and cream cheese, Maui onions, and capers is excellent. The special Saturday-night desserts draw a brisk postmovie business.

3565 Waialae Ave. © 808/735-7717. Most items less than $8. AE, DC, DISC, MC, V. Sun–Mon and Wed–Thurs 10am–10pm; Fri–Sat 10am–11pm.

EAST OF WAIKIKI: KAHALA

Hoku's ⭐⭐⭐ PACIFIC/EUROPEAN   Elegant without being stuffy and creative without being overwrought, the fine-dining room of the Kahala Mandarin offers elegant lunches and dinners combining European finesse with an island touch. This is fusion that really works. The ocean view, open kitchen, and astonishing bamboo floor are stellar features. Reflecting the restaurant's cross-cultural influences, the kitchen is equipped with a *kiawe* grill; an Indian tandoori oven for its chicken and naan bread; and Szechuan woks for the prawn, lobster, tofu, and other stir-fried specialties. The steamed Hong Kong–style whole fresh fish is worthy of a special occasion, and at lunch, the warm Caesar salad, with kiawe-grilled tiger prawns, is smashing. (It's hard to order anything else once you've tried it.) Hoku's Sampler, the chef's daily selection of appetizers, could include sashimi, dim sum, and other dainty tastings, and is a good choice for the curious. Rack of lamb, peppered ahi steak, and the full range of East–West specialties appeal to many tastes.

In the Kahala Mandarin Oriental Hotel, 5000 Kahala Ave. © **808/739-8780.** Reservations recommended. Main courses $20–$33; prix fixe dinner $65. AE, DC, DISC, MC, V. Mon–Fri 11:30am–2pm; daily 5:30–10pm; Sun brunch 10:30am–2:30pm.

Olive Tree Cafe ★★ *Finds* GREEK/EASTERN MEDITERRANEAN Delectables at bargain prices stream out of the tiny open kitchen here. Recently voted "best restaurant in Hawaii under $20" in a local survey, Olive Tree is every neighborhood's dream—a totally hip restaurant with divine Greek fare and friendly prices. There are umbrella tables outside and a few seats indoors, and you order and pay at the counter. Larger parties now have an awning over the sturdy wooden tables on the Koko Head side. The mussel ceviche is broke-the-mouth fabulous, with lemon, lime, capers, herbs, and olive oil—a perfect blend of flavors. The creamy, tender chicken saffron, a frequent special, always elicits groans of pleasure, as does the robust and generous Greek salad, another Olive Tree attraction. We also love the souvlaki, ranging from fresh fish to chicken and lamb, spruced up with the chef's homemade yogurt-dill sauce. A large group can dine here like sultans without breaking the bank, and take in a movie next door, too. BYOB.

4614 Kilauea Ave., next to Kahala Mall. © **808/737-0303.** Main courses $5–$10. No credit cards; checks accepted. Mon–Thurs 5–10pm; Fri–Sun 11am–10pm.

EAST OAHU
HAWAII KAI
Roy's Restaurant ★★★ EUROPEAN/ASIAN This is the first of Roy Yamaguchi's six signature restaurants in Hawaii (he has 2 dozen all over the world). It is still the flagship and many people's favorite, true to its Euro-Asian roots and Yamaguchi's winning formula: open kitchen, fresh ingredients, ethnic touches, and a good dose of nostalgia mingled with European techniques. The menu changes nightly, but you can generally count on individual pizzas, a varied appetizer menu (summer rolls, blackened ahi, hibachi-style salmon), a small pasta selection, and entrees such as lemongrass-roasted chicken, garlic-mustard short ribs, hibachi-style salmon in ponzu sauce, and several types of fresh catch. One of Hawaii's most popular restaurants, Roy's is lit up at night with tiki torches outside; the view from within is of scenic Maunalua Bay. Roy's is also renowned for its high-decibel style of dining—it's always full and noisy. Other Roy's restaurants in Hawaii appear in Poipu, Kauai; Waikoloa, Big Island; Kihei, Maui; and Napili, Maui, where there are two. There's also live music Friday and Saturday evenings from 7:30 to 10:30pm and Sunday from 6:30 to 9:30pm.

6600 Kalanianaole Hwy. © **808/396-7697.** www.roysrestaurant.com. Reservations recommended. Main courses $14–$29. AE, DC, DISC, MC, V. Mon–Thurs 5:30–9:30pm; Fri 5:30–10pm; Sat 5–10pm; Sun 5–9:30pm.

THE WINDWARD COAST
The following restaurants are located on the "Eastern Oahu & the Windward Coast" map on p. 201.

Ahi's Restaurant ⭐ *Finds* AMERICAN/LOCAL   There's no place like Ahi's in Hawaii: beautiful rural setting, tasty local fare, and the generous aloha of Ahi Logan and his three-generation family business. Their restaurant is nothing fancy, a lush roadside oasis with split-level indoor dining and an airy, screened-in room (for larger parties), a charming throwback to pre-resort, pre-plastic Hawaii. A rolling green lawn and towering shade trees surround the wooden structure; it's casual and rural. The shrimp—the menu highlight—comes four ways: steamed, scampi-style, tempura, and spicy, in Ahi's special Hawaiian spicy sauce. The mahimahi and fresh-fish specials are simple but good. On Saturdays, the generous Hawaiian lunch plate includes laulau, grilled fish, shrimp, and *pipikaula* (dried, salted beef). Ask about their Hawaiian Jamborees, with Hawaiian music and hula. Come here when you're hungry for the taste of real Hawaii that resorts long ago abandoned.

53146 Kamehameha Hwy., Punaluu. ℂ **808/293-5650**. Reservations accepted for parties of 8 or more. Main courses $6–$12. No credit cards. Mon–Sat 11am–9pm.

Assaggio ⭐ ITALIAN   This was the mother ship of the Assaggio empire before the Ala Moana branch opened in December 1999 (p. 139). The affordable prices, attentive service, and winning menu items have attracted loyal fans throughout the years. The best-selling homemade hot antipasto has jumbo shrimp, fresh clams, mussels, and calamari in a sauce of cayenne pepper, white wine, and garlic. You can choose linguine, fettuccine, or ziti with 10 different sauces in small or regular portions or any of nine chicken pastas (the chicken Assaggio, with garlic, peppers, and mushrooms, is especially flavorful). Equally impressive is the extensive list of seafood pastas, including the garlic/olive oil sauté. A plus is that servings come in two sizes and prices.

354 Ulunui St., Kailua. ℂ **808/261-2772**. Reservations recommended. Main courses $10–$20. AE, DC, DISC, MC, V. Tues–Sat 11:30am–2:30pm; Sun and Tues–Thurs 5–9:30pm; Fri–Sat 5–10pm.

Good to Go ⭐⭐ DELI   Hidden on the back streets of Kailua is this amazing sandwich/soup/entree deli with healthy food to eat in or take home. Daily specials range from fresh ahi and papaya salsa to teriyaki salmon. Huge salads, just-made sandwiches on homemade bread, and blue plate specials (starting at just $4.50) make this a must-stop for a picnic at the beach or for something to take back to the hotel/condo to eat for dinner.

307 Ulunui St., Kailua. ℂ **808/266-4646**. Sandwiches $5.50–$6.75. No credit cards. Mon–Fri 11am–7pm.

Lucy's Grill 'n Bar ⭐⭐ HAWAIIAN REGIONAL CUISINE   This is one of Kailua's most popular restaurants, not just because of the open-air bar and the outdoor lanai seating, but because the food is terrific. The menu is eclectic Hawaiian Regional Cuisine with lots of choices and giant-size portions. The dress is casual, and the clientele is from the neighborhood. Be sure to order the spicy ahi tower with sushi rice, avocado, wasabi cream and roasted nori to get you started. Any of the fresh fish and seafood is wonderful, especially the Szechwan spiced jumbo tiger prawns with black bean cream and penne pasta or the lemon grass–crusted scallops with yellow Thai curry. Save room for desserts: crème brûleé with Tahitian vanilla bean, dark chocolate soufflé cake, or their "damn fine" apple pie—a la mode, of course.

33 Aulike St., Kailua. ℂ **808/230-8188**. Reservations recommended. Main courses $15–$28. MC, V. Daily 5–10pm.

THE NORTH SHORE

The following restaurants can be located on the "Oahu's North Shore" map on p. 210.

Cafe Haleiwa BREAKFAST/LUNCH/MEXICAN   Haleiwa's legendary breakfast joint is a big hit with surfers, urban gentry with weekend country homes, reclusive artists, and anyone who loves mahimahi plate lunches and heroic sandwiches. It's a wake-up-and-hit-the-beach kind of place, serving generous omelets with names like Off the Wall, Off the Lip, and Breakfast in a Barrel. Surf pictures line the walls, and the ambience is Formica-style casual. And what could be better than an espresso bar to start the day?

66–460 Kamehameha Hwy., Haleiwa. (C) **808/637-5516.** Reservations not accepted. Main courses $6–$11. AE, MC, V. Sunn–Fri 7am–2pm; Sat 7am–12:30pm.

Cholos Homestyle Mexican II (Value) MEXICAN   There's usually a wait at this popular North Shore eatery, where some of the tables have leather stools without backs, and the excellent spinach quesadillas and roasted veggie combination plate are presented with so-so service. Still, this is the unhurried North Shore, and the biggest rush for most folks is getting to and from the beach. We recommend the above-mentioned spinach quesadilla, a generous serving filled with black beans, cheese, and fresh vegetables; the chicken fajita plate, a winner; and the fish taco plate, a steal at $6.75 (just $4 a la carte). There are tables and stools outdoors; indoors, it's dark and cavelike, with loud music, Mexican handicrafts all over the place, and great home-style Mexican, down to the last drop of fresh-tomato salsa.

North Shore Marketplace, 66–250 Kamehameha Hwy. (C) **808/637-3059.** Combination plates $5.25–$9.25. No credit cards. Daily 8am–9pm; breakfast served until 11am.

Haleiwa Joe's AMERICAN/SEAFOOD   Next to the Haleiwa bridge, with a great harbor and sunset view, Haleiwa Joe's serves up fresh local seafood such as whole Hawaiian moi, opakapaka, ahi, and whatever comes in fresh that day. This is a steak-and-seafood harborside restaurant with indoor–outdoor seating and a surf-and-turf menu that could include Parker Ranch New York steak, coconut shrimp, black-and-blue sashimi, and smoked Hawaiian ono. With sandwiches and salads, it's a great lunch stop too. There are only two Haleiwa restaurants close to the ocean, and this is one of them.

66–0011 Kamehameha Hwy., Haleiwa. (C) **808/637-8005.** Reservations not accepted. Main courses $13–$20. V. Mon–Thurs 11:30am–9:30pm (limited menu 4:15–5:30pm); Fri–Sat 11:30am–10:30pm (limited menu 4:15–5:30pm; bar until midnight); Sun 11:30am–9:30pm (limited menu 3:45–5pm).

Jameson's by the Sea SEAFOOD   Duck into this roadside watering hole across the street from the ocean for cocktails, sashimi, and its celebrated salmon paté, or for other hot and cold appetizers, salads, and sandwiches. The grilled crab-and-shrimp sandwich on sourdough bread is a perennial, and it's hard to go wrong with the fresh-fish sandwich of the day, grilled plain and simple. Upstairs, the much pricier dining room opens its doors 5 nights a week for the usual surf-and-turf choices: fresh opakapaka, ulua (Hawaiian jack fish), and mahimahi; scallops in lemon butter and capers; and lobster tail, New York steak, and filet mignon.

62–540 Kamehameha Hwy., Haleiwa. (C) **808/637-4336.** Reservations recommended. Main courses $13–$39 in upstairs dining room; downstairs lunch menu $7–$14. AE, DC, DISC, MC, V. Downstairs, daily 11am–5pm; pub menu Mon–Tues 5–9pm, Sat–Sun 11am–9pm. Upstairs, Wed–Sun 5–9pm.

Kua Aina (★) (Value) AMERICAN   "What's the name of that sandwich shop on the North Shore?" We hear that often. Although this North Shore staple has expanded to the Ward Centre area in Kakaako, you'd never know it by the lines here. It's as busy as ever, and because there are never enough tables, many diners get their burgers to go and head for the beach. Kua Aina's thin and spindly french fries are renowned islandwide and are the perfect accompaniment to its legendary burgers. Fat, moist, and homemade, the burgers can be ordered with avocado, bacon, and many other accompaniments, including Ortega chiles and cheese. The tuna/avocado, roast turkey, and mahimahi sandwiches are excellent alternatives to the burgers. Kua Aina is unparalleled on the island and is a North Shore must, eclipsing its fancier competitors at lunch. Plans call for a move to a larger location just a few hundred feet away on Kamehameha Highway, so call ahead to check.

66–214 Kamehameha Hwy., Haleiwa. (C) **808/637-6067.** Most items less than $6. No credit cards. Daily 11am–8pm.

Paradise Found Cafe VEGETARIAN   A tiny cafe behind Celestial Natural Foods, Paradise Found is a bit of a hunt, but stick with it. For more than a few townies, the North Shore sojourn begins at Paradise, the only pure vegetarian restaurant in these parts. Their smoothies (especially the Waimea Shorebreak) are legendary, and their organic soups, fresh-pressed vegetable juices, sandwiches, and healthy plate lunches are a great launch to a Haleiwa day. Vegan substitutes are willingly made in place of dairy products and to accommodate dietary needs.

66–443 Kamehameha Hwy., Haleiwa. (C) **808/637-4540.** All items less than $7. No credit cards. Mon–Sat 9am–5pm; Sun 10am–5pm.

5 Beaches

THE WAIKIKI COAST
ALA MOANA BEACH PARK ★★
Quite possibly America's best urban beach, gold-sand Ala Moana ("by the sea"), on sunny Mamala Bay, stretches for more than a mile along Honolulu's coast between downtown and Waikiki. This 76-acre midtown beach park, with spreading lawns shaded by banyans and palms, is one of the island's most popular playgrounds. It has a man-made beach, created in the 1930s by filling a coral reef with Waianae Coast sand, as well as its own lagoon, yacht harbor, tennis courts, music pavilion, bathhouses, picnic tables, and enough wide-open green spaces to accommodate 4 million visitors a year. The water is calm almost year-round, protected by black lava rocks set offshore. There's a large parking lot as well as metered street parking.

WAIKIKI BEACH ★★★
No beach anywhere is so widely known or so universally sought after as this narrow, 1½-mile-long crescent of imported sand (from Molokai) at the foot of a string of high-rise hotels. Home to the world's longest-running beach party, Waikiki attracts nearly 5 million visitors a year from every corner of the planet. First-timers are always amazed to discover how small Waikiki Beach actually is, but there's always a place for them under the tropical sun here.

Waikiki is actually a string of beaches that extends between **Sans Souci State Recreational Area,** near Diamond Head to the east, and **Duke Kahanamoku Beach,** in front of the Hilton Hawaiian Village, to the west. Great stretches along Waikiki include **Kuhio Beach,** next to the Sheraton Moana Surfrider, which provides the quickest access to the Waikiki shoreline; the stretch in front of the Royal Hawaiian Hotel known as **Grey's Beach,** which is canted so it

Beaches & Outdoor Pursuits on Oahu

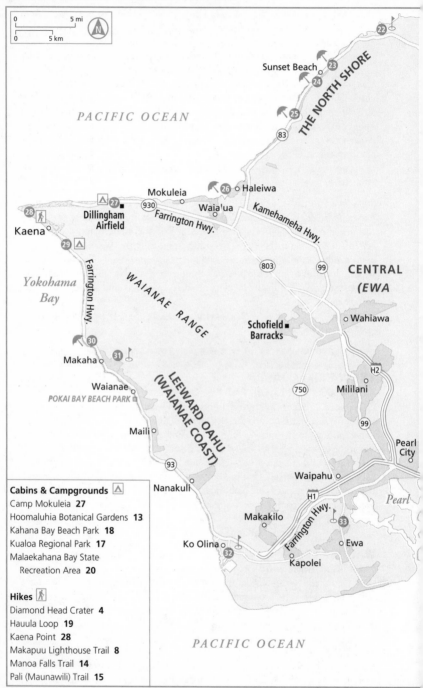

0   5 mi
0   5 km

PACIFIC OCEAN

Sunset Beach **THE NORTH SHORE** 22

23
24

25

83

26 Haleiwa
Mokuleia
27 Waialua
Dillingham 930
Airfield   Farrington Hwy.   Kamehameha Hwy.

28
Kaena   29

Yokohama   WAIANAE RANGE   803   99   **CENTRAL**
Bay   **(EWA**

Farrington Hwy.

Schofield ■   Wahiawa
Barracks

30
Makaha   31

Waianae   LEEWARD OAHU
POKAI BAY BEACH PARK ■   (WAIANAE COAST)   750   Mililani   H2

Maili   99

93   Pearl
City

Waipahu
Nanakuli   H1   Pearl

Makakilo   Farrington Hwy.   33

Ko Olina   32   Ewa
Kapolei

PACIFIC OCEAN

Cabins & Campgrounds △
Camp Mokuleia **27**
Hoomaluhia Botanical Gardens **13**
Kahana Bay Beach Park **18**
Kualoa Regional Park **17**
Malaekahana Bay State
    Recreation Area **20**

Hikes 🚶
Diamond Head Crater **4**
Hauula Loop **19**
Kaena Point **28**
Makapuu Lighthouse Trail **8**
Manoa Falls Trail **14**
Pali (Maunawili) Trail **15**

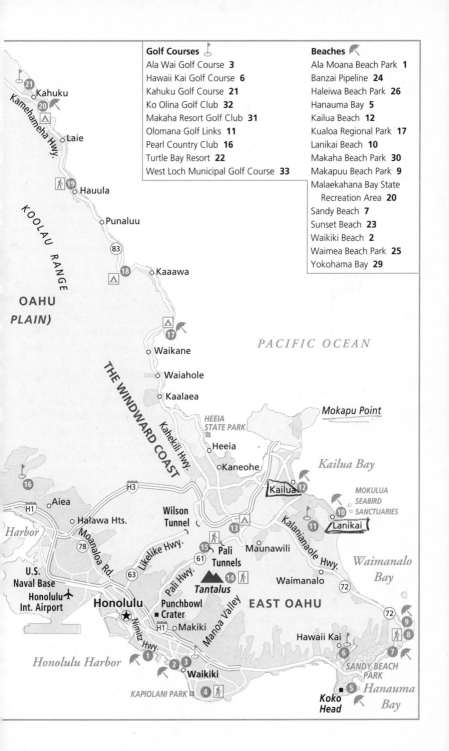

Golf Courses
Ala Wai Golf Course **3**
Hawaii Kai Golf Course **6**
Kahuku Golf Course **21**
Ko Olina Golf Club **32**
Makaha Resort Golf Club **31**
Olomana Golf Links **11**
Pearl Country Club **16**
Turtle Bay Resort **22**
West Loch Municipal Golf Course **33**

Beaches
Ala Moana Beach Park **1**
Banzai Pipeline **24**
Haleiwa Beach Park **26**
Hanauma Bay **5**
Kailua Beach **12**
Kualoa Regional Park **17**
Lanikai Beach **10**
Makaha Beach Park **30**
Makapuu Beach Park **9**
Malaekahana Bay State
  Recreation Area **20**
Sandy Beach **7**
Sunset Beach **23**
Waikiki Beach **2**
Waimea Beach Park **25**
Yokohama Bay **29**

catches the rays perfectly; and **Sans Souci,** the small, popular beach in front of the New Otani Kaimana Beach Hotel that's locally known as "Dig Me" Beach because of all the gorgeous bods who strut their stuff here.

Waikiki is fabulous for swimming, board- and bodysurfing, outrigger canoe-ing, diving, sailing, snorkeling, and pole fishing. Every imaginable type of marine equipment is available for rent here. Facilities include showers, life-guards, restrooms, grills, picnic tables, and pavilions at the **Queen's Surf** end of the beach (at Kapiolani Park, between the zoo and the aquarium). The best place to park is at Kapiolani Park, near Sans Souci.

EAST OAHU
HANAUMA BAY ★★
Oahu's most popular snorkeling spot is this volcanic crater with a broken sea wall; its small, curved, 2,000-foot gold-sand beach is packed elbow-to-elbow with people year-round. The bay's shallow shoreline water and abundant marine life are the main attractions, but this good-looking beach is also popular for sun-bathing and people-watching. Serious divers shoot "the slot" (a passage through the reef) to gain Witch's Brew, a turbulent cove, then brave strong currents in 70-foot depths at the bay mouth to see coral gardens, turtles, and even sharks. (Divers: Beware of the Molokai Express, a strong current.) You can snorkel in the safe, shallow (10 ft.) inner bay, which along with the beach, is almost always crowded. Because Hanauma Bay is a conservation district, you may look at but not touch or take any marine life here. Feeding the fish is also prohibited.

A new $13 million Marine Education Center just opened with exhibits and a 7-minute video orienting visitors on this Marine Life Sanctuary. The 10,000-square-foot center includes a training room, gift shop, public restrooms, snack bar and staging area for the motorized tram, which for a fee (50¢ for 1 ride, or $2 for an all-day pass)will take you down the steep road to the beach. Facilities include parking, restrooms, a pavilion, a grass volleyball court, lifeguards, bar-becues, picnic tables, and food concessions. Alcohol is prohibited in the park; there is no smoking past the visitor center. Expect to pay $1 per vehicle to park and a $3 per person entrance fee (children 12 and under are free). If you're driv-ing, take Kalanianaole Highway to Koko Head Regional Park. Avoid the crowds by going early, about 8am, on a weekday morning; once the parking lot's full, you're out of luck. Alternatively, take TheBus to escape the parking problem: The Hanauma Bay Shuttle runs from Waikiki to Hanauma Bay every ½ hour from 8:45am to 1pm; you can catch it at the Ala Moana Hotel, the Ilikai Hotel, or any city bus stop. It returns every hour from noon to 4:30pm. Hanauma Bay is closed on Tuesdays, so the fish can have a day off.

SANDY BEACH ★
Sandy Beach is one of the best bodysurfing beaches on Oahu; it's also one of the most dangerous. It's better to just stand and watch the daredevils literally risk their necks at this 1,200-foot-long gold-sand beach that's pounded by wild waves and haunted by a dangerous shore break and strong backwash. Weak swimmers and children should definitely stay out of the water here; Sandy Beach's heroic lifeguards make more rescues in a year than those at any other beach. Visitors, easily fooled by experienced bodysurfers who make wave-riding look easy, often fall victim to the bone-crunching waves. Lifeguards post flags to alert beachgoers to the day's surf: Green means safe, yellow caution, and red indicates very dan-gerous water conditions; always check the flags before you dive in.

Facilities include restrooms and parking. Go weekdays to avoid the crowds and weekends to catch the bodysurfers in action. From Waikiki, drive east on the H-1, which becomes Kalanianaole Highway; proceed past Hawaii Kai, up the hill to Hanauma Bay, past the Halona Blow Hole, and along the coast. The next big, gold, sandy beach you see ahead on the right is Sandy Beach. TheBus no. 22 will also get you here.

MAKAPUU BEACH PARK 🐠

Makapuu Beach, the most famous bodysurfing beach in Hawaii, is a beautiful 1,000-foot-long gold-sand beach cupped in the stark black Koolau cliffs on Oahu's easternmost point. Even if you never venture into the water, it's worth a visit just to enjoy the great natural beauty of this classic Hawaiian beach. You've probably already seen it in countless TV shows, from *Hawaii Five-O* to *Magnum, P.I.*

In summer, the ocean here is as gentle as a Jacuzzi, and swimming and diving are perfect; come winter, however, Makapuu is hit with expert bodysurfers, who come for big, pounding waves that are too dangerous for regular swimmers. Small boards—3 feet or less with no skeg (bottom fin)—are permitted; regular board surfing is banned by state law.

Facilities include restrooms, lifeguards, barbecue grills, picnic tables, and parking. To get here, follow Kalanianaole Highway toward Waimanalo, or take TheBus no. 57 or 58.

THE WINDWARD COAST

LANIKAI BEACH 🐠🐠

One of Hawaii's best spots for swimming, gold-sand Lanikai's crystal-clear lagoon is like a giant saltwater swimming pool that you're lucky enough to be able to share with the resident tropical fish and sea turtles. Too gorgeous to be real, this is one of Hawaii's postcard-perfect beaches: It's a mile long and thin in places, but the sand's as soft as talcum powder. Prevailing onshore trade winds make this an excellent place for sailing and windsurfing. Kayakers often paddle out to the two tiny offshore Mokulua islands, which are seabird sanctuaries. Because Lanikai is in a residential neighborhood, it's less crowded than other Oahu beaches; the perfect place to enjoy a quiet day. Sun worshipers should arrive in the morning, though, as the Koolau Range blocks the afternoon rays.

There are no facilities here, just off-street parking. From Waikiki, take the H-1 to the Pali Highway (Hwy. 61) through the Nuuanu Pali Tunnel to Kailua, where the Pali Highway becomes Kailua Road as it proceeds through town. At Kalaheo Avenue, turn right and follow the coast about 2 miles to Kailua Beach Park; just past it, turn left at the T intersection and drive uphill on Aalapapa Drive, a one-way street that loops back as Mokulua Drive. Park on Mokulua Drive and walk down any of the eight public-access lanes to the shore. Or, take TheBus no. 56 or 57 (Kailua) and then transfer to the shuttle bus.

KAILUA BEACH 🐠🐠🐠

Windward Oahu's premier beach is a 2-mile long, wide golden strand with dunes, palm trees, panoramic views, and offshore islets that are home to seabirds. The swimming is excellent, and the azure waters are usually decorated with bright sails; this is Oahu's premier windsurfing beach as well. It's also a favorite spot to sail catamarans, bodysurf the gentle waves, or paddle a kayak. Water conditions are quite safe, especially at the mouth of Kaelepulu Stream, where toddlers play in the freshwater shallows at the middle of the beach park. The water's usually about 78°F (26°C), the views are spectacular, and the setting, at the foot of the sheer, green Koolaus, is idyllic. Best of all, the crowds haven't found it yet.

Frommer's Favorite Oahu Experiences

Getting a Tan on Waikiki Beach.   The best spot for catching the rays on the world-famous beach is in front of the big, pink Royal Hawaiian Hotel—the beach here is set at the perfect angle for sunning. It's also a great spot for people-watching. Get here early; by midday (when the rays are at their peak), it's towel-to-towel out there.

Exploring Oahu's Rain Forests.   In the misty sunbeams, colorful birds flit among giant ferns and hanging vines, while towering tropical trees form a thick canopy that shelters all below in cool shadows. This emerald world is a true Eden. For the full experience, try Manoa Falls Trail, a walk of about a mile that ends at a freshwater pool and waterfall.

Snorkeling the Glistening Waters of Hanauma Bay.   This underwater park, once a volcanic crater, is teeming with a rainbow of tropical fish. Bordered by a 2,000-foot gold-sand beach, the bay's shallow water (10 ft. in places) is perfect for neophyte snorkelers. Arrive early to beat the crowds—and don't forget that the bay is closed on Tuesday. **Aloha Dive Shop,** Koko Marina Shopping Center (© **808/395-5922**), can set you up with fins, mask, and snorkel for just $7 a day.

Hiking to the Top of Diamond Head Crater.   Almost everyone can make this easy hike to the top of Hawaii's most famous landmark. The 1½-mile round-trip goes up to the top of the 750-foot volcanic cone, where you have a 360° view of Oahu. Allow an hour for the trip up and back, bring a buck for the entry fee, and don't forget your camera.

Heading to Waimea Bay When the Surf's Up.   From November to March, monstrous waves—some 30 feet tall—roll into Waimea. When they break on the shore, the ground actually shakes and everyone on the beach is covered with salt spray mist. The best surfers in the world paddle out to challenge these freight trains. It's amazing to see how small they appear in the lip of the giant waves. This is an experience you'll never forget—and the show won't cost you a dime.

Watching the Ancient Hawaiian Sport of Canoe Paddling.   On weekday evenings and weekend days from February to September, hundreds of paddlers gather at Ala Wai Canal and practice taking traditional Hawaiian canoes out to sea. Find a comfortable spot at Ala Wai Park, next to the canal, and watch the canoe paddlers re-create this centuries-old sport.

Finding a Bargain at the Aloha Flea Market.   Just 50¢ will get you into this all-day show at the Aloha Stadium parking lot, where more than 1,000 vendors sell everything from junk to jewels. Go early for the best deals. Open Wednesday, Saturday, and Sunday from 6am to 3pm.

The 35-acre beach park is intersected by a freshwater stream and watched over by lifeguards. Facilities include picnic tables, barbecues, restrooms, a volleyball court, a public boat ramp, free parking, and an open-air cafe. Kailua's new bike path weaves through the park, and Windsurfer and kayak rentals are available as well. To get here, take Pali Highway (Hwy. 61) to Kailua, drive through town,

Attending a Hawaiian-Language Church Service.   Built in 1842, Kawa-iahao Church, 957 Punchbowl St. (near King Street), is the Westminster Abbey of Hawaii; the vestibule is lined with portraits of the Hawaiian monarchy, many of whom were coronated in this very building. The coral church is a perfect setting to experience an all-Hawaiian service, complete with Hawaiian song. Hawaiian-language services are held every Sunday at 10:30am, and admission is free—let your conscience be your guide as to a donation.

Visiting the Lei Sellers in Chinatown.   There's a host of cultural sights and experiences to be had in Honolulu's Chinatown. Wander through this several-square-block area with its jumble of exotic shops offering herbs, Chinese groceries, and acupuncture services. Be sure to check out the lei sellers on Maunakea Street (near N. Hotel Street), where Hawaii's finest leis go for as little as $2.50.

Experiencing a Turning Point in America's History: The Bombing of Pearl Harbor.   Standing on the deck of the USS *Arizona* Memorial at Pearl Harbor, with the ship underneath, is an unforgettable experience. On that fateful day—December 7, 1941—the 608-foot *Arizona* sank in just 9 minutes, killing 1,177 of the men on board, after being bombed during the Japanese air raid that sent the United States to war. Go early; you'll wait 2 to 3 hours if you visit at midday. You must wear closed-toed shoes; no sandals allowed.

Watching the Sun Sink into the Pacific from a Hill Named After a Sweet Potato.   Actually, it's more romantic than it sounds. Puu Ualakaa State Park, at the end of Round Hill Drive, translates into "rolling sweet potato hill." This majestic view of the sunset is not to be missed.

Ordering a Shave Ice in a Tropical Flavor You Can Hardly Pronounce.   In Haleiwa, stop at Matsumoto Shave Ice, 66–087 Kamehameha Hwy., for a snow cone with an exotic flavor poured over the top, such as the local favorite, the fruity *li hing mui,* or try one with sweet Japanese adzuki beans hidden inside. This taste of tropical paradise goes for just $1.

Listening to the Soothing Sounds of Hawaiian Music.   Sit under the huge banyan tree at the Sheraton Moana Surfrider's Banyan Veranda in Waikiki, order a cocktail, and sway to live Hawaiian music any night of the week. Another quintessential sunset oasis is the Halekulani's House Without a Key, a sophisticated oceanfront lounge with wonderful hula and steel-guitar music, a great view of Diamond Head, and the best mai tais on the island.

turn right on Kalaheo Avenue, and go a mile until you see the beach on your left. Or, take TheBus no. 56 or 57 into Kailua, then the no. 70 shuttle.

KUALOA REGIONAL PARK ★★

This 150-acre coco palm–fringed peninsula is the biggest beach park on the windward side and one of Hawaii's most scenic. It's located on Kaneohe Bay's north shore, at the foot of the spiky Koolau Ridge. The park has a broad, grassy lawn and a long, narrow, white-sand beach ideal for swimming, walking, beach-combing, kite-flying, or just enjoying the natural beauty of this once-sacred Hawaiian shore, listed on the National Register of Historic Places. The waters are shallow and safe for swimming year-round. Offshore is Mokolii, the pictur-esque islet otherwise known as Chinaman's Hat. At low tide, you can swim or wade out to the island, which has a small sandy beach and is a bird preserve—so don't spook the red-footed boobies. Lifeguards are on duty.

The park is located on Kamehameha Highway (Hwy. 83) in Kualoa; you can get here via TheBus no. 55.

THE NORTH SHORE
MALAEKAHANA BAY STATE RECREATION AREA ★★

This white-sand crescent, almost a mile long, lives up to just about everyone's image of the perfect Hawaii beach. It's excellent for swimming. On a weekday, you may be the only one here; but should some net fisherman—or kindred soul—intrude upon your delicious privacy, you can swim out to Goat Island (or wade across at low tide) and play Robinson Crusoe. (The islet is a sanctuary for seabirds and turtles, so don't chase 'em, brah.) Facilities include restrooms, bar-becue grills, picnic tables, outdoor showers, and parking.

To get here, take Kamehameha Highway (Hwy. 83) 2 miles north of the Poly-nesian Cultural Center; as you enter the main gate, you'll come upon the wooded beach park. Or, you can take TheBus no. 52.

WAIMEA BEACH PARK ★★

This deep, sandy bowl has gentle summer waves that are excellent for swim-ming, snorkeling, and bodysurfing. To one side of the bay is a huge rock that local kids like to climb up and dive from. In this placid scene, the only clues of what's to come in winter are those evacuation whistles on poles beside the road. But what a difference a season makes: Winter waves pound the narrow bay, sometimes rising to 50 feet high. When the surf's really up, very strong currents and shore breaks sweep the bay—and it seems like everyone on Oahu drives out to Waimea to get a look at the monster waves and those who ride them. Week-ends are great for watching the surfers; to avoid the crowds, go on weekdays. *A safety tip:* Don't get too distracted by the waves and forget to pay attention when parking or crossing the road.

Facilities include lifeguards, restrooms, showers, parking, and nearby restau-rants and shops in Haleiwa town. The beach is located on Kamehameha High-way (Hwy. 83); from Waikiki, you can take TheBus no. 52.

LEEWARD OAHU/THE WAIANAE COAST
MAKAHA BEACH PARK ★★

When surf's up here, it's spectacular: Monstrous waves pound the beach. This is the original home of Hawaii's big-wave surfing championship; surfers today know it as the home of Buffalo's Big Board Surf Classic, where surfers ride the waves on 10-foot-long wooden boards in the old Hawaiian style of surfing.

Impressions

The boldness and address with which we saw them perform these diffi-cult and dangerous maneuvers was altogether astonishing.
— Capt. James Cook's observations of Hawaiian surfers

Nearly a mile long, this half-moon, gold-sand beach is tucked between 231-foot Lahilahi Point, which locals call Black Rock, and Kepuhi Point, a toe of the Waianae mountain range. Summer is the best time to hit this beach—the waves are small, the sand abundant, and the water safe for swimming. Children hug the shore on the north side of the beach, near the lifeguard stand, while surfers dodge the rocks and divers seek an offshore channel full of big fish. *A caveat:* This is a "local" beach; you are welcome, of course, but you can expect "stink eye" (mild approbation) if you are not respectful of the beach and the local residents who use the facility all the time.

Facilities include restrooms, lifeguards, and parking. To get here, take the H-1 freeway to the end of the line, where it becomes Farrington Highway (Hwy. 93), and follow it to the beach; or you can take TheBus no. 51.

YOKOHAMA BAY ★

Where Farrington Highway (Hwy. 93) ends, the wilderness of Kaena Point State Park begins. It's a remote 853-acre coastline park of empty beaches, sand dunes, cliffs, and deep-blue water. This is the last sandy stretch of shore on the northwest coast of Oahu. Sometimes, it's known as Keawalua Beach or Puau Beach, but everybody here calls it Yokohama, after the Japanese immigrants who came from that port city to work the cane fields and fished along this shoreline. When the surf's calm—mainly in summer—this is a good area for snorkeling, diving, swimming, shore fishing, and picnicking. When surf's up, board and bodysurfers are out in droves; don't go in the water then unless you're an expert. There are no lifeguards or facilities, except at the park entrance, where there's a restroom and lifeguard stand. No bus service.

6 Watersports

For general advice on the activities listed below, see "The Active Vacation Planner," in chapter 2.

If you want to rent beach toys (like a mask, snorkel, and fins; boogie boards; surfboards; kayaks; and more), check out the following Waikiki rental shops: **Snorkel Bob's,** on the way to Hanauma Bay at 700 Kapahulu Ave. (at Date Street), Honolulu (© **808/735-7944;** www.snorkelbob.com); and **Aloha Beach Service,** in the Sheraton Moana Surfrider Hotel, 2365 Kalakaua Ave. (© **808/ 922-3111,** ext. 2341) in Waikiki. On Oahu's windward side, try **Kailua Sailboards & Kayaks,** 130 Kailua Rd., a block from the Kailua Beach Park (© **808/262-2555;** www.kailuasailboards.com). On the North Shore, get equipment from **Surf-N-Sea,** 62–595 Kamehameha Hwy., Haleiwa (© **808/ 637-9887;** www.surfnsea.com).

BOATING

A funny thing happens to people when they come to Hawaii: Maybe it's the salt air, the warm tropical nights, or the blue Hawaiian moonlight, but otherwise-rational people who have never set foot on a boat in their life suddenly want to go out to sea. You can opt for a "booze cruise" with a thousand loud, rum-soaked strangers, or you can sail on one of these special yachts, all of which will take you out **whale-watching** in season (roughly Dec–Apr). For fishing charters, see "Sportfishing," below.

Captain Bob's Adventure Cruises ★ See the majestic Windward Coast the way it should be seen—from a boat. Captain Bob will take you on a 4-hour, lazy-day sail of Kaneohe Bay aboard his 42-foot catamaran, which skims across the almost-always calm water above the shallow coral reef, lands at the disappearing sandbar Ahu o Laka, and takes you past two small islands to snorkel spots full of tropical fish and, sometimes, turtles. The color of the water alone is worth the price. This is an all-day affair, but hey, getting out on the water is the reason you came to Hawaii, right? A shuttle will pick you up at your Waikiki hotel between 9 and 9:30am and bring you back at about 4pm—it's a lot quicker than taking TheBus.

Kaneohe Bay. ℂ **808/942-5077.** $69 adults, $59 children 13–17, $49 children 12 and under. Rates include all-you-can-eat barbecue lunch and transportation from Waikiki hotels. No cruises Sun and holidays. Bus 55 or 56.

Dream Cruises ⚓ If you aren't lucky enough to be in Hawaii during humpback-whale season (roughly Jan–Apr), you can go **dolphin-watching** ⚓ instead. Dream Cruises offers year-round dolphin-watching cruises that check out friendly pods of bottle-nosed and spinner dolphins near Yokahama Bay on the northern end of Oahu. This might be your only chance to get "up-close and personal" with these protected marine mammals. During whale season, the company guarantees that if you don't see whales, you can sail again for free. Departing from the Kewalo Basin are a range of cruises, including a snorkel/splash tour that anchors off Waikiki for snorkeling, swimming, and lunch; and a 2-hour sunset dinner-and-dancing cruise with views of the Waikiki skyline.

Kewalo Basin and Waianae Small Boat Harbor. ℂ **800/400-7300** or 808/592-5200. www.dream-cruises. com. $28–$66 adults, $19–$35 children 4–12. Rates include hotel pickup and drop-off, plus some meals.

Honolulu Sailing Co. This company has been in business for 2 decades, offering a variety of sailing activities. Our favorite is the Diamond Head snorkel-picnic sail on the waves. During whale season (roughly Jan–Apr), check out the half- and full-day adventures to see whales, dolphins, flying fish, and sea turtles.

Pier 2, Honolulu Harbor (across from Restaurant Row). ℂ **800/829-0114** or 808/239-3900. Fax 808/ 239-9718. www.honsail.com. $125 adults for full-day cruises, half-price for children 12 and under; $75 adults for half day, half-price for children. For all-day cruises, park at Restaurant Row, 500 Ala Moana Blvd. (entrance on Pohukaina St., between South and Punchbowl sts.), for $6 all day; for half-day cruises, park in metered spaces in front of Pier 2, for 50¢ per hr. Bus: 19, 20, or 47.

Navatek I ⚓⚓ You've never been on a boat, you don't want to be on a boat, but here you are being dragged aboard one. Why are you boarding this weird-looking vessel? It guarantees that you'll be "seasick-free," that's why. The 140-foot-long *Navatek I* isn't even called a boat; it's actually a SWATH (Small Waterplane Area Twin Hull) vessel. That means the ship's superstructure—the part you ride on—rests on twin torpedo-like hulls that cut through the water so you don't bob like a cork and spill your mai tai. It's the smoothest ride on Mamala Bay. In fact, *Navatek I* is the only dinner cruise ship to receive U.S. Coast Guard certification to travel beyond Diamond Head.

Sunset dinner cruises leave Pier 6 (across from the Hawaii Maritime Museum) nightly. If you have your heart set on seeing the city lights, take the royal Sunset Dinner Cruise, which runs from 5:15 to 7:15pm. The best deal is the **lunch cruise,** with full buffet lunch and a great view of Oahu offshore. During the **whale season** (roughly Dec–Apr), you get whales to boot. The lunch cruise lasts from 11:30am to 2pm. Both cruises include live Hawaiian music.

Aloha Tower Marketplace, Pier 6. c/o Hawaiian Cruises Ltd. ℂ **808/973-1311.** www.go-atlantis.com. Dinner cruises $120 adults, $72 children 2–11; lunch cruises $49 adults, $29 children 2–11. Validated parking before 4:30pm $3, after 4:30pm flat parking fee of $2. Bus: 8, 19, 20, 55, 56, or 57; or the Waikiki Trolley to stop no. 7.

12-2:30 (52)

BODYBOARDING (BOOGIE BOARDING) & BODYSURFING

Good places to learn to bodyboard are in the small waves of **Waikiki Beach** and **Kailua Beach,** and **Bellows Field Beach Park,** off Kalanianaole Highway (Hwy. 72) in Waimanalo, which is open to the public on weekends (from noon Fri–midnight on Sun and holidays). To get here, turn toward the ocean on Hughs Road, then right on Tinker Road, which takes you right to the park.

See above for a list of rental shops where you can get a boogie board.

OCEAN KAYAKING

For a wonderful adventure, rent a kayak, arrive at Lanikai Beach just as the sun is appearing, and paddle across the emerald lagoon to the pyramid-shaped islands off the beach called Mokulua—it's an experience you won't forget. Kayak equipment rental starts at $10 an hour, or $37 for a day. In Waikiki, try **Prime Time Sports,** Fort DeRussy Beach (© 808/949-8952); on the windward side, check out **Kailua Sailboards & Kayaks,** 130 Kailua Rd., a block from Kailua Beach Park (© 808/262-2555; www.kailuasailboards.com). On the North Shore, contact **Waimea Falls Park,** 59–864 Kamehameha Hwy., Haleiwa (© 888/973-9200 or 808/638-8511), which also has guided kayak tours in the stream for $35 for 1 hour and in the ocean for $45.

First-timers should go to **Kailua Sailboards & Kayaks,** 130 Kailua Rd., in Kailua (© 808/262-2555; www.kailuasailboards.com), where the company offers a guided tour with the novice in mind in a safe, protected environment. Included in the tour are lunch, all equipment, and transportation from Waikiki hotels for $79.

SCUBA DIVING

Oahu is a wonderful place to scuba dive, especially for those interested in wreck diving. One of the more famous wrecks in Hawaii is the *Mahi,* a 185-foot former minesweeper easily accessible just south of Waianae. Abundant marine life makes this a great place to shoot photos—schools of lemon butterfly fish and taape are so comfortable with divers and photographers that they practically pose. Eagle rays, green sea turtles, manta rays, and white-tipped sharks occasionally cruise by as well, and eels peer out from the wreck.

For nonwreck diving, one of the best dive spots in summer is **Kahuna Canyon.** In Hawaiian, *kahuna* means priest, wise man, or sorcerer; this massive amphitheater, located near Mokuleia, is a perfect example of something a sorcerer might conjure up. Walls rising from the ocean floor create the illusion of an underwater Grand Canyon. Inside the amphitheater, crabs, octopi, slippers, and spiny lobsters abound (be aware that taking them in summer is illegal), and giant trevally, parrot fish, and unicorn fish congregate as well. Outside the amphitheater, you're likely to see an occasional shark in the distance.

Because Oahu's best dives are offshore, your best bet is to book a two-tank dive from a dive boat. Hawaii's oldest and largest outfitter is **Aaron's Dive Shop,** 307 Hahani Street, Kailua (© 808/262-2333; www.hawaii-scuba.com), which offers boat and beach dive excursions off the coast. The boat dives cost from $115 per person, including two tanks and transportation from the Kailua shop. The beach dive off the North Shore in summer or the Waianae Coast in winter is the same price as a boat dive, including all gear and transportation, so Aaron's recommends the boat dive.

In Waikiki, **South Sea Aquatics,** 2155 Kalakaua, Suite 112 (next to Planet Hollywood; © 808/922-0852; www.ssahawaii.com), features two-tank boat dives, with transportation to and from Waikiki hotels, for $80 without gear and

Moments **Experiencing Jaws: Up Close and Personal**

You're 4 miles out from land, which is just a speck on the horizon, with hundreds of feet of open ocean. Suddenly from out of the blue depths a shape emerges: the sleek, pale shadow of a 6-foot-long gray reef shark, followed quickly by a couple of 10-foot-long Galapagos sharks. Within a couple of heart beats, you are surrounded by sharks on all sides. Do you panic? No, you paid $120 to be in the midst of these jaws of the deep. Of course, there is a 6-foot by 6-foot by 10-foot aluminum shark cage separating you from all those teeth.

It happens every day on the **North Shore Shark Adventure** (© 808/ 256-2769, www.hawaiisharkadventures.com), the dream of Captain Joe Pavsek, who decided after some 30 years of surfing and diving to share the experience of seeing a shark with visitors. To make sure that the predators of the deep will show up for the viewing, Captain Pavsek heaves "chum," a not very appetizing concoction of fish trimmings and entrails, over the side of his 26-foot boat, Kailolo. It's sort of like ringing the dinner bell—after a few minutes the sharks (generally gray reef, Galapagos, and sandbars, ranging from 5–15 ft.) show up—sometimes just a few, sometimes a couple dozen. Depending on the sea conditions and the weather, snorkelers can stay in the cage as long as they wish, with the sharks just inches away. The shark cage, connected to the boat with wire line, floats several feet back and holds up to four snorkelers (it's comfortable with 2 but pretty snug at full capacity). You can stay on the boat and view the sharks from a more respectable distance for just $60. The more adventurous, down in the cage with just thin aluminum separating them from the sharks, are sure to create a memory they won't forget.

$96 with all equipment. On the North Shore, **Surf-N-Sea,** 62–595 Kamehameha Hwy., Haleiwa (© **808/637-9887;** fax 808/637-3008; www.surfnsea. com), has dive tours from the shore (starting at $65 for 1 tank), from a boat ($110 for 2 tanks), and at night ($100 for 1 tank). Surf-N-Sea also rents equipment and can point you to the best dive sites in the area.

Another great resource for diving on your own is the University of Hawaii Sea Grant's *Dive Hawaii Guide,* which describes 44 dive sites on the various Hawaiian islands, including Oahu. Send $2 to UH/SGES, Attn: Dive Guide, 2525 Correa Rd., HIG 237, Honolulu, HI 96822.

SNORKELING

Some of the best snorkeling in Oahu is at **Hanauma Bay** ★★. It's crowded—sometimes it seems there are more people than fish—but Hanauma has clear, warm, protected waters and an abundance of friendly reef fish, including Moorish idols, scores of butterfly fish, damsel fish, and wrasses. Hanauma Bay has two reefs, an inner and an outer—the first for novices, the other for experts. The inner reef is calm and shallow (less than 10 ft.); in some places, you can just wade and put your face in the water. Go early: It's packed by 10am and closed on Tuesdays. For details, see "Beaches," earlier.

Braver snorkelers may want to head to **Shark's Cove,** on the North Shore just off Kamehameha Highway, between Haleiwa and Pupukea. Sounds risky, we know, but we've never seen or heard of any sharks in this cove, and in summer, this big, lava-edged pool is one of Oahu's best snorkel spots. Waves splash over the natural lava grotto and cascade like waterfalls into the pool full of tropical fish. To the right of the cove are deep-sea caves to explore.

The uninitiated might prefer a lesson and a snorkel tour. **Surf-N-Sea,** 62–595 Kamehameha Hwy., Haleiwa (© **808/637-9887**), has 2-hour tours, with equipment, starting at $45.

SPORTFISHING

Kewalo Basin, located between the Honolulu International Airport and Waikiki, is the main location for charter fishing boats on Oahu. From Waikiki, take Kalakaua Ewa (west) beyond Ala Moana Center; Kewalo Basin is on the left, across from Ward Centre. Look for charter boats all in a row in their slips; when the fish are biting, the captains display the catch of the day in the afternoon. You can also take TheBus no. 19 or 20 (Airport).

The best way to book a sportfishing charter is through the experts; the best booking desk in the state is **Sportfish Hawaii** ★ (© **877/388-1376** or 808/ 396-2607; www.sportfishhawaii.com), which not only books boats on Oahu, but on all islands. These fishing vessels have been inspected and must meet rigorous criteria to guarantee that you will have a great time. Prices range from $700 to $817 for a full-day exclusive charter (you, plus 5 friends, get the entire boat to yourself), $500 to $625 for a ½-day exclusive, or from $150 for a full-day share charter (you share the boat with 5 other people).

SUBMARINE DIVES

Here's your chance to play Jules Verne and experience the underwater world from the comfort of a submarine, which will take you on an adventure below the surface in high-tech comfort. The entire trip is narrated as you watch tropical fish and sunken ships just outside the sub; if swimming's not your thing, this is a great way to see Hawaii's spectacular sea life. Shuttle boats to the sub leave from Hilton Hawaiian Village Pier. The cost is $90 to $100 for adults (book on the Internet for just $81–$90), $40 ($35 booked online) for kids 12 and under (children must be at least 36 in. tall). Call **Atlantis Submarines** ★ (© **800/548-6262** or 808/973-9811; www.go-atlantis.com) to reserve. To save money, ask about advance purchase for the shorter "Discovery Adventure," which is only $60 ($50 online) for adults, $40 ($35 online) for children. *A word of warning:* The ride is safe for everyone, but skip it if you suffer from claustrophobia.

SURFING

In summer, when the water's warm and there's a soft breeze in the air, the south swell comes up. It's surf season in Waikiki, the best place to learn how to surf on Oahu. For lessons, go early to **Aloha Beach Service,** next to the Sheraton Moana Surfrider, 2365 Kalakaua Ave., Waikiki (© **808/922-3111**). The beach boys offer surfing lessons for $25 an hour; board rentals are $8 for 1 hour and $12 for 2 hours. You must know how to swim.

Surfboards are also available for rent at **Surf-N-Sea,** 62–595 Kamehameha Hwy., Haleiwa (© **808/637-9887;** www.surfnsea.com), for $5 to $7 an hour. They also offer lessons for $65 for 2 hours. For the best surf shops, where you can soak in the culture as well as pick up gear, also see "Shopping A to Z," later in this chapter.

On the windward side, call **Kimo's Surf Hut,** 151 Hekili St., across from Daiei, in Kailua (ℂ **808/262-1644**). Kimo and his wife, Ruth, couldn't be more friendly and helpful. In addition to surfboards ($20 a day) and body board for rent, Kimo has his own personal collection of vintage surfboards, lovingly displayed on the walls of his shop. If you have the time, Kimo will gladly tell you the pedigree and history of each board. Although Kimo doesn't have formal surfing lessons, he'd be happy to give you pointers.

More experienced surfers should drop in on any surf shop around Oahu, or call the **Surf News Network Surfline** (ℂ **808/596-SURF**) to get the latest surf conditions. **The Cliffs,** at the base of Diamond Head, is a good spot for advanced surfers; 4- to 6-foot waves churn here, allowing high-performance surfing.

If you're in Hawaii in winter and want to see the serious surfers catch the really big waves, bring your binoculars and grab a front-row seat on the beach near **Kalalua Point.** To get here from Waikiki, take the H-1 toward the North Shore, veering off at H-2, which becomes Kamehameha Highway (Hwy. 83). Keep going to the funky surf town of Haleiwa and Waimea Bay; the big waves will be on your left, just past Pupukea Beach Park.

WINDSURFING

Windward Oahu's **Kailua Beach** is the home of champion and pioneer windsurfer Robbie Naish; it's also the best place to learn to windsurf. The oldest and most established windsurfing business in Hawaii is **Naish Hawaii/Naish Windsurfing Hawaii,** 155-A Hamakua Dr., Kailua (ℂ **800/767-6068** or 808/262-6068; www.naish.com). The company offers everything: sales, rentals, instruction, repair, and free advice on where to go when the wind and waves are happening. Private lessons start at $55 for one, $75 for two for a 60- to 90-minute lesson (depending on your skill level); beginner equipment rental is $25 for a ½ day and $30 for a full day. Kite surfing lessons are also available ($100 for 1½ hours). **Kailua Sailboards & Kayaks,** 130 Kailua Rd., a block from the Kailua Beach Park (ℂ **808/ 262-2555;** www.kailuasailboards.com), offers 3-hour small-group lessons ($49 per person, including all gear) and rentals of windsurfing equipment, surfboards, snorkel gear, and ocean kayaks.

Windsurfer wannabes on the North Shore can contact **Surf-N-Sea,** 62–595 Kamehameha Hwy., Haleiwa (ℂ **808/637-9887;** www.surfnsea.com), which offers equipment rental ($12 an hour or $45 for the day), as well as private lessons (beginning at $65 for 2–3 hr.).

7 Nature Hikes

People think Oahu is just one big urban island, so they're always surprised to discover that the great outdoors is less than an hour away from downtown Honolulu. Highlights of the island's 33 major hiking trails include razor-thin ridgebacks and deep waterfall valleys.

Check out Stuart Ball's *The Hikers Guide to Oahu* (University of Hawaii Press, 1993) before you go. Another good source of hiking information on Oahu is the state's **Na Ala Hele** (Trails to Go On) Program (ℂ **808/973-9782** or 808/587-0058).

For a free Oahu recreation map listing all 33 trails in the program, write to the **Department of Land and Natural Resources,** 1151 Punchbowl St., Room 131, Honolulu, HI 96813 (ℂ **808/587-0300**). The department will also send free topographic trail maps on request and issue camping permits.

Another good source of information is the *Hiking/Camping Information Packet*, which costs $7 (postage included); to order, contact **Hawaii Geographic Maps and Books,** 49 S. Hotel St., Honolulu, HI 96813 (© **800/538-3950** or 808/538-3952). This store also carries a full line of United States Geographic Survey topographic maps, very handy for hikers.

Also be sure to get a copy of *Hiking on Oahu: The Official Guide,* a hiking safety brochure that includes instructions on hiking preparation, safety procedures, emergency phone numbers, and necessary equipment; for a copy, contact Erin Lau, Trails and Access Manager, **City and County of Honolulu** (© **808/973-9782**); the **Hawaii Nature Center,** 2131 Makiki Heights Dr. (© **808/955-0100**); or **The Bike Shop,** 1149 S. King St. (© **808/596-0588**).

The **Hawaiian Trail and Mountain Club,** P.O. Box 2238, Honolulu, HI 96804, offers regular hikes on Oahu. You bring your own lunch and drinking water and meet up with the club at the Iolani Palace to join them on a hike. The club also has an information packet on hiking and camping in Hawaii, as well as a schedule of all upcoming hikes; send $2 plus a legal-size, self-addressed, stamped envelope to the address above.

Other organizations that offer regularly scheduled hikes are the **Sierra Club,** P.O. Box 2577, Honolulu, HI 96803 (www.hi.sierraclub.org); the **Nature Conservancy,** 1116 Smith St., Suite 201, Honolulu, HI 96817 (© **808/537-4508,** ext. 220); and the **Hawaii Nature Center,** 2131 Makiki Heights Dr. (© **808/955-0100**).

Casual hikers and walkers will enjoy the maps put out by the Hawaii Department of Health on great places to walk. The two brochures are *The Honolulu Walking Map,* with 16 routes in Honolulu ranging from 1½ miles to 3½ miles, and *The Fun Fitness Map,* with 12 walking adventures all over Oahu. To get a free copy of each, send a self-addressed, stamped envelope (with four 37¢ stamps) to Angela Wagner, Health, Promotions and Education Branch, Room 217, 1250 Punchbowl St., Honolulu, HI 96813. For more information, call © **808/586-4661.**

HONOLULU AREA HIKES
DIAMOND HEAD CRATER ★★★
This is a moderate, but steep, walk to the summit of Hawaii's most famous landmark. Kids love to look out from the top of the 760-foot volcanic cone, where they have 360-degree views of Oahu up the leeward coast from Waikiki. The 1½-mile round-trip takes about 1½ hours and the entry fee is $1.

Diamond Head was created by a volcanic explosion about half a million years ago. The Hawaiians called the crater *Leahi* (meaning the brow of the ahi, or tuna, referring to the shape of the crater). Diamond Head was considered a sacred spot; King Kamehameha offered human sacrifices at a *heiau* (temple) on the western slope. It wasn't until the 19th century that Mount Leahi got its current name: A group of sailors found what they thought were diamonds in the crater; it turned out they were just worthless calcite crystals, but the Diamond Head moniker stuck.

Before you begin your journey to the top of the crater, put on some decent shoes (rubber-soled tennies are fine) and gather a flashlight (you'll walk through several dark tunnels), binoculars (for better viewing at the top), water (very important), a hat to protect you from the sun, and a camera. You might want to put all your gear in a pack to leave your hands free for the climb. If you don't have a flashlight or your hotel can't lend you one, you can buy a small one for a few dollars as part of a Diamond Head climbers' "kit" at the gift shop at the **New Otani Kaimana Beach Hotel,** on the Diamond Head end of Kalakaua Avenue, just past the Waikiki Aquarium and across from Kapiolani Park.

Go early, preferably just after the 6:30am opening, before the midday sun starts beating down. The hike to the summit of Diamond Head starts at Monsarrat and 18th avenues on the crater's inland (or mauka) side. To get here, take TheBus no. 58 from the Ala Moana Shopping Center or drive to the intersection of Diamond Head Road and 18th Avenue. Follow the road through the tunnel (which is closed from 6pm–6am) and park in the lot. The trailhead starts in the parking lot and proceeds along a paved walkway (with handrails) as it climbs up the slope. You'll pass old World War I and II pillboxes, gun emplacements, and tunnels built as part of the Pacific defense network. Several steps take you up to the top observation post on Point Leahi. The views are incredible.

If you want to go with a guide, the Clean Air Team leads a guided hike to the top of Diamond Head every Saturday. The group gathers at 9am, near the front entrance to the Honolulu Zoo (look for the rainbow windsock). Hikers should bring a flashlight and a $5 fee. Each person will be given a bag and asked to help keep the trail clean by picking up litter. For more information, call 🕾 **808/ 948-3299.**

MANOA FALLS TRAIL 🌟🌟

This easy, ¾ mile (one-way) hike is terrific for families; it takes less than an hour to reach idyllic Manoa Falls. The trailhead, marked by a footbridge, is at the end of Manoa Road, past Lyon Arboretum. The staff at the arboretum prefers that hikers do not park in their lot, so the best place to park is in the residential area below Paradise Park; you can also get to the arboretum via TheBus no. 5. The often-muddy trail follows Waihi Stream and meanders through the forest reserve past guavas, mountain apples, and wild ginger. The forest is moist and humid and is inhabited by giant bloodthirsty mosquitoes, so bring repellent. As we went to press, the state of Hawaii was still assessing the safety of the trail after a series of landslides. Before you venture out, call 🕾 **808/587-0300** to check if the trail is open.

EAST OAHU HIKES
MAKAPUU LIGHTHOUSE TRAIL 🌟

You've seen this famous old lighthouse on episodes of *Magnum, P.I.* and *Hawaii Five-O.* No longer manned by the Coast Guard (it's fully automated now), the lighthouse is the goal of hikers who challenge a precipitous cliff trail to gain an airy perch over the Windward Coast, Manana (Rabbit) Island, and the azure Pacific. It's about a 45-minute, mile-long hike from Kalanianaole Highway (Hwy. 72), along a paved road that begins across from Hawaii Kai Executive Golf Course and winds around the 646-foot-high sea bluff to the lighthouse lookout.

To get to the trailhead from Waikiki, take Kalanianaole Highway (Hwy. 72) past Hanauma Bay and Sandy Beach to Makapuu Head, the southeastern tip of the island; you can also take TheBus no. 57 or 58. Look for a sign that says NO VEHICLES ALLOWED on a gate to the right, a few hundred yards past the entrance to the golf course. The trail isn't marked, but it's fairly obvious: Just follow the abandoned road that leads gradually uphill to a trail that wraps around Makapuu Point. It's a little precarious, but anyone in reasonably good shape can handle it.

Blowhole alert: When the south swell is running, usually in summer, there are a couple of blowholes on the south side of Makapuu Head that put the famous Halona blowhole to shame.

WINDWARD OAHU HIKES
HAUULA LOOP ⊛

For one of the best views of the coast and the ocean, follow the Hauula Loop Trail on the windward side of the island. It's an easy, 2½-mile loop on a well-maintained path that passes through a whispering ironwood forest and a grove of tall Norfolk pines. The trip takes about 3 hours and gains some 600 feet in elevation.

To get to the trail, take TheBus no. 55 or follow Highway 83 to Hauula Beach Park. Turn toward the mountains on Hauula Homestead Road; when it forks to the left at Maakua Road, park on the side of the road. Walk along Maakua Road to the wide, grassy trail that begins the hike into the mountains. The climb is fairly steep for about 300 yards but turns into easier-on-the-calves switchbacks as you go up the ridge. Look down as you climb: You'll spot wildflowers and mushrooms among the matted needles. The trail continues up, crossing Waipilopilo Gulch, where you'll see several forms of native plant life. Eventually, you reach the top of the ridge, where the views are spectacular.

Camping is permitted along the trail, but it's difficult to find a place to pitch a tent on the steep slopes and in the dense forest growth. There are a few places along the ridge, however, that are wide enough for a tent. Contact the **Division of Forestry and Wildlife,** 1151 Punchbowl St., Honolulu, HI 96813 (© **808/ 587-0166**), for information on camping permits.

PALI (MAUNAWILI) TRAIL ⊛

For a million-dollar view of the Windward Coast, take this easy 11-mile (one-way) foothill trail. The trailhead is about 6 miles from downtown Honolulu, on the windward side of the Nuuanu Pali Tunnel, at the scenic lookout just beyond the hairpin turn of the Pali Highway (Hwy. 61). Just as you begin the turn, look for the scenic overlook sign, slow down, and pull off the highway into the parking lot (sorry, no bus service available).

The mostly flat, well-marked, easy-to-moderate trail goes through the forest on the lower slopes of the 3,000-foot Koolau Mountain range and ends up in the backyard of the coastal Hawaiian village of Waimanalo. Go halfway to get the view and return to your car, or have someone meet you in 'Nalo.

TO LAND'S END: A LEEWARD OAHU HIKE
KAENA POINT ⊛

At the very western tip of Oahu lie the dry, barren lands of Kaena Point State Park, 853 acres consisting of a remote, wild coastline of jagged sea cliffs, deep gulches, sand dunes, endangered plant life, and a wind- and surf-battered coastline. *Kaena* means "red-hot" or "glowing" in Hawaiian; the name refers to the brilliant sunsets visible from the point.

Kaena is steeped in numerous legends. A popular one concerns the demigod Maui: Maui had a famous hook that he used to raise islands from the sea. He decided that he wanted to bring the islands of Oahu and Kauai closer together, so one day he threw his hook across the Kauai Channel and snagged Kauai (which is actually visible from Kaena Point on clear days). Using all his might, Maui was able to pull loose a huge boulder, which fell into the waters very close to the present lighthouse at Kaena. The rock is still called Pohaku o Kauai (the rock from Kauai). Like Black Rock in Kaanapali on Maui, Kaena is thought of as the point on Oahu from which souls depart.

To hike out to the departing place, take the clearly marked trail from the parking lot of Kaena Point State Park. The moderate, 5-mile, round-trip hike to the point will take a couple of hours. The trail along the cliff passes tide pools abundant in marine life and rugged protrusions of lava reaching out to the turbulent sea; seabirds circle overhead. There are no sandy beaches, and the water is nearly always turbulent. In winter, when a big north swell is running, the waves at Kaena are the biggest in the state, averaging heights of 30 to 40 feet. Even when the water appears calm, offshore currents are powerful, so don't plan to swim. Go early in the morning to see the schools of porpoises that frequent the area just offshore.

To get to the trailhead from Honolulu or Waikiki, take the H-1 west to its end; continue on Highway 93 past Makaha and follow Highway 930 to the end of the road. There's no bus service.

8 Camping & Wilderness Cabins

If you don't plan to bring your own camping gear, you can rent or buy it at **Omar The Tent Man,** 94–158 Leole St., (from H-2 take the 2nd Waipahu exit, then at the first light, make a right on to Leole Street), Waipahu (② **808/677-8785**). Also check out "Surf & Sports" under "Shopping A to Z," later in this chapter.

The best places to camp on Oahu are listed below. TheBus's Circle Island route can get you to or near all these sites, but remember: On TheBus, you're allowed only one bag, which has to fit under the seat. If you have more gear, you're going to have to drive or take a cab.

WINDWARD OAHU
HOOMALUHIA BOTANICAL GARDENS 🍀
This windward campground outside Kaneohe is an almost secret place and a real treasure. It's hard to believe that you're just a half-hour from downtown Honolulu.

Hoomaluhia, or "peace and tranquility," accurately describes this 400-acre botanical garden at the foot of the jagged Koolaus. In this lush, tropical setting, gardens are devoted to plants specific to tropical America, native Hawaii, Polynesia, India, Sri Lanka, and Africa. A 32-acre lake sits in the middle of the scenic park (no swimming or boating are allowed, though), and there are numerous hiking trails. The visitor center offers free guided walks Saturday at 10am and Sunday at 1pm.

Facilities for this tent-camp area include restrooms, cold showers, dish-washing stations, picnic tables, and water. A public phone is available at the visitor center. Shopping and gas are available in Kaneohe, 2 miles away. Permits are free, but stays are limited to 3 nights (Fri, Sat, and Sun only); the office is closed on Sunday. The gate is locked at 4pm and doesn't open again until 9am, so you're locked in for the night.

Hoomaluhia Botanical Gardens is at 45–680 Luluku Rd. (at Kamehameha Hwy.), Kaneohe (② **808/233-7323**). From Waikiki, take H-1 to the Pali Highway (Hwy. 61); turn left on Kamehameha Highway (Hwy. 83); at the fourth light, turn left on Luluku Road. TheBus no. 55 and 56 stop nearby on Kamehameha Highway; from here, you have to walk 2 miles to the visitor center.

KUALOA REGIONAL PARK 🍀🍀
This park has a spectacular setting on a peninsula on Kaneohe Bay. The gold-sand beach is excellent for snorkeling, and fishing can be rewarding as well (see section 5 of this chapter, "Beaches."). There are two campgrounds: Campground A—located in a wooded area with a sandy beach and palm, ironwood,

kamani, and monkeypod trees—is mainly used for groups. It does have a few sites for families, except during the summer (Jun–Aug), when the Department of Parks and Recreation conducts a children's camping program here. Campground B is on the main beach; it has fewer shade trees but a great view of Mokolii Island. Facilities at both sites include restrooms, showers, picnic tables, drinking fountains, and a public phone. Campground A also has sinks for dish washing, a volleyball court, and a kitchen building. Gas and groceries are available in Kaaawa, 2½ miles away. The gate hours at Kualoa Regional Park are 7am to 8pm; if you're not back to the park by 8pm, you're locked out for the night.

Permits are free but limited to 5 days (no camping on Wed and Thur). Contact the **Honolulu Department of Parks and Recreation,** 650 S. King St., Honolulu, HI 96713 (© **808/523-4525**), for information and permits. Kualoa Regional Park is located in the 49–600 area of Kamehameha Highway, across from Mokolii Island. Take the Likelike Highway (Hwy. 63); after the Wilson Tunnel, get in the right lane and turn off on Kahakili Highway (Hwy. 83). Or, take TheBus no. 55.

KAHANA BAY BEACH PARK 🛪🛪

Lying under Tahiti-like cliffs, with a beautiful, gold-sand crescent beach framed by pine-needle casuarina trees, Kahana Bay Beach Park is a place of serene beauty. You can swim, bodysurf, fish, hike, and picnic, or just sit and listen to the trade winds whistle through the beach pines. Only tent and vehicle camping are allowed at this oceanside oasis. Facilities include restrooms, picnic tables, drinking water, public phones, and a boat-launching ramp. *Note:* The restrooms are located at the north end of the beach, far away from the camping area, and there are no showers.

There's a $5 fee for camping, and you must get a permit. Permits are limited to 5 nights; contact the **Department of Land and Natural Resources,** State Parks Division, P.O. Box 621, Honolulu, HI 96809 (© **808/587-0300;** www. state.hi.us/dlnr). Kahana Bay Beach Park is located in the 52–222 block of Kamehameha Highway (Hwy. 83) in Kahana. From Waikiki, take the H-1 west to the Likelike Highway (Hwy. 63). Continue north on the Likelike, through the Wilson Tunnel, turning left on Highway 83; Kahana Bay is 13 miles down the road on the right. You can also get here via TheBus no. 55.

THE NORTH SHORE
MALAEKAHANA BAY STATE RECREATION AREA 🛪🛪

This is one of the most beautiful beach-camping areas in the state, with a mile-long, gold-sand beach on Oahu's Windward Coast (see "Beaches," earlier in this chapter, for details). There are two areas for tent camping. Facilities include picnic tables, restrooms, showers, sinks, drinking water, and a phone. For your safety, the park gate is closed between 6:45pm and 7am; vehicles cannot enter or exit during those hours. Groceries and gas are available in Laie and Kahuku, each less than a mile away.

Permits are $5 and limited to 5 nights; they may be obtained at any state park office, including the **Department of Land and Natural Resources,** State Parks Division, P.O. Box 621, Honolulu, HI 96809 (© **808/587-0300;** www.state.hi. us/dlnr). The recreation area is located on Kamehameha Highway (Hwy. 83) between Laie and Kahuku. Take the H-2 to Highway 99 to Highway 83 (both roads are called Kamehameha Hwy.); continue on Highway 83 just past Kahuku. You can also get here via TheBus no. 55.

CAMP MOKULEIA ⭐

The centerpiece of this 9-acre campground is a quiet, isolated beach on Oahu's North Shore, 4 miles from Kaena Point. Camping is available on the beach or in a grassy, wooded area. Activities include swimming, surfing, shore fishing, and beachcombing. This place makes a great getaway. Facilities include tent camping, cabins, and lodge accommodations. The tent-camping site has portable chemical toilets, a water spigot, and outdoor showers; there are no picnic tables or barbecue grills, so come prepared. The cabins sleep up to 22 people in bunk beds. The cabins are $150 per night for the 14-bed cabin and $225 per night for the 22-bed cabin. Rooms at the lodge are $60 for a shared bathroom and $70 for a private bathroom. Tent camping is $6 per person, per night. Many groups use the camp, but there's a real sense of privacy. Parking is $3 per day. Reservations are required; contact **Camp Mokuleia,** 68–729 Farrington Hwy., Waialua, HI 96791 (© **808/637-6241**).

Camp Mokuleia is located on Farrington Highway, west of Haleiwa. From Waikiki, take the H-1 to the H-2 exit; stay on H-2 until the end. Where the road forks, bear left to Waialua on Highway 803, which turns into Highway 930 to Kaena Point. Look for the green fence on the right, where a small sign at the driveway reads CAMP MOKULEIA, EPISCOPAL CHURCH OF HAWAII.

9 Golf & Other Outdoor Pursuits

GOLF

Oahu has nearly 3 dozen golf courses, ranging from bare-bones municipal courses to exclusive country-club courses with membership fees running to six figures a year. Below are the best of a great bunch.

As you play Oahu's courses, you'll come to know that the windward courses play much differently than the leeward courses. On the windward side, the prevailing winds blow from the ocean to shore, and the grain direction of the greens tends to run the same way—from the ocean to the mountains. Leeward golf courses have the opposite tendency: The winds usually blow from the mountains to the ocean, with the grain direction of the greens corresponding.

Tips on beating the crowds and saving money: Oahu's golf courses tend to be crowded, so we suggest that you go midweek if you can. Also, most island courses have twilight rates that offer substantial discounts if you're willing to tee off in the afternoon, usually between 1 and 3pm; these are included in the listings below, where applicable.

Transportation note: TheBus does not allow golf-club bags on board, so if you want to use TheBus to get to a course, you're going to have to rent clubs there.

WAIKIKI

Ala Wai Municipal Golf Course   The Guinness Book of World Records lists this as the busiest golf course in the world; some 500 rounds a day are played on

---

⟨ *Tips* Insider Tip

For last-minute and discount tee times, call **Stand-by Golf** (© **888/ 645-BOOK**), www.stand-bygolf.com, which offers discounted tee times for same-day or next-day golfing. Call between 7am and 11pm for a guaranteed tee time with up to 50% discount off green fees.

this 18-hole municipal course within walking distance of Waikiki's hotels. For years, we've held off recommending this par 70, 6,020-yard course because it was so busy (tee times taken by local retirees), but a recent scandal, involving telephone company employees tapping into the tee time reservation system to get tee times for themselves and their friends, has shaken up the old system, and visitors now have a better chance of playing here. It still is a challenge to get a tee time, and the computerized tee reservations system for all of Oahu's municipal courses will only allow you to book 3 days in advance, but keep trying. Ala Wai basically is a flat layout, bordered by the Ala Wai Canal one side and the Manoa-Palolo Stream on the other. It's less windy than most Oahu courses, but pay attention to the 372-yard, par-4, first hole which demands a straight and long shot to the very tiny green. If you miss, you can make it up on the 478-yard, par-5 10th hole—the green is reachable in two, so with a two-putt, a birdie is within reach.

404 Kapahulu Ave., Waikiki. ✆ **808/733-7387** (golf course) or 808/296-2000 tee time reservations. Greens fee: $12 weekdays, $16 weekends, plus $16 cart for two. From Waikiki turn left on Kapahulu Ave.; the course is on the mauka side of Ala Wai Canal. Bus: 19, 20, 22.

EAST OAHU

Hawaii Kai Golf Course   This is actually two golf courses in one. The par-72, 6,222-yard **Hawaii Kai Championship Golf Course** is moderately challenging, with scenic vistas. The course is forgiving to high-handicap golfers, although it does have a few surprises. The par-3 **Hawaii Kai Executive Golf Course** is fun for beginners and those just getting back in the game after a few years. The course has lots of hills and valleys, with no water hazards and only a few sand traps. Lockers are available.

8902 Kalanianaole Hwy., Honolulu. ✆ **808/395-2358.** www.hawaiikaigolf.com. Greens fees: Champion Course $90 Mon.–Fri., $100 Sat.–Sun, with twilight rates $60; Executive Course $37 Mon.–Fri., $42 Sat.–Sun. Take H-1 east past Hawaii Kai; it's immediately past Sandy Beach on the left. Bus: 58.

THE WINDWARD COAST

Olomana Golf Links   Low-handicap golfers may not find this gorgeous course difficult, but the striking views of the craggy Koolau mountain ridge alone are worth the fees. The par-72, 6,326-yard course is popular with locals and visitors alike. The course starts off a bit hilly on the front nine but flattens out by the back nine. The back nine has its own surprises, including tricky water hazards. The first hole, a 384-yard, par-4 that tees downhill and approaches uphill, is definitely a warm-up. The next hole is a 160-yard, par-3 that starts from an elevated tee to an elevated green over a severely banked, V-shaped gully. Shoot long here—it's longer than you think, and short shots tend to roll all the way back down the fairway to the base of the gully. This course is very, very green; the rain gods bless it regularly with brief passing showers. You can spot the regular players here—they all carry umbrellas, wait patiently for the squalls to pass, and then resume play. Reservations are a must. Facilities include a driving range, practice greens, club rental, pro shop, and restaurant.

41–1801 Kalanianaole Hwy., Waimanalo. ✆ **808/259-7926.** www.olomanagolflinks.com. Greens fees $67; twilight $40 weekdays, $44 weekends. Take H-1 to the Pali Hwy. (Hwy. 61); turn right on Kalanianaole Hwy.; after 5 miles, it will be on the left. Bus: 57.

THE NORTH SHORE

Kahuku Golf Course *Finds*   This nine-hole budget golf course is a bit funky. There are no club rentals, no clubhouse, and no facilities other than a few pull carts that disappear with the first handful of golfers. But a round at this scenic oceanside course amidst the tranquility of the North Shore is quite an experience nonetheless. Duffers will love the ease of this recreational course, and weight watchers will be happy to walk the gently sloping greens. Don't forget to bring your camera for the views (especially at holes 3, 4, 7, and 8, which are right on the ocean). No reservations are taken; tee times are first-come, first-served, and with plenty of retirees happy to sit and wait, the competition is fierce for early tee times. Bring your own clubs and call ahead to check the weather. The cost for this experience? Ten bucks!

56-501 Kamehameha Hwy, Kajuku. © 808/293-5842. Greens fees: $8 weekdays, $10 weekends for 9 holes. Take H-1 west to H-2; follow H-2 through Wahiawa to Kamehameha Hwy. (Hwy. 99, then Hwy. 83); follow it to Kahuku.

Turtle Bay Resort ★   This North Shore resort is home to two of Hawaii's top golf courses. The 18-hole **Arnold Palmer Course** (formerly the Links at Kuilima) was designed by Arnold Palmer and Ed Seay. Turtle Bay used to be labeled a "wind tunnel"; it still is one, though the casuarina (ironwood) trees have matured and dampened the wind somewhat. But Palmer and Seay never meant for golfers to get off too easy; this is a challenging course. The front nine, with rolling terrain, only a few trees, and lots of wind, play like a British Isles course. The back nine have narrower, tree-lined fairways and water. The course circles Punahoolapa Marsh, a protected wetland for endangered Hawaiian waterfowl.

Another option is the **George Fazio–designed Course**—the only one Fazio designed in Hawaii—a par-71, 6,200-yard course. Larry Keil, pro at Turtle Bay, says that people like the Fazio course because it's more of a forgiving resort course, without the water hazards and bunkers of the more challenging Palmer course. The sixth hole has two greens so you can play the hole as a par-3 or a par-4. The toughest hole has to be the par-3, 176-yard second hole, where you tee off across a lake with the trade winds creating a mean crosswind. The most scenic hole is the seventh, where the ocean is on your left; if you're lucky, you'll see whales cavorting in the winter months. Facilities include a pro shop, driving range, putting and chipping green, and snack bar. Weekdays are best for tee times.

57–049 Kamehameha Hwy., Kahuku. © 808/293-8574 or 808/293-9094. www.turtlebayresort.com. Greens fees at the Palmer Course: $160 (Turtle Bay guests pay $115); twilight fees are $85 ($60 for guests). Greens fees at the Fazio: $155 (guests pay $110); twilight fees are $85 ($60 for guests). Take H-1 west past Pearl City; when the freeway splits, take H-2 and follow the signs to Haleiwa; at Haleiwa, take Hwy. 83 to Turtle Bay Resort. Bus: 52 or 55.

LEEWARD OAHU

Ko Olina Golf Club ★★★   *Golf Digest* named this 6,867-yard, par-72 course one of "America's Top 75 Resort Courses" in 1992. The Ted Robinson–designed course has rolling fairways and elevated tee and water features. The signature hole—the 12th, a par-3—has an elevated tee that sits on a rock garden with a cascading waterfall. Wait until you get to the 18th hole, where you'll see and hear water all around you—seven pools begin on the right side of the fairway and slope down to a lake. A waterfall is on your left off the elevated green. You'll have no choice but to play the left and approach the green over the water. Book in advance; this course is crowded all the time. Facilities include a driving range, locker rooms, Jacuzzi, steam rooms, and a restaurant and bar. Lessons are available.

92–1220 Aliinui Dr., Kapolei. © 808/676-5309. www.koolinagolf.com. Greens fees: $145 ($125 for Ihilani Resort guests); twilight rates (after 1pm in winter and 2:30pm in summer) are $75. Men are asked to wear a collared shirt. Take H-1 west until it becomes Hwy. 93 (Farrington Hwy.); turn off at the Ko Olina exit; take the exit road (Aliinui Dr.) into Ko Olina Resort; turn left into the clubhouse. No bus service.

Makaha Resort Golf Club ★★   This challenging course—recently named "The Best Golf Course on Oahu" by *Honolulu* magazine—sits some 45 miles west of Honolulu, in Makaha Valley. Designed by William Bell, the par-72, 7,091-yard course meanders toward the ocean before turning and heading into the valley. Sheer volcanic walls tower 1,500 feet above the course, which is surrounded by swaying palm trees and neon-bright bougainvillea; an occasional peacock will even strut across the fairways. The beauty here could make it difficult to keep your mind on the game if it weren't for the course's many challenges: 8 water hazards, 107 bunkers, and frequent brisk winds. This course is packed on weekends, so it's best to try weekdays. Facilities include a pro shop, bag storage, and snack shop.

84–627 Makaha Valley Rd., Waianae. (*C*) 808/695-7111 or 808/695-5239. www.makahavalleycc.com. Greens fees: $100. Take H-1 west until it turns into Hwy. 93, which winds through the coastal towns of Nanakuli, Waianae, and Makaha. Turn right on Makaha Valley Rd. and follow it to the fork; the course is on the left. Bus: 51. Shuttle: 75.

West Loch Municipal Golf Course *Value*   This par-72, 6,615-yard course located just 30 minutes from Waikiki, in Ewa Beach, offers golfers a challenge at bargain rates. The difficulties on this municipal course are water (lots of hazards), wind (constant trade winds), and narrow fairways. To help you out, the course features a "water" driving range (with a lake) to practice your drives. After a few practice swings on the driving range, you'll be ready to take on this unusual course, designed by Robin Nelson and Rodney Wright. In addition to the driving range, West Loch has practice greens, a pro shop, and a restaurant.

91–1126 Okupe St., Ewa Beach. (*C*) **808/675-6076.** www.gvhawaii.com/westloch/westloch.htm. Greens fees: $40; $20 after 4pm. Booking a week in advance is recommended. Take H-1 west to the Hwy. 76 exit; stay in the left lane and turn left at West Loch Estates, just opposite St. Francis Medical Center. To park, take two immediate right turns. Bus: 50.

CENTRAL OAHU

Pearl Country Club   Looking for a challenge? You'll find one at this popular public course, located just above Pearl City in Aiea. Sure, the 6,230-yard, par-72 looks harmless enough, and the views of Pearl Harbor and the USS *Arizona* Memorial are gorgeous, but around the fifth hole, you'll start to see what you're in for. That par-5, a blind 472-yard hole, doglegs seriously to the left (with a small margin of error between the tee and the steep out-of-bounds hillside on the entire left side of the fairway). A water hazard and a forest await your next two shots. Suddenly, this nice public course becomes not so nice. Oahu residents can't get enough of it, so don't even try to get a tee time on weekends. Stick to weekdays—Mondays are usually the best bet. Facilities include a driving range, practice greens, club rental, pro shop, and restaurant.

98–535 Kaonohi St., Aiea. (*C*) **808/487-3802.** www.pearlcc.com. Greens fees: $65 Mon–Fri.; $75 Sat–Sun. After 4pm, 9 holes are $20. Call for a tee time at least a week in advance. Take H-1 past Pearl Harbor to the Hwy. 78 (Moanalua Freeway), Exit 13A; stay in the left lane, where Hwy. 78 becomes Hwy. 99 (Kamehameha Hwy.); turn right on Kaonohi St., entry on the right. Bus: 32 (stops at Pearlridge Shopping Center at Kaonohi and Moanalua St.; you'll have to walk about a ½ mile uphill from here).

BICYCLING

Bicycling is a great way to see Oahu. Most streets here have bike lanes. For information on biking trails, races, and tours, check out **www.bikehawaii.com**. For information on bikeways and maps, contact the **Honolulu City and County Bike Coordinator** ((*C*) **808/527-5044**).

If you're in Waikiki, you can rent a bike for as little as $10 for a half day and $16 for 24 hours at **Wiki Wiki Wheels,** 1827 Ala Moana, Suite 201 (✆ **808/ 951-5787;** http://lava.net/wikiwiki-wheels). On the North Shore, for a full suspension mountain bike try **Raging Isle,** 66–250 Kamehameha Hwy., Haleiwa (✆ **808/637-7707**), which rents full-suspension mountain bikes for $40 for 24 hours. If you're interested in taking a bicycling tour, **The Parks at Waimea,** 59–864 Kamehameha Hwy., Haleiwa (✆ **888/973-9200** or 808/638-5300), has mountain bikes, for advance and expert riders, starting at $35 for an hour and 45 minutes.

For a bike and hike adventure, call **Bike Hawaii** (✆ **877-MTV-RIDE** or 808/734-4214; www.bikehawaii.com). They have a variety of group tours, like their Downhill Coasting Ride, which gives you a bird's eye view of Oahu from 1800 feet above Waikiki. The tour includes coasting down 5 miles on a paved mountain road with scenic views above Waikiki, Honolulu and Manoa Valley. Listen to the songs of birds and the wind through the trees, and learn about the culture, plants and geology of the Hawaiian Islands. After that, you leave your bike for a 2-mile round-trip hike to a 200-foot waterfall. The 9am to 2pm trip— which includes van transportation from your hotel, continental-style breakfast, bike, helmet, snacks, water bottle and guide—is $74 adults and $59 children 14 and under.

If you'd like to join in on some club rides, contact the **Hawaii Bicycle League** (✆ **808/735-5756**), which offers rides every weekend, as well as several annual events. The league can also provide a schedule of upcoming rides, races, and outings.

HORSEBACK RIDING

You can gallop on the beach at the **Turtle Bay Resort,** 57–091 Kamehameha Hwy., Kahuku (✆ **808/293-8811;** www.turtlebayresort.com, bus: 52 or 55), where 45-minute rides along sandy beaches with spectacular ocean views and through a forest of ironwood trees cost $35 for adults and $22 for children 9 to 12 (they must be at least 54 in. tall). Romantic evening rides take place on Friday, Saturday, and Sunday from 5 to 6:30pm ($65 per person). Advanced riders can sign up for a 40-minute trot-and-canter ride along Kawela Bay ($50).

For guided horseback tours of lush Waimea Valley on the North Shore, contact **The Parks at Waimea,** 59–864 Kamehameha Hwy., Haleiwa (✆ **888/973- 9200** or 808/638-5300; www.go-atlantis.com), which offers a range of tours starting at $35 for 1 hour.

TENNIS

Oahu has 181 free public tennis courts. To get a complete list of all facilities or information on upcoming tournaments, send a self-addressed, stamped envelope to **Department of Parks and Recreation,** Tennis Unit, 650 S. King St., Honolulu, HI 96813. In Waikiki, if you want to check on the Diamond Head courts, 3908 Paki Ave., across from the Kapiolani Park, call (✆ **808/971-7150**). The courts are available on a first-come, first-served basis; playing time is limited to 45 minutes if others are waiting.

If you're staying in Waikiki, try the **Ilikai Tennis Center** at the Renaissance Ilikai Hotel, 1777 Ala Moana Blvd., at Hobron Lane (✆ **808/949-3811;** www. ilikaihotel.com, bus: 19 or 20), which has six courts, equipment rental, lessons, and repair service. Courts cost $8 per person per hour for nonguests of the hotel ($5 for guests); private lessons are $44 per hour.

If you're on the North Shore, the **Turtle Bay Resort,** 57–091 Kamehameha Hwy., Kahuku (© **808/293-8811,** ext. 24; bus: 52 or 55), has 10 courts, four of which are lit for night play. You must reserve the night courts in advance; they're very popular. Court time is $20 for 1½ hours, equipment rental and lessons are also available.

10 Orientation Tours

GUIDED SIGHTSEEING TOURS

If your time is limited, you might want to consider a guided tour. These tours are informative, can give you a good overview of Honolulu or Oahu in a limited amount of time, and are surprisingly entertaining.

E Noa Tours, 1141 Waimanu St., Suite 105, Honolulu (© **800/824-8804** or 808/591-2561; www.enoa.com), offers a range of tours, from island loops to explorations of historic Honolulu. These narrated tours are on air-conditioned, 27-passenger minibuses. The Royal Circle Island tour ($52 for adults, $41 for children 6–11, $35 for children under 6), stops at Diamond Head Crater, Hanauma Bay, Byodo-In Temple, Sunset Beach, Waimea Valley (admission included), and various beach sites along the way. Other tours go to Pearl Harbor/ USS *Arizona* Memorial and the Polynesian Cultural Center.

Waikiki Trolley Tours ⭐, 1141 Waimanu St., Suite 105, Honolulu (© **800/ 824-8804** or 808/596-2199; www.waikikitrolley.com), offers three fun tours of sightseeing, entertainment, dining, and shopping. These tours are a great way to get the lay of the land. You can get on and off the trolley as needed (trolleys come along every 2–20 min.). An all-day pass (from 8:30am–11:35pm) is $20 for adults, $17 for seniors, $14 for teenagers (ages 12–18) and $10 for children (4–11); a 4-day pass is $45 for adults, $42 for seniors, $31 for teenagers (ages 12–18) and $15 for children (4–11). For the same price, you can experience the new 2-hour narrated Ocean Coastline tour of the southeast side of Oahu, an easy way to see the stunning views.

Polynesian Adventure Tours, 1049 Kikowaena Pl., Honolulu (© **808/833-3000;** www.polyad.com), also offers a range of guided excursions. The all-day island tour starts at $53 for adults, $30 for children 6 to 12, and $16 for children 3-5; the half-day scenic shore and rain-forest tour is $24 for adults, $18 for children 3 to 11; the half-day *Arizona* Memorial Excursion is $22 for adults and $18 for children 3 to 11.

WAIKIKI & HONOLULU WALKING TOURS

DOWNTOWN HONOLULU   The **Mission Houses Museum,** 553 S. King St., at Kawaiahao Street (© **808/531-0481;** www.missionhouses.org; bus: 2), offers a guided walking tour of historic downtown Honolulu on Thursday, from 9:30am to 12:45pm. The fee is $15 for adults, $12 for seniors, $10 children 6 and up; age 5 and under free; rates includes the regular Mission Houses tour (see "Attractions in & Around Honolulu & Waikiki," below). The tour also includes the capitol district, making stops at sites such as Iolani Place, the Kamehameha Statue, the Royal Tomb, and James Kekela's grave. Reserve a day ahead in person or by phone.

Kapiolani Community College has a unique series of walking tours into Hawaii's past, including visits to Honolulu's famous cemeteries, the almost-vanished "Little Tokyo" neighborhood, and many more fascinating destinations. Tours, which generally cost about $5, are for groups only, but you may be able to tag along. For information and reservations, call © **808/734-9234.**

Moments A Bird's-Eye View

To understand why Oahu was the island of kings, you need to see it from the air. **Island Seaplane Service** ★★ (© **808/836-6273;** www. islandseaplane.com) operates flights departing from a floating dock in the protected waters of Keehi Lagoon (parallel to Honolulu International Airport's runway) in either a six-passenger DeHavilland Beaver or a four-passenger Cessna 206. There's nothing quite like feeling the slap of the waves as the plane skims across the water and then effortlessly lifts into the air.

Your tour will give you aerial views of Waikiki Beach, Diamond Head Crater, Kahala's luxury estates, and the sparkling waters of Hanauma and Kaneohe bays. The ½-hour tour ($99) ends here, while the 1-hour tour ($159) continues on to Chinaman's Hat, the Polynesian Cultural Center, and the rolling surf of the North Shore. The flight returns across the island, flying over Hawaii's historic wartime sites: Schofield Barracks and the USS *Arizona* and *Missouri* memorials in Pearl Harbor.

Captain Pat Magie, company president and chief pilot, has logged more than 32,000 hours of flight time without an accident (26,000 hours in seaplanes in Alaska, Canada, the Arctic, and the Caribbean). Any day now, he'll break the world record for seaplane hours.

The **Hawaii Geographic Society** (© **808/538-3952**) presents numerous interesting and unusual tours, such as "A Temple Tour," which includes Chinese, Japanese, Christian, and Jewish houses of worship; an archaeology tour in and around downtown Honolulu; and others. Each is guided by an expert from the Hawaii Geographic Society and must have a minimum of three people; the cost is $10 per person. The society's brochure, *Historic Downtown Honolulu Walking Tour,* is a fascinating self-guided tour of the 200-year-old city center. If you'd like a copy, send $3 to **Hawaii Geographic Maps and Books,** 49 S. Hotel St. (P.O. Box 1698), Honolulu, HI 96808.

CHINATOWN HISTORIC DISTRICT   Two 3-hour guided tours of Chinatown are offered Tuesdays at 9:30am by the **Chinese Chamber of Commerce** ★, 42 N. King St., at Smith Street (© **808/533-3181;** bus: 2). The cost is $5 per person; call to reserve. The **Hawaii Heritage Center** (© **808/521-2749**) also conducts 2-hour walking tours that focus on the history, culture, and multicultural aspects of Chinatown. Tours begin Fridays at 9:30am at the Ramsay Gallery, 1128 Smith St., at N. King Street (bus: 2 or 13, get off on Hotel and Smith sts.); the cost is $5 per person.

For a self-guided tour of the neighborhood, see "A Stroll Through Historic Chinatown," on p. 196.

GUIDED ECOTOURS

If you want to explore a hidden, ancient Hawaii that most lifelong residents have never seen, book a tour with **Mauka Makai Excursions** ★, 350 Ward Ave., Honolulu (© **808/593-3525;** www.oahu-ecotours.com), a Hawaiian-owned and operated ecotour company specializing in field trips to off-the-beaten-path (and sometimes hidden in the jungle) ancient temples, sea caves, sacred stones, petroglyphs, and other cultural treasures. Tours range from a half day ($47 adult, $32 children 6–17 years) to a full day ($78 adult, $63 children). They provide bottled water, insect repellent, rain gear, beach gear, fishing tackle, and hotel pickup; you bring your imagination.

11 Attractions in & Around Honolulu & Waikiki

HISTORIC HONOLULU

The Waikiki you see today bears no resemblance to the Waikiki of yesteryear, a place of vast taro fields extending from the ocean to deep into Manoa Valley, dotted with numerous fish ponds and gardens tended by thousands of people. This picture of old Waikiki can be recaptured by following the emerging **Waikiki Historic Trail** ⭐, a meandering 2-mile walk with 20 bronze surfboard markers (standing 6 ft., 5 in. tall—you can't miss 'em), complete with descriptions and archive photos of the historic sites. The markers note everything from Waikiki's ancient fish ponds to the history of the Ala Wai Canal. The trail begins at Kuhio Beach and ends at the King Kalakaua statue, at the intersection of Kuhio and Kalakaua avenues. Free 90-minute walking tours are given Monday to Friday at 9am and on Saturdays at 4:30pm; meet at the beachside surfboard marker ("The Beaches of Waikiki") at the entrance to Kapiolani Park, on Kalakaua Avenue, across from the Honolulu Zoo. For more information, call ℂ 808/841-6442.

A hula performance is a popular way for visitors to get a taste of traditional Hawaiian culture. Unfortunately the **Kodak Hula Show** at the Waikiki Band Shell at Kapiolani Park closed in 2002. For a more genuine Hawaiian hula experience, catch the hula *halau* performed at the **Bishop Museum** (see below).

Bishop Museum ⭐⭐ *(Kids* This forbidding, four-story, Romanesque lava-rock structure (it looks like an Addams family residence) holds safe the world's greatest collection of natural and cultural artifacts from Hawaii and the Pacific. It's a great rainy-day diversion; plan to spend about half a day here. The museum was founded by a Hawaiian princess, Bernice Pauahi, who collected priceless artifacts and in her will instructed her husband, Charles Reed Bishop, to establish a Hawaiian museum "to enrich and delight" the people of Hawaii. Dr. Yosihiko Sinoto, the last in a proud line of adventuring archaeologists who explored more of the Pacific than Captain Cook and traced Hawaii's history and culture through its fish hooks, now works at the museum.

Plan to spend a day here. The Bishop is jam-packed with acquisitions—from insect specimens and ceremonial spears to calabashes and old photos of topless hula dancers. A visit here will give you a good basis for understanding Hawaiian life and culture. You'll see the great feathered capes of kings, the last grass shack in Hawaii, preindustrial Polynesian art, even the skeleton of a 50-foot sperm whale. There are also seashells, koa-wood bowls, nose flutes, and Dr. Sinoto's major collection of fish hooks.

Hula performances ⭐ take place weekdays at 11am and 2pm, and various Hawaiian crafts like lei-making, feather working, and quilting are demonstrated. This daily cultural event is worth making time for. For a look at spectacular artifacts such as the ancient feather cloak of King Kamehameha and other items not shown to the general public, take the "Behind the Scenes Tour" offered weekdays at 1:30pm for an additional fee of $15.

1525 Bernice St., just off Kalihi St. (also known as Likelike Hwy.). ℂ 808/847-3511. www.bishopmuseum. org. Admission $15 adults, $12 children 4–12 and seniors. Daily 9am–5pm. Bus: 2.

Honolulu Attractions

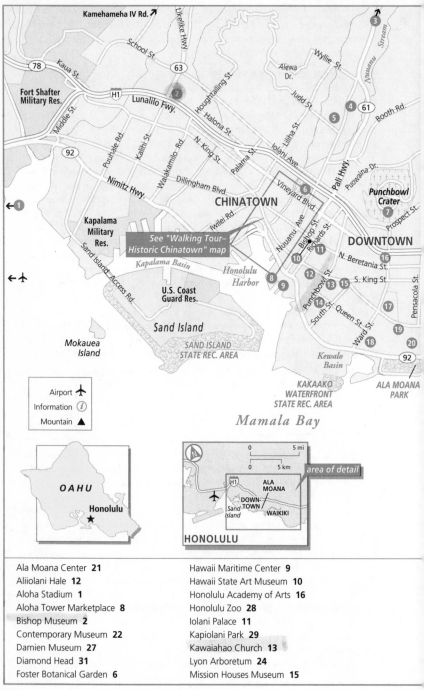

Kamehameha IV Rd.

Likelike Hwy.

School St.

Nuuanu Stream

Wyllie St.

Alewa Dr.

78

Kaua St.

63

Judd St.

61

Booth Rd.

Fort Shafter Military Res.

H1

Lunalilo Fwy.

Houghtailing St.

Halona St.

Iolani Ave

Puowaina Dr.

Pali Hwy.

92

Middle St.

Puuhale Rd.

Kalihi St.

Waiakamilo Rd.

N. King St.

Palama St.

Lililha St.

Punchbowl Crater

Nimitz Hwy.

Dillingham Blvd.

Vineyard Blvd.

CHINATOWN

Prospect St.

Kapalama Military Res.

Kapalama Basin

Iwilei Rd.

Nuuanu Ave.

Bishop St.

Richards St.

See "Walking Tour–Historic Chinatown" map

DOWNTOWN

N. Beretania St.

Pensacola St.

U.S. Coast Guard Res.

Honolulu Harbor

S. King St.

Mokauea Island

Sand Island

SAND ISLAND STATE REC. AREA

Punchbowl St.

South St.

Queen St.

Ward St.

92

Kewalo Basin

KAKAAKO WATERFRONT STATE REC. AREA

ALA MOANA PARK

Airport ✈
Information ⓘ
Mountain ▲

Mamala Bay

0 ___ 5 mi
0 ___ 5 km

area of detail

OAHU

Honolulu ★

H1

ALA MOANA

DOWNTOWN

WAIKIKI

Sand Island

HONOLULU

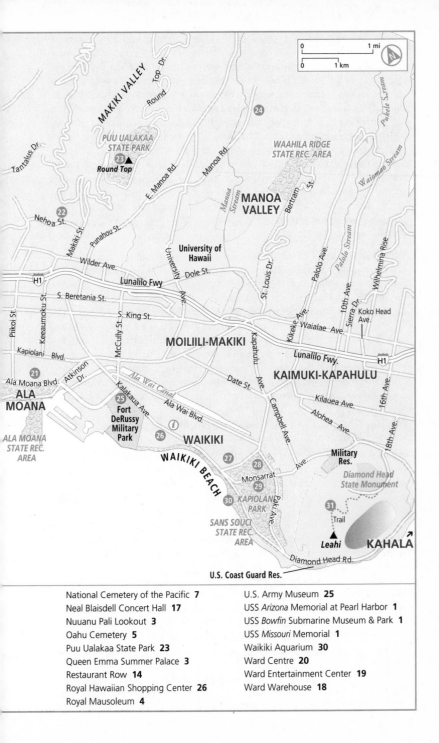

National Cemetery of the Pacific **7**
Neal Blaisdell Concert Hall **17**
Nuuanu Pali Lookout **3**
Oahu Cemetery **5**
Puu Ualakaa State Park **23**
Queen Emma Summer Palace **3**
Restaurant Row **14**
Royal Hawaiian Shopping Center **26**
Royal Mausoleum **4**

U.S. Army Museum **25**
USS *Arizona* Memorial at Pearl Harbor **1**
USS *Bowfin* Submarine Museum & Park **1**
USS *Missouri* Memorial **1**
Waikiki Aquarium **30**
Ward Centre **20**
Ward Entertainment Center **19**
Ward Warehouse **18**

Bishop Museum at Kalia ★★★ *Kids*   Now in Waikiki, this "mini" version of the Bishop Museum is just right for visitors who want to get an insider's view of Hawaiian culture but are pressed for time. Located in the Kalia Tower of the Hilton Hawaiian Village Beach Resort and Spa, the Bishop Musuem at Kalia features cultural interpreters to walk you through the story of life in Waikiki from ancient times to today. Allow at least an hour (1½ hr. would be better). You can participate in a variety of interactive, hands-on-activities, like lei making, weaving cordage from coconut fibers, pounding kapa into cloth, learning the basic motions of the hula, or trying your hand at playing a Hawaiian instrument like the pahu (shark skin drum), ohe hano ihu (nose flute) or uli uli (feathered gourd rattle). As you move from ancient times into the arrival of the missionaries, the royal monarchy, and into Waikiki of the 20th century (with great old surfing movies), you will be amazed at how time flies. Not to be missed!

2005 Kalia Rd. ✆ **808/946-9478.** www.bishopmuseum.org. Admission $9.95 adults, $7.95 children 4–12 years. Daily 9am–5 pm. Bus: 19 or 20.

Hawaii Maritime Center ★ *Finds*   You can easily spend a couple of hours here, wandering around and learning the story of Hawaii's rich maritime past, from the ancient journey of Polynesian voyagers to the nostalgic days of the *Lurline,* which once brought tourists from San Francisco on 4-day cruises. Inside the Hawaii Maritime Center's Kalakaua Boat House, patterned after His Majesty King David Kalakaua's own canoe house, are more than 30 exhibits, including Matson cruise ships (which brought the first tourists to Waikiki), flying boats that delivered the mail, and the skeleton of a Pacific humpback whale that beached on Kahoolawe. Outside, the *Hokulea,* a double-hulled sailing canoe that in 1976 reenacted the Polynesian voyage of discovery, is moored next to the *Falls of Clyde,* a four-masted schooner that once ran tea from China to the West Coast.

Pier 7 (next to Aloha Tower), Honolulu Harbor. ✆ **808/536-6373;** www.bishopmuseum.org. Admission $7.50 adults, $4.50 children 6–17. Daily 8:30am–5pm. Bus: 19, 20.

Iolani Palace ★   If you want to really "understand" Hawaii, this 45-minute tour is well worth the time. The Iolani Palace was built by King David Kalakaua, who spared no expense. The 4-year project, completed in 1882, cost $360,000—and nearly bankrupted the Hawaiian kingdom. This four-story Italian Renaissance palace was the first electrified building in Honolulu (it had electricity before the White House and Buckingham Palace). Royals lived here for 11 years, until Queen Liliuokalani was deposed and the Hawaiian monarchy fell forever, in a palace coup led by U.S. Marines on January 17, 1893, at the demand of sugar planters and missionary descendants.

Cherished by latter-day royalists, the 10-room palace stands as an architectural statement of the monarchy period. Iolani attracts 100,000 visitors a year in groups of 20; everyone must don denim booties to scoot across the royal floors. Tours are either a comprehensive **Grand Tour** ★, which is 90 minutes long and covers the Palace history, the Palace grounds, and the Palace itself; or the **Galleries Tour,** a self-guided tour of the Palace Galleries (complete with crown jewels, the ancient feathered cloaks, the Royal china, etc.).

At S. King and Richards sts. ✆ **800/532-1051** or 808/522-0832. iolanipalace.org. Admission Grand Tour $20 adults, $5 children 5–17; Galleries Tour $10 adults, $5 children 5–17. Tues–Sat 8:30am–2pm; call ahead to reserve the Grand Tour. Children under 5 not permitted. Extremely limited parking on Palace grounds, try off street-metered parking. Bus: 2.

(Kids) Especially for Kids

Pounding a shark-skin drum (p. 186)   The new Bishop Museum at Kalia (in the heart of Waikiki) is made for kids (and those of us who are kids at heart). The interactive minimusuem features a host of activities, from lei making to thumping an ancient Hawaii drum made from shark skin. Cool surf movies too.

Visiting the Honolulu Zoo (p. 191)   Visit Africa in Hawaii at Waikiki's Kapiolani Park. The lions, giraffes, zebras, and elephants delight youngsters and parents alike. But the great new thrill is the Zoo by Moonlight tour—so kids can see and hear what really goes bump in the night.

Shopping Aloha Flea Market (p. 162)   Most kids hate to shop. But the Aloha Flea Market, a giant outdoor bazaar at Aloha Stadium every Wednesday, Saturday, and Sunday, is more than shopping. It's an experience akin to a carnival, full of strange food, odd goods, and bold barkers. Nobody ever leaves this place empty-handed—or without having had lots of fun.

Seeing the World's Only Wholphin (p. 192)   It's a freak of nature, a cross between a whale and a dolphin—and you can see it at Sea Life Park. Kids love this marine amusement park, where trained dolphins, whales, and seals do their thing.

Flying a Kite at Kapiolani Park   Great open expanses of green and constant trade winds make this urban park one of Hawaii's prime locations for kite-flying. You can watch the pros fly dragon kites and stage kite-fighting contests, or join in the fun after checking out the convenient kite shop across the street in New Otani's arcade.

Spending a Day at the Parks at Waimea   What many think is only a botanical garden tucked away on the North Shore is really a child's garden of delight. There are waterfalls and pools for swimming, cliff divers to watch, and much more. Try kayaking the Waimea River or hiking through a junglelike forest.

Eating Shave Ice at Haleiwa (p. 224)   No visit to Hawaii is complete without an authentic shave ice. You can find shave ice in all kinds of tropical flavors throughout the islands, but for some reason, it tastes better in this funky North Shore surf town.

Beating Bamboo Drums in a Fijian Village (p. 205)   The Polynesian Cultural Center introduces kids to the games played by Polynesian and Melanesian children. The activities, which range from face painting to Hawaiian bowling, go on every day from 12:30 to 5:30pm.

Kawaiahao Church ☞   In 1842, Kawaiahao Church stood complete at last, the crowning achievement of missionaries and Hawaiians working together for the first time on a common project. Designed by Rev. Hiram Bingham and supervised by Kamehameha III, who ordered his people to help build it, the project took 5 years. Workers quarried 14,000 coral blocks weighing 1,000 pounds each from the offshore reefs and cut timber in the forests for the beams.

This proud stone church, complete with bell tower and colonial colonnade, was the first permanent Western house of worship in the islands. It became the church of the Hawaiian royalty and remains in use today by Hawaiians who conduct services in the Hawaiian language (which probably sets old Rev. Bingham spinning in his grave). Some fine portraits of Hawaiian royalty hang inside. We recommend seeing this edifice at the **Hawaiian-language services** ⋆⋆, conducted on Sundays at 10:30am.

957 Punchbowl St. (at King St.). ✆ 808/522-1333. Free admission (small donations appreciated). Mon–Fri 8am–4pm; Sun services 8am and 10:30am. Bus: 2.

Mission Houses Museum   This museum tells the dramatic story of cultural change in 19th-century Hawaii. American Protestant missionaries established their headquarters here in 1820. Included in the complex are a visitor center and three historic mission buildings, which have been restored and refurnished to reflect the daily life and work of the missionaries.

Tip: The best way to see the museum is as part of a walking tour of historic downtown buildings, offered on Thursday and Friday mornings (museum admission is included in the tour price); for details, see "Orientation Tours," earlier in this chapter.

553 S. King St. (at Kawaiahao St.). ✆ 808/531-0481. www.missionhouses.org. Admission $10 adults, $8 military personnel, $8 seniors, $6 students and youths 6–18, children under 5 free. Tues–Sat 9am–4pm. Bus: 2.

Queen Emma Summer Palace   Hanaiakamalama, the name of the country estate of Kamehameha IV and Queen Emma, was once in the secluded uplands of Nuuanu Valley. These days, it's adjacent to a six-lane highway full of speeding cars that sound remarkably like surf as they zip by. This simple, seven-room New England–style house, built in 1848 and restored by the Daughters of Hawaii, is worth about an hour of your time to see the interesting blend of Victorian furniture and hallmarks of Hawaiian royalty, including feather cloaks and *kahili,* the feathered standards that mark the presence of *alii* (royalty). Other royal treasures include a canoe-shaped cradle for Queen Emma's baby, Prince Albert, who died at the age of 4. (Kauai's ultraritzy Princeville Resort is named for the little prince.)

2913 Pali Hwy. (at Old Pali Rd.). ✆ 808/595-3167. Admission $5 adults, $4 seniors, $1 children 11 and under. Daily 9am–4pm. Bus: 4, 55, 56, 57, or 65.

WARTIME HONOLULU

USS *Arizona* Memorial at Pearl Harbor ⋆⋆⋆   On December 7, 1941, the USS *Arizona,* while moored here in Pearl Harbor, was bombed in a Japanese air raid. The 608-foot battleship sank in 9 minutes without firing a shot, taking 1,177 sailors and Marines to their deaths—and catapulting the United States into World War II.

Nobody who visits the memorial will ever forget it. The deck of the ship lies 6 feet below the surface of the sea. Oil still oozes slowly up from the Arizona's engine room to stain the harbor's calm, blue water; some say the ship still weeps for its lost crew. The memorial is a stark, white, 184-foot rectangle that spans the sunken hull of the ship; it was designed by Alfred Pries, a German architect interned on Sand Island during the war. It contains the ship's bell, recovered from the wreckage, and a shrine room with the names of the dead carved in stone.

Today, free U.S. Navy launches take visitors to the *Arizona.* Try to arrive at the visitor center, operated jointly by the National Park Service and the U.S. Navy, no later than 1:30pm to avoid the huge crowds; waits of 1 to 3 hours are common, and they don't take reservations. While you're waiting for the shuttle to take you out to the ship—you'll be issued a number and time of departure—you can explore the interesting museum's personal mementos, photographs, and historic documents. A moving 20-minute film precedes your trip to the ship. Allow a total of at least 4 hours for your visit.

Parents: Note that baby strollers, baby carriages, and baby backpacks are not allowed in the theater, on the boat, or on the USS *Arizona* Memorial. All babies must be carried. *One last note:* Most unfortunately, the USS *Arizona* Memorial is a high-theft area—leave your valuables at the hotel.

Pearl Harbor. © 808/422-0561 (recorded info) or 808/422-2771. www.nps.gov/usar. Daily 7:30am–5pm (programs run 8am–3pm). Free admission. Children under 12 should be accompanied by an adult. Shirts and shoes required; no swimsuits or flip-flops allowed (shorts are okay). Wheelchairs gladly accommodated. Drive west on H-1 past the airport; take the USS *Arizona* Memorial exit and follow the green-and-white signs; there's ample free parking. Bus: 20 and 47; or *Arizona* Memorial Shuttle Bus (© 808/839-0911), which picks up at Waikiki hotels 6:50am–1pm ($6 round-trip).

USS *Bowfin* Submarine Museum & Park ✦

The USS *Bowfin* is one of only 15 World War II submarines still in existence today. You can go below deck of this famous submarine—nicknamed the "Pearl Harbor Avenger" for its successful attacks on the Japanese—and see how the 80-man crew lived during wartime. The *Bowfin* Museum has an impressive collection of submarine-related artifacts. The Waterfront Memorial honors submariners lost during World War II.

11 Arizona Memorial Dr. (next to the USS *Arizona* Memorial Visitor Center). © 808/423-1341. www.bowfin. org. Admission $8 adults, $6 active-duty military personnel, $3 children 4–12. Daily 8am–5pm. See USS *Arizona* Memorial, above for driving, bus, and shuttle directions.

USS *Missouri* Memorial ✦

On the deck of this 58,000-ton battleship (the last one the navy built), World War II came to an end with the signing of the Japanese surrender on September 2, 1945. The *Missouri* was part of the force that carried out bombing raids over Tokyo and provided firepower in the battles of Iwo Jima and Okinawa. In 1955, the navy decommissioned the ship and placed it in mothballs at the Puget Sound Naval Shipyard, in Washington State. But the *Missouri* was modernized and called back into action in 1986, eventually being deployed in the Persian Gulf War, before retiring once again in 1992. Here it sat until another battle ensued, this time over who would get the right to keep this living legend. Hawaii won that battle and brought the ship to Pearl Harbor in 1998. The next year, the 887-foot ship, like a phoenix, rose again into the public spotlight; it's now open to visitors as a museum memorial.

If you have the time, take the tour, which begins at the visitor center. Guests are shuttled to Ford Island on military-style buses while listening to a 1940s-style radio program (complete with news clips, wartime commercials, and music). Once on the ship, guests watch an informational film and are then free to explore on their own or take a guided tour. Highlights of this massive (more than 200 ft. tall) battleship include the forecastle (or *foc's'le,* in Navy talk), where the 30,000-pound anchors are "dropped" on 1,080 feet of anchor chain; the 16-inch guns (each 65 ft. long and weighing 116 tons), which can accurately fire a 2,700-pound shell some 23 miles in 50 seconds; and the spot where the Instrument of Surrender was signed as Douglas MacArthur, Chester Nimitz, and "Bull" Halsey looked on.

Battleship Row, Pearl Harbor. © 808/423-2263. www.ussmissouri.com. Admission $16 adults, $8 children 4–12 (hr.-long guided tours available 9:30am–4:30pm; cost $22 adults and $14 children—admission included). Daily 9am–5pm. Check in at the visitor center of the USS *Bowfin* Memorial, next to the USS *Arizona* Memorial. Drive west on H-1 past the airport, take the USS *Arizona* Memorial exit, and follow the green-and-white signs; there's ample free parking. Bus: 20 and 47.

National Cemetery of the Pacific   The National Cemetery of the Pacific (also known as "the Punchbowl") is an ash-and-lava tuff cone that exploded about 150,000 years ago—like Diamond Head, only smaller. Early Hawaiians called it Puowaina, or "hill of sacrifice." The old crater is a burial ground for 35,000 victims of three American wars in Asia and the Pacific: World War II, Korea, and Vietnam. Among the graves, you'll find many unmarked ones with the date December 7, 1941, carved in stone. Some will be unknown forever; others are famous, like that of war correspondent Ernie Pyle, killed by a Japanese sniper in April 1945 on Okinawa; still others buried here are remembered only by family and surviving buddies. The white stone tablets known as the Courts of the Missing bear the names of 28,788 Americans missing in action in World War II.

Survivors come here often to reflect on the meaning of war and to remember those, like themselves, who stood in harm's way to win peace a half-century ago. Some fight back tears, remembering lost buddies, lost missions, and the sacrifices of those who died.

Punchbowl Crater, 2177 Puowaina Dr. (at the end of the road). ℂ **808/541-1434**. Free admission. Daily 8am–5:30pm (Mar–Sept to 6:30pm). Bus: 15.

JUST BEYOND PEARL HARBOR

Hawaiian Railway *Kids*   All aboard! This is a train ride back into history. Between 1890 and 1947, the chief mode of transportation for Oahu's sugar mills was the Oahu Railway and Land Co.'s narrow-gauge trains. The line carried not only equipment, raw sugar, and supplies, but also passengers from one side of the island to the other. You can relive those days every Sunday with a 1½-hour narrated ride through Ko Olina Resort and out to Makaha. As an added attraction, on the second Sunday of the month, you can ride on the nearly 100-year-old, custom-built, parlor-observation car belonging to Benjamin F. Dillingham, founder of the Oahu Railway and Land Co.; the fare is $15 (no kids under 13), and you must reserve in advance.

Ewa Station, Ewa Beach. ℂ **808/681-5461**. www.hawaiianrailway.com. Admission $8 adults, $5 seniors and children 2–12. Departures Sun 1 and 3pm and weekdays by appointment. Take H-1 west to exit 5A; take Hwy. 76 south for 2½ miles to Tesoro Gas; turn right on Renton Rd. and drive 1½ miles to end of paved section. The station is on the left. Bus: C-Express to Kapalei, then transfer to no. 41, which goes through Eva drops you off outside the gate.

Hawaiian Waters Adventure Park *Kids*   If you have kids, you have to take them here! This 29-acre water-theme amusement park opened in spring 1999 with some $14 million in attractions. Plan to spend the day. Highlights are a football field–size wave pool for bodysurfing, two 65-foot-high free-fall slides, two water-toboggan bullet slides, inner-tube slides, body flume slides, a continuous river for floating inner tubes, and separate pools for adults, teens, and children. In addition, there are restaurants, food carts, Hawaiian performances, and shops.

400 Farrington Hwy., Kapolei. ℂ **808/674-9283**. www.hawaiianwaters.com. Admission $33 adults, $22 children 4–11, free for children under 3. Daily 10:30am–5pm in peak season; during nonpeak season Mon–Fri 10:30am–3:30pm, Sat–Sun 10:30am–4pm. Take H-1 west to exit 1 (Campbell Industrial Park). Make an immediate left turn to Farrington Hwy., and you will see the park on your left.

Hawaii's Plantation Village   The hour-long tour of this restored 50-acre village offers a glimpse back in time to when sugar planters from America shaped the land, economy, and culture of territorial Hawaii. From 1852, when the first contract laborers arrived here from China, to 1947, when the plantation era ended, more than 400,000 men, women, and children from China, Japan, Portugal, Puerto Rico, Korea, and the Philippines came to work the sugarcane fields. The "talk story" tour brings the old village alive with 30 faithfully restored camp houses, Chinese and Japanese temples, the Plantation Store, and even a sumo-wrestling ring.

Waipahu Cultural Garden Park, 94–695 Waipahu St. (at Waipahu Depot Rd.), Waipahu. ℭ **808/677-0110**; www.hawaiiplantationvillage.org. Admission (including escorted tour) $7 adults, $5 military personnel, $4 seniors, $3 children 5–12. Mon–Fri 9am–4:30pm; Sat 10am–4:30pm. Take H-1 west to Waikele-Waipahu exit (exit 7); get in the left lane on exit and turn left on Paiwa St.; at the fifth light, turn right onto Waipahu St.; after the second light, turn left. Bus: 47.

FISH, FLORA & FAUNA

Foster Botanical Garden ★★ *Finds*   You could spend days in this unique and historic garden, a leafy oasis amid the high-rises of downtown Honolulu, but your schedule will probably only allow a couple of hours. Combine a tour of the Garden with a trip to Chinatown (just across the street) to maximize your time. The giant trees that tower over the main terrace were planted in the 1850s by William Hillebrand, a German physician and botanist, on royal land leased from Queen Emma. Today, this 14-acre public garden, on the north side of Chinatown, is a living museum of plants, some rare and endangered, collected from the tropical regions of the world. Of special interest are 26 "Exceptional Trees" protected by state law, a large palm collection, a primitive cycad garden, and a hybrid orchid collection.

50 N. Vineyard Blvd. (at Nuuanu Ave.). ℭ **808/522-7066**. Admission $5 adults, $1 children 6–12. Daily 9am–4pm; guided tours Mon–Fri at 1pm (reservations recommended). Bus: 2, 4, or 13.

Honolulu Zoo ★ *Kids*   Nobody comes to Hawaii to see an Indian elephant, or African lions and zebras. Right? Wrong. This 43-acre municipal zoo in Waikiki attracts visitors in droves. If you've got kids, allot at least half a day. The highlight is the new African Savannah, a 10-acre wild preserve exhibit with more than 40 African critters roaming around in the open. The zoo also has a rare Hawaiian nene goose, a Hawaiian pig, and mouflon sheep. (Only the goose, an evolved version of the Canadian honker, is considered to be truly Hawaiian; the others are imported from Polynesia, India, and elsewhere.)

For a real treat, take the **Zoo by Moonlight tour** ★, which offers a rare behind-the-scenes look into the lives of the zoo's nocturnal residents. Tours are offered 2 days before, during, and 2 days after the full moon, from 7 to 9pm; the cost is $7 for adults and $5 for children.

151 Kapahulu Ave. (between Paki and Kalakaua aves.), at entrance to Kapiolani Park. ℭ **808/971-7171**. www.honoluluzoo.org. Admission $6 adults, $1 children 6–12. Daily 9am–4:30pm. Bus: 2, 8, 19, 20, or 47.

Lyon Arboretum ★   Six-story-tall breadfruit trees, yellow orchids no bigger than a bus token, ferns with fuzzy buds as big as a human head. . . . These are just a few of the botanical wonders you'll find at 194-acre Lyon Arboretum. A whole different world opens up to you along the self-guided 20-minute hike through the arboretum to Inspiration Point. You'll pass more than 5,000 exotic tropical plants full of singing birds in this cultivated rain forest (a University of Hawaii research facility) at the head of Manoa Valley. A new children's garden opened in 2002, and in 2003, a new Hawaiian garden was launched.

3860 Manoa Rd. (near the top of the road). ℭ **808/988-0456**. www.hawaii.edu/lyonarboretum. $2.50 donation requested. Mon–Sat 9am–3pm; Public tours Tue 10am and Sat 1 pm, reservations a must for tours. Bus: 5.

Sea Life Park ⭐ *Kids*   This 62-acre ocean theme park, located in East Oahu, is one of the island's top attractions. It features whales from Puget Sound, Atlantic bottle-nosed dolphins, California sea lions, and penguins going through their hoops to the delight of kids of all ages. If you have kids, allow all day to take in the sights. There's also a Hawaiian reef tank full of tropical fish; a "touch" pool, where you can touch a real sea cucumber (commonly found in tide pools); and a bird sanctuary, where you can see birds like the red-footed booby and the frigate bird. The chief curiosity, though, is the world's only "wholphin"—a cross between a false killer whale and an Atlantic bottle-nosed dolphin. On-site, marine biologists operate a recovery center for endangered marine life; during your visit, you'll be able to see rehabilitated Hawaiian monk seals and seabirds.

41–202 Kalanianaole Hwy. (at Makapuu Point), Honolulu. © **808/259-7933**. www.sealifeparkhawaii.com. Admission $24 adults, $12 children 4–12. Daily 9:30am–5pm. Parking $3. Shuttle buses from Waikiki $5. Bus: 22 or 58.

Waikiki Aquarium ⭐⭐⭐ *Kids*   Do not miss this! Half of Hawaii is its underwater world; plan to spend at least 2 hours discovering it. Behold the chambered nautilus, nature's submarine and inspiration for Jules Verne's *20,000 Leagues Under the Sea.* You may see this tropical spiral-shelled cephalopod mollusk—the only living one born in captivity—any day of the week here. Its natural habitat is the deep waters of Micronesia, but aquarium director Bruce Carlson not only succeeded in trapping the pearly-shelled creature in 1,500 feet of water (by dangling chunks of raw tuna), he also managed to breed this ancient relative of the octopus. There are also plenty of other fish in this small but first-class aquarium, located on a live coral reef. The Hawaiian reef habitat features sharks, eels, a touch tank, and habitats for the endangered Hawaiian monk seal and green sea turtle. Recently added: a rotating biodiversity exhibit and interactive displays focusing on corals and coral reefs.

2777 Kalakaua Ave. (across from Kapiolani Park). © **808/923-9741**. www.waquarium.org. Admission $7 adults, $5 active military, seniors, and college students, $3.50 children 13–17, children under 12 free. Daily 9am–5pm. Bus: 2.

OTHER NATURAL WONDERS & SPECTACULAR VIEWS

In addition to the attractions listed below, check out "Diamond Head Crater" under "Nature Hikes," earlier in this chapter; almost everybody can handle this hike, and the 360° views from the top are fabulous.

Nuuanu Pali Lookout ⭐ *Moments*   Gale-force winds sometimes howl through the mountain pass at this 1,186-foot-high perch guarded by 3,000-foot peaks, so hold on to your hat—and small children. But if you walk up from the parking lot to the precipice, you'll be rewarded with a view that'll blow you away. At the edge, the dizzying panorama of Oahu's windward side is breathtaking: Clouds low enough to pinch scoot by on trade winds; pinnacles of the *pali* (cliffs), green with ferns, often disappear in the mist. From on high, the tropical palette of green and blue runs down to the sea. Combine this 10-minute stop with a trip over the Pali to the Windward side.

Near the summit of Pali Hwy. (Hwy. 61); take the Nuuanu Pali Lookout turnoff.

Nuuanu Valley Rain Forest *Finds*   It's not the same as a peaceful nature walk, but if time is short and hiking isn't your thing, Honolulu has a rain forest you can drive through. It's only a few minutes from downtown Honolulu in verdant Nuuanu Valley, where it rains nearly 300 inches a year. And it's easy to reach: As the Pali Highway leaves residential Nuuanu and begins its climb though the forest, the last stoplight is the Nuuanu Pali Road turnoff; turn right for a jungly detour of about 2 miles under a thick canopy strung with liana vines, past giant bamboo that creaks in the wind, Norfolk pines, and wild shell ginger. The road rises and the vegetation clears as you drive, blinking in the bright light of day, past a small mountain reservoir.

Soon the road rejoins the Pali Highway. Kailua is to the right and Honolulu to the left—but it can be a hair-raising turn. Instead, turn right, go a ½ mile to the Nuuanu Pali Lookout (see above), stop for a panoramic view of Oahu's windward side, and return to the town-bound highway on the other side.

Take the Old Nuuanu Pali Rd. exit off Pali Hwy. (Hwy. 61).

Puu Ualakaa State Park ★ (Moments   The best **sunset view** of Honolulu is from a 1,048-foot-high hill named for sweet potatoes. Actually, the poetic Hawaiian name means "rolling sweet potato hill," because of how early planters used gravity to harvest their crop. The panorama is sweeping and majestic. On a clear day—which is almost always—you can see from Diamond Head to the Waianae Range, almost the length of Oahu. At night, several scenic overlooks provide romantic spots for young lovers who like to smooch under the stars with the city lights at their feet. It's a top-of-the-world experience—the view, that is.

At the end of Round Hill Dr. Daily 7am–6:45pm (to 7:45pm in summer). From Waikiki, take Ala Wai Blvd. to McCully St., turn right, and drive mauka (inland) beyond the H-1 on-ramps to Wilder St.; turn left and go to Makiki St.; turn right, and continue onward and upward about 3 miles.

MORE MUSEUMS

For details on Honolulu's three wonderful art museums, **The Contemporary Museum,** the **Honolulu Academy of Arts,** and the **Hawaii State Art Museum** see the box "Oahu's Vibrant Art Scene," below.

Aliiolani Hale   Don't be surprised if this place looks familiar; you probably saw it on *Magnum, P.I.* This gingerbread Italianate building, designed by Australian Thomas Rowe in Renaissance revival style, was built in 1874 and was originally intended to be a palace. Instead, Aliiolani Hale ("chief unto heavens") became the Supreme Court and Parliament government office building. Inside, there's a **Judiciary History Center** ★, which features a multimedia presentation, a restored historic courtroom, and exhibits tracing Hawaii's transition from precontact Hawaiian law to Western law.

417 S. King St. (between Miililani and Punchbowl sts.). ℂ **808/539-4999.** Fax 808/539-4996. www.jhc hawaii.org. Free admission. Mon–Fri 9am–4pm; reservations for group tours only. Bus: 1, 2, 3, 4, 8, 11, or 12. Limited parking meter parking on street.

Damien Museum   This is a tiny museum about a large subject in Hawaii's history: Father Damien's work with leprosy victims on the island of Molokai. The museum contains prayer books used by Father Damien in his ministry as well as his personal items. Don't miss the award-winning video on Damien's story.

130 Ohua St. (between Kuhio and Kalakaua aves., behind St. Augustine's Catholic Church). ℂ **808/923-2690.** Donations accepted. Mon–Fri 9am–3pm. Bus: 8, 19, or 20.

U.S. Army Museum   This museum, a former military fort built in 1909 and used in defense of Honolulu and Pearl Harbor, houses military memorabilia ranging from ancient Hawaiian warfare items to modern-day, high-tech munitions. On the upper deck, the Corps of Engineers Pacific Regional Visitors Center shows how the corps works with the civilian community to manage water resources in an island environment.

Fort DeRussy Park, Waikiki. ℂ **808/438-2822.** Free admission. Tues–Sun 10am–4:30pm. Bus: 8.

Oahu's Vibrant Art Scene

MUSEUMS   Passionate art lovers should head straight to Hawaii's three top cultural resources: The Contemporary Museum, the Honolulu Academy of Arts, and the State Art Museum, which opened in 2002.

The acclaimed **Honolulu Academy of Arts** ★★, 900 S. Beretania St. ((*C* **808/532-8700,** or 808/532-8701 for recording; www.honoluluacademy. org), unveiled its new $28-million Henry R. Luce Pavilion Complex in May 2001 and wowed the state with its new exhibition space, court-yard, expanded outdoor cafe, and gift shop. Making an already mag-nificent space even better, two 4,000-square-foot galleries were added to the existing 30, and the John Dominis and Patches Damon Holt Gallery allowed the display of the museum's Hawaii regional collection in one space for the first time. Considered Hawaii's premier example of *kamaaina*-style architecture, the Academy is the state's only general fine-arts museum. It boasts one of the top Asian art collections in the country. Also on exhibit are American and European masters and pre-historic works of Mayan, Greek, and Hawaiian art. The museum's award-winning architecture is a paragon of graciousness, featuring magnificent courtyards, lily ponds, and sensitively designed galleries. Open Tuesday through Saturday from 10am to 4:30pm, Sunday from 1 to 5pm; tours 11am Tuesday through Saturday and 1:15pm on Sunday. Admission is $7 for adults and $4 for students, seniors, and military personnel; children under 12 enter free.

Set up on the slopes of Tantalus, one of Honolulu's upscale residen-tial communities, The **Contemporary Museum,** 2411 Makiki Heights Dr. ((*C* **808/526-0232;** www.tcmhi.org), is renowned for its 3 acres of Asian gardens (with reflecting pools, sun-drenched terraces, views of Dia-mond Head, and stone benches for quiet contemplation). Its Cades Pavilion houses David Hockney's *L'Enfant et les Sortileges,* an environ-mental installation of his sets and costumes for Ravel's 1925 opera, and six galleries display significant works from the last 4 decades. Equally prominent is the presence of contemporary Hawaii artists in the museum's programs and exhibitions. Open Tuesday through Saturday from 10am to 4pm, Sunday from noon to 4pm. A 1-day membership is $5 for adults, $3 for seniors and students, and free for children 12 and under. The third Thursday of each month is free. Ask about the daily docent-led tours, and check out the excellent cafe and shop.

Just opened in 2002 is the **Hawaii State Art Museum,** housed in the original Royal Hawaiian Hotel built in 1872, during the reign of King Kamehameha V, at 250 South Hotel St (at Richards St.) ((*C* **808/586-0900;** www.state.hi.us.sfca/hawaiistateartmuseum.htm). All of the 360 works currently displayed were created by artists who live in Hawaii. The pieces were all purchased by the state thanks to a 1967 law that said that 1% of the cost of state buildings will be used to acquire works of art. Nearly 4 decades later, the state has amassed some 5,000 pieces. The current exhibit depicts Hawaii and its history, culture, and ideals through a variety of mediums. Open Tuesday to Saturday from 11am to 2pm; admission is free. Take the no. 2 bus from Waikiki. If you are driving, look for street (metered) parking.

GALLERIES   Galleries come and go in Chinatown, where efforts to revitalize the area have moved in fits and spurts. Two exceptions are the **Ramsay Galleries,** Tan Sing Building, 1128 Smith St. (© **808/537-2787**), and the **Pegge Hopper Gallery,** 1164 Nuuanu Ave. (© **808/524-1160**). Both are housed in historic Chinatown buildings that have been renovated and transformed into stunning showplaces.

Nationally known quill-and-ink artist Ramsay, who has drawn everything from the Plaza in New York to most of Honolulu's historic buildings, maintains a vital monthly show schedule featuring her own work, as well as shows of her fellow Hawaii artists.

Pegge Hopper, one of Hawaii's most popular artists, displays her widely collected paintings (usually of Hawaiian women with broad, strong features) in her attractive gallery, which has become quite the gathering place for exhibits that range from Tibetan sand-painting by saffron-robed monks to the most avant-garde printmaking in the islands.

Newcomer **Bibelot,** 1130 Koko Head Ave., Suite 2, in Kaimuki (© **808/ 738-0368**), is small and smart, with an impressive selection of works from new and emerging artists, as well as those well established.

The **Gallery at Ward Centre** in the Ward Centre, 1200 Ala Moana Blvd. (© **808/597-8034**), a cooperative gallery of Oahu artists, features fine works in all media, including paper, clay, scratchboard, oils, watercolors, collages, woodblocks, lithographs, glass, jewelry, and more.

Hawaii's most unusual gallery, listed on the Hawaii Register of Historic Places, is perched on the slopes of Punchbowl. The **Tennent Art Foundation Gallery,** 203 Prospect St. (© **808/531-1987**), is devoted to the oeuvre of artist Madge Tennent, whose paintings hang in the National Museum of Women alongside the work of Georgia O'Keeffe. Tennent's much-imitated style depicts Polynesians from the 1920s to the 1940s. Open limited hours and by appointment, so call before you go.

Art lovers now have a wonderful new resource: a 34-page brochure offering an overview of the music, theater, history, music, and visual arts of Oahu. The free brochure, which includes a map, phone numbers, websites, and more information, is put out by Arts with Aloha, representing 11 major Honolulu cultural organizations. Send a legal-size, self-addressed, stamped (55¢) envelope to **Arts with Aloha,** c/o Honolulu Academy of Arts, 900 S. Beretania St., Honolulu, HI 96814, or call the 24-hour hotline at © **808/532-8713.**

WALKING TOUR	A STROLL THROUGH HISTORIC CHINATOWN

Getting There: From Waikiki, take bus no. 2 or 20 toward downtown; get off on North Hotel Street (after Maunakea St.). If you're driving, take Ala Moana Boulevard and turn right on Smith Street; make a left on Beretania Street and a left again at Maunakea. The city parking garage (50¢ per hr.) is on the Ewa (west) side of Maunakea Street, between North Hotel and North King streets.

Start and Finish: North Hotel and Maunakea streets.

Time: 1 to 2 hours, depending on how much time you spend browsing.

Best Times: Daylight hours.

Chinese laborers from the Guangdong Province first came to work on Hawaii's sugar and pineapple plantations in the 1850s. They quickly figured out that they would never get rich working in the fields; once their contracts were up, a few of the ambitious started up small shops and restaurants in the area around River Street.

Chinatown was twice devastated by fire, once in 1886 and again in 1900. The second fire still intrigues historians. In December 1899, bubonic plague broke out in the area, and the Board of Health immediately quarantined its 7,000 Chinese and Japanese residents. But the plague continued to spread. On January 20, 1900, the board decided to burn down plague-infected homes, starting at the corner of Beretania Street and Nuuanu Avenue. But the fire department wasn't quite ready; a sudden wind quickly spread the flames from one wooden building to another in the densely built area, and soon Chinatown's entire 40 acres were leveled. Many historians believe that the "out-of-control" fire may have been purposely set to drive the Chinese merchants—who were becoming economically powerful and controlled prime real estate—out of Honolulu. If this was indeed the case, it didn't work: The determined merchants built a new Chinatown in the same spot.

Chinatown reached its peak in the 1930s. In the days before air travel, visitors arrived here by cruise ship. Just a block up the street was the pier where they disembarked—and they often headed straight for the shops and restaurants of Chinatown, which mainlanders considered an exotic treat. In the '40s, military personnel on leave flocked here looking for different kinds of exotic treats—in the form of pool halls, tattoo joints, and brothels.

Today, Chinatown is again rising from the ashes. After deteriorating over the years into a tawdry district of seedy bars, drug dealing, and homeless squatters, the neighborhood recently underwent extensive urban renewal. There's still just enough sleaze on the fringes (a few peep shows and a couple of topless bars) to keep it from being some theme park–style tourist attraction, but Chinatown is poised to relive its glory days.

It's not exactly a microcosm of China, however. What you'll find is a mix of Asian cultures, all packed into a small area where tangy spices rule the cuisine, open-air markets have kept out the minimalls, and the way to good health is through acupuncture and herbalists. The jumble of streets comes alive every day with bustling residents and visitors from all over the world; a cacophony of sounds, from the high-pitched bleating of vendors in the market to the lyrical dialects of the retired men "talking story" over a game of mahjong; and brilliant reds, blues, and greens trimming buildings and goods everywhere you look. No trip to Honolulu is complete without a visit to this exotic, historic district.

1 Hotel Street
2 Bank of Hawaii
3 Yat Tung Chow
   Noodle Factory
4 Viet Hoa Chinese
   Herb Shop
5 Oahu Market Place
6 River Street
   Pedestrian Mall
7 Chinatown Cultural
   Plaza
8 Izumo Taisha
   Mission
   Cultural Hall
9 Kuan Yin Temple
10 Maunakea Street
11 Nuuanu Avenue
12 Hawaii Theatre

"Take a Break"

Start your walk on the Ewa (west) side of Maunakea Street at:

① Hotel Street

During World War II, Hotel Street was synonymous with good times. Pool halls and beer parlors lined the blocks, and prostitutes were plentiful. Nowadays, the more nefarious establishments have been replaced with small shops, from art galleries to specialty boutiques, and urban professionals and recent immigrants look for bargains where the sailors once roamed.

Once you're done wandering through the shops, head to the intersection with Smith Street. On the Diamond Head (east) side of Smith, you'll notice stones in the sidewalk; they were taken from the sandalwood ships, which came to Hawaii empty of cargo except for these stones, which were used as ballast on the trip over. The stones were removed and the ships' hulls were filled with sandalwood for the return to the mainland.

From Hotel Street, turn left on Maunakea and proceed to the corner of King Street to the:

② Bank of Hawaii

This unusual-looking bank is not the conservative edifice you'd expect—it's guarded by two fire-breathing dragon statues.

Turn right onto King Street, where you'll pass the shops of various Chinese herbalists. Stop at 150 N. King St., where you'll find the:

③ Yat Tung Chow Noodle Factory

The delicious, delicate noodles that star in numerous Asian dishes are made here, ranging from threadlike noodles (literally no thicker than embroidery thread) to fat udon noodles. There aren't any tours of the factory, but you can look through the window, past the white cloud of flour that hangs in the air, and watch as dough is fed into rollers at one end of the noodle machines; perfectly cut noodles emerge at the other end.

Proceed to 162 N. King St., to the:

❹ Viet Hoa Chinese Herb Shop

Here, Chinese herbalists act as both doctors and dispensers of herbs. Patients come in and tell the herbalist what ails them; the herbalist then decides which of the myriad herbs to mix together. Usually, there's a wall of tiny drawers all labeled in Chinese characters; the herbalist quickly pulls from the drawers various objects that range from dried flowers and ground-up roots to such exotics as mashed antelope antler. The patient then takes the concoction home to brew into a strong tea.

Cross to the south side of King Street, where, just west of Kekaulike Street, you'll come to the most visited part of Chinatown, the open-air market known as:

❺ Oahu Market Place

Those interested in Asian cooking will find all the necessary ingredients here, including pig's heads, poultry (some still squawking), fresh octopi, salted jellyfish, pungent fish sauce, fresh herbs, and thousand-year-old eggs. The friendly vendors are happy to explain their wares and give instructions on how to prepare these exotic treats. The market, which has been at this spot since 1904, is divided into meats, poultry, fish, vegetables, and fruits. Past the open market are several grocery stores with fresh produce on display on the sidewalk. You're bound to spot some goodies here that you're not used to seeing at your local supermarket.

Follow King down to River Street and turn right toward the mountains. A range of

inexpensive restaurants lines River Street from King to Beretania. You can get the best Vietnamese and Filipino food in town in these blocks, but go early—lines for lunch start at 11:15am. Beyond Beretania Street is the:

❻ River Street Pedestrian Mall

Here, River Street ends and the pedestrian mall begins with the **statue of Chinese revolutionary leader Sun Yat-sen.** The wide mall, which borders the Nuuanu Stream, is lined with shade trees, park benches, and tables where seniors gather to play mahjong and checkers. There are plenty of takeout restaurants nearby if you'd like to eat lunch outdoors. If you're up early (5:30am in summer and 6am in winter), you'll see seniors practicing tai chi.

Along the River Street Mall, extending nearly a block over to Maunakea Street, is the:

❼ Chinatown Cultural Plaza

This modern complex is filled with shops featuring everything from tailors to calligraphers (most somewhat more expensive than their street-side counterparts), as well as numerous restaurants—a great idea, but in reality, people seem to prefer wandering Chinatown's crowded streets to venturing into a modern mall. A couple of interesting shops here specialize in Asian magazines; there's also a small post office tucked away in a corner of the plaza, for those who want to mail cards home with the "Chinatown" postmark. The best feature of the plaza is the **Moongate Stage** in the center, the site of many cultural presentations, especially around the Chinese New Year.

Continue up the River Street Mall and cross the Nuuanu Stream via the bridge at Kukui Street, which will bring you to the:

❽ Izumo Taisha Mission Cultural Hall

This small, wooden Shinto shrine, built in 1923, houses a male deity (look for the X-shaped crosses on the top). Members of the faith ring the bell out front as an act of purification when

✓Bargaining: A Way of Life in Chinatown

In Chinatown, nearly every purchase—from haggling over the price of chicken's feet to buying an 18-carat gold necklace—is made by bargaining. It's the way of life for most Asian countries—and part of the fun and charm of shopping in Chinatown.

The main rule of thumb when negotiating a price is **respect.** The customer must have respect for the merchant and understand that he's in business to make money. This respect is coupled with the understanding that the customer does not want to be taken advantage of and would like the best deal possible.

Keep in mind two rules when bargaining: **cash** and **volume.** Don't even begin haggling if you're not planning to pay cash. The second you pull out a credit card (if the merchant or vendor will even accept it), all deals are off. And remember, the more you buy, the better the deal the merchant will extend to you.

Significant savings can be realized for high-ticket items like jewelry. The price of gold in Chinatown is based on the posted price of the tael (a unit of weight, slightly more than an ounce), which is listed for 14-, 18-, and 24-carat gold, plus the value of the labor. There's no negotiating on the tael price, but the cost of the labor is where the bargaining begins.

---

they come to pray. Inside the temple is a 100-pound sack of rice, symbolizing good health. During World War II, the shrine was confiscated by the city of Honolulu and wasn't returned to the congregation until 1962.

If temples interest you, walk a block toward the mountains to Vineyard Boulevard; cross back over Nuuanu Stream, past the entrance of Foster Botanical Gardens, to:

❾ Kuan Yin Temple

This Buddhist temple, painted in a brilliant red with a green ceramic-tiled roof, is dedicated to Kuan Yin Bodhisattva, the goddess of mercy, whose statue towers in the prayer hall. The aroma of burning incense is your clue that the temple is still a house of worship, not an exhibit, so enter with respect and leave your shoes outside. You may see people burning paper "money" for prosperity and good luck, or leaving flowers and fruits at the altar (gifts to the goddess). A common offering is the pomelo, a grapefruit-like fruit that's a fertility symbol as well as a gift, indicating a request for the blessing of children.

Continue down Vineyard and then turn right (toward the ocean) on:

❿ Maunakea Street

Between Beretania and King streets are numerous **lei shops** (with lei-makers working away right on the premises). The air is heavy with the aroma of flowers being woven into beautiful treasures. Not only is this the best place in all of Hawaii to get a deal on leis, but the size, color, and design of the leis made here are exceptional. Wander through the shops before you decide which lei you want.

> **TAKE A BREAK**
> If you have a sweet tooth, stop in at **Shung Chong Yuein** ✦, 1027 Maunakea St. (near Hotel Street), for delicious Asian pastries like moon cakes and almond cookies, all at very reasonable prices. The shop also has a wide selection of dried and sugared candies (like ginger, pineapple, and lotus root) that you can eat as you stroll or give as an exotic gift to friends back home.

Turn left on Hotel Street and walk in the Diamond Head (east) direction to:

⓫ Nuuanu Avenue

You may notice that the sidewalks on Nuuanu are made of granite blocks; they came from the ballasts of ships that brought tea from China to Hawaii in the 1800s. On the corner of Nuuanu Avenue and Hotel Street is **Lai Fong Department Store,** a classic Chinatown store owned by the same family for more than 75 years. Walking into Lai Fong is like stepping back in time. The old store sells everything from precious antiques to god-awful knickknacks to rare turn-of-the-century Hawaiian postcards—but it has built its reputation on its fabulous selection of Chinese silks, brocades, and custom dresses.

Between Hotel and Pauahi streets is the **Pegge Hopper Gallery,** 1164 Nuuanu Ave., where you can admire Pegge's well-known paintings of beautiful Hawaiian women.

At Pauahi Street, turn right (toward Diamond Head) and walk up to Bethel Street and the:

⓬ Hawaii Theatre

This restored 1920 Art Deco theater is a work of art in itself. It hosts a variety of programs, from the Hawaii International Film Festival to beauty pageants (see "Oahu After Dark," later in this chapter, for information on how to find out what's on).

Turn right onto Bethel and walk toward the ocean. Turn right again onto Hotel Street, which will lead you back to where you started.

12 Beyond Honolulu: Exploring the Island by Car

The moment always arrives—usually after a couple of days at the beach, snorkeling in the warm, blue-green waters of Hanauma Bay, enjoying sundown mai tais—when a certain curiosity kicks in about the rest of Oahu, largely unknown to most visitors. It's time to find the rental car in the hotel garage and set out around the island. You can also explore Oahu using **TheBus** (see "Getting Around," earlier in this chapter).

OAHU'S SOUTHEAST COAST

From the high-rises of Waikiki, venture down Kalakaua Avenue through tree-lined Kapiolani Park to take a look at a different side of Oahu, the arid south shore. The landscape here is more moonscape, with prickly cacti onshore and, in winter, spouting whales cavorting in the water. Some call it the South Shore, others Sandy's (after the mile-long beach here), but Hawaiians call it **Ka Iwi,** which means "the bone"—no doubt because of all the bone-cracking shore breaks along this popular bodyboarding coastline. The beaches here are long, wide, and popular with local daredevils.

This open, scenic coast is the best place on Oahu to watch sea, shore, and even land birds. It's also a good whale-watching spot in season, and the night sky is ideal for amateur astronomers on the lookout for meteors, comets, and stars.

To get to this coast, follow Kalakaua Avenue past the multitiered Dillingham Fountain and around the bend in the road, which now becomes Poni Moi Road. Make a right on Diamond Head Road and begin the climb up the side of the old crater. At the top are several lookout points, so if the official Diamond Head Lookout is jammed with cars, try one of the other lookouts just down the road. The view of the rolling waves is spectacular; take the time to pull over.

Diamond Head Road rolls downhill now into the ritzy community of **Kahala.** At the V in the road at the triangular Fort Ruger Park, veer to your right and continue on the palm-tree-lined Kahala Avenue. Make a left on Hunakai

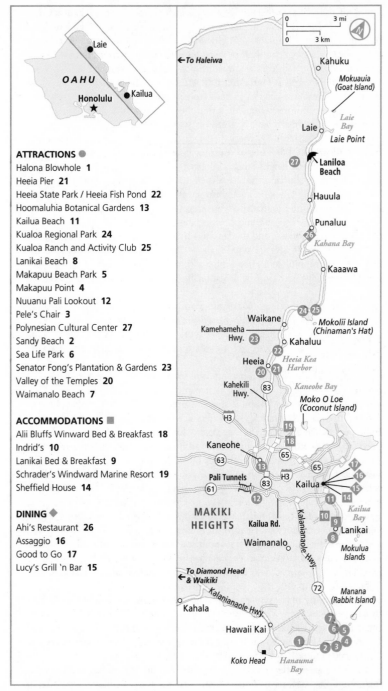

ATTRACTIONS ●
Halona Blowhole **1**
Heeia Pier **21**
Heeia State Park / Heeia Fish Pond **22**
Hoomaluhia Botanical Gardens **13**
Kailua Beach **11**
Kualoa Regional Park **24**
Kualoa Ranch and Activity Club **25**
Lanikai Beach **8**
Makapuu Beach Park **5**
Makapuu Point **4**
Nuuanu Pali Lookout **12**
Pele's Chair **3**
Polynesian Cultural Center **27**
Sandy Beach **2**
Sea Life Park **6**
Senator Fong's Plantation & Gardens **23**
Valley of the Temples **20**
Waimanalo Beach **7**

ACCOMMODATIONS ■
Alii Bluffs Winward Bed & Breakfast **18**
Indrid's **10**
Lanikai Bed & Breakfast **9**
Schrader's Windward Marine Resort **19**
Sheffield House **14**

DINING ◆
Ahi's Restaurant **26**
Assaggio **16**
Good to Go **17**
Lucy's Grill 'n Bar **15**

Street, then a right on Kilauea Avenue, and look for the sign: H-1 WEST—
WAIMANALO. Turn right at the sign, although you won't get on the H-1 freeway;
instead, get on the Kalanianaole Highway, a four-lane highway interrupted every
few blocks by a stoplight. This is the suburban bedroom community to Honolulu, marked by malls on the left and beach parks on the right.

One of these parks is **Hanauma Bay** ⚔⚔ (p. 160); you'll see the turnoff on
the right when you're about a ½ hour from Waikiki. This marine preserve is a
great place to stop for a swim; you'll find the friendliest fish on the island here.
A reminder: The beach park is closed on Tuesdays.

Around mile marker 11, the jagged lava coast itself spouts sea foam at the
Halona Blowhole. Look out to sea from Halona over Sandy Beach and across
the 26-mile gulf to neighboring Molokai and the faint triangular shadow of
Lanai on the far horizon. **Sandy Beach** (p. 160) is Oahu's most dangerous
beach; it's the only one with an ambulance always standing by to whisk injured
wave catchers to the hospital. Bodyboarders just love it.

The coast looks raw and empty along this stretch, but the road weaves past
old Hawaiian fish ponds and the famous formation known as **Pele's Chair,** just
off Kalanianaole Highway (Hwy. 72) above Queen's Beach. From a distance, the
lava-rock outcropping looks like a mighty throne; it's believed to be the fire goddess's last resting place on Oahu before she flew off to continue her work on
other islands.

Ahead lies 647-foot-high **Makapuu Point,** with a lighthouse that once sig-
naled safe passage for steamship passengers arriving from San Francisco. The
automated light now brightens Oahu's south coast for passing tankers, fishing
boats, and sailors. You can take a short hike up here for a spectacular vista
(p. 172).

If you're with the kids, you may want to spend the day at **Sea Life Park** ⚔, a
marine amusement park described earlier in this chapter (p. 192).

Turn the corner at Makapuu, and you're on Oahu's windward side, where
cooling trade winds propel windsurfers across turquoise bays; the waves at
Makapuu Beach Park (p. 161) are perfect for bodysurfing.

Ahead, the coastal vista is a profusion of fluted green mountains and strange
peaks, edged by golden beaches and the blue, blue Pacific. The 3,000-foot-high
sheer green Koolau Mountains plunge almost straight down, presenting an irresistible jumping-off spot for hang-glider pilots, who catch the thermals on
hours-long rides.

Winding up the coast, Kalanianaole Highway (Hwy. 72) leads through rural
Waimanalo, a country beach town of nurseries and stables, fresh-fruit stands,
and some of the island's best conch and triton shell specimens at roadside stands.
Nearly 4 miles long, **Waimanalo Beach** is Oahu's longest beach and the most
popular for bodysurfing. Take a swim here or head on to **Kailua Beach** ⚔⚔, one
of Hawaii's best (p. 161).

If it's still early in the day, you can head up the lush, green Windward Coast
by turning right at the Castle Junction, where Highway 72 meets Highway 61
(which is called Kailua Road on the makai [seaward] side of the junction, and
Kalanianaole Highway on the mauka [inland] side of the junction), and continuing down Kailua Road (Hwy. 61). After Kailua Road crosses the Kaelepulu
Stream, the name of the road changes to Kuulei Road. When Kuulei Road ends,
turn left onto Kalaheo Avenue, which becomes Kaneohe Bay Drive after it
crosses the Kawainui Channel. Follow this scenic drive around the peninsula

until it crosses Kamehameha Highway (Hwy. 83); turn right and continue on Kamehameha Highway for a scenic drive along the ocean.

If you're in a hurry to get back to Waikiki, turn left at Castle Junction and head over the Pali Highway (Hwy. 61), which becomes Bishop Street in Honolulu and ends at Ala Moana. Turn left for Waikiki; it's the second beach on the right.

THE WINDWARD COAST

From the **Nuuanu Pali Lookout** ⚓, near the summit of the Pali Highway (Hwy. 61), you get the first hint of the other side of Oahu, a region so green and lovely that it could be an island sibling of Tahiti. With its many beaches and bays, the scenic 30-mile Windward Coast parallels the corduroy-ridged, nearly perpendicular cliffs of the Koolau Range, which separates the windward side of the island from Honolulu and the rest of Oahu. As you descend on the serpentine Pali Highway beneath often gushing waterfalls, you'll see the nearly 1,000-foot spike of **Olomana,** the bold pinnacle that always reminds us of Devil's Tower National Monument in Wyoming, and beyond, the Hawaiian village of **Waimanalo.**

From the Pali Highway, to the right is Kailua, Hawaii's biggest beach town, with more than 50,000 residents and two special beaches, Kailua and Lanikai, begging for visitors (see "Beaches," earlier in this chapter, for more details). Funky little Kailua is lined with million-dollar houses next to tarpaper shacks, antiques shops, and bed-and-breakfasts. Although the Pali Highway (Hwy. 61) proceeds directly to the coast, it undergoes two name changes, becoming first Kalanianaole Highway—from the intersection of Kamehameha Highway (Hwy. 83)—and then Kailua Road as it heads into Kailua town; but the road remains Highway 61 the whole way. Kailua Road ends at the T intersection at Kalaheo Drive, which follows the coast in a northerly and southerly direction. Turn right on South Kalaheo Drive to get to Kailua Beach Park and Lanikai Beach. No signs point the way, but you can't miss them.

If you spend a day at the beach here, stick around for sunset, when the sun sinks behind the Koolau Range and tints the clouds pink and orange. After a hard day at the beach, you'll work up an appetite, and Kailua has several great, inexpensive restaurants (see "Dining," earlier in this chapter).

If you want to skip the beaches this time, turn left on North Kalaheo Drive, which becomes Kaneohe Bay Drive as it skirts Kaneohe Bay and leads back to Kamehameha Highway (Hwy. 83), which then passes through Kaneohe. The suburban maze of Kaneohe is one giant strip mall of retail excess that mars one of the Pacific's most picturesque bays. After clearing this obstacle, the place begins to look like Hawaii again.

Incredibly scenic Kaneohe Bay is spiked with islets and lined with gold-sand beach parks like **Kualoa** (p. 163), a favorite picnic spot. The bay has a barrier reef and four tiny islets, one of which is known as Moku o loe, or Coconut Island. Don't be surprised if it looks familiar—it appeared in *Gilligan's Island.*

At Heeia State Park is **Heeia Fish Pond,** which ancient Hawaiians built by enclosing natural bays with rocks to trap fish on the incoming tide. The 88-acre fish pond, which is made of lava rock and had four watchtowers to observe fish movement and several sluice gates along the 5,000-foot-long wall, is now in the process of being restored.

Stop by the **Heeia Pier,** which juts onto Kaneohe Bay. You can take a snorkel cruise here, or sail out to a sandbar in the middle of the bay for an incredible view of Oahu that most people, even those who live here, never see. If it's

Tuesday through Sunday between 7am and 5pm, stop in at the **Deli on Heeia Kea Pier** (© 808/235-2192), serving fishermen, sailors, and kayakers the town's best omelettes and plate lunches at reasonable prices since 1979.

Everyone calls it **Chinaman's Hat,** but the tiny island off the eastern shore of Kualoa Regional Park is really named **Mokolii.** It's a sacred *puu honua,* or place of refuge, like the restored Puu Honua Honaunau on the Big Island of Hawaii. Excavations have unearthed evidence that this area was the home of ancient *alii* (royalty). Early Hawaiians believed that Mokolii ("fin of the lizard") is all that remains of a *mo'o,* or lizard, slain by Pele's sister, Hiiaka, and hurled into the sea. At low tide, you can swim out to the island, but keep watch on the changing tide, which can sweep you out to sea. The islet has a small, sandy beach and is a bird preserve, so don't spook the red-footed boobies.

Little poly-voweled beach towns like **Kaaawa, Hauula, Punaluu,** and **Kahaluu** pop up along the coast, offering passersby shell shops and art galleries to explore. Famed hula photographer **Kim Taylor Reece** lives on this coast; his gallery at 53–866 Kamehameha Hwy., near Sacred Falls (© **808/293-2000**), is open Thursday to Saturday from noon to 5pm. You'll also see working cattle ranches, fishermen's wharves, and roadside fruit and flower stands vending ice-cold coconuts (to drink) and tree-ripened mangoes, papayas, and apple bananas.

Sugar, once the sole industry of this region, is gone. But **Kahuku,** the former sugar-plantation town, has found new life as a small aquaculture community with prawn farms that supply island restaurants.

From here, continue along Kamehameha Highway (Hwy. 83) to the North Shore.

ATTRACTIONS ALONG THE WINDWARD COAST

The attractions below are arranged geographically as you drive up the coast from south to north.

Hoomaluhia Botanical Gardens ⋆   This 400-acre botanical garden at the foot of the steepled Koolau Mountains is the perfect place for a picnic. Its name means "a peaceful refuge" and that's exactly what the Army Corps of Engineers created when they installed a flood-control project here, which resulted in a 32-acre freshwater lake and garden. Just unfold a beach mat, lie back, and watch the clouds race across the rippled cliffs of the majestic Koolau Range. This is one of the few public places on Oahu that provides a close-up view of the steepled cliffs. The park has hiking trails and—best of all—the island's only free inland campground (p. 174). If you like hiking and nature, plan to spend at least a half a day here.

45–680 Luluku Rd., Kaneohe. © 808/233-7323. www.co.honolulu.hi.us/parks/hbg/hmbg.htm. Free admission. Daily 9am–4pm. Guided nature hikes Sat 10am and Sun 1pm. Take H-1 to the Pali Hwy. (Hwy. 61); turn left on Kamehameha Hwy. (Hwy. 83); at the fourth light, turn left onto Luluku Rd. Bus: 55 or 56 will stop on Kamehameha Hwy.; it's a 2-mile walk to the visitor center.

Valley of the Temples   This famous cemetery in a cleft of the pali is stalked by wild peacocks and about 700 curious people a day, who pay to see the 9-foot meditation Buddha, acres of ponds full of more than 10,000 Japanese koi carp, and a replica of Japan's 900-year-old Byodo-in Temple of Equality. The original, made of wood, stands in Uji, on the outskirts of Kyoto; the Hawaiian version, made of concrete, was erected in 1968 to commemorate the 100th anniversary of the arrival of the first Japanese immigrants to Hawaii. It's not the same as seeing the original, but it's worth a detour. A 3-ton brass temple bell brings good luck to those who can ring it—although the gongs do jar the Zen-like serenity of this little bit of Japan. If you are in a rush, you can sail through here in an hour, but you'll want to stay longer.

47–200 Kahekili Hwy. (across the street from Temple Valley Shopping Center), Kaneohe. ✆ 808/239-8811. Admission $2 adults, $1 children under 12 and seniors 65 and over. Daily 8:30am–4:30pm. Take the H-1 to the Likelike Hwy. (Hwy. 63); after the Wilson Tunnel, get in the right lane and take the Kahekili Hwy. (Hwy. 63); at the sixth traffic light is the entrance to the cemetery (on the left). Bus: 65.

Senator Fong's Plantation & Gardens   Senator Hiram Fong, the first Chinese American elected to the U.S. Senate, served 17 years before retiring to tropical gardening years ago. Now you can ride an open-air tram through five gardens named for the American presidents he served. His 725-acre private estate includes 75 edible nuts and fruits. It's definitely worth an hour—if you haven't already seen enough botanics to last a lifetime.

47–285 Pulama Rd., Kaneohe. ✆ 808/239-6775. www.fonggarden.net. Admission $10 adults, $8 seniors, $6 children 5–12. Daily 9am–4pm; 45-min. narrated tram tours daily from 10:30am, last tour 3pm. Take the H-1 to the Likelike Hwy. (Hwy. 63); turn left at Kahekili Hwy. (Hwy. 83); continue to Kaneohe and turn left on Pulama Rd. Bus: 55; it's a mile walk uphill from the stop.

Kualoa Ranch and Activity Club   This once-working ranch now has five different adventure packages covering two dozen activities on its 4,000 acres. Activities include horseback riding, mountain-bike riding, shooting a rifle or a .22-caliber handgun, hiking, ATV dune cycling, jet skiing, canoeing, kayaking, snorkeling, freshwater fishing, and more. We highly recommend the beach activities. You'll be shuttled to Molii fish pond's outermost bank, which is decked out like a country club: hammocks on the beach, volleyball courts, horseshoe pits, Ping-Pong tables, and beach pavilions. From here, you can take a 45-foot catamaran to Kaneohe Bay for snorkeling.

49–560 Kamehameha Hwy., Kaaawa. ✆ 800/231-7321 or 808/237-7321. www.kualoa.com. Daily 9:30am–3pm. Various activity packages $15–$139 adults, $15–$79 children 3–11. Reservations required. Take H-1 to the Likelike Hwy. (Hwy. 63), turn left at Kahekili Hwy. (Hwy. 83), and continue to Kaaawa. Bus: 52.

Polynesian Cultural Center ★ *Kids*   Even if you never leave Hawaii, you can still experience the natural beauty and culture of the vast Pacific in a single day at the Polynesian Cultural Center, a kind of living museum of Polynesia. Here, you can see first-hand the lifestyles, songs, dance, costumes, and architecture of seven Pacific islands—Fiji, New Zealand, Marquesas, Samoa, Tahiti, Tonga, and Hawaii—in the re-created villages scattered throughout the 42-acre lagoon park. A recent $1.1 million renovation project remodeled the front entrance and added an exhibit on the story of the Polynesian immigration.

You "travel" through this museum by foot or in a canoe on a man-made freshwater lagoon. Each village is "inhabited" by native students from Polynesia who attend Hawaii's Brigham Young University. The park, which is operated by the Mormon Church, also features a variety of stage shows celebrating the music, dance, history, and culture of Polynesia. There's a luau every evening. Because a visit can take up to 8 hours, it's a good idea to arrive before 2pm. Just beyond the center is the **Hawaii Temple** of the Church of Jesus Christ of Latter-Day Saints, which is built of volcanic rock and concrete in the form of a Greek cross and includes reflecting pools, formal gardens, and royal palms. Completed in 1919, it was the first Mormon temple built outside the continental United States. An optional tour of the Temple Visitors Center, as well as neighboring Brigham Young University, Hawaii, is included in the package admission prices.

55–370 Kamehameha Hwy., Laie. ✆ 800/367-7060, 808/293-3333, or 808/923-2911. www.polynesia.com. Admission $39 adults, $24 children 5–11. Admission, buffet, and nightly show $55 adults, $32 children.

Admission, IMAX, luau, and nightly show $75 adults, $51 children. Ambassador VIP (deluxe) tour $105-$175 adults, $71-$115 children. Mon–Sat 12:30–9:30pm. Take H-1 to Pali Hwy. (Hwy. 61) and turn left on Kamehameha Hwy. (Hwy. 83). Bus: 55. Polynesian Cultural Center coaches $15 round-trip; call numbers above to book.

CENTRAL OAHU & THE NORTH SHORE

If you can afford the splurge, rent a bright, shiny convertible—the perfect car for Oahu, because you can tan as you go—and head for the North Shore and Hawaii's surf city: **Haleiwa** ✪, a quaint turn-of-the-20th-century sugar-plantation town designated a historic site. A collection of faded clapboard stores with a picturesque harbor, Haleiwa has evolved into a surfer outpost and major roadside attraction with art galleries, restaurants, and shops that sell hand-decorated clothing, jewelry, and sports gear (see "Shopping A to Z," later in this chapter).

Getting here is half the fun. You have two choices: The first is to meander north along the lush Windward Coast, through country hamlets with roadside stands selling mangoes, bright tropical pareus, fresh corn, and pond-raised prawns. Attractions along that route are discussed in the previous section.

The second choice is to cruise up the H-2 through Oahu's broad and fertile central valley, past Pearl Harbor and the Schofield Barracks of *From Here to Eternity* fame, and on through the red-earthed heart of the island, where pineapple and sugarcane fields stretch from the Koolau to the Waianae mountains, until the sea reappears on the horizon. If you take this route, the tough part is getting on and off the H-1 freeway from Waikiki, which is done by way of convoluted routing on neighborhood streets. Try McCully Street off Ala Wai Boulevard, which is always crowded but usually the most direct route.

Once you're on H-1, stay to the right side; the freeway tends to divide abruptly. Keep following the signs for the H-1 (it separates off to Hwy. 78 at the airport and reunites later on; either way will get you there), then the H-1/H-2. Leave the H-1 where the two "interstates" divide; take the H-2 up the middle of the island, heading north toward the town of Wahiawa. That's what the sign will say—not North Shore or Haleiwa, but Wahiawa.

The H-2 runs out and becomes a two-lane country road about 18 miles outside downtown Honolulu, near Schofield Barracks (see below). The highway becomes Kamehameha Highway (Hwy. 99 and later Hwy. 83) at Wahiawa. Just past Wahiawa, about a half-hour out of Honolulu, the **Dole Pineapple Plantation,** 64–1550 Kamehameha Hwy. (✆ **808/621-8408;** fax 808/621-1926; www.dole-plantation.com; bus: 52), offers a rest stop with pineapples, pineapple history, pineapple trinkets, and pineapple juice, open daily, 9am to 6pm. This agricultural exhibit/retail area also features a maze kids will love to wander through, open daily from 9:30am to 5pm; admission is $5 for adults and $3 for children 4 to 12 (3 and under are free). The latest attraction is the Pineapple Express, a single-engine diesel locomotive with four cars that takes a 22-minute tour around 2¼ miles of the plantation's grounds, with an educational spiel on the legacy of pineapple and agriculture in Hawaii. The first tour departs at 9:30am, and the last tour gets back to the station at 5:20pm. Cost is $7.50 for adults, $5.50 for children 4 to 12 (3 and under are free). "Kam" Highway, as everyone calls it, will be your road for most of the rest of the trip to Haleiwa.

CENTRAL OAHU ATTRACTIONS

On the central plains of Oahu, tract homes and malls with factory-outlet stores are now spreading across abandoned sugarcane fields, where sandalwood forests used to stand at the foot of Mount Kaala, the mighty summit of Oahu. Hawaiian

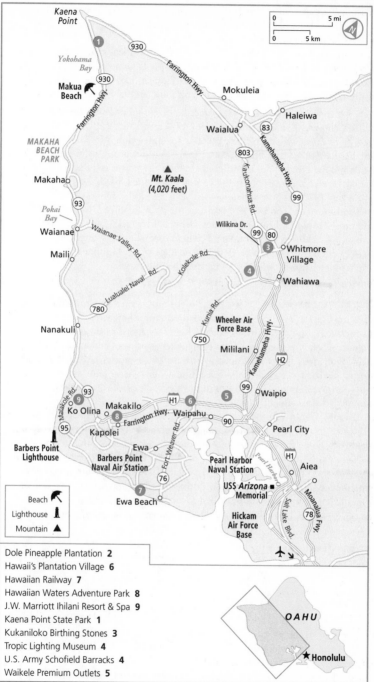

0 — 5 mi
0 — 5 km

Kaena Point

1

(930)

Yokohama Bay

(930)

Makua Beach ☂

Mokuleia

Haleiwa

Waialua (83)

MAKAHA BEACH PARK

(803) Kamehameha Hwy.

Mt. Kaala (4,020 feet) ▲

Makaha o

(99)

Pokai Bay

(93)

2

Waianae o

Wilikina Dr.

(99)(80)

3 Whitmore Village

Maili o

Waianae Valley Rd.

Kolekole Rd.

Lualualei Naval Rd.

Kaukonahua Rd.

4

Wahiawa

(780)

Kunia Rd.

Wheeler Air Force Base

Nanakuli o

(750)

Mililani

Kamehameha Hwy.

(H2)

Malakole Rd.

(99)

Waipio

(93) **9**

Makakilo

(H1) **6**

5

Ko Olina 8

Farrington Hwy.

Waipahu

Pearl City

(95)

Kapolei

(90)

(H1)

Fort Weaver Rd.

Barbers Point Lighthouse ⚓

Ewa

Barbers Point Naval Air Station

Pearl Harbor Naval Station

Aiea

(76)

USS *Arizona* Memorial ■

Salt Lake Blvd.

(78) Moanalua Hwy.

7

Ewa Beach

Hickam Air Force Base

✈

Beach	☂
Lighthouse	⚓
Mountain	▲

Dole Pineapple Plantation **2**
Hawaii's Plantation Village **6**
Hawaiian Railway **7**
Hawaiian Waters Adventure Park **8**
J.W. Marriott Ihilani Resort & Spa **9**
Kaena Point State Park **1**
Kukaniloko Birthing Stones **3**
Tropic Lighting Museum **4**
U.S. Army Schofield Barracks **4**
Waikele Premium Outlets **5**

OAHU

★ Honolulu

chiefs once sent commoners into thick sandalwood forests to cut down trees, which were then sold to China traders for small fortunes. The scantily-clad natives caught cold in the cool uplands, and many died.

On these plains in 1908, the U.S. Army pitched a tent that later became a fort. And on December 7, 1941, Japanese pilots came screaming through Kolekole Pass to shoot up the Art Deco barracks at Schofield, sending soldiers running for cover, and then flew on to sink ships at Pearl Harbor.

U.S. Army Schofield Barracks   James Jones, author of *From Here to Eternity,* called Schofield Barracks "the most beautiful army post the U.S. has or ever had." The *Honolulu Star Bulletin* called it a country club. More than a million soldiers have called Schofield Barracks home. With its broad, palm-lined boulevards and Art Deco buildings, this old army cavalry post is still the largest operated by the U.S. Army outside the continental United States. And it's still one of the best places to be a soldier.

The history of Schofield Barracks and the 25th Infantry Division is told in the small **Tropic Lightning Museum,** Schofield Barracks, Bldg. 361, Waianae Avenue (© **808/655-0438;** troplight1@juno.com). Displays range from a 1917 bunker exhibit to a replica of Vietnam's infamous Cu Chi tunnels. Open Tuesday through Saturday from 10am to 4pm; free admission.

Bus: 52 to Wahiawa; transfer at California Ave. to no. 72, Schofield Barracks Shuttle.

Kukaniloko Birthing Stones   This is the most sacred site in central Oahu. Two rows of 18 lava rocks once flanked a central birthing stone, where women of ancient Hawaii gave birth to potential *alii* (royalty). The rocks, according to Hawaiian belief, held the power to ease the labor pains of childbirth. Birth rituals involved 48 chiefs who pounded drums to announce the arrival of newborns likely to become chiefs. Children born here were taken to the now-destroyed Holonopahu Heiau in the pineapple field, where chiefs ceremoniously cut the umbilical cord.

Used by Oahu's *alii* for generations of births, the *pohaku* (rocks), many in bowl-like shapes, now lie strewn in a grove of trees that stands in a pineapple field here. Some think the site also may have served ancient astronomers—like a Hawaiian Stonehenge. Petroglyphs of human forms and circles appear on some of the stones. The Wahiawa Hawaiian Civic Club recently erected two interpretive signs, one explaining why this was chosen as a birth site and the other telling how the stones were used to aid in the birth process.

Off Kamehameha Hwy. between Wahiawa and Haleiwa, on Plantation Rd. opposite the road to Whitmore Village.

SURF CITY: HALEIWA

Only 28 miles from Waikiki is Haleiwa, the funky ex-sugar-plantation town that's the world capital of big-wave surfing. This beach town really comes alive in winter, when waves rise up, light rain falls, and temperatures dip into the 70s; then, it seems, every surfer in the world is here to see and be seen.

Officially designated a historic cultural and scenic district, Haleiwa thrives in a time warp recalling the turn of the 20th century, when it was founded by sugar baron Benjamin Dillingham, who built a 30-mile railroad to link his Honolulu and North Shore plantations in 1899. He opened a Victorian hotel overlooking Kaiaka Bay and named it Haleiwa, or "house of the Iwa," the tropical seabird often seen here. The hotel and railroad are gone, but Haleiwa, which was rediscovered in the late 1960s by hippies, resonates with rare rustic charm. Tofu, not taro, is a staple in the local diet. Arts and crafts, boutiques, and burger stands line both sides of the town. There's also a busy fishing harbor full of charter boats and captains who hunt the Kauai Channel daily for tuna, mahimahi, and marlin. The bartenders at **Jameson's by the Sea** ☆, 62–540 Kamehameha Hwy. (© **808/637-6272**), make the best mai tais on the North Shore; they use the original recipe by Trader Vic Bergeron.

Once in Haleiwa, the hot and thirsty traveler should report directly to the nearest shave-ice stand, like **Matsumoto Shave Ice** ☆☆, 66–087 Kamehameha Hwy. (© **808/637-4827**). For 40 years, this small, humble shop operated by the Matsumoto family has served a popular rendition of the Hawaii-style snow cone flavored with tropical tastes. The cooling treat is also available at neighboring stores, some of which still shave the ice with a hand-crank device.

Just down the road are some of the fabled shrines of surfing—**Waimea Beach, Banzai Pipeline, Sunset Beach**—where some of the world's largest waves, reaching 20 feet and more, rise up between November and January. They draw professional surfers as well as reckless daredevils and hordes of onlookers, who jump in their cars and head north when word goes out that "surf's up." Don't forget your binoculars. For more details on North Shore beaches, see p. 164.

North Shore Surf and Cultural Museum   Even if you've never set foot on a surfboard, you'll want to visit Oahu's only surf museum to learn the history of this Hawaiian sport of kings. This collection of memorabilia traces the evolution of surfboards from an enormous, weathered redwood board made in the 1930s for Turkey Love, one of Waikiki's legendary beach boys, to the modern-day equivalent—a light, sleek, racy, foam-and-fiberglass board made for big-wave surfer Mark Foo, who drowned while surfing in California in 1994. Other items include classic 1950s surf-meet posters, 1960s surf-music album covers, old beach movie posters with Frankie Avalon and Sandra Dee, the early black-and-white photos by legendary surf photographer LeRoy Grannis, and trophies won by surfing's greatest. Curator Steve Gould is working on a new exhibit of surfing in the ancient Hawaiian culture, complete with Hawaiian artifacts.

North Shore Marketplace, 66–250 Kamehameha Hwy. (behind Kentucky Fried Chicken), Haleiwa. © 808/637-8888. Free admission. Tues–Sun noon–5pm.

MORE NORTH SHORE ATTRACTIONS

Waimea Falls Park ☆ *Kids*   If you have only a day to spend on Oahu and want to see an ancient hula, sniff tropical flowers, go kayaking along the shore, hike to archaeological sites and a waterfall, and play the games of ancient Hawaii (such as spear throwing and lawn bowling), there's only one place to be: Waimea Falls Park. This is the perfect family place. You can also explore remnants of the old Hawaiian settlements in a scenic 1,800-acre river valley that's full of tropical blooms; watch authentic demonstrations of the ancient hula by the park's own *halau* (school); and see cliff divers swan-dive into a pool fed by a 45-foot water-fall. Other activities include riding a mountain bike, paddling a kayak, and walking along the Elehaha River into the jungle.

59–864 Kamehameha Hwy. © 808/638-8511. www.goatlantis.com Admission $24 adults, $12 children 4–12. Various packages available, including kayaking, horseback riding, and mountain biking. Daily 10am–5:30pm. Parking $3. Bus: 52.

Puu o Mahuka Heiau ☆ *Moments*   Go around sundown to feel the *mana* (sacred spirit) of this Hawaiian place. The largest sacrificial temple on Oahu, it's associated with the great Kaopulupulu, who sought peace between Oahu and

Oahu's North Shore

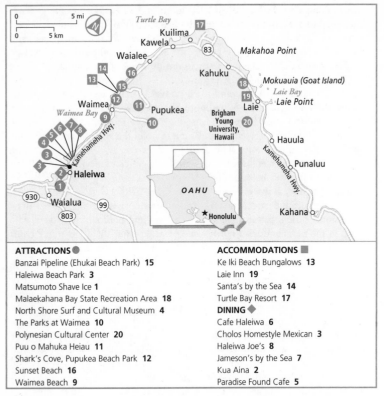

0	5 mi
0	5 km

Turtle Bay

Kuilima **17**

Kawela

Waialee **83** *Makahoa Point*

14 **16** Kahuku

13 **15** **18** *Mokuauia (Goat Island)*

Waimea **12** **11** Pupukea **19** *Laie Bay* *Laie Point*

Waimea Bay **9** **10** Laie

Brigham Young University, Hawaii **20**

4 **5** **6** **7** **8** Hauula

3 *Kamehameha Hwy.* Punaluu

3 **2** Haleiwa

OAHU

930 Waialua **99**

803 ★Honolulu Kahana

Kahana

ATTRACTIONS ●

Banzai Pipeline (Ehukai Beach Park) **15**
Haleiwa Beach Park **3**
Matsumoto Shave Ice **1**
Malaekahana Bay State Recreation Area **18**
North Shore Surf and Cultural Museum **4**
The Parks at Waimea **10**
Polynesian Cultural Center **20**
Puu o Mahuka Heiau **11**
Shark's Cove, Pupukea Beach Park **12**
Sunset Beach **16**
Waimea Beach **9**

ACCOMMODATIONS ■

Ke Iki Beach Bungalows **13**
Laie Inn **19**
Santa's by the Sea **14**
Turtle Bay Resort **17**

DINING ◆

Cafe Haleiwa **6**
Cholos Homestyle Mexican **3**
Haleiwa Joe's **8**
Jameson's by the Sea **7**
Kua Aina **2**
Paradise Found Cafe **5**

Kauai. This prescient *kahuna* predicted that the island would be overrun by strangers from a distant land. In 1794, three of Capt. George Vancouver's men of the *Daedalus* were sacrificed here. In 1819, the year before New England missionaries landed in Hawaii, King Kamehameha II ordered all idols here to be destroyed.

A national historic landmark, this 18th-century heiau, known as the "hill of escape," sits on a 300-foot bluff overlooking Waimea Bay and 25 miles of Oahu's wave-lashed North Coast—all the way to Kaena Point, where the Waianae Range ends in a spirit leap to the other world. The heiau appears as a huge rectangle of rocks twice as big as a football field, with an altar often covered by the flower and fruit offerings left by native Hawaiians.

1 mile past Waimea Bay. Take Pupukea Rd. mauka (inland) off Kamehameha Hwy. at Foodland, and drive 1 mile up a switchback road. Bus: 52, then walk up Pupukea Rd.

13 Shopping from A to Z

Shopping competes with golf, surfing, and sightseeing as a bona fide Honolulu activity. And why not? The proliferation of top-notch made-in-Hawaii products, the vitality of the local crafts scene, and the unquenchable thirst for mementos of the islands lend respectability to shopping here.

Oahu is also a haven for mall mavens. More than 1,000 stores occupy the 11 major shopping centers on this island. From T-shirts to Versace, posh European to down-home local, avant-garde to unspeakably tacky, Oahu's offerings are wide-ranging indeed. But you must sometimes wade through oceans of schlock to arrive at the mother lode. Nestled amid the Louis Vuitton, Chanel, and Tiffany boutiques on Waikiki's Kalakaua Avenue are plenty of tacky booths hawking air-brushed T-shirts, gold by the inch, and tasteless aloha shirts.

The section that follows is not about finding cheap souvenirs or tony items from designer fashion chains; you can find these on your own. Rather, we offer a guide to finding those special treasures that lie somewhere in between.

SHOPPING IN & AROUND HONOLULU & WAIKIKI
ALOHA WEAR

One of Hawaii's lasting afflictions is the penchant tourists have for wearing loud, matching aloha shirts and muumuus. We applaud such visitors' good intentions (to act local), but no local resident would be caught dead in such a get-up. Muumuus and aloha shirts are wonderful, but the real thing is what island folks wear on Aloha Friday (every Fri), to the Brothers Cazimero Lei Day Concert (every May 1), or to work (where allowed). It's what they wear at home and to special parties where the invitation reads "Aloha Attire."

Aside from the vintage Hawaiian wear (1930s–1950s) found in collectibles shops and at swap meets, our favorite contemporary aloha-wear designer is Hawaii's **Tori Richards. Tommy Bahama,** which never calls its shirts "aloha shirts" but claims, instead, a Caribbean influence, is another Hawaii shirt icon, and so is the up-and-coming **Tiki** brand, quirky and distinctive, with elements that hark back to 1950s bowling shirts and Jimmy Dean charisma.

The best aloha shirts are pricey these days, going for $70 to $100. For the vintage look, **Avanti** has a corner on the market with its stunning line of silk shirts and dresses in authentic 1930s to 1950s patterns. The $70 shirts boast all the qualities of a vintage silky but without the high price or the web-thin fragility of an authentic antique. The dresses and other styles are the epitome of comfort and nostalgic good looks. The line is distributed in better boutiques and department stores throughout Hawaii. In Waikiki, the major retail outlet is **Avanti Fashion,** at 2229 Kuhio Ave. (© **808/924-1668**); Waikiki Shopping Plaza, 2250 Kalakaua Ave. (© **808/922-2828**); 307 Lewers St. (© **808/926-6886**); and 2160 Kalakaua Ave. (© **808/924-3232**).

Also popular is **Kahala Sportswear,** a well-known local company established in 1936. Kahala has faithfully reproduced, with astounding success, the linoleum-block prints of noted Maui artist Avi Kiriaty and the designs of other contemporary artists. Kahala is sold in department stores (from Macy's to Nordstrom), surf shops, and stylish boutiques throughout Hawaii and the mainland.

For the most culturally correct aloha wear, and for a graphic identity that is rare in the aloha shirt realm, check out the shirts, dresses, and pareus of **Sig Zane Designs** (p. 343 and 458), available at his Hilo (Big Island) and Wailuku (Maui) stores. Zane, an accomplished hula dancer married to one of Hawaii's most revered hula masters, has an unmistakable visual style and a profound knowledge of Hawaiian culture that brings depth and meaning to his boldly styled renditions. Each Sig Zane pareu and aloha shirt, in pure cotton, tells a story. No wonder it's the garb of the cultural connoisseurs, who also buy fabrics by the yard for cushions, curtains, and interior accents.

Another name to watch for is **Tutuvi,** whose T-shirts, dresses, and pareus are distinctive for their brilliant color combinations and witty juxtaposition of design motifs. Tutuvi can be found in various shops throughout Hawaii (such as

Ⓒ Vintage Clothing

It costs big bucks to wear old clothes if they're in good shape and have a past—$600 to $1,000, say, for a vintage silky in perfect condition. Take a peek in **Bailey's Antiques and Aloha Shirts,** 517 Kapahulu Ave. (Ⓒ **808/734-7628**), and check out vintage finds from the tatty to the sublime: old lamps, cushions, jewelry, fur stoles, and a dizzying selection of clothing for both collectors and neophytes. A vintage rayon Chinese-style muu or any vintage schmatte in perfect condition could fetch $600 and up, but you may be able to turn up some cheaper options. Prices begin below $20, and a lucky hunter could find a velvet dress or sarong skirt for less than $50.

In Kaimuki, **Comme Ci Comme Ça,** 3464 Waialae Ave. (Ⓒ **808/734-8869**), is a cozy, adorable repository of nearly new and vintage treasures, from Donna Karan suits on consignment to nearly new Ferragamo and Prada bags and the occasional retro tea-timer or 1930s dress. This shop is big on 1920s to 1940s sweaters with fur collars, movie-starlet stoles, and other stylish oldies. And the vintage jewelry! Earrings, bracelets, brooches, necklaces, fans—the selection grows and brightens by the year.

Native Books & Beautiful Things; see below), or by appointment at **Tutuvi,** 2850 S. King St. (Ⓒ **808/947-5950**).

Reyn Spooner is another source of attractive aloha shirts and muumuus in traditional and contemporary styles, with stores in Ala Moana Center, Kahala Mall, and the Sheraton Waikiki. Reyn has popularized the reverse-print aloha shirt—the uniform of downtown boardrooms—and has also jumped aboard the vintage-look bandwagon with old-Hawaii cotton prints, some of them in attractive two-color pareu patterns.

Well-known muumuu labels in Hawaii include **Mamo Howell,** with a boutique in Ward Warehouse, and **Princess Kaiulani** and **Bete** for the dressier muus, sold along with many other lines at Macy's and other department stores. **Hilo Hattie's** new Ala Moana store (Ⓒ **808/973-3266**) is a gold mine of affordable aloha wear. Hilo Hattie's also offers free daily shuttle service from Waikiki to its retail outlet on Nimitz Highway (Ⓒ **808/537-2926**), and to Aloha Tower Marketplace, Ala Moana Center, and Waikiki. You'll also find macadamia nuts, Hawaii coffees, and other souvenirs at these Hilo Hattie's stores, as well as live Hawaiian entertainment. Quality and selection have improved noticeably in recent years.

ANTIQUES & COLLECTIBLES

Aloha Antiques and Collectibles   You may find rare Japanese plates or a priceless Lalique among the tchotchkes that fill every square inch of this dizzying miniemporium of seven shops, where the items literally spill out onto the sidewalk. You'll have to look hard, but it's worth it—the prices are good and the rewards substantial. Jewelry, vintage aloha shirts, vases, silver, Asian lacquer, Hawaiian collectibles, and countless eclectic items make up this collection of junk, treasures, and nostalgia. 920 Maunakea St. (at the harbor end of the street by Nimitz Hwy.). © 808/536-1828.

Anchor House Antiques   This highly eclectic collection of Hawaiian, Asian, and European pieces sprawls over thousands of square feet. You'll find wooden calabashes, camphor chests, paintings, Hawaiian artifacts, and trinkets, priced from $10 to $2,000. 471 Kapahulu Ave. © 808/732-3884.

Antique Alley   This narrow shop is chockablock with the passionate collections of several vendors under one roof. With its expanded collection of old Hawaiian artifacts and surfing and hula nostalgia, it's a sure winner for eclectic tastes. The showcases include estate jewelry, antique silver, Hawaiian bottles, collectible toys, pottery, cameras, Depression glass, linens, plantation photos and ephemera, and a wide selection of nostalgic items from Hawaii and across America. At the rear is a small, attractive selection of Soiree clothing, made by Julie Lauster, of antique kimonos and obis. 1347 Kapiolani Blvd. © 808/941-8551.

Antique House   Small but tasteful, the low-profile Antique House is hidden below the lobby level of the illustrious Royal Hawaiian Hotel. Come here for small items, such as Asian antiques, Chinese and Japanese porcelains, and a stunning selection of snuff bottles, bronzes, vases, and china. In the Royal Hawaiian Hotel, 2259 Kalakaua Ave. © 808/923-5101.

Bailey's Antiques & Aloha Shirts   A large selection (thousands) of vintage, secondhand, and nearly new aloha shirts and other collectibles fills this eclectic emporium. It looks as though the owners regularly scour Hollywood movie costume departments for oddball gowns, feather boas, fur stoles, leather jackets, 1930s dresses, and scads of other garments from periods past. Bailey's has one of the largest vintage aloha-shirt collections in Honolulu, with prices ranging from inexpensive to sky-high. Old Levi's jeans, mandarin jackets, vintage vases, household items, shawls, purses, and an eye-popping assortment of bark-cloth fabrics (the real thing, not repros) are among the mementos in this monumental collection. 517 Kapahulu Ave. © 808/734-7628.

Garakuta-Do   This huge warehouse/store at the gateway to Waikiki has a sublime collection of Japanese antiques. In its expanded space on the Ala Wai Canal, across from the Convention Center, it offers ample free parking. It's worth finding for its late-Edo period (1800s–early 1900s) antiques, collected and sold by cheerful owner Wataru Harada. The selection of gorgeous tansus, mingei folk art, Japanese screens, scrolls, Imari plates, bronze sculptures, kimonos, obis, modern woodblock prints, and stone objects makes shopping here a treasure hunt. 1833 Kalakaua Ave., Suite 100. © 808/955-2099.

Kilohana Square   If we had to recommend only one destination for antiques, we'd pick this tiny square in Kapahulu. Kilohana's antiques shops cover a rich range of Asian art, Japanese and European objects, and high-quality collectibles. Many have loyal clients across the country. Our favorites include **T. Fujii Japanese Antiques** (© 808/732-7860), a long-standing icon in Hawaii's antiques world and an impeccable source for ukiyo-e prints, scrolls, obis, Imari porcelain, tansus, tea-ceremony bowls, and screens, as well as contemporary ceramics from Mashiko and Kasama, with prices from $25 to $18,000; **Miko Oriental Art Gallery** (© 808/735-4503), recently moved to a bigger space within Kilohana Square and housing an even larger repository of Chinese, Japanese, Korean, and Southeast Asian ceramics, bronzes, and furniture, ranging in price from $50 to $22,000; and **Silk Winds** (© 808/735-6599), with a wonderful selection of

Asian antiques and beads. Each shop has its own hours; call for details. 1016 Kapahulu Ave.

Robyn Buntin   Robyn Buntin's 5,000-square-foot gallery and picture-framing department, called Robyn Buntin's Picture Framing and Oceania Gallery, and his gallery for Hawaiian art, at 820 S. Beretania St., are among the features of this burgeoning art resource, located three doors from the Honolulu Academy of Art. This is Honolulu's stellar source of museum-quality Asian art and contemporary and traditional Hawaiian art. 848 S. Beretania St. ✆ **808/523-5913.**

BOOKSTORES

Barnes & Noble   With more than 150,000 titles, a respectable music department, and strong Hawaiiana, fiction, and new-release departments, as well as a popular coffee bar, Barnes & Noble has become the second home of Honolulu's casual readers and bibliophiles. Kahala Mall, 4211 Waialae Ave. ✆ **808/737-3323.**

Borders   Borders is a beehive of literary activity, with weekly signings, prominent local and mainland musicians at least monthly, and special events almost daily that make this store a major Honolulu attraction. There's a second Borders at Waikele Center, 94–821 Lumiaina St. (✆ 808/676-6699). Ward Centre, 1200 Ala Moana Blvd. ✆ **808/591-8995.**

Pacific Book House   Denis Perron, connoisseur of rare books, has moved his venerable Pacific Book House to a new location, kept and expanded the rare and out-of-print book inventory, and expanded into paintings, antiques, and estate jewelry, even offering appraisals of rare books and paintings and handling restorations others are afraid to touch. When you tire of book browsing, look into the selection of antique silver and china. Literati still come here for finds in Hawaiiana, rare prints, collectible books, and other out-of-print treasures. 1249 S. Beretania St. ✆ **808/591-1599.**

Rainbow Books and Records   A little weird but totally lovable, especially among students and eccentrics (and insatiable readers), Rainbow Books is notable for its selection of popular fiction, records, and Hawaii-themed books, secondhand and reduced. Because it's located in the university area, it's always bulging with textbooks, Hawaiiana, and popular music. It's about the size of a large closet, but you'll be surprised by what you'll find. 1010 University Ave. ✆ **808/ 955-7994.**

EDIBLES

In addition to the stores listed below, we also recommend **Executive Chef** (✆ **808/596-2433**), in the Ward Warehouse, and **Islands' Best** (✆ **808/949-5345**), in the Ala Moana Center. Both shops contain wide-ranging selections that include Hawaii's specialty food items.

If you're looking for a bakery, **Saint-Germain,** in Shirokiya at Ala Moana Shopping Center (✆ **808/955-1711**), and near Times Supermarket, 1296 S. Beretania St. (✆ **808/593-8711**), sells baguettes, country loaves, and oddball delicacies such as mini mushroom-and-spinach pizzas. The reigning queen of bakers, though, is **Cafe Laufer,** 3565 Waialae Ave. (✆ **808/735-7717;** p. 153). Nearby, old-timers still line up at **Sconees,** 1117 12th Ave. (✆ **808/734-4024**), formerly Bea's Pies. Sconees has fantastic scones, pumpkin-custard pies, and Danishes. And don't forget **Mary Catherine's** (see below), a great place for quality cakes and European pastries.

Asian Grocery   Asian Grocery supplies many of Honolulu's Thai, Vietnamese, Chinese, Indonesian, and Filipino restaurants with authentic spices, rice, noodles, produce, sauces, herbs, and adventurous ingredients. Browse among the kaffir lime leaves, tamarind and fish pastes, red and green chiles, curries, chutneys, lotus leaves, gingko nuts, jasmine and basmati rice, and shelf upon shelf of medium to hot chile sauces. 1319 S. Beretania St. (©) **808/593-8440.** www.Asianfoodtrading.com.

Daiei   Stands offering takeout sushi, Korean *kal bi*, pizza, Chinese food, flowers, Mrs. Fields cookies, and other items for self and home surround this huge emporium. Inside, you'll find household products, a pharmacy, and inexpensive clothing, but it's the prepared foods and produce that excel. The fresh seafood section is one of Honolulu's best, not far from where regulars line up for the bento lunches and individually wrapped sushi. When Kau navel oranges, macadamia nuts, Kona coffee, Chinese taro, and other Hawaii products are on sale, savvy locals arrive in droves to take advantage of the high quality and good value. 801 Kaheka St. (©) **808/973-4800.**

Fujioka's Wine Merchants   Oenophiles flock here for a mouthwatering selection of wines, single-malt Scotches, excellent Italian wines, and affordable, farm-raised caviar—food and libations for all occasions. Everyday wines, special-occasion wines, and esoteric wines are priced lower here than at most places. The wine-tasting bar at the rear of the store is a new attraction. Market City Shopping Center, 2919 Kapiolani Blvd., lower level. (©) **808/739-9463.**

Honolulu Chocolate Co.   Life's greatest pleasures are dispensed here with abandon: expensive gourmet chocolates made in Honolulu, Italian and Hawaiian biscotti, boulder-size turtles (caramel and pecans covered with chocolate), truffles, chocolate-covered coffee beans, jumbo apricots in white and dark

---

(C) Fish Markets

Tamashiro Market, 802 N. King St., Kalihi ((©) **808/841-8047**), is the grandfather of fish markets and the ace in the hole for home chefs with bouillabaisse or paella in mind. A separate counter sells seaweed salad, prepared poke, Filipino and Puerto Rican ti-wrapped steamed rice, and dozens of other ethnic foods.

For more mainstream shoppers, **Safeway** on Beretania Street ((©) **808/ 591-8315**) has a seafood counter with fresh choices and a staff that takes pride in its deftness with prepared foods (like fresh ahi poke, seaweed salad, shrimp cocktail, and marinated crab—don't be shy about asking for a taste).

Neighbor islanders have been known to drive directly from the airport to **Yama's Fish Market,** 2203 Young St., Moiliili ((©) **808/941-9994**), for one of the best plate lunches in town. But Yama's is also known for its inexpensive fresh fish, tasty poke, and lomi salmon. Chilled beer, boiled peanuts, and fresh ahi sliced into sashimi are popular for local-style gatherings, sunset beach parties, and festive *pau hana* (end of work) celebrations. New standouts include a fabulous assortment of chocolate biscotti and chocolate chip cookies, sweet-potato and custard mochi and a *haupia* (coconut pudding) pie layered with bright-purple Okinawan sweet potato.

chocolate, to name a few. There are also tinned biscuits, European candies, and sweets in a million disguises. *Hint:* You pay dearly for them, but the dark-chocolate-dipped macadamia-nut clusters are beyond compare. Ward Centre, 1200 Ala Moana Blvd. ℂ 808/591-2997.

It's Chili in Hawaii This is *the* oasis for chili-heads, a house of heat with endorphins aplenty and good food to accompany the hot sauces from around the world, including a fabulous selection of made-in-Hawaii products. Scoville units (measurements of heat in food) are the topic of the day in this shop, lined with thousands of bottles of hot sauces, salsas, and other chili-based food products. Not everything is scorching, however; some products, like Dave's Soyabi and the limu-habañero sauce called Makai, are everyday flavor enhancers that can be used on rice, salads, meats, and pasta. If you're eating in, the fresh-frozen tamales, in several varieties (including meatless), are now in regular supply. Every Saturday, free samples of green-chili stew are dished up to go with the generous hot-sauce tastings. 2080 S. King St., Suite 105. ℂ 808/945-7070.

Mary Catherine's Bakery This top-notch European bakery sells everything from lavishly tiered wedding cakes to killer carrot cakes and chocolate decadence cake that is moist, rich, and extravagant. Cookies, cakes, scones, pastries, tortes, and all manner of baked sweets line the counters. Long a favorite of locals. 2820 S. King St., across from the Hawaiian Humane Society. ℂ 808/946-4333.

Mauna Kea Marketplace Food Court Hungry patrons line up in front of these no-nonsense food booths that sell everything from pizza and plate lunches to quick, authentic, and inexpensive Vietnamese, Thai, Italian, Chinese, Japanese, and Filipino dishes. The best seafood fried rice comes from the woks of **Malee Thai/Vietnamese Cuisine,** at the mauka (inland) end of the marketplace—perfectly flavored with morsels of fish, squid, and shrimp. Right next to it is Tandoori Chicken Cafe, a fount of Indian culinary pleasures, from curries and jasmine-chicken rice balls to spiced rounds of curried potatoes and a wonderful lentil dal. On the other side of Malee, **Masa's** serves bento and Japanese dishes, such as miso eggplant, that are famous. A few stalls makai, you'll find the best dessert around at **Pho Lau,** which serves haupia (coconut pudding), tapioca, and taro in individual baskets made of pandanus. Walk the few steps down to the produce stalls (pungent odors, fish heads, and chicken feet on counters—not for the squeamish) and join in the spirit of discovery. Vendors sell everything from fresh ahi and whole snapper to yams and taro, seaweed, and fresh fruits and vegetables of every shape and size. 1120 Maunakea St., Chinatown. ℂ 808/524-3409.

Paradise Produce Co. Neat rows of mangoes, top-quality papayas, and reasonably priced and very fresh produce make this a paradise for food lovers. When mangoes are in season, you'll find Yee's Orchard Haydens set apart from the less desirable Mexican mangoes and, if you're lucky, a stash of ambrosial Pirie mangoes (they sell out quickly). Chinese taro, lychee and asparagus in season, local eggplant, and dozens of fruits and vegetables are offered up fresh, neat, and colorful. 83 N. King St., Chinatown. ℂ 808/533-2125.

People's Open Markets Truck farmers from all over the island bring their produce to Oahu's neighborhoods in regularly scheduled, city-sponsored open markets, held Monday through Saturday at various locations. Among the tables of ong choy, choi sum, Okinawan spinach, opal basil, papayas, mangoes, seaweed, and fresh fish, you'll find homemade banana bread, Chinese pomelo (like large grapefruit), fresh fiddleheads (fern shoots) when available, and colorful,

Health-Food Stores

In the university district, **Down to Earth,** 2525 S. King St., Moiliili (© 808/947-7678), is a respectable source of organic vegetables and vegetarian bulk foods, with good prices, a strong selection of supplements and herbs, and a vegetarian juice-and-sandwich bar. But our favorite is nearby **Kokua Market,** 2643 S. King St. (© 808/941-1922), a health-food cooperative and Honolulu's best source for organic vegetables. It also has an excellent variety of cheeses; pastas and bulk grains; sandwiches, salads, and prepared foods; organic wines; and an expanded vitamin section.

Tiny but powerful, with a loyal clientele, **Hou Ola,** 1541 S. Beretania St. (© 808/955-6168), has competitive prices and a wide selection of health-food supplements. There's no produce, but there are frozen vegetarian foods, bulk grains, and healthful snacks. In Nuuanu Valley, mauka (inland) of downtown Honolulu, **Huckleberry Farms,** 1613 Nuuanu Ave. (© 808/524-7960), has a wide range of produce, vitamins, cosmetics, books, and prepared vegetarian foods. A few doors down, the beauty and vitamin retail outlet is stocked with cosmetics, nutritional supplements, and nonperishable, nongrocery health products.

bountiful harvests from land and sea. Various sites around town. © 808/527-5167. Call to find the open market nearest you.

R. Field Wine Co.   Foodland has won countless new converts since Richard Field—oenophile, gourmet, and cigar aficionado—moved his wine shop from Ward Centre to this new location within lower Makiki's Foodland. The thriving gourmet store offers gemlike vine-ripened tomatoes and juicy clementines, sparkling bags of Nalo gourmet greens, designer cheeses, caviar, Langenstein Farms macadamia nuts, vegetarian and salmon mousses, vinegars, and all manner of epicurean delights, including wines and single-malt Scotches. *A huge hit:* the warm, just-baked breads (rosemary–olive oil, whole wheat, organic wheat, and others) baked on the premises with dough flown in from Los Angeles's famous La Brea Bakery. Foodland Super Market, 1460 S. Beretania St. © 808/596-9463.

Sushi Company   It's not easy to find premium grade hamachi (yellowtail tuna), ahi, ikura (salmon roe), ika (cuttlefish), and other top-grade fresh ingredients in anything but a bona-fide sit-down sushi bar. But here it is, a small, sparkling gem of a sushi maker that sells fast-food sushi of non-fast-food quality, at great prices. Order ahead or wait while they make it. The combinations range from minisets (27 pieces) to large-variety sets (43–51 pieces), ideal for picnics and potlucks. Individual hand rolls range from 99¢ to $1.55, and the nigiri comes in orders of two and more. An expanded menu now offers excellent miso soup, salmon skin sushi to go, scallop, sea urchin, and spicy tuna. A newcomer to the neighborhood and already a mainstay, Sushi Company has one small two-person table; most of the business is takeout. 1111 McCully St., McCully. © 808/947-5411.

FLOWERS & LEIS

At most lei shops, simple leis sell for $3 and up, deluxe leis for $10 and up. For a special-occasion designer bouquet or lei, you can't do better than Michael Miyashiro of **Rainforest Plantes et Fleurs** (© **808/942-1550** or 808/591-5999). He's an ecologically aware, highly gifted lei-maker—his leis are pricey, but worth it. He custom-designs the lei for the person, occasion, and even destination. Order by phone or stop by the Ward Warehouse, where his tiny shop is an oasis of green and beauty. Upon request, Miyashiro's leis will come in ti-leaf bundles, called *puʻolo;* custom gift baskets (in woven green coconut baskets), and special arrangements. You can even request the card sentiments in Hawaiian, with English translations.

The other primary sources for flowers and leis are the shops lining the streets of Moiliili and Chinatown. Moiliili favorites include **Rudy's Flowers,** 2722 S. King St. (© **808/944-8844**), a local institution with the best prices on roses, Micronesian ginger lei, and a variety of cut blooms. Across the street, **Flowers for a Friend,** 2739 S. King St. (© **808/955-4227**), has good prices on leis, floral arrangements, and cut flowers. Nearby, **Flowers by Jr. and Lou,** 2652 S. King St. (© **808/941-2022**), offers calla lilies, Gerber daisies, a riot of potted orchids, and the full range of cut flowers along with its lei selection.

In Chinatown, lei vendors line Beretania and Maunakea streets, and the fragrances of their wares mix with the earthy scents of incense and ethnic foods. Our top picks are **Lita's Leis,** 59 N. Beretania St. (© **808/521-9065**), which has fresh puakenikeni, gardenias that last, and a supply of fresh and reasonable leis; **Sweetheart's Leis,** 69 N. Beretania St. (© **808/537-3011**), with a worthy selection of the classics at fair prices; **Lin's Lei Shop,** 1017-A Maunakea St. (© **808/537-4112**), with creatively fashioned, unusual leis; and **Cindy's Lei Shoppe,** 1034 Maunakea St. (© **808/536-6538**), with terrific sources for unusual leis such as feather dendrobiums, firecracker combinations, and everyday favorites like ginger, tuberose, orchid, and pikake. Ask Cindy's about its unique "curb service," available with phone orders. Just give them your car's color and model, and you can pick up your lei curbside—a great convenience on this busy street.

HAWAIIANA & GIFT ITEMS

Our top recommendations are the **Academy Shop,** at the Honolulu Academy of Arts, 900 S. Beretania St. (© **808/523-8703**), and the **Contemporary Museum Gift Shop,** 2411 Makiki Heights Rd. (© **808/523-3447**), two of the finest shopping stops on Oahu and worth a special trip whether or not you want to see the museums themselves. (And you will want to see the museums, especially the recently expanded Honolulu Academy of Arts.) The Academy Shop offers art books, jewelry, basketry, ethnic fabrics, native crafts from all over the world, posters and books, and fiber vessels and accessories. The Contemporary Museum shop focuses on arts and crafts such as avant-garde jewelry, cards and stationery, books, home accessories, and gift items made by artists from Hawaii and across the country. We love the glammy selection of jewelry and novelties, such as the twisted-wire wall hangings.

Hula Supply Center Hawaiiana meets kitsch in this shop's marvelous selection of Day-Glo cellophane skirts, bamboo nose flutes, T-shirts, hula drums, shell leis, feathered rattle gourds, lauhala accessories, fiber mats, and a wide assortment of pareu fabrics. Although hula dancers shop here for their dance accouterments, it's not all serious shopping. This is fertile ground for souvenirs and memorabilia of Hawaii, rooted somewhere between irreverent humor and cultural integrity. A great stop for Hawaiian and Polynesian gift items. 2346 S. King St., Moiliili. ℂ 808/941-5379.

**Macy's Ku`u Home Island Gifts** The fourth-floor island lifestyle department, called Ku`u Home ("my home") Island Gifts, is the best thing this department store has done in recent memory. Cultural/retail wizards Donna Burns and Maile Meyer of the enormously successful Native Books & Beautiful Things (see below) contacted 65 Hawaii artists and created a department of more than 600 unique, made-in-Hawaii products, skillfully displayed in a warm, real-life setting. Furniture, lamps, books, cushions, baskets, Hawaiian implements, quilts, lauhala and coconut home accessories, glassware, fabrics, gifts, personal adornments—the selection is eclectic and wonderful, capturing a distinctive Hawaii flavor that has its own strong identity within the store. The "Hawaii Artist of the Month" series brings the artists into the store to talk about their works. More than a shopping must, Ku`u Home is a cultural and aesthetic eye-opener. Ala Moana Center, 1450 Ala Moana Blvd. ℂ 808/945-5636.

Native Books & Beautiful Things *(Finds* This *hui* (association) of artists and craftspeople features a love of things Hawaiian, from musical instruments to calabashes, jewelry, leis, and books. You'll find contemporary Hawaiian clothing, handmade koa journals, Hawaii-themed home accessories, lauhala handbags and accessories, jams, jellies, and food products, etched glass, hand-painted fabrics and clothing, stone poi pounders, and other high-quality gift items. Some of Hawaii's finest artists in all craft media have their works available here on a regular basis, and the Hawaiian-book selection is tops. The 5,000-square-foot emporium at Ward Warehouse is a browser's paradise. Ward Warehouse, 1050 Ala Moana Blvd. ℂ 808/596-8885.

Nohea Gallery A fine showcase for contemporary Hawaii art, Nohea celebrates the islands with thoughtful, attractive selections in all media, from pit-fired raku and finely turned wood vessels to jewelry, hand-blown glass, paintings, prints, fabrics (including Hawaiian-quilt cushions), and furniture. Nohea's selection is always evolving and growing, with 90% of the works by Hawaii artists. Ward Warehouse, 1050 Ala Moana Blvd. ℂ 808/596-0074. Also at Kahala Mandarin Oriental Hawaii, 5000 Kahala Ave. ℂ 808/737-8688; two Waikiki locations, in Ohana Reef Towers Hotel, 227 Lewers St. ℂ 808/926-2224, and Sheraton Moana Surfrider Hotel, 2365 Kalakaua Ave. ℂ 808/923-6644.

Nui Mono We love this tiny shop's kimono clothing and accessories and the contemporary clothes made from ethnic fabrics. Other items include handbags made of patchwork vintage fabrics and priceless kimono silks, drapey Asian shapes and ikat fabrics, and richly textured vests and skirts. Warm, rich colors are the Nui Mono signature, and everything's moderately priced. 2745 S. King St., Moiliili. ℂ 808/946-7407.

Shop Pacifica Local crafts, lauhala and Cook Island woven coconut, Hawaiian music tapes and CDs, pareus, and a vast selection of Hawaii-themed books anchor this gift shop. Hawaiian quilt cushion kits, jewelry, glassware, seed and Niihau shell leis, cookbooks, and many other gift possibilities will keep you occupied between stargazing in the planetarium and pondering the shells and antiquities of the esteemed historical museum. In the Bishop Museum, 1525 Bernice St. ℂ 808/848-4158.

SHOPPING CENTERS

Ala Moana Center The new third level is abuzz with eateries and shops, while the ponds on the mall level are thriving with taro and Hawaiian plants, and even hapu`u ferns and koa trees. At press time the finishing touches of a recent ambitious expansion are still being applied, but most of the shops are in, and many of them are the familiar names of mainland chains, such as **DKNY, Old Navy,** and **Eddie Bauer.** The three-story, superluxe **Neiman Marcus,** which opened in September 1998, was a bold move in Hawaii's troubled economy and has retained its position as the shrine of the fashionistas. But there are practical touches in the center, too, such as banks, a foreign-exchange service (**Thomas Cook**), a U.S. Post Office, several optical companies (including 1-hr. service by **LensCrafters**), **Foodland Supermarket, Longs Drugs,** and a handful of photo-processing services. The smaller locally-owned stores are scattered among the behemoths, mostly on the ground floor. Nearly 400 shops and restaurants sprawl over several blocks (and 1.8 million sq. ft. of store space), catering to every imaginable need, from over-the-top upscale (**Tiffany, Chanel, Versace**) to mainland chains such as the **Gap** and **Banana Republic.** Department stores such as **Macy's** sell fashion, food, cosmetics, shoes, and household needs. Shoes? They're a kick at **Nordstrom,** and newcomer **Walking Co.** has first-rate comfort styles by Mephisto, Ecco, and Naot.

A good stop for gifts is **Islands' Best,** which spills over with Hawaiian-made foodstuffs, ceramics, fragrances, and more. **Splash! Hawaii** is a good source for women's swimwear; for aloha shirts and men's swimwear, try **Macy's, Town & Country Surf, Reyn's,** or the terminally hip **Hawaiian Island Creations.** Lovers of Polynesian wear and pareus shouldn't miss **Tahiti Imports.** The **food court** is abuzz with dozens of stalls purveying Cajun food, ramen, pizza, plate lunches, vegetarian fare, green tea and fruit freezes (like frozen yogurt), panini, and countless other treats. Open Monday through Saturday 9:30am to 9pm, Sunday 10am to 7pm. 1450 Ala Moana Blvd. ⓒ 808/955-9517. Bus: 8, 19, or 20. Ala Moana Shuttle Bus runs daily every 15 minutes from 7 stops in Waikiki; Waikiki Trolley also stops at Ala Moana (see "Getting Around," on p. 98).

Aloha Tower Marketplace There is a perpetual parking shortage here, and if you do manage to find a parking spot the rates are ridiculously sky high. Take the trolley if you can. Or skip the hassle all together and go somewhere else. Once you get to the new harbor-front complex, you'll find everything from sleek ocean liners to malodorous fishing boats still tied up at the waterfront. The refurbished Aloha Tower stands high over the complex, as it did in the days when it was the tallest structure in Honolulu.

Hawaiian House is a hit with its island-style interiors and home accents. Dining and shopping prospects abound: **Martin & MacArthur** gift shop, **Hawaiian Ukulele Company, Sunglass Hut, Don Ho's Island Grill, Chai's Island Bistro,** and **Gordon Biersch Brewery** (see "Where to Dine," earlier in this chapter). Retail shops are open Monday through Saturday 9am to 9pm, Sunday 9am to 6pm; dining and entertainment, daily 8am to midnight. 1 Aloha Tower Dr., on the waterfront between piers 8 and 11, Honolulu Harbor. ⓒ 808/528-5700; Aloha Tower Entertainment Hotline, ⓒ 808/566-2333. Various Honolulu trolleys stop here; if you want a direct ride from Waikiki, take the free Hilo Hattie's trolley or the Waikiki Red Line trolley, which continues on to Hilo Hattie's in Iwilei.

DFS Galleria "Boat days" is the theme at this newly renovated (to the tune of 65 million dollars) Waikiki emporium, a three-floor extravaganza of shops ranging from the superluxe (**Givenchy, Coach,** and many more) to the very touristy.

There are some great Hawaii food products though, ranging from the incomparable **Big Island Candies** shortbread cookies to a spate of coffees and preserves. Servers bearing warm, fresh-from-the-oven cookies are a nice touch. The Tube, a walk-through aquarium complete with spotted and sting rays, is a big attraction, visible from indoors and on the sidewalk at the corner of Kalakaua and Royal Hawaiian Avenues. There are multitudes of aloha shirts and T-shirts, a virtual golf course, surf and skate equipment, a terrific Hawaiian music department, and a labyrinth of fashionable stores once you get past the Waikiki Walk. Fragrances and cosmetics make a big splash at DFS. **Starbucks** and **Jamba Juice** are always buzzing with coffee and smoothies, and **Kalia Grill** features rotisserie and deli items for casual dining. *Caveat:* Some sections are duty-free and therefore restricted to international travelers only. Free live Hawaiian entertainment, featuring hula styles from the 1920s through the 1940s, takes place nightly at 7pm. Open daily 9am to 11pm. Corner of Kalakaua and Royal Hawaiian aves., 330 Royal Hawaiian Ave. ℭ 808/931-2655.

Kahala Mall   Chic, manageable, and unfrenzied, Kahala Mall is home to some of Honolulu's best shops. Located east of Waikiki in the posh neighborhood of Kahala, the mall has everything from a small **Macy's** to chain stores such as **Banana Republic** and the **Gap**—nearly 100 specialty shops (including dozens of eateries and 8 movie theaters) in an enclosed, air-conditioned area. **Starbucks** is a java magnet, a stone's throw from the **Gourmet Express** with its fast, healthy salads, tortilla wraps, and fresh juices and smoothies. **Jamba Juice** is the hot spot of the mall, with lines of smoothie lovers waiting for their Citrus Squeeze or Kiwi-Berry Burner. For gift, fashion, and specialty stores, our picks of the mall's best and brightest are **Riches,** a tiny kiosk with a big, bold selection of jewelry; the **Compleat Kitchen;** the **Paperie,** with an impressive selection of everything you'll need in stationery, cards, napkins, and paper goods; and the sprawling **Hawaiian House.** Open Monday through Saturday 10am to 9pm, Sunday 10am to 5pm. 4211 Waialae Ave., Kahala. ℭ 808/732-7736.

Royal Hawaiian Shopping Center   *Upscale* is the operative word here. Although there are drugstores, lei stands, restaurants, and food kiosks, the most conspicuous stores are the European designer boutiques (**Chanel, Cartier, Hermès,** and more) that cater largely to visitors from Japan. **Beretania Florist,** located in the hut under the large banyan tree, will ship cut tropical flowers anywhere in the United States.

Waikele Premium Outlets   Just say the word *Waikele* and our eyes glaze over. So many shops, so little time! And so much money to be saved while shopping for what you don't need. There are two sections to this sprawling discount shopping mecca: the **Waikele Premium Outlets,** some 51 retailers offering designer and name-brand merchandise; and the **Waikele Value Center** across the street, with another 25 stores more practical than fashion-oriented (**Eagle Hardware, Sports Authority**). The 64-acre complex has made discount shopping a major activity and a travel pursuit in itself, with shopping tours for visitor groups and carloads of neighbor islanders and Oahu residents making pilgrimages from all corners of the state. They come to hunt down bargains on everything from perfumes, luggage, and hardware to sporting goods, fashions, vitamins, and china. Examples: **Geoffrey Beene, Donna Karan, Saks Fifth Avenue, Anne Klein, Mikasa, Kenneth Cole, Banana Republic,** and dozens of other name brands at a fraction of retail. The ultrachic **Barneys** has added new cachet to this shopping haven. Open Monday through Friday 9am to 9pm,

Sunday 10am to 6pm. 94–790 Lumiaina St., Waikele (about 20 miles from Waikiki). (*C* 808/ 676-5656. www.premiumoutlets.com. Take H-1 west toward Waianae and turn off at exit 7. Bus: no. 42 from Waikiki to Waipahu Transit Center, then 433 from Transit Center to Waikele. To find out which companies offer shopping tours with Waikiki pickups, call the **Information Center** at (*C* 808/678-0786.

Ward Centre   Although it has a high turnover and a changeable profile, Ward Centre is a standout for its concentration of restaurants and shops. **Ryan's** and **Kakaako Kitchen** are as popular as ever, the former looking out over Ala Moana Park and the latter with lanai views of the sprawling **Pier 1 Imports** across the street. Across from **Pier 1, Nordstrom Rack** and **Office Depot** have sprouted in a new development area that also include a 16-theater movie megaplex now being built. All these establishments are part of developer Victoria Ward's Kakaako projects, which take up several blocks in this area: Ward Centre, Ward Farmers Market, Ward Village Shops, Ward Gateway Center, and Ward Warehouse.

Ward Centre's gift shops and galleries include **Kamehameha Garment Company** for aloha shirts, **Paper Roses** for wonderful paper products, **Honolulu Chocolate Company** (see "Edibles," earlier in this chapter), and the very attractive **Gallery at Ward Centre. Handblock** proffers wonderful table linens, clothing, and household accents, while **Borders** is action central, bustling with browsers. Open Monday through Saturday 10am to 9pm, Sunday 10am to 5pm. 1200 Ala Moana Blvd. (*C* 808/591-8411; www.victoriaward.com.

Ward Entertainment Center   This large, multiblock complex includes Ward Centre and Ward Warehouse, mentioned above, at the corner of Auahi and Kamakee streets. The complex has undergone enormous expansion, beginning with a new 16-movie megaplex, and a new retail and restaurant complex, with eateries like **Dave & Buster's** (with virtual golf, games, interactive entertainment, bars, and a restaurant), **Buca di Beppo**, **Wolfgang Puck Express** and **Cold Stone Creamery.** Open Monday through Saturday 10am to 10pm, Sunday 10am to 9pm. Auahi and Kamakee Streets. (*C* 808/591-8411; www.victoriaward.com.

Ward Warehouse   Older than its sister property, Ward Centre, and endowed with an endearing patina, Ward Warehouse remains a popular stop for dining and shopping. **Native Books & Beautiful Things** and the **Nohea Gallery** (see "Hawaiiana & Gift Items," for both) are excellent sources for quality Hawaii-made arts and crafts.

Other recommended stops in the low-rise wooden structure include the ever-colorful **C. June Shoes,** with flamboyant designer women's shoes and handbags (tony, expensive, and oh-so-entertaining!); **Executive Chef,** for gourmet Hawaii food items and household accessories; **Out of Africa,** for pottery, beads, and interior accents; **Mamo Howell,** for distinctive aloha wear; **Private World,** for delicate sachets, linens, and fragrances; and **Bambini,** brimming with tasteful gifts for kids and babies. For T-shirts and swimwear, check out the **Town & Country Surf Shop,** and for an excellent selection of sunglasses, knapsacks, and footwear to take you from the beach to the ridgetops, don't miss **Thongs 'N Things.** Open Monday through Saturday 10am to 9pm, Sunday 10am to 5pm. 1050 Ala Moana Blvd. (*C* 808/591-8411; www.victoriaward.com.

SURF & SPORTS

The surf-and-sports shops scattered throughout Honolulu are a highly competitive lot, with each trying to capture your interest (and dollars). The top sources for sports gear and accessories in town are **McCully Bicycle & Sporting Goods,** 2124 S. King St. ((*C* 808/955-6329), with everything from bicycles and fishing gear to athletic shoes and accessories, along with a stunning selection of sunglasses; and **The Bike Shop,** 1149 S. King St., near Piikoi Street (© **808/596-0588**), excellent for cycling and backpacking equipment for all levels, with major camping lines such as North Face, MSR, and Kelty. Avid cyclists coming to Oahu should make this a definite stop, as it's the hub of cycling news on the island, offering night tours of downtown Honolulu by bicycle and other cycling activities islandwide. The **Sports Authority,** at 333 Ward Ave. (© **808/596-0166**) and at Waikele Center (© **808/677-9933**), is a discount megaoutlet offering clothing, cycles, and equipment.

Surf shops, centers of fashion as well as definers of daring, include **Local Motion,** in Waikiki and Windward Mall (© **808/979-7873**); **Town and Country** in Ala Moana Center and Ward Warehouse; and **Hawaiian Island Creations,** at Ala Moana Center (© **808/941-4491**). Local Motion is the icon of surfers and skateboarders, both professionals and wannabes; the shop offers surfboards, T-shirts, aloha and casual wear, boogie boards, and countless accessories for life in the sun. Hawaiian Island Creations is another supercool surf shop offering sunglasses, sun lotions, surf wear, and accessories galore.

SHOPPING IN WINDWARD OAHU

Windward Oahu's largest shopping complex is **Windward Mall,** 46–056 Kamehameha Hwy., in Kaneohe (© **808/235-1143**), open Monday through Saturday from 10am to 9pm and Sunday from 10am to 5pm. The 100 stores and services at this standard suburban mall include **Macy's** and **Sears,** health stores, airline counters, surf shops, and **LensCrafters.** A small food court serves pizza, Chinese fare, tacos, and other morsels. A new 10-screen theater complex opened in May 2001.

All of the listings below can be found in the town of **Kailua,** whose shopping nexus is formed by **Long's Drugs** and **Macy's** department store, located side by side on Kailua Road.

The *malassada* mecca of Oahu is **Agnes Portuguese Bake Shop,** 46 Hoolai St. (© **808/262-5367**). (Malassadas are sugary Portuguese dumplings, like doughnuts without holes.) With its abundance of free parking and an expanded menu of homemade soups, artisan breads, and unique pastries, Agnes is a Kailua treasure.

Alii Antiques of Kailua II   Abandon all restraint, particularly if you have a weakness for vintage Hawaiiana. Koa lamps and rattan furniture from the 1930s and 1940s, hula nodders, rare 1940s koa tables, Roseville vases, Don Blanding dinnerware, and a breathtaking array of vintage etched-glass vases and trays are some of the items in this unforgettable shop. Across the street, the owner's wife runs **Alii Antiques of Kailua,** which is chockablock with all the things that won't fit here: jewelry, clothing, Bauer and Fiesta Ware, linens, Bakelite bracelets, and floor-to-ceiling collectibles. 9-A Maluniu Ave., Kailua. © 808/261-1705.

BookEnds   BookEnds is the quintessential neighborhood bookstore, run by a pro who buys good books and knows how to find the ones she doesn't have. There are more than 60,000 titles here, new and used, from *Celtic Mandalas* to C. S. Lewis's *Chronicles of Narnia* and the full roster of current best-sellers. Volumes on child care, cooking, and self-improvement; a hefty periodicals section; and mainstream and offbeat titles are among the treasures to be found. 600 Kailua Rd., Kailua. © 808/261-1996.

Heritage Antiques & Gifts   This Kailua landmark is known for its selection of Tiffany-style lamps ($200–$2,000), many of which are hand-carted back to the mainland. The mind-boggling inventory also includes European, Asian, American, local, and Pacific Island collectibles. The shop is fun, the people friendly, and the selection diverse enough to appeal to the casual as well as serious collector. Glassware; china; and estate, costume, and fine jewelry are among the items of note. Heritage has its own jeweler who does custom designs and repairs, plus a stable of woodworkers who turn out custom-made koa rockers and hutches to complement the antique furniture selection. 767 Kailua Rd. © 808/ 261-8700.

SHOPPING ON THE NORTH SHORE: HALEIWA
Like Hilo on the Big Island and Maui's upcountry Makawao, Haleiwa means serious shopping for those who know that the unhurried pace of rural life can conceal vast material treasures. Ask the legions of townies who drive an hour each way just to stock up on wine and clothes at Haleiwa stores. (Of course, a cooler is de rigueur for perishables.) Below are our Haleiwa highlights.

ARTS, CRAFTS & GIFT ITEMS
Haleiwa's shops and galleries display a combination of marine art, watercolors, sculptures, and a plethora of crafts trying to masquerade (quite transparently) as fine art. This is the town for gifts, fashions, and surf stuff—mostly casual, despite some very high price tags. **Haleiwa Gallery** next door to the North Shore Marketplace displays a lot of local art of the nonmarine variety, and some of it is very appealing.

   Global Creations Interiors, 66–079 Kamehameha Hwy. (© **808/637-1505**), offers casual clothes as well as international imports for the home, including Balinese bamboo furniture and colorful Yucatán hammocks. There are gifts and crafts by 115 local potters, painters, and artists of other media.

EDIBLES
Haleiwa is best known for its roadside shave-ice stands: the famous **Matsumoto Shave Ice** ★★, 66–087 Kamehameha Hwy. (© **808/637-4827**), with the perennial queue snaking along Kamehameha Highway, and nearby **Aoki's.** Shave ice is the popular island version of a snow cone, topped with your choice of syrups, such as strawberry, rainbow, root beer, vanilla, or passion fruit. For a real exotic treat order the li hing mui flavor. Aficionados order it with a scoop of ice cream and sweetened black adzuki beans nestled in the middle.

   For food-and-wine shopping, our mightiest accolades go to **Fujioka Super Market,** 66–190 Kamehameha Hwy. (© **808/637-4520**). Oenophiles and tony wine clubs from town shop here for the best prices on California reds, coveted Italian reds, and a growing selection of cabernets, merlots, and French vintages. Fresh produce and no-cholesterol vegetarian health foods round out the aisles.

   Tiny, funky **Celestial Natural Foods,** 66–443 Kamehameha Hwy. (© **808/ 637-6729**), is the health foodies' Grand Central for everything from wooden spine-massagers to health supplements, produce, cosmetics, and bulk foods.

FASHION
Although Haleiwa used to be an incense-infused surfer outpost where zoris and tank tops were the regional uniform and the Beach Boys and Ravi Shankar the music of the day, today it's one of the top shopping destinations for those with unconventional tastes. Specialty shops abound.

   Top-drawer **Silver Moon Emporium,** North Shore Marketplace, 66–250 Kamehameha Hwy. (© **808/637-7710**), is an islandwide phenomenon, featuring the terrific finds of owner Lucie Talbot-Holu. Exquisite clothing and handbags, reasonably priced footwear, hats straight out of *Vogue,* jewelry, scarves, and a full gamut of other treasures pepper the attractive boutique. The entire line of chic Brighton accessories—shoes, handbags, fragrance, belts, and jewelry—are a prized addition.

In addition to Silver Moon, other highlights of the prominent North Shore Marketplace include **Patagonia** (© **808/637-1245**) for high-quality surf, swim, hiking, kayaking, and all-around adventure wear; **North Shore Swimwear** (© **808/637-6859**) for excellent mix-and-match bikinis and one-piece suits, custom ordered or off the rack; **Kama`ainas Haleiwa** (© **808/637-1907**), the new gallery-gift store for quality island crafts, Hawaiian quilts, soaps, hats, accessories, clothing, and food specialties; and **Jungle Gems** (© **808/637-6609**), the mother lode of gemstones, crystals, silver, and beadwork.

Nearby **Oceania,** 66–208 Kamehameha Hwy. (© **808/637-4581**), also has some treasures among its racks of casual and leisure wear. Foldable straw hats, diaphanous dresses, dressy T-shirts, friendly service, and good prices are what we've found here. **Oogenesis Boutique,** 66–249 Kamehameha Hwy. (© **808/ 637-4580**), in the southern part of Haleiwa, features a storefront lined with vintage-looking dresses that flutter prettily in the North Shore breeze.

Amid all these hip Haleiwa newcomers, the perennial favorite remains the old-fashioned, longtime neighborhood staple, **H. Miura Store and Tailor Shop,** 66–057 Kamehameha Hwy. (© **808/637-4845**). You can custom-order swim trunks, an aloha shirt, or a muumuu from bolts of Polynesian-printed fabrics, from tapa designs to two-color pareu prints. The staff will sew, ship, and remember you years later when you return. It's the most versatile tailor shop we've ever seen, with coconut-shell bikini tops, fake hula skirts, and heaps of cheap and glorious tchotchkes lining the aisles.

SURF SHOPS

Haleiwa's ubiquitous surf shops are the best on earth, surfers say. At the top of the heap is **Northshore Boardriders Club,** North Shore Marketplace, 66–250 Kamehameha Hwy. (© **808/637-5026**), the mecca of the board-riding elite, with sleek, fast, elegant, and top-of-the-line boards designed by North Shore legends such as long-board shaper Barry Kanaiaupuni, John Carper, Jeff Bushman, and Pat Rawson. This is a Quicksilver "concept store," which means that it's the testing ground for the newest and hottest trends in surf wear put out by the retail giant. Kanaiaupuni's other store, **B K Ocean Sports,** in the old Haleiwa Post Office, 66–215 Kamehameha Hwy. (© **808/637-4966**), is a more casual version, appealing to surfers and watersports enthusiasts of all levels. Across the street, **Hawaii Surf & Sail,** 66–214 Kamehameha Hwy. (© **808/ 637-5373**), offers new and used surfboards and accessories for surfers, bodyboarders, and sailboarders.

Strong Current Surf Design, North Shore Marketplace (© **808/637-3406**), is the North Shore's nexus for memorabilia and surf nostalgia because of the passion of its owners, Bonnie and John Moore, who expanded the commercial surfshop space to encompass the Haleiwa Surf Museum. From head level down, Strong Current displays shorts, ocean sportswear, hats, jewelry, towels, and popular new items of Hawaiiana; from head level up, the walls and ceilings are lined with vintage boards, posters, and pictures from the 1950s and 1960s. Although Strong Current is a long-board surf shop, the renewed popularity of long boarding has made this a popular stop. World-famous North Shore shapers Dick Brewer and Mike Diffenderfer are among the big names who design the fiberglass and balsa wood boards.

Also in the North Shore Marketplace, **Barnfield's Raging Isle Sports** (© 808/637-7707) is the surf-and-cycle center of the area, with everything from wet suits and surfboards to surf gear and clothing for men, women, and children. The adjoining surfboard factory puts out custom-built boards of high renown. There's also a large inventory of mountain bikes for rent and sale.

A longtime favorite among old-timers is the newly expanded **Surf & Sea Surf Sail & Dive Shop,** 62–595 Kamehameha Hwy. (© **808/637-9887**), a flamboyant roadside structure just over the bridge, with old wood floors, blowing fans, and a tangle of surf and swimwear, T-shirts, surfboards, Boogie Boards, fins, watches, sunglasses, and countless other miscellany; you can also rent surf and snorkel equipment here.

Tropical Rush, 62–620-A Kamehameha Hwy. (© **808/637-8886**), has a huge inventory of surf and swim gear: surfboards, long boards, bodyboards, Sector 9 skateboards, and all the accessories to go with an ocean-minded life, like slippers and swimwear for men and women. T-shirts, hats, sunglasses, and visors are among the scads of cool gear, and you can rent equipment and arrange surf lessons, too. An added feature is the shop's surf report line for the up-to-the-minute lowdown on wave action (© **808/638-7874**); it covers the day's surf and weather details for all of Oahu.

14 Oahu After Dark

Nightlife in Hawaii begins at sunset, when all eyes turn westward to see how the day will end. Sunset viewers always seem to bond in the mutual enjoyment of a natural spectacle. People in Hawaii are fortunate to have an environment that encourages this cultural ritual.

On Fridays and Saturdays at 6:30pm, as the sun casts its golden glow on the beach and surfers and beach boys paddle in for the day, **Kuhio Beach,** where Kalakaua Avenue intersects with Kaiulani, eases into evening with hula dancing and a torch-lighting ceremony. This is a thoroughly delightful, free weekend offering. Start off earlier with a picnic basket and walk along the oceanside path fronting Queen's Surf, near the Waikiki Aquarium. (You can park along Kapiolani Park or near the zoo.) There are few more pleasing spots in Waikiki than the benches at water's edge at this Diamond Head end of Kalakaua Avenue. A short walk across the intersection of Kalakaua and Kapahulu avenues, where the seawall and daring boogie boarders attract hordes of spectators, takes you to the Duke Kahanamoku statue on Kuhio Beach and the nearby Wizard Stones. Here, you can view the torch-lighting and hula and gear up for the strolling musicians who amble down Kalakaua Avenue every Friday from 8 to 10pm. The musicians begin at Beachwalk Avenue at the Ewa (western) end of Waikiki and end up at the statue.

BARS

ON THE BEACH Waikiki's beachfront bars also offer many possibilities, from the Royal Hawaiian Hotel's **Mai Tai Bar** (© **808/923-7311**), a few feet from the sand, to the unfailingly enchanting **House Without a Key,** at the Halekulani (© **808/923-2311**), where the breathtaking **Kanoelehua Miller** dances hula to the riffs of Hawaiian steel-pedal guitar under a century-old kiawe tree. With the sunset and ocean glowing behind her and Diamond Head visible in the distance, the scene is straight out of Somerset Maugham—romantic, evocative, nostalgic. It doesn't hurt, either, that the Halekulani happens to make the best mai tais in the world. This place has the after-dinner hours covered, too, with light jazz by local artists from 10:15pm to midnight nightly (see "Jazz," below).

ALOHA TOWER MARKETPLACE   The landmark Aloha Tower at Honolulu Harbor, once Oahu's tallest building, has always occupied Honolulu's prime downtown location—on the water, at a naturally sheltered bay, near the business and civic center of Honolulu. Since its construction, the Aloha Tower Marketplace, 1 Aloha Tower Dr. (on the waterfront between piers 8 and 11, Honolulu Harbor; ✆ **808/528-5700**), has gained popularity as an entertainment and nightlife spot, with more than 100 shops and restaurants, including several venues for Honolulu's leading musical groups.

Unlike Waikiki, there are no swaying palm trees at your fingertips here, but you will see tugboats and cruise ships from the popular open-air **Pier Bar** (✆ **808/536-2166**) and various other venues in the marketplace offering live music throughout the week. There's live music nightly at the Pier Bar: contemporary Hawaiian, swing, alternative rock, and jazz. The Pier Bar's main stage, the **Gordon Biersch Brewery Restaurant** (p. 145), and the **Atrium Center Court** feature ongoing programs of foot-stomping good times. At the recently expanded Gordon Biersch, where a new stage area was added, diners swing to jazz, blues, and island riffs. Most notable, however, are **Don Ho's Island Grill** and **Chai's Island Bistro,** Honolulu's hottest nightspots (see "Hawaiian Music," below for more on Chai's).

Across the street from Aloha Tower Marketplace, the bar and lounge of **Palomino** (✆ **808/528-2400**) is a magnet for revelers, often two deep at the bar. You'll find great appetizers, pizzas, service, and drinks, and you can order from the full dinner menu as well.

DOWNTOWN   The downtown scene is awakening from a long slumber, thanks to the performances at the Hawaii Theatre and the popular Nuuanu Avenue block parties, courtesy of some tenacious entrepreneurs who want everyone to love Nuuanu as much as they do. New and noteworthy is **Hanks Café,** on Nuuanu between Hotel and King streets (✆ **808/526-1410**), a tiny, kitschy, friendly pub with live music nightly, open-mike nights, and special events that attract great talent and a supportive crowd. On some nights the music spills out into the streets, and it's so packed you have to press your nose against the window to see what you're missing. At the makai end of Nuuanu, toward the pier, **Murphy's Bar & Grill** (✆ **808/531-0422**) and **O'Toole's Irish Pub** (✆ **808/ 536-6360**), which recently built an entertainment stage, are the downtown ale houses and media haunts that have kept Irish eyes smiling for years.

HAWAIIAN MUSIC

Oahu has several key spots for Hawaiian music. A delightful (and powerful) addition to the Waikiki music scene is Hawaii's queen of falsetto, **Genoa Keawe,** who fills the Lobby Bar of the Hawaiian Regent Hotel (✆ **808/922-6611**) with her larger-than-life voice. You'll find her here from 5:30 to 8:30pm every Thursday; the rest of the week, except Monday, other contemporary Hawaiian musicians fill in.

Brothers Cazimero remains one of Hawaii's most gifted duos (Robert on bass, Roland on 12-string guitar), appearing every Wednesday at 7pm at **Chai's Island Bistro** (✆ **808/585-0011**) in the Aloha Tower Marketplace. Also at Chai's: Robert Cazimero plays by himself on the piano on Friday at 7pm; and **Jerry Santos** and **Olomana** perform on Sunday and Monday at 7pm. In the past couple of years, Chai's has emerged as the leading venue for Hawaiian entertainment. But if you're here on May 1, Lei Day, try to make it to the special concert the Brothers Caz give every year at the Waikiki Shell—it's one of the loveliest events in Hawaii. Locals dress up in their leis and best aloha shirts, the air smells like pikake and pakalana, and if you're lucky you'll see the moon rise over Diamond Head.

Impromptu hula and spirited music from the family and friends of the performers are an island tradition at places such as the Hilton Hawaiian Village's **Paradise Lounge** (© 808/949-4321), which, despite its pillars, serves as a large living room for the full-bodied music of **Olomana.** The group plays Friday and Saturday from 8pm to midnight (no cover, 1 drink minimum). At **Duke's Canoe Club** at the Outrigger Waikiki (© 808/922-2268), it's always three deep at the beachside bar when the sun is setting; extra-special entertainment is a given here—usually from 4 to 6pm on Friday, Saturday, and Sunday, and nightly from 10pm to midnight.

Nearby, the Sheraton Moana Surfrider offers a regular nightly program of live Hawaiian music and piano in its **Banyan Veranda** (© 808/922-3111), which surrounds an islet-size canopy of banyan tree and roots where Robert Louis Stevenson loved to linger. The Veranda serves afternoon tea, a sunset buffet, and cocktails. Still sizzling in the Polynesian revue world is Sheraton Princess Kaiulani's new *Creation—A Polynesian Odyssey* (© 808/931-4660), in the hotel's second-floor Ainahau Showroom. Produced by Tihati, the state's largest entertainment company, the show is a theatrical journey of fire dancing, special effects, illusions, and Polynesian dances from Hawaii and the South Pacific. The dinner show is 5:15pm, dinner and admission is $62, and the cocktail show, priced at $32, is 6pm. No shows on Monday and Wednesday.

Our best advice for lovers of Hawaiian music is to scan the local dailies or the *Honolulu Weekly* to see if and where the following Hawaiian entertainers are appearing: **Kekuhi Kanahele,** accomplished chanter and *kahiko* (ancient hula) dancer whose award-winning recordings have redefined Hawaiian music; **Ho'okena,** a symphonically rich quintet featuring **Manu Boyd,** one of the most prolific songwriters and chanters in Hawaii; **Keali'i Reichel,** premier chanter, dancer, and award-winning recording artist; **Robbie Kahakalau,** another award-winning musician; **Kapena,** for contemporary Hawaiian music; **Na Leo Pilimehana,** a trio of angelic Hawaiian singers; the **Makaha Sons of Niihau,** pioneers in the Hawaiian cultural renaissance; **Fiji;** and slack-key guitar master **Raymond Kane.**

Consider the gods beneficent if you happen to be here when the hula halau of **Frank Kawaikapuokalani Hewett** is holding its annual fund-raiser in Windward Oahu. It's a rousing, inspired, family effort for a good cause, and it always features the best in ancient and contemporary Hawaiian music. For the best in ancient and modern hula, check the dailies for halau fund-raisers, which are always authentic, enriching, and local to the core.

Showroom acts that have maintained a following are led by the tireless, disarming **Don Ho,** who still sings "Tiny Bubbles" and remains a fixture at the supper club **Waikiki Beachcomber** (© 808/923-3981). He may be corny, but he's attentive to fans as he accommodates their requests and sings nostalgic favorites. He's also very generous in sharing his stage with other Hawaii performers, so guests are often in for surprise appearances by leading Hawaii performers. The **Outrigger Waikiki on the Beach** (© 808/923-0711), features the **Society of Seven's** nightclub act (a blend of skits, Broadway hits, popular music, and costumed musical acts) is into its 30th year—no small feat for performers.

THE BLUES

The blues are alive and well in Hawaii, with quality acts both local and from the mainland drawing enthusiastic crowds. **Junior Wells, Willie & Lobo, War,** and surprise appearances by the likes of **Bonnie Raitt** are among the past successes of this genre of big-time licks. The best-loved Oahu venue is **Anna Bannanas,** 2440 S. Beretania St. (© **808/946-5190**), still rocking after 30 years in the business, with reggae, blues, and rock—plus video games and darts.

JAZZ

Jazz lovers should watch for the Great Hawaiian Jazz Blow-Out every March (2004 will be its 7th year), at Mid-Pacific Institute's Bakken Hall. At the south end of Honolulu, near Diamond Head, **Diamond Head Grill** (© **808/922-3734;** p. 132) features live music nightly, and **Duc's Bistro** (© **808/531-6325;** p. 145), downtown, presents live jazz nightly except Thursday, when vocalist Mihana Souza brings her style of Hawaiian music to the cozy venue. **Nick's Fishmarket,** Waikiki Gateway Hotel, 2070 Kalakaua Ave. (© **808/955-6333**), still offers live entertainment nightly in its lounge—mild jazz or Top 40 contemporary hits.

Tops in taste and ambience is the perennially alluring **Lewers Lounge,** in the Halekulani, 2199 Kalia Rd. (© **808/923-2311**). Loretta Ables, who played there for years, is now at Kahala Mandarin's Veranda, and it's a good gig.

Around town, watch for **Sandy Tsukiyama,** a gifted singer (Brazilian, Latin, jazz) and one of Honolulu's great assets, and jazz singers **Rachel Gonzales** and **Loretta Ables.** Other groups in jazz, blues, and R&B include **Blue Budda, Bongo Tribe, Secondhand Smoke, Bluzilla, Piranha Brothers,** and the **Greg Pai Trio.**

ALTERNATIVE MUSIC

Anna Bannanas (see "The Blues," above) is the granddaddy of them all, still packing them in, with bands known to generate the most perspiration on the most enthusiastic dance floor in Honolulu. This indomitable club is a venue for groups with roots in reggae, blues, world music, and alternative music. Most shows start at 9:30pm; the cover varies. The under-30s also flock to the **Wave Waikiki** (© **808/941-0424**), two rooms at two levels with two full bars and local, national, and international DJs.

Near the new convention center and down the street from the Wave is that bastion of decibels run amok, the **Hard Rock Cafe,** 1837 Kapiolani Blvd. (© **808/955-7383**), offering live entertainment on many, but not all, Friday and Saturday nights. These no-cover events bring out a hip crowd for the local alternative, reggae, and classic-rock bands.

DISCOS

The nightlife buzz is all about **Blue Tropix,** complete with a jiggy weekend crowd and a live monkey contained in soundproof glass behind the bar. (Its grand opening was a benefit for the Honolulu Zoological Society.) The nightclub opened in early 2001 at 1700 Kapiolani Blvd. (© **808/944-0001**) and features a 100-square-foot dance floor for the lively DJ jams of Top 40, hip-hop, and R&B dance music. There's a $5 cover charge. Open daily from 10pm to 2am.

Downstairs in the lobby of the Ala Moana Hotel, **Rumours Nightclub** (© **808/955-4811**) is the disco of choice for those who remember Paul McCartney as something other than Stella's father. The theme changes by the month, but generally, it's the "Big Chill" '60s, '70s, and '80s music on Friday;

the "Little Chill" on Saturday; ballroom dancing from 5 to 9pm on Sunday; Top 40 on Tuesday; karaoke on Wednesday; and an "after-work office party" to midnight on Thursday. A spacious dance floor, good sound system, and Top 40 music draw a mix of generations.

At Restaurant Row, **Ocean Club,** 500 Ala Moana Blvd. (© **808/526-9888**), is the Row's hottest and hippest spot. Good seafood appetizers, attractive happy-hour prices, a fabulous quirky interior, and passionate DJs in alternative garb make up a dizzyingly successful formula. The minimum age is 23, and the dress code calls for "smart-casual"—no T-shirts, slippers, or beach wear (see also the dining review on p. 146).

Finally, for late-night schmoozing, Restaurant Row's **Row Bar,** 500 Ala Moana Blvd. (© **808/528-2345**), always seems to be full, and somewhat, if impersonally, convivial, especially after the nearby movie theater has let out. Also in Restaurant Row, **Sansei** (© **808/536-6286**) seems to be a hit with its late-night karaoke on Saturday, starting at 10pm.

THE PERFORMING ARTS

"Aloha shirt to Armani" is how we describe the night scene in Honolulu—mostly casual but with ample opportunity to dress up if you dare to part with your flip-flops.

Audiences have stomped to the big Off-Broadway percussion hit *Stomp,* and have enjoyed the talent of *Tap Dogs,* Momix, Forever Tango, Cool Heat, Urban Beat, the Jim Nabors Christmas show, the Hawaii International Jazz Festival, the American Repertory Dance Company, barbershop quartets, and John Ka'imikaua's halau—all at the **Hawaii Theatre,** 1130 Bethel St., downtown (© **808/528-0506**), still basking in its renaissance following a 4-year, $22 million renovation. The neoclassical beaux arts landmark features a 1922 dome, 1,400 plush seats, a hydraulically elevated organ, a mezzanine lobby with two full bars, Corinthian columns, and gilt galore. Breathtaking murals, including a restored proscenium centerpiece lauded as Lionel Walden's "greatest creation," create an atmosphere that's making the theater a leading multipurpose center for the performing arts.

The **Honolulu Symphony Orchestra** has booked some of its performances at the new theater, but it still performs at the Waikiki Shell and the **Neal Blaisdell Concert Hall** (© **808/591-2211**). Meanwhile, the highly successful **Hawaii Opera Theatre,** in its 41st season (past hits have included *La Bohème, Carmen, Turandot, Romeo and Juliet, Rigoletto,* and *Aïda*), still draws fans to the Neal Blaisdell Concert Hall, as do many of the performances of Hawaii's four ballet companies: **Hawaii Ballet Theatre, Ballet Hawaii, Hawaii State Ballet,** and **Honolulu Dance Theatre.** Contemporary performances by **Dances We Dance** and the **Iona Pear Dance Company,** a strikingly creative Butoh group, are worth tracking down if you love the avant-garde.

Top 40 from the Top

Aaron's Atop the Ala Moana, Ala Moana Hotel, 410 Atkinson Dr. ((© **808/955-4466**), has the best view: Take the express elevator to the 36th floor of the hotel (p. 123), then watch the Honolulu city lights wrap around the room and cha-cha-cha to the vertigo! There's live music and dancing nightly, a great dinner menu, and an appetizer menu nightly from 5pm.

Hawaii, the Big Island

The Big Island of Hawaii—the island that lends its name to the entire 1,500-mile-long Hawaiian archipelago—is where Mother Nature pulled out all the stops. Simply put, it's spectacular.

The Big Island has it all: fiery volcanoes and sparkling waterfalls, black-lava deserts and snowcapped mountain peaks, tropical rain forests and alpine meadows, a glacial lake and miles of golden, black, and green (!) sand beaches. The Big Island has an unmatched diversity of terrain and climate. A 50-mile drive will take you from snowy winter to sultry summer, passing through spring or fall along the way. The island looks like the inside of a barbecue pit on one side, and a lush jungle on the other.

The Big Island is the largest island in the Hawaiian chain (4,038 sq. miles—about the size of Connecticut), the youngest (800,000 years), and the least populated (with 30 people per sq. mile). It has the nation's wettest city, the southernmost point in the United States, the world's biggest telescope, the ocean's biggest trophy marlin, and America's greatest collection of tropical luxury resorts. It also has the highest peaks in the Pacific, the most volcanoes of any Hawaiian island, and the newest land on earth.

Five volcanoes—one still erupting—have created this continental island, which is growing bigger daily. At its heart is snowcapped Mauna Kea, the world's tallest sea mountain (measured from the ocean floor), complete with its own glacial lake. Mauna Kea's

nearest neighbor is Mauna Loa (or "Long Mountain"), creator of one-sixth of the island; it's the largest volcano on earth, rising 30,000 feet out of the ocean floor (of course, you can see only the 13,796 ft. that are above sea level). Erupting Kilauea makes the Big Island bigger every day—and, if you're lucky and your timing is good, you can stand just a few feet away and watch it do its work. (In just a week, Kilauea volcano can produce enough lava to fill the Astrodome.)

Steeped in tradition and shrouded in the primal mist of creation, the Big Island called to the Polynesians across 2,000 miles of open ocean. In fact, ancient Hawaiian chants talk about a great burning in the night skies that guided the sojourners to the land of volcanoes. The Big Island radiates what the Hawaiians call *mana,* a sense of spirituality that's still apparent through the acres of petroglyphs etched in the black lava, the numerous *heiau* (ancient temples), burial caves scattered in the cliffs, sacred shrines both on land and in the sea, and even in the sound the wind makes as it blows across the desolate lava fields.

The Big Island is not for everyone, however. It refuses to fit the stereotype of a tropical island. Some tourists are taken aback at the sight of stark fields of lava or black-sand beaches. You must remember that it's *big* (expect to do lots of driving). And you may have to go out of your way if you're looking for traditional tropical beauty, such as a quintessential white-sand beach.

The Big Island

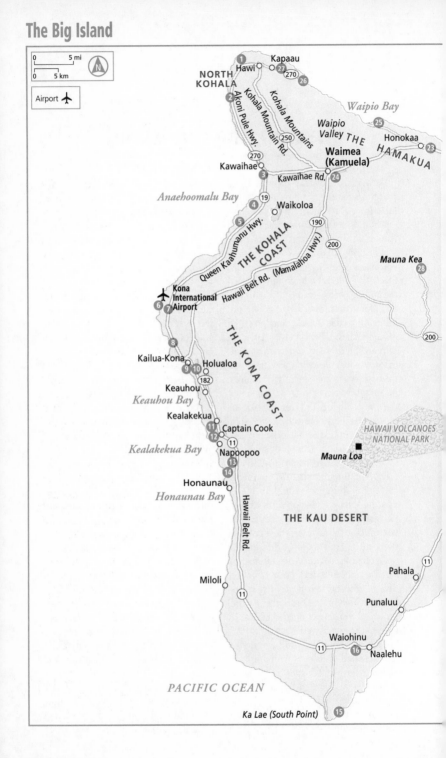

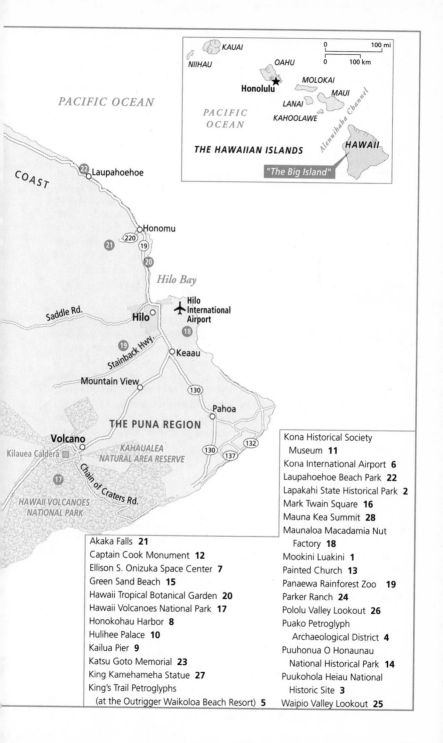

PACIFIC OCEAN

KAUAI

NIIHAU

OAHU

MOLOKAI

Honolulu

LANAI

MAUI

PACIFIC
OCEAN

KAHOOLAWE

Alenuihaha Channel

THE HAWAIIAN ISLANDS

HAWAII

"The Big Island"

0   100 mi
0   100 km

COAST

22 Laupahoehoe

Honomu

21   220   19

20

Hilo Bay

Saddle Rd.

Hilo

Hilo
International
Airport

19

18

Stainback Hwy.

Keaau

Mountain View

130

Pahoa

THE PUNA REGION

Volcano

132

Kilauea Caldera

KAHAUALEA
NATURAL AREA RESERVE

130   137

17

Chain of Craters Rd.

HAWAII VOLCANOES
NATIONAL PARK

Akaka Falls **21**
Captain Cook Monument **12**
Ellison S. Onizuka Space Center **7**
Green Sand Beach **15**
Hawaii Tropical Botanical Garden **20**
Hawaii Volcanoes National Park **17**
Honokohau Harbor **8**
Hulihee Palace **10**
Kailua Pier **9**
Katsu Goto Memorial **23**
King Kamehameha Statue **27**
King's Trail Petroglyphs
  (at the Outrigger Waikoloa Beach Resort) **5**

Kona Historical Society
  Museum **11**
Kona International Airport **6**
Laupahoehoe Beach Park **22**
Lapakahi State Historical Park **2**
Mark Twain Square **16**
Mauna Kea Summit **28**
Maunaloa Macadamia Nut
  Factory **18**
Mookini Luakini **1**
Painted Church **13**
Panaewa Rainforest Zoo   **19**
Parker Ranch **24**
Pololu Valley Lookout **26**
Puako Petroglyph
  Archaeological District **4**
Puuhonua O Honaunau
  National Historical Park **14**
Puukohola Heiau National
  Historic Site **3**
Waipio Valley Lookout **25**

On the other hand, if you're into watersports, this is paradise. The two tall volcanoes mean 350 days of calm water on the leeward side. The underwater landscape of caves, cliffs, and tunnels attracts a stunning array of colorful marine life just waiting to be visited by divers and snorkelers. The island's west coast is one of the best destinations in the world for big-game fishing. And its miles of remote coastline are a kayaker's dream of caves, secluded coves, and crescent-shaped beaches reachable only by sea.

On land, hikers, bikers, and horseback riders can head up and down a volcano, across black-sand beaches, into remote valleys, and through rain forests without seeing another soul. Bird-watchers are rewarded with sightings of the rare, rapidly dwindling native birds of Hawaii. Golfers can find nirvana on top championship courses, less-crowded municipal courses, and even some unusual off-the-beaten-track choices.

This is the least-explored island in the Hawaiian chain, but if you're looking to get away from it all and back to nature in its most primal state, that might be the best thing of all about it. Where else can you witness fiery creation and swim with dolphins; ponder the stars from the world's tallest mountain and catch a blue marlin; downhill ski and surf the waves in a single day? You can do all this, and more, on only one island in the world: the Big Island of Hawaii.

1 Orientation

Most people arrive on the Big Island at Kona International Airport, on the island's West Coast, and discover there are only two ways to go: clockwise or counterclockwise. From the airport, Kilauea volcano is to the right or counterclockwise, and the ritzy Kohala Coast is to the left or clockwise. (If you land in Hilo, of course, the volcano is clockwise, and Kohala is counterclockwise.)

If you think you can "do" the Big Island in a day, forget it. You need about 3 days to really see Hawaii Volcanoes National Park alone. It's best to spend at least a week here.

ARRIVING

The Big Island has two major airports for jet traffic between the islands: **Kona International Airport** and **Hilo International Airport.**

The Kona Airport receives direct overseas flights from Japan (Japan Airlines) and Vancouver (Aloha Airlines) as well as direct mainland flights from Los Angeles and San Francisco on **United Airlines** (✆ **800/241-6522;** www.ual.com); from Los Angeles on **American Airlines** (✆ **800/433-7300;** www.aa.com) and from Oakland on **Aloha Airlines** (✆ **800/367-5250;** www.alohaairlines.com). Otherwise, you'll have to pick up an interisland flight in Honolulu. Both **Aloha Airlines** (see above) and **Hawaiian Airlines** (✆ **800/367-5320;** www.hawaiianair.com) offer jet service to both Big Island airports. All major rental companies have cars available at both airports. See "Getting There & Getting Around," in chapter 2 for more details on interisland travel and car rentals.

VISITOR INFORMATION

The **Big Island Visitors Bureau** has two offices on the Big Island: one at 250 Keawe St., Hilo, HI 96720 (✆ **808/961-5797;** fax 808/961-2126); and on the other side of the island at 250 Waikoloa Beach Dr., Waikoloa, HI 96738 (✆ **808/886-1652**). Its website is www.bigisland.org.

On the west side of the island, there are two additional sources to contact for information: the **Kona–Kohala Resort Association,** 69–275 Waikoloa Beach Dr., Kamuela, HI 96743 (© **800/318-3637** or 808/886-4915; fax 808/886-1044; www.kkra.org); and **Destination Kona,** P.O. Box 2850, Kailua-Kona, HI 96745 (© **808/322-6809;** fax 808/322-8899). On the east side, you can contact **Destination Hilo,** P.O. Box 1391, Hilo, HI 96721 (© **808/935-5294;** fax 808/969-1984). And in the middle, contact the **Waimea Visitor Center,** P.O. Box 6570, Kamuela, HI 96743 (© **808/885-6707;** fax 808/885-0885).

The Big Island's best free tourist publications are *This Week,* the *Beach and Activity Guide,* and *101 Things to Do on Hawaii the Big Island.* All three offer lots of useful information, as well as discount coupons on a variety of island adventures. Copies are easy to find all around the island.

The *Beach and Activity Guide* is affiliated with the **Activity Connection,** Bougainvillea Plaza, Ste. 102, 75-5656 Kuakini Hwy., Kailua-Kona (© **800/ 459-7156** or 808/329-1038; fax 808/327-9411; www.beachactivityguide.com), a discount activity desk offering real savings (no fees, no timeshares) of up to 15% on activities including island tours, snorkel and dive trips, submarine and horseback rides, luaus, and more. The office is open daily from 7:30am to 5:30pm.

THE ISLAND IN BRIEF

The Kona Coast ★★

One Hawaiian word everyone seems to know is Kona, probably because it's synonymous with great coffee and big fish—both of which are found in abundance along this 70-mile-long stretch of black lava–covered coast.

A collection of tiny communities devoted to farming and fishing along the sunbaked leeward side of the island, the Kona Coast has an amazingly diverse geography and climate for such a compact area. The oceanfront town of **Kailua-Kona,** a quaint fishing village that now caters more to tourists than boat captains, is its commercial center. The lands of Kona range from stark, black, dry coastal desert to cool, cloudy upcountry so fertile that it seems anything could grow here. And it does—glossy green coffee, macadamia nuts, tropical fruit, and a riotous profusion of flowers cover the jagged steep slopes. Among the coffee fields, you'll find the funky, artsy village of **Holualoa.** Higher yet in elevation are native forests of giant trees filled

with tiny, colorful birds, some perilously close to extinction. About 7 miles south of Kailua-Kona, bordering the ocean, is the resort area of **Keauhou,** a suburban-like series of upscale condominiums, a shopping center, and homes in the seven-figure range.

Kona means "leeward side" in Hawaiian—and that means full-on summer sun every day of the year. This is an affordable vacation spot; an ample selection of midpriced condo units, peppered with a few older hotels and B&Bs, lines the shore, which is mostly rocky lava reef, interrupted by an occasional pocket beach. Here, too, stand two world-class resorts: Kona Village, the site of one of the best luaus in the islands, and one of Hawaii's luxury retreats, the Four Seasons at Hualalai.

Away from the bright lights of the town of Kailua lies the rural **South Kona Coast,** home to coffee farmers, macadamia-nut growers, and people escaping to the country. The serrated South Kona Coast is indented with numerous bays, from

Kealakekua, a marine-life preserve that's the island's best diving spot and the place where Capt. James Cook met his demise, down to **Honaunau,** where a national historic park recalls the days of old Hawaii. Accommodations in this area are mainly inexpensive B&Bs, everything from the very frugal Japanese Manago Hotel to the very classy Horizon Guest House. This coast is a great place to stay if you want to get away from crowds and experience peaceful country living. You'll be within driving distance of beaches and the sites of Kailua.

The Kohala Coast ★★

Fringes of palms and flowers, brilliant blankets of emerald green, and an occasional flash of white buildings are your only clues from the road that this black-lava coast north of Kona is more than bleak and barren. But, oh, is it! Down by the sea, pleasure domes rise like palaces no Hawaiian king ever imagined. This is where the Lear jet–set escapes to play in world-class beachfront hotels set like jewels in the golden sand. But you don't have to be a billionaire to visit the Waikoloa, Mauna Lani, and Mauna Kea resorts: The fabulous beaches and abundant historic sites are open to the public, with parking and other facilities provided by the resorts, including restaurants, golf courses, and shopping.

North Kohala ★★

Seven sugar mills once shipped enough sugar from three harbors on this knob of land to sweeten all the coffee in San Francisco. **Hawi,** the region's hub and home to the Kohala Sugar Co., was a flourishing town. Today, Hawi's quaint, 3-block-long strip of sun-faded, false-fronted buildings and 1920s vintage shops lives on as a minor tourist stop in one of Hawaii's most

scenic rural regions, located at the northernmost reaches of the island. North Kohala is most famous as the birthplace of King Kamehameha the Great; a statue commemorates the royal site. It's also home to the islands' most sacred site, the 1,500-year-old **Mookini Heiau** (see Mookini Luakini, on p. 312).

Waimea (Kamuela) ★★

This old upcountry cow town on the northern road between the coasts is set in lovely country: rolling green pastures, wide-open spaces dotted by *puu* (hills), and real cowpokes who ride mammoth **Parker Ranch,** Hawaii's largest working ranch. The town is also headquarters for the **Keck Telescope,** the largest and most powerful in the world, bringing world-class, starry-eyed astronomers to town. Waimea is home to several affordable B&Bs, and Merriman's Restaurant is a popular foodie outpost at Opelo Plaza.

The Hamakua Coast ★★

This emerald coast, a 52-mile stretch from Honokaa to Hilo on the island's windward northeast side, was once planted with sugarcane; it now blooms with flowers, macadamia nuts, papayas, and marijuana, also known as *pakalolo* (still Hawaii's number-one cash crop). Resort-free and virtually without beaches, the Hamakua Coast still has a few major destinations, such as spectacular **Waipio Valley,** a picture-perfect valley with impossibly steep sides, taro patches, a green riot of wild plants, and a winding stream leading to a broad, black-sand beach; and the historic plantation town of **Honokaa,** making a comeback as the B&B capital on the coastal trail. Akaka Falls and Laupahoehoe Beach Park are also worth seeking out (see "Seeing the Sights," later in this chapter).

Hilo ★★

When the sun shines in Hilo, it's one of the most beautiful tropical cities in the Pacific. Being here is an entirely different kind of island experience: Hawaii's largest metropolis after Honolulu is a quaint, misty, flower-filled city of Victorian houses overlooking a half-moon bay, with a restored historic downtown and a clear view of Mauna Loa's often snowcapped peak. Hilo catches everyone's eye until it rains—it rains a lot in Hilo—and when it rains, it pours.

Hilo is America's wettest town, with 128 inches of rain annually. It's ideal for growing ferns, orchids, and anthuriums, but not for catching a few rays. But there's lots to see and do in Hilo, so grab your umbrella. The rain is warm (the temperature seldom dips below 70°F/21°C), and there's usually a rainbow afterward.

Hilo's oversize airport and hotels are remnants of a dream: The city wanted to be Hawaii's major port of entry. That didn't happen, but the facilities here are excellent. Hilo is also Hawaii's best bargain for budget travelers. It has plenty of hotel rooms—most of the year, that is. Hilo's magic moment comes in spring, the week after Easter, when hula *halau* (schools) arrive for the annual Merrie Monarch Festival hula competition (see "Hawaii Calendar of Events," in chapter 2 for details). This is a full-on Hawaiian spectacle and a wonderful cultural event. Plan ahead if you want to go: Tickets are sold out the first week in January for the post-Easter event, and the hotels within 30 miles are usually booked solid.

Hilo is also the gateway to Hawaii Volcanoes National Park; it's just an hour's drive away up-slope.

Hawaii Volcanoes National Park ★★★

This is the location of America's most exciting national park, where a live volcano called Kilauea erupts daily. (If you're lucky, it will be a spectacular sight. At other times, you may not be able to see the molten lava at all, but there's still a lot to see and learn.) Ideally, you should plan to spend 3 days at the park exploring the trails, watching the volcano, visiting the rain forest, and just enjoying this most unusual, spectacular place. But even if you have only a day, get here—it's worth the trip. Bring your sweats or jacket (honest!); it's cool up here, especially at night.

If you plan to dally in the park—and you should—you can find a great place to stay in the sleepy hamlet of Volcano Village (located in a rain forest just outside the National Park entrance). Several terrifically cozy B&Bs, some with fireplaces, hide under tree ferns in this cool mountain hideaway. The tiny highland community (elev. 4,000 ft.), first settled by Japanese immigrants, is now inhabited by artists, soul-searchers, and others who like the crisp air of Hawaii's high country. It has just enough civilization to sustain a good life: a few stores, a handful of eateries, a gas station, and a golf course.

Ka Lae: South Point ★★

This is the Plymouth Rock of Hawaii, where the first Polynesians arrived in seagoing canoes, probably from the Marquesas Islands or Tahiti, around A.D. 500. You'll feel like you're at the end of the world on this lonely, windswept place, the southernmost point of the United States (a geographic claim that belonged to Key West, Florida, until 1959, when Hawaii became the 50th state). Hawaii ends in a sharp, black-lava point. Bold 500-foot cliffs stand against the blue sea to the west and shelter the old fishing village of Waiahukini, which was born in A.D. 750 and lasted until the 1860s. Ancient canoe moorings, shelter caves, and *heiau* (temples) poke through windblown pili grass. The East Coast curves inland to reveal a lonely, green-sand beach, a world-famous anomaly that's accessible only by foot or four-wheel-drive. For most, the only reason to venture down to the southern tip is to say you did or to experience the empty vista of land's end.

Everything in **Naalehu** and **Waiohinu,** the two wide spots in the road that pass for towns at South Point, claims to be the southernmost this or that. Except for a monkeypod tree planted by Mark Twain in 1866, there's not much else to crow about. There is, thankfully, a gas station, along with a couple of places to eat, a fruit stand, and a few B&Bs. These end-of-the-world towns are just about as far removed from the real world as you can get.

2 Getting Around

BY CAR   You'll need a rental car on the Big Island; not having one will really limit what you'll be able to see and do. All the major car-rental firms have agencies at the airports and at the Kohala Coast resorts; for a complete list, as well as tips on insurance and driving rules, see "Car Rentals" under "Getting There & Getting Around," in chapter 2.

There are more than 480 miles of paved road on the Big Island. The highway that circles the island is called the **Hawaii Belt Road.** On the Kona side of the island, you have two choices: the scenic "upper" road, **Mamalahoa Highway** (Hwy. 190), or the speedier "lower" road, **Queen Kaahumanu Highway** (Hwy. 19). The road that links east to west is called the **Saddle Road** (Hwy. 200), because it crosses the "saddle" between Mauna Kea and Mauna Loa. Saddle Road looks like a shortcut from Kona to Hilo, but it usually doesn't make for a shorter trip. It's rough, narrow, and plagued by bad weather; as a result, most rental-car agencies forbid you from taking their cars on it.

BY TAXI   Taxis are readily available at both Keahole and Hilo airports. In Hilo, call **Ace-1** (© **808/935-8303**). In Kailua-Kona, call **Kona Airport Taxi** (© **808/329-7779**). Taxis will take you wherever you want to go on the Big Island, but it's prohibitively expensive to use them for long distances.

BY BUS & SHUTTLE   For transportation from the Kona Airport, call **SpeediShuttle** (© **808/329-5433;** www.speedishuttle.com). Some sample rates: From the airport to Kailua-Kona the fare is $18; to the Four Seasons it's also $18; and to Mauna Lani it's $41.

There is an islandwide bus system, but all it does is take passengers from Kona to Hilo and back (and does not stop at the airports). It's the **Hele-On Bus** (© **808/961-8744**), and it leaves Kailua-Kona from the Lanihau Shopping Center, at Palani Road and Queen Kaahumanu Highway, every morning at 6:45am, getting into Hilo at 9:30am. The afternoon return trip leaves the bus terminal on Kamehameha Avenue at Mamo Street, in Hilo, at 1:30pm, arriving back in Kailua-Kona at 4:30pm. The fare is $5.25 each way.

For transportation around Kailua-Kona all the way to Keauhou, take the **Alii Shuttle** (© **808/775-7121**), which travels up and down Alii Drive (the coastal road) and Palani Road (the main entrance to Kailua-Kona) from the Lanihau Shopping Center to Ohana Keauhou Bay Resort, stopping just about anywhere you want on Palai Road or Alii Drive. The cost is $2 one-way; the current hours of operation (subject to change, so call to check) are from 8:30am to 7:40pm.

Ⓒ FAST FACTS: The Big Island

American Express There's an office on the Kohala Coast at the **Hilton Waikoloa Village** (Ⓒ **808/886-7958**). To report lost or stolen traveler's checks, call Ⓒ **800/221-7282**.

Dentists In an emergency, contact **Dr. Craig C. Kimura** at Kamuela Office Center (Ⓒ **808/885-5947**); in Kona, call **Dr. Frank Sayre,** Frame 10 Center, behind Lanihau Shopping Center on Palani Road (Ⓒ **808/329-8067**); in Hilo, call **Hawaii Smile Center,** Hilo Lagoon Center, 101 Aupuni St. (Ⓒ **808/961-9181**).

Doctors In Hilo, the **Hilo Medical Center** is at 1190 Waianuenue Ave. (Ⓒ **808/974-4700**); on the Kona side, call **Hualalai Urgent Care,** 75–1028 Henry St., across the street from Safeway (Ⓒ **808/327-HELP**).

Emergencies For ambulance, fire, and rescue services, dial Ⓒ **911** or call Ⓒ **808/961-6022**. The **Poison Control Center** hot line is Ⓒ **800/362-3585**.

Hospitals Hospitals offering 24-hour urgent-care facilities include the **Hilo Medical Center,** 1190 Waianuenue Ave., Hilo (Ⓒ **808/974-4700**); **North Hawaii Community Hospital,** Waimea (Ⓒ **808/885-4444**); and **Kona Community Hospital,** on the Kona Coast in Kealakekua (Ⓒ **808/322-9311**).

Police Dial Ⓒ **911** in case of emergency; otherwise, call the **Hawaii Police Department** at Ⓒ **808/326-4646** in Kona, Ⓒ **808/961-2213** in Hilo.

Post Office All calls to the U.S. Post Office can be directed to Ⓒ **800/275-8777**. There are local branches in Hilo, at 1299 Kekuanaoa Ave.; in Kailua-Kona, at 74–5577 Palani Rd.; and in Waimea, on Lindsey Road.

Weather For conditions in and around Hilo, call Ⓒ **808/935-8555**; for the rest of the Big Island, call Ⓒ **808/961-5582**. For marine forecasts, call Ⓒ **808/935-9883**.

---

3 Where to Stay

Before you reach for the phone to book your vacation dream house, refer back to "Tips on Accommodations," in chapter 2 to make sure you book the kind of place you want. Also remember that the Big Island is really big; see "The Island in Brief," earlier in this chapter, to make sure you choose the best area in which to base yourself.

If you're interested in additional information on bed-and-breakfasts, contact the **Hawaii Island B&B Association,** P.O. Box 1890, Honokaa, HI 96727 (no phone; **www.stayhawaii.com**).

In the listings below, all rooms come with a full private bathroom (with tub or shower) and free parking unless otherwise noted. Remember to add Hawaii's 11.42% in taxes to your final bill.

THE KONA COAST

IN & AROUND KAILUA-KONA

For a detailed map of central Kailua-Kona, see p. 307.

Very Expensive

Four Seasons Resort Hualalai at Historic Kaupulehu ★★★ *Kids*   This is a great place to relax in the lap of luxury. You're guaranteed to experience Polynesian paralysis after a few days of lying in a hammock and watching the clouds waft across the sky, though there are plenty of diversions available as well. Low-rise clusters of oceanfront villas nestle between the sea and the greens of a new golf course. The Four Seasons has no concrete corridors, and no massive central building—it looks like a two-story town house project, clustered around three seaside swimming pools. The rooms are furnished in Pacific tropical style: beige walls, raffia rugs over clay-colored slate, and Madge Tennent etchings over rattan and bamboo settees. The ground-level rooms have bathrooms with private outdoor gardens (surrounded by black-lava rock), so you can shower naked under the tropical sun or nighttime stars.

This Four Seasons at Hualalai is very different from its cousin on Maui. The low-rise bungalows create an entirely different effect than Maui's palatial mansion by the sea. In fact, the staff calls the Maui property "the palace" and the Big Island property "the village."

If you can afford it, this is the place to go to be pampered (the pool attendants will make sure that you have plenty of ice-cold water to drink and a chilled towel for your brow). Other pluses include: a Hawaiian history and cultural interpretive center, complimentary scuba lessons, complimentary valet, 1-hour pressing, twice-daily maid service, multilingual concierge, free shoe shine and sandal repair, and early/late arrival facilities. The spa here was selected by *Condé Nast Traveler* magazine as the world's best resort spa. One of the five pools is a saltwater pond carved out of black-lava rock with reef fish swimming about.

Your kids will be pampered too—the complimentary Kids for All Seasons program features plenty of activities to keep the little ones busy. The resort also offers children's menus in all restaurants, a game room, videos, and more.

P.O. Box 1269, Kailua-Kona, HI 96745. (© 888/340-5662 or 808/325-8000. Fax 808/325-8100. www.four seasons.com/hualalai. 243 units. $520–$750 double; from $1,100 suite. Extra person $120; children under 18 stay free in parent's room. AE, DC, MC, V. **Amenities:** 3 restaurants (see reviews for Pahu i'a and Beach Tree Bar and Grill on p. 261 and 262); 3 bars (nightly entertainment ranging from Hawaiian to jazz); 5 exquisite outdoor pools (including a giant infinite pool and a gorgeous lap pool); 18-hole Jack Nicklaus signature golf course exclusively for guests and residents; 8 tennis courts (4 lit for night play); complete fitness center; award-winning spa; 6 Jacuzzis; watersports equipment rentals; bike rentals; complimentary, year-round children's program; game room; attentive concierge; activity desk; car-rental desk; business center; top-drawer shopping arcade; salon; 24-hr. room service; both in-room and spa massage; babysitting; complimentary washer/dryers; same-day laundry/dry cleaning. *In room:* A/C, TV, dataport, fridge, coffeemaker, hair dryer, iron, safe.

Kona Village Resort ★★★ *Kids*   For more than 30 years, those seeking the great escape have crossed the black-lava fields to find refuge at this exclusive, one-of-a-kind haven by the sea with its wonderful dark-sand beach. A blissful languor settles in as you surrender to the gentle staff and peaceful, low-key atmosphere. Maybe it's the spirit of the ancients who once lived here. Maybe it's the deluxe summer-camp setup: thatched-roof, island-style bungalows with no air-conditioning and no TVs, a central dining house, and phones only at the office.

Kona Coast Accommodations

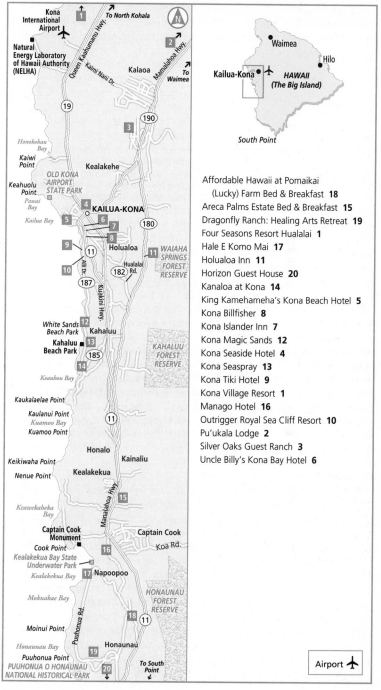

Affordable Hawaii at Pomaikai
  (Lucky) Farm Bed & Breakfast **18**
Areca Palms Estate Bed & Breakfast **15**
Dragonfly Ranch: Healing Arts Retreat **19**
Four Seasons Resort Hualalai **1**
Hale E Komo Mai **17**
Holualoa Inn **11**
Horizon Guest House **20**
Kanaloa at Kona **14**
King Kamehameha's Kona Beach Hotel **5**
Kona Billfisher **8**
Kona Islander Inn **7**
Kona Magic Sands **12**
Kona Seaside Hotel **4**
Kona Seaspray **13**
Kona Tiki Hotel **9**
Kona Village Resort **1**
Manago Hotel **16**
Outrigger Royal Sea Cliff Resort **10**
Pu'ukala Lodge **2**
Silver Oaks Guest Ranch **3**
Uncle Billy's Kona Bay Hotel **6**

The resort resembles an eclectic Polynesian village, with proudly tended palms, historic sites, and beaches on a secluded cove. Its magic frees children of all ages (except during May and Sept, when the resort is reserved for couples only) to relax and play on 82 acres by the sea, behind a lava barrier that keeps the world at bay. The bungalows, renovated in 1998, each have a bedroom, bathroom, and lanai, and the maids replenish the fridge daily with free sodas and bottled water. Some units have an outdoor hot tub and an extra anteroom with a single bed.

The room rate includes breakfast, lunch, and dinner—the Friday-night luau here is fabulous—plus all snorkeling equipment and other beach toys. It also includes scheduled activities throughout the day for kids and teens.

P.O. Box 1299, Kailua-Kona, HI 96745. ⓒ 800/367-5290 or 808/325-5555. Fax 808/325-5124. www.kona village.com. 125 bungalows. $505–$1,095 double. Extra person $193 adult, $38–$143 children. Rates include all meals for 2 adults, tennis, watersports, walking tours, airport transfers, and a Friday-night luau. Packages available. AE, DC, MC, V. **Amenities:** 2 restaurants; 2 bars (with live entertainment most nights); 2 outdoor pools; tennis courts; fitness room; 2 Jacuzzis; complimentary watersports; extensive children's program (especially during the summer, when it extends past dinner); concierge; activity desk; a Polynesian general store; babysitting; complimentary washer/dryers; laundry/dry cleaning. *In room:* Fridge, coffeemaker, hair dryer, iron, safe, no phone.

Expensive

Outrigger Royal Sea Cliff Resort   Families will love these luxuriously appointed apartments and their affordable rates. The architecturally striking, five-story white buildings that make up this resort/condo complex, 2 miles from Kailua-Kona, are stepped back from the ocean for maximum views and privacy. (The downside is that there's no ocean swimming here, but the waves are near enough to lull you to sleep, and if you really want to take a dip there's a decent swimming beach about a mile away.) Atrium gardens and hanging bougainvillea soften the look. Spacious units are furnished in tropical rattan with a large, sunny lanai, a full kitchen, and a washer/dryer. All units have voice mail, and the property also has several barbecue and picnic facilities for oceanfront dining.

75–6040 Alii Dr., Kailua-Kona, HI 96740. ⓒ 800/688-7444 or 808/329-8021. Fax 808/326-1887. www. outrigger.com. 148 units. $183–$233 studio double; $215–$318 1-bedroom apt for 4; $250–$363 2-bedroom apt for 6; $600–$803 villa for 4. AE, DC, DISC, MC, V. **Amenities:** 2 outdoor pools; complimentary tennis courts; Jacuzzi; activity desk; business center; small store. *In room:* A/C, TV, kitchen, fridge, coffeemaker, hair dryer, iron, safe, washer/dryer.

Moderate

King Kamehameha's Kona Beach Hotel   The best deal at this convenient downtown Kailua-Kona hotel is the Package of Aloha, which comes with a double room, a compact car, and breakfast for two, starting at just $148—a price that makes the "King Kam" (as locals call it) attractive to travelers on a budget. This place isn't anything fancy—just a standard hotel in need of a little TLC— but it's well located, right in the heart of town, across the street from the pier, where record Pacific blue marlin are weighed in every afternoon. Rooms are showing their age, but they are clean and can have views of an ancient banyan tree, the Kona Pier, or sparkling Kailua Bay. The hotel's own small, gold-sand beach is right out the front door. All three of the hotel's restaurants are forgettable, but you're within walking distance of dozens of other options.

75–5660 Palani Rd., Kailua-Kona, HI 96740. ⓒ 800/367-6060 or 808/329-2911. Fax 808/922-8061. www. konabeachhotel.com. 460 units. $135–$225 double; from $500 suite. Package of Aloha (including room, car, and breakfast) from $148 (subject to availability). Extra person $30. AE, DC, DISC, MC, V. Parking $5. **Amenities:** 3 restaurants; outdoor bar with Hawaiian entertainment; outdoor pool; 4 tennis courts; Jacuzzi; watersports equipment rentals; activity desk; shopping arcade; salon; limited room service; coin-op washer/dryers; laundry/dry cleaning. *In room:* A/C, TV, dataport, fridge, coffeemaker, iron, safe.

Silver Oaks Guest Ranch ★★ *Finds*   Book this place! Not a bed-and-breakfast or a condo, this is a true "guest ranch," consisting of five separate units spread over a 10-acre working ranch (with friendly horses—no horseback riding, just petting—and wild turkeys that come to get fed once a day). Located at 1,300 feet, where the temperatures are in the 70s year-round, the ranch has units ranging from studios to family-size units. The views are spectacular, some 40 miles of coastline from the ocean to Mauna Loa, yet it's just 5 miles from the airport and 5 miles from all the activities in downtown Kailua-Kona. Hosts Amy and Rick Decker have impeccable taste and every unit is uniquely decorated. All the units have a private bathroom and either a kitchenette or complete kitchen. Amy leaves breakfast items in your unit (fresh bread, just-picked fruit, and Kona coffee), so you can enjoy breakfast at your leisure.

Reservations: 75–1027 Henry St., Suite 310, Kailua-Kona, HI 96740. ⓒ **877-325-2300** or 808/325-2000. Fax 808/325-2200. www.silveroaksranch.com. 5 units. $115–$160 (includes breakfast items). Children under 10 stay free. Extra person $15. 3-night minimum. MC, V. **Amenities:** Outdoor pool; Jacuzzi; washer/dryers. *In room:* TV, dataport, kitchenette or kitchen, fridge, coffeemaker.

Inexpensive

Interested in a B&B? Call **Pu'ukala Lodge** ★ (ⓒ **808/325-1729;** www.puukala-lodge.com), a five-room lodge on the slopes of Hualalai with sweeping views; rates start at $75, which includes full gourmet breakfast.

Kona Billfisher ★ *Kids*   This is our favorite of all the affordable condos on this coast. It's within walking distance of downtown Kailua-Kona, and the big, blue Pacific is just across the street. (Unfortunately, the ocean here is not good for swimming or snorkeling, but there's a pool on-site, and the Kailua Pier, just a mile away, has a good swimming area.) The property is very well maintained (the interiors were renovated in 1998). Each unit comes with a full kitchen and a balcony and features new furnishings and king-size beds. The one-bedroom units have sliding-glass doors that allow you to close off the living room and make it into another private bedroom, so for the price of a one-bedroom unit, you can have a two-bedroom—a real deal. Other on-site facilities include a barbecue area. Book well in advance.

Alii Dr. (across from the Royal Kona Resort), c/o Hawaii Resort Management, P.O. Box 39, Kailua-Kona, HI 96745. ⓒ **800/622-5348** or 808/329-3333. Fax 808/326-4137. www.konahawaii.com. 60 units. High season $95 1-bedroom and $125 for 2-bedroom/1-bath units; low season $80 1-bedroom and $105 for 2-bedroom/1-bath units. AE, DC, DISC, MC, V. **Amenities:** Outdoor pool; nearby coin-op washer/dryer. *In room:* A/C, TV, kitchen, fridge, coffeemaker, iron.

Kona Islander Inn *Value*   This is the most affordable place to stay in Kailua-Kona. These plantation-style, three-story buildings are surrounded by lush, palm tree–lined gardens with torch-lit pathways that make it hard to believe you're smack-dab in the middle of downtown. The central location—across the street from the historic Kona Inn Shops—is convenient but can be noisy. Built in 1962, the complex is showing some signs of age, but the units were recently outfitted with new appliances, new bedspreads and curtains, and a fresh coat of paint. The studios are small, but extras like lanais and kitchenettes outfitted with microwaves, minifridges, and coffeemakers make up for the lack of space.

75–5776 Kuakini Hwy. (south of Hualalai Rd.), Kailua-Kona. c/o Hawaii Resort Management, P.O. Box 39, Kailua-Kona, HI 96745. ⓒ **800/622-5348** or 808/329-3333. Fax 808/326-4137. www.konahawaii.com. 80 studios. $60–$90 double. AE, MC, V. **Amenities:** Outdoor pool; hot tub; activity desk; coin-op washer/dryers. *In room:* A/C, TV, kitchenette, fridge, coffeemaker.

Kona Magic Sands ★ *Value* If you want to stay right on the ocean without spending a fortune, this is the place to do it—it's one of the best oceanfront deals you'll find on a Kona condo, and the only one with a beach for swimming and snorkeling right next door. Every unit in this older complex has a lanai that steps out over the ocean and sunset views that you'll dream about long after you return home. These studio units aren't luxurious; they're small (2 people max) and cozy, great for people who want to be lulled to sleep by the sound of the waves crashing on the shore. Each consists of one long, narrow room with a small kitchen at one end and the lanai at the other, with a living room/dining room/bedroom combo in between.

77–6452 Alii Dr. (next to Magic Sands Beach Park). c/o Hawaii Resort Management, P.O. Box 39, Kailua-Kona, HI 96745. ✆ **800/622-5348** or 808/329-3333. Fax 808/326-4137. www.konahawaii.com. 37 units (shower only). High season $125 double; low season $95 double. DISC, MC, V. **Amenities:** Excellent seafood restaurant (Jameson's by the Sea); bar; oceanfront outdoor pool. *In room:* TV, kitchen, fridge, coffeemaker.

Kona Seaside Hotel The package deal here is great: For just a few dollars more than the regular room rate, you can have a rental car thrown in, too. This budget hotel, located in the heart of Kailua-Kona, is just steps away from Kailua Bay and Kailua-Kona's shopping, restaurants, and historic sites. The rooms are large and comfy (even if they don't have fancy soaps and extra amenities), but they can be noisy (ask for one away from the road). You may want to splurge on one of the 14 rooms with kitchenettes.

75–5646 Palani Rd. (at Kuakini Hwy.), Kailua-Kona, HI 96740. ✆ **800/560-5558** or 808/329-2455. Fax 808/922-0052. www.sand-seaside.com. 225 units. $98–$120 double; $130 double with kitchenette. Extra person $12; children under 12 stay free in parent's room. Room/car packages available from $103. AE, DC, MC, V. **Amenities:** Restaurant; bar; 2 small outdoor pools; coin-op washer/dryers; laundry/dry cleaning. *In room:* A/C, TV, some kitchenettes, fridge.

Kona Tiki Hotel ★★ *Finds* It's hard to believe that places like this still exist. The Kona Tiki, located right on the ocean, away from the hustle and bustle of downtown Kailua-Kona, is one of the best budget deals in Hawaii. All of the rooms are tastefully decorated and feature queen beds, ceiling fans, minifridges, and private lanais overlooking the ocean. Although it's called a hotel, this small, family-run operation is more like a large B&B, with lots of aloha and plenty of friendly conversation at the morning breakfast buffet around the pool. The staff is helpful in planning activities. There are no TVs or phones in the rooms, but there's a pay phone in the lobby. If a double with a kitchenette is available, grab it—the few bucks will save you a bundle in food costs. Book way, way, way in advance.

75–5968 Alii Dr. (about a mile from downtown Kailua-Kona), Kailua-Kona, HI 96740. ✆ **808/329-1425.** Fax 808/327-9402. www.konatiki.com. 15 units. $59–$72 double; $79 double with kitchenette. Rates include continental breakfast. Extra person $8; children 2–12 $6. 3-night minimum. No credit cards. **Amenities:** Outdoor pool. *In room:* Some kitchenettes, fridge, no phone.

Uncle Billy's Kona Bay Hotel An institution in Kona, Uncle Billy's is where visitors from the other islands stay when they come to this coast. A thatched roof hangs over the lobby area, and a Polynesian longhouse restaurant is next door. The rooms are old, but comfortable, and come with large lanais; most also have minifridges (request one at booking if you want one), and 16 are condo-style units with kitchens. This budget hotel is a good place to sleep, but don't expect new furniture or carpets, or fancy soap in the bathroom. It can be noisy at night when big groups book in; avoid Labor Day weekend, when all the canoe paddlers in the state want to stay here and rehash the race into the wee morning hours.

75–5739 Alii Dr., Kailua-Kona, HI 96740. ✆ 800/367-5102 or 808/961-5818. Fax 808/935-7903. www.uncle billy.com. 139 units. $94–$99 double; $99 double with kitchenettes. Breakfast included in the price. Check Internet for specials starting at $84 and car/room deals for just $30 more a night. Extra person $14; children 18 and under stay free in parent's room. AE, DC, DISC, MC, V. **Amenities:** Restaurant (buffet); bar (with Hawaiian entertainment); 2 outdoor pools (1 just for children); watersports equipment rentals; activity desk; coin-op washer/dryers. *In room:* A/C, TV, dataport, some kitchenettes, some fridges.

UPCOUNTRY KONA: HOLUALOA

Holualoa Inn ★★ *Finds*   The quiet, secluded setting of this B&B—40 pastoral acres just off the main drag of the artsy village of Holualoa, 1,350 feet above Kailua-Kona—provides stunning panoramic views of the entire coast. Owned by a *kamaaina* (old-line) family, this contemporary 7,000-square-foot Hawaiian home built of golden woods has six private suites and window-walls that roll back to embrace the gardens and views. Cows graze on the bucolic pastures below the garden Jacuzzi and pool, and the coffee plantation on the property is the source of the morning brew. The inn offers several nice features, such as a gas grill for a romantic dinner beside the pool, a telescope for stargazing, and a billiard table. It's a 15-minute drive down the hill to busy Kailua-Kona and about 20 minutes to the beach, but the pool has a stunning view of Kailua-Kona and the sparkling Pacific below. Children must be 13 or older.

P.O. Box 222 (76–5932 Mamalahoa Hwy.), Holualoa, HI 96725. ✆ 800/392-1812 or 808/324-1121. Fax 808/ 322-2472. www.konaweb.com/HINN. 6 units (1 with shower only). $175–$225 double. Rates include full breakfast and sunset pupu platter. Extra person $30. 15% discount for 7 nights or more. AE, DC, DISC, MC, V. On Mamalahoa Hwy., just after the Holualoa Post Office, look for Paul's Place General Store; the next driveway is the inn. **Amenities:** Huge outdoor pool; Jacuzzi. *In room:* Hair dryer, no phone.

KEAUHOU

Kanaloa at Kona ★★ *Kids*   These big, comfortable, well-managed, and spacious vacation condos border the rocky coast beside Keauhou Bay, 6 miles south of Kailua-Kona. They're exceptional units, ideal for families, with comforts such as huge bathrooms with whirlpool bathtubs, dressing rooms, and bidets. In addition, the spacious lanais, tropical decor, and many appliances make for free and easy living. It's easy to stock up on supplies at the supermarket at the new mall just up the hill, but the oceanfront restaurant offers an alternative to your own cooking. Guests receive discounted rates at the two 18-hole golf courses at a nearby country club.

78–261 Manukai St., Kailua-Kona, HI 96740. ✆ 800/688-7444 or 808/322-9625 Outrigger Resorts. Fax 800/622-4852. www.outrigger.com. 76 units. $205–$290 1-bedroom apt (sleeps up to 4); $220–$330 2-bedroom apt (up to 6); $305-$360 2-bedroom apt with loft (up to 8). AE, DC, DISC, MC, V. **Amenities:** Restaurant; oceanside bar; 3 outdoor pools (1 for adults only); 2 (lighted) tennis courts; 3 Jacuzzis; concierge; activity desk; babysitting; coin-op washer/dryers. *In room:* TV, kitchen, fridge, coffeemaker, hair dryer, iron, safe.

Kona Seaspray ★ *Value*   The Kona Seaspray has a couple of great things going for it: location and price. It's just across from the Kahaluu Beach Park, possibly the best snorkeling area in Kona. The rates are a great deal when you consider that the one-bedroom apartments easily sleep four and the two-bedroom (1-bathroom) unit can sleep six. It's recently under new ownership, and all the units are undergoing renovation with upgraded furniture, new carpets, and a whole new look. All apartments have a full kitchen, complete with all the amenities of home. Plus every unit has a lanai and fabulous ocean view. Golf and tennis are nearby. This is the place to book if you are going to spend a lot of time lounging around or if you need the extra space.

78–6671 Alii Dr. (reservations c/o Johnson Resort Properties, 78–6665 Alii Dr.), Kailua-Kona, HI 96740. ✆ 808/322-2403. Fax 808/322-0105. www.konaseaspray.com. 12 units. $105–$125 1-bedroom apt for 2;

(Kids Family-Friendly Hotels

In addition to our favorites below, also consider the **Kanaloa at Kona** (see above) and **Mauna Lani Bay Hotel and Bungalows** (p. 250) on the Kohala Coast; **Mountain Meadow Ranch Bed & Breakfast** (p. 254) on the Hamakua Coast; **Hiiaka House and Log Cabin** (p. 257), in Volcano; and *Macadamia Meadows Bed & Breakfast* (p. 260) on South Point. *Note:* By state law, hotels can only accept children ages 5 to 12 in supervised activities programs.

Four Seasons Resort Hualalai (p. 240)   This is one of Hawaii's most kid-friendly hotels, offering the complimentary Kids for All Seasons program. The activities center features everything from sand-sculpting to kite-flying. The hotel also offers free milk and cookies on arrival, children's menus in all restaurants, complimentary items for infant needs (cribs, strollers, high chairs, playpens, bottles, car seats), and child safety features. There's even a games room (SuperNintendo!), complimentary scuba clinic for kids 12 and older, videos, and a host of sailing, snorkeling, and other activities.

Kona Village Resort (p. 240)   Here, you'll find a parent's dream: custom-designed programs to entertain your children (ages 6 and up), all at no charge. There's even a dinner seating for children, at 5:30pm every day, with a special menu; the kids can go unescorted so their parents can enjoy an intimate dinner for two later in the evening. *Note:* Children are not permitted in May and September, when the resort features a month of romance for couples only.

Kona Billfisher (p. 243)   This condo complex has well-equipped—and very well-priced—one-bedroom units, which sleep four and are great for families. The ocean is just across the street, and there's a great family-style pizza-and-hamburger joint right next door.

$130–$135 for 1-bedroom/2 bath double; $135 2-bedroom/1 bath apt for 4; $145–$165 2-bedroom/2 bath apt 4. Stays of less than 3 nights add $45 cleaning fee. Extra person $20. AE, DISC, MC, V. **Amenities:** Gorgeous outdoor pool with waterfall; washer/dryers. *In room:* TV, kitchen, full-size fridge, coffeemaker, hair dryer, iron.

SOUTH KONA
Expensive

Horizon Guest House ★★ *(Finds*   Host Clem Classen spent 2 years researching the elements of a perfect bed-and-breakfast. The Horizon Guest House is the result. Its 40 acres of pastureland are located at an altitude of 1,100 feet. You can see 25 miles of coastline from Kealakekua to just about South Point, yet you cannot see another structure or hear any sounds of civilization. The carefully thought-out individual units (all under one roof but positioned at an angle to each other so you don't see any other units) are filled with some $16,000 worth of Hawaiian furnishings, including hand-quilted Hawaiian bedspreads, writing desks, and luxurious robes. Units also include private lanais with coastline views. The property features a spectacular ocean view, top-drawer barbecue facilities, gardens everywhere, outdoor shower, and all the ocean and beach toys you can

Hale E Komo Mai (p. 249)   Large families will love this rambling Victorian just down the street from Kealakekua Bay. The interior is open and airy, and the furnishings can take any punishment the kids dish out. The house sleeps up to six or seven (counting the 2 bedrooms, sofa bed, tiny bed in the alcove, and bed on the lanai). Good swimming beaches line the coastline, dolphins are in the bay nearly every day, and Puuhonua O Honaunau National Historic Park is just a 5-minute drive away.

The Fairmont Orchid, Hawaii (p. 251)   The Keiki Aloha program, for kids 5 to 12 years, features supervised activities like watersports (from kayaking to snorkeling), Hawaiian cultural activities (petroglyph hikes, hula lessons), and just plain fun (face painting, video games, treasure hunts) for $60 for the full day (including lunch) and $40 for a half day. The resort has some great money-saving deals; for example, children 5 and under eat free at various restaurants in the resort (except during holidays). Also ask about Family Package, which includes buffet breakfast for two daily, plus 2 half-day Keiki Aloha programs. If you book a second room, it's half price.

Guest House at Volcano (p. 257)   If you're bringing the little ones to see the volcano, here's the place to stay. A mother herself, hostess Bonnie Gooddell has childproofed her house, and her guest cottage comes complete with toys on the porch and a basketball hoop in the driveway. You can take the kids on a hike along the forest trail in the backyard, which cuts through 2 miles of tropical rain forest to the Thurston Lava Tube in Hawaii Volcanoes National Park.

think of. Clem whips up a gourmet breakfast in the octagonal kitchen in the main house, which also features a media room with library, video collection, TV (which you can take to your room, if you promise to use the headphones so you won't disturb other guests), DVD, VCR, and cordless phone. At first glance, the rate may seem high, but once you're ensconced on the unique property, we think you'll agree it's worth every penny.

P.O. Box 268, Honaunau, HI 96726. (C) **888/328-8301** or 808/328-2540. Fax 808/328-8707. www.horizon guesthouse.com. 4 units. $250 double. Rates include full gourmet breakfast. 2-night minimum. MC, V. 21 miles south of Kailua-Kona on Hwy. 11, just before mile marker 100. Children must be 14 or older. **Amenities:** Large outdoor pool that's worthy of a big resort; Jacuzzi perfectly placed to watch the sunset behind Kealakekua Bay; complimentary washer/dryers. *In room:* Fridge, coffeemaker, hair dryer, no phone.

Inexpensive

Affordable Hawaii at Pomaikai (Lucky) Farm Bed & Breakfast *Value*
True to its name, Affordable Hawaii offers an inexpensive perch from which to explore the South Kona Coast. Come share ex-Californian Nita Isherwood's century-old 4-acre farm, which is overflowing with macadamia-nut trees, coffee, tropical fruits, avocados as big as footballs, and even *jaboticaba,* an exotic fruit

that makes a zingy jam and local wine. The least expensive room is inside the old farm house with private bathroom (hey, at $60 a night, this is a deal!). The recent addition, the Greenhouse wing, has two rooms with wooden floors, big windows with screens, full private bathrooms, and private entrances. The most unique accommodation is the old coffee barn, updated into a rustic room for two with a raised queen bed, a fabulous view of the coastline, a private bathroom (with toilet and sink only), and an outdoor shower. Guests can use a common kitchen with a refrigerator, microwave, hot plate, and barbecue grill.

83–5465 Mamalahoa Hwy. (south of Kailua-Kona, after mile marker 107), Captain Cook, HI 96704. (C) 800/ 325-6427 or 808/328-2112. Fax 808/328-2255. www.luckyfarm.com. 4 units. $60–$75 double. Rates include full farm breakfast. Extra person $10; children 5 and under $5. AE, DISC, M/C, V. In room: No phone.

Areca Palms Estate Bed & Breakfast (formerly Merryman's Bed & Breakfast) ★ (Finds)

Everything about this upcountry B&B is impeccable: the landscaping, the furnishings, the fresh flowers in every room—even breakfast is served with attention to every detail. This charming cedar home, surrounded by immaculate parklike landscaping, sits above the Captain Cook–Kealakekua area, close to beaches, shopping, and restaurants. Guests enjoy watching the sun sink into the ocean from the large lanai or gazing at the starry sky as they soak in the hot tub. Hosts Janice and Steve Glass took over from Don and Penny Merryman but continue the tradition of memorable breakfasts (orange-oatmeal quiche, tropical stuffed French toast, tree-ripened banana cakes), offer daily maid service, provide guests with beach equipment, and gladly help with reservations for activities and dinner.

P.O. Box 489, Captain Cook, HI 96704. (C) 800/545-4390 or 808/323-2276. Fax 808/323-3749. www.konabed andbreakfast.com. 4 units. $85–$125 double. Rates include full breakfast. Extra person $20. 10% discount for 7 nights or more. DISC, MC, V. From Hwy. 11, make a left at the Pacific Island Tire dealer (after mile marker 111) and follow the signs. **Amenities:** Outdoor Jacuzzi. In room: TV, hair dryer, no phone.

Dragonfly Ranch: Healing Arts Retreat

Some may find the Dragonfly Ranch too rustic. But if you want to enjoy Hawaii's tropical outdoors and you're thrilled by the island's most unique architecture—structures that bring the outdoors inside—this may be the place for you. Cabins range from one room (with screens only, no windows or drapes) to suites; you might describe the style as "early hippie." The location is ideal, with Puuhonua o Honaunau National Historic Park just down the road and five bays offering great swimming and diving just minutes away. The place itself, with freestanding cabins tucked away on 2 acres of fruit trees and exotic flowers, truly is a tropical fantasy.

P.O. Box 675 (19 miles south of Kailua-Kona on Hwy. 160), Honaunau, HI 96726. (C) 800/487-2159 or 808/ 328-2159. Fax 808/328-9570. www.dragonflyranch.com. 5 units (4 with private bathroom; 1 with shower only). $85–$100 double; $150–$200 suite. Rates include continental breakfast. Extra person $20. MC, V. From Hwy. 11, turn onto Hwy. 160 (the road to Puuhonua o Honaunau National Historic Park), between mile markers 103 and 104; after 1½ miles, look for the Dragonfly Ranch mailbox. **Amenities:** Yoga studio and fitness room; watersports equipment rentals; activity desk; car-rental desk; massage; babysitting; laundry service. In room: TV, some dataports, some kitchenettes, fridge, coffeemaker, hair dryer, iron.

Manago Hotel (Value)

If you want to experience the history and culture of the 50th state, the Manago Hotel may be the place for you. This living relic is still operated by the third generation of the same Japanese family that opened it in 1917. It offers clean accommodations, tasty home cooking (Manago Hotel Restaurant, p. 269), and generous helpings of aloha, all at budget prices. The older rooms (with community bathrooms) are ultraspartan—strictly for desperate budget travelers. The rooms with private bathrooms in the new wing are still pretty sparse (freshly painted walls with no decoration and no TV), but they're spotlessly clean and surrounded by Japanese gardens with a koi pond. The room prices increase as you go up; the third-floor units have the most spectacular views of the Kona coastline. Adventuresome travelers might want to try the Japanese rooms with tatami mats to sleep on and *furo* (deep hot tubs) in each room to soak in. By the end of your stay, you may leave with new friends (the Manago family is very friendly).

P.O. Box 145, Captain Cook, HI 96704. © 808/323-2642. Fax 808/323-3451. www.managohotel.com. 64 units (some with shared bathroom). $29 double without bathroom; $47–$52 double with private bathroom; $66 double Japanese room with small *furo* tub and private bathroom. Extra person $3. DISC, MC, V. **Amenities:** Restaurant; bar. *In room:* No phone.

For Long-Term Family Stays

Hale E Komo Mai *(Kids)*   If you have a big family and want to spend time at the beach, this Victorian-style custom-designed home is your best bet. Shoe-horned onto a small lot just steps from Kealakekua Bay, this three-story house rents out either as two separate units, each on its own floor, or as an entire house (we recommend the entire house, so you can have it all to yourself). The best feature is the third-floor rooftop lanai, which runs the entire length of the house and has a 360° view. The first floor has a full kitchen and bedroom with queen bed, plus a queen-size sofa bed in the living room. The second floor has a bed-room/sitting room, outdoor kitchen, and another bed out on the lanai. Amenities include a picnic table and barbecue, beach toys, and manicured lawn. Good swimming beaches line the coastline, dolphins visit the bay nearly every day, and Puuhonua O Honaunau National Historic Park is just a 5-minute drive away.

Napoopoo Rd., Kealakakua Bay. Reservations: 1392 Coast Meridian Rd., Port Coquitlam, B.C., Canada V3C 3V4. © 604/462-8315. www.hawaiikbaybeach.com. 2 units. $780 a week double; entire house, $1,200 per week double (sleeps up to 6). Extra person charge $50 and up. 1-week minimum. V. **Amenities:** Complimentary use of watersports equipment; washer/dryers. *In room:* TV, kitchen, fridge, coffeemaker, hair dryer, iron.

THE KOHALA COAST

Note: You'll find Kohala coast accommodations on the "North Kohala & Waimea" map on p. 313.

VERY EXPENSIVE

Hapuna Beach Prince Hotel ⋆   This hotel enjoys one of the best locations on the Kohala Coast, adjacent to the magnificent white sands of Hapuna Beach. The Hapuna Beach Prince is a bit more formal than other hotels on the Kohala Coast; guests, many from Japan, dress up here, some in the latest Tokyo fashions. You won't feel comfortable parading around the lobby and public areas in your T-shirt and flip-flops.

The rooms are comfortable, all attuned to the fabulous ocean view and the sea breezes. Although the rooms are small for a luxury hotel, the sprawling grounds make up for it (some guests, however, complain about the long walk from the lobby to their rooms). And the service is friendly and caring, with an unassuming confidence that springs from the Japanese ownership's low-key, hands-on managerial approach.

There is also a wealth of activities on the property, from the 18-hole championship links-style golf course (designed by Arnold Palmer and Ed Seay, and reserved for guests and residents) to the state-of-the-art fitness center and world-class spa.

At Mauna Kea Resort. 62–100 Kaunaoa Dr., Kohala Coast, HI 96743. ☎ **800/882-6060** or 808/880-1111. Fax 808/880-3112. www.hapunabeachprincehotel.com. 350 units. $360–$610 double; from $1,225 suite. Extra person $35; children 17 and under stay free in parent's room using existing bedding. AE, DC, MC, V. **Amenities:** 5 restaurants (including the Coast Grille, serving seafood, and the Ocean Terrace, with Continental cuisine); 2 bars (evenings, a local trio sings Hawaiian songs in the open-air, beachfront Reef Lounge); huge outdoor pool; golf course; 13 tennis courts; fitness center; Paul Brown Salon and Spa; Jacuzzi; watersports equipment rentals; year-round Keiki Kamp children's program; concierge; activity desk; car-rental desk; business center; shopping arcade; 24-hr. room service; massage; babysitting; same-day laundry/dry cleaning. *In room:* A/C, TV, dataport, fridge, coffeemaker, hair dryer, iron, safe.

Mauna Lani Bay Hotel & Bungalows ★★ *(Kids)*

Burned out? In need of tranquility and gorgeous surroundings? Look no further. Sandy beaches and lava tide pools are the focus of this serene seaside resort, where gracious hospitality is dispensed in a setting that's exceptional for its historic features. From the lounge chairs on the pristine beach to the turndown service at night, everything here is done impeccably.

Louvered doors open onto the plush guest rooms, which are outfitted in natural tones with teak accents, each with a lanai. They're arranged to capture maximum ocean views, and they surround interior atrium gardens and pools in which endangered baby sea turtles are raised for a Fourth of July "Independence Day" release to the sea. A shoreline trail leads across the whole 3,200-acre resort, giving you an intimate glimpse into the ancient past, when people lived in lava caves and tended the large complex of spring-fed and tidal fish ponds.

In addition to their very complete children's programs, plus "kid friendly" restaurants, this is a great place for kids to explore. The salt water stream that meanders through the hotel and out onto the property outside is filled with reef fish and even a shark. The fish ponds on the property are a great educational experience for "keiki," and the beach has plenty of room for the youngsters to run and play. Next door to the resort are ancient Hawaiian petroglyph fields, where older kids can learn about Hawaii's past.

The hotel's CanoeHouse restaurant (p. 271), featuring Pacific Rim, pan-Asian cuisine, is one of the most visually appealing beachside restaurants on the coast. You can also nibble on appetizers and dessert items at the bar while you listen to live music nightly.

68–1400 Mauna Lani Dr., Kohala Coast, HI 96743. ☎ **800/327-8585** or 808/885-6622. Fax 808/885-1484. www.maunalani.com. 350 units. $385–$750 double; $1,200 suite; $550–$910 villa (3-day minimum); $4,900–$5,600 bungalow (sleeps up to 4). AE, DC, DISC, MC, V. **Amenities:** 5 excellent restaurants; bar; large outdoor pool; 2 celebrated 18-hole championship golf courses; 10 Plexipave tennis courts; full-service fitness facility; range of massage treatment at the spa; Jacuzzi; watersports equipment rentals; bike rentals; year-round children's program; game room; concierge; activity desk; car-rental desk; business center; shopping arcade; salon; room service; massage; babysitting; coin-op washer/dryers; laundry/dry cleaning. *In room:* A/C, TV, dataport, minibar, coffeemaker, hair dryer, iron, safe.

Mauna Kea Beach Hotel ★

Laurance S. Rockefeller was sailing around Hawaii ("looking for a place to swim," as he tells it) when he spotted a perfect crescent of gold sand and dropped anchor. In 1965, he built the Mauna Kea on the spot. Over the years, all the new luxury hotels have eclipsed this grande dame in architectural style and amenities. Still, the beach out front is divine, and the landscaped grounds have a maturity seen nowhere else on this coast. Also, no other hotel has been able to claim the loyalty of its old-money guests, who keep returning to savor the relaxed clubby ambience, remote setting, world-class golf course, and old Hawaii ways. The next generation is welcome to find themselves a new and better beach hotel somewhere else.

The formal atmosphere extends to the Provençal-inspired restaurant Batik (p. 270), where collared shirts for men are required for dinner. The two championship golf courses—Robert Trent Jones Sr.'s famous Mauna Kea course and the Arnold Palmer–designed Hapuna course—are both award winners.

The rooms are huge by today's standards. The hotel is positioned to catch the cooling trade winds, and the view from the large lanais are breathtaking. We do like this place but have a few reservations: After years, they finally put TVs in every room, but the TVs are so tiny you need a pair of binoculars to watch from bed; the staff did not display the usual aloha spirit during our last visit; and access to ocean activities (such as scuba diving, sailing, and so on) was not from the beautiful beach outside the hotel—instead, we were bused down the road to another hotel. At these prices, we expect more.

62–100 Mauna Kea Beach Dr., Kohala Coast, HI 96743. ℂ 800/882-6060 or 808/882-7222. Fax 808/880-3112. www.maunakeabeachhotel.com. 310 units. $360–$630 double; from $600 suite. Extra person using roll-away bed $35; children 17 and under stay free in parent's room using existing bedding. AE, DC, MC, V. **Amenities:** 6 restaurants; 3 bars with live music; large outdoor pool; 2 championship golf courses; 13-court oceanside tennis complex; excellent fitness center; Jacuzzi; watersports equipment rentals; children's program; concierge; activity desk; car-rental desk; shopping arcade; salon; room service; massage; babysitting; coin-op washer/dryers; laundry/dry cleaning. *In room:* A/C, TV, dataport, minibar, hair dryer, iron, safe.

Waikoloa Beach Marriott, an Outrigger Resort ✸   This resort has always had one outstanding attribute: an excellent location on Anaehoomalu Bay (or A-Bay, as the locals call it), one of the best ocean sports bays in the Kohala coast. The gentle sloping beach has everything: swimming, snorkeling, diving, kayaking, windsurfing, and even old royal fish ponds. In 1999, Outrigger purchased the property and spent $23 million and 5 months redesigning and rebuilding it into one of the premier full-service resorts of the Kohala Coast. The Outrigger still isn't as posh as other luxury hotels along the Kohala coast, but it also isn't nearly as expensive. The size and layout of the guest rooms remain the same—perfectly nice, but not in the luxurious category of some of the other Kohala hotels. The guest rooms have all-new rattan furniture, carpeting, and bathroom fixtures.

The excellent Hawaii Calls restaurant (p. 271) serves Pacific Regional cuisine in a dining room with decor that harks back to the days of the 1940s radio show. Guests may use the two championship golf courses at the adjacent Hilton Waikoloa Village.

69–275 Waikoloa Beach Dr., Waikoloa, HI 96738. ℂ 888/924-5656 or 808/886-6789. Fax 808/886-7852. www.mariott.com or www.outrigger.com. 555 units. $315–$535 double; from $965 suite. Extra person $40; children 17 and under stay free in parent's room. AE, DC, DISC, MC, V. Valet Parking $5. **Amenities:** 2 restaurants; bar with nightly live entertainment; 2 outdoor pools (a huge pool with water slide and separate children's pool); 6 tennis courts; small fitness center and spa; Jacuzzi; watersports equipment rentals; year-round children's program; game room; concierge; activity desk; small shopping arcade; salon; limited room service; massage; babysitting; coin-op washer/dryers; laundry/dry cleaning; concierge-level rooms. *In room:* A/C, TV, dataport, fridge, coffeemaker, hair dryer, iron, safe.

Expensive

The Fairmont Orchid, Hawaii ✸✸ *Kids*   Located on 32 acres of oceanfront property, the Orchid is the place for watersports nuts, cultural explorers, families with children, or those who just want to lie back and soak up the sun. This elegant beach resort takes full advantage of the spectacular ocean views and historical sites on its grounds. The sports facilities here are extensive, and there's an excellent Hawaiiana program: The "beach boys" demonstrate how to do everything from creating drums from the trunks of coconut trees to paddling a Hawaiian canoe or strumming a ukulele.

We recommend spending a few dollars more to book a room with an ocean view, so you can watch that magnificent aqua-blue surf roll onto the white-sand beach. The spacious guest rooms feature big lanais, sitting areas, and marble bathrooms, each with a double vanity and separate shower. The Spa Without Walls allows you to book a massage just about anywhere on the property—overlooking the ocean, nestled deep in the lush vegetation, or simply in your room. The Orchid's three restaurants—The Grill, the Orchid Court, and the fabulous Brown's Beach House (p. 270)—are all wonderful, with a casual, relaxed, necktie-free atmosphere.

The Keiki Aloha program, for kids 5 to 12 years, features supervised activities like watersports and Hawaiian cultural activities. Some special money-saving family packages are also available.

1 N. Kaniku Dr., Kohala Coast, HI 96743. ⓒ **800/845-9905** or 808/885-2000. Fax 808/885-1064. www. fairmont.com. 539 units. $297–$600 double; from $665 suite. Daily Resort Fee of $12.50 for local newspaper, local phone calls, bottled water, access to fitness center, use of snorkeling gear, tennis clinics, and 10% off at selected shops. Extra person $75; children 17 and under stay free in parent's room. AE, DC, DISC, MC, V. Valet parking $10. **Amenities:** 3 restaurants; 5 bars (with evening entertainment in the Paniolo Lounge); large outdoor pool; 2 championship golf courses; award-winning tennis with 10 tennis (Plexipave) courts (7 lit for night play); well-equipped fitness center; outstanding spa; 2 lava rock whirlpools; watersports equipment rentals; bike rentals; year-round children's program ($40 for a ½ day and $60 for a full day, which includes lunch); concierge; activity desk; car-rental desk; business center; shopping arcade; salon; 24-hr. room service; babysitting; same-day laundry/dry cleaning. *In room:* A/C, TV, dataport, minibar, hair dryer, iron, safe.

Hilton Waikoloa Village ⭐ This is not just another beach hotel (it actually has no real beach)—it's a fantasy world all its own, perfect for those who love Vegas and Disneyland. Its high-rise towers are connected by silver-bullet trams, boats, and museum-like walkways lined with $7 million in Asian/Pacific reproductions. The kids will love it, but Mom and Dad may get a little weary waiting for the tram or boat to take them to breakfast (sometimes a 20-min. ordeal or a mile long walk). The 62 acres feature tropical gardens, cascading waterfalls, exotic wildlife, exaggerated architecture, a 175-foot water slide twisting into a 1-acre pool, hidden grottos, and man-made lagoons. The biggest hit of all (for some) is the dolphin lagoon, where, if you're lucky enough to be selected by lottery, you can pay to swim with real dolphins.

The recently updated, contemporary guest rooms are spacious and luxurious, with built-in platform beds, lanais, and loads of amenities, from spacious dressing areas with comfy bathrobes to a second phone and second line in all units. With nine—yes nine!—restaurants to choose from (everything from Japanese to family style buffets), you'll never lack for culinary choices. One of the two championship golf courses was designed by Robert Trent Jones Jr.; the other by Tom Weiskopf.

425 Waikoloa Beach Dr., Waikoloa, HI 96738. ⓒ **800/HILTONS** or 808/886-1234. Fax 808/886-2900. www. hiltonwaikoloavillage.com. 1,240 units. $199–$659 double; from $995 suite. Daily resort fee $18 for local phone calls, coffee in room, use of safe, use of spa for two and $25 credit towards beach rental and tennis. Extra person (roll-away bed) $35; children 18 and under stay free in parent's room. AE, DC, DISC, MC, V. Valet parking $8. **Amenities:** 9 restaurants; 8 bars, many with entertainment; 3 huge outdoor pools (with waterfalls, slides, and even a quiet adults-only pool); 2 18-hole golf courses; 8 tennis courts; 25,000-sq. ft. spa with cardio machines, weights, and a multitude of massages and body treatments; Jacuzzi; watersports equipment rentals; bike rentals; fabulous children's program; game room; concierge; activity desk; car-rental desk; business center; shopping arcade; salon; room service; in-room massage; babysitting; coin-op washer/dryers; same-day laundry/dry cleaning; concierge-level rooms. *In room:* A/C, TV, dataport, minibar, coffeemaker, hair dryer, iron, safe.

WAIMEA
MODERATE

Waimea Garden Cottages ★★ *Finds*   Imagine rolling hills on pastoral ranch land. Then add a babbling stream. Now set two cozy Hawaiian cottages in the scene, and complete the picture with mountain views—and you have Waimea Garden Cottages. One unit has the feel of an old English country cottage, with oak floors, a fireplace, and French doors opening onto a spacious brick patio. The other is a remodeled century-old Hawaiian wash house, filled with antiques, eucalyptus-wood floors, and a full kitchen. Extra touches keep guests returning again and again: plush English robes, sandalwood soaps in the bathroom, mints next to the bed, and fresh flower arrangements throughout. Hosts Barbara and Charlie Campbell live on the spacious property.

Off Mamalahoa Hwy., 2 miles west of Waimea town center. Reservations c/o Hawaii's Best Bed & Breakfasts, P.O. Box 758, Volcano, HI 96785. ℰ **800/262-9912** or 808/985-7488. Fax 808/967-8610. www.bestbnb.com. 2 cottages. $145–$155 double. Rates include continental breakfast. Extra person $15. 3-night minimum. No credit cards. *In room:* TV/VCR, kitchen, fridge, coffeemaker, hair dryer, iron, whirlpool bath in 1 unit, fireplace in 1 unit.

INEXPENSIVE

Aaah the Views Bed & Breakfast ★ *Value*   In the land of rainbows, you have the choice of a two-bedroom apartment (with private entrance), a separate new garden cottage, or a room in the main house of this quiet B&B, just 15 minutes from the fabulous beaches of the Kohala coast and 5 minutes from the cowboy town of Waimea. Host Mare Grace, who ran a successful bed-and-breakfast on Oahu for years, was very particular about the precise location of the two-bedroom apartment. She wanted her guests to be able to watch the moon rise from the large picture window, to fall asleep to the babble of the stream outside, and to awaken to the sounds of birds in the surrounding trees. The apartment can be rented as two separate rooms, but we don't recommend it—it's a little too crowded. Continental breakfast is served next door at Mare's house.

P.O. Box 6593, Kamuela, HI 96743. ℰ **808/885-3455.** Fax 808/885-4031. www.beingsintouch.com. 4 units. $65–$110 double. Rates include continental breakfast. Extra person $15. 2-night minimum. No credit cards. *In room:* TV, kitchenette, fridge, coffeemaker, hair dryer, iron.

Belle Vue ★   This two-story vacation rental has a truly beautiful view. Sitting in the hills overlooking Waimea and surrounded by manicured gardens, the charming home is just 15 minutes from the Kohala Coast beaches. The penthouse unit is a large, cathedral-ceilinged studio apartment with a small kitchen, huge bedroom, luxurious bathroom, and view of Mauna Loa and Mauna Kea mountains down to the Pacific Ocean. The one-bedroom apartment has a full kitchen, fireplace, and sofa bed. Each unit has a separate entrance. The rates include breakfast fixings (toast, juice, fruit, cereal, coffee) inside the kitchenettes.

1351 Konokohuu Rd., off Opelo Rd. (P.O. Box 1295), Kamuela, HI 96743. ℰ **800/772-5044,** or 808/885-7732 local phone and fax. www.hawaii-bellevue.com. 2 units. $85–$165 double. Extra person $25. AE, MC, V. *In room:* TV, dataport, kitchenette, fridge, coffeemaker, hair dryer, iron.

Cook's Discoveries Waimea Suite ★★ *Finds*   Not exactly a bed-and-breakfast, this bottom floor apartment, in a large, two-story, 40-year-old gracious upcountry home, is more of an intimate, romantic hideaway. The two-bedroom, 1,100-square-foot unit has a huge, full kitchen (with everything a gourmet cook could want), living room with fireplace, and an outdoor lanai surrounded by giant ohia, koa, jacaranda, magnolia, and avocado trees. There's even oatmeal-coconut-macadamia nut cookies from the Cook's Discoveries Store for a bed-time snack. Breakfast fixings (from eggs, sausage, breads, fruit, hot and cold cereal to a half a dozen different teas) are stocked in the kitchen when you arrive. Hostess Patti Cook is the owner and inspiration behind Cook's Discoveries, one of the best boutique shops on the island (if you book this property direct, she gives you a $20 gift certificate to her wonderful shop). She has decorated this suite with her favorite antique and island paraphernalia. It's so cozy here, you'll find it hard to leave.

P.O. Box 6960, Kamuela, HI 96743 ℂ 808/937-2833. cookshi@aol.com. 1 unit. $135 double. Extra person $25; children under 12 years $15. 2-night minimum. AE, DISC, MC, V. *In room:* TV/VCR, full kitchen, fridge, coffeemaker, hair dryer, iron.

THE HAMAKUA COAST

In addition to those listed below, another B&B in this area is **Waipio Ridge Vacation Rental** (ℂ 808/775-0603; www.cyberrentals.com/HI/LaskoBIGI.html), with two studios priced at $75 to $85 for two and just minutes from the Waipio Lookout. In Ahualoa, a mountain community a short drive from Waipio, is **Mountain Meadow Ranch Bed & Breakfast** (ℂ 808/775-9376; www.mountainmeadowranch.com), offering both a private cottage ($135 for 4) and rooms in a house, $80 double.

Note: You'll find the following hotels on the "North Kohala & Waimea" map on p. 313.

The Cliff House ★★ *(Finds)*   Perched on the cliffs above the ocean is this romantic two-bedroom getaway, surrounded by horse pastures and million-dollar views. A large deck takes in that ocean vista, where whales frolic offshore in winter. Impeccably decorated (the owner also owns Waipio Valley Artworks), the unit features a full kitchen (stocked with everything you could possibly want—even a salad spinner), two large bedrooms, and a full bathroom. Lots of little touches make this property stand out from the others: an answering machine for the phone, a pair of binoculars, a chess set, and even an umbrella for the rain squalls. Four people could comfortably share this unit.

P.O. Box 5070, Kukuihaele, HI 96727. ℂ 800/492-4746 or 808/775-0005. Fax 808/775-0058. www.cliffhouse hawaii.com. 1 unit. $185 double. Extra person $25. 2-night minimum. MC, V. *In room:* TV, dataport, kitchen, fridge, coffeemaker, hair dryer, iron.

Waipio Wayside B&B Inn ★★ *(Finds)*   Jackie Horne's restored Hamakua Sugar supervisor's home, built in 1938, sits nestled among fruit trees and surrounded by sweet-smelling ginger, fragile orchids, and blooming birds-of-paradise. The comfortable house, done in old Hawaii style, abounds with thoughtful touches, such as the help-yourself tea-and-cookies bar with 26 different kinds of tea. A sunny lanai with hammocks overlooks a yard lush with five kinds of banana trees, plus lemon, lime, tangerine, and avocado trees; the cliff-side gazebo has views of the ocean 600 feet below. There are five vintage rooms to choose from: Our favorite is the master bedroom suite (dubbed the "bird's-eye" room) with double doors that open onto the deck; we also love the Library Room, which has an ocean view, hundreds of books, and a skylight in the shower. Jackie's friendly hospitality and excellent breakfasts (such as pesto scrambled eggs with blueberry muffins) round out the experience.

P.O. Box 840, Honokaa, HI 96727. ℂ 800/833-8849 or 808/775-0275. Fax 808/775-0275. www.waipio wayside.com. 5 units. $95–$155 double. Rates include full breakfast. Extra person $25. MC, V. On Hwy. 240,

2 miles from the Honokaa Post Office; look on the right for a long white picket fence and sign on the ocean side of the road; the second driveway is the parking lot. **Amenities:** Concierge. *In room:* TV.

HILO

Just outside Hilo is a terrific B&B, **Lihi Kai** (© **808/935-7865**), a beautifully designed house with mahogany floors, perched on the edge of a cliff with a wide-angle view of Hilo Bay; rooms start at $55 double (with a 3-night minimum, otherwise it is $60 a night).

Note: You'll find the following accommodations on the "Hilo" map on p. 321.

EXPENSIVE

The Palms Cliff House ★★ *(Finds)*   The newest accommodation in the Hilo area actually is a 15-minute drive north of Hilo town, at Honomu (where Akaka Falls is located). Perched on the side of a cliff, this grand old Victorian-style inn is surrounded by manicured lawns and macadamia nut, lemon, banana, lime, orange, avocado, papaya, star fruit, breadfruit, grapefruit, and mango trees. Eight oversize suites, filled with antiques, DVD players, fireplaces, and private lanais, all overlook the ocean. Four rooms have private Jacuzzis; other extras include custom-made Italian lace sheets, cooking classes, yoga classes, and private massage. A gourmet hot breakfast (fresh fruit, home-baked bread, and entrees ranging from banana–mac nut pancakes to asparagus–sweet potato quiche) is served on the wrap-around lanai overlooking the rolling surf. This magnificent getaway is not to be missed.

Honomu. Reservation c/o Hawaii's Best Bed and Breakfasts, P.O. Box 758, Volcano, HI 96785. © **800/262-9912** or 808/985-7488. Fax 808/967-8610. www.bestbnb.com. 8 units. $175–$275. Rates include full gourmet breakfast. No credit cards. **Amenities:** Hot tub. *In room:* TV/DVD, dataport, hair dryer, iron, and in some rooms, Jacuzzi.

MODERATE

Shipman House Bed & Breakfast ★★ *(Finds)*   Built in 1900, the Shipman House is on both the national and state registers of historic places. This Victorian mansion has been totally restored by Barbara Andersen, the great-granddaughter of the original owner, and her husband, Gary. Despite the home's historic appearance, Barbara has made sure that its conveniences are strictly 21st century, including full bathrooms with all the amenities. All five guest bedrooms are large, with 10- to 12-foot ceilings and extras like cotton kimonos, heirloom furnishings, hand-woven lauhala mats, ceiling fans, and fresh flowers. In addition to a large continental-breakfast buffet, Barbara serves afternoon tea with nibbles on the enclosed lanai. *Tip:* For a real Hawaiian experience stay on a Wednesday, when guests can join in with the hula class practicing on the lanai.

131 Kaiulani St., Hilo, HI 96720. © **800/627-8447** or 808/934-8002. Fax 808/934-8002. www.shipman house.com. 5 units. $154–$184 double (plus $25 for a single night stay). Rates include continental breakfast and afternoon tea. Extra person $25. AE, MC, V. From Hwy. 19, take Waianuenue Ave.; turn right on Kaiulani St. and go 1 block over the wooden bridge; look for the large house on the left. *In room:* No phone.

INEXPENSIVE

The Bay House ★ *(Finds)*   Overlooking Hilo Bay, this new B&B offers immaculate rooms (each with oak-wood floors, king-size bed, sofa, private bathroom, and oceanview lanai) at reasonable prices. A full breakfast (fruit, yogurt, eggs, granola, muffins, and so on) is set out in a common area every morning (which also has a refrigerator, coffeemaker, toaster, and microwave for common use); you can take all you want to eat back to your lanai and watch the sun rise over

Hilo Bay. In the evening, relax in the cliffside Jacuzzi as the stars come out. The only minus is the lack of laundry facilities, but there are plenty in nearby Hilo.

42 Pukihae St., Hilo, HI 96720. ℂ **888/235-8195**, or 808/961-6311 local phone and fax. www.bayhouse hawaii.com. 3 units. $105–$120 double. Rates include continental breakfast. AE, MC, V. *In room:* TV, hair dryer.

Dolphin Bay Hotel 👨 *(Value)*   This two-story, motel-like building, 4 blocks from downtown, is a clean, family-run property that offers good value in a quiet garden setting. Ripe star fruit hang from the trees, flowers abound, and there's a junglelike trail by a stream. The tidy concrete-block apartments are small and often breezeless, but they're equipped with ceiling fans and jalousie windows. Rooms are brightly painted and outfitted with rattan furniture and Hawaiian prints. There are no phones in the rooms, but there's one in the lobby. You're welcome to all the papayas and bananas you can eat.

333 Iliahi St., Hilo, HI 96720. ℂ **808/935-1466**. Fax 808/935-1523. www.dolphinbayhilo.com. 18 units. $69–$79 studio double; $89 1-bedroom apt double; $99 2-bedroom apt double. Extra person $10. From Hwy. 19, turn mauka (toward the mountains) on Hwy. 200 (Waianuenue St.), then right on Puueo St.; go over the bridge and turn left on Iliahi St. **Amenities:** Concierge; car-rental desk; coin-op washer/dryer. *In room:* TV, kitchenette, fridge, coffeemaker, hair dryer, iron.

Hale Kai Bjornen 👨   An eye-popping view of the ocean runs the entire length of this house; you can sit on the wide deck and watch the surfers slide down the waves. Staying here is like a visit to your favorite aunt and uncle's house—only in this case, your uncle is a Hawaiian who knows the best deals on the island (and will get on the phone to make sure that you're treated like royalty). All rooms have that fabulous ocean view through sliding-glass doors. There's one suite, with a living room, kitchenette, and separate bedroom. Guests have access to a pool, hot tub, large living room, bar room, and small family room with VCR, movies, small fridge, telephone, and library. For $3 a load, hostess Evonne will do your laundry. Breakfast is a treat: homemade macadamia-nut waffles, a double cheese soufflé, or banana pancakes.

111 Honolii Pali, Hilo, HI 96720. ℂ **808/935-6330**. Fax 808/935-8439. www.interpac.net/~halekai. 4 units. $90–$100 double; $110 suite. Rates include gourmet breakfast. Extra person $15. 2-night minimum. No credit cards. **Amenities:** Oceanfront outdoor pool; Jacuzzi. *In room:* TV, no phone.

Hawaii Naniloa Resort   Hilo's biggest hotel offers nice rooms with lanais and enjoys a quiet, leafy Banyan Drive setting on the ocean. The hotel is a little old and tired, but so are all the other hotels on Banyan drive; in terms of comfort and amenities, this is one of the best that Hilo has to offer. Although it needs work (new carpet, a paint job, and overall remodeling), the rooms are clean and the oceanfront views are spectacular. Not only can you see the ocean, but on a cloudless day, you can see to the top of Mauna Kea. The rack rates are on the high side, but it's usually pretty easy to secure one of the cheapest rooms (which have only partial ocean views and no balconies).

93 Banyan Dr. (off Hwy. 19), Hilo, HI 96720. ℂ **800/367-5360** or 808/969-3333. Fax 808/969-6622. www. naniloa.com. 325 units. $100–$160 double. Internet rates from $70. AE, DC, DISC, MC, V. **Amenities:** 2 restaurants; bar; 2 outdoor pools; 18-hole golf course nearby with special rates for guests; $5 fee for fitness center with Jacuzzi and sauna; salon; very limited room service; coin-op washer/dryers; laundry/dry cleaning. *In room:* A/C, TV, fridge, coffeemaker, hair dryer, iron, safe.

Uncle Billy's Hilo Bay Hotel   Uncle Billy's is the least expensive place to stay along Hilo's hotel row, Banyan Drive. This oceanfront budget hotel boasts a dynamite location, and the car/room package offers an extra incentive to stay here. You enter via a tiny lobby, gussied up Polynesian style; it's slightly overdone, with sagging fishnets and tapa-covered walls. The guest rooms are simple: bed, TV, phone, closet, and soap and clean towels in the bathroom—that's about it. The walls seem paper thin, and it can get very noisy at night (you may want to bring ear plugs), but at rates like these, you're still getting your money's worth.

87 Banyan Dr. (off Hwy. 19), Hilo, HI 96720. © **800/367-5102** or 808/961-5818. Fax 808/935-7903. www. unclebilly.com. 144 units. $84–$89 double; $94 studio with kitchenette. Car/room packages and special senior rates available. Extra person $14; children 18 and under stay free in parent's room. AE, DC, DISC, MC, V. **Amenities:** Restaurant; bar with hula show nightly; oceanfront outdoor pool; activity desk; coin-op washer/dryers. *In room:* A/C, TV, some kitchenettes, fridge.

HAWAII VOLCANOES NATIONAL PARK

Since Hawaii Volcanoes was officially designated National Park in 1916, a village has popped up at its front door. Volcano Village isn't so much a town as a wide spot in Old Volcano Road: a 10-block area with two general stores, a couple of restaurants, a post office, a coffee shop, a new firehouse, and even an ATM. Volcano has no stoplights or jail, and not even a church or a cemetery, though it does have a winery.

Except for Volcano House (see below), which is within the National Park, all of the accommodations in this section are in Volcano Village. It gets cool here at night—Volcano Village is located at 3,700 feet above sea level—so while air-conditioning is not an issue, a fireplace or space heater might be an attractive amenity. It also rains a lot in Volcano—100 inches a year—which makes everything grow Jack-and-the-Beanstalk style.

A great B&B on the way to the Park is **Bed & Breakfast Mountain View** (© **888/698-9896** or 808/968-6868; www.bbmtview.com), a 7,000-square-foot home overlooking a 10,000-square-foot fish pond; rooms start at $55. It's located on South Kulani Road, between mile markers 13 and 14 off Highway 11.

The **Guest House at Volcano** ★ (© **808/967-7775;** fax 808/967-8295; www.volcanoguesthouse.com) is a terrific cottage that rents for just $75 double. It's an ideal place to stay with the kids: completely childproofed and complete with toys (even a basketball hoop). It has two twin beds and a queen in the upstairs bedroom, a sofa bed in the living room, a full kitchen, and a backyard forest trail that goes all the way through 2 miles of tropical rain forest to the Thurston Lava Tube in Hawaii Volcanoes National Park.

Hiiaka House (© **877/967-7990** or 808/967-7990; www.volcanoplaces. com) is a 1930s three-bedroom home that sleeps up to six. It's tucked in the rain forest and rents for $135 double (2-night minimum). The **Log Cabin** (© **808/ 262-7249;** www.crubinstein.com) is a century-old ohia log cabin for the young at heart, for just $100 for four and $125 for six. And the **Volcano Teapot Cottage** (© **808/967-7112;** www.volcanoteapot.com) is a quaint, renovated 1914 two-bedroom cottage, decorated with one-of-a-kind antiques, complete with hot tub spa in the forest out back and renting for $150 double.

MODERATE

Carson's Volcano Cottage ★★ In 1988, friends of Tom and Brenda Carson came to visit from Alaska, so the Carsons renovated their 1925 tin-roofed cabin, under giant tree ferns in the rain forest, to accommodate them. That was the beginning of the Carson's B&B business, and today they're quite a success story. They have six units on their spacious property in the rain forest: three guest rooms with private entrances and private bathrooms, done in Asian, 1940s, and 1950s Hawaiiana themes; and three cottages, each with its own decor (Asian, American, and a quaint Victorian English cottage); plus another three houses in the neighborhood. Several of the deluxe cottages even have their own hot tubs and freestanding fireplaces. The property also has a hot tub tucked under the ferns for guests' use. Tom and Brenda serve a hearty breakfast in the dining room.

P.O. Box 503 (in Mauna Loa Estates, 501 Sixth St., at Jade Ave.), Volcano, HI 96785. ℂ **800/845-5282** or 808/967-7683. Fax 808/967-8094. www.carsonscottage.com. 3 units (shower only), 6 cottages (3 with shower only). $105–$125 double; $125–$165 cottage. Rates include full buffet breakfast. Extra person $15. AE, DISC, MC, V. **Amenities:** Hot tub. *In room:* Some kitchens, fridge, coffeemaker.

Kilauea Lodge ⋆ This crowded and popular roadside lodge, built in 1938 as a YMCA camp, sits on 10 wooded and landscaped acres. Its rooms offer heating systems and hot-towel warmers, beautiful art on the walls, fresh flowers, and, in some, fireplaces. There's also a 1929 two-bedroom cottage with a fireplace and a full kitchen, just a couple of blocks down the street. A full gourmet breakfast is served to guests at the restaurant, which is open to the public for dinner (p. 282).

P.O. Box 116 (1 block off Hwy. 11 on Old Volcano Rd.), Volcano, HI 96785. ℂ **808/967-7366.** Fax 808/967-7367. www.kilauealodge.com. 14 units, 3 cottages. $125–$175 double. Rates include full breakfast. Extra person $15. AE, MC, V. **Amenities:** Restaurant; hot tub. *In room:* Coffeemaker, no phone.

Volcano Rainforest Retreat This charming property is on a large lot of fern-filled land. The "guest" cottage has a full kitchen, a sleeping loft, and a bathroom that looks right into the jungle. The eight-sided "Forest Hale" studio is a new addition with a private forest entrance, queen bed, gas fireplace, kitchenette, skylight dome, and private bathroom. The six-sided "sanctuary" cottage started out as a meditation house, but once guests saw it, they begged the Goldens to rent it out. The only drawback is the half-bathroom, but next door, open to the forest, is a handcrafted Japanese *furo* (hot tub) with an outdoor shower.

P.O. Box 957, Volcano, HI 96785. ℂ **800/550-8696,** or 808/985-8696 local phone and fax. www.volcanoretreat.com. 3 units (1 with half-bathroom). $110–$185 cottage double. Rates include continental breakfast. 2-night minimum. Extra person $15. MC, V. **Amenities:** Hot tub. *In room:* Kitchenette, fridge, coffeemaker; phones in cottages only.

INEXPENSIVE

Hale Ohia Cottages ⋆ *Finds* Take a step back in time to the 1930s. Here you'll have a choice of suites, each with private entrance, located in the main residence or a cottage. There are also four guest cottages, ranging from one bedroom to three. The surrounding botanical gardens contribute to the overall tranquil ambience of the estate. They were groomed in the 1930s by a resident Japanese gardener, who worked with the natural volcanic terrain but gently tamed the flora into soothing shapes and designs. The lush grounds are just a mile from Hawaii Volcanoes National Park. New this year is a romantic, cozy cottage with fireplace, hot tub, and bedroom made from a round, redwood water tank.

P.O. Box 758 (Hale Ohia Rd., off Hwy. 11), Volcano, HI 96785. ℂ **800/455-3803** or 808/967-7986. Fax 808/967-8610. www.haleohia.com. 4 units, 4 cottages. $95–$150 double. Rates include continental breakfast. Extra person $15. MC, V. *In room:* Fridge, coffeemaker, hair dryer, no phone.

Volcano Bed & Breakfast *Value* If you are on a tight-tight budget this charming restored 1912 historic home offers comfortable, clean, quiet rooms, all with shared bathrooms. The restored house sits on beautifully landscaped grounds and has new carpeting throughout, new furnishings in the common

Volcano Area Accommodations & Dining

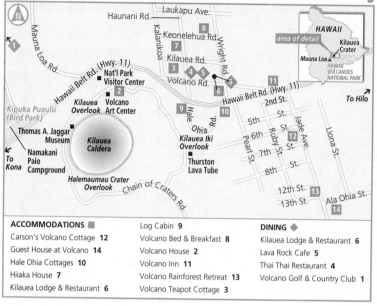

ACCOMMODATIONS ◼

Carson's Volcano Cottage **12**
Guest House at Volcano **14**
Hale Ohia Cottages **10**
Hiiaka House **7**
Kilauea Lodge & Restaurant **6**

Log Cabin **9**
Volcano Bed & Breakfast **8**
Volcano House **2**
Volcano Inn **11**
Volcano Rainforest Retreat **13**
Volcano Teapot Cottage **3**

DINING ◆

Kilauea Lodge & Restaurant **6**
Lava Rock Cafe **5**
Thai Thai Restaurant **4**
Volcano Golf & Country Club **1**

area, and other recent upgrades. The rooms are small, but clean and inviting. The common rooms include a living room with TV, VCR, and piano; a reading room; and a sunroom.

P.O. Box 998 (on Keonelehua St., off Hwy. 11 on Wright Rd.), Volcano, HI 96785. ☎ **800/937-7786** or 808/967-7779. Fax 808/967-8660. www.volcano-hawaii.com. 6 units (none with private bathroom). $49–$69 double. Rates include continental breakfast. Extra person $15. AE, DC, DISC, MC, V. From Hwy. 11, turn north onto Wright Rd.; go 1 mile to Chalet Kilauea on the right, where you'll check in. *In room:* No phone.

Volcano House   Volcano House has a great location—inside the boundaries of the national park—and that's about all. This mountain lodge, which evolved out of a grass lean-to in 1865, is Hawaii's oldest visitor accommodation. It stands on the edge of Halemaumau's bubbling crater, and while its edgy view of the crater is still an awesome sight, don't expect the Ritz here. The rooms are very plain, but who cares with that fabulous view. Rooms are heated with volcanic steam. *Tip:* Book only if you can get a room facing the volcano; if they are filled, don't bother—you can do better elsewhere.

P.O. Box 53 (Hawaii Volcanoes National Park), HI 96718. ☎ **808/967-7321.** Fax 808/967-8429. volcano house@earthlink.net. 42 units. $85–$185 double. AE, DC, DISC, MC, V. **Amenities:** Restaurant with great view; bar.

Volcano Inn   Located in the rain forest, this AAA-rated property is a combination of a five-room inn in the heart of Volcano Village and four fully equipped cedar cabins (with complete kitchens) a few blocks away. Guests in all units (both the inn rooms and the cottages) enjoy a family-style breakfast with eggs, granola, breads, pastries, and coffee, tea, and juice. The rooms at the inn are quite luxurious for the price; each comes with a fireplace, daily maid service, and even comfy robes for the cool mornings. The cottages are best for families.

19–3820 Old Volcano Rd., Volcano, HI 96785. ☎ **800/997-2292** or 808/967-7293. Fax 808/985-7349. www.volcanoinn.com. 8 units. $90–$130 double. Rates include full breakfast. 3-night minimum. AE, DC, DISC,

MC, V. **Amenities:** Bike rentals; car-rental desk. *In room:* TV, kitchen (cottages only), fridge, coffeemaker, hair dryer.

SOUTH POINT

Bougainvillea Bed & Breakfast ★ *(Finds* Don and Martie Jean Nitsche bought this 3-acre property in the Hawaiian Rancho subdivision of Ocean View and had a *Field of Dreams* experience: They decided that if they built a bed-and-breakfast, people would come. Where some people just saw lava, the Nitsches saw the ancient Hawaiian path that went from the mountain to the sea. So they built. And out of the lava came gardens—first colorful bougainvillea, then flowers and a pineapple patch, then a fish pond to add to the pool and hot tub, and finally a barbecue area and satellite for TV reception. Word got out. Martie's breakfast—her secret-recipe banana-nut pancakes, plus sausage, fruit, and coffee—drew people from all over. Things got so good, they had to add more rooms (all with their own private entrances) and expand the living room (complete with TV, VCR, and video library) and dining room. Guests usually take their breakfast plates out to the lanai, which boasts ocean views.

P.O. Box 6045, Ocean View, HI 96737. © 800/688-1763 or 808/929-7089. Fax 808/929-7089. www.hi-inns. com/bouga. 4 units. $65 double. Rates include full breakfast. Extra person $15. AE, DC, DISC, MC, V. **Amenities:** Big outdoor pool; Jacuzzi; concierge; car-rental desk; massage in-room or outdoors. *In room:* Hair dryer, no phone.

Macadamia Meadows Bed & Breakfast ★ *(Kids* Near the southernmost point in the United States and just 45 minutes from Volcanoes National Park lies one of the Big Island's most welcoming B&Bs. It's located on an 8-acre working macadamia-nut farm, in a great place for stargazing. The warmth and hospitality of hosts Charlene and Cortney Cowan are unsurpassed: Each guest is treated like a favorite relative. This is an excellent place for children; because the owner has children herself, the entire property is very kid-friendly. In addition to exploring the groves of mac-nut trees, kids can swim in the pool or play tennis. Owner Charlene also has puzzles, games, and other "rainy day" items to entertain children. Accommodations include a two-bedroom suite, a private room, and a honeymoon suite, which has an antique claw-foot tub on a private lanai. All rooms have private entrances and are immaculately clean.

94–6263 Kamaoa Rd., Waiohinu. Reservations: P.O. Box 756, Naalehu, HI 96772. © 888/929-8118 or 808/929-8097. Fax 808/929-8097. www.macadamiameadows.com. 5 units. $65–$125 double. Rates include continental breakfast. Extra person $10; children under 2 stay free. AE, DISC, MC, V. **Amenities:** Resort-size outdoor pool; tennis courts; activity desk; washer/dryers. *In room:* TV, fridge, no phone, microwave.

South Point Banyan Tree House ★ *(Finds* Couples looking for an exotic place to nest should try this tree house, nestled inside a huge Chinese banyan tree. The cottage comes complete with see-through roof that lets the outside in, plus a comfy, just-for-two hot tub on the wraparound deck. Inside, there's a queen bed and a kitchen with microwave and two-burner stove. The scent of ginger brings you sweet dreams at night, while the twitter of birds greets you in the morning.

At Hwy. 11 and Pinao St., Waiohinu. c/o Janette LeGault, 11172 W. Edwards Rd., Saxon, WI 54559. © 888/ 451-0880 or 715/893-2419. www.ifb.com/hawaii-banyan/. 1 cottage. $140 double; $165 for 4. 2-night minimum. No credit cards. **Amenities:** Hot tub; washer/dryer. *In room:* TV, kitchen, fridge, coffeemaker.

4 Where to Dine

So many restaurants, so little time. What's a traveler to do? The Big Island's delicious dilemma is its daunting size and abundant offerings. Its gastronomic environment—the fruitful marriage of creative chefs, good soil, and rich cultural traditions—has made this island as much a culinary destination as a recreational one. And from the Big Island Festival to the Kona Coffee Festival to the Sam Choy Poke Recipe Contest, the Big Island is host to extraordinary, world-renowned culinary events.

Rather than an afterthought, dining is an authentic attraction here. The Big Island's volcanic soil produces fine tomatoes, lettuces, beets, beans, fruit, and basic herbs and vegetables that were once difficult to find locally. Southeast Asian fruit, such as mangosteen and rambutan, are beginning to appear in markets, along with the sweet white pineapple that is by now a well-established Big Island crop. Along with the lamb and beef from Big Island ranches and seafood from local fishermen, the freshness of the produce forms the backbone of ethnic cookery and Hawaii Regional Cuisine.

Among the star chefs who claim roots here are Peter Merriman (the visionary behind the eponymous Merriman's in Waimea), Sam Choy (the Kona chef who prepares local food with a gourmet twist), and Alan Wong (who put the Mauna Lani's Canoe House on the map before moving to open his own place, now Honolulu's most popular).

Kailua-Kona is teeming with restaurants for all pocketbooks. The haute cuisine of the island is concentrated in the Kohala Coast resorts, where the decade-old Hualalai Resort and, within it, the tony Four Seasons hotel; the Mauna Lani Bay Hotel and Bungalows; the Orchid at Mauna Lani; the Mauna Kea Beach Hotel; and the Hapuna Beach Prince Hotel claim their share of the action for deep pockets and special-occasion tastes.

Waimea, known as Kamuela, is a thriving upcountry community, a haven for yuppies, techies, and retirees who know a good place when they see one. In Hawi, North Kohala, expect bakeries, neighborhood diners, and one tropical-chic restaurant that's worth a special trip. In Hilo in eastern Hawaii, you'll find pockets of trendiness among the precious old Japanese and ethnic restaurants that provide honest, tasty, and affordable meals in unpretentious surroundings.

In the listings below, reservations are not necessary unless otherwise noted.

THE KONA COAST
IN & AROUND KAILUA-KONA
Note: Hualalai Club Grille, Pahu i'a, and Beach Tree Bar and Grill are located north of Kailua-Kona, 6 miles north of the airport and just south of the Kohala Coast.

Very Expensive
Pahu i'a ✴ ISLAND SEAFOOD/INTERNATIONAL   You can't find a better oceanfront location on the Big Island (maybe in the entire state). Just feet from the lapping waves is this icon of culinary masterpieces. A small bridge of natural logs leads to this oceanfront dining room, where views on three sides expand on the aquatic theme (*pahu i'a* is Hawaiian for "aquarium," and there's a large one at the entrance); dining here is a completely enchanting experience. The food features fresh produce and seafood from the island—and even from the resort's own aquaculture ponds, teeming with shrimp and *moi* (threadfish), a rich, Island fish. The day begins with the excellent breakfast buffet, the coast's most elegant presentation of omelets, meats, fresh fruit, and regional specialties; and the a la carte menu, a fabulous selection that includes huevos rancheros and lemon-ricotta pancakes. At dinner, part of the menu changes daily and always includes several fresh seafood preparations, such as steamed opakapaka with

shiitake mushrooms, cilantro, ginger, garlic, and ginger-soy sauce, a flawless balance of flavors; and fine meats, such as lamb loin from Kahua Ranch in the uplands of Kohala. The finale—Hualalai flourless chocolate cake—comes warm and sublime, not too sweet, and accompanied with chocolate sorbet. From ambience to execution to presentation, Pahu i`a is top-drawer.

In the Four Seasons Resort Hualalai, Queen Kaahumanu Hwy., Kaupulehu-Kona. 📞 **808/325-8000.** Reservations recommended. Breakfast $9–$24; dinner main courses $30–$48. AE, DC, DISC, MC, V. Daily 6–11:30am (buffet 7–11:30am) and 5:30–10pm.

Expensive

Beach Tree Bar and Grill ⭐ CASUAL GOURMET   Here's an example of outstanding cuisine in a perfect setting, without being fancy, fussy, or prohibitively expensive. The bar on the sand is a sunset paradise, and the sandwiches, seafood, and grilled items at the casual outdoor restaurant (a few ft. from the bar) are in a class of their own—simple, excellent, prepared with no short cuts and imagination that overflows. The menu, which varies, features such items as grilled fresh fish sandwiches, steaks, alternative healthy cuisine, and vegetarian specialties. On Saturdays there is a "Surf, Sand and Stars" feast, which has an array of buffet-style items from fresh fish to grilled New York sirloin to mouthwatering desserts for $46 ($15 for kids 6–12), and on Wednesday a special buffet featuring Hawaiian cuisine for $58 ($28 kids). An added attraction is entertainment from 5 to 8pm nightly.

In the Four Seasons Resort Hualalai, Queen Kaahumanu Hwy., Kaupulehu-Kona. 📞 **808/325-8000.** Reservations recommended for dinner. Lunch main courses $12–$18; dinner main courses $22–$40. AE, DC, DISC, MC, V. Daily 11am–8:30pm.

The Dining Room at Keauhou Beach Resort PACIFIC RIM   A new menu in an attractive, open-air dining room (formerly a Sam Choy's restaurant) bodes well for this greatly improved Kailua-Kona resort. Keauhou Beach Resort is a part of Kona history, peppered with historic sites and situated on one of the best locations in Kona, the Kahalu`u bay, where turtles swim freely and the snorkeling is breathtaking. The reefy flats surrounding the area afford stunning views of sea life: From the cocktail lounge sitting over the water, you can see turtles, seabirds and, in the evening, husky herons stalking their reef-bound dinners. It's a great place for breakfast, not only for the view, but for the Punaluu raisin bread French toast or the pineapple upside-down pancakes. Dinner features creative dishes like ancho-chili crusted ahi with a ginger lemon sauce, wasabi-sesame tempura fresh fish in a lilikoi plum sauce, and jerk marinated grilled lamb chops with a butter plum shiitake demi sauce. Unfortunately, they're closed for lunch.

In the Keauhou Beach Resort, 78–6740 Alii Dr. 📞 **808/322-3441.** Reservations recommended. Breakfast under $10. Main courses $18–$27; Fri prime rib/seafood buffet $30. AE, DISC, MC, V. Daily 7–11am and 5:30–9pm.

Hualalai Club Grille ⭐⭐ CONTEMPORARY PACIFIC   The Grille is a part of the golf clubhouse, but even nongolfers make a special trip here for lunch or dinner. You can sit in the open-air dining room or on the deck overlooking the 18th hole and nosh on the signature Makalapua onion, a large "flower" of sweet fried onions. The Kona Coast lobster (flown in from Maine and fattened in the aquaculture farm nearby) comes as a salad, an entree, or a pizza topping, hot and savory from the brick oven in the exhibition kitchen. The mango baby back ribs are tender and smoky, while the black-and-blue seared ahi is a classic, spiced up with hot mustard. Even the salads are special, gathered from upland

Kona Coast Dining

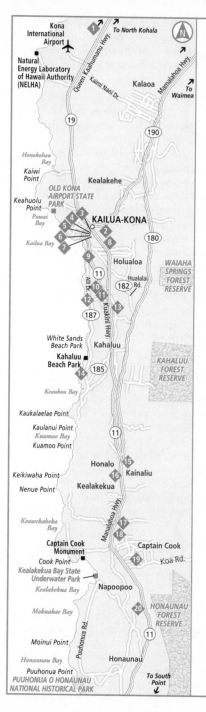

Aloha Angel Cafe **16**

Basil's Pizzeria **7**

Beach Tree Bar & Grill **1**

Bianelli's Pizza **4**

Big Island Grill **9**

The Coffee Shack **20**

The Dining Room
   at Keauhou Beach Resort **14**

Hualalai Club Grille **1**

Huggo's **12**

Ka'upena **10**

Keei Cafe **18**

Kona Inn Restaurant **8**

La Bourgogne **13**

Lu Lu's **11**

Manago Hotel Restaurant **19**

Martini Yacht Club **11**

Nasturtium Café **17**

Ocean View Inn **5**

Oodles of Noodles **2**

Pahu i'a **1**

Quinn's Almost by the Sea **3**

Sibu Cafe **6**

Teshima's **15**

and coastal farms on the Big Island and prepared with such heavenly accompaniments as wild mushrooms and Molokai sweet potato curls.

In the Hualalai Resort, Queen Kaahumanu Hwy., Kaupulehu-Kona. (C) **808/325-8525**. www.hualalairesort. com. Reservations recommended. Main courses $10–$18 lunch, $14–$56 dinner. AE, DC, MC, V. Daily 11am–3pm; bar menu 3–9pm; dinner 5–9pm.

Huggo's (F) PACIFIC RIM/SEAFOOD   The main Huggo's dining room still hums with diners murmuring dreamily about the view, but it's the thatched-bar fantasy that's *really* on the rocks. **Huggo's on the Rocks** (F), a mound of thatch, rock, and grassy-sandy ground right next to Huggo's, is a sunset-lover's nirvana. At sundown, it's choked with people either on chaises or at the 50-seat thatched bar, sipping mai tais and noshing on salads, poke, sandwiches, plate lunches, sashimi, and fish-and-chips. From 6:30 to 11am, this same location turns into the Java on the Rocks espresso bar. Island-style pupus are offered here from 11:30am to 10pm, and from 5:30pm to 1am there's dancing at the water's edge.

At the senior Huggo's, fresh seafood remains the signature, as does the coral-strewn beach with tide pools just beyond the wooden deck. The tables are so close to the water, you can see the entire curve of Kailua Bay. Feast on garlic chicken and wild mushroom pasta, sautéed mahimahi or steamed clams, seared ahi or imu-style chicken cooked in ti leaves. At lunch, specialties include kalua chicken quesadillas, brick-oven pizzas, and sandwiches ranging from hot turkey to prime rib and fresh fish.

75–5828 Kahakai Rd. (C) **808/329-1493.** www.huggos.com. Reservations requested. Main courses $9–$23 lunch, $18–$46 dinner. AE, DC, DISC, MC, V. Daily 11:30am–2pm and 5:30–10pm.

Kona Inn Restaurant (F) AMERICAN/SEAFOOD   This is touristy, but it can be a very pleasant experience if the sun is setting or you've just arrived from the airport and don't want your hotel's offerings. The wide-ranging menu and fresh seafood in the open-air oceanfront setting tell you why you have come to Kailua-Kona. The large, open room and panoramic view of the Kailua shoreline are the most attractive features, especially for sunset cocktails and appetizers. It's a huge menu, so the choices are vast, everything from nachos and chicken Caesar salad to sandwiches, pasta, stir-fried dishes, and the highlight: the fresh fish served Cajun-style or broiled and basted in lemon butter. Watch for the daily specials on the less expensive Cafe Grill menu.

In Kona Inn Shopping Village, 75–5744 Alii Dr. (C) **808/329-4455.** Reservations recommended at dinner. Main courses $13–$36; Cafe Grill $7–$13. AE, MC, V. Dinner menu daily 5:30–9:30pm; Cafe Grill daily 11:30am–10:30pm.

La Bourgogne (★★) *(Finds)* CLASSIC FRENCH   Come to this cozy French inn to satisfy your Gallic urgings. An intimate spot with 10 tables, La Bourgogne serves classic French fare with simple, skillful elegance. Baked Brie in puff pastry is a taste treat, and the fresh Maine lobster salad, served on a bed of greens with mango slices and a passion-fruit vinaigrette, is a master stroke. Other offerings include: classic onion soup, fresh catch of the day (market price), and osso buco, a former special added to the menu by popular demand. Also in demand are the New Zealand mussels steamed in apple cider, thyme, shallots, and cognac. The roast duck breast with raspberries and pine nuts is exactly the kind of dish that characterizes La Bourgogne—done to perfection, presented attractively and with an unbeatable match of flavors and textures. Classically trained chef Ron Gallaher expresses his allegiance to *la cuisine Française* down to the last morsel of flourless chocolate cake and lemon tartlette.

Hwy. 11, 3 miles south of Kailua-Kona. © 808/329-6711. Reservations required. Main courses $24–$32. AE, DC, DISC, MC, V. Tues–Sat 6–10pm.

Martini Yacht Club HAWAIIAN/ASIAN/AMERICAN Chef Stephan Schoembs took over the former location of the Palm Café in the Coconut Grove Market Place in 2002. His eclectic cuisine is a wonderful combination of Hawaii Regional Cuisine (seared ahi in blackening spice with a mango salad); Asian (grilled ono with sticky rice, bok choy and Okinawa spinach, in a honey-miso sauce); and American (ribeye steak in a skillet with potatoes and stuffed tomatoes). The decor is nautical (World Cup memorabilia) with sandstone floors, wood trim, and a baby grand in the middle of the room. Live music from 9pm on.

Coconut Grove Market Place, 75–8200 Alii Dr., Kailua-Kona. © 808/329-8200. Reservations suggested. Main courses $25–$58. AE, MC, V. Tues–Sun 5:30–10pm.

Moderate

Bianelli's Pizza PIZZA/ITALIAN This always-crowded, very popular pizza and Italian eatery recently moved from the Pines Plaza to its new location where the old Kona Ranch House resided for decades. The draw here is pizza, made with wholesome ingredients and cheeses. The full bar features an international beer selection, including the local Kona Brew. The sensational Ricotta pizza is dripping with garlic, Parmesan, and ricotta, yet it's 40% less fatty than most pizzas. The house specialty, the Buffala, is redolent with garlic and buffalo-milk mozzarella. Make reservations or be prepared to wait; this is a local favorite.

Hwy. 11, at corner of Kuakini and Palani. © 808/326-4800. Reservations recommended for dinner. Pizzas $9–$23; main courses $8–$23. DC, DISC, MC, V. Mon–Fri 11am–10pm; Sat–Sun 5–10pm.

Lu Lu's AMERICAN As it often is with joints that are popular, Lu Lu's has fallen prey to the deadly sin of self-importance. Service is brisk and can be downright rude. It is casual, noisy, and corny (black velvet paintings at the entrance!), but it's undeniably popular, with open-air dining, ocean views, and a sports-bar atmosphere. Other elements include capiz-shell lamps, clam-shell sconces, and hula girl replicas. The offerings include: appetizers, sandwiches, salads, burgers, fresh-fish tacos, and fresh fish and meats in the evening.

In the Coconut Grove Market Place, 75–5819 Alii Dr. © 808/331-2633. Reservations not accepted. Main courses $10–$14. AE, DISC, MC, V. Daily 11am–10pm; appetizers until midnight; bar until 2am.

Oodles of Noodles ✪ NOODLES The short-lived Paradise Spice Cafe is no more, and the space has become an extra dining room for Amy Ferguson-Ota's wildly popular gourmet noodle house. The menu offers a staggering assortment of noodles from far-flung cultures and countries, so diners can tuck into udon, cake noodles, saimin, ramen, spaghetti, orzo, somen, spring rolls, chow mein, linguine, vermicelli, and other noodle wonders. If you're looking for the world's best tuna casserole (with wok-seared ahi), saimin with Peking duck broth, miso ramen with shiitake mushrooms, summer rolls, pad Thai noodles, fettuccine Alfredo, veggie teriyaki chow funn, coconut tapioca, or shaved ice with fresh fruit or adzuki beans, look no further. They have recently brought back breakfast with gourmet grinds, espresso drinks, and yummy pastries.

In Crossroads Shopping Center, 75–1027 Henry St. © 808/329-9222. Noodle dishes $8–$14 lunch; main course $9–23 dinner. AE, DC, DISC, MC, V. Daily 8am–9pm.

Quinn's Almost by the Sea ✪ STEAK/SEAFOOD If you are hungry late at night, this is one of the few places you can grab a bite to eat in Kona after 9pm. The newly renovated Quinn's, located at the northern gateway to town,

Ⓒ Kona Coffee Craze!

Coffeehouses are booming on the Big Island. Why not? This is, after all, the home of Kona coffee, and it's a wide-open field for the dozens of vendors competing for your loyalty and dollars.

Most of the farms are concentrated in the North and South Kona districts, where coffee remains a viable industry. Notable among them is the **Kona Blue Sky Coffee Company,** in Holualoa (Ⓒ **877/322-1700** or 808/322-1700), which handles its own beans exclusively. The Christian Twigg-Smith family and staff grow, hand-pick, sun-dry, roast, grind, and sell their coffee, whole or ground, on a 400-acre estate. There are only a few retail locations for Kona Blue Sky coffee. One of them is the farm itself, where visitors are welcome to see the operation from field to final product. You can also find Blue Sky at the cheerful outdoor market, Alii Marketplace Gardens in Kailua-Kona, open Wednesday through Sunday.

Also in Holualoa, 10 minutes above Kailua-Kona, **Holualoa Kona Coffee Company** (Ⓒ **800/334-0348** or 808/322-9937) purveys organic Kona from its own farm and other growers: unsprayed, hand-picked, sun-dried, and carefully roasted. Not only can you buy premium, unadulterated Kona coffee here, but you can also witness the hulling, sorting, roasting, and packaging of beans on a farm tour, Monday through Friday from 8am to 4pm. Also in this upcountry village, the **Holuakoa Cafe,** Highway 180 (Ⓒ **808/322-2233**), is famous for its high-octane espresso, ground from fresh-roasted pure Kona Blue Sky beans.

Some other coffees to watch for: **Bong Brothers** (Ⓒ **808/328-9289**) thrives with its coffees, roadside fruit stand, B&B, and natural-foods deli

has changed its theme so it now has a nautical/sports bar atmosphere. Quinn's offers casual alfresco dining on a garden lanai, with an air-conditioned, non-smoking area now available. The menu is surf-and-turf basic: burgers, sandwiches, and a limited dinner menu of dependably good fresh fish, filet mignon, and a few shrimp dishes. There are six burger selections, and, when available, fresh ahi or ono sandwiches.

75–5655A Palani Rd. Ⓒ **808/329-3822.** Main courses $7–$19. MC, V. Daily 11am–midnight.

Inexpensive

Basil's Pizzeria PIZZA/ITALIAN   Two dining rooms seat 100 in a garlic-infused atmosphere where pizza is king, sauces sizzle, and pasta is cheap. The oceanview restaurant, in a prime location in Kailua-Kona, is redolent with cheeses, garlic, and fresh organic herbs (a big plus). Shrimp pesto and the original barbecue-chicken pizzas are long-standing favorites, as is the artichoke-olive-caper version, a Greek-Italian hybrid. Very popular with the 20-something crowd.

75–5707 Alii Dr. Ⓒ **808/326-7836.** Individual pizzas $5.95–$9.95; main courses $8–$15. MC, V. Daily 11am–10pm.

Big Island Grill ★★ *Finds* AMERICAN   One of the best-kept secrets among local residents is the Big Island Grill, where you get huge servings of home cooking at 1970s prices. The place is always packed from the first cup of coffee that sells smoothies and healthful foods. Aficionados know that **Langenstein Farms** (📞 808/328-8356), a name associated with quality and integrity, distributes excellent Kona coffee and distinctively tasty macadamia nuts in the town of Honaunau. New products include fresh honey (in limited supply) and chocolate-covered macadamia nuts and coffee beans. **Rooster Farms,** also in Honaunau (📞 808/328-9173), enjoys an excellent reputation for the quality of its organic coffee beans. The **Bad Ass Coffee Company** has franchises in Kainaliu, Kawaihae, Honokaa, Keauhou, and Kailua-Kona, all selling its 100% Kona as well as coffees from Molokai, Kauai, and other tropical regions.

In Waimea, the **Waimea Coffee Company,** Parker Square, Highway 19 (📞 808/885-4472), a deli/coffeehouse/retail operation, is a whirl of activity. The owners are friendly and their coffee is top-of-the-line: organic pure Kona from Sakamoto Estate, organic Hamakua Coast coffee from Carter's Coffee Farm, pure water-processed decaf—an impressive selection of the island's best estate-grown coffees, plus signature blends and coffee from Molokai Plantation. The homemade quiches, sandwiches, and pastas draw a lively lunchtime crowd. Island-made gourmet foods make great gift baskets, and local artists display their work on the walls.

A good bet in Hilo is **Bears' Coffee,** 106 Keawe St. (📞 808/935-0708), the quintessential sidewalk coffeehouse and a Hilo stalwart. Regulars love to start their day here, with coffee and specialties such as souffléed eggs, cooked light and fluffy in the espresso machine and served in a croissant. It's a great lunchtime spot as well.

at breakfast to the last bite of dessert at night. Chef Bruce Goold has been cooking in Kona for decades and has a loyal following for his "localized" American cuisine. This is a place to take the family for dinner (excellent fresh salmon, generous-size salads, and the world's tastiest mashed potatoes) without having to go into debt. There's a drive-up window for coffee, cappuccino, smoothies, fresh baked pastries, and lunch specials.

75–5702 Kuakini Hwy. 📞 808/326-1153. Main courses under $12. MC, V. Mon–Fri 6am–10am breakfast; Mon–Sat 11am–2pm lunch and 5–9pm dinner.

Ka'upena *Finds* HAWAIIAN   For authentic Hawaii food, this is the "home of the foot-long laulau," (pork, chicken, or fish steamed in ti leaves). Owner Kalae Ah Chin and his wife, Kali'i Kanoe, have been making foot-long lauluas for the Hilo community for years; after repeated requests, they recently opened a second restaurant in Kona. These so-called "plate lunches" look like a luau; each "plate" includes three scoops of rice or bowl of poi, a ¼ pound of lomi salmon, a ¼ pound of macaroni salad, and entree. No one leaves here hungry. Their special laulaus are the foot-long pork/fish, the pork, chicken, fish, kalo (taro), 'uala (sweet potato) and ulu (breadfruit) combination, and the chicken combination with pork, chicken, kalo, 'uala, and 'ulu.

Alii Sunset Plaza, 75–5799 Alii Dr. 📞 808/329-4764. Plate lunches $8.95. Daily 10 am–8pm.

Ocean View Inn AMERICAN/CHINESE/HAWAIIAN   The Hawaiian food and the local color are reasons enough to come here, not to mention the budget prices. This is a no-nonsense, unpretentious restaurant that's been a Kailua landmark for as long as anyone can remember. Don't expect epicurean fare; concentrate instead on the ocean view, because the Ocean View Inn is as much a Kona fixture as the sunsets that curl around Kailua Pier across the street. Stew and rice, roast pork, kalua pork and cabbage, a vegetarian selection, and local staples such as shoyu chicken and broiled ahi appear on a menu with dozens of Chinese dishes. It's definitely a refreshing change from the more touristy waterfront eateries and is especially appealing on Sundays, when old-timers from along the coast appear in their haku leis and muumuu.

75–5683 Alii Dr. ⒸⒸ **808/329-9998.** Main courses $8–$11. No credit cards. Tues–Sun 6:30am–2:45pm and 5:15–9pm.

Sibu Cafe ⭐ *Finds* INDONESIAN/SOUTHEAST ASIAN   An affordable favorite for many years, Sibu offers curries, homemade condiments, and a very popular spicy grilled Balinese chicken with peanut sauce. Fresh catch is available daily, and weekday lunch specials are a good value, especially the Kona Combo: spring roll, chicken or beef satay, vegetable stir-fry, and cucumber salad with rice. We recommend the vegetarian combo or a gado gado (a large, peanut-sauced Indonesian salad). The Indonesian decor, courtyard dining, and excellent satays (traditional grilled skewers of vegetables, seafood, and meats) are the Sibu signature. Wine and beer are available; white sugar and MSG are not. Come with cash as they don't accept credit cards.

In Banyan Court, 75–5695 Alii Dr. ⒸⒸ **808/329-1112.** Most items less than $14. No credit cards. Daily 11:30am–3pm and 5–9pm.

SOUTH KONA
Moderate

Aloha Angel Cafe ISLAND CUISINE   The former Aloha Cafe is under new management, but they kept the trademark large servings, heroic burgers and sandwiches, and a home-style menu for vegetarians and carnivores. Breakfast and lunch are served on the veranda that wraps around the old Aloha Theatre with sweeping views down from the coffee fields to the shoreline. Dinner is in the tiny dining room (which unfortunately has no view); space is limited so phone ahead to assure that you get a table. The cheaper daytime staples include omelets, burritos, tostadas, quesadillas, and home-baked goods. Most of the produce is organic, and fresh-squeezed orange juice and fresh-fruit smoothies are served daily. Sandwiches, from turkey to tofu-avocado and a wonderful fresh ahi, are heaped with vegetables on tasty whole-wheat buns, still generous after all these years. The dinner entrees cover the basics, from fresh catch to grilled New York steak and Cajun chicken with tropical salsa.

Hwy. 11, Kainaliu. ⒸⒸ **808/322-3383.** Reservations recommended for large parties. Most items less than $7 during day; dinner main courses $14–$21. MC, V. Daily 8am–3pm and 5–9pm.

Keei Cafe ⭐⭐⭐ *Finds* MEDITERRANEAN/LATINO/ISLAND   The darling of South Kona is still going strong. Formerly a fish market, Keei Cafe is about as far as you can get from the famous dining rooms of the Kohala resorts. But the food is "so much more ono" as we say in Hawaii, that people gladly drive the long distance to eat at Hawaii's version of a bistro. A friendly, casual ambience, great food, and affordable prices are only part of its appeal. The concrete floors, plastic chairs, and local art create a quirky setting, and the menu roams the globe, from spicy fajitas (chicken or tofu) to excellent vegetarian black-bean soup; and Brazilian seafood chowder to Greek salad with Maui onions. Peanut-miso salad and piquant red curry sauces are a nod to Thailand. The fresh catch and roasted chicken are highlights, sometimes accompanied by caramelized onions and whipped potatoes. Everything is made from scratch, and virtually everything is grown or harvested in the Honaunau Valley area. Save room for dessert: The tropical bread pudding (with bananas and pineapple) and coconut flan with lilikoi sauce, made by the owner's Portuguese mother-in-law, are tops.

Close to the 113 mile marker on Hwy. 11, in Kealakekua. © 808/328-8451. Main courses $10–$19. No credit cards. Tues–Sat 5:15–9pm.

Inexpensive

The Coffee Shack ★ *Kids* COFFEEHOUSE/DELI   Great food, crisp air, and a sweeping ocean view make the Coffee Shack one of South Kona's great finds. It's an informal place with counter service, pool chairs, and white trellises on the deck framed by ferns, palms, and banana trees. Especially charming is the wooden deck near a towering old tree that droops with the weight of avocados. The fare is equally inviting: French toast made with homemade poi bread; lemon bars and carrot cake; eggs Benedict with a delectable Hollandaise. At lunch: a cheerful assortment of imported beers; excellent sandwiches on home-baked breads; and fresh, hearty salads made with organic lettuces. Let the kids order peanut-butter-and-jelly or grilled-cheese sandwiches while you head for the smoked Alaskan salmon sandwich or the hot, authentic Reuben (complete with sauerkraut and tangy Russian dressing).

Hwy 11, 1 mile south of Captain Cook. © 808/328-9555. Most items less than $6.95; pizzas $10–$14. MC, V. Daily 7am–5pm.

Manago Hotel Restaurant *Value* AMERICAN   The dining room of the decades-old H. Manago Hotel is a local legend, greatly loved for its unpretentious, tasty food at bargain prices. At breakfast, $4.50 buys you eggs, bacon, papaya, rice, and coffee. At lunch or dinner, you can dine handsomely on local favorites: a 12-ounce T-bone, fried ahi, opelu, or the house specialty, pork chops—Manago T-shirts announce "the best pork chops in town," and the restaurant serves nearly 1,500 pounds monthly. When the akule or opelu are running, count on a rush by the regular customers. This place is nothing fancy, and there's a lot of frying going on in the big kitchen, but the local folks would riot if anything were to change after so many years.

In the Manago Hotel, Hwy. 11, Captain Cook. © 808/323-2642. Reservations recommended for dinner. Main courses $7–$12. DISC, MC, V. Tues–Sun 7–9am, 11am–2pm, and 5–7:30pm.

Nasturtium Café ★★ *Finds* HEALTHY GOURMET   This tiny cafe, now serving lunch only, but with plans for breakfast in the future, is a true find for those who love healthy gourmet food, with an international flair, at budget prices. Chef Diane Tomac-Campogan is in the kitchen cooking up interesting dishes like Moroccan chicken wrap (with range-fed, hormone- and antibiotic-free chicken), a to-die-for fresh-fish burger, a mean Mexican corn soup, and a Korean spinach salad that will keep you smiling all afternoon. Do not leave this culinary heaven without dessert: ginger macadamia nut tart (wheat and dairy free), fresh ginger spice cake, homemade fruit crisp ala mode, or the very yummy chocolate mousse (which Chef Diane claims in cholesterol free). They also have takeout, so you can take your mouth-watering treats and go to the beach for a picnic.

79-7491-B Mamalaloa Hwy. (Hwy. 11), Kainaliu © 808/322-2193. Reservations recommended. Most items under $10. MC, V. Mon–Fri 11am–2:30pm.

Teshima's JAPANESE/AMERICAN   This is local style all the way. Shizuko Teshima has a strong following among those who have made her miso soup and sukiyaki an integral part of their lives. The early morning crowd starts gathering while it's still dark for omelets or Japanese breakfasts (soup, rice, and fish). As the day progresses, the orders pour in for shrimp tempura and sukiyaki. By dinner, Number 3 teishoku trays—miso soup, sashimi, sukiyaki, shrimp, pickles, and other delights—are streaming out of the kitchen. Other combinations include steak and shrimp tempura; beef teriyaki and shrimp tempura; and the deep-sea trio of shrimp tempura, fried fish, and sashimi.

Hwy. 11, Honalo. ℂ 808/322-9140. Reservations recommended for large parties. Complete dinners $16 and under. No credit cards. Daily 6:30am–1:45pm and 5–9pm.

THE KOHALA COAST

Note: You'll find the following restaurants on the "North Kohala & Waimea" map on p. 313.

VERY EXPENSIVE

Batik ★★ EURO-ASIAN   This is a room of hushed tones and great restraint, with high, dark-wood ceilings, sedate (and loyal) guests, and sensitive lighting—a shrine to fine dining. The artichoke salad—its leaves spread out flamboyantly, like a flower—is one of several standouts on the appetizer menu. Fresh snapper in various exotic preparations (with Kona mushrooms and lobster), grilled fresh fish with seaweed-herb sauces, and Keahole lobster Provençale are among the elegant entrees blending local ingredients and Asian preparations with Continental techniques. If your tastes run hotter, try one of the curries—vegetable, chicken, or shrimp, prepared in mild Indonesian or spicy Thai styles and offered with excellent chutneys. Naan from the tandoori oven comes warm and fresh. The only drawback is that the restaurant is only open seasonally (generally closed in Sept, open 3 or 4 nights a week Oct–Christmas, usually open 5 nights a week Christmas–Apr).

In the Mauna Kea Beach Hotel, 62–100 Mauna Kea Beach Dr. ℂ 808/882-7222. www.maunakeabeach hotel.com. Reservations recommended. Collared, button-down shirts and dress slacks requested for men. Main courses $32–$45; prix fixe from $65. AE, DC, MC, V. Seasonally 6:30–9pm.

Brown's Beach House ★★ HAWAII REGIONAL   The nearby lagoon takes on the pink-orange glow of sunset, while torches flicker between the coconut trees. With white tablecloths, candles, and seating near the lagoon, this is a spectacular

---

Tropical Dreams of Ice Cream

Tropical Dreams ice creams have spread out over the island, and North Kohala is where the line began. Across the street from Bamboo, **Kohala Coffee Mill and Tropical Dreams Ice Cream,** Highway 270, Hawi (ℂ **808/ 889-5577**), serves their upscale ice creams along with sandwiches, pastries, and a selection of island coffees, including 100% Kona. The Tahitian vanilla and lychee ice creams are local legends, but we also love the macadamia-nut torte and lilikoi bars, made by a Kohala Coast pastry chef. Jams, jellies, herb vinegars, Hawaiian honey, herbal salts, and macadamia-nut oils are among the gift items for sale. Residents meet here to start the day, in the afternoon for an espresso pick-me-up, and at all times in between. They are open Monday to Friday, 6:30am to 6pm and Saturday and Sunday, 7:30am to 5:30pm.

setting, complemented by a menu that keeps getting better by the year. At lunch, the seared ahi poke sprinkled with kukui nuts is a winner; so is the fresh island taco, a brilliant take on the local favorite, enlivened with the fresh catch of the day with homemade fire-roasted tomato salsa, poblano cream, and pepper jack cheese. There are sandwiches and wraps, from the vegetables to a gourmet burger. Dinner faves include bouillabaisse "etsuji-style" with a steamed bowl of shellfish, mussels, crab and local fish on perciatelli pasta, or osso buco with pumpkin risotto. Don't miss their yummy soufflés. Day or night, it's an elegant affair.

At the Fairmont Orchid, Hawaii, 1 N. Kaniku Dr. © **808/885-2000.** Reservations recommended for dinner. Lunch main courses $12–$17; dinner main courses $28–$58. AE, DC, DISC, MC, V. Daily 6–10pm.

CanoeHouse ★★ HAWAII REGIONAL   The setting is as gorgeous as ever, but it is not the same restaurant as it was when Alan Wong was the chef and the food coming out of the kitchen was nothing short of extraordinary. However, Wong didn't take the ambience with him, and the legendary sunset views remain, along with a koa canoe still hanging from the ceiling in the open-air dining room. *Tip:* Ask for a table outside and go at sunset to get the real flavor of this incredible setting. The menu still offers Wong's nori-wrapped tempura ahi and wasabi lobster tempura on a stick, in addition to an array of seafood, from seared and peppered ono to mahimahi wrapped in pancetta and a grilled salmon misoyaki. Save room for dessert, especially the chocolate pillar, a rich chocolate torte with vanilla sauce and fresh berries, or white chocolate li hing mui mousse, a classic white chocolate mouse with a local Asian flavoring, served in a phyllo cup.

At Mauna Lani Bay Hotel and Bungalows, 68–1400 Mauna Lani Dr. © **808/885-6622.** Reservations recommended. Main courses $27–$50. AE, DC, DISC, MC, V. Daily, summer 5:30–9pm; winter 6–9:30pm.

Coast Grille ★★ STEAK/SEAFOOD/HAWAII REGIONAL   It's a 3-minute walk from the main lobby to the open-air Grille, but the view along the way is nothing to complain about and will help you work up an appetite. The split-level dining room has banquettes and wicker furniture, open-air seating, and an oyster bar that is famous. The extensive seafood selection includes poke, clams, and fresh oysters from all over the world, as well as fresh seafood from Island waters, served in multicultural preparations. Kona lobster tempura sushi and an excellent clam chowder are among the finer pleasures.

In the Hapuna Beach Prince Hotel. © **808/880-1111.** www.hapunabeachprincehotel.com. Reservations recommended. Main courses $28–$34. AE, DC, MC, V. Daily 6–9:30pm.

Expensive

Hawaii Calls ★ PACIFIC RIM   Hawaii of the 1930s and '40s comes to mind in the retro decor of this Waikoloa dining room: John Kelly prints, Pan Am Clipper posters, old RCA record covers, and mementos of Hawaii's boat days. Hawaii Calls is one of the most pleasing features of this resort. Breakfast and lunch are an outdoor experience, open-air with views of Anaehoomalu Bay and the surrounding ponds. At night come the tablecloths and lighting and indoor tables. Hula Sunsets, 1½ hours of Hawaiian song and dance on the nearby poolside lawn, are nostalgic and picturesque. They take place weekly, from 5:30 to 7pm Fridays. Hula Sunset and the Friday night seafood buffet are a festive way to launch the weekend. The array of appetizers (such as clams, and the "hukilau sampler" of Keahole lobster claw, seared ahi, and poke on a bed of greens) and the signature Kamuela Lamb are among the menu highlights. There's live entertainment nightly in the adjoining Clipper Lounge, where diners can order from a special bistro menu from 5:30 to 11pm.

In the Outrigger Waikoloa Beach Resort, 69–275 Waikoloa Beach Dr. ⓒ 808/886-6789. Reservations recommended. Lunch $10–$18; dinner main courses $19–$49. AE, DC, DISC, MC, V. Daily 6am–2pm and 5:30–9:30pm; Clipper Lounge 5–11:30pm.

Roy's Waikoloa Bar & Grill ⭐⭐ PACIFIC RIM/EURO-ASIAN   Don't let the strip mall location fool you. Roy's Waikoloa has several distinctive and inviting features: a golf-course view, large windows overlooking part of a 10-acre lake, and the East–West cuisine and upbeat service that are Roy Yamaguchi signatures. This is a clone of his Oahu restaurant, offering dishes we've come to love: Szechuan baby back ribs, blackened island ahi, and six other types of fresh fish prepared charred, steamed, or seared, and topped with exotic sauces such as shiitake miso and gingered lime-chile butter. Always in demand are the hibachi-style salmon and, at lunch, the "lumpia basket" of fresh fish and stir-fried vegetables. Yamaguchi's tireless exploration of local ingredients and world traditions produces food that keeps him at Hawaii's culinary cutting edge.

In the Waikoloa Beach Resort, Kings' Shops, 250 Waikoloa Beach Dr. ⓒ 808/886-4321. www.roysrestaurant. com. Reservations recommended. Main courses $8–$14 at lunch, $17–$27 at dinner. AE, DC, DISC, MC, V. Daily 11:30am–2pm and 5:30–9:30pm.

Moderate

Cafe Pesto ⭐⭐ MEDITERRANEAN/ITALIAN   Fans drive long miles for these gourmet pizzas, calzones, and fresh organic greens grown from Kealakekua to Kamuela. The herb-infused Italian pies are adorned with lobster from the aquaculture farms on Keahole Point, shiitake mushrooms from a few miles mauka (inland), and fresh fish, shrimp, and crab. Honey-miso crab cakes, Santa Fe chicken pasta, sweet roasted peppers, and herb-garlic Gorgonzola dressing are other favorites.

In Kawaihae Shopping Center, at Kawaihae Harbor, Pule Hwy. and Kawaihae Rd. ⓒ 808/882-1071. Main courses $7–$26. AE, DC, DISC, MC, V. Sun–Thurs 11am–9pm; Fri–Sat 11am–10pm.

NORTH KOHALA

Note: You'll find the following restaurants on the "North Kohala & Waimea" map on p. 313.

Bamboo ⭐⭐ *Finds* PACIFIC RIM   Serving fresh fish and Asian specialties in a turn-of-the-century building, Hawi's self-professed "tropical saloon" is a major attraction on the island's northern coastline. The exotic interior is a nod to nostalgia, with high wicker chairs from Waikiki's historic Moana Hotel, works by local artists, and old Matson liner menus accenting the bamboo-lined walls. The fare, island favorites in sophisticated presentations, is a match for all this style: imu-smoked pork quesadillas, fish prepared several ways, sesame nori-crusted or tequila-lime shrimp, and selections of pork, beef, and chicken. There are even some local faves, such as teriyaki chicken and fried noodles served vegetarian, with chicken, or with shrimp. Produce from nearby gardens and fish fresh off the chef's own hook are among the highlights. At Sunday brunch, diners gather for eggs Bamboo (eggs Benedict with a lilikoi-hollandaise sauce) and the famous passion-fruit margaritas. Hawaiian music wafts through the Bamboo from 7pm to closing on weekends. Next door and upstairs is a gallery of furniture and arts and crafts, some very good and most locally made.

Hwy. 270, Hawi. ⓒ 808/889-5555. Reservations recommended. Main courses $10–$24 (full- and half-size portions available). DC, MC, V. Tues–Sat 11:30am–2:30pm and 6–9pm; Sun 11am–2pm (brunch).

Jen's Kohala Cafe ⭐ *Value* GOURMET DELI   Jen's is loved for its healthful fare and made-with-care wraps. Fresh soups and salads, homemade burgers and veggie burgers, an award-winning black-bean and red-onion chili served with fresh homemade corn bread—it's all good stuff. But most in demand are Jen's wraps, herb-garlic flat bread filled with local organic baby greens and vine-ripened organic tomatoes, cheese, and various fillings. The Kamehameha Wrap features kalua pork, two different cheeses, and a Maui onion dressing. Our favorite: the Greek Wrap of greens, feta and Parmesan, olives, peppers, and red onions, with balsamic vinaigrette. There are about 30 seats indoors and a few outdoors next to an art gallery with a striking mural.

Hwy. 270, Kapaau, in front of the King Kamehameha Statue. ℭ 808/889-0099. Main courses $2.50–$6.50. MC, V. Daily 10am–6pm.

WAIMEA

Note: You'll find the following restaurants on the "North Kohala & Waimea" map on p. 313.

EXPENSIVE

Daniel Thiebaut Restaurant ✿ FRENCH-ASIAN   It took two years to renovate the 100-year-old Chock Inn Store, but when it finally opened, it did not disappoint. Chef Daniel Thiebaut's menu highlights Big Island products (Kamuela Pride beef, Kahua Ranch lettuces, Hirabara Farms field greens, herbs and greens from Adaptations in South Kona) interpreted by the French-trained Thiebaut, formerly executive chef at Mauna Kea Beach Resort. Highlights include a greaseless, perfect kalua-duck lumpia; vegetarian spring rolls; wok-fried scallops; and fresh mahimahi in kaffir lime reduction. The restaurant, with a gaily lit plantation-style veranda, is full of intimate enclaves allowing all kinds of demographics, from the intimate tête-à-tête to groups of 40 or more. In the past couple of years, we have become increasingly disappointed at the alarming rise in prices and the corresponding decrease in the amount of food on your plate. Reluctantly, we have lowered the star rating of this once-sterling eatery in hopes that the management will bring prices to a more reasonable level.

65–1259 Kawaihae Rd. (the Historic Yellow Building). ℭ 808/887-2200. www.danielthiebaut.com. Reservations recommended. Main courses $21–$25; desserts $4.50–$8. AE, DISC, MC, V. Mon–Fri 11:30am–1:30pm; daily 5:30–9:30pm.

Merriman's ✿✿✿ HAWAII REGIONAL   Merriman's is peerless. Although founder/owner/chef Peter Merriman now commutes between the Big Island and Maui, where he runs the Hula Grill, he manages to maintain the sizzle that has made Merriman's a premier Hawaii attraction. Order anything from saimin to poisson cru for lunch; at dinner, choose from the signature wok-charred ahi, kung pao shrimp, lamb from nearby Kahua Ranch, and a noteworthy vegetarian selection. Peter's Caesar with sashimi, Pahoa corn and shrimp fritters, and sautéed, sesame-crusted fresh catch with spicy lilikoi sauce are among our many favorites. An organic spinach salad (like most things on the menu, grown nearby), Lokelani tomatoes, kalua pig quesadillas, and his famous platters of seafood and meats are among the many reasons this is still the best, and busiest, dining spot in Waimea.

In Opelu Plaza, Hwy. 19. ℭ 808/885-6822. Reservations recommended. Main courses $7–$13 lunch, $17–$35 dinner (market price for ranch lamb or ahi). AE, MC, V. Mon–Fri 11:30am–1:30pm; daily 5:30–9pm.

Moderate

Edelweiss ✿ CONTINENTAL   Diners with a hankering for Wiener schnitzel, bratwurst, sauerkraut, Black Forest cake, and richly adorned fowl and meats are known to drive all the way from Kona or Hilo for the traditional

German offerings at this chalet-like bistro. The upscale ranch burgers and chicken aux champignons have a following, though they may require a siesta after lunch. In the evening, complete dinners include sautéed veal, rack of lamb, roast pork, roast duck, and other Continental classics. Although heavy on the meats and sauces, and certainly not a magnet for vegetarians or those on a low-fat diet, Edelweiss has anchored itself firmly in the hearts of Hawaii islanders. "We do not believe in all these changes," sniffs chef/owner Hans Peter Hager. "When you enjoy something, you come back for it." The menu has barely changed in his 14 years in Waimea, and the tables are always full, so who's arguing?

Kawaihae Rd. (C) 808/885-6800. Reservations recommended for dinner. Lunch $8–$12; complete dinners $20–$25 (most around $21). MC, V. Tues–Sat 11:30am–1:30pm and 5–8:30pm. Closed Sept and first week of Oct.

Inexpensive

Aioli's ★ AMERICAN ECLECTIC   Most of the breads for the sandwiches are homemade, the turkey is roasted in Aioli's own kitchen, the prices are reasonable, and on Saturday mornings, the scent of fresh-baked cinnamon rolls wafts through the neighborhood. Specialty salads, homemade cookies and desserts, and daily hot sandwich specials (fresh catch on fresh bread can hardly be beat!) have kept the diners coming. Lunch is informal: order, pay at the counter, and find a table. The evening bistro menu changes every 3 weeks; recent offerings include herb-crusted Black Angus prime rib with baked potato and vegetables, seared sea scallops with a coconut curry sauce, rack of lamb with cranberry orange sauce, and vegetarian items.

Opelo Plaza, Hwy. 19. (C) 808/885-6325. Main courses $3.95–$8.95 lunch, $12–$23 dinner. DISC, MC, V. Tues 11am–4pm; Wed–Thurs 11am–8pm; Fri–Sat 11am–9pm; Sun 8am–2pm.

The Little Juice Shack JUICE BAR/DELI   When you want a sudden jolt of energy that isn't caffeine, Juice Shack comes to the rescue. There's nothing like fresh-squeezed carrot-apple juice to put a spring in your step, and this is the place to get it. The smoothies and sandwiches here are wholesome and the produce fresh, green, and varied. All juices are made fresh to order: orange, pear, apple, pineapple, carrot, tomato, and many combinations, including vegetable drinks and spirulina powder. Smoothies (Bananarama, Nutty Monkey, Hawaii 5-0) are witty, creamy, and healthful, made with low-fat yogurt mix. Bagels with luscious toppings (like pesto, smoked salmon, or tapenade); vegetarian chili; and hearty soups, salads, and sandwiches (Thai curry vegetable soup, Greek salad, ahi-tuna sandwich) are guiltless and guileless.

In Parker Ranch Shopping Center, Hwy. 19. (C) 808/885-1686. Most items less than $6. No credit cards. Mon–Fri 7am–4pm; Sat 9am–4pm.

Maha's Cafe ★★ (Finds) COFFEEHOUSE/SANDWICHES   More like a cozy living room than a restaurant, Maha's serves breakfast (a small selection, but each item is top-quality) and impressive sandwiches in a wood-floored room of Waimea's first frame house, built in 1852. Harriet-Ann Namahaokalani (Maha) Schutte dispenses poi pancakes, granola for breakfast, and very fluffy scrambled eggs in a flour tortilla, served with salsa and bananas with yogurt on the side— delectable, and for only $5! Sandwiches prevail at lunch, and cookies, tea, and coffee are available all day long. Everything is made to order using fresh local ingredients, and the menu reads like a map of the island: smoked-ahi sandwiches with lilikoi salsa, fresh roasted turkey with mushroom stuffing and squaw bread, fresh fish with Waipio taro and Kahua greens, vine-ripened tomatoes with local feta cheese, and bread made from Waimea sweet corn. Lunch has never been grander, served at cozy wooden tables on lauhala mats.

In Spencer House, Hwy. 19. © 808/885-0693. Main courses $6–$14. MC, V. Thurs–Mon 8am–4pm.

Zappas *Value* LOCAL/ITALIAN   At the rear of a small grocery store across from Opelo Plaza (where Merriman's is located), tantalizing aromas of garlic, tomato sauce, pizza, and puttanesca emit radar signals to those in search of good, cheap pizza and pasta. You order at the counter for takeout or eat at one of six booths. There are cream sodas, root beer, black cherry soda, and all the elements of a Little Italy deli: cold cuts, eggplant Parmesan, burgers, antipasto, caprese (local tomatoes and buffalo mozzarella), bruschetta, penne arrabbiata, and a linguine puttanesca (with whole olives) that was respectable, especially for a budget-friendly $8.95. The pizzas are also popular, especially the Zappas Special, pepperoni, mushrooms, olives, bell peppers, and sausage; and the pesto pizza with Asiago cheese, vine-ripened tomatoes, and the buffalo mozzarella that the chef likes so much. At breakfast, the omelets, eggs, and loco moco are a magnet for early risers with big appetites.

64–1210 Hwy. 19. © **808/885-1511.** Main dishes $7.95–$8.95; small pizzas $9–$21. MC, V. Daily 6:30am–8pm.

THE HAMAKUA COAST

Cafe Il Mondo ✦ PIZZA/ESPRESSO BAR   A tiny cafe with a big spirit has taken over the Andrade Building in the heart of Honokaa. Tropical watercolors and local art, the irresistible aromas of garlic sauces and pizzas, and a 1924 koa bar meld gracefully in Sergio and Dena Ramirez's tribute to the Old World. A classical and flamenco guitarist, Sergio occasionally plays solo guitar in his restaurant while contented drinkers tuck into the stone oven–baked pizzas. The Waipio vegetable pizza is a best-seller, but the Sergio—pesto with marinated artichokes and mushrooms—is the one folks remember. Sandwiches come cradled in fresh French, onion, or rosemary buns, all made by local bakeries. There's fresh soup daily, roasted chicken, and other specials; all greens are fresh, local, and organic.

Mamane St., Honokaa. © **808/775-7711.** Pizzas $8.50–$18; sandwiches $4.75–$5; pasta $8.95. No credit cards. Mon–Sat 11am–9pm.

Jolene's Kau Kau Korner AMERICAN/LOCAL   It's homey and friendly, nothing fancy, with eight tables and windows that look out into a scene much like an old western town, but for the cars. The Hawaiian food has been dropped from the menu, leaving us with saimin, stir-fried tempeh with vegetables, sandwiches (including a good vegetarian tempeh burger), and plate lunches—mahimahi, fried chicken, shrimp, beef stew, and familiar selections of local food.

At Mamane St. and Lehua, Honokaa. © **808/775-9498.** Plate lunches $5.95–$7.95; dinner main courses $7.95–$18.95. No credit cards. Mon–Fri 10am–3pm.

Mamane Street Bakery BAKERY/CAFE   Honokaa's gourmet bake shop serves espresso, cappuccino, sandwiches, and snacks, including a legendary focaccia. Most sandwich lovers on the island have tasted these breads, as the Mamane Street Bakery also wholesales breads and pastries, including its well-known burger buns, to the Big Island's most prominent eateries. Portuguese sweet bread and honey-nut muffins are the big sellers in this easygoing, informal coffeehouse with lower-than-coffeehouse prices: Breads sell for $2.25 to $3.25, and most pastries are less than $1.50. The Danishes are to die for. Edible gift products made on the island, such as Lilikoi Gold jams and local coffees, are a recent addition.

Mamane St., Honokaa. ℭ 808/775-9478. Most items less than $3. MC, V. Mon–Sat 7am–5:30pm.

Simply Natural ⋆ *(Value)* HEALTH FOOD/SANDWICH SHOP   Simply Natural is a superb find on Honokaa's main street. We love this charming deli with its friendly staff, wholesome food, and vintage interior. It offers a counter and a few small tables with bright tablecloths and fresh anthuriums. Don't be fooled by the unpretentiousness of the place; we had the best smoked chicken sandwich we've ever tasted here. The owner's mother proudly displayed the gloriously plump whole chicken, smoked by her neighbor in Honokaa, before slicing and serving it on freshly baked onion bread from the Big Island Bakery. The menu is wholesome, with no sacrifice in flavor: sautéed mushroom-onion sandwich, tempeh burger, and breakfast delights that include taro-banana pancakes. Even a simple vegetable-mushroom sandwich is special, made to order with grilled mushrooms and onions, luscious fresh tomato, and your choice of squaw, onion, or rosemary bread. Top it off with premium ice cream by Hilo Homemade (another favorite) or a smoothie. The mango-pineapple-banana-strawberry version is sublime.

Mamane St., Honokaa. ℭ 808/775-0119. Deli items $3–$7.50. MC, V. Mon–Sat 9am–4pm.

Tex Drive In & Restaurant AMERICAN/LOCAL ETHNIC   When Ada Lamme bought the old Tex Drive In, she made significant changes, such as improving upon an ages-old recipe for Portuguese *malassadas,* a cakelike doughnut without a hole. Tex sells tens of thousands of these sugar-rolled morsels a month, including malassadas filled with pineapple/papaya preserves, pepper jelly, or Bavarian cream. The menu has a local flavor and features ethnic specialties: Korean chicken, teriyaki meat, kalua pork with cabbage, and Filipino specials. Hamburgers, on buns baked by Mamane Street Bakery, are a big seller. New on the menu are Tex wraps, served with homemade sweet-potato chips. With its gift shop and visitor center, Tex is a roadside attraction and a local hangout; residents have been gathering there for decades over early morning coffee and breakfast.

Hwy. 19, Honokaa. ℭ 808/775-0598. Main courses $6.95–$9.95. DC, DISC, MC, V. Daily 6am–8:30pm.

What's Shakin' ⋆ *(Finds)* HEALTH FOOD   Look for the cheerful, plantation-style, wooden house in yellow and white with a green roof, 2 miles north of the Hawaii Tropical Botanical Garden. This is where many of the bananas and papayas from Patsy and Tim Withers's 20-acre farm end up: in fresh-fruit smoothies with names like Papaya Paradise, an ambrosial blend of pineapples, coconuts, papayas, and bananas, one of the eight different types of smoothies offered. If you're in the mood for something more substantial, try the Blue Hawaii blue-corn tamale with homemade salsa, or the teriyaki-ginger tempeh burger. There are several lunch specials daily, and every plate arrives with fresh fruit and a green salad topped with Patsy's Oriental sesame dressing. You can sit outdoors in the garden, where bunches of bananas hang for the taking and the ocean view is staggering.

27–999 Old Mamalahoa Hwy. (on the 4-mile scenic drive), Pepeekeo. ℭ 808/964-3080. Most items less than $6.95; smoothies $3.85–$4.25. No credit cards. Daily 10am–5pm.

HILO

Note: You'll find the following restaurants on the "Hilo" map on p. 321.

EXPENSIVE

Harrington's ☆ SEAFOOD/STEAK   This is arguably the prettiest location in Hilo, on a clear rocky pool teeming with koi (carp) at Reeds Bay, close to the waterfront but not on it. The house specialty, thinly sliced Slavic steak swimming in butter and garlic, is part of the old-fashioned steak-and-seafood formula that makes the Harrington's experience a predictable one. But the Caesar salad is zesty and noteworthy, and for those oblivious to calories, the escargots—baked en casserole on a bed of spinach and topped with lightly browned cheeses—are a rewarding choice. The meunière-style fresh catch, sautéed in white wine and topped with a lightly browned lemon-butter sauce, is also popular. The strongest feature of Harrington's is the tranquil beauty of Reeds Pond (also known as Ice Pond), one of Hilo's visual wonders. The open-air restaurant perches on the pond's shores, creating a sublime ambience.

135 Kalanianaole. ℂ **808/961-4966.** Reservations recommended. Lunch main courses $6–$15; dinner main courses $16 to market price. MC, V. Mon–Fri 11am–4pm; Mon–Sat 4–5:30pm sunset cocktails and dinner 5:30–9:30pm; Sun 5:30–9pm.

Pescatore ☆ SOUTHERN ITALIAN   In a town of ethnic eateries and casual mom-and-pop diners, this is a special-occasion restaurant, dressier and pricier than most of the Hilo choices. It's ornate, especially for Hilo, with gilded frames on antique paintings, chairs of vintage velvet, koa walls, and a tile floor. The fresh catch is offered in several preparations, including reduced-cream and Parmesan or capers and wine. The paper-thin ahi carpaccio is garnished with capers, red onion, garlic, lemon, olive oil, and shaved Parmesan—and it's superb. Chicken, veal, and fish Marsala, a rich and garlicky scampi Alfredo, and the Fra Diavolo (a spicy seafood marinara) are among the dinner offerings, which come with soup and salad. Lighter fare, such as simple pasta marinara and chicken Parmesan, prevails at lunch.

235 Keawe St. ℂ **808/969-9090.** Reservations recommended for dinner. Main courses $5–$12 lunch, $16–$29 dinner. AE, DC, DISC, MC, V. Daily 11am–2pm and 5:30–9pm; Sat–Sun buffet 7:30–11am.

MODERATE

Nihon Restaurant & Cultural Center ☆ JAPANESE   The room offers a beautiful view of Hilo Bay on one side and the soothing green sprawl of Liliuokalani Gardens on the other. This is a magnificent part of Hilo that's often overlooked because of its location away from the central business district. The reasonably priced menu features steak-and-seafood combination dinners and selections from the sushi bar, including the innovative poke and lomi salmon hand rolls. The "Businessman's Lunch," a terrific deal, comes with sushi, potato salad, soup, vegetables, and two choices from the following: butterfish, shrimp tempura, sashimi, chicken, and other morsels. This isn't inexpensive dining, but the value is sky-high, with a presentation that matches the serenity of the room and its stunning view of the bay.

Overlooking Liliuokalani Gardens and Hilo Bay, 123 Lihiwai St. ℂ **808/969-1133.** Reservations recommended. Main courses $9–$20; combination dinner $17. AE, DC, DISC, MC, V. Mon–Sat 11am–1:30pm and 5–8pm.

Ocean Sushi Deli ☆ *(Finds* SUSHI   Now that sister restaurant Tsunami (p. 281) has opened across the street, the lines aren't so long at Ocean Sushi Deli, Hilo's nexus of affordable sushi. This tiny takeout sushi shop, Hilo's spot for poetic-license sushi at friendly prices, is very popular. Local-style specials stretch purist boundaries but are so much fun: lomi salmon, oyster nigiri, opihi nigiri, unagi avocado hand roll, ahi poke roll, and special new rolls that use thin sheets of tofu skins and cooked egg. For traditionalists, there are ample shrimp, salmon, hamachi, clam, and other sushi delights—a long menu of them, including handy ready-to-cook sukiyaki and shabu-shabu sets.

239 Keawe St. ✆ **808/961-6625.** Sushi boxes $4–$23; sushi family platters $20–$50. MC, V. Mon–Sat 10am–2:30pm and 4:30–9pm.

Queen's Court Restaurant AMERICAN/BUFFET   Many of those with a "not me!" attitude toward buffets have been disarmed by the Hilo Hawaiian's generous and well-rounded offerings at budget-friendly prices. A la carte menu items are offered Monday through Thursday, but the Hawaiian, seafood, and Dungeness crab/prime rib buffets throughout the week (particularly the seafood buffet) cover the bases and draw throngs of local families. Hawaiian food–lovers also come for the Wednesday and Friday Hawaiian lunch buffet.

In the Hilo Hawaiian Hotel, 71 Banyan Dr. ✆ **808/935-9361.** Reservations recommended. Wed and Fri Hawaiian lunch buffet $14; Mon–Thurs prime rib/crab buffet $25; Fri–Sun seafood buffet $27. AE, DC, DISC, MC, V. Mon–Sat 6:30am–9:30am and 11:15am–1:15pm; Sun 6:30am–9am and 10:30am–1:30pm (brunch); daily 5:30–9pm.

Restaurant Miwa ★ JAPANESE   Duck around a corner of the shopping center and discover sensational seafood in this quintessential neighborhood sushi bar. This self-contained slice of Japan is a pleasant surprise in an otherwise unremarkable mall. Shabu-shabu (you cook your own ingredients in a heavy pot), tempura, fresh catch, and a full sushi selection are among the offerings. The top-of-the-line dinner, the steak-and-lobster combination, is a splurge you can enjoy without dressing up. Some items, such as the fresh catch, may be ordered American style. The haupia (coconut pudding) cream-cheese pie is a Miwa signature but is not offered daily; blueberry cream-cheese is the alternative.

In the Hilo Shopping Center, 1261 Kilauea Ave. ✆ **808/961-4454.** Reservations recommended. Main courses $9–$37 (most $10–$15). AE, DC, DISC, MC, V. Mon–Sat 11am–2pm and 5–10pm; Sun 5–9pm.

Seaside Restaurant ★★ STEAK/SEAFOOD   This is a casual local favorite, not fancy but quite an experience—a Hilo signature with a character all its own. How fresh are the trout, catfish, mullet, golden perch, and *aholehole,* the silvery mountain bass devoured passionately by island fish lovers? Fished out of the pond shortly before you arrive, that's how fresh. The restaurant has large windows overlooking the glassy ponds that spawned your dinner, so you can't be sentimental. Colin Nakagawa and his family raise the fish and cook them in two unadorned styles: fried or steamed in ti leaves with lemon juice and onions. Daily specials include steamed opakapaka, onaga (snapper), steak and lobster, paniolo-style prime rib, salmon encrusted with a nori-wasabi sprinkle, New York steak, and shrimp. If you want fish from the pond, *you must call ahead* so your order can be caught and whisked from the pond to kitchen to your table. The outdoor tables are fabulous at dusk when the light reflects on the ponds with an otherworldly glow.

1790 Kalanianaole Ave. ✆ **808/935-8825.** Reservations recommended. Main courses $11–$24. AE, DC, MC, V. Tues–Sun 5–8:30pm.

INEXPENSIVE

Cafe Pesto Hilo Bay ★★ PIZZA/PACIFIC RIM   The Italian brick oven burns many bushels of ohia and kiawe wood to turn out its toothsome pizzas, topped with fresh organic herbs and island-grown produce. The high-ceilinged 1912 room, with windows looking out over Hilo's bay front, is filled with seductive aromas. It's difficult to resist the wild mushroom–artichoke pizza or the chipotle and tomato-drenched southwestern. But go with the Four Seasons—dripping with prosciutto, bell peppers, and mushrooms—it won't disappoint. Some of our other favorites are the Milolii, a crab-shrimp-mushroom sandwich with basil pesto; the chile-grilled shrimp pizza; and the flash-seared poke salad on a bed of spinach. There are many raves on this tried-and-true menu.

In the S. Hata Building, 308 Kamehameha Ave. (C) **808/969-6640.** Pizzas $8–$18. AE, DC, DISC, MC, V. Mon–Thurs 11am–9pm; Fri–Sat 11am–10pm.

Honu's Nest *(Value)* JAPANESE/AMERICAN   Home-cooked Japanese fare at friendly prices and a location on the bay front of Hilo make Honu's a solid hit. There are only four tables and a small wooden counter; the place is usually full, and you'll see why. It's not just the prices that are winners—this is good home cooking, tasty without being greasy, light on the pocketbook as well as the waistline. The teishoku dishes—served with a fresh salad, miso soup, and rice—are inexpensive; they include broiled fresh fish, tofu steak (excellent, with a ginger sauce), sautéed squid, sautéed vegetables, broiled spicy chicken, sesame chicken, and other worthy choices. Tempura is also recommended. The rice dishes called *donburi* come in nine varieties (we like the ahi version), the curries in four, and the soups in seven, including chicken soup, udon, and miso. Sashimi, bought from Suisan Fish Market just down the street, is translucent and fresh.

270 Kamehameha Ave. (C) **808/935-9321.** Main courses $5–$11. No credit cards. Mon–Sat 11am–3pm.

Ken's House of Pancakes AMERICAN/LOCAL   You never know whom you'll bump into at Ken's after an important convention, concert, or the Merrie Monarch Hula Festival. The only 24-hour coffee shop on the Big Island, Ken's fulfills basic dining needs simply and efficiently, with a good dose of local color. Lighter servings and a concession towards health-conscious meals and salads have been added to the menu, a clever antidote to the more than dozen pies available. Omelets, pancakes, French toast made with Portuguese sweet bread, saimin, sandwiches, and soup—what they call a "poi dog menu"—stream out of the busy kitchen. Other affordable selections include fried chicken, steak, prime rib, and grilled fish. Wednesday is prime rib night, and Sunday is the "All-You-Can-Eat Spaghetti Night." Very local, very Hilo.

1730 Kamehameha Ave. (C) **808/935-8711.** Most items less than $7. AE, DC, DISC, MC, V. Daily 24 hours.

Kilauea Kitchen *(★) (Value)* AMERICAN/HAWAIIAN/ASIAN   The latest success of Chef Russell Siu, chef and owner of Honolulu's 3660 On the Rise and the Kakaako Kitchen, is this family restaurant featuring excellent local, oriental, and American food at very reasonable prices. Inside this typical-looking diner is Siu's classic cooking at Hilo prices: fresh mahimahi with soup or salad, rice or mashed potatoes, and veggies for under $10, or sweet chili chicken ($6.95), grilled vegetable wrap ($6.25), and butter croissant French toast ($4.25).

1438 Kilauea Ave. (C) **808/935-6664.** www.kilaueakitchen.com. Breakfast under $5; lunch under $8; dinners under $10. AE, MC, V. Sun–Thurs 7–10:30am, 11am–2:30pm, and 5–8pm; Fri 7–10:30am, 11am–2:30pm, and 5–9pm; Sat 7–10:30am, 11am–2:30pm, and 5–8:30pm.

Kuhio Grille AMERICAN/HAWAIIAN   The "home of the 1-pound laulau" is quite the local hangout, a coffee/saimin shop with a few tables outdoors and a bustling business indoors. Taro and taro leaves from Waipio Valley are featured in the popular Hawaiian plate, but there are other local specialties: saimin, miso-saimin, taro-corned-beef hash, chicken yakitori, burgers, fried rice (famous!), and eclectic selections such as nacho salad and spaghetti. The famous "Kanak Atak" is a 1-pound lau, kalua pig, lomi salmon, pickled onions, haupia, rice and poi, for $11.95. Habitués make a beeline for the counter, where desserts (such as the superb chocolate cake with custard filling) are ordered apace before they run out.

In Prince Kuhio Plaza. © 808/959-2336. Main courses $6–$17. MC, V. Sun–Thurs 6am–10pm; Fri–Sat 6am–2am.

Miyo's JAPANESE   Often cited by local publications as the island's "best Japanese restaurant," Miyo's offers home-cooked, healthy food, served in an open-air room on Wailoa Pond, where an idyll of curving footpaths and greenery fills the horizon. Sliding shoji doors bordering the dining area are left open so you can take in the view and gaze at Mauna Kea on a clear day. Although sesame chicken (deep-fried and boneless with a spine-tingling sesame sauce) is a best-seller, the entire menu is appealing. For vegetarians, there are constantly changing specials such as vegetable tempura, vegetarian shabu-shabu (cooked in a chafing dish at your table, then dipped in a special sauce), and noodle and sea-weed dishes. Other choices include mouthwatering sashimi, beef teriyaki, fried oysters, tempura, ahi donburi (seasoned and steamed in a bowl of rice), sukiyaki, and generous combination dinners. All orders are served with rice, soup, and pickled vegetables. The miso soup is a wonder, and the ahi tempura plate is one of Hilo's stellar buys. Special diets (low-sodium, sugarless) are cheerfully accommodated, and no MSG is used.

In Waiakea Villas, 400 Hualani St. © 808/935-2273. Lunch main courses $4.50–$8.95, combinations $7.50–$9.25; dinner main courses $5–$11, combinations $8–$11. MC, V. Mon–Sat 11am–2pm and 5:30–8:30pm.

Naung Mai *Value* THAI   This quintessential hole-in-the-wall has gained an extra room, but even with 26 seats, it fills up quickly. In a short time, Naung Mai has gained the respect of Hilo residents for its curries and pad Thai noodles and its use of fresh local ingredients. The flavors are assertive, the produce comes straight from the Hilo Farmers Market, and the prices are good. The four curries—green, red, yellow, and Mussaman (Thai Muslim)—go with the jasmine, brown, white, and sticky rice. The pad Thai rice noodles, served with tofu and fresh vegetables, come with a choice of chicken, pork, or shrimp, and are sprinkled with fresh peanuts. You can order your curry Thai-spicy (incendiary) or American-spicy (moderately hot), but even mild, the flavors are outstanding. Known for her magic with spices, owner-chef Alisa Rung Khongnok makes wonderful spring rolls and a Tom Yum spicy soup that is legendary. Lunch

Ice Cream Treats

Fresh, creamy, homemade ice cream made in paradise flavors fresh from the island—that's what you'll get at **Hilo Homemade Ice Cream,** 1477 Kalanianaole Ave., in the Keaukaha area of Hilo (© 808/933-9399). Young Hilo ginger is used for the ginger ice cream, a best-seller; other winners include mango, lilikoi (passion fruit), local banana, green tea, Kona coffee, macadamia nut, coconut-cream, banana-poha (gooseberry), and many others. Some loyal regulars come several times a week for the same flavor.

specials are a steal. Naung Mai is obscured behind the Garden Exchange, so it may take some looking.

86 Kilauea Ave. © **808/934-7540.** Reservations recommended. Main dishes $10–$13. MC, V. Mon–Tues and Thurs–Fri 11am–2pm; Thurs 5–8:30pm; Fri–Sat 5–9pm.

Nori's Saimin & Snacks ★ *Finds* SAIMIN/NOODLE SHOP   Like Naung Mai, Nori's requires some looking, but it's worth it. Unmarked and not visible from the street, it's located across from the Hilo Lanes bowling alley, down a short driveway into an obscure parking lot. You'll wonder what you're doing here, but stroll into the tiny noodle house with the neon sign of chopsticks and a bowl, grab a plywood booth or Formica table, and prepare to enjoy the best saimin on the island. Saimin comes fried or in a savory homemade broth—the key to its success—with various embellishments, from seaweed to wonton dumplings. Ramen, soba, udon, and *mundoo* (a Korean noodle soup) are among the 16 varieties of noodle soups. Barbecued chicken or beef sticks are part of the saimin ritual, smoky and marvelous. Cold noodles, plate lunches (teriyaki beef, ahi, Korean short ribs), and sandwiches give diners ample choices from morning to late night, but noodles are the star. The "big plate" dinners feature ahi, barbecue beef, fried noodles, kal bi ribs, and salad—not for junior appetites. The desserts at Nori's are also legendary, with its signature pies—haupia and sweet potato—flying out the door almost as fast as the famous chocolate mochi cookies and cakes.

688 Kinoole St. © **808/935-9133.** Most items less than $7.95; "big plate" dinner for 2 $15. MC, V. Mon 10:30am–3pm; Tues–Thurs 10:30am–3pm and 4pm–midnight; Fri–Sat 4pm–1am; Sun 10:30am–9:30pm.

Royal Siam Thai Restaurant ★ THAI   A popular neighborhood restaurant, the Royal Siam serves consistently good Thai curries in a simple room just off the sidewalk. Fresh herbs and vegetables from the owner's gardens add an extra zip to the platters of noodles, soups, curries, and specialties that pour out of the kitchen in clouds of spicy fragrance. The Buddha Rama, a wonderful concoction of spinach, chicken, and peanut sauce, is a scene-stealer and a personal favorite. The Thai garlic chicken, in sweet basil with garlic and coconut milk, is equally superb.

70 Mamo St. © **808/961-6100.** Main courses $5–$12. AE, DC, DISC, MC, V. Mon–Sat 11am–2pm and 5–9pm.

Tsunami Grill & Tempura ★ *Value* JAPANESE/AMERICAN   This place is so popular, they don't even bother to put a sign out front. Like its sister restaurant across the street, Ocean Sushi Deli, Tsunami proves that you can dine well in Hilo without breaking the bank. You'll discover here what local residents love to eat: cheap, tasty appetizers such as gyoza and steamed clams for under $5; complete dinners of ahi tempura, chicken yakitori, mahimahi, or beef teriyaki, accompanied by rice, miso soup, and salad, all for an astonishing $6.50; bentos (lavish assortments of sushi, tempura, salmon, noodles, tofu, and other treats) for $8.45; donburi (meats and fish steamed atop rice in a bowl) for under $7; and Japanese curries and tempura for just $4.95 and up. What a find! If you want to get fancier, there are stuffed seafood dinners and New York steak. The lunch and dinner buffets are a top value, and the Sunday seafood buffet includes sushi from Ocean Sushi Deli.

250 Keawe St. © **808/961-6789.** Main courses $5–$10; lunch buffet $11, $9 for seniors, $7 for children; dinner buffet $15, $13 for seniors, $9 for children; Sun seafood buffet $25, $17 for seniors, $10 for children. AE, DISC, MC, V. Mon–Sat 10:30am–2pm and 4:30–9pm; Sun 4:30–8pm.

HAWAII VOLCANOES NATIONAL PARK

Note: You'll find the following restaurants on the "Volcano Area Accommodations & Dining" map on p. 259.

EXPENSIVE

Kilauea Lodge & Restaurant ✪ CONTINENTAL   Diners travel long distances to escape from the crisp upland air into the warmth of this high-ceilinged lodge. The decor is a cross between chalet-cozy and volcano-rugged; the sofa in front of the 1938 fireplace is especially inviting when a fire is roaring. The European cooking is a fine culinary act on the big volcano. Favorites include the fresh catch, hasenpfeffer, potato-leek soup (all flavor and no cream), and Alsatian soup. All dinners come with soup, a loaf of freshly baked bread, and salad.

Hwy. 11 (Volcano Village exit). ✆ **808/967-7366.** Reservations recommended. Main courses $17–$38. MC, V. Daily 5:30–9pm.

MODERATE

Lava Rock Café ✪ ECLECTIC/LOCAL   Volcano Village's newest favorite spot isn't actually a rocky lava cave, but a cheerful, airy oasis in knotty pine, with tables and booths indoors and semi-outdoors, under a clear corrugated-plastic ceiling. The cross-cultural menu includes everything from chow fun to fajitas. The choices include three-egg omelets and pancakes with wonderful house-made lilikoi butter, teriyaki beef and chicken, serious desserts (lilikoi, mango, or ohelo cheesecake), fresh catch, T-bone steak, and steak-and-shrimp combos. The lunchtime winners are the "seismic sandwiches" (which the cafe will pack for hikers), chili, quarter-pound burgers, and a host of salads, plate lunches, and "volcanic" heavies such as Southern-fried chicken and grilled meats.

Hwy. 11 (Volcano Village exit, next to Kilauea Kreations). ✆ **808/967-8526.** Main courses $4.50–$6.99 lunch, $7–$18 dinner. MC, V. Sun 7:30am–4pm; Mon 7:30am–5pm; Tues–Sat 7:30am–9pm.

INEXPENSIVE

Thai Thai Restaurant ✪✪ THAI   Volcano's first Thai restaurant adds warming curries to the chill of upcountry life. The menu features spicy curries and rich satays, coconut-rich soups, noodles and rice, and sweet-and-sour stir-fries of fish, vegetables, beef, cashew chicken, and garlic shrimp. A big hit is the green papaya salad made with tomatoes, crunchy green beans, green onions, and a heap of raw and roasted peanuts—heat and texture and a full symphony of color, aroma, and flavor. There are five types of curries, each with its own array of choices and each quite rich with coconut milk and spices.

19-4084 Old Volcano Rd. ✆ **808/967-7969.** Main courses $9–$15. AE, DISC, MC, V. Daily 5–9pm.

Volcano Golf & Country Club AMERICAN/LOCAL   One of the first two eateries in the area, this golf-course clubhouse has kept its niche as a low-key purveyor of local favorites. The food ranges from okay to good, while the room—looking out over a fairway—is cordial. It's not as clichéd as it sounds, especially when the mists are rolling in and the greens and grays assume an eye-popping intensity; we've even seen nene geese from our table. In the typically cool Volcano air, local favorites such as chili, saimin, and Hawaiian stew with rice become especially comforting. Also featured are prime rib or corned beef and cabbage on special occasions; teriyaki beef or chicken; and stir-fry.

Hwy. 11 (at mile marker 30). ✆ **808/967-8228.** Reservations recommended for large groups. Breakfast items under $6.50; lunch items under $9.75. AE, DC, DISC, MC, V. Mon–Fri 8–10am; Sat–Sun 6:30–10am; daily 10:30am–2pm; bar until 4pm.

NAALEHU/SOUTH POINT

Naalehu Fruit Stand ★ AMERICAN/PIZZA   This little roadside attraction is a bright spot on the long southern route, the liveliest nook in pleasingly sleepy Naalehu. You can buy sandwiches, pizza, fresh salads, and baked goods—the best-loved items here—and then nosh away at one of the few tables on the front porch while panting canines stare longingly from truck beds. Big Island macadamia nuts, hefty quiches, fresh local papayas, and Ka'u navel oranges are usually good here, and the pastries are famous, especially the macadamia-nut pie and the new mac-nut bars and passion fruit–cream cheese bars.

Hwy. 11, Naalehu. ℂ 808/929-9009. Most items less than $10. No credit cards. Mon–Thurs 9am–6pm; Fri–Sat 9am–7pm; Sun 9am–5pm.

Shaka Restaurant AMERICAN/LOCAL   You can't miss the Shaka sign from the highway. This welcome addition to the very slim Naalehu restaurant scene has white tile floors, long tables, an espresso machine, and a friendly, casual atmosphere (including a new "garden room" for smokers). The service-able menu of plate lunches and American fare will seem like foie gras on the long drive through the Ka'u desert. The servings are humongous, especially the Mauna Loa–size burrito, brimming with cheese, beans, olives, onions, and zucchini—highly recommended if you have a hefty appetite. Locals come here for the plate lunches, sandwiches (the shaka burger is very popular), and honey-dipped fried chicken; and at dinner, for the fresh catch—grilled, deep-fried, or prepared in a special potato crust with a ginger-mango sauce.

Hwy. 11. Naalehu. ℂ 808/929-7404. Reservations recommended for dinner. Main courses $6.50–$8.95 lunch, $110–$17 dinner. MC, V. Tues–Sun 10am–9pm.

5 Beaches

Too young geologically to have many great beaches, the Big Island instead has an odd collection of unusual ones: brand-new black-sand beaches, green-sand beaches, salt-and-pepper beaches, and even a rare (for this island) white-sand beach.

THE KONA COAST
KAHALUU BEACH PARK ★★

This is the most popular beach on the Kona Coast; these reef-protected lagoons attract 1,000 people a day almost year-round. Kahaluu is the best all-around beach on Alii Drive, with coconut trees lining a narrow salt-and-pepper sand shore that gently slopes to turquoise pools. The schools of brilliantly colored tropical fish that weave in and out of the well-established reef make this a great place to snorkel. It's also an ideal spot for children and beginning snorkelers to get their fins wet; the water is so shallow that you can just stand up if you feel uncomfortable. Be careful in winter, though: The placid waters become tur-bulent, and there's a rip current when high surf rolls in; look for the lifeguard warnings.

Kahaluu isn't the biggest beach on the island, but it's one of the best equipped, with off-road parking, beach-gear rentals, a covered pavilion, and a food con-cession. It gets crowded, so come early to stake out a spot.

KEKAHA KAI STATE PARK (KONA COAST STATE PARK) ★
You'll glimpse this beach as your plane makes its final approach to Kona Airport. It's about 2 miles north of the airport on Queen Kaahumanu Highway; turn left

Beaches & Outdoor Pursuits on the Big Island

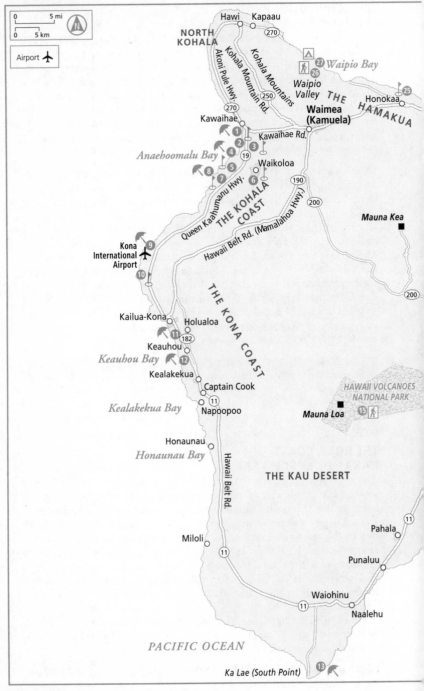

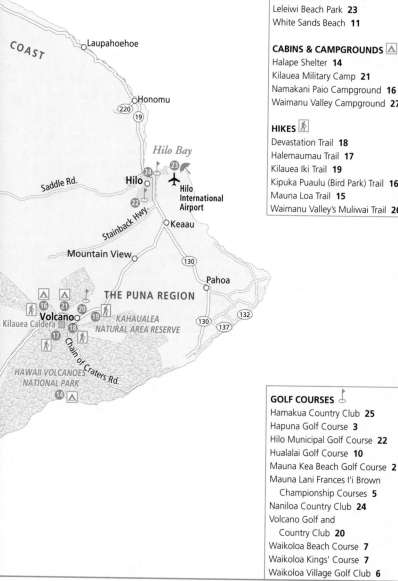

PACIFIC OCEAN

COAST

Laupahoehoe

Honomu

220
19

Hilo Bay

Saddle Rd.

Hilo
24
23
Hilo
International
Airport

22

Stainback Hwy.

Keaau

Mountain View

130

Pahoa

THE PUNA REGION

16
21
20
Volcano
19
KAHAUALEA
NATURAL AREA RESERVE

Kilauea Caldera
17
18

130
137
132

Chain of Craters Rd.

HAWAII VOLCANOES
NATIONAL PARK

14

BEACHES
Anaehoomalu Bay (A-Bay) **8**
Green Sand (Papakolea) Beach **13**
Hapuna Beach **4**
Kahuluu Beach Park **12**
Kaunaoa (Mauna Kea) Beach **1**
Kekaha Kai State Park **9**
Leleiwi Beach Park **23**
White Sands Beach **11**

CABINS & CAMPGROUNDS △
Halape Shelter **14**
Kilauea Military Camp **21**
Namakani Paio Campground **16**
Waimanu Valley Campground **27**

HIKES 🚶
Devastation Trail **18**
Halemaumau Trail **17**
Kilauea Iki Trail **19**
Kipuka Puaulu (Bird Park) Trail **16**
Mauna Loa Trail **15**
Waimanu Valley's Muliwai Trail **26**

GOLF COURSES ⛳
Hamakua Country Club **25**
Hapuna Golf Course **3**
Hilo Municipal Golf Course **22**
Hualalai Golf Course **10**
Mauna Kea Beach Golf Course **2**
Mauna Lani Frances I'i Brown
   Championship Courses **5**
Naniloa Country Club **24**
Volcano Golf and
   Country Club **20**
Waikoloa Beach Course **7**
Waikoloa Kings' Course **7**
Waikoloa Village Golf Club **6**

at a sign pointing improbably down a bumpy road. You won't need a four-wheel-drive vehicle to make it down here—just drive slowly and watch out for potholes. What you'll find at the end is 5 miles of shoreline with a half-dozen long, curving beaches and a big cove on Mahaiula Bay, as well as archaeological and historical sites. The series of well-protected coves is excellent for swimming, and there's great snorkeling and diving offshore; the big winter waves attract surfers.

Facilities include restrooms, picnic tables, and barbecue pits; you'll have to bring your own drinking water. Because it's a state park, the beach is open daily from 8am to 8pm (the closing is strictly enforced, and there's no overnight camping).

WHITE SANDS BEACH ⊛

Don't blink as you cruise Alii Drive, or you'll miss White Sands Beach. This small, white-sand pocket beach about 4½ miles south of Kailua-Kona—very unusual on this lava-rock coast—is sometimes called Disappearing Beach because it does just that, especially at high tide or during storms. It vanished completely when Hurricane Iniki hit in 1991, but it's now back in place. (At least it was the last time we looked.) On calm days, the water is perfect for swimming and snorkeling. Locals use the elementary waves to teach their children how to surf and boogie board. In winter, the waves swell to expert levels, attracting both surfers and spectators. Facilities include restrooms, showers, lifeguards, and a small parking lot.

THE KOHALA COAST
HAPUNA BEACH ⊛⊛⊛

Just off Queen Kaahumanu Highway, south of the Hapuna Beach Prince Hotel, lies this crescent of gold sand—big, wide, and a ½ mile long. In summer, when the beach is widest, the ocean calmest, and the crowds biggest, this is the island's best beach for swimming, snorkeling, and bodysurfing. But beware of Hapuna in winter, when its thundering waves, strong rip currents, and lack of lifeguards can be dangerous. Facilities include A-frame cabins for camping, pavilions, restrooms, showers, and plenty of parking.

KAUNAOA BEACH (MAUNA KEA BEACH) ⊛⊛⊛

For nearly 40 years, this gold-sand beach at the foot of Westin Mauna Kea Beach Hotel has been the top vacation spot among America's corporate chiefs. Everyone calls it Mauna Kea Beach, but its real name is Hawaiian for "native dodder," a lacy, yellow-orange vine that once thrived on the shore. A coconut grove sweeps around this golden crescent, where the water is calm and protected by two black-lava points. The sandy bottom slopes gently into the bay, which often fills with schools of tropical fish, green sea turtles, and manta rays, especially at night, when the hotel lights flood the shore. Swimming is excellent year-round, except in rare winter storms. Snorkelers prefer the rocky points, where fish thrive in the surge. Facilities include restrooms, showers, and ample parking, but there are no lifeguards.

ANAEHOOMALU BAY (A-BAY) ⊛⊛

The Big Island makes up for its dearth of beaches with a few spectacular ones, like Anaehoomalu, or A-Bay, as the locals call it. This popular gold-sand beach, fringed by a grove of palms and backed by royal fish ponds still full of mullet, is one of Hawaii's most beautiful. It fronts the Marriott Waikoloa Beach Resort and is enjoyed by guests and locals alike (it's a little busier in summer, but doesn't ever get truly crowded). The beach slopes gently from shallow to deep water; swimming, snorkeling, diving, kayaking, and windsurfing are all excellent here. Equipment rental and snorkeling, scuba, and windsurfing instruction are available at the north end of the beach. At the far edge of the bay is a rare turtle cleaning station, where snorkelers and divers can watch endangered green sea turtles line up, waiting their turn to have small fish clean them. Facilities include restrooms, showers, picnic tables, and plenty of parking.

HILO
LELEIWI BEACH PARK ✪

Hilo's beaches may be few, but Leleiwi is one of Hawaii's most beautiful. This unusual cove of palm-fringed black-lava tide pools fed by freshwater springs and rippled by gentle waves is a photographer's delight—and the perfect place to take a plunge. In winter, big waves can splash these ponds, but the shallow pools are generally free of currents and ideal for families with children, especially in the protected inlets at the center of the park. Leleiwi often attracts endangered sea turtles, making this one of Hawaii's most popular snorkeling spots. The beach is 4 miles out of town on Kalanianaole Avenue. Facilities include restrooms, showers, lifeguards, picnic pavilions, and paved walkways. There's also a marine-life facility here.

SOUTH POINT
GREEN SAND BEACH (PAPAKOLEA BEACH) ✪

Hawaii's famous green-sand beach is located at the base of Puu o Mahana, an old cinder cone spilling into the sea. The place has its problems: It's difficult to reach; the open bay is often rough; there are no facilities, fresh water, or shade from the relentless sun; and howling winds scour the point. Nevertheless, each year the unusual emerald-green sands attract thousands of oglers, who follow a well-worn four-wheel-drive-only road for 2½ miles to the top of a cliff, which you have to climb down to reach the beach (the south end offers the safest path). The "sand" is actually crushed olivine, a green semiprecious mineral found in eruptive rocks and meteorites. If the surf's up, just check out the beach from the cliff's edge; if the water's calm, it's generally safe to swim and dive.

To get to Green Sand Beach from the boat ramp at South Point, follow the four-wheel-drive trail; even if you have a four-wheel-drive vehicle, you may want to walk, because the trail is very, very bad in parts. Make sure you have appropriate closed-toed footwear: tennis shoes or hiking boots. The trail is relatively flat, but you're usually walking into the wind as you head toward the beach. The beginning of the trail is lava. After the first 10 to 15 minutes of walking, the lava disappears and the trail begins to cross pastureland. After about 30 to 40 minutes more, you'll see an eroded cinder cone by the water; continue to the edge, and there lie the green sands below.

The best way to reach the beach is to go over the edge from the cinder cone. (It looks like walking around the south side of the cone would be easier, but it's not.) From the cinder cone, go over the overhang of the rock, and you'll see a trail.

Going down to the beach is very difficult and treacherous, as you'll be able to see from the top. You'll have to make it over and around big lava boulders, dropping down 4 to 5 feet from boulder to boulder in certain spots. And don't forget that you'll have to climb back up. Look before you start; if you have any hesitation, don't go down (you get a pretty good view from the top, anyway).

Warning: When you get to the beach, watch the waves for about 15 minutes and make sure they don't break over the entire beach. If you walk on the beach, always keep one eye on the ocean and stick close to the rock wall. There can be strong rip currents here, and it's imperative to avoid them. Allow a minimum of 2 to 3 hours for this entire excursion.

6 Watersports

For general advice on the activities listed below, see "The Active Vacation Planner," in chapter 2.

If you want to rent beach toys, like snorkel gear or boogie boards, the beach concessions at all the big resorts, as well as tour desks and dive shops, offer equipment rentals and sometimes lessons for beginners. The cheapest places to get great rental equipment are **Snorkel Bob's,** in the parking lot of Huggo's Restaurant at 75–5831 Kahakai Rd., at Alii Drive, Kailua-Kona (© **808/ 329-0770;** www.snorkelbob.com), and **Planet Ocean Watersports,** 200 Kaneolehua Ave. (© **800/265-6819** or 808/935-7277; www.hawaiidive.com).

BOATING

For fishing charters, see "Sportfishing: The Hunt for Granders," later in this chapter.

Body Glove Cruises ✦   The *Body Glove,* a 55-foot trimaran that carries up to 100 passengers, runs an adventurous sail-snorkel-dive cruise at a reasonable price. You'll be greeted with fresh Kona coffee, fruit, and breakfast pastries; you'll then sail north of Kailua to Pawai Bay, a marine preserve where you can snorkel, scuba dive, swim, or just hang out on the deck for a couple of hours. After a buffet deli lunch spread, you might want to take the plunge off the boat's water slide or diving board before heading back to Kailua Pier. The boat departs daily from the pier at 9am and returns at 1:30pm. The only thing you need to bring is a towel; snorkeling equipment (and scuba equipment, if you choose to dive) is provided. *Money-saving tip:* The afternoon trip is $32 cheaper for adults.

Kailua Pier. © 800/551-8911 or 808/326-7122. www.bodyglovehawaii.com. Morning cruise $84 adults, $46 children 6–12, free for children under 5; afternoon cruise $52 adults, $32 children 6–12, free for children under 5; additional $40 for certified scuba divers with own equipment ($50 without own equipment) and $60 additional for introductory scuba; whale-watching with Greenpeace Hawaii (Dec–Apr) $52 adults, $32 children 6–12, free for children under 5.

Captain Beans' Cruises   Captain Beans' runs Kona's most popular dinner sails on a 150-foot catamaran, which can accommodate about 290 passengers. The 2-hour cruise includes dinner, cocktails, dancing, and Hawaiian entertainment.

Kailua Pier. © 800/831-5541 or 808/329-2955. www.robertshawaii.com. $52 per person; you must be 21 to board the boat.

Captain Dan McSweeney's Year-Round Whale-Watching Adventures ✦✦✦   Hawaii's most impressive visitors—45-foot humpback whales— return to the waters off Kona every winter. Captain Dan McSweeney, a whale researcher for more than 25 years, is always here to greet them, as well as other whales who spend the warmer months in Hawaiian waters. Because Captain Dan works daily with the whales, he has no problem finding them. Frequently, he drops an underwater microphone into the water so you can listen to their songs. If the whales aren't singing, he may use his underwater video camera to show you what's going on. In humpback season—roughly December to April— Dan makes two 3-hour trips daily. From July 1 to December 20, he schedules one morning trip on Tuesday, Thursday, and Saturday to look for pilot, sperm, false killer, melon-headed, pygmy killer, and beaked whales. Captain Dan guarantees a sighting, or he'll take you out again for free. There are no cruises in May and June; that's when he goes whale-watching in Alaska.

Honokohau Harbor. © **888/WHALE6** or 808/322-0028. www.ilovewhales.com. $55 adults, $5 children under 11.

Captain Zodiac   If you'd prefer to take a **snorkel cruise to Kealakekua Bay** in a small boat, go in Captain Zodiac's 16-passenger, 24-foot inflatable rubber life raft. The boat takes you on a wild ride 14 miles down the Kona Coast to Kealakekua, where you'll spend about an hour snorkeling in the bay and then enjoy snacks and beverages at the picnic snorkel site. Trips are twice daily, from 8am to 12:15pm and from 12:45 to 5pm. *Warning:* Pregnant women and those with bad backs should avoid this often-bumpy ride.

Gentry's Marina, Honokohau Harbor. © **808/329-3199.** www.captainzodiac.com. $78 adults, $63 children 3–12.

Fair Wind Snorkeling and Diving Adventures ★★★ *(Kids)*   One of the best ways to snorkel Kealakekua Bay, the marine-life preserve that's one of the best snorkel spots in Hawaii, is on Fair Wind's half-day **sail-and-snorkel cruise to Kealakekua.** The company's 60-foot catamaran holds up to 100 passengers. The morning cruise, which leaves from Keauhou Bay at 9am and returns at 1:30pm, includes breakfast, lunch, snorkel gear, and lessons; it goes for $87 for adults and $50 for children ages 4 to 12 (free for those 3 and under). The afternoon cruise is a little shorter and a little cheaper: It runs from 2 to 5:30pm and includes snacks, sailing, and snorkeling, at a cost of $55 for adults and $35 for kids 4 to 12.

Fair Wind also has daily 3- and 4-hour **Inflatable Raft snorkel cruises** from Kailua Pier, aboard a 28-foot hard-bottom Ridged Inflatable boat. The trip includes stops at two snorkel sites (Kealakekua Marine Preserve and Honaunua), snacks, and a historical/cultural tour on the return (including stops to look in sea caves and lava tubes). Only 14 people are booked at a time. The cost for the morning cruise is $73 for adults and $60 for children ages 6 to 12 (you must be 6 years or older to go); the afternoon cruise is $55 for adults and $45 for children ages 6 to 12.

© **800/677-9461** or 808/322-2788. www.fair-wind.com. $55–$87 adults, $35–$60 children (prices vary depending on cruise).

Kamanu Charters ★★   This sleek catamaran, 36 feet long and 22 feet wide, provides a laid-back sail-snorkel cruise from Honokohau Harbor to Pawai Bay. The 3½-hour trip includes a tropical lunch (deli sandwiches, chips, fresh island fruit, and beverages), snorkeling gear, and personalized instruction for first-time snorkelers. The *Kamanu* sails Monday through Saturday (weather permitting) at 9am and 1:30pm; it can hold up to 24 people.

Honokohau Harbor. © **800/348-3091** or 808/329-2021. www.kamanu.com. $65 adults, $45 children under 12.

BODYBOARDING (BOOGIE BOARDING) & BODYSURFING

On the Kona side of the island, the best beaches for bodyboarding and bodysurfing are **Hapuna Beach, White Sands Beach,** and **Kekaha Kai State Park.** On the east side, try **Leleiwi Beach.**

KAYAKING

OCEAN KAYAKING   Imagine sitting at sea level, eye-to-eye with a turtle, a dolphin, even a whale—it's possible in an oceangoing kayak. Anyone can kayak: Just get in, find your balance, and paddle. After a few minutes of instruction and

Frommer's Favorite Big Island Experiences

Creeping Up to the Ooze. Hawaii Volcanoes National Park is a work in progress, thanks to Kilauea Volcano, which pours red-hot lava into the sea and adds land to the already-big Big Island every day. Since the ongoing eruption began in 1983, Kilauea's been bubbling and oozing in a mild-mannered way that lets you walk right up to the creeping lava flow for an up-close-and-personal encounter.

Going Underwater at Kealakekua Bay. The islands have lots of extraordinary snorkel and dive sites, but none are so easily accessible or have as much to offer as mile-wide Kealakekua Bay, an uncrowded marine preserve on the South Kona Coast. Here, you can swim with dolphins, sea turtles, octopi, and every species of tropical fish that calls Hawaii's waters home.

Discovering Old Hawaii at Puuhonua O Honaunau National Historical Park. Protected by a huge rock wall, this sacred Honaunau site was once a refuge for ancient Hawaiian warriors. Today, you can walk the consecrated grounds and glimpse a former way of life in a partially restored 16th-century village, complete with thatched huts, canoes, forbidding idols, and a temple that holds the bones of 23 Hawaiian chiefs.

Stargazing from Mauna Kea. A jacket, beach mat, and binoculars are all you need to see every star and planet in this ultra-clean atmosphere, where the visibility is so keen that 11 nations have set up telescopes (2 of them the biggest in the world) to probe deep space.

Watching for Whales. Humpback whales pass through waters off the Kona Coast every December through April. To spot them from shore, head down to the Keahole National Energy Lab, just south of the Kona airport, and keep your eyes peeled as you walk the shoreline. To get here, follow Queen Kaahumanu Highway (Hwy. 19) toward the Keahole airport; 6 miles outside of town, look for the sign NATURAL ENERGY LAB, and turn left. Just after the road takes a sharp turn to the right, there's a small paved parking area with restrooms; a beach trail is on the ocean side of the lot.

Savoring a Cup of Kona Coffee. It's just one of those things you have to do while you're on the Big Island. For a truly authentic cup of java, head upcountry to **Holuakoa Cafe,** on Mamalahoa Highway (Hwy. 180) in

---

a little practice in a calm area (like the lagoon in front of the **King Kamehameha's Kona Beach Hotel**), you'll be ready to explore. Beginners can practice their skills in **Kailua** and **Kealakekua bays;** intermediates might try paddling from **Honokohau Harbor** to **Kekaha Kai Beach Park;** the **Hamakua Coast** is a challenge for experienced kayakers.

You can rent one- and two-person kayaks (and other ocean toys) from **Kona Beach Shack,** on the beach in front of the King Kamehameha's Kona Beach Hotel (© **808/329-7494**), starting at $15 for 2 hours and $5 for each additional hour. The price is the same for one- and two-person kayaks.

Holualoa (© 808/322-2233), where owner Meggi Worbach buys green coffee beans from local farmers, roasts and grinds them, and pours you the freshest cup of coffee you've ever had.

Hanging Out in Waipio Valley. Pack a picnic and head for this gorgeously lush valley that time forgot. Delve deep into the jungle on foot, comb the black-sand beach, or just laze the day away by a babbling stream, the tail end of a 1,000-foot waterfall.

Chasing Rainbows at Akaka Falls. When the light is right, a perfect prism is formed and a rainbow leaps out of this spectacular 442-foot waterfall, about 11 miles north of Hilo. Take time to roam through the surrounding rain forest, where you're sure to have close encounters with exotic birds, aromatic plumeria trees, and shocking red-torch ginger.

Gawking at the Day's Catch in Honokohau Harbor. Every afternoon between 4 and 5pm, local fishermen pull into the fuel dock to weigh in their big-game fish. And when we say big, we mean it: We're talking 1,000-pound blue marlins and 150-pound yellowfin tunas, plus plenty of scale-tipping mahimahi, ono (also known as wahoo), and others. Sit in the bleachers and check out these magnificent creatures. Afterward, you can walk the docks, inspect the boats, and chat with captains and crew.

Hunting for Petroglyphs. Archaeologists still aren't sure who's responsible for these ancient rock carvings, but the majority of Hawaii's are found in the 233-acre Puako Petroglyph Archaeological District, near Mauna Lani Resort. The best time to go looking for canoes, turtles, dancers, and family groups is in the cool early morning or late afternoon. There are more than 3,000 petroglyphs in this area alone—see how many you can spot!

Shopping at the Hilo Farmers Market. For less than $10, you can buy a pound of rambutan (a sweet Indonesian fruit), a bouquet of tropical orchids, and a couple of tasty foot-long Hawaiian laulaus (pork, chicken, or fish steamed in ti leaves). But be sure to arrive early—the market opens at sunrise—because many of the 60 or so vendors quickly sell out.

Aloha Kayak ★★★ (© 877/322-1441 or 808/322-2868; www.alohakayak. com) has a unique tour from Keauhou Bay and the Captain Cook Monument, with Hawaiian guides showing you their "secret" spots (including sea caves) and snorkeling areas, abundant with fish and turtles. The tours are either 4 hours ($65 adults, $3 for children ages 12 and under) or 2½ hours ($50 adults, $25 children 12 and under) and include all equipment, beverages, snorkeling gear, and snacks.

FRESHWATER FLUMING Years ago, the best thing to do on a hot summer day was to grab an old inner tube and go "fluming" down the Kohala Sugar

Plantation irrigation system. There were only two problems: You had to trespass to get to the elaborate ditch system, and the water was cold. But the opportunity to float past a pristine rain forest, over ravines, and under waterfalls was worth the risk of getting caught (and worth a numb rear end). You no longer have to worry about either problem. **Flumin' da Ditch** (© 877/449-6922 or 808/889-6922; www.flumindaditch.com) offers perfectly legal access to this North Kohala area, and guided tours in high-tech, double-hulled inflatable kayaks, with knowledgeable guides talking story about the history, culture, and legends of the area. The tour includes snacks. When the operation first started years ago it was fabulous, but on our last trip we were somewhat disappointed. To ensure a good trip, tell them you want to be in the kayak with the guide (otherwise you will miss out on all the history, culture, and so on). Wear a swimsuit or bring a change of clothing, because the kayaks pass under waterfalls and through water pouring in from the intake systems—getting wet is part of the fun, and the whole experience is one you won't forget. The 2½-hour cruises are $85 for adults, $65 for kids 5 to 18. No experience is necessary, but children must be at least 5.

PARASAILING

Get a bird's-eye view of Hawaii's pristine waters with **UFO Parasail** (© 800/ FLY-4UFO or 808/325-5836; www.ufoparasail.net). UFO offers parasail rides daily from 8am to 2pm from Kailua Pier. The cost is $50 for the standard flight of 7 minutes of air time at 400 feet and $60 for a deluxe 10-minute ride at 800 feet. You can go up alone or with a friend; no experience is necessary. *Tip:* Take the early-bird special (when the light is fantastic and the price is right) at 8am for just $45 (for 400 ft.) and $55 (for 800 ft.).

SCUBA DIVING

The Big Island's leeward coast offers some of the best diving in the world; the water is calm (protected by the two 13,000-ft. volcanoes), warm (75–81°F/24–27°C), and clear (visibility is more than 100 ft. year-round). Want to swim with fast-moving game fish? Try **Ulua Cave** at the north end of the Kohala Coast. There are nearly 2 dozen dive operators on the west side of the Big Island, plus a couple in Hilo. They offer everything from scuba certification courses to guided boat dives.

One of Kona's most popular dive operators is **Eco Adventures** (★, King Kamehameha's Kona Beach Hotel, Kailua-Kona (© 800/949-3483 or 808/ 329-7116; www.eco-adventure.com). A two-tank morning dive (ask to go on one of the 36-ft. or 50-ft. boats, which have bathrooms and hot showers) costs $102 with your own gear and includes lunch. The late-afternoon two-tank dive, including a one-tank manta-ray dive, is $102. Gear is available for $5 per item. Note that validated parking in the hotel parking lot is $4 for 6 hours.

Another popular dive operator is **Jack's Diving Locker,** 75–5819 Alii Dr. (© 800/345-4807 or 808/329-7585; www.jacksdivinglocker.com), which offers two-tank morning or sunset dives off either a 23-foot boat or a 38-foot boat, starting at $90 per person with your own gear or $100 with rental equipment. Jack's also offers shore dives for those who tend to get seasick on a boat; the cost is $50 per person for one tank, including gear.

On the Hilo side, check out **Planet Ocean Watersports** (★, 200 Kanoelehua Ave., Hilo (© 800/265-6819 or 808/935-7277; www.hawaiidive.com), which offers two-tank boat dives ($75 for the 1st person, $60 each for 2, and $50 each for 3 or more) and also rents scuba and snorkeling gear and other equipment.

HOT-LAVA DIVES   Hilo's **Nautilus Dive Center,** 382 Kamehameha Ave., between Open Market and the Shell Gas Station (© **808/935-6939;** www. nautilusdivehilo.com), offers a very unusual opportunity for advanced divers: diving where the lava flows into the ocean. For $150 to $200 each, four divers can take two-tank dives where the molten lava pours into the ocean. "Sometimes you can feel the pressure from the sound waves as the lava explodes," owner Bill De Rooy says. "Sometimes you have perfect visibility to the color show of your life." As we went to press, these hot lava dives were currently on hold (an unstable collapse of recent lava field sent 20 acres of lava into the ocean, fortunately no one was injured). Call to see if the dives have resumed.

NIGHT DIVING WITH MANTA RAYS ★★   A little less risky—but still something you'll never forget—is swimming with manta rays on a night dive. These giant, harmless creatures, with wingspans that reach up to 14 feet, glide gracefully through the water to feed on plankton. **Eco Adventures** ★, King Kamehameha's Kona Beach Hotel, Kailua-Kona (© **800/949-3483** or 808/329-7116; www.eco-adventure.com), will take you on a two-tank afternoon/evening dive for $102. **Sandwich Isle Divers,** 75–5729 Alii Dr., in the back of the Kona Market Place (© **888/743-3483** or 808/329-9188; www. sandwichisledivers.com), offers one-tank nighttime manta dives for $75, including equipment ($65 if you have your own gear).

WEEKLONG DIVES   If you're looking for an all-diving vacation, you might think about spending a week on the 80-foot ***Kona Aggressor II*** ★ (© **800/344-5662** or 808/329-8182; www.pac-aggressor.com), a live-aboard dive boat that promises to provide you with unlimited underwater exploration, including day and night dives, along 85 miles of the Big Island's coastline. You may spot harmless 70-foot whale sharks, plus not-so-harmless tiger and hammerhead sharks, as well as dolphins, whales, monk seals, and sea turtles. You'll navigate through caves and lava tubes, glide along huge reefs, and take on the open ocean, too. Ten divers are accommodated in five staterooms. Guided dives are available, but as long as you're certified, just log in with the dive master and you're free to follow the limits of your dive computer. It's $1,995 for 7 days (without gear), which isn't so bad when you consider the excellent accommodations and the all-inclusive meals. Rental gear, from cameras (starting at $175 a week) to dive gear ($120) to computers ($100), is available.

SNORKELING

If you come to Hawaii and don't snorkel, you'll miss half the fun. The year-round calm waters along the Kona and Kohala coasts are home to spectacular marine life. Some of the best snorkeling areas on the Kona-Kohala Coast include **Hapuna Beach Cove,** at the foot of the Hapuna Beach Prince Hotel, a secluded little cove where you can snorkel not only with schools of yellow tangs, needlefish, and green sea turtles, but also, once in a while, with somebody rich and famous. But if you've never snorkeled in your life, **Kahaluu Beach Park** is the best place to start. Just wade in and look down at the schools of fish in the bay's black-lava tide pools. Another "hidden" snorkeling spot is off the rocks north of the boat launch ramp at **Honaunau Bay.** Other great snorkel sites include **White Sands Beach,** as well as **Kekaha Kai State Park, Hookena, Honaunau, Puako,** and **Spencer** beach parks.

In addition to **Snorkel Bob's** and **Planet Ocean Watersports,** mentioned in the intro to this section, you can also rent gear from **Kona Coast Divers** ★, 74–5614 Palani Rd., Kailua-Kona (© **808/329-8802**).

SNORKELING CRUISES TO KEALAKEKUA BAY ★★★   Probably the best snorkeling for all levels can be found in **Kealakekua Bay.** The calm waters of this underwater preserve teem with a wealth of marine life. Coral heads, lava tubes, and underwater caves all provide an excellent habitat for Hawaii's vast array of tropical fish, making mile-wide Kealakekua the Big Island's best accessible spot for snorkeling and diving. Without looking very hard, you can see octopi, free-swimming moray eels, parrot fish, and goat fish; once in a while, a pod of spinner dolphins streaks across the bay. Kealakekua is reachable only by boat; in addition to **Fair Wind** ★★★ and **Captain Zodiac** (p. 289), check out **Sea Quest Snorkeling and Rafting Adventures** (© 808/329-RAFT; www.seaquest hawaii.com), which offers unique coastal adventures through sea caves and lava tubes on the Kona Coast, as well as snorkeling plunges into the ocean at the Historic Place of Refuge in Honaunau and at the Captain Cook Monument at Kealakekua. The small size of the rigid-hull, inflatable rafts allows the six-passenger vessels to go where larger boats can't. The 4-hour morning tour is $77, while the 3-hour afternoon tour goes for $58.

SNUBA

If you're not quite ready to make the commitment to scuba but you want more time underwater than snorkeling allows, **Big Island Snuba** (© 808/326-7446; www.snubabigisland.com) may be the answer. Just like in scuba, the diver wears a regulator and mask; however, the tank floats on the surface on a raft, and is connected to the diver's regulator by a hose that allows the diver to go 20 to 25 feet down. Snuba can actually be easier than snorkeling, as the water is calmer beneath the surface. With just 15 minutes of instruction, neophytes can be down under. It costs $69 for a 1½-hour dive from the beach, $110 for one day aboard a boat, and $135 for two dives; children must be at least 8.

SPORTFISHING: THE HUNT FOR GRANDERS ★★

If you want to catch fish, it doesn't get any better than the Kona Coast, known internationally as the marlin capital of the world. Big-game fish, including gigantic blue marlin and other Pacific billfish, tuna, mahimahi, sailfish, swordfish, ono (also known as wahoo), and giant trevellies (ulua) roam the waters here. When anglers here catch marlin that weighs 1,000 pounds or more, they call them *granders;* there's even a "wall of fame" on Kailua-Kona's Waterfront Row, honoring 40 anglers who've nailed more than 20 tons of fighting fish.

Nearly 100 charter boats with professional captains and crew offer fishing charters out of **Keauhou, Kawaihae, Honokohau,** and **Kailua Bay harbors.** If you're not an expert angler, the best way to arrange a charter is through a booking agency like the **Charter Desk at Honokohau Marina** (© 888/KONA-4-US or 808/329-5735; charter@aloha.net) or **Charter Services Hawaii** (© 800/567-2650 or 808/334-1881; www.konazone.com). Either one will sort through the more than 40 different types of vessels, fishing specialties, and personalities to match you with the right boat. Prices range from $525 to $750 or so for a full-day exclusive charter (you and up to 5 of your friends have the entire boat to yourself) and about $325 to $424 for a half-day charter on a six-passenger boat.

Serious sportfishers should call the boats directly. They include *Anxious* (© 808/326-1229; www.alohazone.com), *Marlin Magic* (© 808/325-7138), and *Ihu Nui* (© 808/325-1513). If you aren't into hooking a 1,000-pound marlin or 200-pound tuna and just want to go out to catch some smaller fish and have fun, we recommend **Reel Action Light Tackle Sportfishing** ★★

(© 808/325-6811). Light-tackle anglers and saltwater fly fisherman should contact *Sea Genie II* ★★ (© 808/325-5355), which has helped several anglers set world records. All of the above outfitters operate out of Honokohau Harbor.

Most big-game charter boats carry six passengers max, and the boats supply all equipment, bait, tackle, and lures. No license is required. Many captains now tag and release marlins; other fish caught belong to the boat (not to you, the charter)—that's island style. If you want to eat your catch or have your trophy marlin mounted, tell the captain before you go.

SUBMARINE DIVES

This is the stuff movies are made of: venturing 100 feet below the sea in a high-tech, 65-foot submarine. On a 1-hour trip, you'll be able to explore a 25-acre coral reef that's teeming with schools of colorful tropical fish. Look closely, and you may catch glimpses of moray eels—or even a shark—in and around the reef. On selected trips, you'll watch as divers swim among these aquatic creatures, luring them to the view ports for face-to-face observation. Call **Atlantis Submarines** ★, 75–5669 Alii Dr. (across the street from Kailua Pier, underneath Flashback's Restaurant), Kailua-Kona (© 800/548-6262; www.go-atlantis.com). Trips leave daily between 10am and 3pm. The cost is $84 for adults and $42 for children under 12. *Note:* The ride is safe for everyone, but skip it if you suffer from claustrophobia.

SURFING

Most surfing off the Big Island is for the experienced only. As a general rule, the beaches on the north and west shores of the island get northern swells in winter, while those on the south and east shores get southern swells in summer. Experienced surfers should check out the waves at **Pine Trees** (north of Kailua-Kona), **Lyman's** (off Alii Dr. in Kailua-Kona), and **Banyan's** (also off Alii Dr.); reliable spots on the east side of the island include **Honolii Point** (outside Hilo), **Hilo Bay Front Park,** and **Keaukaha Beach Park.** But there are a few sites where beginners can catch a wave, too: You might want to try **Kahuluu Beach,** where the waves are manageable most of the year; other surfers are around to give you pointers, and there's a lifeguard on shore.

Ocean Eco Tours (© 808/324-SURF; www.oceanecotours.com), owned and operated by veteran surfers Rob Hemshere and Steve Velonza, is the only company on the Big Island that teaches surfing. Private lessons cost $125 per person (including all equipment) and usually last a minimum of 2 hours; 2- to 3-hour group lessons go for $85 (also including all equipment), with a maximum of four students. Both guys love this ancient Hawaiian sport, and their enthusiasm is contagious. The minimum age is 8, and you must be a fairly good swimmer.

Your only Big Island choice for surfboard rentals is **Pacific Vibrations,** 75–5702 Likana Lane (just off Alii Dr., across from the pier), Kailua-Kona (© 808/329-4140; www.laguerdobros.com/pacvib/pacificv.html), where they have short boards for $10 for 24 hours and long boards for $10 to $20.

WINDSURFING

Anaehoomalu Bay (A-Bay), on the Kohala Coast, is one of the best beaches for windsurfing because there are constant 5- to 25-knot winds blowing toward the beach. If you get into trouble, the wind brings you back to shore, instead of taking you out to sea. **Ocean Sports,** at the Outrigger Waikoloa Beach Hotel (© 808/885-5555; www.hawaiioceansports.com), starts beginners on a land simulator to teach them how to handle the sail and "come about" (turn around and come back). Instruction is $50 an hour; after a ½ hour or so of instruction on land, you're ready to hit the water. If you already know how to windsurf, equipment rental is $25 an hour. Advanced windsurfers should head to **Puako** and **Hilo Bay.**

7 Hiking & Camping

For information on camping and hiking, contact **Hawaii Volcanoes National Park,** P.O. Box 52, Hawaii National Park, HI 96718 (© 808/985-6000; www. nps.gov/havo); **Puuhonua O Honaunau National Historic Park,** Honaunau, HI 96726 (© 808/328-2288; www.nps.gov/puho); the **State Division of Forestry and Wildlife,** P.O. Box 4849, Hilo, HI 96720 (© 808/947-4221; www.hawaii.gov); the **State Division of Parks,** P.O. Box 936, Hilo, HI 96721 (© 808/974-6200; www.hawaii.gov); the **County Department of Parks and Recreation,** 25 Aupuni St., Hilo, HI 96720 (© 808/961-8311; www.hawaii-county.com); or the **Hawaii Sierra Club** (© 808/959-0452;www.hi.sierraclub. org). For other sources and general tips on hiking and camping in Hawaii, see "The Active Vacation Planner," in chapter 2.

Camping equipment is *not* available for rent on the Big Island. Plan to bring your own or buy it at **C&S Outfitters,** in Waimea (© 808/885-5005), or the **Surplus Store,** in Hilo (© 808/935-6398).

GUIDED DAY HIKES   If you'd like to discover natural Hawaii off the beaten path but don't necessarily want to sleep under a tree to do it, a day hike is your ticket. Call the following outfitters ahead of time (even before you arrive) for a schedule of trips; they fill up quickly.

A long-time resident of Hawaii, Dr. Hugh Montgomery of **Hawaiian Walkways** ★, Honokaa (© **800/457-7759** or 808/775-0372; www.hawaiian walkways.com), who was recently named the "Tour Operator of the Year," by the Hawaii Ecotourism Association of Hawaii, offers a variety of options on a scheduled or custom basis, ranging from excursions that skirt the rim of immense valleys to hikes through the clouds on the volcano. Half-day hikes are $95 (50% off for children 12 and younger) and custom hikes are $175 for the first hiker, then $100 each additional hiker (10% discount for 4 or more), 50% off for children 12 and younger. Prices include food, beverages, and equipment.

Naturalist and educator Rob Pacheco of **Hawaii Forest & Trail** ★★, 74–5035-B Queen Kaahumanu Hwy. (behind the Chevron Station), Kailua-Kona (© **800/464-1993** or 808/331-8505; www.hawaii-forest.com), will take you out for day trips to some of the island's most remote, pristine, natural areas, some of which he has exclusive access to. Rob's fully trained staff narrates the entire trip, offering extensive natural, geological, and cultural history inter-pretation (and more than a little humor). Because the tours are limited to a max-imum of 10 people, they are highly personalized to meet the group's interests and abilities. A day with Hawaii Forest & Trail may just be the highlight of your Big Island experience. Options include waterfall adventures, rain-forest discov-ery hikes, birding tours, a caving adventure, and even a mule ride on the rim of Pulolu Valley (see the box "Riding a Mule on the Big Island," on p. 303). Each tour involves 2 to 4 hours of easy-to-moderate walking, over terrain man-ageable by anyone in average physical condition. Half-day trips, including snacks, beverages, water, and gear, start at $89 for adults, $69 for children ages 8 to 12.

GUIDED NIGHT HIKES   For an off-the-beaten-track experience, **Arnott's Lodge,** 98 Apapane Rd., Hilo (© **808/969-7097;** www.arnottslodge.com), offers a day-long tour of Hawaii Volcanoes National Park, followed by a night lava hike right up to the fiery flow. The 9½-hour tour leaves the lodge at noon and spends most of the afternoon in the park. The lava hike (a 4-hour round-trip and somewhat strenuous experience) takes place as the sun is setting, so you can see the glow of the flow both during and after sunset. The cost is $75.

HAWAII VOLCANOES NATIONAL PARK ★★★

This national park is a wilderness wonderland. Miles of trails not only lace the lava but also cross deserts, rain forests, beaches, and, in winter, snow at 13,650 feet. Trail maps are sold at park headquarters and are highly recommended. Check conditions before you head out. Come prepared for hot sun, cold rain, and hard wind any time of year. Always wear sunscreen and bring plenty of drinking water.

Warning: If you have heart or respiratory problems or if you're pregnant, don't attempt any hike in the park; the fumes will bother you.

TRAILS IN THE PARK

KILAUEA IKI TRAIL   You'll experience the work of the volcano goddess, Pele, firsthand on this hike. The 4-mile trail begins at the visitor center, descends through a forest of ferns into still-fuming Kilauea Iki Crater, and then crosses the crater floor past the vent where a 1959 lava blast shot a fountain of fire 1,900 feet into the air for 36 days. Allow 2 hours for this fair-to-moderate hike.

HALEMAUMAU TRAIL   This moderate 3½-mile hike starts at the visitor center, goes down 500 feet to the floor of Kilauea crater, crosses the crater, and ends at Halemaumau Overlook.

DEVASTATION TRAIL   Up on the rim of Kilauea Iki Crater, you can see what an erupting volcano did to a once-flourishing ohia forest. The scorched earth with its ghostly tree skeletons stands in sharp contrast to the rest of the nearby lush forest that escaped the rain of hot molten lava, cinder, and debris. Everyone can—and should—take this ½-mile hike on a paved path across the eerie bed of black cinders. The trailhead is on Crater Rim Road at Puu Puai Overlook.

KIPUKA PUAULU (BIRD PARK) TRAIL   This easy, 1½-mile, hour-long hike lets you see native Hawaiian flora and fauna in a little oasis of living nature in a field of lava. For some reason (gravity or rate of flow or protection from the volcano goddess, Pele, perhaps), the once red-hot lava skirted this miniforest and let it survive. At the trailhead on Mauna Loa Road is a display of plants and birds you'll see on the walk. Go early in the morning or in the evening (or even better, just after a rain) to see native birds like the *apapane* (a small, bright-red bird with black wings and tail that sips the nectar of the red-blossom ohia lehua trees) and the iiwi (larger and orange-vermilion colored, with a curved orange bill). Native trees along the trail include giant ohia, koa, soapberry, kolea, and mamani.

MAUNA LOA TRAIL   Probably the most challenging hike in Hawaii, this 7½-mile trail goes from the lookout to a cabin at the Red Hill at 10,035 feet, then 12 more miles up to the primitive Mauna Loa summit cabin at 13,250 feet, where the climate is called subarctic, whiteouts are common, and overnight temperatures are below freezing year-round; there's often snow in July. This 4-day round-trip requires advance planning, great physical condition, and registration at the visitor center. Call ☏ **808/985-6000** for maps and details. The trailhead begins where Mauna Loa Road ends, 14 miles north of Highway 11.

CAMPGROUNDS & WILDERNESS CABINS IN THE PARK

The only park campground accessible by car is **Namakani Paio,** which has a pavilion with picnic tables and a fireplace (no wood is provided). Tent camping is free; no reservations are required. Stays are limited to 7 days per year. Backpack camping at hiker shelters and cabins is available on a first-come, shared basis, but you must register at the visitor center.

Kilauea Military Camp, a mile from the visitor center, is a rest-and-recreation camp for active and retired military personnel. Facilities include 75 one- to three-bedroom cabins with fireplaces (some with a Jacuzzi), cafeteria, bowling alley, bar, general store, weight room, and tennis and basketball courts. Rates are based on rank, ranging from $46 to $120 a night. Call ☏ **808/967-8333** on the Big Island, or 808/438-6707 on Oahu (www.kmc-volcano.com).

The following cabins and campgrounds are the best of what the park and surrounding area have to offer:

HALAPE SHELTER   This backcountry site, about 7 miles from the nearest road, is the place for those who want to get away from it all and enjoy their own private white-sand beach. The small, three-sided stone shelter, with a roof but no floor, can accommodate two people comfortably, but four's a crowd. You could pitch a tent inside, but if the weather is nice, you're better off setting up outside. There's a catchment water tank, but check with rangers on the water situation before hiking in (sometimes they don't have accurate information on the water level; bring extra water just in case). The only other facility is a pit toilet. Go on weekdays if you're really looking for an escape. It's free to stay here, but you're limited to 3 nights. Permits are available at the visitor center on a first-come, first-served basis, no earlier than noon on the day before your trip. For more information, call ☏ **808/985-6000.**

NAMAKANI PAIO CAMPGROUNDS & CABINS   Just 5 miles west of the park entrance is a tall eucalyptus forest where you can pitch a tent in an open grassy field. The trail to Kilauea Crater is just a ½ mile away. No permit is needed, but stays are limited to 7 days. Facilities include pavilions with barbecues and a fireplace, picnic tables, outdoor dish-washing areas, restrooms, and drinking water. There are also 10 cabins that accommodate up to four people each. Each cabin has a covered picnic table at the entrance and a fireplace with a grill. Toilets, sinks, and hot showers are available in a separate building. You can get groceries and gas in the town of Volcano, 4 miles away. Make cabin reservations through **Volcano House,** P.O. Box 53, Hawaii National Park, HI 96718 (☏ **808/967-7321**); the cost is $40 per night for two adults (and 2 children), $48 for three adults, and $56 for four adults.

WAIMANU VALLEY'S MULIWAI TRAIL

This difficult 2- to 3-day backpacking adventure—only for the hardy—takes you to a hidden valley some call Eden. It probably looks just as it did when Captain James Cook first saw it, with virgin waterfalls and pools and spectacular views. The trail, which goes from sea level to 1,350 feet and down to the sea again, takes more than 9 hours to hike in and more than 10 hours to hike out. Be prepared for clouds of bloodthirsty mosquitoes, and look out for wild pigs. If it's raining, forget it: You'll have 13 streams to cross before you reach the rim of Waimanu Valley, and rain means flash floods.

You must get permission to camp in Waimanu Valley from the **Division of Forestry and Wildlife,** P.O. Box 4849, Hilo, HI 96720-0849 (© **808/974-4221**). Permits to the nine designated campsites are assigned by number. They're free, but you're limited to a 7-day stay. Facilities are limited to two composting pit toilets. The best water in the valley is from the stream on the western wall, a 15-minute walk up a trail from the beach. All water must be treated before drinking. The water from the Waimanu Stream drains from a swamp, so skip it. Be sure to pack out what you take in.

To get to the trailhead, take Highway 19 to the turnoff for Honokaa; drive 9½ miles to the Waipio Valley Lookout. Unless you have four-wheel-drive, this is where your hike begins. Walk down the road and wade the Wailoa Stream; then cross the beach and go to the northwest wall. The trail starts here and goes up the valley floor, past a swamp, and into a forest before beginning a series of switchbacks that parallel the coastline. These switchbacks go up and down about 14 gulches. At the ninth gulch, about two-thirds of the way along the trail, is a shelter. After the shelter, the trail descends into Waimanu Valley, which looks like a smaller version of Waipio Valley but without a sign of human intrusion.

8 Golf & Other Outdoor Pursuits

The not-for-profit group **Friends for Fitness,** P.O. Box 1671, Kailua-Kona, HI 96745 (© **808/322-0033**), offers a free brochure on physical activities (from aerobic classes to dancing to yoga) in West Hawaii; they will gladly mail it to you upon request.

GOLF

For last-minute and discount tee times, call **Stand-by Golf** (© **888/645-BOOK** or 808/322-BOOK) between 7am and 11pm. Stand-by offers discounted (10%–40%), guaranteed tee times for same-day or next-day golfing.

If your game's a little rusty, you might head for the **Swing Zone,** 74–5562 Makala Blvd. (corner of Kuikuni Hwy., by the Old Airport Park), Kailua-Kona (© **808/329-6909**), which has everything to polish up your game. The driving range has 27 mats and 10 grass tee spaces; the practice putting green and chipping area is free with a bucket of balls (60 balls for $6); and the pro shop sells limited supplies (rental clubs are available too for just $2). For $6, you can play a round on the 18-hole, all-grass putting course built in the shape of the Big Island (they'll even supply the putter and a ball for free).

In addition to the courses below, we love the fabulous **Hualalai Golf Course** ★★★, at Four Seasons Resort Hualalai (p. 240). Unfortunately, it's open only to resort guests—but for committed golfers, this Jack Nicklaus–designed championship course is reason enough to pay the sky-high rates.

THE KOHALA COAST

Hapuna Golf Course ★★★ Since its opening in 1992, this 18-hole championship course has been named the most environmentally sensitive course by *Golf* magazine, as well as "Course of the Future" by the U.S. Golf Association. Designed by Arnold Palmer and Ed Seay, this 6,027-yard, links-style course extends from the shoreline to 700 feet above sea level, with views of the pastoral Kohala Mountains and the Kohala coastline. The elevation changes on the course keep it challenging (watch out for the wind at the higher elevations!). There are a few elevated tee boxes and only 40 bunkers. Facilities include putting greens, driving ranges, lockers, showers, a pro shop, and restaurants.

Hapuna Beach Prince Hotel, off Hwy. 19 (near mile marker 69). ✆ **808/880-3000**. www.hapunabeach princehotel.com. Greens fees: $145 ($95 for resort guests).

Mauna Kea Golf Course ★★★   This breathtakingly beautiful, par-72, 7,114-yard championship course, designed by Robert Trent Jones Jr., is consistently rated one of the top golf courses in the United States. The signature third hole is 175 yards long; the Pacific Ocean and shoreline cliffs stand between the tee and the green, giving every golfer, from beginner to pro, a real challenge. Another par-3 that confounds duffers is the 11th hole, which drops 100 feet from tee to green and plays down to the ocean, into the steady trade winds. When the trades are blowing, 181 yards might as well be 1,000 yards. Facilities include putting greens, a driving range, lockers and showers, a pro shop, and a restaurant. The course is very popular, especially for early weekend tee times, so book ahead.

Mauna Kea Beach Resort, Hwy. 19 (near mile marker 68). ✆ **808/882-5400**. www.maunakeabeachhotel. com. Greens fees: $195 ($125 for resort guests); twilight rates (after 3pm in the summer and 2pm in the winter) are $110 for everyone.

Mauna Lani Frances I'i Brown Championship Courses ★★★   The **Mauna Lani South Course,** a 7,029-yard, par-72, has an unforgettable ocean hole: the downhill, 221-yard, par-3 seventh, which is bordered by the sea, a salt-and-pepper sand dune, and lush kiawe trees. Depending on the wind, you may need anything from a wood to a wedge to hit the green. The **North Course** may not have the drama of the oceanfront holes, but because it was built on older lava flows, the more extensive indigenous vegetation gives the course a Scottish feel. The hole that's cursed the most is the 140-yard, par-3 17th: It's absolutely beautiful but plays right into the surrounding lava field. Facilities include two driving ranges, a golf shop (with teaching pros), a restaurant, and putting greens.

Mauna Lani Dr., off Hwy. 19 (20 miles north of Kona Airport). ✆ **808/885-6655**. www.maunalani.com. Greens fees: $185 ($120 for resort guests); twilight rates are $75 for everyone all year.

Waikoloa Beach Course ★   This pristine 18-hole, par-70 course certainly reflects designer Robert Trent Jones Jr.'s motto: "Hard par, easy bogey." Most golfers remember the par-5, 505-yard 12th hole, a sharp dogleg left with bunkers in the corner and an elevated tee surrounded by lava. Facilities include a golf shop, restaurant, and driving range.

1020 Keana Pl. (adjacent to the Outrigger Waikoloa and Hilton Waikoloa Village), Waikoloa. ✆ **877/ WAIKOLOA** or 808/886-6060. www.waikoloagolf.com. Greens fees: $165 ($115 for resort guests); twilight fees: $75.

Waikoloa Kings' Course ★   This sister course to the Waikoloa Beach Course is about 500 yards longer. Designed by Tom Weiskopf and Jay Morrish, the 18-hole links-style tract features a double green at the third and sixth holes and several carefully placed bunkers that often come into play due to the ever-present trade winds. Facilities include a pro shop and showers.

600 Waikoloa Beach Dr. (adjacent to the Outrigger Waikoloa and Hilton Waikoloa Village), Waikoloa. ✆ **877/WAIKOLOA** or 808/886-7888. www.waikoloagolf.com. Greens fees: $165 ($115 for resort guests); twilight fees: $75.

Waikoloa Village Golf Club   This semiprivate 18-hole course, with a par-72 for each of the three sets of tees, is hidden in the town of Waikoloa and usually overshadowed by the glamour resort courses along the Kohala Coast. Not only is it a beautiful course with great views, but it also offers some great golfing. The wind can play havoc with your game here (like most Hawaii golf courses), so choose your clubs with caution. Robert Trent Jones Jr. designed this challenging course, inserting his trademark sand traps, slick greens, and great fairways. We're particularly fond of the 18th hole: This par-5, 490-yard thriller doglegs to the left, and the last 75 yards up to the green are water, water, water—always a great way to end the day. Take time to check out the fabulous views of Mauna Kea and Mauna Loa, and—on a very clear day—Maui's Haleakala in the distance.

Waikoloa Rd., Waikoloa Village, off Hwy. 19 (18 miles north of Kona Airport). (C) **808/883-9621**. www. waikoloa.org. Turn left at the Waikoloa sign; it's about 6 miles up, on your left. Greens fees: $100 before 1pm, $55 after 1pm.

THE HAMAKUA COAST

Hamakua Country Club *Value*   As you approach the sugar town of Honokaa, you can't miss this funky nine-hole course, built in the 1920s on a very steep hill overlooking the ocean. It's a par-33, 2,520-yard course that really has room for only about 4½ holes; but somehow, architect Frank Anderson managed to squeeze in nine by crisscrossing holes across fairways—you may never see a lay-out like this again. The best part about Hamakua, though, is the price, just $15. The course is open to nonmembers on weekdays only; you don't need a tee time—just show up. If no one's around, simply drop your $15 in the box and head right to the first tee. Carts aren't allowed because of the steep hills.

On the ocean side of Hwy. 19 (41 miles from Hilo), Honokaa. (C) **808/775-7244**. Greens fees: $15 for 18 holes.

HILO

Hilo Municipal Golf Course   This is a great course for the casual golfer: It's flat, scenic, and often fun. *Warning:* Don't go after a heavy rain (especially in winter), when the fairways can get really soggy and play can slow way down. The rain does keep the course green and beautiful, though. Wonderful trees (monkeypods, coconuts, eucalyptus, banyans) dot the grounds, and the views—of Mauna Kea on one side and Hilo Bay on the other—are breathtaking. This is a course where you can challenge yourself. There are four sets of tees, with a par-71 from all; if you carry a medium handicap, go ahead and play from the back (black) tees (6,325 yd. of play). Getting a tee time can be a challenge as well, because lots of Hilo golfers love this course; weekdays are your best bet.

340 Haihai St. (between Kinoole and Iwalani sts.), Hilo. (C) **808/959-7711**. www.gvhawaii.com. From Hilo, take Hwy. 11 toward Volcano; turn right at Puainako St. (at Prince Kuhio Shopping Center), left on Kinoole, then right on Haihai St. Greens fees: $20 weekdays, $25 Sat–Sun and holidays; cart fee is $15.

Naniloa Country Club   At first glance, this semiprivate, nine-hole course looks pretty flat and short, but once you get beyond the first hole—a wide, straightforward 330-yard par-4—the challenges come. The tree-lined fairways require straight drives, and the huge lake on the second and fifth holes is sure to haunt you. This course is very popular with locals and visitors alike. Rental clubs are available.

120 Banyan Dr. (at the intersection of Hwy. 11 and Hwy. 19). (C) **808/935-3000**. www.gvhawaii.com. Green fees: $25 ($15 Naniloa Hotel guests) Mon–Fri; $30 ($20 Naniloa Hotel guests) Sat–Sun (if you can get a tee time); twilight rates (after 3pm) are $10 less; cart fee is $14.

VOLCANO VILLAGE

Volcano Golf and Country Club   Located at an altitude of 4,200 feet, this public course got its start in 1922, when the Blackshear family put in a green, using old tomato cans for the holes. It now has three sets of tees to choose from, all with a par of 72. The course is unusually landscaped, making use of a few ancient lava flows among the pine and ohia trees. It's considered challenging by locals. *Some tips from the regulars:* Because the course is at such a high altitude, the ball travels farther than you're probably used to, so club down. If you hit the ball off the fairway, take the stroke—you don't want to look for your ball in the lava. Also, play a pitch-and-run game—the greens are slick and your ball just won't stick.

Hwy. 11, on the right side, just after the entrance to Hawaii Volcanoes National Park. © **808/967-7331.** www.gvhawaii.com. Greens fees: $63; includes a shared cart.

BICYCLING & MOUNTAIN BIKING

For mountain-bike and cross-training bike rentals in Kona, see **Dave's Bike and Triathlon Shop,** 75–5669 Alii Dr., across from the Kailua Pier underneath Flashback's Restaurant, behind Atlantis Submarine (© **808/329-4522**). Dave rents brand-name mountain bikes (with full-suspension) for $15 a day or $60 a week (including helmet and water bottle). Feel free to ask Dave for riding advice (such as which routes are the most scenic) and local weather reports. To carry your rented bike around, be sure to get a bike rack for your car ($10 a week).

Hawaiian Pedals ✦, Kona Inn Shopping Village, Alii Drive, Kailua-Kona (© **808/329-2294**), and **Hawaiian Pedals Bike Works,** 75–5599 Lihua St., Kailua-Kona (© **808/326-2453**), www.hawaiianpedals.com, have a huge selection of bikes, from mountain bikes and hybrids ($20 a day, $65 a week) to racing bikes and front-suspension mountain bikes ($25 a day, $105 a week) to full-suspension mountain bikes ($30 a day, $140 a week). Bike racks go for $5 a day, and you pay only for the days you actually use it (the honor system): if you have the rack for a week but only use it for 2 days, you'll be charged just $10. The folks at the shops are friendly and knowledgeable about cycling routes all over the Big Island.

In Waimea, contact **Mauna Kea Mountain Bikes** (© **888/MTB-TOUR,** 808/883-0130, or cell 808/936-TOUR, www.bikehawaii.com). Grant Mitchell can set you up with a mountain bike (starting at $25 for 5 hours or $30 a day) and have it delivered free to your hotel room, along with a helmet, pump, tube, and patch kit. Mitchell also offers guided bike tours (see below).

BIKING AROUND THE BIG ISLAND   When was the last time you bicycled around a tropical island? Jump on a 21-speed mountain bike and do it here. A novice can complete the 225-mile Circle Island tour in 6 days or less; serious bikers do it in 2.

Some tips if you're going to make your way around the island: Plan your trip. Make advance reservations. Get a bike that fits. Get started early in the day— just after sunrise is best. Wear lightweight bike togs and a helmet. Take two water bottles and sunscreen. Bring rain gear. Bring a patch kit, cables, and a lock. And finally, stay on the road, because razor-sharp lava and kiawe thorns can cause blowouts.

GUIDED TOURS   Mauna Kea Mountain Bikes, Inc. (© **888/MTB-TOUR** or 808/883-0130, or cell 808/936-TOUR) offers everything from 3-hour downhill cruises in the historic Kohala mountains to advanced rides down monstrous Mauna Kea. Prices range from $75 to $115.

On the Hilo side, **Aquatic Perceptions,** 111 Banyan Dr., Hilo (© **808/935-9997**), has a number of guided bike tours; a favorite is the Jungle Coast Tour, a 3-hour ride (with some short hikes) along an undulating serpentine road through the "jungles" of Puna down to Lava Trees State Park, then on to the

Kids Riding a Mule on the Big Island

Mule rides used to be done only on Molokai, until 1998, when **Hawaii Forest & Trail Guided Nature Adventures** ★★, 74–5035-B Queen Kaahumanu Hwy. (behind the Chevron), Kailua-Kona (© **800/464-1993** or 808/322-8881; www.hawaii-forest.com), began the **Kohala Mule Trail Adventure**. This unique tour on the rim of historic Pololu Valley, where teams of mules were once used as transportation, is not only a trail-riding adventure but also a rare opportunity to step back in time. The trip begins at the historic Kohala Ditch Company Mule Station. After a brief orientation, riders head out to the rim of Pololu Valley, wander through a native ohia-lehua forest, discover three waterfalls, meander across gentle streams, and even stop at a section of the historic Kohala Ditch trail. There are two 3-hour trips a day, at 8:30am and 12:30pm. The cost is $89 for adults, $69 for children ages 8 to 12. Snacks, water, and rain gear are provided.

ocean, with a stop for lunch and a short hike to the lava flow and the newly created black-sand beach. The tour starts at $96 per person.

Contact the **Big Island Mountain Bike Association,** P.O. Box 6819, Hilo, HI 96720 (© **808/961-4452;** www.interpac.net/~mtbike), for its free brochure, *Big Island Mountain Biking,* which has useful safety tips on biking as well as great off-road trails for both beginner and advanced riders. Check out www.bikehawaii.com for information on trails and access. Another good contact for biking information and maps is **PATH** (© **808/326-9495**).

BIRDING

Native Hawaiian birds are few—and dwindling. But though Hawaii may be the endangered bird capital of the world, it still offers extraordinary birding for anyone nimble enough to traverse tough, mucky landscape. And the best birding is on the Big Island; birders the world over come here hoping to see three Hawaiian birds in particular: *akiapolaau,* a woodpecker wannabe with a war club–like head; *nukupuu,* an elusive little yellow bird with a curved beak, one of the crown jewels of Hawaiian birding; and *alala,* the critically endangered Hawaiian crow that's now almost impossible to see in the wild.

Good spots to see native Hawaiian and other birds include the following:

HAWAII VOLCANOES NATIONAL PARK   The best places for accomplished birders to go on their own are the ohia forests of this national park, usually at sunrise or sunset, when the little forest birds seem to be most active. The Hawaiian nene goose can be spotted at the park's Kipuka Nene Campground, a favorite nesting habitat. Geese and pheasants sometimes appear on the Volcano Golf Course in the afternoon. The white-tailed tropical bird often rides the thermals caused by steam inside Halemaumau Crater.

HAKALAU FOREST NATIONAL WILDLIFE REFUGE   The first national wildlife refuge established solely for forest bird management is on the eastern slope of Mauna Kea above the Hamakua Coast. It's open for birding on Saturdays and Sundays, using the public access road only. You must call ahead of time to get the gate combinations of the locked gates and to register. Contact Refuge Manager Richard Wass, Hakalau Forest, 154 Waianuenue Ave., Room 219, Hilo, HI 96720 (© **808/933-6915;** Richard_Wass@mail.fws.gov).

HILO PONDS   Ducks, coots, herons (night and great blue), cattle egrets, and even Canada and snow geese fly into these popular coastal wetlands in Hilo, near the airport. Take Kalanianaole Highway about 3 miles east, past the industrial port facilities to Loko Waka Pond and Waiakea Pond.

BIRDING TOURS
If you don't know an apapane from a nukupuu, go with someone who does. Even rank amateurs can see Hawaii's *rara avis* in the wild. Contact Hawaii Forest & Trail, 74–5035-B Queen Kaahumanu Hwy. (behind the Chevron Station), Kailua-Kona (© **800/464-1993** or 808/331-8505; www.hawaii-forest.com), to sign up for the **Rainforest Birdwatching Adventure tour** 🎯🎯, led by naturalist Rob Pacheco. On this tour, you'll venture into pristine rainforest to see rare and endangered Hawaiian birds. Immersed in this world of giant ferns and crisp mountain air, the guide will also point out Hawaii's unique botany and evolution. This full-day adventure costs $145 for adults or $105 for children 5 to 12 years, and includes pick up, mid-morning snack with coffee, lunch, beverages, daypacks, bottled water, binoculars, walking sticks, warm wear, and rain gear.

HORSEBACK RIDING
Kohala Na'alapa 🎯, on Kohala Mountain Road (Hwy. 250) at mile marker 11 (ask for directions to the stables at the security-guard station; © **808/889-0022;** www.naalapastables.com), offers unforgettable journeys into the rolling hills of Kahua and Kohala ranches, past ancient Hawaiian ruins, through lush pastures with grazing sheep and cows, and along mountaintops with panoramic coastal views. The horses and various riding areas are suited to everyone from first-timers to experienced equestrians. There are two trips a day: a 2½-hour tour at 9am for $75 and a 1½-hour tour at 1:30pm for $55. No riders over 230 pounds, no pregnant riders, and no children under 8 permitted.

Experienced riders should sign up for a trip with **King's Trail Rides, Tack, and Gift Shop** 🎯🎯, Highway 11 at mile marker 111, Kealakekua (© **808/323-2388;** www.konacowboy.com). These 4-hour trips, with 2 hours of riding, are limited to four people. The trip heads down the mountain along Monument Trail to the Captain Cook Monument in Kealakekua Bay, where you'll stop for lunch and an hour of snorkeling. The $95 price tag isn't so bad when you consider that it includes both lunch and gear.

To see Waipio Valley on horseback, call **Waipio Na'alapa Trail Rides** 🎯 (© **808/775-0419;** www.naalapastables.com). The 2-hour tours of this gorgeous tropical valley depart Monday through Saturday at 9:30am and 1pm (don't forget your camera). The guides are well versed in Hawaiian history and provide running commentary as you move through this historic place. The cost is $75 for adults. No kids under 8, no pregnant riders, and no riders over 230 pounds.

RIDING PARKER RANCH   To ride Parker Ranch, call the **Cowboys of Hawaii** (© **808/885-5006**) for a ride back in time. They have two, 2-hour rides for $79 per person, which explores parts of the 225,000 acre ranch. For a real treat they offer a 1½ hour sunset ride, also $79.

TENNIS
You can play for free at any Hawaii County tennis court; for a detailed list of all courts on the island, contact **Hawaii County Department of Parks and Recreation,** 25 Apuni St., Hilo, HI 96720 (© **808/961-8720**). The best courts in

Hilo are at the Hoolulu Tennis Stadium, located next to the Civic Auditorium on Manono Street; in Kona, the best courts are at Old Airport Park.

Most of the resorts in the Kona-Kohala area do not allow nonguests to use their tennis facilities.

9 Seeing the Sights

THE KONA COAST

GUIDED WALKING TOURS   The **Kona Historical Society** (© 808/323-2005; www.konahistorical.org) hosts two historic walking tours in the Kona region. All walks must be booked in advance; call for reservations and departure locations. The 75-minute **Historic Kailua Village Walking Tour** ★ is the most comprehensive tour of the Kona Coast. It takes you all around Kailua-Kona, from King Kamehameha's last seat of government to the summer palace of the Hawaiian royal family and beyond, with lots of Hawaiian history and colorful lore along the way. Tours depart from the King Kamehameha Hotel lobby Monday through Friday, at 9 and 11 am. Tickets are $15 for adults, $10 for children ages 5 to 12. For reservations, call © 808/323-3222.

The 1-hour **Living History Tour** takes you through the everyday life of a Japanese family on the historic Uchida Coffee Farm during the 1900s. Interact with costumed interpreters as they go about life on a coffee farm. The tour is offered Monday through Friday, on the hour from 9am to 1pm, at a cost of $15 for adults ($30 with transportation from your hotel) and $10 for kids ages 5 to 12 ($25 with transportation from hotel). Meet at the Kona Historical Society office, 81–6551 Mamalahoa Hwy. (next to Kona Specialty Meats), Kealakekua, or call for transportation. For reservations, call © 808/323-2006.

A SELF-GUIDED DRIVING TOUR   If you're interested in seeing how your morning cup of joe goes from beans to brew, get a copy of the **Coffee Country Driving Tour.** This self-guided drive will take you farm by farm through Kona's famous coffee country; it also features a fascinating history of the area, the lowdown on coffeemaking lingo, some insider tips on how to make a great cup, and even a recipe for Kona coffee macadamia-nut chocolate-chunk pie (goes great with a cup of java). The free brochure is available at the **Big Island Visitors Bureau,** 250 Waikoloa Beach Dr., Waikoloa, HI 96738 (© 808/886-1652).

IN & AROUND KAILUA-KONA ★★★

Ellison S. Onizuka Space Center (Kids)   This small museum has a real moon rock and memorabilia in honor of Big Island–born astronaut Ellison Onizuka, who died in the 1986 *Challenger* space shuttle disaster. Fun displays in the museum include a gravity well, which illustrates orbital motion, and an interactive rocket-propulsion exhibit, where you can launch your own miniature space shuttle.

At Kona International Airport, Kailua-Kona. © 808/329-3441. Admission $3 adults, $1 children 12 and under. Daily 8:30am–4:30pm. Parking in airport lot, $2 per hour.

Hulihee Palace ★★   This two-story New England–style mansion of lava rock and coral mortar, erected in 1838 by the governor of the island of Hawaii, John Adams Kuakini, overlooks the harbor at Kailua-Kona. The largest, most elegant residence on the island when it was erected, Hulihee (the name means "turn and flee") was the gracious summer home of Hawaii's royalty, making it the other royal palace in the United States (the most famous being Oahu's Iolani Palace). Now run by Daughters of Hawaii, it features many 19th-century mementos and gorgeous koa furniture. You'll get lots of background and royal lore on the guided tour. No photography is allowed.

The Palace hosts 12 **Hawaiian music and hula concerts** a year, each dedicated to a Hawaiian monarch, at 4pm on the last Sunday of the month (except June and Dec, when the performances are held in conjunction with King Kamehameha Day and Christmas).

Across the street is **Mokuaikaua Church** (© 808/329-1589), the oldest Christian church in Hawaii. It's constructed of lava stones, but its architecture is New England–style all the way. The 112-foot steeple is still the tallest man-made structure in Kailua-Kona.

75–5718 Alii Dr., Kailua-Kona. © 808/329-1877. www.daughtersofhawaii.org/hulihee, Admission $5 adults, $4 seniors, $1 students. Daily 9am–4pm. Daily tours held throughout the day (arrive at least an hr. before closing).

Kamehameha's Compound at Kamakahonu Bay ★★

On the ocean side of the Kona Beach Hotel is a restored area of deep spiritual meaning to Hawaiians. This was the spot that King Kamehameha the Great chose to retreat to in 1812 after conquering the Hawaiian islands. He stayed until his death in 1819. The king built a temple, Ahuena Heiau, and used it as a gathering place for his *kahuna* (priests) to counsel him on governing his people in times of peace. In 1820, it was on this sacred ground that Kamehameha's son Liholiho, as king, sat down to eat with his mother, Keopuolani, and Kamehameha's principal queen, Kaahumanu, thus breaking the ancient *kapu* (taboo) against eating with women; this act established a new order in the Hawaiian kingdom. Although the temple grounds are now just a third of their original size, they're still impressive. You're free to come and wander the grounds, envisioning the days when King Kamehameha appealed to the gods to help him rule with the spirit of humanity's highest nature.

On the grounds of King Kamehameha's Kona Beach Hotel, 75–5660 Palani Rd., Kailua-Kona. © 808/329-2911. www.konabeachhotel.com. Free admission. Daily 9am–4pm; guided tours Mon–Fri at 1:30pm.

Kona Brewing Co. and Brewpub

This microbrewery is the first of its kind on the Big Island. Spoon and Pops, a father-and-son duo from Oregon, brought their brewing talents here and now produce about 25 barrels (about 124,000 gal.) per year. Drop by any time during their business hours and take a quick, informal tour of the brewery, after which you get to taste the product. A brewpub on the property serves gourmet pizza, salads, and fresh brewed Hawaiian ales.

75–5629 Kuakini Hwy. (at Palani Rd.), Kailua-Kona. © 808/334-BREW. www.konabrewingco.com. Free tours and tastings. Tours Mon–Fri 10:30am and 3pm. Turn into Firestone's parking lot on Palani Rd. at Kuakini Hwy; the brewery is at the back of the shopping center (behind Zac's Photo)—look for the orange gecko on the door.

Kona Pier

This is action central for water adventures. Fishing charters, snorkel cruises, and party boats all come and go here. Stop by around 4pm, when the captains weigh in with the catch of the day, usually huge marlin—the record-setters often come in here. It's also a great place to watch the sunset.

On the waterfront outside Honokohau Harbor, Kailua-Kona. © 808/329-7494.

Natural Energy Laboratory of Hawaii Authority (NELHA)

Technology buffs should consider a visit to NELHA, the only site in the world where the hot tropical sun, in combination with a complex pumping system that brings 42°F (6°C) ocean water from 2,000 feet deep up to land, is used to develop

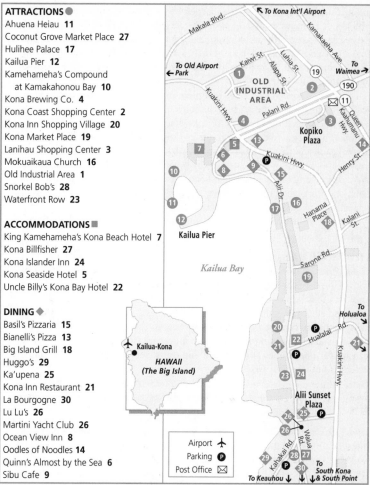

ATTRACTIONS ●
Ahuena Heiau **11**
Coconut Grove Market Place **27**
Hulihee Palace **17**
Kailua Pier **12**
Kamehameha's Compound
   at Kamakahonou Bay **10**
Kona Brewing Co. **4**
Kona Coast Shopping Center **2**
Kona Inn Shopping Village **20**
Kona Market Place **19**
Lanihau Shopping Center **3**
Mokuaikaua Church **16**
Old Industrial Area **1**
Snorkel Bob's **28**
Waterfront Row **23**

ACCOMMODATIONS ■
King Kamehameha's Kona Beach Hotel **7**
Kona Billfisher **27**
Kona Islander Inn **24**
Kona Seaside Hotel **5**
Uncle Billy's Kona Bay Hotel **22**

DINING ◆
Basil's Pizzaria **15**
Bianelli's Pizza **13**
Big Island Grill **18**
Huggo's **29**
Ka'upena **25**
Kona Inn Restaurant **21**
La Bourgogne **30**
Lu Lu's **26**
Martini Yacht Club **26**
Ocean View Inn **8**
Oodles of Noodles **14**
Quinn's Almost by the Sea **6**
Sibu Cafe **9**

innovations in agriculture, aquaculture, and ocean conservation. The interesting 1½-hour tour takes in all areas of the high-tech ocean science and technology park, including the seawater delivery system, the energy-conversion process, and some of the park's more interesting tenants, from Maine lobsters to giant clams.

73–4460 Queen Kaahumanu Hwy. (at mile marker 94), Kailua-Kona. ℂ 808/329-7341. www.nelha.org. Public presentation tours $3 adults, children under 11 years free. Thurs 10am and 1pm; reservations required.

UPCOUNTRY KONA: HOLUALOA ✦✦

On the slope of Hualalai volcano above Kailua-Kona sits the small village of Holualoa, which attracts travelers weary of super-resorts. Here you'll find a little art and culture—and shade.

This funky upcountry town, centered on two-lane Mamalaloa Highway, is nestled amid a lush, tropical landscape where avocados grow as big as footballs. Little more than a wide spot in the road, Holualoa is a cluster of brightly painted, tin-roofed plantation shacks enjoying a revival as B&Bs, art galleries, and quaint shops (see "Shops & Galleries," later in this chapter, for details). In 2 blocks, it manages to pack in two first-rate galleries, a frame shop, a potter, a glassworks, a goldsmith, an old-fashioned general store, a vintage 1930s gas station, a tiny post office, a Catholic church, and the **Kona Hotel,** a hot-pink clapboard structure that looks like a western movie set—you're welcome to peek in, and you should.

The cool upslope village is the best place in Hawaii for a coffee break. That's because Holualoa is in the heart of the coffee belt, a 20-mile long strip at an elevation of between 1,000 and 1,400 feet, where all the Kona coffee in the world is grown in the rich volcanic soil of the cool uplands (see the box "Kona Coffee Craze," earlier in this chapter). Everyone's backyard seems to teem with glossy green leaves and ruby-red cherries (which contain the seeds, or beans, used to make coffee), and the air smells like a San Francisco espresso bar. The **Holuakoa Cafe,** on Mamalahoa Highway (Hwy. 180) in Holualoa (② **808/322-2233**), is a great place to get a freshly brewed cup.

To reach Holualoa, follow narrow, winding Hualalai Road up the hill from Highway 19; it's about a 15-minute drive.

SOUTH KONA ✪✪✪

Kona Historical Society Museum ✪✪   This well-organized museum is housed in the historic Greenwell Store, built in 1875 by Henry Nicholas Greenwell out of native stone and lime mortar made from burnt coral. Antiques, artifacts, and photos tell the story of this fabled coast. The museum is filled with items that were common to everyday life here in the last century, when coffee-growing and cattle-raising were the main industries. Serious history buffs should sign up for one of the museum's walking tours; see "Guided Walking Tours," earlier in this chapter.

Hwy. 11, between mile markers 111 and 112, Kealakekua. ② **808/323-3222** or 808/323-2006. www.kona historical.org. Admission $2. Mon–Fri 9am–3pm. Parking on grassy area next to Kona Specialty Meats parking lot.

Kula Kai Caverns and Lava Tubes ✪✪ *Finds*   Before you trudge up to Pele's volcanic eruption, take a look at her underground handiwork. Ric Elhard and Rose Herrera have explored and mapped out the labyrinth of lava tubes and caves, carved out over the last 1,000 years or so, that crisscross their property on the southwest rift zone on the slopes of Mauna Loa near South Point. As soon as you enter their thatched yurt field office (which resembles something out of an Indiana Jones movie), you know you're in for an amazing tour. Choices range from an easy ½-hour tour on a well-lit underground route ($12 for adults, $8 for children ages 5–12) to a more adventuresome 2-hour caving trip ($45 for adults, $25 for children ages 8–12) to a deluxe ½-day exploration ($65, minimum age 12 years). Helmets, lights, gloves, and knee pads are all included. Sturdy shoes are recommended for caving.

Off Hwy. 11, Ocean View. ② **808/929-7539**. www.kulakaicaverns.com. Tours by appointment. Between mile markers 79 and 78 off Hwy. 11.

The Painted Church ✪ *Finds*   Oh, those Belgian priests—what a talented lot. At the turn of the century, Father John Berchman Velghe borrowed a page from Michelangelo and painted biblical scenes inside St. Benedict's Catholic Church, so the illiterate Hawaiians could visualize the white man's version of creation.

Hwy. 19, Honaunau. ② **808/328-2227**.

Kids Especially for Kids

Walking through Thurston Lava Tube at Hawaii Volcanoes National Park (p. 323)   It's scary, it's spooky, and most kids love it. You hike downhill through a rain forest full of little chittering native birds to enter this huge, silent black hole full of drips, cobwebs, and tree roots that stretch underground for almost ½ mile. At the end, there's a fork in the tunnel, which leads either up a stairway to our world or—here's the best part—down an unexplored hole that probably goes all the way to China.

Snorkeling Kahaluu Beach Park (p. 283)   The shallow, calm waters off Kahaluu Beach are the perfect place to take kids snorkeling. The waters are protected by a barrier reef, and the abundance of fish will keep the kids' attention. You can pick up a fish identification card at any dive shop and make a game out of seeing how many fish the kids can find.

Riding a Submarine into the Underwater World (p. 295)   The huge viewing windows will have the kids enthralled as the high-tech sub leaves the surface and plunges 120 feet down through the mysterious Neptunian waters. The trip isn't too long—just an hour—and there are plenty of reef fish and prehistoric-looking corals to hold the young ones' attention.

Launching Your Own Space Shuttle (p. 305)   Okay, it's a model of a space shuttle, but it's close enough to the real thing to be a real blast. The Ellison S. Onizuka Space Center has dozens of interactive displays to thrill budding young astronauts, such as a hands-on experience with gyroscopic stabilization. Great video clips of astronauts working and living in space may inspire your kids as well.

Hunting for Petroglyphs (p. 311)   There's plenty of space to run around and discover ancient stone carvings at either the Puako Petroglyph Archaeological District, at Mauna Lani Resort, or at the King's Trail, by the Outrigger Waikoloan. And finding the petroglyphs is only part of the game—once you find them, you have to guess what the designs mean.

Watching the Volcano (p. 323)   Any kid who doesn't get a kick out of watching a live volcano set the night on fire has been watching too much television. Take hot dogs, bottled water, flashlights, and sturdy shoes and follow the ranger's instructions on where to view the lava safely. You might want to make the trip during daylight first so the kids can see the Technicolor difference in experiencing a lava flow in the dark.

Puuhonua O Honaunau National Historical Park ★★★   With its fierce, haunting idols, this sacred site on the black-lava Kona Coast certainly looks forbidding. To ancient Hawaiians, however, it must have been a welcome sight, for Puuhonua O Honaunau served as a 16th-century place of refuge, providing sanctuary for defeated warriors and *kapu* (taboo) violators. A great rock wall—1,000 feet long, 10 feet high, and 17 feet thick—defines the refuge where Hawaiians found safety. On the wall's north end is Hale O Keawe Heiau, which holds the bones of 23 Hawaiian chiefs. Other archaeological finds include burial sites, old trails, and a portion of an ancient village. On a self-guided tour of the 180-acre site—which has been restored to its precontact state—you can see and learn about reconstructed thatched huts, canoes, and idols and feel the *mana* (power) of old Hawaii.

A cultural festival, usually held in June, allows you to join in games, learn crafts, sample Hawaiian food, see traditional hula, and experience life in the islands before outsiders arrived in the late 1700s. Every Labor Day weekend, one of Hawaii's major outrigger canoe races starts here and ends in Kailua-Kona. Call for details on both events.

Hwy. 160 (off Hwy. 11 at mile marker 104), Honaunau. (℗ **808/328-2288**. www.nps.gov/puho. Admission $5 per vehicle or $3 per person; children 16 and under free. Visitor center daily 8am–4:30pm; park Mon–Thurs 6am–8pm, Fri–Sun 6am–11pm. From Hwy. 11, it's 3½ miles to the park entrance.

SOUTH POINT: LAND'S END ★★★

The history of Hawaii is condensed here, at the end of 11 miles of bad road that peters out at Kaulana Bay, in the lee of a jagged, black-lava point—the tail end of the United States. No historic marker marks the spot or gives any clue as to the geographical significance of the place. If you walk out to the very tip, beware of the big waves that lash the shore.

The nearest continental landfall is Antarctica, 7,500 miles away.

It's a 2½-mile, four-wheel-drive trip and a hike down a cliff from South Point to the anomaly known as **Green Sand Beach** ★ (see "Beaches," earlier in this chapter).

Back on the Mamalahoa Highway (Hwy. 11), about 20 miles east is the small town of Pahoa; turn off the highway and travel about 5 miles through this once-thriving sugar plantation and beyond to the **Wood Valley Temple and Retreat Center** ★ (℗ **808/928-8539**), also known as *Nechung Drayang Ling* ("Island of Melodious Sound"). It's an oasis of tranquility tucked into the rain forest. Built by Japanese sugarcane workers, the temple, retreat center, and surrounding gardens were rededicated by the Dalai Lama in 1980 to serve as a spiritual center for Tibetan Buddhism. You can walk the beautiful grounds, attend morning or evening services, and breathe in the quiet mindfulness of this serene area.

THE KOHALA COAST ★★★

Puukohola Heiau National Historic Site ★★★   This seacoast temple, called "the hill of the whale," is the single most imposing and dramatic structure of the ancient Hawaiians. It was built by Kamehameha I from 1790 to 1791. The temple stands 224 feet long by 100 feet wide, with three narrow terraces on the seaside and an amphitheater to view canoes. Kamehameha built this temple of sacrifice with mortarless stone after a prophet told him he would conquer and unite the islands if he did so; 4 years later, he fulfilled his kingly goal. The site also includes the house of John Young, a trusted advisor of Kamehameha, and, offshore, the submerged ruins of Hale O Ka Puni, a shrine dedicated to the shark gods.

Hwy. 270, near Kawaihae Harbor. (℗ **808/882-7218**. www.nps.gov/puhe. Free admission. Daily 7:30am–4pm. The visitor center is on Hwy. 270; the heiau is a short walk away. The trail is closed when it's too windy, so call ahead if you're in doubt.

ANCIENT HAWAIIAN FISH PONDS

Like their Polynesian forebears, Hawaiians were among the first aquaculturists on the planet. Scientists still marvel at the ways they used the brackish ponds along the shoreline to stock and harvest fish. There are actually two different types of ancient fish ponds (or *loko i'a*). Closed ponds, inshore and closed off from the ocean, were used to raise mullet and milkfish, while open ponds were open to the sea, with rock walls as a barrier to the ocean and sluice gates that connected the ponds to the ocean. The gates were woven vines, with just enough room for juvenile fish to swim in at high tide while keeping the bigger, fatter fish from swimming out. Generally, the Hawaiians kept and raised mullet, milkfish, and shrimp in these open ponds; juvenile manini, papio, eels, and barracuda occasionally found their way in too.

The **Kalahuipuaa Fish Ponds,** at Mauna Lani Resort (© **808/885-6622**), are great examples of both types of ponds in a lush tropical setting. South of the Mauna Lani Resort are **Kuualii** and **Kahapapa Fish Ponds,** at the Marriott Waikoloa Beach Resort (© **808/885-6789**). Both resorts have taken great pains to restore the ponds to their original state and to preserve them for future generations; call ahead to arrange a free guided tour.

KOHALA COAST PETROGLYPHS

The Hawaiian petroglyph is a great enigma of the Pacific. No one knows who made them or why, only that they're here. The petroglyphs appear at 135 different sites on six inhabited islands, but most of them are found on the Big Island.

At first glance, the huge slate of pahoehoe looks like any other smooth black slate of lava on the seacoast of the Big Island—until gradually, in slanting rays of the sun, a wonderful cast of characters leaps to life before your eyes. You might see dancers and paddlers, fishermen and chiefs, hundreds of marchers all in a row. Pictures of the tools of daily life are everywhere: fish hooks, spears, poi pounders, canoes. The most common representations are family groups: father, mother, and child. There are also post–European contact petroglyphs of ships, anchors, goats, horses, and guns.

The largest concentration of these stone symbols in the Pacific lies within the 233-acre **Puako Petroglyph Archaeological District** ⊛, near Mauna Lani Resort. Once hard to find, the enigmatic graffiti is now easily reachable. The 1½ mile **Malama Trail** starts north of Mauna Lani Resort; take Highway 19 to the resort turnoff and drive toward the coast on North Kaniku Drive, which ends at a parking lot; the trailhead is marked by a sign and interpretive kiosk. Go in the early morning or late afternoon, when it's cool. A total of 3,000 designs have been identified, including paddlers, sails, marchers, dancers, and family groups, as well as dog, chicken, turtle, and deity symbols.

The **Kings' Shops** (© **808/886-8811**), at the Waikoloa Beach Resort, offers a free tour of the surrounding petroglyphs Tuesday through Friday at 10:30am and Saturday at 8:30am; it meets in front of the Food Pavilion. For the best viewing go Saturday morning.

Visitors with disabilities, as well as others, can explore petroglyphs at **Kaupulehu Petroglyphs** ⊛ in the **Kona Village Resort,** Queen Kaahumanu Highway. © **808/325-5555.** Free guided tours are offered three times a week, but reservations are required (or you won't get past the gatehouse). Here you can see some of the finest images in the Hawaiian islands. There are many petroglyphs of sails, canoes, fish, and chiefs in headdresses, plus a burial scene with three stick figures. Kite motifs—rare in rock art—similar to those found in New Zealand are also here. This is Hawaii's only ADA accessible petroglyph trial.

Warning: The petroglyphs are thousands of years old and easily destroyed. Do not walk on them or attempt to take a "rubbing" (there's a special area in the Puako Preserve for doing so). The best way to capture a petroglyph is with a photo in the late afternoon, when the shadows are long.

NORTH KOHALA ★★★

The Original King Kamehameha Statue ★★   Here stands King Kamehameha the Great, right arm outstretched, left arm holding a spear, as if guarding the seniors who have turned a century-old New England–style courthouse into an airy center for their golden years. The center is worth a stop just to meet the town elders, who are quick to point out the local sights, hand you a free *Guide to Historic North Kohala,* and give you a brief tour of the courthouse, where a faded photo of FDR looms over the judge's dais and the walls are covered with the faces of innocent-looking local boys killed in World War II, Korea, and Vietnam.

But the statue's main attraction here. There's one just like it in Honolulu, across the street from Iolani Palace, but this is the original: an 8-foot, 6-inch bronze by Thomas R. Gould, a Boston sculptor. It was cast in Europe in 1880 but was lost at sea on its way to Hawaii. A sea captain eventually recovered and returned the statue, which was finally placed here, near Kamehameha's Kohala birthplace, in 1912.

Kamehameha was born in 1750, became ruler of Hawaii in 1810, and died in Kailua-Kona in 1819. His burial site remains a mystery.

Hwy. 270, Kapaau.

Pololu Valley Lookout ★★★   At this end-of-the-road scenic lookout, you can gaze at the vertical jade-green cliffs of the Hamakua Coast and two islets offshore. The view may look familiar once you get here—it often appears on travel posters. Most people race up, jump out, take a snapshot, and turn around and drive off; but it's a beautiful scene, so linger if you can. For the more adventurous, a switchback trail leads to a secluded black-sand beach at the mouth of a wild valley once planted in taro; bring water and bug spray.

At the end of Hwy. 270, Makapala.

Lapakahi State Historical Park ★ (Kids)   This 14th-century fishing village, on a hot, dry, dusty stretch of coast, offers a glimpse into the lifestyle of the ancients. Lapakahi is the best-preserved fishing village in Hawaii. Take the self-guided, 1-mile loop trail past stone platforms, fish shrines, rock shelters, salt pans, and restored *hale* (houses) to a coral-sand beach and the deep blue sea (good snorkeling). Wear good hiking shoes or tennies; it's a hearty 45-minute walk. Go early or later in the afternoon; during most of the day the sun is hot and shade is at a premium.

Hwy. 270, Mahukona. ✆ 808/889-5566. Free admission. Daily 8am–4pm. Guided tours by appointment.

Mookini Luakini ★★ (Moments)   On the coast where King Kamehameha the Great was born stands Hawaii's oldest, largest, and most sacred religious site, now a national historic landmark—the 1,500-year-old Mookini Heiau ★, used by kings to pray and offer human sacrifices. The road is rough, so you'll need four-wheel-drive to get here, but it's worth the trip. The massive three-story stone temple, dedicated to Ku, the Hawaiian god of war, was erected in A.D. 480;

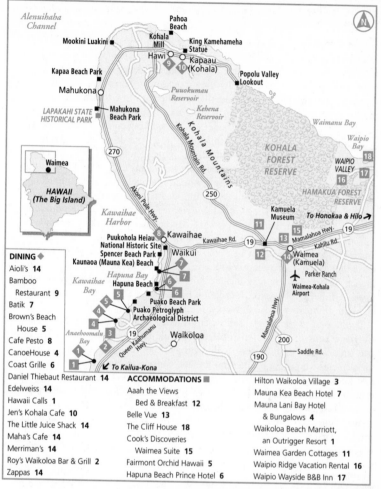

DINING ◆

Aioli's **14**
Bamboo
  Restaurant **9**
Batik **7**
Brown's Beach
  House **5**
Cafe Pesto **8**
CanoeHouse **4**
Coast Grille **6**
Daniel Thiebaut Restaurant **14**
Edelweiss **14**
Hawaii Calls **1**
Jen's Kohala Cafe **10**
The Little Juice Shack **14**
Maha's Cafe **14**
Merriman's **14**
Roy's Waikoloa Bar & Grill **2**
Zappas **14**

ACCOMMODATIONS ■

Aaah the Views
  Bed & Breakfast **12**
Belle Vue **13**
The Cliff House **18**
Cook's Discoveries
  Waimea Suite **15**
Fairmont Orchid Hawaii **5**
Hapuna Beach Prince Hotel **6**

Hilton Waikoloa Village **3**
Mauna Kea Beach Hotel **7**
Mauna Lani Bay Hotel
  & Bungalows **4**
Waikoloa Beach Marriott,
  an Outrigger Resort **1**
Waimea Garden Cottages **11**
Waipio Ridge Vacation Rental **16**
Waipio Wayside B&B Inn **17**

each stone is said to have been passed hand to hand from Pololu Valley, 14 miles away, by 18,000 men who worked from sunset to sunrise. Kamehameha, born nearby under Halley's Comet, sought spiritual guidance here before embarking on his campaign to unite Hawaii. Go in the late afternoon when the setting sun strikes the lava-rock walls and creates a primal mood.

The heiau can be tricky to find; it's on a dirt road that branches off the highway, and there may or may not be a sign up marking the turnoff. Your best bet is to ask for directions at a store or gas station in the area.

On the north shore, near Upolu Point Airport.

WAIMEA (KAMUELA) ✿✿✿

Kamuela Museum It takes only about an hour to explore tiny Kamuela Museum. Its eclectic collection includes an early Hawaiian dogtooth death cup, which sits next to a piece of rope used on the *Apollo* mission, which in turn sits near ancient artifacts from the royal family.

At the junction of Hwy. 19 and Hwy. 250, Waimea. (✆ **808/885-4724.** Admission $5 adults, $2 children under 12. Daily 8am–5pm.

Parker Ranch ⭐   The *paniolo* (cowboy) tradition began here in 1809, when John Parker, a 19-year-old New England sailor, jumped ship and rounded up wild cows for King Kamehameha. There's some evidence that Hawaiian cowboys were the first to be taught by the great Spanish horsemen, the *vaqueros;* they were cowboying 40 years before their counterparts in California, Texas, and the Pacific Northwest. The Parker Ranch, after six generations of cowboys, is smaller today than it in its glory, but it still is a working ranch of some 12 cowboys work 250 horses and 30,000 to 35,000 head of cattle on 200,000 acres.

The **Visitor Center,** located at the Parker Ranch Shopping Center on Highway 190 (✆ **808/885-7655**), is open daily from 9am to 5pm and houses the **Parker Ranch Museum,** which displays items that have been used throughout the ranch's history, dating from 1847, and illustrates six generations of Parker family history. An interesting video takes you inside the ranch and captures the essence of day-to-day life of what it was like when it was a working ranch.

You can also tour two historic homes on the ranch. In 1989, the late Richard Smart—the sixth-generation heir who sought a career on Broadway—opened his 8,000-square-foot yellow Victorian home, **Puuopelu,** to art lovers. The French Regency gallery here includes original works by Renoir, Degas, Dufy, Corot, Utrillo, and Pissarro. Next door is **Mana Hale,** a little New England saltbox built from koa wood 140 years ago.

If you want to get out and see the ranch itself, a 45-minute narrated **Kohala Carriage Tour** (Tues–Sat) takes place in an old-fashioned wagon—pulled by two large Belgian draft horses—with seating for 20, roll-down protection from the elements, and warm blankets for the upcountry temperatures. The tour rolls past ancient Hawaiian artifacts, 19th-century stone corrals (still in use), and miles of vast rolling hills; it stops at a working cowboy station, where visitors can get out, take photos, and stretch their legs.

See "Horseback Riding" under "Golf & Other Outdoor Pursuits," earlier in this chapter, for details on riding tours of Parker Ranch.

Parker Ranch Center, Waimea. (✆ **808/885-7655** for visitor center. www.parkerranch.com. Admission $6 to museum only ($4.50 for children younger than 12 years); $8.50 tour of ranch homes ($6 for children); $15 adults for the Wagon Tour ($12 for children). Visitor Center and Museum open 9am–5pm. If you're seeing the museum only, you can arrive as late as 4pm; the last museum/ranch homes tickets are sold at 4pm; the final museum/Wagon Tour tickets are sold at 2pm. Allow about 1½ hours to see everything.

MAUNA KEA ⭐⭐⭐

Some people just have to be on top of things. If you're one of them, head for the summit of Mauna Kea, which is the world's tallest mountain if you measure it from its base on the ocean floor.

Cowboy Culture

For more information on the Big Island's *paniolo* (cowboy) past, contact the **Hawaii Island Economic Board,** 200 Kanoelehua Ave., Suite 103, Hilo, HI 96720 (✆ **808/966-5416**; www.rodeohawaii.com), which offers a free brochure on the paniolo lifestyle and history, tips on where to meet the paniolos of today, and information on ranches, outfitters, activities, shops, and more.

Mauna Kea's summit is the best place on earth for astronomical observations, because its mid-Pacific site is near the equator and because it enjoys clear, pollution-free skies and pitch-black nights with no urban light to interfere. That's why Mauna Kea is home to the world's largest telescope. Needless to say, the stargazing from here is fantastic, even with the naked eye.

SETTING OUT   You'll need a four-wheel-drive vehicle to climb to the peak, **Observatory Hill.** A standard car will get you as far as the visitor center, but check your rental agreement before you go; some agencies prohibit you from taking your car on the Saddle Road, which is narrow and rutted, and has a soft shoulder.

SAFETY TIPS   Always check the weather and Mauna Kea road conditions before you head out (© 808/969-3218). Dress warmly; the temperatures drop into the 30s after dark. Drink as much liquid as possible, avoiding alcohol and coffee, in the 36 hours surrounding your trip to avoid dehydration. Don't go within 24 hours of scuba diving—you could get the bends. The day before you go, avoid gas-producing foods, such as beans, cabbage, onions, soft drinks, or starches. If you smoke, take a break for 48 hours before to allow the carbon monoxide in your bloodstream to dissipate—you need all the oxygen you can get. Wear dark sunglasses to avoid snow blindness, and use lots of sunscreen and lip balm. Pregnant women and anyone under 16 or with a heart condition or lung ailment are advised to stay below. Once you're at the top, don't overexert yourself; it's bad for your heart. Take it easy up here.

ACCESS POINTS & VISITOR CENTERS   Before you climb the mountain, you've got to find it. It's about an hour from Hilo or Waimea to the visitor center and another 30 to 45 minutes from here to the summit. Take the Saddle Road (Hwy. 200) from Highway 190; it's about 19 miles to Mauna Kea State Recreation Area, a good place to stop and stretch your legs. Go another 9 miles to the unmarked Summit Road turnoff, at mile marker 28 (about 9,300 ft.), across from the Hunter's Check-in Station. The higher you go, the more lightheaded you get, sometimes even dizzy; it usually sets in after the 9,600-foot marker (about 6¼ miles up the Summit Road), the site of the last comfort zone and the **Onizuka Visitor Center** (© 808/961-2180; www.ifa.hawaii.edu/info/vis). Named in memory of Hawaii's fallen astronaut, a native of the Big Island and a victim of the *Challenger* explosion, the center is open daily from 9am to 10pm.

TOURS & PROGRAMS   If you'd rather not go it alone to the top, you can caravan up as part of a **free summit tour,** offered Saturday and Sunday at 1pm from the visitor center (returns at 5pm). You must be 16 or older and in good health (no cardiopulmonary problems), not be pregnant, and have a four-wheel-drive vehicle. The tours explain the development of the facilities on Mauna Kea and include a walking tour of an observatory at 13,796 feet. Call © 808/961-2180 if you'd like to participate.

Every night from 6 to 10pm, you can do some serious **stargazing** from the Onizuka Visitor Center. There's a free lecture at 6pm, followed by a video, a question-and-answer session, and your chance to peer through 11-inch, 14-inch, and 16-inch telescopes. Bring a snack and, if you've got them, your own telescope or binoculars, along with a flashlight (with a red filter). Dress for 30° to 40°F (-1–4°C) temperatures, but call for the weather report first (© 808/961-5582). Families are welcome.

> **_Moments_ Experiencing Where the Gods Live**
>
> "The ancient Hawaiians thought of the top of Mauna Kea as heaven, or at least where the Gods and Goddess lived," according to Monte "Pat" Wright, owner and chief guide of **Mauna Kea Summit Adventures.**
>
> Wright, the first guide to take people up to the top of the Mauna Kea, world's tallest mountain when measured from the base and an astonishing 13,796 feet when measured from the sea, says he fell in love with this often-snow capped peak the first time he saw it.
>
> Mauna Kea Summit Adventures offer a luxurious trip to the top of the world. The 7- to 8-hour adventure actually begins mid-afternoon with pick up along the Kona-Kohala coast in a brand-new, $65,000, custom Ford 4-wheel-drive, turbo-diesel van.
>
> As the passengers make the drive up the mountain, the extensively-trained guides discuss the geography, geology, natural history and Hawaiian culture along the way.
>
> The first stop is at the Onizuka Visitor's Center, at the 9,000 foot level.
>
> "We let people out to stretch, get acclimatized to the altitude and to eat dinner," Wright says.
>
> As guests gear up with Mauna Kea Summit's heavy, arctic-style hooded parkas and gloves (30°F/-1°C is the average temperature on the mountain), the guide describes why the world's largest telescopes are located on Mauna Kea and also tells stores about the lifestyle of astronomers who live for a clear, night sky.
>
> After a dinner of gourmet sandwiches (turkey, Black Forest ham or lacto-veggie on a fresh baguette roll), vegetarian onion soup, and hot chocolate, coffee or tea, everyone climbs back into the van for the half-hour ride to the summit.
>
> Arriving in time to catch the sun sinking into the Pacific nearly 14,000 feet below, the guide points out the various world-renowned

You can see a model of the world's largest telescope, which sits atop Mauna Kea, at the **Keck Control Center,** 65–1120 Mamalahoa Hwy. (Hwy. 19), across from the North Hawaii Community Hospital, Waimea (© **808/885-7887**), open Monday through Friday from 8am to 4:30pm. A 10-minute video explains the Keck's search for objects in deep space.

MAKING THE CLIMB If you're heading up on your own, stop at the visitor center for about a half-hour to get acquainted with the altitude. Walk around, eat a banana, drink some water, and take deep breaths of the crystal-clear air before you press onward and upward in low gear, engine whining. It takes about 30 to 45 minutes to get to the top from here. The trip is a mere 6 miles, but you climb from 9,000 to nearly 14,000 feet.

AT THE SUMMIT Up here, 11 nations, including Japan, France, and Canada, have set up peerless infrared telescopes to look into deep space. Among them sits the **Keck Telescope,** the world's largest. Developed by the University of California and the California Institute of Technology, it's eight stories high, weighs telescopes as the observatories open and the high-tech, multi-mirrored telescopes rotate into position for the night viewing.

After the last trace of sunset colors has disappeared from the sky, the tour again descends down to mid-mountain, where the climate is more agreeable, for stargazing. Each tour has Celestron Celestar 8 deluxe telescopes, which are capable of 30-175x magnification and gather up to 500x more light than the unaided eye.

Wright does caution people to book the adventure early in their vacation.

"Although we do cancel about 25 trips a year due to weather, we want to be able to accommodate everyone," he said. Extensive series of live Web cameras, live weather stats, and a full-time meteorologist constantly feed weather information on the mountain. If guests book at the beginning of their holiday and the trip is canceled due to weather, then Mauna Kea Summit will attempt to reschedule another day.

Wright also points out that due to the summit's low oxygen level (40% less oxygen than sea level) and the diminished air pressure (also 40% less air pressure than sea level), the lack of oxygen can be a serious problem for people with heart or lung problems or for scuba divers who have been diving in the previous 24 hours.

Pregnant woman, children under 13, and obese people should not travel to the summit due to the decreased oxygen. Because the roads to the summit are bumpy, anyone with a bad back might want to reconsider the trip.

The cost for this celestial adventure is $150 (discounted if you book on the Internet, www.maunakea.com, two weeks in advance). For more information, call ℂ **1-888-322-2366** or 808-322-2366.

150 tons, and has a 33-foot-diameter mirror made of 36 perfectly attuned hexagon mirrors, like a fly's eye, rather than one conventional lens.

Also at the summit, up a narrow footpath, is a **cairn of rocks;** from it, you can see across the Pacific Ocean in a 360° view that's beyond words and pictures. When it's socked in (and that can happen while you're standing here), you get a surreal look at the summits of Mauna Loa and Maui's Haleakala poking through the puffy white cumulus clouds beneath your feet.

Inside a cinder cone just below the summit is **Lake Waiau,** the only glacial lake in the mid-Pacific, and at 13,020 feet above sea level, one of the highest lakes in the world. The lake never dries up, even though it gets only 15 inches of rain a year and sits in porous lava where there are no springs. Nobody quite knows what to make of this, but scientists suspect the lake is replenished by snowmelt and permafrost from submerged lava tubes. You can't see the lake from Summit Road; you must take a brief, high-altitude hike. But it's easy: On the final approach to the summit area, upon regaining the blacktop road, go about 200 yards to the major switchback and make a hard right turn. Park on the shoulder of the road (which, if you brought your altimeter, is at 13,200 ft.). No sign points the way, but there's an obvious half-mile trail that goes down to the lake about 200 feet across the lava. Follow the base of the big cinder cone on your left; you should have the summit of Mauna Loa in view directly ahead as you walk.

THE HAMAKUA COAST ★★★

The rich history of 117 years of the sugar industry, along the scenic 45-mile coastline from Hilo to Hamakua, comes alive in the interpretive *Hilo-Hamakua Heritage Coast* drive guide, produced by the **Hawaii Island Economic Development Board,** 200 Kanoelehua Ave., Suite 103, Hilo, HI 96720 (© **808/966-5416**).

The free guide not only points out the historic sites and museums, scenic photo opportunities, restaurants and stores, and even restrooms along the Hawaii Belt Road (Hwy. 19), but also has corresponding brown-and-white, points-of-interest signs on the highway. Visitor information centers anchored at either end in Hilo and in Hamakua offer additional information on the area.

NATURAL WONDERS ALONG THE COAST

Akaka Falls ★★★   See one of Hawaii's most scenic waterfalls via an easy, 1-mile paved loop through a rain forest, past bamboo and ginger and down to an observation point. You'll have a perfect view of 442-foot Akaka and nearby Kahuna Falls, which is a mere 100-footer. Keep your eyes peeled for rainbows.

On Hwy. 19, Honomu (8 miles north of Hilo). Turn left at Honomu and head 3½ miles inland on Akaka Falls Rd. (Hwy. 220).

Hawaii Tropical Botanical Garden ★★   More than 1,800 species of tropical plants thrive in this little-known Eden by the sea. The 40-acre garden, nestled between the crashing surf and a thundering waterfall, has the world's largest selection of tropical plants growing in a natural environment, including a torch ginger forest, a banyan canyon, an orchid garden, a banana grove, a bromeliad hill, and a golden bamboo grove, which rattles like a jungle drum in the trade winds. The torch gingers tower on 12-foot stalks. Each spectacular specimen is named by genus and species, and caretakers point out new or rare buds in bloom. Some endangered Hawaiian specimens, such as the rare *Gardenia remyi,* are flourishing in this habitat. The gardens are seldom crowded; you can wander around by yourself all day.

Off Hwy. 19 on the 4-mile Scenic Route, Onomea Bay (8 miles north of Hilo). © **808/964-5233.** www.htbg.com. Admission $15 adults, $5 children 6–16. Daily 8:30am–4pm.

World Botanical Garden ★★   Just north of Hilo is Hawaii's largest botanical garden in the state, with some 5,000 species, and, still growing. When the fruits are in season, they hand out free chilled juices. One of the most spectacular sites is the ¼-mile rainforest walk, which is also wheelchair accessible, along a stream, on a path lined with flowers, to the viewing area of the three-tiered, 300 foot Umauma Falls. Parents will appreciate the children's maze, nearly the size of a football field, where the "prize" is a playing field near the exit. The mock orange hedge, which defines the various paths in the maze, is only 5 feet tall, so most parents can peer over the edge to keep an eye on their keiki. Under construction (when we went to press) are an educational visitor center, scheduled to be open by the end of the year, a Hawaii wellness garden with medicinal Hawaiian plants, an etho-botanical garden, an arboretum, and a phylogenetic garden with various plants and trees arranged in roughly the same sequence they first appeared on earth.

Off Hwy. 19 near the 16 mile marker in Umauma. P.O. Box 411, Honomu, HI 96728 (C) **808/963-5427.** www.wbgi.com. Admission is $8 adults, $4 teens ages 13–19, free for children 12 and under. Mon–Sat 9am–5:30pm.

Laupahoehoe Beach Park ⭐ This idyllic place holds a grim reminder of nature's fury. In 1946, a tidal wave swept across the village that once stood on this lava-leaf (that's what *laupahoehoe* means) peninsula and claimed the lives of 20 students and four teachers. A memorial in this pretty little park recalls the tragedy. The land here ends in black sea stacks that resemble tombstones. It's not a place for swimming, but the views are spectacular.
Laupahoehoe Point exit off Hwy. 19.

HONOKAA ⭐⭐⭐
Honokaa is worth a visit to see the remnants of plantation life when sugar was king. This is a real place that hasn't yet been boutiqued into a shopping mall; it looks as if someone has kept it in a bell jar since 1920. There's a real barber shop, a real Filipino store, some good shopping (see "Shops & Galleries," later in this chapter), and a hotel with creaky floorboards that dishes up hearty food. The town also serves as the gateway to spectacular Waipio Valley (see below).

Honokaa has no attractions per se, but you might want to check out the **Katsu Goto Memorial,** next to the library at the Hilo end of town. Katsu Goto, one of the first indentured Japanese immigrants, arrived in Honokaa in the late 1800s to work on the sugar plantations. He learned English, quit the plantation, and aided his fellow immigrants in labor disputes with American planters. On October 23, 1889, he was hanged from a lamppost in Honokaa, a victim of local-style justice. Today, a memorial recalls Goto's heroic human-rights struggle.

THE END OF THE ROAD: WAIPIO VALLEY ⭐⭐⭐
Long ago, this lush, tropical place was the valley of kings, who called it the valley of "curving water" (which is what *Waipio* means). From the black-sand bay at its mouth, Waipio sweeps back 6 miles between sheer, cathedral-like walls that reach almost a mile high. Here, 40,000 Hawaiians lived amid taro, red bananas, and wild guavas in an area etched by streams and waterfalls. Only about 50 Hawaiians live in the valley today, tending taro, fishing, and soaking up the ambience of this old Hawaiian place.

Many of the ancient royals are buried in Waipio's hidden crevices; some believe they rise up to become Marchers of the Night, whose chants reverberate through the valley. It's here that the caskets of Hawaiian chiefs Liloa and Lono Ika Makahiki, recently stolen from Bishop Museum, are believed to have been returned by Hawaiians. The sacred valley is steeped in myth and legend, some of which you may hear—usually after dark in the company of Hawaiian elders.

To get to Waipio Valley, take Highway 19 from Hilo to Honokaa, then Highway 240 to **Waipio Valley Lookout** ⭐⭐⭐, a grassy park on the edge of Waipio Valley's sheer cliffs with splendid views of the wild oasis below. This is a great place for a picnic; you can sit at old redwood picnic tables and watch the white combers race upon the black-sand beach at the mouth of Waipio Valley.

From the lookout, you can hike down into the valley. Do not, we repeat, *do not* attempt to drive your rental car down into the valley (even if you see someone else doing it). The problem is not so much going down as coming back up. Every day, rental cars have to be "rescued" and towed back up to the top, at great expense to the driver. Instead, take the **Waipio Valley Shuttle** (C) **808/775-7121**) on a 90-minute guided tour. The shuttle runs Monday through Saturday from 9am to 4pm; tickets are $40 for adults, $20 for kids 4 to 11. Get your tickets at **Waipio Valley Art Works,** on Highway 240, 2 miles from the lookout (© **808/775-0958**).

You can also explore the valley on a narrated, 90-minute **Waipio Valley Wagon Tour** (© **808/775-9518;** www.waipiovalleywagontours.com), a historical ride by mule-drawn surrey. Tours are offered Monday through Saturday at 9:30am, 11:30am, 1:30pm, and 3:30pm. It costs $40 for adults, $20 for children ages 4 to 12; call for reservations.

If you want to spend more than a day in the valley, plan ahead. A few simple B&Bs are situated on the ridge overlooking the valley and require advance reservations (see "Where to Stay," earlier in this chapter). While it's possible to camp, it does put a strain on the natural environment here.

HILO ★★★

Contact or stop by the **Downtown Hilo Improvement Association,** 252 Kamehameha Ave., Hilo, HI 96720 (© **808/935-8850**); www.downtownhilo. com) for a copy of its very informative self-guided walking tour of 18 historic sites in Hilo, focusing on various sites from the 1870s to the present.

ON THE WATERFRONT

Old banyan trees shade **Banyan Drive** ★★, the lane that curves along the waterfront to the Hilo Bay hotels. Most of the trees were planted in the mid-1930s by memorable visitors like Cecil B. DeMille (who was here in 1933 filming *Four Frightened People*), Babe Ruth (his tree is in front of Hilo Hawaiian Hotel), King George V, and Amelia Earhart, but many were planted by celebrities whose fleeting fame didn't last as long as the trees themselves.

It's worth a stop along Banyan Drive—especially if the coast is clear and the summit of Mauna Kea is free of clouds—to make the short walk across the concrete-arch bridge in front of the Naniloa Hotel to **Coconut Island** ★, if only to gain a panoramic sense of the place.

Also along Banyan Drive is **Liliuokalani Gardens** ★★, the largest formal Japanese garden this side of Tokyo. This 30-acre park, named for Hawaii's last monarch, Queen Liliuokalani, is as pretty as a postcard from the East, with bonsai, carp ponds, pagodas, and a moon-gate bridge. Admission is free; open 24 hours.

OTHER HILO SIGHTS

Lyman Museum & Mission House ★ *Kids* The oldest wood-frame house on the island was built in 1839 by David and Sarah Lyman, a missionary couple who arrived from New England in 1832. This hybrid combined New England– and Hawaiian–style architecture with a pitched thatch roof. Built of hand-hewn koa planks and timbers, it's crowned by Hawaii's first corrugated zinc roof, imported from England in 1856. Here, the Lymans served as the spiritual center of Hilo, receiving such guests as Mark Twain, Robert Louis Stevenson, and Hawaii's own monarchs. The well-preserved house is the best example of missionary life and times in Hawaii. You'll find lots of artifacts from the last century, including furniture and clothing from the Lymans and one of the first mirrors in Hawaii. The 21st century has also entered the museum, which now offers online computers and interactive, high-tech exhibits.

The **Earth Heritage Gallery** next door continues the story of the islands with geology and astronomy exhibits, a mineral rock collection that's rated one of the top 10 in the country, and a section on local flora and fauna. Upstairs is the

Hilo

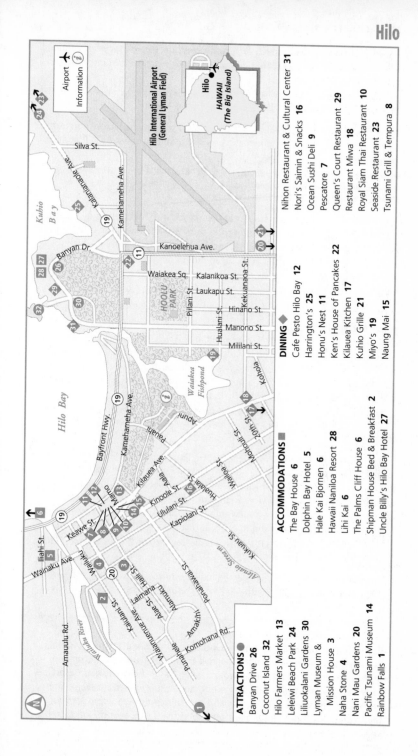

Airport ✈
Information ⓘ

Hilo International Airport
(General Lyman Field)

HAWAII
(The Big Island)
Hilo ●

ATTRACTIONS ●
Banyan Drive **26**
Coconut Island **32**
Hilo Farmers Market **13**
Leleiwi Beach Park **24**
Liliuokalani Gardens **30**
Lyman Museum &
  Mission House **3**
Naha Stone **4**
Nani Mau Gardens **20**
Pacific Tsunami Museum **14**
Rainbow Falls **1**

ACCOMMODATIONS ■
The Bay House **6**
Dolphin Bay Hotel **5**
Hale Kai Bjornen **6**
Hawaii Naniloa Resort **28**
Lihi Kai **6**
The Palms Cliff House **6**
Shipman House Bed & Breakfast **2**
Uncle Billy's Hilo Bay Hotel **27**

DINING ◆
Cafe Pesto Hilo Bay **12**
Harrington's **25**
Honu's Nest **11**
Ken's House of Pancakes **22**
Kilauea Kitchen **17**
Kuhio Grille **21**
Miyo's **19**
Naung Mai **15**

Nihon Restaurant & Cultural Center **31**
Nori's Saimin & Snacks **16**
Ocean Sushi Deli **9**
Pescatore **7**
Queen's Court Restaurant **29**
Restaurant Miwa **18**
Royal Siam Thai Restaurant **10**
Seaside Restaurant **23**
Tsunami Grill & Tempura **8**

Island Heritage Gallery, which features displays on native Hawaiian culture, including a replica of a grass hut, as well as on other cultures transplanted to Hawaii's shores.

276 Haili St. (at Kapiolani St.), Hilo. ℂ 808/935-5021. www.lymanmuseum.org. Admission $7 adults, $5 seniors over 60, $3 children under 18, $15 per family. Mon–Sat 9am–4:30pm.

Maunaloa Macadamia Nut Factory   Explore this unique factory and learn how Hawaii's favorite nut is grown and processed. And, of course, you'll want to sample the tasty mac nuts, too.

Macadamia Nut Rd. (8 miles from Hilo, off Hwy. 11), Hilo. ℂ 888/MAUNA LOA or 808/966-8618. www. maunaloa.com. Free admission; self-guided factory tours. Daily 8:30am–5pm. From Hwy. 11, turn on Macadamia Nut Rd.; go 3 miles down the road to the factory.

Naha Stone   This 2½-ton stone was used as a test of royal strength: Ancient legend said that whoever could move the stone would conquer and unite the islands. As a 14-year-old boy, King Kamehameha the Great moved the stone— and later fulfilled his destiny. The Pinao stone, next to it, once guarded an ancient temple.

In front of Hilo Public Library, 300 Waianuenue Ave.

Nani Mau Gardens ⋆   Just outside Hilo is Nani Mau ("forever beautiful"), where Makato Nitahara, who turned a 20-acre papaya patch into a tropical garden, claims to have every flowering plant in Hawaii. His collection includes more than 2,000 varieties, from fragile hibiscus, whose blooms last only a day, to durable red anthuriums imported from South America. There are also Japanese gardens, an orchid walkway, a botanical museum, a house full of butterflies, and a restaurant that's open for lunch and dinner.

421 Makalika St., Hilo. ℂ 808/959-3500. www.nanimau.com. Admission $10 adults, $5 children 4–10. Tram tours $8 extra. Daily 8:30am–5pm. Go 3 miles south of Hilo Airport on Hwy. 11, turn on Makalika St., and continue ¾ mile.

Pacific Tsunami Museum ⋆   The most interesting artifacts here are not the exhibits, but the volunteers who survived Hawaii's most deadly "walls of water" in 1946 and 1960, both of which reshaped the town of Hilo. Visitors can listen to their stories of terror and view a range of exhibits, from interactive computers to a children's section to a display on what happens when a local earthquake triggers a seismic wave, as it did in 1975 during the Big Island's last tsunami.

130 Kamehameha Ave., Hilo. ℂ 808/935-0926. www.tsunami.org. Admission $5 adults, $4 seniors, $2 students and children. Mon–Sat 9am–4pm.

Panaewa Rainforest Zoo ⋆ *Kids*   This 12-acre zoo, nestled in the heart of the Panaewa Forest Reserve south of Hilo, is the only outdoor rain-forest zoo in

---

A Desert Crossing

If you follow Highway 11 counterclockwise from Kona to the Volcano, you'll get a preview of what lies ahead in the national park: Hot, scorched, quake-shaken, bubbling-up, new/dead land: This is the great Kau Desert, layer upon layer of lava flows, fine ash, and fallout. As you traverse the desert, you cross the Great Crack and the Southwest Rift Zone, a major fault zone that looks like a giant groove in the earth, before you reach Kilauea Volcano.

the United States. Some 50 species of animals from rain forests around the globe call Panaewa home—including several endangered Hawaiian birds. All of them are exhibited in a natural setting. This is one of the few zoos where you can observe Sumatran tigers, Brazilian tapirs, and the rare pygmy hippopotamus, an endangered "minihippo" found in Western Africa.

Stainback Highway (off Hwy. 11), Hilo. © **808/959-7224**. www.hilozoo.com. Free admission. Daily 9am–4pm.

Rainbow Falls ★ *(Moments*   Go in the morning, around 9 or 10am, just as the sun comes over the mango trees, to see Rainbow Falls at its best. The 80-foot falls spill into a big round natural pool surrounded by wild ginger. According to legend, Hina, the mother of Maui, lives in the cave behind the falls. In the old days, before liability suits and lawyers, people swam in the pool, but that's now prohibited.

West on Waianuenue Ave., past Kaumana Dr.

HAWAII VOLCANOES NATIONAL PARK ★★★

Yellowstone, Yosemite, and other national parks are spectacular, no doubt about it. But in our opinion, they're all ho-hum compared to this one: Here, nothing less than the miracle of creation is the daily attraction.

In the 19th century, before tourism became Hawaii's middle name, the islands' singular attraction for world travelers wasn't the beach, but the volcano. From the world over, curious spectators gathered on the rim of Kilauea's Halemaumau crater to see one of the greatest wonders of the globe. Nearly a century after it was named a national park (in 1916), Hawaii Volcanoes remains the state's premier natural attraction.

Hawaii Volcanoes has the only rain forest in the U.S. National Park system—and it's the only park that's home to an active volcano. Most people drive through the park (it has 50 miles of good roads, some of them often covered by lava flows) and call it a day. But it takes at least 3 days to explore the whole park, including such oddities as **Halemaumau Crater** ★★★, a still-fuming pit of steam and sulfur; the intestinal-looking **Thurston Lava Tube** ★★★; **Devastation Trail** ★★★, a short hike through a desolated area destroyed by lava; and finally, the end of **Chain of Craters Road** ★★★, where lava regularly spills across the man-made two-lane blacktop to create its own red-hot freeway to the sea. In addition to some of the world's weirdest landscapes, the park also has hiking trails, rain forests, campgrounds, a historic old hotel on the crater's rim, and that spectacular, still-erupting volcano.

NOTES ON THE ERUPTING VOLCANO   In Hawaii, volcanoes aren't violent killers like Mount Pinatubo in the Philippines or even Mount St. Helens in Washington State. Vulcanologists refer to Hawaii's volcanic eruptions as "quiet" eruptions, because gases escape slowly instead of building up and exploding violently all at once. Hawaii's eruptions produce slow-moving, oozing lava that provides excellent, safe viewing most of the time. In Hawaii, people run to volcanoes instead of fleeing from them.

Since the current eruption of Kilauea began on January 3, 1983, lava has covered some 16,000 acres of lowland and rain forest, threatening rare hawks, honeycreeper birds, spiders, and bats, while destroying power and telephone lines and eliminating water service possibly forever. Some areas have been mantled repeatedly and are now buried underneath 80 feet of lava.

Even though people haven't had to run from this flow, it has still caused its share of destruction. At last count, the lava flow had destroyed nearly 200 homes and businesses; wiped out Kaimu Black Sand Beach (once Hawaii's most photographed beach) and Queen's Bath; obliterated entire towns and subdivisions (Kalapana, Royal Gardens, Kalapana Gardens, and Kapaahu Homesteads); and buried natural and historic landmarks (a 12th-century heiau, the century-old Kalapana Mauna Kea Church, Wahaulu Visitor Center, and thousands of archaeological artifacts and sites). The cost of the destruction—so far—is estimated at $100 million. But how do you price the destruction of a 700-year-old temple or a 100-year-old church?

However, Kilauea has not only destroyed parts of the island, it has also added to it—more than 560 acres of new land. The volume of erupted lava over the last two decades measures nearly two billion cubic yards—enough new rock to pave a two-lane highway 1¼ million miles long, circling the earth some 50 times. Or, as a spokesperson for the park puts it: "Every 5 days, there is enough lava coming out of Kilauea volcano's eruption to place a thin veneer over Washington, D.C.—all 63 square miles."

The most prominent vent of the eruption has been Puu Oo, a 760-foot-high cinder-and-spatter cone. The most recent flow—the one you'll be able to see, if you're lucky—follows a 7-mile long tube from the Puu Oo vent area to the sea. This lava flow has extended the Big Island's shoreline seaward and added hundreds of acres of new land along the steep southern slopes. Periodically, the new land proves unstable, falls under its own weight, and slides into the ocean. (These areas of ground gained and lost are not included in the tally of new acreage—only the land that sticks counts.)

Scientists are also keeping an eye on Mauna Loa, which has been swelling since its last eruption in 1983. If there's a new eruption, there could be a fast-moving flow down the southwest side of the island, possibly into South Kona or Kau.

WHAT YOU'RE LIKELY TO SEE   With luck the volcano will still be streaming rivers of red lava when you visit the park, but a continuous eruption of this length (more than 2 decades) is setting new ground, so to speak. Kilauea continues to perplex vulcanologists, because most major eruptions in the past have ended abruptly after only several months.

But neither Mother Nature nor Madame Pele (the volcano goddess) runs on a schedule. The volcano could be shooting fountains of lava hundreds of feet into the air on the day you arrive, or it could be completely quiet—there are no guarantees with nature. On many days, the lava flows right by accessible roads, and you can get as close as the heat will allow; sometimes, however, the flow is miles away from the nearest access point, visible only in the distance or in underground tubes where you can't see it. Always ask the park rangers before you set out on any lava-viewing expeditions.

VOLCANO VOCABULARY   The volcano has its own unique, poetic vocabulary that describes in Hawaiian what cannot be said so well in English. The lava that looks like swirls of chocolate cake frosting is called **pahoehoe** (pa-*hoy*-hoy); it results from a fast-moving flow that curls artistically as it flows. The big, blocky, jumbled lava that looks like a chopped-up parking lot is called **aa** (ah-ah); it's caused by lava that moves slowly, pulling apart as it overruns itself.

Newer words include **vog,** which is volcanic smog made of volcanic gases and smoke from forests set on fire by aa and pahoehoe. **Laze** results when sulfuric

Hawaii Volcanoes National Park

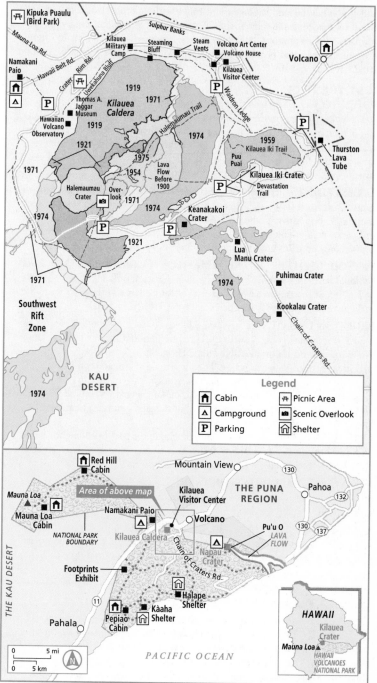

acid hits the water and vaporizes and mixes with chlorine to become, as any chemistry student knows, hydrochloric acid. Both vog and laze sting your eyes and can cause respiratory illness; don't expose yourself to either for too long. Anyone with heart or breathing trouble, or women who are pregnant, should avoid both vog and laze.

JUST THE FACTS

WHEN TO GO   The best time to go is when Kilauea is really pumping. If you're lucky, you'll be in the park when the volcano is active and there's a fountain of lava; mostly, the lava runs like a red river downslope into the sea. If you're on another island and hear a TV news bulletin that the volcano is acting up, catch the next flight to Hilo to see the spectacle. You won't be sorry—and your favorite beach will still be there when you get back.

ACCESS POINTS   Hawaii Volcanoes National Park is 29 miles from Hilo, on Hawaii Belt Road (Hwy. 11). If you're staying in Kailua-Kona, it's 100 miles, or about a 2½-hour drive, to the park. Admission is $10 per vehicle; you can come and go as often as you want for 7 days. Hikers and bicyclists pay $5; bikes are allowed only on roads and paved trails.

VISITOR CENTERS & INFORMATION   Contact **Hawaii Volcanoes National Park,** P.O. Box 52, Hawaii Volcanoes National Park, HI 96718 (© **808/ 985-6000;** www.nps.gov/havo). **Kilauea Visitor Center** is at the entrance to the park, just off Highway 11; it's open daily from 7:45am to 5pm.

ERUPTION UPDATES   Everything you wanted to know about Hawaii's volcanoes, from what's going on with the current eruptions to where the next eruption is likely to be, is now available on the Hawaiian Volcano Observatory's new website, at **http://hvo.wr.usgs.gov.** The site is divided into areas on Kilauea (the currently erupting volcano), Mauna Loa (which last erupted in 1984), and Hawaii's other volcanoes (including Lo'ihi, the submerged volcano off the coast of the Big Island). Each section provides photos, maps, eruption summaries, and historical information.

You can also get the latest on volcanic activity in the park by calling the park's **24-hour hotline** (© **808/985-6000**). Updates on volcanic activity are also posted daily on the bulletin board at the visitor center.

HIKING & CAMPING IN THE PARK   Hawaii Volcanoes National Park offers a wealth of hiking and camping possibilities. See "Hiking & Camping," earlier in this chapter, for details.

ACCOMMODATIONS IN & AROUND THE PARK   If camping isn't your thing, don't worry. There's a hotel, **Volcano House,** within the park boundary, on the rim of Halemaumau Crater; Volcano Village, just outside the park, has

---

Tips   A Volcano-Visiting Tip

Thanks to its higher elevation and windward (rainier) location, this neck of the woods is always colder than it is at the beach. If you're coming from the Kona side of the island in summer, expect it to be at least 10° to 20°F cooler at the volcano; bring a sweater or light jacket. In the winter months, expect temperatures to be in the 40s or 50s, and dress accordingly. Always have rain gear on hand, especially in winter.

plenty of comfortable and convenient hotels and restaurants (see "Where to Stay" and "Where to Dine," earlier in this chapter).

SEEING THE HIGHLIGHTS

Your first stop should be **Kilauea Visitor Center** ★★, a rustic structure in a shady grove of trees just inside the entrance to the park. Here, you can get up-to-the-minute reports on the volcano's activity, learn how volcanoes work, see a film showing blasts from the past, get information on hiking and camping, and pick up the obligatory postcards.

Filled with a new understanding of vulcanology and the volcano goddess, Pele, you should then walk across the street to **Volcano House;** go through the lobby and out the other side, where you can get a look at **Kilauea Caldera** ★★★, a 2½-mile wide, 500-foot-deep pit. The caldera used to be a bubbling pit of fountaining lava; today, you can still see wisps of steam that might, while you're standing there, turn into something more.

Now get out on the road and drive by the **Sulphur Banks** ★, which smell like rotten eggs, and the **Steam Vents** ★★★, where trails of smoke, once molten lava, rise from within the inner reaches of the earth. This is one of the few places where you feel that the volcano is really alive. Stop at the **Thomas A. Jaggar Museum** ★★★ (open daily from 8:30am to 5pm; free admission) for a good look at Halemaumau Crater, which is ½ mile across and 1,000 feet deep. On a clear day, you might also see Mauna Loa, 20 miles to the west. The museum shows video from days when the volcano is really spewing, explains the Pele legend in murals, and monitors earthquakes (a precursor of eruptions) on a seismograph, recording every twitch in the earth.

Once you've seen the museum, drive around the caldera to the south side, park, and take the short walk to Halemaumau Crater's edge, past stinky sulfur banks and steam vents, to stand at the overlook and stare in awe at this once-fuming old fire pit, which still generates ferocious heat out of vestigial vents.

If you feel the need to cool off now, go to the **Thurston Lava Tube** ★★★, the coolest place in the park. You'll hike down into a natural bowl in the earth, a forest preserve the lava didn't touch—full of native bird songs and giant tree ferns. Then you'll see a black hole in the earth; step in. It's all drippy and cool here, with bare roots hanging down. You can either resurface into the bright daylight or, if you have a flashlight, poke on deeper into the tube, which goes for another ½ mile or so.

If you're still game for a good hike, try **Kilauea Iki Crater** ★, a 4-mile, 2-hour hike across the floor of the crater, which became a bubbling pool of lava in 1959 and sent fountains of lava 1,900 feet in the air, completely devastating a nearby ohia forest and leaving another popular hike ominously known as **Devastation Trail** ★★★. This ½-mile walk is a startling look at the powers of a volcanic eruption on the environment. (See "Hiking & Camping," earlier in this chapter, for details on these and other park hikes.)

Check out ancient Hawaiian art at the **Puu Loa Petroglyphs** ★, around the 15-mile marker down Chain of Craters Road. Look for the stack of rocks on the road. A brief, ½-mile walk will bring you to a circular boardwalk where you can see thousands of mysterious Hawaiian petroglyphs carved in stone. *Warning:* It's very easy to destroy these ancient works of art. Do not leave the boardwalk, and do not walk on or around the petroglyphs. Rubbings of petroglyphs will destroy them; the best way to capture them is by taking a photo.

Moments   Driving up to an Erupting Volcano

When the hot tropical sun quits for the day, do not miss seeing the eruption—after dark. At night, it's the greatest show on earth: Red rivers of fire flow just below the surface, visible through the fissures between your feet, and Jell-O–like globs of molten lava inch their way down the mountain and pour into the steaming Pacific, creating the newest land on earth. The ongoing eruption has been pouring out lava for more than 20 years, with no sign of it stopping. Visitors wanting to see the lava flow have had difficulties in the past, as Madame Pele would roll her lava across the very roads leading to the eruption. Be sure to call ahead (© 808/985-6000) to check where the current eruption is and how to get there.

Every time you go, the eruption will be different. The best plan is to go about an hour or two before sunset. Before you jump in your car, be sure to bring a flashlight, plenty of water, sturdy closed-toed shoes and a jacket for after the sun has set. Some even pack sandwiches and juice, and a banana and an apple (for later, to rid your mouth of the lingering sulfur taste), plus an extra jug of water because it's hot out there on the lava, even after dark.

By the time you can see the telltale plume of smog that rises 1,000 feet in the sky, like a giant exclamation point, you will be near the end of Highway 130. Follow the signs to the newly constructed road, where you will be directed to park. From there you usually can see ruby rivers of lava running to the sea. Close to the parking area is a pile of steaming black pillowy-looking stuff with a silvery sheen—it's actually rock-hard pahoehoe lava, like swirls of chocolate frosting.

The first step onto the hardened lava is scary. It crunches like crushed glass under your heels (you'll be happy you have closed-toed shoes or hiking boots). In the distance you can see a red road map of molten lava glowing in the cracks and flowing in fiery rivulets about a foot below the surface. Depending on where the eruption is, you will have to walk a ¼-mile to a mile, in pitch-black darkness (except for your flashlight), to the intersection of lava and sea—but it's a walk that is well worth the trouble.

Silhouetted against the fire, visitors stand at the edge of the earth witnessing the double act of creation and destruction. The lava hisses and spits and crackles as it moves, snakelike, in its perpetual flow to the sea, dripping like candle wax into the wavy surf—fire and water, the very stuff of the islands. The lava still burns underwater until the vast Pacific Ocean finally douses the fire and transforms the flow into yet more black-sand beach.

It's a sight you will never forget.

This area, Puu Loa, was a sacred place for generations. Fathers came here to bury their newborns' umbilical cords in the numerous small holes in the lava, thus ensuring a long life for the child.

THE VOLCANO AFTER DARK   If the volcano is erupting, be sure to see it after dark as brilliant red lava snakes down the side of the mountain and pours into the sea. It's a vivid display you'll never forget. About 1½ hours before sunset, head out of the park and back down Volcano Highway (Hwy. 11). Turn onto Highway 130 at Keaau, go past Pahoa to the end of the road. (The drive takes the better part of an hour.) From here (depending on the flow), it's about a mile walk over sharp crusted lava; park rangers will tell you how to get to the best viewing locations. Be forewarned that the flow changes constantly, and on same days may be too far from the road to hike, in which case you'll have to be content with seeing it from a distance. Be sure to heed the rangers: In the past, a handful of hikers who ignored these directions died en route; new lava can be unstable and break off without warning. Take water, a flashlight, and your camera, and wear sturdy shoes.

A BIRD'S-EYE VIEW   The best way to see Kilauea's bubbling caldera is from on high, in a helicopter. This bird's-eye view puts the enormity of it all into perspective. We recommend **Blue Hawaiian Helicopter** ★★★ (© **800/745-BLUE** or 808/886-1768; www.bluehawaiian.com), a professionally run, locally based company with an excellent safety record; comfortable, top-of-the-line copters; and pilots who are extremely knowledgeable about everything from vulcanology to Hawaii lore. The company flies out of both Hilo and Waikoloa (Hilo is cheaper because it's closer). From Hilo, the 45-minute **Circle of Fire tour** ★★ takes you over the boiling volcano and then on to a bird's-eye view of the destruction the lava has caused and remote beaches ($165 per person). From Waikoloa, the 2-hour **Big Island Spectacular** ★★★ stars the volcano, tropical valleys, Hamakua Coast waterfalls, and the Kohala Mountains (from $340, but worth every penny).

10 Shops & Galleries

While chefs and farmers tout this island as fertile ground for crops and food, artists point to its primal, volcanic energy as a boost to their creative endeavors. Art communities and galleries are sprinkled across the Big Island, in villages like Holualoa and Volcano, where fine works in pottery, wood-turning, handmade glass, and other two- and three-dimensional media are sold in serene settings.

Although the visual arts are flourishing on this island, the line between shop and gallery can often be too fine to determine. Too many self-proclaimed "galleries" sell schlock or a mixture of arts, crafts, and tacky souvenirs. T-shirts and Kona coffee mugs are a souvenir staple in many so-called galleries.

The galleries and shops below offer a broad mix in many media. Items for the home, jewelry and accessories, vintage Hawaiiana, and accouterments at various prices and for various tastes can make great gifts to go, as can locally made food products such as preserves, cookies, flowers, Kona coffee, and macadamia nuts. You'll find that bowls made of rare native woods such as koa are especially abundant on the Big Island. This is an area in which politics and art intersect: Although reforestation efforts are underway to plant new koa trees, the decline of old-growth forests is causing many artists to turn to equally beautiful, and more environmentally sensitive, alternative woods.

Shops in resort areas generally open around 9 to 10am and close around 9pm. Shops in nonresort areas open around 9am and close about 5pm.

THE KONA COAST
IN & AROUND KAILUA-KONA

Kailua-Kona's shopping prospects pour out into the streets in a festival atmosphere of T-shirts, trinkets, and dime-a-dozen souvenirs, with Alii Drive at the center of this activity. But the **Coconut Grove Market Place,** on Alii Drive, across the street from the seawall, has changed that image and added some great new shops around a sand volleyball court. The **Rift Zone** gallery (② **808/331-1100**) pulled up its Hilo stakes and moved to this prime location, offering a large selection of ceramics and crafts by island artists. Oil paintings, Niihau shells, etched and blown glass, koa furniture, photography, and bronze sculptures are among the works represented. (Expect everything from koa wood compacts and Hawaiian coffee to a $4,800 koa executive desk by Frank Chase and a $3,000 koa rocker.) Also in Coconut Grove, **Kane Coconut Grove** (② **808/334-1717**) is a good source of aloha wear for men and women, mostly made by local manufacturer Malia. And who can resist the lighthearted appeal of **Giggles** (② **808/329-7763**), also in the Grove, with a collection of "fun and fancy fashions for kids" that will have you reeling—and reaching for your pocketbook. Next door in the Alii Sunset Plaza, next to Hard Rock Cafe, beaders can make a beeline for **Mana Beads** (② **808/331-2161**) and peruse a dizzying—and handsome—collection of beads from all over the world.

Shopping stalwarts in Kona, in more familiar shopping territory, are the **Kona Square,** across from **King Kamehameha's Kona Beach Hotel;** the hotel's shopping mall, with close to two dozen shops, including the sprawling new emporium called **Big Island Outlet;** and the **Kona Inn Shopping Village,** on Alii Drive. All include the usual assortment of T-shirt shops. One highlight is **Alii Gardens Marketplace** at the southern end of Kailua-Kona, a pleasant, tented outdoor marketplace with fresh fruit, flowers, imports, local crafts, and a wonderful selection of orchid plants. There's cheesy stuff there too, but somehow it's less noticeable outdoors.

Alapaki's Hawaiian Gifts   Lovers of Polynesian crafts will appreciate this selection of gift items, made by more than 100 craftspeople from five of the Hawaiian Islands, with a small percentage of the inventory from Fiji, Samoa, Tonga, Tahiti, and other Polynesian islands. Alapaki's includes jewelry, original paintings, feather hat bands, ceramics, and handblown glass. Works by noted Big Island photographer G. Brad Lewis, who specializes in volcanoes, are among the items for sale. In Keauhou Shopping Center, Alii Dr. ② 808/322-2007.

Hawaiian Country   Noe Kimi Buchanan and her husband, Alika Buchanan, make a fine team on the main drag of Kailua-Kona. He does all the weaving of the fans and hats, while she makes the trims. Their colorful display, in the open air across from the Kailua Bay seawall, is a celebration of things Hawaiian: good weather, generosity of spirit, love of fibers and textures, and old-fashioned ingenuity. The hats are visible from up and down the street—and they're wonderfully affordable (you can find a great one for $12). Lauhala, raffia, straw, you name it—it's here, just waiting to soothe the sunburned brow. And every woman who buys one gets a free lauhala hat pin, made by the Buchanans. 75–5693 Alii Dr., outdoors below Stan's Restaurant. No phone.

Honolua Surf Company   This shop targets the surf-and-sun enthusiast with good things for good times: towels, flip-flops, body boards, sunglasses, swimsuits, and everything else you need for ocean and shore action. Quiksilver, Tommy Bahama, Roxy, Billabong, and Kahala are among the top menswear labels here, but we also like the quirky, colorful Toes on the Nose. Also popular is the full line of products with the Honolua Surf Co. label, including T-shirts, hats, bags, dresses, sweatshirts, aloha shirts, and swimwear. At Kona Inn Shopping Village, Alii Dr. ℰ 808/329-1001.

Hula Heaven   Neighbor islanders make special trips to Kona just to shop for vintage Hawaiian gems at Hula Heaven. It has the island's best collection of aloha shirts and muumuus from the 1920s through '50s, and even the items that aren't vintage have a stylish retro look. Owners Gwen and Evan Olins are passionate collectors whose treasure-laden shop is a nexus for serious and casual collectors of Hawaiiana. Give yourself time to browse the vintage aloha shirts, nodding hula-girl dolls, out-of-print books, lauhala bags, Mundorff prints, Matson liner menus, vintage ukuleles and guitars, Don Blanding dinnerware, koa perfume bottles, Ming's jewelry (the *ne plus ultra* of vintage jewelry), and accessories made of authentic vintage bark cloth. Gwen's fondness for textiles is reflected in the window displays, which often feature one-of-a-kind 1940s fabrics. In Kona Inn Shopping Village, Alii Dr. (next to Hulihee Palace). ℰ 808/329-7885.

Kailua Village Artists Gallery   A co-op of 4 dozen Hawaii island artists, plus a few guest artists, display their works in various media: watercolors, paintings, prints, handblown and blasted glass, and photography. Books, pottery, and an attractive assortment of greeting cards are among the lower-priced items. In King Kamehameha's Kona Beach Hotel, 75–5660 Palani Rd. ℰ 808/329-6653; also at the Lanihau Center ℰ 808/334-0457 and Keauhou Beach Resort ℰ 808/324-7060.

Noelani Farms   Noelani Whittington's grandfather planted the coffee trees on this farm when he was 85 years old. The trees are still yielding tasty coffee beans that Noelani and her husband, Rick, sell wholesale and retail. The 100% Kona coffee is available by phone order, and there are tastings from 4 to 8pm daily at DFS Galleria at King's Shops Waikoloa. The beans are hand-roasted—only 15 pounds at a time—and packed with lots of TLC. You can also order the seasonally available pincushion and miniature king protea, and the dazzling Telopa protea, which resemble torch gingers in all red and all white. Protea are sturdy, showy flowers with a long afterlife—they dry beautifully. The selection varies, depending on the time of year, so there are always surprises. Whittington also sells gift baskets and wreaths, and ships just about anywhere. Phone orders only; ℰ 877/322-3579 or 808/322-3579.

Edibles & Everyday Things

The Big Island's **green markets** are notable for the quality of produce and the abundance of island specialties at better-than-usual prices. Look for the cheerful

Art Appreciation

The finest art on the Kona Coast hangs in, of all places, a bank. Award-winning **First Hawaiian Bank**, 74–5593 Palani Rd. (ℰ 808/329-2461), has art lovers making special trips to view Hiroki Morinoue's mural, John Buck's prints, Chiu Leong's ceramic sculpture, Franco Salmoiraghi's photographs, Setsuko Morinoue's abstract fiber wallpiece, and other works that were incorporated as part of the bank's design, rather than added on as an afterthought. Artists Yvonne Cheng and Sharon Carter Smith, whose works are included, assembled this exhibition, a sterling example of corporate sponsorship of the arts.

green kiosks of the **Alii Gardens Marketplace,** 75–6129 Alii Dr. (at the south end), where local farmers and artists set up their wares daily from 8am to 5pm. This is not your garden-variety marketplace; some vendors are permanent, some drive over from Hilo, and the owners have planted shade trees and foliage to make the 5-acre plot a Kona landmark. There are 40 to 50 vendors on any given day, selling jewelry, woodcrafts, produce, macadamia nuts, orchids, and—our favorite—the fresh juices of Kay Reeves, owner of Wau, who gets up before dawn to make her sensational fresh lilikoi and lime juices with healthful ingredients. Kona Blue Sky Coffee is also here, as is Lynn Cappell, a fine painter of island landscapes, and Laura de Rosa's sensational A'ala Dreams lotions and oils.

From 6am to 3pm on Wednesday and Saturday, look for the loosely assembled tarps of the **Kailua Village Farmers Market,** in the Kona Inn parking lot on Alii Drive. (Go as early as possible to avoid the heat.) Local farmers sell organic corn and tomatoes, anthuriums of every hue, star fruit, breadfruit, papayas, sugarcane, Ka'u oranges, locally made crafts, and macadamia nuts. It's a great way to sample the region's specialties, some of which also make affordable souvenirs. On a recent visit, I found the best prices for macadamia nuts there.

Java junkies jump-start their day at **Island Lava Java** (© 808/327-2161), the hot new magnet for coffee lovers at the Coconut Grove Market Place, on Alii Drive. At the other end of Kailua-Kona, the handmade candies of **Kailua Candy Company** (© 808/329-2522, or 800/622-2462 for orders) also beckon, especially the macadamia-nut clusters with ground ginger or the legendary macadamia-nut *honu* (turtle). Other products include truffles, pure Kona coffee, shortbread cookies, toffee, T-shirts, mugs, mustards, and other gift items.

Kona Wine Market, in the King Kamehameha Mall (© 808/329-9400), has a noteworthy selection, including some esoteric vintages, at prices you'll love. This is a wine lover's store, with selections from California, Europe, and points beyond, as well as gift baskets, cheeses, cigars, oils and vinegars, specialty pastas and condiments, Riedel glassware, and friendly, knowledgeable service.

For everyday grocery needs, **KTA Stores** (in the Kona Coast Shopping Center, at Palani Road and the Queen Kaahumanu Highway, and in the Keauhou Shopping Village, on Alii Drive) are always our first choice. Through its Mountain Apple brand, KTA sells hundreds of top-notch local products—from Kona smoked marlin and Hilo-grown rainbow trout to cookies, breads, jams and jellies, taro chips, and *kulolo,* the decadently dense taro-coconut steamed pudding—by dozens of local vendors. The fresh-fish department is always an adventure; if anything esoteric is running, such as the flashy red aweoweo, it's sure to be on KTA's counters, along with a large spread of prepared foods for sunset picnics and barbecues.

Our other favorite is **Kona Natural Foods,** in the Crossroads Center (© 808/329-2296). It's been upgraded from a health-food store to a full-on healthful supermarket. And it's the only full-service health-food store for miles, selling bulk grains and cereals, vitamins, snacks, fresh-fruit smoothies, and sandwiches and salads from its takeout deli. Organic greens, grown in the South Kona area, are a small but strong feature of the produce section.

For produce and flowers straight from the farm, go to the **Kona Farmers Market in Kaiwi Square,** in Kona's old industrial area (follow the sign on the Queen Kaahumanu Highway). Open on Saturday and Sunday from 8:30am to 2:30pm, it teems with dedicated vendors and eager shoppers. You'll find live catfish, taro, organic vine-ripened tomatoes, Kamuela string beans, lettuces, potatoes, and just-picked blooms, such as anthuriums and feathery, sturdy protea.

UPCOUNTRY KONA: HOLUALOA

Charming Holualoa, 1,400 feet and 10 minutes above Kailua-Kona at the top of Hualalai Road, is a place for strong espresso, leisurely gallery hopping, and nostalgic explorations across several cultural and time zones. One narrow road takes you across generations and cultures.

Paul's Place is Holualoa's only all-purpose general store, a time warp tucked between frame shops, galleries, and studios.

Prominent Holualoa artists include the jewelry maker/sculptor Sam Rosen, who years ago set the pace for found-object art and today makes beautiful pieces at the rear of Chestnut Gallery; the furniture maker and wood sculptor Gerald Ben; the printmaker Nora Yamanoha; the glass artist Wilfred Yamazawa; the sculptor Cal Hashimoto; and Hiroki and Setsuko Morinoue of Studio 7 gallery. All galleries listed are on the main street, Mamalahoa Highway, and all are within walking distance of each other.

Chestnut & Co.   Chestnut is a gallery of great things, inside and out, and worth a special trip to Holualoa. Artists Peggy Chestnut and Sam Rosen took the quaint architecture of the old Holualoa Post Office (which closed in 1961) and turned it into a top-notch gallery of works by Big Island artists. Rosen's studio within Chestnut & Co., Hale O Kula Gallery, displays the jewelry and ceramic/copper/bronze sculptures and vessels that have made him a top name in Big Island art. The eclectic selection includes Chestnut's handwoven table runners, tansus, Asian and South American furniture, hand-turned bowls by Renee Fukumoto Ben and furniture and bowls by her husband Gerald, handmade dolls by Linda Wolfsberg, journals by Ira Ono, and more jewelry ranging from $2 into the thousands. Mamalahoa Hwy. © **808/324-1446.**

Cinderella Unlimited (*Finds*   Most of the treasures here are tucked away, so don't be shy about asking the owner, Cindi Nespor, where she keeps her prized antique engravings or her out-of-print naturalists' books of hand-painted engravings. There are engravings of old Hawaii, rare prints and vases, kimono, lamps, and home accessories. The rare books will quicken a book lover's heart, while the estate jewelry, vintage linens, rattan furniture, and hats make this a brilliant browse. Gorgeous antique shawls, long-extinct Chanel perfumes, and 1940s Garbo-style hats are among the treasures found here. Call ahead, though; the owner keeps flexible, island-style hours. Mamalahoa Hwy. © **808/322-2474;** plus another location: 65-1275 Kawaihae Rd., Waimea © **808/887-6466.**

Holualoa Gallery   Owners Matthew and Mary Lovein show their own work as well as the work of selected Hawaii artists in this roadside gallery in Holualoa. Sculptures, paintings, koa furniture, fused-glass bowls, raku ceramics, and creations in paper, bronze, metal, and glass are among the gallery's offerings. 76–5921 Mamalahoa Hwy. © **808/322-8484.**

Kimura Lauhala Shop   Tsuruyo Kimura, looking 2 decades younger than her 90 years, presides over a labor-intensive legacy—lauhala—that's increasingly difficult to maintain. All the better, because everyone loves Kimura's and the masterpieces of weaving that spill out of the tiny shop. It's lined with lauhala, from rolled-up mats and wide-brimmed hats to tote bags, coasters, and coin purses. The fragrant, resilient fiber, woven from the spiny leaves of the *hala* (pandanus) tree, is smooth to the touch and becomes softer with use. Lauhala also varies in color, according to region and growing conditions. Although Kimura employs a covey of local weavers who use the renowned hala leaves of Kona, some South Pacific imports bolster the supply. At Mamalahoa Hwy. and Hualalai Rd. ✆ 808/ 324-0053.

Studio 7 *Finds* Some of Hawaii's most respected artists, among them gallery owners Setsuko and Hiroki Morinoue, exhibit their works in this serenely beautiful studio. Smooth pebbles, stark woods, and a garden setting provide the backdrop for Hiroki's paintings and prints and Setsuko's pottery, paper collages, and wall pieces. The Main Gallery houses multimedia art, the Print Gallery sculptural pieces and two-dimensional works, and the Ceramic Gallery the works of Clayton Amemiya, Chiu Leong, and Gerald Ben, whose mixed-media sculptures made of ceramic raku and wood continue to be a pleasing attraction. This is the hub of the Holualoa art community; activities include workshops, classes, and special events by visiting artists. Mamalahoa Hwy. ✆ 808/324-1335.

SOUTH KONA

In Kealakekua, the **Kamigaki Market,** on Highway 11, also called Mamalahoa Highway, is a reliable source of food items, especially for regional specialties such as macadamia nuts and Kona coffee.

In Honaunau, farther south, keep an eye out for the **Bong Brothers Store,** on Highway 11, and its eye-catching selections of fresh local fruit—from cherimoya (in season) to star fruit and white **Sugarloaf pineapples.** The Bongs are known for their deli items, produce, and Kona coffee fresh from their own roasting room, but we think their black, very hip Bong Brothers and Bong Sistah T-shirts are the find of the region and season. The juice bar offers homemade soups and smoothies made with fresh local fruit.

In Captain Cook, look for the big "Banana Bread" sign (you can't miss it) across the street from the fire station on Highway 11 and you'll come across the **Captain Cook Baking Company,** which bakes excellent banana bread with macadamia nuts, under the "Auntie Helen's" label. The bread is made with Big Island bananas and macadamia nut honey, and baked right there in the kitchen. This bakery-sandwich shop also sells Lilikoi Gold passion butter, cheesecake-brownies, and submarine sandwiches on its own house-made breads.

Antiques and Orchids Beverly Napolitan and her husband took over the oldest building in Captain Cook (built in 1906) and filled it with an eclectic array of antiques, collectibles, and fresh orchids. There are a few vintage Hawaiian items, lots of tea cups, raspberry-colored walls, linens, old kimonos, celadon, etched glass and crystal lamps, a Queen Liliuokalani lanai sofa from the 1800s, and a red wooden veranda where high tea is served on Saturday (11am–4pm), complete with homemade scones, Devonshire cream, and English tea cups. You can't miss this green building with white trim, on the mauka side of the highway in Captain Cook. Hwy. 11, Captain Cook. ✆ 808/323-9851.

The Grass Shack Grass Shack has been here for more than 3 decades with its large selection of local woodcrafts, Niihau shell and wiliwili-seed leis, packaged coffee, pahu drums, nose flutes, and lauhala (woven pandanus leaves) in every form. Bowls, boxes, and accessories of Norfolk pine, the rare kou, and other local woods also take up a sizable portion of the shop. Lauhala baskets, made of fiber from the region and the Hamakua Coast, are among the Shack's finest offerings, as are the custom ukuleles and feather gourds for hula dancing. Hwy. 11, Kealakekua. ✆ 808/323-2877.

Island Framing Company and Gifts   The owners of this tiny frame shop have great taste, and they've filled their shop with their favorite things: excellent soaps and candles (including Votivo, very chichi), line lights in fabulous designs (such as Japanese lanterns), framed prints, koa frames, Indonesian imports, umbrellas, and household accessories and accents that would liven up any home. Look closely and you might spot a treasure, such as the beautiful lacquer chest I saw for $1,285. The shop is in a charming green plantation house with a small veranda, on the ocean side of the street at the border of Kainaliu and Kealakekua. 79-7506 Hwy. 11, Kealakekua. ✆ **808/322-4397.**

Kimura Store *(Finds*   This old-fashioned general store is one of those places you'll be glad you found—a store with spirit and character, plus everything you need and don't need. You'll see Hawaii's finest selection of yardage, enough cookware for a multicourse dinner, aspirin, Shiseido cosmetics, and an eye-popping assortment of buttons, zippers, and quilting materials. Irene Kimura, the family matriarch, who presided over the store for more than 60 years until she passed away recently, says she quit counting the fabric bolts at 8,000 but knows she has more than 10,000. Kimura's is the spot for pareu and Hawaiian fabrics, brocades, silks, and offbeat gift items, such as Japanese china and *tabi*, the comfortable cloth footwear. Hwy. 11, Kainaliu. ✆ **808/322-3771.**

THE KOHALA COAST

Shops on the Kohala Coast are concentrated in and around the resorts, listed below.

HILTON WAIKOLOA VILLAGE   Among the hotel's shops, **Sandal Tree** carries footwear with style and kick: Italian sandals at non-Italian prices, designer pumps, and other footwear to carry you from dockside to dance floor.

KING'S SHOPS   These stores are located near the Hilton. A recent find here is **Walking in Paradise** (✆ **808/886-2600**). The footwear—much of it made in France (Mephisto, Arche)—can be expensive, but it's worthwhile for anyone seeking comfort while exploring the harsh lava terrain of this island or the pedestrian culture of Kailua's Alii Drive. Toward the mauka (mountainside) end is **Noa Noa,** filled with exotic artifacts from Java and Borneo and tropical clothing for easygoing life on the Pacific Rim. **Kunah's** offers Kahala, Kamehameha, and other hip aloha shirts, as well as baseball caps, flip-flops, and tropical-print canvas bags. At **Under the Koa Tree,** some of the island's finest artists display their prints, woodcrafts, and paintings. For snacks, ice, sunscreen, wine, postcards, newspapers, and everyday essentials, there's the **Whalers General Store,** and for dining on the run, a small Food Court with pizza, plate lunches, and the **Wild Boar Juice & Java** bar for fresh-pressed carrot/ginger juice or a steaming cup of brew.

HUALALAI RESORT   **Ka'upulehu Store,** in the Four Seasons Resort Hualalai, is a perfect blend of high quality and cultural integrity. Located within the award-winning Ka'upulehu Cultural Center, the store carries items made in Hawaii: handmade paper, hand-painted silks, seed lei, greeting cards, koa bowls, wreaths, John Kelly prints, and a selection of Hawaii-themed books. **Hualalai Sports Club and Spa,** in the same resort, has a winning retail section of beauty, aromatherapy, and treatment products, including Hana Nai'a Aromatherapy Products. The products include mango and jasmine perfumes, Bulgarian rose water, and herbal lotions and potions.

MAUNA LANI RESORT   In the Fairmont Orchid, **Collectors Fine Art** is a fine place to wander. We saw a breathtaking milo bowl, about 28 inches tall, made by Hilo's Elmer Adams from a 100-year-old stump found in nearby Puako. Cook pine bowls and Murano glass artist Dino Rosin's extraordinary pieces are the types of treasures you'll find here. Amrit Sakshina's wonderful baskets of local fibers convey the quiet reverence she holds for her art, materials, and environment. At **Spa Without Walls,** the finest European beauty treatments, a well-trained staff, and products using seaweeds, salts, herbs, and essential oils make it hard to resist the spa's refined allure.

NORTH KOHALA

Ackerman Gallery   Crafts and fine arts are housed in two separate galleries a few blocks apart. Artist Gary Ackerman and his wife, Yesan, display gifts, crafts, and the works of award-winning Big Island artists, including Ackerman's own Impressionistic paintings. There are Kelly Dunn's hand-turned Norfolk pine bowls, Jer Houston's heirloom-quality koa-and-ebony desks, and Wilfred Yamazawa's handblown-glass perfume bottles and sculptures. Primitive artifacts, Asian antiques, jewelry, and Cal Hashimoto's bamboo sculptures are also among the discoveries here. The crafts-and-gifts gallery, across from the King Kamehameha statue, has recently doubled in size; it features gift ideas in all media and price ranges. Hwy. 270 (across from the Kamehameha statue; also 3 blocks away, on the opposite side of the street), Kapaau. ⓒ 808/889-5971.

As Hawi Turns   You never know what you'll find in this whimsical, delightful shop of women's clothing and accessories. The windows may be filled with painted paper lanterns in the shapes of stars, or retro painted switch plates, or kicky straw hats paired with bias-cut silk dresses and quirky jewelry. This is the perfect place to pamper yourself with such fripperies as tatami zoris and flamboyant accessories for a colorful tropical life. Hwy. 270 (Akoni Pule Hwy.), Hawi. ⓒ 808/889-5023.

Elements   John Flynn designs jewelry and his wife, Prakash, assembles fountains and other treasures, and together they've filled their quiet gallery with an assortment of arts and crafts from the Big Island, including local artist Margaret Ann Hoy's wonderful watercolors of island scenes. The lauhala accessories, jewelry, and fountains—simple bowls filled with smooth gemstones such as amethyst and rose quartz, with a water pump for the movement—make great gifts and accessories. Hwy. 270 (Akoni Pule Hwy.), Kapaau. ⓒ 808/889-0760.

Harbor Gallery   Formerly Kohala Kollection, this two-story gallery seems to have made a seamless transition, remaining a big draw next to the Cafe Pesto in this industrial harbor area of Kawaihae. Harry Wishard paintings, Miles Fry's museum-quality model canoes and ships, Kathy Long pencil drawings, and Frances Dennis's painted island scenes on canvas are among the works by more than 150 artists, primarily from the Big Island. The range is vast—from jewelry to basketry to ceramics, carved native woods, and heirloom-quality koa furniture. In Kawaihae Shopping Center, Hwy. 270, just north of Hwy. 19. ⓒ 808/882-1510.

Kohala Book Shop   Jan and Frank Morgan's new and used book store—the largest such store in Hawaii—is a huge success and a major attraction in the town's historic Hotel Nanbu building. The yellow building with red-and-green trim is beautifully and faithfully restored, all the better to house a priceless collection that includes out-of-print first editions, the $22,500 set of *Captain Cook's Journals, The Morals of Confucius* (dated 1691 and priced at $350), and

Art Appreciation

The **Mauna Kea Beach Hotel,** 62–100 Mauna Kea Beach Dr. (✆ **808/882-7222**), is home to one of the world's most impressive collections of Asian and Oceanic art. It's displayed unpretentiously, in public and private spaces. Laurance Rockefeller planned his resort so that the art would be totally integrated into the environment: indoors, outdoors, and in hallways, lounges, and alcoves. The result is a spiritually and aesthetically uplifting view in every direction. A 7th-century granite Buddha is the oldest work in a collection that incorporates art from China, Japan, India, Southeast Asia, and Polynesia, including Hawaii. The Lloyd Sexton Gallery and John Young paintings throughout the hotel reflect Rockefeller's commitment to the finest.

thousands of other treasures. You'll see popular fiction and everyday books, too, along with titles on Hawaii and Oceania; at last count, the inventory was 20,000 and climbing. Thoughtful signs, good prices, and an attractive and welcoming environment are only some of the winning features. Hwy. 270 (Akoni Pule Hwy.), a block from the Kamehameha statue, Kapaau. ✆ 808/889-6732.

Sugar Moon   Tom and Julie Kostes display their ceramics and woodworks in a tidy gallery on Kapaau's main street. Ceramic wall sconces, bowls made of banyan wood, mirrors with ceramic frames, koa chopsticks, ceramic basins, custom tiles and lamps, and Julie McCue original watercolors are some of the finds here. Hwy. 270 (Akoni Pule Hwy.), Kapaau. ✆ 808/889-0994.

WAIMEA

Waimea is lei country as well as the island's breadbasket, so look for protea, vegetables, vine-ripened tomatoes, and tuberose stalks here at reasonable prices. Mainstays include **Honopua Farm** and **Hufford's Farm,** side by side, selling flowers and organic vegetables. The selection of flowers often includes freesias, irises, heather, stars-of-Bethlehem, Australian teas, and cleomes, all freshly clipped. You'll find **Marie McDonald,** one of Hawaii's premier lei-makers, at the booth. (If you want one of her designer Waimea leis, you have to order ahead; call ✆ 808/885-4148.) Also here is **Bernice Berdon,** considered the best maker of akulikuli leis, a Waimea signature that comes in yellows, oranges, and fuchsias. Ask about her bat-face kika, the cigar-flower lei with bat-faced blossoms. If you're here around Christmas, you'll find phenomenal protea wreaths.

Small and sublime, the **Waimea Farmers Market,** Highway 19, at mile marker 55 on the Hamakua side of Waimea town (on the lawn in front of the Department of Hawaiian Home Lands, West Hawaii office), draws a loyal crowd from 7am to noon on Saturdays.

At the other end of Waimea, the **Parker School Farmers Market,** held Saturdays from 7:30am to noon, is smaller and more subdued, but with choice items as well. The Kalopa macadamia nuts are the sweetest and tastiest we've ever had. Hilo's wonderful **Dan De Luz Woods** (p. 342) has a branch at 64-1013 Mamamlahoa Hwy., in front of the True Value hardware store.

Other shops in Waimea range from the small roadside storefronts lining Highway 19 and Highway 190, which intersect in the middle of town, to complexes such as **Waimea Center,** where you'll find the trusty old **KTA Super Store,** the one-stop shop for all your basic necessities, plus a glorious profusion of interesting local foods.

Cook's Discoveries, at a prominent corner on the Hamakua side of town, is better than ever. With its upscale galleries and shops, **Parker Square** will likely be your most rewarding stop.

Adasa Boutique at Opelo Plaza   Former entertainer Donna Loren brought her other talents to Waimea and unveiled them in this high-style boutique. Her original designs appear in lavish fabrics, along with a small selection of cashmere separates, Anna Sui and Vivienne Tam designs, Versace cosmetics, Donald Pliner and Robert Clergerie shoes, Rocket Dog sandals, and extraordinary beaded cushions, lamps, and purses. From beaded duvets to dragon-print rubber zoris, the collection includes dangerously seductive items. Scarves, hats, handbags, swimwear, eyewear, lingerie, party dresses—it's hard to imagine all this in a boutique the size of Adasa, a welcome softening of Waimea's cowboy style. The handmade Italian sandals by Don Ciccillo are crafted in the old-fashioned cobbler tradition, using hand-staked hides, precious silks, glove leather, and modern adornments such as Swarovsky crystal and silk flowers. Three Opelo Plaza (in the same complex as Merriman's), Mamalahoa Hwy. ✆ 808/887-0067.

Bentley's Home & Garden Collection   To its lavish list of glassware, linens, chenille throws, home fragrances, stuffed animals, and Wild West gift-wraps, Bentley's has added casual country clothing in linens and cottons. Dresses, sweaters, raffia hats, top-drawer Western shirts, handbags, woven shoes, and all things Martha Stewart adorn this fragrant, gardenlike shop. This is for people who like to raise flowers and herbs, cook with them, breathe potpourried air, take relaxing baths (with expensive designer soaps), and make everything from scratch. In Parker Square, Hwy. 19. ✆ 808/885-5565.

Cook's Discoveries _Finds_   It's a heady mix: Hawaii-themed wearables, fine collectibles, locally made crafts, books, Hawaiian quilts, gift baskets, and ranching memorabilia. One of the few places to carry feather hat lei, Cook's Discoveries has expanded its selection to include quilted slippers, Hawaiian music, cards, framed prints, excellent soaps and beauty products by Island Apothecary, and Niihau shell lei. Other treasures: coconut fiber purses, Hawaiian quilt kits, palaka nightshirts and house slippers, kupe'e shell necklaces, the rare miniature kukui-nut lei, locally designed pareus, lauhala baskets, and hundreds of other surprises. Lauhala hats made of Kona and rare Puna hala leaves are fashioned into 1930s and '40s designs, and are wonderful. Muumuu, silkscreened dresses, and a fabulous assortment of food items—from mango chutney to Hamakua coffee, lemon butter, and condiments—attest to owner Patti Cook's nose for the good things of Hawaii. Her own line of triple-chocolate-chunk cookies and macadamia-nut ginger snaps should claim a fair share of the shopping basket. Cook's Corner, 64-1066 Mamalahoa Hwy. (Hwy. 190). ✆ 808/885-3633.

Gallery of Great Things   Here's an eye-popping assemblage of local art and Pacific Rim artifacts. Browse under the watchful gaze of an antique Tongan war club (not for sale) and authentic rhinoceros- and deer-horn blowguns from Borneo among the plethora of treasures from Polynesia, Micronesia, and Indonesia. You'll find jewelry, glassware, photographs, greeting cards, fiber baskets, and hand-turned bowls of beautifully grained woods. Photos by Victoria McCormick, Kathy Long sketches, feather masks by Bety McCormick, and the paintings of Yvonne Cheng are among the treasures by local artists. There are a few pieces of etched glass and vintage clothing, too, along with a small, gorgeous collection of antique kimono. In Parker Square, Hwy. 19. ✆ 808/885-7706.

Imagination   This children's shop is stacked high with upscale toys, dolls, books, games, and other upper-end diversions. The selection includes a first-rate collection of educational toys and European and Asian imports. In Parker Square, Hwy. 19. ✆ **808/885-0430**.

Mauna Kea Galleries *(Finds*   This is the new and expanded version of the gallery we've come to know and love in Hilo, which is now open by appointment only. Mark Blackburn, who wrote *Hawaiiana: The Best of Hawaiian Design,* has made this his showcase for the treasures he loves to collect. He and his wife, Carolyn, amass vintage Hawaiiana in mint condition from estate sales and collectors all over the country and then respectfully display it. Their collection includes monarchy and Ming jewelry; mint-condition Santa Anita and Don Blanding dinnerware, including very rare pieces; adz-hewn, not lathed, koa- and kou-wood bowls; and vintage photography and menus, all individually stored in plastic sleeves ($10–$300). Rare books and prints, including hand-colored 1870s lithographs; old koa furniture; original Hawaiian fish prints from the early 1900s; and limited-edition, museum-quality reproductions of hula-girl photos from the 1890s are also among the finds. 65-1298 Kawaihae Rd. (across the street from Edelweiss Restaurant), Waimea. ✆ **808/969-1184**.

Silk Road Gallery   Now doubled in size from its original location, Silk Road offers a rare experience of beauty in a large corner of Parker Square. It's worth a special stop if you love Asian antiques: porcelain tea cups, jade cups, kimono, lacquerware, Buddhas, tansus, bronze bells and chimes, Indonesian woven baskets, Japanese screens, and all manner of delights for elevated living. Fine textiles and baskets, antique dolls, rare woodblock prints, and books, cards, and prints are some of its offerings. You can part with $15 for a bronze bell, thousands for an antique tansu, or something in between. The gallery overflows with Asian treasures, so leave time for an unhurried look. In Parker Square, Hwy. 19. ✆ **808/885-7474**.

Sweet Wind   Because the owner loves beauty and harmonious things, you'll find chimes, carved dolphins, crystals, geodes, incense (an excellent selection), beads, jewelry, gems, essential oils, and thoughtfully selected books worth more than a casual glance. The books cover self-help, health, metaphysics, Hawaiian spirituality, yoga, meditation, and other topics for wholesome living. In Parker Square, Hwy. 19. ✆ **808/885-0562**.

Upcountry Connection   This warm, gleaming gallery and gift shop offers an even mix of fine art, antiques, and crafts, all of impeccable taste, plus a recently expanded collection of home accessories, gifts, and decorative pieces. You may not be looking for a koa chest, but it's here, along with antique koa mirrors, Ed Kayton originals, fine crocheted linens, jewelry boxes, and all kinds of collectibles and contemporary art. One-of-a-kind finds have included a $1,200 coconut-wood Polynesian drum, Hawaiian musical instruments of feathers and coconut shells, Jerry Kotz's hand-turned Norfolk pine bowls, and raku-fired ceramic vases for under $100. Other great discoveries: the original oils, limited prints, cards, and books of Herb Kawainui Kane, a living treasure of Hawaii; and the vibrant paintings of Harry Wishard. The gallery has expanded its line of sterling and hand-beaded jewelry, accessories, and clothing. In Mauna Kea Center, Hwy. 19 and Hwy. 190. ✆ **808/885-0623**.

Waimea General Store   This charming, unpretentious country store has always offered a superb assortment of Hawaii-themed books, soaps and toiletries, cookbooks and kitchen accessories, candles, linens, greeting cards, dolls, Japanese hapi coats, island teas, rare kiawe honey, preserves, and countless gift items from the practical to the whimsical. This is a great stop for Crabtree and Evelyn soaps, fragrances, and cookies—and 1,000 other delights. In Parker Square, Hwy. 19. ✆ 808/885-4479.

THE HAMAKUA COAST

Waipio Valley Artworks *Finds*   Housed in an old wooden building at the end of the road before the Waipio Valley, this gallery/boutique offers treasures for the home. The focus here is strictly local, with a strong emphasis on woodwork—one of the largest selections, if not the largest, in the state. A recent expansion has brought more chests and tables and gift items by Big Island artists. All the luminaries of wood-turning have works here: Jack Straka, Robert Butts, Scott Hare, Kevin Parks. Their bowls, rocking chairs, and jewelry boxes exhibit flawless craftsmanship and richly burnished grains. More affordable are the pens and hair accessories. Deli sandwiches and Tropical Dreams ice cream are served in the expanded cafe. In Kukuihaele. ✆ 808/775-0958.

HONOKAA

Mamane Street Bakery, on the main drag, will fill all your coffee-shop needs. Fresh-baked breads, pies, and pastries (including melt-in-your-mouth Danishes) are served with good coffee in a tiny cafe lined with old photographs.

Honokaa Market Place   We've noticed a proliferation of Balinese imports (not a good sign) mingling with the old and new Hawaiiana. The eclectic selection of Hawaiian, Asian, and Indonesian handicrafts includes wood crafts, Hawaiian prints, and Hawaiian quilts, from wall hangings and pillows to the full-size quilts, plus a few pieces of jewelry. 45–3321 Mamane St. ✆ 808/775-8255.

Honokaa Trading Company   "Rustic, tacky, rare—there's something for everyone," says owner Grace Walker. Every inch of this labyrinthine, 2,200-square-foot bazaar is occupied by antiques and collectibles, new and used goods, and countless treasures. You'll find plantation memorabilia, Hawaiiana, barkcloth fabrics from the 1940s, rhinestone jewelry and rattan furniture from the 1930s, vintage ukuleles, Depression glass, dinnerware from Honolulu's landmark Willows restaurant, koa lamps, Francis Oda airbrush paintings, vintage kimono and linens. This is a Honokaa landmark, a plantation museum, and a major attraction for treasure hunters. It's an unbelievable conglomeration, with surprises in every corner. Vigilant collectors make regular forays here to scoop up the 1950s ivory jewelry and John Kelly prints. Mamane St. ✆ 808/775-0808.

Kamaaina Woods   The showroom is adjacent to the workshop, so visitors can watch the craftspeople at work on the other side of the glass panel. Local woods are the specialty here, with a strong emphasis on koa and milo bowls. Boxes, carvings, albums, and smaller accessories are also included in the mix, but bowl-turning is clearly the focus. Prices begin at about $10. Lehua St. (down the hill from the post office). ✆ 808/775-7722.

Maya's Clothing and Gifts   The Hawaiian-print table runners and locally made soaps and ceramics are only part of the growing selection at this Honokaa newcomer. Napkins, place mats, hula girl lamps, koa accessories, quilted Hawaiian pot holders, aloha shirts, jams and jellies, T-shirts, sportswear, jewelry boxes—it's an eclectic selection for all tastes. Mamane St. ✆ 808/775-1016.

Seconds to Go   Elaine Carlsmith spends a lot of time collecting vintage pottery, glassware, kimono, fabrics, and other treasures, only to release them to eager seekers of nostalgia. Many beautiful things have passed through her doors, including antique koa furniture, old maps, music sheets, rare and out-of-print books, and reams of ephemera. The vintage ivory jewelry and Don Blanding dinnerware are grabbed up quickly. The main store is a few doors away from the warehouse, where furniture and larger pieces are displayed. Mamane St. © **808/ 775-9212.**

Starseed   Shop here for offbeat holographic bumper stickers, jewelry, beads, incense, and New Age amulets. The selection of beads and crystals is impressive. The owner has a special camera that purportedly photographs people's auras, or electromagnetic fields. Find out what your colors are, or look for them in the hundreds of boxes of beads, some of them rare European and Asian imports. 45–3551 A-2 Mamane St. © **808/775-9344.**

Taro Patch Gifts   Taro Patch carries an eclectic assortment of Hawaiian music tapes and CDs, switch plates printed with Hawaiian labels, Ka'u coffee, local jams and jellies, soaps, pareus, books, ceramics, sushi candles, essential oils, and sportswear, such as Hawaiian-print cowboy shirts. The Hawaiian seed lei selection is the best in town: kamani, blue marble, wiliwili, double sheep eye, betel nut, and several other attractive native species. Mamane St. © **808/776-1602.**

HILO

Shopping in Hilo is centered on the **Kaiko'o Hilo Mall,** 777 Kilauea Ave., near the state and county buildings; the **Prince Kuhio Shopping Plaza,** 111 E. Puainako, just off Highway 11 on the road north to Volcano, where you'll find a supermarket, drugstore, Macy's, and other standards; the **Bayfront area** downtown, where the hippest new businesses have taken up residence in the historic buildings lining Kamehameha Avenue; and the new **Waiakea Plaza,** where the big-box retailers (Ross, Office Max, Borders, Wal-Mart) have moved in. For practical needs, there's a **KTA Super Store** at 323 Keawe St. and another at 50 E. Puainako St.

Basically Books   Our favorite Hilo bookstore, affectionately called "the map shop," is a sanctuary for lovers of books, maps, and the environment. They have expanded their selection of Hawaii-themed gift items while they maintain the engaging selection of printed materials covering geology, history, topography, botany, mythology, and more. Get your bearings by browsing among the nautical charts, U.S. Geological Survey maps, street maps, raised relief maps, atlases,

---

A Special Arts Center & Gallery

Part gallery, part retail store, and part consortium of the arts, the **East Hawaii Cultural Center,** 141 Kalakaua St., across from Kalakaua Park (© **808/961-5711**), is run by volunteers in the visual and performing arts. Keep it in mind for gifts of Hawaii, or if you have any questions regarding the **Hawaii Concert Society, Hilo Community Players, Big Island Dance Council,** or **Big Island Art Guild.** The art gallery and gift shop exhibit locally made cards, jewelry, handmade books, sculptures, and wood objects, including museum-quality works.

and compasses, and books on travel, natural history, music, spirituality, and countless other topics. Specializing in Hawaii and the Pacific, this is a bountiful source of information that will enhance any visit. Even the most knowledgeable residents stop by here to keep current and conscious. 160 Kamehameha Ave. © **808/ 961-0144.**

Dan De Luz Woods The unstoppable Dan De Luz has been turning bowls for more than 30 years. His studio, on the highway on the way to Volcano, is a larger, more stunning showcase than his previous location in Hilo. He turns koa, milo, mango, kamani, kou, sandalwood, hau, and other island woods, some very rare, into bowls, trays, and accessories of all shapes and sizes. You can find bookmarks, rice and stir-fry paddles, letter openers, and calabashes, priced from $3 to $1,000. Hwy. 11, Kurtistown. © **808/935-5587.**

Dragon Mama *Finds* For a dreamy stop in Hilo, head for this haven of all-natural comforters, cushions, futons, meditation pillows, hemp yarns and shirts, antique kimono and obi, tatami mats sold by the panel, and all manner of comforts in the elegantly spare Japanese esthetic. The bolts of lavish silks and pure, crisp cottons, sold by the yard, can be used for clothing or interior decorating. Dragon Mama also offers custom sewing, and you know she's good: She sewed the futon and bedding for the Dalai Lama when he visited the island a few years ago. 266 Kamehameha Ave. © **808/934-9081.**

Ets'ko Shop and be entertained by the dizzying selection of loungewear, porcelains, teapots, home accessories, purses, and miscellaneous good things the owner collects from the design centers of the world. Hand-painted cards, unique jewelry and a teapot collection that is out of this world are among the treasurers here. Futuristic wine racks, one-of-a-kind clothes, neckties, photo frames, handblown-glass pens, Japanese furniture and accessories, and ultraluxe candles are included in the glittering assortment. Espresso bar with yummy coffee drinks in the back. 35 Waianuenue Ave. © **808/961-3778.**

Hana Hou *Finds* Michele Zane-Faridi has done a superlative job of assembling, designing, and collecting objects of beauty that evoke old and new Hawaii. If you are looking for Hawaiian lauhala weaving, this is the place for mats, hats, purses, place mats, slippers, even tissue box covers. But that's not all: vintage shirts, china, books, women's dresses, jewelry, handbags, accessories, and fabrics are displayed in surprising corners. The feathered leis and collector's dreams—such as vintage silver-and-ivory jewelry by Ming—disappear quickly. Mundorff prints, 1940s sheet music, and the nicest dressing room on the island (with a mango-wood bench made from the same tree as the desk) are more reasons for a standing ovation. 164 Kamehameha Ave. © **808/935-4555.**

Hawaiian Force Artist Craig Neff and his wife, Luana, hang their shingle at the original location of Sig Zane Designs (good karma), where they sell bold, wonderful T-shirt dresses, mamaki tea they gather themselves, lauhala fans and trivets, surf wear, aloha shirts, and jewelry made of opihi and Niihau shells. Everything here is Hawaiian, most of it made or designed by the Neffs. Their handsome two-toned T-shirt dresses are a Hawaiian Force signature, ideal for Island living, and very popular. 140 Kilauea Ave. © **808/934-7171.**

Rain Clayton Amemiya, revered master of pottery, has opened his studio in Hilo, and it is a gem. Tatami, ceramic accessories and sconces, and walls lined with ceramic vases imbue his gallery with a Zen-like purity and beauty. The gallery features his distinctive works and understated style, which have established him as one of Hawaii's most prominent ceramicists. 86 Mamo St. © 808/934-9134.

Sig Zane Designs *Finds*   Our favorite stop in Hilo, Sig Zane Designs evokes such loyalty that people make special trips from the outer islands for this inspired line of authentic Hawaiian wear. The spirit of this place complements the high esthetic standards; everyone involved is completely immersed in Hawaiian culture and dance. The partnership of Zane and his wife, the revered hula master Nalani Kanaka'ole, is stunningly creative. The shop is awash in gleaming woods, lauhala mats, and clothing and accessories—handmade house slippers, aloha shirts, pareus, muumuus, T-shirts, and high-quality, made-in-Hawaii crafts. They all center on the Sig Zane fabric designs. New designs appear constantly, yet the classics remain fresh and compelling: ti, koa, kukui, taro, the lehua blossoms of the ohia tree. The Sig Zane bedcovers, cushions, fabrics, clothing and custom-ordered upholstery bring the rain forest into your room. To add to the delight, Sig and his staff take time to talk story and explain the significance of the images, or simply chat about Hilo, hula, and Hawaiian culture. 122 Kamehameha Ave. © 808/935-7077.

EDIBLES

Abundant Life Natural Foods   Stock up here on healthful snacks, fresh organic produce, vitamins and supplements, bulk grains, baked goods, and the latest in health foods. There's a sound selection of natural remedies and herbal body, face, and hair products. The takeout deli makes fresh-fruit smoothies and sprout- and nutrient-rich sandwiches and salads. Seniors get a 10% discount. 292 Kamehameha Ave. © 808/935-7411.

Big Island Candies   Abandon all restraint. The smell of butter mixing with chocolate is as thick as honey, and the chocolate-dipped shortbread and macadamia nuts will make it very hard to be sensible. And the free samples when you walk in the door let you know that you have entered heaven. Owner Alan Ikawa has turned cookie-making into an art and spectator sport. Large viewing windows allow you to watch the hand-dipping from huge vats of chocolate while the aroma of butter fills the room. Ikawa uses eggs straight from a nearby farm, pure butter, Hawaiian cane sugar, no preservatives, and premium chocolate. Gift boxes are available, and they're carted interisland—or shipped all over the country—in staggering volumes. The Hawaiian Da Kine line is irrepressibly local: mochi crunch, fortune cookies, animal crackers, and other morsels—all dipped in chocolate. By far the best are the shortbread cookies, dipped in chocolate, peanut butter, and white chocolate. If you get thirsty, there's a juice and smoothie bar. Outside are picnic tables on the manicured grounds. 585 Hinano St. © 800/935-5510 or 808/935-8890; www.bigislandcandies.com for mail orders.

Hilo Farmers Market *Finds*   This has grown into the state's best farmers market, embodying what we love most in Hawaii: local color, good soil and weather, the mixing of cultures, and new adventures in taste. More than 120 vendors from around the island bring their flowers, produce, and baked goods to this teeming corner of Hilo every Wednesday and Saturday from sunrise to 4pm. Because many of the vendors sell out early, go as early as you can. Expect to find a stunning assortment: fresh, homegrown oyster mushrooms from Kona—three or four different colors and sizes—for about $5 a pound; the creamy, sweet, queenly Indonesian fruit called mangosteen; warm breads, from focaccia to walnut; an array of flowers; fresh aquacultured seaweed; corn from Pahoa; Waimea strawberries; taro and taro products; foot-long, miso-flavored, and traditional Hawaiian laulau; made-from-scratch tamales; and fabulous ethnic vegetables with unpronounceable names. The selection changes by the week, but it's always reasonable, fresh, and appealing, with a good cross-section of the island's specialties. Although it's open daily, Wednesday and Saturday are the days when all the vendors are there. Kamehameha Ave. at Mamo St. ⓒ 808/933-1000.

O'Keefe & Sons   You can enjoy O'Keefe's breads throughout the island, served in the best delis, coffee shops, and restaurants. But come to the source, this friendly Hilo bakery, for the full selection or artisan breads and pastries hot from the oven: Hilo nori bread, black-pepper/cilantro bread, focaccia in many flavors, cracked rye, challah, three types of sourdough, carrot-herb bread, and the classic French country loaf. Located opposite the Hawaii Tribune Herald building, O'Keefe's serves sandwiches, soups, and quiche for lunch. 374 Kinoole St. ⓒ 808/934-9334.

HAWAII VOLCANOES NATIONAL PARK

Kilauea Kreations   This is the quilting center of Volcano, a co-op made up of local Volcano artists and crafters who make quilts, jewelry, feather leis, ceramics, baskets, and fiber arts. Gift items made by Volcano artists are also sold here, but it's the quilts and quilting materials that distinguish the shop. Starter kits are available to initiate the needleworthy into this Hawaiian and American craft. We also like the Hawaiian seed leis and items made of lauhala, as well as the locally made soaps and bath products and the greeting cards, picture frames, and candles. Old Volcano Rd. ⓒ 808/967-8090.

Volcano Art Center   The Volcano Island's frontier spirit and raw, primal energy have spawned a close-knit community of artists. Although their works appear in galleries and gift shops throughout the island, the Volcano Art Center (VAC) is the hub of the island's arts activity. Housed in the original 1877 Volcano House, VAC is a not-for-profit art-education center that offers exhibits and shows that change monthly, as well as workshops and retail space. Marian Berger's watercolors of endangered birds, Dietrich Varez oils and block prints, Avi Kiriaty oils, Kelly Dunn and Jack Straka woods, Brad Lewis photography, Harry Wishard paintings, Ira Ono goddess masks, and Mike Riley furnishings are among the works you'll see. Of the 300 artists represented, 90% come from the Big Island. The fine crafts include baskets, jewelry, mixed-media pieces, stone and wood carvings, and the journals and wood diaries of Jesus Sanchez, a third-generation Vatican bookbinder who has turned his skills to the island woods. In Hawaii Volcanoes National Park. ⓒ 808/967-8222.

Volcano Store   Walk up the wooden steps into a wonderland of flowers and local specialties. Tangy lilikoi butter (transportable, and worth a special trip) and flamboyant sprays of cymbidiums, tuberoses, dendrobiums, anthuriums, hanging plants, mixed bouquets, and calla lilies (splendid when grown in Volcano) make a breathtaking assemblage in the enclosed front porch. Volcano residents are lucky to have these blooms at such prices. The flowers can also be shipped (orders are taken by phone); Marie and Ronald Onouye and their staff pack them meticulously. If mainland weather is too humid or frosty for reliable shipping, they'll let you know. Produce, stone cookies (as in hard-as-stone) from Mountain View, Hilo taro chips, bottled water (a necessity in Volcano), local poha (gooseberry) jam, and bowls of chili rice (a local favorite) round out the selection. Even if you're just visiting the park for the day, it's worth turning off

to stop for gas here; kindly clerks give directions. At Huanani and Old Volcano Hwy.
© 808/967-7210.

Volcano Winery   Lift a glass of Volcano Blush or Macadamia Nut Honey and
toast Pele at this boutique winery, where the local wines are made from tropical
honey (no grapes) and tropical fruit blends (half-grape and half-fruit). It's open
daily from 10am to 5:30pm; tastings are free. Pii Mauna Dr., off Hwy. 11 at mile marker
30, all the way to the end. © 808/967-7479.

STUDIO VISITS

The airy Volcano studio/showroom of **Phan Barker** (© 808/985-8636), an
international artist, is a mountain idyll and splendid backdrop for her art, which
ranges from batik paintings on silk, acrylic painting on wood, oil on paper, dye
on paper, and mixed media sculptures. Her work has been exhibited in galleries
and museums ranging from the Smithsonian to Saigon. In addition to studio
visits (by appointment only), she also offers classes in painting on silk and drawing for beginners.

Adding to the vitality of the Volcano arts environment are the studio visits
offered by the **Volcano Village Art Studios.** Several respected artists in various
media open their studios to the public by appointment. Artists in the hui
include **Ira Ono** (© 808/967-7261), who makes masks, water containers,
fountains, paste-paper journals, garden vessels, and goddesses out of clay and
found objects; **Pam Barton** (© 808/967-7247), who transforms vines, leaves,
roots, bark, and tree sheddings into stunning fiber sculptures and vessels, from
baskets to handmade paper and books; raku and jewelry artist **Zeke Israel**
(© 808/965-8820); and sculptor **Randy Takaki** (© 808/985-8756), who
works in wood, metal, and ceramics. These artists, as well as other members Ron
Hanatani (functional stoneware), Cynee Gillette-Wenner (ethnic textiles and
clothing), Dina Kageler (quilts, fabrics, beads), and Hans Ladislaus (painting,
sculpture) are well known in their fields and have their work displayed throughout the islands.

11 The Big Island After Dark

Jokes abound about neighbor-island nightlife being an oxymoron, but there are
a few pockets of entertainment here, largely in the Kailua-Kona and Kohala
Coast resorts. Your best bet is to check the local newspapers—*Honolulu Advertiser* and *West Hawaii Today*—for special shows, such as fund-raisers, that are
held at local venues. Other than that, regular entertainment in the local clubs
usually consists of mellow Hawaiian music at sunset, small hula groups, or jazz
trios.

Some of the island's best events are held at **Kahilu Theatre,** in Waimea
(© 808/885-6017; www.kahilutheatre.org), so be on the lookout for any mention of it during your stay. Hula, the top Hawaiian music groups from all over
Hawaii, drama, and all aspects of the performing arts use Kahilu as a venue.

LUAUS IN & AROUND KAILUA-KONA

Kona Village Luau *(Moments*   The longest continuously running luau on the
island is still the best—a combination of an authentic Polynesian venue with a
menu that works, impressive entertainment, and the spirit of old Hawaii. The
feast begins with a ceremony in a sandy kiawe grove, where the pig is unearthed
after a full day of cooking in a rock-heated underground oven. In the open-air

dining room, next to prehistoric lagoons and tropical gardens, you'll sample a Polynesian buffet: poisson cru, poi, laulau (butterfish, seasoned pork, and taro leaves cooked in ti leaves), lomi salmon, squid luau (cooked taro leaves with steamed octopus and coconut milk), ahi poke, *opihi* (fresh limpets), coconut pudding, taro chips, sweet potatoes, chicken long rice, steamed breadfruit, and the shredded kalua pig. The generosity is striking. The Polynesian revue, a fast-moving, mesmerizing tour of South Pacific cultures, manages—miraculously—to avoid being clichéd or corny. In Kona Village Resort. ℂ 808/325-5555. Reservations required. Part of the full American plan for Kona Village guests; for nonguests, $76 adults, $46 children 6–12, $22 children 2–5. AE, DC, MC, V. Fri 5:30pm.

THE KOHALA COAST RESORTS

Evening entertainment here usually takes the form of a luau or indistinctive lounge music at scenic terrace bars with scintillating sunset views. But newcomer Marriott Waikoloa's **Hawaii Calls** restaurant and adjoining **Clipper Lounge** are a bright new venue for local musicians, with live music nightly from 8:30 to 11:30pm (see also "Where to Dine," earlier in this chapter).

The Friday luau at the **Kona Village Resort** (see above) is the best choice on the island. Otherwise, the resort roundup includes the Hilton Waikoloa Village's **Legends of the Pacific** Friday dinner show, $68 adults, $34 children ages 5 to 12 (ℂ **808/885-1234**) and the Tuesday luau at the **Mauna Kea Beach Hotel** (ℂ **808/882-7222**) $76 adults $38 children ages 5 to 12.

A popular night spot on the Kohala Coast is the **Honu Bar** (ℂ **808/885-6622**) at the Mauna Lani Bay Hotel, a sleek, chic place for light supper, live light jazz with dancing, gourmet desserts, fine wines, and after-dinner drinks. You can order toothsome pastas and light suppers with fine wines by the glass when most other restaurants are closing.

If you get a chance to see the **Lim Family,** don't miss them. Immensely talented in hula and song, members of the family perform in the intimate setting of the Mauna Lani Bay Hotel's **Atrium Bar** (ℂ **808/885-6622**), at the Hapuna Beach Prince Hotel's open-air **Reef Lounge** (ℂ **808/880-1111**), and at the Ohana Keauhou's oceanfront luau (see above).

HILO

Hilo's most notable events are special or annual occasions such as the **Merrie Monarch Hula Festival,** the state's largest, which continues for a week after Easter Sunday. The festivities include hula competitions from all over the world, demonstrations, and crafts fairs. A staggering spirit of pageantry takes over the entire town. Tickets are always hard to come by; call ℂ **808/935-9168** well ahead of time, and see the "Hawaii Calendar of Events," in chapter 2, for further information.

A special new venue is the old **Palace Theater,** 38 Haili St. (ℂ **808/934-7010**), restored and in action thanks to the diligent Friends of the Palace Theater. The neoclassical wonder first opened in 1925, was last restored in 1940, and has reopened for first-run movies while restoration continues. Film festivals, art movies, hula, community events, concerts (including the Slack Key Guitar Festival), and all manner of special entertainment take place at this historical marvel.

Special concerts are also held at the **Hawaii Naniloa Hotel's Crown Room** (ℂ **808/969-3333**), the Hilo venue for name performers from Oahu and the outer islands. You can always count on a great act here, whether it's the Brothers Cazimero or Willie K.

Moments **Old-Style Hawaiian Entertainment**

The plaintive drone of the conch shell pierces the air, calling all to assemble. A sizzling orange sun sinks slowly towards the cobalt waters of the Pacific. In the distance the majestic mountain, Mauna Kea, reflects the waning sun's light with a fiery red, that fades to a hazy-purple and finally to an inky black as a voluptuous full moon dramatically rises over her shoulder.

It's **"Twilight at Kalahuipua'a,"** a monthly Hawaiian cultural celebration, which includes story-telling, singing, and dancing, on the oceanside, grassy lawn, fronting a turn-of-the-century-style wooden cottage at Mauna Lani Bay Resort (© **808/885-6622**). These full-moon events, created by Daniel Akaka, Jr., who is Mauna Lani Resort's Director of Cultural Affairs, hearken back to another time in Hawaii, when family and neighbors would gather on back porches (in carports and yards) to sing, dance and "talk story."

Each month guests, ranging from the ultra-well-known in the world of Hawaiian entertainment to the virtually unknown local kupuna (elder), gather to perpetuate the traditional folk art of storytelling, with plenty of music and dance thrown in.

For more than a half a decade, Twilight at Kalahuipua'a, always set on a Saturday closest to the full moon, really gets underway at least an hour before the 5:30 start. People from across the island, and guests staying at the hotel, begin arriving. They carry picnic baskets, mats, coolers, babies, and cameras. A sort of oceanside, pre-music, tailgate party takes place with kama'aina (local resident) families sharing their plate lunches, sushi, and beverages with visitors, who have catered lunches, packaged sandwiches and taro chips, in a truly old-fashioned demonstration of aloha.

JAZZ

The best jazz on the island takes place every Friday night from 7 to 9:30pm at the **Blue Dolphin Restaurant,** 61–3616 Kawaihae Rd., Kawaihae, © **808/882-7771,** when local residents (many of them retired studio musicians) jam with well-known stars, who just happen to be in the neighborhood (usually on vacation).

6

Maui, the Valley Isle

Maui meets all the criteria for a tropical paradise: swaying palm trees bordering perfect white-sand coves; free-falling waterfalls etching the faces of mountains; voluptuous jungles bursting with bright color and birdsong; and moonlight sparkling on calm, turquoise seas.

And everybody, it seems, knows it. Next to Waikiki, Maui is Hawaii's most popular destination, welcoming 2½ million people each year to its sunny shores. As soon as you arrive at Kahului Airport, a huge banner will tell you that readers of *Condé Nast Traveller* voted Maui the best island *in the world*—and they've done so 9 years running. *Travel and Leisure's* readers also ranked Maui as their favorite island and top travel destination.

Maui has become *the* hip travel destination. Indeed, sometimes it feels a little too well-known—especially when you're stuck in bumper-to-bumper traffic or the wall-to-wall boat jam at Maui's popular snorkeling-diving atoll, Molokini Crater. However, the congestion here pales in comparison to big-city Honolulu; Maui is really just a casual collection of small towns. Once you move beyond the resort areas, you'll find a slower, more peaceful way of life, where car horns are used only to greet friends, posted store hours mean nothing if the surf's up, and taking time to watch the sunset is part of the daily routine.

Visitors from other small towns in America and elsewhere find Maui just right: warm and friendly and not too foreign, with an easygoing lifestyle that's perfect for relaxing. But Maui also has an underlying energy that can nudge devout sunbathers right off the beach. People get inspired to do things they might not do otherwise, like rise before dawn to catch the sunrise over Haleakala Crater, then mount a bicycle to coast 37 switchbacked miles down to sea level; head out to sea on a kayak to look for wintering humpback whales; swim in the clear pool of a waterfall; or discover a whole new world of exotic flowers and tropical fish.

On a map, Maui doesn't look like much, but it's bigger than you might think. The 727-square-mile island has three peaks more than a mile high, thousands of waterfalls, 120 miles of shoreline, and more than 80 golden-sand beaches (including 2 more than a mile long). The island is the result of a marriage of two shield volcanoes, 10,023-foot-high Haleakala and 5,788-foot-high Puu Kukui, that spilled enough lava between them to create a valley—and inspire the island's nickname. Thanks to this unusual makeup, Maui packs a lot of nature in and around its landscape, and its microclimates offer distinct variations on the tropical-island theme: The island's as lush as an equatorial rain forest in Hana, as dry as the Arizona desert in Makena, as hot as Mexico in Lahaina, and as cool and misty as Oregon up in Kula. The shores of Hookipa are ideal for windsurfers, while channel breezes challenge golfers in Kapalua.

1 Orientation

ARRIVING

If you think of the island of Maui as the shape of a person's head and shoulders, you'll probably arrive on its neck, at **Kahului Airport.**

As of press time, six airlines fly directly from the mainland to Maui. **United Airlines** (© 800/241-6522; www.ual.com) has nonstop service from Los Angeles and San Francisco; **Hawaiian Airlines** (© 800/367-5320; www.hawaiian air.com) offers direct flights from Los Angeles, San Francisco and Seattle; **American Airlines** (© 800/433-7300; www.aa.com) has direct service from Los Angeles; **Delta Airlines** (© 800/221-1212; www.delta.com) flies direct from San Francisco and Los Angeles; **Aloha Airlines** (© 800/367-5250 or 808/484-1111; www.alohaair.com) has direct flights from Oakland and Orange County, California; and **American Trans Air** (© 808/435-9282; www.ata.com) offers direct flights from San Francisco, Los Angeles, and Phoenix several times a week.

The other major carriers fly to Honolulu, where you'll have to pick up an interisland flight to Maui. **Aloha Airlines** (© 800/367-5250 or 808/484-1111; www.alohaair.com) and **Hawaiian Airlines** (© 800/367-5320 or 808/838-1555; www.hawaiianair.com) both offer jet service from Honolulu and the other neighbor islands. *Note:* As we went to press, a merger was pending that would combine Aloha and Hawaiian Airlines into one air carrier.

LANDING AT KAHULUI   If there's a long wait at baggage claim, step over to the state-operated **Visitor Information Center** and pick up brochures and the latest issue of *This Week Maui*, which features great regional maps of the islands. After collecting your bags from the poky automated carousels, step out, take a deep breath, and proceed to the curbside rental-car pickup area (at the ocean end, to your right as you stand with your back to the terminal) and wait for the appropriate rental-agency shuttle van to take you a half-mile away to the rental-car check-out desk. (All the major rental companies have branches at Kahului; see "Getting There & Getting Around," in chapter 2 for details on renting in Hawaii.)

If you're not renting a car, the cheapest way to get to your hotel is via **Speedi-Shuttle** (© 800/977/2605 or 808/661-6667; www.speedishuttle.com), which can take you between Kahului Airport and all the major resorts between 6am and 11pm daily. Rates vary, but figure on $30 for one to Wailea (one-way); $41 one-way to Kaanapali and $57 one-way to Kapalua. Be sure to call ahead of time to arrange pickup.

If possible, avoid landing on Maui between 3 and 6pm, when the working stiffs on the island are "pau work" (finished with work) and a major traffic jam occurs.

AVOIDING KAHULUI   If you're planning to stay at any of the hotels in Kapalua or at the Kaanapali resorts, you might consider flying **Island Air** (© 800/323-3345; www.islandair.com) from Honolulu to **Kapalua–West Maui Airport.** From this airport, it's only a 10- to 15-minute drive to most hotels in West Maui, as opposed to an hour from Kahului. **Pacific Wings** (© 888/873-0877 or 808/575-4546; fax 808/873-7920; www.pacificwings.com) flies eight-passenger, twin-engine Cessna 402C aircraft into tiny **Hana Airport,** and also flies into Kahului.

Maui

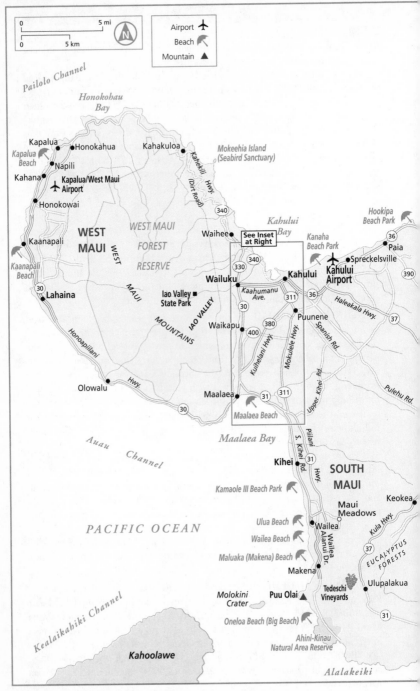

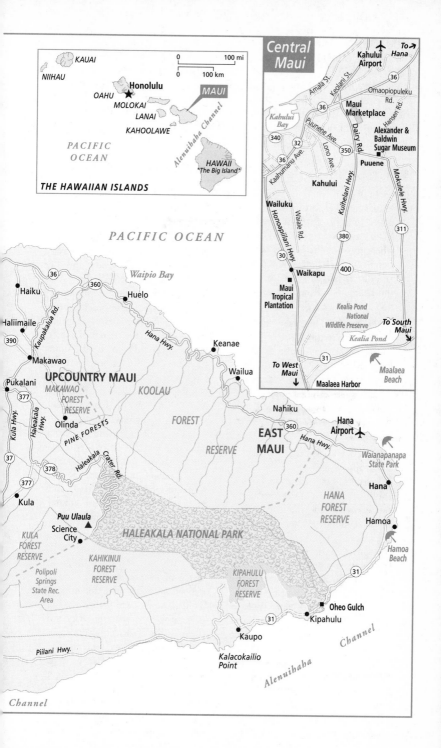

THE HAWAIIAN ISLANDS

KAUAI

NIIHAU

Honolulu

OAHU

MOLOKAI

LANAI

KAHOOLAWE

MAUI

PACIFIC OCEAN

Alenuihaha Channel

HAWAII "The Big Island"

0   100 mi
0   100 km

Central Maui

To Hana

Kahului Airport

Amala St.

Keolani St.

Omaopiopuleku Rd.

36

Maui Marketplace

Puunene Ave.

Kabului Bay

Hansen Rd.

Alexander & Baldwin Sugar Museum

340

32

Lono Ave.

350

Puunene

Kaahumanu Ave.

Dairy Rd.

Kahului

Mokulele Hwy.

36

Wailuku

Waiale Rd.

Kuihelani Hwy.

311

Honoapiilani Hwy.

30

380

Waikapu

400

Maui Tropical Plantation

Kealia Pond National Wildlife Preserve

To South Maui

Kealia Pond

To West Maui

31

Maalaea Harbor

Maalaea Beach

PACIFIC OCEAN

Waipio Bay

36

360

Haiku

Huelo

Haliimaile

Kaupakalua Rd.

Hana Hwy.

Keanae

390

Makawao

Wailua

Pukalani

UPCOUNTRY MAUI

MAKAWAO FOREST RESERVE

KOOLAU

377

Haleakala Hwy.

Kula Hwy.

Olinda

PINE FORESTS

FOREST

Nahiku

EAST MAUI

Hana Airport

Hana Hwy.

360

37

378

Haleakala

Crater Rd.

RESERVE

Waianapanapa State Park

377

Hana

Kula

Puu Ulaula

Science City

HALEAKALA NATIONAL PARK

HANA FOREST RESERVE

Hamoa

KULA FOREST RESERVE

KAHIKINUI FOREST RESERVE

Hamoa Beach

Polipoli Springs State Rec. Area

KIPAHULU FOREST RESERVE

31

Oheo Gulch

Kipahulu

Kaupo

Piilani Hwy.

31

Kalacokailio Point

Channel

Alenuihaha

Channel

VISITOR INFORMATION

The **Maui Visitors Bureau** is at 1727 Wili Pa Loop, Wailuku, Maui, HI 96793 (© **800/525-MAUI** or 808/244-3530; fax 808/244-1337; www.visitmaui.com). To get here from the airport, go right on Highway 36 (Hana Hwy.) to Kaahumanu Avenue (Hwy. 32); follow it past Maui Community College and Wailuku War Memorial Park onto East Main Street in Wailuku. At North Market Street, turn right, and then right again on Mill Street; go left on Imi Kala Street and left again onto Wili Pa Loop.

THE ISLAND IN BRIEF

Central Maui

Maui's main airport lies in this flat, often windy corridor between Maui's two volcanoes, and this is where most of the island's population lives. You'll find good shopping and dining bargains here, as well as the heart of the business community and the local government.

KAHULUI This is "Dream City," home to thousands of former sugarcane workers whose dream in life was to own their own home away from the sugar plantation. There's wonderful shopping here (especially at discount stores), but this is not a place to spend your vacation.

WAILUKU Wailuku is like a time capsule, with its faded wooden storefronts, old plantation homes, shops straight out of the 1950s, and relaxed way of life. While most people race through on their way to see the natural beauty of **Iao Valley**, this quaint little town is worth a brief visit, if only to see a real place where real people actually appear to be working at something other than a suntan. This is the county seat, so you'll see men in neckties and women in dressy suits on important missions in the tropical heat. The town has a spectacular view of Haleakala Crater, great budget restaurants, some interesting bungalow architecture, a Frank Lloyd Wright building on the outskirts, a wonderful historic B&B, and the always-endearing Bailey House Museum.

West Maui

This is the fabled Maui you see on postcards. Jagged peaks, green velvet valleys, a wilderness full of native species—the majestic West Maui Mountains are the epitome of earthly paradise. The beaches here are some of the islands' best. And it's no secret: This stretch of coastline along Maui's "forehead," from Kapalua to the historic port of Lahaina, is the island's most bustling resort area (with South Maui close behind). Expect a few mainland-style traffic jams.

If you want to book into a resort or condo on this coast, first consider what community you'd like to base yourself in. Starting at the southern end of West Maui and moving northward, the coastal communities look like this:

LAHAINA This old seaport is a tame version of its former self, when whalers swaggered ashore in search of women and grog. Today, the village teems with restaurants, T-shirt shops, and galleries, and parts of it are downright tacky, but there's still lots of real history to be found amid the gimcrackery. Lahaina is a great place to stay; accommodation choices include a few old hotels (such as the newly restored 1901 Pioneer Inn on the harbor), quaint bed-and-breakfasts, and a handful of oceanfront condos.

KAANAPALI ✹ Farther north along the West Maui Coast is Hawaii's first master-planned family resort. Pricey midrise hotels line nearly 3 miles of gold-sand beach; they're linked by a landscaped parkway and a walking path along the sand. Golf greens wrap around the slope between beachfront and hillside properties. **Whalers Village**— a seaside mall with 48 shops and restaurants, including such fancy names as Tiffany and Louis Vuitton, plus the best little whale museum in Hawaii—and other restaurants are easy to reach on foot along the oceanfront walkway or by resort shuttle, which also serves the small West Maui airport just to the north. Shuttles also go to Lahaina (see above), 3 miles to the south, for shopping, dining, entertainment, and boat tours. Kaanapali is popular with meeting groups and families—especially those with teenagers, who like all the action.

HONOKOWAI, KAHANA & NAPILI In the building binge of the 1970s, condominiums sprouted along this gorgeous coastline like mushrooms after a rain. Today, these older oceanside units offer excellent bargains for astute travelers. The great location—along sandy beaches, within minutes of both the Kapalua and Kaanapali resort areas, and close enough to the goings-on in Lahaina town—makes this area an accommodations heaven for the budget-minded.

In **Honokowai** and **Mahinahina,** you'll find mostly older units that tend to be cheaper. There's not much shopping here (mostly convenience stores), but you'll have easy access to the shops and restaurants of Kaanapali.

Kahana is a little more upscale than Honokowai and Mahinahina. Most of its condos are big high-rise types, newer than those immediately to the south. You'll find a nice selection of shops and restaurants (including the Maui branch of Roy's) in the area, and Kapalua–West Maui Airport is nearby.

Napili is a much-sought-after area for condo seekers: It's quiet; has great beaches, restaurants, and shops; and is close to Kapalua. Units are generally more expensive here (although we've found a few hidden gems at affordable prices).

KAPALUA ✹✹ North beyond Kaanapali and the shopping centers of Napili and Kahana, the road starts to climb and the vista opens up to fields of golden-green pineapple and manicured golf fairways. Turn down a country lane lined with Pacific pines that leads toward the sea, and you could only be in Kapalua. It's the very exclusive domain of two gracious—and expensive—hotels set on one of Hawaii's best white-sand beaches, next to two bays that are marine-life preserves (with fabulous surfing in winter).

Even if you don't stay here, you're welcome to come and enjoy Kapalua. Both of the fancy hotels here provide public parking and beach access. The resort champions innovative environmental programs; it also has an art school where you can learn local crafts, as well as three favorite golf courses, historic features, a collection of swanky condos and homes (many available for vacation rental at astronomical prices), and wide-open spaces that include a rain-forest preserve—all open to the general public.

South Maui

This is the hottest, sunniest, driest, most popular coastline on Maui for sun lovers—Arizona by the sea. Rain rarely falls here, and temperatures stick around 85°F (29°C) year-round. On this former scrubland from Maalaea to Makena, where cacti once grew wild and cows grazed, there are now four distinctive areas—Maalaea, Kihei, Wailea, and Makena—and a surprising amount of traffic.

MAALAEA If West Maui is the island's head, Maalaea is just under the chin. This windy, oceanfront village centers on the small boat harbor (with a general store and a couple of restaurants) and the **Maui Ocean Center** ★★, an aquarium/ocean complex. Visitors staying here should be aware that it's often—like, 350 days a year—very windy. All the wind from the Pacific is funneled between the West Maui Mountains and Haleakala and comes out in Maalaea.

KIHEI Kihei is less a proper town than a nearly continuous series of condos and minimalls lining South Kihei Road. This is Maui's best vacation bargain. Budget travelers swarm like sun-seeking geckos over the eight sandy beaches along this scalloped, condo-packed, 7-mile stretch of coast. Kihei is neither charming nor quaint; what it lacks in aesthetics, though, it more than makes up for in sunshine, affordability, and convenience. If you want a latte in the morning, the beach in the afternoon, and Hawaii Regional Cuisine in the evening—all at budget prices—head to Kihei.

WAILEA ★★ Just 3 decades ago, this was wall-to-wall scrub kiawe trees, but now Wailea is a manicured oasis of multimillion-dollar resort hotels along 2 miles of palm-fringed gold coast—sort of Beverly Hills by the sea, except California never had it so good: warm, clear water full of tropical fish; year-round golden sunshine and clear blue skies; and hedonistic pleasure palaces on 1,500 acres of black-lava

shore indented by five beautiful beaches. Amazing what a billion dollars can do.

This is the playground of the stretch-limo set. The planned resort development—practically a well-heeled town—has a shopping village, three prized golf courses of its own and three more in close range, and a tennis complex. A growing number of large homes sprawl over the upper hillside, some offering excellent bed-and-breakfast units at reasonable prices. The resorts along this fantasy coast are spectacular, to say the least. Next door to the Four Seasons, the most elegant, is the Grand Wailea Resort and Spa, a public display of ego by Tokyo mogul Takeshi Sekiguchi, who dropped 600 million dollars in 1991 to create his own minicity. There's nothing like it in Hawaii, maybe even on the planet. Stop in and take a look—it's so gauche you've gotta see it.

Appealing natural features include the coastal trail, a 3-mile round-trip path along the oceanfront with pleasing views everywhere you look—out to sea and to the neighboring islands, or inland to the broad lawns and gardens of the hotels. The trail's south end borders an extensive native coastal plant garden, as well as ancient lava-rock house ruins juxtaposed with elegant oceanfront condos. But the chief attractions, of course, are those five outstanding beaches (the best is Wailea).

MAKENA ★★ Suddenly, the road enters raw wilderness. After Wailea's overdone density, the thorny landscape is a welcome relief. Although beautiful, this is an end-of-the-road kind of place: It's a long drive from Makena to anywhere on Maui. If you're looking for an activity-filled vacation, you might want to try somewhere else, or you'll spend most of your vacation in the car. But if you want a quiet, relaxing respite, where the biggest trip of the day is from your bed to the beach, Makena is the place.

Beyond Makena, you'll discover Haleakala's last lava flow, which ran to the sea in 1790; the bay named for French explorer La Pérouse; and a chunky lava trail known as the King's Highway, which leads around Maui's empty south shore past ruins and fish camps. Puu Olai stands like Maui's Diamond Head on the shore, where a sunken crater shelters tropical fish, and empty golden-sand beaches stand at the end of dirt roads.

Upcountry Maui

After a few days at the beach, you'll probably take notice of the 10,000-foot mountain in the middle of Maui. The slopes of Haleakala ("House of the Sun") are home to cowboys, growers, and other country people who wave back as you drive by. They're all up here enjoying the crisp air, emerald pastures, eucalyptus, and flower farms of this tropical Olympus—there's even a misty California redwood grove. You can see a thousand tropical sunsets reflected in the windows of houses old and new, strung along a road that runs like a loose hound from Makawao to Kula, where the road leads up to the crater and **Haleakala National Park** ★★★. The rumpled, two-lane blacktop of Highway 37 narrows on the other side of Tedeschi Winery, where wine grapes and wild elk flourish on the Ulupalakua Ranch, the biggest on Maui. A stay upcountry is usually affordable and a nice contrast to the sizzling beaches and busy resorts below.

MAKAWAO ★★ Until recently, this small, two-street upcountry town was little more than a post office, a gas station, a feed store, a bakery, and a restaurant/bar serving the cowboys and farmers living in the surrounding community; the hitching posts outside storefronts were really used to tie up horses. As the population of Maui started expanding in the 1970s, a health-food store sprang up, followed by boutiques, a chiropractic clinic, and a host of health-conscious restaurants. The result is an eclectic amalgam of old paniolo Hawaii and the baby-boomer trends of transplanted mainlanders. **Hui No'Eau Visual Arts Center** ★, Hawaii's premier arts collective, is definitely worth a peek. The only accommodations here are reasonably priced bed-and-breakfasts, perfect for those who enjoy great views and don't mind slightly chilly nights.

KULA A feeling of pastoral remoteness prevails in this upcountry community of old flower farms, humble cottages, and new suburban ranch houses with million-dollar views that take in the ocean, the isthmus, the West Maui Mountains, and, at night, the lights that run along the gold coast like a string of pearls, from Maalaea to Puu Olai. Everything flourishes at a cool 3,000 feet (bring a jacket), just below the cloud line, along a winding road on the way up to Haleakala National Park. Everyone here grows something—Maui onions, carnations, orchids, and proteas, that strange-looking blossom that looks like a *Star Trek* prop—and B&Bs cater to guests seeking cool tropic nights, panoramic views, and a rural upland escape. Here you'll find the true peace and quiet that only rural farming country can offer—yet you're still just 30 to 40 minutes away from the beach and an hour's drive from Lahaina.

East Maui

ON THE ROAD TO HANA

★★★ When old sugar towns die, they usually fade away in rust and red dirt. Not **Paia** ★★. The tangled spaghetti of electrical, phone, and cable wires hanging overhead symbolizes the town's ability to adapt to the times—it may look messy, but it works. Here, trendy restaurants, eclectic boutiques, and high-tech windsurf shops stand next door to a ma-and-pa grocery, a fish market, and stores that have been serving customers since plantation days. Hippies took over in the 1970s; although their macrobiotic restaurants and old-style artists' co-op have made way for Hawaii Regional Cuisine and galleries featuring the works of renowned international artists, Paia still manages to maintain a pleasantly granola vibe. The town's main attraction, though, is **Hookipa Beach Park** ★★, where the wind that roars through the isthmus of Maui brings windsurfers from around the world. A few B&Bs are located just outside Paia in the tiny community of **Kuau.**

Ten minutes down the road from Paia and up the hill from the Hana Highway—the connector road to the entire east side of Maui—is **Haiku.** Once a pineapple-plantation village, complete with working cannery (which is now a shopping complex), Haiku offers vacation rentals and B&Bs in a quiet, pastoral setting: the perfect base for those who want to get off the beaten path and experience the quieter side of Maui, but don't want to feel too removed (the beach is only 10 min. away).

About 15 to 20 minutes past Haiku is the largely unknown community of **Huelo** ★. Every day, thousands of cars whiz by on the road to Hana; most barely glance at the double row of mailboxes overseen by a fading Hawaii Visitors Bureau sign. But down the gunmetal road lies a hidden Hawaii: a Hawaii of an earlier time, where Mother Nature is still sensual and wild, where ocean waves pummel soaring lava cliffs, and where an indescribable sense of serenity prevails. Huelo is not for everyone—but those who hunger for the magic of a place still largely untouched by "progress" should check into a B&B or vacation rental here.

HANA ★★ Set between an emerald rain forest and the blue Pacific is a village probably best defined by what it lacks: golf courses, shopping malls, and McDonald's. Except for a gas station and a bank with an ATM, you'll find little of what passes for progress here. Instead, you'll discover the simple joys of fragrant tropical flowers, the sweet taste of backyard bananas and papayas, and the easy calm and unabashed small-town aloha spirit of old Hawaii. What saved "Heavenly" Hana from the inevitable march of progress? The 52-mile **Hana Highway,** which winds around 600 curves and crosses more than 50 one-lane bridges on its way from Kahului. You can go to Hana for the day— it's a 3-hour drive from Kihei and Lahaina (and a half century away)—but 3 days are better.

2 Getting Around

BY CAR The only way to really see Maui is by rental car; there's no island-wide public transit. All of the major car-rental firms have agencies on Maui, usually at both Kahului and West Maui airports (for a complete list as well as tips on insurance and driving rules, see "Getting There & Getting Around," in chapter 2).

Maui has only a handful of major roads, and you can expect to encounter a traffic jam or two in the major resort areas. Two of them follow the coastline around the two volcanoes that form the island, Haleakala and Puu Kukui (the West Maui Mountain); one road goes up to Haleakala's summit; one road goes to Hana; one goes to Wailea; and one goes to Lahaina. It sounds simple, right? Well, it isn't, because the names of the few roads change en route. Study a map before you set out.

A Traffic Advisory: The road from Central Maui to Kihei and Wailea, Mokulele Highway (Hwy. 311), is a dangerous strip that's often the scene of head-on crashes involving intoxicated and speeding drivers; be careful. Also, be alert on the Honoapiilani Highway (Hwy. 30) en route to Lahaina, because drivers who spot whales in the channel between Maui and Lanai often slam on the brakes and cause major tie-ups and accidents. Since this is the only main road connecting the west side to the rest of the island, if there is an accident, flooding, rock slide, or any other road hazard, traffic can back up for 1 to 8 hours (no joking)—plan accordingly.

If you get into trouble on Maui's highways, look for the flashing blue strobe lights on 12-foot poles; at the base are emergency solar-powered call boxes (programmed to dial 911 as soon as you pick up the handset). There are 29 emergency call boxes on the island's busiest highways and remote areas, including along the Hana and Haleakala highways and on the north end of the island in the remote community of Kahakuloa.

BY MOPED   Mopeds are available for rent from **Wheels USA** at either of its two locations: 578 Front St., Lahaina (© **808/667-7751**); and in the Rainbow Mall, 2439 S. Kihei Rd., Kihei (© **808/875-1221**). Mopeds, which start at $10 for 2 hours or $22 per 24-hours, are little more than motorized bicycles that get up to around 35 mph (with a good wind at your back), so we suggest using them only locally (to get to the beach or to go shopping). Don't take them out on the highway; they can't keep up with traffic.

BY TAXI & SHUTTLE   Alii Taxi (© **808/661-3688**) offers 24-hour service islandwide. You can also call **Kihei Taxi** (© **808/879-3000**), **Islandwide Taxi & Tours** (© **808/874-TAXI,** or **Sushine Cabs of Maui** (© **808/879-2220**) if you need a ride.

Free shuttle vans operate within the resort areas of Kaanapali, Kapalua, and Wailea.

Ⓒ *FAST FACTS:* **Maui**

American Express Offices are located in South Maui, at the **Grand Wailea Resort** (© **808/875-4526**), and in West Maui, at the **Westin Maui** at Kaanapali Beach (© **808/661-7155**).

Dentists Emergency dental care is available at **Kihei Dental Center,** 1847 S. Kihei Rd., Kihei (© **808/874-8401**) or in Lahaina at the **Aloha Lahaina Dentists,** 134 Luakini St. (in the Maui Medical Group Buidling), Lahaina (© **808/661-4005**).

Doctors **West Maui Healthcare Center,** Whalers Village, 2435 Kaanapali Pkwy., Suite H-7 (near Leilani's Restaurant), Kaanapali (℃ **808/667-9721;** fax 808/661-1584), is open 365 days a year until 10pm nightly; no appointment is necessary. In Kihei, call **Urgent Care Maui,** 1325 S. Kihei Rd, Suite 103 (at Lipoa St., across from Star Market), Kihei (℃ **808/879-7781**), which is open daily from 6am to midnight.

Emergencies Call ℃ **911** for police, fire, and ambulance service. District stations are located in Lahaina (℃ **808/661-4441**) and in Hana (℃ **808/ 248-8311**).

Hospitals In Central Maui, **Maui Memorial Hospital** is at 221 Mahalani, Wailuku (℃ **808/244-9056**). East Maui's **Hana Medical Center** is on Hana Highway (℃ **808/248-8924**). In upcountry Maui, **Kula Hospital** is at 204 Kula Hwy., Kula (℃ **808/878-1221**).

Post Office To find the nearest post office, call ℃ **800/ASK-USPS.** In Lahaina, there are branches at the Lahaina Civic Center, 1760 Honoapiilani Hwy., and at the Lahaina Shopping Center, 132 Papalaua St. In Kahului, there's a branch at 138 S. Puunene Ave.; and in Kihei, there's one at 1254 S. Kihei Rd.

Weather For the current weather, call ℃ **808/871-5054;** for Haleakala National Park weather, call ℃ **808/572-9306;** for marine weather and surf and wave conditions, call ℃ **808/877-3477.**

3 Where to Stay

Maui has accommodations to fit every kind of vacation, from deluxe oceanfront resorts to reasonably priced condos to historic bed-and-breakfasts. Before you book, be sure to read "The Island in Brief," earlier in this chapter, which will help you settle on a location. Also check out "Tips on Accommodations," in chapter 2 for useful advice and reliable booking agents that can help you plan your trip.

Remember that Hawaii's 11.42% accommodations tax will be added to your final bill. Parking is free unless otherwise noted. Also, if you're booking a stay at an upscale hotel, be sure to ask if there is a "resort fee" (which can range from $10–$15 a day) tacked onto your bill.

For an even wider selection of places to stay, check out *Frommer's Maui.*

CENTRAL MAUI

If you're arriving late at night or you have an early morning flight out, the best choice near Kahului Airport is the **Maui Beach Hotel,** 170 Kaahumanu Ave. (℃ **888/649-3222**). The nondescript, motel-like rooms go for $98 to $175 and include free airport shuttle service. It's okay for a night, but not a place to spend your vacation.

WAILUKU

Old Wailuku Inn at Ulupono ★★ *Finds* This 1924 former plantation manager's home, lovingly restored by innkeepers Janice and Thomas Fairbanks, offers a genuine old Hawaii experience. The theme is Hawaii of the 1920s and '30s, with decor, design, and landscaping to match. The spacious rooms are gorgeously outfitted with exotic ohia-wood floors, high ceilings, and traditional Hawaiian quilts. The mammoth bathrooms (some with claw-foot tubs, others with Jacuzzis) have plush towels and earth-friendly toiletries on hand. A full gourmet breakfast is served on the enclosed back lanai or, if you prefer, delivered to your room. You'll feel right at home lounging on the generously sized living-room sofa or watching the world go by from an old wicker chair on the lanai. The inn is located in the old historic area of Wailuku, just a few minutes' walk from the Maui County Seat Government Building, the courthouse, and a wonderful stretch of antiques shops.

2199 Kahookele St. (at High St., across from the Wailuku School), Wailuku, HI 96732. (© 800/305-4899 or 808/244-5897. Fax 808/242-9600. www.mauiinn.com. 7 units. $120–$180 double. Rates include full breakfast. Extra person $20. AE, DC, DISC, MC, V. **Amenities:** Jacuzzi; laundry service; dry cleaning. In room: A/C, TV, dataport.

WEST MAUI
LAHAINA

In addition to the following choices, you may want to consider the oceanfront condos at **Lahaina Shores Beach Resort,** 475 Front St. (© **800/642-6284;** www.lahainashores.com); studio and one-bedroom units go for $180 to $315. Value-priced **Old Lahaina House** (© **800/847-0761** or 808/667-4663; fax 808/667-5615; www.oldlahaina.com) features comfy twin- and king-bedded doubles for just $69 to $125; it's only a block from the water.

Moderate

Best Western Pioneer Inn This once-rowdy home-away-from-home for sailors now seems almost respectable—even charming. The hotel is a two-story plantation-style structure with big verandas that overlook the streets of Lahaina and the harbor, which is just 50 feet away. All rooms have been totally remodeled, with vintage bathrooms and new curtains and carpets. The quietest rooms face either the garden courtyard—devoted to refined outdoor dining accompanied by live (but quiet) music—or the square-block-size banyan tree next door. We recommend room no. 31, over the banyan court, with a view of the ocean and the harbor. If you want a front-row seat for all the Front Street action, book no. 49 or 36.

658 Wharf St. (in front of Lahaina Pier), Lahaina, HI 96761. (© **800/457-5457** or 808/661-3636. Fax 808/667-5708. www.pioneerinnmaui.com. 34 units. $115–$200 double. Extra person $10. AE, DC, DISC, MC, V. Parking $4 in lot 2 blocks away. **Amenities:** Restaurant (good for breakfast); bar with live music; outdoor pool; big shopping arcade; laundry service. In room: A/C, TV/VCR, fridge, coffeemaker, hair dryer, iron, safe.

Guest House ★★ *Finds* This is one of Lahaina's great bed-and-breakfast deals: a charming house with more amenities than the expensive Kaanapali hotels just down the road. The roomy home features parquet floors and floor-to-ceiling windows; its swimming pool—surrounded by a deck and comfortable lounge chairs—is larger than some at high-priced condos. Every guest room has a quiet lanai and a romantic Jacuzzi. The large kitchen (with every gadget imaginable) is available for guests' use. The Guest House also operates Trinity Tours and offers discounts on car rentals and just about every island activity. Tennis courts are nearby, and the nearest beach is about a block away.

1620 Ainakea Rd. (off Fleming Rd., north of Lahaina town), Lahaina, HI 96761. (© **800/621-8942** or 808/661-8085. Fax 808/661-1896. www.mauiguesthouse.com. 4 units. $129 double. Rates include full breakfast. AE, DC, DISC, MC, V. Take Fleming Rd. off Hwy. 30; turn left on Ainakea; it's 2 blocks down. **Amenities:** Huge outdoor pool; watersports equipment rentals; concierge; activity desk; car-rental desk; self-service washers/dryers. In room: A/C, TV/VCR, fridge, hair dryer, Jacuzzi.

House of Fountains Bed & Breakfast *(Finds)* This 7,000-square-foot contemporary home, in a quiet residential subdivision at the north end of town, is popular with visitors from around the world. This place is immaculate (hostess Daniela Atay provides daily maid service). The oversize rooms are fresh and quiet, with white ceramic-tile floors, handmade koa furniture, Hawaiian quilt bedspreads, and Hawaiiana theme; the four downstairs rooms all open onto flower-filled private patios. In fact in 2002, Daniela won the prestigious "Most Hawaiian Accommodation" award from the Hawaii Visitors and Convention Bureau. Guests share the fully equipped guest kitchen and barbecue area, and are welcome to curl up on the living-room sofa facing the fireplace (not really needed in Lahaina) with a book from the library. The nearest beach is about a 5-minute drive away, and tennis courts are nearby. Around the pool is a thatch hut for weekly hula performances, an imu pit for luaus, and an area that's perfect for Hawaiian weddings.

1579 Lokia St. (off Fleming Rd., north of Lahaina town), Lahaina, HI 96761. (C) **800/789-6865** or 808/667-2121. Fax 808/667-2120. www.alohahouse.com. 6 units (shower only). $95–$145 double. Rates include full breakfast. Extra person $20. DISC, MC, V (additional 5% charge if using credit card). From Hwy. 30, take the Fleming Rd. exit; turn left on Ainakea; after 2 blocks, turn right on Malanai St.; go 3 blocks, and turn left onto Lokia St. **Amenities:** Outdoor pool; Jacuzzi; washer/dryers. *In room:* A/C, TV, fridge, hair dryer, no phone.

Lahaina Inn *(★)* If you like old hotels that have genuine historic touches, you'll love this place. As in many old hotels, some of these Victorian antique–stuffed rooms are small; if that's a problem for you, ask for a larger unit. All come with private bathrooms and lanais. The best room in the house is no. 7, which overlooks the beach, the town, and the island of Lanai; you can watch the action below or close the door and ignore it. There's an excellent, though unaffiliated, restaurant in the same building (David Paul's Lahaina Grill, p. 394), with a bar downstairs.

127 Lahainaluna Rd. (near Front St.), Lahaina, HI 96761. (C) **800/669-3444** or 808/661-0577. Fax 808/667-9480. www.lahainainn.com. 12 units (most bathrooms have shower only). $109–$169 double. Rates include continental breakfast. AE, DC, MC, V. Next-door parking $5. No children under age 15. **Amenities:** Bar; concierge; activity desk. *In room:* A/C.

Lahaina Roads *(Value)* If you dream of an oceanfront condo but your budget is on the slim side, here's your place. This condominium complex offers small, reasonably priced units in an older building located in the quiet part of Lahaina, away from the noisy, crowded downtown area, overlooking the boats in the Mala Wharf roadstead (a protected place to anchor near the shore). The compact units come with full kitchens. The bedrooms face the road, while the living rooms and lanais overlook the ocean and the island of Lanai. The soundproofed walls are a real plus. The building is about 35 years old, but well maintained. The only drawback is that there are no laundry facilities.

1403 Front St. (1 block north of Lahaina Cannery Shopping Center). Reservations c/o Klahani Travel, Lahaina Cannery Mall, 1221 Honoapiilani Hwy., Lahaina, HI 96761. (C) **800/669-MAUI** or 808/667-2712. Fax 808/661-5875. www.klahani-travel.com. 17 units. $125 1-bedroom (sleeps up to 4);. 3-night minimum. AE, DC, DISC, MC, V. **Amenities:** Oceanside outdoor pool. *In room:* TV, kitchen, fridge, coffeemaker, hair dryer, iron.

Ohana Maui Islander *(★)* *(Value)* This wooden complex's units, especially those with kitchenettes, are one of Lahaina's great buys. The larger ones are great for families on a budget. The property isn't on the beach, but on a quiet side street (a rarity in Lahaina) and within walking distance of restaurants, shops, attractions,

Lahaina & Kaanapali Accommodations & Attractions

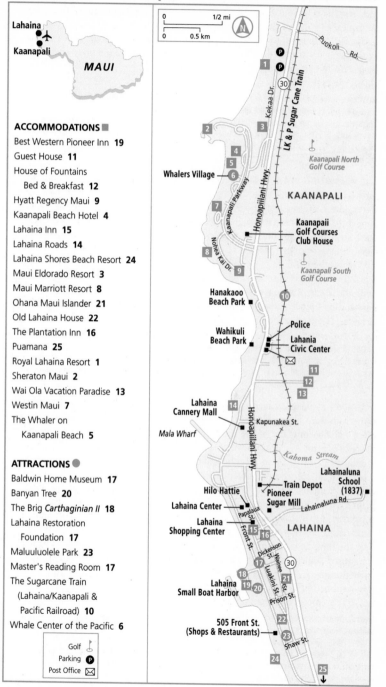

Lahaina
Kaanapali

MAUI

ACCOMMODATIONS ■
Best Western Pioneer Inn **19**
Guest House **11**
House of Fountains
   Bed & Breakfast **12**
Hyatt Regency Maui **9**
Kaanapali Beach Hotel **4**
Lahaina Inn **15**
Lahaina Roads **14**
Lahaina Shores Beach Resort **24**
Maui Eldorado Resort **3**
Maui Marriott Resort **8**
Ohana Maui Islander **21**
Old Lahaina House **22**
The Plantation Inn **16**
Puamana **25**
Royal Lahaina Resort **1**
Sheraton Maui **2**
Wai Ola Vacation Paradise **13**
Westin Maui **7**
The Whaler on
   Kaanapali Beach **5**

ATTRACTIONS ●
Baldwin Home Museum **17**
Banyan Tree **20**
The Brig *Carthaginian II* **18**
Lahaina Restoration
   Foundation **17**
Maluuluolele Park **23**
Master's Reading Room **17**
The Sugarcane Train
   (Lahaina/Kaanapali &
   Pacific Railroad) **10**
Whale Center of the Pacific **6**

Golf
Parking ●
Post Office ✉

Whalers Village

Kaanapali North
Golf Course

KAANAPALI

Kaanapaii
Golf Courses
Club House

Kaanapali South
Golf Course

Hanakaoo
Beach Park

Police
Wahikuli
Beach Park
Lahania
Civic Center

Lahaina
Cannery Mall

Mala Wharf

Kapunakea St.

Kahoma Stream

Lahainaluna
School
(1837)

Hilo Hattie
Train Depot
Pioneer
Sugar Mill

Lahaina Center
Lahaina
Shopping Center

LAHAINA

Lahaina
Small Boat Harbor

505 Front St.
(Shops & Restaurants)

Shaw St.

and, yes, the beach (just 3 blocks away). All of the good-size rooms, decorated in tropical-island style, are comfortable and quiet. The entire complex is spread across 10 landscaped acres and includes a sun deck, a barbecue, and a picnic area. The aloha-friendly staff will take the time to answer all of your questions. *Budget tip:* When booking, ask about "SimpleSaver Rates;" you can save a bundle off the rack rates.

660 Wainee St. (between Dickenson and Prison sts.), Lahaina, HI 96761. © 800/462-6262 or 808/667-9766. Fax 808/661-3733. www.ohanahotels.com. 317 units. $149 double; $179 studio with kitchenette; $199 1-bedroom with kitchen (sleeps up to 4); $279 2-bedroom with kitchen (sleeps 6). Extra rollaway bed $18, cribs free. AE, DC, DISC, MC, V. Parking $3. **Amenities:** Outdoor pool; tennis courts (lit for night play until 10pm); activity desk; coin-op washer/dryers. *In room:* A/C, TV, kitchenettes (in some units), fridge, coffeemaker, hair dryer, iron, safe.

The Plantation Inn ★★ *Finds* Attention, romance-seeking couples: Look no further. This charming Victorian-style inn, located a couple of blocks from the water, looks like it's been here 100 years or more, but it's actually of 1990s vintage—an artful deception. The rooms are romantic to the max, tastefully done with period furniture, hardwood floors, stained glass, and ceiling fans. There are four-poster canopy beds and armoires in some rooms, brass beds and wicker in others. All units are soundproofed (a plus in Lahaina) and come with a private lanai; the suites have kitchenettes. The rooms wrap around the large pool and deck. Also on the property are a pavilion lounge and Gerard's, an outstanding French restaurant (hotel guests get a discount on dinner; p. 394). Breakfast is served around the pool and in the elegant pavilion lounge.

174 Lahainaluna Rd. (between Wainee and Luakini sts., 1 block from Hwy. 30), Lahaina, HI 96761. © 800/ 433-6815 or 808/667-9225. Fax 808/667-9293. www.theplantationinn.com. 19 units (some bathrooms with shower only). $152–$245 double. Rates include full breakfast. Extra person $20. AE, DC, DISC, MC, V. **Amenities:** Acclaimed restaurant and bar; large outdoor pool; Jacuzzi; concierge; activity desk; coin-op washer/dryers. *In room:* A/C, TV/VCR, kitchenettes (in suites), fridge, hair dryer, iron, safe.

Puamana These 28 acres of town houses set right on the water are ideal for those who want to be able to retreat from the crowds and cacophony of downtown Lahaina into the serene quiet of an elegant neighborhood. Private and peaceful are apt descriptions for this complex: Each unit is a privately owned individual home, with no neighbors above or below. Most are exquisitely decorated, and all come with full kitchen, lanai, barbecue, and at least two bathrooms. Puamana was once a private estate in the 1920s, part of the sugar plantations that dominated Lahaina; the plantation manager's house has been converted into a clubhouse with an oceanfront lanai, library, card room, sauna, table-tennis tables, and office. We've found the best rates by booking through Klahani Travel (contact information below), but their office is not on-site, which has caused some problems with guests getting assistance. If you'd rather book with the on-site Puamana association office, contact Puamana Community Association, 34 Puailima Place, Lahaina, HI 96761 (© **808/661-3423;** fax 808/ 667-0398; info@Puamana.info).

Front St. (at the extreme southern end of Lahaina, ½ mile from downtown). Reservations c/o Klahani Travel, Lahaina Cannery Mall, 1221 Honoapiilani Hwy., Lahaina, HI 96761. © 800/669-6284 or 808/667-2712. Fax 808/661-5875. www.klahani-travel.com. 40 units. $125–$200 1-bedroom unit; $150–$275 2-bedroom; $300–$500 3-bedroom. 3-night minimum. AE, DC, DISC, MC, V. **Amenities:** 3 pools (1 for adults only); tennis court; Jacuzzi; game room; activity desk; on-site laundry. *In room:* TV, kitchen, fridge, coffeemaker, hair dryer, iron, washer/dryer (in some units).

Wai Ola Vacation Paradise on Maui ★ Just 2 blocks from the beach, in a quiet, residential development behind a tall concrete wall, lies this lovely retreat, with shade trees, sitting areas, gardens, a pool, an ocean mural, and a range of accommodations (a suite inside the 5,000 sq. ft. home, a separate studio cottage, a one-bedroom apartment to the entire house). Hostess Julie Frank is a veteran innkeeper who knows how to provide comfortable accommodations and memorable vacations. You'll also find a deck, barbecue facilities, and an outdoor wet bar on the property; tennis courts are nearby. Ask about her honeymoon package.

Kuuipo St. (P.O. Box 12580), Lahaina, HI 96761. © 800/492-4652 or 808/661-7901. Fax 808/661-7901. www.waiola.com. 5 units. $135 suite; $150 1-bedroom apt.; $175 cottage; $550-$850 house; 5-night minimum. Extra person $15. AE, DC, DISC, MC, V. **Amenities:** Outdoor pool/Jacuzzi; complimentary use of watersports equipment; free self-service washer/dryers. *In room:* A/C, TV/DVD/VCR, dataport, kitchenette, fridge, coffeemaker, hair dryer, iron.

KAANAPALI

Note: You'll find Kaanapali hotels on the "Lahaina & Kaanapali Accommodations & Attractions" map on p. 361.

Very Expensive

Another option to consider, in addition to those below, is the **Royal Lahaina Resort** (© 800/44-ROYAL or 808/661-3611; fax 808/661-6150; www.hawaii hotels.com). But skip the overpriced hotel rooms; only stay here if you can get one of the 122 cottages tucked among the well-manicured grounds. *Tip:* Book on the Internet, where rates are $195 to $250 double; rack rates are double that price. The **Maui Marriott Resort and Ocean Club** (© 800/228-9290 or 808/667-1200; fax 808/667-8300; www.marriott.com) is wonderful if you like the Marriott style; not so wonderful if you're looking for something a little more Hawaiian. It's a big hit with conventions and incentive groups. Rates are $269 to $550 double; ask about packages. Both properties are located right on the beach.

Hyatt Regency Maui ★★ Kids   Spa goers will love this resort. Hawaii's first oceanfront spa, the Spa Moana, opened here in 2000 with some 9,000 square feet of facilities, including an exercise floor with an ocean view, 11 treatment rooms, sauna and steam rooms, and a huge menu of massages, body treatments, and therapies. Book your treatment before you leave home, this place is popular.

The management has poured some $19 million in renovations to rooms in this fantasy resort, the southernmost of the Kaanapali beachfront properties. It certainly has lots of imaginative touches: a collection of exotic species (flaming pink flamingoes, unhappy-looking penguins, and an assortment of loud parrots and macaws in the lobby), nine waterfalls, and an eclectic Asian and Pacific art collection. This huge place covers some 40 acres; even if you don't stay here, you might want to walk through the expansive tree-filled atrium and the parklike grounds, with their dense riot of plants and the half-acre outdoor pool with a 150-foot lava tube slide, a cocktail bar under the falls, a "honeymooner's cave," and a swinging rope bridge. There's even a children-only pool with its own beach, tidal pools and fountains.

The rooms, spread out among three towers, are pleasantly outfitted with an array of amenities, and have very comfortable separate sitting areas and private lanais with eye-popping views. The latest, most comfortable bedding is now standard in every room (you will sleep like a baby in these fluffy, feather beds). The very romantic Swan Court (p. 400) is not to be missed for a special dinner. Two Regency Club floors have a private concierge, complimentary breakfast, sunset cocktails, and snacks.

200 Nohea Kai Dr., Lahaina, HI 96761. © 800/233-1234 or 808/661-1234. Fax 808/667-4714. www.maui. hyatt.com. 806 units. $345–$565 double; $585–$650 Regency Club; from $850 suite. All rooms are charged

Kids Family-Friendly Hotels

If you're traveling with the kids, you'll be welcomed with open arms at many of Maui's resorts, condos, vacation rentals, and B&Bs (condos are a particularly good choice for families). Our favorite family friendly accommodations are listed below. In addition to these, you might also consider the **Sheraton Maui** (p. 364), the **Westin Maui** (p. 365), the **Kaanapali Beach Hotel** (p. 366), the **Maui Eldorado Resort** (p. 366), **Kahana Sunset** (p. 368), **Noelani Condominium Resort** (p. 370), **Kapalua Bay Hotel & Ocean Villas** (p. 372), **Koa Resort** (p. 374), and **Hotel Hana-Maui** (p. 388), all of which are great for families.

Our Favorite: Four Seasons Resort Maui at Wailea (p. 379) This is the most kid-friendly hotel on Maui. Its complimentary Kids for All Seasons program features activities from sand-sculpting to kite-flying. The resort goes out of its way to make the *keikis* feel welcome, with complimentary milk and cookies on the first day, children's menus in all restaurants (including room service), free infant supplies (cribs, strollers, high chairs, playpens, and car seats), and child-safety features (like toilet-seat locks and security gates). The resort can also prepurchase a range of necessities (such as diapers and baby food) for you before your arrival. Kids and teens have a huge list of diversions to choose from, including a game room (with Super Nintendo, Sony PlayStation, foosball, billiards, and more), a scuba clinic (for ages 12 and older), videos, and more.

Hyatt Regency Maui (p. 363) The Camp Hyatt program, one of the few programs that takes children as young as 3 years old (and as old as 12), operates daily from 9am to 3pm and offers young guests a

a mandatory $12 "resort fee" for access to spa, local phone calls, daily local paper, in-room coffee and tea, in-room safe, and 1-hr. tennis court time. Extra person $35 ($50 in Regency Club rooms). Children 18 and under stay free in parent's room using existing bedding. Packages available. AE, DC, DISC, MC, V. Valet parking $10, free self-parking. **Amenities:** 5 restaurants; 2 bars; a ½-acre-size outdoor pool with lava tube slide, a cocktail bar under the falls, a "honeymooner's cave," and a swinging rope bridge; 36-hole golf course; 6 tennis courts; health club with weight room; brand-new, state-of-the-art spa; Jacuzzi; watersports equipment rentals; bike rentals; Camp Hyatt kids' program, offering supervised activities for 3- to 12-year-olds; game room; concierge; activity desk; car-rental desk; business center; big shopping arcade; salon; 24-hr. room service; in-room spa massage; coin-op washer/dryers; laundry service; dry-cleaning; concierge-level rooms. *In room:* A/C, TV, dataport, 2-line phone, minibar, fridge (on request), coffeemaker, hair dryer, iron, safe.

Sheraton Maui ★★ Kids Terrific facilities for families and fitness buffs and a premier beach location make this beautiful resort an all-around great place to stay. The grande dame of Kaanapali Beach is built into the side of a cliff on the curving, white-sand cove next to Black Rock (a lava formation that rises 80 ft. above the beach), where there's excellent snorkeling. After its recent renovation, the resort is virtually new, with six buildings of six stories or less set in well-established tropical gardens. The lobby has been elevated to take advantage of panoramic views, while a new lagoonlike pool features lava-rock waterways, wooden bridges, and an open-air whirlpool. But not everything has changed, thankfully. Cliff divers still swan-dive off the torch-lit lava-rock headland in a range of activities, from "Olympic Games" to a scavenger hunt. The cost is $75 for a full day (includes lunch and snacks), $38 for a half day.

Hale Kai (p. 368)   This small condo complex in Honokowai is ideally located for families. It's right on the beach, next door to a county park, and within a 10-minute drive of Lahaina's shops, restaurants, and attractions. Kids can hang out at the pool, swim in the ocean, or play in the park next door. There's a TV and VCR in every unit, and the well-equipped kitchens (with dishwasher, disposal, microwave, and even a blender) allow Mom and Dad to save money on eating out.

Ritz-Carlton Kapalua (p. 372)   The Ritz Kids is a year-round daytime activities center for kids ages 5 to 12 that features both educational programs (from exploring the ecosystems in streams to learning the hula) and sports (from golf to swimming). The cost is $15 for hotel guests for a full day (9am–4pm), including lunch, and $70 for Kapalua Villa guests for a full day (with the second child $35). The half-day program (9am–noon or 1–4pm) is complimentary for hotel guests (covered by the $12 daily resort fee) and $35 for Kapalua Villa guests ($18 for the second child).

Mana Kai Maui Resort (p. 377)   This eight-story complex, an unusual combination of hotel and condominium, sits on a beautiful white-sand cove in Kihei that's one of the best snorkeling beaches on Maui's South Coast. Families should consider the condo units, which feature full kitchens and open living rooms; sliding-glass doors lead to small lanais overlooking the sandy beach and ocean.

traditional sunset ceremony—a sight to see. And the views of Kaanapali Beach, with Lanai and Molokai in the distance, are some of the best around.

The new emphasis is on family appeal, with a class of rooms dedicated to those traveling with kids. Every unit is outfitted with amenities galore, right down to toothbrushes and toothpaste. Other pluses include a "no-hassle" check-in policy: The valet takes you and your luggage straight to your room—no time wasted standing in line at registration. One downside is the "resort fee," of $10 per day.

2605 Kaanapali Pkwy., Lahaina, HI 96761. ℂ **800/782-9488** or 808/661-0031. Fax 808/661-0458. www.sheraton-maui.com. 510 units. $350–$750 double; from $825 suite. Extra person $50. Children 17 and under stay free in parent's room using existing bedding. "Resort fee" of $10 for self-parking, "free" local calls and credit-card calls, in-room safe, daily coffee and newspaper, and use of fitness center. AE, DC, DISC, MC, V. Valet parking $5. **Amenities:** 3 restaurants; 2 bars (one poolside); lagoon-style pool; 36-hole golf course; 3 tennis courts; fitness center; Jacuzzi; watersports equipment rentals; children's program; concierge; activity desk; car-rental desk; business center; shopping arcade; salon; limited room service (breakfast and dinner); babysitting; coin-op washer/dryers; same-day laundry service and dry cleaning. *In room:* A/C, TV, dataport, fridge, coffeemaker, hair dryer, iron, safe.

Westin Maui ⭐ *Kids*   The latest addition to the rooms here are fabulous new beds (Westin's custom-designed, pillow-top "heavenly beds"), plus a choice of five different pillows. If that doesn't give you sweet dreams, nothing will. Once you get up, head to the "aquatic playground"—an 87,000-square-foot pool area with five free-form heated pools joined by swim-through grottoes, waterfalls, and a 128-foot-long water slide—which sets this resort apart from its peers along lovely Kaanapali Beach. This is the Disney World of water-park resorts, and your kids will be in water-hog heaven. The fantasy theme extends from the estatelike grounds into the interior's public spaces, which are filled with the shrieks of tropical birds and the splash of waterfalls. The oversize architecture, requisite colonnade, and $2 million art collection make a pleasing backdrop for all the action. Most of the rooms in the two 11-story towers overlook the aquatic playground, the ocean, and the island of Lanai in the distance. Like the Sheraton, the Westin has instituted an obnoxious and not-very-hospitable "resort fee."

2365 Kaanapali Pkwy., Lahaina, HI 96761. ⓒ 888-625-4949 or 808/667-2525. Fax 808/661-5764. www.westinmaui.com. 758 units. $350–$630 double; from $800 suite. Extra person $45. "Resort fee" of $10 for "free" local calls, use of fitness center, coffee and tea, parking, and local paper. AE, DC, DISC, MC, V. Valet Parking $5. **Amenities:** 5 restaurants; 3 bars; 5 free-form outdoor pools with swim-through grotto with twin waterfalls and two water slides; 36-hole golf course; tennis courts; health club and spa with aerobics, steam baths, sauna, massage, and body treatments; Jacuzzi; watersports equipment rentals; bike rental; children's program; game room; concierge; activity desk; car-rental desk; business center; shopping arcade; salon; limited room service; in-room and spa massage; babysitting; coin-op washer/dryers; same-day laundry service and dry cleaning; concierge-level rooms. *In room:* A/C, TV, dataport, minibar, fridge, coffeemaker, hair dryer, iron, safe.

Expensive

Kaanapali Beach Hotel ⭐ *Value* *Kids*   It's older and less high-tech than its upscale neighbors, but the Kaanapali has an irresistible local style and a real Hawaiian warmth that's missing from many other Maui hotels. Three low-rise wings, bordering a fabulous stretch of beach, are set around a wide, grassy lawn with coco palms and a whale-shaped pool. The spacious, spotless motel-like rooms are done in wicker and rattan, with Hawaiian-style bedspreads and a lanai that looks toward the courtyard and the beach. The beachfront rooms are separated from the water only by Kaanapali's landscaped walking trail.

Old Hawaii values and customs are always close at hand, and the service is some of the friendliest around. Tiki torches, hula, and Hawaiian music create a festive atmosphere in the expansive open courtyard every night. As part of the hotel's extensive Hawaiiana program, you can learn to cut pineapple, weave lauhala, or even dance the *real* hula. There's also an arts-and-crafts fair 3 days a week, a morning welcome reception on weekdays, and a Hawaiian library.

2525 Kaanapali Pkwy., Lahaina, HI 96761. ⓒ 800/262-8450 or 808/661-0011. Fax 808/667-5978. www.kbhmaui.com. 430 units. $195–$290 double; from $235 suite. Extra person $25. Car, golf, bed-and-breakfast, and romance packages available, as well as senior discounts. AE, DC, DISC, MC, V. Valet parking $7, self-parking $5. **Amenities:** 3 restaurants; 1 bar (a poolside bar that fixes a mean piña colada); outdoor pool; 36-hole golf course; access to tennis courts; Jacuzzi; watersports equipment rentals; children's program; game room; concierge; activity desk; car-rental desk; business center; convenience store; salon; limited room service; babysitting; coin-op washer/dryers. *In room:* A/C, TV, fridge, coffeemaker, iron, safe.

Maui Eldorado Resort ⭐ *Kids*   These spacious condominium units—each with full kitchen, washer/dryer, and daily maid service—were built at a time when land in Kaanapali was cheap, contractors took pride in their work, and visitors expected large, spacious units with views from every window. You'll find it hard to believe that this was one of Kaanapali's first properties in the late 1960s; this first-class choice still looks like new. The Outrigger chain has managed to keep prices down to reasonable levels, especially if you come in spring or fall. This is a great choice for families, with its big units, grassy areas that are perfect for running off excess energy, and a beachfront (with beach cabanas and a barbecue area) that's usually safe for swimming. Tennis courts are nearby.

2661 Kekaa Dr., Lahaina, HI 96761. (C) **800/688-7444** or 808/661-0021. Fax 808/667-7039. www.outrigger. com. 98 units. $195–$240 studio double; $245–$295 1-bedroom (rates for up to 4); $355–$425 2-bedroom (rates for up to 6). Numerous packages available, including fifth night free, rental-car packages, senior rates, and more. AE, DC, DISC, MC, V. **Amenities:** 3 outdoor pools; 36-hole golf course; concierge; activity desk; car-rental desk; some business services; babysitting; coin-op washer/dryers. *In room:* A/C, TV, dataport, kitchen, fridge, coffeemaker, hair dryer, iron, safe, washer/dryer (in some units).

The Whaler on Kaanapali Beach ★★ In the heart of Kaanapali, right on the world-famous beach, lies this oasis of elegance, privacy, and luxury. The relaxing atmosphere strikes you as soon as you enter the open-air lobby, where light reflects off the dazzling koi in the meditative lily pond. No expense has been spared on these gorgeous accommodations; each unit has a full kitchen, washer/dryer, marble bathroom, 10-foot beamed ceilings, and blue-tiled lanai. Every unit boasts spectacular views of Kaanapali's gentle waves or the humpback peaks of the West Maui Mountains. Next door is Whalers Village, with numerous restaurants, bars, and shops; Kaanapali Golf Club's 36 holes are across the street.

2481 Kaanapali Pkwy. (next to Whalers Village), Lahaina, HI 96761. (C) Aston Hotels **800/922-7866** or 808/661-4861. Fax 808/661-8315. www.whalermaui.com. 360 units. High season $235–$255 studio double; $330–$485 1-bedroom (rate for up to 4 people); $535–$700 2-bedroom (up to 6). Low season $205–$230 studio; $275–$415 1-bedroom; $435–$573 2-bedroom. Check Internet for specials. Extra person $20; crib $12. 2-night minimum. AE, DC, DISC, MC, V. **Amenities:** Outdoor pool; 5 tennis courts; fitness room; Jacuzzi; watersports equipment rentals; concierge; activity desk; car-rental desk; babysitting; coin-op washer/dryers; laundry service; dry cleaning. *In room:* A/C, TV, dataport, kitchen, fridge, coffeemaker, hair dryer, iron, safe, washer/dryer.

HONOKOWAI, KAHANA & NAPILI
Expensive

Also consider **Sands of Kahana** ((C) **800/326-9874** or 808/669-0423; www. sands-of-kahana.com), an eight-story condo/timeshare complex that's great for families. The one- to three-bedroom units have small kitchens and washer/dryers. The property is loaded with kid-friendly extras, including a large children's pool, a playground, and a stretch of beach that's safe for swimming. Rates start at $130 for one bedroom, $180 for two bedrooms, and $275 for three bedrooms (5-night minimum).

Napili Kai Beach Resort ★★ *(Finds)* Just south of the Bay Club restaurant in Kapalua, nestled in a small white-sand cove, lies this comfortable oceanfront complex. The one- and two-story units with double-hipped Hawaii-style roofs face their very own gold-sand beach, which is safe for swimming. Many units have a view of the Pacific, with Molokai and Lanai in the distance. The older beachfront Lahaina Building units—with ceiling fans only—are a good buy at $225. Those who prefer air-conditioning should book into the Honolua Building, where, for the same price, you'll get a fully air-conditioned room set back from the shore around a grassy, parklike lawn and pool. Every unit (except 8 hotel rooms) has a fully stocked kitchenette with full-size fridge, cooktop, microwave, toaster oven, washer/dryer, and coffeemaker; some have dishwashers as well. On-site pluses include daily maid service, even in the condo units; two shuffleboard courts; barbecue areas; complimentary coffee at the beach pagoda every morning; free tea in the lobby every afternoon; weekly lei making, hula lessons, and horticultural tours; and a free weekly mai tai party. There are three nearby championship golf courses and excellent tennis courts at next-door Kapalua Resort.

5900 Honoapiilani Rd. (at the extreme north end of Napili, next to Kapalua), Lahaina, HI 96761. ℭ **800/ 367-5030** or 808/669-6271. Fax 808/669-0086. www.napilikai.com. 163 units. $190–$225 hotel room double; $220–$305 studio double; $360–$425 1-bedroom suite (sleeps up to 4); $525–$675 2-bedroom (sleeps 6). Packages available. Extra person $15. AE, MC, V. **Amenities:** Well-recommended restaurant; bar; 4 outdoor pools; two 18-hole putting greens (with free golf putters for guest use); complimentary use of tennis racquets; good-size fitness room, filled with the latest equipment; Jacuzzi; complimentary watersports equipment; free children's activities at Easter, June 15–Aug 31, and at Christmas; concierge; activity desk; babysitting; coin-op washer/dryers; laundry service; dry cleaning. *In room:* A/C (in most units, but not all), TV, kitchenette, fridge, coffeemaker, hair dryer, iron, safe.

Moderate

Hale Kai ★ *Kids* This small, two-story condo complex is ideally located, right on the beach and next door to a county park, which is great for those traveling with kids. Shops, restaurants, and ocean activities are all within a 6-mile radius. The units are older but in excellent shape, and come with well-equipped kitchens (with dishwasher, disposal, microwave, even a blender), and louvered windows that open to the trade winds. Lots of guests clamor for the oceanfront pool units, but we find the park-view units cooler, and they still have ocean views (upstairs units also have cathedral ceilings). This place fills up fast, so book early; repeat guests make up most of the clientele.

3691 Lower Honoapiilani Rd. (in Honokowai), Lahaina, HI 96761. ℭ **800/446-7307** or 808/669-6333. Fax 808/669-7474. www.halekai.com. 23 units. High season $120 1-bedroom double, $150–$155 2-bedroom (rates for up to 4), $200 3-bedroom (up to 6). Low season $105 1-bedroom, $135–$140 2-bedroom, $200 3-bedroom. Extra person $15. 3-night minimum. MC, V. **Amenities:** Outdoor pool; concierge; car-rental desk; coin-op washer/dryers. *In room:* TV/VCR, kitchen, fridge, coffeemaker, hair dryer, iron.

Kahana Sunset ★★ *Kids* Lying in the crook of a sharp horseshoe curve on Lower Honoapiilani Road is this series of wooden condo units, stair-stepping down the side of a hill to a postcard-perfect white-sand beach. The unique location, nestled between the coastline and the road above, makes this a very private place to stay. In the midst of the buildings sits a grassy lawn with a small pool and Jacuzzi; down by the sandy beach are gazebos and picnic areas. The units feature full kitchens (complete with dishwashers), washer/dryers, large lanais with terrific views, and sleeper sofas. This is a great complex for families: The beach is safe for swimming, the grassy area is away from traffic, and the units are roomy. The two-bedroom units have parking just outside, making carrying luggage and groceries that much easier.

4909 Lower Honoapiilani Hwy. (at the northern end of Kahana, almost in Napili). c/o P.O. Box 10219 Lahaina, HI 96761. ℭ **800/669-1488** or 808/669-8011. Fax 808/669-9170. www.kahanasunset.com. 79 units, 49 in rental pool. $130–$240 1-bedroom (sleeps up to 4); $175–$370 2-bedroom (sleeps 6). 2-night minimum. AE, MC, V. From Hwy. 30, turn *makai* (toward the ocean) at the Napili Plaza (Napilihau St.), then left on Lower Honoapiilani Rd. **Amenities:** 2 outdoor pools (1 just for children); concierge. *In room:* TV, kitchen, coffeemaker, hair dryer, iron, safe (in some units), washer/dryer.

Maui Sands The Maui Sands was built back when property wasn't as expensive and developers took the extra time and money to surround their condos with lush landscaping. It's hard to get a unit with a bad view: All face either the ocean (with views of Lanai and Molokai) or tropical gardens blooming with brilliant heliconia, flowering hibiscus, and sweet-smelling ginger. Each roomy unit has a big lanai and a full kitchen. With two big bedrooms, plus space in the living room for a fifth person (or even a 6th), the larger units are good deals fo families. There's a narrow beach out front.

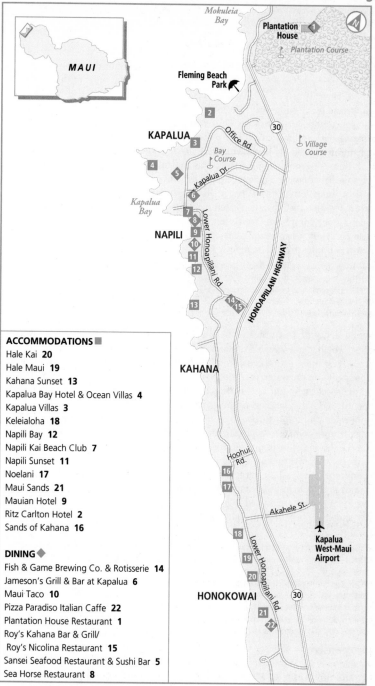

ACCOMMODATIONS ◼

Hale Kai **20**
Hale Maui **19**
Kahana Sunset **13**
Kapalua Bay Hotel & Ocean Villas **4**
Kapalua Villas **3**
Keleialoha **18**
Napili Bay **12**
Napili Kai Beach Club **7**
Napili Sunset **11**
Noelani **17**
Maui Sands **21**
Mauian Hotel **9**
Ritz Carlton Hotel **2**
Sands of Kahana **16**

DINING ◆

Fish & Game Brewing Co. & Rotisserie **14**
Jameson's Grill & Bar at Kapalua **6**
Maui Taco **10**
Pizza Paradiso Italian Caffe **22**
Plantation House Restaurant **1**
Roy's Kahana Bar & Grill/
 Roy's Nicolina Restaurant **15**
Sansei Seafood Restaurant & Sushi Bar **5**
Sea Horse Restaurant **8**

Maui Resort Management, 3600 Lower Honoapiilani Rd. (in Honokowai), Lahaina, HI 96761. ℂ 800/367-5037 or 808/669-1902. Fax 808/669-8790. www.mauigetaway.com. 76 units. $105–$145 1-bedroom (sleeps up to 3); $150–$210 2-bedroom (sleeps 5). Extra person $10. 7-night minimum. MC, V. **Amenities:** Outdoor pool; coin-op washer/dryer. *In room:* A/C, TV, kitchen, fridge, coffeemaker.

Mauian Hotel on Napili Beach ⭐

The family that built this low-rise hotel in 1961 now owns it again, and they've restored the studio units to their original old Hawaiian style. The Mauian is perched above a beautiful half-mile long white-sand beach with great swimming and snorkeling; there's a pool with chaise lounges, umbrellas, and tables on the sun deck; and the verdant grounds are bursting with tropical color. The rooms feature hardwood floors, Indonesian-style furniture, and big lanais with great views. Thoughtful little touches include fresh flowers in rooms upon arrival, plus chilled champagne for guests celebrating a special occasion. There are no phones and no TVs in the rooms (this place really is about getting away from it all), but the large Ohana (family) room does have a TV with a VCR and an extensive library for those who can't bear the solitude. There's complimentary coffee; phones and fax service are available in the business center. Great restaurants are just a 5-minute walk away, and Kapalua Resort is up the street. The nightly sunsets off the beach are spectacular.

5441 Lower Honoapiilani Rd. (in Napili), Lahaina, HI 96761. ℂ 800/367-5034 or 808/669-6205. Fax 808/669-0129. www.mauian.com. 44 units. High season $165–$195 double; low season $145–$180 double. Rates include continental breakfast. Extra person $10. Children under 5 stay free in parent's room. AE, DISC, MC, V. **Amenities:** Outdoor pool; golf course; tennis courts; concierge; activity desk; business center; coin-op washer/dryer. *In room:* Kitchen, fridge, coffeemaker, no phone.

Noelani Condominium Resort ⭐⭐ *Kids*

This oceanfront condo is a great value, whether you stay in a studio or a three-bedroom unit (ideal for large families). Everything is first class, from the furnishings to the oceanfront location. Though it's on the water, there's no sandy beach here (despite the photos posted on their website)—but next door is a sandy cove at the new county park, just opened in 2001. There's good snorkeling off the cove, which is frequented by spinner dolphins and turtles in summer and humpback whales in winter. All units feature complete kitchens, entertainment centers, and spectacular views (the 1-, 2-, and 3-bedroom units also have their own washer/dryers and dishwashers). Our favorites are in the Anthurium Building, where the condos have oceanfront lanais just 20 feet from the water. Frugal travelers will love the deluxe studios in the Orchid Building, with great ocean views and all the amenities for just $119. Guests are invited to a continental breakfast orientation on their first day and mai tai parties at night; there are also oceanfront barbecue grills for guest use.

4095 Lower Honoapiilani Rd. (in Kahana), Lahaina, HI 96761. ℂ 800/367-6030 or 808/669-8374. Fax 808/669-7904. www.noelani-condo-resort.com. 50 units. $107–$135 studio double; $147–$165 1-bedroom (sleeps up to 4); $207–$217 2-bedroom (sleeps 4); $267 3-bedroom (sleeps 6). Rates include continental breakfast on first morning. Extra person $10. Children under 18 stay free in parent's room. Packages for honeymooners, seniors, and AAA members available. 3-night minimum. AE, MC, V. **Amenities:** 2 freshwater swimming pools (1 heated for night swimming); access to nearby health club; oceanfront Jacuzzi; concierge; activity desk; car-rental desk; coin-op washer/dryers. *In room:* TV/VCR, kitchen, fridge, coffeemaker, hair dryer, iron, safe, washer/dryer (in larger units).

Inexpensive

In addition to the choices below, consider **Hale Maui Apartment Hotel** (ℂ **808/669-6312;** fax 808/669-1302; www.maui.net/~halemaui), a wonderful tiny place run by Hans and Eva Zimmerman, whose spirit is 100% aloha. The one-bedroom suites, which run from $85 to $95 for a double, come with ceiling fans, private lanais, and complete kitchens. There's no pool, but a private path leads to a great swimming beach.

Kaleialoha   This condo complex for the budget-minded has recently been upgraded, with new paint, bedspreads, and drapes in each apartment. The one-bedroom units each have a sofa bed in the living room, which allows you to comfortably sleep four. All of the island-style units feature fully equipped kitchens, with everything from dishwashers to washer/dryers (the only thing not supplied is beach towels; bring your own). There's great ocean swimming just off the rock wall (no sandy beach); a protective reef mows waves down and allows even timid swimmers to relax.

3785 Lower Honoapiilani Rd. (in Honokowai), Lahaina, HI 96761. © **800/222-8688** or 808/669-8197. Fax 808/669-2502. www.mauicondosoceanfront.com. 26 units. $95 or $125 1-bedroom double. Extra person $10. 3-night minimum. MC, V. **Amenities:** Outdoor pool; concierge; activity desk; coin-op washer/dryers. *In room:* TV, kitchen, fridge, coffeemaker, washer/dryer.

Napili Bay ⭐ *Finds*   One of Maui's best secret bargains is this small, two-story complex right on Napili's beautiful half-mile white-sand beach. It's perfect for a romantic getaway: The atmosphere is comfortable and relaxing, the ocean lulls you to sleep at night, and birdsong wakes you in the morning. The beach here is one of the best on the coast, with great swimming and snorkeling—in fact, it's so beautiful that people staying at much more expensive resorts down the road frequently haul all their beach paraphernalia here for the day. The studio apartments are definitely small, but they pack in everything you need to feel at home, from a full kitchen to a comfortable queen bed, and a roomy lanai that's great for watching the sun set over the Pacific. There's no air-conditioning, but louvered windows and ceiling fans keep the units fairly cool during the day. There are lots of restaurants and a convenience store within walking distance, and you're about 10 to 15 minutes away from Lahaina and some great golf courses. All this for as little as $110 a night—unbelievable! Book early, and tell 'em Frommer's sent you.

33 Hui Dr. (off Lower Honoapiilani Hwy., in Napili). c/o Maui Beachfront Rentals, 256 Papalaua St., Lahaina, HI 96767. © **888/661-7200** or 808/661-3500. Fax 808/661-2649. www.mauibeachfront.com. 33 units. $110–$140 studio for up to 4. 5-night minimum. MC, V. **Amenities:** Coin-op washer/dryers. *In room:* TV, kitchen, fridge, coffeemaker.

Napili Sunset *Value*   Housed in three buildings (2 on the ocean and 1 across the street) and located just down the street from Napili Bay (see above), these clean, older, well-maintained units offer good value. At first glance, the plain two-story structures don't look like much, but the location, the bargain prices, and the friendly staff are the real hidden treasures here. In addition to daily maid service, the units all have full kitchens (with dishwashers), ceiling fans (no A/C), sofa beds, small dining rooms, and small bedrooms. The beach—one of Maui's best—can get a little crowded, because the public beach access is through this property (and everyone on Maui seems to want to come here). The studio units are all located in the building off the beach and a few steps up a slight hill; they're good-size, with a full kitchen and either a sofa bed or a Murphy bed, and they overlook the small pool and garden. The one- and two-bedroom units are all on the beach (the downstairs units have lanais that lead right to the sand). The staff makes sure each unit has the basics—paper towels, dishwasher soap, coffee filters, condiments—to get your stay off to a good start. There are restaurants within walking distance.

46 Hui Rd. (in Napili), Lahaina, HI 96761. © 800/447-9229 or 808/669-8083. Fax 808/669-2730. www.
napilisunset.com. 42 units. High season $120 studio double; $225 1-bedroom double; $315 2-bedroom
(sleeps up to 4). Low season $105 studio; $205 1-bedroom; $265 2-bedroom. Extra person $12. Children
under 3 stay free in parent's room. 3-night minimum. MC, V. **Amenities:** Small outdoor pool; coin-op
washer/dryers (free detergent supplied). *In room:* TV, kitchen, fridge, coffeemaker.

KAPALUA

If you're interested in a luxurious condo or town house, consider **Kapalua Villas** (© **800/545-0018** or 808/669-8088; www.kapaluavillas.com). The palatial
units dotting the oceanfront cliffs and fairways of this idyllic coast are a (relative) bargain, especially if you're traveling with a group. The one- and two-bedroom condos go for $199 to $279; two-bedrooms for $299 to $469; plus there
are numerous package deals (which include golf, tennis, honeymoon amenities
and car) to save even more money.

Note: You'll find the following hotels on the "West Maui Accommodations
and Dining" map on p. 369.

Very Expensive

Kapalua Bay Hotel & Ocean Villas ★★ *(Kids)*   Few Hawaiian resorts have so
much open space. The Kapalua Bay sits seaward of 23,000 acres of green fields
lined with spiky Norfolk pine windbreaks. The 1970s-style rectilinear building,
down by the often-windy shore, is full of angles that frame stunning views of the
ocean, mountains, and blue sky. The tastefully designed maze of oversize rooms
fronts a palm-fringed gold-sand beach that's one of the best in Hawaii, and
there's an excellent Ben Crenshaw golf course. Each guest room has a sitting area
with sofa, a king or two double beds, and an entertainment center. Plantation-
style shutter doors open onto private lanais with views of Molokai across the
channel. The renovated bathrooms feature two granite vanities, a large soaking
tub, and a glass-enclosed shower.

The good news is that unlike some other luxury resorts, the Kapalua Bay has
waved the obnoxious and not-very-hospitable "resort fee"; the bad news is that
they now charge for parking (self or valet) at the outrageous rate of $15 a day
(the highest not only on Maui, but the highest rate of all the neighbor islands,
rivaling parking in Waikiki).

1 Bay Dr., Kapalua, HI 96761. © 800/367-8000 or 808/669-5656. Fax 808/669-4694. www.kapaluabay
hotel.com. 206 units. $350–$600 double; from $500 1- and 2-bedroom bay villas; from $1200 suites. Extra
person $75. Children 17 and under stay free in parent's room using existing bedding. AE, DC, MC, V. Parking:
$15. **Amenities:** 3 restaurants; 3 bars; 2 outdoor pools; access to the Kapalua Resort's acclaimed trio of golf
courses (each with its own pro shop); 10 Plexipave tennis courts for day and night play; 24-hr. fitness facilities; small spa; Jacuzzi; watersports equipment rentals; children's program for kids age 5–12, offering activities ranging from snorkeling and surfing to lei-making and cookie-baking; concierge; activity desk; car-rental
desk; business center; shopping arcade; salon; 24-hr. room service; in-room and spa massage; babysitting;
same-day laundry service and dry cleaning; concierge-level rooms. *In room:* A/C, TV, dataport, minibar, fridge,
coffeemaker, hair dryer, iron, safe.

Ritz-Carlton Kapalua ★★ *(Kids)*   In our opinion, this is the best Ritz-Carlton
in the world. It's in the best place (Hawaii), near a great beach (Kapalua), and
has a friendly staff that goes above and beyond the call of duty. The Ritz is a
complete universe, one of those resorts where you can happily sit by the ocean
with a book for 2 whole weeks and never leave the grounds. It rises proudly on
a knoll, in a singularly spectacular setting between the rain forest and the sea.
During construction, the burial sites of hundreds of ancient Hawaiians were discovered in the sand, so the hotel was moved inland to avoid disrupting the

graves. The setback improved the hotel's outlook, which now has a commanding view of Molokai.

The style is fancy plantation, elegant but not imposing. The public spaces are open, airy, and graceful, with plenty of tropical foliage and landscapes by artist Sarah Supplee that recall the not-so-long-ago agrarian past. Rooms are up to the usual Ritz standard, outfitted with marble bathrooms, private lanais, and in-room fax capability. Hospitality is the keynote here; you'll find the exemplary service you expect from Ritz-Carlton seasoned with good old-fashioned Hawaiian aloha. If you can afford it, stay on the **Club Floor** ★★★—it offers the best amenities in the state, from French roast coffee in the morning to a buffet at lunch to cookies in the afternoon to pupus and drinks at sunset. The Ritz Kids program offers a variety of activities and is very reasonable for hotel guests—only $15 for a full day, including lunch. Our only complaint about this fabulous property is the "resort fee" you're charged.

1 Ritz-Carlton Dr., Kapalua, HI 96761. ℂ **800/262-8440** or 808/669-6200. Fax 808/665-0026. www.ritz carlton.com. 548 units. $375–$535 double; from $635 suite. Extra person $50 ($125 in Club Floor rooms). "Resort fee" of $15 for "complimentary" use of fitness center and children's program. Wedding/honeymoon, golf, and other packages available. AE, DC, DISC, MC, V. Valet parking $10, free self-parking. **Amenities:** 4 restaurants; 4 bars (including 1 serving drinks and light fare on the sand); outdoor pool; access to the Kapalua Resort's 3 championship golf courses (each with its own pro shop) and its deluxe tennis complex; fitness room; spa; Jacuzzi; watersports equipment rentals; bike rentals; children's program; game room; concierge; activity desk; car-rental desk; business center; shopping arcade; salon; room service; in-room and spa massage; babysitting; same-day laundry and dry cleaning; concierge-level rooms (some of Hawaii's best, with top-drawer service and amenities). *In room:* A/C, TV, dataport, minibar, coffeemaker, hair dryer, iron, safe.

SOUTH MAUI

We recommend two booking agencies that rent a host of condominiums and unique vacation homes in the Kihei/Wailea/Maalaea area: **Kihei Maui Vacation** (ℂ **800/541-6284** or 808/879-7581; www.kmvmaui.com) and **Condominium Rentals Hawaii** (ℂ **800/367-5242** or 808/879-2778; www.crhmaui.com).

KIHEI

In addition to the choices below, also consider the **Aston at the Maui Banyan** (ℂ **800/92-ASTON** or 808/875-0004; www.aston-hotels.com), a condo property across the street from Kamaole Beach Park II. The one- to three-bedroom units are very nicely done and feature full kitchens, air-conditioning, and washer/dryers. Rates start at $145 for hotel rooms, $180 for one-bedroom units, and $245 for two-bedrooms; be sure to ask about packages.

Expensive

Maalaea Surf Resort ★   This is the place for people who want a quiet, relaxing vacation on a well-landscaped property, with a beautiful white-sand beach right outside. Located at the quiet end of Kihei Road, this two-story complex sprawls across 5 acres of lush tropical gardens. The luxury town houses all have ocean views, big kitchens (with dishwashers), cable TV, and VCRs. Amenities include maid service (Mon–Sat), shuffleboard, barbecue grills, and discounts on tee times at nearby golf courses; restaurants and shops are within a 5-minute drive.

12 S. Kihei Rd. (at S. Kihei Rd. and Hwy. 350), Kihei, HI 96753. ℂ **800/423-7953** or 808/879-1267. Fax 808/874-2884. www.maalaeasurfresort.com. 34 units. $205–$230 1-bedroom unit; $277–$307 2-bedroom (sleeps up to 6). Extra person $15. MC, V. **Amenities:** 2 outdoor pools; 2 tennis courts; concierge; activity desk; car-rental desk; coin-op washer/dryers. *In room:* A/C, TV/VCR, kitchen, fridge, coffeemaker, hair dryer, iron, safe.

Maui Hill ⋆ If you can't decide between the privacy of a condo and the conveniences of a hotel, try this place. Managed by the respected Aston chain, Maui Hill gives you the best of both worlds. Located on a hill above the heat of Kihei town, this large, Spanish-style resort (with stucco buildings, red-tile roofs, and arched entries) combines all the amenities and activities of a hotel—pool, hot tub, tennis courts, Hawaiiana classes, maid service, and more—with large luxury condos that have full kitchens and plenty of privacy. Nearly all units have ocean views, dishwashers, washer/dryers, queen sofa beds, and big lanais. Beaches, restaurants, and shops are within easy walking distance, and a golf course is nearby. The management here goes out of its way to make sure your stay is perfect.

2881 S. Kihei Rd. (across from Kamaole Park III, between Keonekai St. and Kilohana Dr.), Kihei, HI 96753. ☎ 800/92-ASTON, or 808/879-6321. Fax 808/879-8945. www.aston-hotels.com. 140 units. High season $280 1-bedroom apt; $365 2-bedroom; $495 3-bedroom. Low season $215 1-bedroom; $280 2-bedroom; $385 3-bedroom. AE, DC, DISC, MC, V. **Amenities:** Outdoor pool; putting green; tennis courts; Jacuzzi; concierge; activity desk; car-rental desk; coin-op washer/dryers; laundry service; dry cleaning. *In room:* A/C, TV, kitchen, fridge, coffeemaker, hair dryer, iron, safe, washer/dryer (in most units).

Moderate

Kamaole Nalu Resort This six-story condominium complex is located between two beach parks, Kamaole I and Kamaole II, and right across the street from a shopping complex. Units have fabulous ocean views, large living rooms, and private lanais; the kitchens are a bit small but come fully equipped. We recommend no. 306 for its wonderful bird's-eye view. The property also has an oceanside pool and great barbecue facilities. Restaurants, bars, a golf course, and tennis courts are nearby; shopping is across the street. *Warning:* Because the building is right on Kihei Road, it can be noisy.

2450 S. Kihei Rd. (between Kanani and Keonekai rds., next to Kamaole Beach Park II), Kihei, HI 96753. ☎ 800/767-1497 or 808/879-1006. Fax 808/879-8693. www.kamaolenalu.com. 36 units. High season $155–$215 double. Low season $135–$195 double. Extra person $15. 5-night minimum. MC, V. **Amenities:** Outdoor pool; activity desk; car-rental desk. *In room:* TV, kitchen, fridge, coffeemaker, hair dryer, iron, safe, washer/dryer.

Koa Resort ⋆ *Kids* Located just across the street from the ocean, Koa Resort consists of five two-story wooden buildings on more than 5½ acres of landscaped grounds. The spacious, privately owned one-, two-, and three-bedroom units are decorated with care and come fully equipped, right down to the dishwasher and disposal in the kitchens. The larger condos have both showers and tubs; the smaller units have showers only. All feature large lanais, ceiling fans, and washer/dryers. For maximum peace and quiet, ask for a unit far from Kihei Road. Bars, restaurants, and a golf course are nearby.

811 S. Kihei Rd. (between Kulanihakoi St. and Namauu Place). c/o Bello Realty, P.O. Box 1776, Kihei, HI 96753. ☎ 800/541-3060 or 808/879-3328. Fax 808/875-1483. www.bellomaui.com. 54 units (some with shower only). High season $110 one-bedroom; $120-$130 two-bedroom; $155-$180 three-bedroom. Low season $85 one-bedroom; $100-$110 two-bedroom; $135-$160 three-bedroom. No credit cards. **Amenities:** Outdoor pool; 18-hole putting green; 2 tennis courts; Jacuzzi. *In room:* TV, kitchen, fridge, coffeemaker, hair dryer, iron, safe, washer/dryer.

Maui Coast Hotel ⋆⋆ This place stands out as one of the only moderately priced hotels in Kihei (which is largely full of affordable condo complexes rather than traditional hotels or resorts). That's big news—especially on Maui, where luxury abounds. Ask about the room/car packages: For the price of a room (or a 1- or 2-bedroom), the Maui Coast's Extra Value package gives you a rental car for just a few dollars more. The other chief advantage of this hotel is its location,

South Maui Accommodations & Dining

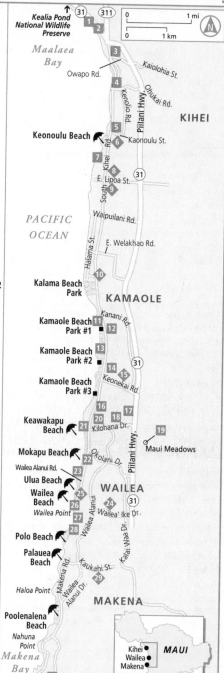

ACCOMMODATIONS ■

Aloha Pualani **4**
Ann and Bob Babson's B&B **19**
Aston at the Maui Banyan **14**
Fairmont Kea Lani Maui **28**
Four Seasons Resort Maui
   at Wailea **27**
Grand Wailea Resort Hotel **25**
Kamaole Nalu Resort **13**
Kealia Resort **1**
Koa Resort **5**
Leinaala **7**
Maàlaea Surf Resort **2**
Mana Kai Maui Resort **21**
Maui Coast Hotel **12**
Maui Hill **20**
Maui Kamaole **16**
Maui Prince Hotel **29**
Nona Lani Cottages **3**
Punahoa Beach Apts. **11**
Renaissance Wailea Beach Resort **22**
Two Mermaids B&B **18**
Wailea Marriott,
   an Outrigger Resort **23**
What a Wonderful World B&B **17**

DINING ◆

Bubba's Burgers **10**
Caffe Ciao **28**
Cheeseburger, Mai Tai's,
   and Rock-n-Roll **25**
Coffee Company Café Wailea **25**
The Coffee Store **8**
Ferraro's at Seaside **27**
Five Palms **21**
Hula Moons **26**
Joe's Bar & Grill **24**
Longhi's **25**
Maui Tacos **1 5**
Nick's Fishmarket Maui **28**
Peggy Sue's **8**
Prince Court **30**
Ruth's Chris Steak House **25**
SeaWatch **29**
Shaka Sandwich & Pizza **9**
Spago **27**
Stella Blues Cafe **6**
Tommy Bahama's Tropical Cafe
   & Emporium **25**

about a block from Kamaole Beach Park I, with plenty of bars, restaurants, and shopping within walking distance and a golf course nearby. A $2.5 million renovation of all the furniture, linens, and upholstery in the rooms has this moderately priced hotel looking better than ever. The rooms offer extras such as sitting areas, whirlpool tubs, ceiling fans, and private lanais.

2259 S. Kihei Rd. (1 block from Kamaole Beach Park I), Kihei, HI 96753. *C* 800/325-4000 or 808/874-6284. Fax 808/875-4731. www.mauicoasthotel.com. 265 units. $155–$165 double; $175–$195 suite; $230 1-bedroom (sleeps up to 4). Children 17 and under stay free in parent's room using existing bedding. Roll-away bed $20. Packages including rental car available. AE, DC, DISC, MC, V. **Amenities:** Restaurant; pool bar with nightly entertainment; outdoor pool (plus children's wading pool); 2 night-lit tennis courts; fitness room; concierge; activity desk; limited room service; free use of self-serve washer/dryers; laundry service; dry cleaning. *In room:* A/C, TV, fridge, coffeemaker, hair dryer, iron, safe.

Maui Kamaole You'll find this condo complex right across the street from the Kihei Public Boat Ramp and beautiful Kamaole Beach Park III, which is great for swimming, snorkeling, and beachcombing. Each roomy, fully furnished unit comes with a private lanai, two bathrooms (even in the 1-bedroom units), and an all-electric kitchen. The one-bedroom units—which can comfortably accommodate four—are quite a deal, especially if you're traveling in the off season. The grounds are nicely landscaped and offer barbecues. Restaurants and bars are within walking distance; a golf course and tennis courts are also nearby.

2777 S. Kihei Rd. (between Keonekai and Kilohana rds., at the Wailea end of Kihei), Kihei, HI 96753. *C* 800-822-4409 or 808/874-8467. Fax 808/875-9117. www.mauikamaole.com. 210 units. High season $170–$195 1-bedroom double (sleeps up to 4); $220–$250 2-bedroom (rates for 4, sleeps up to 6). Low season $135–$150 1-bedroom; $175–$200 2-bedroom. 4-night minimum. AE, MC, V. **Amenities:** 2 outdoor pools; Jacuzzi; concierge; laundry service; dry cleaning. *In room:* A/C, TV, kitchen, fridge, coffeemaker, iron, safe, washer/dryer.

Inexpensive

In addition to the choices below, six suites are available at **Aloha Pualani** (*C* **800/PUALANI** or 808/874-9265; www.mauigateway.com/~pualani), which manages to combine the personal service of a B&B with the independent living arrangements of a condo—and the beach is just across the street. Rates are $89 to $150 (3-night minimum).

Ann and Bob Babson's Bed & Breakfast and Sunset Cottage ★ *Value* We highly recommend staying right here on this spacious landscaped property, which boasts 180° views of the islands of Lanai, Kahoolawe, and Molokini; sunsets are not to be missed. Accommodations include two rooms in the main house (1 with panoramic ocean views, skylights, and a whirlpool tub), a one-bedroom suite downstairs, and a two-bedroom cottage with a kitchen. The Babsons have three adorable cats—if you're allergic, you might want to book elsewhere.

3371 Keha Dr. (in Maui Meadows), Kihei, HI 96753. *C* 800/824-6409 or 808/874-1166. Fax 808/879-7906. www.mauibnb.com. 4 units. $100–$130 double (including breakfast Mon–Sat); $135 cottage double (sleeps up to 4). Extra person $15. 5-night minimum in house, 7-night minimum for cottage. MC, V. *In room:* TV, kitchen (in cottage only), fridge, coffeemaker.

Kealia Resort *Value* This oceanfront property at the northern end of Kihei is well maintained and nicely furnished—and the price is excellent. As tempting as the $75 studio units may sound, don't give in: They face noisy Kihei Road and are near a major junction, so big trucks downshifting can be especially noisy at night. Instead, go for one of the oceanview units, which all have full kitchens and private lanais. The grounds face a 5-mile stretch of white-sand beach. The management goes out of its way to provide opportunities for guests to meet; social gatherings include free coffee-and-doughnut get-togethers every Friday morning and pupu parties on Wednesdays.

191 N. Kihei Rd. (north of Hwy. 31, at the Maalaea end of Kihei), Kihei, HI 96753. © **800/265-0686** or 808/879-0952. Fax 808/875-1540. www.kealiaresort.com. 51 units. $75–$99 studio double; $100–$150 1-bedroom double; $165–$195 2-bedroom (sleeps up to 4). Extra person $10. Children 12 and under stay free in parent's room. 4-night minimum. MC, V. **Amenities:** Recently retiled outdoor pool. *In room:* TV, kitchen, fridge, coffeemaker, hair dryer, iron, washer/dryer.

Leinaala ⭑ From Kihei Road, you can't see Leinaala amid the jumble of buildings, but this oceanfront boutique condo offers excellent accommodations at moderate prices. The building is set back from the water, with a county park—an oasis of green grass and tennis courts—in-between. A golf course lies nearby. The units are compact, but filled with everything you need: a full kitchen, sofa bed, and oceanview lanai. (Hideaway beds are available if you need one.)

998 S. Kihei Rd., Kihei, HI 96753. © **800/822-4409** or 808/879-2235. Fax 808/879-8366. www.mauicondo. com. 24 units. $135 1-bedroom double; $180 2-bedroom (sleeps up to 4). Extra person $10. 4-night minimum. No cards. **Amenities:** Outdoor pool; coin-op washer/dryers. *In room:* A/C, TV, kitchen, fridge, coffeemaker.

Mana Kai Maui Resort ⭑ *Kids* This eight-story complex, situated on a beautiful white-sand cove, is an unusual combination of hotel and condominium. The hotel rooms, which account for half of the total number of units, are small but nicely furnished. The condo units feature full kitchens and open living rooms with sliding-glass doors that lead to small lanais overlooking the sandy beach and ocean. Some units are beginning to show their age (the building is more than 30 years old), but they're all clean and comfortable. One of the best snorkeling beaches on the coast is just steps away; a golf course and tennis courts are nearby.

2960 S. Kihei Rd. (between Kilohana and Keonekai rds., at the Wailea end of Kihei), Kihei, HI 96753. © **800/367-5242** or 808/879-2778. Fax 808/879-7825. www.crhmaui.com. 105 units. $95–$135 hotel room double; $175–$245 1-bedroom (sleeps up to 4); $234–$300 2-bedroom (up to 6). AE, DC, DISC, MC, V. **Amenities:** Restaurant (Five Palms, p. 403); bar; outdoor pool; concierge; coin-op washer/dryers. *In room:* A/C (in hotel rooms only), TV, kitchen (in condo units), fridge, coffeemaker, safe.

Nona Lani Cottages ⭑ *Finds* Picture this: a grassy expanse dotted with eight cottages tucked among palm, fruit, and sweet-smelling flower trees, right across the street from a white-sand beach. This is one of the great hidden deals in Kihei. The cottages are tiny, but contain everything you'll need: a small but complete kitchen, twin beds that double as couches in the living room, a separate bedroom with a queen bed, and a lanai with table and chairs. The cottages were renovated in 2002 with new ceramic flooring. The real attraction, however, is the garden setting next to the beach. There are no phones in the cabins (a blessing if you're trying to escape civilization), but there's a public one by the registration/check-in area.

If the cabins are booked, or if you want a bit more luxury, you might opt for one of the private guest rooms, with private entrance and private bath. These beautiful units feature plush carpet, koa bed frames, air-conditioning, lanais, and private entrances. As we went to press, the industrious Kong family, hosts here, were working on hostel accommodations on the other side of the island in Happy Valley, next to Wailuku, with very low rates.

455 S. Kihei Rd. (just south of Hwy. 31), P.O. Box 655, Kihei, HI 96753. © **800/733-2688** or 808/879-2497. www.nonalanicottages.com. 11 units. $75–$85 double; $90–$99 cottage. Extra person $12–$15. 3-night minimum for rooms, 4-night minimum for cottages. No credit cards. **Amenities:** Coin-op washer/dryers. *In room:* A/C, TV, kitchen (in cottages), fridge, coffeemaker, no phone.

Punahoa Beach Apts ★ *Value*   Book this place! We can't put it any more simply than that. The location—off noisy, traffic-ridden Kihei Road, on a quiet side street with ocean frontage—is fabulous. A grassy lawn rolls about 50 feet down to the beach, where there's great snorkeling just offshore and a popular surfing spot next door; shopping and restaurants are all within walking distance. All of the beautifully decorated units in this small, four-story building have fully equipped kitchens and lanais with great ocean views. Rooms go quickly in winter, so reserve early.

2142 Iliili Rd. (off S. Kihei Rd., 100 yards from Kamaole Beach I), Kihei, HI 96753. © **800/564-4380** or 808/879-2720. Fax 808/875-9147. www.punahoa.com. 13 units. High season $130 studio double; $185–$198 1-bedroom double; $220 2-bedroom double. Low season $94 studio; $130–$145 1-bedroom; $160 2-bedroom. Extra person $15. 5-night minimum. AE, MC, V. **Amenities:** Coin-op washer/dryer. *In room:* TV, kitchen, fridge, coffeemaker, iron.

Two Mermaids on the Sunnyside of Maui B&B ★ *Finds*   The two mermaids, Juddee and Miranda, both avid scuba divers, have a friendly accommodation, professionally decorated in brilliant, tropical colors, complete with hand painted art of the island (above and below the water) in a quiet neighborhood just a 10-minute walk from the beach. Our favorite is the "ocean ohana," a large one-bedroom (with option of a 2nd connecting bedroom) apartment, complete with kitchenette (full-size fridge, microwave, coffeemaker), huge private deck, private entryway and your own giant hot tub. Equally cute is the "poolside suite," with private entry next to the outdoor pool. This studio (with the option of a separate connecting bedroom) is a living room during the day; at night it converts to a bedroom with a pull-down hide-a-bed. Continental breakfast, with some of the best homemade bread on the island, is placed on your doorstep every morning (so you can sleep in). Amenities include guitars in every unit (in case you get the urge to strum a few songs), a range of complimentary beach equipment, microwave popcorn, a barbecue area, and a swimming pool. Juddee is also a licensed minister and performs weddings and vow renewal.

Kihei. Reservations c/o Hawaii's Best Bed & Breakfast, P.O. Box 758, Volcano, HI 96785. © **800/262-9912** or 808/985-7488. Fax 808/967-8610. www.bestbnb.com. 2 units. $95 studio double; $150 studio plus connecting bedroom double; $135 one-bedroom apartment; $175 with connecting 2nd bedroom. Rates include continental breakfast. No credit cards. **Amenities:** Outdoor pool; golf nearby; tennis courts nearby; barbecue; child care available and massage available. *In room:* digital TV/VCR, kitchen, fridge, coffeemaker, iron, hair dryer, free local phone calls.

What a Wonderful World B&B ★ *Value*   We couldn't believe what we'd discovered here: an impeccably done B&B with a great location, excellent rates, and thought and care put into every room. Then we met hostess Eva Tantillo, who has not only a full-service travel agency, but also a master's degree—along with several years of experience—in hotel management. The result? One of Maui's finest bed-and-breakfasts, centrally located in Kihei (½ mile to Kamaole II Beach Park, 5 min. from Wailea golf courses, and convenient to shopping and restaurants). Choose from one of four units: the master suite (with small fridge, coffeemaker, and barbecue grill on the lanai); studio apartment (with fully equipped kitchen); or two one-bedroom apartments (also with full kitchens). All come with private bathroom, phone, and entrance. You're also welcome to use the communal barbecue. Eva serves a gourmet family-style breakfast (eggs Benedict, Alaskan waffles, skillet eggs with mushroom sauce, fruit blintzes, and more) on her lanai, which boasts views of white-sand beaches, the West Maui Mountains, and Haleakala.

2828 Umalu Place (off Keonakai St., near Hwy. 31), Kihei, HI 96753. ✆ 800/943-5804 or 808/879-9103. Fax 808/874-9352. www.amauibedandbreakfast.com. 4 units. $75 double; $89 studio double; $99 1-bedroom apt. (5% discount for cash). Rates include full breakfast. Children 11 and under stay free in parent's room. AE, MC, V. **Amenities:** Hot tub; laundry facilities. *In room:* TV, kitchenette, fridge, coffeemaker, hair dryer, iron.

WAILEA

For a complete selection of condo units throughout Wailea and Makena, contact **Destination Resorts Hawaii** (✆ **800/367-5246** or 808/879-1595; fax 808/874-3554; www.destinationresortshi.com). Its luxury units include studio doubles starting at $180; one-bedroom doubles from $170; two-bedrooms from $205; and three-bedrooms from $585. Children under 16 stay free; minimum stays vary by property.

Note: You'll find the following hotels on the "South Maui Accommodations & Dining" map on p. 375.

Very Expensive

The Fairmont Kea Lani Maui ★★★ At first glance, this blinding white complex of arches and turrets may look a bit out of place in tropical Hawaii (it's actually a close architectural cousin of Las Hadas, the Arabian Nights fantasy resort in Manzanillo, Mexico). But once you enter the flower-filled lobby and see the big blue Pacific outside, there's no doubt you're in Hawaii.

This is the place to get your money's worth; for the price of a hotel room you get an entire suite—plus a few extras. Each unit in this all-suite luxury hotel has a kitchenette (with microwave and coffeemaker), a living room with entertainment center and sofa bed (great if you have the kids in tow), a marble wet bar, an oversize marble bathroom with separate shower big enough for a party, a spacious bedroom, and a large lanai that overlooks the pools, lawns, and white-sand beach.

The villas are definitely out of a fantasy. The rich and famous stay in these 2,000-square-foot, two- and three-bedroom beach bungalows, each with its own plunge pool and gourmet kitchen.

4100 Wailea Alanui Dr., Wailea, HI 96753. ✆ **800/659-4100** or 808/875-4100. Fax 808/875-1200. www.kealani.com. 450 units. $339–$729 suite (sleeps up to 4); from $1,400 villa. AE, DC, DISC, MC, V. **Amenities:** 4 restaurants (including Nick's Fishmarket Maui and Caffé Ciao; p. 405); 3 bars (with sunset cocktails and nightly entertainment at the Lobby Lounge); 2 large swimming "lagoons" connected by a 140-ft. water slide and swim-up bar, plus an adult lap pool; use of Wailea Golf Club's 3 18-hole championship golf courses, as well as the nearby Makena and Elleair golf courses; use of Wailea Tennis Center's 11 courts (3 lit for night play and a pro shop); fine 24-hr. fitness center; excellent full-service spa offering the latest in body treatments, facials, and massage; Jacuzzi; watersports equipment rentals; bike rentals; children's program; game room; concierge; activity desk; car-rental desk; business center; shopping arcade; salon; 24-hr. room service; in-room and spa massage; babysitting; same-day laundry service and dry-cleaning. *In room:* A/C, TV, dataport, kitchenette, minibar, fridge, coffeemaker, hair dryer, iron, safe.

Four Seasons Resort Maui at Wailea ★★★ *Kids* If money's no object, this is the place to spend it. It's hard to beat this modern version of a Hawaiian palace by the sea, with a relaxing, casual atmosphere. Although it sits on a glorious beach between two other hotels, you won't feel like you're on chockablock resort row: The Four Seasons inhabits its own separate world, thanks to an open courtyard of pools and gardens. Amenities are first rate here, including outstanding restaurants, an excellent spa, and a complete activities program for kids (complimentary, of course).

The spacious (about 600 sq. ft.) rooms feature furnished lanais (nearly all with ocean views) that are great for watching whales in winter and sunsets year-round. The grand bathrooms contain deep marble tubs, showers for two, and lighted French makeup mirrors.

Service is attentive but not cloying. At the pool, guests lounge in Casbah-like tents, pampered with special touches like iced Evian and chilled towels. And you'll never see a housekeeping cart in the hall: The cleaning staff works in teams, so they're as unobtrusive as possible and in and out of your room in minutes.

Wolfgang Puck recently opened his Spago restaurant (p. 405) at the resort. It features a fusion of Hawaiian and California cuisine in a dreamy open-air setting. Ferraro's at Seaside Restaurant offers a casual atmosphere overlooking the Pacific by day; by night, it's transformed into a romantic atmosphere featuring authentic Italian cucina rustica with great sunset views and dining under the stars. The poolside Pacific Grill offers lavish breakfast buffets and dinners featuring Pacific Rim cuisine.

The ritzy neighborhood surrounding the hotel is home to great restaurants and shopping, the Wailea Tennis Center (known as Wimbledon West), and six golf courses—not to mention that great beach, with gentle waves and islands framing the view on either side.

3900 Wailea Alanui Dr., Wailea, HI 96753. © **800/334-MAUI** or 808/874-8000. Fax 808/874-2222. www.fourseasons.com/maui. 380 units. $335–$590 double; from $630 suite. Packages available. Extra person $90 ($160 in Club Floor rooms). Children under 18 stay free in parent's room. AE, DC, MC, V. **Amenities:** 3 restaurants; 3 bars (with nightly entertainment); 3 fabulous outdoor pools; putting green; use of Wailea Golf Club's 3 18-hole championship golf courses, as well as the nearby Makena and Elleair golf courses; 2 on-site tennis courts (lit for night play); use of Wailea Tennis Center's 11 courts (3 lit for night play and a pro shop); health club featuring outdoor cardiovascular equipment (with individual televison/videoplayers); excellent spa (offering a variety of treatments in the spa, in-room, and ocean side); 2 whirlpools (1 for adults only); beach pavilion with watersports gear rentals and 1 hour free use of snorkel equipment; complimentary use of bicycles; fabulous year-round kids' program, plus a teen recreation center and a children's video library and toys; game room (with shuffleboard, pool tables, jukebox, big-screen TV, and video games); one of Maui's best concierge desks; activity desk; car-rental desk; business center; shopping arcade; salon; 24-hr room service; in-room, spa, or oceanside massage; babysitting; same-day laundry service and dry cleaning; concierge-level rooms. *In room:* A/C, TV, dataport, minibar, fridge, coffeemaker, hair dryer, iron, safe.

Grand Wailea Resort Hotel & Spa ✸✸ Here's where grand becomes grandiose. The pinnacle of Hawaii's brief fling with fantasy megaresorts, this monument to excess is extremely popular with families, incentive groups, and conventions; it's the grand prize in Hawaii vacation contests and the dream of many honeymooners. It has a Japanese restaurant decorated with real rocks hewn from the slopes of Mount Fuji; 10,000 tropical plants in the lobby; an intricate pool system with slides, waterfalls, rapids, and a water-powered elevator to take you up to the top; Hawaii's most elaborate spa; a restaurant in a man-made tide pool; a floating New England–style wedding chapel; and nothing but oceanview rooms, outfitted with every amenity you could ask for. And it's all crowned with a $30 million collection of original art, much of it created expressly for the hotel by Hawaii artists and sculptors. Though minimalists may be put off, there's no denying that the Grand Wailea is plush, professional, and pampering, with all the diversions you could imagine. Oh, and did we mention the fantastic beach out front?

3850 Wailea Alanui Dr., Wailea, HI 96753. ⓒ 800/888-6100 or 808/875-1234. Fax 808/874-2442. www.
grandwailea.com. 780 units. $450–$760 double; from $1575 suite. Concierge tower from $800. Resort fee
$15 for "complimentary" lei greeting on arrival, welcome drink, local calls, coffee in room, use of spa, admis-
sion to scuba diving clinics and water aerobics, art and garden tours, nightly turndown service, self parking,
and shuttle service to Wailea area. Extra person $25 ($75 in concierge tower). AE, DC, DISC, MC, V.
Amenities: 6 restaurants; 12 bars (including a nightclub with laser-light shows and a hydraulic dance floor);
2,000-ft.-long Action Pool, featuring a 10-min. swim/ride through mountains and grottoes; use of Wailea Golf
Club's 3 18-hole championship golf courses, as well as the nearby Makena and Elleair golf courses; use of
Wailea Tennis Center's 11 courts (3 lit for night play and a pro shop); complete fitness center; Hawaii's largest
spa, the 50,000 sq. ft. Spa Grande, with a blend of European-, Japanese-, and American-style techniques;
Jacuzzi; watersports equipment rentals; complimentary dive and windsurf lessons; bike rentals; children's program (including a computer center, video game room, arts and crafts, children's theater, outdoor playground,
and infant-care center); game room; activity desk; car-rental desk; business center; shopping
arcade; salon; 24-hr. room service; in-room and spa massage; babysitting; same-day laundry service and dry-
cleaning; concierge-level rooms. *In room:* A/C, TV, dataport, kitchenette, minibar, fridge ($25 per stay fee), cof-
feemaker, hair dryer, iron, safe.

Renaissance Wailea Beach Resort ★★ This is the place for visitors in
search of Wailea-style luxury, but in a smaller, more intimate setting. Located on
15 acres of rolling lawn and tropical gardens, the Renaissance Wailea has the air
of a small boutique hotel. Perhaps it's the resort's U-shaped design, the series of
small coves and beaches, or the spaciousness of the rooms—whatever the reason,
you just don't feel crowded here.

Each room has a sitting area, a large lanai, and three phones. The bathrooms
include such extras as double vanities (1 with lighted make-up mirror) and *hapi*
coats (Japanese-style cotton robes). All bedspreads, drapes, and towels have been
recently upgraded. Rooms in the Mokapu Beach Club, an exclusive two-story
building just steps from a crescent-shaped beach, feature such extras as private
check-in, in-room continental breakfast, and access to a private pool and beach
cabanas.

3550 Wailea Alanui Dr., Wailea, HI 96753. ⓒ 800/9-WAILEA or 808/879-4900. Fax 808/874-5370. www.
renaissancehotels.com. 345 units. $360–$600 double; from $1,050 suite. Extra person $40. Children 18 and
under stay free in parent's room using existing bedding. Package rates available. AE, DC, DISC, MC, V. Parking $4. **Amenities:** 3 restaurants; 2 bars; 2 freshwater outdoor pools; use of Wailea Golf Club's 3 18-hole
championship golf courses, as well as the nearby Makena and Elleair golf courses; use of Wailea Tennis Center's 11 courts (3 lit for night play and a pro shop); fitness center; small spa; 2 Jacuzzis; watersports equipment rentals; children's program; game room; concierge; activity desk; car-rental desk; business center;
shopping arcade; salon; room service (6am–11pm); massage; babysitting; laundry service; dry-cleaning;
concierge-level rooms. *In room:* A/C, TV/VCR, dataport, fridge, coffeemaker, hair dryer, iron, safe.

Expensive

Wailea Marriott, an Outrigger Resort ★★ Yes, it is confusing and yes, it
seems ridiculous to have two brand names tacked on to a Hawaiian resort, but
it seems that the Outrigger people entered into a "franchise agreement" with
Marriott in 2002 to increase sales (through Marriott), yet still retain the same
management (Outrigger). The bottom line: this classic open-air, 1970s-style
hotel in a tropical garden by the sea gives you a sense of what Maui was like
before the big resort boom. It was the first resort built in Wailea (in 1976), yet
it remains the most Hawaiian of them all. Airy and comfortable, with touches
of Hawaiian art throughout and a terrific aquarium that stretches forever behind
the front desk, it just feels right.

What's truly special about this hotel is how it fits into its environment without overwhelming it. Eight buildings, all low-rise except for an eight-story
tower, are spread along 22 gracious acres of lawns and gardens spiked by coco

palms, with lots of open space and a half-mile of oceanfront on a point between Wailea and Ulua beaches. The vast, parklike expanses are a luxury on this now-crowded coast.

In 2000, the resort went through a $25 million renovation that expanded the entrance into an open-air courtyard with a waterfall and carp pond, transformed the south pool into a water-activities area complete with two water slides, and refurbished and upgraded the guest rooms.

3700 Wailea Alanui Dr., Wailea, HI 96753. © **800/367-2960** or 808/879-1922. Fax 808/874-8331. www.outriggerwailea.com. 524 units. $325–$525 double. Suites from $650. Extra person $40. Packages available. AE, DC, DISC, MC, V. **Amenities:** 2 restaurants; 2 bars; 3 outdoor pools; use of Wailea Golf Club's 3 18-hole championship golf courses, as well as the nearby Makena and Elleair golf courses; use of Wailea Tennis Center's 11 courts (3 lit for night play and a pro shop); fitness room; Mandora Spa; Jacuzzi; watersports equipment rentals; children's program (plus kids-only pool and recreation center); game room; concierge; activity desk; business center; shopping arcade; salon; room service (6am–11pm); in-room and spa massage; babysitting; coin-op washer/dryers; same-day laundry service and dry cleaning; concierge-level rooms. *In room:* A/C, TV, dataport, fridge, coffeemaker, hair dryer, iron, safe.

MAKENA
Expensive
Maui Prince Hotel ★★   If you're looking for a vacation in a beautiful, tranquil spot with a golden-sand beach, here's your place. But if you plan to tour Maui, you might try another hotel. The Maui Prince is at the end of the road, far, far away from anything else on the island, so sightseeing in other areas would require a lot of driving.

When you first see the stark-white hotel, it looks like a high-rise motel stuck in the woods—but only from the outside. Inside, you'll discover an atrium garden with a koi-filled waterfall stream, an ocean view from every room, and a simplicity to the furnishings that makes some people feel uncomfortable and others blissfully clutter-free. Rooms are small but come with private lanais with great views.

5400 Makena Alanui, Makena, HI 96753. © **800/PRINCE-4** or 808/874-1111. Fax 808/879-8763. www.mauiprincehotel.com. 310 units. $310–$480 double; from $600 suite. Extra person $40. Packages available. AE, DC, MC, V. **Amenities:** 4 restaurants (including the excellent Prince Court, p. 407); 2 bars with local Hawaiian music nightly; 2 outdoor pools (adults' and children's); 36 holes of golf (designed by Robert Trent Jones); 6 Plexipave tennis courts (2 lit for night play); fitness room; Jacuzzi; watersports equipment rentals; children's program; concierge; activity desk; business center; shopping arcade; salon; room service; in-room massage; babysitting; same-day laundry service and dry cleaning. *In room:* A/C, TV, dataport, fridge, hair dryer, iron, safe.

UPCOUNTRY MAUI
You'll find it cool and peaceful up here; be sure to bring a sweater.

MAKAWAO & OLINDA
Here you'll be (relatively) close to Haleakala National Park; Makawao and Olinda are approximately 90 minutes from the entrance to the park at the 7,000-foot level (you still have 3,000 ft. and another 30–45 min. to get to the top). Accommodations in Kula are the only other options that will get you closer to the park so you can make the sunrise.

Banyan Tree House ★ *(Finds)*   Huge monkeypod trees (complete with swing and hammock) extend their branches over this 2½-acre property like a giant green canopy. The restored 1920s plantation manager's house is decorated with Hawaiian furniture from the 1930s. The house can accommodate a big family or a group of friends; it has three spacious bedrooms with big, comfortable beds and three private, marble-tiled bathrooms. A fireplace stands at one end of the huge

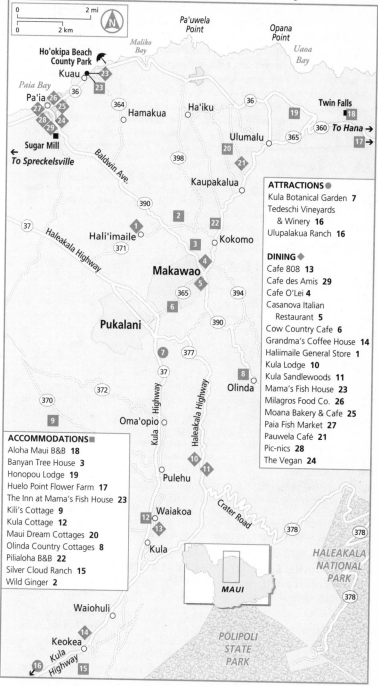

0 2 mi
0 2 km

Pa'uwela Point

Opana Point

Maliko Bay

Uaoa Bay

Ho'okipa Beach County Park

Kuau **23**
23

Paia Bay

Pa'ia **26**
27 **25**
28 **24**
29

Sugar Mill

← To Spreckelsville

364

Hamakua

36

Ha'iku

36

Twin Falls **18**

19

To Hana →

360

365

17 →

Ulumalu **20**

21

398

Baldwin Ave.

37

Haleakala Highway

390

Hali'imaile **1**

371

2

22

3

Kokomo

4

Makawao

5

365

394

6

Pukalani

390

7 377

37

372

370

9

Oma'opio

8

Olinda

Kula Highway

Haleakala Highway

10

11

Pulehu

Crater Road

12

13

Waiakoa

378

378

Kula

MAUI

HALEAKALA NATIONAL PARK

Waiohuli

14

Keokea

Kula Highway

16 **15**

378

POLIPOLI STATE PARK

ATTRACTIONS ●
Kula Botanical Garden **7**
Tedeschi Vineyards & Winery **16**
Ulupalakua Ranch **16**

DINING ◆
Cafe 808 **13**
Cafe des Amis **29**
Cafe O'Lei **4**
Casanova Italian Restaurant **5**
Cow Country Cafe **6**
Grandma's Coffee House **14**
Haliimaile General Store **1**
Kula Lodge **10**
Kula Sandlewoods **11**
Mama's Fish House **23**
Milagros Food Co. **26**
Moana Bakery & Cafe **25**
Paia Fish Market **27**
Pauwela Café **21**
Pic-nics **28**
The Vegan **24**

ACCOMMODATIONS ■
Aloha Maui B&B **18**
Banyan Tree House **3**
Honopou Lodge **19**
Huelo Point Flower Farm **17**
The Inn at Mama's Fish House **23**
Kili's Cottage **9**
Kula Cottage **12**
Maui Dream Cottages **20**
Olinda Country Cottages **8**
Pilialoha B&B **22**
Silver Cloud Ranch **15**
Wild Ginger **2**

living room, a large lanai runs the entire length of the house, and the hardwood floors shine throughout. The four smaller guest cottages have been totally renovated and also feature hardwood floors and marble bathrooms. The small cottage has a queen bed, private bathroom, microwave, coffee pot, and access to the refrigerator in the laundry room. Each of the larger cottages has two beds, a private bathroom, and a TV. One cottage has a kitchenette, the other a full kitchen.

New additions to this grand property include a full-size swimming pool and Jacuzzi. The quiet neighborhood and old Hawaii ambience give this place a comfortable, easygoing atmosphere. Restaurants and shops are just minutes away in Makawao, and the beach is a 15-minute drive away—but this place is so relaxing that you may find yourself wanting to do nothing more than lie in the hammock and watch the clouds float by.

3265 Baldwin Ave. (next to Veteran's Cemetery, less than a mile below Makawao), Makawao, HI 96768. ⓒ 808/572-9021. Fax 808/573-5072. www.banyantreehouse.com. 1 house, 4 cottages. $85–$110 cottage for 2; $300 3-bedroom house (sleeps up to 9). Extra person $15. Children age 12 and under stay free in parent's room. 3-night minimum for house. MC, V. **Amenities:** Outdoor pool; Jacuzzi; babysitting; small charge for self-serve washer/dryer. *In room:* Kitchen or kitchenette, fridge, coffeemaker.

Olinda Country Cottages & Inn 🌟🌟 *Finds*   This charming B&B is set on the slopes of Haleakala in the crisp, clean air of Olinda, on an 8½-acre protea farm, surrounded by 35,000 acres of ranch lands (with miles of great hiking trails). The 5,000-square-foot country home, outfitted with a professional eye to detail, has large windows with incredible panoramic views of all of Maui. Upstairs are two guest rooms with antique beds, private full bathrooms, and separate entryways. Connected to the main house but with its own private entrance, the Pineapple Sweet has a full kitchen, an antique-filled living room, and a marble-tiled full bath. A separate 1,000-square-foot cottage is the epitome of cozy country luxury, with a fireplace, a queen bedroom, cushioned window seats (with great sunset views), and cathedral ceilings. The 950-square-foot Hidden Cottage (located in a truly secluded spot surrounded by protea flowers) features three decks, 8-foot French glass doors, a full kitchen, a washer/dryer, and a private tub for two on the deck.

Restaurants are a 15-minute drive away in Makawao, and beaches are another 15 minutes beyond that. Once ensconced, however, you may never want to leave this enchanting inn.

2660 Olinda Rd. (near the top of Olinda Rd., a 15-min. drive from Makawao), Makawao, HI 96768. ⓒ 800/932-3435 or 808/572-1453. Fax 808/573-5326. www.mauibnbcottages.com. 5 units. $140 double (includes continental breakfast); $140 suite double (includes 1st morning's breakfast in fridge); $195–$245 cottage for 2 (sleeps up to 5; includes 1st morning's breakfast in fridge). Extra person $25. 2-night minimum for rooms and suite, 3-night minimum for cottages. No credit cards. *In room:* TV, kitchen (in cottages), fridge, coffeemaker.

KULA (AT THE BASE OF HALEAKALA NATIONAL PARK)

Lodgings in Kula are the closest options to the entrance of Haleakala National Park (about 60 min. away).

Kili's Cottage 🌟 *Value*   If you're looking for a quiet getaway in the cool elevation of Kula, this sweet cottage, situated on 2 acres, is the place. The amenities are numerous: large lanai, full kitchen, gas barbecue, washer/dryer, views, even toys for the kids. The hostess, Kili Namau'u, who is the director of a Hawaiian-language immersion school, greets each guest with royal aloha—from the flowers (picked from the garden) that fill the house to the welcome basket filled with tropical produce grown on the property.

Kula. Reservations c/o Hawaii's Best Bed & Breakfast, P.O. Box 758, Volcano, HI 96785. ☏ **800/262-9912** or 808/985-7488. Fax 808/967-8610. www.bestbnb.com. 1 3-bedroom/2-bathroom house. $105 double. Extra person $15. 2-night minimum. No credit cards. *In room:* TV, kitchen, fridge, coffeemaker, washer/dryer.

Kula Cottage ⭐ *Finds*   We can't imagine having a less-than-fantastic vacation here. Tucked away on a quiet street amid a large grove of blooming papaya and banana trees, Cecilia and Larry Gilbert's romantic honeymoon cottage is very private—it even has its own driveway and carport. The 700-square-foot cottage has a full kitchen (complete with dishwasher), and three huge closets that offer enough storage space for you to move in permanently. An outside lanai has a big gas barbecue and an umbrella table and chairs. Cecilia delivers a continental breakfast daily. Groceries and a small takeout lunch counter are within walking distance; it's a 30-minute drive to the beach.

40 Puakea Place (off Lower Kula Rd.), Kula, HI 96790. ☏ **808/878-2043** or 808/871-6230. Fax 808/871-9187. www.gilbertadvertising.com/kulacottage. 1 cottage. $95 double. Rate includes continental breakfast. 2-night minimum. No credit cards. *In room:* TV, kitchen, fridge, coffeemaker, washer/dryer.

Silver Cloud Ranch   Old Hawaii lives on at Silver Cloud Ranch, founded in 1902 by a sailor who jumped ship when he got to Maui. The former working cattle spread has a commanding view of four islands, the West Maui Mountains, and the valley and beaches below. The Lanai Cottage, a honeymoon favorite nestled in a flower garden, has an oceanview lanai, claw-foot tub, full kitchen, and wood-burning stove to warm chilly nights; a futon is available for a third person. The best rooms in the main house are on the second floor: the King Kamehameha Suite (with king bed) and the Queen Emma Suite (with queen bed). One-lane Thompson Road makes an ideal morning walk (about 3 miles roundtrip), and you can go horseback riding next door at Thompson Ranch. There's a TV available if you feel visually deprived, but after a few Maui sunsets, you won't even remember why you bothered to ask.

Old Thompson Rd. (1¼ miles past Hwy. 37). RR 2, Box 201, Kula, HI 96790. ☏ **800/532-1111** or 808/878-6101. Fax 808/878-2132. www.silvercloudranch.com. 12 units. $110–$162 double in main house; $136–$188 double studio in mauka hale; $195 double cottage. Rates include full breakfast. Extra person $15. 2 night minimum or $15 surcharge. AE, DC, DISC, MC, V. *In room:* TV, Kitchen (in cottage), fridge (in cottage), coffeemaker (in cottage); no phone.

EAST MAUI: ON THE ROAD TO HANA

Note: You'll find the accommodations in this section on the "Upcountry & East Maui" map on p. 383.

KUAU

The Inn at Mama's Fish House ⭐   The fabulous location (nestled in a coconut grove on secluded Kuau Beach), beautifully decorated interior (with island-style rattan furniture and works by Hawaiian artists), full kitchen, and extras (Weber gas barbecue, huge 27-in. TVs, and all the beach toys you can think of) make this place a gem for those seeking a centrally located vacation rental. It has everything, even Mama's Fish House next door, where guests get a discount of 20% off lunch and dinner. The one-bedrooms are nestled in tropical jungle (red ginger surrounds the garden patio), while the two-bedrooms face the beach. Both have terra-cotta floors, complete kitchens (even dishwashers), sofa beds, and laundry facilities.

799 Poho Place (off the Hana Hwy. in Kuau), Paia, HI 96779. ☏ **800/860-HULA** or 808/579-9764. Fax 808/579-8594. www.mamasfishhouse.com. 6 units. $140–$160 1-bedroom (sleeps up to 4); $350 2-bedroom (up to 6). 3-night minimum stay. AE, DISC, MC, V. *In room:* A/C, TV/VCR, kitchen, fridge, coffeemaker, iron, hair dryer.

HAIKU

Honopou Lodge ✦ *Finds*   Hidden on Maui's north shore, next door to a 750-acre ranch, is this upscale vacation retreat. The Lodge is a unique 4,000 square foot, architect-designed, octagonal house with native ohia posts and cedar wood. The three rooms in the house can be rented separately or the entire complex as a whole. Downstairs, two spacious octagonal studios share the deluxe, gourmet kitchen. Upstairs, a smaller studio has its own private entrance and a small kitchenette. Outside is a huge (32 ft. × 16 ft.), ozone-filtered swimming pool, Jacuzzi, and satellite TV. Awe-inspiring ocean views greet you from every room, and sculptures and paintings created by the owners fill the house. Honopou Lodge is minutes from hiking trails and waterfalls.

Honopou Rd., Haiku. Reservations c/o Hawaii's Best Bed & Breakfasts, P.O. Box 758, Volcano, HI 96785. © **800/262-9912** or 808/985-7488. Fax 808/967-8610. www.bestbnb.com. 3 units. $125–$150 studio double, $300 two-bedroom downstairs of house, $400 entire house. Additional person $25. 3-night minimum. No credit cards. **Amenities:** Outdoor pool; Jacuzzi. *In room:* TV, kitchen (downstairs), kitchenette (upstairs), fridge, coffeemaker, iron, hair dryer.

Maui Dream Cottages *Value*   Essentially a vacation rental, this country estate is located atop a hill overlooking the ocean. The grounds are dotted with fruit trees (bananas, papayas, and avocados, all free for the picking), and the front lawn is comfortably equipped with a double hammock, chaise lounges, and table and chairs. One cottage has two bedrooms, a full kitchen, a washer/dryer, and an entertainment center. The other is basically the same, but with only one bedroom (plus a sofa bed in the living room). They're both very well maintained and comfortably outfitted with furniture that's attractive but casual. The Haiku location is quiet and restful and offers the opportunity to see how real islanders live. However, you'll have to drive a good 20 to 25 minutes to restaurants in Makawao or Paia. Hookipa Beach is about a 20-minute drive, and Baldwin Beach (good swimming) is 25 minutes away.

265 W. Kuiaha Rd. (1 block from Pauwela Cafe), Haiku, HI 96708. © **808/575-9079.** Fax 808/575-9477. www.planet-hawaii.com/haiku. 2 cottages (shower only). $70 for 2. 7-night minimum. MC, V. *In room:* TV kitchen, fridge, coffeemaker, washer/dryer.

Pilialoha B&B Cottage ✦   The minute you arrive at this split-level country cottage, located on a large lot with half-century-old eucalyptus trees, you'll see owner Machiko Heyde's artistry at work. Just in front of the quaint cottage (which is great for couples but can sleep up to 5) is a garden blooming with some 200 varieties of roses. You'll find more of Machiko's handiwork inside. There's a queen bed in the master bedroom, a twin bed in a small adjoining room, and a queen sofa bed in the living room. A large lanai extends from the master bedroom. There's a great movie collection for rainy days or cool country nights, and a garage. Machiko delivers breakfast daily; if you plan on an early morning ride to the top of Haleakala, she'll make sure you go with a thermos of coffee and her homemade bread.

2512 Kaupakalua Rd. (½ mile from Kokomo intersection), Haiku, HI 96708. © **808/572-1440.** Fax 808/572-4612. www.pilialoha.com. 1 cottage. $130 double. Rates include continental breakfast. Extra person $20. 3-night minimum. MC, V. **Amenities:** Complimentary use of beach paraphernalia (including snorkel equipment); complimentary use of washer/dryer. *In room:* TV, kitchenette, fridge, coffeemaker.

Wild Ginger ✦✦ *Finds*   This cozy, romantic intimate cottage, hidden in Miliko Gulch, overlooking a stream with a waterfall, bamboo, sweet smelling ginger and banana trees, is perfect for honeymooners, lovers and fans of Hawaiiana art. The moment you step into this 400-square-foot, artistically decorated

Hawaiian cottage (with additional 156 sq. ft. screened deck) you will be delighted at the carefully placed memorabilia (ukulele tile, canoe paddle, etc.) found throughout. The cottage has a full kitchen with everything you could possibly need for cooking. The Hawaiian theme carries into the living room with VCR behind a tropical painted cabinet and stereo. The comfy queen bed opens to the living area. The screened porch has table, chairs, and couch, perfect for curling up with a good book. Outside there's a barbecue, plus all the beach toys you could want to borrow. Your hosts are Bob, a ceramic artist (with his creations throughout the cottage) and his wife, Sonny, who manages Dolphin Galleries (where she has selected the best of the best artwork for the cottage).

Haiku. Reservations c/o Hawaii's Best Bed & Breakfasts, P.O. Box 758, Volcano, HI 96785. ℂ **800/262-9912** or 808/985-7488. Fax 808/967-8610. www.bestbnb.com. 1 unit. $125 double, 3-night minimum. No credit cards. *In room:* VCR, kitchen, fridge, coffeemaker, iron, hair dryer, washer and dryer.

TWIN FALLS

Aloha Maui B&B *(Finds)*   On 2 acres of jungle, tucked away in the Twin Falls area, is this budget traveler accommodation. Four separate bungalows offer a back to nature experience. The rustic, but clean and well outfitted cabins, are all landscaped to offer privacy and offer good value for the price. The cabins range from the $110 Mango cottage with hardwood floors, full kitchen, big bedroom with ocean view, with continental breakfast included (for an extra $5 a night, you can get satellite TV) to the Banana Room, a small room with kitchenette (2 burners, full fridge, microwave, toaster, coffeemaker), a CD player, even a phone for $65, including breakfast (the only drawback to this room is a shared bathroom). Host Ken knows all the hiking and biking trails (he will loan you his mountain bikes to go exploring) and secret waterfalls. This is the perfect place if you are on a tight budget and looking for a vacation in Maui's rainforest.

P.O. Box 790210, Paia, HI 96779. ℂ **808/572-0298.** kenred101@yahoo.com. 4 units. $65–$110, including continental breakfast. Extra person $5 plus $5 for breakfast. 3 night minimum. No credit cards. *In room:* CD player, TV on request ($5 per night).

HUELO

Huelo Point Flower Farm *(★ Finds)*   Here's a little Eden by the sea on a spectacular, remote, 300-foot sea cliff near a waterfall stream. This estate overlooking Waipio Bay has two guest cottages, a guesthouse, and a main house available for rent. The studio-size Gazebo Cottage has a glass-walled oceanfront, a koawood captain's bed, a TV, a stereo, a kitchenette, a private oceanside patio, a private hot tub, and a half-bathroom with outdoor shower. The new 900-square-foot Carriage House apartment sleeps four and has glass walls facing the mountain and sea, plus a kitchen, a den, decks, and a loft bedroom. The two-bedroom main house contains an exercise room, a fireplace, a sunken Roman bath, cathedral ceilings, and other extras. On-site is a natural pool with a waterfall and an oceanfront hot tub. You're welcome to pick fruit, vegetables, and flowers from the extensive garden. Homemade scones, tree-ripened papayas, and fresh-roasted coffee start your day. Despite its seclusion, off the crooked road to Hana, it's just a half-hour to Kahului, or about 20 minutes to Paia's shops and restaurants.

Off Hana Hwy., between mile markers 3 and 4. P.O. Box 791808, Paia, HI 96779. ℂ **808/572-1850.** www.mauiflowerfarm.com. 4 units. $150 cottage double; $175 carriage house double; $325 guesthouse double; $425 main house double (sleeps 6). Extra person $20–$35. 2-night minimum, except for 7-night minimum for main house. No credit cards. **Amenities:** Outdoor pool; 3 Jacuzzis; self-serve washer/dryer. *In room:* TV, kitchenette (in cottage), kitchen (in houses), fridge, coffeemaker, hair dryer.

AT THE END OF THE ROAD IN EAST MAUI: HANA

Note: You'll find Hana accommodations on the map on p. 213.

EXPENSIVE

Hotel Hana-Maui ★★★ *(Kids)*   Picture Shangri-La, Hawaiian-style: 66 acres rolling down to the sea in a remote Hawaiian village, with a wellness center, two pools, and access to one of the best beaches in Hana. This is the atmosphere, the landscape, and the culture of old Hawaii set in 21st-century accommodations. Every unit is excellent, but our favorites are the Sea Ranch Cottages (especially units 215–218 for the best views of turtles frolicking in the ocean), where individual duplex bungalows look out over the craggy shoreline to the rolling surf. You step out of the over-size, open, airy units (with floor-to-ceiling sliding doors) onto a huge lanai with views that will stay with you long after your tan has faded. These comfy units have been totally redecorated with every amenity you can think of, and you won't be nickle-and-dimed for things like coffee, water, etc.—everything they give you, from the homemade banana bread to the bottled water, is complimentary. Cathedral ceilings, a plush feather bed, a giant-size soaking tub, Hawaiian art work, bamboo hardwood floors—this is luxury. The white sand beach (just a 5 min. shuttle away), top notch wellness center with some of the best massage therapists in Hawaii, and numerous activities (horseback riding, mountain biking, tennis, pitch-and-putt golf) all add up to make this one of the top resorts in the state. There's no TV in the rooms, but the Club Room has a giant screen TV, plus VCR and Internet access. We highly recommend this little slice of paradise.

Hana, Maui 96713. ⓒ **800/321-HANA** or 808/248-8211; fax 808/248-7202; www.hotelhanamaui.com. 78 units. $295–$365 Bay Cottages double; $395-$725 Sea Ranch Cottages double; 2-bedroom Plantation Guest House from $1,500. $50 extra person. AE, DC, DISC, MC, V. **Amenities:** 1 restaurant (with Hawaiian entertainment twice a week); 1 bar (with nightly entertainment); two outdoor pools; complimentary use of the three-hole practice golf courses (clubs are complimentary); complimentary tennis courts; fitness center; game room; concierge; activity desk; car-rental desk; business center; small shopping arcade; salon; room service (11:30am–2pm and 6–9pm); in-room and spa massage; babysitting; laundry service. *In room:* dataport, kitchenette, fridge, coffeemaker, hair dryer, iron, safe.

MODERATE

Ekena ★   Just one glance at the 360 degree view, and you can see why hosts Robin and Gaylord gave up their careers on the mainland and moved here. This 8½-acre piece of paradise in rural Hana boasts ocean and rain-forest views; the floor-to-ceiling glass doors in the spacious Hawaiian-style pole house bring the outside in. The elegant two-story home is exquisitely furnished, from the comfortable U-shaped couch that invites you to relax and take in the view to the top-of-the-line mattress on the king bed. The kitchen is fully equipped with every high-tech convenience you can imagine (guests have made complete holiday meals here). Only one floor (and 1 two-bedroom unit) is rented at any one time to ensure privacy. The grounds are impeccably groomed and dotted with tropical plants and fruit trees. Hiking trails into the rain forest start right on the property, and beaches and waterfalls are just minutes away. Robin places fresh flowers in every room and makes sure you're comfortable; after that, she's available to answer questions, but she also respects your privacy.

P.O. Box 728 (off Hana Hwy., above Hana Airport), Hana, HI 96713. ⓒ **808/248-7047.** Fax 808/248-7047. www.ekenamaui.com. 2 units. $185 for 2; $250–$350 for 4. Extra person $25. 3-night minimum. No credit cards. **Amenities:** Complimentary use of washer/dryers. *In room:* TV, kitchen, fridge, coffeemaker, iron.

Hamoa Bay Bungalow ★ *(Finds)*   Down a country lane guarded by two Balinese statues stands a little bit of Indonesia in Hawaii: a carefully crafted bungalow and an Asian-inspired two-bedroom house overlooking Hamoa Bay. This enchanting retreat is just 2 miles beyond Hasegawa's general store on the way to Kipahulu. It sits on 4 verdant acres within walking distance of Hamoa Beach (which James Michener considered one of the most beautiful in the Pacific). The 600-square-foot Balinese-style cottage is distinctly tropical, with giant Elephant bamboo furniture from Indonesia, batik prints, a king bed, a full kitchen, and a screened porch with hot tub and shower. Hidden from the cottage is a 1,300-square-foot home with a soaking tub and private outdoor stone shower. It offers an Elephant bamboo king bed in one room, a queen bed in another, a screened-in sleeping porch, a full kitchen, and wonderful ocean views.

P.O. Box 773, Hana, HI 96713. ℂ 808/248-7884. Fax 808/248-7047. www.hamoabay.com. 2 units. $195 cottage (sleeps only 2); $250 house for 2; $350 house for 4. 3-night minimum. No credit cards. **Amenities:** Hot tub; complimentary use of washer/dryers. *In room:* TV, kitchen, fridge, coffeemaker, iron.

Hana Ocean Front ★★ Just across the street from Hamoa Bay, Hana's premier white sand beach, lie these two plantation style units, impeccably decorated in old Hawaii decor and outfitted with everything you could possibly desire during your vacation. Our favorite unit is the romantic cottage, complete with old-fashioned front porch where you can sit and watch the ocean; separate bedroom (with a bamboo sleigh bed), plus pull out sofa for extra guests; top-notch kitchen appliances (Jenn-Air stove); and comfy living room. The 1,000-square-foot vacation suite, located downstairs from hosts Dan and Sandi's home (but totally soundproof—you'll never hear them) has an elegant master bedroom with polished bamboo flooring, spacious bath with custom hand-painted tile, and a fully appointed gourmet kitchen. Outside is a 320-square-foot lanai. The units sit on the road facing Hana's most popular beach, so there is traffic during the day. At night, the traffic disappears, the stars come out, and the sound of the ocean lulls you to sleep.

Hana. Reservations c/o Hawaii's Best Bed & Breakfasts, P.O. Box 758, Volcano, HI 96785. ℂ 800/262-9912 or 808/985-7488. Fax 808/967-8610. www.bestbnb.com. 2 units. $190–$225 double, 2-night minimum. No credit cards. *In room:* TV/VCR, kitchen, fridge, coffeemaker, iron, hair dryer.

Heavenly Hana Inn ★★ *Finds* Owners Robert Filippi and Sheryl Murray humbly describe their B&B as a "Japanese-style inn at secluded and beautiful Hana." That's like saying a Four Seasons Hotel is a big building with rooms. This place on the Hana Highway, just a stone's throw from the center of Hana town, is a little bit of heaven, where no attention to detail has been spared. Each suite has a sitting room with futon and couch, polished hardwood floors, and separate bedroom with a raised platform bed (with an excellent, firm mattress). The black-marble bathrooms have huge tubs. Flowers are everywhere, ceiling fans keep the rooms cool, and the delicious gourmet breakfast—worth splurging for—is served in a setting filled with art. The grounds are done in Japanese style with a bamboo fence, tiny bridges over a meandering stream, and Japanese gardens.

P.O. Box 790, Hana, HI 96713. ℂ and fax **808/248-8442.** www.heavenlyhanainn.com. 3 units. $185–$250 suite. Full gourmet breakfast available for $15 per person. Ask about special rates. 2-night minimum. AE, DISC, MC, V. No children under age 15 accepted. **Amenities:** Laundry service. *In room:* TV, no phone.

INEXPENSIVE

Mrs. Nakamura has been renting her **Aloha Cottages** (ℂ **808/248-8420**) since the 1970s. Located in residential areas near Hana Bay, these five budget rentals are simple but adequately furnished, varying in size from a roomy studio with kitchenette to a three-bedroom, two-bathroom unit. They're all fully equipped, clean, and fairly well kept. Rates run from $62 to $95 double. Not all units have TVs, and none have phones, but Mrs. N. is happy to take messages.

Baby Pigs Crossing Bed & Breakfast ★★ *Finds*   If you're looking for a quiet, romantic little cottage, nestled away from it all in Old Hawaii, but close enough to drive into Hana for dinner, this is your place. International artist Gail Bakutis has created a lovely retreat on her one-acre parcel of land, which is landscaped in a "fragrance" garden with Hawaii's best sweet-smelling plants carefully planted throughout the property. The separate guesthouse, with an ocean view from the lanai, is professionally decorated with comfort in mind, from the very cozy rattan furniture to the snug king-size sofa bed. There's a separate bedroom with a queen bed and a small but utilitarian kitchenette (refrigerator, microwave, toaster and coffeemaker). But the surprise is the unique bathroom with glass ceiling and walls (with discreet privacy curtains), which opens out to a garden area.

P.O. Box 667, Hana, HI 96713. ⓒ **808/248-8890.** Fax 808/248-4865. www.mauibandb.com. 1 unit. $125 double. 2 nights minimum. AE, DISC, MC, V. *In room:* TV/VCR, kitchenette, fridge, coffeemaker, cellphone.

Hana's Tradewinds Cottage ★ *Value*   Nestled among the ginger and heliconias on a 5-acre flower farm are two separate cottages, each with full kitchen, carport, barbecue, private hot tub, TV, ceiling fans, and sofa bed. The studio cottage sleeps up to four; a bamboo shoji blind separates the sleeping area (with queen bed) from the sofa bed in the living room. The Tradewinds cottage has two bedrooms (with a queen bed in 1 room and 2 twins in the other), one bathroom (shower only), and a huge front porch. The atmosphere is quiet and relaxing, and hostess Rebecca Buckley, who has been in business for a decade, welcomes families (she has 2 children, a cat, and a very sweet golden retriever). You can use the laundry facilities at no extra charge.

135 Alalele Place (the airport road), P.O. Box 385, Hana, HI 96713. ⓒ **800/327-8097** or 808/248-8980. Fax 808/248-7735. www.hanamaui.net. 2 cottages. $120 studio double; $145 2-bedroom double. Extra person $10. 2-night minimum. AE, DISC, MC, V. *In room:* TV, kitchen, fridge, coffeemaker, no phone.

Waianapanapa State Park Cabins *Value*   These 12 rustic cabins are the best lodging deal on Maui. Everyone knows it, too—so make your reservations early (up to 6 months in advance). The cabins are warm and dry and come complete with kitchen, living room, bedroom, and bathroom with hot shower; furnishings include bedding, linen, towels, dishes, and very basic cooking and eating utensils. Don't expect luxury—this is a step above camping, albeit in a beautiful tropical jungle setting. The key attraction at this 120-acre state beach park is the unusual horseshoe-shaped black-sand beach on Pailoa Bay, popular for shore fishing, snorkeling, and swimming. There's a caretaker on-site, along with restrooms, showers, picnic tables, shoreline hiking trails, and historic sites. But bring mosquito protection—this *is* the jungle, after all.

Off Hana Hwy. c/o State Parks Division, 54 S. High St., Rm. 101, Wailuku, HI 96793. ⓒ **808/984-8109.** 12 cabins. $45 for 4 (sleeps up to 6). Extra person $5. 5-night maximum. No credit cards. *In room:* Kitchen, fridge, coffeemaker, no phone.

4 Where to Dine

With soaring visitor statistics and a glamorous image, the Valley Isle is fertile ground for Hawaii's famous enterprising chefs (like Roy Yamaguchi from Roy's and Nicolina, Gerard Reversade of Gerard's, James McDonald of I'o and Pacific'o, Peter Merriman of Hula Grill, Mark Ellman of Maui Taco, D.K. Kodoma of Sansei Seafood, and Beverly Gannon of Haliimaile General Store and Joe's

Bar and Grill), as well as an international name or two (Wolfgang Puck of Spago). Plus a few newcomers who are cooking up a storm and getting a well deserved following (Jennifer Nguyen of A Saigon Café, Tom Lelli of Manana Garage, Dana Pastula of Café O'Lei and Don Ritchey of Moana Bakery and Café).

In this dizzying scenario, some things haven't changed: You can still dine well at Lahaina's open-air waterfront watering holes, where the view counts for 50% of the experience. There are still budget eateries, but not many; Maui's old-fashioned, multigenerational mom-and-pop diners are disappearing, eclipsed by the flashy newcomers, or clinging to the edge of existence in the older neighborhoods of central Maui, such as lovable Wailuku. Although you'll have to work harder to find them in the resort areas, you won't have to go far to find creative cuisine, pleasing style, and stellar dining experiences.

In the listings below, reservations are not necessary unless otherwise noted.

CENTRAL MAUI

The **Queen Kaahumanu Center,** the structure that looks like a white *Star Wars* umbrella in the center of Kahului, at 275 Kaahumanu Ave. (5 min. from Kahului Airport on Hwy. 32), has a very popular food court. Busy shoppers seem more than willing to dispense with fine china and other formalities to enjoy a no-nonsense meal on foam plates. **Edo Japan** teppanyaki is a real find, its flat Benihana-like grill dispensing marvelous, flavorful mounds of grilled fresh vegetables and chicken teriyaki for $4.15. **Maui Mixed Plate** dishes out "local style" cuisine of meat with rice and macaroni salad in the $5 to $7 range. **Yummy Korean B-B-Q** offers the assertive flavors of Korea; **Panda Express** serves tasty Chinese food; and the **Coffee Store** (p. 404) sells sandwiches, salads, pasta, and nearly 2 dozen different coffee drinks. When you leave Kaahumanu Center, take a moment to gaze at the West Maui Mountains to your left from the parking lot. They are one of Maui's wonders.

There's a branch of **Maui Tacos** (p. 401) in Kaahumanu Center, Kahului (© **808/871-7726**).

MODERATE

A Saigon Cafe ★★ (Finds VIETNAMESE Jennifer Nguyen has stuck to her guns and steadfastly refused to erect a sign, but diners find their way here anyway. That's how good the food is. Fans drive from all over the island for her crisped, spiced Dungeness crab, her steamed opakapaka with ginger and garlic, and her wok-cooked Vietnamese specials tangy with spices, herbs, and lemongrass. There are a dozen different soups, cold and hot noodles (including the popular beef noodle soup called *pho*) and chicken and shrimp cooked in a clay pot. You can create your own Vietnamese "burritos" from a platter of tofu, noodles, and vegetables that you wrap in rice paper and dip in garlic sauce. Among our favorites are the shrimp lemongrass, savory and refreshing, and the tofu curry, swimming in herbs and vegetables straight from the garden. The Nhung Dam—a hearty spread of basil, cucumbers, mint, romaine, bean sprouts, pickled carrots, turnips, and vermicelli, wrapped in rice paper and dipped in a legendary sauce—is cooked at your table.

1792 Main St., Wailuku. (Heading into Wailuku from Kahului, go over the bridge and take the 1st right onto Central Ave, then the 1st right on Nani St. At the next stop sign, look for the building with the neon sign that says OPEN) © **808/243-9560**. Main courses $6.50–$17. DC, MC, V. Mon–Sat 10am–9:30pm; Sun 10am–8:30pm.

Class Act ★ GLOBAL   Part of a program run by the distinguished Food Service Department of Maui Community College (soon to be housed in a new state-of-the-art, $15 million culinary facility), this restaurant has a following. Student chefs show their stuff with a flourish in their "classroom," where they pull out all the stops. Linen, china, servers in ties and white shirts, and a four-course lunch make this a unique value. The appetizer, soup, salad, and dessert are set, but you can choose between the regular entrees and a heart-healthy main course prepared in the culinary tradition of the week. The menu roams the globe with highlights of Italy, Mexico, Maui, Napa valley, France, New Orleans, and other locales. The filet mignon of French week is popular, as are the New Orleans gumbo and Cajun shrimp; the sesame-crusted mahimahi on taro leaf pasta; the polenta flan with eggplant; and the bean- and green-chile chilaquile. Tea and soft drinks are offered—and they can get pretty fancy, with fresh fruit and spritzers—but otherwise it's BYOB.

Maui Community College, 310 Kaahumanu Ave., Wailuku. ℂ **808/984-3480.** Reservations recommended. 4-course lunch $15. No credit cards. Wed and Fri 11am–12:15pm (last seating); closed June–Aug for summer vacation. Menu and cuisine type change weekly.

Ichiban *Finds* JAPANESE/SUSHI   What a find: an informal neighborhood restaurant that serves inexpensive, home-cooked Japanese food *and* good sushi at realistic prices. Local residents consider Ichiban a staple for breakfast, lunch, or dinner and a haven of comforts: egg-white omelets; great saimin; combination plates of teriyaki chicken, teriyaki meat, *tonkatsu* (pork cutlet), rice, and pickled cabbage; chicken yakitori; and sushi—everything from unagi and scallop to California roll. The sushi items may not be cheap, but like the specials, such as steamed opakapaka, they're a good value. We love the tempura, miso soup, and spicy ahi hand roll.

Kahului Shopping Center, 47 Kaahumanu Ave., Kahului. ℂ **808/871-6977.** Main courses $4.25–$5.25 breakfast; $5.50–$9.50 lunch (combination plates $8); $5.95–$28 dinner (combination dinner $12, dinner specials from $8.95). AE, DC, MC, V. Mon–Fri 6:30am–2pm and 5–9pm; Sat 10:30am–2pm and 5–9pm; closed 2 weeks around Christmas and New Year.

Mañana Garage ★ ★ *Finds* LATIN AMERICAN   Chef Tom Lelli, formerly of Haliimaile General Store, is serving up some incomparable fare at this central Maui hot spot. The industrial motif features table bases like hubcaps, a vertical garage door as a divider for private parties, blown-glass chandeliers, and gleaming chrome and cobalt walls with orange accents. The menu is brilliantly conceived and executed. Fried green tomatoes are done just right and served with slivered red onions. The ceviche perfectly balances flavors and textures: lime, cilantro, chile, coconut, and fresh fish. Arepas (cornmeal and cheese griddle cakes with smoked salmon and wasabi sour cream) meld the flavors and textures of many traditions. Mañana Garage has raised the bar and introduced exciting new flavors to Maui's dining options.

33 Lono Ave., Kahului. ℂ **808/873-0220.** Reservations recommended. Lunch main courses $7–$13; dinner main courses $12–$26. AE, DC, DISC, MC, V. Mon 11am–9pm; Tues–Fri 11am–10:30pm; Sat 5–10:30pm; Sun 5–9pm.

Marco's Grill & Deli ITALIAN   Located in the thick of central Maui, where the roads to upcountry, west, and south Maui converge, Marco's is popular among area residents for its homemade Italian fare and friendly informality. Everything—from the meatballs, sausages, and burgers to the sauces, salad dressings, and raviolis—is made in-house. The 35 different choices of hot and cold sandwiches and entrees are served all day, and they include vodka rigatoni with imported prosciutto; pasta e' fagiolo (a house specialty: smoked ham hock simmered for hours in tomato sauce, with red and white beans); and simple pasta with marinara sauce. This is one of those comfortable neighborhood fixtures favored by all generations. Locals stop here for breakfast, lunch, and dinner; before and after movies; on the way to and from baseball games and concerts. The antipasto salad, vegetarian lasagna, and roasted peppers are taste treats, but the meatballs and Italian sausage are famous in central Maui.

Dairy Center, 395 Dairy Rd., Kahului. ✆ 808/877-4446. Main courses $11–$26. AE, DC, DISC, MC, V. Daily 7:30am–10pm.

INEXPENSIVE

Cafe O'Lei on Main ★ (*Value* AMERICAN/ISLAND Dana Pastula, who managed fancy restaurants on Lanai and in Wailea before opening her own, has cloned her wonderful Makawao eatery for lucky Wailuku diners. The menu is expanded here, with seating for 50 and daily lunch specials that have the same imaginative, attentive touches of her Makawao gem. The cafe is on the main street of Wailuku, with a menu that features fresh Island ingredients: taro salad with crisp Molokai sweet potato, seared ahi sandwich with wasabi mayonnaise, fresh fish, and Aloha Friday crab cakes with sweet chili aioli. Sandwiches (crab club, roast turkey breast, roasted Maui vegetables) and salads (like the popular curry chicken; hot chicken with peanuts, chiles, ginger, and veggies) complement daily specials such as chicken fettuccine and blackened mahimahi. The plate lunch, a terrific deal at $5.50, is always a surprise. *Tip:* You can get a great picnic lunch here for your outing in Iao Valley. Look for the sister restaurants in Makawao, Maalaea and Lahaina.

2051 Main St., Wailuku. ✆ 808/244-6816. Sandwiches $4.95–$6.95; lunch specials $5.50–$7.50. No credit cards. Mon–Fri 10:30am–2:30pm.

Maui Bake Shop BAKERY/DELI Sleepy Vineyard Street has seen many a mom-and-pop business come and go, but Maui Bake Shop is here to stay. Maui native Claire Fujii-Krall and her husband, baker José Krall (who was trained in the south of France), are turning out buttery brioches, healthful nine-grain and two-tone rye breads, focaccia, strudels, sumptuous fresh-fruit gâteaux, puff pastries, and dozens of other baked goods and confections. The breads are baked in one of Maui's oldest brick ovens, installed in 1935; a high-tech European diesel oven handles the rest. The front window displays more than 100 bakery and deli items, among them salads, a popular eggplant marinara focaccia, homemade quiches, and an inexpensive calzone filled with chicken, pesto, mushroom, and cheese. Homemade soups (clam chowder, minestrone, cream of asparagus) team up nicely with sandwiches on freshly baked bread. The food here is light enough (well, almost) to justify the Ultimate Dessert: white-chocolate macadamia-nut cheesecake.

2092 Vineyard St. (at N. Church St.), Wailuku. ✆ 808/242-0064. Most items under $5. AE, DISC, MC, V. Mon–Fri 6am–4pm; Sat 7am–2pm.

Restaurant Matsu JAPANESE/LOCAL Customers have come from Hana (more than 50 miles away) just for Matsu's California rolls, while regulars line up for the cold saimin (julienned cucumber, egg, Chinese-style sweet pork, and red ginger on noodles) and for the bento plates, various assemblages of chicken, teriyaki beef, fish, and rice. The nigiri sushi items are popular, especially among the don't-dally lunch crowd. The katsu pork and chicken, breaded and deep-fried, are other specialties of this casual Formica-style diner. We love the tempura udon and the saimin, steaming mounds of wide and fine noodles swimming in homemade broths and topped with condiments. The daily specials are a changing lineup of home-cooked classics: oxtail soup, roast pork with gravy, teriyaki ahi, miso butterfish, and breaded mahimahi.

Maui Mall, 161 Alamaha St., Kahului. (✆ 808/871-0822. Most items less than $6. No credit cards. Mon–Sat 10am–8pm.

WEST MAUI
LAHAINA
There's a **Maui Tacos** (p. 401) in Lahaina Square (✆ **808/661-8883**). Maui's branch of the **Hard Rock Cafe** is in Lahaina at 900 Front St. (✆ **808/667-7400**).

Very Expensive
David Paul's Lahaina Grill ✿ NEW AMERICAN   Even after David Paul Johnson's departure, this Lahaina hot spot has maintained its popularity. It's still filled with chic, tanned diners in stylish aloha shirts, and there's still attitude aplenty at the entrance. The signature items remain: tequila shrimp and firecracker rice, Kona coffee–roasted rack of lamb, Maui onion–crusted seared ahi, and Kalua duck quesadilla. As always, a special custom-designed chef's table can be arranged with 72-hour notice for larger parties. The ambience—black-and-white tile floors, pressed tin ceilings, eclectic 1890s decor—is striking, and the bar, even without an ocean view, is the busiest spot in Lahaina.

127 Lahainaluna Rd. (✆ 808/667-5117. Reservations required. Main courses $22–$38. AE, DC, DISC, MC, V. Daily 5:30–10pm. Bar daily 5:30pm–midnight.

The Feast at Lele ✿✿ POLYNESIAN   The owners of Old Lahaina Luau (see the box "A Night to Remember: Luau, Maui Style," later in this chapter), have teamed up with Chef James McDonald's culinary prowess (I'o, and Pacific'o) placed it in a perfect outdoor oceanfront setting, and added the exquisite dancers of the Old Lahaina Luau, the result: a culinary and cultural experience that sizzles. As if the sunset weren't heady enough, dances from Hawaii, Tonga, Tahiti, and Samoa are presented, up close and personal, in full costumed splendor. Chanting, singing, drumming, dancing, the swish of ti-leaf skirts, the scent of plumeria—it's a full adventure, even for the most jaded luau aficionado. Guests sit at white-clothed, candlelit tables set on the sand (unlike the luau, where seating is en masse) and dine on entrees from each island: kaluapig, tasty steamed moi, and savory pohole ferns and hearts of palm from Hawaii. From Tonga come lobster-ogo (seaweed) salad and grilled steak, from Tahiti steamed chicken and taro leaf in coconut milk, and from Samoa grilled fish in banana leaf. Particularly mesmerizing is the evening's opening: A softly lit canoe carries three people ashore to the sound of conch shells.

505 Front St. (✆ 886/244-5353 or 808/667-5353. www.feastatlele.com. Reservations a must. Set 5-course menu $89 for adults, $59 for children 2–12; gratuity not included. AE, MC, V. April 1–Sept 30 Tues–Sat 6–9pm; Oct 1–Mar 31 5:30–8:30pm.

Expensive
Gerard's ✿✿✿ *Finds* FRENCH   The charm of Gerard's—soft lighting, Edith Piaf on the sound system, excellent service—is matched by a menu of uncompromising standards. After more than 2 decades in Lahaina, Gerard Reversade never runs out of creative offerings, yet stays true to his French roots. A frequent winner of the *Wine Spectator* Award of Excellence, Gerard's offers roasted opakapaka with star anise, fennel fondue, and hints of orange and ginger, a stellar

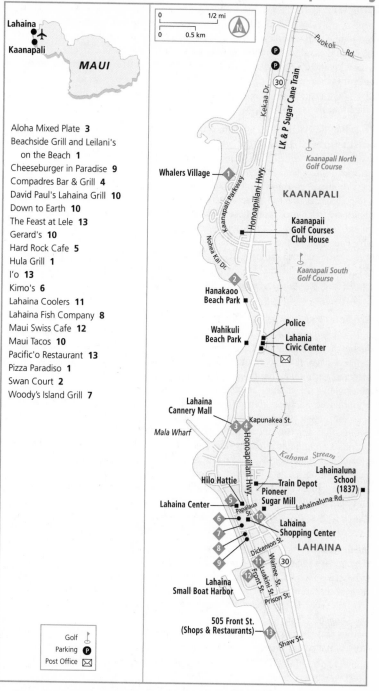

Lahaina & Kaanapali Dining

Lahaina
Kaanapali

MAUI

Aloha Mixed Plate **3**

Beachside Grill and Leilani's
on the Beach **1**

Cheeseburger in Paradise **9**

Compadres Bar & Grill **4**

David Paul's Lahaina Grill **10**

Down to Earth **10**

The Feast at Lele **13**

Gerard's **10**

Hard Rock Cafe **5**

Hula Grill **1**

I'o **13**

Kimo's **6**

Lahaina Coolers **11**

Lahaina Fish Company **8**

Maui Swiss Cafe **12**

Maui Tacos **10**

Pacific'o Restaurant **13**

Pizza Paradiso **1**

Swan Court **2**

Woody's Island Grill **7**

0   1/2 mi
0   0.5 km

Puokoli Rd.

LK & P Sugar Cane Train

Kekaa Dr.

Honoapiilani Hwy.

*Kaanapali North
Golf Course*

KAANAPALI

Whalers Village

Kaanapali Parkway

Nohea Kai Dr.

**Kaanapaii
Golf Courses
Club House**

*Kaanapali South
Golf Course*

**Hanakaoo
Beach Park**

**Wahikuli
Beach Park**

Police

**Lahania
Civic Center**

**Lahaina
Cannery Mall**

Kapunakea St.

Mala Wharf

Honoapiilani Hwy.

Kahoma Stream

**Lahainaluna
School
(1837)**

Hilo Hattie

Train Depot

**Pioneer
Sugar Mill**

Lahainaluna Rd.

Lahaina Center

Papalaua St.

**Lahaina
Shopping Center**

LAHAINA

Dickenson St.

Wainee St.

Luakini St.

Front St.

Prison St.

**Lahaina
Small Boat Harbor**

**505 Front St.
(Shops & Restaurants)**

Shaw St.

Golf
Parking
Post Office

entree on a menu of winners. If you're feeling extravagant, the Kona lobster ragout with pasta and morels promises ecstasy, and the spinach salad with scallops is among the finest we've tasted. Gerard's has an excellent appetizer menu, with shiitake and oyster mushrooms in puff pastry, fresh ahi and smoked salmon carpaccio, and a very rich, highly touted escargot ragout with burgundy butter and garlic cream.

In the Plantation Inn, 174 Lahainaluna Rd. © **808/661-8939.** www.gerardsmaui.com. Reservations recommended. Main courses $27–$33. AE, DC, DISC, MC, V. Daily 6–9pm.

I'o ★ PACIFIC RIM   I'o is a fantasy of sleek curves and etched glass, co-owned by chef James McDonald. He offers an impressive selection of appetizers (his strong suit) and some lavish Asian-Polynesian interpretations of seafood, such as stir-fried lobster with mango-Thai curry sauce, fresh ahi in a nori panko crust, and lemongrass coconut fish. Unless you're sold on a particular entree, our advice is to go heavy on the superb appetizers, especially the silken purse, a brilliant concoction of tricolored pot stickers stuffed with roasted peppers, mushrooms, spinach, macadamia nuts, and silken tofu. Oyster lovers, take heed: The memorable Pan Asian Rockefellers are baked on a bed of spinach and served with a hint of star anise coconut cream. Chef McDonald also owns Pacific'o, the restaurant next door, and is the chef for the Feast at Lele, which is ocean-side of I'o.

505 Front St. © **808/661-8422.** www.iomaui.com. Reservations recommended. Main courses $18–$30. AE, DC, MC, V. Daily 5:30–10pm.

Pacific'o Restaurant ★ PACIFIC RIM/CONTEMPORARY PACIFIC You can't get any closer to the ocean than the tables here, which are literally on the beach. With good food complementing this sensational setting, foodies and aesthetes have much to enjoy. The split-level dining starts at the top, near the entrance, with a long bar (where you can also order lunch or dinner) and a few tables along the railing. Steps lead to the outdoor tables, where the award-winning seafood dishes come to you with the backdrop of Lanai across the channel. The prawn and basil wontons, fresh fish over wilted arugula and bean sprouts, and ahi and ono tempura with miso and lime-basil sauce are among Pacific'o's memorable offerings. The vegetarian special, a marinated, roasted tofu steak crowned with quinoa, Maui onions, red lentils, and a heavenly dose of shiitake mushrooms, is a long-time favorite. If you like seafood, sunsets, and touches of India and Indonesia in your fresh-from-the-sea dining choices, you should be happy here.

505 Front St. © **808/667-4341.** www.pacificomaui.com. Reservations recommended. Main courses $9–$14 lunch, $19–$38 dinner. AE, DC, MC, V. Daily 11am–4pm and 5:30–10pm.

Moderate

Compadres Bar & Grill MEXICAN   Despite its concrete floor and high industrial ceilings, Compadres exudes good cheer. And that cheer has burgeoned lately with a new open-air seating area and a takeout taqueria window for diners on the run. The food is classic Tex-Mex, good any time of the day, beginning with huevos rancheros, egg burritos, hotcakes, and omelets (the Acapulco is heroic) and progressing to enchiladas and appetizers for the margarita-happy crowd. Stay spare (vegetable enchilada in fresh spinach tortilla) or get hefty (Texas T-bone and enchiladas). This is a carefree place with a large capacity for merrymaking.

Lahaina Cannery Mall, 1221 Honoapiilani Hwy. © **808/661-7189.** Main courses $10–$20. AE, DC, DISC, MC, V. Daily 8am–10pm.

Kimo's STEAK/SEAFOOD   Kimo's has a loyal following that keeps it from falling into the faceless morass of waterfront restaurants serving surf-and-turf with great sunset views. It's a formula restaurant (sibling to Leilani's and Hula Grill) that works not only because of its oceanfront patio and upstairs dining room, but also because, for the price, there are some satisfying choices. It's always crowded, buzzing with people on a deck offering views of Molokai, Lanai, and Kahoolawe. Burgers and sandwiches are affordable and consistent, and the fresh catch in garlic-lemon and a sweet-basil glaze is a top seller. The waistline-defying hula pie—macadamia-nut ice cream in a chocolate-wafer crust with fudge and whipped cream—originated here.

845 Front St. © **808/661-4811**. www.kimosmaui.com. Reservations recommended for dinner. Main courses $7–$11 lunch, $15–$24 dinner. AE, DC, DISC, MC, V. Daily 11am–3pm and 5–10:30pm; bar open 11am–1:30am.

Lahaina Fish Company SEAFOOD   The open-air dining room is literally over the water, with flickering torches after sunset and an affordable menu that covers the seafood-pasta basics. Head to an oceanside table and order a cheeseburger, chicken burger, fish burger, generous basket of peel-and-eat shrimp, or sashimi—lingering is highly recommended. The light lunch/grill menu offers appetizers (sashimi, seared ahi, spring rolls, and pot stickers), salads, and soups. The restaurant has spiffed up its dinner selections to include hand-carved steaks, several pasta choices, and local fare such as stir-fry dishes, teriyaki chicken, and luau-style ribs. The specialty, though, remains the fresh seafood: four types of fresh fish are offered nightly, in three preparations. Pacific Rim specials include fresh ahi, seared spicy or cooked in a sweet ginger-soy sauce.

831 Front St. © **808/661-3472**. Main courses $10–$26. AE, MC, V. Daily 11am–midnight.

Woody's Island Grill AMERICAN   The owners of Cheeseburger in Paradise closed Aloha Cantina and replaced it with Woody's, a big improvement. You'll walk through a socko aloha-shirt shop to enter the open-air oceanfront room, where a wood-burning grill cooks fresh ono, mahimahi (with mango ginger butter), ribs, New York steak, and other surf-and-turf choices. Other options include sandwiches, such as an excellent blackened ahi with wasabi aioli, Cajun fish tacos, and coconut shrimp with sweet-sour sauce. Very popular is the grilled opakapaka with a lemon-caper-butter sauce, teamed with the coconut shrimp for $20.

839 Front St. © **808/661-8788**. Reservations recommended. Main courses $8–$22. AE, DISC, MC, V. Daily 11am–10pm.

Inexpensive

Aloha Mixed Plate ★ *Value* PLATE LUNCHES/BEACHSIDE GRILL   Look for the festive turquoise-and-yellow, plantation-style front with the red corrugated-iron roof and adorable bar, tiny and busy, directly across from the Lahaina Cannery Mall. Grab a picnic table at ocean's edge, in the shade of large kiawe and milo trees, where you can watch the bobbing sailboats and two islands on the near horizon. (On the upper level, there are umbrellas and plumeria trees—just as charming.) Then tuck into inexpensive mahimahi, kalua pig and cabbage, shoyu chicken, teriyaki beef, and other local plate-lunch specials, all at budget-friendly prices, served with macaroni salad and rice. The shoyu chicken is the best we've had, fork tender and tasty, and the spicy chicken drumettes come from a fabled family recipe. (The bestsellers are the coconut prawns and Aloha Mixed Plate of shoyu chicken, teriyaki beef, and mahimahi.) We don't know of anywhere else where you can order a mai tai with a plate lunch and enjoy table service with an ocean view.

1285 Front St. ✆ **808/661-3322.** www.alohamixedplate.com. Main courses $4.95–$9.95. MC, V. Daily 10:30am–10pm.

Cheeseburger in Paradise AMERICAN Wildly successful, always crowded, highly visible, and very noisy with its live music in the evenings, Cheeseburger is a shrine to the American classic. The home of three-napkin cheeseburgers with attitude, this is burger country, tropical style, with everything from tofu and garden burgers to the biggest, juiciest beef and chicken burgers, served on whole-wheat and sesame buns baked fresh daily. There are good reasons why the two-story green-and-white building next to the seawall is always packed: good value, good grinds, and a great ocean view. The Cheeseburger in Paradise—a hefty hunk with Jack and cheddar cheeses, sautéed onions, lettuce, fresh tomatoes, and Thousand Island dressing—is a paean to the basics. You can build your own burger by adding sautéed mushrooms, bacon, grilled Ortega chilies, and other condiments for an extra charge. Onion rings, chili-cheese fries, and cold beer complete the carefree fantasy.

811 Front St. ✆ **808/661-4855.** www.cheeseburgermaui.com. Burgers $7.50–$8.50. AE, DISC, MC, V. Daily 8am–10pm.

Down to Earth *(Value* ORGANIC HEALTH FOOD Formerly Westside Natural Foods, this is one of the best deals in West Maui. Healthful organic ingredients, 90% vegan, appear in scrumptious salads, lasagna, chili, curries, and dozens of tasty dishes, presented at hot and cold serve-yourself stations. Stools line the abundant windows in the simple dining area, where a few tables are available for those who don't want takeout. (For all you cyberjunkies, there's Internet access too.) The food is great: millet cakes, mock tofu chicken, curried tofu, and Greek salad, everything organic and tasty, with herb-tamari marinades and pleasing condiments such as currants or raisins, apples, and cashews. (The tofu curry has apples, raw cashews, and raisins, and is fabulous.) Because the food is sold by the pound, you can buy a hearty, wholesome plate for $7. Vitamin supplements, health food products, fresh produce, and cosmetics fill the rest of the store.

193 Lahainaluna Rd. ✆ **808/667-2855.** Self-serve hot buffet and salad bar; food sold by the pound. Average $6–$8 for a plate. AE, MC, V. Mon–Sat 7:30am–9pm; Sun 8:30am–8pm.

Lahaina Coolers ⍟ AMERICAN/INTERNATIONAL A huge marlin hangs above the bar, epic wave shots and wall sconces made of surfboard fins line the walls, and open windows on three sides of this ultracasual indoor/outdoor restaurant take advantage of the shade trees to create a cheerful ambience. This is a great breakfast joint, with feta-cheese Mediterranean omelets, huevos rancheros, and fried rice made with jasmine rice, Kula vegetables and Portuguese sausage. There are three types of eggs Benedict: the classic, a vegetarian version (with Kula vegetables, excellent), and the Local, with Portuguese sausage and sweet bread. At lunch, burgers rule and the sandwiches, from grilled portobellos to the classic tuna melt, are ideal for casual Lahaina. Made fresh daily, the pasta is prepared Asian style (chicken breast in a spicy Thai peanut sauce), with pesto, or vegetarian (in a spicy Creole sauce). Pizzas, pastas, fresh catch, steak, and enchiladas round out the entrees, and everything can be prepared vegetarian upon request.

180 Dickensen St. ✆ **808/661-7082.** www.lahainacoolers.com. Lunch main courses $7.50–$11; dinner main courses $11–$19. AE, DC, DISC, MC, V. Daily 8am–2am (full menu to midnight).

Maui Swiss Cafe SANDWICHES/PIZZA Newly renovated and double its original size (which was tiny), Swiss Cafe now has five Internet stations (3 of them with flat-screen monitors!) and continues to serve excellent sandwiches and continental breakfast. Having gone from a sandwich-and-pizza shop to a European-style sidewalk Internet cafe, it still serves $5 lunch specials and two scoops of ice cream for $2.50 (and sometimes the ice cream is free with the lunch special), and remains a welcome stop in hot Lahaina. Top-quality breads baked fresh daily, Dijon mustard, good Swiss cheese, and keen attention to sandwich fillings and pizza toppings make this a very special sandwich shop. The Swiss owner, Dominique Martin, has imbued this corner of Lahaina with a European flavor, down to the menus printed in English and German and the Swiss breakfast of sliced ham, Emmentaler cheese, hard-boiled egg, and freshly baked croissant. *Tip:* The "signature melt" sandwiches, with imported Emmentaler cheese baked on an Italian Parmesan crust, are something to watch for, and there are excellent vegetarian and turkey sandwiches as well.

640 Front St. ⓒ **808/661-6776.** www.swisscafe.net. Sandwiches and 8-inch pizzas $5.50–$6. No credit cards. Daily 9am–6pm.

KAANAPALI

Whalers Village has a food court where you can buy pizza, very good Japanese food (including tempura soba and other noodle dishes), Korean plates, and fast-food burgers at serve-yourself counters and courtyard tables. It's an inexpensive alternative and a quick, handy stop for shoppers and Kaanapali beachgoers.

Beachside Grill and Leilani's on the Beach STEAK/SEAFOOD The Beachside Grill is the informal, less-expensive room downstairs on the beach, where folks wander in off the sand for a frothy beer and a beachside burger. Leilani's is the dinner-only room, with more expensive but still not outrageously priced steak and seafood offerings. At Leilani's, you can order everything from affordable spinach, cheese, and mushroom ravioli to lobster and steak. Children can get a quarter-pound hamburger for under $5 or a broiled chicken breast for a couple of dollars more—a value, for sure. Pasta, rack of lamb, filet mignon, and Alaskan king crab at market price are among the choices in the upstairs room. Although the steak-and-lobster combinations can be pricey, the good thing about Leilani's is the strong middle range of entree prices, especially the fresh fish for around $20 to $25. All of this, of course, comes with an ocean view. There's live Hawaiian music every afternoon except Fridays, when the Rock 'n' Roll Aloha Friday set gets those decibels climbing. Free concerts are usually offered on a stage outside the restaurant on the last Sunday of the month.

In Whalers Village, 2435 Kaanapali Pkwy. ⓒ **808/661-4495.** www.leilanis.com. Reservations suggested for dinner. Lunch and dinner (Beachside Grill) $6.95–$13; dinner (Leilani's) from $18. AE, DC, DISC, MC, V. Beachside Grill daily 11am–11pm (bar daily until 12:30am); Leilani's daily 5–10pm.

Hula Grill ⭐ HAWAII REGIONAL/SEAFOOD Who wouldn't want to be tucking into crab-and-corn cakes, banana-glazed opah, mac-nut-roasted opakapaka, or crab won tons under a thatched umbrella, with a sand floor and palm trees at arm's length and a view of Lanai across the channel? Peter Merriman, one of the originators of Hawaii Regional Cuisine, segued seamlessly from his small-ish, Big Island upcountry enclave to this large, high-volume, open-air dining room on the beach. Hula Grill offers a wide range of prices and choices; it can be expensive but doesn't have to be. The menu includes Merriman's signature firecracker mahimahi, seafood pot stickers, and several different fresh-fish preparations, including his famous ahi poke rolls—lightly sautéed rare ahi wrapped in rice paper with Maui onions. At lunch the menu is more limited, with a choice of sandwiches, entrees, pizza, appetizers, and salads. There's happy-hour entertainment and Hawaiian music daily. For those wanting a more casual atmosphere, the Barefoot Bar, located on the beach, offers burgers, fish, pizza, and salads.

In Whalers Village, 2435 Kaanapali Pkwy. ℂ **808/667-6636.** www.hulagrill.com. Reservations recommended for dinner. Lunch and Barefoot Bar menus $5.95–$12; dinner main courses from $13. AE, DC, DISC, MC, V. Daily 11am–11pm.

Pizza Paradiso PIZZA   Pizza Paradiso took over the ice cream counter next door and expanded to include a full menu of pastas, pizzas, and desserts, including smoothies, coffee, and ice cream. This is a welcome addition to the Kaanapali scene, where casual is king and good food doesn't have to be fancy. The pizza reflects a simple and effective formula that has won acclaim through the years: good crust, true-blue sauces, and toppings loyal to tradition but with just enough edge for those who want it. Create your own pizza with roasted eggplant, mushrooms, anchovies, artichoke hearts, spicy sausages, cheeses, and a slew of other toppings. Pizza Paradiso offers some heroic choices, from the Veg Wedge to the Maui Wowie (ham and Maui pineapple) and the Godfather (roasted chicken, artichoke hearts, sun-dried tomatoes). At Pizza Paradiso's Honokowai location (see below), award-winning pastas are also part of the draw.

In Whalers Village, 2435 Kaanapali Pkwy. ℂ **808/667-0333.** www.pizzaparadiso.com. Gourmet pizza $3.65–$4.45 (by the slice); whole pizzas $12–$26. MC, V. Daily 11am–10pm.

Swan Court ✿✿ CONTINENTAL   What could be better than a fantasy restaurant in a fantasy resort? It's not exactly a hideaway (this is, after all, a Hyatt), but Swan Court is wonderful in a resorty sort of way, with a dance floor, waterfalls, flamingos, and an ocean view adding to the package. Come here as a splurge or on a bottomless expense account, and enjoy Pacific lobster coconut soup, rock shrimp crab cake, Maui sugar cane skewered ahi, and sautéed opakapaka in striking surroundings. The menu sticks to the tried-and-true, making Swan Court a safe choice for those who like a respectable and well-executed selection in a romantic setting with candlelight, a Japanese garden, and swans gliding by serenely. A year-round Valentine dinner.

In the Hyatt Regency Maui, 200 Nohea Kai Dr. ℂ **808/661-1234.** Reservations recommended for dinner. Main courses $30–$38. AE, DC, DISC, MC, V. Daily 6:30–11:30am; Tues–Sat 6–10pm.

HONOKOWAI, KAHANA & NAPILI

Note: You'll find the restaurants in this section on the "West Maui Accommodations & Dining" map on p. 369.

Fish & Game Brewing Co. & Rotisserie SEAFOOD/STEAK   This restaurant consists of an oyster bar, deli counter and retail section, and tables. The small retail section sells fresh seafood, while the sit-down menu covers basic tastes: salads (Caesar, Oriental chicken with wontons), fish and chips, fresh-fish sandwiches, cheeseburgers, and beer—lots of it. At dinner, count on heavier meats and the fresh catch of the day (ahi, mahimahi, ono), with rotisserie items such as grilled chicken, steaks, and duck. The late-night menu offers shrimp, cheese fries, quesadillas, and lighter fare.

In the Kahana Gateway Shopping Center, 4405 Honoapiilani Hwy. ℂ **808/669-3474.** Reservations recommended for dinner. Main courses $6.95–$13 lunch, $14–$31 dinner. AE, DC, DISC, MC, V. Daily 11am–10pm; late-night menu 10:30pm–1am. During football season (Sept–Jan) brunch Sat–Sun 7:30am–3pm.

Maui Tacos MEXICAN   Mark Ellman's Maui Tacos chain has grown faster than you can say "Haleakala." Ellman put gourmet Mexican on paper plates and on the island's culinary map long before the island became known as Hawaii's center of salsa and chimichangas. Barely more than a takeout counter with a few tables, this and the six other Maui Tacos in Hawaii (4 on Maui alone) are the rage of hungry surfers, discerning diners, burrito buffs, and Hollywood glitterati, like Sharon Stone, whose picture adorns a wall or two. Choices include excellent fresh-fish tacos (garlicky and flavorful), chimichangas, and mouth-breaking compositions such as the Hookipa (a personal favorite): a "surf burrito" of fresh fish, black beans, and salsa. The green-spinach burrito contains four kinds of beans, rice, and potatoes—it's a knockout, requiring a siesta afterwards. Expect good food but not very fast service.

In Napili Plaza, 5095 Napili Hau St. *C* 808/665-0222. www.mauitacos.com. Items range from $1.65–$7. No credit cards. Daily 9am–9pm.

Pizza Paradiso Italian Caffe PIZZA/ITALIAN   Owner Paris Nabavi had such success with his Pizza Paradiso in Whalers Village (p. 400) that he opened up in the marketplace—and can hardly keep up with demand. Order at the counter (pastas, gourmet pizza whole or by the slice, salads, and desserts) and find a seat at one of the few tables. The pasta sauces—marinara, pescatore, Alfredo, Florentine, and pesto, with options and add-ons—are as popular as the pizzas and panini sandwiches. The Massimo, a pesto sauce with artichoke hearts, sun-dried tomatoes, and capers, comes with a choice of chicken, shrimp, or clams, and is so good it was a Taste of Lahaina winner in 1999. Takeout or dine in, this is a hot spot in the neighborhood, with free delivery.

In the Honokowai Marketplace, 3350 Lower Honoapiilani Rd. *C* 808/667-2929. www.pizzaparadiso.com. Pastas $6.95–$8.95; pizzas $12–$26. MC, V. Daily 11am–10pm.

Roy's Kahana Bar & Grill/Roy's Nicolina Restaurant ★★ EURO-ASIAN   These sibling restaurants are next door to each other, offer the same menu, and are busy, busy, busy. They bustle with young, hip servers impeccably trained to deliver blackened ahi or perfectly seared lemongrass *shutome* (broadbill swordfish) hot to your table, in rooms that sizzle with cross-cultural tastings. Both are known for their rack of lamb and fresh seafood (usually 8 or 9 choices), and for their large, open kitchens that turn out everything from pizza to sake-grilled New York steak. If polenta is on the menu, don't resist; on my last visit, the polenta was rich and fabulous, with garlic, cream, spinach, and wild mushrooms. Large picture windows open up Roy's Kahana but don't quell the noise, another tireless trait long ago established by Roy's Restaurant in Honolulu, the flagship of Yamaguchi's burgeoning empire. The restaurant has banquet facilities for up to 70 people, while Roy's Nicolina features dining on the lanai.

In the Kahana Gateway Shopping Center, 4405 Honoapiilani Hwy. *C* 808/669-6999. www.roysrestaurant. com. Reservations strongly suggested. Main courses $14–$31. AE, DC, DISC, MC, V. Roy's Kahana daily 5:30–10pm; Roy's Nicolina daily 5:30–9:30pm.

Sea House Restaurant ASIAN/PACIFIC   The Sea House is not glamorous, famous, or hip, but it's worth mentioning for its gorgeous view of Napili Bay. It is spectacular. The Napili Kai Beach Club, where Sea House is located, is a charming throwback to the days when hotels blended in with their surroundings, had lush tropical foliage, and were sprawling rather than vertical. Dinner entrees come complete with soup or salad, vegetables, and rice or potato. The lighter appetizer menu is a delight—more than a dozen choices ranging from sautéed or blackened crab cake to crisp Pacific Rim sushi of ahi capped in nori and cooked tempura-style. On Friday nights, a Polynesian dinner show features the children of the Napili Kai Foundation, an organization devoted to supporting Hawaiian culture. They share top billing with the million-dollar view.

In Napili Kai Beach Resort, 5900 Honoapiilani Hwy. ⓒ **808/669-1500.** Reservations required for dinner. Main courses $18–$49; appetizer menu $5–$14. AE, DISC, MC, V. Sun–Fri 8–10:30am, noon–2pm, and 5:30–9pm (6–9pm in summer); pupu menu Sat–Thurs 2–9pm and Fri 2–7:30pm; Fri Polynesian Show 6–9pm.

KAPALUA

Note: You'll find the restaurants in this section on the "West Maui Accommodations & Dining" map on p. 369.

Jameson's Grill & Bar at Kapalua AMERICAN   This is the quintessential country-club restaurant, open-air with mountain and ocean views. The glass-enclosed room is across from the Kapalua pro shop, a short lob from the tennis courts and golf course. The familiar Jameson's mix of fresh fish (sautéed, wok-seared, or grilled), stuffed shrimp, prawns, rack of lamb, ahi steak, and other basic surf-and turf selections prevail at dinner. At lunch, duffers dashing to make tee time can opt for inexpensive "golf sandwiches" (roast beef, turkey, tuna salad). Other choices: fish and chips, crab cakes, and an affordable cafe menu of gourmet appetizers. Breakfasts are terrific—eggs Benedict, eggs Elizabeth (marlin on a muffin with all the trimmings), or eggs Kapalua (crab cakes topped with poached egg and wild-mushroom sauce).

200 Kapalua Dr. (at the 18th hole of the Kapalua Golf Course). ⓒ **808/669-5653.** Reservations recommended for dinner. Lunch $5.95–$12; cafe menu (3–10pm) $6.95–$13; dinner main courses $18–$33. AE, DC, DISC, MC, V. Daily 8am–10pm.

Plantation House Restaurant ✸✸ SEAFOOD/HAWAIIAN-MEDITER-RANEAN   With its teak tables, fireplace, and open sides, Plantation House gets stellar marks for atmosphere. The 360° view from high among the resort's pine-studded hills takes in Molokai and Lanai, the ocean, the rolling fairways and greens, the northwestern flanks of the West Maui Mountains, and the daily sunset spectacular. Readers of the *Maui News* have deemed this the island's "Best Ambience"—a big honor on an island of wonderful views. It's the best place for breakfast in West Maui, hands down, and one of my top choices for dinner. The menu changes constantly but may include fresh fish prepared several ways—among them, Mediterranean (seared), Upcountry (sautéed with Maui onions and vegetable sauté), Island (pan-seared in sweet sake and macadamia nuts), and Rich Forest (with roasted wild mushrooms), the top seller. At breakfast, the Eggs Mediterranean is superb, and at lunch, sandwiches (open-faced smoked turkey, roasted vegetable, and goat cheese wrap) and salads rule. When the sun sets, the menu expands to marvelous starters such as polenta and scampi-style shrimp, crab cakes, Kula and Mediterranean salads, and a hearty entree selection of fish, pork tenderloin, roast duck, and filet mignon with apple-smoked Maui onion.

2000 Plantation Club Dr. (at Kapalua Plantation Golf Course). ⓒ **808/669-6299.** www.theplantationhouse. com. Reservations recommended. Main courses $19–$30. AE, DC, MC, V. Daily 8am–3pm and 5:30–10pm.

Sansei Seafood Restaurant and Sushi Bar ✸✸ PACIFIC RIM   Perpetual award-winner Sansei offers an extensive menu of Japanese and East-West delicacies. Furiously fusion, part Hawaii Regional Cuisine, and all parts sushi, Sansei is tirelessly creative, with a menu that scores higher with adventurous palates than with purists (although there are endless traditional choices as well). Maki is the mantra here. If you don't like cilantro, watch out for those complex spicy crab rolls. Other choices include Panko-crusted ahi sashimi, sashimi trio, ahi carpaccio, noodle dishes, lobster, Asian rock-shrimp cakes, traditional Japanese tempura, and sauces that surprise, in creative combinations such as ginger-lime chile butter and cilantro pesto. But there's simpler fare as well, such as shrimp tempura, noodles, and wok-tossed upcountry vegetables. Desserts are not to be missed. If it's autumn, don't pass up persimmon crême brûlée made with Kula persimmons. In other seasons, opt for tempura-fried ice cream with chocolate sauce. There's karaoke every night 10pm to 1am. *Budget-saving tip:* Eat early; all food is 25% off between 5:30 and 6pm.

At the Kapalua Shops, 115 Bay Dr. ⓒ **808/669-6286.** www.sanseihawaii.com. Reservations recommended. Main courses $19–$29. AE, DISC, MC, V. Daily 5:30–10pm

SOUTH MAUI
KIHEI/MAALAEA
There's a **Maui Tacos** at Kamaole Beach Center in Kihei (ⓒ **808/879-5005**).

Expensive

Buzz's Wharf AMERICAN   Buzz's is another formula restaurant that offers a superb view, substantial sandwiches, meaty french fries, and surf-and-turf fare—in a word, satisfying but not sensational. Still, this bright, airy dining room is a fine way-station for whale-watching over a cold beer and a fresh mahimahi sandwich with fries. Some diners opt for several appetizers (stuffed mushrooms, steamer clams, clam chowder, onion soup) and a salad, then splurge on dessert. Buzz's prize-winning Tahitian Baked Papaya is a warm, fragrant melding of fresh papaya with vanilla and coconut—the pride of the house.

Maalaea Harbor, 50 Hauoli St. ⓒ **808/244-5426.** Reservations suggested. Main courses $20–$33. AE, DC, DISC, MC, V. Daily 11am–9pm.

Five Palms ⭑ PACIFIC RIM   This is the best lunch spot in Kihei—open-air, with tables a few feet from the beach and up-close-and-personal views of Kahoolawe and Molokini. You'll have to walk through a nondescript parking area and the modest entrance of the Mana Kai Resort to reach this unpretentious place. At lunch, salads, sandwiches, and pasta are the hot items: Kula greens; burgers; sandwiches on homemade focaccia; capellini with shiitake mushrooms, sun-dried tomatoes, and white wine sauce; and other appealing choices, including a perfectly grilled vegetable platter. At dinner, with the torches lit on the beach and the main dining room open, the ambience shifts to evening romantic, but still casual.

In the Mana Kai Resort, 2960 S. Kihei Rd. ⓒ **808/879-2607.** Reservations recommended for dinner. Main courses $19–$49. AE, DC, MC, V. Daily 8am–2:30pm and 5–9pm.

The Waterfront at Maalaea ⭑⭑ SEAFOOD   The family-owned Waterfront has won many prestigious awards for wine excellence, service, and seafood, but its biggest boost is word of mouth. Loyal diners rave about the friendly staff and seafood, fresh off the boat in nearby Maalaea Harbor and prepared with care. The bay and harbor view is one you'll never forget, especially at sunset. You have nine choices of preparations for the several varieties of fresh Hawaiian fish, ranging from *en papillote* (baked in buttered parchment) to southwestern (smoked chile and cilantro butter) to Cajun spiced and Island style (sautéed, broiled, poached, or baked and paired with tiger prawns). Other choices: Kula onion soup, an excellent Caesar salad, the signature lobster chowder, and grilled eggplant layered with Maui onions, tomatoes, and spinach, served with red-pepper coulis and Big Island goat cheese. Like the seafood, it's superb.

Maalaea Harbor, 50 Hauoli St. ⓒ **808/244-9028.** Reservations recommended. Main courses $18–$35. AE, DC, DISC, MC, V. Daily 5pm–closing; last seating at 8:30pm.

Moderate

Stella Blues Cafe ⋆ AMERICAN   Stella Blues gets going at breakfast and continues through to dinner with something for everyone—vegetarians, kids, pasta and sandwich lovers, hefty steak eaters, and sensible diners who go for the inexpensive fresh Kula green salad. Grateful Dead posters line the walls, and a covey of gleaming motorcycles is invariably parked outside. It's loud and lively, irreverent, and unpretentious. Sandwiches are the highlight, ranging from Tofu Extraordinaire to Mom's egg salad on croissant to garden burgers and grilled chicken. Tofu wraps and mountain-size Cobb salads are popular, and for the reckless, large coffee shakes with mounds of whipped cream. Daily specials include fresh seafood and other surprises—all home-style cooking, made from scratch, down to the pesto mayonnaise and herb bread. At dinner, selections are geared toward good-value family dining, from affordable full dinners to pastas and burgers.

In Long's Center, 1215 S. Kihei Rd. ⓒ **808/874-3779.** Main courses $9.95–$18. DISC, MC, V. Daily 8am–9pm.

Inexpensive

Bubba's Burgers BURGERS   On the heels of his remarkable success on Kauai, Bubba has sprouted in South Maui. Half-pound Big Bubbas, Budweiser chili, and Hubba Bubbas (with rice, hot dogs, and chili) are among the heroic offerings fueling the beach-going crowd from this roadside cafe in Kihei. Fish and chips, tempeh burgers, and fresh fish specials are among the offerings of this house of Bubba, where plate lunches, burgers, and attitude aplenty provide good grinds with irreverent entertainment. (Bubba T-shirts are hilarious.)

1945 S. Kihei Rd. ⓒ **808/891-2600.** www.bubbaburger.com. Burgers $2.75–$6.75. MC, V. Daily 10:30am–9pm.

The Coffee Store COFFEEHOUSE   This simple, classic coffeehouse for caffeine connoisseurs serves 2 dozen different types of coffee and coffee drinks, from mochas and lattes to cappuccinos, espressos, and toddies. Breakfast items include smoothies, lox and bagels, quiches, granola, and assorted pastries. Pizza, salads, vegetarian lasagna, veggie-and-shrimp quesadillas, and sandwiches (garden burger, tuna, turkey, ham, grilled veggie panini) also move briskly from the takeout counter. The turkey-and-veggie wraps are a local legend. There are only a few small tables and they fill up fast, often with musicians and artists who've spent the previous evening entertaining at the Wailea and Kihei resorts.

In Azeka Place II, 1279 Kihei Rd. ⓒ **808/875-4244.** www.mauicoffee.com. All items less than $8.50. AE, MC, V. Daily 6am–6pm.

Peggy Sue's AMERICAN   Just for a moment, forget that diet and take a leap. It's Peggy Sue's to the rescue! This 1950s-style diner has oodles of charm and is a swell place to spring for the best chocolate malt on the island. You'll also find sodas, shakes, floats, egg creams, milkshakes, and scoops of made-on-Maui Roselani brand gourmet ice cream—14 flavors. Old-fashioned soda-shop stools, an Elvis Presley Boulevard sign, and jukeboxes on every Formica table serve as a backdrop for the famous burgers (and garden burgers), brushed with teriyaki sauce and served with all the goodies. The fries are great, too.

In Azeka Place II, 1279 S. Kihei Rd. ⓒ **808/875-8944.** Burgers $6–$11; plate lunches $5–$12. DC, MC, V. Sun–Thurs 11am–9pm; Fri–Sat 11am–10pm.

Shaka Sandwich & Pizza PIZZA   How many "best pizzas" are there on Maui? It depends on which shore you're on, the west or the south. At this south-shore old-timer, award-winning pizzas share the limelight with New York–style heroes and Philly cheese steaks, calzones, salads, homemade garlic bread, and homemade meatball sandwiches. Shaka uses fresh Maui produce, long-simmering sauces, and homemade Italian bread. Choose thin or Sicilian thick crust with gourmet toppings: Maui onions, spinach, anchovies, jalapeños, and a spate of other vegetables. Don't be misled by the whiteness of the white pizza; with the perfectly balanced flavors of olive oil, garlic, and cheese, you won't even miss the tomato sauce. Clam-and-garlic pizza, spinach pizza (with olive oil, spinach, garlic, and mozzarella), and the Shaka Supreme (with at least 10 top-pings) will satisfy even the insatiable.

1295 S. Kihei Rd. Ⓒ **808/874-0331**. Sandwiches $4.35–$11; pizzas $13–$26. No credit cards. Sun–Thurs 10:30am–9pm; Fri–Sat 10:30am–10pm.

WAILEA

The Shops at Wailea, a sprawling location between the Grand Wailea Hotel and Outrigger Wailea Resort, has added a spate of new shops and restaurants to this stretch of south Maui. Five restaurants and dozens of shops, most of them upscale, are among the new tenants of this complex. **Ruth's Chris Steak House** is here, as well as **Tommy Bahama's Tropical Cafe & Emporium, Honolulu Coffee Company Café Wailea, Cheeseburger, Mai Tai's and Rock-n-Roll,** and **Longhi's.** Next door at the Outrigger Wailea, **Hula Moons,** the retro-Hawaiian-themed restaurant, has reopened after a $3 million renovation and moved to the upper level of the lobby building, where it serves midpriced steak and seafood with an ocean view.

Note: You'll find the restaurants in this section on the "South Maui Accommodations & Dining" map on p. 375.

Very Expensive

Nick's Fishmarket Maui ★★★ SEAFOOD   We do love Nick's. The ambience is spectacular, the stephanotis have grown in on the terrace, and the seafood is fresh. This is a classic seafood restaurant that sticks to the tried and true (i.e. *not* an overwrought menu) but stays fresh with excellent ingredients and a high degree of professionalism in service and preparation. The Greek Maui Wowie salad gets my vote as one of the top salads in Hawaii. The blackened mahimahi has been a Nick's signature for eons, and why not—it's wonderful. Fresh opah (moonfish), salmon, scallops, Hawaiian lobster tails, and chicken, beef, and lamb choices offer ample choices for diners, who find themselves in a fantasy setting on the south Maui shoreline. A private room with attractive murals seats 50, and the round bar, where you can sit facing the ocean, is highlighted with minimalist dangling amber lights, one of the friendliest touches in Wailea. I love the onion vichyssoise with taro swirl and a hint of *tobiko* (flying-fish roe), and the bow-tied servers with almond-scented cold towels.

In the Fairmont Kea Lani Hotel, 4100 Wailea Alanui. Ⓒ **808/879-7224**. www.tri-star-restaurants.com. Reservations recommended. Main courses $25–$50. Prix Fixe dinners $55–$85. AE, DC, DISC, MC, V. Mon–Thurs 5:30–10pm; Fri–Sat 5:30–10:30pm, bar until 11pm.

Spago ★★★ HAWAIIAN/CALIFORNIA/PACIFIC REGIONAL   California meets Hawaii in this contemporary-designed eatery featuring fresh, local Hawaii ingredients prepared under the culinary watch of master chef Wolfgang Puck. The room, formerly Seasons Dining Room, has been stunningly transformed into a sleek modern layout using stone and wood in the open-air setting overlooking the Pacific Ocean. The cuisine lives up to Puck's reputation of using traditional Hawaiian dishes with his own brand of cutting-edge innovations. Open for dinner only, the menu features an unbelievable coconut soup with local lobster, keffir, chili and galangal; for entrees try the whole steamed fish served with chili, ginger and baby choy sum; the incredible Kona lobster with sweet and sour banana curry, coconut rice and dry-fried green beans; or the grilled cote de bouef with braised celery, armagnac, peppercorns and pommes aligot. The wine and beverage list is well-thought-out and extensive. Save room for dessert (don't pass up the warm guanaja chocolate tart with Tahitian vanilla bean ice cream). Make reservations as soon as you land on the island (if not before); this place is popular. And bring plenty of cash, or your platinum card.

Four Seasons Resort Maui, 3900 Wailea Alanui Dr., Wailea, 96753. © **808/879-2999.** www.fourseasons. com/maui. Reservations required. Main courses $30–$50. AE, DC, DISC, MC, V. Daily 5:30–9pm; bar with pupu daily 5–11pm.

Expensive

Ferraro's at Seaside ★ ITALIAN   This was a master stroke for Four Seasons: authentic Italian fare in a casual outdoor tropical setting, with a drop-dead gorgeous view of the ocean and the West Maui Mountains. Ferraro's is not inexpensive, but the food is first-rate, including dishes such as oregano-marinated shrimp with avocado and linguine puttanesca. Mango margaritas, generous salads such as the Maine lobster with avocado and toasted sourdough, and sandwiches and half-pound burgers cater to the poolside crowd at lunch, but at dinnertime, the choices intensify. The fish selection is noteworthy: pepper-crusted ahi, grilled sea scallops and steamed mussels with saffron risotto cake, and poached snapper with red onion–orange marmalade. It won't be easy to choose.

In the Four Seasons Resort Maui at Wailea, 3900 Wailea Alanui Dr. © **808/874-8000.** www.fourseasons. com/maui. Reservations recommended. Main courses $21–$39. AE, DC, DISC, MC, V. Daily 11:30am–3pm, 3–6pm (pupu menu), and 6–9pm.

Moderate

Caffé Ciao ★ ITALIAN   There are two parts to this charming trattoria: the deli, with takeout section, and the cafe, with tables under the trees, next to the bar. Rare and wonderful wines, such as Vine Cliff, are sold in the deli, along with ultraluxe rose soaps and other bath products, assorted pastas, pizzas, roasted potatoes, vegetable panini, vegetable lasagna, abundant salads, and an appealing selection of microwavable and takeout goodies. On the terrace under the trees, the tables are cheerfully accented with Italian herbs growing in cachepots. *A fave:* the linguine pomodoro, with fresh tomatoes, spinach-tomato sauce, and a dollop of mascarpone.

In the Kea Lani Hotel, 4100 Wailea Alanui. © **808/875-4100.** Reservations recommended. Main courses $15–$30; pizzas $16–$22. AE, DC, DISC, MC, V. Daily 11am–10pm.

Joe's Bar & Grill ★★ AMERICAN GRILL   The 270 degree view spans the golf course, tennis courts, ocean, and Haleakala—a worthy setting for Beverly Gannon's style of American home cooking with a regional twist. The hearty staples include excellent mashed potatoes, lobster, fresh fish, and filet mignon, but the meat loaf (a whole loaf, like Mom used to make) seems to upstage them all. The Tuscan white bean soup is superb, and the tenderloin, with roasted portobellos, mashed potatoes with whole garlic, and a pinot noir demi glace, is

American home cooking at its best. Daily specials could be grilled ahi with white truffle–Yukon gold mashed potatoes or sautéed mahimahi with shrimp bisque and sautéed spinach. If chocolate cake is on the menu, you should definitely spring for it.

In the Wailea Tennis Club, 131 Wailea Ike Place. © **808/875-7767.** www.joesbarandgrill.com. Reservations recommended. Main courses $17–$30. AE, DC, DISC, MC, V. Daily 5:30–9pm.

SeaWatch ⭐ ISLAND CUISINE   Under the same ownership as Kapalua's Plantation House (p. 402), SeaWatch is a good choice from morning to evening, and it's one of the more affordable stops in tony Wailea. You'll dine on the terrace or in a high-ceilinged room, on a menu that carries the tee-off-to-19th-hole crowd with ease. From breakfast on, it's a celebration of island bounty: Maui onions on the bagels and lox, kalua pork and Maui onions in the scrambled eggs, crab cake Benedict with roasted pepper hollandaise. Lunchtime sandwiches, pastas, salads, wraps, and soups are moderately priced, and you get 360° views to go with them. The cashew chicken wrap with mango chutney is a winner, but if that's too Pan-Asian for you, try the tropical fish quesadilla or the grilled fresh-catch sandwich with Kula lime aioli. Save room for the bananas Foster.

100 Wailea Golf Club Dr. © **808/875-8080.** www.seawatchrestaurant.com. Reservations required for dinner. Breakfast $3–$10; lunch $6.50–$12; dinner main courses $23–$28. AE, MC, V. Daily 8am–3pm, 3–5:30pm (grill menu), and 5:30–10pm.

MAKENA

Prince Court ⭐⭐ CONTEMPORARY ISLAND   Half of the Sunday brunch experience here is the head-turning view of Makena Beach, Molokini islet, and Kahoolawe island. The other half is the fabled Sunday buffet, bountiful and sumptuous, spread over several tables: pasta, omelets, cheeses, pastries, sashimi, crab legs, smoked salmon, fresh Maui produce, and a smashing array of ethnic and Continental foods. The dinner menu changes regularly; the current winners are the steamed Manila Clams Scampi with roasted garlic, diced tomatoes, and fried basil; Dungeness crab and goat cheese won ton with Maui onion guacamole; and the Prince Court Sampler with Kona lobster cakes, kalua duck lumpia, and sugar-cane speared grilled prawns. New game entrees (venison, rack of lamb, breast of duck) come in highly acclaimed preparations, such as poha compote and black cherry Cabernet sauce.

In the Maui Prince Hotel, 5400 Makena Alanui. © **808/874-1111.** Reservations recommended. Main courses $17–$30; Fri prime rib and seafood buffet $38 ($23 child); Sun brunch $36. AE, MC, V. Sun 9am–1pm; daily 6–9:30pm.

UPCOUNTRY MAUI

Note: You'll find the restaurants in this section on the "Upcountry & East Maui" map on p. 383.

HALIIMAILE (ON THE WAY TO UPCOUNTRY MAUI)

Haliimaile General Store ⭐⭐⭐ AMERICAN   More than a decade later, Bev Gannon, one of the 12 original Hawaii Regional Cuisine chefs, is still going strong at her foodie haven in the pineapple fields. You'll dine at tables set on old wood floors under high ceilings (sound ricochets fiercely here), in a peach-colored room emblazoned with works by local artists. The food, a blend of eclectic American with ethnic touches, puts an innovative spin on Hawaii Regional Cuisine. Even the fresh-catch sandwich on the lunch menu is anything but prosaic. Sip the lilikoi lemonade and nibble the sashimi napoleon or the house salad—island greens with mandarin oranges, onions, toasted walnuts, and blue-cheese crumble—all are notable items on a menu that bridges Hawaii with Gannon's Texas roots.

Haliimaile Rd., Haliimaile. © 808/572-2666. www.haliimailegeneralstore.com. Reservations recommended. Lunch $7–$14; dinner $14–$28. DC, MC, V. Mon–Fri 11am–2:30pm; daily 5:30–9:30pm.

MAKAWAO & PUKALANI

Cafe O' Lei ★ AMERICAN/ISLAND   Dana Pastula managed restaurants at Lanai's Manele Bay Hotel and the Four Seasons Resort Wailea before opening her tiny, charming outdoor cafe in this sunlit sliver of Makawao. And the alfresco dining is just part of it: From the sandwiches (roast chicken breast, turkey breast, prosciutto) and salads to the soup of the day, the offerings are homemade and excellent. The chic Makawao shopkeepers who lunch here never tire of the quinoa salad, the ginger chicken soup, the roasted-beet-and-potato soup, the curry chicken salad, and the talk of the town—a towering Asian salad of Oriental vegetables, tofu, and baby greens, tossed in a sesame vinaigrette with fresh mint, ginger, and lemongrass, and served over Chinese noodles. Our favorite? The shiitake mushroom soup with chicken long rice and the snow crab–avocado sandwich—too good to be true.

In the Paniolo Courtyard, 3673 Baldwin Ave. © 808/573-9065. Sandwiches and salads $4.95–$6.95. No credit cards. Mon–Sat 11am–4pm.

Casanova Italian Restaurant ★ ITALIAN   Look for the tiny veranda with a few stools, always full, in front of a deli at Makawao's busiest intersection—that's the most visible part of the Casanova restaurant and lounge. Makawao's nightlife center contains a stage, dance floor, restaurant, and bar—and food to love and remember. This is pasta heaven; try the spaghetti fra diavolo or the spinach gnocchi in a fresh tomato-Gorgonzola sauce. Other choices include a huge pizza selection, grilled lamb chops in an Italian mushroom marinade, every possible type of pasta, and luscious desserts. Our personal picks on a stellar menu: garlic spinach topped with Parmesan and pine nuts, polenta with radicchio (the mushrooms and cream sauce are fabulous!), and tiramisu, the best on the island.

1188 Makawao Ave. © 808/572-0220. www.casanovamaui.com. Reservations recommended for dinner. Main courses $10–$24; 12-inch pizzas from $10. DC, DISC, MC, V. Mon–Sat 11:30am–2pm and 5:30–9pm; Sun 5:30–9pm; dancing Wed–Sat 9:45pm–1am. Lounge daily 5:30pm–12:30am or 1am; deli daily 8am–6:30pm.

Cow Country Cafe AMERICAN/LOCAL   Pukalani's inexpensive, casual, and very popular cafe features cows everywhere—on the walls, chairs, menus, aprons, even the exterior. But the real draw is the simple, home-cooked comfort food, such as meat loaf, roast pork, and humongous hamburgers, plus home-baked bread, oven-fresh muffins, and local faves such as saimin and Chinese chicken salad. Soups (homemade cream of mushroom), salads, and shrimp scampi with bow-tie pasta are among the cafe's other pleasures. The signature dessert is the cow pie, a naughty pile of chocolate cream cheese with macadamia nuts in a cookie crust, shaped like you-know-what.

In the Andrade Building, 7–2 Aewa Place (just off Haleakala Hwy.), Pukalani. © 808/572-2395. Lunch $5.95–$8.95; most dinner items less than $15. MC, V. Mon–Sat 7am–3pm and 5:30–9pm; Sun 7am–1pm.

KULA (AT THE BASE OF HALEAKALA NATIONAL PARK)

Cafe 808 AMERICAN/LOCAL   Despite its out-of-the-way location (or perhaps because of it), Cafe 808 has become the universal favorite among upcountry residents of all ages. The breakfast coffee group, the lunchtime crowd, kids after school, and dinner regulars all know it's the place for tasty home-style cooking with no pretensions: chicken lasagna, smoked-salmon omelette, famous burgers (teriyaki, hamburger, cheeseburger, garden burger, mahimahi, taro), roast pork, smoked turkey, and a huge selection of local-style specials. Regulars rave about the chicken katsu, saimin, and beef stew. The few tables are sprinkled around a room with linoleum-tile floors, hardwood benches, plastic patio chairs, and old-fashioned booths—rough around the edges in a pleasing way, and very camp.

Lower Kula Rd., past Holy Ghost Church, across from Morihara Store. ☎ **808/878-6874**. Burgers from $3.50; main courses $4.50–$9.95. No credit cards. Daily 6am–8pm.

Grandma's Coffee House ☞ COFFEEHOUSE/AMERICAN   Alfred

Franco's grandmother started what is now a five-generation coffee business back in 1918, when she was 16 years old. Today, this tiny wooden coffeehouse, still fueled by homegrown Haleakala coffee beans, is the quintessential roadside oasis. Grandma's offers espresso, hot and cold coffees, home-baked pastries, inexpensive pasta, sandwiches (including sensational avocado and garden burgers), homemade soups, fresh juices, and local plate-lunch specials that change daily. Rotating specials include Hawaiian beef stew, ginger chicken, saimin, chicken curry, lentil soup, and sandwiches piled high with Kula vegetables. While the coffee is legendary, we think the real standouts are the lemon squares and the pumpkin bread.

At the end of Hwy. 37, Keokea (about 6 miles before the Tedeschi Vineyards in Ulupalakua). ☎ **808/ 878-2140**. Most items less than $8.95. MC, V. Daily 7am–5pm.

Kula Lodge ☞ HAWAII REGIONAL/AMERICAN   Don't let the dinner

prices scare you; the Kula Lodge is equally enjoyable, if not more so, at breakfast and lunch, when the prices are lower and the views through the picture windows have an eye-popping intensity. The million-dollar vista spans the flanks of Haleakala, rolling 3,200 feet down to central Maui, the ocean, and the West Maui Mountains. The Kula Lodge has always been known for its breakfasts: fabulous eggs Benedict, including a vegetarian version with Kula onions, shiitake mushrooms, and scallions; legendary banana-mac nut pancakes; and a highly recommended tofu scramble with green onions, Kula vegetables, and garlic chives. If possible, go for sunset cocktails and watch the colors change into deep end-of-day hues. When darkness descends, a roaring fire and lodge atmosphere add to the coziness of the room. The dinner menu features "small plates" of Thai summer rolls, seared ahi, and other starters. Sesame-seared ono, Cuban-style spicy swordfish with rum-soaked bananas, and miso salmon with wild mushrooms are seafood attractions, but there's also pasta, rack of lamb, filet mignon, and free-range chicken breast.

Haleakala Hwy. (Hwy. 377). ☎ **808/878-2517**. Reservations recommended for dinner. Breakfast $7.50–$18; lunch $11–$18; dinner main courses $14–$28. AE, MC, V. Daily 6:30am–9pm.

Kula Sandalwoods Restaurant ☞ AMERICAN   Chef Eleanor Loui, a

graduate of the Culinary Institute of America, makes hollandaise sauce every morning from fresh upcountry egg yolks, sweet butter, and Myers lemons, which her family grows in the yard above the restaurant. This is Kula cuisine, with produce from the backyard and everything made from scratch, including French toast with home-baked Portuguese sweet bread; hotcakes or Belgian waffles with fresh fruit; baguettes; open-faced country omelets; hamburgers drenched in a special cheese sauce made with grated sharp cheddar; and an out-standing veggie burger. The grilled chicken breast sandwich is marvelous, served with soup of the day and Kula mixed greens. Dine in the gazebo or on the ter-race, with dazzling views in all directions, including, in the spring, a yard dusted with lavender jacaranda flowers and a hillside ablaze with fields of orange aku-likuli blossoms.

15427 Haleakala Hwy. (Hwy. 377). (© 808/878-3523. Breakfast $6.95–9.75; lunch $7.25–$13; Sunday Brunch $6.95–$9.75. MC, V. Mon–Sat 6:30am–2pm; Sun brunch 6:30am–noon.

EAST MAUI

Note: You'll find the restaurants in this section on the "Upcountry & East Maui" map on p. 383.

PAIA

Cafe des Amis ☆ CREPES/SALADS   This Paia newcomer quickly became known as the place for healthy and tasty lunches that are kind to the pocket-book. Crepes are the star here, and they are popular: spinach with feta cheese, scallops with garlic and chipotle chile; shrimp curry with coconut milk; and dozens more choices, including breakfast crepes and dessert crepes (like banana and chocolate, strawberries and cream, or caramelized apples with rum). Equally popular are the salads (including niçoise, Greek, and Caesar) and smoothies (like peach/banana/raspberry and mango/banana/pineapple). The crepes come with a house salad—a great deal.

42 Baldwin Ave. (© 808/579-6323. Crepes $5.90–$7.50. DISC, MC, V. Mon–Sat 8:30am–8:30pm.

Milagros Food Company ☆ SOUTHWESTERN/SEAFOOD   Milagros has gained a following with its great home-style cooking, upbeat atmosphere, and highly touted margaritas. Sit outdoors and watch the parade of Willie Nel-son look-alikes ambling by as you tuck into the ahi creation of the evening, a combination of southwestern and Pacific Rim styles and flavors accompanied by fresh veggies and Kula greens. Blackened ahi taquitos, pepper-crusted ono pasta, blue shrimp tostadas, and sandwiches, salads, and combination plates are some of the offerings here. For breakfast, we recommend the Olive Oyl spinach omelet or the huevos rancheros, served with home fries. We love Paia's tie dyes, beads, and hippie flavor, and this is the front row seat for it all. Watch for happy hour, with cheap and fabulous margaritas.

Hana Hwy. and Baldwin Ave., Paia. (© 808/579-8755. Breakfast around $7; lunch $6–$10; dinner $15–$20. DC, MC, V. Daily 8am–11pm.

Moana Bakery & Cafe ☆☆ LOCAL/EUROPEAN   Moana gets high marks for its stylish concrete floors, high ceilings, booths and cafe tables, and fabulous food. Don Ritchey, formerly a chef at Haliimaile General Store, has created the perfect Paia eatery, a casual bakery-cafe that highlights his stellar skills. All the bases are covered: saimin, omelets, wraps, pancakes, and fresh-baked goods in the morning; soups, sandwiches, pasta, and satisfying salads for lunch; and for dinner, varied selections with Asian and European influences and fresh island ingredients. The lemongrass-grilled prawns with green papaya salad are an explosion of flavors and textures, the roasted vegetable napoleon is gourmet fare, and the Thai red curry with coconut milk, served over vegetables, seafood, or tofu, comes atop jasmine rice with crisp rice noodles and fresh sprouts to cool the fire. Ritchey's Thai-style curries are richly spiced and intense. We also vouch for his special gift with fish: The nori-sesame crusted opakapaka, with wasabi beurre blanc, is cooked, like the curry, to perfection.

71 Baldwin Ave. ✆ 808/579-9999. Reservations recommended for dinner. Breakfast $4.60–$9.95; lunch $5.95–$9.95; dinner main courses $7.95–$24. MC, V. Daily 8am–9pm.

Paia Fish Market ⭐ SEAFOOD This really is a fish market, with fresh fish to take home and cooked seafood, salads, pastas, fajitas, and quesadillas to take out or enjoy at the few picnic tables inside the restaurant. It's an appealing and budget-friendly selection: Cajun-style fresh catch, fresh-fish specials (usually ahi or salmon), fresh-fish tacos and quesadillas, and seafood and chicken pastas. You can also order hamburgers, cheeseburgers, fish and chips (or shrimp and chips), and wonderful lunch and dinner plates, cheap and tasty. Peppering the walls are photos of the number-one sport here, windsurfing.

110 Hana Hwy. ✆ 808/579-8030. Lunch and dinner plates $6.95–$20. DISC, MC, V. Daily 11am–9:30pm.

Pic-nics SANDWICHES/PICNIC LUNCHES Breakfast is terrific here— omelets, eggs made to order, Maui Portuguese sausage, Hawaiian pancakes— and so is lunch. Pic-nics is famous for many things, among them the spinach-nut burger, an ingenious vegetarian blend topped with vegetables and cheddar cheese. Stop here to refresh yourself with a plate lunch or smoothie for the drive to Hana or upcountry Maui. The gourmet sandwiches (Kula vegetables, home-baked breast of turkey, Cajun chicken, Cajun fish) are worthy of the most idyllic picnic spot. The rosemary herb-roasted chicken can be ordered as a plate lunch or as part of the Hana Bay picnic, which includes sandwiches, meats, Maui-style potato chips, and home-baked cookies and muffins. You can order old-fashioned fish and chips, too, or shrimp-and-chips. Fresh breads and pastries add to the appeal, and several coffee drinks made with Maui-blend coffee may give you the jolt you need for the drive ahead.

30 Baldwin Ave. ✆ 808/579-8021. Most items less than $6.95. MC, V. Daily 7am–3pm.

The Vegan GOURMET VEGETARIAN/VEGAN Wholesome foods with ingenious soy substitutes and satisfying flavors appear on a menu that dares you to feel healthy *without* feeling deprived. Pad Thai noodles are the best-selling item, cooked in a creamy coconut sauce and generously seasoned with garlic and spices. Curries, grilled polenta, pepper steak made of seitan (a meat substitute), and organic hummus are among the items that draw vegetarians from around the island. Proving that desserts are justly deserved, Vegan offers a carob cake and coconut milk–flavored tapioca pudding that hint of Thailand yet are dairy-free.

115 Baldwin Ave. ✆ 808/579-9144. Main courses $7.95–$9.95. MC, V. Daily 11am–9pm.

ON THE ROAD TO HANA

Mama's Fish House ⭐⭐ The restaurant's entrance, a cove with windsurfers, tide pools, white sand, and a canoe resting under palm trees, is a South Seas fantasy worthy of Gauguin. The interior features curved lauhala-lined ceilings, walls of split bamboo, lavish arrangements of tropical blooms, and picture windows to let in the view. With servers wearing Polynesian prints and flowers behind their ears, and the sun setting in Kuau Cove, Mama's mood is hard to beat. The fish is fresh (the fishermen are even credited by name on the menu) and prepared Hawaiian style, with tropical fruit or baked in a macadamia nut and vanilla bean crust, or in a number of preparations involving ferns, seaweed, Maui onions, and roasted kukui nut. Menu items include mahimahi laulau with luau leaves (taro greens) and Maui onions, baked in ti leaves and served with kalua pig and Hanalei poi—the best. Deep-water ahi could be seared with coconut and lime, while ono "caught by Keith Nakamura along the 40-fathom ledge near Hana" comes in Hana ginger teriyaki with mac nuts and crisp Maui onion. Other special touches include the use of Molokai sweet potato, Hana breadfruit, organic lettuces, Haiku bananas, and fresh coconut, which evoke the mood and tastes of old Hawaii.

799 Poho Place, just off the Hana Hwy., Kuau. © **808/579-8488.** Reservations recommended for lunch, required for dinner. Main courses $29–$59. AE, DC, DISC, MC, V. Daily 11am–3pm, light menu 3–4:45pm, and 4:45–9pm last seating.

Nahiku Coffee Shop, Smoked Fish Stand, and Ti Gallery ★ *(Finds)*
SMOKED KEBABS   What a delight to stumble across this trio of comforts on the long drive to Hana! The small coffee shop purveys locally made baked goods, several flavors of Maui-grown coffee, banana breads made in the neighborhood, organic tropical fruit smoothies, and the Original and Best Coconut Candy made by Hana character Jungle Johnny. Next door, the Ti Gallery sells locally made Hawaiian arts and crafts, such as pottery and koa wood vessels.

The barbecue smoker, though, is our favorite part of the operation. It puts out superb smoked and grilled fish, fresh and locally caught, sending seductive aromas out into the moist Nahiku air. These are not jerky-like smoked meats; the process keeps the kebabs moist while retaining the smoke flavor. The breadfruit—sliced, wrapped in banana leaf, and baked—can be bland and starchy (like a baked potato), but it's a stroke of genius to give visitors a taste of this important Polynesian staple. The teriyaki-based marinade, made by the owner, adds a special touch to the fish (ono, ahi, marlin). One of the biggest sellers is the kalua pig sandwich. Also a hit are the island-style, two-hand tacos of fish, beef, and chicken, served with about six condiments, including cheese, jalapeños, and salsa. When available, fresh corn on the cob from Kipahulu is served, and grabbed up apace. There are a few roadside picnic tables, or you can take your lunch to go for a beachside picnic in Hana.

Hana Hwy., ½ mile past mile marker 28. No phone. Kebabs $3 each. No credit cards. Coffee shop daily 9am–5:30pm; fish stand Fri–Wed 10am–5pm; gallery daily 10am–5pm.

Pauwela Cafe ★ *(Finds)* INTERNATIONAL   It's easy to get lost while searching out this wonderful cafe, but it's such a find. We never dreamed you could dine so well with such pleasing informality. The tiny cafe with a few tables indoors and out has a strong local following for many reasons. Becky Speere, a gifted chef, and her husband, Chris, a former food-service instructor at Maui Community College and a former sous chef at the Maui Prince Hotel, infuse every sandwich, salad, and muffin with finesse.

All breads are prepared in-house, including rosemary potato, Scottish country, French baguette, and green onion and cheese. The scene-stealing kalua turkey sandwich is one success layered upon another: moist, smoky shredded turkey, served with cheese on home-baked French bread and covered with a green-chili and cilantro sauce. For breakfast, eggs chilaquile are a good starter, with layers of corn tortillas, pinto beans, chiles, cheese, and herbs, topped with egg custard and served hot with salsa and sour cream. At lunch, the Greek salad and veggie burrito are excellent. Because this cafe is located in an industrial center of sailboard and surfboard manufacturers, you may find a surf legend dining at the next table. The cafe is a little less than 1½ miles past the Haiku turn-off and a half-mile up on the left.

375 W. Kuiaha Rd., off Hana Hwy., past Haiku Rd., Haiku. ℂ 808/575-9242. Most items less than $6.50. No credit cards. Mon–Sat 7am–3pm; Sun 8am–2pm.

HANA

Hana Ranch Restaurant AMERICAN   Part of the Hotel Hana-Maui operation, the Hana Ranch Restaurant is the informal alternative to the hotel's dining room. Dinner choices include New York steak, prawns and pasta, and Pacific Rim options like spicy shrimp wontons or the predictable fresh-fish poke. The warmly received Wednesday Pizza Night and the luncheon buffets are the most affordable prospects: baked mahimahi, pita sandwiches, chicken stir-fry, cheeseburgers, and club and fresh-catch sandwiches. It's not an inspired menu, and the service can be practically nonexistent when the tour buses descend during lunch rush. There are indoor tables as well as two outdoor pavilions that offer distant ocean views. At the adjoining takeout stand, fast-food classics prevail: teriyaki plate lunch, mahimahi sandwich, cheeseburgers, hot dogs, and ice cream.

Hana Hwy. ℂ 808/248-8255. Reservations required Fri–Sat. Main courses $18–$33. AE, DC, DISC, MC, V. Daily 7am–10am and 11am–2pm; Fri–Sat 6–8pm. Takeout counter daily 6–10am and 11am–4pm.

5 Beaches

For beach toys and equipment, head to **Activity Warehouse** (ℂ 800/923-4004; www.travelhawaii.com), which has branches in Lahaina at 578 Front St., near Prison Street (ℂ 808/661-1970), and in Kihei at Azeka Place II, on the mountain side of Kihei Road near Lipoa Street (ℂ 808/875-4050). Beach chairs rent for $2 a day, coolers (with ice!) for $2 a day, and a host of toys (Frisbees, volleyballs, and more) for $1 a day.

WEST MAUI

KAANAPALI BEACH 🌴

Four-mile long Kaanapali is one of Maui's best beaches, with grainy gold sand as far as the eye can see. The beach parallels the sea channel through most of its length, and a paved walk links hotels and condos, open-air restaurants, and the Whalers Village shopping center. Because Kaanapali is so long and broad, and because most hotels have adjacent swimming pools, the beach is crowded only in pockets—there's plenty of room to find seclusion. Summertime swimming is excellent. The best snorkeling is around Black Rock, in front of the Sheraton, where the water's clear, calm, and populated with clouds of tropical fish.

Facilities include outdoor showers; you can also use the restrooms at the hotel pools. Various beach-activities vendors line up in front of the hotels. Parking is a problem, though. There are two public entrances: At the south end, turn off Honoapiilani Highway into the Kaanapali Resort, and pay for parking here; or continue on Honoapiilani Highway, turn off at the last Kaanapali exit at the stoplight near the Maui Kaanapali Villas, and park next to the beach signs indicating public access.

KAPALUA BEACH 🌴🌴🌴

The beach cove that fronts the Kapalua Bay Hotel and the Coconut Grove Villas is the stuff of dreams: a golden crescent bordered by two palm-studded points. The sandy bottom slopes gently to deep water at the bay mouth; the water's so clear that you can see where the gold sands turn to green and then deep blue. Protected from strong winds and currents by the lava-rock promontories, Kapalua's calm waters are ideal for swimmers of all ages and abilities, and

Beaches & Outdoor Pursuits on Maui

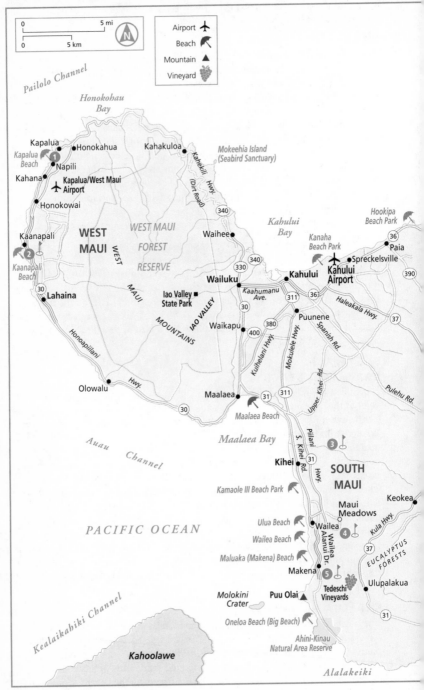

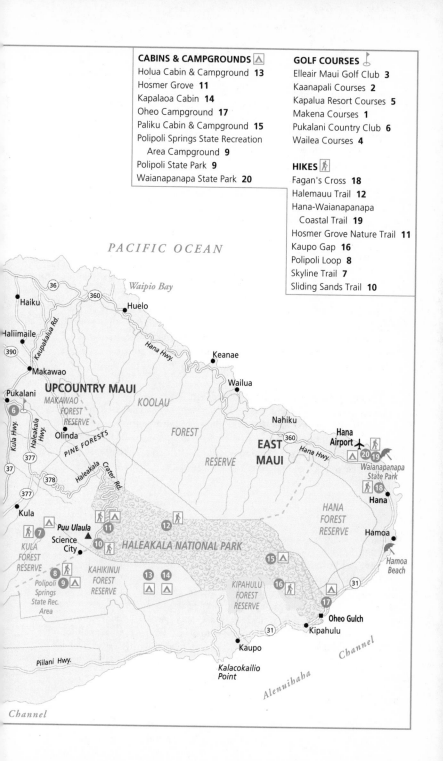

CABINS & CAMPGROUNDS △
Holua Cabin & Campground **13**
Hosmer Grove **11**
Kapalaoa Cabin **14**
Oheo Campground **17**
Paliku Cabin & Campground **15**
Polipoli Springs State Recreation
 Area Campground **9**
Polipoli State Park **9**
Waianapanapa State Park **20**

GOLF COURSES ⛳
Elleair Maui Golf Club **3**
Kaanapali Courses **2**
Kapalua Resort Courses **5**
Makena Courses **1**
Pukalani Country Club **6**
Wailea Courses **4**

HIKES 🥾
Fagan's Cross **18**
Halemauu Trail **12**
Hana-Waianapanapa
 Coastal Trail **19**
Hosmer Grove Nature Trail **11**
Kaupo Gap **16**
Polipoli Loop **8**
Skyline Trail **7**
Sliding Sands Trail **10**

PACIFIC OCEAN

Waipio Bay

Haiku

Huelo

Haliimaile

Makawao

Keanae

Pukalani

UPCOUNTRY MAUI

MAKAWAO
FOREST
RESERVE

KOOLAU

Wailua

Olinda

PINE FORESTS

FOREST

Nahiku

Hana
Airport ✈

EAST
MAUI

Hana Hwy.

Waianapanapa
State Park

RESERVE

Kula

Haleakala

Hana

Puu Ulaula
Science
City

HALEAKALA NATIONAL PARK

HANA
FOREST
RESERVE

Hamoa

KULA
FOREST
RESERVE

Hamoa
Beach

KAHIKINUI
FOREST
RESERVE

Polipoli
Springs
State Rec.
Area

KIPAHULU
FOREST
RESERVE

Oheo Gulch

Kipahulu

Piilani Hwy.

Kaupo

Kalacokailio
Point

Channel

Alenuihaha

Channel

Frommer's Favorite Maui Experiences

Greeting the Rising Sun from atop Haleakala. Bundle up, fill a thermos with hot java, and drive up the 37 miles from sea level to 10,000 feet to witness the birth of yet another day. Breathing in the rarefied air and watching the first rays of light streak across the sky makes the Haleakala sunrise a mystical experience.

Watching for Whales. No need to head out in a boat—in winter, you can see these majestic mammals breach and spy hop from shore. One of the best places is scenic McGregor Point, at mile marker 9 along Honoapiilani Highway, just outside Maalaea in south Maui. The humpbacks arrive as early as November, but the majority travel through Maui's waters from mid-December to mid-April.

Snorkeling off Makena Landing. Calm waters and an abundance of marine life make Makena Bay one of Hawaii's best places to swim with the fishes. Don a mask and snorkel and paddle with turtles, watch clouds of butterfly fish flitter past, and search for tiny damsel fish in the coral.

Taking a Dip in the Seven Sacred Pools. There are actually more than seven of these fern-shrouded waterfall pools, and they're all beautiful. They spill seaward at Oheo Gulch, on the rainy eastern flanks of Haleakala. Some people try to swim in the pools nearest the ocean; if you do, keep an eye on the sky overhead so that a sudden cloudburst doesn't send you cascading out to sea.

Venturing Back in Time in a Historic Port Town. In the 1800s, when whaling was at its height, seafarers swarmed into Lahaina and missionaries fought to stem the spread of their sinful influence. It was a wild time, and this tiny town was an exciting place. The Lahaina Restoration Society, in the Master's Reading Room on Front and Dickenson streets, will give you a free map that will let you discover those wild whaling days for yourself.

---

the bay is big enough to paddle a kayak around in without getting into the more challenging channel that separates Maui from Molokai. Waves come in just right for riding, and fish hang out by the rocks, making it great for snorkeling.

The beach is accessible from the hotel on one end, which provides shaded sun chairs and a beach-activities center for its guests, and a public access way on the other. It isn't so wide that you burn your feet getting in or out of the water, and the inland side is edged by a shady path and cool lawns. Outdoor showers are stationed at both ends. Parking is limited to about 30 spaces in a small lot off Lower Honoapiilani Road, by Napili Kai Beach Club, so arrive early. Next door is a nice but pricey oceanfront restaurant, Kapalua's Bay Club. Facilities include showers, restrooms, lifeguards, a rental shack, and plenty of shade.

SOUTH MAUI

Wailea's beaches may seem off-limits, hidden from plain view as they are by an intimidating wall of luxury resorts, but they're all open to the public by law. Look for the SHORELINE ACCESS signs along **Wailea Alanui Drive,** the resort's main boulevard.

Watching Windsurfers Ride the Waves at Hookipa. Just off the Hana Highway past Paia is Hookipa Beach, known the world over as a windsurfing mecca. The great waves and consistent wind draw top windsurfers from around the globe. Watch spellbound as these colorful sailboarders ride, sail, and pirouette over the waves, turning into the wind and flipping into the air while rotating 360°. It's the best free show in town.

Exploring Iao Valley. When the sun strikes Iao Valley in the West Maui Mountains, an almost ethereal light sends rays out in all directions. This really may be Eden.

Walking the Shoreline Trail at Waianapanapa. A 6-mile trail follows the shoreline, bordered on one side by lava cliffs and a forest of lauhala trees, on the other by the open ocean. As you go, you'll pass an ancient *heiau* (temple), some fascinating caves, a pretty cool blowhole, jungly native Hawaiian plants, and the ever-changing sea.

Heading to Kula to Bid the Sun Aloha. Harold Rice Park, just off Kula Highway, is the perfect vantage point for watching the sun set over the entire island: down the side of Haleakala, out across the isthmus, and over to the West Maui Mountains, with Molokai and Lanai in the distance. As the sun sinks in the sky, the light shifts from bright yellow to mellow red. Once the sun drops below the horizon, the sky puts on its own Technicolor show in a dazzling array of colors.

Experiencing Art Night in Lahaina. Every Friday after the sun goes down, most of the town's galleries open their doors, serve pupu and refreshments, and hope you'll wander in. This is a fun, festive way to see what's going on in Maui's creative community. You may even be able to meet the artists; many are on hand to talk about their works.

KAMAOLE III BEACH PARK ✸

Three beach parks—Kamaole I, II, and III—stand like golden jewels in the front yard of the funky seaside town of Kihei, which all of a sudden is sprawling like suburban blight. The beaches are the best thing about Kihei. These three are popular with local residents and visitors alike because they're easily accessible. On weekends, they're jam-packed with fishermen, picnickers, swimmers, and snorkelers. The most popular is Kamaole III, or "Kam-3." The biggest of the three beaches, with wide pockets of gold sand, it's the only one with a children's playground and a grassy lawn. Swimming is safe here, but scattered lava rocks are toe-stubbers at the water line, and parents should make sure their kids don't venture too far out, because the bottom slopes off quickly. Both the north and south shores are rocky fingers with a surge big enough to attract fish and snorkelers; the winter waves appeal to bodysurfers. Kam-3 is also a wonderful place to watch the sunset. Facilities include restrooms, showers, picnic tables, barbecue grills, and lifeguards. There's plenty of parking on South Kihei Road across from the Maui Parkshore condos.

WAILEA BEACH ✦

Wailea is the best golden-sand crescent on Maui's sunbaked southwestern coast. One of five beaches within Wailea Resort, Wailea is big, wide, and protected on both sides by black-lava points. It's the front yard of the Four Seasons Wailea and the Grand Wailea Resort Hotel and Spa, Maui's most elegant and outrageous beach hotels, respectively. From the beach, the view out to sea is magnificent, framed by neighboring Kahoolawe and Lanai and the tiny crescent of Molokini, probably the most popular snorkel spot in these parts. The clear waters tumble to shore in waves just the right size for gentle riding, with or without a board. From shore, you can see Pacific humpback whales in season (Dec–Apr) and unreal sunsets nightly. Facilities include restrooms, outdoor showers, and limited free parking at the blue SHORELINE ACCESS sign, which points toward Wailea Alanui Drive.

ULUA BEACH ✦

One of the most popular beaches in Wailea, Ulua is a long, wide, crescent-shaped gold-sand beach between two rocky points. When the ocean's calm, Ulua offers Wailea's best snorkeling; when it's rough, the waves are excellent for body-surfers. The ocean bottom is shallow and gently slopes down to deeper waters, making swimming generally safe. The beach is usually occupied by guests of nearby resorts. In high season (Christmas–Mar and June–Aug), it's carpeted with beach towels and packed with sunbathers like sardines in cocoa butter. Facilities include showers and restrooms. Beach equipment is available for rent at the nearby Wailea Ocean Activity Center. Look for the blue SHORELINE ACCESS sign on South Kihei Road, near Renaissance Wailea Beach Resort; a tiny parking lot is nearby.

MALUAKA BEACH (MAKENA BEACH) ✦

On the southern end of Maui's resort coast, development falls off dramatically, leaving a wild, dry countryside of green kiawe trees. The Maui Prince sits in isolated splendor, sharing Makena Resort's 1,800 acres with only a couple of first-rate golf courses and a necklace of perfect beaches. The strand nearest the hotel is Maluaka Beach, often called Makena, notable for its beauty and its views of Molokini Crater, the offshore islet, and Kahoolawe, the so-called "target" island (it was used as a bombing target from 1945 until the early 1990s). This is a short, wide, palm-fringed crescent of golden, grainy sand set between two black-lava points and bounded by big sand dunes topped by a grassy knoll. The swimming in this mostly calm bay is considered the best on Makena Bay, which is bordered on the south by Puu Olai Cinder Cone and historic Keawalai Congregational Church. The waters around Makena Landing, at the north end of the bay, are particularly good for snorkeling. Facilities include restrooms, showers, a landscaped park, lifeguards, and roadside parking. Along Makena Alanui, look for the SHORELINE ACCESS sign near the hotel, turn right, and head down to the shore.

ONELOA BEACH (BIG BEACH) ✦✦

Oneloa, meaning "long sand" in Hawaiian, is one of the most popular beaches on Maui. Locals call it "Big Beach"—it's 3,300 feet long and more than 100 feet wide. Mauians come here to swim, fish, sunbathe, surf, and enjoy the view of Kahoolawe and Lanai. Snorkeling is good around the north end, at the foot of Puu Olai, a 360-foot cinder cone. During storms, however, big waves lash the shore, and a strong rip current sweeps the sharp drop-off, posing a danger for inexperienced open-ocean swimmers. There are no facilities except for portable toilets, but there's plenty of parking. To get here, drive past the Maui Prince Hotel to the second dirt road, which leads through a kiawe thicket to the beach.

On the other side of Puu Olai is **Little Beach,** a small pocket beach where assorted nudists work on their all-over tans, to the chagrin of uptight authorities. You can get a nasty sunburn and a lewd-conduct ticket, too.

EAST MAUI
HOOKIPA BEACH PARK 🏄

Two miles past Paia, on the Hana Highway, is one of the most famous windsurfing sites in the world. Because of its hard, constant wind and endless waves, Hookipa attracts top windsurfers and wave jumpers from around the globe. Surfers and fishermen also enjoy this small, gold-sand beach at the foot of a grassy cliff, which provides a natural amphitheater for spectators. Except when competitions are being held, weekdays are the best times to watch the daredevils fly over the waves. When waves are flat, snorkelers and divers explore the reef. Facilities include restrooms, showers, pavilions, picnic tables, barbecues, and parking.

WAIANAPANAPA STATE PARK 🏄

Four miles before Hana, off the Hana Highway, is this beach park, which takes its name from the legend of the Waianapanapa Cave, where Chief Kaakea, a jealous and cruel man, suspected his wife, Popoalaea, of having an affair. Popoalaea left her husband and hid herself in a chamber of the Waianapanapa Cave. She and her attendant ventured out only at night for food. Nevertheless, a few days later, Kaakea was passing by the area and saw the shadow of the servant. Knowing he had found his wife's hiding place, Kaakea entered the cave and killed her. During certain times of the year, the water in the tide pool turns red, commemorating Popoalaea's death. (Scientists claim, less imaginatively, that the water turns red due to the presence of small red shrimp.)

Waianapanapa State Park's 120 acres contain 12 cabins (p. 390), a caretaker's residence, a beach park, picnic tables, barbecue grills, restrooms, showers, a parking lot, a shoreline hiking trail, and a black-sand beach (the sand is actually small, black pebbles). This is a wonderful area for shoreline hikes (bring insect repellent—the mosquitoes are plentiful) and picnicking. Swimming is generally unsafe, though, due to strong waves and rip currents. Because Waianapanapa is crowded on weekends with local residents and their families, as well as tourists, weekdays are generally a better bet.

HAMOA BEACH 🏄

This half moon–shaped, gray-sand beach (a mix of coral and lava) in a truly tropical setting is a favorite of sunbathers seeking rest and refuge. The Hotel Hana-Maui maintains the beach and acts as though it's private, which it isn't— so just march down the lava-rock steps and grab a spot on the sand. James Michener called it "a beach so perfectly formed that I wonder at its comparative obscurity." The 100-foot-wide beach is three football fields long and sits below 30-foot black-lava sea cliffs. Surf on this unprotected beach breaks offshore and rolls in, making it a popular surfing and bodysurfing area. Hamoa is often swept by powerful rip currents, so be careful. The calm left side is best for snorkeling in summer. The hotel has numerous facilities for guests; there's an outdoor shower and restrooms for nonguests. Parking is limited. Look for the Hamoa Beach turnoff from Hana Highway.

6 Watersports

For general advice on the activities listed below, see "The Active Vacation Planner," in chapter 2.

Activity Warehouse (© **800/923-4004;** www.travelhawaii.com), which has branches in Lahaina at 578 Front St., near Prison Street (© **808/661-1970**), and in Kihei at Azeka Place II, on the mountain side of Kihei Road near Lipoa Street (© **808/875-4050**) rents everything from beach chairs and coolers to kayaks, boogie boards, and surf boards.

Snorkel Bob's (www.snorkelbob.com) has snorkel gear, boogie boards, and other ocean toys at three locations: 1217 Front St., Lahaina (© **808/661-4421**); Napili Village, 5425-C Lower Honoapiilani Hwy., Napili (© **808/669-9603**); and Kamaole Beach Center, 2411 S. Kihei Rd., Kihei (© **808/879-7449**). All locations are open daily from 8am to 5pm. If you're island hopping, you can rent from a Snorkel Bob's location on one island and return to a branch on another.

BOATING

Maui is big on snorkel cruises. The crescent-shaped islet called **Molokini** is one of the best snorkel and scuba spots in Hawaii. Trips to the island of **Lanai** (see chapter 8) are also popular for a day of snorkeling. Always remember to bring a towel, swimsuit, sunscreen, and hat on a snorkel cruise; everything else is usually included. If you'd like to go a little deeper than snorkeling allows, consider trying **Snuba.** Most of these snorkel boats offer it for an additional cost; it's usually around $50 for a half-hour or so.

For fishing charters, see "Sportfishing," later in this chapter.

America II ✫   This U.S. contender in the 1987 America's Cup race is a true racing boat, a 65-foot, 12-meter sailing yacht offering four different 2-hour trips in winter, three in summer: a **morning sail,** an **afternoon sail,** and a **sunset sail,** plus **whale-watching** in winter. These are sailing trips. No snorkeling—just the thrill of racing with the wind. Complimentary bottled water, soda, and chips are available.

Lahaina Harbor, slip 5. © **888/667-2133** or 808/667-2195. www.galaxymall.com/stores/americaii. Trips $33 adults, $16 children 12 and under, whale watching $30 adults and $15 children.

Maui Classic Charters ✫✫   Maui Classic Charters offers morning and afternoon **snorkel-sail cruises to Molokini** on *Four Winds II,* a 55-foot, glass bottom catamaran for $72 adults ($47 children 3–12 years) for the morning sail and $40 adults ($30 children) in the afternoon. *Four Winds* trips include a continental breakfast; a barbecue lunch; complimentary beer, wine, and soda; complimentary snorkeling gear and instruction; and sportfishing along the way.

Those looking for speed should book a trip on the fast, state-of-the-art catamaran, *Maui Magic.* The company offers a 5-hour snorkel journey to both Molokini and La Perouse for $99 for adults and $79 for children ages 5 to 12, including a continental breakfast; barbecue lunch; beer, wine, soda; snorkel gear; and instruction. During **whale season** (Dec 22–Apr 22), the Maui Magic Whale Watch, an hour and a half trip with beverages, is $29 for adults and $24 for children ages 3 to 12 years.

Maalaea Harbor, slip 55 and slip 80. © **800/736-5740** or 808/879-8188. www.mauicharters.com. Prices vary depending on cruise.

Ocean Activities Center ⚓ In season, this activities center runs 2-hour **whale-watching cruises** on its own spacious 65-foot catamaran; trips range from $25 to $32 for adults and $15 to $20 for children ages 3 to 12. The best deal to **Molokini** is the 5-hour Maka Kai cruise, which includes a continental breakfast, deli lunch, snorkel gear, and instruction; it's $60 for adults, $50 for teenagers, and $40 for children ages 3 to 12. Trips leave from Maalaea Harbor, slip 62. They also have a sportfishing charter boat (a 6 hr. trip on a shared boat starts at $135) and bottom fishing cruises for $95 per angler.

1847 S. Kihei Rd., Kihei. ℂ **800/798-0652** or 808/879-4485. www.mauioceanactivities.com. Prices vary depending on cruise.

Pacific Whale Foundation This not-for-profit foundation supports its whale research by offering **whale-watch cruises** and **snorkel tours,** some to Molokini and Lanai. It operates a 65-foot power catamaran called *Ocean Spirit,* a 50-foot sailing catamaran called *Manute'a,* and a sea kayak. There are 15 daily trips to choose from, offered from December through May, out of both Lahaina and Maalaea harbors.

101 N. Kihei Rd., Kihei. ℂ **800/942-5311** or 808/879-8811. www.pacificwhale.org. Trips from $20 adults, $15 children ages 7-12; 6 years and under free; snorkeling cruises from $30.

Pride of Maui For a high-speed, action-packed snorkel-sail experience, consider the *Pride of Maui.* These 5½-hour **snorkel cruises** take in not only **Molokini,** but also Turtle Bay and Makena for more snorkeling. Continental breakfast, barbecue lunch, gear, and instruction are included.

Maalaea Harbor. ℂ **877/TO-PRIDE** or 808/875-0955. Trips $86 adults, $53 children 3–12.

Scotch Mist Sailing Charters This 50-foot Santa Cruz sailboat offers 2-hour sailing adventures. Prices include snorkel gear, juice, fresh pineapple spears, Maui chips, beer, wine, and soda.

Lahaina Harbor, slip 2. ℂ **808/661-0386.** www.scotchmistsailingcharters.com. Sail trips $35 adults, $18 children ages 5-12; sunset sail $45.

Trilogy ⚓⚓⚓ *Kids*   Trilogy offers our favorite **snorkel-sail trips.** Hop aboard its 50-foot catamaran for a 90-mile sail from Lahaina Harbor to **Lanai's Hulopoe Beach,** a terrific marine preserve, for a fun-filled day of sailing, snorkeling, swimming, and **whale-watching** (in season, of course). This is the only cruise that offers a personalized ground tour of the island, and the only one with rights to take you to Hulopoe Beach. The full-day trip costs $169 for adults, half-price for children ages 3 to 12. Ask about overnighters to Lanai.

Trilogy also offers snorkel-sail trips to **Molokini,** one of Hawaii's best snorkel spots. This half-day trip leaves from Maalaea Harbor and costs $95 for adults, half-price for kids ages 3 to 12, including breakfast and a barbecue lunch. There's also a late-morning half-day snorkel-sail off Kaanapali Beach for the same price.

These are the most expensive sail-snorkel cruises on Maui, but they're worth every penny. The crews are fun and knowledgeable, and the boats comfortable and well-equipped. All trips include breakfast (Mom's homemade cinnamon buns) and a very good barbecue lunch (shipboard on the half-day trip, on land on the Lanai trip). Note, however, that you will be required to wear a flotation device no matter how good your swimming skills are; if this bothers you, go with another outfitter.

ℂ **888/MAUI-800** or 888/628-4800. www.sailtrilogy.com. Prices and departure points vary with cruise.

DAY CRUISES TO MOLOKAI

You can travel across the seas by ferry from Maui's Lahaina Harbor to Molokai's Kaunakakai Wharf on the *Molokai Princess* (© **800/275-6969** or 808/667-6165; www.mauiprincess.com). The 100-foot yacht, certified for 149 passengers, is fitted with the latest generation of gyroscopic stabilizers, making the ride smoother. The ferry makes the 90-minute journey from Lahaina to Kaunakakai daily; the cost is $40 adult one-way and $20 children one-way. Or you can choose to tour the island from two different package options: Cruise-Drive, which includes round-trip passage and a rental car for $149 for the driver, $80 per additional adult passenger and $40 for children; or the Alii Tour, which is a guided tour in an air-conditioned van plus lunch for $149 for adults and $89 for children.

They also offer ferry transportation and a hike-tour of the Kalaupapa Leprosy Settlement for $215 per person. See "The Legacy of Father Damien: Kalaupapa National Historic Park," in chapter 7 for more information about the settlement.

DAY CRUISES TO LANAI

In addition to **Trilogy** (see above), the following boats specialize in day trips to the island of Lanai.

Expeditions Lahaina/Lanai Passenger Ferry ★ *Value* The cheapest way to Lanai is the ferry, which runs five times a day, 365 days a year. It leaves Lahaina at 6:45am, 9:15am, 12:45, 3:15, and 5:45pm; the return ferry from Lanai's Manele Bay Harbor leaves at 8am, 10:30am, 2, 4:30, and 6:45pm. The 9-mile channel crossing takes between 45 minutes and an hour, depending on sea conditions. Reservations are strongly recommended. Baggage is limited to two checked bags and one carry-on. Call **Lanai City Service** (© **800/800-4000** or 808/565-7227) to arrange a car rental or bus ride when you arrive.

Boat: Lahaina Harbor, office: 658 Front St., Suite 127, Lahaina, HI 96761. © **808/661-3756**. www.go-lanai. com. Round-trip from Maui to Lanai $52 adult, $42 children 2–11 (children under 2 years are free).

BODYBOARDING (BOOGIE BOARDING) & BODYSURFING

In winter, Maui's best bodysurfing spot is **Mokuleia Beach,** known locally as Slaughterhouse because of the cattle slaughterhouse that once stood here, not because of the waves—although these waves are for expert bodysurfers only. Take Honoapiilani Highway just past Kapalua Bay Resort; various trails will take you down to the pocket beach.

Good bodyboarding can be found at **Baldwin Beach Park,** just outside Paia. Storms from the south bring fair bodysurfing conditions and great bodyboarding to the lee side of Maui: **Oneloa Beach** (or Big Beach) in Makena, **Ulua** and **Kamaole III** in Kihei, and **Kapalua** beaches are all good choices.

OCEAN KAYAKING

Gliding silently over the water, propelled by a paddle, seeing Maui from the sea the way the early Hawaiians did—that's what ocean kayaking is all about. One of Maui's best kayak routes is along the **Kihei Coast,** where there's easy access to calm water. Mornings are always best; the wind comes up around 11am, making seas choppy and paddling difficult.

For beginners, our favorite kayak-tour operator is **Makena Kayak Tours** ★ (© **877/879-8426** or 808/879-8426; makenakayak@aol.com). Professional guide Dino Ventura leads a 2½-hour trip from Makena Landing and loves taking first-timers over the secluded coral reefs and into remote coves. His wonderful tour will be a highlight of your vacation. It costs $55, including refreshments and snorkel and kayak equipment.

South Pacific Kayaks, 2439 S. Kihei Rd., Kihei (© **800/776-2326** or 808/875-4848; www.mauikayak.com), is Maui's oldest kayak-tour company. Its expert guides lead ocean-kayak trips that include lessons, a guided tour, and snorkeling. Tours run from 2½ to 5 hours and range in price from $55 to $89. South Pacific also offers kayak rentals starting at $30 a day.

In Hana, **Hana-Maui Sea Sports,** www.hana-maui-seasports.com (© **808/248-7711**) runs 2-hour tours of Hana's coastline on wide, stable "no roll" kayaks, with snorkeling, for $79 per person. They also feature kayak surfing lessons for $89.

OCEAN RAFTING

If you're semiadventurous and looking for a more intimate experience with the sea, try ocean rafting. The inflatable rafts hold 6 to 24 passengers. Tours usually include snorkeling and coastal cruising. One of the best (and most reasonable) outfitters is **Hawaiian Ocean Raft** (© **888/677-RAFT** or 808/667-2191; www.hawaiioceanrafting.com), which operates out of Lahaina Harbor. The best deal is the 5-hour morning tour which is $70 for adults and $50 for children ages 5 to 12 (book online and save $10); it includes three snorkeling stops and time spent searching for dolphins, not to mention continental breakfast and mid-morning snacks.

SCUBA DIVING

Everyone dives **Molokini,** a marine-life park and one of Hawaii's top dive spots. This crescent-shaped crater has three tiers of diving: a 35-foot plateau inside the crater basin (used by beginning divers and snorkelers), a wall sloping to 70 feet just beyond the inside plateau, and a sheer wall on the outside and backside of the crater that plunges 350 feet. This underwater park is very popular, thanks to calm, clear, protected waters and an abundance of marine life, from manta rays to clouds of yellow butterfly fish.

Stop by any location of **Maui Dive Shop** ★ (www.mauidiveshop.com), Maui's largest diving retailer, with everything from rentals to scuba-diving instruction to dive-boat charters, for a free copy of the 24-page *Maui Dive Guide.* Inside are maps of and details on the 20 best shoreline and offshore dives and snorkel sites, each ranked for beginner, intermediate, or advanced snorkelers/divers. Maui Dive Shop has branches in Kihei at Azeka Place II Shopping Center, 1455 S. Kihei Road (© **808/879-3388**), and Kamaole Shopping Center (© **808/879-1533**); in Lahaina at Lahaina Cannery Mall (© **808/661-5388**); and in the Honokowai Market Place (© **808/661-6166**). Other locations include Whalers Village, Kaanapali (© **808/661-5117**), Maalaea Village (© **808/244-5514**) and Kahana Gateway, Kahana (© **808/669-3800**).

For personalized diving, **Ed Robinson's Diving Adventures** ★ (© **800/635-1273** or 808/879-3584; www.mauiscuba.com) is the only Maui company rated one of *Scuba Diver* magazine's top 10 best dive operators for 5 years straight. Ed, a widely published underwater photographer, offers specialized charters for small groups. Two-tank dives are $110 ($125 with equipment); his dive boats depart from Kihei Boat Ramp.

If Ed is booked, call **Mike Severns Diving** (© **808/879-6596;** www.mikesevernsdiving.com), for small (maximum 12 people, divided into 2 groups of 6), personal diving tours on a 38-foot Munson/Hammerhead boat with freshwater

An Expert Shares His Secrets: Maui's Best Dives

Ed Robinson, of Ed Robinson's Diving Adventures (see above), knows what makes a great dive. Here are five of his favorites on Maui:

Hawaiian Reef This area off the Kihei-Wailea Coast is so named because it hosts a good cross-section of Hawaiian topography and marine life. Diving to depths of 85 feet, you'll see everything from lava formations and coral reef to sand and rubble, plus a diverse range of both shallow and deep-water creatures. It's clear why this area was so popular with ancient Hawaiian fishermen: Large helmet shells, a healthy garden of antler coral heads, and big schools of snapper are common.

Third Tank Located off Makena Beach at 80 feet, this World War II tank is one of the most picturesque artificial reefs you're likely to see around Maui. It acts like a fish magnet: Because it's the only large solid object in the area, any fish or invertebrates looking for a safe home come here. Surrounding the tank is a cloak of schooling snapper and goat fish just waiting for a photographer with a wide-angle lens. For its small size, the Third Tank is loaded with more marine life per square inch than any site off Maui.

Molokini Crater The backside is always done as a live boat-drift dive. The vertical wall plummets from more than 150 feet above sea level to around 250 feet below. Looking down to unseen depths gives you a feeling for the vastness of the open ocean. Pelagic fish and sharks are often sighted, and living coral perches on the wall, which is home to lobsters, crabs, and a number of photogenic black-coral trees at 50 feet.

There are actually two great dive sites around Molokini Crater. Named after common chub or rudderfish, **Enenue Side** gently slopes from the surface to about 60 feet, then drops rapidly to deeper waters.

shower. Mike and his wife, Pauline Fiene-Severns, are both biologists who make diving in Hawaii not only fun but also educational (they have a spectacular underwater photography book, *Molokini Island*). In their 25 years of operation, they have been accident-free. Two-tank dives are $120 (with equipment).

SNORKELING

Snorkeling on Maui is easy—there are so many great spots where you can just wade in the water with a face mask and look down to see the tropical fish. Mornings are best; local winds kick in around noon. Maui's best snorkeling beaches include **Kapalua Beach;** along the Kihei coastline, especially at **Kamaole Beach Park III;** and along the Wailea coastline, particularly at **Ulua Beach.** For an off-the-beaten track experience, head south to **Makena Beach;** the bay is filled with clouds of tropical fish, and on weekdays, the waters are virtually empty.

The snorkeling at **Black Rock at Kaanapali** is worth the inflated rates at the parking lots that buffer this beach. The prominent craggy cliff at the Sheraton Maui Hotel doesn't just end when it plunges into the ocean. Underwater, the sheer wall continues, creating one of the west side's best snorkeling areas: Turtles, rays, and a variety of snappers and goat fish cruise along the sandy

The shallower area is an easy dive, with lots of tame butterfly fish. It's also the home of Morgan Bentjaw, one of our friendliest moray eels. Enenue Side is often done as a live boat-drift dive to extend the range of the tour. Diving depths vary. Divers usually do a 50-foot dive, but on occasion, advanced divers drop to the 130-foot level to visit the rare boarfish and the shark condos.

Almost every kind of fish found in Hawaii can be seen in the crystalline waters of **Reef's End**. It's an extension of the rim of the crater, which runs for about 200 yards underwater, barely breaking the surface. Reef's End is shallow enough for novice snorkelers and exciting enough for experienced divers. The end and outside of this shoal drop off in dramatic terraces to beyond diving range. In deeper waters, there are shark ledges at varying depths and dozens of eels, some of which are tame, including moray, dragon, snowflake, and garden eels. The shallower inner side is home to Garbanzo, one of the largest and first eels to be tamed. The reef is covered with cauliflower coral; in bright sunlight, it's one of the most dramatic underwater scenes in Hawaii.

La Pérouse Pinnacle   In the middle of scenic La Pérouse Bay, site of Haleakala's most recent lava flow, is a pinnacle rising from the 60-foot bottom to about 10 feet below the surface. Getting to the dive site is half the fun: The scenery above water is as exciting as that below the surface. Underwater, you'll enjoy a very diversified dive. Clouds of damselfish and triggerfish will greet you on the surface. Divers can approach even the timid bird wrasse. There are more porcupine puffers here than anywhere else, as well as schools of goat fish and fields of healthy finger coral. La Pérouse is good for snorkeling and long, shallow second dives.

bottom. In the crevices, ledges, and holes of the rock wall, you can find eels, shrimp, lobster, and a range of rainbowed tropical fish.

Two truly terrific snorkel spots are difficult to get to but worth the effort—as they're home to Hawaii's tropical marine life at its best:

MOLOKINI ★★   This sunken crater sits like a crescent moon fallen from the sky, almost midway between Maui and the uninhabited island of Kahoolawe. Molokini stands like a scoop against the tide and serves, on its concave side, as a natural sanctuary and marine-life preserve for tropical fish. Snorkelers commute daily in a fleet of dive boats. Molokini is accessible only by boat; see "Boating," above, for outfitters that can take you here. Expect crowds in the high season.

AHIHI-KINAU NATURAL PRESERVE ★★   In Ahihi Bay, you can't miss this 2,000-acre state natural area reserve in the lee of Cape Kinau, on Maui's rugged south coast, where, in 1790, Haleakala spilled red-hot lava that ran to the sea. Fishing is strictly forbidden here, and the fish know it; they're everywhere in this series of rocky coves and black-lava tide pools. To get here, drive south of Makena past Puu Olai to Ahihi Bay, where the road turns to gravel (and sometimes seems like it'll disappear under the waves). At Cape Kinau, three four-wheel-drive trails lead across the lava flow; take the shortest one, nearest La Pérouse Bay. If you have a standard car, drive as far as you can, park, and walk the remainder of the way. Après-snorkel, check out La Pérouse Bay on the south side of Cape Kinau, where the French admiral La Pérouse became the first European to set foot on Maui. A lava-rock pyramid known as Pérouse Monument marks the spot.

When the whales aren't around, **Capt. Steve's Rafting Excursions** (© 808/667-5565; www.captainsteves.com) offers 7-hour snorkel trips from Mala Wharf in Lahaina to the waters around **Lanai** (you don't actually land on the island). Rates of $130 for adults and $95 for children 12 and under include breakfast, lunch, snorkel gear, and wet suits.

Snorkel Bob's (www.snorkelbob.com) and the **Activity Warehouse** (© 800/923-4004; www.travelhawaii.com), will rent you everything you need; see the introduction to this section for locations. Also see "Scuba Diving" (above) for information on Maui Dive Shop's free booklet on great snorkeling sites.

SPORTFISHING

Marlin, tuna, ono, and mahimahi await the baited hook in Maui's coastal and channel waters. No license is required; just book a sportfishing vessel out of Lahaina or Maalaea harbors. Most charter boats that troll for big-game fish carry six passengers max.

The best way to book a sportfishing charter is through the experts; the best booking desk in the state is **Sportfish Hawaii** ✯ (© 877/388-1376 or 808/396-2607; www.sportfishhawaii.com), which not only books boats on Maui, but on all islands. These fishing vessels have been inspected and must meet rigorous criteria to guarantee that you will have a great time. Prices range from $800 to $975 for a full day exclusive charter (you, plus 5 friends, get the entire boat to yourself); it's $600 to $675 for a half-day exclusive.

SUBMARINE DIVES

Plunging 100 feet below the surface of the sea in a state-of-the-art, high-tech submarine is a great way to experience Maui's magnificent underwater world, especially if you're not a swimmer. **Atlantis Submarines** ✯, 658 Front St., Lahaina (© 800/548-6262 or 808/667-2224; www.goatlantis.com), offers trips out of Lahaina Harbor every hour on the hour from 9am to 2pm; tickets range from $70 to $80 for adults and $40 for children under 12 (children must be at least 3 ft. tall). Allow 2 hours for this underwater adventure. This is not a good choice if you're claustrophobic.

SURFING

Expert surfers visit Maui in winter, when the surf's really up. The best surfing beaches include **Honolua Bay,** north of the Kapalua Resort (the 3rd bay past the Ritz-Carlton Kapalua, off the Honoapiilani Hwy., or Hwy. 30); **Lahaina Harbor** (in summer, there'll be waves just off the channel entrance with a south swell); **Maalaea,** just outside the breakwall of the Maalaea Harbor (a clean, world-class left); and **Hookipa Beach,** where surfers get the waves until noon (after that—in a carefully worked-out compromise to share this prized surf spot—the windsurfers take over).

Always wanted to learn to surf, but didn't know whom to ask? Call the **Nancy Emerson School of Surfing** (© 808/244-SURF or 808/874-1183;

www.surfclinics.com). Nancy has been surfing since 1961, and has even been a stunt performer for various movies, including *Waterworld*. She's pioneered a new instructional technique called "Learn to Surf in One Lesson"—you can, really. It's $75 per person for a 2-hour group lesson; private 2-hour classes are $150.

In Hana, **Hana-Maui Sea Sports,** www.hana-maui-seasports.com (© **808/ 248-7711**) has 2-hour long-board lessons taught by a certified ocean lifeguard for $89.

WHALE-WATCHING

The humpback is the star of the annual whale-watching season, which usually begins in December and can last until May.

WHALE-WATCHING FROM SHORE   The best time to whale watch is between mid-December and April: Just look out to sea. There's no best time of day, but it seems that when the sea is glassy and there's no wind, the whales appear. Once you see one, keep watching in the same vicinity; they may stay down for 20 minutes. Bring a book. And binoculars, if you can. You can rent a pair for $2 a day at **Activity Warehouse** (© **800/923-4004;** www.travel hawaii.com), which has branches in Lahaina at 578 Front St., near Prison Street (© **808/661-1970**), and in Kihei at Azeka Place II, on the mountain side of Kihei Road near Lipoa Street (© **808/875-4050**).

Some good whale-watching spots on Maui are:

McGregor Point   On the way to Lahaina, there's a scenic lookout at mile marker 9 (just before you get to the Lahaina Tunnel); it's a good viewpoint to scan for whales.

Outrigger Wailea Beach Resort   On the Wailea coastal walk, stop at this resort to look for whales through the telescope installed as a public service by the Hawaii Island Humpback Whale National Marine Sanctuary.

Olowalu Reef   Along the straight part of Honoapiilani Highway, between McGregor Point and Olowalu, you'll sometimes see whales leap out of the water. Their appearance can bring traffic to a screeching halt: People abandon their cars and run down to the sea to watch, causing a major traffic jam. If you stop, pull off the road so others may pass.

Puu Olai   It's a tough climb up this coastal landmark near the Maui Prince Hotel, but you're likely to be well rewarded: This is the island's best spot for off-shore whale-watching. On the 360-foot cinder cone overlooking Makena Beach, you'll be at the right elevation to see Pacific humpbacks as they dodge Molokini and cruise up Alalakeiki Channel between Maui and Kahoolawe. If you don't see one, you'll at least have a whale of a view.

WHALE-WATCHING CRUISES   For a closer look, take a whale-watching cruise. Just about all of Hawaii's snorkel and dive boats become whale-watching boats in season; some of them even carry professional naturalists on board so you'll know what you're seeing. For the best options, see "Boating," earlier in this chapter.

WHALE-WATCHING BY KAYAK & RAFT   Seeing a humpback whale from an ocean kayak or raft is awesome. **Capt. Steve's Rafting Excursions** (© **808/667-5565;** www.captainsteves.com) offers 2-hour whale-watching excursions out of Lahaina Harbor for $45 adults, $35 for children 12 and under. *Tip:* Save $10 by booking the "Early Bird" adventure, which leaves at 7:30am.

WINDSURFING

Maui has Hawaii's best windsurfing beaches. In winter, windsurfers from around the world flock to the town of **Paia** to ride the waves; **Hookipa Beach,** known all over the globe for its brisk winds and excellent waves, is the site of several world-championship contests. **Kanaha,** west of Kahului Airport, also has dependable winds. When the winds turn northerly, **Kihei** is the spot to be; some days, you can spot whales in the distance behind the windsurfers. The northern end of Kihei is best: **Ohukai Park,** the first beach as you enter South Kihei Road from the northern end, has not only good winds, but also parking, a long strip of grass to assemble your gear, and good access to the water. Experienced windsurfers here are found in front of the **Maui Sunset** condo, 1032 S. Kihei Rd., near Waipuilani Street (a block north of McDonald's), which has great windsurfing conditions but a very shallow reef (not good for beginners).

Hawaiian Island Surf and Sport, 415 Dairy Rd., Kahului (© **800/ 231-6958** or 808/871-4981; www.hawaiianisland.com), offers lessons, rentals, and repairs. Other shops that offer rentals and lessons are **Hawaiian Sailboarding Techniques,** 425 Koloa St., Kahului (© **800/968-5423** or 808/871-5423; www.hstwindsurfing.com), with 2½-hour lessons from $79; and **Maui Windsurf Co.,** 22 Hana Hwy., Kahului (© **800/872-0999** or 808/877-4816; www. maui-windsurf.com), which has complete equipment rental (board, sail, rig harness, and roof rack) from $45 and 1- or 2½-hour lessons ranging from $69 to $75.

For daily reports on wind and surf conditions, call the **Wind and Surf Report** at © **808/877-3611.**

7 Hiking & Camping

In the past 3 decades, Maui has grown from a rural island to a fast-paced resort destination, but its natural beauty remains largely inviolate; there are still many places that can be explored only on foot. Those interested in seeing the backcountry—complete with virgin waterfalls, remote wilderness trails, and quiet, meditative settings—should head for Haleakala's upcountry or the tropical Hana Coast.

Camping on Maui can be extreme (inside a volcano) or benign (by the sea in Hana). It can be wet, cold, and rainy; or hot, dry, and windy—often, all on the same day. If you're heading for Haleakala, remember that U.S. astronauts trained for the moon inside the volcano; bring survival gear. You'll need your swimsuit and rain gear if you're bound for Waianapanapa. Bring your own gear, as there are no places to rent camping equipment on Maui.

For more information on Maui camping and hiking trails, and to obtain free maps, contact **Haleakala National Park,** P.O. Box 369, Makawao, HI 96768 (© **808/572-4400;** www.nps.gov/hale); and the **State Division of Forestry and Wildlife,** 54 S. High St., Wailuku, HI 96793 (© **808/984-8100;** www. hawaii.gov). For information on trails, hikes, camping, and permits for state parks, contact the **Hawaii State Department of Land and Natural Resources,** State Parks Division, P.O. Box 621, Honolulu, HI 96809 (© **808/587-0300;** www.state.hi.us/dlnr); note that you can get information from the website, but cannot obtain permits there. For Maui County Parks, contact the **Department of Parks and Recreation,** 1580-C Kaahumanu Ave., Wailuku, HI 96793 (© **808/243-7132;** www.mauimapp.com).

GUIDED HIKES If you'd like a knowledgeable guide to accompany you on a hike, call **Maui Hiking Safaris** ✦ (© **888/445-3963** or 808/573-0168; fax 808/572-3037; www.mauihikingsafaris.com). Owner Randy Warner takes visitors on half- and full-day hikes into valleys, rain forests, and coastal areas. Randy's been hiking around Maui for more than 22 years and is wise in the ways of Hawaiian history, native flora and fauna, and vulcanology. His rates are $49 for a half day and $79 to $89 for a full day and include day packs, rain parkas, snacks, water, and, on full-day hikes, sandwiches.

Maui's oldest hiking guide company is **Hike Maui** ✦ (© **808/879-5270;** fax 808/893-2515; www.hikemaui.com), headed by Ken Schmitt, who pioneered guided hikes on the Valley Isle. Hike Maui offers five different hikes a day, ranging from an easy 1-mile, 3-hour hike to a waterfall ($59), to a strenuous, full-day hike in Haleakala Crater ($135). All prices include equipment and transportation.

Venture into the lush West Maui Mountains with an experienced guide on one of the numerous hikes offered by **Maui Eco-Adventures** (© **877/661-7720** or 808/661-7720; www.ecomaui.com). After a continental breakfast, you'll hike by streams and waterfalls, through native trees and plants, and on to breathtaking vistas. The tour includes a picnic lunch, swims in secluded pools, and memorable photo ops. The 6-hour excursion costs $110 per person, including meals, a fanny pack with bottled water, and rain gear if necessary. No children under 13 are allowed. For those more "on vacation," an easy hour jaunt costs just $70.

About 1,500 years ago, the verdant Kahakuloa Valley was a thriving Hawaiian village. Today, only a few hundred people live in this secluded hamlet, but old Hawaii still lives on here. Explore the valley with **Ekahi Tours** (© **888/ 292-2422** or 808/877-9775; www.ekahi.com). Your guide, a Kahakuloa resident and a Hawaiiana expert, walks you through a taro farm, explains the mystical legends of the valley, and provides you with a peek into ancient Hawaii. The 7½-hour Kahakuloa Valley Tour is $65 for adults, $50 for children under 12; snacks, beverages, and hotel pickup are included.

For information on hikes given by the **Hawaii Sierra Club** on Maui, call © **808/573-4147;** www.hi.sierraclub.org.

HALEAKALA NATIONAL PARK ✦✦✦

For complete coverage of the national park, see p. 445.

INTO THE WILDERNESS: SLIDING SANDS & HALEMAUU TRAILS

Hiking into Maui's dormant volcano is the best way to see it. The terrain inside the wilderness area of the volcano, which ranges from burnt-red cinder cones to ebony-black lava flows, is simply spectacular. There are some 27 miles of hiking trails, two camping sites, and three cabins.

Entrance to Haleakala National Park is $10 per car. The rangers offer free guided hikes, which are a great way to learn about the unusual flora and geological formations here. Briefing sessions on culture, history, and flora are given daily at 9:30, 10:30, and 11:30am at the Summit Visitors Building, 11 miles up from the Visitor's Information Center. Every Tuesday and Friday at 9am, there's a 2-hour, 2-mile guided cinder desert hike (meet at Sliding Sands Trailhead, next to the summit parking lot). Every Monday and Thursday at 9am, there's a 3-hour, 3-mile guided Waikamoi Cloud Forest hike (meet at Hosmer Grove) to view rare native birds and plants. Wear sturdy shoes and be prepared for wind, rain, and intense sun. Bring water and a hat. Additional options include full-moon hikes and star program hikes. For details, call the park at ℂ **808/572-4400** or www.nps.gov/hale.

Try to arrange to stay at least 1 night in the park; 2 or 3 nights will allow you more time to explore the fascinating interior of the volcano (see below for details on the cabins and campgrounds in the wilderness area of the valley). If you want to venture out on your own, the best route takes in two trails: into the crater along **Sliding Sands Trail,** which begins on the rim at 9,800 feet and descends into the belly of the beast, to the valley floor at 6,600 feet; and back out along **Halemauu Trail.** Hardy hikers can consider making the 11-mile, one-way descent, which takes 9 hours, and the equally-as-long returning ascent, in a day. The rest of us can extend this steep hike to 2 days. The descending and ascending trails aren't loops; the trailheads are miles (and several thousand feet in elevation) apart, so you'll need to make transportation arrangements in advance. Before you set out, stop at park headquarters to get camping and hiking updates.

The trailhead for Sliding Sands is well marked and the trail is easy to follow over lava flows and cinders. As you descend, look around: the view is breathtaking. In the afternoon, waves of clouds flow into the Kaupo and Koolau gaps. Vegetation is spare to nonexistent at the top, but the closer you get to the valley floor, the more vegetation you'll see: bracken ferns, pili grass, shrubs, even flowers. On the floor, the trail travels across rough lava flows, passing by rare silversword plants, volcanic vents, and multicolored cinder cones.

The Halemauu Trail goes over red and black lava and past vegetation, like evening primrose, as it begins its ascent up the valley wall. Occasionally, riders on horseback use this trail. The proper etiquette is to step aside and stand quietly next to the trail as the horses pass.

Some shorter and easier hiking options include the half-mile walk down the **Hosmer Grove Nature Trail,** or the first mile or two down **Sliding Sands Trail,** which gives you a hint of what lies ahead. (Even this short hike is exhausting at the high altitude.) A good day hike is **Halemauu Trail** to Holua Cabin and back, an 8-mile, half-day trip.

STAYING IN THE WILDERNESS AREA Most people stay at one of two tent campgrounds, unless they get lucky and win the lottery—the lottery, that is, for one of the three wilderness cabins. For more information, contact **Haleakala National Park,** P.O. Box 369, Makawao, HI 96768 (ℂ **808/572-4400;** www.nps.gov/hale).

⌠Tips **A Word of Warning About the Weather**

The weather at nearly 10,000 feet can change suddenly and without warning. Come prepared for cold, high winds, rain, and even snow in winter. Temperatures can range from 77°F (25°C) down to 26°F (-3°C), and high winds are frequent. Daytime temperatures can be 30° colder than at sea level. Sunrise and sunset temperatures average 30° to 40° in winter (-1–4°C) and 40° to 50° (4–10°C) in summer. Rainfall varies from 40 inches a year on the western end of the crater to more than 200 inches on the eastern side. Bring boots, waterproof gear, warm clothes, extra layers, and lots of sunscreen—the sun shines very brightly up here. For the latest weather information, call ℂ **808/871-5054.**

Cabins It can get really cold and windy down in the valley (see "A Word of Warning About the Weather," above), so try for a cabin. They're warm, protected from the elements, and reasonably priced. Each has 12 padded bunks (but no bedding; bring your own), a table, chairs, cooking utensils, a two-burner propane stove, and a wood-burning stove with firewood (you may also have a few cockroaches). The cabins are spaced so that each one is an easy walk from the other: Holua cabin is on the Halemauu Trail, Kapalaoa cabin on Sliding Sands Trail, and Paliku cabin on the eastern end by the Kaupo Gap. The rates are $40 a night for groups of one to six, $80 a night for groups of 7 to 12.

The cabins are so popular that the National Park Service has a lottery system for reservations. Requests for cabins must be made 3 months in advance (be sure to request alternate dates). You can request all three cabins at once; you're limited to 2 nights in one cabin and 3 nights total in the wilderness each month.

Campgrounds If you don't win the cabin lottery, all is not lost—there are three tent-camping sites that can accommodate you: two in the wilderness and one just outside at Hosmer Grove. There is no charge for tent camping.

Hosmer Grove, located at 6,800 feet, is a small, open, grassy area surrounded by a forest. Trees protect campers from the winds, but nights still get very cold; sometimes there's ice on the ground up here. This is the best place to spend the night in a tent if you want to see the Haleakala sunrise. Come up the day before, enjoy the park, take a day hike, then turn in early. The enclosed-glass summit building opens at sunrise for those who come to greet the dawn—a welcome windbreak. Facilities at Hosmer Grove include a covered pavilion with picnic tables and grills, chemical toilets, and drinking water. No permits are needed, and there's no charge—but you can only stay for 3 nights in a 30-day period.

The two tent-camping areas inside the volcano are **Holua,** just off Halemauu at 6,920 feet; and **Paliku,** just before the Kaupo Gap at the eastern end of the valley, at 6,380 feet. Facilities at both campgrounds are limited to pit toilets and nonpotable catchment water. Water at Holua is limited, especially in summer. No open fires are allowed inside the volcano, so bring a stove if you plan to cook. Tent camping is restricted to the signed area. No camping is allowed in the horse pasture. The inviting grassy lawn in front of the cabin is off-limits. Camping is free, but limited to 2 consecutive nights, and no more than 3 nights a month inside the volcano. Permits are issued at Park Headquarters, daily from 8am to 3pm, on a first-come, first-served basis on the day you plan to camp. Occupancy is limited to 25 people in each campground.

HIKING & CAMPING AT KIPAHULU (NEAR HANA)

In the East Maui section of Haleakala National Park, you can set up at **Oheo Campground,** a first-come, first-served, drive-in campground with tent sites for 100 near the ocean. It has a few tables, barbecue grills, and chemical toilets. No permit is required, but there's a 3-night limit. No food or drinking water is available, so bring your own. Bring a tent as well—it rains 75 inches a year here. Contact **Kipahulu Ranger Station,** Haleakala National Park, HI 96713 (© **808/ 248-7375;** www.nps.gov/hale), for information.

HIKING FROM THE SUMMIT If you hike from the crater rim down **Kaupo Gap** to the ocean, more than 20 miles away, you'll pass through several climate zones. On a clear day, you can see every island except Kauai on the trip down.

APPROACHING KIPAHULU FROM HANA If you drive to Kipahulu, you'll have to approach it from the Hana Highway, because it's not accessible from the summit. From the ranger station, it's a short hike above the famous **Oheo Gulch** (which was misnamed the Seven Sacred Pools in the 1940s) to two spectacular waterfalls. The first, **Makahiku Falls,** is easily reached from the central parking area; the trailhead begins near the ranger station. Pipiwai Trail leads you up to the road and beyond for a half-mile to the overlook. If you hike another 1½ miles up the trail across two bridges and through a bamboo forest, you reach **Waimoku Falls.** It's a good uphill hike, but press on to avoid the pool's crowd. In hard rain, streams swell quickly. Always be aware of your surroundings.

SKYLINE TRAIL, POLIPOLI SPRINGS STATE RECREATION AREA

This is some hike—strenuous but worth every step if you like seeing the big picture. It's 8 miles, all downhill, with a dazzling 100-mile view of the islands dotting the blue Pacific, plus the West Maui Mountains, which seem like a separate island.

The trail is just outside Haleakala National Park at Polipoli Springs Recreation Area; however, you access it by going through the national park to the summit. It starts just beyond the Puu Ulaula summit building on the south side of Science City and follows the southwest rift zone of Haleakala from its lunarlike cinder cones to a cool redwood grove. The trail drops 3,800 feet on a 4-hour hike to the recreation area in the 12,000-acre Kahikinui Forest Reserve. If you'd rather drive, you'll need a four-wheel-drive vehicle.

There's a campground at the recreation area at 6,300 feet. No fee or reservations are required, but your stay must be limited to 5 nights. Tent camping is free, but you'll need a permit. One 10-bunk cabin is available for $45 a night for one to four guests ($5 for each additional guest); it has a cold shower and a gas stove, but no electricity or drinking water (bring your own). To reserve, write the **State Parks Division,** 54 High St., Rm. 101, Wailuku, HI 96793, or call ✆ **808/984-8109** Monday through Friday between 8am and 4pm.

POLIPOLI STATE PARK ✦

One of the most unusual hiking experiences in the state can be found at Polipoli State Park, part of the 21,000-acre Kula and Kahikinui Forest Reserve on the slope of Haleakala. At Polipoli, it's hard to believe that you're in Hawaii: First of all, it's cold, even in summer, because the elevation is 5,300 to 6,200 feet; second, this former forest of native koa, ohia, and mamane trees, which was overlogged in the 1800s, was reforested in the 1930s with introduced species: pine, Monterey cypress, ash, sugi, red adler, redwood, and several varieties of eucalyptus. The result is a cool area, with muted sunlight filtered by towering trees.

The **Polipoli Loop** is an easy 5-mile hike that takes about 3 hours; dress warmly for it. Take the Haleakala Highway (Hwy. 37) to Keokea and turn right onto Highway 337; after less than a half-mile, turn on Waipoli Road, which climbs swiftly. After 10 miles, Waipoli Road ends at the Polipoli State Park campgrounds. The well-marked trailhead is next to the parking lot, near a stand of Monterey cypresses; the tree-lined trail offers the best view of the island.

Polipoli Loop is really a network of three trails: Haleakala Ridge, Plum Trail, and Redwood Trail. After a half-mile of meandering through groves of eucalyptus, blackwood, swamp mahogany, and hybrid cypress, you'll join the Haleakala Ridge Trail, which, about a mile into the trail, joins with the Plum Trail (named for the plums that ripen in June and July). This trail passes through massive redwoods and by an old Conservation Corps bunkhouse and a run-down cabin before joining up with the Redwood Trail, which climbs through Mexican pine, tropical ash, Port Orford cedar, and—of course—redwood.

Camping is allowed with a $5-per-night permit from the **State Parks Division,** 54 S. High St., Rm. 101, Wailuku, HI 96793 (© **808/984-8109**). There's one cabin, available by reservation.

KANAHA BEACH PARK CAMPING

One of the few Maui County camping facilities on the island is Kanaha Beach Park, located next to the Kahului Airport. The county has two separate areas for camping: seven tent sites on the beach and an additional 10 tent sites inland. This well-used park is a favorite of windsurfers, who take advantage of the strong winds that roar across this end of the island. Facilities include a paved parking lot, portable toilets, outdoor showers, barbecue grills, and picnic tables. Camping is limited to no more than three consecutive days; the permit fee is $3 per adult and 50 cents for children, per night, and can be obtained from the **Maui County Parks and Recreation Department,** 1580-C Kaahumanu Ave., Wailuku, HI 96793 (© **808/243-7389;** www.mauimapp.com). The 17 sites book up quickly; reserve your dates far in advance (the county will accept reservations a year in advance).

WAIANAPANAPA STATE PARK ★★

Tucked in a tropical jungle, on the outskirts of the little coastal town of Hana, is Waianapanapa State Park, a black-sand beach set in an emerald forest.

The **Hana-Waianapanapa Coast Trail** is an easy 6-mile hike that takes you back in time. Allow 4 hours to walk along this relatively flat trail, which parallels the sea, along lava cliffs and a forest of lauhala trees. The best time to take the hike is either in the early morning or late afternoon, when the light on the lava and surf makes for great photos. Midday is the worst time; not only is it hot (lava intensifies the heat), but there's also no shade or potable water available.

There's no formal trailhead; join the route at any point along the Waianapanapa Campground and go in either direction. Along the trail, you'll see remains of an ancient *heiau* (temple), stands of lauhala trees, caves, a blowhole, and a remarkable plant, *naupaka,* that flourishes along the beach. Upon close inspection, you'll see that the naupaka have only half blossoms; according to Hawaiian legend, a similar plant living in the mountains has the other half of the blossoms. One ancient explanation is that the two plants represent never-to-be-reunited lovers: As the story goes, the couple bickered so much that the gods, fed up with their incessant quarreling, banished one lover to the mountain and the other to the sea.

Waianapanapa has 12 cabins and a tent campground. Go for the cabins (see "Where to Stay," earlier in this chapter), as it rains torrentially here, sometimes turning the campground into a mud-wrestling arena. Tent-camping is $5 per night but limited to 5 nights in a 30-day period. Permits are available from the **State Parks Division,** 54 S. High St., Rm. 101, Wailuku, HI 96793 (© **808/984-8109**). Facilities include restrooms, outdoor showers, drinking water, and picnic tables.

HANA: THE HIKE TO FAGAN'S CROSS

This 3-mile hike to the cross erected in memory of Paul Fagan, the founder of Hana Ranch and Hotel Hana-Maui, offers spectacular views of the Hana Coast, particularly at sunset. The uphill trail starts across Hana Highway from the Hotel Hana-Maui. Enter the pastures at your own risk; they're often occupied by glaring bulls with sharp horns and cows with new calves. Watch your step as you ascend this steep hill on a Jeep trail across open pastures to the cross and the breathtaking view.

8 Golf & Other Outdoor Pursuits

GOLF

For last-minute and discount tee times, call **Stand-by Golf** (✆ **888/645-BOOK** or 808/874-0600; www.stand-bygolf.com) between 7am and 9pm. Stand-by offers discounted (up to 50% off green fees), guaranteed tee times for same-day or next-day golfing.

Golf Club Rentals (✆ **808/665-0800;** www.maui.net/~rentgolf) has custom-built clubs for men, women, and juniors (both right- and left-handed), which can be delivered islandwide; the rates are just $15 to $25 a day. The company also offers lessons with pros starting at $150 for 9 holes plus greens fees.

WEST MAUI

Kaanapali Courses ⚐ Both courses at Kaanapali offer a challenge to all golfers, from high handicappers to near-pros. The par-72, 6,305-yard **North Course** is a true Robert Trent Jones design: an abundance of wide bunkers; several long, stretched-out tees; and the largest, most contoured greens on Maui. The tricky 18th hole (par 4, 435 yd.) has a water hazard on the approach to the green. The par-72, 6,250-yard **South Course** is an Arthur Jack Snyder design; although shorter than the North Course, it requires more accuracy on the narrow, hilly fairways. It also has a water hazard on its final hole, so don't tally up your scorecard until you sink the final putt.

Facilities include a driving range, putting course, and clubhouse with dining. You'll have a better chance of getting a tee time on weekdays.

Off Hwy. 30, Kaanapali. ✆ **808/661-3691.** www.kaanapali-golf.com. Greens fees: $150 (North Course), $142 (South Course); Kaanapali guests pay $130 (North), $117 (South); twilight rates after 2pm are $77 (North), $74 (South) for everyone. At the first stoplight in Kaanapali, turn onto Kaanapali Pkwy.; the first building on your right is the clubhouse.

Kapalua Resort Courses ⚐⚐⚐ The views from these three championship courses are worth the greens fees alone. The par-72, 6,761-yard **Bay Course** (✆ **808/669-8820**) was designed by Arnold Palmer and Ed Seay. This course is a bit forgiving, with its wide fairways; the greens, however, are difficult to read. The often-photographed fifth overlooks a small ocean cove; even the pros have trouble with this rocky par-3, 205-yard hole. The par-71, 6,632-yard **Village Course** (✆ **808/669-8830**), another Palmer/Seay design, is the most scenic of the three courses. The hole with the best vista is the sixth, which overlooks a lake with the ocean in the distance. But don't get distracted by the view—the tee is between two rows of Cook pines. The **Plantation Course** (✆ **808/669-8877**), site of the Mercedes Championships, is a Ben Crenshaw/Bill Coore design. This 6,547-yard, par-73 course, set on a rolling hillside, is excellent for developing your low shots and precise chipping.

Facilities for all three courses include locker rooms, a driving range, and an excellent restaurant. Weekdays are your best bet for tee times.

Off Hwy. 30, Kapalua. ✆ **877/KAPALUA.** www.kapaluamaui.com. Greens fees: $180 ($125 for hotel guests) at the Village and Bay courses ($80 after 2pm); $220 ($135 for guests) at the Plantation Course ($85 after 2pm).

SOUTH MAUI

Elleair Maui Golf Club (formerly Silversword Golf Club) Sitting in the foothills of Haleakala, just high enough to afford spectacular ocean vistas from every hole, this is a course for golfers who love the views as much as the fairways and greens. It's very forgiving. *Just one caveat:* Go in the morning. Not only is it cooler, but more important, it's also less windy. In the afternoon, the winds bluster down Haleakala with great gusto. This is a fun course to play, with some challenging holes; the par-5 second hole is a virtual minefield of bunkers, and the par-5 eighth hole shoots over a swale and then uphill.

1345 Piilani Hwy. (near Lipoa St. turnoff), Kihei. © 808/874-0777. Greens fees: $85; twilight rates (after 2pm) are $65; 9-hole rates (after 3:30pm) are $45.

Makena Courses ★★ Here you'll find 36 holes of "Mr. Hawaii Golf"— Robert Trent Jones Jr.—at its best. Add to that spectacular views: Molokini islet looms in the background, humpback whales gambol offshore in winter, and the tropical sunsets are spectacular. The par-72, 6,876-yard **South Course** has a couple of holes you'll never forget. The view from the par-4 15th hole, which shoots from an elevated tee 183 yards downhill to the Pacific, is magnificent. The 16th hole has a two-tiered green that's blind from the tee 383 yards away (that is, if you make it past the gully off the fairway). The par-72, 6,823-yard **North Course** is more difficult and more spectacular. The 13th hole, located partway up the mountain, has a view that makes most golfers stop and stare. The next hole is even more memorable: a 200-foot drop between tee and green.

Facilities include a clubhouse, a driving range, two putting greens, a pro shop, lockers, and lessons. Beware of weekend crowds.

On Makena Alanui Dr., just past the Maui Prince Hotel. © 808/879-3344. www.maui.net/~makena/. Greens fees: North Course $155 ($90–$135 for Makena Resort guests), twilight fees (after 2pm) are $80–$90 ($70–$80 for guests); South Course $175 ($100–$145 for resort guests), twilight fees (after 2 pm) are $100 ($80–$90 for guests); guest rates vary seasonally, with higher rates in the winter.

Wailea Courses ★★ There are three courses to choose from at Wailea. The **Blue Course,** a par-72, 6,758-yard course designed by Arthur Jack Snyder and dotted with bunkers and water hazards, is for duffers and pros alike. The wide fairways appeal to beginners, while the undulating terrain makes it a course everyone can enjoy. A little more difficult is the par-72, 7,078-yard championship **Gold Course,** with narrow fairways, several tricky dogleg holes, and the classic Robert Trent Jones Jr. challenges: natural hazards, like lava-rock walls, and native Hawaiian grasses. The **Emerald Course,** also designed by Robert Trent Jones Jr., is Wailea's newest, with tropical landscaping and a player-friendly design.

With 54 holes to play, getting a tee time is slightly easier on weekends than at other resorts, but weekdays are best (the Emerald Course is usually the toughest to book). Facilities include two pro shops, restaurants, locker rooms, and a complete golf training facility.

Wailea Alanui Dr. (off Wailea Iki Dr.), Wailea. © 888/328-MAUI or 808/875-7450. www.waileagolf.com. Greens fees: Blue Course $140 ($115 resort guests), twlight $90 ($80 resort guests); Gold Course $160 ($115 resort guests); Emerald Course $150 ($125 resort guests).

UPCOUNTRY MAUI

Pukalani Country Club This cool, par-72, 6,962-yard course at 1,100 feet offers a break from the resorts' high greens fees, and it's really fun to play. The third hole offers golfers two different options: a tough (especially into the wind) iron shot from the tee, across a gully (yuck!) to the green; or a shot down the side of the gully across a second green into sand traps below. (Most people choose to shoot down the side of the gully; it's actually easier than shooting across a ravine.) High handicappers will love this course, and more experienced players can make it more challenging by playing from the back tees. Facilities include club and shoe rentals, practice areas, lockers, a pro shop, and a restaurant.

360 Pukalani St., Pukalani. (✆ 808/572-1314. www.pukalanigolf.com. Greens fees, including cart, are $60 for 18 holes before 11am; $50 11am–2pm; $40 after 2pm. Take the Hana Hwy. (Hwy. 36) to Haleakala Hwy. (Hwy. 37) to the Pukalani exit; turn right onto Pukalani St. and go 2 blocks.

BICYCLING

If you want to venture out on your own, cheap rentals—$10 a day for cruisers and $25 a day for mountain bikes—are available from **Activity Warehouse** (✆ **800/923-4004;** www.travelhawaii.com), which has branches in Lahaina at 578 Front St., near Prison Street (✆ **808/661-1970**), and in Kihei at Azeka Place II, on the mountain side of Kihei Road near Lipoa Street (✆ **808/875-4050**).

For information on bikeways and maps, check out **www.bikehawaii.com** or get a copy of the *Maui County Bicycle Map,* which has information on road suitability, climate, mileage, elevation changes, bike shops, safety tips, and various bicycling routes. The map is available for $7.50 ($6.25 for the map and $1.25 for postage), bank checks or money orders only, from **Tri Isle R, C, and D Council,** Attn: Bike Map Project, 200 Imi Kala St., Suite 208, Wailuku, HI 96793.

CRUISING HALEAKALA ✮ It's not even close to dawn, but here you are, rubbing your eyes awake, riding in a van up the long, dark road to the top of Maui's dormant volcano. It's colder than you ever thought possible for a tropical island. The air is thin. You stomp your chilly feet while you wait, sipping hot coffee. Then comes the sun, exploding over the yawning Haleakala Crater, big enough to swallow Manhattan—a mystic moment you won't soon forget. Now you know why Hawaiians named the crater the House of the Sun. But there's no time to linger: Decked out in your screaming-yellow parka, you mount your mechanical steed and test its most important feature, the brakes—because you're about to coast 37 miles down a 10,000-foot volcano.

Cruising down Haleakala, from the lunarlike landscape at the top past flower farms, pineapple fields, and eucalyptus groves, is quite an experience—and just about anybody can do it. This is a safe, no-strain bicycle trip that requires some stamina in the colder, wetter winter months but is fun for everyone in the warmer months—the key word being *warmer.* In winter and the rainy season, conditions can be harsh, especially on the top, with below-freezing temperatures and 40 mile-per-hour winds.

Maui's oldest downhill company is **Maui Downhill** ✮ (✆ **800/535-BIKE** or 808/871-2155; www.mauidownhill.com), which offers a sunrise safari bike tour, including continental breakfast and brunch, starting at $150 (book online and save $48). If it's all booked up, try **Maui Mountain Cruisers** (✆ **800/232-6284** or 808/871-6014; www.mauimountaincruisers.com), which has sunrise trips at $125 (book online and save 15%), or **Mountain Riders Bike Tours** (✆ **800/706-7700** or 808/242-9739; www.mountainriders.com), with sunrise rides for $115 (book online for $98). All rates include hotel pickup, transport to the top, bicycle, safety equipment, and meals. Wear layers of warm clothing—there may be a 30°F change in temperature from the top of the mountain to the ocean. Generally, the tour groups will not take riders under 12, but younger children can ride along in the van that accompanies the groups. Pregnant women should also ride in the van.

If you want to avoid the crowd and go down the mountain at your own pace, call **Haleakala Bike Company** (© **888/922-2453;** www.bikemaui.com), which will outfit you with the latest gear and take you up to the top, then after making sure you are secure on the bike will let you ride down by yourself at your own pace. Trips range from $65 to $85; they also have bicycle rentals to tour other parts of Maui on your own (from $45 a day).

HORSEBACK RIDING

Maui offers spectacular adventure rides through rugged ranchlands, into tropical forests, and to remote swimming holes. For a 5½-hour tour on horseback—complete with swimming and lunch—call **Adventure on Horseback** (© **808/242-7445** or 808/572-6211; www.mauihorsewhisperer.com); the cost is $185 per person, including a hearty lunch. The day begins over coffee and pastries, while owner Frank Levinson matches the horses to the riders, in terms of both skill and personality. Frank leads small groups across pastures, through thick rain forests, alongside streams, and up to waterfalls and pools. He recently added a "Maui Horse Whisperer Experience" which includes a seminar on the language of the horse, $200 for half day and $300 for full day workshops. No horse lover should pass it up.

If you're out in Hana, **Oheo Stables,** Kipahulu Ranch (a mile past Oheo Gulch), Kipahulu (© **808/667-2222;** www.mauihorse.com), offers two daily rides through the mountains above Oheo Gulch (Seven Sacred Pools). The best deal is the 10:30am ride ($129), which includes a snack during the 3-hour adventure (2½ hours in the saddle) into Haleakala National Park. You'll stop at scenic spots like Pipiwai Lookout, where you can glimpse the 400-foot Waimoku Falls.

If you enjoy your ride, remember to kiss your horse and tip your guide.

HALEAKALA ON HORSEBACK   If you'd like to ride down into Haleakala's crater, contact **Pony Express Tours** ✦ (© **808/667-2200** or 808/878-6698; www.ponyexpresstours.com), which offers a variety of rides down to the crater floor and back up, from $155 to $190 per person. Shorter 1- and 2-hour rides are also offered at Haleakala Ranch, located on the beautiful lower slopes of the volcano, for $60 and $105. If you book via the Internet, you get 10% off. Pony Express provides well-trained horses and experienced guides, and accommodates all riding levels. You must be at least 10 years old, weigh no more than 230 pounds, and wear long pants and closed-toe shoes.

WAY OUT WEST ON MAUI: RANCH RIDES   We recommend riding with **Mendes Ranch & Trail Rides** ✦, 3530 Kahekili Hwy., 4 miles past Wailuku (© **808/244-7320;** www.mendesranch.com). The 300-acre Mendes Ranch is a real-life working cowboy ranch that has the essential elements of an earthly paradise—rainbows, waterfalls, palm trees, coral-sand beaches, lagoons, tide pools, a rain forest, and its own volcanic peak (more than a mile high). Allan Mendes, a third-generation wrangler, will take you from the edge of the rain forest out to the sea. On the way, you'll cross tree-studded meadows where Texas longhorns sit in the shade and pass a dusty corral where Allan's father, Ernest, a champion roper, may be breaking in a wild horse. Allan keeps close watch, turning often in his saddle to make sure everyone is happy. He points out flora and fauna and fields questions, but generally just lets you soak up Maui's natural splendor in golden silence. The morning ride, which lasts 3 hours and ends with a barbecue

Kids Especially for Kids

Taking a Submarine Ride Atlantis Submarines takes you and the kids down into the shallow coastal waters off Lahaina in a real sub, where you'll see plenty of fish (and maybe even a shark!). They'll love it, and you'll stay dry the entire time.

Riding the Sugarcane Train Small kids love this ride, as do train buffs of all ages. A steam engine pulls open-passenger cars of the Lahaina/Kaanapali and Pacific Railroad on a 30-minute, 12-mile round-trip through sugarcane fields between Lahaina and Kaanapali while the conductor sings and calls out the landmarks. Along the way, you can see the hidden parts of Kaanapali, and the islands of Molokai and Lanai beyond. Tickets are $16 for adults, $8.75 for kids ages 3 to 12; call ℂ 808/661-0080 for details.

Searching for Stars After sunset, the stars over Kaanapali shine big and bright, because the tropical sky is almost pollutant-free and no big-city lights interfere with the cosmic view. Amateur astronomers can probe the Milky Way, see the rings of Saturn and Jupiter's moons, and scan the Sea of Tranquillity in a 60-minute star search on the world's first recreational computer-driven telescope. This cosmic adventure takes place nightly at the **Hyatt Regency Maui,** 200 Nohea Kai Dr. (ℂ **808/661-1234**), at 8, 9, and 10pm. If you are staying at the hotel it is $20 for adults and $10 for children 12 and under, and $25 for nonguests (adults) and $15 for children of nonguests.

back at the corral (the perfect ranch-style lunch after a morning in the saddle), is $130; the 2½-hour afternoon ride costs $85, including snacks.

TENNIS

Maui has excellent public tennis courts; all are free and available from daylight to sunset (a few are even lit for night play until 10pm). The courts are available on a first-come, first-served basis; when someone's waiting, limit your play to 45 minutes. For a complete list of public courts, call **Maui County Parks and Recreation** (ℂ 808/243-7230). But most public courts require a wait and are not conveniently located near the major resort areas, so most visitors are likely to play at their own hotels for a fee. The exceptions to this are in Kihei (which has courts in Kalama Park on South Kihei Road, and in Waipualani Park on West Waipualani Road, behind the Maui Sunset Condo), in Lahaina (courts are in Malu'uou o lele Park, at Front and Shaw sts.), and Hana (courts are in Hana Park, on the Hana Hwy.).

Private tennis courts are available at most resorts and hotels on the island. The **Kapalua Tennis Garden and Village Tennis Center,** Kapalua Resort (ℂ 808/669-5677; www.kapaluamaui.com), is home to the Kapalua Open, which features the largest purse in the state, on Labor Day weekend. Court rentals are $10 an hour for resort guests and $12 an hour for nonguests. The staff will match you up with a partner if you need one. In Wailea, try the **Wailea Tennis Club,** 131 Wailea Iki Place (ℂ **808/879-1958;** www.wailea-resort.com), with 11 Plexipave courts. Court fees are $30 for Wailea resort guests and $35 for non-guests.

9 Seeing the Sights

CENTRAL MAUI

Central Maui isn't exactly tourist central; this is where real people live. Most likely, you'll land here and head directly to the beach. However, there are a few sights worth checking out if you feel like a respite from the sun 'n' surf.

KAHULUI

Under the airport flight path, next to Maui's busiest intersection and across from Costco and Kmart in Kahului's new business park, is a most unlikely place: the **Kanaha Wildlife Sanctuary,** Haleakala Highway Extension and Hana Highway (© **808/984-8100**). Look for the parking area off Haleakala Highway Extension (behind the mall, across the Hana Hwy. from Cutter Automotive), and you'll find a 50-yard trail that meanders along the shore to a shade shelter and lookout. Look for the sign proclaiming this the permanent home of the endangered black-neck Hawaiian stilt, whose population is now down to about 1,000. Naturalists say this is a good place to see endangered Hawaiian Koloa ducks, stilts, coots, and other migrating shorebirds. For a quieter, more natural-looking wildlife preserve, see the **Kealia Pond National Wildlife Preserve,** in Kihei (below).

WAILUKU & WAIKAPU

Wailuku, the historic gateway to Iao Valley, is worth a visit for a little antiquing and a visit to the **Bailey House Museum** ✦, 2375-A Main St. (© **808/244-3326**). Missionary and sugar planter Edward Bailey's 1833 home—an architectural hybrid of stones laid by Hawaiian craftsmen and timbers joined in a display of Yankee ingenuity—is a treasure trove of Hawaiiana. Inside, you'll find an eclectic collection, from precontact artifacts like scary temple images, dogtooth necklaces, and a rare lei made of tree snail shells to latter-day relics like Duke Kahanamoku's 1919 redwood surfboard and a koa-wood table given to Pres. Ulysses S. Grant, who had to refuse it because he couldn't accept gifts from foreign countries. There's also a gallery devoted to a few of Bailey's landscapes, painted from 1866 to 1896, which capture on canvas a Maui we can only imagine today. It's open Monday through Saturday from 10am to 4pm; admission is $4 for adults, $3.50 for seniors, and $1 for children ages 6 to 12.

About 3 miles south of Wailuku lies the tiny, one-street village of Waikapu, which has two attractions that are worth a peek. Relive Maui's past by taking a 40-minute narrated tram ride around fields of pineapple, sugarcane, and papaya trees at **Maui Tropical Plantation,** 1670 Honoapiilani Hwy. (© **800/451-6805** or 808/244-7643), a real working plantation open daily from 9am to 5pm. A shop sells fresh and dried fruit, and a restaurant serves lunch. Admission is free; the tram tours, which start at 10am and leave about every 45 minutes, are $9.50 for adults, $3.50 for kids ages 3 to 12.

Marilyn Monroe and Frank Lloyd Wright meet for dinner every night at one of Maui's most unusual buildings, the **Waikapu Golf and Country Club,** 2500 Honoapiilani Hwy. (© **808/244-2011**). Neither actually set foot on Maui, but these icons of architecture and glamour share a Hawaiian legacy. Wright designed this place for a Pennsylvania family in 1949, but it was never constructed. In 1957, Marilyn and her husband, Arthur Miller, wanted it built for them in Connecticut, but they separated the following year. When Tokyo billionaire Takeshi Sekiguchi went shopping at Taliesen West for a signature building to adorn his 18-hole golf course, he found the blueprints and had Marilyn's

Wright house cleverly redesigned as a clubhouse. A horizontal in a vertical landscape, it doesn't quite fit the setting, but it's still the best-looking building on Maui today.

IAO VALLEY ✦

A couple of miles north of Wailuku, where the little plantation houses stop and the road climbs ever higher, Maui's true nature begins to reveal itself. The transition from suburban sprawl to raw nature is so abrupt that most people who drive up into the valley don't realize they're suddenly in a rain forest. The moist, cool air, and the shade a welcome comfort after the hot tropic sun. This is Iao Valley, a 6¼-acre state park whose great nature, history, and beauty have been enjoyed by millions of people from around the world for more than a century. Iao ("Supreme Light") Valley, 10 miles long and encompassing 4,000 acres, is the eroded volcanic caldera of the West Maui Mountains. The head of the valley is a broad circular amphitheater where four major streams converge into Iao Stream. At the back of the amphitheater is rain-drenched Puu Kukui, the West Maui Mountains' highest point. No other Hawaiian valley lets you go from seacoast to rain forest so easily. This peaceful valley, full of tropical plants, rainbows, waterfalls, swimming holes, and hiking trails, is a place of solitude, reflection, and escape for residents and visitors alike.

To get here from Wailuku, take Main Street to Iao Valley Road to the entrance to the state park.

Two paved walkways loop into the massive green amphitheater, across the bridge of Iao Valley Stream, and along the stream itself. This paved, ⅓-mile loop is Maui's easiest hike—you can take your grandmother on this one. The leisurely walk will allow you to enjoy lovely views of the Iao Needle and the lush vegetation. Others often proceed beyond the state park border and take two trails deeper into the valley, but the trails enter private land, and NO TRESPASSING signs are posted.

The feature known as **Iao Needle** is an erosional remnant consisting of basalt dikes. This phallic rock juts an impressive 2,250 feet above sea level. Youngsters play in **Iao Stream,** a peaceful brook that belies its bloody history. In 1790, King Kamehameha the Great and his men engaged in the bloody battle of Iao Valley to gain control of Maui. When the battle ended, so many bodies blocked Iao Stream that the battle site was named Kepaniwai, or "damming of the waters."

Moments Flying High: Helicopter Rides

Only a helicopter can bring you face to face with volcanoes, waterfalls, and remote places like Maui's little-known Wall of Tears, up near the summit of Puu Kukui in the West Maui Mountains. A helicopter trip on Maui isn't a wild ride; it's more like a gentle zip into a seldom-seen Eden. Today's pilots are part Hawaiian historian, part DJ, part amusement-ride operator, and part tour guide, telling you about Hawaii's flora and fauna, history, and culture. **Blue Hawaiian Helicopters** ✦✦✦ (© **800/745-BLUE** or 808/871-8844; www.bluehawaiian.com) is the Cadillac of helicopter-tour companies. They have the latest, high-tech, environmentally friendly (and quiet) Eco-Star helicopter, specially designed for air-tour operators. Flights vary from 30 minutes to 100 minutes and range from $125 to $335.

An architectural heritage park of Hawaiian, Japanese, Chinese, Filipino, and New England–style houses stands in harmony by Iao Stream at **Kepaniwai Heritage Garden.** This is a good picnic spot, with plenty of tables and benches. You can see ferns, banana trees, and other native and exotic plants in the **Iao Valley Botanic Garden** along the stream.

WHEN TO GO   The park is open daily from 7am to 7pm. Go early in the morning or late in the afternoon, when the sun's rays slant into the valley and create a mystical mood. You can bring a picnic and spend the day, but be prepared at any time for a tropical cloudburst, which often soaks the valley and swells both waterfalls and streams.

INFORMATION & VISITOR CENTERS   For information, contact **Iao Valley State Park,** State Parks and Recreation, 54 High St., Rm. 101, Wailuku, HI 96793 (© **808/984-8100**). The **Hawaii Nature Center,** 875 Iao Valley Rd. (© **808/244-6500;** www.hawaiinaturecenter.org), home to the Iao Valley Nature Center, features hands-on, interactive exhibits and displays relating the story of Hawaiian natural history; it's an important stop for all who want to explore Iao Valley. Hours are daily from 10am to 4pm; admission is $6 for adults and $4 for children ages 4 to 12.

THE SCENIC ROUTE TO WEST MAUI: THE KAHEKILI HIGHWAY

The usual road to West Maui from Wailuku is the Honoapiilani Highway, which takes you across the isthmus to Maalaea and around to Lahaina, Kaapanali, and Kapalua. But those wanting a back-to-nature driving experience should go the other way, along the **Kahekili Highway** (Hwy. 340). (*Highway* is a bit of a euphemism for this paved but somewhat precarious road.)

Drive north from Wailuku to Waiehu and onto this road named for King Kahekili, who built houses out of the skulls of his enemies. The true wild nature of Maui is on full display here. The narrow and winding road weaves for 20 miles along an ancient Hawaiian coastal footpath to Honokohau Bay, at the island's northernmost tip, past blowholes, sea stacks, seabird rookeries, and the imposing 636-foot Kahakaloa headland. On the land side, you'll pass high cliffs, deep valleys dotted with plantation houses, cattle grazing on green plateaus, old wooden churches, taro fields, and houses hung with fishing nets. It's slow going (you can drive only about 10 mph along the road), but it's probably the most beautiful drive in Maui. Your rental-car company might try to deter you, but it's not really a hard drive (don't go if it has been raining), and the views are spectacular.

At Honokohau, pick up Highway 30 and continue on to the West Maui resorts; the first one you'll reach is Kapalua (see below).

WEST MAUI

For a map of attractions in Lahaina and Kaanapali, see p. 361.

KAPALUA

For generations, West Maui meant one thing: pineapple. Hawaii's only pineapple cannery today, **Maui Pineapple Co.,** offers tours of its plantation through the Kapalua Resort Activity Center, www.kapaluamaui.com (© **808/669-8088**). Real plantation workers lead the 2½-hour tours. You'll learn about the history of West Maui, facts about growing and harvesting pineapple, and lots of trivia about plantation life; you can even pick and harvest your own pineapple.

The tours, which depart from the Kapalua Villas Reception Center, 500 Office Rd., are offered twice daily Monday through Friday, at 9:30am and 1pm. It costs $26; children must be at least 12.

A WHALE OF A PLACE IN KAANAPALI

If you haven't seen a real whale yet, go to **Whalers Village,** 2435 Kaanapali Pkwy., an oceanfront shopping center that has adopted the whale as its mascot. You can't miss it: A huge, almost life-size metal sculpture of a mother whale and two nursing calves greets you. A few more steps, and you're met by the looming, bleached-white bony skeleton of a 40-foot sperm whale; it's pretty impressive.

On the second floor of the mall is the **Whale Center of the Pacific** (© **808/661-5992**), a museum celebrating the "Golden Era of Whaling" (1825–60). Harpoons and scrimshaw are on display; the museum has even re-created the cramped quarters of a whaler's seagoing vessel. It's open daily from 9:30am to 10pm; admission is free.

HISTORIC LAHAINA

Back when "there was no God west of the Horn," Lahaina was the capital of Hawaii and the Pacific's wildest port. Today, it's a milder version of its old self—mostly a hustle-bustle of whale art, timeshares, and "Just Got Lei'd" T-shirts. We're not sure the rowdy whalers would be pleased. But if you look hard, you'll still find the historic port town they loved, filled with the kind of history that inspired James Michener to write his best-selling epic novel *Hawaii.*

Baldwin Home Museum ☆ The oldest house in Lahaina, this coral-and-rock structure was built in 1834 by Rev. Dwight Baldwin, a doctor with the fourth company of American missionaries to sail 'round the Horn to Hawaii. Like many missionaries, he came to Hawaii to do good—and did very well for himself. After 17 years of service, Baldwin was granted 2,600 acres in Kapalua for farming and grazing. His ranch manager experimented with what Hawaiians called *hala-kahiki,* or pineapple, on a 4-acre plot; the rest is history. The house looks as if Baldwin has just stepped out for a minute to tend a sick neighbor down the street.

Next door is the **Master's Reading Room,** Maui's oldest building. This became visiting sea captains' favorite hangout once the missionaries closed down all of Lahaina's grog shops and banned prostitution. By 1844, once hotels and bars started reopening, it lost its appeal. It's now the headquarters of the **Lahaina Restoration Foundation** (© **808/661-3262**), a plucky band of historians who try to keep this town alive and antique at the same time. Stop in and pick up a self-guided walking-tour map, which will take you to Lahaina's most historic sites.

120 Dickenson St. (at Front St.). © **808/661-3262.** Admission $3 adults, $2 seniors, $5 family. Daily 10am–4:30pm.

Banyan Tree Of all the banyan trees in Hawaii, this is the greatest of all—so big that you can't get it in your camera's viewfinder. It was only 8 feet tall when it was planted in 1873 by Maui Sheriff William O. Smith to mark the 50th anniversary of Lahaina's first Christian mission. Today, the big old banyan from India is more than 50 feet tall, has 12 major trunks, and shades two-thirds of an acre in Courthouse Square.

At the Courthouse Building, 649 Wharf St.

Day Trips to Molokai

It's possible to visit Molokai's famous leper colony (officially known as Kalaupapa National Historic Park) as a day trip from Maui. You won't be able to squeeze in the exhilarating mule ride down the 1,600-foot cliffs (they start at 8am), but you didn't want to sit on your own ass all day long anyway, now did you? (Sorry, bad pun.) **Pacific Wings** (© **808/873-0877;** www.pacificwings.com) offers daily scheduled flights to Kalaupapa from Honolulu for $163 round-trip or check out **Paragon Air,** www.paragon-air.com (© **808/244-3356**), which offers a $210 package deal that includes round-trip airfare from Kahului Airport to Molokai's Kalaupapa airport, a 4-hour tour, lunch, and drinks. All visitors must be at least 16 years old. Or you can take a ferry ride over to Molokai and then hike down to Kalaupapa and tour the legendary peninsula on the **Molokai Princess** (© **800/275-6969** or 808/667-6165 or www.mauiprincess.com) for $215 per person, including lunch.

The Brig *Carthaginian* ★ *Kids*   This restored square-rigged brigantine, an authentic replica of a 19th-century whaling ship, the kind that brought the first missionaries to Hawaii was closed for "repairs" when we went to press. Apparently the old vessel has become a liability and the people in charge were leaning towards getting rid of the old boat vs. repairing her. As we went to press, history lovers were frantically trying to raise funds to either restore the old ship or purchase another replica of the same era. If you don't see her proud masts at the foot of the Lahaina Pier, then you know her fate. If the ship is still there, drop by, the floating museum features exhibits on whales and 19th-century whaling life. You won't believe how cramped the living quarters were—they make today's cruise-ship cabins look downright roomy.

Lahaina Harbor. © **808/661-8527.** Admission $3 adults, $2 seniors, $5 family. Daily 10am–4:30pm.

Maluuluolele Park   At first glance, this Front Street park appears to be only a hot, dry, dusty softball field. But under home plate is an edge of Mokuula, where a royal compound once stood more than 100 years ago, now buried under tons of red dirt and sand. Here, Prince Kauikeaolui, who ascended the throne as King Kamehameha III when he was only 10, lived with the love of his life, his sister, Princess Nahienaena. Missionaries took a dim view of incest, which was acceptable to Hawaiian nobles in order to preserve the royal bloodline. Torn between love for her brother and the new Christian morality, Nahienaena grew despondent and died at the age of 21. King Kamehameha III, who reigned for 29 years—longer than any other Hawaiian monarch—presided over Hawaii as it went from kingdom to constitutional monarchy, and as power over the islands began to shift from island nobles to missionaries, merchants, and sugar planters. Kamehameha died in 1854; he was 39. In 1918, his royal compound, containing a mausoleum and artifacts of the kingdom, was demolished and covered with dirt to create a public park. The baseball team from Lahainaluna School, the first American school founded by missionaries west of the Rockies, now plays games on the site of this royal place, still considered sacred to many Hawaiians.

Front and Shaw sts.

SOUTH MAUI
MAALAEA

Maui Ocean Center ★★★ *(Kids*   This 5-acre facility houses the largest aquarium in Hawaii and features one of Hawaii's largest predators: the tiger shark. As you walk past the 3 dozen or so tanks and countless exhibits, you'll slowly descend from the "beach" to the deepest part of the ocean, without ever getting wet. Start at the surge pool, where you'll see shallow-water marine life like spiny urchins and cauliflower coral, then move on to the reef tanks, turtle pool, "touch" pool (with starfish and urchins), and eagle-ray pool before reaching the star of the show: the 100-foot-long, 600,000-gallon main tank featuring tiger, gray, and white-tip sharks, as well as tuna, surgeonfish, triggerfish, and numerous other tropicals. The most phenomenal thing about this tank is that the walkway goes right through it—so you'll be surrounded on three sides by marine creatures. A very cool place, and well worth the time.

Maalaea Harbor Village, 192 Maalaea Rd. (the triangle between Honoapiilani Hwy. and Maalaea Rd.) *©* **808/270-7000.** www.mauioceancenter.com. Admission $19 adults, $17 seniors, $13 children 3–12, $12 military adults ($6.50 for their children ages 3-12). Daily 9am–5pm (until 6 pm in July and Aug).

KIHEI

Capt. George Vancouver "discovered" Kihei in 1778, when it was only a collection of fishermen's grass shacks on the hot, dry, dusty coast (hard to believe, eh?). A **totem pole** stands today where he's believed to have landed, across from Aston Maui Lu Resort, 575 S. Kihei Rd. Vancouver sailed on to "discover" British Columbia, where a great international city and harbor now bear his name.

West of the junction of Piilani Highway (Hwy. 31) and Mokulele Highway (Hwy. 350) is **Kealia Pond National Wildlife Preserve** (*©* **808/875-1582**), a 700-acre U.S. Fish and Wildlife wetland preserve where endangered Hawaiian stilts, coots, and ducks hang out and splash. These ponds work two ways: as bird preserves and as sedimentation basins that keep the coral reefs from silting from runoff. You can take a self-guided tour along a boardwalk dotted with interpretive signs and shade shelters, through sand dunes, and around ponds to Maalaea Harbor. The boardwalk starts at the outlet of Kealia Pond on the ocean side of North Kihei Road (near mile marker 2 on Piilani Hwy.). Among the Hawaiian waterbirds seen here are the black-crowned high heron, Hawaiian coot, Hawaiian duck, and Hawaiian stilt. There also are shorebirds like sanderlings, Pacific golden plovers, ruddy turnstones, and wandering tattlers. From July to December, the hawksbill turtle comes ashore here to lay her eggs.

WAILEA

The best way to explore this golden resort coast is to rise with the sun and head for Wailea's 1½-mile **coastal nature trail** ★, stretching between the Kea Lani Hotel and the kiawe thicket just beyond the Renaissance Wailea. It's a great morning walk, a serpentine path that meanders uphill and down past native plants, old Hawaiian habitats, and a billion dollars' worth of luxury hotels. You can pick up the trail at any of the resorts or from clearly marked SHORELINE ACCESS points along the coast. The best time to go is when you first wake up; by midmorning, the coastal trail is too often clogged with pushy joggers, and it grows crowded with beachgoers as the day wears on. As the path crosses several bold black-lava points, it affords new vistas of islands and ocean; benches allow you to pause and contemplate the view across Alalakeiki Channel, where you may see jumping whales in season. Sunset is another good time to hit the trail.

MAKENA

A few miles south of Wailea, the manicured coast turns to wilderness; now you're in Makena. Once cattle were driven down the slope from upland ranches, lashed to rafts, and sent into the water to swim to boats that waited to take them to market. Now, **Makena Landing** ✯ is the best place to launch kayaks bound for La Pérouse Bay and Ahihi-Kinau preserve.

From the landing, go south on Makena Road; on the right is **Keawali Congregational Church** (✆ **808/879-5557**), built in 1855, with walls 3 feet thick. Surrounded by ti leaves, which by Hawaiian custom provide protection, and built of lava rock with coral used as mortar, this church sits on its own cove with a gold-sand beach. It always attracts a Sunday crowd for its 9:30am Hawaiian-language service.

A little farther south on the coast is **La Pérouse Monument,** a pyramid of lava rocks that marks the spot where French explorer Admiral Comte de la Pérouse set foot on Maui in 1786. The first Westerner to "discover" the island, he described the "burning climate" of the leeward coast, observed several fishing villages near Kihei, and sailed on into oblivion, never to be seen again; some believe he may have been eaten by cannibals in what now is Vanuatu. To get here, drive south past Puu Olai to Ahihi Bay, where the road turns to gravel. Go another 2 miles along the coast to La Pérouse Bay; the monument sits amid a clearing in black lava at the end of the dirt road.

HOUSE OF THE SUN: HALEAKALA NATIONAL PARK ✯✯✯

At once forbidding and compelling, Haleakala ("House of the Sun") National Park is Maui's main natural attraction. More than 1.3 million people a year go up the 10,023-foot-high mountain to peer down into the crater of the world's largest dormant volcano. (Haleakala is officially considered active, even though it has not rumbled since 1790.) That hole would hold Manhattan.

But there's more to do here than stare into a big black hole: Just going up the mountain is an experience. Where else on the planet can you climb from sea level to 10,000 feet in just 37 miles, or a 2-hour drive? The snaky road passes through big, puffy, cumulus clouds to offer magnificent views of the isthmus of Maui, the West Maui Mountains, and the Pacific Ocean.

Many drive up to the summit in predawn darkness to watch the **sunrise over Haleakala** ✯✯; others coast down the 37-mile road from the summit on a bicycle with special brakes (see "Bicycling," earlier in this chapter). Hardy adventurers hike and camp inside the crater's wilderness (see "Hiking & Camping," earlier in this chapter). Those bound for the interior should bring their survival gear, for the terrain is raw, rugged, and punishing—not unlike the moon.

JUST THE FACTS

Haleakala National Park extends from the summit of Mount Haleakala down the volcano's southeast flank to Maui's eastern coast, beyond Hana. There are

---

Impressions

There are few enough places in the world that belong entirely to themselves. The human passion to carry all things everywhere, so that every place is home, seems well on its way to homogenizing our planet, save for the odd unreachable corner. Haleakala Crater is one of those corners.
—Barbara Kingsolver, *The New York Times*

actually two separate and distinct destinations within the park: **Haleakala Summit** and the **Kipahulu** coast (see "Tropical Haleakala: Oheo Gulch at Kipahulu," later in this chapter). The summit gets all the publicity, but Kipahulu draws crowds, too—it's lush, green, and tropical, and home to Oheo Gulch (also known as Seven Sacred Pools). No road links the summit and the coast; you have to approach them separately, and you need at least a day to see each place.

WHEN TO GO   At the 10,023-foot summit, weather changes fast. With wind chill, temperatures can be freezing any time of year. Summer can be dry and warm; winter can be wet, windy, and cold. Before you go, get current weather conditions from the park (© **808/572-4400**) or the **National Weather Service** (© **808/871-5054**).

From sunrise to noon, the light is weak, but the view is usually free of clouds. The best time for photos is in the afternoon, when the sun lights the crater and clouds are few. Go on full-moon nights for spectacular viewing.

But here's a note of caution: This is Mother Nature, not Disneyland, so there are no guarantees or schedules. Especially in winter, some mornings may be misty or rainy, and sunrise viewing may be obscured. It's the luck of the draw.

ACCESS POINTS   Haleakala Summit is 37 miles, or a 1½- to 2-hour drive, from Kahului. To get here, take Highway 37 to Highway 377 to Highway 378. For details on the drive, see "The Drive to the Summit," below. Pukalani is the last town for water, food, and gas.

The **Kipahulu** section of Haleakala National Park is on Maui's east end near Hana, 60 miles from Kahului on Highway 36 (Hana Hwy.). Due to traffic and rough road conditions, plan on 4 hours for the drive, one-way. For complete information, see "The Road to Hana," below and "Tropical Haleakala: Oheo Gulch at Kipahulu," later in this chapter.

At both entrances to the park, the admission fee is $5 per person or $10 per car, good for a week of unlimited entry.

INFORMATION, VISITOR CENTERS & RANGER PROGRAMS   For information before you go, contact **Haleakala National Park,** Box 369, Makawao, HI 96768 (© **808/572-4400;** www.nps.gov/hale).

One mile from the park entrance, at 7,000 feet, is **Haleakala National Park Headquarters** (© **808/572-4400**), open daily from 7:30am to 4pm. Stop here to pick up information on park programs and activities, get camping permits, and, occasionally, see a Hawaiian nene bird. Restrooms, a pay phone, and drinking water are available.

The **Haleakala Visitor Center,** open daily from sunrise to 3pm, is near the summit, 11 miles past the park entrance. It offers a panoramic view of the volcanic landscape, with photos identifying the various features, and exhibits that explain the area's history, ecology, geology, and vulcanology. Park staff members are often on hand to answer questions. Restrooms and water are available.

Rangers offer excellent, informative, and free **naturalist talks** at 9:30, 10:30, and 11:30am daily in the summit building. For information on **hiking** and **camping** possibilities, including wilderness cabins and campgrounds, see "Hiking & Camping," earlier in this chapter.

THE DRIVE TO THE SUMMIT

If you look on a Maui map, almost in the middle of the part that resembles a torso, there's a black, wiggly line that looks like this: WWWWW. That's

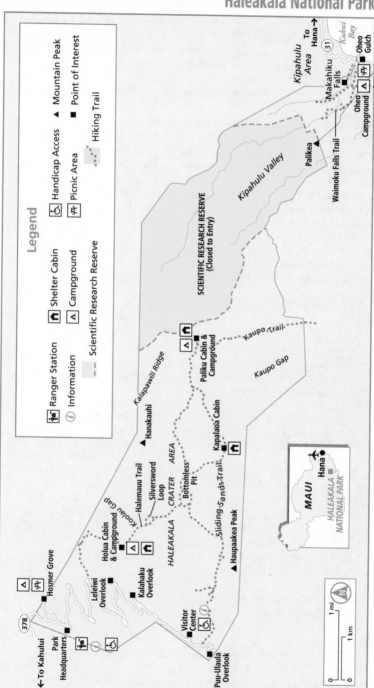

Haleakala National Park

Legend

- 👤 Ranger Station
- ⛺ Shelter Cabin
- 👤 Handicap Access
- ▲ Mountain Peak
- ℹ️ Information
- ▲ Campground
- 🪑 Picnic Area
- ■ Point of Interest
- ⸱⸱⸱ Hiking Trail
- Scientific Research Reserve

Hosmer Grove

← To Kahului

Park Headquarters

378

Leleiwi Overlook

Kalahaku Overlook

Holua Cabin & Campground

Koolau Gap

Kalapawili Ridge

Halemauu Trail

Silversword Loop

▲ Hanakauhi

HALEAKALA CRATER AREA

Bottomless Pit

Visitor Center

Puu-Ulaula Overlook

Sliding Sands Trail

Kapalaoa Cabin

▲ Haupaakea Peak

Paliku Cabin & Campground

Kaupo Trail

Kaupo Gap

SCIENTIFIC RESEARCH RESERVE (Closed to Entry)

Kipahulu Valley

Kipahulu Area

Makahiku Falls

▲ Palikea

Waimoku Falls Trail

Oheo Gulch

Oheo Campground

To Hana →

Kukui Bay

31

MAUI

Hana

HALEAKALA NATIONAL PARK

1 mi

1 km

0

Tips Descending from the Crater

When driving down the Haleakala Crater Road, be sure to put your car in low gear; that way, you won't destroy your brakes by riding them the whole way down.

Highway 378, also known as **Haleakala Crater Road**—one of fastest-ascending roads in the world. This grand corniche has at least 33 switchbacks; passes through numerous climate zones; goes under, in, and out of clouds; takes you past rare silversword plants and endangered Hawaiian geese sailing through the clear, thin air; and offers a view that extends for more than 100 miles.

Going to the summit takes 1½ to 2 hours from Kahului. No matter where you start out, you'll follow Highway 37 (Haleakala Hwy.) to Pukalani, where you'll pick up Highway 377 (aka Haleakala Hwy.), which you'll take to Highway 378. Along the way, expect fog, rain, and wind. You may encounter stray cattle and downhill bicyclists. Fill up your gas tank before you go—the only gas available is 27 miles below the summit at Pukalani. There are no facilities beyond the ranger stations—not even a coffee urn in sight. Bring your own food and water.

Remember, you're entering a high-altitude wilderness area. Some people get dizzy due to the lack of oxygen; you might also suffer lightheadedness, shortness of breath, nausea, or worse: severe headaches, flatulence, and dehydration. People with asthma, pregnant women, heavy smokers, and those with heart conditions should be especially careful in the rarefied air. Bring water and a jacket or a blanket, especially if you go up for sunrise. Or you might want to go up to the summit for sunset, which is also spectacular.

At the **park entrance,** you'll pay an entrance fee of $10 per car (or $2 for a bicycle). About a mile from the entrance is **Park Headquarters,** where an endangered **nene,** or Hawaiian goose, may greet you with its unique call. With its black face, buff cheeks, and partially webbed feet, the gray-brown bird looks like a small Canada goose with zebra stripes; it brays out "nay-nay" (thus its name), doesn't migrate, and prefers lava beds to lakes. More than 25,000 nenes once inhabited Hawaii, but habitat destruction and predators (hunters, pigs, feral cats and dogs, and mongooses) nearly caused their extinction. By 1951, there were only 30 left. Now protected as Hawaii's state bird, the number of wild nene on Haleakala numbers fewer than 250—the species remains endangered.

Beyond headquarters are **two scenic overlooks** on the way to the summit; stop at Leleiwi on the way up and Kalahaku on the way back down, if only to get out, stretch, and get accustomed to the heights. Take a deep breath, look around, and pop your ears. If you feel dizzy, drowsy, or get a sudden headache, consider turning around and going back down.

Leleiwi Overlook ✦ is just beyond mile marker 17. From the parking area, a short trail leads you to a panoramic view of the lunarlike crater. When the clouds are low and the sun is in the right place, usually around sunset, you may experience a phenomenon known as the "Specter of the Brocken"—you can see a reflection of your shadow, ringed by a rainbow, in the clouds below. It's an optical illusion caused by a rare combination of sun, shadow, and fog that occurs in only three places on the planet: Haleakala, Scotland, and Germany.

Two miles farther along is **Kalahaku Overlook** ⭐, the best place to see a rare **silversword.** You can turn into this overlook only when you are descending from the top. The silversword is the punk of the plant world, its silvery bayonets displaying tiny, purple bouquets—like a spacey artichoke with attitude. This botanical wonder proved irresistible to humans, who gathered them in gunnysacks for Chinese potions, British specimen collections, and just for the sheer thrill of having something so rare. Silverswords grow only in Hawaii, take from 4 to 50 years to bloom, and then, usually between May and October, send up a 1- to 6-foot stalk with a purple bouquet of sunflower-like blooms. They're now very rare, so don't even think about taking one home.

Continue on, and you'll quickly reach **Haleakala Visitor Center,** which offers spectacular views. You'll feel as if you're at the edge of the earth, but the actual summit's a little farther on, at **Puu Ulaula Overlook** ⭐⭐⭐ (also known as Red Hill), the volcano's highest point, where you'll find a mysterious cluster of buildings officially known as Haleakala Observatories, but unofficially called **Science City.** If you go up for sunrise, the building at Puu Ulaula Overlook, a triangle of glass that serves as a windbreak, is the best viewing spot. After the daily miracle of sunrise—the sun seems to rise out of the vast ocean (hence the name "House of the Sun")—you can see all the way across Alenuihaha Channel to the often snowcapped summit of Mauna Kea on the Big Island.

UPCOUNTRY MAUI

Come upcountry and discover a different side of Maui: On the slopes of Haleakala, cowboys, planters, and other country people make their homes in serene, neighborly communities like **Makawao** and **Kula,** a world away from the bustling beach resorts. Even if you can't spare a day or two in the cool, upcountry air, there are some sights that are worth a look on your way to or from the crater. Shoppers and gallery hoppers might want to spend more time here; see "Shopping," later in this chapter.

Kula Botanical Garden ⭐   You can take a self-guided, informative, leisurely stroll through more than 700 native and exotic plants—including three unique collections of orchids, proteas, and bromeliads—at this 5-acre garden. It offers a good overview of Hawaii's exotic flora in one small, cool place.

Hwy. 377, south of Haleakala Crater Rd. (Hwy. 378), ½ miles from Hwy. 37. ℂ **808/878-1715.** Admission $5 adults, $1 children 6–12. Daily 9am–4pm.

Tedeschi Vineyards and Winery ⭐   On the southern shoulder of Haleakala is **Ulupalakua Ranch,** a 20,000-acre spread once owned by legendary sea captain James Makee, celebrated in the Hawaiian song and dance *Hula O Makee.* Wounded in a Honolulu waterfront brawl in 1843, Makee moved to Maui and bought Ulupalakua. He renamed it Rose Ranch, planted sugar as a cash crop, and grew rich. Still in operation, the ranch is now home to Maui's only winery, established in 1974 by Napa vintner Emil Tedeschi, who began growing California and European grapes here and producing serious still and sparkling wines, plus a silly wine made of pineapple juice. The rustic grounds are the perfect place for a picnic. Pack a basket before you go, but don't BYOB: There's plenty of great wine to enjoy at Tedeschi. Settle in under the sprawling camphor tree, pop the cork on a Blanc du Blanc, and toast your good fortune in being here.

Off Hwy. 37 (Kula Hwy.). ℂ **808/878-6058.** www.mauiwine.com. Free tastings. Daily 9am–5pm. Tours given 10:30am and 1:30pm.

EAST MAUI & HEAVENLY HANA

Hana is Paradise on Earth—or just about as close as you can get to it, anyway. In and around Hana, you'll find a lush tropical rain forest dotted with cascading waterfalls and sparkling blue pools, skirted by red- and black-sand beaches.

THE ROAD TO HANA 🞶🞶🞶

Top down, sunscreen on, radio tuned to a little Hawaiian music on a Maui morning—it's time to head out to Hana along the Hana Highway (Hwy. 36), a wiggle of a road that runs along Maui's northeastern shore. The drive takes at least 3 hours from Lahaina or Kihei—but take all day. Going to Hana is about the journey, not the destination.

There are wilder roads, steeper roads, and more dangerous roads, but in all of Hawaii, no road is more celebrated than this one. It winds 50 miles past taro patches, magnificent seascapes, waterfall pools, botanical gardens, and verdant rain forests, and ends at one of Hawaii's most beautiful tropical places.

The outside world discovered the little village of Hana in 1926, when the narrow coastal road, carved by pickax-wielding convicts, opened. The mud-and-gravel road, often subject to landslides and washouts, was paved in 1962, when tourist traffic began to increase; it now sees 1,000 cars and dozens of vans a day, according to storekeeper Harry Hasegawa. That translates into half a million people a year, which is way too many. Go at the wrong time, and you'll be stuck in a bumper-to-bumper rental-car parade—peak traffic hours are midmorning and midafternoon year-round, especially on weekends.

In the rush to "do" Hana in a day, most visitors spin around town in 10 minutes and wonder what all the fuss is about. It takes time to take in Hana, play in the waterfalls, sniff the tropical flowers, hike to bamboo forests, and view the spectacular scenery. Stay overnight if you can, and meander back in a day or two. If you really must do the Hana Highway in a day, go just before sunrise and return after sunset.

Tips: Practice aloha. Give way at one-lane bridges, wave at oncoming motorists, let the big guys in 4×4s have the right of way—it's just common sense, brah. If the guy behind you blinks his lights, let him pass. And don't honk your horn—in Hawaii, it's considered rude.

THE JOURNEY BEGINS IN PAIA   Before you even start out, fill up your gas tank. Gas in Paia is expensive, and it's the last place for gas until you get to Hana, some 54 bridges and 600 hairpin turns down the road.

Paia was once a thriving sugar-mill town. The mill is still here, but the population shifted to Kahului in the 1950s when subdivisions opened there, leaving Paia to shrivel up and die. But the town refused to give up, and it has proven its ability to adapt to the times. Now chic eateries and trendy shops stand next door to the old ma-and-pa establishments. Plan to be here early, around 7am, when **Charley's** 🞶, 142 Hana Hwy. (✆ **808/579-9453**), opens. Enjoy a big, hearty breakfast for a reasonable price. Stop by **Pic-nics** 🞶, 30 Baldwin Ave. (✆ **808/ 579-8021**), to stock up on—what else?—a picnic lunch for the road (p. 411).

WINDSURFING MECCA   Just before mile marker 9 is **Hookipa Beach Park** 🞶, where top-ranked windsurfers come to test themselves against the forces of nature: thunderous surf and forceful wind. On nearly every windy day, after noon (the board surfers have the waves in the morning), you can watch dozens of windsurfers twirling and dancing in the wind like colored butterflies. To watch them, do not stop on the highway, but go past the park and turn left at the entrance on the far side of the beach. You can either park on the high grassy bluff or drive down to the sandy beach and park alongside the pavilion. Facilities include restrooms, a shower, picnic tables, and a barbecue area.

INTO THE COUNTRY Past Hookipa Beach, the road winds down into **Maliko Gulch** at mile marker 10. At the bottom of the gulch, look for the road on your right, which will take you out to **Maliko Bay.** Take the first right, which goes under the bridge and past a rodeo arena and on to the rocky beach. There are no facilities here except a boat-launch ramp. In the 1940s, Maliko had a thriving community at the mouth of the bay, but its residents rebuilt farther inland after a strong tidal wave wiped it out.

Back on the Hana Highway, for the next few miles, you'll pass through the rural area of **Haiku,** where you'll see banana patches, forests of guavas and palms, and avocados. Just before mile marker 15 is the **Maui Grown Market and Deli** (© 808/572-1693), a good stop for drinks or snacks for the ride.

At mile marker 16, the curves begin, one right after another. Slow down and enjoy the view of bucolic rolling hills, mango trees, and vibrant ferns. After mile marker 16, the road is still called the Hana Highway, but the number changes from Highway 36 to Highway 360, and the mile markers go back to 0.

A GREAT PLUNGE ALONG THE WAY A dip in a waterfall pool is everybody's tropical-island fantasy. A great place to stop is **Twin Falls** ⚘, at mile marker 2. Just before the wide, concrete bridge, pull over on the mountain side and park. Ignore the NO TRESPASSING sign and hop over the ladder on the right side of the red gate. From here you can walk 3 to 5 minutes to the waterfall and pool, or continue on another 10 to 15 minutes to the second, larger waterfall and pool (don't go in if it has been raining).

HIDDEN HUELO Just before mile marker 4 on a blind curve, look for a double row of mailboxes on the left-hand side by the pay phone. Down the road lies a hidden Hawaii of an earlier time, where an indescribable sense of serenity prevails. Hemmed in by Waipo and Hoalua bays is the remote community of **Huelo** ⚘. This fertile area once supported a population of 75,000; today, only a few hundred live among the scattered homes here, where a handful of B&Bs and exquisite vacation rentals cater to a trickle of travelers (see "Where to Stay," earlier in this chapter).

The only reason Huelo is even marked is the historic 1853 **Kaulanapueo Church.** Reminiscent of New England architecture, this coral-and-cement church, topped with a plantation-green steeple and a gray tin roof, is still in use, although services are held just once or twice a month. It still has the same austere, stark interior of 1853: straight-backed benches, a no-nonsense platform for the minister, and no distractions on the walls to tempt you from paying

---

Tips Travel Tip

If you'd like to know exactly what you're seeing as you head down the road to Hana, rent a cassette tour, available from **Activity Warehouse** (© 800/923-4004; www.travelhawaii.com), which has branches in Lahaina at 578 Front St., near Prison Street (© 808/661-1970), and in Kihei at Azeka Place II, on the mountain side of Kihei Road near Lipoa Street (© 808/875-4050), for $10 a day.

attention to the sermon. Next to the church is a small graveyard, a personal history of this village in concrete and stone.

KOOLAU FOREST RESERVE   After Huelo, the vegetation seems lusher, as though Mother Nature had poured Miracle-Gro on everything. This is the edge of the **Koolau Forest Reserve.** *Koolau* means "windward," and this certainly is one of the greatest examples of a lush windward area: The coastline here gets about 60 to 80 inches of rain a year, as well as runoff from the 200 to 300 inches that falls farther up the mountain. Here you'll see trees laden with guavas, as well as mangoes, java plums, and avocados the size of softballs. The spiny, long-leafed plants are hala trees, which the Hawaiians used for weaving baskets, mats, even canoe sails.

From here on out, there's a waterfall (and one-lane bridge) around nearly every turn in the road, so drive slowly and be prepared to stop and yield to oncoming cars.

DANGEROUS CURVES   About a half-mile after mile marker 6, there's a sharp U-curve in the road, going uphill. The road is practically one-lane here, with a brick wall on one side and virtually no maneuvering room. Sound your horn at the start of the U-curve to let approaching cars know you're coming. Take this curve, as well as the few more coming up in the next several miles, very slowly.

Just before mile marker 7 is a forest of waving **bamboo.** The sight is so spectacular that drivers are often tempted to take their eyes off the road. Be very cautious. Wait until just after mile marker 7, at the **Kaaiea Bridge** and stream below, to pull over and take a closer look at the hand-hewn stone walls. Then turn around to see the vista of bamboo.

A GREAT FAMILY HIKE   At mile marker 9, there's a small state wayside area with restrooms, picnic tables, and a barbecue area. The sign says Koolau Forest Reserve, but the real attraction here is the **Waikamoi Ridge Trail** *, an easy ¾-mile loop. The start of the trail is just behind the QUIET TREES AT WORK sign. The well-marked trail meanders through eucalyptus, ferns, and hala trees.

ANOTHER GREAT PLUNGE   Thirty-foot **Puohokamoa Falls** spill into an idyllic pool in a fern-filled amphitheater. Park at mile marker 11, clamber over river rocks, scramble up a trail through dense jungle, and—bingo!—plunge into the ice-cold pool of upper Puohokamoa Falls.

CAN'T-MISS PHOTO OPS   Just past mile marker 12 is the **Kaumahina State Wayside Park** *. This is not only a good pit stop (restrooms are available) and a wonderful place for a picnic (with tables and a barbecue area), but also a great vista point. The view of the rugged coastline makes an excellent shot—you can see all the way down to the jutting Keanae Peninsula.

Another mile and a couple of bends in the road, and you'll enter the Honomanu Valley, with its beautiful bay. To get to the **Honomanu Bay County Beach Park** *, look for the turnoff on your left, just after mile marker 14, as you begin your ascent up the other side of the valley. The rutted dirt-and-cinder road takes you down to the rocky black-sand beach. There are no facilities here. Because of the strong rip currents offshore, swimming is best in the stream inland from the ocean. You'll consider the drive down worthwhile as you stand on the beach, well away from the ocean, and turn to look back on the steep cliffs covered with vegetation.

KEANAE PENINSULA & ARBORETUM   At mile marker 17, the old Hawaiian village of **Keanae** ** stands out against the Pacific like a place time forgot. Here, on an old lava flow graced by an 1860 stone church and swaying palms, is one of the last coastal enclaves of native Hawaiians. They still grow taro in patches and pound it into poi, the staple of the old Hawaiian diet; and they still pluck *opihi* (limpet) from tide pools along the jagged coast and cast throw-nets at schools of fish.

At nearby **Keanae Arboretum,** Hawaii's botanical world is divided into three parts: native forest; introduced forest; and traditional Hawaiian plants, food, and medicine. You can swim in the pools of Piinaau Stream, or press on along a mile long trail into Keanae Valley, where a lovely tropical rain forest waits at the end.

WAIANAPANAPA STATE PARK ★★   On the outskirts of Hana, shiny black-sand Waianapanapa Beach appears like a vivid dream, with bright-green jungle foliage on three sides and cobalt blue water lapping at its feet. The 120-acre park on an ancient lava flow includes sea cliffs, lava tubes, arches, and that beach—plus a dozen rustic cabins. If you're interested in staying here, see "Where to Stay," earlier in this chapter. Also see "Beaches" and "Hiking & Camping."

HANA ★★★

Green, tropical Hana, which some call heavenly, is a destination all its own, a small coastal village in a rain forest inhabited by 2,500 people, many part-Hawaiian. Beautiful Hana enjoys more than 90 inches of rain a year—more than enough to keep the scenery lush. Banyans, bamboo, breadfruit trees—everything seems larger than life, especially the flowers, like wild ginger and plumeria. Several roadside stands offer exotic blooms for $1 a bunch. Just "put money in box." It's the Hana honor system.

The last unspoiled Hawaiian town on Maui is, oddly enough, the home of Maui's first resort, which opened in 1946. Paul Fagan, owner of the San Francisco Seals baseball team, bought an old inn and turned it into the **Hotel Hana-Maui,** which gave Hana its first and, as it turns out, last taste of tourism. Others have tried to open hotels and golf courses and resorts, but Hana, which is interested in remaining Hana, always politely refuses. There are a few B&Bs here, though; see "Where to Stay," earlier in this chapter.

A wood-frame 1871 building that served as the old Hana District Police Station now holds the **Hana Museum Cultural Center,** 4974 Uakea Rd. (© **808/248-8622;** www.planet-hawaii.com/hana). The center tells the history of the area, with some excellent artifacts, memorabilia, and photographs. Also stop in at **Hasegawa General Store,** a Maui institution.

On the green hills above Hana stands a 30-foot-high white cross made of lava rock. The cross was erected by citizens in memory of Paul Fagan, who helped keep the town alive. The 3-mile hike up to **Fagan's Cross** provides a gorgeous view of the Hana coast, especially at sunset, when Fagan himself liked to climb this hill. See p. 433 for details.

Most day-trippers to Hana miss the most unusual natural attraction of all: **Red Sand Beach** ★, officially named Kaihalulu Beach, which means "roaring sea." It's truly a sight to see. It's on the ocean side of Kauiki Hill, just south of Hana Bay, in a wild, natural setting in a pocket cove. Kauiki, a 390-foot-high volcanic cinder cone, lost its seaward wall to erosion and spilled red cinders everywhere, creating the red sands. To get here, walk south on Uakea Road, past the Hotel Hana-Maui to the end of the parking lot for Sea Ranch Cottages. Turn left, cross an open field past an old cemetery, and follow a well-worn path down a narrow cliff trail. In this private, romantic setting, some beachgoers shed their clothes, so try not to be offended.

TROPICAL HALEAKALA: OHEO GULCH AT KIPAHULU

If you're thinking about heading out to the so-called Seven Sacred Pools, out past Hana at the Kipahulu end of Haleakala National Park, let's clear this up right now: There are more than seven pools—about 24, actually—and *all* water in Hawaii is considered sacred. It's all a PR campaign that has spun out of control. Folks here call it by its rightful name, **Oheo Gulch** ★★★, and visitors sometimes refer to it as Kipahulu, which is actually the name of the area where Oheo Gulch is located. No matter what you call it, it's beautiful. This dazzling series of pools and cataracts is so popular that it has its own roadside parking lot.

From the ranger station, it's just a short hike above the famous Oheo Gulch to two spectacular **waterfalls.** Check with park rangers before hiking up to or swimming in the pools, and always keep an eye on the water in the streams. The sky can be sunny near the coast, but flood waters travel 6 miles down from the Kipahulu Valley, and the water level can rise 4 feet in less than 10 minutes. It's not a good idea to swim in the pools in winter.

Makahiku Falls is easily reached from the central parking area; the trailhead begins near the ranger station. **Pipiwai Trail** leads up to the road and beyond for a half-mile to the overlook. If you hike another 1½ miles up the trail across two bridges and through a bamboo forest, you reach **Waimoku Falls.** It's a hard uphill hike, but press on to avoid the pool's crowd.

ACCESS POINTS   Even though Oheo is part of Haleakala National Park, you cannot drive here from the summit. Oheo is about 30 to 50 minutes beyond Hana town, along Highway 31. The admission fee to enter is $5 per person or $10 per car. The Highway 31 bridge passes over some of the pools near the ocean; the others, plus magnificent 400-foot Waimoku Falls, are uphill, via an often-muddy but rewarding, hour-long hike (see "Hiking & Camping," earlier in this chapter). Expect showers on the Kipahulu coast.

VISITOR CENTER   The **Kipahulu Ranger Station** (✆ 808/248-7375) is staffed from 9am to 5pm daily. Restrooms are available, but there's no drinking water. Here you'll find park-safety information, exhibits, and books. Rangers offer a variety of walks and hikes year-round; check at the station for current activities. Tent camping is permitted in the park; see "Hiking & Camping," earlier in this chapter, for details.

BEYOND OHEO GULCH

A mile past Oheo Gulch on the ocean side of the road is **Lindbergh's Grave.** First to fly across the Atlantic Ocean, Charles A. Lindbergh (1902–74) found peace in the Pacific; he settled in Hana, where he died of cancer in 1974. The famous aviator is buried under river stones in a seaside graveyard behind the 1857 **Palapala Hoomau Congregational Church.**

Those of you who are continuing on around Maui to the fishing village of **Kaupo** and beyond should be warned that Kaupo Road, or Old Piilani Highway (Hwy. 31), is rough and unpaved, often full of potholes and ruts. There are no goods or services until you reach **Ulupalakua Ranch,** where there's a winery, a general store, and a gas station, which is likely to be closed. Before you attempt this journey, ask around about road conditions, or call the **Maui Public Works Department** (✆ 808/248-8254) or the **Police Department** (✆ 808/248-8311). This road frequently washes out in the rain. Most rental car companies

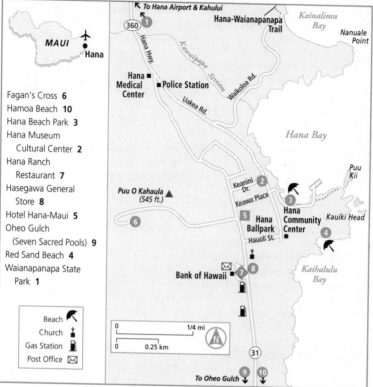

Fagan's Cross **6**
Hamoa Beach **10**
Hana Beach Park **3**
Hana Museum
 Cultural Center **2**
Hana Ranch
 Restaurant **7**
Hasegawa General
 Store **8**
Hotel Hana-Maui **5**
Oheo Gulch
 (Seven Sacred Pools) **9**
Red Sand Beach **4**
Waianapanapa State
 Park **1**

forbid you from taking their cars on this road (they don't want to trek all the way out here to get you if your car breaks down), so you'd really be better off retracing your route back through Hana. But if conditions are good, it can be a pretty drive in the spring (it tends to be dry and boring in summer).

10 Shops & Galleries

The island of Maui is a shopaholic's dream as well as an arts center, with a large number of resident artists who show their works in dozens of galleries and countless gift shops. Maui is also the queen of specialty products, an agricultural cornucopia that includes Kula onions, upcountry proteas, Kaanapali coffee, world-renowned potato chips, and many other taste treats that are shipped worldwide.

As with any popular visitor destination, you'll have to wade through bad art and mountains of trinkets, particularly in Lahaina and Kihei, where touristy boutiques line the streets between rare pockets of treasures. If you shop in South or West Maui, expect to pay resort prices, clear down to a bottle of Evian or sunscreen.

With a well-heeled flourish, the upscale shopping and restaurant complex called The Shops at Wailea recently opened in south Maui. The 16.4-acre complex features more than 50 shops and five restaurants, everything from an ABC store to Louis Vuitton and The Gap. This is resort shopping much in the vein of Whalers Village in Kaanapali, where shopping and restaurant activity is concentrated in a single oceanfront complex, livening up what was an arid retail landscape. The Shops at Wailea signals a repositioning of the resort as a place of heightened commercial activity.

Central Maui is home to some first-rate boutiques: Watch Wailuku, which is poised for a resurgence—if not now, then soon. The town has its own antiques alleys, the new Sig Zane Designs has brought a delightful infusion of creative and cultural energy, and a major promenade/emporium on Main Street is in the works. The Kaahumanu Center, in neighboring Kahului, is becoming more fashionable by the month.

Upcountry, Makawao's boutiques are worth seeking out, despite some attitude and high prices. The charm of shopping on Maui has always rested in the small, independent shops and galleries that crop up in surprising places.

CENTRAL MAUI
KAHULUI

Kahului's best shopping is concentrated in two places. Almost all of the shops listed below are at one of the following centers:

The once rough-around-the-edges **Maui Mall,** 70 E. Kaahumanu Ave. (© 808/877-7559), is the talk of Kahului. Newly renovated, it's now bigger and better, and has retained some of our favorite stores while adding a 12-screen movie megaplex that features current releases as well as art-house films. The mall is still a place of everyday good things, from **Long's Drugs** to **Star Market** to **Tasaka Guri Guri,** the decades-old purveyor of inimitable icy treats that are neither ice cream nor shave ice, but something in-between.

Queen Kaahumanu Center, 275 Kaahumanu Ave. (© 808/877-3369), 5 minutes from the Kahului Airport on Highway 32, offers more than 100 shops, restaurants, and theaters. Its second-floor Plantation District offers home furnishings and accessories, fabulous Naot and Kenneth Cole shoes (**Native Soles & Things**), and gift and accessories shops. Kaahumanu covers all the bases, from the arts and crafts to a **Foodland Supermarket** and everything in-between: a thriving food court; the island's best beauty supply, **Lisa's Beauty Supply & Salon** (© 808/877-6463), and its sister store for cosmetics, **Madison Avenue Day Spa and Boutique** (© 808/873-0880); mall standards like **Sunglass Hut, Radio Shack,** and **Local Motion** (surf and beach wear—including the current fad, women's board shorts, a combination of hot pants and men's surf trunks); attractive gift shops such as **Maui Hands** and standard department stores like **Macy's** and **Sears.**

Cost Less Imports   Natural fibers are ubiquitous in this newly expanded corner of the Maui Mall, three times larger than before. Household accessories include lauhala, bamboo blinds, grassy floor and window coverings, shoji-style lamps, burlap yardage, baskets, Balinese cushions, Asian imports, and top-of-the-line, made-on-Maui soaps and handicrafts. Japanese folk curtains, called *noreng,* are among the diverse items you'll find here; it's a good source of tropical and Asian home decor. In the Maui Mall. © 808/877-0300.

Maui Hands   Maui hands have made 90% of the items in this shop/gallery. Because it's a consignment shop, you'll find Hawaii-made handicrafts and prices that aren't inflated. The selection includes paintings, prints, jewelry, glass marbles, native-wood bowls, and tchotchkes for every budget. This is an ideal stop for made-on-Maui products and crafts of good quality.

The original Maui Hands is in Makawao at the Courtyard, 3620 Baldwin Ave. (© 808/572-5194); another Maui Hands can be found in Paia, at 84 Hana Hwy. (© 808/ 579-9245). In Kaahumanu Center. © **808/877-0368**.

Maui Swap Meet   The Maui Swap Meet is a large and popular event. After Thanksgiving and throughout December, the number of booths nearly explodes into the hundreds and the activity reaches fever pitch. The colorful Maui specialties include vegetables from Kula and Keanae, fresh taro, plants, proteas, crafts, household items, homemade ethnic foods, and baked goods, including some fabulous fruit breads. Every Saturday from 7am to noon, vendors spread out their wares in booths and under tarps, in a festival-like atmosphere that is pure Maui with a touch of kitsch. Between the cheap Balinese imports and New Age crystals and incense, you may find some vintage John Kelly prints and 1930s collectibles. Admission is 50¢, and if you go early while the vendors are setting up, no one will turn you away. S. Puunene Ave. (next to the Kahului Post Office). © **808/877-3100**.

Summer House   Sleek and chic, tiny Summerhouse is big on style: casual and party dresses, separates by Russ Berens, FLAX, Kiko, and Tencel jeans by Signatur—the best. During the holiday season the selection gets dressy and sassy, but it's a fun browse year-round. We adore the hats, accessories, easy-care clothing, and up-to-the-minute evening dresses that Summerhouse carries in abundance. The high-quality T-shirts are always a cut above. The casual selection is well suited to the island lifestyle. Also on the west side at 4405 Honoapiilani Hwy., © 808/669-6616. In the Dairy Center, 395 Dairy Rd. © **808/871-1320**.

WAILUKU

Wailuku's attractive vintage architecture, numerous antiques shops, and mom-and-pop eateries imbue the town with a charm noticeably absent in the resort areas of west, south, and upcountry Maui. There is no plastic aloha in Wailuku. Of course there's junk, but a stroll along Main and Market streets usually turns up a treasure or two. It's a mixed bag, but a treasure hunt, too.

Bailey House Gift Shop   For made-in-Hawaii items, Bailey House is a must-stop. It offers a thoroughly enjoyable browse through authoritative Hawaiiana, in a museum that's one of the finest examples of missionary architecture, dating from 1833. Gracious gardens, rare paintings of early Maui, wonderful programs in Hawaiian arts and culture, and a restored hand-hewn koa canoe await visitors. The shop, a small space of discriminating taste, packs a wallop with its selection of remarkable gift items, from Hawaiian music to exquisite woods; traditional Hawaiian games to pareus and books. Prints by the legendary Hawaii artist Madge Tennent, lauhala hats hanging in midair, hand-sewn pheasant hatbands, jams and jellies, Maui cookbooks, and an occasional Hawaiian quilt are some of the treasures to be found here. Bailey House Museum Shop, 2375-A Main St. © **808/244-3326**.

Bird of Paradise Unique Antiques   Owner Joe Myhand loves furniture, old Matson liner menus, blue willow china, kimono for children, and anything nostalgic that happens to be Hawaiian. The furniture in the strongly Hawaiian collection ranges from 1940s rattan to wicker and old koa—those items tailor-made for informal island living and leisurely moments on the lanai. Myhand also collects bottles and mails his license plates all over the world. The collection ebbs and flows with his finds, keeping buyers waiting in the wings fo his Depression glass, California pottery from the 1930s and 1940s, old dinnerware, perfume bottles, vintage aloha shirts, and vintage Hawaiian music on cassettes. 56 N. Market St. ℂ 808/242-7699.

Brown-Kobayashi   Graceful living is the theme here. Prices range from a few dollars to the thousands in this 750-square-foot treasure trove. The owners have added a fabulous selection of antique stone garden pieces that mingle quietly with Asian antiques and old and new French, European, and Hawaiian objects. Although the collection is eclectic, there is a strong cohesive aesthetic that sets Brown-Kobayashi apart from other Maui antique stores. Japanese kimono and obi, Bakelite and Peking glass beads, breathtaking Japanese lacquerware, cricket carriers, and cloisonne are among the delights here. Exotic and precious Chinese woods (purple sandalwood and huanghauali) glow discreetly from quiet corners, and an occasional monarchy-style lidded milo bowl comes in and flies out. 160-A N. Market St. ℂ 808/242-0804.

Gottling Ltd.   Karl Gottling's shop specializes in Asian antique furniture, but you can also find smaller carvings, precious stones, jewelry, netsuke, opium weights, and finds in all sizes. One cabinet had 350-year-old doors; a 17th-century Buddha lent an air of serenity next to a 150-year-old Chinese cabinet. Ming dynasty ceramics, carved wooden apples ($15), and a Persian rug ($65,000) give you an idea of the range of possibilities here. 34 N. Market St. ℂ 808/244-7779.

Sig Zane Designs Wailuku   Sig Zane is synonymous with the best in aloha wear. Whether it's a T-shirt, pareu, duffel bag, aloha shirt, or muumuu, a Sig Zane design has depth and sizzle. So when Hilo-based Sig Zane Designs opened in Wailuku, Maui retailers perked up. Zane and co-owner Punawai Rice have redefined Hawaiian wear by creating an inimitable style in clothing, textiles, furnishings, and bedding. The Maui store has already proven enormously successful. The staff is helpful and willing to share the background of each design, so you will learn much about the culture, botany, mythology, and beauty of the Islands. 53 Market St. ℂ 808/249-8997.

CENTRAL MAUI EDIBLES

Down to Earth Natural Foods, 305 Dairy Rd. (ℂ **808/877-2661**), has fresh organic produce, a bountiful salad bar, sandwiches and smoothies, vitamins and supplements, fresh-baked goods, chips and snacks, whole grains, and more.

Established in 1941, the **Ooka Super Market,** 1870 Main St., Wailuku (ℂ **808/244-3931**), Maui's ultimate home-grown supermarket, is a mom-and-pop business that has grown by leaps and bounds but still manages to keep its neighborhood flavor. Ooka sells inexpensive produce (fresh Maui mushrooms for a song), fresh island seafood, and Maui specialties such as manju and mochi. Proteas cut the same day, freesias in season, hydrangeas, fresh leis, torch ginger from Hana, upcountry calla lilies in season, and multicolored anthuriums are offered at what is one of Maui's finest and most affordable retail flower selections. Prepared foods are also a hit: bentos and plate lunches, roast chicken and laulau, and specialties from all the islands. The fish is fresh, and the seaweed, poi, Kula persimmons in fall, fresh Haiku mushrooms, and dried marlin from Kona are among the local delicacies that make Ooka a Maui favorite.

Maui's produce has long been a source of pride for islanders, and **Ohana Farmers Market,** Kahului Shopping Center, next to Ah Fook's Super Market (ℂ **808/878-3189**), is where you'll find a fresh, inexpensive selection of Maui-grown fruit, vegetables, flowers, and plants. Crafts and gourmet foods add to the event, and the large monkeypod trees provide welcome shade.

Located in the northern section of Wailuku, **Takamiya Market,** 359 N. Market St. (© **808/244-3404**), is much loved by local folks and visitors with adventurous palates, who often drive all the way from Kihei to stock up on picnic fare and mouthwatering ethnic foods for sunset gatherings. Unpretentious home-cooked foods from East and West are prepared daily and served on plastic-foam plates. From the chilled-fish counter come fresh sashimi and poke, and in the renowned assortment of prepared foods are mounds of shoyu chicken, tender fried squid, roast pork, kalua pork, laulau, Chinese noodles, fiddlehead ferns, and Western comfort foods, such as corn bread and potato salad.

WEST MAUI
LAHAINA

Lahaina's merchants and art galleries go all out from 7 to 9pm on Fridays, when **Art Night** ⚜ brings an extra measure of hospitality and community spirit. The Art Night openings are usually marked with live entertainment and refreshments and a livelier-than-usual street scene.

If you're in Lahaina on the second or last Thursday of the month, stroll by the front lawn of the **Baldwin Home,** 120 Dickenson St. (at Front St.), for a splendid look at the craft of lei-making (you can even buy the results).

What was formerly a big, belching pineapple cannery is now a maze of shops and restaurants at the northern end of Lahaina town, known as the **Lahaina Cannery Mall,** 1221 Honoapiilani Hwy. (© **808/661-5304**). Find your way through the T-shirt and sportswear shops to **Lahaina Printsellers,** home of antique originals, prints, paintings, and wonderful 18th- to 20th-century cartography, representing the largest collection of engravings and antique maps in Hawaii. Follow your nose to **Sir Wilfred's Coffee House,** where you can unwind with espresso and croissants, or head for **Compadres Bar & Grill,** where the margaritas flow freely and the Mexican food is tasty (p. 396). **Roland's** may surprise you with its selection of footwear, everything from Cole Haan sophisticates to inexpensive sandals. At the recently expanded food court, the new **Compadres Taqueria** sells Mexican food to go, while **L & L Drive-Inn** sells plate lunches near Greek, pizza, Vietnamese, and Japanese food booths. There's also a **Long's Drugs** and a **Safeway.**

The **Lahaina Center,** 900 Front St. (© **808/667-9216**), is fairly new and still a work in progress. It's located north of Lahaina's most congested strip, where Front Street begins. Across the street from the center, the seawall is a much-sought-after front-row seat to the sunset. There's plenty of free validated parking and easy access to more than 30 shops, a salon, restaurants, a nightclub, and a four-plex movie-theater complex. **Ruth's Chris Steak House** has opened its doors in Lahaina Center, and **Maui Brews** serves lunch and dinner and offers live music nightly except weekends. Among the shopping stops: **Banana Republic,** the **Hilo Hattie** (a dizzying emporium of aloha wear), **ABC Discount Store,** and a dozen other recreational, dining, and entertainment options.

The conversion of 10,000 square feet of parking space into the re-creation of a traditional Hawaiian village is a welcome touch of Hawaiiana at Lahaina Center. With the commercialization of modern Lahaina, it's easy to forget that it was once the capital of the Hawaiian kingdom and a significant historic site. The village, called **Hale Kahiko,** features three main *hale,* or houses: a sleeping house; the men's dining house; and the crafts house, where women pounded lauhala for mats and baskets. Construction of the houses consumed 10,000 feet of ohia wood from the island, 20 tons of pili grass, and more than 4 miles of handwoven coconut sennit for the lashings. Artifacts, weapons, a canoe, and indigenous trees are among the authentic touches in this village; you can take a free guided tour daily between 9am and 6pm..

David Lee Galleries This gallery is devoted to the works of David Lee, who uses natural powder colors to paint on silk. The pigments and technique create a luminous, ethereal quality. 712 Front St. ℂ 808/667-7740.

Down to Earth Formerly Westside Natural Foods, this longtime Lahaina staple, is serious about providing tasty food that's healthy and affordable. Its excellent food bar offers vegetarian lasagna, marinated tofu strips, vegetarian pot pie, crisp salads, grains, curries, and gorgeous organic produce. The selection changes regularly, and includes produce, cosmetics, and healthful food staples. 193 Lahainaluna Rd. ℂ 808/667-2855.

Lahaina Arts Society Galleries With its membership of more than 185 Maui artists, the nonprofit Lahaina Arts Society is an excellent community resource. Changing monthly exhibits in the Banyan Tree and Old Jail galleries offer a good look at the island's artistic well: two-dimensional art, fiber art, ceramics, sculpture, prints, jewelry, and more. In the shade of the humongous banyan tree in the square across from Pioneer Inn, "Art in the Park" fairs are offered every second and fourth weekend of the month. 648 Wharf St. ℂ 808/661-3228.

Lei Spa Maui The Lei Spa Maui has expanded to include two massage rooms and shower facilities, making it a day spa offering facials and other therapies. It's a good sign that 95% of the beauty and bath products sold are made on Maui, and that includes Hawaiian Botanical Pikake shower gel; kukui and macadamia-nut oils; Hawaiian potpourris; mud masks with Hawaiian seaweed; and a spate of rejuvenating potions for hair and skin. Aromatherapy body oils and perfumes are popular, as are the handmade soaps and fragrances of torch ginger, plumeria, coconut, tuberose, and sandalwood. Scented candles in coconut shells, inexpensive and fragrant, make great gifts. 505 Front St. ℂ 808/661-1178.

The Old Lahaina Book Emporium What a bookstore! Chockablock with used books in stacks, shelves, counters and aisles, this bookstore is a browser's dream. More than 25,000 quality used books are lovingly housed in this shop, where owner JoAnn Carroll treats books and customers well. Prices are low, the selection diverse, everything from *Li'l Abner* to *Genius and Lust,* old *Mad* magazines, *Aphrodisiac Cookery, Baghavad Gita, A History of Bicycles,* and *The Cockroach Combat Manual,* the store is 95% used books and 100% delight. Specialties include Hawaiiana, fiction, mystery, sci-fi, and military history, with substantial selections in cookbooks, children's books, and philosophy/religion. You could pay as little as $2 for a quality read, or a whole lot more for that rare first edition. Books on tape, videos, the classics, and old guitar magazines are among the treasures of this two-story emporium. 834 Front St. ℂ 808/661-1399.

Totally Hawaiian Gift Gallery This gallery makes a good browse for its selection of Niihau shell jewelry, excellent Hawaiian CDs, Norfolk pine bowls, and Hawaiian quilt kits. Hawaiian quilt patterns sewn in Asia (at least they're honest about it) are labor-intensive, less expensive, and attractive, although not totally Hawaiian. Hawaiian-quilt-patterned gift wraps and tiles, perfumes and soaps, handcrafted dolls, and koa accessories are of good quality, and the artists, such as Kelly Dunn (Norfolk wood bowls), Jerry Kermode (wood) and Pat Coito (wood) are among the tops in their fields. Also in the Maui Marriott in

Kaanapali ℭ 808/667-2171. In the Lahaina Cannery Mall, 1221 Honoapiilani Hwy. ℭ **808/ 667-2558.**

Village Galleries in Lahaina   The nearly 30-year-old Village Galleries is the oldest continuously running gallery on Maui, and it's esteemed as one of the few galleries with consistently high standards. Art collectors know this as a respectable showcase for regional artists; the selection of mostly original two- and three-dimensional art offers a good look at the quality of work originating on the island. The newer contemporary gallery offers colorful gift items and jewelry. An additional location is in the Ritz-Carlton Kapalua, 1 Ritz-Carlton Dr. (ℭ 808/669-1800). 120 and 180 Dickenson St. ℭ **808/661-4402** and 808/661-5559.

KAANAPALI

On a recent trip we were somewhat disappointed with upscale **Whalers Village,** 2435 Kaanapali Pkwy. (ℭ **808/661-4567**), although it offers everything from whale blubber to Prada and Ferragamo, it is short on local shops and parking at the nearby lot is expensive. The complex is home to the Whalers Village Museum with its interactive exhibits and 40-foot sperm whale skeleton, and sand castles on perpetual display, built by artists of the shifting sands., but shoppers come for the designer thrills and beachfront dining.

Our favorite shoe store, **Sandal Tree,** has its third store in Whalers Village. (The other two are at Hyatt Regency Maui and Grand Wailea Resort in Wailea.) **Martin & MacArthur,** a mainstay of the village, offers a dizzying array of Hawaii crafts: Hawaiian-quilt cushion covers, jewelry, soaps, books, and a stunning selection of woodworks. The always wonderful **Lahaina Printsellers** has a selection of antique prints, maps, paintings, and engravings, including 18th- to 20th-century cartography, all of which offer great browsing and gift potential. You can find award-winning **Kimo Bean** coffee at a kiosk, an expanded **Reyn's** for aloha wear, and **Cinnamon Girl,** a hit in Honolulu for its matching mother-daughter clothing. The return of **Waldenbooks** makes it that much easier to pick up the latest best-seller on the way to the beach. Once you've stood under the authentic whale skeleton at the **Whalers Village Museum** (p. 442), you can blow a bundle at **Tiffany, Prada, Chanel, Coach, Dolphin Galleries,** or any of the more than 60 shops and restaurants that have sprouted in this open-air shopping center. The posh Euro trend continues; despite obvious efforts to offer more of a balance between island-made and designer goods, it's still open season for the chain luxury stores.

Other mainstays: The **Eyecatcher** has an extensive selection of sunglasses; it's located just across from the busiest **ABC** store in the state. The former **Maui Yogurt Company** has been taken over by **Pizza Paradiso,** which sells ice cream and smoothies in a food court of other dine-and-dash goodies. Whalers Village is open daily from 9:30am to 10pm.

Ki'i Gallery   Some of the works are large and lavish, such as the Toland Sand prisms for just under $5,000 and the John Stokes hand-blown glass. Those who love glass in all forms, from hand-blown vessels to jewelry, will love a browse through Ki'i. We found Pat Kazi's work in porcelain and found objects, such as the mermaid in a teacup, inspired by fairy tales and mythology, both fantastic and compelling. The gallery is devoted to glass and original paintings and drawings; roughly half of the artists are from Hawaii. Also at the Grand Wailea Resort ℭ 808/874-3059 and the Shops at Wailea ℭ 808/874-1181. In the Hyatt Regency Maui, 200 Nohea Kai Dr. ℭ **808/661-4456.**

Sandal Tree   It's unusual for a resort shop to draw local customers on a regular basis, but the Sandal Tree attracts a flock of footwear fanatics who come here from throughout the islands for rubber thongs and Top-Siders, sandals and dressy pumps, athletic shoes and hats, designer footwear, and much more. Sandal Tree also carries a generous selection of Mephisto and Arche comfort sandals, Donald Pliner, Anne Klein, Charles Jourdan, and beach wear and casual footwear for all tastes. Accessories range from fashionable knapsacks to avant-garde geometrical handbags—for town and country, day and evening, kids, women, and men. Prices are realistic, too. In Whalers Village, 2435 Kaanapali Pkwy. © 808/667-5330; also in Grand Wailea Resort, 3850 Wailea Alanui Drive, Wailea; and in the Hyatt Regency Maui, 200 Nohea Kai Drive.

HONOKOWAI, KAHANA & NAPILI

Those driving north of Kaanapali toward Kapalua will notice the **Honokowai Marketplace** on Lower Honoapiilani Road, only minutes before the Kapalua Airport. There are restaurants and coffee shops, a dry cleaner, the flagship **Star Market,** a few clothing stores, and the sprawling **Hawaiian Interiors.**

Nearby **Kahana Gateway** is an unimpressive mall built to serve the condominium community that has sprawled along the coastline between Honokowai and Kapalua. If you need women's swimsuits, however, **Rainbow Beach Swimwear** is a find. It carries a selection of suits for all shapes, at lower-than-resort prices, slashed even further during the frequent sales. **Hutton's Fine Jewelry** offers high-end jewelry from designers around the country (lots of platinum and diamonds), reflecting discerning taste for those who can afford it. Tahitian black pearls and jade (some hundreds of years old, all certified) are among Hutton's specialties.

KAPALUA

Honolua Store   Walk on the old wood floors peppered with holes from golf shoes and find your everyday essentials: bottled water, stationery, mailing tape, jackets, chips, wine, soft drinks, paper products, fresh fruit and produce, and aisles of notions and necessities. With picnic tables on the veranda and a take-out counter offering deli items—more than a dozen types of sandwiches, salads, and budget-friendly breakfasts—there are always long lines of customers. Golfers and surfers love to come here for the morning paper and coffee. 502 Office Rd. (next to the Ritz-Carlton Kapalua). © 808/669-6128.

Kapalua Shops   Shops have come and gone in this small, exclusive, and once-chic shopping center, now much quieter than in days past. The closing of

---

A Creative Way to Spend the Day

Make a bowl from clay or paint a premade one, then fire it and take it home. The **Art School at Kapalua,** www.kapaluamaui.com (© **808/665-0007**), in a charming 1920s plantation building that was part of an old cannery operation, features local and visiting instructors and is open daily for people of all ages and skill levels. Projects, classes, and workshops at this not-for-profit organization highlight creativity in all forms, including photography, figure drawing, ceramics, landscape painting, painting on silk, and the performing arts (ballet, yoga, creative movement, Pilates). Classes are inexpensive. Call the school to see what's scheduled while you're on Maui.

elegant Mandalay is a big loss. The **Elizabeth Dole Gallery** has loads of Dale Chihuly studio glass, fabulous and expensive, a dramatic counterpoint to **South Seas Trading Post** and its exotic artifacts such as New Guinea masks, Balinese beads, tribal jewelry, lizard-skin drums, and coconut-shell carvings with mother-of-pearl inlay. Otherwise, it's slim pickings for shoppers in Kapalua. In the Kapalua Bay Hotel and Villas. ✆ 808/669-1029.

Village Galleries Maui's finest exhibit their works here and in the other two Village Galleries in Lahaina. Take heart, art lovers: There's no clichéd marine art here. Translucent, delicately turned bowls of Norfolk pine gleam in the light, and George Allan, Betty Hay Freeland, Fred KenKnight, and Pamela Andelin are included in the pantheon of respected artists represented in the tiny gallery. Watercolors, oils, sculptures, handblown glass, Niihau shell leis, jewelry, and other media are represented. The Ritz-Carlton's monthly Artist-in-Residence program features gallery artists in demonstrations and special hands-on workshops—free, including materials. In the Ritz-Carlton Kapalua, 1 Ritz-Carlton Dr. ✆ 808/669-1800.

SOUTH MAUI
KIHEI

Kihei is one long strip of strip malls. Most of the shopping here is concentrated in the **Azeka Place Shopping Center** on South Kihei Road. Across the street, **Azeka Place II** houses several prominent attractions, including the **Coffee Store** and a cluster of specialty shops with everything from children's clothes to shoes, sunglasses, and swimwear.

Hawaiian Moons Natural Foods Hawaiian Moons is an exceptional health-food store, as well as a minisupermarket with one of the best selections of Maui products on the island. The tortillas are made on Maui (and good!), and much of the produce here, such as organic vine-ripened tomatoes and organic onions, is grown in the fertile upcountry soil of Kula. There's also locally grown organic coffee, gourmet salsas, Maui shiitake mushrooms, organic lemongrass and okra, Maui Crunch bread, free-range Big Island turkeys and chickens (no antibiotics or artificial nasties), and fresh Maui juices. Cosmetics are top-of-the-line: a staggering selection of sunblocks, fragrant floral oils, kukui-nut oil from Waialua on Oahu, and Island Essence made-on-Maui mango-coconut and vanilla-papaya lotions, the ultimate in body pampering. The salad bar is one of the most popular food stops on the coast. Also on the West Side at 3636 Lower Honoapiilani Rd., ✆ 808/665-1339. 2411 S. Kihei Rd. ✆ 808/875-4356.

Pua's Lei Stand *(Finds* Surprise! Fresh plumeria lei in hot Kihei! Located at the far mauka (mountainside) end of the shopping village, Pua's Lei Stand is an oasis of fragrance, freshness, and the spirit of Hawaii. You'll see lavish wiliwili and seed lei, hula implements, Hawaiian-printed flaxseed eye pillows, Hawaiian angels made from fibers found in Kihei, and all manner of made-on-Maui gems. The hard-to-find Maui Herbal soaps are generous blocks in fabulous fragrances of pikake, tuberose, guavaberry, tropical sea, and—our favorite—plumeria. These soaps lather richly and contain pure ingredients; their simple packaging belie the fact that they are of top quality, and not widely available. In Kihei Kalama Village, 1941 S. Kihei Rd. No phone.

Tuna Luna There are treasures to be found in this small cluster of tables and booths where Maui artists display their work. Ceramics, raku, sculpture, glass, koa-wood books and photo albums, jewelry, soaps, handmade paper, and fiber-art accessories make great gifts to go. Something to watch for: Maui Metal hand-crafted journals, aluminum books with designs of hula girls, palms, fish, and sea horses. Tuna Luna also has a new booth in the back pavilion. Also in Lahaina at 658 Front St., (C) 808/661-8662. In Kihei Kalama Village, 1941 S. Kihei Rd. (C) 808/874-9482.

WAILEA

The Shops at Wailea   This is the big shopping boost that resort-goers have been awaiting for years. Chains still rule (**The Gap, Louis Vuitton, Banana Republic, Tiffany, Crazy Shirts, Honolua Surf Co.**), but there is still fertile ground for the inveterate shopper in the nearly 60 shops in the complex. **Martin & MacArthur** (furniture and gift gallery; see Whalers Village, above) has landed in Wailea as part of a retail mix that is similar to Whalers Village. The high-end resort shops sell expensive souvenirs, gifts, clothing, and accessories for a life of perpetual vacations.

One store of particular note in this complex is **CY Maui** ((C) 808/891-0782). Women who like washable, flowing clothing in silks, rayons, and natural fibers will love this shop, formerly the popular Manikin in Kahului. If you don't find what you want on the racks of simple bias-cut designs, you can have it made from the bolts of stupendous fabrics lining the shop. Except for a few hand-painted silks, everything in the shop is washable. 3750 Wailea Alanui. (C) 808/ 891-6770.

Grand Wailea Shops   The sprawling Grand Wailea Resort is known for its long arcade of shops and galleries tailored to hefty pocketbooks. However, gift items in all price ranges can be found at Lahaina Printsellers (for old maps and prints), Dolphin Galleries, H. F. Wichman, Sandal Tree, and Napua Gallery, which houses the private collection of the resort owner. Ki'i Gallery is luminous with studio glass and exquisitely turned woods, and Sandal Tree (p. 462) raises the footwear bar. At Grand Wailea Resort, 3850 Wailea Alanui Dr. (C) 808/875-1234.

UPCOUNTRY MAUI
MAKAWAO

Besides being a shopper's paradise, Makawao is the home of the island's most prominent arts organization, the **Hui No'eau Visual Arts Center,** 2841 Baldwin Ave. ((C) 808/572-6560). Designed in 1917 by C. W. Dickey, one of Hawaii's most prominent architects, the two-story, Mediterranean-style stucco home that houses the center is located on a sprawling 9-acre estate called Kaluanui. Its tree-lined driveway features two of Maui's largest hybrid Cook and Norfolk Island pines. A legacy of Maui's prominent kamaaina (old-timers), Harry and Ethel Baldwin, the estate became an art center in 1976. Visiting artists offer lectures, classes, and demonstrations, all at reasonable prices, in basketry, jewelry making, ceramics, painting, and other media. Classes on Hawaiian art, culture, and history are also available. Call ahead for schedules and details. The exhibits here are drawn from a wide range of disciplines and multicultural sources, and include both contemporary and traditional art from established and emerging artists. The gift shop, featuring many one-of-a-kind works by local artists and artisans, is worth a stop. Hours are Monday through Saturday from 10am to 4pm.

Collections   This long-time Makawao attraction is showing renewed vigor after more than 2 decades on Baldwin Avenue. It's one of my favorite Makawao stops, full of gift items and spirited clothing reflecting the ease and color of island living. Its selection of sportswear, soaps, jewelry, candles, and tasteful, marvelous miscellany reflects good sense and style. Dresses (including up-to-the-moment Citron in cross-cultural and vintage-looking prints), separates, home and bath accessories, sweaters, and a shop full of good things make this a Makawao must. 3677 Baldwin Ave. ⓒ 808/572-0781.

Cuckoo for Coconuts   The owner's quirky sense of humor pervades every inch of this tiny shop, barely bigger than a walk-in closet and brimming with vintage collectibles, gag gifts, silly coconuts, 1960s and '70s aloha wear, tutus, sequined dresses, vintage wedding gowns, and all sorts of oddities. Things we've seen here: an Elvira wig, very convincing; a raffia hat looking suspiciously like a nest, with blue eggs on top; and some vintage aloha shirts that would make a collector drool. New items include crazy sunglasses, colored wigs, tie-dyes, and party hats. Vintage aloha wear gets grabbed up fast. The new services—singing telegrams, balloon deliveries, costumes, makeup, and gag gifts—keep the laughs coming. 1158 Makawao Ave. ⓒ 808/573-6887.

Gallery Maui   Follow the sign down the charming shaded pathway to a cozy gallery of top-notch art and crafts. Most of the works here are by Maui artists, and the quality is outstanding. About 30 artists are represented: Wayne Omura and his Norfolk pine bowls, Pamela Hayes's watercolors, Martha Vockrodt and her wonderful paintings, a stunning Steve Hynson dresser of curly koa and ebony. The two- and three-dimensional original works reflect the high standards of gallery owners Deborah and Robert Zaleski (a painter), who have just added to their roster the talented ceramic artist David Stabley, a two-time American Craft Council juror. 3643-A Baldwin Ave. ⓒ 808/572-8092.

Gecko Trading Co. Boutique   The selection here is eclectic and always changing: One day it's St. John's Wort body lotion and mesh T-shirts in a dragon motif, the next it's Provence soaps and antique lapis jewelry. You never know what you'll find in this tiny boutique; we've seen everything from handmade crocheted bags from New York to Mexican hammered-tin candle holders. The prices are reasonable, the service is friendly, and it's more homey than glammy, and not as self-conscious as some of the other local boutiques. 3621 Baldwin Ave. ⓒ 808/572-0249.

Holiday & Co.   Attractive women's clothing in natural fibers hangs from racks, while jewelry to go with it beckons from the counter. Recent finds include elegant fiber evening bags, luxurious bath gels, easygoing dresses and separates, Dansko clogs, shawls, shoes, soaps, aloha shirts, books, picture frames, and jewelry. 3681 Baldwin Ave. ⓒ 808/572-1470.

Hot Island Glassblowing Studio & Gallery   You can watch the artist transform molten glass into works of art and utility in this studio in Makawao's Courtyard, where an award-winning family of glassblowers built its own furnaces. It's fascinating to watch the shapes emerge from glass melted at 2,300°F (1,260°C). The colorful works displayed range from small paperweights to large vessels. Four to five artists participate in the demonstrations, which begin when the furnace is heated, about half an hour before the studio opens at 9am. 3620 Baldwin Ave. ⓒ 808/572-4527.

Hurricane   This boutique carries clothing, gifts, accessories, and books that are two steps ahead of the competition. Tommy Bahama aloha shirts and aloha print dresses; Sigrid Olsen's knitted shells, cardigans, and extraordinary silk tank dresses; hats; art by local artists; a notable selection of fragrances for men and women; and hard-to-find, eccentric books and home accessories are part of the Hurricane appeal. 3639 Baldwin Ave. ℭ 808/572-5076.

The Mercantile The jewelry, home accessories (especially the Tiffany-style glass-and-shell lamps), dinnerware, Italian linens, plantation-style furniture, and clothing here are a salute to the good life. There's exquisite bedding, rugs, furniture including hand-carved armoires, down-filled furniture and slipcovers, and a large selection of Kiehl's products. The clothing—comfortable cottons and upscale European linens—is for men and women, as are the soaps, which include Maui Herbal Soap products and some unusual finds from France. Maui-made jams, honey, soaps and ceramics, and Jurlique organic facial and body products are among the new winners. 3673 Baldwin Ave. ℭ 808/572-1407.

Tropo Tropo is a magnet for stylish, sensitive, *and* rugged men searching for tasteful aloha wear and comfortable basics. Books, clothing, Tilley hats, and Crabtree & Evelyn products are among the finds here. Men can shop for Tommy Bahama trousers and shorts, tasteful T-shirts, stylish winter wovens by Toes on the Nose, and aloha shirts by Reyn Spooner, Tori Richards, Que, and Kahala. 3643 Baldwin Ave. ℭ 808/573-0356.

Viewpoints Gallery Maui's only fine-arts cooperative showcases the work of 20 established artists in an airy, attractive gallery located in a restored theater with a courtyard, glassblowing studio, and restaurants. The gallery features two-dimensional art, jewelry, fiber art, stained glass, paper, sculpture, and other media. This is a fine example of what can happen in a collectively supportive artistic environment. 3620 Baldwin Ave. ℭ 808/572-5979.

FRESH FLOWERS IN KULA

Like anthuriums on the Big Island, proteas are a Maui trademark and an abundant crop on Haleakala's rich volcanic slopes. They also travel well, dry beautifully, and can be shipped worldwide with ease. Among Maui's most prominent sources is **Sunrise Protea** (ℭ 808/876-0200; www.sunriseprotea.com), in Kula. It offers a walk-through garden and gift shops, friendly service, and a larger-than-usual selection. Freshly cut flowers arrive from the fields on Tuesday and Friday afternoons. You can order individual blooms, baskets, arrangements, or wreaths for shipping all over the world. (Next door, the Sunrise Country Market offers fresh local fruits, snacks, and sandwiches, with picnic tables for lingering.)

Proteas of Hawaii (ℭ 808/878-2533; www.proteasofhawaii.com), another reliable source, offers regular walking tours of the University of Hawaii Extension Service gardens across the street in Kula.

Outside of Kula, **Ooka Super Market** (p. 458) and the Saturday-morning **Maui Swap Meet** (p. 457) are among the best and least expensive places for tropical flowers of every stripe.

UPCOUNTRY EDIBLES

Working folks in Makawao pick up spaghetti and lasagna, sandwiches, salads, and changing specials from the **Rodeo General Store,** 3661 Baldwin Ave. (ℭ 808/572-7841). At the far end of the store is the oenophile's bonanza, a superior wine selection housed in its own temperature-controlled cave.

Down to Earth Natural Foods, 1169 Makawao Ave. (ℭ 808/572-1488), always has fresh salads and sandwiches, a full section of organic produce (Kula onions, strawberry papayas, mangos, and lychees in season), bulk grains, beauty aids, herbs, juices, snacks, tofu, seaweed, soy products, and aisles of vegetarian and health foods. Whether it's a smoothie or a salad, Down to Earth has fresh, healthful, vegetarian offerings.

In the more than 6 decades that the **T. Komoda Store and Bakery,** 3674 Baldwin Ave. (© **808/572-7261**), has spent in this spot, untold numbers have creaked over the wooden floors to pick up Komoda's famous cream puffs. Old-timers know to come early, or they'll be sold out. Then the cinnamon rolls, doughnuts, pies, and chocolate cake take over. Pastries are just the beginning; poi, macadamia-nut candies and cookies, and small bunches of local fruit keep the customers coming.

EAST MAUI
PAIA

Hemp House   Clothing and accessories made of hemp, a sturdy and sensible fiber, are finally making their way into the mainstream. The Hemp House has as complete a selection as you can expect to see in Hawaii, with "denim" hemp jeans, lightweight linen-like trousers, dresses, shirts, and a full range of sensible, easy-care wear. 16 Baldwin Ave. © 808/579-8880.

Maui Crafts Guild   The old wooden storefront at the gateway to Paia houses crafts of high quality and in all price ranges, from pit-fired raku to bowls of Norfolk pine and other Maui woods, fashioned by Maui hands. Artist-owned and -operated, the guild claims 25 members who live and work on Maui. Basketry, hand-painted fabrics, jewelry, beadwork, traditional Hawaiian stone work, pressed flowers, fused glass, stained glass, copper sculpture, banana bark paintings, pottery of all styles, and hundreds of items are displayed in the two-story gift gallery. Upstairs, sculptor Arthur Dennis Williams displays his breathtaking work in wood, bronze, and stone. Everything can be shipped. **Aloha Bead Co.** (© **808/579-9709**), in the back of the gallery, is a treasure trove for beadworkers. 43 Hana Hwy. © 808/579-9697.

Moonbow Tropics   If you're looking for a tasteful aloha shirt, go to Moonbow. The selection consists of a few carefully culled racks of the top labels in aloha wear, in fabrics ranging from the finest silks and linens to Egyptian cotton and spun rayons. Silk pants, silk shorts, vintage print neckwear, and an upgraded women's selection hang on colorful racks. The jewelry pieces, ranging from tanzanite to topaz, rubies to moonstones, are mounted in unique settings made on-site. 36 Baldwin Ave. © 808/579-8592.

HANA

Hana Coast Gallery *Finds*   This gallery is a good reason to go to Hana: It's an esthetic and cultural experience that informs as it enlightens. Tucked away in the posh hideaway hotel, the gallery is known for its high level of curatorship and commitment to the cultural art of Hawaii. There are no jumping whales or dolphins here—and except for a section of European and Asian masters (Renoir, Japanese woodblock prints), the 3,000-square-foot gallery is devoted entirely to Hawaii artists. Dozens of well-established local artists display their sculptures, paintings, prints, feather work, stone work, and carvings in displays that are so natural they could well exist in someone's home. Director-curator Patrick Robinson (of impeccable artistic integrity) has expanded the selection of koa wood furniture in response to the ongoing revival of the American Crafts Movement with a Hawaiian/Japanese influence. Stellar artists Tai Lake from the Big Island and Randall Watkins from Maui are among those represented.

Connoisseurs of hand-turned bowls will find the crème de la crème of the genre here: J. Kelly Dunn, Ron Kent, Todd Campbell, Ed Perrira, and Gary Stevens. You won't find a better selection elsewhere under one roof. The award-winning gallery has won accolades from the top travel and arts magazines in the country (*Travel & Leisure, Arts & Antiques* magazine) and has steered clear of trendiness and unfortunate tastes. In the Hotel Hana-Maui. © **808/248-8636.**

Hasegawa General Store   Established in 1910, immortalized in song since 1961, burned to the ground in 1990, and back in business in 1991, this legendary store is indefatigable and more colorful than ever in its fourth generation in business. The aisles are choked with merchandise: coffee specially roasted and blended for the store, Ono Farms organic dried fruit, fishing equipment, every tape and CD that mentions Hana, the best books on Hana to be found, T-shirts, beach and garden essentials, baseball caps, film, baby food, napkins, and other necessities for the Hana life. Hana Hwy. © **808/248-8231.**

11 Maui After Dark

The island's most prestigious entertainment venue is the $28 million **Maui Arts and Cultural Center,** in Kahului (© **808/242-7469;** www.mauiarts.org). Bonnie Raitt has performed here, as have B. B. King, Hiroshima, Pearl Jam, Ziggy Marley, Lou Rawls, the American Indian Dance Theatre, Jonny Lang, and Tony Bennett, not to mention Keali`i Reichel and the finest in local and Hawaii talent. The center is as precious to Maui as the Met is to New York, with a visual-arts gallery, an outdoor amphitheater, offices, rehearsal space, a 300-seat theater for experimental performances, and a 1,200-seat main theater. Whether it's hula, the Iona Pear Dance Company, Willie Nelson, or the Maui Symphony Orchestra, only the best appear here. The center's activities are well publicized locally, so check the *Maui News* or ask your hotel concierge what's going on during your visit.

HAWAIIAN MUSIC   Except for **Casanova** in Makawao and **Maui Brews** in Lahaina, nightlife options on this island are limited. The major hotels generally have lobby lounges offering Hawaiian music, soft jazz, or hula shows beginning at sunset. If **Hapa, Willie K. and Amy Gilliom,** or the soloist **Keali'i Reichel** are playing anywhere on their native island, don't miss them; they're among the finest Hawaiian musicians around today.

WEST MAUI: LAHAINA

The buzz in Lahaina is **Ulalena** ✦, Maui Myth and Magic Theatre, 878 Front St. (© **877/688-4800** or 808/661-9913; www.ulalena.com), a riveting evening of entertainment that weaves Hawaiian mythology with drama, dance, and state-of-the-art multimedia capabilities in a brand-new, multimillion-dollar theater. Polynesian dance, original music, acrobatics, and chant, performed by a local and international cast, combine to create an evocative experience that often leaves the audience speechless. It's interactive, with dancers coming down the aisles, drummers and musicians in surprising corners, and mind-boggling stage and lighting effects that draw the audience in. Some special moments: the goddesses dancing on the moon, the white sail of the first Europeans, the wrath of the volcano goddess Pele, the labors of the field-worker immigrants. The story unfolds seamlessly; at the end, you'll be shocked to realize that not a single word of dialogue was spoken. Performances are Tuesday, 6pm and 8:30pm, and Wednesday to Saturday 6pm only. Tickets are $48 to $58 for adults and $28 to $38 for children (ages 3-10).

Moments   A Night to Remember: Luau, Maui Style

Most of the larger hotels in Maui's major resorts offer luaus on a regular basis. You'll pay about $65 to $70 to attend one. To protect yourself from disappointment, don't expect it to be a homegrown affair
prepared in the traditional Hawaiian way. There are, however, commercial luaus that capture the romance and spirit of the luau with
quality food and entertainment in outdoor settings.

Maui's best luau is indisputably the nightly **Old Lahaina Luau** ★★
(© 800/248-5828 or 808/667-1998; www.oldlahainaluau.com). Located
just oceanside of the Lahaina Cannery, the Old Lahaina Luau maintains
its high standards in food and entertainment, in a oceanfront setting
that is peerless. Local craftspeople display their wares only a few feet
from the ocean. Seating is provided on lauhala mats for those who
wish to dine as the traditional Hawaiians did, but there are tables for
everyone else. There's no fire dancing in the program, but you won't
miss it (for that, go to the Feast at Lele, p. 394). This luau offers a
healthy balance of entertainment, showmanship, authentic high-quality food, educational value, and sheer romantic beauty. (No watered-
down mai tais, either; these are the real thing.)

The luau begins at sunset and features Tahitian and Hawaiian entertainment, including ancient hula, hula from the missionary era, modern hula, and an intelligent narrative on the dance's rocky course of
survival into modern times. The entertainment is riveting, even for
jaded locals. The food, which is served from an open-air thatched
structure, is as much Pacific Rim as authentically Hawaiian: imu-roasted
kalua pig, baked mahimahi in Maui onion cream sauce, guava chicken,
teriyaki sirloin steak, lomi salmon, poi, dried fish, poke, Hawaiian
sweet potato, sautéed vegetables, seafood salad, and the ultimate
taste treat, taro leaves with coconut milk. The cost is $79 for adults,
$49 for children 12 and under , plus tax.

A very different type of live entertainment is **Warren & Annabelle's,** 900
Front St., Lahaina (©808/667-6244, www.hawaiimagic.com), a mystery/magic
cocktail show with illusionist Warren Gibson and "Annabella," a ghost from the
1800s who plays the grand piano (even taking requests from the audience) as
Warren dazzles you with his sleight-of-hand magic. Pre-show entertainment
begins at 6:45pm nightly. Tickets (book in advance) are $40, cocktails and food
are extra. You must be 21 years old to attend, although they occasionally have a
5pm family show (minimum age is 6 years) without food or cocktails; call for
details.

Maui Brews, 900 Front St. (© 808/667-7794), draws the late-night crowd
to its corner of the Lahaina Center with swing, salsa, reggae, and jams. There's
live music Friday and Monday nights. Hours are daily from 11:30am, with
happy hour from 3 to 6pm and nightclub hours from 9pm to 1:30am.

At **Longhi's,** 888 Front St. (© 808/667-2288), live music spills out into the
streets from 9:30pm on weekends. It's usually salsa or jazz, but call ahead to

confirm. Other special gigs can be expected if rock-and-rollers or jazz musicians who are friends of the owner happen to be passing through.

You won't have to ask what's going on at **Cheeseburger in Paradise,** 811 Front St. (© **808/661-4855**), the two-story green-and-white building at the corner of Front and Lahainaluna streets. Just go outside and you'll hear it. Loud, live, and lively tropical rock blasts into the streets and out to sea nightly from 4:30 to 11pm.

UPCOUNTRY MAUI

Upcountry in Makawao, the party never ends at **Casanova,** 1188 Makawao Ave. (© 808/572-0220), the popular Italian ristorante where the good times roll with the pasta. The newly renovated bar area has large booths, all the better for socializing around the stage and dance floor. If a big-name mainland band is resting up on Maui following a sold-out concert on Oahu, you may find its members setting up for an impromptu night here. DJs take over on Wednesday (ladies' night) and, on Thursday, Friday, and Saturday, live entertainment draws fun-lovers from even the most remote reaches of the island. Entertainment starts at 9:45pm and continues to 1:30am. Expect good blues, rock-and-roll, reggae, jazz, Hawaiian, and the top names in local and visiting entertainment. Elvin Bishop, the local duo Hapa, Los Lobos, and many others have filled Casanova's stage and limelight. The cover is usually $5. Sunday afternoons, 3 to 6pm, is excellent live jazz.

7

Molokai, the Most Hawaiian Isle

Born of volcanic eruptions 1½ million years ago, Molokai remains a time capsule on the dawn of the 21st century. It has no deluxe resorts, no stoplights, and no buildings taller than a coconut tree. Molokai is the least developed, most "Hawaiian" of all the islands, making it especially attractive to adventure travelers and peace seekers.

Molokai lives up to its reputation as the most Hawaiian place chiefly through its lineage; there are more people here of Hawaiian blood than anywhere else. This slipper-shaped island was the cradle of Hawaiian dance (the hula was born here) and the ancient science of aquaculture. An aura of ancient mysticism clings to the land here, and the old ways still govern life. The residents survive by taking fish from the sea and hunting wild pigs and axis deer on the range. Some folks still catch fish in throw nets and troll the reef for squid.

Modern Hawaii's high-rise hotels, shopping centers, and other trappings of tourism haven't been able to gain a foothold here. The lone low-rise resort on the island, Kaluakoi—a temporarily closed, empty hotel built nearly 30 years ago—is Molokai's token attempt at contemporary tourism. The only "new" developments since Kaluakoi are the Molokai Ranch's eco-tourism project of upscale "camping" in semipermanent "tentalows" (a combination of a bungalow and a tent)

and an upscale 22-room lodge on the 53,000-acre ranch, now managed by Sheraton. The focus of both is on outdoor recreation and adventure, with all the comforts of home.

Not everyone will love Molokai. The slow-paced, simple life of the people and the absence of contemporary landmarks attract those in search of the "real" Hawaii. We got a letter from a New York City resident who claimed that any "big city resident" would "blanche" at the lack of "sophistication." But that is exactly the charm of the "Friendly Isle." This is a place where Mother Nature is wild and uninhibited, with very little intrusion by man. Forget sophistication, this is one of the few spots on the planet where one can stand in awe of the island's diverse natural wonders: Hawaii's highest waterfall and greatest collection of fish ponds; the world's tallest sea cliffs; sand dunes, coral reefs, rain forests, and hidden coves; and gloriously empty beaches.

EXPLORING THE "MOST HAWAIIAN" ISLE Only 38 miles from end to end and just 10 miles wide, Molokai stands like a big green wedge in the blue Pacific. It has an east side, a west side, a backside, and a topside. This long, narrow island is like yin and yang: One side is a flat, austere, arid desert; the other is a lush, green, steepled tropical Eden. Three volcanic eruptions formed Molokai; the last produced the island's "thumb"—a peninsula jutting out of the steep cliffs of the north shore, like a punctuation mark on the island's geological story.

On the red-dirt southern plain, where most of the island's 6,000 residents live, the rustic village of **Kaunakakai** ✴ looks like the set of an old Hollywood Western, with sun-faded clapboard houses and horses tethered on the side of the road. Mile marker 0, in the center of town, divides the island into east and west; an arid cactus desert lies on one side and a lush coco-palm jungle on the other.

Eastbound, along the **coastal highway** ✴✴✴ named for King Kamehameha V, are Gauguin-like, palm-shaded cottages set on small coves or near fish ponds; spectacular vistas that take in Maui, Lanai, and Kahoolawe; and a fringing coral reef visible through the crystal-clear waves.

Out on the sun-scorched West End is the island's lone destination resort, **Kaluakoi** (where the hotel is currently closed), overlooking a gold-sand beach with water usually too rough to swim in. The old hilltop plantation town of **Maunaloa** has been razed and rebuilt as a gentrified plantation community, complete with an expensive country lodge with a pricey dining room. Cowboys still ride the range on **Molokai Ranch,** a 53,000-acre spread, while adventure travelers and outdoor-recreation buffs stay at the tentalows on the ranch property and spend their days mountain biking, kayaking, horseback riding, sailing, hiking, snorkeling, and just vegetating on the endless white-sand beaches.

Elsewhere around the island, in hamlets like **Kualapuu,** old farmhouses with pickup trucks in the yards and sleepy dogs under the shade trees stand amid row crops of papaya, coffee, and corn—just like farm towns in Anywhere, USA.

But that's not all there is. The "backside" of Molokai is a rugged wilderness of spectacular beauty. On the outskirts of **Kaunakakai,** the land rises gradually from sea-level fish ponds to cool uplands and the Molokai Forest, long ago stripped of sandalwood for the China trade. All that remains is an indentation in the earth that natives shaped like a ship's hull, a crude matrix that gave them a rough idea of when they'd cut enough sandalwood to fill a ship (it's identified on good maps as *Luanamokuiliahi,* or Sandalwood Boat).

The land inclines sharply to the lofty mountains and the nearly mile-high summit of Mount Kamakou, then ends abruptly with emerald-green cliffs, which plunge into a lurid aquamarine sea dotted with tiny deserted islets. These breathtaking 3,250-foot **sea cliffs** ✴✴, the highest in the world, stretch 14 majestic miles along Molokai's north shore, laced by waterfalls and creased by five valleys—Halawa, Papalaua, Wailau, Pelekunu, and Waikolu—once occupied by early Hawaiians who built stone terraces and used waterfalls to irrigate taro patches.

Long after the sea cliffs were formed, a tiny volcano erupted out of the sea at their feet and spread lava into a flat, leaflike peninsula called **Kalaupapa** ✴✴✴—the 1860s leper exile where Father Damien de Veuster of Belgium devoted his life to care for the afflicted. A few people remain in the remote colony by choice, keeping it tidy for the daily company that arrives on mules and by small planes.

WHAT A VISIT TO MOLOKAI IS *REALLY* **LIKE** There's plenty of aloha on Molokai, but the so-called "friendly island" remains ambivalent about vacationers. One of the least visited Hawaiian islands, Molokai welcomes about 70,000 visitors annually on its own take-it-or-leave-it terms, and makes few concessions beyond that of gracious host; it never wants to attract too big of a crowd, anyway.

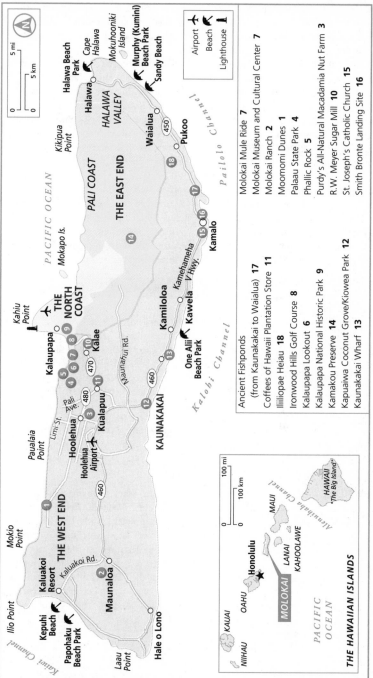

Airport
Beach
Lighthouse

Molokai Mule Ride **7**
Molokai Museum and Cultural Center **7**
Molokai Ranch **2**
Moomomi Dunes **1**
Palaau State Park **4**
Phallic Rock **5**
Purdy's All-Natural Macadamia Nut Farm **3**
R.W. Meyer Sugar Mill **10**
St. Joseph's Catholic Church **15**
Smith Bronte Landing Site **16**

Ancient Fishponds
(from Kaunakakai to Waialua) **17**
Coffees of Hawaii Plantation Store **11**
Ililiopae Heiau **18**
Ironwood Hills Golf Course **8**
Kalaupapa Lookout **6**
Kalaupapa National Historic Park **9**
Kamakou Preserve **14**
Kapuaiwa Coconut Grove/Kiowea Park **12**
Kaunakakai Wharf **13**

A sign at the airport offers the first clue: SLOW DOWN, YOU ON MOLOKAI NOW—wisdom to heed on this island, where life proceeds at its own pace.

Rugged, red-dirt Molokai isn't for everyone, but those who like to explore remote places and seek their own adventures should love it. The best of the island can be seen only on foot, bicycle, mule, horseback, kayak, or boat. The sea cliffs are accessible only by sea in summer, when the Pacific is calm, or via a 10-mile trek through the Wailau Valley—an adventure only a handful of hardy hikers attempt each year. The great Kamakou Preserve is open just once a month, by special arrangement with the Nature Conservancy. Even Moomomi, which holds bony relics of prehistoric flightless birds and other creatures, requires a guide to divulge the secrets of the dunes.

Those in search of nightlife have come to the wrong place; Molokai shuts down after sunset. The only public diversions are softball games under the lights of Mitchell Pauole Field, movies at Maunaloa, and the few restaurants that stay open after dark, often serving local brew and pizza.

The "friendly" island may enchant you as the "real" Hawaii of your dreams. On the other hand, you may leave shaking your head, never to return. Regardless of how you approach Molokai, remember our advice: Take it slow.

1 Orientation

ARRIVING

BY PLANE Molokai has two airports, but you'll most likely fly into **Hoolehua Airport,** which everyone calls "the Molokai Airport." It's on a dusty plain about 6 miles from Kaunakakai town. Jet service to Lanai is now available, but only on **Hawaiian Airlines** (✆ 800/367-5320 or 808/565-6977; www.hawaiianair.com), which offers one flight a day. Twin-engine planes take longer and are sometimes bumpier, but they offer great views because they fly lower: **Island Air** (✆ 800/323-3345 from the mainland, or 800/652-6541 interisland; www.islandair.com), with eight to nine direct flights a day from Honolulu and two direct flights from Maui; **Molokai Air Shuttle** (✆ 808/545-4988); and **Pacific Wings** (✆ 888/575-4546 from the mainland, or 808/873-0877 from Maui; www.pacificwings.com), with one daily flight from Honolulu to Hoolehua and one flight a day from Kahului, Maui to Molokai.

BY BOAT You can travel across the seas from Maui's Lahaina Harbor to Molokai's Kaunakakai Wharf on Island Marine's *Molokai Princess* ferry (✆ 800/275-6969 or 808/667-6165; www.mauiprincess.com). The 100-foot yacht, certified for 149 passengers, is fitted with the latest generation of gyroscopic stabilizers, making the ride smoother. The ferry makes the 90-minute journey from Lahaina to Kaunakakai daily; the cost is $40 adult one-way and $20 children one-way. Or you can choose to tour the island from two different package options: Cruise-Drive, which includes round-trip passage and a rental car for $149 for the driver, $80 per additional adult passenger and $40 for children; or the Alii Tour, which is a guided tour in an air-conditioned van plus lunch for $149 for adults and $89 for children.

They also offer ferry transportation and a hike-tour of the Kalaupapa Leprosy Settlement for $215 per person. See "The Legacy of Father Damien: Kalaupapa National Historic Park," later in this chapter, for more information about the settlement.

VISITOR INFORMATION

Look for a sun-faded, yellow building on the main drag, Kamehameha V Highway (Hwy. 460), on the right just past the town's first stop sign, at mile marker 0; it houses the **Molokai Visitors Association,** P.O. Box 960, Kaunakakai, HI 96748 (© **800/800-6367** from the U.S. mainland and Canada, 800/553-0404 interisland, or 808/553-3876; www.molokai-hawaii.com). The staff can give you all the information you need on what to see and do while you're on Molokai.

THE ISLAND IN BRIEF

Kaunakakai ★

Dusty vehicles—mostly pickup trucks—are parked diagonally along Ala Malama Street. It could be any small town, except it's Kaunakakai, the closest thing Molokai has to a business district. Friendly Isle Realty and Friendly Isle Travel offer islanders dream homes and vacations; Rabang's Filipino Food posts bad checks in the window; antlered deer-head trophies guard the grocery aisles at Misaki's Market; and Kanemitsu's, the town's legendary bakery, churns out fresh loaves of onion-cheese bread daily.

Once an ancient canoe landing, Kaunakakai was the royal summer residence of King Kamehameha V. The port town bustled when pineapple and sugar were king, but those days, too, are gone. With its Old West–style storefronts laid out in a 3-block grid on a flat, dusty plain, Kaunakakai is a town from the past. At the end of Wharf Road is Molokai Wharf, a picturesque place to fish, photograph, and just hang out.

Kaunakakai is the dividing point between the lush, green east end and the dry, arid West End. On the west side of town stands a cactus and on the east side of town, there's thick, green vegetation.

The North Coast ★★

Upland from Kaunakakai, the land tilts skyward and turns green, with scented plumeria in yards and glossy coffee trees all in a row, until it blooms into a true forest—and then abruptly ends at a great precipice, falling 3,250 feet to the sea. The green sea cliffs are creased with five V-shaped crevices so deep that light is seldom seen (to paraphrase a Hawaii poet). The north coast is a remote, forbidding place, with a solitary peninsula—**Kalaupapa** ★★★—that was once the home for exiled lepers (it's now a national historical park). This region is easy on the eyes but difficult to visit. It lies at a cool elevation, and frequent rain squalls blow in from the ocean. In summer, the ocean is calm, providing great opportunities for kayaking, fishing, and swimming, but during the rest of the year, giant waves come rolling onto the shores.

The West End ★

This end of the island, home to **Molokai Ranch,** is miles of stark desert terrain, bordered by the most beautiful white-sand beaches in Hawaii. The rugged rolling land slopes down to Molokai's only destination resort, **Kaluakoi,** a cul-de-sac of condos clustered around a nearly 3-decades old seafront hotel (which closed in 2001 and was still closed when we went to press) near 3-mile long Papohaku, the island's biggest beach. On the way to Kaluakoi, you'll find **Maunaloa,** a 1920s-era pineapple-plantation town that's in the midst of being transformed into a master-planned community, Maunaloa Village, with an upscale lodge, triplex theater, restaurants, and shops. The West End is dry, dry, dry. It hardly ever rains, but when it does (usually in the winter), expect a downpour and lots of red mud.

The East End ★★★

The area east of Kaunakakai becomes lush, green, and tropical, with golden pocket beaches and a handful of cottages and condos that are popular with thrifty travelers. With this voluptuous landscape comes rain. However, most storms are brief (15-min.) affairs that blow in, dry up, and disappear. Winter is Hawaii's rainy season, so expect more rain during January to March, but even then, the storms usually are brief and the sun comes back out.

Beyond Kaunakakai, the two-lane road curves along the coast past piggeries, palm groves, and a 20-mile string of fish ponds as well as an ancient heiau, Damien-built churches, and a few contemporary condos by the sea. The road ends in the glorious **Halawa Valley** ★, one of Hawaii's most beautiful valleys.

FAST FACTS

Molokai and Lanai are both part of Maui County. For **local emergencies,** call ℂ 911. For nonemergencies, call the **police** at ℂ 808/553-5355, the **fire department** at ℂ 808/553-5601, or **Molokai General Hospital,** in Kaunakakai, at ℂ 808/553-5331.

Downtown Kaunakakai has a **post office** (ℂ 808/553-5845) and several banks, including the **Bank of Hawaii** (ℂ 808/553-3273), which has a 24-hour ATM.

2 Getting Around

Getting around Molokai isn't easy if you don't have a rental car, and rental cars are often hard to find here. On holiday weekends—and remember, Hawaii celebrates different holidays than the rest of the United States (p. 33)—car-rental agencies simply run out of cars. Book before you go. There's no municipal transit or shuttle service, but a 24-hour taxi service is available (see below).

CAR-RENTAL AGENCIES   Rental cars are available from **Budget** (ℂ 808/567-6877) and **Dollar** (ℂ 808/567-6156); both agencies are located at the Molokai Airport. Non-chain operators include: **Molokai Rentals and Tours,** Kaunakakai (ℂ 800/553-9071 or 808/553-5663; www.molokai-rentals.com), prices range from $32 a day ($203 a week) for a compact to $65 a day ($420 a week) for a 4×4 Jeep. We also recommend **Island Kine** (ℂ 808/553-5242; fishin@aloha.net)—not only are the cars cheaper, but Barbara Shonely and her son, Steve, also give personalized service. They'll meet you at the Molokai Airport, take you to their office in Kaunakakai, and recommend specific outfitters for your activities. The used cars are in perfect condition (to quote Barbara: "I would drive every one of them with my grandkids") and are air-conditioned. Vans and pickup trucks are also available. You won't need a four-wheel-drive vehicle unless you're planning some specialized hiking, but if that's the case, Island Kine has what you're looking for.

TAXI & TOUR SERVICES   Molokai Off-Road Tours & Taxi (ℂ 808/553-3369) offers regular taxi service, an airport shuttle ($7 per person, one-way, to Sheraton Molokai Lodge, based on 4 people; otherwise it is $28 for 2, one-way; and $7.50 per person to Kaunakakai, based on 3 people), and island tours (6 hours for $59 per person, 3-person minimum).

3 Where to Stay

Molokai is Hawaii's most affordable island, especially for hotels. And because the island's restaurants are few, most hotel rooms and condo units come with kitchens, which can save you a bundle on dining costs.

There aren't a ton of accommodations options on Molokai—mostly B&Bs, condos, a few quaint oceanfront vacation rentals, an aging resort, and a very expensive lodge. For camping on Molokai, you have two options: the upscale tentalows offered by Sheraton Molokai Lodge and Beach Village, or, for hardy souls, camping with your own tent at the beach or in the cool upland forest (see "Hiking & Camping," later in this chapter). We've listed our top picks below; for additional options, contact **Molokai Visitors Association** (see "Visitor Information" under "Orientation," above).

Note: Taxes of 11.42% will be added to your hotel bill. Parking is free.

KAUNAKAKAI

A'ahi Place *Value* Just outside of the main town of Kaunakakai and up a small hill lies this dream vacation cottage (recently sold and now under new management), complete with a wicker-filled sitting area, a kitchen, and two full-size beds in the bedroom. Two lanais make great places to just sit and enjoy the stars at night. The entire property is surrounded by tropical plants, flowers, and fruit trees. You can choose to forgo breakfast or for $10 more per night (for 2) get all the fixings for a continental breakfast (home-grown Molokai coffee, fresh-baked goods, and fruit from the property) placed in the kitchen, so you can enjoy it at your leisure. For those who seek a quiet vacation, with no phone or TV to distract you, this is the place. And for those who wish to explore Molokai, the central location is perfect.

P.O. Box 2006, Kaunakakai, HI 96748. © 808/553-8033. www.molokai.com/aahi. 1 unit. $85–$95 double including continental breakfast, $75–$85 double without breakfast. Extra person $20. 2-night minimum for continental breakfast, 3-night minimum without breakfast. No credit cards. *In room:* Kitchen, fridge, coffeemaker, no phone.

Hotel Molokai *★* This nostalgic Hawaiian motel complex is composed of a series of modified A-frame units, nestled under coco palms along a gray-sand beach with a great view of Lanai. The rooms are basic (be sure to ask for one with a ceiling fan), with a lanai. The mattresses are on the soft side, the sheets thin, and the bath towels rough, but you're on Molokai—and this is the only hotel in Kaunakakai. The kitchenettes, with coffeemaker, toaster, pots, and two-burner stove, can save you money on eating out. The front desk is open only from 7am to 8pm; late check-ins or visitors with problems have to go to security.

Kamehameha V Hwy. (P.O. Box 1020), Kaunakakai, HI 96748. © 800/367-5004 on the mainland, 800/272-5275 in Hawaii, or 808/553-5347. Fax 800/477-2329. www.hotelmolokai.com. 45 units. $82–$132 double; $137 suite with kitchenette (sleeps 4). Extra bed/crib $17. AE, DC, DISC, MC, V. **Amenities:** Fairly good and reasonably priced restaurant with bar; outdoor pool; watersports equipment rentals; bike rentals; activity desk; babysitting; coin-op washer/dryers. *In room:* A/C, TV, dataport, some kitchenettes, fridge, coffeemaker, hair dryer, iron, safe.

Ka Hale Mala Bed & Breakfast *Value* In a subdivision just outside town (off Kamehameha V Hwy., before mile marker 5) is this large four-room unit, with a private entrance through the garden and a Jacuzzi just outside. Inside, you'll find white rattan furnishings, room enough to sleep four, and a full kitchen. The helpful owners, Jack and Cheryl, meet all guests at the airport like long-lost relatives. They'll happily share their homegrown, organic produce; we recommend paying the extra $5 each for breakfast here. The owners can also supply a couple of bikes and snorkel and picnic gear.

7 Kamakana Place (P.O. Box 1582), Kaunakakai, HI 96748. 📞 and fax **808/553-9009**. www.molokai-bnb. com. 1 unit. $70 double without breakfast, $80 double with breakfast. Extra person $10. No credit cards. **Amenities:** Jacuzzi. *In room:* TV, kitchen, fridge, coffeemaker.

Molokai Shores Suites *(Kids)*   Basic units with kitchens and large lanais face a small gold-sand beach in this quiet complex of three-story Polynesian-style buildings, less than a mile from Kaunakakai. Alas, the beach is mostly for show (offshore, it's shallow mud flats underfoot), fishing, or launching kayaks, but the swimming pool and barbecue area come with an ocean view, and the spacious units make this a good choice for families. Well-tended gardens, spreading lawns, and palms frame a restful view of fish ponds, offshore reefs, and neighbor islands. The central location can be a plus, minimizing driving time from the airport or town, and it's convenient to the mule ride, as well as the lush East End countryside. There's no daily maid service. Check the website for Internet-only discounts. We have gotten some letters complaining about the lack of maintenance and cleanliness; the management swears that they are taking steps to correct these deficiencies.

Kamehameha V Hwy. (P.O. Box 1037), Kaunakakai, HI 96748. 📞 **800/535-0085** or 808/553-5954. Fax 808/ 553-5954. www.marcresorts.com. 102 units. $155 1-bedroom apt (sleeps up to 4); $199 2-bedroom apt (up to 6). Discounted rates for weekly and extended stays, plus corporate, military, and senior discounts. AE, DC, MC, V. **Amenities:** Putting green; salon; coin-op washer/dryers. *In room:* TV, kitchen, fridge, coffeemaker, iron.

THE WEST END

Ke Nani Kai Resort *(star) (Kids)*   This place is great for families, who will appreciate the space. The large apartments are set up for full-time living with real kitchens, washer/dryers, VCRs, attractive furnishings, and breezy lanais. There's a huge pool, a volleyball court, tennis courts, and golf on the neighboring Kaluakoi course. These condos are farther from the sea than other local accommodations but are still just a brief walk from the beach. The two-story buildings are surrounded by parking and garden areas. The only down side: Maid service is only every third day.

In the Kaluakoi Resort development, Kaluakoi Rd., off Hwy. 460 (P.O. Box 289), Maunaloa, HI 96770. 📞 **800/535-0085** or 808/552-2761. Fax 808/552-0045. www.marcresorts.com. 100 units. $155–$169 1-bedroom apt (sleeps up to 4); $189–$209 2-bedroom apt (up to 6). AE, DISC, DC, MC, V. **Amenities:** Outdoor pool; golf course; 2 tennis courts; Jacuzzi; washer/dryers in units. *In room:* TV, kitchen, fridge, coffeemaker.

Paniolo Hale *(star)(star) (Finds)*   This is far and away Molokai's most charming lodging and probably its best value—be sure to ask about discounted weekly rates and special condo/car packages when making your reservations. The two-story, old Hawaii ranch-house design is airy and homey, with oak floors and walls of folding-glass doors that open to huge screened verandas, doubling your living space. The one- and two-bedrooms come with two bathrooms and accommodate three or four easily. Some units have hot tubs on the lanai. All are spacious, comfortably furnished, and well equipped, with full kitchens and washer/dryers.

The whole place overlooks the Kaluakoi Golf Course (recently reopened), a green barrier that separates these condos from the rest of Kaluakoi Resort. Out front, Kepuhi Beach is a scenic place for walkers and beachcombers, but the seas

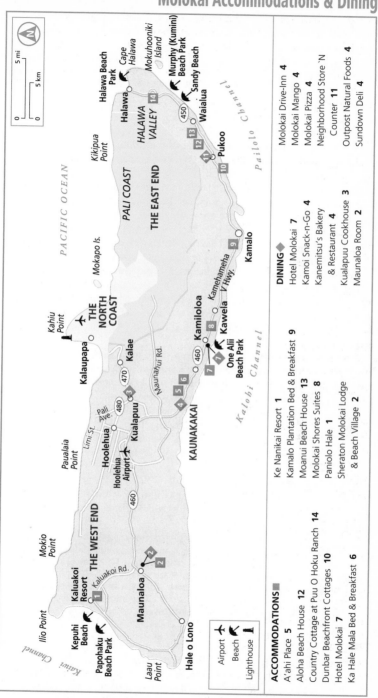

ACCOMMODATIONS

A'ahi Place **5**
Aloha Beach House **12**
Country Cottage at Puu O Hoku Ranch **14**
Dunbar Beachfront Cottages **10**
Hotel Molokai **7**
Ka Hale Mala Bed & Breakfast **6**
Ke Nanikai Resort **1**
Kamalo Plantation Bed & Breakfast **9**
Moanui Beach House **13**
Molokai Shores Suites **8**
Paniolo Hale **1**
Sheraton Molokai Lodge & Beach Village **2**

DINING ◆

Hotel Molokai **7**
Kamoi Snack-n-Go **4**
Kanemitsu's Bakery & Restaurant **4**
Kualapuu Cookhouse **3**
Maunaloa Room **2**
Molokai Drive-Inn **4**
Molokai Mango **4**
Molokai Pizza **4**
Neighborhood Store 'N Counter **11**
Outpost Natural Foods **4**
Sundown Deli **4**

are too hazardous for most swimmers. A pool, paddle tennis, and barbecue facilities are on the property, which adjoins open grassland countryside.

Next door to Kaluakoi Resort, Lio Place (P.O. Box 190), Maunaloa, HI 96770. © **800/367-2984** or 808/552-2731. Fax 808/552-2288. www.paniolohaleresort.com. 77 units. $95–$155 double studio; $115–$230 1-bedroom apt (sleeps up to 4); $145–$265 2-bedroom apt (up to 6). Extra person $10. 2-night minimum; 1-week minimum Dec 20–Jan 5. AE, MC, V. **Amenities:** Outdoor pool; nearby golf course. *In room:* TV, kitchen, fridge, coffeemaker, washer/dryers.

Sheraton Molokai Lodge & Beach Village ★ Sheraton took over the beachside camping village (see "Believe it or Not: High-Priced Camping," below) and the quaint 22-room inn in Maunaloa in 2002, which was previously run by the Molokai Ranch, owner of 53,000 acres on the west side of the island. Located in a cool upcountry climate of the tiny village of Maunaloa, the attractive, two-story lodge sits on 8 nicely landscaped acres located 6 miles and a 20- to 25-minute shuttle ride to the nearest beach. Designed to resemble a 1930s-style Hawaii ranch owner's private home, the Lodge features a giant fireplace, huge wooden beam construction, panoramic views, and lots of details—cuffed cowboy boots beside the door, old books lining the shelves—to make it look and feel like a real ranch. Guests step back in time to a Hawaii of yesteryear.

The guest rooms, each with individual country decor, are of two types: deluxe ($360) and luxury ($425). The luxury rooms are spacious corner units that feature either greenhouse-type skylights or a cozy king daybed nestled in a comfy alcove. Our luxury room was wonderful, with a free-standing four-poster bed, 270° view, and a TV that hydraulically lifted out of a credenza, then magically disappeared again.

Other amenities include a dining room (p. 486), the option of dining at buffets at the beach pavilion, a small but practical spa (with massage treatments, men and women's sauna and locker facilities), outdoor heated swimming pool, and access to a host of activities. The Lodge is geared toward outdoorsy types, with a complimentary shuttle to the beach and to activities (horseback riding, mountain biking, hiking, kayaking, snorkeling, beach activities, and more, ranging in price from $30–$125). There's also wonderful local entertainment in the Great Room in the evening; even if you don't stay here, come for the free entertainment.

This is the most expensive place to stay on Molokai and is priced as high as oceanfront resorts on Maui. Despite some nice features, it cannot compete with the amenities (not to mention the beach location) offered by other, similarly priced Hawaii resorts.

P.O. Box 259, Maunaloa, HI 96770. © **800/782-9488** or 808/660-2710. Fax 808/5520-2908. www.sheraton-hawaii.com. 22 units. $360–$425 double, plus $10 per day resort fee for transportation to beach, use of facilities at Lodge, and use of beach equipment at the beach camp. Extra person $45; children 12 and under stay and eat free with adult. AE, DISC, DC, MC, V. **Amenities:** Restaurant (see Maunaloa Dining Room. p. 486); bar with entertainment Tues–Sat evenings; gorgeous outdoor "infinity" pool heated to a perfect temperature for the cool climate; workout room; small spa with massage room; bike rentals; game room; concierge; activity desk; car-rental desk; shopping arcade; massage; laundry service. *In room:* A/C, TV, dataport, fridge, coffeemaker, hair dryer, iron, safe.

THE EAST END

Aloha Beach House ★★ *Finds* This is a great place to stay on Molokai. Nestled on the lush East End lies this Hawaiian-style beach house sitting right on the white sand beach of Waialua. Perfect for families, this impeccably decorated, two-bedroom, 1,600-square-foot beach house has a huge open living/dining/kitchen area that opens out to an old-fashioned porch for meals or just sitting in

Believe It or Not: High-Priced Camping

This was a great idea: a unique ecoadventure that combines camping and outdoor activities with the amenities of a resort. **Sheraton Molokai Lodge and Beach Village** (© 800/782-9488 or 808/660-2710; fax 808/552-2908; www.sheraton-hawaii.com) recently took over the Molokai Ranch's camping on an exclusive private beach, with very upscale "camping" accommodations. The Beach Village offers "ten-talows" (safari-type tents mounted on wooden platforms). This is yuppie camping—with queen or twin beds, ceiling fans, solar-powered lights, private bathrooms with composting toilets, and solar hot-water showers, plus big decks with lounge chairs, personal hammocks for two and picnic tables. There's even daily maid service! A big pavilion down at the beach has all-you-can-eat buffet meals three times a day, plus nightly entertainment under the stars.

When the Ranch first opened these camps, the price included airport pick up, meals, and a large menu of outdoor activities (horseback riding, mountain biking, hiking, sailing, snorkeling, kayaking, and other adventures). It was all-inclusive and quite a deal at $185 per person.

Today, the prices have risen to an astounding $275 (near the beach) to $320 (directly on the beach) double or single occupancy (plus the ubiquitous "Resort Fee" of $10 a day). Children 17 and under do stay free (when accompanied by an adult) and children 12 and under also eat free, when accompanied by an adult. Meal prices are: $12 for breakfast, $15 for lunch and $29 for dinner. It starts to add up: Two adults staying in the least expensive room will spend $318 a day—including tax and $10 daily resort fee—just on the room! With meals, tax and tip, it comes out to $452 a day for two—and that's not including any activities you may want to do. That's pretty expensive "camping."

---

the comfy chairs and watching the clouds roll by. It's fully equipped, from the complete kitchen (including a dishwasher), to a VCR (plus a library of videos), to all the beach toys you can think of. Located close to the Neighborhood Store in case you need to pick up something or don't feel like cooking and want to eat out.

Located just after mile marker 19. Reservations c/o The Rietows, P.O. Box 79, Kilauea, Hi 96754. © 888/828-1008 or 808/828-1100. Fax 808/828-2199. www.molokaivacation.com. 1 2-bedroom house (sleeps up to 5). $180 (for up to 5) plus $95 cleaning fee. 3-night minimum. No credit cards. *In room:* TV, kitchen, fridge, coffeemaker, washer/dryer.

Country Cottage at Pu'u O Hoku Ranch 🌟 *Kids*   Escape to a working cattle ranch! *Pu'u O Hoku* ("Star Hill") Ranch, which spreads across 14,000 acres of pasture and forests, is the last place to stay before Halawa Valley—it's at least an hour's drive from Kaunakakai along the shoreline. Two acres of tropically landscaped property circle the ranch's rustic cottage, which boasts breathtaking views of rolling hills and the Pacific Ocean. The wooden cottage features comfortable country furniture, a full kitchen, two bedrooms (1 with a double bed,

1 with 2 twins), two bathrooms, and a separate dining room on the enclosed lanai. TVs and VCRs are available on request. We recommend stargazing at night, watching the sunrise in the morning, and hiking, swimming, or a game of croquet in the afternoon. For larger parties, there's a four-bedroom, three-bathroom house (sleeps up to 8) on the property. Horseback riding is available at the ranch; see p. 495 for details.

Kamehameha V Hwy., at mile marker 25. Reservations: P.O. Box 1889, Kaunakakai, HI 96748. (℅ **808/558-8109.** Fax 808/558-8100. www.puuohoku.com. 1 unit. $125 double for two-bedroom cottage. Extra person $10. 2-night minimum. No credit cards. **Amenities:** Swimming pool. *In room:* TV/VCR available on request, kitchen, fridge, coffeemaker.

Dunbar Beachfront Cottages ★★ *(Kids)*　This is one of the most peaceful, comfortable, and elegant properties on Molokai's East End, and the setting is simply stunning. Each of these two green-and-white plantation-style cottages sits on its own secluded beach (good for swimming)—you'll feel like you're on your own private island. The Puunana Cottage has a king bed and two twins, while the Pauwalu has a queen and two twins. Each has a full kitchen, VCR, ceiling fans, comfortable tropical furniture, a large furnished deck (perfect for whale-watching in winter), and views of Maui, Lanai, and Kahoolawe across the channel.

Kamehameha V Hwy., past mile marker 18. Reservations c/o Kip and Leslie Dunbar, HC01 Box 901, Kaunakakai, HI 96748. (℅ **800/673-0520** or 808/558-8153. Fax 808/558-8153. www.molokai-beachfront-cottages.com. 2 two-bedroom cottages (each sleeps up to 4). $140 cottage, plus one-time $75 cleaning charge. 3-night minimum. No credit cards. *In room:* TV, kitchen, fridge, coffeemaker, washer/dryer.

(Kids) Family-Friendly Hotels

Molokai Shores Suites (p. 478)　At this great central location, just outside Kaunakakai, families can choose from large one- and two-bedroom units in a tropical garden complex with great views of the fish ponds, offshore reefs, and neighbor islands. Amenities include a swimming pool and laundry facilities.

Ke Nani Kai Resort (p. 478)　Located in Kaluakoi Resort, these one- and two-bedroom condo units offer lots of space, with complete kitchens, washer/dryers, VCRs, attractive furnishings, and breezy lanais. For active families, there's a huge pool, a volleyball court, tennis courts, and golf at neighboring Kaluakoi.

Country Cottage at Pu'u O Hoku Ranch (p. 481)　Take the kids to a working cattle ranch! *Pu'u o Hoku* ("Star Hill") has plenty of room for the kids to spread out and play, plus its own secluded, private beach on the shoreline. If you have a really big family (or you're staging a family reunion), there's an 11-room lodge on the property, too.

Dunbar Beachfront Cottages (p. 482)　These private two-bedroom cottages are located on the beach in the lush East End—the perfect spot for a family getaway. Each cottage sits on its own secluded beach and features a complete kitchen, washer/dryer, VCR, large deck, and breathtaking views (great for watching whales in winter).

Moanui Beach House (p. 483)　This spacious, 2-bedroom house across the street from a secluded beach is a great place for families to spread out and relax.

Kamalo Plantation Bed & Breakfast ✦ *Value*   Glenn and Akiko Foster's (no relation to the author) 5-acre spread includes an ancient heiau ruin in the front yard, plus leafy tropical gardens and a working fruit orchard. Their Eden-like property is easy to find: It's right across the East End road from Father Damien's historic St. Joseph church. The plantation-style cottage is tucked under flowering trees and surrounded by swaying palms and tropical foliage. It has its own lanai, a big living room with a queen sofa bed, and a separate bedroom with a king bed, so it can sleep four comfortably. The kitchen is fully equipped (it even has spices), and there's a barbecue outside. A breakfast of fruit and freshly baked bread is served every morning. There's no TV reception, but the cottage does have a VCR, radio, and a CD and cassette player.

Kamehameha V Hwy., just past mile marker 10 (HC01, Box 300), Kaunakakai, HI 96748. Ⓒ and fax **808/558-8236**. www.molokai.com/kamalo. 1 unit. $85 cottage. Rate includes continental breakfast. Extra person $10. 2-night minimum. No credit cards. *In room:* Kitchen, fridge, coffeemaker, hair dryer.

Moanui Beach House ✦ *Kids*   If you're looking for a quiet, remote beach house, this is it. The genial Fosters, who have lived in the islands for many years, run the popular Kamalo Plantation Bed & Breakfast (see above). They recently purchased and renovated this two-bedroom beach house, right across the street from a secluded white-sand cove beach. The A-frame has a shaded lanai facing the ocean, a screened-in lanai on the side of the house, a full kitchen, and an ocean view that's worth the price alone. The Fosters leave a "starter supply" of breakfast foods for guests (fruit basket, home-baked bread, tropical fruit juices, tea, and coffee).

Kamehameha V Hwy., at mile marker 20. Reservations c/o Glenn and Akiko Foster, HC01, Box 300, Kaunakakai, HI 96748. Ⓒ and fax **808/558-8236**. www.molokai.com/kamalo. 1 two-bedroom unit. $140 double. Extra person $20. 3-night minimum. No credit cards. *In room:* TV, kitchen, fridge, coffeemaker, hair dryer, iron, washer and dryer.

4 Where to Dine

Molokai is strong on adventure, the outdoors, and the get-away-from-it-all feeling. No traffic lights and honking horns here, nor long lines at overbooked, self-important restaurants. But when it comes to dining, Molokai is not nirvana. Even with the first upscale hotel and dining room open in Maunaloa, Molokai's culinary offerings are spare.

A lot of people like it that way and acknowledge that the island's character is unchangeably rugged and natural. But a few years ago, when the renovated Hotel Molokai unveiled a tropical fantasy of an oceanfront dining room, the islanders thought this was the height of culinary pleasure. And it quickly became the island's busiest restaurant.

In 1999, when the Molokai Ranch opened the Lodge (now renamed the Sheraton Molokai Lodge & Beach Village), it introduced the concept of Molokai having its own gourmet culinary cuisine, using local ingredients in not only traditional Molokai preparations but also in other ethnic styles of cooking.

Even with these new developments, Molokai has retained its glacial pace of change. The culinary offerings of the island are dominated by mom-and-pop eateries, nothing fancy, most of them fast-food or takeout places and many of them with a home-cooked touch. Lovers of the fast lane might consider this aspect of the island's personality a con rather than a pro, but they wouldn't choose to come here, anyway. Molokai is for those who want to get away from it all, who consider the lack of high-rises and traffic lights a welcome change from the urban chaos that keeps nibbling at the edges of the more popular and populated islands. Sybarites, foodies, and pampered oenophiles had best lower their expectations upon arrival, or turn around and leave the island's natural beauty to nature lovers.

Personally, we like the unpretentiousness of the island; it's an oasis in a state where plastic aloha abounds. Most Molokai residents fish, collect seaweed, grow potatoes and tomatoes, and prepare for backyard luaus. Unlike Lanai (see chapter 8), which is small and rural but offers sophisticated dining in the two classy hotels, Molokai provides no such mix of innocence and erudition. Molokai doesn't pretend to be anything more than a combination of old ways and an informal lifestyle that's closer to the land than to a chef's toque.

You'll even find a certain defiant stance against the trappings of modernity. Although some of the best produce in Hawaii is grown on this island, you're not likely to find much of it served in its restaurants, other than in the takeout items at Outpost Natural Foods, or at the Molokai Pizza Cafe (one of the most pleasing eateries on the island), and the Hotel Molokai. The rest of the time, content yourself with ethnic or diner fare—or by cooking for yourself. The many visitors who stay in condos find that it doesn't take long to sniff out the best sources of produce, groceries, and fresh fish to fire up at home when the island's other dining options are exhausted. The "Edibles" sections in "Shopping" (later in this chapter) will point you to the places where you can pick up foodstuffs for your own island-style feast.

Molokai's restaurants are inexpensive or moderately priced, and several of them do not accept credit cards. Regardless of where you eat, you certainly won't have to dress up. In most cases, we've listed just the town rather than the street address because, as you'll see, street addresses are as meaningless on this island as fancy cars and sequins. Reservations are not accepted unless otherwise noted.

Note: You'll find the restaurants reviewed in this chapter on the "Molokai Accommodations & Dining" map on p. 479.

KAUNAKAKAI

Hotel Molokai ⭐ AMERICAN/ISLAND   On the ocean, with a view of Lanai, torches flickering under palm trees, and tiny fairy lights lining the room and the neighboring pool area, the Hotel Molokai's dining room evokes the romance of a South Seas fantasy. It's a casual room, and since its 1999 reopening, provides the only nightlife in Kaunakakai (see "Molokai After Dark," later in this chapter) and the most pleasing ambience on the island. Lunch choices stick to the basics; most promising are salads (Big Island organic greens) and sandwiches, from roast beef to grilled mahimahi. As the sun sets and the torches are lit for dinner, the menu turns to heavier meats, ribs, fish, and pasta. Try the fresh catch, Korean kalbi ribs, barbecued pork ribs, New York steak, coconut shrimp, or garlic chicken. Temper your expectations of culinary excellence, and you're sure to enjoy a pleasing dinner in an atmosphere that's unequaled on the island.

On Kamehameha V Hwy. ℂ 808/553-5347. Reservations recommended for dinner. Main courses $7–$8 lunch, $12–$19 dinner. AE, DC, MC, V. Daily 7–10am, 11am–2pm, and 6–9pm; bar until 10:30pm.

Kamoi Snack-N-Go ICE CREAM/SNACKS   The Kamoi specialty: sweets and icy treats. Ice cream made by Dave's on Oahu comes in flavors such as green tea, lychee sherbet, *ube* (a brilliant purple color, made from Okinawan sweet potato), haupia, mango, and many other tropical—and traditional—flavors. Schoolchildren and their parents line up for the cones, shakes, sundaes, and popular Icee floats served at this tiny snack shop. If the ice cream doesn't tempt you, maybe something in the aisles full of candies will. It's takeout only; no tables.

In Kamoi Professional Center. (© 808/553-3742. Ice cream $1.65–$3.40. MC, V. Mon–Sat 9am–9pm; Sun noon–9pm.

Kanemitsu's Bakery & Restaurant ☆ BAKERY/DELI   Morning, noon, and night, this local legend fills the Kaunakakai air with the sweet smells of baking. Taro lavosh is the hot seller, joining Molokai bread—developed in 1935 in a cast-iron, kiawe-fired oven—as a Kanemitsu signature. Flavors range from apricot-pineapple to mango (in season), but the classics remain the regular white, wheat, cheese, sweet, and onion-cheese breads. For those who like their bread warm, the bread mixes offer a way to take Molokai home. In the adjoining coffee shop/deli, all sandwiches come on their own freshly baked buns and breads. The hamburgers, egg-salad sandwiches, mahi burgers, and honey-dipped fried chicken are popular and cheap.

Kanemitsu's has a life after dark, too. Whenever anyone on Molokai mentions "hot bread," he's talking about the hot-bread run at Kanemitsu's, the surreal late-night ritual for die-hard bread lovers. Those in the know line up at the bakery's back door beginning at 10:30pm, when the bread is whisked hot out of the oven and into waiting hands (see the box "The Hot Bread Run," later in this chapter). You can order your fresh bread with butter, jelly, cinnamon, or cream cheese, and the bakers will cut the hot loaves down the middle and slather on the works so it melts in the bread. The cream cheese and jelly bread makes a fine substitute for dessert.

79 Ala Malama St. (© 808/553-5855. Most items less than $5.50. No credit cards. Restaurant Wed–Mon 5:30–11:30am; bakery Wed–Mon 5:30am–6:30pm.

Molokai Drive-Inn AMERICAN/TAKEOUT   It is a greasy spoon, but it's one of the rare drive-up places with fresh *akule* (mackerel) and ahi (when available), plus fried saimin at budget-friendly prices. The honey-dipped fried chicken is a favorite among residents, who also come here for the floats, shakes, and other artery-clogging choices. But don't expect much in terms of ambience: This is a fast-food takeout counter that smells like fried food—and it doesn't pretend to be otherwise.

Kaunakakai. (© 808/553-5655. Most items less than $7.75. No credit cards. Mon–Thurs 5:30am–10pm; Fri–Sun 6am–10:30pm.

Molokai Mango DELI/AMERICAN   The former owner of JoJo's restaurant in Maunaloa opened this video store and popular sandwich shop in downtown Kaunakakai, where he sells sandwiches and nachos from the takeout counter. Turkey, ham, and roast beef are served on five different breads, and all are popular. The inexpensive nachos are a hit, too. Molokai Mango also rents and sells videos, games, and equipment, including TV sets.

93-D Ala Malama St. (© 808/553-3981. Most items $2–$4. MC, V. Mon–Sat 9am–8pm.

Molokai Pizza Cafe ☆ PIZZA   It's still the gathering place, with excellent pizzas and sandwiches that have made it a Kaunakakai staple as well as one of our favorite eateries on the island. The best-selling pies are the Molokai (pepperoni and cheese), the Big Island (pepperoni, ham, mushroom, Italian sausage, bacon, and vegetables), and the Molokini (plain cheese slices). Pasta, sandwiches, and specials round out the menu. Our personal fave is the vegetarian Maui pizza, but others tout the fresh-baked submarine and pocket sandwiches and the gyro pocket with spinach pie. Sunday is prime-rib day, Wednesday is Mexican, and Hawaiian plates are sold on Thursdays.

Coin-operated cars and a toy airplane follow the children's theme, but adults should feel equally at home with the very popular barbecued baby-back rib plate and the fresh fish dinners. Children's art and letters in the tiled dining room add an entertaining and charming touch. Free delivery to Hotel Molokai is a welcome development.

In Kahua Center, on the old Wharf Rd. ℂ 808/553-3288. Large pizzas $13–$23. No credit cards. Sun 11am–10pm; Mon–Thurs 10am–10pm; Fri–Sat 10am–11pm.

Outpost Natural Foods ⚘ VEGETARIAN   The healthiest and freshest food on the island is served at the lunch counter of this health food store, around the corner from the main drag on the ocean side of Kaunakakai town. The tiny store abounds in Molokai papayas, bananas, herbs, potatoes, watermelon, and other local produce, complementing its selection of vitamins, cosmetics, and health aids, as well as bulk and shelf items. But the real star is the closet-size lunch counter. The salads, burritos, tempeh sandwiches, vegetarian pot pie, tofu-spinach lasagna, and mock chicken, turkey, and meat loaf (made from oats, sprouts, seeds, and seasonings) are testament to the fact that vegetarian food need not be boring. A must for health-conscious diners and shoppers.

70 Makaena Place. ℂ 808/553-3377. Most items less than $5. AE, DISC, MC, V. Sun–Fri 10am–3pm.

Sundown Deli DELI   From "gourmet saimin" to spinach pie, Sundown's offerings are home-cooked and healthful, with daily specials that include vegetarian quiche, vegetarian lasagna, and club sandwiches. The sandwiches (like smoked turkey and chicken salad) and several salads (Caesar, Oriental, stuffed tomato) are served daily, with a soup that changes by the day (clam chowder, Portuguese bean, cream of broccoli). Vitamins, T-shirts, and snacks are sold in this tiny cafe, but most of the business is takeout.

145 Puali St. (across the street from Veteran's Memorial Park). ℂ 808/553-3713. Sandwiches, soups, and salads $3.95–$7.50. AE, MC, V. Mon–Fri 7am–4pm; Sat 10:30am–2pm.

EN ROUTE TO THE NORTH COAST

Kualapuu Cook House ⚘ AMERICAN   An old wagon in front of a former plantation house marks this down-home eatery, now takeout only. Local residents flock here, not only for the family atmosphere, but for the oversize servings. Breakfasts feature giant omelets, homemade corned beef hash, and, for those who dare, The Works—buttermilk pancakes, eggs and home fries (you'll either be fueled for the day or ready to take a nap). Lunch can either be a burger or sandwich or one of their humongous plate lunches of pork katsu or chicken, served up with rice, of course.

Farrington Hwy., 1 block west of Hwy. 470, Kalapuu. ℂ 808/567-9655. Most items under $15. No credit cards. Mon–Sat 7am–3pm.

THE WEST END

Maunaloa Dining Room ⚘ MOLOKAI REGIONAL   Molokai has never had anything resembling fine dining, but this restaurant changes the picture. It's in the island's first upscale hotel, the Sheraton Molokai Lodge, a 22-room lodge fashioned after a ranch owner's private home in the cool hills of Maunaloa, where you can see Oahu (Diamond Head under the best of conditions) past the rolling ranchlands and the ocean. Fresh Molokai ingredients come in cross-cultural preparations. Breakfast features banana-stuffed Molokai sweetbread French toast or eggs with taro hash. The dinner menu includes entrees like fresh fish with roasted corn; Molokai prawns and Pacific snapper; and lemon-grass mango chicken with avocado relish and spiced tortillas. The room's rustic, lodge-like ambience fits the paniolo surroundings, and Hawaiian proverbs stenciled on the walls are a nice cultural touch.

Sheraton Molokai Lodge, Maunaloa. ✆ 808/660-2725. Reservations recommended for dinner. Breakfast entrees $6–$12; dinner main courses $20–$28. AE, DC, DISC, MC, V. Daily 7–10am and 6–9pm; Sunday brunch ($23) 11am–1:30pm. Lunch served 10am–4pm in the bar, most sandwiches under $10.

THE EAST END

Neighborhood Store 'N Counter 🏹 AMERICAN The Neighborhood Store is nothing fancy, and that's what we love about it. This store/lunch counter appears like a mirage near mile marker 16 in the Pukoo area en route to the East End. Picnic tables under a royal poinciana tree are a wonderful sight, and the food does not disappoint. The place serves omelets, Portuguese sausage, and other breakfast specials (brunch is very popular), then segues into sandwiches, salads, mahimahi plates, and varied over-the-counter lunch offerings. Favorites include the mahimahi plate lunch, the chicken katsu, and the Mexican plate, each one with a tried-and-true home-cooked flavor. There are daily specials, ethnic dishes, and some vegetarian options, as well as burgers (including a killer veggie burger), saimin, and legendary desserts. Made-on-Maui Roselani ice cream is a featured attraction, and customers rave over the Portuguese doughnut dessert, a deep-fried doughnut filled with ice cream. A Molokai treasure, the Neighborhood Store is also the only grocery store on the East End (see "Shopping," later in this chapter).

Pukoo. ✆ 808/558-8498. Most items less than $6.95; bento $7.30. No credit cards. Daily 8am–6pm.

5 Beaches

With imposing sea cliffs on one side and lazy fish ponds on the other, Molokai has little room for beaches along its 106-mile coast. Still, a big gold-sand beach flourishes on the West End, and you'll find tiny pocket beaches on the East End. The emptiness of Molokai's beaches is both a blessing and a curse: The seclusion means no lifeguards on any of the beaches.

See the "Molokai" map on p. 473 for locations of these beaches.

KAUNAKAKAI
ONE ALII BEACH PARK

This thin strip of sand, once reserved for the *alii* (chiefs), is the oldest public beach park on Molokai. You'll find One Alii Beach Park (*One* is pronounced *o-nay*, not *won*) by a coconut grove on the outskirts of Kaunakakai. Safe for swimmers of all ages and abilities, it's often crowded with families on weekends, but it can be all yours on weekdays. Facilities include outdoor showers, restrooms, and free parking.

THE WEST END
PAPOHAKU BEACH 🏹🏹

Nearly 3 miles long and 100 yards wide, gold-sand Papohaku Beach is one of the biggest in Hawaii (17-mile long, Polihale Beach on Kauai is the biggest). It's great for walking, beachcombing, picnics, and sunset watching year-round. The big surf and rip tides make swimming risky except in summer, when the waters are calmer. Go early in the day when the tropic sun is less fierce and the winds calm. The beach is so big that you may never see another soul except at sunset, when a few people gather on the shore in hopes of spotting the elusive green flash, a natural wonder that takes place when the horizon is cloud free. Facilities include outdoor showers, restrooms, picnic grounds, and free parking.

KEPUHI BEACH

Golfers see this picturesque golden strand in front of the Kaluakoi Resort and Golf Course as just another sand trap, but sunbathers like the semiprivate grassy dunes; they're seldom, if ever, crowded. Beachcombers often find what they're looking for here, but swimmers have to dodge lava rocks and risk rip tides. Oh, yes—look out for errant golf balls. There are no facilities or lifeguards, but cold drinks and restrooms are handy at the resort.

THE EAST END
SANDY BEACH ✵

Molokai's most popular swimming beach—ideal for families with small kids— is a roadside pocket of gold sand protected by a reef, with a great view of Maui and Lanai. You'll find it off the King Kamehameha V Highway (Hwy. 450) at mile marker 20. There are no facilities—just you, the sun, the sand, and the surf.

MURPHY BEACH PARK (KUMIMI BEACH PARK)

In 1970, the Molokai Jaycees wanted to create a sandy beach park with a good swimming area for the children of the East End. They chose a section known as Kumimi Beach, which was owned by the Puu o Hoku Ranch. The beach was a dump, literally. The ranch owner, George Murphy, immediately gave his permission to use the site as a park; the Jaycees cleaned it up and built three small pavilions, plus picnic tables and barbecue grills. Officially, the park is called the George Murphy Beach Park (shortened to Murphy Beach Park over the years), but some old-timers still call it Kumimi Beach, and, just to make things real confusing, some people call it Jaycees Park.

No matter what you call it, this small park is shaded by ironwood trees that line a white-sand beach. It's generally a very safe swimming area. On calm days, snorkeling and diving are great outside the reef. Fishermen are also frequently spotted here looking for papio and other island fish.

HALAWA BEACH PARK ✵

At the foot of scenic Halawa Valley is this beautiful black-sand beach with a palm-fringed lagoon, a wave-lashed island offshore, and a distant view of the West Maui Mountains across the Pailolo Channel. The swimming is safe in the shallows close to shore, but where the waterfall stream meets the sea, the ocean is often murky and unnerving. A winter swell creases the mouth of Halawa Valley on the north side of the bay and attracts a crowd of local surfers. Facilities are minimal; bring your own water. To get here, take King Kamehameha V Highway (Hwy. 450) east to the end.

6 Watersports

The best places to rent beach toys (snorkels, boogie boards, beach chairs, fishing poles, and more) are **Molokai Rentals and Tours,** Kaunakakai (© **800/553-9071** or 808/553-5663; www.molokai-rentals.com) and **Molokai Outdoors Activities,** in the lobby of Hotel Molokai, just outside Kaunakakai (© **877/553-4477** or 808/553-4477; www.molokai-outdoors.com). Both operators have everything you'll need for a day at the beach and can also give you advice on where to find a great swimming beach or where the waves are breaking. Another good place to check out is **Molokai Fish & Dive,** Kaunakakai

(© **808/553-5926;** http://molokai-aloha.com/fishdiv/), a mind-boggling store filled with outdoor gear. You can rent snorkels, fishing gear, even ice chests here. This is also a hot spot for fishing news and tips on what's running where.

For general advice on the activities listed below, see "The Active Vacation Planner," in chapter 2.

BODYBOARDING (BOOGIE BOARDING) & BODYSURFING

Molokai has only three beaches that offer ridable waves for bodyboarding and bodysurfing: Papohaku, Kepuhi, and Halawa. Even these beaches are only for experienced bodysurfers, due to the strength of the rip currents and undertows. You can rent boogie boards with fins for $7 a day or $21 a week from **Molokai Rentals and Tours,** Kaunakakai (© **808/553-5663;** www.molokai-rentals. com). Boards with fins go for just $2.95 a day at **Molokai Outdoors Activities,** in the lobby of Hotel Molokai, just outside Kaunakakai (© **877/553-4477** or 808/553-4477; www.molokai-outdoors.com).

OCEAN KAYAKING

During the summer months, when the waters on the north shore are calm, Molokai offers some of the most spectacular kayaking in Hawaii. You can paddle from remote valley to remote valley, spending a week or more exploring the exotic terrain. However, most of Molokai is for the experienced kayaker only. You must be adept in paddling through open ocean swells and rough waves. **Molokai Rentals and Tours,** Kaunakakai (© **808/553-5663;** www. molokai-rentals.com) has a kayak tour of the south side of Molokai for $45 adults and $25 children under 16, which includes snorkeling. They also offer kayak rentals, singles $25 a day ($100 a week) and doubles $40 a day ($160 a week), which include life jackets, roof rack, paddles, and leashes.

Molokai Outdoors Activities, in the lobby of Hotel Molokai, just outside Kaunakakai (© **877/553-4477** or 808/553-4477; www.molokai-outdoors.com), has sunset tours of the ancient Hawaii fish ponds and the inshore reefs for beginners or nature lovers ($45–$75 per person) and a coastline tour for more experienced kayakers with snorkeling ($55–$75 per person). They also rent kayaks; rates start at $10 a day.

On the West End, the **Sheraton Molokai Lodge and Beach Village** (© **800/ 782-9488** or 808/660-2710; www.molokai-ranch.com) offers ocean kayaking ($65 for nonguests, $45 for guests) and ocean expeditions ($35 for nonguests, $30 for guests).

SAILING

Molokai Charters ☆ (© **808/553-5852**) offers a variety of sailing trips on *Satan's Doll,* a 42-foot sloop: 2-hour sunset sails for $40 per person, a ½ day of sailing and whale-watching for $50 (mid-Dec to mid-Mar), and a full-day sail to Lanai with swimming and snorkeling for $90 (which includes lunch, cold drinks, snacks, and all equipment). Owners Richard and Doris Reed have been sailing visitors around Molokai's waters since 1975.

SCUBA DIVING

Want to see turtles or manta rays up close? How about sharks? Molokai resident Bill Kapuni has been diving the waters around the island his entire life; he'll be happy to show you whatever you're brave enough to encounter. **Bill Kapuni's Snorkel and Dive,** Kaunakakai (© **808/553-9867**), can provide gear, a boat, and even instruction. Two-tank dives in his 22-foot Boston whaler cost $110 and include Bill's voluminous knowledge of the legends and lore of Hawaii.

C **Molokai's Best Snorkel Spots**

Most Molokai beaches are too dangerous for snorkeling in winter, when big waves and strong currents are generated by storms that sweep down from Alaska. From mid-September to April, stick to Murphy Beach Park (also known as Kumimi Beach Park) on the East End. In summer, roughly May to mid-September, when the Pacific Ocean takes a holiday and turns into a flat lake, the whole west coast of Molokai opens up for snorkeling. Mike Holmes, of Molokai Ranch & Fun Hogs Hawaii, says the best spots are as follows:

Kawaikiunui, Ilio Point, and **Pohaku Moiliili** (West End)   These are all special places seldom seen by even those who live on Molokai. You can reach Kawaikiunui and Pohaku Moiliili on foot after a long, hot, dusty ride in a four-wheel-drive vehicle, but it's much easier and quicker to go by sea. See above for places to rent a kayak and get advice. It's about 2 miles as the crow flies from Pohaku Moiliili to Ilio Point.

Kapukahehu (Dixie Maru) Beach (West End)   This gold-sand family beach is well protected, and the reef is close and shallow. The name Dixie Maru comes from a 1920s Japanese fishing boat stranded off the rocky shore. One of the Molokai Ranch cowboys hung the wrecked boat's nameplate on a gate by Kapukahehu Beach, and the name Dixie Maru stuck. To get here, take Kaluakoi Road to the end of the pavement, and then take the footpath 100 yards to the beach.

Murphy (Kumimi) Beach Park ⭐ (East End)   This beach is located between mile markers 20 and 21, off Kamehameha V Highway. The reef here is easily reachable, and the waters are calm year-round.

SNORKELING

When the waters are calm, Molokai offers excellent snorkeling; you'll see a wide range of butterfly fish, tangs, and angelfish. Good snorkeling can be found—when conditions are right—at many of Molokai's beaches (see the box titled "Molokai's Best Snorkel Spots," below). **Molokai Rentals and Tours** (© 808/553-5663; www.molokai-rentals.com) and **Molokai Outdoors Activities** (© 877/553-4477 or 808/553-4477; www.molokai-outdoors.com) offer the least-expensive snorkel gear for rent ($6 a day or $24 a week).

For snorkeling tours, contact **Bill Kapuni's Snorkel & Dive,** Kaunakakai (© 808/553-9867), which charges $65 for a 2½-hour trip. They also rent snorkeling gear for $10 a day (see "Scuba Diving," above). Walter Naki of **Molokai Action Adventures** (© 808/558-8184) offers leisurely snorkeling, diving, and swimming trips in his 21-foot Boston whaler for $100 per person for a 4- to 6-hour custom tour.

SPORTFISHING

Molokai's waters can provide prime sporting opportunities, whether you're looking for big-game sportfishing or bottom fishing. When customers are scarce, Capt. Joe Reich, who has been fishing the waters around Molokai for decades, goes commercial fishing, so he always knows where the fish are biting. He runs *Alyce* **C Sportfishing** out of Kaunakakai Harbor (© 808/558-8377). A full day of fishing for up to six people is $400, a ¾ day is $350, and a ½ day is $300. You can usually persuade him to do a whale-watching cruise during the winter months.

For fly-fishing or light-tackle reef-fish trolling, contact Walter Naki at **Molokai Action Adventures** (© **808/558-8184**). Walter's been fishing his entire life and loves to share his secret spots with visiting fishermen—he knows *the* place for bonefishing on the flats. A full-day trip in his 21-foot Boston whaler, for up to four people, is $300.

For deep-sea fishing, **Fun Hogs Hawaii** (© **808/567-6789**; www.molokai-rentals.com/funhogs.html) has fishing excursions on a 27-foot, fully equipped sportfishing vessel. Prices are $350 for six passengers for 4 hours; $400 for 6 hours; and $450 for 8 hours.

If you just want to try your luck casting along the shoreline, **Molokai Outdoors Activities,** in the lobby of Hotel Molokai, just outside Kaunakakai (© **877/553-4477** or 808/553-4477; www.molokai-outdoors.com), rents fishing poles for $4.95 a day and can tell you where they're biting.

7 Hiking & Camping

HIKING MOLOKAI'S PEPEOPAE TRAIL

Molokai's most awesome hike is the **Pepeopae Trail** ★★, which takes you back a few million years. On the cloud-draped trail (actually a boardwalk across the bog), you'll see mosses, sedges, native violets, knee-high ancient ohias, and lichens that evolved in total isolation over eons. Eerie intermittent mists blowing in and out will give you an idea of this island at its creation.

The narrow boardwalk, built by volunteers, protects the bog and keeps you out of the primal ooze. Don't venture off it; you could damage this fragile environment or get lost. The 3-mile round-trip takes about 90 minutes to hike—but first you have to drive about 20 miles from Kaunakakai, deep into the Molokai Forest Preserve on a four-wheel-drive road. *Warning:* Don't try this with a regular rental car. Plan a full day for this outing. Better yet, go on a guided nature hike with the **Nature Conservancy of Hawaii,** which guards this unusual ecosystem. For information, write to the Nature Conservancy at 1116 Smith St., Suite 201, Honolulu, HI 96817. No permit is required for this easy hike. Call ahead (© **808/537-4508** or 808/553-5236) to check on the condition of the ungraded, four-wheel-drive, red-dirt road that leads to the trailhead and to let people know that you'll be up there.

To get here, take Highway 460 west from Kaunakakai for 3½ miles and turn right before the Maunawainui Bridge onto the unmarked Molokai Forest Reserve Road (sorry, there aren't any road signs). The pavement ends at the cemetery; continue on the dirt road. After about 2 to 2½ miles, you'll see a sign telling you that you are now in the Molokai Forest Reserve. At the Waikolu Lookout and picnic area, which is just over 9 miles on the Molokai Forest Reserve Road, sign in at the box near the entrance. Continue on the road for another 5 miles to a fork in the road with the sign PUU KOLEKOLE pointing to the right side of the fork. Do not turn right; instead, continue straight at the fork, which will lead to the clearly marked trailhead. The drive will take about 45 minutes.

HIKING TO KALAUPAPA ★★

This hike to the site of Molokai's famous leper colony is like going down a switchback staircase with what seems like a million steps. You don't always see the breathtaking view because you're too busy watching your step. It's easier

Frommer's Favorite Molokai Experiences

Riding a Mule into a Leper Colony. Don't pass up the opportunity to see this hauntingly beautiful peninsula. Buzzy Sproat's mules go up and down the 3-mile Kalaupapa Trail (with 26 switchbacks) to Molokai's famous leper colony. The views are breathtaking: You'll see the world's highest sea cliffs (taller than a 300-story skyscraper) and waterfalls plunging thousands of feet into the ocean. If you're afraid of heights, catch the views from the Kalaupapa Lookout.

Venturing into the Garden of Eden. Drive the 30 miles along Molokai's East End. Take your time. Stop to smell the flowers and pick guavas by the side of the road. Pull over for a swim. Wave at every car you pass and every person you see. At the end of the road, stand on the beach at Halawa Valley and see Hawaii as it must have looked in A.D. 650, when the first people arrived in the islands.

Celebrating the Ancient Hula. Hula is the heartbeat of Hawaiian culture, and Molokai is its birthplace. Although most visitors to Hawaii never get to see the real thing, it's possible to see it here—once a year, on the third Saturday in May, when Molokai celebrates the birth of the hula at its **Ka Hula Piko Festival.** The daylong affair includes dance, music, food, and crafts; see the "Hawaii Calendar of Events," in chapter 2 for details.

Strolling the Sands at Papohaku. Go early, when the tropical sun isn't so fierce, and stroll this 3-mile stretch of unspoiled golden sand on Molokai's West End. It's one of the longest beaches in Hawaii. The big surf and rip tides make swimming somewhat risky, but Papohaku is perfect for walking, beachcombing, and, in the evening, sunset watching.

Traveling Back in Time on the Pepeopae Trail. This awesome hike takes you through the Molokai Forest Reserve and back a few million years in time. Along the misty trail (actually a boardwalk across the bog), expect close encounters of the botanical kind: mosses, sedges, violets, lichens, and knee-high ancient ohias.

Soaking in the Warm Waters off Sandy Beach. On the East End, about 20 miles outside Kaunakakai—just before the road starts to climb to Halawa Valley—lies a small pocket of white sand known as Sandy Beach. Submerging yourself here in the warm, calm waters (an outer reef protects the cove) is a sensuous experience par excellence.

Snorkeling Among Clouds of Butterfly Fish. The calm waters off Murphy (Kumimi) Beach, on the East End, are perfect for snorkelers. Just

going down (surprise!)—in about an hour, you'll go 2½ miles, from 2,000 feet to sea level. The trip up sometimes takes twice as long. The trailhead starts on the *mauka* (inland) side of Highway 470, just past the Mule Barn (you can't miss it). Check in here at 7:30am, get a permit, and go before the mule train departs. You must be 16 or older (it's an old state law that kept kids out of the leper colony) and should be in good shape. Wear good hiking boots or sneakers; you won't make it past the first turn in sandals.

don your gear and head to the reef, where you'll find lots of exotic tropical fish, including long-nosed butterfly fish, saddle wrasses, and convict tangs.

Kayaking Along the North Shore. This is the Hawaii of your dreams: waterfalls thundering down sheer cliffs, remote sand beaches, miles of tropical vegetation, and the sounds of the sea splashing on your kayak and the wind whispering in your ear. The best times to go are late March and early April, or in summer, especially August to September, when the normally galloping ocean lies down flat.

Watching the Sunset from a Coconut Grove. Kapuaiwa Coconut Beach Park, off Maunaloa Highway (Hwy. 460), is a perfect place to watch the sunset. The sky behind the coconut trees fills with a kaleidoscope of colors as the sun sinks into the Pacific. Be careful where you sit, though: Falling coconuts could have you seeing stars well before dusk.

Sampling the Local Brew. Saunter up to the Espresso Bar at the Coffees of Hawaii Plantation Store in Kualapuu for a fresh cup of java made from beans that were grown, processed, and packed on this 450-acre plantation. While you sip, survey the vast collection of native crafts.

Tasting Aloha at a Macadamia Nut Farm. It could be the owner, Tuddie Purdy, and his friendly disposition that make the macadamia nuts here taste so good. Or it could be his years of practice in growing, harvesting, and shelling them on his 1½-acre farm. Either way, Purdy produces a perfect crop. See how he does it on a short, free tour of Purdy's All-Natural Macadamia Nut Farm in Hoolehua, just a nut's throw from the airport.

Talking Story with the Locals. The number-one favorite pastime of most islanders is "talking story," or exchanging experiences and knowledge. It's an old Hawaiian custom that brings people, and generations, closer together. You can probably find residents more than willing to share their wisdom with you while fishing from the wharf at Kaunakakai, hanging out at Molokai Fish & Dive, or having coffee at any of the island's restaurants.

Posting a Nut. Why send a picturesque postcard to your friends and family back home when you can send a fresh coconut? The Hoolelua Post Office will supply the free coconuts, if you'll supply the $3.95 postage fee.

HIKING THE WEST END

Molokai's entire West End, some 53,000 acres, is opening to hike tours through the **Sheraton Molokai Lodge and Beach Village** (© **800/782-9488** or 808/660-2710, www.molokai-ranch.com), which offers a range of hikes to fit different abilities. Prices range from $45 for nonguests ($30 for guests) for an easy 2- to 3-hour hike to $125 ($85 for guests) for advanced hikes along the sea cliff coast.

CAMPING

Camping equipment is available for rent from **Molokai Rentals and Tours** (© **808/553-5663;** www.molokai-rentals.com). A two-person camping package is $20 a day or $80 a week. **Molokai Outdoors Activities,** in the lobby of Hotel Molokai, just outside Kaunakakai (© **877/553-4477** or 808/553-4477; www.molokai-outdoors.com), also rents all kinds of tents and camping gear from $5 up.

AT THE BEACH

One of the best year-round places to camp on Molokai is **Papohaku Beach Park** ⚘, on the island's West End. This drive-up seaside site makes a great get-away. Facilities include restrooms, drinking water, outdoor showers, barbecue grills, and picnic tables. Groceries and gas are available in Maunaloa, 6 miles away. Kaluakoi Resort is a mile away. Get camping permits by contacting **Maui County Parks Department,** P.O. Box 526, Kaunakakai, HI 96748 (© **808/ 553-3204**). Camping is limited to 3 days, but if nobody else has applied, the time limit is waived. The cost is $3 a person per night.

IN AN IRONWOOD FOREST

At the end of Highway 470 is the 234-acre piney woods known as **Palaau State Park** ⚘⚘, home to the Kalaupapa Lookout (the best vantage point for seeing the historic leper colony if you're not hiking or riding a mule in). It's airy and cool in the park's ironwood forest, where many love to camp at the designated state campground. Camping is free, but you'll need a permit from the **State Division of Parks** (© **808/567-6618**). For more on the park, see p. 497.

8 Golf & Other Outdoor Pursuits

GOLF

If you didn't bring your clubs, you can rent them from **Molokai Rentals and Tours,** Kaunakakai, (© **808/553-5663;** www.molokai-rentals.com). Prices start at $6 a day ($24 for the week).

Golf is one of Molokai's best-kept secrets; it's challenging and fun, tee times are open, and the rates are lower than your score will be. After being closed for a number of years, the **Kaluakoi Golf Course** (© **808/552-0255**) is open again. After extensive renovation (repairs to irrigation, new grass planted, redesigned bunkers and narrower fairways), the 18-hole course went back online in 2003. Most of the work was cosmetic, and the Ted Robinson designed course is still as challenging as ever, especially the par 3, 16th hole, where you tee off over a gulch or the distraction of the incredible Papohaku Beach from the 3rd tee. Green fees are $35 without cart, $55 with cart, or $45 each for two players

---

A Tip for the Adventurous

If it's action you crave, call **Molokai Action Adventures** (© **808/558-8184**). Island guide Walter Naki will take you skin diving, reef trolling, kayaking, hunting, or hiking into Molokai's remote hidden valleys. Hiking tours are $50 per person for 4 hours; the number of participants is limited to no more than four. Not only does Walter know Molokai like the back of his hand, but he also loves being outdoors and talking story with visitors; he'll tell you about the island, the people, the politics, the myths, and anything else you want to know.

with cart. The real find is the **Ironwood Hills Golf Course,** off Kalae Highway (© **808/567-6000**). It's located just before the Molokai Mule Ride Mule Barn, on the road to the Lookout. One of the oldest courses in the state, Ironwood Hills (named after the two predominant features of the course, ironwood trees and hills) was built in 1929 by Del Monte Plantation for its executives. This unusual course, which sits in the cool air at 1,200 feet, delights with its rich foliage, open fairways, and spectacular views of the rest of the island. If you play here, use a trick developed by the local residents: After teeing off on the sixth hole, just take whatever clubs you need to finish playing the hole and a driver for the seventh hole, and park your bag under a tree. The climb to the seventh hole is steep—you'll be glad that you're only carrying a few clubs. Greens fees are $15 for 9 holes or $20 for 18 holes. Cart fees are $7 for 9 holes or $14 for 18. You can also rent a hand cart for just $2.50. Club rentals are $7 for 9 holes and $12 for 18.

BICYCLING

Molokai is a great place to see by bicycle. The roads are not very busy and there are great places to pull off the road and take a quick dip. **Molokai Rentals and Tours,** Kaunakakai (© **800/553-9071** or 808/553-5663; www.molokai-rentals.com) offers a great tour of the 500 cultivated acres of coffee of Hawaii's fields. With numerous ups and downs, the tour rounds the perimeter of the coffee fields and ventures up to an overlook and back to the plant where you get a walking tour that shows you the coffee-making process. Included in the tour are a taste-testing of different varieties, a delicious Mocha Mama or Smoothie, and a complimentary 2 oz. bag of coffee. The 2½ hour tours are Monday to Friday at 8:30am; the cost is $45 for adults and $25 for children under 16. The more adventurous may want to try Molokai Rentals' All Day Bike Tours, which either go up to the Forest Reserve or explore Molokai's off-the-beaten-track paths. Both tours start at 8am and end around 3pm; lunch is also provided. Cost is $80.00 and includes bikes, helmets, and water bottles. If you'd rather explore the island on your own, you can rent a bike for $20 a day or $80 a week.

Molokai Outdoors Activities, in the lobby of Hotel Molokai, just outside Kaunakakai (© **877/553-4477** or 808/553-4477; www.molokai-outdoors.com), offers a bike/kayak tour of the East End of Molokai, with snorkeling. All gear, lunch, guide and transportation is $135. Bike rentals range from a beach cruiser ($10 a day) to MTB front shocks ($35 a day), and include a complimentary bicycle rack for your rental.

The best mountain biking in the state is on the trails of **Sheraton Molokai Lodge and Beach Village** (© **800/782-9488** or 808/660-2710; www.molokai-ranch.com). Imagine 53,000 acres with inter-crossing trails that weave up and down the West End to the beach—simply spectacular. The equipment is good, the guides excellent, and they even have courses on how to mountain bike, conducted on specially-constructed wooden trails for teaching ($50 for nonguests and $35 for guests). Guided tours range from $50 ($35 for guests) for 2 to 3 hours to full-day rides with a guide and lunch for $100 ($80 guests).

HORSEBACK RIDING

One of the most scenic places to go riding on Molokai is **Pu'u O Hoku Ranch** (© **808/558-8109;** www.puuohoku.com), about 25 miles outside Kaunakakai on the East End. Guided trail rides pass through green pasture on one of the largest working ranches on Molokai, then head up into the high mountain forest. Don't forget your camera: There are plenty of scenic views of waterfalls, the

Pacific Ocean, and the islands of Maui and Lanai in the distance. Rates are $55 for an hour-long ride, $75 for a 2-hour ride, and $120 for a beach adventure.

For those looking for a little more than just a horseback ride, **Sheraton Molokai Lodge and Beach Village** (© 800/782-9488 or 808/660-2710; www.molokai-ranch.com) offers a "Paniolo Roundup." You can learn horsemanship from the ranch's working cowboys and compete in traditional rodeo games; the ½-day adventure is $105 ($80 guests). Trail rides range from $105 ($80 guests) to $150 ($125 guests).

TENNIS

The only two tennis courts on Molokai are located at the **Mitchell Pauole Center,** in Kaunakakai (© 808/553-5141). Both are lit for night play and are available free on a first-come, first-served basis, with a 45-minute time limit if someone is waiting. If you left your racket at home, you can rent one for just $4 a day ($16 a week) from **Molokai Rentals and Tours,** HC01 Box 28, Kaunakakai (© 808/553-5663; www.molokai-rentals.com). You can also rent tennis rackets and balls from **Molokai Outdoors Activities,** in the lobby of Hotel Molokai, just outside Kaunakakai (© 877/553-4477 or 808/553-4477; www.molokai-outdoors.com).

9 Seeing the Sights

Note: You'll find the following attractions on the "Molokai" map on p. 473.

IN & AROUND KAUNAKAKAI

Kapuaiwa Coconut Grove/Kiowea Park ★ *Kids*   This royal grove—1,000 coconut trees on 10 acres planted in 1863 by the island's high chief Kapua'iwa (later, King Kamehameha V)—is a major roadside attraction. The shoreline park is a favorite subject of sunset photographers and visitors who delight in a hand-lettered sign that warns: DANGER: FALLING COCONUTS. In its backyard, across the highway, stands Church Row: seven churches, each a different denomination—clear evidence of the missionary impact on Hawaii.

Along Maunaloa Hwy. (Hwy. 460), 2 miles west of Kaunakakai.

Post-A-Nut ★   Postmaster Margaret Keahi-Leary will help you say "Aloha" with a dried Molokai coconut. Just write a message on the coconut with a felt-tip pen, and she'll send it via U.S. mail over the sea. Coconuts are free but postage is $3.95 for a mainland-bound, 2-pound coconut.

Hoolehua Post Office, Puu Peelua Ave. (Hwy. 480), near Maunaloa Hwy. (Hwy. 460). © 808/567-6144. Mon–Fri 7:30–11:30am and 12:30–4:30pm.

Purdy's All-Natural Macadamia Nut Farm (Na Hua O'Ka Aina) ★ *Finds* The Purdys have made macadamia-nut buying an entertainment event, offering tours of the homestead and giving lively demonstrations of nutshell-cracking in the shade of their towering trees. The tour of the 70-year-old nut farm explains the growth, bearing, harvesting, and shelling processes, so that by the time you bite into the luxurious macadamia nut, you'll have more than a passing knowledge of its entire life cycle.

Lihi Pali Ave. (behind Molokai High School), Hoolehua. © 808/567-6601. www.visitmolokai.com. Free admission. Mon–Fri 9:30am–3:30pm; Sat 10am–2pm; closed on holidays.

THE NORTH COAST

Even if you don't get a chance to see Hawaii's most dramatic coast in its entirety—not many people do—you shouldn't miss the opportunity to glimpse

(**Kids** Especially for Kids

Flying a Kite (p. 505) Not only can you get a guaranteed-to-fly kite at the **Big Wind Kite Factory** (✆ **808/552-2634**) in Maunaloa, but kite designer Jonathan Socher offers free kite-flying classes to kids, who'll learn how to make their kites soar, swoop, and, most important, stay in the air for more than 5 minutes.

Spending the Day at Murphy (Kumimi) Beach Park (p. 488) Just beyond Wailua on the East End is this small wayside park that's perfect for kids. You'll find safe swimming conditions, plenty of shade from the ironwood trees, and small pavilions with picnic tables and barbecue grills.

Watching Whales (p. 489) From mid-December to mid-March, kids of all ages can go whale-watching on Molokai Charters's 42-foot sloop, *Satan's Doll*.

it from the **Kalaupapa Lookout** at Palauu State Park. On the way, there are a few diversions (arranged here in geographical order).

EN ROUTE TO THE NORTH COAST

Coffees of Hawaii Plantation Store The defunct Del Monte pineapple town of Kualapuu is rising again—only this time, coffee is the catch, not pineapple. Located in the cool foothills, Coffees of Hawaii has planted coffee beans on 600 acres of former pineapple land. The plantation is irrigating the plants with a high-tech, continuous water and fertilizer drip system. You can see it all on the walking tour; call 24 hours in advance to set it up. The Plantation Store sells arts and crafts from Molokai. Stop by the Espresso Bar for a Mocha Mama (Molokai coffee, ice, chocolate ice cream, chocolate syrup, whipped cream, and chocolate shavings on top). It'll keep you going all day—maybe even all night.

Hwy. 480 (near the junction of Hwy. 470). ✆ **800/709-BEAN** or 808/567-9241, www.molokaicoffee.com. Walking tour $7 adults, $3.50 children 5–12. Tours Mon–Sat. 9:30 am and 11:30 am; Sun 11:30 am only. Store open Mon–Fri 7am–4pm; Sat 8am–4pm; Sun 10am–4pm.

Molokai Museum and Cultural Center En route to the California Gold Rush in 1849, Rudolph W. Meyer, a German professor, came to Molokai, married the high chieftess Kalama, and began to operate a small sugar plantation near his home. Now on the National Register of Historic Places, this restored 1878 sugar mill, with its century-old steam engine, mule-driven cane crusher, copper clarifiers, and redwood evaporating pan (all in working order), is the last of its kind in Hawaii. The mill also houses a museum that traces the history of sugar growing on Molokai and features special events, such as wine tastings every 2 months, taro festivals, an annual music festival, and occasional classes in ukulele making, loom weaving, and sewing. Call for a schedule.

Meyer Sugar Mill, Hwy. 470 (just after the turnoff for the Ironwood Hills Golf Course and 2 miles below Kalaupapa Overlook), Kalae. ✆ **808/567-6436**. Admission $2.50 adults, $1 students. Mon–Sat 10am–2pm.

Palauu State Park ✵ This 234-acre piney-woods park, 8 miles out of Kaunakakai, doesn't look like much until you get out of the car and take a hike, which literally puts you between a rock and a hard place. Go right, and you end up on the edge of Molokai's magnificent sea cliffs, with its panoramic view of the well-known Kalaupapa leper colony; go left, and you come face to face with a stone phallus.

If you have no plans to scale the cliffs by mule or on foot (see "Hiking & Camping," earlier in this chapter), the **Kalaupapa Lookout** ☆☆☆ is the only place from which to see the former place of exile. The trail is marked, and historic photos and interpretive signs will explain what you're seeing.

It's airy and cool in the ironwood forest, where camping is free at the designated state campground. You'll need a permit from the **State Division of Parks** (℃ **808/567-6618**). Not many people seem to camp here, probably because of the legend associated with the **Phallic Rock** ☆. Six feet high, pointed at an angle that means business, Molokai's famous Phallic Rock is a legendary fertility tool that appears to be working today. According to Hawaiian legend, a woman who wishes to become pregnant need only spend the night near the rock and, *voilà!* It's probably just a coincidence, of course, but Molokai does have a growing number of young, pregnant women.

Phallic Rock is at the end of a well-worn uphill path that passes an ironwood grove and several other rocks that vaguely resemble sexual body parts. No mistaking the big guy, though. Supposedly, it belonged to Nanahoa, a demigod who quarreled with his wife, Kawahuna, over a pretty girl. In the tussle, Kawahuna was thrown over the cliff, and both husband and wife were turned to stone. Of all the phallic rocks in Hawaii and the Pacific, this is the one to see. It's featured on a postcard with a tiny, awestruck Japanese woman standing next to it.

At the end of Hwy. 470.

THE LEGACY OF FATHER DAMIEN: KALAUPAPA NATIONAL HISTORIC PARK ☆☆☆

An old tongue of lava that sticks out to form a peninsula, Kalaupapa became infamous because of man's inhumanity to victims of a formerly incurable contagious disease.

King Kamehameha V sent the first lepers—nine men and three women—into exile on this lonely shore, at the base of ramparts that rise like temples against the Pacific, on January 6, 1866. By 1874, more 11,000 lepers had been dispatched to die in one of the world's most beautiful—and lonely—places. They called Kalaupapa "The Place of the Living Dead."

Leprosy is actually one of the world's least contagious diseases, transmitted only by direct, repetitive contact over a long period of time. It's caused by a germ, *Mycobacterium leprae,* that attacks the nerves, skin, and eyes, and is found mainly, but not exclusively, in tropical regions. American scientists found a cure for the disease in the 1940s.

Before science intervened, there was Father Damien. Born to wealth in Belgium, Joseph de Veuster traded a life of excess for exile among lepers; he devoted himself to caring for the afflicted at Kalaupapa. Father Damien, as he became known, volunteered to go out to the Pacific in place of his ailing brother. Horrified by the conditions in the leper colony, Father Damien worked at Kalaupapa for 11 years, building houses, schools, and churches, and giving hope to his patients. He died on April 15, 1889, in Kalaupapa, of leprosy. He was 49.

A hero nominated for Catholic sainthood, Father Damien is buried not in his tomb next to Molokai's St. Philomena Church but in his native Belgium. Well, most of him anyway. His hand was recently returned to Molokai, and was reinterred at Kalaupapa as a relic of his martyrdom.

This small peninsula is probably the final resting place of more than 11,000 souls. The sand dunes are littered with grave markers, sorted by the religious affiliation—Catholic, Protestant, Lutheran, Buddhist—of those who died here. But so many are buried in unmarked graves that no accurate census of the dead exists.

Kalaupapa is now a National Historic Park (© **808/567-6802;** www.nps.gov/kala) and one of Hawaii's richest archaeological preserves, with sites that date from A.D. 1000. About 60 former patients chose to remain in the tidy village of whitewashed houses with statues of angels in their yards. The original name for their former affliction, leprosy, was officially banned in Hawaii by the state legislature in 1981. The name used now is "Hansen's disease," for Dr. Gerhard Hansen of Norway, who discovered the germ in 1873. The few remaining residents of Kalaupapa still call the disease leprosy, although none are too keen on being called lepers.

Kalaupapa welcomes visitors who arrive on foot, by mule, or by small plane. Father Damien's St. Philomena church, built in 1872, is open to visitors, who can see it from a yellow school bus driven by resident tour guide Richard Marks, an ex-seaman and sheriff who survived the disease. You won't be able to roam freely, and you'll be allowed to enter only the museum, the craft shop, and the church.

MULE RIDES TO KALAUPAPA   The first turn's a gasp, and it's all downhill from there. You can close your eyes and hold on for dear life, or slip the reins over the pommel and sit back, letting the mule do the walking down the precipitous path to Kalaupapa National Historic Park.

Even if you have only 1 day to spend on Molokai, spend it on a mule. This is a once-in-a-lifetime ride. The cliffs are taller than a 300-story skyscraper, but Buzzy Sproat's mules go safely up and down the narrow 3-mile trail daily, rain or shine. Starting at the top of the nearly perpendicular ridge (1,600 ft. high), the surefooted mules step down the muddy trail, pausing often on the 26 switchbacks to calculate their next move—and always, it seems to us, veering a little too close to the edge. Each switchback is numbered; by the time you get to number four, you'll catch your breath, put the mule on cruise control, and begin to enjoy Hawaii's most awesome trail ride.

The mule tours are offered once daily starting at 8am, and they last until about 3:30pm. It costs $150 per person for the all-day adventure, which includes the round-trip mule ride, a guided tour of the settlement, a visit to Father Damien's church and grave, lunch at Kalawao, and souvenirs. To go, you must be at least 16 years old and physically fit. Contact **Molokai Mule Ride** ★★★, 100 Kalae Highway, Suite 104, on Highway 470, 5 miles north of Highway 460 (© **800/567-7550,** or 808/567-6088 between 8 and 10pm; www. muleride.com). Advance reservations (at least 2 weeks ahead) are required.

SEEING KALAUPAPA BY PLANE   The fastest and easiest way to get to Kalaupapa is by hopping on a plane and zipping to Kalaupapa airport. From here, you can pick up the same Kalaupapa tour that the mule riders and hikers take. **Father Damien Tours** (© and fax **808/567-6171**), picks you up at Kalaupapa airport and takes you to some of the area's most scenic spots, including Kalawao, where Father Damien's church still stands, and the town of Kalaupapa. Packages including a round-trip flight to Kalaupapa, entry permits, historical park tour with Damien Tours, and a light picnic lunch cost $119 from the Molokai Airport, $279 from Maui; and $215 from Honolulu. All visitors must be at least 16 years old. From Maui (either Kahului, Kapalua or Hana), call

Paragon Air (© **808/244-3356;** www. paragon-air.com). For flights from either Maui or Honolulu to both the Molokai airport and to Kalaupapa, call **Pacific Wings** (© **888/575-4546** or 808/873-0877; www.pacificwings.com).

SEEING KALAUPAPA BY FERRY/HIKING   From Maui take the *Molokai Princess* Ferry to Molokai (© **800/275-6969** or 808/667-6165; www.maui princess.com), where you are met and transported by van to the top of the 1700-foot sea cliffs. Here you hike down the 3-mile trail to the Kalaupapa National Historic Park; at the park you are met by Damien tours and given a van tour of the peninsula, during which you'll visit Father Damien's St. Philomena Church, see his early gravesite, and hear the stories of struggle and courage of the residents of Kalaupapa. The only catch is you have to hike back up the 1,700-foot cliffs, where you are picked up by the van and returned to the ferry dock for the trip back to Maui. This fabulous experience really should be undertaken only by the physically fit (it will take about an hour hiking down and another 1½ hours to hike back up). Cost for ferry, transportation, tour, and lunch is $215 (participants must be 16 years and older).

THE WEST END
MAUNALOA
In the first and only urban renewal on Molokai, the 1920s-era pineapple-plantation town of Maunaloa is being reinvented. Streets are getting widened and paved, and curbs and sidewalks are being added to serve a new tract of houses. Historic Maunaloa is becoming Maunaloa Village—there's already a town center with a park, a restaurant, a triplex movie theater, a gas station, a KFC, and an upscale lodge.

This master-planned village will also have a museum and artisans' studios—uptown stuff for Molokai. Jonathan Socher of **Big Wind Kite Factory** (p. 505) is keeping his kites and books wrapped in cellophane against constant clouds of red dust raised by construction crews.

ON THE NORTHWEST SHORE: MOOMOMI DUNES
Undisturbed for centuries, the Moomomi Dunes, on Molokai's northwest shore, are a unique treasure chest of great scientific value. The area may look like just a pile of sand as you fly over on the final approach to Hoolehua Airport, but Moomomi Dunes is much more than that. Archaeologists have found adz quarries, ancient Hawaiian burial sites, and shelter caves; botanists have identified five endangered plant species; and marine biologists are finding evidence that endangered green sea turtles are coming out from the waters once again to lay eggs here. The greatest discovery, however, belongs to Smithsonian Institute ornithologists, who have found bones of prehistoric birds—some of them flightless—that existed nowhere else on earth.

Accessible by Jeep trails that thread downhill to the shore, this wild coast is buffeted by strong afternoon breezes. It's hot, dry, and windy, so take water, sunscreen, and a windbreaker.

At Kawaaloa Bay, a 20-minute walk to the west, there's a broad golden beach that you can have all to yourself. *Warning: Due to the rough seas, stay out of the water.* Within the dunes, there's a 920-acre preserve accessible via monthly guided nature tours led by the **Nature Conservancy of Hawaii;** call © **808/553-5236** or 808/524-0779 for an exact schedule and details.

To get here, take Highway 460 (Maunaloa Hwy.) from Kaunakakai; turn right onto Highway 470, and follow it to Kualapuu. At Kualapuu, turn left on Highway 480 and go through Hoolehua Village; it's 3 miles to the bay.

THE EAST END

The East End is a cool and inviting green place that's worth a drive to the end of King Kamehameha V Highway (Hwy. 450). Unfortunately, the trail that leads into the area's greatest natural attraction, Halawa Valley, is now off-limits.

A HORSEBACK RIDE TO ILIILIOPAE HEIAU

On horseback (where the elevated view is magnificent), you bump along a dirt trail through an incredible mango grove, bound for an ancient temple of human sacrifice. This temple of doom—right out of *Indiana Jones*—is Iliiliopae, a huge rectangle of stone made of 90 million rocks, overlooking the once-important village of Mapulehu and four ancient fish ponds. The horses trek under the perfumed mangoes, then head uphill through a kiawe forest filled with Java plums to the *heiau* (temple), which stands across a dry stream bed under cloud-spiked Kaunolu, the 4,970-foot island summit.

Hawaii's most powerful heiau attracted *kahuna* (priests) from all over the islands. They came to learn the rules of human sacrifice at this university of sacred rites. Contrary to Hollywood's version, historians say that the victims here were always men, not young virgins, and that they were strangled, not thrown into a volcano, while priests sat on lauhala mats watching silently. Spooky, eh?

This is the biggest, oldest, and most famous heiau on Molokai. The massive 22-foot-high stone altar is dedicated to Lono, the Hawaiian god of fertility. The heiau resonates with *mana* (power) strong enough to lean on. Legend says Iliiliopae was built in a single night by a thousand men who passed rocks hand over hand through the Wailau Valley from the other side of the island; in exchange for the rock (*ili'ili*), each received a shrimp (*'opae*). Others say it was built by *menehune*, mythic elves who accomplished Herculean feats.

After the visit to the temple, your horse takes you back to the mango grove. Contact **Molokai Wagon Rides,** King Kamehameha V Highway (Hwy. 450), at mile marker 15, Kaunakakai, HI 96748 (© **808/558-8380**). The tour and horseback ride is $50 per person. The hour-long ride goes up to the heiau, then beyond it to the top of the mountain for those breathtaking views, and finally back down to the beach.

KAMAKOU PRESERVE

It's hard to believe, but close to the nearly mile-high summit here, it rains more than 80 inches a year—enough to qualify as a rain forest. The Molokai Forest, as it was historically known, is the source of 60% of Molokai's water. Nearly 3,000 acres, from the summit to the lowland forests of eucalyptus and pine, are now held by the Nature Conservancy, which has identified 219 Hawaiian plants that grow here exclusively. The preserve is also the last stand of the endangered Molokai thrush (*olomao*) and Molokai creeper (*kawawahie*).

To get to the preserve, take the Forest Reserve road from Kaunakakai. It's a 45-minute, four-wheel-drive trip on a dirt trail to Waikolu Lookout Campground; from here, you can venture into the wilderness preserve on foot across a boardwalk on a 1½-hour hike (see "Hiking Molokai's Pepeopae Trail," earlier in this chapter). For more information, contact the **Nature Conservancy** (© **808/553-5236**).

EN ROUTE TO HALAWA VALLEY

No visit to Molokai is complete without at least a passing glance at the island's **ancient fish ponds,** a singular achievement in Pacific aquaculture. With their hunger for fresh fish and lack of ice or refrigeration, Hawaiians perfected aquaculture in A.D. 1400, before Christopher Columbus "discovered" America. They built gated, U-shaped stone and coral walls on the shore to catch fish on the incoming tide; they would then raise them in captivity. The result: a constant, ready supply of fresh fish.

The ponds, which stretch for 20 miles along Molokai's south shore and are visible from Kamehameha V Highway (Hwy. 450), offer insight into the island's ancient population. It took something like a thousand people to tend a single fish pond, and more than 60 ponds once existed on this coast. All the fish ponds are named; a few are privately owned. Some are silted in by red-dirt runoff from south coast gulches; others have been revived by folks who raise fish and seaweed.

The largest, 54-acre **Keawa Nui Pond,** is surrounded by a 3-foot-high, 2,000-foot-long stone wall. **Alii Fish Pond,** reserved for kings, is visible through the coconut groves at One Alii Beach Park (p. 487). From the road, you can see **Kalokoeli Pond,** 6 miles east of Kaunakakai on the highway.

Our Lady of Sorrows Catholic Church, one of five built by Father Damien on Molokai and the first outside Kalaupapa, sits across the highway from a fish pond. Park in the church lot (except on Sun) for a closer look.

St. Joseph's Catholic Church   The afternoon sun strikes St. Joseph's Church with such a bold ray of light that it looks as if God is about to perform a miracle. This little 1876 wood-frame church is one of four Father Damien built "topside" on Molokai. Restored in 1971, the church stands beside a seaside cemetery, where feral cats play under the gaze of a Damien statue amid gravestones decorated with flower leis.

King Kamehameha V Hwy. (Hwy. 450), just after mile marker 10.

Smith Bronte Landing Site   In 1927, Charles Lindbergh soloed the Atlantic Ocean in a plane called *The Spirit of St. Louis* and became an American hero. That same year, Ernie Smith and Emory B. Bronte took off from Oakland, California, on July 14, in a single-engine Travelair aircraft named *The City of Oakland,* headed across the Pacific Ocean for Honolulu, 2,397 miles away. The next day, after running out of fuel, they crash-landed upside-down in a kiawe thicket on Molokai, but emerged unhurt to become the first civilians to fly to Hawaii from the U.S. mainland. The 25-hour, 2-minute flight landed Smith and Bronte a place in aviation history—and on a roadside marker on Molokai.

King Kamehameha V Hwy. (Hwy. 450), at mile marker 11, on the *makai* (ocean) side.

HALAWA VALLEY ⍟

Of the five great valleys of Molokai, only Halawa, with its two waterfalls, golden beach, sleepy lagoon, great surf, and offshore island, is easily accessible. Unfortunately, the trail through fertile Halawa Valley, which was inhabited for centuries, and on to the 250-foot Moaula Falls has been closed for some time. There is one operator who conducts very expensive tours, but we have received so many letters of complaint (and have been personally stood up by him after a confirmed reservation) that we no longer recommend you use him.

You can spend a day at the county beach park (described under "Beaches," earlier in this chapter), but do not venture into the valley on your own. In a kind of 21st-century *kapu,* the private landowners in the valley, worried about slip-and-fall lawsuits, have posted NO TRESPASSING signs on their property.

To get to Halawa Valley, drive north from Kaunakakai on Highway 450 for 30 miles along the coast to the end of the road, which descends into the valley past Jersalema Hou Church. If you'd just like a glimpse of the valley on your way to the beach, there's a scenic overlook along the road: After Puuo Hoku Ranch at mile marker 25, the narrow two-lane road widens at a hairpin curve, and you'll find the overlook on your right; it's 2 miles more to the valley floor.

10 Shopping

KAUNAKAKAI

Molokai Surf, Molokai Island Creations, and **Lourdes** are clothing and gift shops in close proximity to one another in downtown Kaunakakai, where most of the retail shops sell T-shirts, muumuus, surf wear, and informal apparel. For food shopping, there are several good options. Because many visitors stay in condos, knowing the grocery stores is especially important. Other than that, serious shoppers will be disappointed, unless they love kites or native wood vessels. The following are Kaunakakai's notable stores.

Imamura Store   Wilfred Imamura, whose mother founded this store, recalls the old railroad track that stretched from the pier to a spot across the street. "We brought our household things from the pier on a hand-pumped vehicle," he recalls. His store, appropriately, is a leap into the past, a marvelous amalgam of precious old-fashioned things. Rubber boots, Hawaiian-print tablecloths, Japanese tea plates, ukulele cases, plastic slippers, and even coconut bikini tops line the shelves. But it's not all nostalgia: The Molokai T-shirts, jeans, and palaka shorts are of good quality and inexpensive, and the pareu fabrics are a find. In Kaunakakai. ✆ **808/553-5615.**

Molokai Drugs   David Mikami, whose father-in-law founded this pharmacy in 1935, has made this more than a drugstore. It's a gleaming, friendly stop full of life's basic necessities, with generous amenities such as a phone and a restroom for passersby. Here you'll find the best selection of guidebooks, books about Molokai, and maps, as well as greeting cards, paperbacks, cassette players, flip-flops, and every imaginable essential. The Mikamis are a household name on the island not only because of their pharmacy, but also because the family has shown exceptional kindness to the often economically strapped Molokaians. In Kamoi Professional Center. ✆ **808/553-5790.**

Molokai Fish & Dive   Here you'll find the island's largest selection of T-shirts and souvenirs, crammed in among fishing, snorkeling, and outdoor gear that you can rent or buy. Find your way among the fish nets, boogie boards, diving equipment, bamboo rakes, beach towels, postcards, juices and soft drinks, disposable cameras, and staggering miscellany of this chockablock store. One entire wall is lined with T-shirts, and the selection of Molokai books and souvenirs is extensive. The staff is happy to point out the best snorkeling spots of the day. In Kaunakakai. ✆ **808/553-5926.**

Molokai Surf   This brand-new wooden building now houses Molokai Surf and its selection of skateboards, surf shorts, sweatshirts, sunglasses, T-shirts, footwear, boogie boards, backpacks, and a broad range of clothing and accessories for life in the surf and sun. In Kaunakakai. 130 Kamehameha V Hwy. ✆ **808/ 553-5093.**

Take's Variety Store   If you need luggage tags, buzz saws, toys, candy, cloth dolls, canned goods, canteens, camping equipment, hardware, batteries, candles, pipe fittings, fishing supplies—whew!—and other products for work and play,

---

Moments The Hot Bread Run

For years, local residents have lined up waiting for Molokai Bread to be taken from the oven. Molokai's well-known and well loved export, Molokai Bread—developed in 1935 in a cast-iron, kiawe-fired oven—is **Kanemitsu Bakery's** signature product. Flavors range from apricot-pineapple to mango (in season), but the classics remain the regular white, wheat, cheese, sweet, and onion-cheese breads. Kanemitsu's is part of Molokai's night life, too. Whenever anyone on Molokai mentions "hot bread," he's talking about the hot-bread run at Kanemitsu's, the surreal late-night ritual for die-hard bread lovers. Those in the know line up at the bakery's back door beginning at 10:30pm, when the bread is whisked hot out of the oven and into waiting hands. You can order your fresh bread with butter, jelly, cinnamon, or cream cheese, and the bakers will cut the hot loaves down the middle and slather on the works so it melts in the bread. The cream cheese and jelly bread makes a fine substitute for dessert.

If you are a little hesitant to venture out by yourself for this only-on-Molokai experience, now you can go on a tour with **Molokai Outdoors Activities,** in the lobby of Hotel Molokai, just outside Kaunakakai (© 877/553-4477 or 808/553-4477; www.molokai-outdoors.com). The Hot Bread Run "tour" starts at 9:30pm, when they whisk you through the back streets of Kaunakakai to line up in a dimly-lit alley to wait for the bread to come out. After getting the still-hot bread, they take you on a night tour of the town and down the wharf, where you enjoy a cup of hot cocoa and your hot bread. The tour costs $25 and includes a loaf of the Molokai bread of your choice. If you forgo the tour and get bread on your own, a loaf will cost you $2.15.

---

this 54-year-old variety store is the answer. You may suffer from claustrophobia in the crowded, dusty aisles, but Take's carries everything. In Kaunakakai. © 808/553-5442.

EDIBLES

Friendly Market Center   You can't miss this salmon-colored wooden storefront on the main drag of "downtown" Kaunakakai, where people of all generations can be found just talking story in the Molokai way. Friendly's has an especially good selection of produce and healthy foods—from local poi to Glenlivet. Blue-corn tortilla chips, soy milk, organic brown rice, a good selection of pasta sauces, and Kumu Farms macadamia-nut pesto, the island's stellar gourmet food, are among the items that surpass standard grocery-store fare. In Kaunakakai. © 808/553-5595.

Misaki's Grocery and Dry Goods   Established in 1922, this third-generation local legend is one of Kaunakakai's two grocery stores. Some of its notable items: chopped garlic from Gilroy, California, fresh luau leaves (taro greens), fresh okra, Boca Burgers, large Korean chestnuts in season, gorgeous bananas, and an ATM. The fish section includes akule and ahi, fresh and dried, but the stock consists mostly of meats, produce, baking products, and a humongous array of soft drinks. Liquor, stationery, candies, and paper products round out the selection of this full-service grocery. In Kaunakakai. ✆ 808/553-5505.

Molokai Wines & Spirits   This is your best bet on the island for a decent bottle of wine. The shop offers 200 labels, including Caymus, Silver Oak, Joseph Phelps, Heitz, Bonny Doon, and a carefully culled European selection. *Wine Spectator* reviews are tacked to some of the selections, which always helps, and the snack options include imported gourmet cheeses, salami, and Carr's biscuits. In Kaunakakai. ✆ 808/553-5009.

EN ROUTE TO THE NORTH COAST

Coffees of Hawaii Plantation Store and Espresso Bar   This is a fairly slick—for Molokai—combination coffee bar, store, and gallery for more than 30 artists and craftspeople from Molokai, Maui, and the Big Island. Sold here are the Malulani Estate and Muleskinner coffees that are grown, processed, and packed on the 500-acre plantation surrounding the shop, as well as Hawaii-grown flavored coffees. (See p. 497 for details on plantation tours.) You may find better prices on coffee at other retail outlets, but the gift items are worth a look: pikake and plumeria soaps from Kauai, perfumes and pure beeswax candles from Maui, koa bookmarks and hair sticks, pottery, woods, and baskets. Hwy. 480 (near the junction of Hwy. 470), Kualapuu. ✆ 800/709-BEAN or 808/567-9023.

Molokai Museum Gift Shop   The restored 1878 sugar mill sits 1,500 feet above the town of Kualapuu. It's a considerable drive from town, but a good cause for those who'd like to support the museum and the handful of local artisans who sell their crafts, fabrics, cookbooks, quilt sets, and other gift items in the tiny shop. There's also a modest selection of cards, T-shirts, coloring books, and, at Christmas, handmade ornaments made of lauhala and koa. Meyer Sugar Mill, Hwy. 470 (just after the turnoff for the Ironwood Hills Golf Course, and 2 miles below Kalaupapa Overlook), Kalae. ✆ 808/567-6436.

EDIBLES

Kualapuu Market   This market, in its third generation, is a stone's throw from the Coffees of Hawaii store. It's a scaled-down, one-stop shop with wine, food, and necessities—and a surprisingly presentable, albeit small, assortment of produce, from Molokai sweet potatoes to Ka'u navel oranges in season. The shelves are filled with canned goods, propane, rope, hoses, paper products, and baking goods, reflecting the uncomplicated, rural lifestyle of the area. In Kualapuu. ✆ 808/567-6243.

THE WEST END

Big Wind Kite Factory & the Plantation Gallery   Jonathan and Daphne Socher, kite designers and inveterate Bali-philes, have combined their interests in a kite factory/import shop that dominates the commercial landscape of Maunaloa, the reconstituted plantation town. Maunaloa's naturally windy conditions make it ideal for kite-flying classes, which are offered free when conditions are right. The adjoining Plantation Gallery features local handicrafts such as milo-wood bowls, locally made T-shirts, Hawaii-themed sandblasted glassware, baskets of lauhala and other fibers, and Hawaiian-music CDs. There are also many Balinese handicrafts, from jewelry to clothing and fabrics. In Maunaloa. ✆ 808/552-2364.

Maunaloa General Store   Maunaloa's only general store sells everything from paper products to batteries, dairy products, frozen and fresh meats, wine, canned goods, and a cross-section of necessities. In Maunaloa. ✆ 808/552-2346.

Sheraton Molokai Lodge & Beach Village Logo Shop Located between the front desk check in and the bike rentals in a recently renovated wooden building, this shop can outfit you for life's great adventures. Heavy-duty sweat-shirts, Bullfrog sunscreens, sandals, swimwear, T-shirts, walking sticks, and fash-ionable dresses line the shelves. The food items and souvenirs are also diverse: mugs, magnets, CDs and cassettes, Molokai jams and jellies, mobiles, toys, plas-tic buckets, lidded koa boxes, fine wines, cold beer, Muleskinner coffees, coconut-shell soap dishes, picture frames, and other attractive gifts to go. In Mau-naloa. © 808/552-2791.

A Touch of Molokai Even though the Kalaukoi Hotel is closed, this fabulous shop remains open. It is well worth the drive. The surf shorts and aloha shirts sold here are better than the norm, with attractive, up-to-date choices by Jams, Quiksilver, and other name brands. Tencel dresses, South Pacific shell necklaces (up to $400), and a magnificent, hand-turned milo bowl also caught our atten-tion. Most impressive are the wiliwili, kamani, and soap-berry leis and a hand-some array of lauhala bags, all made on Molokai. At Kaluakoi Hotel & Golf Club. © 808/552-0133.

THE EAST END
EDIBLES
The Neighborhood Store 'N Counter The Neighborhood Store, the only grocery on the East End, sells batteries, film, aspirin, cookies, beer, Molokai pro-duce, candies, paper products, and other sundries. There's good food pouring out of the kitchen for the breakfast and lunch counter, too. See p. 487 for a restaurant review. In Pukoo. © 808/558-8498.

11 Molokai After Dark

Hotel Molokai, in Kaunakakai (© 800/367-5004 or 808/553-5347), offers live entertainment from local musicians poolside and in the dining room on Fri-day from 4 to 11pm and Saturday from 6 to 10pm. With its South Seas ambi-ence and poolside setting, it's become the island's premier venue for local and visiting entertainers.

Molokai musicians to watch for include **Pound for Pound,** a powerful group of artists, each over 250 pounds. The members are lead vocalist Jack Stone, Shane Dudoit, Danny Reyes, John Pele, and Alika Lani. As popular off-island as on, they perform Hawaiian, reggae, country, and contemporary Hawaiian numbers, many of them originals. Their CD, *100% Molokai,* has become a local legend.

Darryl Labrado is a teen phenom and the island's rising star; he sings and plays the ukulele to a huge local following. And **Pa'a Pono,** with its contempo-rary Hawaiian and reggae sounds, is a familiar name on the local nightlife cir-cuit. *Molokai Now,* a CD anthology of original music from Molokai, is a terrific memento for those who love the island and its music.

Movie buffs, too, finally have a place to call their own on Molokai. **Maunaloa Cinemas** (© 808/552-2707) is a triplex theater that shows first-run movies in the middle of Maunaloa town—four screenings a day at each of the three theaters.

Also in Maunaloa, the lounge at the **Sheraton Molokai Lodge and Beach Village** (© 800/782-9488 or 808/660-2710; fax 808/552-2908; www.sheraton-hawaii.com) offers live music Friday and Saturday, from 7 to 9pm, ranging from Phil Stevens and his lively Hawaiian songs and stories about the Hawaiian cow-boys to keiki hula, acoustic classical guitar, and contemporary Hawaiian music.

8

Lanai, a Different Kind of Paradise

Lanai is not an easy place to reach. There are no direct flights from the mainland. It's almost as if this quiet, gentle oasis—known, paradoxically, for both its small-town feel and its celebrity appeal—demands that its visitors go to great lengths to get here in order to ensure that they will appreciate it.

Lanai (pronounced lah-*nigh*-ee), the nation's biggest defunct pineapple patch, now claims to be one of the world's top tropical destinations. It's a bold claim because so little is here. Don't expect a lot of dining or accommodations choices (Lanai has even fewer than Molokai). There are no stoplights here and barely 30 miles of paved road. This almost virgin island is unspoiled by what passes for progress, except for a tiny 1920s-era plantation village—and, of course, the village's fancy new arrivals: two first-class luxury hotels where room rates hover around $400 a night.

As soon as you arrive on Lanai, you'll feel the small-town coziness. People wave to every car; residents stop to "talk story" with their friends; fishing and working in the garden are considered priorities in life; and leaving the keys in the car's ignition is standard practice.

For generations, Lanai was little more than a small village, owned and operated by the pineapple company, surrounded by acres of pineapple fields. The few visitors to the island were either relatives of the mainly Filipino residents or occasional weekend hunters. Life in the 1960s was pretty much the same as in the 1930s. But all that changed in 1990, when the Lodge at Koele, a 102-room hotel resembling an opulent English Tudor mansion, opened its doors, followed a year later by the 250-room Manele Bay Hotel, a Mediterranean-style luxury resort overlooking Hulopoe Bay. Overnight, the isolated island was transformed: Corporate jets streamed into tiny Lanai Airport, former plantation workers were retrained in the art of serving gourmet meals, and the population of 2,500 swelled with transient visitors and outsiders coming to work in the island's new hospitality industry. Microsoft billionaire Bill Gates chose the island for his lavish wedding, buying up all of its hotel rooms to fend off the press—and uncomplicated Lanai went on the map as a vacation spot for the rich and powerful.

But this island is also a place where people come looking for dramatic beauty, quiet, solitude, and an experience with nature away from the bright lights of Waikiki, the publicity of Maui, and the hoopla surrounding most resorts. The sojourners who find their way to Lanai come seeking the dramatic views, the tropical fusion of stars at night, and the chance to be alone with the elements.

They also come for the wealth of activities: snorkeling and swimming in the marine preserve known as Hulopoe Bay; hiking on 100 miles of remote trails; talking story with the friendly locals; and beachcombing and whale-watching along stretches of otherwise deserted sand. For the adventurous, there's horseback riding in the forest, scuba diving in caves, playing golf on courses with stunning ocean views, or renting a four-wheel-drive vehicle for the day and discovering wild plains where spotted deer run free.

In a single decade, a plain red-dirt pineapple patch has become one of Hawaii's top fantasy destinations. But the real Lanai is a multifaceted place that's so much more than a luxury resort—and it's the traveler who comes to discover the island's natural wonders, local lifestyle, and other inherent joys who's bound to have the most genuine island experience.

1 Orientation

ARRIVING

BY PLANE   No matter where you're coming from, you'll have to make a connection in Honolulu or Kahului (on Maui), where you can easily catch a small plane for the 25-minute flight to Lanai's airport. Jet service to Lanai is now available, but only on **Hawaiian Airlines** (© 800/367-5320 or 808/565-6977; www.hawaiianair.com), which offers one flight a day. Twin-engine planes take longer and are sometimes bumpier, but they offer great views because they fly lower. **Island Air** (© 800/652-6541 or 808/565-6744; www.islandair.com) offers six flights a day. For more details on these airlines—including details on how to get the cheapest fares—see "Getting There & Getting Around" and "Money-Saving Package Deals," in chapter 2.

Prop or jet, you'll touch down in Puuwai Basin, once the world's largest pineapple plantation; it's about 10 minutes by car to Lanai City and 25 minutes to Manele Bay.

BY BOAT   A round-trip on **Expeditions Lahaina/Lanai Passenger Ferry** (© 808/661-3756) takes you between Maui and Lanai for $52. The ferry service runs five times a day, 365 days a year, between Lahaina and Lanai's Manele Bay harbor. The ferry leaves Lahaina at 6:45and 9:15am, 12:45, 3:15, and 5:45pm; the return ferry from Lanai's Manele Bay Harbor leaves at 8and 10:30am, 2, 4:30, and 6:45pm. The 9-mile channel crossing takes 45 minutes to an hour, depending on sea conditions. Reservations are strongly recommended. Baggage is limited to two checked bags and one carry-on.

VISITOR INFORMATION

Destination Lanai (© 800/947-4774 or 808/565-7600; fax 808/565-9316; www.visitlanai.net) and the **Hawaii Visitors and Convention Bureau** (© 800/ GO-HAWAII or 808/923-1811; www.gohawaii.com) will both provide brochures, maps, and island guides. For a free *Road and Site Map* of hikes, archaeological sites, and other sights, contact the **Castle and Cooke Resorts,** P.O. Box 310, Lanai, HI 96763 (© 808/565-3000; www.lanai-resorts.com).

THE ISLAND IN BRIEF

Inhabited Lanai is divided into three parts—Lanai City, Koele, and Manele— and two distinct climate zones: hot and dry, and cool and misty.

Lanai City (pop. 2,800) sits at the heart of the island at 1,645 feet above sea level. It's the only place on the island where you'll find services. Built in 1924, this plantation village is a tidy grid of quaint tin-roofed cottages in bright pastels, with roosters penned in tropical gardens of banana, lilikoi, and papaya. Many of the residents are Filipino immigrants who worked the pineapple fields

Lanai

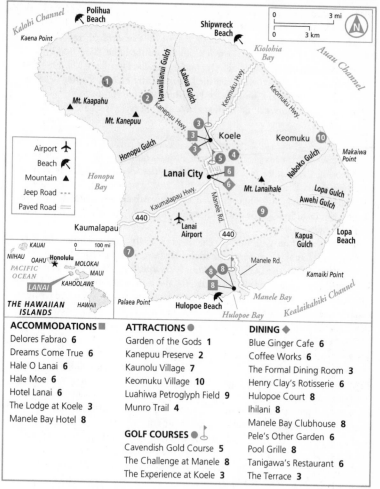

and imported the art, culture, language, food, and lifestyle of the Philippines. Their clapboard homes, now worth $150,000 or more, are excellent examples of historic preservation; the whole town looks like it's been kept under a bell jar.

Around Dole Park Square, a charming village square lined with towering Norfolk and Cook Island pines, plantation buildings house general stores with basic necessities as well as a U.S. Post Office (where people stop to chat), two banks, and a police station with a jail that consists of three blue-and-white wooden outhouse-size cells with padlocks.

In the nearby cool upland district of **Koele** is the Lodge at Koele, standing alone on a knoll overlooking pastures and the sea at the edge of a pine forest, like a grand European manor. The other bastion of indulgence, the Manele Bay Hotel, is on the sunny southwestern tip of the island at **Manele.** You'll get more of what you expect from Hawaii here—beaches, swaying palms, mai tais, and the like.

FAST FACTS

Lanai is part of Maui County. In case of **emergencies,** call the police, fire department, or ambulance services at *℃* 911, or the **Poison Control Center** at *℃* 800/362-3585. For nonemergencies, call the **police** (*℃* 808/565-6428).

For emergency dental care, call **Dr. Nick's Family Dentistry** (*℃* 808/565-7801). If you need a doctor, contact the **Lanai Family Health Center** (*℃* 808/565-6423) or the **Lanai Community Hospital** (*℃* 808/565-6411).

For a weather report, call the **National Weather Service** at *℃* 808/565-6033.

2 Getting Around

With so few paved roads here, you'll need a four-wheel-drive vehicle if you plan on exploring the island's remote shores, its interior, or the summit of Mount Lanaihale. Even if you have only 1 day on Lanai, rent one and see the island. You can also arrange a 4×4 adventure tour from **Adventure Lanai Ecocentre Centre** (*℃* **808/565-7373;** www.adventurelanai.com), which offers 3- to 4-hour off-road tours for $99.

Both cars and four-wheel-drive vehicles are available at the **Dollar Rent-A-Car** desk at **Lanai City Service/Lanai Plantation Store,** 1036 Lanai Ave. (*℃* **800/588-7808** for Dollar reservations, or **808/565-7227** for Lanai City Service). Expect to pay about $60 a day for the least expensive car available, a Nissan Sentra, and up to $129 a day for a four-wheel-drive Jeep. **Adventure Lanai Ecocentre Centre** (*℃* **808/565-7373;** www.adventurelanai.com), has 4×4 Jeeps for rent (complete with towels, masks, fins, snorkel, ice chest and an island map) for $124.

Be warned: Gas is expensive on Lanai and those four-wheel-drive vehicles get terrible gas mileage. Because everything in Lanai City is within walking distance, it makes sense to rent a Jeep only for the days you want to explore the island.

Though it's fun to rent a car and explore the island, it's possible to stay here and get to the beach without one. The two big resort hotels run shuttle vans around the island, but only for their guests. If you are staying at The Lodge at Koele or Hotel Lanai, the shuttles to Manele Bay Hotel run every hour. From the Manele Bay Hotel, you walk over to Hulopoe Beach. When you want to return, you just catch the hourly shuttle (it may run on the half-hour from Manele Bay Hotel) back to Lanai City.

If you're staying elsewhere, you can walk to everything in Lanai City and take a taxi to the beach. **Lanai Plantation Store** (*℃* **808/565-7227**) will provide transportation from Lanai City to Hulopoe Beach for $10 per person one-way (you can arrange with them when you want to be picked up, or you can walk over to the Manele Bay Hotel and phone them to come and get you—or you can most likely get a ride back up to Lanai City with a local). Whether or not you rent a car, sooner or later, you'll find yourself at Lanai City Service/Lanai Plantation Store. This all-in-one grocery store, gas station, rental-car agency, and souvenir shop serves as the island's Grand Central Station; here you can pick up information, directions, maps, and all the local gossip.

3 Where to Stay

The majority of the accommodations are located "in the village," as residents call Lanai City. Above the village is the luxurious Lodge at Koele, while down the hill at Hulopoe Bay are two options: the equally luxurious Manele Bay Hotel or tent camping under the stars at the park.

In addition to the choices listed below, also consider the B&B accommodations offered by **Delores Fabrao** (© 808/565-6134; dmfabrao@hotmail.com), who has two guest rooms in her home: a double with a shared bathroom and a family room that sleeps up to six ($55 double, $100 for 4) with a private bathroom. She doesn't provide breakfast, but you'll have the run of the entire house, including the kitchen. At **Hale Moe** (© 808/565-9520), host and Lanai native Momi Suzuki makes three bedrooms in her Lanai City home available to guests; all have private bathrooms ($80 to $90 double). Guests are welcome to use the entertainment center, large deck, and Momi's two bicycles. For a fully equipped, two-bedroom vacation rental that sleeps up to six, call **Hale O Lanai,** in Lanai City (© 808/247-3637; www.hibeach.com); rates range from $115 to $135.

Don't forget to add 11.42% in taxes to all accommodation bills. Parking is free.

Note: You'll find the hotels reviewed in this chapter on the map on p. 509.

VERY EXPENSIVE

The Lodge at Koele ★   In the past few years, we have been dismayed to watch this once grand resort (one of the best in the state) start to slip from its once very high standards, especially in the area of maintenance of the grounds and the hotel itself. Once a sterling property in every respect, the management appears to be not as diligent as it once was. At these prices we expect higher standards. Hopefully this current downward trend will reverse itself.

It still is a great place to stay for a quiet vacation in the cool mist of the mountains. Most guests here are looking for relaxation: sitting out on the porch, reading or watching the turkeys mosey across the manicured lawns, strolling through the Japanese hillside garden, or watching the sun sink into the Pacific and the stars light up at night. The Lodge, as folks here call it, stands in a 21-acre grove of Norfolk Island pines at 1,700 feet above sea level, 8 miles inland from any beach. The atmosphere is informal during the day and more formal after sunset (jackets are required in the main dining room; see review on p. 513).

The 102-room resort resembles a grand English country estate. Inside, heavy timbers, beamed ceilings, and the two huge stone fireplaces of the Great Hall complete the look. Overstuffed furniture sits invitingly around the fireplaces, richly patterned rugs adorn the floor, and museum-quality art hangs on the walls. Cushioned wicker chairs on the long porches are perfect for a long afternoon with a good book. The guest rooms continue the English theme with four-poster beds, sitting areas (complete with window seats), flowery wallpaper, formal writing desks, and luxury bathrooms with oversize tubs. There are plenty of activities here and at the sister resort down the hill, Manele Bay, so you'll get the best of both hotels. Other pluses include: complimentary shuttle to the golf courses, beach, and Manele Bay Hotel; complimentary coffee and tea in the lobby; formal tea every afternoon; twice-daily maid service; turndowns; and some rooms with butler service. Additional activities include croquet lawns, horse riding stables, upcountry hiking trails, and garden walks.

The hotel sponsors periodic guest appearances by celebrities who chat informally about their work in a drawing-room setting (see the box "'Talk Story' with the Greats," later in this chapter).

P.O. Box 630310, Lanai City, HI 96793. © 800/321-4666 or 808/565-7300. Fax 808/565-4561. www.lanai-resorts.com. 102 units. $375–$525 double; from $725 suites. Extra person $75. Children under 15 stay free in parent's room. Numerous packages (such as 5th night free, adventure, golf, and wedding) available. AE, DC, MC, V. Airport shuttle $25 round-trip. **Amenities:** 2 restaurants; bar (with quiet live music, hula, and occasional talks by celebrities); outdoor pool; golf at the Experience at Koele, an 18-hole championship Greg Norman/Ted Robinson–designed course, and executive putting green; tennis courts; fitness room; Jacuzzi; watersports equipment rentals at sister hotel Manele Bay Hotel; bike rentals; children's program; game room; concierge; activity desk; car-rental desk; business center; shopping arcade; room service; massage; babysitting; laundry service; dry cleaning. *In room:* A/C, TV, dataport, minibar, fridge, coffeemaker, hair dryer, iron, safe.

Manele Bay Hotel ⭐   We have the same complaints at this oceanside property as we do with the resort's sister property, the Lodge at Koele (reviewed above): in the past we have given both properties high marks, but we have been disappointed over the last few years at the downturn in the level of maintenance and housekeeping at both properties. Hopefully, this trend will reverse itself in the coming year.

Located on a sun-washed southern bluff overlooking Hulopoe Beach, one of Hawaii's best stretches of golden sand, this U-shaped hotel steps down the hillside to the pool and that great beach, then fans out in oceanfront wings separated by gardens with lush flora, manmade waterfalls, lotus ponds, and streams. On the other side, it's bordered by golf greens on a hillside of dry land scrub. The place is a real oasis against the dry Arizona-like heat of Lanai's arid South Coast.

Designed as a traditional luxury beachfront hotel, the Manele Bay features open, airy rooms situated so that each one has a peek of the big blue Pacific. The lobby is filled with murals depicting scenes from Hawaiian history, sea charts, potted palms, soft camel-hued club chairs, and handwoven kilim rugs. The oversize guest rooms are done in the style of an English country house on the beach: sunny chintz fabrics, mahogany furniture, Audubon prints, huge marble bathrooms, and semiprivate lanais. This resort is much less formal than the Lodge up the hill. Its attracts more families, and because it's warmer here, people wander through the lobby in shorts and T-shirts.

The 10-year old small spa was given a facelift in 2001 with a redesign of the six treatment rooms. In addition to a variety of massages, facials, and wraps, the center, open from 8am to 8pm daily, also has a fitness center with cardiovascular equipment, free weights, a multi-station gym, and yoga classes.

P.O. Box 630310, Lanai City, HI 96793. ℂ **800/321-4666** or 808/565-7700. Fax 808/565-2483. www.lanai-resorts.com. 250 units. $350–$695 double; $725–$3,000 suite. Additional person $75. Numerous packages (such as 5th night free, adventure, golf, and wedding) available. AE, DC, MC, V. Airport shuttle $25 round-trip. **Amenities:** 3 restaurants (the Ihilani, p. 514; the Hulopoe Court, p. 514; and the Pool Grille, p. 515); bar with breathtaking views; large outdoor pool; golf at the Jack Nicklaus–designed Challenge at Manele; tennis courts; fitness room; small spa; Jacuzzi; watersports equipment rentals; children's program; game room; concierge; activity desk; business center; shopping arcade; salon; room service; massage; babysitting; laundry/dry cleaning. *In room:* A/C, TV, dataport, minibar, coffeemaker, hair dryer, iron, safe.

MODERATE

Hotel Lanai ⭐ *Kids*   This hotel lacks the facilities of the two resorts described above, but it's perfect for families and other vacationers who can't afford to spend $375 to $700 a night. In fact, if you are looking for the old-fashioned aloha that Lanai City is famous for, this is the place to stay. Just a few years ago, the Hotel Lanai, on a rise overlooking Lanai City, was the only place to stay and eat, unless you knew someone who lived on the island. Built in the 1920s for VIP plantation guests, this clapboard plantation-era relic has retained its quaint character and lives on as a country inn. A well-known chef from Maui, Henry Clay Richardson, is the inn's owner and the dining room's executive chef (see review on p. 514).

The guest rooms are extremely small but clean and newly decorated with Hawaiian quilts, wood furniture, and ceiling fans (but no air-conditioning or televisions). The most popular are the lanai units, which feature a shared lanai with the room next door. All rooms have ceiling fans and private, shower-only bathrooms. The small, one-bedroom cottage, with a TV and bathtub, is perfect for a small family.

The hotel serves as a down-home crossroads where total strangers meet local folks on the lanai to drink beer and talk story or play the ukulele and sing into the dark, tropical night. Often, a curious visitor in search of an authentic experience will join the party and discover Lanai's very Hawaiian heart. Guests have the use of the complimentary shuttle to the Lodge at Koele, the Manele Bay Hotel, the golf courses (at which they get the same low rates given to guests at the 2 resorts), and the beach.

828 Lanai Ave. (P.O. Box 630520), Lanai City, HI 96763. © 800/795-7211 or 808/565-7211. Fax 808/565-6450. www.hotellanai.com. 11 units. $105–$135 double; $175 cottage double. Rates include continental breakfast. Extra person $10. AE, MC, V. Airport shuttle $25 round-trip. **Amenities:** Excellent restaurant; intimate bar; access to 2 resort courses on the island and the 9-hole golf course in town; nearby tennis courts; complimentary snorkeling equipment.

INEXPENSIVE

Dreams Come True ★ *Finds*   This quaint plantation house is tucked away among papaya, banana, lemon, and avocado trees in the heart of Lanai City, at 1,620 feet. Hosts Susan and Michael Hunter have filled their house with Southeast Asian antiques collected on their travels. Both are jewelers, and they operate a working studio on the premises. Two of the four bedrooms feature a four-poster canopied bed, with an additional single bed (perfect for a small family), while the other rooms have just one queen bed. The common area looks out on the garden and is equipped with both TV and VCR. Breakfast usually consists of freshly-baked bread with homemade jellies and jams, tropical fruit, juice, and coffee. The Hunters also rent nearby two-, three-, and four-bedroom homes for $250 to $350 a night.

547 12th St. (P.O. Box 525), Lanai City, HI 96763. © 800/566-6961 or 808/565-6961. Fax 808/565-7056. http://circumvista.com/dreamscometrue.html. 4 units. $99 double. Rates include continental breakfast. Extra person $25. AE, DISC, MC, V. *In room:* No phone.

4 Where to Dine

Lanai is a curious mix of innocence and sophistication, with strong cross-cultural elements that liven up its culinary offerings. You can dine like a sultan on this island, but be prepared for high prices. The tony hotel restaurants require deep pockets (or bottomless expense accounts), and there are only a handful of other options.

Note: You'll find the restaurants reviewed in this chapter on the map on p. 509.

VERY EXPENSIVE

Formal Dining Room ★★ RUSTIC AMERICAN/UPCOUNTRY HAWAIIAN   The setting: a roaring fire, bountiful sprays of orchids, sienna-colored walls, and well-dressed women in pearls sitting across from men in jackets, with wine buckets tableside. The menu highlights American favorites with intense flavors. Foie gras has a strong presence on the seasonally changing menu, as do venison, local seafood, wild mushrooms, rack of lamb, and the vaunted threadfish. During fall and winter months, expect to see pumpkins, beans, ragouts, and braised items offered in creative seasonal preparations. The Dining Room is known for its use of fresh herbs, vegetables, and fruit grown on the island, harvested just minutes away.

In the Lodge at Koele. © 808/565-4580. Reservations required. Jackets requested for men. Main courses $42 and up. AE, DC, MC, V. Daily 6–9:30pm.

Ihilani ★★ MEDITERRANEAN   Master chef Edwin Goto, ranked at the top in national surveys, has left his post at the Manele Bay Hotel's formal dining room, but his replacement, Executive Chef Mark Tsuchiyama, has continued Goto's style of melding Mediterranean with Island styles. Standouts include appetizers like homemade goat cheese and spinach ravioli with roasted eggplant and asparagus salad in a sun-dried tomato cilantro sauce ($13), or terrine of foie gras with pear d'anjou, Madeira wine gelee, and warm toasted black truffle brioche ($23). Entrees include baked onaga and citrus in a sea-salt crust ($38) and lavender-honey glazed duck breast ($34). The prix fixe menu is very complete and comes with selected wines.

In the Manele Bay Hotel. © 808/565-2296. Reservations strongly recommended. Jackets requested for men. Main courses $21–$40; set menu $100 without wine, $150 with wine. AE, DC, MC, V. Tues–Sat 6–9:30pm.

EXPENSIVE

Hulopoe Court ★★ HAWAII REGIONAL   Hulopoe is casual compared to the hotel's fine dining room, Ihilani, but more formal than the Pool Grille, the hotel's lunchtime spot. The 17th-century palanquin in the adjoining lower lobby, the Asian accents, the tropical murals by gifted Lanai artists, and the high vaulted ceilings add up to an eclectic ambience. The new menu showcases local ingredients such as Maui asparagus, hearts of palm, locally caught fresh fish, and gourmet breakfasts, including an impressive buffet. If crab-coconut soup is on the menu or mahimahi on poblano mashed potatoes, they're a good bet.

In the Manele Bay Hotel. © 808/565-2290. Reservations recommended. Collared shirt required for men. Main courses $20–$29. AE, DC, MC, V. Daily 7–11am and 6–9:30pm.

The Terrace ★★ AMERICAN   Located next to the Formal Dining Room in the Lodge at Koele, between the 35-foot-high Great Hall and a wall of glass looking out over prim English gardens, the Terrace is far from your typical hotel dining room. The menu may be fancy for comfort food, but it does, indeed, comfort. Hearty breakfasts of waffles and cereals, fresh pineapple from the nearby Palawai Basin, frittata, and Kauai Shrimp Benedict (sautéed Kauai shrimp, grilled taro bread, and wilted spinach with poached eggs and blue crab hollandaise) are a grand start to the day. Dinner choices are the American classics, created by Executive Chef Andrew Manion-Copley, such as roasted veal chop on herb mashed potatoes with fava beans and carrots, ($30), pepper roasted rib-eye steak with blue cheese mashed potatoes ($30), and garlic-herb roasted chicken with potato onion cake ($28).

In the Lodge at Koele. © 808/565-4580. Reservations recommended. Main courses $12–$15 breakfast, $19–$30 dinner. AE, DC, MC, V. Daily 6am–9:30pm.

MODERATE

Henry Clay's Rotisserie ★★ COUNTRY CUISINE   Henry Clay Richardson, a New Orleans native, has made some welcome changes to Lanai's dining landscape with his rustic inn in the middle of Lanai City. It's very popular and always full. Maybe that's because it's the only option on Lanai that occupies the vast gap between deli-diner and upscale-luxe.

The menu focuses on French country fare: fresh meats, seafood, and local produce in assertive preparations. Appetizers and entrees reflect Cajun, regional, and international influences, particularly the Rajun Cajun Clay's shrimp, a fiery concoction of hefty shrimp in a spiced tomato broth or the "Almost Grandma's Gumbo," straight from his New Orleans roots. The meats, which could be rabbit, duck, quail, venison, osso bucco, beef, or chicken, are spit-roasted on the rotisserie. Gourmet pizzas and salads occupy the lighter end of the spectrum. Diners rave about the fresh catch in lemon butter caper sauce; we loved the eggplant Creole, presented with perfect sugar snap peas on a bed of herbed angelhair pasta. Don't leave without a piece of the New Orleans-style pecan pie. The decor consists of plates on the pine-paneled walls, chintz curtains, peach tablecloths and hunter-green napkins, and fireplaces in both rooms.

In the Hotel Lanai. 828 Lanai Ave., Lanai City. © **808/565-7211.** Main courses $14–$38. MC, V. Daily 5:30–9pm.

Manele Bay Clubhouse ★ PACIFIC RIM   The view from the alfresco tables here may be the best on the island, encompassing Kahoolawe, Haleakala on Maui, and, on an especially clear day, the peaks of Mauna Kea and Mauna Loa on the Big Island. Lighter fare prevails at lunch: salads and sandwiches, burgers, Caesar with chicken, herbed chicken sandwich on sourdough, fish and chips, and excellent dim sum and calamari salad. The clubhouse is casual, specializing in cold and warm pupu (appetizers), which can be enjoyed as a light meal or can be combined to create a large feast, such as soft shell crab sushi rolls ($12), crispy calamari with fried sea greens ($10), Chinese barbecue chicken salad ($11) and pan seared foie gras with sushi rice ($14).

In the Challenge at Manele Clubhouse. © **808/565-2230.** Reservations recommended. Main courses $10–$16. AE, DC, MC, V. Lunch 11am–5pm; dining 5–9pm.

Pool Grille ★ ECLECTIC   At this, the most casual of the hotel's restaurants, you'll dine poolside under beach umbrellas, feasting on huge hamburgers (homemade buns, of course) and gourmet salads. Salad choices include spicy chicken ($13), grilled tiger prawns ($15) and cobb ($14). Lanai venison pastrami sandwich ($12) and grilled Hawaiian taro burger ($11) are among the popular sandwich choices. Even nonguests drop by, as this is one of only two restaurants on the beach open for lunch.

In the Manele Bay Hotel. © **808/565-7700.** Main courses $11–$16. AE, DC, MC, V. Daily 11am–5pm.

INEXPENSIVE

Blue Ginger Cafe COFFEE SHOP   Famous for its mahimahi sandwiches and inexpensive omelets, Blue Ginger is a very local, very casual, and inexpensive alternative to Lanai's fancy hotel restaurants. The four tables on the front porch face the cool Norfolk pines of Dole Park and are always filled with locals who talk story from morning to night. The tiny cafe is often jammed from 6 to 7am with construction workers on their way to work. The offerings are solid, no-nonsense, everyday fare: fried saimin (no MSG, a plus), very popular hamburgers on homemade buns, and mahimahi with capers in a white-wine sauce. Blue Ginger also serves a tasty French toast made with homemade bread, vegetable lumpia (the Filipino version of a spring roll), and Mexican specials. The stir-fried vegetables—a heaping platter of fresh, perfectly cooked veggies, including summer squash and fresh mushrooms—are a hit.

409 Seventh St. (at Lilima St), Lanai City. © **808/565-6363.** Breakfast items under $6.50; lunch under $10; dinner under $12. No credit cards. Daily 6am–8pm.

Coffee Works ★ COFFEE HOUSE   Oahu's popular Ward Warehouse coffeehouse has opened a new branch in Lanai City with a menu of espresso coffees and drinks, ice cream (from gelatos to local brands like Lapperts and Roselani), and a small selection of pastries. It's Lanai City's new gathering place, a tiny cafe with tables and benches on a pleasing wooden deck surrounded by tall pines and a stone's throw from Dole Park. Formerly a plantation house, the structure fits in with the surrounding plantation homes in the heart of Lanai City. There are some nice gift items available, including T-shirts, tea infusers, Chai, teapots, cookies, and gourmet coffees.

604 Ilima, Lanai City (across from Post Office). © 808/565-6962. Most items under $5. MC, V. Mon–Fri 7am–6pm; Sat 7am–2pm.

Pele's Other Garden ★★ DELI/PIZZERIA/JUICE BAR This popular Lanai City eatery has added a patio with umbrella tables outside and expanded the kitchen in the back, so there's a lot more seating—and a fuller menu to match. Pele's Other Garden is now a full-scale, New York–style deli, and you can also get box lunches and picnic baskets to go. Dinner is now served on china, not paper, with tablecloths under sconces—a real dining room! At lunch the pizzas and sandwiches are still top-drawer and popular; in the evening you can also order pastas (butterfly pasta with garlic shrimp, fettuccine with smoked salmon) and salads. Daily soup and menu specials, excellent pizza, fresh organic produce, fresh juices, and special touches such as top-quality black-bean burritos, roasted red peppers, and stuffed grape leaves are some of the features that make Pele's Other Garden a Lanai City must. Sandwiches are made with whole-wheat, rye, sourdough, or French bread, which are baked on the island and delivered fresh daily; the turkey is free-range. The fire-truck-yellow building is easy to spot along tree-shaded Dole Park.

Dole Park, 811 Houston St., Lanai City. © 808/565-9628. Most items less than $7. AE, DISC, MC, V. Mon–Sat 9:30am–3pm and 5–9pm.

Tanigawa's Restaurant LOCAL Formerly S. T. Properties, Tanigawa's has changed its name but remains the landmark that it's been since the 1920s. In those days, the tiny storefront sold canned goods and cigarettes; the 10 tables, hamburgers, and Filipino food came later. Jerry Tanigawa has kept his hole-in-the-wall a local institution, with a reputation for serving local-style breakfasts. The fare—fried rice, omelets, short stack, and simple ham and eggs—is more greasy spoon than gourmet, but it's friendly to the pocketbook.

419 Seventh St., Lanai City. © 808/565-6537. Reservations not accepted. Breakfast less than $7.50; lunch sandwiches $2.50–$7; burgers $2–$4.75. No credit cards. Thurs–Tues 6:30am–1pm.

5 Beaches

If you like big, wide, empty, gold-sand beaches and crystal-clear, cobalt-blue water full of bright tropical fish—and who doesn't?—go to Lanai. With 18 miles of sandy shoreline, Lanai has some of Hawaii's least crowded and most interesting beaches. One spot in particular is perfect for swimming, snorkeling, and watching spinner dolphins play: Hulopoe Beach, Lanai's best.

HULOPOE BEACH ★★★

In 1997, Dr. Stephen Leatherman of the University of Maryland (a professional beach surveyor who's also known as "Dr. Beach") ranked Hulopoe the best beach in the United States. It's easy to see why. This palm-fringed, gold-sand beach is bordered by black-lava fingers, protecting swimmers from the serious ocean currents that sweep around Lanai. In summer, Hulopoe is perfect for swimming, snorkeling, or just lolling about; the water temperature is usually in the mid-70s. Swimming is usually safe, except when swells kick up in winter. The bay at the foot of the Manele Bay Hotel is a protected marine preserve, and the schools of colorful fish know it. So do the spinner dolphins that come here to play, as well as the humpback whales that cruise by in winter. Hulopoe is also Lanai's premier

Frommer's Favorite Lanai Experiences

Snorkeling Hulopoe Beach. Crystal-clear waters teem with brilliant tropical fish off one of Hawaii's best beaches. There are tide pools to explore, waves to play in, and other surprises—like a pod of spinner dolphins that often makes a splashy entrance.

Exploring the Garden of the Gods. Eroded by wind, rain, and time, these geologic badlands are worth visiting at sunrise or sunset, when the low light plays tricks on the land—and your mind.

Hiking the Munro Trail. The 11-mile Munro Trail is a lofty, rigorous hike along the rim of an old volcano. You'll get great views of the nearby islands. Take a four-wheel-drive vehicle if you want to spend more time on top of the island.

Four-Wheeling It. Four-wheeling is a way of life on Lanai because there are only 30 miles of pavement. Plenty of rugged trails lead to deserted beaches, abandoned villages, and valleys filled with wild game. No other island offers off-road adventures like this one.

Camp Under the Stars. The campsites at Hulopoe Beach Park are about as close to the heavens as you can get. The sound of the crashing surf will lull you to sleep at night, while the chirping of the birds will wake you in the morning. If you're into roughing it, this is a great way to experience Lanai.

Watching the Whales at Polihua Beach. Located on the north shore, this beach—which gets its name from the turtles that nest here—is a great place to spend the day scanning the ocean for whales during the winter months.

beach park, with a grassy lawn, picnic tables, barbecue grills, restrooms, showers, and ample parking. You can camp here, too.

HULOPOE'S TIDE POOLS Some of the best lava-rock tide pools in Hawaii are found along the south shore of Hulopoe Bay. These miniature Sea Worlds are full of strange creatures: asteroids (sea stars) and holothurians (sea cucumbers), not to mention spaghetti worms, Barber Pole shrimp, and Hawaii's favorite local delicacy, the opihi, a tasty morsel also known as the limpet. Youngsters enjoy swimming in the enlarged tide pool at the eastern edge of the bay. When you explore tide pools, do so at low tide. Never turn your back on the waves. Wear tennis shoes or reef walkers, as wet rocks are slippery. Collecting specimens in this marine preserve is forbidden, so don't take any souvenirs home.

SHIPWRECK BEACH

This 8-mile long windswept strand on Lanai's northeastern shore—named for the rusty ship *Liberty* stuck on the coral reef—is a sailor's nightmare and a beachcomber's dream. The strong currents yield all sorts of flotsam, from Japanese handblown-glass fish floats and rare pelagic paper nautilus shells to lots of junk. This is also a great place to spot whales from December to April, when the Pacific humpbacks cruise in from Alaska to winter in the calm offshore waters. The road to the beach is paved most of the way, but you really need a four-wheel-drive to get down here.

POLIHUA BEACH ⟨★⟩

So many sea turtles once hauled themselves out of the water to lay their eggs in the sunbaked sand on Lanai's northwestern shore that Hawaiians named the beach here *Polihua*, or "egg nest." Although the endangered green sea turtles are making a comeback, they're seldom seen here now. You're more likely to spot an offshore whale (in season) or the perennial litter that washes up onto this deserted beach at the end of Polihua Road, a 4-mile Jeep trail. There are no facilities except fishermen's huts and driftwood shelters. Bring water and sunscreen. Beware of the strong currents, which make the water unsafe for swimming. This strand is ideal for beachcombing (those little green-glass Japanese fishing-net floats often show up here), fishing, or just being alone.

6 Watersports

Lanai has Hawaii's best water clarity because it lacks major development, because it has low rainfall and runoff, and because its coast is washed clean daily by the sea current known as "The Way to Tahiti." But the strong sea currents pose a threat to swimmers, and there are few good surf breaks. Most of the aquatic adventures—swimming, snorkeling, scuba diving—are centered on the somewhat protected south shore, around Hulopoe Bay.

The two main outfitters for watersports are: **Trilogy Lanai Ocean Sports,** ⟨★⟩ www.visitlanai.com (**©** **888/MAUI-800** or 808/565-9303), and **Adventure Lanai Ecocentre** (**©** **808/565-7373;** www.adventurelanai.com).

BODYBOARDING (BOOGIE BOARDING), BODYSURFING & BOARD SURFING

When the surf's up on Lanai, it's a real treat. Under the right conditions, Hulopoe and Polihua are both great for catching waves. Boogie boards ($10 a day) are available through **Adventure Lanai Ecocentre** (see contact information above). The beach shack at Hulopoe Beach has complimentary boogie boards for hotel guests (Manele Bay and the Lodge at Koele) only.

OCEAN KAYAKING

Discover the thrill of kayaking with **Trilogy's** guided trips into Lanai's complex eco-systems and unique flora and fauna (see contact information above). Monday to Saturday, from 7:30am to 2pm, you'll either paddle along Lanai's magnificent south shore to explore the water and sea caves at Kahekili Ho'e, where thousand-foot sea cliffs still hide the bones of ancient Hawaiians; or you'll travel along the north shore at Shipwreck Beach, one of the longest barrier reefs in Hawaii, where you can explore the shipwreck and paddle your kayak amongst the numerous turtles who frequent the reef. Both trips offer lunch, sodas and snacks, single and double kayaks, and snorkeling gear. Cost is $125 (half-price for children 3–15).

Adventure Lanai Ecocentre (see contact information above), offers ½-day sea kayak/snorkel adventures (as well as kayak/scuba trips; see below) aimed at introducing beginners to the world of ocean kayaking. The center provides state-of-the-art kayaks (with lightweight graphite paddles and full back-support seats), life vests, the latest in snorkel equipment, dry bags, towels, water, and snacks. After receiving instruction on how to kayak, your group will set off to explore the waters around Lanai, with stops for snorkeling, snacks, and beachcombing. The 4-hour trip costs $99. Rental kayaks are also available, starting at $30 a day for a single kayak or $50 a day for a double kayak.

SAILING

Trilogy Lanai Ocean Sports, ✦ (see contact information above), which has built a well-deserved reputation as the leader in sailing/snorkeling cruises in Hawaii, has a morning snorkel sailing trip on Monday, Wednesday, and Friday from 8:45am to 1pm and on Saturday from 10am to 2:30pm on board their luxury custom sailing catamarans. The trips along Lanai's protected coastline include sailing past hundreds of spinner dolphins and into some of the best snorkeling sites in the world. The $110 price (half-price for children 3–15) includes breakfast, lunch, sodas, snacks, snorkel gear and instruction.

SCUBA DIVING

Two of Hawaii's best-known dive spots are found in Lanai's clear waters, just off the south shore: **Cathedrals I** and **II,** so named because the sun lights up an underwater grotto like a magnificent church. **Trilogy Lanai Ocean Sports** ✦ (see above for contact information) offers several different kinds of sailing, diving, and snorkeling trips on catamarans and from their new 32-foot, high-tech, jet-drive ocean raft. At the crack of dawn (6:30am–8am) on Tuesday, Thursday and Saturday, Trilogy has its own version of "sunrise services" at the Cathedrals. Not only is this the best time of day to dive this incredible area, but there are virtually no other dive boats in the water at this time. Cost is $95.

For those wanting to sleep in, **Trilogy** offers an afternoon dive (3–6pm) on Monday, Wednesday, and Friday for the serious diver looking for a two tank dive in the areas that have made Lanai famous. Cost is $130 and includes sodas, snacks, scuba gear and dive master. Non-certified divers can check out Trilogy's Daily Beach Dives (Mon–Fri, 10 am) from the beach at Hulopoe Bay, for $75; certified divers can join in for $65.

Adventure Lanai Ecocentre (see contact information above), has a 4-hour diving tour, with instructor, to the top dive spots on Lanai, for $99; scuba gear rental a la carte or package deals are available also at their store, 338 Eight St. in Lanai City. ↓

SNORKELING

Hulopoe is Lanai's best snorkeling spot. Fish are abundant and friendly in the marine-life conservation area. Try the lava-rock points at either end of the beach and around the lava pools. Snorkel gear is free to guests of the two resorts and also can be rented from $10 a day from **Adventure Lanai Ecocentre;** see above for information on the center's ocean kayaking/snorkeling trips and contact information.

On Sundays, from 7:45am to 1pm, **Trilogy** (see contact information above) offers an extraordinary adventure called **In the Footsteps of Royalty.** Captain Dustin Kaopuiki, a direct descendent of Lanai's royalty, takes a group on a snorkeling tour of the waters around the southern coast of Lanai, where King Kamehameha the Great had his summer retreat. The pristine waters are teaming with tropical fish and lava tubes; spinner dolphins are usually present. Masks, fins, juice, sodas and lunch are included in the $125 price (half-price for children 3–15).

SPORTFISHING

Jeff Menze will take you out on the 28-foot Omega boat ***Spinning Dolphin*** (✆ **808/565-6613**). His fishing charters cost $400 for six people for 4 hours, or $600 for six people for 8 hours. He also offers exclusive 3-hour whale-watching trips in season, which cost $300 for six passengers.

SURFING

Adventure Lanai Ecocentre (see contact information above), specializes in teaching everyone from small kids to grandparents how to surf using lightweight wooden long boards. The 4-hour "Surf Safari" is $99, and surfboard rental is $45 a day.

WHALE-WATCHING

Year-round, **Trilogy** offers 1½-hour adventures on a 32-foot, 26-passenger, rigid-hulled inflatable boat. From late December through April, they are on the lookout for whales, but the remainder of the year schools of spinner dolphins are featured on this Blue Water Marine Mammal Watch. The cost is $75 (half-price for children 3-15).

7 Hiking & Camping

HIKING

A LEISURELY MORNING HIKE

The 3-hour self-guided **Koele Nature Hike** starts by the reflecting pool in the backyard of the Lodge at Koele and takes you on a 5-mile loop through a cathedral of Norfolk Island pines, into Hulopoe Valley, past wild ginger, and up to Koloiki Ridge, with its panoramic view of Maunalei Valley and Molokai and Maui in the distance. You're welcome to take the hike even if you're not a guest at the Lodge. The trailhead isn't obvious—just keep going mauka (inland) toward the trees—and the path isn't clearly marked, but the concierge will give you a free map. We suggest doing this hike in the morning; by afternoon the clouds usually roll in, marring visibility at the top and increasing your chance of being caught in a downpour.

THE CHALLENGING MUNRO TRAIL

This tough, 11-mile (round-trip) uphill climb through the groves of Norfolk pines is a lung-buster, but if you reach the top, you'll be rewarded with a breathtaking view of Molokai, Maui, Kahoolawe, the peaks of the Big Island, and—on a really clear day—Oahu in the distance. Figure on 7 hours. The trail begins at Lanai Cemetery along Keomoku Road (Hwy. 44) and follows Lanai's ancient caldera rim, ending up at the island's highest point, Lanaihale. Go in the morning for the best visibility. After 4 miles, you'll get a view of Lanai City. The weary retrace their steps from here, while the more determined go the last 1¼ miles to the top. Diehards head down Lanai's steep south-crater rim to join the highway to Manele Bay. For more details on the Munro Trail—including information on four-wheel-driving it to the top—see p. 523.

A SELF-GUIDED NATURE TRAIL

This self-guided nature trail in the Kanepuu Preserve is about a 10- to 15-minute walk through eight stations, with interpretive signs explaining the natural or cultural significance of what you're seeing. The trailhead is clearly marked on the Polihua Road on the way to the Garden of the Gods. Kanepuu is one of the last remaining examples of the type of forest that once covered the dry lowlands throughout the state. There are some 49 plant species here that are found only in Hawaii. The **Nature Conservancy** (© **808/565-7430**) conducts guided hikes every month; call for details.

GUIDED HIKES

Adventure Lanai Ecocentre (© **808/565-7373;** www.adventurelanai.com), offers a 4×4 Adventure Trek that combines hiking and four-wheeling. The trips include such destinations as the Munro Trail, Poiaiwa Gulch, Garden of the Gods, and more. The cost is $99 per person, which includes fruit, drinks, snacks, and transportation.

The **Lodge at Koele** (℃ **808/5657300;** www.lanai-resorts.com) has a 2½-hour Koloiki Ridge Nature hike through 5 miles of the upland forests of Koele at 11am daily. Fee is $15, and snacks and drinks are included.

The **Manele Bay Hotel** (℃ **808/565-7700;** www.lanai-resorts.com) has a 1½-hour fitness hike along an old fisherman's trail at 9am every morning. The fee is $20.

CAMPING AT HULOPOE BEACH PARK

There is only one "legal" place to camp on Lanai: Hulopoe Beach Park, which is owned by Castle and Cooke Resorts. To camp in this exquisite beach park, with its crescent-shaped, white-sand beach bordered by kiawe trees, contact **Castle and Cooke Resorts,** P.O. Box 310, Lanai City, HI 96763 (℃ **808/565-3978;** www.lanai-resorts.com). There's a $5 registration fee, plus a charge of $5 per person, per night. Hulopoe has six campsites; each can accommodate up to six people. Facilities include restrooms, running water, showers, barbecue areas, and picnic tables.

You can rent camping equipment from **Adventure Lanai Ecocentre** (see contact information above), which has everything from backpacks to tents. Castle and Cooke Resorts recommends a tent (rain can be expected year-round), a cooking stove or hibachi (the number of barbecues are limited), and insect repellent (mosquitoes are plentiful).

8 Golf & Other Outdoor Pursuits

GOLF

Cavendish Golf Course *Finds* This quirky par-36, nine-hole public course has not only no clubhouse or club pros, but also no tee times, scorecards, or club rentals. To play, just show up, put a donation into the little wooden box next to the first tee ($5–$10 would be nice), and hit away. The 3,071-yard, E. B. Cavendish–designed course was built by the Dole plantation in 1947 for its employees. The greens are a bit bumpy, but the views of Lanai are great, and the temperatures usually quite mild.

Next to the Lodge at Koele in Lanai City. No phone.

The Challenge at Manele ★★ This target-style, desert-links course, designed by Jack Nicklaus, is one of the most challenging courses in the state. Check out the local rules: "No retrieving golf balls from the 150-foot cliffs on the ocean holes 12, 13, or 17," and "All whales, axis deer, and other wild animals are considered immovable obstructions." That's just a hint of the uniqueness of this course, which is routed among lava outcroppings, archaeological sites, kiawe groves, and ilima trees. The five sets of staggered tees pose a challenge to everyone from the casual golfer to the pro. Facilities include a clubhouse, a pro shop, rentals, a practice area, lockers, and showers.

Next to the Manele Bay Hotel in Hulopoe Bay. ℃ 800/321-4666 or 808/565-2222. Greens fees: $205 ($165 for guests).

The Experience at Koele ★★ This traditional par-72 course, designed by Greg Norman with fairway architecture by Ted Robinson, has very different front and back 9 holes. Mother Nature reigns throughout: You'll see Cook Island and Norfolk pines, indigenous plants, and water—lots of water, including seven lakes, flowing streams, cascading waterfalls, and one green (the 17th) completely surrounded by a lake. All goes well until you hit the signature hole, number eight, where you tee off from a 250-foot elevated tee to a fairway bordered by a lake on the right and trees and dense shrubs on the left. After that, the back 9 holes drop dramatically through ravines filled with pine, koa, and eucalyptus trees. The grand finale, the par-five 18th, features a green rimmed by waterfalls that flow into a lake on the left side. To level the playing field, there are four different sets of tees. Facilities include a clubhouse, a pro shop, rentals, a practice area, lockers, and showers.

Next to the Lodge at Koele in Lanai City. 📞 800/321-4666 or 808/565-4653. Greens fees: $205 ($165 for guests).

BICYCLING

Road-bike treks are available through **Adventure Lanai Ecocentre** (📞 **808/565-7373;** www.adventurelanai.com), for $99 per person for 4 hours and are perfect for beginners—they're all downhill. A 4×4 van meets you at the bottom with snacks, takes you on a tour of the petroglyphs, and then gives you a ride back up to the top. Trips for more advanced riders are also available. The center also rents 21-speed front suspension mountain bikes starting at $25 a day.

The **Lodge at Koele** (📞 **808/565-7300**) also has mountain bikes to rent for $8 an hour, $35 for 4 hours, and $40 to $55 for 8 hours.

For general information about bike trails, check out **www.bikehawaii.com**.

HORSEBACK RIDING

Horses can take you to many places in Lanai's unique landscape that are otherwise unreachable, even in a four-wheel-drive vehicle. The **Stables at Koele** (📞 **808/565-4424**) offers various rides, including group rides that are a slow, gentle walk, starting at $50 for a 1½-hour trip. We recommend the 2-hour **Paniolo Trail Ride,** which takes you into the hills surrounding Koele. You'll meander through guava groves and patches of ironwood trees; catch glimpses of axis deer, quail, wild turkeys, and Santa Getrudis cattle; and end with panoramic views of Maui and Lanai. The cost is $75. Private rides (where you can canter, gallop, and trot) are $75 per person for 1 hour and $130 per person for 2 hours. Long pants and shoes are required; safety helmets are provided. Bring a jacket; the weather is chilly and rain is frequent. Children must be at least 9 years old and 4 feet tall. The maximum weight limit is 250 pounds.

TENNIS

Public courts, lit for night play, are available in Lanai City at no charge; call 📞 **808/565-6979** for reservations. Guests staying at the Lodge at Koele or the Manele Bay Hotel have tennis privileges at either the Tennis Center at Manele, with its six Plexipave courts, a fully equipped pro shop, and tournament facilities; or at the courts at Koele. Instruction is available for $25 for a clinic, $65 for a private 1-hour lesson. Court fees are $25 an hour. For information, call 📞 **808/565-2072.**

9 Seeing the Sights

You'll need a four-wheel-drive vehicle to reach all the sights listed below. Renting a Jeep is an expensive proposition on Lanai—from $129 to $179 a day—so we suggest that you rent one just for the day (or days) you plan on sightseeing; otherwise, it's easy enough to get to the beach and around Lanai City without your own wheels. For details on vehicle rentals, see "Getting Around," earlier in this chapter.

Kids **Especially for Kids**

Exploring Hulopoe Tide Pools (p. 517)   An entire world of marine life lives in the tide pools on the eastern side of Hulopoe Bay. Everything in the water, including the tiny fish, is small—kid-size. After examining the wonders of the tide pool, check out the larger swimming holes in the lava rock, perfect for children.

Hunting for Petroglyphs (p. 524)   The Luahiwa Petroglyphs Field, located just outside Lanai City, is spread out over a 3-acre site. Make it a game: Whoever finds the most petroglyphs gets ice cream from the Pine Isle Market.

Listening to Storytellers   Check with the Lanai Library, Fraser Avenue near Fifth Street, Lanai City (© 808/565-6996), to see if any storytelling or other children's activities are scheduled. The events are usually free and open to everyone.

For a guided 4×4 tour, contact **Adventure Lanai Ecocentre** (© 808/565-7373; www.adventurelanai.com), which offers 4-hour off-road tours for $99 per person.

Note: You'll find the following attractions on the map on p. 509.

GARDEN OF THE GODS ⊛

A dirt four-wheel-drive road leads out of Lanai City, through the now uncultivated pineapple fields, past the Kanepuu Preserve (a dry-land forest preserve teeming with rare plant and animal life) to the so-called Garden of the Gods, out on Lanai's north shore. This place has little to do with gods, Hawaiian or otherwise. It is, however, the ultimate rock garden: a rugged, barren, beautiful place full of rocks strewn by volcanic forces and shaped by the elements into a variety of shapes and colors—brilliant reds, oranges, ochers, and yellows.

Ancient Hawaiians considered this desolate, windswept place an entirely supernatural phenomenon. Scientists, however, have other, less colorful explanations. Some call the area an "ongoing posterosional event"; others say it's just "plain and simple badlands." Take a four-wheel-drive ride out here and decide for yourself.

Go early in the morning or just before sunset, when the light casts eerie shadows on the mysterious lava formations. Drive west from the Lodge on Polihua Road; in about 2 miles, you'll see a hand-painted sign that'll point you in the right direction, left down a one-lane, red-dirt road through a kiawe forest and past sisal and scrub to the site.

FIVE ISLANDS AT A SINGLE GLANCE: THE MUNRO TRAIL ⊛

In the first golden rays of dawn, when lone owls swoop over abandoned pineapple fields, hop into a 4×4 and head out on the two-lane blacktop toward Mount Lanaihale, the 3,370-foot summit of Lanai. Your destination is the Munro Trail, the narrow, winding ridge trail that runs across Lanai's razorback spine to the summit. From here, you may get a rare Hawaii treat: On a clear day, you can see all of the main islands in the Hawaiian chain except Kauai.

When it rains, the Munro Trail becomes slick and boggy with major washouts. Rainy-day excursions often end with a rental Jeep on the hook of the island's lone tow truck—and a $250 tow charge. You could even slide off into a major gulch and never be found, so don't try it. But in late August and September, when trade winds stop and the air over the islands stalls in what's called a *kona* condition, Mount Lanaihale's suddenly visible peak becomes an irresistible attraction.

When you're on Lanai, look to the summit. If it's clear in the morning, get a four-wheel-drive vehicle and take the Munro Trail to the top. Look for a red-dirt road off Manele Road (Hwy. 440), about 5 miles south of Lanai City; turn left and head up the ridge line. No sign marks the peak, so you'll have to keep an eye out. Look for a wide spot in the road and a clearing that falls sharply to the sea.

From here you can see Kahoolawe, Maui, the Big Island of Hawaii, and Molokini's tiny crescent. Even the summits show. You can also see the silver domes of Space City on Haleakala in Maui; Puu Moaulanui, the tongue-twisting summit of Kahoolawe; and, looming above the clouds, Mauna Kea on the Big Island. At another clearing farther along the thickly forested ridge, all of Molokai, including the 4,961-foot summit of Kamakou, and the faint outline of Oahu (more than 30 miles across the sea) are visible. You actually can't see all five in a single glance anymore because a thriving pine forest blocks the view. For details on hiking the trail, see p. 520.

LUAHIWA PETROGLYPH FIELD

With more than 450 known petroglyphs in Hawaii at 23 sites, Lanai is second only to the Big Island in its wealth of prehistoric rock art, but you'll have to search a little to find it. Some of the best examples are on the outskirts of Lanai City, on a hillside site known as Luahiwa Petroglyph Field. The characters you'll see incised on 13 boulders in this grassy 3-acre knoll include a running man, a deer, a turtle, a bird, a goat, and even a rare, curly-tailed Polynesian dog (a latter-day wag has put a leash on him—some joke).

To get here, take the road to Hulopoe Beach. About 2 miles out of Lanai City, look to the left, up on the slopes of the crater, for a cluster of reddish-tan boulders (believed to form a rain *heiau*, or shrine, where people called up the gods Ku and Hina to nourish their crops). A cluster of spiky century plants marks the spot. Look for the Norfolk pines on the left side of the highway, turn left on the dirt road that veers across the abandoned pineapple fields, and after about 1 mile, take a sharp left by the water tanks. Drive for another ½ mile and then veer to the right at the V in the road. Stay on this upper road for about a ¼ mile; you'll come to a large cluster of boulders on the right side. It's just a short walk up the cliffs (wear walking or hiking shoes) to the petroglyphs. Exit the same way you came. Go between 3pm and sunset for ideal viewing and photo ops.

KAUNOLU VILLAGE

Out on Lanai's nearly vertical, Gibraltar-like sea cliffs is an old royal compound and fishing village. Now a national historic landmark and one of Hawaii's most treasured ruins, it's believed to have been inhabited by King Kamehameha the Great and hundreds of his closest followers about 200 years ago. It's a hot, dry, dusty, slow-going 3-mile 4×4 drive from Lanai City to Kaunolu, but the mini-expedition is worth it. Take plenty of water, don a hat for protection against the sun, and wear sturdy shoes.

Ruins of 86 house platforms and 35 stone shelters have been identified on both sides of Kaunolu Gulch. The residential complex also includes the Halulu Heiau temple, named after a mythical man-eating bird. The king's royal retreat is thought to have stood on the eastern edge of Kaunolu Gulch, overlooking the

---

Perfect for a Rainy Day: Lanai Art Program

A perfect activity for a rainy day in Lanai City is the **Lanai Arts Program,** 339 Seventh St., located in the heart of the small town. Frequently, top artists from across Hawaii visit this home-grown art program and teach a variety of classes ranging from raku (Japanese pottery), silk printing, silk screening, paero making (creating your own design on this islanders' wrap), gyotaku (printing a real fish on your own T-shirt), and watercolor drawing to a variety of other island crafts. The cost is usually in the $60 range for the 2- to 3-hour classes and includes all materials. For more information call ⓒ **808/565-7503.**

---

rocky shore facing Kahekili's Leap, a 62-foot-high bluff named for the mighty Maui chief who leaped off cliffs as a show of bravado. Nearby are burial caves, a fishing shrine, a lookout tower, and many warrior-like stick figures carved on boulders. Just offshore stands the telltale fin of little Shark Island, a popular dive spot that teems with bright tropical fish and, frequently, sharks.

Excavations are underway to discover more about how ancient Hawaiians lived, worked, and worshipped on Lanai's leeward coast. Who knows? The royal fishing village may yet yield the bones of King Kamehameha. His burial site, according to legend, is known only to the moon and the stars.

KANEPUU PRESERVE

Don't expect giant sequoias big enough to drive a car through; this ancient forest on the island's western plateau is so fragile, you can only visit once a month, and even then, only on a guided hike. Kanepuu, which has 48 species of plants unique to Hawaii, survives under the Nature Conservancy's protective wing. Botanists say the 590-acre forest is the last dry lowland forest in Hawaii; the others have all vanished, trashed by axis deer, agriculture, or "progress." Among the botanical marvels of this dry forest are the remains of *olopua* (native olive), *lama* (native ebony), *mau hau hele* (a native hibiscus), and the rare *'aiea* trees, which were used for canoe parts.

Due to the forest's fragile nature, guided hikes are led only 12 times a year, on a monthly, reservations-only basis. Contact the **Nature Conservancy Oahu Land Preserve** manager at 1116 Smith St., Suite 201, Honolulu, HI 96817 (ⓒ **808/537-4508**), to reserve.

OFF THE TOURIST TRAIL: KEOMOKU VILLAGE

If you're sunburned lobster red, have read all the books you packed, and are starting to get island fever, take a little drive to Keomoku Village, on Lanai's east coast. You'll really be off the tourist trail. All that's in Keomoku, a ghost town since the mid-1950s, is a 1903 clapboard church in disrepair, an overgrown graveyard, an excellent view across the 9-mile Auau Channel to Maui's crowded Kaanapali Beach, and some very empty beaches that are perfect for a picnic or a snorkel. This former ranching and fishing village of 2,000 was the first non-Hawaiian settlement on Lanai, but it dried up after droughts killed off the Maunalei Sugar Company. The village, such as it is, is a great little escape from Lanai City. Follow Keomoku Road for 8 miles to the coast, turn right on the sandy road, and keep going for 5¾ miles.

10 Shopping

Central Bakery This is the mother lode of the island's baked delights, the bakery that is, well, central to Lanai's dining pleasure. If you've noshed on the fantastic sandwiches at Lodge at Koele's Terrace or any of the stellar desserts at its Formal Dining Room or at Manele Bay Hotel, you've enjoyed the good-time goodies from Central Bakery. The bakery supplies all breads, all breakfast pastries, specialty ice creams and sorbets, all banquet desserts, and restaurant desserts on the island. Although it's not your standard retail outlet, you can call in advance, place your order, and pick it up. They prefer as much notice as possible, and it's worth it. The guava chiffon and chocolate chantilly cakes are in great demand, and the breads are legendary. 1311 Fraser Ave., Lanai City. © 808/565-3920.

Gifts with Aloha Phoenix and Kimberly Dupree's store of treasures has blossomed since they moved to a larger location on the other side of Dole Park. They are now shipping minigardens, fountains, and lamps to the mainland, and are selling fabulously stylish hats and hatbands, T-shirts, swimwear, quilts, Jams World dresses, children's books and toys, Hawaii-themed books, pareus, candles, aloha shirts, picture frames, handbags, ceramics, dolls, and art by local artists (including some of the most beautiful wooden bowls in the islands). The sumptuous white lehua honey from the Big Island is available here, as are jams and jellies by Lanai's Fabrao House. The made-on-Maui soaps and bath products—in gardenia, pikake, and plumeria fragrances—make great gifts to go. Dole Park, 363 Seventh St. (at Ilima St.) © 808/565-6589.

International Food & Clothing This store sells the basics: groceries, housewares, T-shirts, hunting and fishing supplies, over-the-counter drugs, wine and liquor, paper goods, and hardware, even a take-out lunch counter. We were pleasantly surprised by the extraordinary candy and bubble-gum section, the beautiful local bananas in the small produce section, the surprisingly extensive selection of yuppie soft drinks (Sobe, Snapple, and others), and the best knife-sharpener we've seen—handy for the Lanai lifestyle. 833 Ilima Ave. © 808/565-6433.

Lanai Marketplace Everyone on Lanai, it seems, is a backyard farmer. From 7 to 11am or noon on Saturday, they all head to this shady square to sell their dewy-fresh produce, home-baked breads, plate lunches, and handicrafts. This is Lanai's version of the green market: petite in scale (like the island) but charming, and growing.

Dolores Fabrao's jams and jellies, under the **Fabrao House** label (© 808/565-6134 for special orders), are a big seller at the market and at the resort gift shops where they're sold. The exotic flavors include pineapple-coconut, pineapple-mango, papaya, guaivi (strawberry guava), poha (gooseberry) in season, passion fruit, Surinam cherry, and the very tart karamay jelly. All fruits are grown on the island. Dole Square.

The Local Gentry *Finds* Open since December 1999, Jenna Gentry's wonderful boutique is the first of its kind on the island, featuring clothing and accessories that are not the standard resort-shop fare. (Visiting and local women alike make a beeline for this store.) You'll find fabulous silk aloha shirts by Iolani; mahogany wood lamps; mermaids and hula girls; Putumayo separates (perfect for Hawaii) in easy-care fabrics; a fabulous line of silk aloha shirts by Tiki; top-quality hemp-linen camp shirts; inexpensive sarongs; fabulous socks; and the Tommy Bahama line for men and women. There are also great T-shirts, swimwear, jewelry, bath products, picture frames, jeans, chic sunglasses, and off-beat sandals. 363 Seventh St. (behind Gifs of Aloha, facing Ilima St.) © 808/565-9130.

C "Talk Story" with the Greats: Lanai's Visiting Artists Program

Not so very long ago—before CNN, e-mail, faxes, and modems—news spread in person, on the lips of those who chanced by these remote islands. Visitors were always welcome, especially if they had a good story to tell. The *ha'i mo'olelo,* or storyteller, was always held in high regard; Hawaii's kings invited them to the grass palace to discuss topics of contemporary life. Maybe you've seen the pictures in history books: King Kalakaua and Robert Louis Stevenson sitting on the beach at Waikiki, the famous author regaling His Majesty with bons mots. Or jaunty Jack London describing the voyage of his *Snark* to Queen Lili-uokalani. In Hawaiian pidgin, it's called "talk story."

The tradition continues. When the Lodge at Koele opened, David Murdock invited a few friends over. The "friends" just happened to be the late Henry Mancini, Sidney Sheldon, and Michael York, and they all had a fabulous time in the Great Hall, singing, playing the piano, and reciting poetry. Kurt Matsumoto, general manager at the Lodge then, liked what he saw and scheduled more informal gatherings of creative people. "We never had anything like this on this island before," said Matsumoto, who was born and reared on Lanai.

Today, the **Lanai Visiting Artists Program** ★★★ is dedicated to bringing the literati of America to Lanai, in a new version of "talk story." On any given weekend, you could find yourself in the company of poets, musicians, writers, actors, filmmakers, chefs, and other creative types. You might find yourself vacationing with, say, classical pianist Andre Watts, humorist Dave Barry, author Tom Robbins, "A Prairie Home Companion" host Garrison Keillor, or who knows which Pulitzer Prize or Academy Award winner, each sharing his or her talent and insights in a casual, living-room atmosphere.

The program takes place about a dozen times a year either at the Lodge or the Manele Bay Hotel. It's free and open to everyone. There's a constantly changing schedule, so contact either of those resorts to see who's visiting while you're on Lanai (*C* **800/321-4666;** www.lanai-resorts.com).

Pele's Garden Even if nothing ails you, Pele's Garden is the Eden of the island for health products, with an assortment of vitamins, herbs, homeopathics, and supplements. Shop here for health-related reference books, greeting cards and magazines, natural and organic groceries, baby food, natural pet products, organic seeds, and natural health and beauty aids. With the addition of **Pele's Other Garden,** the deli that serves up guiltless gourmet fare in the front of the store (p. 516), this corner of Lanai is a place you'll want to find. 811 Houston St. *C* **808/565-9629.**

Petroglyphs Located between Richard's and Pine Isle on Dole Park, the former Akamai, under new ownership, sells espresso, Icee floats, T-shirts, jewelry, clothes, candles, Lanai jams and jellies, coffee mugs, newspapers and magazines, fresh pastries, and souvenirs. 408 Eighth St. *C* **808/565-6587.**

Pine Isle Market   A local landmark for two generations, Pine Isle specializes in locally caught fresh fish, but you can also find fresh herbs and spices, canned goods, electronic games, ice cream, toys, zoris, diapers, paint, cigars, and other basic essentials of work and play. The fishing section is outstanding, with every lure imaginable. 356 Eighth St. ⓒ **808/565-6488.**

Richard's Shopping Center   The Tamashiros' family business has been on the square since 1946; not much has changed over the years. This "shopping center" is, in fact, a general store with a grocery section, paper products, ethnic foods, meats (mostly frozen), liquor, toys, film, cosmetics, fishing gear, sunscreens, clothing, kitchen utensils, T-shirts, and other miscellany. Half a wall is lined with an extraordinary selection of fish hooks and anglers' needs. Aloha shirts, aloha-print zoris, inexpensive brocade-covered writing tablets, fold-up lauhala mats, and gourmet breads from the Central Bakery (see above) are among the countless good things at Richard's. 434 Eighth St. ⓒ **808/565-6047.**

11 Lanai After Dark

Except for special programs such as the annual **Pineapple Festival** in May, when some of Hawaii's best musicians arrive to show their support for Lanai (see "Hawaii Calendar of Events," in chapter 2), the only regular nightlife venues are the Lanai Playhouse, at the corner of Seventh and Lanai avenues in Lanai City, and the two resorts, the Lodge at Koele and Manele Bay Hotel.

The **Lanai Playhouse** (ⓒ **808/565-7500**) is a historic 1920s building that has won awards for its renovations. When it opened in 1993, the 150-seat venue stunned residents by offering first-run movies with Dolby sound—quite contemporary for anachronistic Lanai. Lanai Playhouse usually, but not always, shows two movies each evening from Friday to Tuesday (to Wed in summer), at 6:30 and 8:30pm, with occasional Sunday and Monday matinees; if a 3-hour movie is on, it's shown at 7:30pm. Tickets are $7 for adults and $4.50 for kids and seniors. The playhouse is also the venue for occasional special events.

The **Lodge at Koele** has stepped up its live entertainment. In the lodge's **Great Hall,** in front of its manorial fireplaces, visiting artists bring contemporary Hawaiian, jazz, Broadway, classical, and other genres to listeners who sip port and fine liqueurs while sinking into plush chairs. The special programs are on weekends, but throughout the week, some form of nightly entertainment takes place from 7 to 10pm. Both the Lodge at Koele and Manele Bay Hotel are known for their **Visiting Artists Program** (see the box titled "'Talk Story' with the Greats," above), which brings acclaimed literary and performing artists from across the country to this tiny island. These are scheduled throughout the year, usually on a monthly or bimonthly basis. Other than that, what happens after dark in Lanai is really up to you. You can linger over your evening meal, letting dinner become extended leisurely entertainment. Afterward, you can retire to your room with a book or find an after-dinner crowd in the Tea Room at Koele or a game of billiards at Manele. And the local folks out on the veranda of the Hotel Lanai will be happy to welcome you. All the nightlife options in the hotels are open to nonguests.

9

Kauai, the Garden Isle

On any list of the world's most spectacular islands, Kauai ranks right up there with Bora Bora, Huahine, and Rarotonga. All the elements are here: moody rain forests, majestic cliffs, jagged peaks, emerald valleys, palm trees swaying in the breeze, daily rainbows, and some of the most spectacular golden beaches you'll find anywhere. Soft tropical air, sunrise birdsong, essence of ginger and plumeria, golden sunsets, sparkling waterfalls—you don't just go to Kauai, you absorb it with every sense. It may get more than its fair share of tropical downpours, but that's what makes it so lush and green—and creates an abundance of rainbows.

Kauai is essentially a single large shield volcano that rises 3 miles above the sea floor. The island lies 90 miles across the open ocean from Oahu, but it seems at least a half-century removed in time. It's often called "the separate kingdom" because it stood alone and resisted King Kamehameha's efforts to unite Hawaii. In the end, it required a royal kidnapping to take the garden isle. After King Kamehameha died, his son, Liholiho, ascended the throne. He gained control of Kauai by luring Kauai's king, Kaumualii, aboard the royal yacht and sailing to Oahu; once there, Kaumualii was forced to marry Kaahumanu, Kamehameha's widow, thereby uniting the islands.

Today the independent spirit lives on in Kauai, which refuses to surrender its island to wholesale tourism, preferring instead to take care of residents first (though it takes good care of visitors, too). A Kauai rule is that no building may exceed the height of a coconut tree—between three and four stories. As a result, the island itself, not its palatial beach hotels, is the attention-grabber. There's no real nightlife here, no opulent shopping malls. But there is the beauty of the verdant jungle, the endless succession of spectacular beaches, the grandeur of Waimea Canyon, and the drama of the Na Pali Coast. Even Princeville, an opulent marble-and-glass luxury hotel, does little more than frame the natural glory of Hanalei's spectacular 4,000-foot-high Namolokama mountain range.

Kauai's beauty has played a supporting role in more than 40 Hollywood films, from *South Pacific* to *Jurassic Park*. But this island is not just another pretty face: Its raw wilderness is daunting, its seas challenging, its canyons forbidding—two-thirds of the island is impenetrable. This is the place for active visitors: There's watersports galore; miles of trails through rain forests and along ocean cliffs for hikers, bikers, and horseback riders; and golf options that range from championship links to funky local courses where chickens roam the greens and balls wind up embedded in coconut trees.

But Kauai is also great for those who need to relax and heal jangled nerves. Here you'll find miles of sandy beaches, perfect for just sitting and meditating. There are also quiet spots in the forest where you can listen to the rain dance on the leaves as well as an endless supply of laid-back, lazy days that end with the sun sinking into the Pacific amid a blaze of glorious tropical color.

1 Orientation

ARRIVING

The final approach to Lihue Airport is dramatic; try to sit on the left side of the aircraft, where passengers are treated to an excellent view of the Hauupu Ridge, Nawiliwili Bay, and Kilohana Crater. **United Airlines** (© 800/225-5825; www. ual.com) offers direct service to Kauai, with daily flights from Los Angeles. **Pleasant Holidays** (© 800/742-9244; www.pleasantholidays.com), one of Hawaii's largest travel companies offering low-cost airfare and package deals, has two weekly non-stop flights from Los Angeles and San Francisco using American Trans Air. All other airlines land in Honolulu, where you'll have to connect to a 30-minute interisland flight to Kauai's Lihue Airport. Between the two inter-island carriers, **Aloha Airlines** (© 800/367-5250, 808/245-3691, or 808/484-1111; www.alohaair.com) and **Hawaiian Airlines** (© 800/367-5320, 808/245-1813, or 808/838-1555; www.hawaiianair.com), there is a flight at least every hour to Lihue.

All of the major car-rental companies have branches at Lihue Airport; see "Getting Around," below, and "Getting There & Getting Around," in chapter 2, for details on renting in Hawaii. If you're not renting a car (although you should be), call **Kauai Taxi Company** (© 808/246-9554) for airport pickup.

VISITOR INFORMATION

The **Kauai Visitors Bureau** is located on the first floor of the Watumull Plaza, 4334 Rice St., Suite 101, Lihue, HI 96766 (© 808/245-3971; fax 808/246-9235; www.kauaivisitorsbureau.org). For a free official *Kauai Vacation Planner* or recorded information, call © 800/262-1400. The **Poipu Beach Resort Association,** P.O. Box 730, Koloa, HI 96756 (© 888/744-0888 or 808/742-7444; http://poipu-beach.org), will also send you a free guide to accommodations, activities, shopping, and dining in the Poipu Beach area.

If you'd like to learn more about Kauai before you go, contact the **Kauai Historical Society,** 4396 Rice St., Lihue, HI 96766 (© 808/245-3373; khs@hawaiian.net). The group maintains a video-lending library that includes material on a range of topics, including Hawaiian legends, ghost stories, archaeology, and travelogues on individual areas around Kauai. Mainland residents can borrow tapes for up to 3 weeks. Rates are $1 for society members, $2.50 for nonmembers; shipping and handling costs $5.

THE ISLAND IN BRIEF

Kauai's three main resort areas, where nearly all the island's accommodations are located, are all quite different in climate, price, and type of accommodations offered, but it's a wide, wonderful range. On the south shore, dry and sunny **Poipu** is anchored by perfect beaches. This is the place to stay if you like the ocean, watersports, and plenty of sunshine. The **Coconut Coast,** on the east coast of Kauai, has the most condos, shops, and traffic—it's where all the action is. Hanalei, up on the **North Shore,** is rainy, lush, and quiet, with spectacular beaches and deep wilderness. Because of its remote location, the North Shore is a great place to get away from it all—but not a great place from which to explore the rest of the island.

Lihue & Environs

Lihue is where most visitors first set foot on the island. This red-dirt farm town, the county seat, was founded by sugar planters and populated by descendants of Filipino and Japanese cane cutters. It's a plain and simple place, with used-car lots and mom-and-pop shops. It's also the source of bargains: inexpensive lodging, great deals on dining, and some terrific shopping

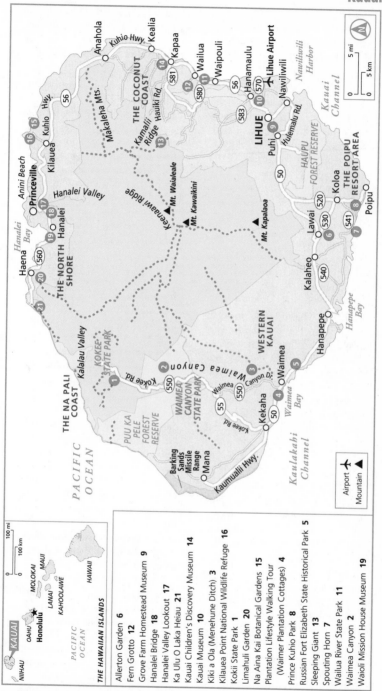

Kauai

Kuhio Hwy.
Anahola
Kealia
Kuhio Hwy.
Kapaa **14**
Wailua
Waipouli **11**
581
12 **580**
THE COCONUT
COAST
Makaleha Mts.
Kamalii
Ridge
Hauiki Rd.
13
Kilauea **15**
16 Kuhio Hwy.
Kilauea
Anini Beach
Princeville **17**
18
19
Hanalei Valley
Hanalei Bay
Haena
560
20
THE NORTH SHORE
21
Kalalau Valley
KOKEE STATE PARK
1
THE NA PALI COAST
Kokee Rd.
2 Waimea Canyon
WAIMEA CANYON STATE PARK
550
Waimea Canyon Dr.
3
Waimea **550**
Canyon Dr.
Kekaha **4**
55
Kokee Rd.
50
Waimea
Waimea Bay
5
WESTERN KAUAI
PACIFIC OCEAN
PUU KA PELE FOREST RESERVE
Barking Sands Missile Range
Mana
Kaumualii Hwy.
Kaulakahi Channel

Mt. Waialeale
Mt. Kawaikini
Mt. Kapalaoa
Keanawai Ridge

Hanamaulu
56
Lihue Airport
570 Nawiliwili
10
583
LIHUE
Puhi **9**
Hulemalu Rd.
HAUPU FOREST RESERVE
50
Koloa
THE POIPU RESORT AREA
Kalaheo **520**
Lawai **530**
6
540
541
7
Poipu
8
Hanapepe
Hanapepe Bay

Nawiliwili Harbor
Kauai Channel

Airport ✈
Mountain ▲

0   5 mi
0   5 km

THE HAWAIIAN ISLANDS

NIIHAU
KAUAI
OAHU
Honolulu
MOLOKAI
MAUI
LANAI
KAHOOLAWE
HAWAII
PACIFIC OCEAN

0   100 mi
0   100 km

Allerton Garden **6**
Fern Grotto **12**
Grove Farm Homestead Museum **9**
Hanalei Bridge **18**
Hanalei Valley Lookout **17**
Ka Ulu O Laka Heiau **21**
Kauai Children's Discovery Museum **14**
Kauai Museum **10**
Kiki a Ola (Menehune Ditch) **3**
Kilauea Point National Wildlife Refuge **16**
Kokii State Park **1**
Limahuli Garden **20**
Na Aina Kai Botanical Gardens **15**
Plantation Lifestyle Walking Tour (Waimer Plantation Cottages) **4**
Prince Kuhio Park **8**
Russian Fort Elizabeth State Historical Park **5**
Sleeping Giant **13**
Spouting Horn **7**
Wailua River State Park **11**
Waimea Canyon **2**
Waioli Mission House Museum **19**

buys. One of the island's most beautiful beaches, **Kalapaki Beach** ⋆⋆, is just next door at **Nawiliwili,** by the island's main harbor.

The Poipu Resort Area

POIPU BEACH ⋆⋆⋆ On Kauai's sun-soaked south shore, this is a pleasant if sleepy resort destination of low-rise hotels set on gold-sand pocket beaches. Well-done, master-planned Poipu is Kauai's most popular resort, with the widest variety of accommodations, from luxury hotels to B&Bs and condos. It offers 36 holes of golf, 38 tennis courts, and outstanding restaurants. This is a great place for watersports, and a good base from which to tour the rest of Kauai. The only drawback is that the North Shore is about 1 to 1½ hours away.

KOLOA This tiny old town of gaily painted sugar shacks just inland from Poipu Beach is where the Hawaiian sugar industry was born more than a century and a half ago. The mill is closed, but this showcase plantation town lives on as a tourist attraction, with delightful shops, an old general store, and a vintage Texaco gas station with a 1930s Model A truck in place, just like in the good old days.

KAHALEO/LAWAI Just a short 10- to 15-minute drive inland from the beach at Poipu lie the more residential communities of Lawai and Kalaheo. Quiet subdivisions line the streets, restaurants catering to locals dot the area, and life revolves around family and work. Good bargains on B&Bs and a handful of reasonably priced restaurants can be found here.

Western Kauai

This region, west of Poipu, is more remote than its eastern neighbor and lacks its terrific beaches. But it's home to one of Hawaii's most spectacular natural wonders, **Waimea**

Canyon ⋆⋆⋆ (the "Grand Canyon of the Pacific"); and farther upland and inland, one of its best parks, **Kokee State Park** ⋆⋆.

HANAPEPE For a quick trip back in time, turn off Highway 50 at Hanapepe, once one of Kauai's biggest towns. Founded by Chinese rice farmers, it's so picturesque that it was used as a backdrop for the miniseries *The Thornbirds.* Hanapepe makes a good rest stop on the way to or from Waimea Canyon. It has galleries selling antiques as well as local art and crafts, including Georgio's surfboard art and coconut-grams. It's also home to one of the best restaurants on Kauai, the Hanapepe Cafe & Espresso Bar (p. 563). Nearby, at **Salt Pond Beach Park** ⋆ (p. 572), Hawaiians since the 17th century have dried a reddish sea salt in shallow, red-clay pans. This is a great place to swim, snorkel, and maybe even observe an ancient industry still in practice.

WAIMEA This little coastal town, the original capital of Kauai, seems to have quit the march of time. Dogs sleep in the street while old pickups rust in front yards. The ambience is definitely laid-back. A stay in Waimea is peaceful and quiet (especially at the Waimea Plantation Cottages on the beach), but the remote location means this isn't the best base if you want to explore the other regions of Kauai, such as the North Shore, without a lot of driving.

On his search for the Northwest Passage in 1778, British explorer Capt. James Cook dropped anchor at Waimea and discovered a sleepy village of grass shacks. In 1815, the Russians arrived and built a fort here (now a national historic landmark), but they didn't last long: A scoundrel named George Anton Scheffer tried to claim Kauai for Russia, but he was exposed as an

Niihau: The Forbidden Island

Just 17 miles across the Kaulakahi Channel from Kauai lies the arid island of Niihau, "The Forbidden Island." Visitors are not allowed on this privately owned island, which is a working cattle and sheep ranch with about 200 residents living in the single town of Puuwai.

In 1864, after an unusually wet winter that turned the dry scrub land of the small island (18 miles by 6 miles) into green pasture, Eliza Sinclair, a Scottish widow, decided to buy Niihau and move her family here. King Kamehameha IV agreed to sell the island for $10,000. The next year, normal weather returned, and the green pastures withered into sparse semi-desert vegetation.

Today, Sinclair's great-great-grandson, Bruce Robinson, continues to run the ranching operation and fiercely protects the privacy of the island residents. From the outside, life on Niihau has not changed much in 140 years: There's no running water, indoor plumbing, or electrically generated power. The Hawaiian language is still spoken. Most of the men work for the ranch when there is work, and fish and hunt when there is no work. The women specialize in gathering and stringing *pupu Niihau,* prized, tiny white seashells (found only on this island), into Niihau's famous leis, which fetch prices in the thousands of dollars.

impostor and expelled by King Kamehameha I.

Today, even Waimea's historic relics are spare and simple: a statue of Cook alongside a bas-relief of his ships, the rubble foundation of the Russian fort, and the remains of an ancient aqueduct unlike any other in the Pacific. Except for an overabundance of churches for a town this size, there's no sign that Waimea was selected as the first landing site of missionaries in 1820.

The Coconut Coast

The eastern shore of Kauai north of Lihue is a jumble of commerce and condos strung along the coast road named for Prince Kuhio, with several small beaches beyond. Almost anything you need, and a lot of stuff you can live without, can be found along this coast, which is known for its hundreds of coconut trees waving in the breeze. It's popular with budget travelers because of the myriad B&Bs and affordable

hotels and condos to choose from, and it offers great restaurants and the island's major shopping areas.

KAPAA   The center of commerce on the east coast and the capital of the Coconut Coast condo-and-hotel district, this restored plantation town looks just like an antique. False-front wooden stores line both sides of the highway; it looks as though they've been here forever—until you notice the fresh paint and new roofs and realize that everything has been rebuilt since Hurricane Iniki smacked the town flat in 1992. Kapaa has made an amazing comeback without losing its funky charm.

The North Shore

Kauai's North Shore may be the most beautiful place in Hawaii. Exotic seabirds, a half-moon bay, jagged peaks soaring into the clouds, and a mighty wilderness lie around the bend from the Coconut Coast, just beyond a series of one-lane bridges traversing the tail ends of waterfalls. There's only one road in and out, and only two towns, Hanalei and Kilauea—the former by the sea, the latter on a lighthouse cliff that's home to a bird preserve. Sun seekers may fret about all the rainy days, but Princeville Resort offers elegant shelter and two golf courses where you can play through rainbows.

KILAUEA ✦   This village is home to an antique lighthouse, tropical-fruit stands, little stone houses, and Kilauea Point National Wildlife Refuge, a wonderful seabird preserve. The rolling hills and sea cliffs are hideaways for the rich and famous, including Bette Midler and Sylvester Stallone. The village itself has its charms: The 1892 Kong Lung Company, Kauai's oldest general store, sells antiques, art, and crafts; and you can order a jazzy Billie Holiday Pizza to go at Kilauea Bakery and Pau Hana Pizza.

ANINI BEACH ✦   This little-known residential district on a 2-mile reef (the biggest on Kauai) offers the safest swimming and snorkeling on the island. A great beach park is open to campers and day-trippers, and there's a boat ramp where locals launch sampans to fish for tuna. On Sundays, there's polo in the park and the sizzle of barbecue on the green. Several residents host guests in nearby B&Bs.

PRINCEVILLE ✦   A little overwhelming for Kauai's wild North Shore, Princeville Resort is Kauai's biggest project, an 11,000-acre development set on a high plain overlooking Hanalei Bay. This resort community includes a luxury Sheraton hotel, 10 condo complexes, new timeshare units around two championship golf courses, cliff-side access to pocket beaches, and one B&B right on the golf course.

HANALEI ✦✦✦   Picture-postcard Hanalei is the laid-back center of North Shore life and an escapist's dream; it's also the gateway to the wild Na Pali Coast. Hanalei is the last great place on Kauai yet to face the developer's blade of progress. At **Hanalei Bay,** sloops anchor and surfers play year-round. The 2-mile-long crescent beach, the biggest indentation on Kauai's coast, is ideal for kids in summer, when the wild surf turns placid. Hanalei still retains the essence of its original sleepy, end-of-the-road charm. On either side of two-lane Kuhio Highway, you'll find just enough shops and restaurants to sustain you for a week's visit—unless you're a hiker, surfer, or sailor, or have some other preoccupation that just might keep you here the rest of your life.

HAENA ✦✦   Emerald-green Haena isn't a town or a beach but an ancient Hawaiian district, a place of exceptional natural beauty and the gateway to the Na Pali Coast. It's the perfect tropical escape, and everybody knows it: Old house foundations and temples, now covered by jungle, lie in the shadow of new million-dollar homes of movie stars and musicians like Jeff Bridges and Graham Nash. This idyllic, 4-mile coast has lagoons, bays, great beaches, spectacular snorkeling, a botanical garden, and the only North Shore resort that's right on the sand, the Hanalei Colony Resort.

The Na Pali Coast ✦✦✦

The road comes to an end, and now it begins: the Hawaii you've been dreaming about. Kauai's Na Pali Coast (*na pali* means "the cliffs") is a place of extreme beauty and Hawaii's last true wilderness. Its majestic splendor will forever remain unspoiled because no road will ever traverse it. You can enter this state park only on foot or by sea. Serious hikers—and we mean very serious—tackle the ancient 11-mile-long trail down the forbidding coast to Kalalau Valley (see "Hiking & Camping," later in this chapter). The lone, thin trail that creases these cliffs isn't for the faint of heart or anyone afraid of heights. Those of us who aren't up to it can explore the wild coast in an inflatable rubber Zodiac, a billowing sailboat, a high-powered catamaran, or a hovering helicopter, which takes you for the ride of your life.

2 Getting Around

DRIVING AROUND KAUAI

You need a car to see and do everything on Kauai. Luckily, driving here is easy. There are only two major highways, each beginning in Lihue. From Lihue Airport, turn right, and you'll be on Kapule Highway (Hwy. 51), which eventually merges into Kuhio Highway (Hwy. 56) a mile down. This road will take you to the Coconut Coast and through the North Shore, before reaching a dead end at Kee Beach, where the Na Pali Coast begins.

If you turn left from Lihue Airport and follow Kapule Highway (Hwy. 51), you'll pass through Lihue and Nawiliwili. Turning on Nawiliwili Road (Hwy. 58) will bring you to the intersection of Kaumualii Highway (Hwy. 50), which will take you to the south and southwest sections of the island. This road doesn't follow the coast, however, so if you're heading to Poipu (and most people are), take Maluhia Road (Hwy. 520) south.

Kaumualii Highway (Hwy. 50) continues all the way to Waimea, where it then dwindles to a secondary road before reaching a dead end at the other end of the Na Pali Coast.

To get to Waimea Canyon, take either Waimea Canyon Road (Hwy. 550), which follows the western rim of the canyon and affords spectacular views, or Kokee Road (Hwy. 55), which goes up through Waimea Canyon to Kokee State Park (4,000 ft. above sea level); the roads join up about halfway.

CAR RENTALS　　All of the major car-rental agencies are represented on Kauai; for a complete list, as well as tips on insurance and driving rules, see "Getting There & Getting Around," in chapter 2. The rental desks are just across the street from Lihue Airport, but you must go by van to collect your car. For deep discounts on weekly car-rental rates, call **Hookipa Haven Vacation Services** (© **800/398-6284;** www.hookipa.com). Rates in low season (Jan, Apr 16–June, and Aug 21–Dec 18) are $148 a week; they jump up to $160 in high season.

MOTORCYCLE RENTALS　　The best place to find a customized, cherried-out Harley is **Pacific Island Rentals,** across the street from the Chevron Station in Kapaa (© **808/821-9090**), which has Harleys from $69 a day.

OTHER TRANSPORTATION OPTIONS　　**Kauai Taxi Company** (© **808/246-9554**) offers taxi, limousine, and airport shuttle service. **Kauai Bus** (© **808/241-6410**) operates a fleet of 15 buses that serve the entire island. Taking the bus may be practical for day trips if you know your way around the island, but you can't take anything larger than a shopping bag aboard, and the buses don't stop at any of the resort areas—but they do serve more than a dozen coastal towns between Kekaha, on the southwest shore, all the way to Hanalei. Buses run more or less hourly from 5:30am to 6pm. The fare is $1, or 50¢ for seniors, students, and passengers with disabilities.

FAST FACTS: **Kauai**

American Express There's no local office on the island.

Dentists Emergency dental care is available from **Dr. Mark A. Baird,** 4–9768 Kuhio Hwy., Kapaa (© **808/822-9393**), and **Dr. Michael Furgeson,** 4347 Rice St., Lihue (© **808/246-6960**).

Doctors Walk-ins are accepted at **Kauai Medical Clinic,** 3–3420 Kuhio Hwy., Suite B, Lihue (© **808/245-1500,** or 808/245-1831 after hours). You can also try the **North Shore Clinic,** Kilauea and Oka roads, Kilauea (© **808/828-1418**); **Koloa Clinic,** 5371 Koloa Rd. (© **808/742-1621**); **Eleele Clinic,** 3292 Waialo Rd. (© **808/335-0499**); or **Kapaa Clinic,** 3–1105 Kuhio Hwy. (© **808/822-3431**).

Emergencies Dial © **911** for police, fire, and ambulance service. The **Poison Control Center** can be reached at © **800/362-3585.**

Hospitals **Wilcox Health System,** 3420 Kuhio Hwy., Lihue (© **808/245-1100**), has emergency services available around the clock.

Police For nonemergencies, call © **808/245-9711.**

Post Office The main post office is at 4441 Rice St., Lihue. To find the branch office nearest you, call © **800/ASK-USPS.**

Weather For current weather conditions, call © **808/245-6001.** For marine conditions, call © **808/245-3564.**

3 Where to Stay

You don't want to be stuck with long drives every day, so be sure to review "The Island in Brief," earlier in this chapter, to choose the location that best fits your vacation needs.

Taxes of 11.42% are added to all hotel bills. Parking is free unless otherwise noted.

LIHUE & ENVIRONS

If you need to stay overnight near the airport, try the **Garden Island Inn** (see below).

VERY EXPENSIVE

Kauai Marriott Resort & Beach Club ★★ *Kids* Once upon a time, this was a glitzy megaresort (the Westin Kauai) with ostentatious fantasy architecture, but then a hurricane (and new owners) toned it down. The result is grand enough to be memorable, but it's now grounded in reality—it looks like a Hawaiian hotel rather than a European palace. Water is everywhere throughout the resort: lagoons, waterfalls, fountains, a 5-acre circular swimming pool (some 26,000 sq. ft., the largest on the island), and a terrific stretch of beach. The lagoons are home to six islands that serve as an exotic minizoo, which still lends an air of fantasy to the place and, along with the enormous pool and children's program, makes the resort popular with families.

Guest rooms are comfortable, with fabulous views of gold-sand Kalapaki Beach, verdant gardens, and palm trees, and a recent refurbishment has them all looking brand-new. The location—Lihue Airport is only a mile away—allows

for easy arrival and departure, but it also means you can hear the takeoff and landing of every jet. Fortunately, air traffic stops by 9pm, but it begins bright and early in the morning.

Kalapaki Beach, Lihue, HI 96766. ✆ **800/220-2925** or 808/245-5050. Fax 808/245-5049. www.marriott.com/marriott/LIHHI. 356 units. $329–$444 double; from $649 suite. Also consider their Paradise Plus Packages include accommodations and a choice of car or daily breakfast for 2 for just $269-$349 (cheaper than rack rates, and you get a car thrown in). Extra person $35. AE, DC, DISC, MC, V. Valet parking $8. Free airport shuttle. **Amenities:** 4 restaurants (Duke's Canoe Club on p. 555 and Whalers Brewpub on p. 558); 2 bars; the largest pool on the island; 36-hole Jack Nicklaus golf course; 8 tennis courts; state-of-the-art fitness center; 5 Jacuzzis; watersports equipment rentals; children's program; game room; concierge; activity desk; car-rental desk; business center; shopping arcade; salon; room service; massage; babysitting; coin-op washer/dryers; laundry/dry cleaning. *In room:* A/C, TV/VCR, dataport, fridge, coffeemaker, hair dryer, iron, safe.

EXPENSIVE

Radisson Kauai Beach Resort   Radisson took over this oceanfront property in late 2000. They spent $10 million remodeling all guest rooms, creating a new sand pool, and building a health-club facility. The property, located 4 miles north of Lihue, commands a beachfront setting next door to a top-ranked municipal golf course. The location is good, about equidistant from both north- and south-shore activities, and also close to the Wailua River and its kayaking, water-skiing, river tours, historic sites, and drive-by waterfalls. The only problems here are the windy conditions and the lack of safe swimming on the beautiful white-sand beach.

Kids Family-Friendly Hotels

In addition to the places described below, you might also consider the **Sheraton Kauai Resort** (which allows children under 12 to eat free in the Shell Restaurant when accompanied by an adult), the **Princeville Resort Kauai,** and the **Holiday Inn SunSpree.**

Kauai Marriott Resort & Beach Club (p. 536) This place has Hawaii's largest pool (26,000 sq. ft.) in addition to a new kids' pool—but that's just the beginning. Freshwater lagoons with six islands serve as a mini-zoo, with kangaroos, monkeys, llamas, and other exotic creatures; horses lead carriages through tropical gardens; and a high-energy beach beside Nawiliwili Harbor, Kauai's port of call, provides surfside fun. The informal Kalapaki Kids program (ages 5–12), offers activities ranging from boogie boarding to treasure hunting ($45 for a full day, which includes lunch, or $25 for a half day).

Hyatt Regency Kauai Resort & Spa (p. 539) It's the collection of swimming pools here—freshwater and salt, with slides, waterfalls, and secret lagoons—that makes this oceanfront Hyatt a real kids' paradise. Camp Hyatt (ages 3–12) offers arts and crafts, scavenger hunts, and other special activities for $45 for a full day (9am–4pm), including lunch and a T-shirt; it's $25 for a ½ day with lunch, and $20 for a ½ day without lunch. Plus, the Hyatt is one of the few hotels to offer "camp" in the evening, from 6 to 10pm at $10 an hour. Babysitting and activities on weekend evenings give Mom and Dad some time alone. In summer and holiday season, there's Rock Hyatt, an activities room where teens can gather and play electronic games. Also in summer, Family Fun Theatre Nights show some of the more than 400 movies filmed on Kauai.

Waimea Plantation Cottages (p. 546) Among groves of towering coco palms are these clusters of meticulously restored plantation cottages that offer families the opportunity to relax off the beaten track. Some people may find Waimea a little too out of the way (it's a 1½-hour drive to the North Shore), but it is close to Waimea Canyon and Kokee State Park. The re-created village allows kids plenty of room to wander and play away from traffic and crowds; there's also a pool and tennis courts.

Kauai Coconut Beach Resort (p. 548) Not only do children 17 and under stay free, but children 11 and under also eat free when dining with an adult. Situated on 10½ acres in front of Waipouli Beach, this resort offers kids plenty of room to play, and it throws a wonderful nightly luau.

Hanalei Colony Resort (p. 552) These spacious two-bedroom condos come equipped with full kitchens. Management has badminton and croquet sets on hand for the whole family, as well as toys, puzzles, and games for the kids.

4331 Kauai Beach Dr., Lihue, HI 96766. © 888/805-3843 or 808/245-1955. Fax 808/245-3956. www.radissonkauai.com. 347 units. $239–$349 double; from $399 suite. Numerous packages available, including car packages, senior rates, and more. AE, DC, DISC, MC, V. **Amenities:** Restaurant and bar; 4 outdoor pools; tennis courts; fitness room; Jacuzzi; watersports equipment rentals; concierge; activity desk; car-rental desk; business center; shopping arcade; salon; massage; babysitting; coin-op washer/dryers; laundry/dry cleaning. *In room:* A/C, TV/VCR, dataport, fridge, coffeemaker, hair dryer, iron, safe.

MODERATE

Resort Quest Kauai   These beachfront condos are a good option for families and others seeking more space and privacy than they'd get elsewhere in Lihue. The only drawback is the unsafe swimming conditions on the beautiful but windy white-sand beach. All units are outfitted with tropical decor and bamboo-style furniture, a fully equipped kitchen, a washer/dryer, and a lanai big enough for two lounge chairs, a table, and four chairs. The two-bedroom units have a lanai off each bedroom, too. The immaculately landscaped grounds contain pools, tennis courts, barbecue areas, and a volleyball court. The Wailua Municipal golf course is next door.

4330 Kauai Beach Dr., Lihue, HI 96766. © 800/743-7108 or 808/245-7711. Fax 808/245-3612. www.resortquestkauai.com. 150 units. $140–$170 1-bedroom for 4; $210–$260 2-bedroom for 6. AE, DC, DISC, MC, V. **Amenities:** Outdoor pools; tennis courts; access to nearby health club; Jacuzzi; activity desk; laundry/dry cleaning. *In room:* A/C, TV/VCR, dataport, kitchen, fridge, coffeemaker, hair dryer, iron, safe, coin-op washer/dryers.

INEXPENSIVE

Garden Island Inn ★ *Finds*   This bargain-hunter's delight is located 2 miles from the airport, 1 mile from Lihue, and within walking distance of shops and restaurants. The spacious rooms are decorated with island-style furniture, bright prints, and fresh tropical flowers (grown right on the grounds). Each unit contains a fridge, microwave, wet bar, TV, coffeemaker, and ocean view; some have private lanais, and the suites have sitting areas. The grounds are filled with flowers and banana and papaya trees (and you're welcome to help yourself to the fruit at the front desk). Owner Steve Layne offers friendly service, lots of advice on activities (the entire staff happily uses their connections to get you discounts), and even complimentary use of beach gear, golf clubs (a course is nearby, as are tennis courts), and coolers.

3445 Wilcox Rd. (across the street from Kalapaki Beach, near Nawiliwili Harbor), Lihue, HI 96766. © 800/648-0154 or 808/245-7227. Fax 808/245-7603. www.gardenislandinn.com. 21 units (private bathrooms have shower only). $75–$125 double. Extra person $5. AE, DC, MC, V. **Amenities:** Complimentary watersports equipment; activity desk. *In room:* A/C, TV, fridge, coffeemaker, hair dryer, iron, safe.

THE POIPU RESORT AREA

In addition to the accommodations listed below, you can try **South Shore Vista** (© 808/322-9339; www.planet-hawaii.com/vista), which offers a centrally located one-bedroom apartment for just $64 double; **Surf Song** (© 877/373-2331), with four units from $65 to $120; and, closer to the beach, **Pua Hale at Poipu** (© 800/745-7414 or 808/742-1700; www.kauai-puahale.com), with an intimate cottage within walking distance of the beach for $120 double. And at the **Garden Isle Cottages** (© 800/742-6711 or 808/742-6717; www.oceancottages.com), you'll overlook Koloa Landing and Waikomo Stream in an oceanfront, one-bedroom apartment for $149 to $170 double.

VERY EXPENSIVE

Hyatt Regency Kauai Resort & Spa ★★★ *Kids*   This is one of Hawaii's best luxury hotels and one of the top-ranked tropical resorts in *Condé Nast Traveler's* annual readers' poll. The four-story resort, built into the oceanside bluffs, spreads over 50 acres that overlook Shipwreck Beach (which is too rough for most swimmers) at the end of the road in Poipu. The $250 million Hyatt uses the island architecture of the mid-1920s to recapture the old Hawaii of the Matson Line steamship era.

The airy atmosphere replicates the casual elegance of a grand plantation overlooking the sea. The result is a comfortable, unostentatious place where you can bring the kids and Grandma. The rooms are large (nearly 600 sq. ft.) and elegantly outfitted. All have marble bathrooms and spacious private lanais; most have ocean views. (The most distant quarters are a good 5-min. hike from the lobby.) Club floors have their own concierge and a lounge serving continental breakfast, drinks, and snacks. The hotel is next door to the Robert Trent Jones Jr.–designed Poipu Golf Course. If you stay here, don't leave without a treatment from the **ANARA Spa** ✦✦✦, the best spa on Kauai (also check out the large selection of classes—some of them free—at the fitness center).

1571 Poipu Rd., Koloa, HI 96756. ✆ **800/55-HYATT** or 808/742-1234. Fax 808/742-1557. www.kauai-hyatt. com. 602 units. $395–$670 double; from $1000 suite. Packages available. Extra person $35, $50 in Regency Club room; children 18 and under stay free in parent's room. AE, DC, DISC, MC, V. Self-park $6, valet parking $8. **Amenities:** 6 restaurants (see review of Dondero's on p. 560); 6 bars (the partially open-air Stevenson's Library has mellow jazz in the evenings; Thurs–Sat nights, the Poipu Bay Grill & Bar features live music); an elaborate freshwater fantasy pool complex, plus 2 more pools and 5 acres of saltwater swimming lagoons with islands and a man-made beach; 4 tennis courts; one of the best fitness centers on the island; 25,000-sq.-ft. ANARA Spa is reason enough to stay here, with lava-rock shower gardens, a 10-headed Swedish shower, and indoor-outdoor treatment rooms offering everything from Hawaiian massage to seaweed body wraps; 3 Jacuzzis; watersports equipment rentals; bike rental; extensive Camp Hyatt kids' program; game room; concierge; activity desk; car-rental desk; business center; shopping arcade; salon; room service; massage; babysitting; complimentary washer/dryers; same-day laundry/dry cleaning; concierge-level rooms. *In room:* A/C, TV/VCR, dataport, minibar, fridge, coffeemaker, hair dryer, iron, safe.

Sheraton Kauai Resort ✦✦ *Kids*   This modern Sheraton (since 1997) has the feeling of old Hawaii and a dynamite location on one of Kauai's best beaches. It features buildings on both the ocean side and the mountain side of the road. The horseshoe-shaped, Polynesian-style lobby has shell chandeliers dangling from the ceiling. You have a choice of three buildings: one nestled in tropical gardens with koi-filled ponds; one facing the palm-fringed, white-sand beach (our favorite); and one looking across green grass to the ocean, with great sunset views. The rooms overlook either the tropical gardens or the rolling surf.

The bar here is fabulous. Even if you don't stay here, come by to order a cocktail and an appetizer, and take in the view and the Hawaiian music. A golf course is nearby. *And families, take note:* Kids eat free with a paying adult at the Shell Restaurant, at both breakfast and dinner.

An obnoxious daily "resort amenities" fee of $15 is tacked on to your bill for the following "free" services: continental breakfast, sunset mai tai punch hour with a torch-lighting ceremony, guest library with daily newspapers and three computers with Internet access, use of the fitness center and tennis courts, and shuttle services to Kaloa town, the Poipu Shopping Center, and two nearby golf courses.

2440 Hoonani Rd., Koloa, HI 96756. ✆ **800/782-9488** or 808/742-1661. Fax 808/742-4041. www.sheraton-kauai.com. 413 units. $325–$550 double (max. 4 in room); from $575 suite for 4–5; plus $15 a day "resort amenity" fee. Extra person $50. AE, DC, DISC, MC, V. **Amenities:** 3 restaurants; extraordinary bar; 2 outdoor pools (1 with water playground, 1 for children); 3 tennis courts (2 night-lit); fitness room facing the ocean (one of the most scenic places to work out on Kauai); small massage and skin-care center; Jacuzzi; watersports equipment rentals; children's program; game room; concierge; activity desk; shopping arcade; salon; room service; babysitting; coin-op washer/dryers; same-day laundry/dry cleaning. *In room:* A/C, TV/VCR, dataport, fridge, coffeemaker, hair dryer, iron, safe.

Poipu Resort Area Accommodations & Dining

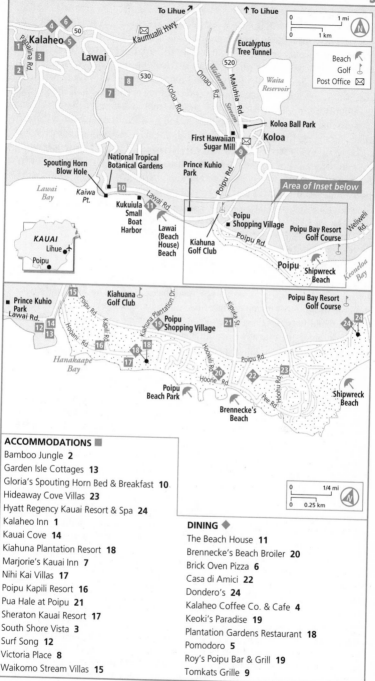

ACCOMMODATIONS ■

Bamboo Jungle **2**
Garden Isle Cottages **13**
Gloria's Spouting Horn Bed & Breakfast **10**
Hideaway Cove Villas **23**
Hyatt Regency Kauai Resort & Spa **24**
Kalaheo Inn **1**
Kauai Cove **14**
Kiahuna Plantation Resort **18**
Marjorie's Kauai Inn **7**
Nihi Kai Villas **17**
Poipu Kapili Resort **16**
Pua Hale at Poipu **21**
Sheraton Kauai Resort **17**
South Shore Vista **3**
Surf Song **12**
Victoria Place **8**
Waikomo Stream Villas **15**

DINING ◆

The Beach House **11**
Brennecke's Beach Broiler **20**
Brick Oven Pizza **6**
Casa di Amici **22**
Dondero's **24**
Kalaheo Coffee Co. & Cafe **4**
Keoki's Paradise **19**
Plantation Gardens Restaurant **18**
Pomodoro **5**
Roy's Poipu Bar & Grill **19**
Tomkats Grille **9**

EXPENSIVE

Gloria's Spouting Horn Bed & Breakfast ★★ *Finds*   As one guest put it, "Staying here makes you want to get married again!" The price is a little high, but a stay here could be the highlight of your trip. All three spacious guest rooms are oceanfront, with huge private lanais overlooking the secluded beach. Our favorite is the Punana Aloha ("love nest") room, furnished in willow, including a romantic queen bed with a woven willow canopy overhead. All of the private bathrooms feature Japanese-style deep soaking tubs and separate showers. Each unit also has a wet bar, microwave, toaster, and blender. Breakfasts are elaborate affairs served on linen, crystal, and English china in the dining room (or for lovers who'd rather stay in bed, on a tray with flowers). The food is five-star quality, and the ambience nothing if not romantic. At sunset, Gloria offers an open bar and pupu, while Bob plays classical music on his guitar. A golf course, tennis courts, and several bars and restaurants are nearby.

4464 Lawai Beach Rd. (just before Spouting Horn Park), Koloa, HI 96756. © and fax **808/742-6995.** www. gloriasbedandbreakfast.com. 3 units. $275 double. Rates include full breakfast, afternoon drinks, and pupu. 3-night minimum. No credit cards. **Amenities:** Solar-heated outdoor pool right next to the ocean. *In room:* TV/VCR, dataport, fridge, coffeemaker, hair dryer, iron, safe.

Kiahuna Plantation Resort ★★   This complex consists of several plantation-style buildings, loaded with Hawaiian style, and sprinkled about a 35-acre garden setting with lagoons, lawns, and a gold-sand beach. Golf, shopping, and restaurants are within easy walking distance. Two different management companies handle the rental pool: Outrigger oversees about two-thirds of the units, Castle the remaining third (despite any price differences, the units are quite comparable). Both companies are excellent and have numerous package deals to fit your budget. All condo units are spacious, with full kitchens, daily maid service, and lanais.

2253 Poipu Rd., Koloa, HI 96756. 333 units. Under 2 different management groups: Outrigger, © **800/OUT-RIGGER** or 808/742-6411. Fax 808/742-1689. www.outrigger.com. $215–$495 1-bedroom apt (sleeps up to 4); $345–$535 2-bedroom apt (sleeps up to 6). Packages available, including 5th night free, car packages, senior rates, and more. AE, DC, DISC, MC, V. Castle Resorts & Hotels, © **800/367-5004** or 808/742-2200. Fax 800/477-2329 or 808/742-1047. www.castleresorts.com. $225–$470 1-bedroom apt; $390–$725 2-bedroom apt. Ask about packages like 5th night free or free car. AE, DC, DISC, MC, V. **Amenities:** Restaurant (see review of Plantation Gardens on p. 560); bar; outdoor pool; tennis courts; watersports equipment rentals; children's program; activity desk; shopping arcade nearby; coin-op washer/dryers. *In room:* TV/VCR, kitchen, fridge, coffeemaker, hair dryer, iron, safe.

MODERATE

Poipu Kapili Resort ★★   This quiet, upscale oceanfront cluster of condos is outstanding in every area. We like the home-away-from-home comforts and special touches: a video and book library, a spacious pool, several barbecues, tennis courts lit for night play, and an herb garden (you're welcome to take samples if you're cooking). A golf course is also nearby. The apartments are large (1-bedroom/2-bathroom units are 1,150 sq. ft.; 2-bedroom/3-bathroom units are 1,820 sq. ft.) and have fully equipped kitchens, tropical furnishings, ceiling fans, and private lanais. The oceanfront two-story town houses are our favorites because they catch the trade winds. The two-bedroom units also have washer/dryers (common laundry facilities are available on the property as well). Although the Pacific is right out your window, the nearest sandy beach is a block away (which can be a blessing because it means more privacy).

2221 Kapili Rd., Koloa, HI 96756. © **800/443-7714** or 808/742-6449. Fax 808/742-9162. www.poipukapili. com. 62 units. $210–$275 1-bedroom apt (sleeps up to 4); $280–$550 2-bedroom apt (up to 6). Discounts for longer stays; package rates available; 7th night free May 1–Dec 20. Rates include Fri continental breakfast by

Value The Queen of Condos

One of the easiest ways to find lodging in the Poipu Beach area is to contact **Grantham Resorts**, 3176 Poipu Rd., Koloa, HI 96756 (© **800/325-5701** or 808/742-2000; fax 808/742-9093; www.poipuaccommodations.com), which handles some 150 rental units for nine different condo developments, plus dozens of vacation homes. Owner Nancy Grantham has high standards for her rental units and offers extremely fair prices. In 2003, Nancy dropped several units and entire condominium projects because they simply did not meet her standards. The condos start at $95 for a basic one-bedroom unit in low season and vacation homes start at $150 for two bedroom and go up to $400 for five bedrooms. Five-night minimums apply for both homes and condos.

If you're staying on Kauai for 7 days, ask Grantham about the *Frommer's* "Casual Rates": large one- and two-bedroom condos, well furnished and equipped (full kitchen, washer/dryer, wet bar, TV, phone), starting as low as $89 a night for one-bedrooms and $119 for two-bedrooms (see Nihi Kai Villas and Waikomo Stream Villas, below). There's not a better deal on Kauai. Kudos to Nancy for these fabulous vacation bargains.

the pool. MC, V. **Amenities:** Oceanside pool; championship tennis courts lighted for night use; activity desk; washer/dryers. *In room:* TV/VCR, dataport, kitchen, fridge, coffeemaker, loaner hair dryer from front desk, iron.

INEXPENSIVE

Bamboo Jungle *Finds*   Step onto this property and into a jungle of verdant plants, a quaint gazebo, a 25-meter lap pool, and an impeccably decorated old plantation-era house. Every room has a private entrance and French doors opening onto a private lanai with an ocean view. The netting over the beds creates a romantic mood and serves a functional purpose (it keeps Hawaii's insects on their side of the sleeping quarters). Accommodations range from a single room with deck to a studio with mini-kitchen. There are no phones in the units, but you can use the house phone. Golf and tennis courts are nearby. Note that there is not air-conditioning, which 350 days of the year is great, but on the days the trade winds stop blowing, it's not so great.

3829 Waha Rd. Reservations: P.O. Box 1301, Koloa, HI 96756. © **888/332-5115** or 808/332-5515. www.kauai-bedandbreakfast.com. 3 units. $110–$130 double. 3-night minimum. No credit cards. From Hwy. 50, turn left at the traffic light onto Papalina Rd., then right on Waha Rd. **Amenities:** Outdoor pool; Jacuzzi; washer/dryers. *In room:* TV, 1 room with kitchenette, fridge, coffeemaker, no phone.

Hideway Cove Villas ★★ *Value*   Just a block from the beach, and next door to an excellent restaurant, are these gorgeous condominiums in a plantation setting. Amenities are top-drawer, and no expense was spared in the interior decorations. Units have hardwood floors, TV/VCR/DVD, comfy furniture, roomy beds (either four-poster beds or wood sleigh designs), spacious living areas, kitchenettes with the best appliances and granite top counters, and big outdoor lanais. You get all of this in a lush, landscaped tropical jungle at affordable prices. Owner Herb Lee is always on hand to guide you to Kauai's best spots and hand out his collection of (free) beach toys and beach cruiser bicycles. A few of the units have Jacuzzis, so ask when you book.

2307 Nalo Rd, reservations P.O. Box 1113, Kaloa, HI 96756. © **886-849-2426** or 808/653-8785. www. hideawaycove.com. 7 units. $110–$120 studio double; $145 one-bedroom double; $175–$225 two-bedroom for 4; $250 3-bedroom for 4. Extra person $10. 2-night minimum. AE, DISC, MC, V. **Amenities:** Restaurant and bar next door; free beach toys and bicycles; washer/dryers. *In room:* TV/VCR/DVD, kitchen, fridge, coffee-maker, hair dryer, iron, phone answering machine.

Kalaheo Inn ⭐ *Value*   What a deal! Located in the town of Kalaheo, a 12-minute drive from world-famous Poipu Beach, a 5-minute drive from the Kukuiolono Golf Course, and within walking distance of shops and restaurants, the inn is a comfortable 1940s motel totally remodeled in 1999 and converted into apartment units with kitchens. Owners Chet and Tish Hunt couldn't be friendlier, handing out complimentary beach towels, beach toys, and even golf clubs to guests (links are nearby). They love families and have a storeroom full of games to keep the kids entertained. This is a must-stay for vacationers on a budget.

444 Papaline Rd. (just behind the Kalaheo Steakhouse), Koloa, HI 96756. © **888/332-6023** or 808/332-6023. Fax 808/742-6432. www.kalaheoinn.com. 14 units. $55–$75 1-bedroom; $95 2-bedroom. 2-night min-imum. **Amenities:** Complimentary watersports equipment; children's games; coin-op washer/dryers. *In room:* TV, kitchen, fridge, coffeemaker, iron, no phone.

Kauai Cove ⭐ *Finds*   These immaculate cottages, located just 300 feet from the Koloa Landing, next to the Waikomo Stream, are the perfect private get-away. Each studio has a full kitchen, private lanai (with barbecue grill), and big bamboo four-poster bed. The cozy rooms feature beautiful hardwood floors, tropical decor, and cathedral ceilings. It's close enough that you can walk to sandy beaches, great restaurants, and shopping, yet far enough off the beaten path that privacy and quiet are assured.

2672 Puuholo Rd., Poipu, HI 96756. © and fax **800/624-9945** or 808/742-2562. www.kauaicove.com. 3 units. $95–$105 double. 4-night minimum. DISC, MC, V. *In room:* TV, dataport, kitchen, fridge, coffeemaker.

Marjorie's Kauai Inn ⭐ *Finds*   This quiet property, perched on the side of a hill, is just 10 minutes from Poipu Beach and 5 minutes from Old Koloa Town. From its large lanai, it offers stunning views over the rolling pastures and the Lawai Valley. Every unit has a kitchenette dining table, ceiling fan, and lanai. The new Sunset View unit has a separate sitting area and a futon sofa for extra guests. On the hillside is a huge, 50-foot swimming pool, perfect for lap swimming. But the best reason to stay here is Marjorie Ketcher herself. "Do more than one fun thing a day!" is Marjorie's motto, and she makes sure that her guests are out diving, snorkeling, sightseeing, hiking, dining, dancing, or enjoying one of the hundreds of other things she can recommend. Not recommended for families with children.

P.O. Box 866 (off Hailima Rd., adjacent to the National Tropical Botanical Garden), Lawai, HI 96765. © **800/ 717-8838** or 808/332-8838. Fax 808/332-8838. www.marjorieskauaiinn.com. 3 units. $88–$115 double. Rates include continental breakfast on first day. Extra person $15. 2-night minimum. No credit cards. **Amenities:** Jacuzzi, swimming pool. *In room:* TV, kitchenette, fridge, coffeemaker, hair dryer, iron.

Nihi Kai Villas ⭐ *Value*   Nancy Grantham (see the box titled "The Queen of Condos," above) is a marketing genius. She's offering the deal of the decade on these large, two-bedroom units just 200 yards from the beach. If you stay 7 nights, the rate for these big, well-equipped two-bedroom, ocean-view apart-ments starts at an unbelievable $127 a night (for 4, which works out to just $64 a couple). You may not be getting new carpet, new furniture, new drapes, or a prime beachfront location, but you *are* getting a clean, well-cared-for unit with a full kitchen, washer/dryer, and TV/VCR, all at an unbeatable price. The prop-erty is a 2-minute walk from world-famous Brennecke's Beach (great for body surfing) and a block from Poipu Beach Park. On-site amenities include an oceanfront swimming pool, tennis and paddle courts, and a barbecue and picnic area. Within a 5-minute drive are two great golf courses, several restaurants, and loads of shopping.

1870 Hoone Rd. Reservations c/o Grantham Resorts, 3176 Poipu Rd., Suite 1, Koloa, HI 96756. ℂ **800/325-5701** or 808/742-2000. Fax 808/742-9093. www.poipuaccommodations.com. 70 units. Regular rates (5-night minimum): $169–$189 2-bedroom for 4. *Frommer's* "Casual Rate" (7-night minimum): $127–$152 2-bedroom for 4. DC, DISC, MC, V. From Poipu Rd., turn toward the ocean on Hoowili Rd., then left on Hoone Rd.; Nihi Kai Villas is just past Nalo Rd. on Hoone Rd. **Amenities:** Outdoor pool; nearby golf course; tennis courts; Jacuzzi; activity desk. *In room:* TV/VCR, dataport, kitchen, coffeemaker, iron, washer/dryer.

Victoria Place ⭐⭐ *(Finds)*   This is our favorite Bed and Breakfast on Kauai. The reason to stay here? Two words: Edee Seymour. It's easy to see why she won the Kauai Chamber of Commerce's Aloha Spirit Award. Her motto is "We pamper!" She lavishes her guests with attention and aloha. Her spacious, skylit, U-shaped house wraps around the swimming pool and garden. Three bedrooms, located in one wing of the home, open onto the pool area, which is surrounded by flowering walls of bougainvillea, hibiscus, gardenia, and ginger. So why is the price is so low? Guests share the TV, the phone, and a refrigerator in the common area. Edee also rents a secluded studio apartment (dubbed "Victoria's Other Secret") down a private path; it contains a king bed, shower-only bathroom, kitchen, and TV. Edee's breakfasts are truly a big deal: at least five different tropical fruits, followed by something from the oven, such as homemade bread, scones, or muffins. Most of her guests are returnees. As a couple from Germany told us, "Once you stay with Edee, every place else is cold and indifferent."

3459 Lawai Loa Lane (off Koloa Rd./Hwy. 530), Koloa. c/o P.O. Box 930, Lawai, HI 96765. ℂ **808/332-9300.** Fax 808/332-9465. www.hshawaii.com/kvp/victoria. 4 units. $70–$90 double; $125 studio apt. Rates include breakfast. Extra person $15. No credit cards. Children under 15 not accepted. **Amenities:** Outdoor pool. *In room:* No phone.

Waikomo Stream Villas ⭐ *(Value)*   Nancy Grantham has one more fabulous trick up her sleeve: these 800- to 900-square-foot one-bedroom apartments, which comfortably sleep four, and larger two-bedroom units, which sleep six. Tucked into a lush tropical garden setting, these spacious, well-decorated units have everything you could possibly need on your vacation: full kitchen, VCR, washer/dryer, and private lanai. The complex—which has both adults' and children's pools, tennis courts, and a barbecue area—is adjacent to the Kiahuna Golf Club and just a 5-minute walk from restaurants, shopping, and Poipu's beaches and golf courses.

2721 Poipu Rd. (just after entry to Poipu, on ocean side of Poipu Rd.), Poipu. c/o Grantham Resorts, 3176 Poipu Rd., Suite 1, Koloa, HI 96756. ℂ **800/325-5701** or 808/742-2000. Fax 808/742-9093. www.poipu accommodations.com. 60 units. Regular rates (5-night minimum): $105–$125 1-bedroom for 4, $135–$155 2-bedroom for 6. *Frommer's* "Casual Rates" (7-night minimum): $89–$109 1-bedroom for 4; $119-$139 2-bedroom for 6. DC, DISC, MC, V. **Amenities:** 2 outdoor pools (1 for children and 1 for adults); complimentary tennis courts; Jacuzzi; activity desk. *In room:* TV/VCR, dataport, kitchen, fridge, coffeemaker, washer/dryer.

WESTERN KAUAI

Kokee Lodge *(Value)*   This is an excellent choice, especially if you want to do some hiking in Waimea Canyon and Kokee State Park. There are two types of cabins here: The older ones have dormitory-style sleeping arrangements (and resemble a youth hostel), while the new ones have two separate bedrooms each. Both styles sleep six and come with cooking utensils, bedding, and linens. We recommend the newer units, which have wood floors, cedar walls, and more modern kitchen facilities (some are wheelchair-accessible as well). There are no phones or TVs in the units, but there is a pay phone at the general store. You can purchase firewood for the cabin stove at Kokee Lodge, where there's a restaurant that's open for continental breakfast and lunch every day. There's also a cocktail lounge, a general store, and a gift shop. *Warning for light sleepers:* This area is home to lots of roosters, which crow at dawn's first light.

P.O. Box 819, Waimea, HI 96796. (©) **808/335-6061.** 12 cabins. $35 studio; $45 2-bedroom. 5-night maximum. DC, DISC, MC, V. *In room:* Kitchen, fridge, coffeemaker, no phone.

Waimea Plantation Cottages (*Kids*) This beachfront vacation retreat is like no other in the islands: Among groves of towering coco palms sit clusters of restored sugar-plantation cottages, dating from the 1880s to the 1930s and bearing the names of their original plantation-worker dwellers. The lovely cottages have been transformed into cozy, comfortable guest units with period rattan and wicker furniture and fabrics from the 1930s, sugar's heyday on Kauai. Each has a furnished lanai and a fully equipped modern kitchen and bathroom; some units are oceanfront. Facilities include an oceanfront pool, tennis courts, and laundry. The seclusion of the village makes it a nice place for kids to wander and explore, away from traffic. The only downsides: the black-sand beach, which is lovely but not conducive to swimming (the water is often murky at the Waimea River mouth), and the location, at the foot of Waimea Canyon Drive—its remoteness can be very appealing, but the North Shore is 1½ hours away. Golf courses and tennis courts, however, are much closer.

9400 Kaumualii Hwy. (P.O. Box 367), Waimea, HI 96796. (©) Aston Hotels and Resorts **800/92-ASTON** or 808/338-1625. Fax 808/338-2338. www.astonhotels.com. 48 units. $115–$130 hotel room double; $130–$145 studios double; $180–$270 1-bedroom double; $225–$290 2-bedroom (sleeps up to 4); $260–$365 3-bedroom (up to 5); $360–$405 4-bedroom (up to 8); $545–$625 5-bedroom (up to 9). AE, DC, DISC, MC, V. **Amenities:** Restaurant and bar; large outdoor pool; activity desk; coin-op washer/dryers; dry cleaning. *In room:* TV, dataport, kitchen, fridge, coffeemaker, iron, safe.

THE COCONUT COAST

This is the land of B&Bs and inexpensive vacation rentals. In addition to those reviewed below, we also recommend **Opaeka'a Falls Hale,** which has two exquisite units with pool and hot tub for $90 to $110; reservations are available through **Hawaii's Best Bed & Breakfasts** ((©) **800/262-9912;** www.bestbnb.com).

Another excellently priced choice is **Kakalina's B&B** ((©) **800/662-4330;** www.kakalina.com), on a 3-acre flower farm nestled in the foothills of Mount Waialeale, offering rates from $90. For a very reasonable $65 double, the intimate **Surf & Ski Cottage** ((©) **800/344-7915** or 808/822-3574), right on the Wailua River, is the place for watersports nuts; it's owned by the people who run Kauai Water Ski & Surf Co., who'll give you 20% off on rental of all water toys. And one of the very best deals on Kauai is **Hibiscus Hollow** ((©) **808/823-0925;** www.hawaiian.net/~hollow), a private studio for two for just $50 a night.

EXPENSIVE

Lae Nani Outrigger Resort Condominium (★) The Lae Nani ("beautiful promontory point") offers a quiet, relaxing setting right on the beach, next door to restaurants and bars. On the point is the Kukui Heiau, where an ancient temple once stood. The one- and two-bedroom units are roomy, with large living rooms, separate dining rooms, complete kitchens, and generous lanais. The two-bedroom/two-bathroom units can easily fit a family of six. Maid service is provided daily. Extras include a swimming pool, lava-rock-protected swimming area, barbecue facilities, tennis courts, and self-service laundry facilities. Next

Coconut Coast Accommodations & Dining

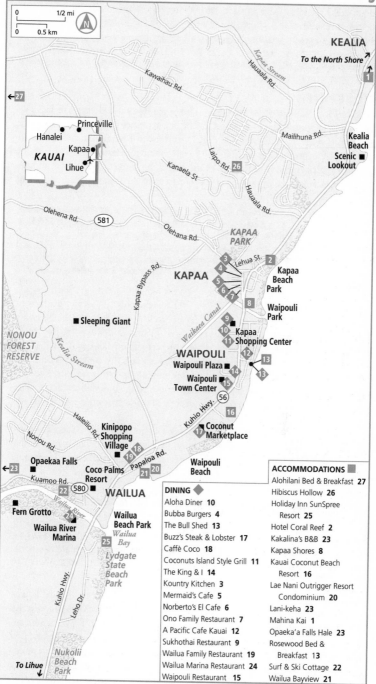

DINING ◆
Aloha Diner **10**
Bubba Burgers **4**
The Bull Shed **13**
Buzz's Steak & Lobster **17**
Caffè Coco **18**
Coconuts Island Style Grill **11**
The King & I **14**
Kountry Kitchen **3**
Mermaid's Cafe **5**
Norberto's El Cafe **6**
Ono Family Restaurant **7**
A Pacific Cafe Kauai **12**
Sukhothai Restaurant **9**
Wailua Family Restaurant **19**
Wailua Marina Restaurant **24**
Waipouli Restaurant **15**

ACCOMMODATIONS ■
Alohilani Bed & Breakfast **27**
Hibiscus Hollow **26**
Holiday Inn SunSpree Resort **25**
Hotel Coral Reef **2**
Kakalina's B&B **23**
Kapaa Shores **8**
Kauai Coconut Beach Resort **16**
Lae Nani Outrigger Resort Condominium **20**
Lani-keha **23**
Mahina Kai **1**
Opaeka'a Falls Hale **23**
Rosewood Bed & Breakfast **13**
Surf & Ski Cottage **22**
Wailua Bayview **21**

door is the Coconut Marketplace, with shops, restaurants, and nightlife; a golf course is nearby.

410 Papaloa Rd., Kapaa, HI 96746. © **800/OUTRIGGER** or 808/822-4938. Fax 808/822-1022. www.outrigger. com. 50 units. $207–$285 1-bedroom for 4; $225–$345 2-bedroom for 6. Roll-away bed/crib $10. 2-night minimum. AE, DC, DISC, MC, V. **Amenities:** Oceanfront outdoor pool; complimentary tennis courts; coin-op washer/dryers. *In room:* TV, dataport, kitchen, fridge, coffeemaker, iron.

MODERATE

Holiday Inn SunSpree Resort *(Kids)*   SunSpree Resorts, a division of Holiday Inn, emphasizes moderate rates and lots of free activities for families. The result is a family-friendly choice located right next door to Lydgate Beach Park (with Kamalani Playground for the kids) and convenient to nearby golf. Every room features a refrigerator, iron/ironing board, hair dryer, and coffeemaker. And kids 12 and under eat free when dining with a parent in the restaurant and ordering from the "keiki" (child) menu.

3–5920 Kuhio Hwy., Kapaa, HI 96746 © **888/823-5111** or 808/823-6000. Fax 808/823-6666. www.holiday inn-kauai.com. 216 units. $239–$309 unit for up to 4; $339 suite for up to 4; 2-room cottages $375 for 4. Roll-away beds/cribs $15. Additional adult $10; children 19 and under stay free with parents. AE, DC, DISC, MC, V. **Amenities:** Restaurant with deli for takeout; bar; 2 outdoor pools; complimentary tennis courts; small fitness room; Jacuzzi; complimentary snorkel gear; children's program; game room; activity desk; babysitting; coin-op washer/dryers; laundry/dry cleaning. *In room:* A/C, TV/VCR, dataport, fridge, coffeemaker, hair dryer, iron, safe.

Kauai Coconut Beach Resort ★ *(Kids)*   This is the only full-service oceanfront resort on this stretch of the coast. It offers an excellent deal for families: Not only do children 17 and under stay free, but those 11 and under also eat free when dining with an adult. This well-landscaped resort sits on 10½ acres in front of Waipouli Beach, next door to the Coconut Marketplace. It's centrally located for shops, restaurants, and great golf, and is 10 minutes from Lihue Airport. The spacious guest rooms feature lanais, refrigerators, safes, and coffeemakers. The oceanview and oceanfront rooms are decorated with custom-designed, hand-carved furniture from Indonesia.

In addition to theme buffets at the Flying Lobster Restaurant, there's a wonderful nightly luau (the Hawaii Visitors and Convention Bureau named it the most authentic in the state). Amenities include a jogging path, shuffleboard, a children's program in summer, a nightly torch-lighting ceremony, and daily Hawaiiana demonstrations.

P.O. Box 830, Kapaa, HI 96746. © **800/22-ALOHA** or 808/822-3455. Fax 808/822-1830. www.kcb.com. 307 units. Special "Internet-only booking" rates from $110, including breakfast and car. Regular rack rates: $160–$280 double. Extra person $15; children 17 and under stay free in parent's room. AE, DC, MC, V. **Amenities:** Full-service restaurant and bar; outdoor pool; complimentary tennis on 3 championship courts, plus pro shop; Jacuzzi; watersports equipment rentals; children's program (summer only); activity desk; car-rental desk; room service; babysitting; coin-op washer/dryers; laundry/dry cleaning. *In room:* A/C, TV/VCR, dataport, fridge, coffeemaker, iron, safe.

Mahina Kai *(Finds)*   Mahina Kai ("moon over the water") is a traditional Japanese villa (complete with teahouse next door) on 2 landscaped acres just across the road from one of the most picturesque white-sand beaches on Kauai. There are three rooms in the main house that come complete with shoji screen doors, private bathrooms and lanais, and use of the gorgeous living room (with fish pond, vintage Hawaiian furniture, and views of Japanese gardens and Aliomanu Beach), and shared kitchenette. Although this place is undeniably unique, the rooms are tiny and sparsely furnished (no TVs or phones), and the walls paper-thin. Also available are a large one-bedroom suite with private entrance and a separate cottage (with kitchenette) next to the saltwater pool. Landscaped into the gardens are a lagoon-style pool and a hot tub. Sitting in the hot tub, listening to the surf across the street, and watching the stars move slowly across the sky is pretty darn close to heaven on earth.

4933 Aliomanu Rd. (off Kuhio Hwy. at mile marker 14). c/o P.O. Box 699, Anahola, HI 96703. ✆ **800/337-1134** or 808/822-9451. www.mahinakai.com. 5 units. $125–$225 double. Rates include continental breakfast. Extra person $25. 3-night minimum. MC, V. **Amenities:** Saltwater lagoon-like swimming pool; hot tub; complimentary beach equipment and snorkel; massage available. *In room:* No phone.

INEXPENSIVE

Alohilani Bed & Breakfast ★ *Finds* Owner Sharon Mitchell has furnished her B&B, which sits amid 6 peaceful acres at the very end of a country road, with antiques and other beautiful pieces. Her separate cottage is a large room decorated in country charm with a full kitchen, sleeper sofa, and adorable antique bed with its own teddy bear. Our favorite suite is the open, airy Sunshine Atrium, with its floor-to-ceiling windows and arched French glass doors opening onto a lanai that overlooks the entire valley. The white-tiled room has a queen bed, a sleeper sofa, a small fridge, and a microwave.

1470 Wanaao Rd., Kapaa, HI 96746. ✆ **800/533-9316** or 808/823-0128. Fax 808/823-0128. www.hawaiilink.net/~alohila. 3 units. $99–$109 double suite; $109 double cottage. Rates include continental breakfast. Extra person $10. 3-night minimum. MC, V. From Kuhio Hwy. (Hwy. 56), turn left onto Kawaihau Rd.; go about 4 miles, then turn left again on Wanaao Rd. **Amenities:** Jacuzzi. *In room:* TV, kitchenette, fridge, coffeemaker, hair dryer, no phone.

Hotel Coral Reef *Value* Here's a budget choice right on the beach. This small, unpretentious hotel faces a grassy lawn, coconut trees, and a white-sand beach. It offers economical rooms and friendly service in an ideal location, within walking distance of shops, restaurants, golf, and tennis, and just 50 yards away from good swimming and snorkeling. There's even an 8-mile bike path that starts right on the grounds. Of the two wings in the hotel, we prefer the oceanfront one, which has big rooms that overlook the beach through sliding-glass lanai doors. The two-room units have a separate bedroom and a living room with a sofa bed—perfect for families. Linda Warriner, owner and gracious hostess of this quaint hotel, is always happy to give you pointers on how to stretch your budget and still have a good time on Kauai.

1516 Kuhio Hwy. (at the northern end of Kapaa, between mile markers 8 and 9), Kapaa, HI 96746. ✆ **800/843-4659** or 808/822-4481. Fax 808/822-7705. www.hotelcoralreef.com. 24 units. $59–$110 double. Rates include continental breakfast. Extra person $10; children 12 and under stay free in parent's room. Room/car packages available. MC, V. **Amenities:** Watersports equipment rentals; activity desk; coin-op washer/dryers. *In room:* TV, fridge, no phone.

Kapaa Shores ★ These apartments are located right on the beach in the heart of Kapaa. Even the budget units have a partial view of the ocean, but oceanfront units are available for a bit more money. The one-bedrooms can comfortably sleep four, while the two-bedrooms can sleep as many as six (the sofa in each unit pulls out into a queen-size bed). All units are in excellent shape and come with fully equipped modern kitchens and large lanais, where you can enjoy a sunrise breakfast or sunset cocktails. On-site amenities include a large pool, a tennis court, a family-size hot tub, a shuffleboard court, laundry facilities, and barbecues. Golf courses, restaurants, and bars are nearby.

900 Kuhio Hwy. (between mile markers 7 and 8), reservations c/o Garden Island Properties, 4–928 Kuhio Hwy., Kapaa, HI 96746. ✆ **800/801-0378** or 808/822-4871. Fax 808/822-7984. www.kauaiproperties.com. 81 units. $115–$125 1-bedroom; $145–$155 2-bedroom. 3-night minimum. MC, V. **Amenities:** Outdoor pool;

complimentary tennis courts; Jacuzzi; salon; coin-op washer/dryers. *In room:* TV, dataport, kitchen, fridge, coffeemaker, iron.

Lani-keha ★ *Finds*

Step back in time to the 1940s, when old Hawaiian families lived in open, airy, rambling homes on large plots of land lush with fruit trees and sweet-smelling flowers. This gracious age is still alive and well in Lani-keha, a *kamaaina* (old-timer) home with an open living/game/writing/dining room, with oversize picture windows to take in the views, and bedrooms with private bathrooms. The house is elegant yet casual, with old-style rattan furniture—practicality and comfort outweigh design aesthetics. The large communal kitchen has everything a cook could want, even a dishwasher. All the guests share the TV/VCR and single phone in the living area.

848 Kamalu Rd. (Hwy. 581), Kapaa, HI 96746. Ⓒ 800/821-4898 or 808/822-1605. Fax 808/822-2429. www.lanikeha.com. 3 units. $55–$65 double. Rates include continental breakfast. Extra person $15. 2-night minimum. No credit cards. From Kuhio Hwy. (Hwy. 56), turn left at the stoplight at Coco Palms onto Hwy. 580 (Kuamoo Rd.); go 3 miles; turn right at Hwy. 581 (Kamalu Rd.) and go 1 mile. **Amenities:** Washer/dryer. *In room:* No phone.

Rosewood Bed & Breakfast ★ *Finds*

This lovingly restored century-old plantation home, set amid tropical flowers, lily ponds, and waterfalls, has accommodations to suit everyone. There's a Laura Ashley–style room in the main house along with two private cottages: one a miniature of the main house, with oak floors and the same Laura Ashley decor; the other a little grass shack set in a tropical garden, with an authentic thatched roof and an outside shower. There's also a bunkhouse with three separate small rooms with a shared shower and toilet. Hostess Rosemary Smith also has a list of other properties she manages. *Note:* Smoking is not permitted on the property.

872 Kamalu Rd., Kapaa, HI. 96746. Ⓒ 808/822-5216. Fax 808/822-5478. www.rosewoodkauai.com. 6 units (3 with shared bathroom). $85 double in main house (includes continental breakfast); $40–$50 double in bunkhouse; $105–$150 cottage double (sleeps up to 4). Extra person $10. No credit cards. From Kuhio Hwy. (Hwy. 56), turn left at the stoplight at Coco Palms onto Hwy. 580 (Kuamoo Rd.); go 3 miles; at junction of Hwy. 581 (Kamalu Rd.), turn right; go 1 mile and look for the yellow house on the right with the long picket fence in front. *In room:* No phone. *In cottages:* TV, kitchen, fridge, coffeemaker, hair dryer, iron, no phone. *In bunkhouse:* Kitchenette, fridge, coffeemaker, no phone.

Wailua Bayview ★ *Value*

Located right on the ocean, these spacious one-bedroom apartments offer excellent value. All units have ceiling fans, full kitchens (including microwave and dishwasher), washer/dryers, and large lanais. Some have air-conditioning as well. The bedrooms are roomy, and the sofa bed in the living room allows you to sleep up to four. Several of the units were renovated in 1998 with new carpet and reupholstered furniture. Some of the $110 garden units are close to the road and can be noisy; ask for one with air-conditioning, which generally drowns out the street sounds. The oceanview units are more expensive but still a great deal. On-site facilities include a pool and barbecue area. Restaurants, bars, shopping, golf, and tennis are nearby.

320 Papaloa Rd., Kapaa, HI 96746. Ⓒ 800/882-9007. Fax 425/391-9121. www.wailuabay.com. 45 units. $110–$120 double. Apr 15–Dec 15, 7th night free. Discount car rentals available. MC, V. **Amenities:** Small outdoor pool; coin-op washer/dryers. *In room:* A/C (most units), TV/VCR, dataport, kitchen, fridge, coffeemaker, iron.

THE NORTH SHORE

Want to rent a rock star's tree house? How about coochy-coochy entertainer Charo's beachfront estate? **Hanalei North Shore Properties** (Ⓒ **800/488-3336** or 808/826-9622; fax 808/826-1188; www.kauai-vacation-rentals.com) handles all kinds of weekly rentals—from beachfront cottages and condos to romantic hideaways and ranch houses—along the North Shore. Renting a home is a great way to enjoy the area's awesome nature, especially for those who like to avoid resorts and fend for themselves. Shopping, restaurants, and nightlife are abundant in nearby Hanalei. The company does not accept credit cards.

In addition to the B&Bs reviewed below, you might also consider **North Country Farms** (© 808/828-1513; www.northcountryfarms.com) a private, handcrafted, redwood cottage on a 4-acre organic farm. It's a great place for families ($110 for 2; children under 15 stay free with parents).

Note: You'll find the following accommodations, on the "Kauai's North Shore: Princeville & Hanalei" map on p. 602.

VERY EXPENSIVE

Princeville Resort Kauai ★★★ *Kids* This resort is the jewel in the Sheraton crown, a palace full of marble and chandeliers. It enjoys one of the world's finest settings, between Hanalei Bay and Kauai's steepled mountains. Nearby are outstanding surfing and windsurfing areas, as well as a wonderful reef for snorkeling. The panoramic view from the lobby has to be the most dramatic vista from any hotel in the state. The Princeville is Kauai's most popular setting for weddings; more than 300 a year are performed outdoors by the pool.

This grand hotel steps down a cliff; the entrance is actually on the ninth floor, and you take elevators down to your room and the beach. Each opulent room has such extras as a door chime, dimmer switches, bedside control panels, a safe, original oil paintings, an oversize bathtub, and a "magic" bathroom window: a liquid-crystal shower window that you can switch in an instant from clear to opaque. There are no lanais, but oversize windows allow you to admire the awesome view from your bed.

In addition to a great children's program, this property has oodles of activities not only for children, but for the entire family, from horseback riding to adventures exploring the island. The hotel grounds are a fantasy land for children (and some adults) with a huge swimming pool, next to a sandy beach.

Other great amenities here: twice-daily fresh towels, daily newspaper, complimentary resort shuttle, comprehensive Hawaiiana program, riding stables, in-house cinema, arts program (from photography to painting), and a wealth of outdoor activities. Golfers may choose from two courses, both designed by Robert Trent Jones Jr.; the whirlpools, steam baths, 35-meter lap pool, and multitude of treatments will delight spa-goers.

P.O. Box 3069 (5520 Kahaku Rd.), Princeville, HI 96722-3069. © 800/826-4400 or 808/826-9644. Fax 808/826-1166. www.princeville.com. 252 units. $405–$615 double; from $705 suite. Extra person $75; children under 18 stay free in parent's room. AE, DC, DISC, MC, V. Parking $15. **Amenities:** 3 restaurants (1 with excellent nightly entertainment; also see the review for La Cascata on p. 568); 3 bars; huge, oceanside outdoor pool; outstanding golf on 2 courses; 25 tennis courts; first-rate health club and spa; 3 outdoor Jacuzzis (including a really palatial one); watersports equipment rentals; bike rental; children's program; game room; concierge; activity desk; car-rental desk; business center; shopping arcade; salon; 24-hr. room service; massage; babysitting; same-day laundry/dry cleaning. *In room:* A/C, TV/VCR, dataport, minibar, fridge, coffeemaker, hair dryer, iron, safe.

EXPENSIVE

Hanalei Bay Resort & Suites ★★ This 22-acre resort is just up the street from ritzy Princeville Resort (see above), overlooking the fabled Bali Ha'i cliffs and Hanalei Bay. It has the same majestic view, but for as little as half the price. The place recaptures the spirit of old Hawaii, especially in the three-story stucco units that angle down the hill to the gold-sand, palm-fringed beach it shares with its neighbor. Rooms are decorated in island style, with rattan furnishings and lanais overlooking the bay, the lush grounds, and the distant mountains. Shuttle service is available for those who may have problems walking on steep hillside.

The Happy Talk Lounge is one of our favorite places on Kauai for sunset cocktails, while the open-air restaurant, Bali Ha'i, has a view that is so distractingly gorgeous that you can hardly concentrate on the food.

P.O. Box 220 (5380 Honoiki St.), Princeville, HI 96722. ℂ **800/827-4427** or 808/826-6522. Fax 808/826-6680. www.hanaleibayresort.com. 236 units. $185–$275 (up to 4); $215–$240 studio with kitchenette (up to 4); $350–$390 1-bedroom apt (up to 4). Suites include full breakfast and afternoon cocktails. AE, DC, DISC, MC, V. **Amenities:** Restaurant; bar; 2 inviting outdoor freshwater pools; complimentary shuttle to Princeville Resort's top-ranked golf courses; 8 tennis courts, pro shop, and tennis school; Jacuzzi; concierge; activity desk; salon; massage; babysitting; coin-op washer/dryers (apartments have washer/dryers in units); laundry/dry cleaning. *In room:* A/C, TV/VCR, dataport, kitchenette, fridge, coffeemaker, hair dryer, iron, safe.

Moloa'a Beach House ★★ *Finds*   Off the beaten track, hidden in the not-so-well-known beach community of Moloa'a, this modern, just-built, multi-million home is located right on the beach with unbelievable rates of $225 for the studio and $275 for the one-bedroom unit (or $500 for the entire house). When Hurricane Iniki hit Kauai in 1992, the former beach house at this location was swept out to sea. The owner spent 10 years building this high-tech home, which is engineered to withstand anything Mother Nature can dish out. Everything in this two-unit home is first-class, from the marble floors to the granite kitchen countertop to the top-of-the-line kitchen appliances to the furniture. But the real reason to stay here is the eye-popping ocean view, just steps outside your door. On the 1,600-square-foot flat roof are a sun deck, Jacuzzi, and wet bar. You may never want to leave.

Moloa'a Rd., Moloa'a. Reservations c/o Hawaii's Best Bed and Breakfast, P.O. Box 758, Volcano, HI 96785. ℂ **800/262-9912** or 808/985-7488. Fax 808/967-8610. www.bestbnb.com. 2 units. $225–$275 or $500 for entire house, double. No credit cards. **Amenities:** Jacuzzi; washer and dryer. *In room:* A/C, TV/VCR, kitchen, fridge, coffeemaker, hair dryer, and iron.

MODERATE

Aloha Sunrise Inn/Aloha Sunset Inn ★★ *Finds*   Hidden on the North Shore are these two unique cottages nestled on a quiet 7-acre farm with horses, fruit trees, flowers, and organic vegetables. We highly recommend both of these darling bungalows. Each is fully furnished with hardwood floors, top of the line bedding, tropical island–style decor, a complete kitchen, washer/dryer, and everything you can think of to make your stay heavenly (from all the great videos you have been meaning to watch to an excellent CD library). It's close to activities, restaurants, and shopping, yet far enough away to feel the peace and quiet of a Hawaii of yesteryears. Hosts Allan and Catherine Rietow, who have lived their entire lives in the islands, can help you plan your stay, give you money-saving tips, and even hand out complimentary masks, snorkels, boogie boards and other beach toys and point you to their favorite beaches. *Note to parents:* These cottages are not appropriate for children.

P.O. Box 79, Kilauea, HI 96754. ℂ **888/828-1008** or 808/828-1100. Fax 808/828-2199. www.kauaisunrise. com. 2 1-bedroom cottages. $125–$130 double (plus a 1-time $60 cleaning fee). 3-night minimum. No credit cards. **Amenities:** Washer and dryer. *In room:* TV/VCR, kitchen, fridge, coffeemaker, hair dryer, iron.

Hanalei Colony Resort ★ *Kids*   Picture this: A perfect white-sand beach just steps from your door, with lush tropical gardens, jagged mountain peaks, and fertile jungle serving as your backdrop. Welcome to Haena, Kauai's northernmost town and gateway to the famous Na Pali Coast, with miles of hiking trails, fabulous sunset views, and great beaches. This 5-acre resort is the place to stay if you're looking to experience the magic of the enchanting North Shore. The units are unbelievably spacious—six people could sleep here comfortably—making them great for families. Each has a private lanai (the less-expensive budget units face the garden), a full kitchen, a dining area, a living room, and ceiling fans (the area is blessed with cooling trade winds, so air-conditioning isn't necessary). The atmosphere is quiet and relaxing: no TVs, stereos, or phones. The property has a large pool, laundry facilities, and a barbecue and picnic area. Guests have access to complimentary beach mats and towels, a lending library, and children's toys, puzzles, and games (plus badminton and croquet for the entire family). A restaurant and deli are next door. The entire property is undergoing a massive renovation and when it is completed, the rates will probably increase, so book it while it is still affordable.

5–7130 Kuhio Hwy. c/o P.O. Box 206, Hanalei, HI 96714. ✆ **800/628-3004** or 808/826-6235. Fax 808/826-9893. www.hcr.com. 48 units. $180 $335 2-bedroom apt for 4. Rate includes continental breakfast once a week. Seventh night free. Minimum 5 nights May 1–Sept 30 and Dec 12–Jan 4. Extra person $15. AE, MC, V. **Amenities:** Good-size outdoor pool; Jacuzzi; coin-op washer/dryers. *In room:* Kitchen, fridge, coffeemaker, no phone.

INEXPENSIVE

Bed, Breakfast & Beach at Hanalei Bay *(Finds* On a quiet street in a residential area just 150 yards from Hanalei Bay lies one of the best deals on the North Shore. The three guest rooms in Carolyn Barnes's three-story house range from a 700-square-foot suite with a 360° view to a mini-apartment on the ground floor with a kitchenette and an outdoor shower. The location couldn't be better (some guests don't even bother to rent a car). It's a 4-minute walk to Hanalei Bay's 2-mile long beach and a 10-minute walk to the shops and restaurants of Hanalei. For families, Carolyn also has a cozy two-bedroom, one-bathroom house a couple of blocks away.

P.O. Box 748, Hanalei, HI 96714. ✆ **808/826-6111.** Fax 808/826-6111. www.bestofhawaii.com/hanalei. 4 units. TV. $80–$135 double room (includes full breakfast); extra person $15. $950/week cottage for 2; extra person $100/week. 2- to 3-night minimum for rooms, 7-night minimum in cottage. No credit cards. *In room:* No phone.

Hale Ho'o Maha *(Finds* Kirby Guyer and her husband, Toby, have a spacious four-bedroom, three-bathroom home on 5 acres. It's filled with Hawaiian and South Pacific artifacts and features a fireplace, a library, and a 150-gallon saltwater aquarium (it's more entertaining than TV). The rooms are uniquely decorated and priced with budget travelers in mind. We recommend the Pineapple Room, with its 7-foot round bed (with custom quilted pineapple spread and matching handmade area rug) and an ocean view from the large picture window. The landscaped grounds feature a stream and a pond, and there's a waterfall across the street. Kirby has everything you need, from beach chairs to surfboards; you'll also have access to a complete kitchen. Within spitting distance are two remarkable white-sand beaches; also close by are golf courses, riding stables, restaurants, and markets. *Warning:* The property is next to the main highway; light sleepers may be bothered by traffic noise.

P.O. Box 422 (on Kalihiwai Rd., off Kuhio Hwy. at mile marker 24), Kilauea, HI 96754. ✆ **800/851-0291** or 808/828-1341. Fax 808/828-2046. www.aloha.net/~hoomaha. 4 units (2 with shared bathroom). $65–$90 double. Rates include continental breakfast. Extra person $15. AE, DC, MC, V. **Amenities:** Complimentary use of laundry facilities. *In room:* TV, hair dryer.

Historic Bed & Breakfast *(Finds* This building used to house Kauai's oldest Buddhist temple (built in 1901), which served the Japanese Buddhist community for 85 years. In 1986, slated for demolition, the wooden structure was given a last-minute reprieve and moved from Lihue to Hanalei. The temple was totally restored, and today it's a four-room B&B. The location is great—right in the middle of Hanalei and an easy walk to shops, restaurants, and Hanalei Bay. Highly polished wooden floors run throughout the building; the atmosphere is peaceful and quiet (in fact there's no TV anywhere on the property, and only 1 house phone). Two of the rooms feature four-poster bamboo queen beds (with antique Hawaiian quilts), and one room has a king bed and a queen futon. All three share one bathroom, with an additional shower outside. New owner Kelly Sato is newly married to a Japanese chef, who whips out gourmet breakfasts with ingredients from his organic farm and can prepare a complete Japanese breakfast on request.

5–5067 Kuhio Hwy. (on mountain side of road, 3rd building on left as you enter Hanalei). P.O. Box 1684, Hanalei, HI 96714. ☎ 808/826-4622. www.historicbnb.com. 4 units. $85 double with shared bathroom. $105 double with private bath. Rates include full breakfast. Extra person $15. 2-night minimum. Credit cards not accepted. *Note:* No maid service. **Amenities:** Laundry facilities; use of a refrigerator. *In room:* Hair dryer in bathroom, no phone.

4 Where to Dine

Kauai's best dining spots ring the shores: Poipu on the south, Kapaa on the east, and Hanalei on the north. And that's a good thing because on Kauai street names seem irrelevant, and locations are determined by trees, erstwhile mom-and-pop stores, and other landmarks of rural life. Follow the winding road and you'll find the tried-and-true temples of Hawaii Regional Cuisine amid plate lunch palaces and a new, post-hippie breed of affordable, top-quality eateries that cook healthful, fresh, and tasty cuisine.

While Roy's in Poipu, Beach House in neighboring Lawai, and A Pacific Cafe in Kapaa remain Kauai's foodie stalwarts, there are some excellent choices at all levels of the food chain. Most of the island's newcomers are moderately priced and have cropped up along the island's one main road.

On your jaunt across the island, you'll find affordable choices in every town, from hamburger joints to *saimin* (noodles in broth topped with scrambled eggs, onions, and sometimes pork) stands to busy neighborhood diners. As long as you don't expect filet mignon on a fish-and-chips budget, it shouldn't be difficult to please both your palate and your pocketbook. But if you're looking for lobster, rack of lamb, or risotto to write home about, you'll find those pleasures, too.

For condo dwellers who are preparing their own meals, we've featured a variety of markets and shops around Kauai—including some wonderful green markets and fruit stands—where you can pick up the island's best foodstuffs. These are listed in "Shops & Galleries," later in this chapter. If you're looking for fresh island fruit, also see the box "Fruity Smoothies & Other Exotic Treats," on p. 606.

In the listings below, reservations are not required unless otherwise noted.

LIHUE & ENVIRONS
You'll find the restaurants in this section on the "Lihue Accommodations & Dining" map on p. 537.

EXPENSIVE
Gaylord's ★★ CONTINENTAL/PACIFIC RIM   One of Kauai's most splendid examples of kamaaina architecture, Gaylord's is the anchor of a 1930s plantation manager's estate on a 1,700-acre sugar plantation. You'll enter a complex

of shops, galleries, and a living room of Hawaiian artifacts and period furniture. The private dining room has a lavish table, always elegantly set, as if Queen Lil-iuokalani were expected at any minute; another room accommodates private parties. The main dining room, which winds around a flagstone courtyard overlooking rolling lawns and purple mountains, serves American classics (New York steak, rack of lamb, prime rib) along with pasta, fresh seafood, and lavish desserts. The ambience, historic surroundings, and soothing views from the terrace make Gaylord's a special spot for lunch—salads, soups, fresh fish, Oliver Shagnasty's signature baby back ribs, burgers, sandwiches, and lighter fare predominate. Daily specials include international dishes, such as kalua pork and Mexican fajitas, and fresh island fish in various cross-cultural preparations.

At Kilohana, 3–2087 Kaumualii Hwy., Lihue. ⓒ 808/245-9593. Reservations recommended. Main courses $8–$11 lunch, $19–$30 dinner. AE, DC, DISC, MC, V. Mon–Sat 11am–3pm and 5–9pm; Sun 9:30am–3pm (brunch) and 5–9pm.

JJ's Broiler ⭐ AMERICAN Famous for its Slavonic steak (tenderloin in butter, wine, and garlic), herb-crusted ahi, and the lazy Susan of salad greens that's brought to your table, JJ's is a lively spot on Kalapaki Bay, with open-air dining and a menu that covers more than the usual surf-and-turf. I have found the service to be either laudable or lamentable, but the quality of the food is consistent. The coconut shrimp and Manila clams are big sellers, and the Mauna Kea scallops (which look like a mountain on a heap of rice with nori) are an imaginative twist on seafood. Lunchtime appetizers include potato skins, calamari rings, quesadillas, and wontons—the United Nations of pupu! The high ceilings, two-story dining, Kenwood Cup posters, and nautically designed rooms are enhanced by stellar views of the bay.

3416 Rice St., Nawiliwili. ⓒ 808/246-4422. Reservations recommended for dinner. Lunch sandwiches $9–$11; dinner main courses $18–$25. DISC, MC, V. Daily 11am–10pm.

MODERATE

Barbecue Inn ⭐ AMERICAN/JAPANESE/PACIFIC RIM Watch for the specials at this 63-year-old family restaurant, where everything from soup to dessert is made in the Sasakis' kitchen. You can get an inexpensive hamburger for lunch, but there are also fancier specials on the wide-ranging menu, including complete dinners for $9 to $19 and entrees such as grilled fresh ahi or ono and macadamia-nut chicken. The familiar favorites remain as well (oxtail soup, Japanese-style dinners, chow mein, roast turkey). Locally grown organic greens are a big hit, and specialty salads are a welcome addition. Several-course dinner combinations of Japanese and American favorites draw long lines.

2982 Kress St. (off Rice St.), Lihue. ⓒ 808/245-2921. Main courses $7–$13 lunch, $8–$24 dinner. MC, V. Mon–Thurs 7:30am–1:30pm and 5–8:30pm; Fri–Sat 7:30am–1:30pm and 4:30–8:45pm.

Duke's Canoe Club ⭐ STEAK/SEAFOOD It's hard to go wrong at Duke's. Part of a highly successful restaurant chain (including Duke's Canoe Club in Waikiki, and 3 similar restaurants on Maui), this oceanfront oasis is the hippest spot in town, with a winning combination of great view, affordable menu, attractive salad bar, popular music, and a very happy happy hour. The noontime best-seller is stir-fried cashew chicken, but the fresh mahi burger and the grilled chicken quesadilla are front-runners, too. The inexpensive fish tacos are a major attraction, and the five or six varieties of fresh catch a night are a highlight, served in several different preparations—a great value. Hawaiian musicians serenade diners nightly, while downstairs in the Barefoot Bar, traditional

Plate Lunch Pointers

If you haven't yet come face to face with the local phenomenon called *plate lunch,* Kauai is a good place to start. Like saimin, the plate lunch is more than a gastronomic experience—it's a part of the local culture. Lihue is peppered with affordable plate-lunch counters that serve this basic dish: two scoops of rice, potato or macaroni salad, and a beef, chicken, fish, or pork entree—all on a single plate. Although heavy gravies are usually de rigueur, some of the less traditional purveyors have streamlined their offerings to include healthier touches, such as lean grilled fresh fish. Pork cutlets and chicken or beef soaked in teriyaki sauce, however, remain staples, as does the breaded and crisply fried method called *katsu,* as in chicken katsu. Most of the time, *fried* is the operative word; that's why it's best to be ravenously hungry when you approach a plate lunch, or it can overpower you. At its best, a plate lunch can be a marvel of flavors, a saving grace after a long hike; at its worst, it's a plate-size grease bomb.

The following are the best plate-lunch counters on Kauai. How fortunate that each is in a different part of the island!

The **Koloa Fish Market** ⋆, 5482 Koloa Rd. (© 808/742-6199), is in southern Kauai, on Koloa's main street. A tiny corner stand with plate lunches, prepared foods, and two stools on a closet-size veranda, it sells excellent fresh fish poke, Hawaiian-food specials, and seared ahi to go. It's gourmet fare masquerading as takeout. Daily specials may include sautéed ahi or fresh opakapaka with capers, and regular treats include crisp-on-the-outside, chewy-on-the-inside poi dumplings (when poi is available), one of life's consummate pleasures. For a picnic or outing on the south shore, this is a good place to start.

On the Hanamaulu side of Lihue, across the street from Wal-Mart, look for the prim, gray building that reads **Fish Express** ⋆ (3343 Kuhio Hwy.; © 808/245-9918). It's astonishing what you'll find here for under $10: Cajun-style grilled ahi with guava basil, fresh fish grilled in a passion-orange-tarragon sauce, fresh fish tacos in garlic and herbs, and many other delectables, all served with rice, salad, and vegetables. The Hawaiian plate lunch (laulau or kalua pork, lomi salmon, ahi poke, rice or poi) is a top seller, as are the several varieties of smoked fish, everything from ahi to swordfish. The owners marinate the fish in soy sauce, sugar, ginger, and garlic (no preservatives), and smoke it with kiawe wood. The fresh fish specials, at $7.95, come in six preparations and are done and flavored to perfection. At the chilled counter you can choose freshly sliced sashimi and many styles of poke, from scallop, ahi, and octopus to exotic marinated crab. This is a potluck bonanza that engages even newcomers, who point and order while regulars pick up sweeping assortments of seafood appetizers on large platters. They're all fresh and reasonably priced, great for Friday-afternoon *pau hana* (after-work) parties.

and contemporary Hawaiian music adds to the cheerful atmosphere. On Tropical Fridays, tropical drinks go for $3.50 from 4 to 6pm, when live music stirs up the joint.

In east Kauai's Kapaa town, the indispensable **Pono Market,** 4–1300 Kuhio Hwy. (© **808/822-4581**), has similarly enticing counters of sashimi, poke, Hawaiian food, sushi, and a diverse assortment of take-out fare. It's known for its flaky *manju* (sweet potato and other fillings in baked crust), apple turnovers, sandwiches, excellent boiled peanuts, pork and chicken laulau, and plate lunches—shoyu chicken, sweet-and-sour spareribs, pineapple-glazed chicken, teriyaki fish, and so on. The potato-macaroni salad (regulars buy it by the pound for barbecues and potlucks) and roast pork are top sellers. Pono Market is as good as they come. If they're available, pick up Taro Ko taro chips. They're made in Hanapepe, hard to find, and worth hand-carrying home.

At **Mark's Place,** 1610 Haleukana St. in Puhi Industrial Park (© **808/245-2722**), just southwest of Lihue, island standards (Korean-style chicken, teriyaki beef, beef stew, chicken katsu) come with brown rice (or white) and salad for $5 or $5.50. The selection, which changes daily, always includes two salad and three entree choices as well as hot sandwiches (chicken, beef, and hamburgers) and the ever-popular *bento* (rice with beef, chicken, or fish, arranged in a lidded box). Mark's is a takeout and catering operation, so don't expect table seating.

Lihue, the island's county and business seat, is full of ethnic eateries serving inexpensive plate lunches, everything from *bento* to Hawaiian, Korean, and Chinese food. **Local Boy's Restaurant & Deli,** 3204 Kuhio Hwy. (just past the old Lihue Theater; © **808/246-8898**), is a budget bonanza and a popular stop for jumbo-size appetites. They offer generous servings of noodles (ramen, several types of chow mein, vegetarian fried noodles); barbecued chicken, beef, and spare ribs by the pound; sandwiches; plate lunches; and local favorites such as chili and beef stew. The Korean plate is very popular, a heroic serving of short ribs, chicken, and teriyaki beef, and kim chee for a mere $6.75. The $4 miniplate of teriyaki chicken is very large for a mini, and, although not boneless and skinless, tasty. They also are open for breakfast, where you are hard pressed to find anything over $5. **Po's Kitchen,** 4100 Rice St. (© **808/246-8617**), offers Japanese specials: cone sushi, chicken katsu, teriyaki beef plates, and bentos. One block away, **Garden Island BBQ,** 4252-A Rice St. (© **808/245-8868**), is the place for Chinese plate lunches and local staples such as barbecued or lemon chicken and teriyaki steak, as well as soups and tofu dishes.

In the Kukui Grove Center, at Kaumualii Highway (Hwy. 50) and Old Nawiliwili Road, **Joni-Hana** (© **808/245-5213**) is famous for its specials—nearly 20 a day! The tiny counter serves fried noodles, lemon-shoyu *ono* (wahoo), teriyaki everything, and many other local dishes. It's arguably the busiest place on the mall.

In the Kauai Marriott Resort & Beach Club, 3610 Rice St., Nawiliwili. © 808/246-9599. Reservations recommended for dinner. Lunch $4–$11; dinner $8–$24. Taco Tuesdays 4–6pm, with $2 fish tacos and $2 draft beer. AE, DISC, MC, V. Barefoot Bar daily 11am–11:30pm; main dining room daily 5–10pm.

Whalers Brewpub ⭐ SEAFOOD   The brewpub, located where the road into the Marriott ends at Ninini Point, opens to a view of Kalapaki Bay and the Kauai Lagoons golf course. The yellow-and-white wooden building hangs on a perch over the harbor, with gazebo-like decks that are a good place to be at sunset. (Check out the whales during the winter season.) The environment and the fare are both surf-and-turf, and appetizers rule: fried flowering onion with ranch dip, egg rolls, chicken skewers, and nachos. At lunch and dinner, diners gasp when the 20-ounce Whale of a Burger comes to the table with its giant bun, lettuce, sautéed onions, mushrooms, and cheeses, enough for two whale-size appetites. Fish and chips in beer batter are accompanied by Cajun coleslaw, and the house fresh fish comes with a choice of soy-ginger, fruit salsa, and lemon-thyme beurre blanc sauces. Steamed whole local snapper with shoyu and ginger, baby back ribs, fresh catch, and vegetarian lasagna are some of the dinner choices. On Sundays, the beer brunch is a beer fest (all you can drink), with omelets, smoked salmon, and more seafood pub fare than you can shake a stick at. With live Hawaiian music on Tuesday, Friday, Saturday, and Sunday nights, it's a lively place all day.

In the Kauai Marriott Resort & Beach Club, 3132 Ninini Point. ✆ **808/245-2000.** Reservations recommended. Main courses $15–$25 lunch, $17–$25 dinner. AE, DC, DISC, MC, V. Mon–Sat 11am–11pm; Sun 10am–9:30pm.

INEXPENSIVE

Dani's Restaurant AMERICAN/HAWAIIAN   Formica all the way and always packed for breakfast, Dani's is the pancake palace of Lihue: banana, pineapple, papaya, and buttermilk, plus sweet-bread French toast and kalua-pig omelets. Regulars know that fried rice is offered on Thursday only and that the papaya hotcakes are always a deal. At lunch, Hawaiian specials—laulau, kalua pig, lomi salmon, and beef stew in various combinations—dominate the otherwise standard American menu of fried foods and sandwiches.

4201 Rice St., Lihue. ✆ **808/245-4991.** Main courses $3.30–$8.50. MC, V. Mon–Fri 5am–1:30pm; Sat 5am–1pm.

Hamura's Saimin Stand ⭐ SAIMIN   If there were a saimin hall of fame, Hamura's would be it. It's a cultural experience, a renowned saimin stand where fans line up to take their place over steaming bowls of this island specialty at a few U-shaped counters that haven't changed in decades. The saimin and teriyaki barbecue sticks attract an all-day, late-night, pre- and post-movie crowd. The noodles come heaped with vegetables, wontons, hard-boiled eggs, sweetened pork, vegetables, and several condiment combinations. We love the casualness of Hamura's and the simple pleasures it consistently delivers.

2956 Kress St., Lihue. ✆ **808/245-3271.** Most items less than $5. No credit cards. Mon–Thurs 10am–11pm; Fri–Sat 10am–midnight; Sun 10am–9pm.

Hanamaulu Restaurant CHINESE/JAPANESE/SUSHI   When passing this restaurant, you'd never know that serene Japanese gardens with stone pathways and tatami-floored teahouses are hidden within. You can dine at the sushi bar, American style, or in the teahouses for lunch or dinner, but you must call ahead for teahouse dining. At lunch, enter a world of chop suey, wontons, teriyaki chicken, and sukiyaki (less verve than value), with many other choices in budget-friendly Japanese and Chinese plate lunches. Special Japanese and Chinese menus can be planned ahead for groups of up to 60 people, who can dine at low tables on tatami floors in a Japanese-garden setting. Old-timers love this place, and those who came here in diapers are now stopping in for after-golf pupu and beer.

3–4291 Kuhio Hwy., Hanamaulu. ℂ **808/245-2511**. Reservations recommended. Main courses $6–$15. MC, V. Tues–Fri 10am–1pm; daily 4:30–8:30pm.

Kako's ✮ SAIMIN   Wonderful home-cooked broth and noodles are the Kako's signature. Kako's Saimin was a west-side phenomenon for years until Hurricane Iniki turned out the lights, so saimin aficionados are ecstatic that this former Hanapepe fixture has reopened, this time in Lihue. After a long absence, the new installation—just as tiny and just as good as the original—is cause for applause. Owner Dorothea Hayashi uses a secret recipe to make her broth from scratch, and the noodles, also house-made and fresh, are the perfect accompaniment. When teamed with her teriyaki chicken sticks, the saimin and wonton min are pure heaven for noodle lovers. The saimin comes with a choice of toppings, such as barbecued chicken, cabbage, sliced eggs, and green onions. Old-fashioned, home-style hamburgers like Mom used to make, flavored with onions mixed into the patties, are flying out the door at a miraculous $1.75.

2980 Ewalu St. ℂ **808/246-0404**. Saimin $3–$5.50. No credit cards or checks. Mon–Sat 10:30am–2pm.

Kauai Chop Suey CANTONESE   With the large, unremarkable dining room here and the so-so service, the food had better be good. And as legions of local regulars will tell you, it is. The huge menu has something for everyone: chow mein, Cantonese shrimp, roast duck, lemon chicken, and hundreds of choices of Cantonese noodles, soups, sweet-and-sours, foo-yongs, and stir-fries.

In the Harbor Mall, 3501 Rice St., Nawiliwili. ℂ **808/245-8790**. Most dishes $7–$10. AE, MC, V. Tues–Sat 11am–2pm and 4:30–9pm; Sun 4:30–9pm.

Restaurant Kiibo JAPANESE   Neither a sleek sushi bar nor a plate-lunch canteen, Kiibo is a neighborhood staple with inexpensive, unpretentious, tasty, home-style Japanese food served in a pleasant room accented with Japanese folk art. You can dine on sushi, ramen, sukiyaki, tempura, teriyaki, or the steamed egg-rice-vegetable marvel called *oyako donburi.* There are satisfying, affordable lunch specials and teishoku specials of mackerel, salmon, soup, dessert, and other condiments.

299 Umi St., Lihue. ℂ **808/245-2650**. Main courses $5–$19. MC, V. Mon–Fri 11am–1:30pm; Mon–Sat 5:30–9pm.

THE POIPU RESORT AREA

You'll find the restaurants in this section on the "Poipu Resort Area Accommodations & Dining" map on p. 541.

EXPENSIVE

The Beach House ✮✮✮ HAWAII REGIONAL   All reports are good from this beachfront magnet in Lawai, formerly owned by Jean-Marie Josselin, who sold it to smart Maui restaurateurs who know a good thing when they see it. Subscribing to the if-it-ain't-broke-don't-fix-it philosophy, the new owners left the staff and operation intact. There has been a major cosmetic overhaul, the food is as good as ever, and Beach House remains the south shore's premier spot for sunset drinks, appetizers, and dinner—a treat for all the senses. The ocean-front room is large, accented with oversize sliding-glass doors, with old Hawaii Regional favorites on the menu. Come for cocktails or early dinner, when you can still see the sunset and perhaps a turtle or two bobbing in the waves. Menus change daily and include Kauai asparagus salad, seared crusted macadamia-nut mahimahi with miso sauce, sea scallops with lemongrass and kaffir lime, and the Beach House crab cake with mint sambal butter sauce and grilled tomato compote. "Local boy paella" features fresh seafood with home-style fried rice and seafood saffron broth. Desserts shine too, like the molten chocolate desire—a hot chocolate tart that comes warm and wonderful, and the kahlua taro cheese cake—tangy, with lilikoi crème fraîche.

5022 Lawai Rd., Poipu. ℂ 808/742-1424. Reservations recommended. Main courses $22–$27. AE, MC, V. Daily 5:30–9:30pm.

Casa di Amici ★★ ITALIAN/INTERNATIONAL   It was hard to see terrific Italian food leave the north shore for the south, but hey, risotto happens. Chef Randall Yates and his wife, Joanna, took over a freestanding wood and stone building in Poipu and turned it into a storybook restaurant with fairy lights, high ceilings, beveled glass, and a generous open deck where you can dine among palms and heliotropes. (There's live classical music on Friday and Saturday evenings from 6:30–9:30pm on the baby grand piano.) It's worth seeking out: It's the third left turn past Brennecke's Beach, not more than 2 minutes from Poipu Beach Park, in an enclave of condos and vacation rentals.

The memorable Italian food has strong Mediterranean and cross-cultural influences. You'll find organic greens from Kilauea, several risotto choices (quattro formaggi and smoked salmon are outstanding), black tiger prawns with ravioli of lobster thermidor, chicken angelica (a favorite, served on farfalle), and surprises, such as Thai lobster bisque and duck kalua carbonara. Among the nearly 2 dozen pasta selections is a classic fettuccine Alfredo for which Yates is deservedly famous. While the set menu is Italian, the specials showcase international influences, such as soy-sauce reductions, furikake (seaweed sprinkle), and the assertive touches of jalapeño tequila aioli on salmon and grilled tiger prawns. This is flamboyant, joyful Italian fare.

2301 Nalo Rd., Poipu. ℂ 808/742-1555. Reservations recommended. Main courses $19–$25. AE, DC, MC, V. Daily 6pm–closing.

Dondero's ★★★ ITALIAN   If you are looking for a romantic dinner either under the stars overlooking the ocean or tucked away in an intimate table surrounded by inlaid marble floors, ornate imported floor tiles, and Franciscan murals, this is the place for you. You get all this atmosphere at Dondero's, plus the best Italian cuisine on the island, served with efficiency. It's hard to have a bad experience here. Our recommendations for a meal to remember: start with either the fresh mozzarella cheese with tomatoes and roasted peppers or the warm goat cheese, roasted eggplant, cannellini beans, and fried basil leaves. Then move on to the black ink linguine with scallops, shrimp, mussels, salmon, clams, and lobster; the risotto with porcini mushrooms and taleggio cheese; or the grilled snapper with roasted vegetables and balsamic glaze. Save room for dessert, especially the chocolate crème brûlée with fresh berries. Dinners are pricey, but worth every penny.

Hyatt Regency Kauai Resort and Spa, 1571 Poipu Rd., Poipu. ℂ 808/742-1234. Reservations a must. Main courses $18–$36. AE, DISC, DC, MC, V. Daily 6–10pm.

Plantation Gardens Restaurant ★★ HAWAII REGIONAL   Eat here. That's as plain as we can make it. The former Piatti is now Plantation Gardens Restaurant, a mix of irresistible garden ambience and a well-executed menu fashioned around fresh local ingredients and a respect for Island traditions. Plantation Gardens has the same owner, management team, and stellar location, plus a new menu under the culinary genius of Chef Brenda Silva-Morando, a local islander, who performs magic with seafood laulau (served with chutney made from Kekaha mangoes), macadamia lamb chops, sugarcane pork, miso shiitake risotto, Kekaha prawns with asparagus over fettuccine, and many other delights. The seaweed, fish, and shellfish are from local waters, and many of the fruits, herbs, and vegetables are grown on the restaurant premises. Other greats include the shrimp and wasabi ravioli, made with fresh local shrimp, ricotta and goat cheese, and kaffir lime and lemongrass—a reminder of forerunner Piatti's well-known pasta prowess. The historic architecture includes a generous veranda, koa trim and Brazilian cherry floors, and gracious details of a 1930s estate that belonged to the manager of Hawaii's first sugar plantation. A sprawling horti-cultural marvel, the property includes koi ponds, shade-giving coconut and kou trees, orchids, bromeliads, and a cactus and succulent garden.

In Kiahuna Plantation Resort, 2253 Poipu Rd. © 808/742-2216. Reservations recommended. Main courses $14–$29. AE, DC, MC, V. Daily 5:30–10pm dinner (open at 4pm for pupu, pizza, and cocktails).

Roy's Poipu Bar & Grill ★★ EURO-ASIAN   This is a loud, lively room with ceiling fans, marble tables, works by local artists, and a menu tailor-made for foodies. The signature touches of Roy Yamaguchi (of Roy's restaurants in Oahu, Big Island, Maui, Tokyo, New York, and Guam) are abundantly present: an excellent, progressive, and affordable wine selection; fresh local ingredients pre-pared with a nod to Europe, Asia, and the Pacific; and service so efficient it can be overbearing. Because appetizers (such as nori-seared ahi with black-bean sauce, spinach-shiitake ravioli, and crisp shrimp cakes with butter sauce) are a major part of the menu, you can sample Roy's legendary fare without breaking the bank. The 3 dozen nightly specials invariably include eight fresh-fish dishes a night, prepared at least five or six different ways.

In Poipu Shopping Village, 2360 Kiahuna Plantation Dr. © 808/742-5000. www.roysrestaurant.com. Reser-vations recommended. Main courses $20–$27. AE, DC, DISC, MC, V. Daily 5:30–9:30pm.

MODERATE

Brennecke's Beach Broiler ★ AMERICAN/SEAFOOD   Cheerful petunias in window boxes and second-floor views of Poipu Beach are pleasing touches at this seafood-burger house, a longtime favorite for more than 15 years. The view alone is worth the price of a drink and pupu, but it helps that the best ham-burgers on the south shore are served here, as well as excellent vegetarian selec-tions. Quality is consistent in the kiawe-broiled steak, fresh fish, and vegetarian gourmet burger. It's so casual that you can drop in before or after the beach and dine on nachos and peppers, fresh-fish sandwiches, kiawe-broiled fish and kebabs, prime rib, pasta, build-your-own gourmet burgers, and the salad bar. Look for the early dinner (from 4–6pm), happy-hour specials daily, and the Alaskan king crab and prime rib nights.

2100 Hoone Rd. (across from Poipu Beach Park). © 808/742-7588. www.brenneckes.com. Main courses $9–$30. AE, DC, DISC, MC, V. Daily 11am–10pm (street-side deli takeout, daily 8am–9pm).

Keoki's Paradise STEAK/SEAFOOD   Keoki's Paradise is sprawling and lively and has improved with the years, with lunch favorites that include a fresh ahi sandwich, fresh-fish tacos, Thai shrimp sticks, and chicken Caesar salad—all good and affordable. In the evenings, regulars tout the fresh fish crusted in lemongrass, basil, and bread crumbs. When it's time for dessert, the original Hula pie from Kimo's in Lahaina is an ever-sinful presence. The cafe in the bar area serves lighter fare and features live Hawaiian music on Thursday and Friday nights and Sunday afternoon.

In Poipu Shopping Village, 2360 Kiahuna Plantation Dr. ✆ 808/742-7534. Reservations recommended. Main courses $6–$12 lunch, $15–$24 dinner. AE, DC, DISC, MC, V. Daily 5–10pm in the main dining room and cafe menu daily 11am–midnight.

Pomodoro ★ ITALIAN   Pomodoro is the Italian magnet of the west side, a small, casual, and intimate second-floor dining room with a bar, potted plants, soft lighting, and pleasing Italian music. It's a warm, welcoming place where Hawaiian hospitality meets European flavors: homemade garlic focaccia, home-made mozzarella, chicken saltimbocca, and homemade pastas (cannelloni, man-icotti, and excellent lasagna, the house specialty). Whether you order the veal, chicken, scampi, calamari, or very fresh, organic green salads, you'll appreciate the wonderful home-style flavor and the polite, efficient servers.

In Rainbow Plaza, Kaumualii Hwy. (Hwy. 50), Kalaheo (inland from Poipu). ✆ 808/332-5945. Reservations recommended. Main courses $11–$20. MC, V. Daily 5:30–10pm.

INEXPENSIVE

Brick Oven Pizza PIZZA   A Kalaheo fixture for nearly 25 years, Brick Oven is the quintessential mom-and-pop business, serving pizza cooked directly on the brick hearth, brushed with garlic butter and topped with real cheeses and long-simmering sauces. This is the real thing! You have a choice of whole-wheat or white crust, plus many toppings: house-made Italian sausage, Portuguese sausage, bay shrimp, anchovies, smoked ham, vegetarian options, and more. The result: very popular pizza, particularly when topped with fresh garlic and served with Gordon Biersch beer. The seafood-style pizza-bread sandwiches are big at lunch, and the "Super Pizza" with everything on it—that's *amore.*

2–2555 Kaumualii Hwy. (Hwy. 50), Kalaheo (inland from Poipu). ✆ 808/332-8561. Sandwiches less than $6.70; pizzas $9–$29. Tues–Sun 11am–10pm.

Kalaheo Coffee Co. & Cafe COFFEEHOUSE/CAFE   John Ferguson has long been one of our favorite Kauai chefs, and his cafe is a coffee lover's fantasy: Kauai Estate Peaberry, Kona dark roast, Maui's Kaanapali Estate, Molokai Estate, Guatemalan French roast, Colombian, Costa Rican, Sumatran, and African coffees—you can visit the world on a coffee bean! The coffeehouse also serves masterful breakfasts: Bonzo Breakfast Burritos (sautéed ham, peppers, mushrooms, onions, and olives scrambled with cheese and served with salsa and sour cream); veggie omelets with sun-dried tomatoes and mushrooms; Belgian waffles; and bagels. At lunch, the fabulous grilled-turkey burgers (heaped with grilled onions and mushrooms on a sourdough bun) are the headliner on a list of winners. Fresh-from-the-garden salads brighten up the day. The tasty, inex-pensive soup changes daily. The cinnamon "knuckles" (baked fresh daily), lilikoi cheesecake, and fresh apple pie and carrot cake are more reasons to stop by.

2–2436 Kaumualii Hwy. (Hwy. 50), Kalaheo (inland from Poipu). ✆ 808/332-5858. Most items less than $7.95. DISC, MC, V. Mon–Fri 6am–3pm; Sat 6:30am–3pm; Sun 6:30am–2pm.

Tomkats Grille AMERICAN/GRILL   Fried appetizers, inexpensive New York steak, rotisserie chicken, seafood salad with fresh catch, and sandwiches and burgers are among the offerings at the Grille, in a serene garden setting in Old Koloa Town. Old-fashioned brews are big here—everything from Watney's to Samuel Adams to Guinness Stout plus 2 dozen others, all the better to wash down the spicy jalapeños stuffed with cream cheese. For the reckless: the Cats' Combo, a basket of jumbo onion rings, mozzarella sticks, zucchini, and mush-rooms, all dangerously fried.

5404 Koloa Rd., Old Koloa Town. ℂ 808/742-8887. Main courses $6–$17. DC, MC, V. Daily 11am–10pm. Bar daily until midnight. Main courses $5–$18. DC, MC, V. Daily 11am–10pm. Happy hour daily 4–6pm; bar daily until midnight.

WESTERN KAUAI

Green Garden AMERICAN/ISLAND   This Hanapepe landmark continues a decades-old tradition of offering local fare amid layers of foliage inside and out. A riot of fishing balls suspended in nets, plants everywhere, and a labyrinthine dining room make for a unique environment. The Green Garden is known for its inexpensive fresh-fish sandwiches, lilikoi-cream pies, and, at dinner, the kiawe-grilled fresh-fish specials (onaga, opakapaka, and ehu) that come with soup and salad.

Hwy. 50, Hanapepe. ℂ 808/335-5422. Reservations recommended for dinner. Sandwiches and plate lunches $6.50; dinner main courses $15–$28. AE, MC, V. Mon and Wed–Sat 10:30am–2pm and 5–9pm; Sun 7:30am–2pm and 5–9pm.

Hanapepe Cafe & Espresso Bar ★★ GOURMET VEGETARIAN/ITALIAN The big pluses: excellent slack-key guitar music on the sound system and delectable, wholesome vegetarian fare in a casual, winning ambience. The espresso, pancakes (multigrain with bananas, multigrain with apple-spice, and so on), and homemade sourdough French toast served with fresh bananas and real maple syrup are major morning attractions. The several varieties of garden burger elevate this modest staple to gourmet status: You can top yours with sautéed mushrooms, grilled onions, pesto, fresh-grated Parmesan, and other choices. Other notables: fresh rosemary home fries, a heroic grilled vegetable sandwich, and whole roasted garlic heads. On the Friday night dinner menu, the Italian specialties shine: southwestern-style lasagna (with green chiles, polenta, and sun-dried tomatoes); lasagna quattro formaggio with spinach, mushrooms, and four cheeses; crepes; and the nightly special with the cafe's famous marinara sauce—terrific choices all.

3830 Hanapepe Rd., Hanapepe. ℂ 808/335-5011. Reservations recommended for dinner. Lunch main courses $6–$9; dinner main courses $18–$19. DISC, MC, V. Tues–Sat 9am–2pm (coffee and dessert until 3pm); Fri 6–9pm.

Toi's Thai Kitchen THAI/AMERICAN   A west Kauai staple, Toi's has gained a following for its affordable, authentic Thai food and a casual atmosphere. Tucked into a corner of a small shopping complex (look for the McDonald's on the highway), Toi's serves savory dishes utilizing fresh herbs and local ingredients, many of them from the owner's garden. Popular items include the house specialty, Toi's Temptation (homegrown herbs, coconut milk, lemongrass, and your choice of seafood, meat, or tofu); the vegetable curries; shrimp satay; and ginger-sauce nua (your choice of seafood, meat, or tofu in a fresh ginger stir-fry). Most of the rice, noodle, soup, curry, and main-course selections allow you to choose from among pork, chicken, seafood, beef, or vegetarian options. Buttered garlic nua, peanut-rich satays, and stir-fried Basil Delight are among Toi's many tasty preparations. All dishes come with green-papaya salad, dessert, and a choice of jasmine, sticky, or brown rice.

In the Eleele Shopping Center, Eleele. ℂ 808/335-3111. Main courses $9–$17. DC, MC, V. Mon–Sat 10:30am–2pm and 5:30–9:30pm.

Waimea Brewing Company ECLECTIC   This popular brewery in the Waimea Plantation Cottages is a welcome addition to the dry west side, serving pub fare with a multiethnic twist. "Small plates" for grazing are composed of ale-steamed shrimp, taro leaf and goat cheese dip with warm pita bread, or ahi-roasted corn chowder. "Big plates" come with roasted chicken, steak, short ribs, or kalua pork. In between are soups, salads, and sandwiches, including fresh catch. The beer is brewed on the premises. It's a pleasant stop, one of the top two places in Waimea for dinner.

In Waimea Plantation Cottages, 9400 Kaumualii Hwy., Waimea. © 808/338-9733. Main courses $8–$19. AE, MC, V. Daily 11am–9pm.

Wrangler's Steakhouse STEAKHOUSE   Good service and pleasant veranda seating are among the pluses of this family-run operation. Western touches abound: a wagon in the loft, log-framed booths with gas lanterns, and lauhala paniolo hats in the made-in-Hawaii gift shop. A combination of cowboy, plantation, and island traditions, Wrangler's serves steak, and lots of it—big, hand-selected cuts—and adds some island touches, from vegetable tempura to grilled steak to ahi with penne pasta. Families like Wrangler's because of its multi-course dinners that won't break the bank.

9852 Kaumualii Hwy., Waimea. © 808/338-1218. Lunch $8–$12; dinner main courses $17–$30. AE, MC, V. Mon–Thurs 11am–8:30pm; Fri 11am–9pm; Sat 5–9pm.

THE COCONUT COAST

You'll find the restaurants in this section on the "Coconut Coast Accommodations & Dining" map on p. 547.

EXPENSIVE

A Pacific Cafe Kauai ★★★ HAWAII REGIONAL/MEDITERRANEAN This is foodie central on Kauai: casual, chic, crowded, and buzzing with energy. It was Jean-Marie Josselin's first Hawaii restaurant, and it remains (along with the Pacific Cafe in Kihei, Maui) a bright star in Josselin's culinary empire. Here you'll find light-as-air, deep-fried tiger-eye sushi with wasabi beurre blanc; wok-charred mahimahi with garlic-sesame crust and lime-ginger-butter sauce; scallop ravioli in lime-ginger sauce; and firecracker salmon—the Josselin signatures. The menu, which changes by the day, offers a hearty selection from the wood-burning grill, such as opah with olives and feta, fire-roasted ono with Thai coconut green curry sauce, and spicy pork tenderloin with banana barbecue sauce. Josselin has a marvelous way with clams, rice, fish, sauces, meats, and fresh Kauai products. There are always ample appetizers in all price ranges, making this a restaurant that can be expensive, but doesn't have to be.

In Kauai Shopping Village, 4–831 Kuhio Hwy., Kapaa. © 808/822-0013. Reservations recommended. Main courses $20–$24. AE, DC, DISC, MC, V. Daily 5:30–9:30pm.

MODERATE

The Bull Shed STEAK/SEAFOOD   The informality and oceanfront location are big pluses, but Kauai regulars also tout the steaks and chops—prime rib, Australian rack of lamb, garlic tenderloin—and the fresh catch. The seafood selection includes broiled shrimp, Alaskan king crab, and Parmesan-drenched scallops. Dinner orders include rice and the salad bar, and combination dinners target the ambivalent, with chicken, steak, seafood, and lobster pairings. The salad bar alone is a value, and the entrees are so big they're often shared.

796 Kuhio Hwy., Waipouli. © 808/822-3791. Reservations recommended for parties of 6 or more. Main courses $12–$30. AE, DC, DISC, MC, V. Daily 5:30–10pm.

Buzz's Steak & Lobster STEAK/SEAFOOD   For years an anchor of the Coconut Marketplace, Buzz's buzzes with happy-hour celebrants who gather for the cheap exotic drinks and vegetable crudités, or whatever appetizers the chef pulls out of his toque. Soup and salad and a fresh ahi sandwich are lunchtime staples in this steak-and-seafood restaurant. But it's popular for dinner, too, when choices range from an early-bird dinner special to the ever-popular mahimahi amandine, fresh fish, and steak-and-lobster combinations. With the $6.95 salad bar, this is a budget-friendly place.

In the Coconut Marketplace, 484 Kuhio Hwy., Kapaa. ℂ 808/822-0041. Reservations recommended for dinner. Main courses $7.50 and less at lunch, $8–$39 at dinner. AE, DC, DISC, MC, V. Daily 12–2:30pm and 4:30–9pm. Bar daily until 11:30pm; happy hour daily 3–4:30pm.

Caffè Coco ★★ GOURMET BISTRO   This gets our vote for the most charming ambience on Kauai, with gourmet fare cooked to order, and at cafe prices. Food gets a lot of individual attention here. Caffè Coco appears just off the main road at the edge of a cane field in Wailua, its backyard shaded by pomelo, avocado, mango, tangerine, lychee, and banana trees, with a view of the Sleeping Giant Mountain. The trees provide many of the ingredients for the muffins, chutneys, salsas, and fresh-squeezed juices that Ginger Carlson whips up in her kitchen. Seats are indoors (beyond the black-light art gallery) or on the gravel-floored back courtyard, where tiki torches flicker at night. From interior design to cooking, this is clearly a showcase for Carlson's creativity. The food is excellent, with vegetarian and other healthful delights such as spanakopita, homemade chai, Greek salad and fish wraps, macadamia nut-black sesame ahi with wasabi cream, and an excellent tofu-and-roast-veggie wrap. Although the regular menu is limited, there are many impressive specials. Service can be, to say the least, laid-back. Next door, Carlson's sister runs **Bambulei,** a vintage shop of treasures (see "Shops & Galleries," later in this chapter).

4–369 Kuhio Hwy., Wailua. ℂ 808/822-7990. Reservations recommended for dinner. Main courses $7–$18; specials usually less than $20. MC, V. dinner Tues–Sun 5–9pm.

Coconuts Island Style Grill ★ AMERICAN/ECLECTIC   Kauai's newest sensation is right on the highway, next to Taco Bell, where fans line up for the happy-hour pupu and affordable, tasty fare. Coconuts is upbeat and busy, with a cheerfully tropical dining room of bamboo ceilings and coconut everything: bar floor, fixtures, furniture, and lights. There are lots of wines by the glass, good beers on tap, and a wide-ranging menu, including the best-selling teriyaki-dipped fresh salmon, a fresh catch for only $15 (oven-roasted, with kaffir lime broth and wasabi mashed potatoes), and an excellent seafood chowder. Grilled polenta with herb pesto and braised spinach, the burger with house-made potato chips, and shrimp cakes are also popular. The appetizer menu—nine items, from baby back ribs to lobster ravioli—is a hit from the time the doors open at 4pm.

4–919 Kuhio Hwy. ℂ 808/823-8777. Reservations accepted only for 6 or more. Main courses $8–$22. AE, DC, MC, V. Mon–Sat beginning at 4pm for pupu, 5:30–10pm dinner.

Wailua Family Restaurant AMERICAN/LOCAL   The salad bars, efficient service, and family-friendly feeling here are legendary. Seniors and kids get discounts on the huge menu and a cross-cultural salad bar that includes a Mexican bar, pasta bar, sushi section, homemade soups, and ethnic samplings from Korean, Japanese, Filipino, and Hawaiian traditions. Everything, from the menu to the servings to the budget-friendly prices, winds up generous and big at Wailua Family Restaurant. The papaya is always freshly sliced at breakfast (there's a breakfast buffet on Sat and Sun), the cornbread is good, and the eggs Benedict comes with a choice of ham or turkey. You can also order mahimahi or ono with the eggs for a high-protein start. The all-you-can-eat buffet (soup, salad, pasta, taco, and desserts) is a steal for $12, and the seafood, sandwiches, stir-fries, teriyaki steak, and seafood combo are among the American and ethnic classics on the menu. There is outdoor seating now, too.

4361 Kuhio Hwy, across from Kinipopo Shopping Village. © 808/822-3325. Reservations not accepted. Breakfast $6–$8; lunch most items under $8; dinner main courses $9–$16. MC, V. Sun–Thurs 6:30am–9:30pm; Fri–Sat 6:30am–10pm.

Wailua Marina Restaurant AMERICAN   This is a strange but lovable place, anti-nouvelle to the end. We recommend the open-air seating along the Wailua River, where you can watch the riverboats heading for the Fern Grotto over sandwiches (mahimahi is a favorite) and salads. The interior is cavernous, with a high ceiling and stuffed fish adorning the upper walls—bordering on weird, but we love it anyway. The salad bar makes the place friendlier to dieters and vegetarians; otherwise, you'll find the Alaskan king crab legs with filet mignon (or filet paired with lobster tail), stuffed prawns, famous hot lobster salad, steamed mullet, teriyaki spareribs, and some 40 other down-home items heavy in the sauces and gravies. Although the open salad bar is a meal in itself, the more reckless can try the mayo-laden minilobster salad appetizer, the crab-stuffed mushrooms, or the baked stuffed island chicken. *Money-saving tip:* the early bird specials (5–6pm) start at $9 for spaghetti dinner and go up to $11 for a mixed plate of shrimp tempura, chicken yakitori, and teriyaki top sirloin.

5971 Kuhio Hwy., Wailua. © 808/822-4311. Reservations recommended. Lunch $7–$10; dinner main courses $9–$28. AE, MC, V. Tues–Sun 10:30am–2pm and 5–8:30pm.

INEXPENSIVE

Aloha Diner HAWAIIAN   It's funky and quirky and claims legions of fans for its authentic Hawaiian plates. Lunch and dinner specials offer samplings of kalua pig, laulau, lomi salmon, fried whole *akule* (big-eyed scad, hooked not netted), and other Hawaiian dishes. Saimin and wonton min are the other favorites at this tiny diner, where steaming dishes and perspiring faces are cooled by electric fans whirring over Formica tables. Although the Aloha Diner may intimidate the uninitiated, it's pure comfort for lovers of Hawaiian food.

971–F Kuhio Hwy., Waipouli. © 808/822-3851. Most items less than $7.50. No credit cards. Mon–Sat 10:30am–2:30pm; Tues–Sat 5:30–9pm.

Bubba Burgers AMERICAN   Here at the house of Bubba they dish out humor, great T-shirts, and burgers nonpareil, along with tempeh burgers for vegetarians. Grilled fresh-fish sandwiches cater to the sensible, fish and chips to the carefree, and fish burgers to the undecided. But old-fashioned hamburgers are still the main attraction. You can order the Slopper (open-faced with chili), the half-pound Big Bubba (3 patties), the Hubba Bubba (with rice, hot dog, and chili—a Bubba's plate lunch), and others. Chicken burgers, Bubba's famous Budweiser chili, and other American standards are also served up here, where the burger is king, attitude reigns, and lettuce and tomato cost extra. For a burger joint, it's big on fish, too, with a daily trio of fresh-fish specials, fish burgers, and fish and chips.

4–1421 Kuhio Hwy., Kapaa. © 808/823-0069. All items less than $6.95. MC, V. Daily 10:30am–8pm.

The King and I THAI   This medium-size restaurant, in a small and nondescript roadside complex, serves reasonably priced specials and vegetarian selections, including spring rolls, salads, curries, and stir-fries. The owners grow their own herbs for the savory curries and seasonings on the menu. At dinner, the pad

Thai noodles with shrimp have a special touch and are a popular counterpoint to the red, green, and yellow curries. The vegetarian menu is generous—everything from noodles to spring rolls to curries and eggplant/tofu—but most diners come back for the Evil Jungle Prince, your choice of veggies, chicken, or fish in a sauce of coconut milk, spices, and kaffir-lime leaves.

In Waipouli Plaza, 4–901 Kuhio Hwy. © 808/822-1642. Reservations recommended for dinner. Main courses $6–$11. AE, DC, DISC, MC, V. Mon–Fri 11am–1:30pm; daily 4:30–9:30pm.

Kountry Kitchen AMERICAN Forget counting calories when you sit down to the brawny omelets here. You can choose your own fillings from several possibilities, among them a kimchi omelet with cream cheese and several vegetable, meat, and cheese combinations. Sandwiches and American dinners (steak, fish, and chicken) are standard coffeehouse fare, but there are sometimes fresh-fish specials that stand out. *Warning:* Sit as far away from the grill as possible; the smell of grease travels—and clings to your clothes.

1485 Kuhio Hwy., Kapaa. © 808/822-3511. Main courses$5–$8.95. MC, V. Daily 6am–2pm.

Mermaids Cafe ⭑ HEALTHFUL/ISLAND STYLE Don't you love these places that use fresh local ingredients, make everything to order, and barely charge anything for all that trouble? A tiny sidewalk cafe with brisk takeout and a handful of tables on Kapaa's main drag, Mermaids takes kaffir lime, lemongrass, local lemons (Meyers when available), and organic herbs, when possible, to make the sauces and beverages to go with its toothsome dishes. Sauces are lively and healthful, such as the peanut satay made with lemon juice instead of fish sauce. It's served in the tofu or chicken satay, chicken coconut curry plate, and chicken satay wrap. The seared ahi wrap is made with the chef's special blend of garlic, jalapeño, lemongrass, kaffir lime, basil, and cilantro, then wrapped in a spinach tortilla—fabulous. The fresh-squeezed lemonade is made daily, and you can choose white or organic brown rice. These special touches elevate the simple classics to dreamy taste sensations; if you don't believe me, try the coconut custard French toast, made with Hawaiian guava-taro bread and served with fresh local fruit—divine.

1384 Kuhio Hwy, Kapaa. © 808/821-2026. Main courses $6.95–$8.95. No credit cards. Mon–Sat 9am–9pm.

Norberto's El Cafe MEXICAN The lard-free, home-style Mexican fare here includes top-notch chiles rellenos with homemade everything, vegetarian selections by request, and, if you're lucky, fresh-fish enchiladas. All of the sauces are made from scratch, and the salsa comes red-hot with homegrown chili peppers fresh from the chef's garden. Norberto's signature is the spinachy Hawaiian taro-leaf enchiladas, a Mexican version of laulau, served with cheese and taro or with chicken.

4–1373 Kuhio Hwy., Kapaa. © 808/822-3362. Reservations recommended for parties of 6 or more. Main courses $3.25–$8.45; complete dinners $13–$17. MC, V. Mon–Sat 5:30–9pm.

Ono Family Restaurant AMERICAN Breakfast is a big deal here, with eggs Florentine (2 poached eggs, blanched spinach, and hollandaise sauce) leading the pack, and eggs Canterbury (much like eggs Benedict, but with more ingredients) following close behind. The Garden Patch, a dollop of fried rice topped with fresh steamed vegetables, scrambled eggs, and hollandaise sauce, is a real conscience-buster. Steak and eggs; banana, coconut, and macadamia-nut pancakes; and dozens of omelet choices also attract throngs of loyalists.

Lunch is no slouch either, with scads of fish, veggie, steak, tuna, and turkey sandwiches to choose from, and Ono beef or buffalo burgers with various toppings highlighting the menu. The gourmet hamburger with fries and soup demands an after-lunch siesta.

4–1292 Kuhio Hwy., Kapaa. (C) 808/822-1710. Most items less than $8. AE, DC, DISC, MC, V. Daily 7am–2pm.

Sukhothai Restaurant THAI/VIETNAMESE/CHINESE Curries, saimin, Chinese soups, satays, Vietnamese pho, and a substantial vegetarian menu are a few of the features of this unobtrusive—but extremely popular—Thai restaurant. Menu items appeal to many tastes and include 85 Vietnamese, Chinese, and Thai choices, along with much-loved curries and the best-selling pad Thai noodles. The coconut/lemongrass/kaffir lime soups (8 choices) are the Sukhothai highlights, along with the red and green curries.

In the Kapaa Shopping Center (next to Kapaa's Big Save Market), 4–1105 Kuhio Hwy., Kapaa. (C) 808/821-1224. Main courses $8–$17. AE, DISC, MC, V. Daily 10:30am–3pm and 5–9pm.

Waipouli Restaurant AMERICAN/JAPANESE Modest home-style cooking at low, low prices attracts throngs of local folks who love the saimin, pancakes, and $3 "rice bowls" with chili, teriyaki beef, chicken katsu, or "anything," says the owner. The saimin is great here, especially the miso saimin special, a hefty bowl of steaming noodles with tofu, vegetables, and a boiled egg (but hold the Spam, please!). There are always inexpensive dinner specials, ranging from sukiyaki to roast chicken. This place is crowded from breakfast to closing.

In Waipouli Town Center, Waipouli. (C) 808/822-9311. Most lunch items less than $7; dinner less than $9. No credit cards. Daily 7am–2pm; Tues–Sat 5–8:30pm.

EN ROUTE TO THE NORTH SHORE

Duane's Ono-Char Burger HAMBURGER STAND We can't imagine Anahola without this roadside burger stand; it's been serving up hefty, all-beef burgers for generations. (And now there are Boca burgers, for vegetarians.) The teriyaki sauce and blue cheese are only part of the secret of Duane's beefy, smoky, and legendary ono-char burgers, which come in several styles: teriyaki, mushroom, cheddar, barbecue, and the Special, with grilled onions, sprouts, and two cheeses. The broiled fish sandwich (another marvel of the seasoned old grill) and the marionberry ice-cream shake, a three-berry combo, are popular as well.

On Kuhio Hwy., Anahola. (C) 808/822-9181. Hamburgers $3.90–$6.20. MC, V. Mon–Sat 10am–6pm; Sun 11am–6pm.

THE NORTH SHORE

You'll find the restaurants in this section on the "Kauai's North Shore: Princeville & Hanalei" map on p. 602.

EXPENSIVE

La Cascata (★★★) MEDITERRANEAN/SOUTHERN ITALIAN The North Shore's special-occasion restaurant is sumptuous—a Sicilian spree in Eden. Try to get here before dark, so you can enjoy the views of Bali Hai, the persimmon-colored sunset, and the waterfalls of Waialeale, all an integral part of the feast. Click your heels on the terra-cotta floors, take in the trompe l'oeil vines, train your eyes through the concertina windows, and pretend you're being served on a terrazzo in Sicily. The menu dazzles quietly with its Mediterranean-inspired offerings and fresh local ingredients. Polenta, charred peppers, Kauai asparagus, organic Kauai vegetables, risottos, ragouts, grilled fresh fish, and vegetable napoleons are colorful and tasty, and beautifully presented.

In the Princeville Resort, 5520 Ka Haku Rd. ℂ **808/826-9644.** Reservations recommended for dinner. Main courses $24–$34; 3-course prix fixe dinner $50. AE, DC, DISC, MC, V. Daily 6–10pm.

MODERATE

Hanalei Dolphin Restaurant & Fish Market ✦ SEAFOOD Hidden behind a gallery called Ola's are this fish market and adjoining steak-and-seafood restaurant, on the banks of the Hanalei River. Particularly inviting are the fresh-fish sandwiches, served under umbrellas at river's edge. Most appealing (besides the river view) are the appetizers: artichokes steamed or stuffed with garlic, but-ter, and cheese; buttery stuffed mushrooms; and ceviche fresh from the fish mar-ket, with a jaunty dash of green olives. From fresh catch to baked shrimp to Alaskan king crab and chicken marinated in soy sauce, the Dolphin has stayed with the tried and true.

5144 Kuhio Hwy., Hanalei. ℂ **808/826-6113.** Main courses $15–$36. MC, V. Daily 11am–10pm. (Fish mar-ket daily 11am–7pm.)

Hanalei Gourmet AMERICAN The wood floors, wooden benches, and blackboards of the old Hanalei School, built in 1926, are a haven for today's Hanalei hipsters noshing on the Tu Tu Tuna (far-from-prosaic tuna salad with green beans, potatoes, niçoise olives, and hard-boiled eggs); fresh grilled ahi sand-wiches; roasted eggplant sandwiches; chicken-salad boats (in papaya or avocado, with macadamia nuts and sans mayonnaise); and other selections. This is an informal cross-cultural tasting, from stir-fried veggies over udon to Oriental ahi-pasta salad to artichoke hearts fried in beer batter. Big Tim's burger is, unsurpris-ingly, big, and the sandwich selection, on fresh-baked bread, hits the timeless deli faves, from roast beef and pastrami to smoked turkey and chicken salad. The TV over the bar competes with the breathtaking view of the Hanalei mountains and waterfalls, and the wooden floors keep the noise level high (the music on the sound system can be almost deafening). Nightly live music adds to the fun.

In the Old Hanalei Schoolhouse, 5–5161 Kuhio Hwy., Hanalei. ℂ **808/826-2524.** Main courses $7–$23. DC, DISC, MC, V. Sun–Thurs 8am–10:30pm; Fri–Sat 8am–11:30pm.

Kilauea Bakery & Pau Hana Pizza ✦ PIZZA/BAKERY When owner, baker, and avid diver Tom Pickett spears an ono and smokes it himself, his catch appears on the Billie Holiday pizza, guaranteed to obliterate the blues with its brilliant notes of Swiss chard, roasted onions, Gorgonzola-rosemary sauce, and moz-zarella. And the much-loved bakery puts out guava sourdough; Hanalei poi sour-dough; fresh chive, goat-cheese, and sun-dried-tomato bread; blackberry–white chocolate scones; and other fine baked goods. The breads go well with the soups and hot lunch specials, and the pastries with the new full-service espresso bar, which serves not only the best of the bean, but also blended frozen drinks and such up-to-the-minute voguish things as iced chai and Mexican chocolate smoothies (with cinnamon). We also love the fresh vegetables in olive oil and herbs, baked in a baguette; the olive tapenade; and the classic scampi pizza with tiger prawns, roasted garlic, capers, and cheeses. The Picketts have added a small dining room, and the few outdoor picnic tables under umbrellas are as inviting as ever. The macadamia nut butter cookies and lilikoi fruit Danishes are sublime.

In Kong Lung Center, Kilauea Rd. (off Hwy. 56 on the way to the Kilauea Lighthouse), Kilauea. ℂ **808/828-2020.** Pizzas $11–$26. MC, V. Daily 6:30am–9pm.

Lighthouse Bistro Kilauea ✦✦✦ CONTINENTAL/PACIFIC RIM/ ITALIAN Even if you're not on your way to the legendary Kilauea Lighthouse, this bistro is so good it's worth a special trip. The charming green-and-white wooden building next to Kong Lung Store has open sides, old-fashioned plantation architecture, open-air seating, trellises, and high ceilings. The ambience is wonderful, with a retro feeling; it's not as polished as Poipu's Plantation Gardens but has its own casual appeal. (In fact, it's the North Shore version of Casa di Amici in Poipu, p. 560.) The food is excellent, an eclectic selection that highlights local ingredients in everything from fresh fish tacos and fresh fish burgers to mac-nut-crusted ahi and four preparations of fresh catch. The mango-cherry chicken in light lilikoi sauce is a tropical delight, and the last time I visited, the ahi quesadilla came beautifully presented with rice, black beans, and spicy condiments on a plate painted with purple cabbage shavings and herbs—much more elegant than usual lunchtime fare.

In Kong Lung Center, Kilauea Rd. (off Hwy. 56 on the way to the Kilauea Lighthouse), Kilauea. ⓒ 808/828-0481. Reservations recommended. Lunch $7–$11; dinner main courses $11–$27. MC, V. Daily 11am–2pm and 5:30–9:30pm.

Postcards Cafe ★★ GOURMET SEAFOOD/NATURAL FOODS The charming plantation-style building that used to be the Hanalei Museum is now Hanalei's gourmet central. Postcards is known for its use of healthful ingredients, fresh from the island and creatively prepared and presented (like fresh fish, grilled or blackened, with macadamia-nut butter, honey Dijon, or peppered-pineapple sage), and for its imaginative use of local ingredients (as in taro fritters served with papaya salsa). Other choices include Thai summer rolls, sautéed prawns, nori rolls (filled with rice, vegetables, and tempeh), and ever-popular laulau-style fish tacos and seafood specials. Omelets, bagels, eggs Florentine, hotcakes, and muffins are some of the day's starters. In the front yard, an immense, mossy, hollowed-out stone serves as a freestanding lily pond and roadside landmark. Great menu, presentation, and ambience—a winner.

On Kuhio Hwy. (at the entrance to Hanalei town). ⓒ 808/826-1191. Reservations recommended for dinner. Main courses $13–$26. AE, DC, MC, V. Daily 8–11am (later on weekends) and 6–9pm.

Sushi & Blues ★ SUSHI/PACIFIC RIM This second-floor oasis has copper tables and a copper-topped bar, large picture windows for gazing at the Hanalei waterfalls, and, most important, chefs who know their sushi. Traditional sushi, fusion sushi, and hot Pacific Rim dishes for those who aren't sushi lovers please diners of every stripe. Big hits: the temaki hand rolls; the Las Vegas roll, a heroic composition of ahi, hamachi, and avocado, dipped in tempura batter and quickly fried, hot on the outside and chilled on the inside; the Rainbow Roll, a super-duper California roll with eight different types of fish; and fresh fish prepared several ways, in fusion flavorings involving mango, garlic, sake, sesame, coconut, passion fruit, and other Pacific Rim preparations. The action fires up Wednesday, Thursday, Saturday, and Sunday from 8:30pm on, with live music, from Hawaiian to blues, jazz to rock and roll.

In Ching Young Village, Hanalei. ⓒ 808/826-9701. www.sushiandblues.com. Reservations recommended for parties of 6 or more. Main courses $18–$23; sushi rolls $4 and up. MC, V. Tues–Sun 6–10pm.

Zelo's Beach House ★ STEAK/SEAFOOD Good food, concrete floors, window tables with flower boxes, seating on the deck with mountain views—what's not to like? Along with Sushi & Blues, Zelo's is the hippest, most popular spot in Hanalei, a "beach house" spiced up with South Pacific kitsch, a wide variety of coffee drinks, excellent mai tais, and sliding doors all around. The congenial bar area has a tin roof and ironwood poles, and a one-person canoe hangs overhead. Gourmet burgers, pastas, steaks, 50 different microbrews and 30 tropical drinks, a wonderful salad in a large clam-shaped bowl, warm bread, seafood chimichangas, and a good seafood chowder are some of the attractions. Zelo's is always packed, and when happy hour rolls around (from 3:30–5:30pm), the inexpensive tap beers and tacos start flowing. A children's menu, appetizers and entrees in all price ranges, and the new Martini Madness menu make Zelo's a Hanalei must, especially if you can snag a table on the deck.

Kuhio Hwy. and Aku Rd., Hanalei. ℂ 808/826-9700. Reservations recommended for parties of 6 or more. Main courses $8–$12 lunch, $9–$25 dinner. MC, V. Winter daily 11am–9:30pm; summer daily 11am–10pm.

INEXPENSIVE

Bubba Burgers AMERICAN   Green picnic tables and umbrellas thatched with coconut leaves stand out against the yellow walls of Bubba's, the burger joint with attitude. The burgers are as flamboyant as the exterior. This North Shore version of the Kapaa fixture (p. 566) has the same menu, same ownership, and same high-quality, all-beef burgers that have made the original such a smashing success.

In Hanalei Center (on the town's main road), Hanalei. ℂ 808/826-7839. All items less than $6.95. MC, V. Daily 10:30am–6pm.

Starvin Marvin's Kilauea Deli AMERICAN   In the same building where the former Roadrunner Café once operated, this creative new deli now serves perfect picnic treats like scrumptious, oversize sandwiches (fresh grilled fish, roasted turkey, black forest ham, curried chicken and basil, and grilled veggies); mouth watering quiches (grilled veggie with gorgonzola and sundried tomatoes); an array of salads; and ono desserts (a selection of cheese cakes, cakes, and truffles). They also serve breakfast (mac nut pancakes, breakfast burrito, and on Saturday their famous eggs benedict, either vegetarian style or the classic). All this is offered at wallet-pleasing prices. You can eat in the dining room or take out. The wonderful assortment of unique drinks includes fresh lemon-grass ginger brew, chai spiced greet tea, and a killer lemonade.

2430 Oka St., Kilauea. ℂ 808/828-0726. Breakfast under $9. Sandwiches (with salad and a fresh-baked cookie) $8. MC, V. Mon–Fri 7:30am–6pm; Sat 7:30am–3pm.

5 Beaches

Eons of wind and rain have created this geological masterpiece of an island, with its fabulous beaches, like Hanalei, Kee, and Kalapaki. All are accessible to the public, as stipulated by Hawaii law, and many have facilities. For beach toys and equipment, head to **Activity Warehouse,** 788 Kuhio Hwy. (across from McDonald's), Kapaa (ℂ **800/688-0580** or 808/822-4000; www.travelhawaii.com); or **Chris the Fun Lady,** 4–746 Kuhio Hwy. (across from Waipouli Town Center), Kapaa (ℂ **808/822-7759;** www.christhefunlady.com).

LIHUE'S BEST BEACH
KALAPAKI BEACH 🐾

Any town would pay a fortune to have a beach like Kalapaki, one of Kauai's best, in its backyard. But little Lihue turns its back on Kalapaki; there's not even a sign pointing the way through the labyrinth of traffic to this graceful half moon of golden sand at the foot of the Marriott Resort & Beach Club. Fifty yards wide and a quarter-mile long, Kalapaki is protected by a jetty and patrolled by lifeguards, making it very safe for swimmers. The waves are good for surfing when there's a winter swell, and the view from the sand—of the steepled, 2,200-foot peaks of the majestic Haupu Ridge that shield Nawiliwili Bay—is awesome. Kalapaki is the best beach not only in Lihue but also on the whole east coast.

From Lihue Airport, turn left onto Kapule Highway (Hwy. 51) to Rice Street; turn left and go to the entrance of the Marriott; pass the hotel's porte cochere and turn right at the SHORELINE ACCESS sign. Facilities include lifeguards, free parking, restrooms, and showers; food and drink are available nearby at JJ's Broiler (p. 555).

THE POIPU RESORT AREA
MAHAULEPU BEACH ★★
Mahaulepu is the best-looking unspoiled beach in Kauai and possibly in the whole state. Its 2 miles of reddish-gold, grainy sand line the southeastern shore at the foot of 1,500-foot-high Haupu Ridge, just beyond the Hyatt Regency Poipu and McBryde sugarcane fields, which end in sand dunes and a forest of casuarina trees. Almost untouched by modern life, Mahaulepu is a great escape from the real world. It's ideal for beachcombing and shell hunting, but swimming can be risky, except in the reef-sheltered shallows 200 yards west of the sandy parking lot. There's no lifeguard, no facilities—just great natural beauty everywhere you look. (This beach is where George C. Scott portrayed Ernest Hemingway in the movie *Islands in the Stream.*) While you're here, see if you can find the Hawaiian petroglyph of a voyaging canoe carved in the beach rock.

To get here, drive past the Hyatt Regency Poipu 3 miles east on a red-dirt road, past the golf course and stables. Turn right at the T intersection; go 1 mile to the big sand dune, turn left, and drive a half-mile to a small lot under the trees.

POIPU BEACH PARK ★
Big, wide Poipu is actually two beaches in one; it's divided by a sandbar, called a *tombolo*. On the left, a lava-rock jetty protects a sandy-bottom pool that's perfect for children; on the right, the open bay attracts swimmers, snorkelers, and surfers. And everyone likes to picnic on the grassy lawn graced by coconut trees. You'll find excellent swimming, small tide pools for exploring, great reefs for snorkeling and diving, good fishing, nice waves for surfers, and a steady wind for windsurfers. Poipu attracts a daily crowd, but the density seldom approaches Waikiki levels, except on holidays. Facilities include restrooms, showers, picnic areas, Brennecke's Beach Broiler nearby (p. 561), and free parking in the red-dirt lot. To get here, turn on Poipu Beach Road, then turn right at Hoowili Road.

WESTERN KAUAI
SALT POND BEACH PARK
Hawaii's only salt ponds still in production are at Salt Pond Beach, just outside Hanapepe. Generations of locals have come here to swim, fish, and collect salt crystals that are dried in sunbeds. The tangy salt is used for health purposes and to cure fish and season food. The curved reddish-gold beach lies between two rocky points and features a protected reef, tide pools, and gentle waves. Swimming here is excellent, even for children; this beach is also good for diving, windsurfing, and fishing. Amenities include a lifeguard, showers, restrooms, camping area, picnic area, pavilion, and parking lot. To get here, take Highway 50 past Hanapepe and turn on Lokokai Road.

POLIHALE STATE PARK ★
This mini-Sahara on the western end of the island is Hawaii's biggest beach: 17 miles long and as wide as three football fields. This is a wonderful place to get away from it all, but don't forget your flip-flops—the midday sand is hotter than a lava flow. The golden sands wrap around Kauai's northwestern shore from

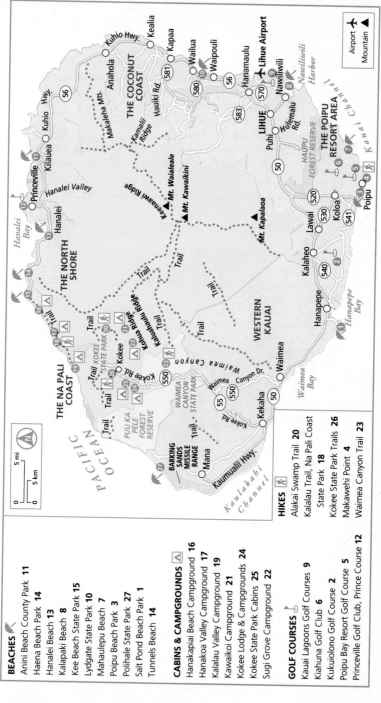

Beaches & Outdoor Pursuits on Kauai

BEACHES

Anini Beach County Park **11**
Haena Beach Park **14**
Hanalei Beach **13**
Kalapaki Beach **8**
Kee Beach State Park **15**
Lydgate State Park **10**
Mahaulepu Beach **7**
Poipu Beach Park **3**
Polihale State Park **27**
Salt Pond Beach Park **1**
Tunnels Beach **14**

CABINS & CAMPGROUNDS

Hanakapiai Beach Campground **16**
Hanakoa Valley Campground **17**
Kalalau Valley Campground **19**
Kawaikoi Campground **21**
Kokee Lodge & Campgrounds **24**
Kokee State Park Cabins **25**
Sugi Grove Campground **22**

GOLF COURSES

Kauai Lagoons Golf Courses **9**
Kiahuna Golf Club **6**
Kukuiolono Golf Course **2**
Poipu Bay Resort Golf Course **5**
Princeville Golf Club, Prince Course **12**

HIKES

Alakai Swamp Trail **20**
Kalalau Trail, Na Pali Coast State Park **18**
Kokee State Park Trails **26**
Makawehi Point **4**
Waimea Canyon Trail **23**

573

Frommer's Favorite Kauai Experiences

Snorkeling Kee Beach. Rent a mask, fins, and snorkel and enter a magical underwater world. Face down, you'll float like a leaf on a pond, watching brilliant fish dart here and there in water clear as day; a slow-moving turtle may even stop by to check you out. Face up, you'll contemplate green-velvet cathedral-like cliffs under a blue sky, with long-tailed tropical birds riding the trade winds. See p. 581.

Hiking Waimea Canyon, the Grand Canyon of the Pacific. Ansel Adams would have loved this ageless desert canyon, carved by an ancient river. Sunlight plays against its rustic red cliffs, burnt-orange pinnacles, and blue-green valleys. There's nothing else like it in the islands. See p. 585.

Wandering Around a High Mountain Forest. Kokee State Park, through Waimea Canyon at the end of Highway 550, is a combination rain forest and bog up around 4,000 feet. The park's 45 miles of trails offer everything from casual nature strolls to hardy camping and hiking adventures among the redwoods. See p. 585.

Strolling Through Hawaiian History. Old Waimea town looks so unassuming that you'd never guess it stood witness to a great many key events in Hawaii's history. This is the place where Capt. James Cook "discovered" the Hawaiian islands, where Russians once built a fort, and where New England missionaries arrived in 1820 to save the heathens. A self-guided walking-tour guide is available at **Waimea Public Library,** Kaumualii Highway (© **808/338-6848**). See "Waimea Town" under "Seeing the Sights," later in this chapter.

Taking a Long Walk on a Short (but Historic) Pier. First built in 1910, Hanalei's Pier was once a major shipping port for local farmers. Today, the rebuilt pier makes a great platform for swimming, fishing, and diving. It's at Black Pot Beach, where, in the olden days, local families would camp out all summer and always have something cooking in a

Kekaha plantation town, just beyond Waimea, to where the ridgebacks of the Na Pali Coast begin. The state park includes ancient Hawaiian *heiau* (temple) and burial sites, a view of the "forbidden" island of Niihau, and the famed **Barking Sands Beach,** where footfalls sound like a barking dog. (Scientists say that the grains of sand are perforated with tiny echo chambers, which emit a "barking" sound when they rub together.) Polihale also takes in the Pacific Missile Range Facility, a U.S. surveillance center that snooped on Russian subs during the Cold War, and Nohili Dune, which is nearly 3 miles long and 100 feet high in some places.

Be careful in winter, when high surf and rip currents make swimming dangerous. The safest place to swim is **Queen's Pond,** a small, shallow, sandy-bottom inlet protected from waves and shore currents. There are facilities for camping, as well as restrooms, showers, picnic tables, and pavilions. To get here, take Highway 50 past Barking Sands Missile Range and follow the signs through the sugarcane fields to Polihale. Local kids have been known to burgle rental cars out here, so don't leave tempting valuables in your car.

"black pot" on the shore. Black Pot—and all of Hanalei Beach—is great for swimming, snorkeling, and surfing. See p. 576.

Watching for Whales. Mahaulepu Beach, in the Poipu area, offers excellent land-based viewing conditions to spot whales that cruise by from December through April. See p. 572.

Journeying into Eden. For a glimpse of the spectacularly remote Na Pali Coast, all you need to do is hike the first 2 miles along the well-maintained Kalalau Trail into the first tropical valley, Hanakapiai. Hardier hikers can venture another 2 miles to the Hanakapiai waterfalls and pools. *Warning:* Na Pali's natural beauty is so enticing that you may want to keep going—but the trail turns rugged and extremely challenging after the 2-mile mark. Contact the State Division of Parks for a permit if you want to camp along the Trail. See "Hiking and Camping," later in this chapter.

Catching a Poipu Wave. Vividly turquoise, curling and totally tubular, big enough to hang ten yet small enough to bodysurf, the waves at Poipu are endless in their attraction. Grab a Boogie Board—you can rent one for just dollars a day—or simply jump in and go with the flow. See p. 572.

Watching the Hula. The Coconut Marketplace, on Kuhio Highway (Hwy. 56) between mile markers 6 and 7, hosts free shows every day at 5pm. Arrive early to get a good seat for the hour-long performances of both *kahiko* (ancient) and *auwana* (modern) hula. The real show-stoppers are the *keiki* (children) who perform. Don't forget your camera!

Bidding the Sun Aloha. Polihale State Park hugs Kauai's western shore for some 17 miles. It's a great place to bring a picnic dinner, stretch out on the sand, and toast the sun as it sinks into the Pacific, illuminating the island of Niihau in the distance. Queen's Pond has facilities for camping as well as restrooms, showers, picnic tables, and pavilions. See p. 572.

THE COCONUT COAST
LYDGATE STATE PARK ⊛

This seacoast park has a rock-wall fish pond that blunts the open ocean waves and provides the only safe swimming and the best snorkeling on the eastern shore. The 1-acre beach park, near the mouth of the Wailua River, is named for the Rev. J. M. Lydgate (1854–1922), founder and first pastor of Lihue English Union Church, who likely would be shocked at the public display of flesh here. This popular park is a great place for a picnic or for kite flying on the green. It's 5 miles north of Lihue on Kuhio Highway (Hwy. 56); look for the turnoff just before the Kauai Resort Hotel. Facilities include a pavilion, restrooms, outdoor showers, picnic tables, barbecue grills, lifeguards, and parking.

THE NORTH SHORE
ANINI BEACH COUNTY PARK ⊛⊛

Anini is Kauai's safest beach for swimming and windsurfing. It's also one of the island's most beautiful: It sits on a blue lagoon at the foot of emerald cliffs, looking more like Tahiti than almost any other strand in the islands. This 3-mile-long, gold-sand beach is shielded from the open ocean by the longest, widest fringing reef in Hawaii. With shallow water, 4 to 5 feet deep, it's also the very best snorkel spot on Kauai, even for beginners; on the northwest side, a channel in the reef runs out to the deep blue water with a 60-foot drop that attracts divers. Beachcombers love it, too: Seashells, cowries, and sometimes even rare Niihau shells can be found here. Anini has a park, a campground, picnic and barbecue facilities, and a boat-launch ramp; several B&Bs and vacation rentals are nearby. Follow Kuhio Highway (Hwy. 56) to Kilauea; take the second exit, called Kalihiwai Road (the 1st dead-ends at Kalihiwai Beach), and drive a half-mile toward the sea; turn left on Anini Beach Road.

HANALEI BEACH 🦀

Gentle waves roll across the face of half-moon Hanalei Bay, running up to the wide, golden sand; sheer volcanic ridges laced by waterfalls rise to 4,000 feet on the other side, 3 miles inland. Is there any beach with a better location? Celebrated in song and hula and featured on travel posters, this beach owes its natural beauty to its age—it's an ancient sunken valley with posterosional cliffs. Hanalei Bay indents the coast a full 1 mile inland and runs 2 miles point to point, with coral reefs on either side and a patch of coral in the middle—plus a sunken ship that belonged to a king, so divers love it. Swimming is excellent year-round, especially in summer, when Hanalei Bay becomes a big, placid lake. The aquamarine water is also great for bodyboarding, surfing, fishing, windsurfing, canoe paddling, kayaking, and boating (there's a boat ramp on the west bank of the Hanalei River). The area known as **Black Pot,** near the pier, is particularly good for swimming, snorkeling, and surfing. Facilities include a pavilion, restrooms, picnic tables, and parking. This beach is always packed with both locals and visitors, but you can usually find your own place in the sun by strolling down the shore; the bay is big enough for everyone.

To get here, take Kuhio Highway (Hwy. 56), which becomes Highway 560 after Princeville. In Hanalei town, make a right on Aku Road just after Tahiti Nui, then turn right again on Weke Road, which dead-ends at the parking lot for the Black Pot section of the beach; the easiest beach access is on your left.

TUNNELS BEACH & HAENA BEACH PARK 🦀🦀

Postcard-perfect, gold-sand Tunnels Beach is one of Hawaii's most beautiful. When the sun sinks into the Pacific along the fabled peaks of Bali Ha'i, there's no better-looking beach in the islands: You're bathed in golden rays that butter-up

---

Moments Stargazing

Any Kauai beach is great for stargazing, almost any night of the year. Once a month, on the Saturday nearest the new moon, when the skies are darkest, the **Kauai Educational Association for the Study of Astronomy** sponsors a star watch at three different locations around the island: the Pioneer Seed Company's parking lot, about 1 mile past the intersection of Highways 50 and 580 in Kekaha; the Hyatt Regency Hotel, in Poipu; and at the Princeville Hotel, in Princeville. For information on the next star watch, contact KEASA, P.O. Box 161, Waimea, HI 96796 (© **808/245-8250,** www.keasa.org). The 2-hour stargazing starts at 7pm in winter and 8pm in summer.

the blue sky, bounce off the steepled ridges, and tint the pale clouds hot pink. Catch the sunset from the pebbly sand beach or while swimming in the emerald-green waters, but do catch it. Tunnels is excellent for swimming nearly year-round and is safe for snorkeling because it's protected by a fringing coral reef (the waters can get rough in winter, though). The long, curvy beach is sheltered by a forest of ironwoods that provides welcome shade from the tropic heat.

Around the corner is grainy-gold-sand Haena Beach Park, which offers excellent swimming in summer and great snorkeling amid clouds of tropical fish. But stay out of the water in winter, when the big waves are dangerous. Haena also has a popular grassy park for camping. Noise-phobes will prefer Tunnels.

Take Kuhio Highway (Hwy. 56), which becomes Highway 560 after Princeville. Tunnels is about 6 miles past Hanalei town, after mile marker 8 on the highway (look for the alley with the big wood gate at the end), and Haena is just down the road. Tunnels has no facilities, but Haena has restrooms, outdoor showers, barbecue grills, picnic tables, and free parking (no lifeguard, though).

KEE BEACH STATE PARK ★★

Where the road ends on the North Shore, you'll find a dandy little reddish-gold beach almost too beautiful to be real. Don't be surprised if it looks familiar; it was featured in *The Thornbirds*. Kee (*kay*-ay) is on a reef-protected cove at the foot of fluted volcanic cliffs. Swimming and snorkeling are safe inside the reef but dangerous outside; those North Shore waves and currents can be killers. This park has restrooms, showers, and parking—but no lifeguard. To get here, take Kuhio Highway (Hwy. 56), which becomes Highway 560 after Princeville; Kee is about 7½ miles past Hanalei.

6 Watersports

Several outfitters on Kauai not only offer equipment rentals and tours, but also give out expert information on weather forecasts, sea and trail conditions, and other important matters for hikers, kayakers, sailors, and other backcountry adventurers. For watersports questions and equipment rental, contact **Kayak Kauai Outbound,** 1 mile past Hanalei Bridge on Hwy. 560, in Hanalei (© **800/ 437-3507** or 808/826-9844; www.kayakkauai.com), the outfitters' center in Hanalei. They also have their own private dock (the only one on Kauai) for launching kayaks and canoes. In Kapaa, contact **Kauai Water Ski & Surf Co.,** Kinipopo Shopping Village, 4–356 Kuhio Hwy. (on the ocean side of the highway), Kapaa (© **808/822-3574**). In the Lihue and Poipu areas, go with **Snorkel Bob's Kauai** at 4–734 Kuhio Hwy. (just north of Coconut Plantation Marketplace), Kapaa (© **800/262-7725** or 808/823-9433; www.snorkelbob.com), and in Koloa at 3236 Poipu Rd. (just south of Poipu Shopping Village), near Poipu Beach (© **808/742-2206**).

For general advice on the activities listed below, see "The Active Vacation Planner," in chapter 2.

BODYBOARDING (BOOGIE BOARDING) & BODYSURFING

The best places for bodysurfing and boogie boarding are **Kalapaki Beach** (near Lihue) and **Poipu Beach.** In addition to the rental shops listed above, one of the most inexpensive places to rent boogie boards is the **Activity Warehouse,** 788 Kuhio Hwy. (across from McDonald's), Kapaa (© **800/343-2087** or 808/822-4000; www.travelhawaii.com), where they go for $2 to $6 a day or **Snorkel Bob's** (see above) for just $15 a week.

BOATING

One of Hawaii's most spectacular natural attractions is Kauai's **Na Pali Coast.** Unless you're willing to make an arduous 22-mile hike (p. 588), there are only two ways to see it: by helicopter (see "Helicopter Rides over Waimea Canyon & the Na Pali Coast," p. 597) or by boat. Picture yourself cruising the rugged Na Pali coastline in a 42-foot ketch-rigged yacht under full sail, watching the sunset as you enjoy a tropical cocktail, or speeding through the aquamarine water in a 40-foot trimaran as porpoises play off the bow.

When the Pacific humpback whales make their annual visit to Hawaii from December to March, they swim right by Kauai. In season, most boats on Kauai—including sail and powerboats—combine **whale-watching** with their regular adventures.

Kauai has many freshwater areas that are accessible only by boat, including the Fern Grotto, Wailua State Park, Huleia and Hanalei national wildlife refuges, Menehune Fish Pond, and numerous waterfalls. If you want to strike out on your own, **Paradise Outdoor Adventures,** 4–1596 Kuhio Hwy., Kapaa (© **800/66-BOATS** or 808/822-0016; www.kayakers.com), has 40 different rental boats to choose from, like the popular Boston whaler (6-person capacity) for $295 a day, plus kayaks and sea cycles. Included are all the amenities, such as safety equipment, coolers, dry bags (for cameras, wallets, towels), and a comprehensive orientation on where to go. The staff will even deliver the boat to the Wailua River at no extra charge.

For sportfishing charters, see "Fishing," below. For tours of the Fern Grotto, see p. 598.

Captain Andy's Sailing Adventures ✦ Captain Andy operates a 55-foot, 49-passenger catamaran out of two locations on the south shore. The **snorkel/ picnic cruise,** a 5½-hour cruise to the **Na Pali Coast,** from May to October, costs $109 for adults and $79 for children 4 to 12, and includes a deli-style lunch, snorkeling, and drinks. Also there's a 4-hour Na Pali Coast **dinner sunset cruise** that sets sail for $109 for adults and $79 for children, and a 2-hour pupu cocktail sunset sail with drinks and pupu for $59 adults and $40 children.
Kukuiula Small Boat Harbor, Poipu; and Port Allen, Eleele. © **800-535-0830** or 808/335-6833. www.capt-andys.com. Prices vary depending on trip.

Holoholo Charters This outfitter has taken over several boats and features both swimming/snorkeling sailing charters as well as powerboat charters to the Na Pali Coast. The 5-hour sailing trips take place on a 48-foot catamaran, *Leila*, and are offered both in the morning (with a continental breakfast and lunch) or afternoon (big buffet lunch) for $109 adults and $79 children. The 7-hour power boat trip is on the 61-foot vessel *Holoholo*, and not only cruises the Na Pali Coast, but then crosses the channel to the forbidden island of Niihau, where they stop to snorkel. A continental breakfast, buffet lunch and snorkel equipment is included in the price: $156 adults, $109 children. They also provide complimentary shuttle service to and from your hotel.
Port Allen, Eleele. © **800/ 848-6130** or 808/335-0815. www.holoholocharters.com. Prices and departure points vary depending on trip.

Liko Kauai Cruises ✦ *Kids* Liko offers more than just a typical whale-watching cruise; this is a 4-hour combination **Na Pali Coast tour**–deep-sea fishing–historical lecture–whale-watching extravaganza with lunch. It all happens on a 49-foot power catamaran (with only 24 passengers). In addition to viewing the whales, you'll glimpse sea caves, waterfalls, lush valleys, and miles of white-sand beaches; you'll also make stops along the way for snorkeling.

Kekaha Small Boat Harbor, Waimea. © 888/SEA-LIKO or 808/338-0333. Fax 808/338-1327. www.liko-kauai. com. Na Pali Trips $110 adults, $75 children 4–12 (lunch included).

FISHING

DEEP-SEA FISHING Kauai's fishing fleet is smaller and less well recognized than others in the islands, but the fish are still out there. All you need to bring is your lunch and your luck. The best way to book a sportfishing charter is through the experts; the best booking desk in the state is **Sportfish Hawaii** ★ (© 877/388-1376 or 808/396-2607; www.sportfishhawaii.com), which books boats not only on Kauai, but on all islands. These fishing vessels have been inspected and must meet rigorous criteria to guarantee that you will have a great time. Prices range from $775 for a full-day exclusive charter (you and 5 of your closest friends get the entire boat to yourself), $575 for a three-quarter day to $495 for a half-day exclusive, or from $119 for a share charter (you share the boat with 5 other people).

FRESHWATER FISHING Freshwater fishing is big on Kauai, thanks to its dozens of "lakes," which are really man-made reservoirs. Regardless, they're full of large-mouth, small-mouth, and peacock bass (also known as *tucunare*). The **Puu Lua Reservoir,** in Kokee State Park, also has rainbow trout and is stocked by the state every year. Fishing for rainbow trout in the reservoir has a limited season: It begins on the first Saturday in August and lasts for 16 days, after which you can only fish on weekends and holidays through the last Sunday in September.

Before you rush out and get a fishing pole, you have to have a **Hawaii Freshwater Fishing License,** available through the **State Department of Land and Natural Resources,** Division of Aquatic Resources, P.O. Box 1671, Lihue, HI 96766 (© 808/241-3400), or through any fishing-supply store like **Lihue Fishing Supply,** 2985 Kalena St., Lihue (© 808/245-4930); or **Rainbow Paint and Fishing Supplies,** Hanapepe (© 808/335-6412); or **Waipouli Variety,** 4–901 Kuhio Hwy., Kapaa (© 808/822-1014). A 1-month license costs $3.75; a 1-year license is $7.50. When you get your license, pick up a copy of the booklet *State of Hawaii Freshwater Fishing Regulations.* Another great little book to get is *The Kauai Guide to Freshwater Sport Fishing,* by Glenn Ikemoto, available for $2.50 plus postage from **Magic Fishes Press,** P.O. Box 3243, Lihue, HI 96766. If you would like a guide, **Sportfish Hawaii** ★ (© 877/388-1376 or 808/396-2607; www.sportfishhawaii.com), has guided bass fishing trips from $100 per person for a half day and up.

KAYAKING

Kauai is made for kayaking. You can take the Huleia River into **Huleia National Wildlife Refuge** (located along the eastern portion of the Huleia Stream where it flows into Nawiliwili Bay). It's the last stand for Kauai's endangered birds, and the only way to see it is by kayak. The adventurous can head to the Na Pali Coast, featuring majestic cliffs, empty beaches, open-ocean conditions, and monster waves. Or you can just go out and paddle around Hanalei Bay.

Kayak Kauai Outbound ★, a mile past Hanalei Bridge on Highway 560, in Hanalei (© 800/437-3507 or 808/826-9844; www.kayakkauai.com), has a range of tours for independent souls. The shop's experts will be happy to take you on a guided kayaking trip or to tell you where to go on your own. Equipment rental starts at $40 for a one person kayak and $60 for a two-person ocean kayak per day. Kayak lessons are $40 per person per hour. Tours (some including snacks) start at $60 adults and $45 children 12 and under. Kayak Kauai also has its own private dock (the only one on Kauai) for launching kayaks and canoes.

Rick Haviland, who gained fame after he was mentioned in Paul Theroux's book *The Happy Isles of Oceania,* is the owner of **Outfitters Kauai** ✸, 2827A Poipu Rd. (Poipu Plaza, a small 5-shop mall before the road forks to Poipu/ Spouting Horn), Poipu (✆ **888/742-9887** or 808/742-9667; www.outfitters kauai.com), which has a bunch of different kayaking tours. A full-day trip along the entire Na Pali Coast (summer only) costs $165 per person and includes a guide, lunch, drinks, and equipment. Another kayak tour takes you up a jungle stream and involves a short hike to waterfalls and a swimming hole; it's $94 (children $72) including lunch, snacks, and drinks. Outfitters Kauai also rents river kayaks by the day ($30 for a single, $45 for a double).

The cheapest place to rent kayaks is the **Activity Warehouse,** 788 Kuhio Hwy. (across from McDonald's), Kapaa (✆ **808/822-4000**), where a one-person kayak goes for $10 a day and a two-person kayak is $15. You can also rent from **Chris the Fun Lady,** 4–746 Kuhio Hwy. (across from Waipouli Town Center), Kapaa (✆ **808/882-7447**; www.christhefunlady.com); **Kauai Water Ski & Surf Co.,** Kinipopo Shopping Village, 4–356 Kuhio Hwy. (on the ocean side), Kapaa (✆ **808/822-3574**); or **Pedal 'n Paddle,** Ching Young Village Shopping Center, Hanalei (✆ **808/826-9069**; http://pedalnpaddle.com).

PADDLING INTO HULEIA NATIONAL WILDLIFE REFUGE Ride the Huleia River through Kauai's 240-acre Huleia National Wildlife Refuge, the last stand of Kauai's endangered birds, with **Island Adventures,** Nawiliwili Harbor (✆ **888/245-1707** or 808/245-9662; www.kauaifun.com). You paddle up the picturesque Huleia (which appeared in *Raiders of the Lost Ark* and the remake of *King Kong*) under sheer pinnacles that open into valleys full of lush tropical plants, bright flowers, and hanging vines. Look for great blue herons and Hawaiian gallinules taking wing. The 2½-hour voyage, which starts at Nawiliwili Harbor, is a great trip for all—but especially for movie buffs, birders, and great adventurers under 12. It's even safe for nonswimmers. Wear a swimsuit, T-shirt, and boat shoes. The cost is $52 for adults, $31 for children 2 to 12. The prices include a picnic snack, juice, kayak, life vest, and guide services.

SCUBA DIVING

Diving on Kauai is dictated by the weather. In winter, when heavy swells and high winds hit the island, it's generally limited to the more protected south shore. Probably the best-known site along the south shore is **Caverns,** located off the Poipu Beach resort area. This site consists of a series of lava tubes interconnected by a chain of archways. A constant parade of fish streams by (even shy lionfish are spotted lurking in crevices), brightly-hued Hawaiian lobsters hide in the lava's tiny holes, and turtles swim past.

In summer, when the north Pacific storms subside, the magnificent North Shore opens up, and you can take a boat dive locally known as the **Oceanarium,** northwest of Hanalei Bay, where you'll find a kaleidoscopic marine world in a horseshoe-shaped cove. From the rare (long-handed spiny lobsters) to the more common (taape, conger eels, and nudibranches), the resident population is one of the more diverse on the island. The topography, which features pinnacles, ridges, and archways, is covered with cup corals, black-coral trees, and nooks and crannies enough for a dozen dives.

Because the best dives on Kauai are offshore, we recommend booking a two-tank dive off a dive boat. **Bubbles Below Scuba Charters,** 6251 Hauaala Rd., Kapaa (© **808/822-3483;** www.aloha.net/~kaimanu), specializes in highly personalized, small-group dives, with an emphasis on marine biology. The 35-foot boat, *Kaimanu,* is a custom-built Radon dive boat that comes complete with a hot shower. Two-tank boat dives cost $105 ($130 if you need gear); nondivers can come along for the ride for $50. In summer (May–Sept), Bubbles Below offers a three-tank trip for experienced divers only to the "forbidden" island of Niihau, 90 minutes by boat from Kauai. You should be comfortable with vertical drop-offs, huge underwater caverns, possibly choppy surface conditions, and significant currents. You should also be willing to share water space with the resident sharks. The all-day, 3-tank trip costs $245, including tanks, weights, dive computer, lunch, drinks, and marine guide (if you need gear, it's $260). Nondivers can tag along for $100.

On the south side, call **Fathom Five Adventures,** 3450 Poipu Rd. (next to the Chevron), Koloa (© **808/742-6991**).

GREAT SHORE DIVES FROM KAUAI If you want to rent your own equipment for shore dives, it will probably cost around $25 to $40 a day. Try **Dive Kauai,** 4–976 Kuhio Hwy., Kapaa (© **808/822-0452**); or **Fathom Five Adventures,** 3450 Poipu Rd. (next to the Chevron), Koloa (© **808/742-6991**).

Spectacular shoreline dive sites on the North Shore include **Kee Beach/Haena Beach Park** (where the road ends), one of the most picturesque beaches on the island. On a calm summer day, the drop-off near the reef begs for underwater exploration. Another good bet is **Tunnels Beach,** also known as Makua Beach. It's off Highway 560, just past mile marker 8; look for the short dirt road (less than a half-mile) to the beach. The wide reef here makes for some fabulous snorkeling and diving, but again, only during the calm summer months. **Cannons Beach,** east of Haena Beach Park (use the parking for Haena, located across the street from the Dry Cave near mile marker 9 on Hwy. 560), has lots of vibrant marine life in its sloping offshore reef.

On the south shore, head to **Tortugas** (located directly in front of Poipu Beach Park) if you want to catch a glimpse of sea turtles. **Koloa Landing** has a horseshoe-shaped reef that's teeming with tropical fish. **Sheraton Caverns** (located off the Sheraton Kauai) is also popular, due to its three large underwater lava tubes, which are usually filled with marine life.

SNORKELING
See the intro to this section for locations of **Snorkel Bob's.**

For great shoreline snorkeling, try the reef off **Kee Beach/Haena Beach Park,** located at the end of Highway 560. **Tunnels Beach,** about a mile before the end of Highway 560 in Haena, has a wide reef that's great for poking around in search of tropical fish. Be sure to check ocean conditions—don't go if the surf is up or if there's a strong current. **Anini Beach,** located off the northern Kalihiwai Road (between mile markers 25 and 26 on Kuhio Hwy., or Hwy. 56), just before the Princeville Airport, has a safe, shallow area with excellent snorkeling. **Poipu Beach Park** has some good snorkeling to the right side of Nukumoi Point—the tombolo area, where the narrow strip of sand divides the ocean, is best. If this spot is too crowded, wander down the beach in front of the old Waiohai resort; if there are no waves, this place is also hopping with marine life. **Salt Pond Beach Park,** off Highway 50 near Hanapepe, has good snorkeling around the two rocky points, home to hundreds of tropical fish.

Kids   Especially for Kids

Surfing with an Expert (p. 583)   If seven-time world champ Margo Oberg, a member of the Surfing Hall of Fame, can't get your kid—or you—up on a board riding a wave, nobody can. She promises same-day results even for klutzes.

Paddling up the Huleia River (p. 580)   Indiana Jones ran for his life up this river to his seaplane in *Raiders of the Lost Ark*. You and the kids can venture down it yourself in a kayak. The picturesque Huleia winds through tropically lush Huleia National Wildlife Refuge, where endangered species like great blue herons and Hawaiian gallinules take wing. It's ideal for everyone.

Climbing the Wooden Jungle Gyms at Kamalani Playground (p. 575) Located in Lydgate Beach Park, Wailua, this unique playground has a maze of jungle gyms for children of all ages. You can whip down slides, explore caves, hang from bars, and climb all over. It's a great place to spend the afternoon.

Cooling Off with a Shave Ice (p. 561)   On a hot, hot day, stop by **Brennecke's Beach Broiler,** across from Poipu Beach Park (© **808/742-1582**), and order a traditional Hawaiian shave ice. This local treat consists of crushed ice stuffed into a paper cone and topped with a tropical-flavored syrup. If you can't decide on a flavor, go for the "rainbow"— three different flavors in one cone.

Exploring a Magical World (p. 604)   **Na Aina Kai Botanical Gardens** on some 240 acres, sprinkled with some 70 life-size (some larger than life size) whimsical bronze statues, hidden off the beaten path of the North Shore is perfect for kids. The tropical children's garden features a gecko hedge maze, a tropical jungle gym, a tree house in a rubber tree, and a 16-foot tall Jack-in-the-Bean Stalk Giant with a 33-foot wading pool below. Only open 3 days a week, so book before you leave for Hawaii, so you won't be disappointed.

Experiencing a Hands-on Learning Adventure (p. 600)   The **Kauai Children's Discovery Museum,** located in Kapaa (© **808/823-8222,** www.kcdm.org), arose out of a grass roots community effort. In addition to the exhibits, which range from playing with Hawaiian musical instruments to participating in virtual reality television to hiding out in a "magic tree house" and reading a book (there's even a baby area for kids 4 and under), there also are Keiki Camps (Children Camps), where you can leave the kids all day and they will take them out to various outings to the beach and to points of interest.

SURFING

Hanalei Bay's winter surf is the most popular on the island, but it's for experts only. **Poipu Beach** is an excellent spot to learn to surf; the waves are small and— best of all—nobody laughs when you wipe out. Check with the local surf shops or call the **Weather Service** (© **808/245-3564**) to find out where surf's up.

Surf lessons are available for $60 for a 1½-hour session, including all-day use of equipment (board, wet suit top, and carrying rack for your car), from **Windsurf Kauai,** in Hanalei (© **808/828-6838**). Poipu is also the site of numerous surfing schools; the oldest and best is **Margo Oberg's School of Surfing,** at the Nukumoi Surf Shop, across from Brennecke's Beach (© **808/742-8019**). Margo charges $45 for 90 minutes of instruction and a half-hour of practice, including surfboard and leash; she guarantees that by the end of the lesson, you'll be standing and catching a wave.

Equipment is available for rent (ranging from $5 an hour or $20 a day for "soft" beginner boards to $7 an hour or $25 a day for hard boards) from **Nukumoi Surf Shop,** across from Brennecke's Beach, Poipu Beach Park (© **888/384-8810** or 808/742-8019); **Hanalei Surf Co.,** 5–5161 Kuhio Hwy. (across from Zelo's Beach House Restaurant in Hanalei Center), Hanalei (© **808/826-9000**); and **Pedal 'n Paddle,** Ching Young Village Shopping Center, Hanalei (© **808/826-9069**). The cheapest place to rent a board is the **Activity Warehouse,** 788 Kuhio Hwy. (across from McDonald's), Kapaa (© **808/822-4000**), where they start at $10 a day.

WATER-SKIING

Hawaii's only freshwater water-skiing is on the Wailua River. Ski boats launch from the boat ramp in Wailua River State Park, directly across from the marina. **Kauai Water Ski & Surf Co.,** Kinipopo Shopping Village, 4–356 Kuhio Hwy., Kapaa (© **800/344-7915** or 808/822-3574), rents equipment and offers lessons and guided tours; it's $55 for a half-hour trip and $110 for an hour.

WINDSURFING

Anini Beach is one of the safest beaches for beginners to learn windsurfing. Lessons and equipment rental are available at **Windsurf Kauai,** in Hanalei (© **808/828-6838**). A 3-hour lesson costs $75, including equipment; rentals are $25 an hour or $50 for a half day and $75 for a full day. Serious windsurfers should head to **Hanalei Bay** or **Tunnels Beach** on the North Shore.

7 Hiking & Camping

Kauai is an adventurer's delight. The island's greatest tropical beauty isn't easily reachable; you've got to head out on foot and find it. For more information on Kauai's hiking trails, contact the **State Division of Parks,** P.O. Box 1671, Lihue, HI 96766 (© **808/274-3446**); the **State Division of Forestry and Wildlife,** P.O. Box 1671, Lihue, HI 96766 (© **808/274-3077**); **Kauai County Parks and Recreation,** 4193 Hardy St., Lihue, HI 96766 (© **808/241-6670**); or the **Kokee Lodge Manager,** P.O. Box 819, Waimea, HI 96796 (© **808/335-6061**).

Kayak Kauai Outbound ⚐, a mile past Hanalei Bridge on Highway 560, in Hanalei (© **800/437-3507** or 808/826-9844; fax 808/822-0577; www.kayak kauai.com), is the premier all-around outfitter on the island. It's staffed by local experts who keep track of weather forecasts and sea and trail conditions; they have a lot more pertinent information that hikers, campers, and other backcountry adventurers need to know. Plus they have guided hiking tours starting at $105 per person. If you don't plan to bring your own gear, you can rent it here or at **Pedal 'n Paddle,** in Hanalei (© **808/826-9069**). If you want to buy camping equipment, head for **Ace Island Hardware,** at Princeville Shopping Center (© **808/826-6980**).

Tips   A Warning About Flash Floods

When it rains on Kauai, the waterfalls rage and rivers and streams overflow, causing flash floods on roads and trails. If you're hiking, avoid dry
streambeds, which flood quickly and wash out to sea. Before going hiking, camping, or sailing, especially in the rainy season (Nov–Mar), check
the weather forecast by calling ⓒ **808/245-6001.**

GUIDED HIKES   You can join a guided hike with the Kauai chapter of the
Sierra Club, P.O. Box 3412, Lihue, HI 96766 (ⓒ **808/246-8748;** www.hi.sierra
club.org), which offers four to seven different hikes every month, varying from
an easy family moonlit beach hike to a moderate 4-mile trip up some 1,100 feet
to 8-mile-plus treks for serious hikers only. The club also does guided hikes of
Kokee State Park (see below), usually on weekends. Because there's no staffed
office, the best way to contact the chapter is to check the website; outings are
usually listed 3 to 6 months in advance, with complete descriptions of the hike,
the hike leader's phone number, and what to wear and bring. You can also check
the daily newspaper, the *Garden Island,* for a list of hikes in the Community Calendar section. Generally, the club asks for a donation of $3 per person per hike
for nonmembers, $1 for members. It also does service work (clearing trails, pick-
ing up trash) on the hikes, so you may spend an hour doing service work, then
2 to 3 hours hiking. Last year, the club took three service-work trips along the
Na Pali Coast trail to help maintain it.

   Hawaiian Wildlife Tours ⚡ (ⓒ **808/639-2968;** cberg@pixi.com) is environmental education in action. Biologist Dr. Carl Berg will take you out into the
woods and down to the shoreline to see Kauai's native and vanishing species,
from forest birds and flora to hoary bats, monk seals, and green sea turtles. His
personalized tours last from 1 hour to a week and are tailored around the season
and weather, your physical abilities, and what you want to see. He leads tours to
Hanalei taro fields to see wetland birds, to Crater Hill to see nene geese, to
Mahaulepu to see wildflowers in the sand dunes, to Kilauea Lighthouse to see
oceanic birds, and much more. Rates are $45 per couple, per hour.

   Other options for guided hikes include **Princeville Ranch Hiking Adventures** (ⓒ **808/826-7669,** www.kauai-hiking.com), which offers various hikes
on 2,000 acres of private property, such as a 3-hour hike to a waterfall (plus
another hour swimming) for $79; and **Kauai Nature Adventures** (ⓒ **888/233-
8365** or 808/742-8305; www.kauainaturetours.com), which leads a geological-
history excursion, a tour of Kauai's environments from the mountain to the
ocean, and a Mahaulepu coast hike, all lead by scientists and costing $82 for
adults and $49 for children 12 and under, plus a host of other tours ranging in
price up to $97 for adults and $64 for children.

THE POIPU RESORT AREA
MAKAWEHI POINT ⚡
Like a ship's prow, Makawehi Point juts out to sea on the east side of Keoneloa
Beach (known locally as Shipwreck Beach), which lies in front of the Hyatt
Regency Poipu. This 50-foot-high sand-dune bluff attracts a variety of people:
pole fishers, whale-watchers, those who just like the panoramic views of the
Pacific, and daredevils who test their courage by leaping off the cliff into the
waves (don't try it).

The trailhead begins on the east end of Shipwreck Beach, past the Hyatt. It's an easy 10-minute walk up to Makawehi Point; after you take in the big picture, keep going uphill along the ridge of the sand dunes (said to contain ancient Hawaiian burial sites), past the coves frequented by green sea turtles and endangered Hawaiian monk seals, through the coastal pine forest, and past World War II bunkers to the very top. Now you can see Hauupu Ridge and its 2,297-foot peak, the famously craggy ridgeline that eerily resembles Queen Victoria's profile, and, in the distance, Mahaulepu Beach, one of the best looking in Hawaii. Inland, three red craters dimple the green fields; the one in the middle, the biggest, Pu'u Huni Huni, is said to have been the last volcano to erupt on Kauai—but it was so long ago that nobody here can remember when.

WESTERN KAUAI
WAIMEA CANYON TRAILS

On a wet island like Kauai, a dry hike is hard to find. But in the desert-dry gulch of Waimea Canyon, known as the Grand Canyon of the Pacific (once you get here, you'll see why—it's pretty spectacular), you're not likely to slip and slide in the muck as you go.

CANYON TRAIL   You want to hike Hawaii's Grand Canyon, but you don't think you have time? Well, then, take the Canyon Trail to the east rim for a breathtaking view into the 3,000-foot-deep canyon. Park your car at the top of Halemanu Valley Road (located between mile markers 14 and 15 on Waimea Canyon Road, about a mile down from the museum). Walk down the not very clearly marked trail on the 3½-mile round-trip, which takes 2 to 3 hours and leads to Waipoo Falls (as does the hike below) and back. We suggest going in the afternoon, when the light is best.

HIKE TO WAIPOO FALLS ⚑   The 3-hour round-trip hike to Waipoo Falls is one of Kauai's best hikes. The two-tiered, 800-foot waterfall that splashes into a natural pool is worth every step it takes to get here. To find the trail, drive up Kokee Road (Hwy. 550) to the Puu Hina Hina Outlook; a quarter mile past the lookout, near a NASA satellite tracking station on the right, a two-lane dirt road leads to the Waipoo Falls trailhead. From here, the trail winds gently through a jungle dotted with wild yellow orchids and flame-red torch ginger before it leads you out on a descending ridgeback that juts deep into the canyon. At the end of the promontory, take a left and push on through the jungle to the falls; at the end, reward yourself with a refreshing splash in the pool.

KOKEE STATE PARK

At the end of Highway 550, which leads through Waimea Canyon to its summit, lies a 4,640-acre state park of high-mountain forest wilderness (3,600–4,000 ft. above sea level). The rain forest, bogs, and breathtaking views of the Na Pali coastline and Waimea Canyon are the draw at Kokee. This is the place for hiking—among the 45 miles of maintained trails are some of the best hikes in Hawaii. Official trail maps of all the park's trails are for sale for 50¢ at the **Kokee Natural History Museum** (✆ 808/335-9975).

A few words of advice: Always check current trail conditions; up-to-date trail information is available on a bulletin board at the Kokee Natural History Museum. Stay on established trails; it's easy to get lost here. Get off the trail well before dark. Carry water and rain gear—even if it's perfectly sunny when you set out—and wear sunscreen.

For complete coverage of the state park, see p. 596.

AWAAWAPUHI TRAIL This 3¼-mile hike (6½ miles round-trip) takes about 3 hours each way and is considered strenuous by most, but it offers a million-dollar view. Look for the trailhead at the left of the parking lot, at mile marker 17 between the museum and Kalalau Lookout. The well-marked and maintained trail now sports quarter-mile markers, and you can pick up a free plant guide for the trail at the museum. The trail drops about 1,600 feet through native forests to a thin precipice right at the very edge of the Na Pali cliffs for a dramatic and dizzying view of the tropical valleys and blue Pacific 2,500 feet below. It's not recommended for anyone with vertigo (although a railing will keep you from a major slip and fall). Go early, before clouds obscure the view, or late in the day; the chiaroscuro sunsets are something to behold.

The Awaawapuhi can be a straight-out-and-back trail or a loop that connects with the **Nualolo Trail** (3¾ miles), which provides awesome views and leads back to the main road between the ranger's house and the Kokee cabins, which is about a mile and a half from where you started. So you can hike the remaining 1½ miles along the road or hitch a ride if you decide to do the entire loop but can't make it all the way.

HALEMANU-KOKEE TRAIL This trail takes you on a pleasant, easy-to-moderate 2½-mile round-trip walk through a native koa and ohia forest inhabited by native birds. The trailhead is near mile marker 15; pick up the Faye Trail, which leads to this one. The Halemanu-Kokee links Kokee Valley to Halemanu Valley (hence the name); along the way, you'll see a plum orchard, valleys, and ridges.

PIHEA TRAIL This is the park's flattest trail, but it's still a pretty strenuous 7½-mile round-trip. A new boardwalk on a third of the trail makes it easier, especially when it's wet. The trail begins at the end of Highway 550 at Puu o Kila Lookout, which overlooks Kalalau Valley; it goes down at first, then flattens out as it traces the back ridge of the valley. Once it enters the rain forest, you'll see native plants and trees. It intersects with the Alakai Swamp Trail (below). If you combine both trails, figure on about 4 hours in and out.

ALAKAI SWAMP TRAIL ✿ If you want to see the "real" Hawaii, this is it—a big swamp that's home to rare birds and plants. The trail allows a rare glimpse into a wet, cloud-covered wilderness preserve where 460 inches of rainfall a year is common. This 7-mile hike used to take 5 hours of sloshing through the bog, with mud up to your knees. Now a boardwalk protects you from the shoe-grabbing mud. Come prepared for rain. (The only silver lining is that there are no mosquitoes above 3,000 ft.)

The trailhead is off Mohihi (Camp 10) Road, just beyond the Forest Reserve entrance sign and the Alakai Shelter picnic area. From the parking lot, the trail follows an old World War II four-wheel-drive road. Stick to the boardwalk; this is a fragile ecoarea (not to mention the mud). At the end of the 3½-mile slog, if you're lucky and the clouds part, you'll have a lovely view of Wainiha Valley and Hanalei from Kilohana Lookout.

CAMPGROUNDS & WILDERNESS CABINS IN KOKEE

CABINS & TENT CAMPGROUNDS Camping facilities include state campgrounds (1 next to Kokee Lodge, and 4 more primitive backcountry sites), one private tent area, and the **Kokee Lodge,** which has 12 cabins for rent at very reasonable rates. At 4,000 feet, the nights are cold, particularly in winter, because no open fires are permitted at Kokee, the best deal is the cabins (see "Where to Stay," earlier in this chapter, for details). The **Kokee Lodge Restaurant** is open daily from 9am to 3:30pm for continental breakfast and lunch. Groceries and gas aren't available in Kokee, so stock up in advance, or you'll have to make the long trip down the mountain.

The **state campground** at Kokee allows tent camping only. Permits can be obtained from a state parks office on any island; on Kauai, it's at 3060 Eiwa St., Room 306, Lihue, HI 96766 (© **808/274-3444**). The permits are $5 per night; the time limit is 5 nights in a single 30-day period. Facilities include showers, drinking water, picnic tables, a pavilion with tables, restrooms, barbecues, sinks for dishwashing, and electric lights.

Tent camping at **Camp Sloggett,** owned by the Kauai YWCA, 3094 Elua St., Lihue, HI 96766 (© **808/335-6060;** fax 808/245-5961; kauaiyw@pixi.com), is available for $10 per person per night (children under 5 stay free). The sites are on 1½ acres of open field, with a covered pit for fires and a barbecue area, plus volleyball and badminton nets. There's also a hostel-style accommodation at the **Weinburg Bunkhouse,** with bunk beds, separate toilets, showers, and kitchenettes ($20 per person). To get here, continue on the highway past park headquarters and take the first right after the Kokee Lodge. Follow the dirt road and look for the wooden CAMP SLOGGETT sign; turn right and follow the bumpy road past the state cabins into a large clearing.

BACKCOUNTRY CAMPING   The more primitive backcountry campgrounds include **Sugi Grove** and **Kawaikoi,** located about 4 miles from park headquarters on the Camp 10 Road, an often muddy and steep four-wheel-drive road. Sugi Grove is located across the Kawaikoi Stream from the Kawaikoi campsite. The area is named for the sugi pines, which were planted in 1937 by the Civilian Conservation Corps. This is a shady campsite with a single picnic shelter, a pit toilet, a stream, and space for several tents. The Kawaikoi site is a 3-acre open grass field, surrounded by Kokee plum trees and forests of koa and ohia. Facilities include two picnic shelters, a composting toilet, and a stream that flows next to the camping area. There is no potable water—bring in your own or treat the stream water.

Permits are available from the **State Forestry and Wildlife Division,** 3060 Eiwa St., Room 306, Lihue, HI 96766 (© **808/274-3444**). There's no fee for the permits, but camping is limited to 3 nights. You can also request the *Kauai Recreation Map* (with illustrations of all roads; trails; and picnic, hunting, and camping areas) by mail; contact the Forestry and Wildlife Division at the number above to find out how.

BEACH CAMPING AT POLIHALE STATE PARK

Polihale holds the distinction of being the westernmost beach in the United States. The beach is spectacular—some 300 feet wide in summer, with rolling sand dunes (some as high as 100 ft.), and the islands of Niihau and Lehua just offshore. Bordered by a curtain of Na Pali Coast cliffs on the north, razor-sharp ridges and steep valleys to the east, and the blue Pacific on the south and west, this is one of the most dramatic camping areas in the state.

The campgrounds for tent camping are located at the south end of the beach, affording privacy from the daytime beach activities. There's great swimming in summer (even then, be on the lookout for waves and rip currents—there are no lifeguards), some surfing (the rides are usually short), and fishing. The camping is on sand, although there are some kiawe trees for shade. (*Warning:* Kiawe trees drop long thorns, so make sure you have protective footwear.) Facilities include restrooms, showers, picnic tables, barbecues, and a spigot for drinking water. You can purchase supplies about 15 miles away in Waimea.

Permits, which are $5 per night, are available through the **State Parks Office,** 3060 Eiwa St., Lihue, HI 96766 (© **808/241-3444**). You're limited to 5 nights in any 30-day period. To reach the park from Lihue, take Highway 50 west to Barking Sands Pacific Missile Range. Bear right onto the paved road, which heads toward the mountains. There will be small signs directing you to Polihale; the second sign will point to a left turn onto a dirt road. Follow this for about 5 miles; at the fork in the road, the campgrounds are to the left and the beach park is to the right.

THE COCONUT COAST
THE SLEEPING GIANT TRAIL

This moderate hike takes you up the fabled mountain known as Sleeping Giant (which really does look like a giant resting on his back) to a fabulous view. The trail will gain 1,000 feet in altitude on a clearly marked trail (be sure to stay on the trail). The climb is steadily uphill (remember you are climbing up a mountain), but the view at the top is well worth the constant incline. To get to the trailhead, turn *mauka* (toward the mountain) off Kuhio Highway (Hwy. 56) onto Haleilio Road (between Wailua and Kapaa, just past mile marker 6); follow Haleilio Road for 1¼ miles to the parking area, at telephone pole number 38. From here, signs posted by the State of Hawaii Division of Forestry and Wildlife lead you over the 1¾-mile trail, which ends at a picnic table and shelter. The panoramic view is breathtaking. Be sure to bring water—and a picnic, if you like.

THE NORTH SHORE
NA PALI COAST STATE PARK

Simply put, the Na Pali Coast is the most beautiful part of the Hawaiian Islands. Hanging valleys open like green-velvet accordions, and waterfalls tumble to the sea from the 4,120-foot-high cliffs; the experience is both exhilarating and humbling. Whether you hike in, fly over, or take a boat cruise past, be sure to see this park.

Established in 1984, Na Pali Coast State Park takes in a 22-mile stretch of fluted cliffs that wrap around the northwest shore of Kauai between Kee Beach and Polihale State Park. Volcanic in origin, carved by wind and sea, "the cliffs" (*na pali* in Hawaiian), which heaved out of the ocean floor 200 million years ago, stand as constant reminders of majesty and endurance. Four major valleys—Kalalau, Honopu, Awaawapuhi, and Nualolo—crease the cliffs.

Unless you boat or fly in (see "Boating," on p. 578, or "Helicopter Rides over Waimea Canyon & the Na Pali Coast," on p. 597), the park is accessible only on foot—and it's not easy. An ancient footpath, the **Kalalau Trail,** winds through this remote, spectacular, 6,500-acre park, ultimately leading to Kalalau Valley. Of all the green valleys in Hawaii, and there are many, only Kalalau is a true wilderness—probably the last wild valley in the islands. No road goes here, and none ever will. The remote valley is home to long-plumed tropical birds, golden monarch butterflies, and many of Kauai's 120 rare and endangered species of plants. The hike into the Kalalau Valley is grueling and takes most people 6 to 8 hours one-way.

Despite its inaccessibility, this journey into Hawaii's wilderness has become increasingly popular since the 1970s. Overrun with hikers, helicopters, and boaters, the Kalalau Valley was in grave danger of being loved to death. Strict rules about access have been adopted. The park is open to hikers and campers only on a limited basis, and you must have a permit (though you can hike the first 2 miles, to Hanakapiai Beach, without a permit). Permits are $10 per night and are issued in person at the **Kauai State Parks Office,** 3060 Eiwa St., Room

306, Lihue, HI 96766 (© **808/274-3444**). You can also request one by writing **Kauai Division of State Parks,** at the address above. For more information, contact **Hawaii State Department of Land and Natural Resources,** 1151 Punchbowl St., Room 130, Honolulu, HI 96813 (© **808/587-0320**).

HIKING THE KALALAU TRAIL ★★
The trailhead is at Kee Beach, at the end of Highway 560. Even if you only go as far as Hanakapiai, bring water.

THE FIRST 2 MILES: TO HANAKAPIAI BEACH Do not attempt this hike unless you have adequate footwear (closed-toe shoes at least; hiking shoes are best), water, a sun visor, insect repellent, and adequate hiking clothes (shorts and T-shirt are fine, your bikini is not). It's only 2 miles to Hanakapiai Beach, but the first mile is all uphill. This tough trail takes about 2 hours one-way and dissuades many, but everyone should attempt at least the first half-mile, which gives a good hint of the startling beauty that lies ahead. Day hikers love this initial stretch, so it's usually crowded. The island of Niihau and Lehua Rock are often visible on the horizon. At mile marker 1, you'll have climbed from sea level to 400 feet; now it's all downhill to Hanakapiai Beach. Sandy in summer, the beach becomes rocky when winter waves scour the coast. There are strong currents and no lifeguards, so swim at your own risk. You can also hike another 2 miles inland from the beach to **Hanakapiai Falls,** a 120-foot cascade. Allow 3 hours for that stretch.

THE REST OF THE WAY Hiking the Kalalau is the most difficult and challenging hike in Hawaii, and one you'll never forget. Even the Sierra Club rates the 22-mile round-trip into Kalalau Valley and back as "strenuous"—this is serious backpacking. Follow the footsteps of ancient Hawaiians along a cliff-side path that's a mere 10 inches wide in some places, with sheer 1,000-foot drops to the sea. One misstep, and it's *limu* (seaweed) time. Even the hardy and fit should allow at least 2 days to hike in and out (see below for camping information). Although the trail is usually in good shape, go in summer when it's dry; parts of it vanish in winter. When it rains, the trail becomes super slippery, and flash floods can sweep you away.

A park ranger is now on-site full time at Kalalau Beach to greet visitors, provide information, oversee campsites, and keep trails and campgrounds in order.

CAMPING IN KALALAU VALLEY & ALONG THE NA PALI COAST
You must obtain a camping permit; see above for details. The camping season runs roughly from May or June to September (depending on the site). All campsites are booked almost a year in advance, so call or write well ahead of time. Stays are limited to 5 nights. Camping areas along the Kalalau Trail include **Hanakapiai Beach** (facilities are pit toilets, and water is from the stream), **Hanakoa Valley** (no facilities, water from the stream), **Milolii** (no facilities, water from the stream), and **Kalalau Valley** (composting toilets, several pit toilets, and water from the stream). Keep your camping permit with you at all times.

8 Golf & Other Outdoor Pursuits

You can rent clubs from **Activity Warehouse,** 788 Kuhio Hwy. (across from McDonald's), Kapaa (© **800/343-2087** or 808/822-4000; www.travelhawaii. com), where top-quality clubs go for $15 a day, not-so-top-quality for $10 a day. For last-minute and discount tee times, call **Stand-by Golf** (© **888/645-BOOK;**

www.stand-bygolf.com) between 7am and 9pm. Stand-by offers discounted (up to 50% off green fees), guaranteed tee times for same-day or next-day golfing.

In the listings below, the cart fee is included in the greens fee unless otherwise noted.

LIHUE & ENVIRONS

Kauai Lagoons Golf Courses Choose between two excellent Jack Nicklaus–designed courses: the **Mokihana Course** (formerly known as the Lagoons Course), for the recreational golfer, or the **Kauai Kiele Championship Course** 🏌, for the low handicapper. The 6,942-yard, par-72 Mokihana is a links-style course with a bunker that's a little less severe than Kiele; emphasis is on the short game. The Kiele is a mixture of tournament-quality challenge and high-traffic playability; it winds up with one of Hawaii's most difficult holes, a 431-yard, par-4 played straightaway to an island green.

Facilities include a driving range, lockers, showers, a restaurant, a snack bar, a pro shop, practice greens, a clubhouse, and club and shoe rental; transportation from the airport is provided.

Kalapaki Beach, Lihue (less than a mile from Lihue Airport). ✆ **800/634-6400** or 808/241-5061. www.kauai lagoonsgolf.com. From the airport, make a left on Kapule Hwy. (Hwy. 51) and look for the sign on your left. Greens fees at Mokihana Course: $120 ($75 for guests of the Kauai Marriott; $85 for guests of other hotels and condos on Kauai); for the Kiele Course: $170 ($125 for Marriott guests; $135–$140 for guests of other hotels and condos on Kauai).

THE POIPU RESORT AREA

Kiahuna Golf Club This par-70, 6,353-yard Robert Trent Jones Jr.–designed course plays around four large archaeological sites, ranging from an ancient Hawaiian temple to the remains of a Portuguese home and crypt built in the early 1800s. This Scottish-style course has rolling terrain, undulating greens, 70 sand bunkers, and near-constant winds. The third hole, a par-3, 185-yarder, goes over Waikomo Stream. At any given time, about half the players on the course are Kauai residents, the other half visitors. Facilities include a driving range, practice greens, and a snack bar.

2545 Kiahuna Plantation Dr. (adjacent to Poipu Resort area), Koloa. ✆ **808/742-9595**. www.kiahunagolf. com.Take Hwy. 50 to Hwy. 520, bear left into Poipu at the fork in the road, and turn left onto Kiahuna Plantation Dr. Greens fees: $75 7am–11am, $65 11am–2:30pm, twilight rates (after 2:30pm) $45 (times for twilight rates may vary throughout the year).

Kukuiolono Golf Course 🔍*Finds* This is a fun nine-hole course in a spectacular location with scenic views of the entire south coast. You can't beat the price— $7 for the day, whether you play 9 holes or 90. The course is in Kukuiolono Park, a beautiful wooded area donated by the family of Walter McBryde. In fact, you'll see McBryde's grave on the course, along with some other oddities, like wild chickens, ancient Hawaiian rock structures, and Japanese gardens. Of course, there are plenty of trees to keep you on your game. When you get to the second tee box, check out the coconut tree dotted with yellow, pink, orange, and white golf balls that have been driven into the bark. Don't laugh—your next shot might add to the decor! This course shouldn't give you many problems— it's excellently maintained and relatively straightforward, with few fairway hazards. Facilities include a driving range, practice greens, club rental, a snack bar, and a clubhouse.

Kukuiolono Park, Kalaheo. ✆ **808/332-9151**. Take Hwy. 50 into the town of Kalaheo; turn left on Papaluna Rd., drive up the hill for nearly a mile, and watch for the sign on your right; the entrance has huge iron gates and stone pillars—you can't miss it. Greens fees: $7 for the day; optional cart rental is $6 for 9 holes, $12 for 18.

Poipu Bay Golf Course ★★   This 6,959-yard, par-72 course with a links-style layout is the home of the PGA Grand Slam of Golf. Designed by Robert Trent Jones Jr., this challenging course features undulating greens and water hazards on eight of the holes. The par-4 16th hole has the coastline weaving along the entire left side. You can take the safe route to the right and maybe make par (but more likely bogey), or you can try to take it tight against the ocean and possibly make it in two. The most striking (and most disrespectful) hole is the 201-yard, par-3 on the 17th, which has a tee built on an ancient Hawaiian stone formation. Facilities include a restaurant, a locker room, a pro shop, a driving range, and putting greens.

2250 Ainako St. (across from the Hyatt Regency Kauai), Koloa. © 808/742-8711. www.kauai-hyatt.com. Take Hwy. 50 to Hwy. 520; bear left into Poipu at the fork in the road; turn right on Ainako St. Greens fees: $185 ($125 Hyatt Regency guest); $120 afternoon play noon–3pm ($110 Hyatt Regency guest); $65 twilight rate after 3pm.

THE NORTH SHORE

Princeville Golf Club, Prince Course ★★   Here's your chance to play one of the best golf courses in Hawaii. This Robert Trent Jones Jr.–designed devil of a course sits on 390 acres molded to create ocean views from every hole. Some holes have a waterfall backdrop to the greens, others shoot into the hillside, and the famous par-4 12th has a long tee shot off a cliff to a narrow, jungle-lined fairway 100 feet below. This is the most challenging course on Kauai; accuracy is key here. Most of the time, if you miss the fairway, your ball's in the drink. "The average vacation golfer may find the Prince Course intimidating, but they don't mind because it's so beautiful," Jones says. Facilities include a restaurant, a health club and spa, lockers, a clubhouse, a golf shop, and a driving range.

Princeville. © 800/826-1105 or 808/ 826-5070. Take Hwy. 56 to mile marker 27; the course is on your right. Greens fees: $175 ($150 for Princeville resort guests and $130 for Princeville Hotel guests) for the Prince Course; $125 ($110 for Princeville resort guests and $105 for Princeville Hotel guests) for the Makai Course.

BIKING

There are a couple of great places on Kauai for two-wheeling: the **Poipu area,** which has wide, flat roads and several dirt-cane roads (especially around Mahaulepu); and the cane road (a dirt road used for hauling sugar cane) between **Kealia Beach** and **Anahola,** north of Kapaa.

The following places rent mountain bikes, usually for $10 to $20 a day (with big discounts for multiple-day rentals): **Activity Warehouse,** 788 Kuhio Hwy. (across from McDonald's), Kapaa (© **800/343-2087** or 808/822-4000; www.travelhawaii.com); **Ray's Rentals & Activities,** 4–1345 Kuhio Hwy., Kapaa (© **808/822-5700**); **Outfitters Kauai,** 2827A Poipu Rd. (look for the small 5-shop mall before the road forks to Poipu/Spouting Horn), Poipu (© **808/742-9667**); and **Kauai Cycle and Tour,** 1379 Kuhio Hwy., Kapaa (© **808/821-2115;** www.bikehawaii.com/kauaicycle). For a great selection of high-quality mountain bikes at reasonable prices, it's worth the drive to **Pedal 'n Paddle,** in Hanalei (© **808/826-9069;** pedalnpaddle.com), which has not only high-grade Kona mountain bikes with Shimano components but also bikes with front-end suspension systems. Rentals start at $10 a day or $30 a week and include helmet, bike lock, and car rack. The shop even has kids' 20-inch BMX bikes. The knowledgeable folks here are more than happy to provide you with free maps and tell you about the best biking spots on the island.

GUIDED BIKE TOURS   **Outfitters Kauai** ★ (© **808/742-9667;** www.outfitterskauai.com) offers a fabulous downhill bike ride from Waimea Canyon to the ocean. The 12-mile trip (mostly coasting) begins at 6am, when the van leaves the shop in Poipu and heads up to the canyon. By the time you've scarfed down the fresh-baked muffins and coffee, you're at the top of the canyon, just as the sun is rising over the rim—it's a remarkable moment. The tour makes a couple of stops on the way down for short, scenic nature hikes. You'll be back at the shop around 10am. The sunset trip follows the same route. Both tours cost $80 per adult; $60 children 10 to 14.

BIRDING

Kauai provides some of Hawaii's last sanctuaries for endangered native birds and oceanic birds, such as the albatross. If you didn't bring your binoculars, you can rent some at **Activity Warehouse,** 788 Kuhio Hwy. (across from McDonald's), Kapaa (© **800/343-2087** or 808/822-4000; www.travelhawaii.com), where rentals start at 99¢ a day.

At **Kokee State Park,** a 4,345-acre wilderness forest at the end of Highway 550 in southwest Kauai, you have an excellent chance of seeing some of Hawaii's endangered native birds. You might spot the apapane, a red bird with black wings and a curved black bill; or the iwi, a red bird with black wings, orange legs, and a salmon-colored bill. Other frequently seen native birds are the honeycreeper, which sings like a canary; the amakihi, a plain, olive-green bird with a long, straight bill; and the anianiau, a tiny yellow bird with a thin, slightly curved bill. The most common native bird at Kokee is the moa, or red jungle fowl, brought as domestic stock by ancient Polynesians. Ordinarily shy, they're quite tame in this environment. David Kuhn leads custom hikes, pointing out Hawaii's rarest birds on his **Terran Tours** (© **808/335-3313**), which range from a half day to 3 days and feature endemic and endangered species.

Kilauea Point National Wildlife Refuge 🐾, a mile north of Kilauea on the North Shore (© **808/828-1413**), is a 200-acre headland habitat that juts above the surf and includes cliffs, two rocky wave-lashed bays, and a tiny islet that serves as a jumping-off spot for seabirds. You can easily spot red-footed boobies, which nest in trees, and wedge-tailed shearwaters, which burrow in nests along the cliffs. You may also see the great frigate bird, the Laysan albatross, the red-tailed tropic bird, and the endangered nene. Native plants and the Kilauea Point Lighthouse are highlights as well. The refuge is open from 10am to 4pm daily (closed on Thanksgiving, Christmas, and New Year's Day); admission is $3. The refuge also offers 1-hour **guided hikes** up to the 568-foot summit of Crater Hill, which affords spectacular views. You can join a hike Monday through Thursday at 10am (the only fee is the $3 admission to the refuge), but you must make a reservation (© **808/828-0168**). To get here, turn right off Kuhio Highway (Hwy. 56) at Kilauea, just after mile marker 23; follow Kilauea Road to the refuge entrance.

Peaceful Hanalei Valley is home to Hawaii's endangered Koloa duck, gallinule, coot, and stilt. The **Hanalei National Wildlife Refuge** (© **808/828-1413**) also provides a safe habitat for migratory shorebirds and waterfowl. It's not open to the public, but an interpretive overlook along the highway serves as an impressive vantage point. Along Ohiki Road, which begins at the west end of the Hanalei River Bridge, you'll often see white cattle egrets hunting crayfish in streams.

HORSEBACK RIDING

Only in Kauai can you ride a horse across the wide-open pastures of a working ranch under volcanic peaks and rein up near a waterfall pool. No wonder Kauai's paniolos smile and sing so much. Near the Poipu area, **CJM Country Stables,** 1731 Kelaukia St. (2 miles beyond the Hyatt Regency Kauai), Koloa (© **808/ 742-6096;** www.cjmstables.com), offers both 2- and 3-hour escorted Hidden Valley beach rides. You'll trot over Hidden Valley ranch land, past secluded beaches and bays, along the Hauupu Ridge, across sugarcane fields, and to Mahaulepu Beach; it's worth your time and money just to get out to this seldom seen part of Kauai. The Secret Beach and Breakfast Ride costs $85 and includes breakfast. The 2-hour Hidden Beach Ride is $75. There's also a 3½-hour swim/ beach/picnic ride for $95.

Princeville Ranch Stables, Highway 56 (just after the Princeville Airport), Hanalei (© **808/826-6777;** www.princevilleranch.com), has a variety of outings. The 1½-hour country ride takes in views of the Hanalei mountains and the vista of Anini Beach ($65), while the 3-hour adventure meanders along the bluffs of the North Shore to Anini Beach, where you tie off your horse and take a short stroll to the beach ($110). The 4-hour Waterfall Picnic Ride crosses ranch land, takes you on a short (but steep) hike to swimming pools at the base of waterfalls, and then feeds you a picnic lunch for $120. Riders must be in good physical shape, and don't forget to put your swimsuit on under your jeans. The Princeville Ranch Stables also offers other adventures, ranging from the less strenuous wagon rides to a cattle-drive ride.

TENNIS

The **Kauai County Parks and Recreation Department,** 4444 Rice St., Suite 150, Lihue (© **808/241-6670**), has a list of the nine county tennis courts around the island, all of which are free and open to the public. Private courts that are open to the public include the **Princeville Tennis Club,** Princeville Hotel (© **808/826-3620,** www.princeville.com), which has six courts available for $15 per person ($12 for guests) for 90 minutes. On the south side, try **Hyatt Regency Kauai Resort and Spa,** Poipu Resort (© **808/742-1234**), which has four courts, available for $20 an hour; and **Kiahuna Tennis Club,** Poipu Road (just past the Poipu Shopping Village on the left), Poipu Resort (© **808/742- 9533**), which has 10 courts renting for $10 per person per hour.

9 Seeing the Sights

No matter how much time you have on Kauai, make it a priority to see the North Shore. No doubt about it—this is Hawaii at its best.

A TOUR OF THE ISLAND

Four-Wheel-Drive Backroad Adventure ☆ Great for getting off the beaten path and seeing the "hidden" Kauai, this 4-hour tour follows a figure-eight path around Kauai, from Kilohana Crater to the Mahaulepu coastline. The tour, done in a four-wheel-drive van, not only stops at Kauai's well-known scenic spots, but also travels on sugarcane roads (on private property), taking you to places most people who live on Kauai have never seen. The guides are well versed in everything from native plants to Hawaiian history. Bring plenty of film for your camera.

Aloha Kauai Tours, 1702 Haleukana St., Lihue, HI 96766. © **800/452-1113** or 808/245-8809. www.aloha kauaitours.com. Tours $65 adults, $50 children ages 5–12.

LIHUE & ENVIRONS

Grove Farm Homestead Museum You can experience a day in the life of an 1860s sugar planter on a visit to Grove Farm Homestead, which shows how good life was (for some, anyway) when sugar was king. This is Hawaii's best

Fun Fact **Discover the Legendary Little People**

According to ancient Hawaiian legend, among Kauai's earliest settlers were the *menehune,* a race of small people who worked at night to accomplish magnificent feats. Above Nawiliwili Harbor, the **Menehune Fish Pond**—which at one time extended 25 miles—is said to have been built in just 1 night, with two rows of thousands of menehune passing stones hand to hand. The menehune were promised that no one would watch them work, but one person did; when they discovered the spy, they stopped working immediately, leaving two gaps in the wall. From Nawiliwili Harbor, take Hulemalu Road above Huleia Stream; look for the HAWAII CONVENTION AND VISITORS BUREAU marker at a turnoff in the road, which leads to the legendary fish pond. Kayakers can paddle up Huleia Stream to see it up close.

remaining example of a sugar-plantation homestead. Founded in 1864 by George N. Wilcox, a Hanalei missionary's son, Grove Farm was one of the earliest of Hawaii's 86 sugar plantations. A self-made millionaire, Wilcox died a bachelor in 1933, at age 94. His estate looks much like it did when he lived here, complete with period furniture, plantation artifacts, and Hawaiiana.

4050 Nawiliwili Rd. (Hwy. 58) at Pikaka St. (2 miles from Waapa Rd.), Lihue. (© 808/245-3202. www.kauai-hawaii.com/lihue/grove_fhm.html. Requested donation $5 adults, $2 children under 12. Tours offered Mon and Wed–Thurs at 10am and 1pm; reservations required.

Kauai Museum ★ *Kids* The history of Kauai is kept safe in an imposing Greco-Roman building that once served as the town library. This great little museum is worth a stop before you set out to explore the island. It contains a wealth of historical artifacts and information tracing the island's history from the beginning of time through Contact (when Capt. James Cook "discovered" Kauai in 1778), the monarchy period, the plantation era, and the present. You'll hear tales of the *menehune* (the mythical elflike people who were said to build massive stoneworks in a single night) and see old poi pounders and idols, relics of sugar planters and paniolos, a nice seashell collection, old Hawaiian quilts, feather leis, a replica of a plantation worker's home, and much more—even a model of Cook's ship, the HMS *Resolution,* riding anchor in Waimea Bay. Vintage photographs by W. J. Senda, a Japanese immigrant, show old Kauai, while a contemporary video, shot from a helicopter, captures the island's natural beauty.

4428 Rice St., Lihue. (© 808/245-6931. Admission $5 adults, $4 seniors, $3 students 13–17, $1 children 6–12. Mon–Fri 9am–4pm; Sat 10am–4pm. First Sat of every month is "Family Day," when admission is free.

THE POIPU RESORT AREA

No Hawaii resort has a better entrance: On Maluhia Road, eucalyptus trees planted in 1911 as a wind break for sugarcane fields now form a monumental **tree tunnel.** The leafy green, cool tunnel starts at Kaumualii Highway; you'll emerge at the golden-red beach.

Prince Kuhio Park This small roadside park is the birthplace of Prince Jonah Kuhio Kalanianaole, the "People's Prince," whose March 26 birthday is a holiday in Hawaii. He opened the beaches of Waikiki to the public in 1918 and served as Hawaii's second territorial delegate to the U.S. Congress. What remains here are the foundations of the family home, a royal fish pond, and a shrine where tributes are still paid in flowers.

Lawai Rd., Koloa. Just after mile marker 4 on Poipu Rd., veer to the right of the fork in the road; the park is on the right side.

Spouting Horn ✯ *Kids*   This natural phenomenon is second only to Yellowstone's Old Faithful. It's quite a sight—big waves hit Kauai's south shore with enough force to send a spout of funneled saltwater 10 feet or more up in the air; in winter, the water can get as high as six stories.

Spouting Horn is different from other blowholes in Hawaii, in that it has an additional hole that blows air that sounds like a loud moaning. According to Hawaiian legend, this coastline was once guarded by a giant female lizard (*Mo'o*); she would gobble up any intruders. One day, along came Liko, who wanted to fish in this area. Mo'o rushed out to eat Liko. Quickly, Liko threw a spear right into the giant lizard's mouth. Mo'o then chased Liko into a lava tube. Liko escaped, but legend says Mo'o is still in the tube, and the moaning sound at Spouting Horn is her cry for help.

At Kukuiula Bay, beyond Prince Kuhio Park (see above).

Allerton Garden of the National Tropical Botanical Garden ✯   Discover an extraordinary collection of tropical fruit and spice trees, rare Hawaiian plants, and hundreds of varieties of flowers at the 186-acre preserve known as **Lawai Gardens,** said to be the largest collection of rare and endangered plants in the world. Adjacent **McBryde Garden,** a royal home site of Queen Emma in the 1860s, is known for its formal gardens, a delicious kind of colonial decadence. It's set amid fountains, streams, waterfalls, and European statuary. Endangered green sea turtles can be seen here (their home in the sea was wiped out years ago by Hurricane Iniki). The tours are fascinating for green thumbs and novices alike.

Visitor Center, Lawai Rd. (across the street from Spouting Horn), Poipu. ✆ 808/742-2623. www.ntbg.org. Admission $30. Guided 2½-hour tours by reservation only, Mon–Sat at 9am, 10am, 1pm, and 2pm. Self-guided tours of McBryde Garden, Mon–Sat 9am–4pm, $15 (trams into the valley leave once an hour on the half-hour, last tram 2:30pm); guided tour Mon. 9:30am, $30. Reserve a week in advance in peak months of July, Aug, and Sept.

WESTERN KAUAI
WAIMEA TOWN
If you'd like to take a self-guided tour of this historic town, stop at the **Waimea Library,** at mile marker 23 on Highway 50, to pick up a map and guide to the sites.

Kiki a Ola (Menehune Ditch)   Hawaiians were expert rock builders, able to construct elaborate edifices without using mortar. They formed long lines and passed stones hand over hand, and lifted rocks weighing tons with ropes made from native plants. Their feats gave rise to fantastic tales of *menehune,* elflike people hired by Hawaiian kings to create massive stoneworks in a single night— reputedly for the payment of a single shrimp (see the box "Discover the Legendary Little People," above). An excellent example of ancient Hawaiian construction is Kiki a Ola, the so-called Menehune Ditch, with cut and dressed stones that form an ancient aqueduct that still directs water to irrigate taro ponds. Historians credit the work to ancient Hawaiian engineers who applied their knowledge of hydraulics to accomplish flood control and irrigation. Only a 2-foot-high portion of the wall can be seen today; the rest of the marvelous stonework is buried under the roadbed.

From Hwy. 50, go inland on Menehune Rd.; a plaque marks the spot about 1½ miles up.

Russian Fort Elizabeth State Historical Park To the list of those who tried to conquer Hawaii, add the Russians. In 1815, a German doctor tried to claim Kauai for Russia. He even supervised the construction of a fort in Waimea, but he and his handful of Russian companions were expelled by Kamehameha I a couple of years later. Now a state historic landmark, the Russian Fort Elizabeth (named for the wife of Russia's Czar Alexander I) is on the eastern headlands overlooking the harbor, across from Lucy Kapahu Aukai Wright Beach Park. The fort, built Hawaiian style with stacked lava rocks in the shape of a star, once bristled with cannons; it's now mostly in ruins. You can take a free, self-guided tour of the site, which affords a keen view of the west bank of the Waimea River, where Captain Cook landed, and of the island of Niihau across the channel.

Hwy. 50 (on the ocean side, just after mile marker 22), east of Waimea.

THE GRAND CANYON OF THE PACIFIC: WAIMEA CANYON ★★★

The great gaping gulch known as Waimea Canyon is quite a sight. This valley, known for its reddish lava beds, reminds everyone who sees it of the Grand Canyon. Kauai's version is bursting with ever-changing color, just like its namesake, but it's smaller—only a mile wide, 3,567 feet deep, and 12 miles long. A massive earthquake sent all the streams flowing into a single river that ultimately carved this picturesque canyon. Today, the Waimea River—a silver thread of water in the gorge that's sometimes a trickle, often a torrent, but always there—keeps cutting the canyon deeper and wider, and nobody can say what the result will be 100 million years from now.

You can stop by the road and look at the canyon, hike down into it, or swoop through it in a helicopter. For more information, see "Hiking & Camping," earlier in this chapter, and "Helicopter Rides over Waimea Canyon & the Na Pali Coast," below.

THE DRIVE THROUGH WAIMEA CANYON & UP TO KOKEE

By car, there are two ways to visit Waimea Canyon and reach Kokee State Park, 20 miles up from Waimea. From the coastal road (Hwy. 50), you can turn up Waimea Canyon Drive (Hwy. 550) at Waimea town, or you can pass through Waimea and turn up Kokee Road (Hwy. 55) at Kekaha. The climb is very steep from Kekaha, but Waimea Canyon Drive, the rim road, is narrower and rougher. A few miles up, the two merge into Kokee Road.

The first good vantage point is **Waimea Canyon Lookout,** located between mile markers 10 and 11 on Waimea Canyon Road. From here, it's another 6 miles to Kokee. There are a few more lookout points along the way that also offer spectacular views, such as **Puu Hina Hina Lookout,** between mile markers 13 and 14, at 3,336 feet; be sure to pull over and spend a few minutes pondering this natural wonder. (The giant white object that looks like a golf ball and defaces the natural landscape is a radar station left over from the Cold War.)

KOKEE STATE PARK

It's only 16 miles from Waimea to Kokee, but it's a whole different world because the park is 4,345 acres of rain forest. You'll enter a new climate zone, where the breeze has a bite and trees look quite continental. You're in a cloud forest on the edge of the Alakai Swamp, the largest swamp in Hawaii, on the summit plateau of Kauai. Days are cool and wet, with intermittent bright sunshine, not unlike Seattle on a good day. Bring your sweater, and, if you're staying over, be sure you know how to light a fire (overnight lows dip into the 40s).

The forest is full of native plants, such as mokihana berry, ohia lehua tree, iliau (similar to Maui's silversword), and imports like Australia's eucalyptus and California's redwood. Pigs, goats, and black-tailed deer thrive in the forest, but the moa, or Polynesian jungle fowl, is the cock of the walk.

Right next to Kokee Lodge (which lies on the only road through the park, about a mile before it ends) is the **Kokee Natural History Museum** ⚐ (© **808/ 335-9975;** www.aloha.net/~kokee), open daily from 10am to 4pm (free admission). This is the best place to learn about the forest and Alakai Swamp before you set off hiking in the wild. The museum shop has great trail information and local books and maps, including the official park trail map. We recommend getting the *Pocket Guide on Native Plants on the Nature Trail for Kokee State Park* and the *Road Guide to Kokee and Waimea Canyon State Park.*

A **nature walk** is the best intro to this rain forest; it starts behind the museum at the rare Hawaiian koa tree. This easy, self-guided walk of about a ¼ mile takes about 20 minutes if you stop and look at all the plants identified along the way.

Two miles above Kokee Lodge is **Kalalau Lookout** ⚐, the spectacular climax of your drive through Waimea Canyon and Kokee. When you stand at the lookout, below you is a work in progress that began at least 5 million years ago. It's hard to stop looking; the view is breathtaking, especially when light and cloud shadows play across the red-and-orange cliffs.

There's lots more to see and do up here: Anglers fly-fish for rainbow trout, and hikers tackle the 45 trails that lace the Alakai Swamp (see "Watersports" and "Hiking & Camping," earlier in this chapter). That's a lot of ground to cover, so you might want to plan on staying over. If pitching a tent is too rustic for you, the wonderful **cabins** set in a grove of redwoods are one of the best lodging bargains in the islands (see "Where to Stay," earlier in this chapter). The restaurant at **Kokee Lodge** is open for continental breakfast and lunch, daily from 9am to 3:30pm.

For advance information, contact the **State Division of Parks,** P.O. Box 1671, Lihue, HI 96766 (© **808/335-5871**); and the **Kokee Lodge Manager,** P.O. Box 819, Waimea, HI 96796 (© **808/335-6061**). The park is open daily year-round. The best time to go is early in the morning, to see the panoramic view of Kalalau Valley from the lookout at 4,000 feet, before clouds obscure the valley and peaks.

HELICOPTER RIDES OVER WAIMEA CANYON & THE NA PALI COAST ⚐⚐⚐

Don't leave Kauai without seeing it from a helicopter. It's expensive but worth the splurge. You can take home memories of the thrilling ride up and over the Kalalau Valley on Kauai's wild North Shore and into the 5,200-foot vertical temple of Mount Waialeale, the most sacred place on the island and the wettest spot on earth (and in some cases, you can even take a video of your ride home). All flights leave from Lihue Airport.

Island Helicopters ⚐   Curt Lofstedt has been flying helicopter tours of Kauai for nearly 3 decades. He personally selects and trains professional pilots with an eye not only to their flying skills but also to their ability to share the magic of Kauai. All flights are in either the four-passenger Bell Jet Ranger III or the six-passenger Aerospatiale A-Star, with extra large windows and stereo headsets to hear the pilot's personal narration.

Lihue Airport. © 800/829-5999 or 808/245-8588. www.islandhelicopters.com. 55-minute island tour $212. Mention *Frommer's* and receive 37% off.

Jack Harter ⭐   The pioneer of helicopter flights on Kauai, Jack was the guy who started the sightseeing-via-helicopter trend. On the 60-minute tour, he flies a four-passenger Bell Jet Ranger Model 204 (with "scenic view" windows), a six-seater A-star, or a Eurocopter AS350BA A-star. The 90-minute tour (in the Bell Jet Ranger only) hovers over the sights a bit longer than the 60-minute flight, so you can get a good look, but we found the shorter tour sufficient.

4231 Ahukini Rd., Lihue. ℭ **888/245-2001** or 808/245-3774. www.helicopters-kauai.com. 60-minute tour $189; 90-minute tour $249 (book on the Internet and save up to 15%).

Ohana Helicopter Tours   Hawaiian-born pilot Bogart Kealoha delights in showing his island his way—aboard one of his four-passenger Bell Jet Rangers or his six-passenger Aerospatiale A-Star helicopter. You're linked to a customized audio entertainment system through individual headsets with narration as you swoop over and through 12-mile long Waimea Canyon on a memorable sightseeing flight that also includes the valleys and waterfalls of the Na Pali Coast.

Anchor Cove Shopping Center, 3416 Rice St., Lihue. ℭ **800/222-6989** or 808/245-3996. www.ohana helicopters.com. 50- to 55-minute tour $153; 65- to 70-minute tour $192.

Will Squyres Helicopter Tours   The 60-minute flight starts in Lihue and takes you through Waimea Canyon, along the Na Pali Coast, and over Waialeale Crater and the two sets of waterfalls that appeared in *Fantasy Island*. Will's A-star six-passenger copter has side-by-side seats (nobody sits backward and everybody gets a window seat) and enlarged windows. A veteran pilot, Will has flown several thousand hours over Kauai since 1984 and knows the island, its ever-changing weather conditions, and his copters.

3222 Kuhio Hwy., Lihue. ℭ **888/245-4354** or 808/245-8881. www.helicopters-hawaii.com. 60-minute Grand Tour of Kauai $165.

THE COCONUT COAST

Fern Grotto   This is one of Kauai's oldest ("since 1947") and most popular tourist attractions. Several times daily, **Smith's Motor Boats** (ℭ **808/821-6892**) and **Waialeale Boat Tours** (ℭ **808/822-4908**) take 150 people up and down the river on a 90-minute, 2½-mile, motorized river trip to a natural amphitheater filled with ferns. The grotto is the source of many Hawaiian legends and a popular site for weddings.

Wailua Marina, at the mouth of the Wailua River; turn off Kuhio Hwy. (Hwy. 56) into Wailua Marine State Park. Daily 9am–3:30pm. Admission $15 adults, $7.50 children 3–12; reservations recommended.

WAILUA RIVER STATE PARK

Ancients called the Wailua River "the river of the great sacred spirit." Seven temples once stood along this 20-mile river, which is fed by 5,148-foot Mount Waialeale, the wettest spot on earth. You can go up Hawaii's biggest navigable river by boat or kayak (see "Boating" and "Kayaking," earlier in this chapter), or drive Kuamoo Road (Hwy. 580, sometimes called the King's Highway), which goes inland along the north side of the river from Kuhio Highway (Hwy. 56)—from the northbound lane, turn left at the stoplight just before the ruins of Coco Palms Resort. Kuamoo Road goes past the *heiau* (temple) and historical sites to Opaekaa Falls and Keahua Arboretum, a State Division of Forestry attempt to reforest the watershed with native plants.

The entire district from the river mouth to the summit of Waialeale was once royal land. This sacred, historical site was believed to be founded by Puna, a Tahitian priest who, according to legend, arrived in one of the first double-hulled voyaging canoes to come to Hawaii, established a beachhead, and

Hollywood Loves Kauai

More than 50 major Hollywood productions have been shot on Kauai since the studios discovered the island's spectacular natural beauty. Here are just a few:

- Manawaiopu Falls, Mount Waialeale, and other scenic areas around the island doubled for *Jurassic Park*.
- Kauai's lush rain forests formed a fantastic backdrop for Harrison Ford in both *Raiders of the Lost Ark* and *Indiana Jones and the Temple of Doom*.
- Mitzi Gaynor sang "I'm Gonna Wash That Man Right Outta My Hair" on Lumahai Beach in *South Pacific*.
- Jessica Lange, Jeff Bridges, and Charles Grodin tangled with Hollywood's most famous gorilla in Honopu Valley, in the remake of *King Kong* (1976).
- Elvis Presley married costar Joan Blackman near the Wailua River in *Blue Hawaii* (1961).
- Beautiful Kee Beach, on the North Shore, masqueraded as Australia in the miniseries *The Thornbirds,* starring Richard Chamberlain and Rachel Ward.
- Kauai appeared as the backdrop for *Outbreak,* the 1994 thriller about the spread of a deadly virus on a remote tropical island, starring Dustin Hoffman. Hoffman also appeared with Robin Williams and Julia Roberts in *Hook* (1991), in which Kauai appeared as Never-Never Land.
- James Caan, Nicholas Cage, Sarah Jessica Parker, and Pat Morita shared laughs on Kauai (which appeared as itself) in *Honeymoon in Vegas*.

Now you can visit these and other Kauai locations that made it to the silver screen, plus locations from such TV classics as *Fantasy Island* and *Gilligan's Island,* with **Hawaii Movie Tours** (© **800/628-8432** or 808/822-1192; www.hawaiimovietour.com). The commentary and sightseeing stops are supplemented by video clips of the location shots (complete with surround sound); in addition, a guide leads sing-alongs of movie and TV themes as you go from locale to locale in the new 16-passenger minivan (for comfort, only 11 passengers are carried). All in all, there's a whole lot of fun to be had, especially for families. You'll see more of Kauai on this tour (including private estates not open to the public) than you would if you explored the island yourself. Tickets are $95 for adults and $76 for children 11 and under; lunch is included.

declared Kauai his kingdom. All of Kauai's *alii* (royalty) are believed to be descended from Puna. Here, in this royal settlement, are remains of the seven temples, including a sacrificial heiau, a planetarium (a simple array of rocks in a celestial pattern), the royal birthing stones, and a stone bell to announce a royal birth. (You can still ring the bell—many people have—but make sure you have an announcement to make when it stops ringing.)

There's a nice overlook view of 40-foot **Opaekaa Falls** ★★ 1½ miles up Highway 580. This is probably the best-looking drive-up waterfall on Kauai. With the scenic peaks of Makaleha mountains in the background and a restored Hawaiian village on the riverbanks, these falls are what the tourist-bureau folks call an "eye-popping" photo op.

Near Opaekaa Falls overlook is **Poliahu Heiau,** the large lava-rock temple of Kauai's last king, Kaumualii, who died on Oahu in 1824 after being abducted by King Kamehameha II. If you stop here, you'll notice two signs. The first, an official 1928 bronze territorial plaque, says that the royal heiau was built by menehunes, which it explains parenthetically as "Hawaiian dwarves or brownies." A more recent, hand-painted sign warns visitors not to climb on the rocks, which are sacred to the Hawaiian people.

SLEEPING GIANT

If you squint your eyes just so as you pass the 1,241-foot-high Nounou Ridge, which forms a dramatic backdrop to the coastal villages of Wailua and Waipouli, you can see the fabled Sleeping Giant. On Kuhio Highway, just after mile marker 7, around the minimall complex Waipouli Town Center, look *mauka* (inland) and you may see what appears to be the legendary giant named Puni, who, as the story goes, fell asleep after a great feast. If you don't see it at first, visualize it this way: His head is Wailua and his feet are Kapaa. For details on an easy hike to the top of the Sleeping Giant, see "The Sleeping Giant Trail," p. 588.

PARADISE FOUND: THE NORTH SHORE ★★★
ON THE ROAD TO HANALEI

The first place everyone should go on Kauai is Hanalei. The drive along **Kuhio Highway** (Hwy. 56, which becomes Hwy. 560 after Princeville to the end of the road), displays Kauai's grandeur at its absolute best. Just before Kilauea, the air and the sea change, the light falls in a different way, and the last signs of development are behind you. Now there are roadside fruit stands, a little stone church

---

Kids Kauai Children's Discovery Museum

This is every parent's dream: an enthralling, hands-on learning adventure to take kids on rainy days (hey, it's so much fun, the kids will beg to come back even on sunny days). The **Kauai Children's Discovery Museum,** located under the Whale Tower, in the Kauai Village Shopping Center, in Kapaa (© **808/823-8222,** www.kcdm.org), arose out of a grass roots community effort to have a fun place where kids could learn about science, culture, arts, technology and nature. Not only are the hands-on, interactive exhibits thrilling to kids, but it's a great place for your kids to interact and meet children from Kauai. The 7,000-square-foot play center is open Tuesday to Saturday from 9am to 5pm; during school breaks they also are open on Monday from 7am to 5pm. In addition to the exhibits, which range from playing with Hawaiian musical instruments to participating in virtual reality television to hiding out in a "magic tree house" and reading a book (there's even a baby area for kids 4 and under), there also are Keiki Camps (Children Camps), where you can leave the kids all day for various outings to the beach and to points of interest. Admission is $3.50 for kids and $4.50 for adults, with family memberships available.

Tips **Bridge Etiquette: Showing Aloha on Kauai's One Lane Bridges**

Contrary to the aggressive driving you see on the Mainland, Hawaii's drivers are much more laid back and courteous than most. Hanalei has a series of one-lane bridges where it is not only proper etiquette to be courteous, but it also is the law. When you approach a one-lane bridge, slow down and YIELD if a vehicle, approaching in the opposite direction, is either on the bridge or just about to enter the bridge (this is not a contest of chicken). If you are in a long line of vehicles approaching the bridge, don't just join the train crossing the bridge. The local "rule of thumb" is about seven to eight cars over the bridge, then yield and give the cars waiting on the other side of the bridge a chance to come across. Of course, not everyone will adhere to these rules, but then, not everyone visiting Hawaii truly feels the spirit of aloha.

---

in Kilauea, two roadside waterfalls, and a long, stiltlike bridge over the Kalihiwai Stream and its green river valley.

If you don't know a guava from a mango, stop in Kilauea at the cool, shady **Guava Kai Plantation,** at the end of Kuawa Road (© **808/828-6121**), for a refreshing, free treat. After you take a walk through the orchards and see what a guava looks like on the tree, you can sample the juice of this exotic pink tropical fruit (which also makes a great jam or jelly—sold here, too). For other sweet treats along the way, check out the box "Fruity Smoothies & Other Exotic Treats," on p. 606. The plantation is open daily from 9am to 5pm.

Birders might want to stop off at **Kilauea Point National Wildlife Refuge,** a mile north of Kilauea, and the **Hanalei National Wildlife Refuge,** along Ohiki Road, at the west end of the Hanalei River Bridge. (For details, see "Birding," earlier in this chapter.) In the Hanalei Refuge, along a dirt road on a levee, you can see the **Hariguchi Rice Mill,** now a historic treasure.

Now the coastal highway heads due west and the showy ridgelines of Mount Namahana create a grand amphitheater. The two-lane coastal highway rolls through pastures of grazing cattle and past a tiny airport and the luxurious Princeville Hotel.

Five miles past Kilauea, just past the Princeville Shopping Center, is **Hanalei Valley Lookout.** Big enough for a dozen cars, this lookout attracts crowds of people who peer over the edge into the 917-acre Hanalei River Valley. So many shades of green: rice green, taro green, and green streams lace a patchwork of green ponds that back up to green-velvet Bali Ha'i cliffs. Pause to catch the first sight of taro growing in irrigated ponds; maybe you'll see an endangered Hawaiian black-necked stilt. Don't be put off by the crowds; this is definitely worth a look.

Farther along, a hairpin turn offers another scenic look at Hanalei town and then you cross the **Hanalei Bridge.** The Pratt truss steel bridge, pre-fabbed in New York City, was erected in 1912; it's now on the National Registry of Historic Landmarks. If it ever goes out, the nature of Hanalei will change forever; currently, this rusty, one-lane bridge (which must violate all kinds of Department of Transportation safety regulations) isn't big enough for a tour bus to cross.

You'll drive slowly past the **Hanalei River banks** and Bill Mowry's **Hanalei Buffalo Ranch,** where 200 American bison roam in the tropic sun; you may even see buffalo grazing in the pastures on your right. The herd is often thinned

Kauai's North Shore: Princeville & Hanalei

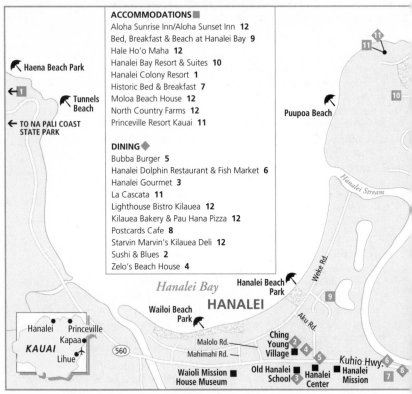

ACCOMMODATIONS ■
Aloha Sunrise Inn/Aloha Sunset Inn **12**
Bed, Breakfast & Beach at Hanalei Bay **9**
Hale Ho'o Maha **12**
Hanalei Bay Resort & Suites **10**
Hanalei Colony Resort **1**
Historic Bed & Breakfast **7**
Moloa Beach House **12**
North Country Farms **12**
Princeville Resort Kauai **11**

DINING ◆
Bubba Burger **5**
Hanalei Dolphin Restaurant & Fish Market **6**
Hanalei Gourmet **3**
La Cascata **11**
Lighthouse Bistro Kilauea **12**
Kilauea Bakery & Pau Hana Pizza **12**
Postcards Cafe **8**
Starvin Marvin's Kilauea Deli **12**
Sushi & Blues **2**
Zelo's Beach House **4**

Haena Beach Park

Tunnels
Beach

← TO NA PALI COAST
STATE PARK

Puupoa Beach

Hanalei Stream

Hanalei Bay
HANALEI

Hanalei Beach
Park

Wailoi Beach
Park

Weke Rd.

Aku Rd.

Hanalei
Princeville
Kapaa
KAUAI
Lihue

560

Malolo Rd.
Mahimahi Rd.

Ching
Young
Village

Kuhio Hwy.

Waioli Mission
House Museum

Old Hanalei
School

Hanalei
Center

Hanalei
Mission

to make buffalo patties. (You wondered why there was a Buffalo Burger on the Ono Family Restaurant menu, didn't you?)

Just past Tahiti Nui, turn right on Aku Road before Ching Young Village, then take a right on Weke Road; **Hanalei Beach Park,** one of Hawaii's most gorgeous, is a ½ block ahead on your left. Swimming is excellent here year-round, especially in summer, when Hanalei Bay becomes a big, placid lake; for details, see "Beaches," earlier in this chapter.

If this exquisite 2-mile-long beach doesn't meet your expectations, head down the highway, where the next 7 miles of coast yield some of Kauai's other spectacular beaches, including **Lumahai Beach,** of *South Pacific* movie fame, as well as **Tunnels Beach** (p. 576), where the 1960s puka-shell necklace craze began, and **Haena Beach Park** (p. 576), a fabulous place to kick back and enjoy the waves, particularly in summer. Once you've found your beach, stick around until sundown, then head back to one of the North Shore's restaurants for a mai tai and a fresh seafood dinner (see "Where to Dine," earlier in this chapter). Another perfect day in paradise.

ATTRACTIONS ALONG THE WAY

Ka Ulu O Laka Heiau   On a knoll above the boulders of Kee Beach (p. 577) stands a sacred altar of rocks, often draped with flower leis and ti-leaf offerings, dedicated to Laka, the goddess of hula. It may seem like a primal relic from the days of idols, but it's very much in use today. Often, dancers (men and women)

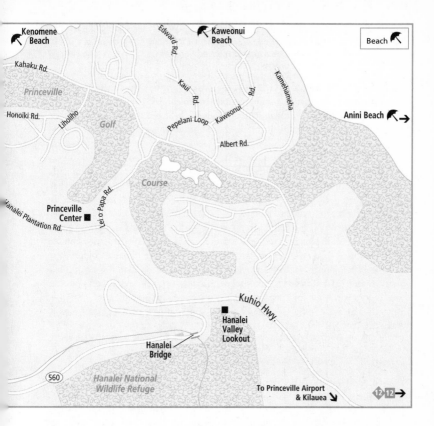

of Hawaii's hula *halau* (schools) climb the cliff, bearing small gifts of flowers. In Hawaiian myths, Lohiau, a handsome chief, danced here before the fire goddess Pele; their passion became *Haena*, which means "the heat." Sometimes, in a revival of the old Hawaiian ways (once banned by missionaries), a mother of a newborn will deposit the umbilical cord of her infant at this sacred shrine. The site is filled with what Hawaiians call *mana*, or power.

From the west side of Kee Beach, take the footpath across the big rocks almost to the point; then climb the steep grassy hill.

Limahuli Garden of the National Tropical Botanical Garden ★
Out on Kauai's far North Shore, beyond Hanalei and the last wooden bridge, there's a mighty cleft in the coastal range where ancestral Hawaiians lived in what can only be called paradise. Carved by a waterfall stream known as Limahuli, the lush valley sits at the foot of steepled cliffs that Hollywood portrayed as Bali Ha'i in the film classic *South Pacific*. This small, almost secret garden is ecotourism at its best. It appeals not just to green thumbs but to all who love Hawaii's great outdoors. Here botanists hope to save Kauai's endangered native plants. You can take the self-tour to view the plants, which are identified in Hawaiian and English. From taro to sugarcane, the mostly Polynesian imports tell the story of the people who cultivated the plants for food, medicine, clothing, shelter, and decoration. In addition, Limahuli's stream is sanctuary to the last five species of Hawaiian freshwater fish.

Visitor Center, ½ mile past mile marker 9 on Kuhio Hwy. (Hwy. 560), Haena. © **808/826-1053.** Fax 808/826-1394. www.ntbg.org. Admission $10 self-guided, $15 guided; free for children 12 and under. Open Tues–Fri and Sun 10am–4pm. Advance reservations required for 2½-hour guided tours. During peak seasons of July, Aug, and Sept, book at least a week ahead.

Na Aina Kai Botanical Gardens ★★★ *Finds*   Do not miss this incredible, magical garden on some 240 acres, sprinkled with some 70 life-size (some larger than life size) whimsical bronze statues, hidden off the beaten path of the North Shore. Recently opened, this is the place for both avid gardeners as well as people who think they don't like botanical gardens. They have everything: waterfalls, pools, arbors, topiaries, colonnades, gazebos, a maze you will never forget, a lagoon with spouting fountains, a Japanese teahouse, and an enchanting path along a bubbling stream to the ocean. The imaginary, fairy-tale creativity that has gone into these grounds will be one of your fondest memories of Kauai. A host of different tours are available, from 1½ hours ($25) to 5 hours ($70) long, ranging from casual, guided strolls to riding in the covered CarTram to treks from one end of the gardens to the ocean. A tropical children's garden was under construction as this book went to press with a gecko hedge maze, a tropical jungle gym, a tree house in a rubber tree, and a 16-foot tall Jack-in-the-Bean Stalk Giant with a 33-foot wading pool below. It's only open 3 days a week; book a tour before you leave for Hawaii, so you won't be disappointed.

4101 Wailapa Rd., (write: P.O. Box 1134), Kilauea, HI 96754. © **808/828-0525.** Fax 808/828-0815. www.na ainakai.com. Open Tues–Thurs, 8am–5pm. Tours vary. Advance reservations strongly recommended. To get there from Lihue, drive north past mile marker 21 and turn right on Waiapa Rd. At the road's end drive through the iron gates. From Princeville, drive south 6½ miles and take the second left past mile marker 22 on Wailapa Rd. At the road's end drive through the iron gates.

Waioli Mission House Museum   If you're lucky and time your visit just right, you can visit this 150-year-old mission house, which serves today as a living museum. It's a real treasure. Others in Honolulu are easier to see, but the Waioli Mission House retains its sense of place and most of its furnishings, so you can really get a clear picture of what life was like for the New England missionaries who came to Kauai to convert the heathens to Christianity.

Most mission houses are small, dark Boston cottages that violate the tropical sense of place. This two-story, wood-frame house, built in 1836 by Abner and Lucy Wilcox of New Bedford, Massachusetts, is an excellent example of hybrid architecture. The house features a lanai on both stories, with a cookhouse in a separate building. It has a lava-rock chimney, ohia-wood floors, and Hawaiian koa furniture.

Kuhio Hwy. (Hwy. 560), just behind the green Waioli Huia Church, Hanalei. © **808/245-3202.** Free admission (donations gratefully accepted). Tours: Mon and Wed–Thurs, 10am and 1pm. Reservations required.

THE END OF THE ROAD

The real Hawaii begins where the road stops. This is especially true on Kauai— for at the end of Highway 56, the spectacular **Na Pali Coast** begins. To explore it, you have to set out on foot, by boat, or by helicopter. For details on experiencing this region, see "Hiking & Camping," "Boating," and "Helicopter Rides over Waimea Canyon & the Na Pali Coast," earlier in this chapter.

10 Shops & Galleries

Shopping is a pleasure on this island. Where else can you browse vintage Hawaii-ana practically in a cane field, buy exquisite home accessories in an old stone building built in 1942, and get a virtual agricultural tour of the island through city-sponsored green markets that move from town to town throughout the week, like a movable feast? At Kauai's small, tasteful boutiques, you can satisfy your shopping ya-yas in concentrated spurts around the island. This is a bonanza for the boutique shopper—particularly the one who appreciates the thrill of the hunt.

"Downtown" Kapaa continues to flourish, and Hanalei, touristy as it is, is still a shopping destination. (Ola's and Yellowfish make up for the hurricane of trinkets and trash in Hanalei.) Kilauea, with Kong Lung Store and the fabulous new Lotus Gallery, is the style center of the island. The Kauai Heritage Center of Hawaiian Culture & the Arts makes it possible for visitors to escape the usual imitations, tourist traps, and clichés in favor of authentic encounters with the real thing: Hawaiian arts, Hawaiian cultural practices, and Hawaiian elders and artists. What else can you expect on Kauai? Anticipate great shops in Hanalei, a few art galleries and boutiques, and a handful of shopping centers—not much to distract you from an afternoon of hiking or snorkeling. The gift items and treasures you'll find in east and north Kauai, however, may be among your best Hawaiian finds.

GREEN MARKETS & FRUIT STANDS   The county of Kauai sponsors regular weekly **Sunshine Markets** throughout the island, featuring fresh Kauai **Sunrise papayas** (sweeter, juicier, and redder than most), herbs and vegetables used in ethnic cuisines, exotic fruit such as rambutan and atemoya, and the most exciting development in pineapple agriculture, the low-acid white pineapple called **Sugarloaf,** rarer these days but still spottily available. These markets, which sell the full range of fresh local produce and flowers at rock-bottom prices, present the perfect opportunity to see what's best and what's in season. Farmers sell their bounty from the backs of trucks or at tables set up under tarps. Mangoes during the summer, lettuces all year, fleshy bananas and juicy papayas, the full range of Filipino vegetables (wing beans, long beans, exotic squashes, and melons), and an ever-changing rainbow of edibles are all on offer.

The biggest market is at **Kapaa New Town Park,** in the middle of Kapaa town, on Wednesday at 3pm. The Sunshine Market in **Lihue,** held on Friday at 3pm at the Vidhina Stadium Parking Lot, is close in size and extremely popular. The schedule for the other markets: **Koloa Ball Park,** Monday at noon; **Kalaheo Neighborhood Center,** Tuesday at 3:30pm; **Hanapepe Park,** Thursday at 3pm; **Kilauea Neighborhood Center,** Thursday at 4:30pm; and **Kekaha Neighborhood Center,** Saturday at 9am. For more information on Sunshine Markets, call © **808/241-6390.** Especially at the Koloa Market, which draws hundreds of shoppers, go early and shop briskly.

Those who miss the Sunshine Markets can shop instead at the privately run **Sunnyside Farmers Market** (© **808/822-0494**), on Kuhio Highway in the middle of Kapaa, open Monday through Saturday from 7am to 7:30pm and Sunday from 10am to 6pm. You'll find several varieties of papayas (grown by the same farmer they've used for 20 years), mangoes, lilikoi (passion fruit), Sugarloaf pineapples, locally grown organic lettuces, Maui onions, purple Molokai sweet potatoes, Molokai watermelons, and exotic fruits, such as soursop and rambutan in season. Fruit preserves, gourmet breads, **Taro Ko chips,** and Kauai macadamia-nut cookies are among the made-on-Kauai products that are shipped and carried all over the United States. The expanded **Dori's Garden Cafe** adjoining the market serves sandwiches, soups, salads, and smoothies—everything from fresh juices to Lappert's ice cream.

Fruity Smoothies & Other Exotic Treats

Fruit stands have sprouted on this island, and smoothies are gaining ground as the milk shake of the new millennium. New crops of exotic trees imported from southeast Asia are maturing on Kauai, creating anticipation among residents and fruitful ideas for the smoothie world. "Everyone's waiting for the mangosteens and durians," comments Joe Halasey, who, with his wife, Cynthia, runs **Banana Joe's** (© **808/828-1092**), the granddaddy of Kauai's roadside fruit-and-smoothie stands. "They take about 12 years to start bearing, so there are a lot of maturing trees. We're all waiting for the fruit. Rambutans [with a hairy, red exterior and a translucent, lycheelike flesh] are good for the farmers here because they're available, and they're a winter fruit. In the summer, mangoes and lychees are always in high demand."

Banana Joe's has been a Kilauea landmark since it opened in 1986 at 52719 Kuhio Hwy., between mile markers 23 and 24 heading north, on the mauka (mountain) side of the street. Sapodilla, star apple (round, purple, and sweet, like a creamy Concord grape), macadamia nuts, Anahola Granola, and homemade breads—like banana and mango-coconut—are among Banana Joe's attractions. The Halaseys have expanded their selection of organic vegetables and exude a quiet aloha from their roadside oasis.

Mangosteen, reputedly the favorite fruit of Queen Victoria, has a creamy, custardy flesh of ambrosial sweetness. When mangosteen starts appearing at Hawaii fruit stands, it will no doubt be in high demand, like mangoes and lychees during their summer season. In the meantime, Banana Joe has a hit on his hands with Sugarloaf, the white, nonacidic, ultra-sweet, organically grown pineapple popularized on the Big Island. Whether made into smoothies or frostees (frozen fruit put through the Champion juicer), or just sold plain, fresh, and whole, the Sugarloaf is pineapple at its best. For lychee lovers, who must wait for their summer appearance, new varieties such as Kaimana and Brewster are adding to

On the North Shore, Kilauea is the agricultural heart of the island, with two weekly green markets: the county-sponsored **Sunshine Market,** Thursday at 4:30pm at the Kilauea Neighborhood Center; and the private Kilauea Quality Farmers Association (mostly organic growers) **Farmers Market,** Saturday from 11:30am to 1:30pm behind the Kilauea Post Office. Everything in the wide-ranging selection is grown or made on Kauai, from rambutan and long beans to sweet potatoes, corn, lettuce, and salsas and chutneys. This is a dramatic, colorful tableau of how farming activity and enterprises are growing by leaps and bounds in Kilauea.

Also on the North Shore, about a quarter mile past Hanalei in an area called Waipa, the **Hawaiian Farmers of Hanalei**—anywhere from a dozen to 25 farmers—gather along the main road with their budget-friendly, just-picked produce. This market is held every Tuesday at 2pm. You'll find unbelievably priced papayas (in some seasons, several for a dollar, ready to eat), organic vegetables, inexpensive tropical flowers, avocados and mangoes in season, and, the pleasures of the season. In addition to fresh fruit, fruit smoothies, and frostees, Banana Joe's sells organic greens, tropical-fruit salsas, jams and jellies, drinking coconuts (young coconuts containing delicious drinking water), gift items, and baked goods such as papaya-banana bread. Its top-selling smoothies are papaya, banana, and pineapple.

Mango Mama's, 4660 Hookui St. (© **808/828-1020**), is another favorite on the Kilauea roadside. Recently expanded, it's now a full-service cafe serving espresso, smoothies, fresh-squeezed juices, sandwiches, bagels, coffee, coffee smoothies, and fresh fruit. The Kauai Breeze (fresh mango, pineapple, passion fruit, and guava) is a big winner here.

At the north end of Kapaa town, **Killer Juice Bar,** 4–1586 Kuhio Hwy. (© **808/821-1905**), is a sight for sore eyes after a drive through commercial Kapaa. Smoothies are $2.50 to $5.50, fresh juices are $1.25 (wheat grass) to $5 (carrot)—and they're good! An attractive selection of fresh fruit—gemlike tomatoes, atemoyas, starfruit, papayas—is displayed in the front. Queen of the smoothies is the Amazing Mango Memory, made with fresh local mangoes in season or, when they're not available, fresh mangoes from Mexico. The Killer Bars, chocolate-chip squares for $1.50, live up to their name.

On the Coconut Coast, just before you reach the center of Kapaa town heading north on Kuhio Highway, keep an eye out to the left for **Sunnyside Farmers Market,** 4–1345 Kuhio Hwy. (© **808/822-0494** or 808/822-1154; see above). Here you can always find realistically priced Sunrise papayas, pineapples, local bananas, tomatoes, and other Kauai produce. You can also get preinspected Sunrise papayas for travel out of state, local apple bananas, coconuts, mangoes in season, and pineapples from Maui and Kauai.

Near the Lihue Airport, Pammie Chock at **Kauai Fruit & Flower** (© **808/245-1814**; see below) makes a pineapple–passion fruit smoothie that gets our vote as the best on the island.

when possible, fresh seafood. The best of the best, in season, are rose apples, mountain apples, and the orange-colored papaya lilikoi.

On the south shore, we're hearing great things about the two adorable fruit stands in Lawai, where you can find inexpensive bananas (sometimes $1.25 a hand!), papayas, and avocados along an old country road. The fruit are cheerfully displayed, and sometimes it's the honor system—leave the money if no one is there. This is country style nonpareil. (From Kaumualii Hwy., turn at the corner where Mustard's Last Stand is—Lauoho Rd.—then take the first right.) In Kauai jargon, directions would be: "Go to that old road where the old post office was, near Matsuura Store, the old manju place . . . ."

Closer to the resorts, in Poipu, with a view across asparagus fields and the chiseled ridges of Haupu Mountain, the **Poipu Southshore Market** sells produce, some of it by Haupu Growers, daily from 10am to 6pm on Koloa Bypass Road. Haupu Growers is the major supplier of Kauai asparagus, and this is where you'll find it. Asparagus season begins in October.

LIHUE & ENVIRONS

DOWNTOWN LIHUE   The gift shop of the **Kauai Museum,** 4428 Rice St. (© **808/245-6931**), is your best bet for made-on-Kauai arts and crafts, from Niihau-shell leis to woodwork, lauhala and coconut products, and more. The master of lauhala weaving, Esther Makuaole, weaves regularly in the gallery on Monday and Wednesday from 9am to 1:30pm.

About a mile north of the Lihue Airport, on Highway 56 (Kuhio Hwy.), **Kauai Fruit & Flower** is a great stop for flowers, including the rare Kauai maile in season, coconut drums the owner makes himself, Hawaiian gourds (*ipu*), cut flowers for shipping, and Kauai fruit, such as papayas and pineapples. Other products include lauhala gift items, teas, Kauai honey, Kauai salad dressings, jams and jellies, and custom-made gift baskets.

In the **Kukui Grove Center,** at Kaumualii Highway (Hwy. 50) and Old Nawiliwili Road, is the **Kauai Products Store** (© **808/246-6753**). It's a fount of local handicrafts (about 60% Kauai artists) and a respectable showcase for made-on-the-island products, such as soaps, paintings, clothing, coffee, Kukui guava jams, fabrics, and Niihau-shell leis. The Hawaiian quilts are made in the Philippines but designed by Kauai families. You'll find everything from a $10,750 bronze sculpture to bamboo chairs and koa ukulele by Raymond Rapozo in Kealia, who does stunning work. Beware of the macadamia nut fudge, found only at Kauai Products Store: It's rich, sweet, and irresistible. Across the mall is the **Deli and Bread Connection** (© **808/245-7715**), which sells soups, sandwiches (in the $4–$5 range), and deli items as well as pots, china, and hundreds of kitchen gadgets.

KILOHANA PLANTATION   Kilohana, the 35-acre Tudor-style estate that sprawls across the landscape in Puhi, on Highway 50 between Lihue and Poipu, is an architectural marvel that houses a sprinkling of galleries and shops. At the **Country Store,** on the ground level, you'll find island and American crafts of decent quality, koa accessories, pottery, and Hawaii-themed gift items. On the other side of Gaylord's, the **Kilohana and Kahn galleries** offer a mix of crafts and two-dimensional art, from originals to affordable prints, at all levels of taste.

THE POIPU RESORT AREA

Expect mostly touristy shops in Poipu, the island's resort mecca; here you'll find T-shirts, souvenirs, black pearls, jewelry, and the usual quota of tired marine art and trite hand-painted silks.

Exceptions: The formerly characterless **Poipu Shopping Village,** at 2360 Kiahuna Plantation Dr., is shaping up to be a serious shopping stop. **Hale Mana** is a glorious collection of hard-to-find gift items of excellent taste: fabulous incense sticks from Provence (lavender, amber, vanilla), antique picture frames, lacquer boxes, beaded bags, unique candles, sterling-silver chopsticks, sake sets, pillows, masks, Hawaiian handmade paper, and jewelry by Kauai artist Adove. The staggering selection also includes dramatic acrylic jewelry that looks like elk horn, one-of-a-kind jewelry and purses by Maya, gemlike sake cups, cotton yukatas, silk kimono, snuff bottles, and diaphanous silk dresses that you won't find elsewhere in Hawaii. Also in Poipu Shopping Village, the tiny **Bamboo Lace** boutique lures the fashionistas; its resort wear and accessories can segue from Hawaii to the south of France in one easy heartbeat. Across the courtyard, **Sand People** is great for understated resort wear (such as Tencel jeans) and Indonesian coconut picture frames, while the newly renovated **Overboard** rides the wave of popularity in aloha wear and surf stuff.

The shopping is surprisingly good at the **Hyatt Regency Kauai,** with the footwear mecca **Sandal Tree, Water Wear Hawaii** for swim stuff, **Reyn's** for top-drawer aloha shirts, **Kauai Kids** for the underage and **McInery,** an institution in Hawaii for aloha wear.

Across the street from Poipu Beach, on Hoone Road, **Nukumoi Surf Shop** is a pleasant surprise: an excellent selection of sunglasses, swimwear, surf equipment, and watersports regalia, and not just for the under-20 crowd.

In neighboring **Old Koloa Town,** you'll find everything from **Lappert's Ice Cream** and **Island Soap and Candle Works** (where you can watch them make soap and candles) to **Crazy Shirts** and **Sueoka Store** on Koloa's main drag, Koloa Road. Just walk the long block for gifts, souvenirs, sun wear, groceries, soaps and bath products, and everyday necessities, but don't expect dazzling temptations.

On Poipu Road between Koloa and Poipu, in the tiny Poipu Plaza minimall, nestled next to **Sea Sport Divers** and **Outfitters Kauai,** the **Kukuiula Store** is a stop for everything from produce and sushi to paper products, sunscreen, beverages, and groceries. Occasionally, when the fishermen drop by, the store offers fresh sliced sashimi and poke, quite delicious and popular for sunset picnickers and nearby condo residents. In Kalaheo, condo dwellers and locals are flocking to the nondescript, single building, **Medeiros Farms** (4365 Papalina Rd.; ✆ **808/332-8211**) for everything they raise and make: chicken, range-fed beef, eggs, Italian pork, and Portuguese sausages. The meats are hailed across the island, and the prices are good. Medeiros Farms chicken is so good it's mentioned on some of the chichi menus on the island. Just up the street is **The Bread Box** (4447 Papalina Rd., ✆ **808/332-9000**) for just-baked breads (a deal at $3.25), gooey mac-nut rolls ($1.50), a huge variety of muffins (poppyseed, blueberry, honey oat, etc.) and wonderfully light and flaky croissants (only $1).

WESTERN KAUAI

HANAPEPE   This West Kauai hamlet is becoming a haven for artists but finding them requires some vigilance. The center of town is off Highway 50; turn right on Hanapepe Road just after Eleele if you're driving from Lihue. First, you'll smell the sumptuous lavender **Taro Ko Chips Factory** ✦, located in an old green plantation house, 3940 Hanapape Rd. Cooking in a tiny, modest kitchen at the east end of town, these famous taro chips are handmade by the farmers who grow the taro in a nearby valley. Despite their breakable nature, these chips make great gifts to go. To really impress them back home, get the lihi mung-flavored chips.

Farther on, Hanapepe Road is lined with gift shops and galleries, including **Koa Wood Gallery** and its koa furniture, koa photo albums, and Norfolk pine bowls; and the corny but cherubic **Aloha Angels,** where everything is angel-themed or angel-related. The **Kauai Village Gallery** offers abstract and surreal paintings by Kauai artist Lew Shortridge, while nearby **Kauai Fine Arts** offers an odd mix that works: antique maps and prints of Hawaii, authentic Polynesian tapa, rare wiliwili-seed leis, old Matson liner menus, and a few pieces of contemporary island art. Down the street, the **Kim Starr Gallery,** showing only Kim Starr's oil paintings, pastels, drawings, and limited-edition graphics, is a strong positive note in Hanapepe's art community. Taking a cue from Maui's Lahaina, where every Friday night is Art Night, Hanapepe's gallery owners and artists recently instituted the **Friday Night Art Walk** every Friday from 6 to 9pm. Gallery owners take turns hosting this informal event along Hanapepe Road.

WAIMEA   Neighboring Waimea is filled more with edibles than art, with Kauai's favorite native supermarket, **Big Save,** serving as the one-stop shop for area residents and passersby heading for the uplands of Kokee State Park, some 4,000 feet above this sea-level village. A cheerful distraction for lovers of Hawaiian collectibles is **Collectibles and Fine Junque,** on Highway 50, next to the fire station on the way to Waimea Canyon. This is where you'll discover what it's like to be the proverbial bull in a china shop (even a knapsack makes it hard to get through the aisles). Heaps of vintage linens, choice aloha shirts and muumuus, rare glassware (and junque, too), books, ceramics, authentic 1950s cotton chenille bedspreads, and a back room full of bargain-priced secondhand goodies always capture our attention. You never know what you'll find in this tiny corner of Waimea.

Up in Kokee State Park, the gift shop of the **Kokee Natural History Museum** (© **808/335-9975**) is *the* stop for botanical, geographical, historical, and nature-related books and gifts, not only on Kauai, but on all the islands. Audubon bird books, hiking maps, and practically every book on Kauai ever written line the shelves.

THE COCONUT COAST

As you make your way from Lihue to the North Shore, you'll pass **Bambulei** (© **808/823-8641**), bordering the canefield in Wailua next to Caffè Coco. Watch for the sign just past the Wailua intersection, across from Kintaro's Restaurant. Bambulei houses a charming collection of 1930s and 1940s treasures—everything from Peking lacquerware to exquisite vintage aloha shirts to lamps, quilts, jewelry, parrot figurines, and zany salt and pepper shakers. If it's not vintage, it will look vintage, and it's bound to be fabulous. Vintage muumuus are often in perfect condition, and dresses go for $20 to $2,000.

Wood turner **Robert Hamada** works in his studio at the foot of the Sleeping Giant, quietly producing museum-quality works with unique textures and grains. His skill, his lathe, and more than 60 years of experience have brought luminous life to the kou, milo, kauila, camphor, mango, and native woods he logs himself. Hamada was honored by the Kauai Museum in May 2001, when his private collection of woods was displayed in the main lobby in honor of his 80th birthday.

KAPAA   Moving toward Kapaa on Highway 56 (Kuhio Hwy.), don't get your shopping hopes up; until you hit Kapaa town, quality goods are slim in this neck of the woods. The **Coconut Marketplace** features the ubiquitous Elephant Walk gift shop, Gifts of Kauai, and various other underwhelming souvenir and clothing shops sprinkled among the sunglass huts. Our favorite shop here is the unassuming **Overboard,** a small but tasteful boutique with great aloha shirts by Kahala, Tommy Bahama, Duke Kahanamoku, and other top labels for men and women.

Nearby, set back from the main road across from Foodland supermarket, **Marta's Boat** is one of the island's more appealing boutiques for children and women. The shop is a tangle of accessories, toys, chic clothing, and unusual gift items.

In the green-and-white wooden storefronts of nearby **Kauai Village,** you'll find everything from **Wyland Galleries'** trite marine art to yin chiao Chinese cold pills and organic produce at **Papayas Natural Foods.** Although its prepared foods are way overpriced, Papayas carries the full range of health-food products and is your only choice in the area for vitamins, prepared health foods to go, health-conscious cosmetics, and bulk food items.

Less than a mile away on the main road, the **Waipouli Variety Store** is Kapaa's version of Maui's fabled Hasegawa General Store—a tangle of fishing supplies, T-shirts and thongs, beach towels, and souvenirs. Fishermen love this store as much as cookie lovers swear by nearby **Popo's Cookies,** the *ne plus ultra* of store-bought cookies on the island. Popo's chocolate-chip, macadamia-nut, chocolate–macadamia nut, chocolate-coconut, almond, peanut butter, and other varieties of butter-rich cookies are among the most sought-after food items to leave the island.

And Kapaa town is full of surprises. On the main strip, across from Sunny-side Market, you'll find the recently expanded **Kela's Glass Gallery** (© 808/ 822-4527), the island's showiest showplace for handmade glass in all sizes, shapes, and prices, with the most impressive selection in Hawaii. Go nuts over the vases and studio glass pieces, functional and nonfunctional, and then stroll along this strip of storefronts to **Kebanu Gallery** (© 808/823-6820), **Hula Girl** (© 808/822-1950), and **South China Sea Trading Company** (© 808/ 823-8655), and see if you can resist their wares. While Kebanu's pottery, foun-tains, candleholders, jewelry, wood works, and glass works are attractive gifts to go, South China's Asian accents make you want to move in for good. You'll find everything from mosquito netting to carved doors or inexpensive bead necklaces to a coconut inlaid armoire for $2,500. We love the fragrance of rush and reed; the amber tones of Indonesian, Vietnamese and Philippine crafts; the coconut rice paddles and kitchen accessories; and the sumptuous Indonesian silk sarongs, of high quality and reasonable prices. Meanwhile, at **Hula Girl,** a wonderful whimsy prevails: aloha shirts (very pricey), vintage-looking luggage covered with decals of old Hawaii, Patrice Pendarvis prints, zoris, sunglasses, and shells.

Down the street, **Earth Beads,** on the main drag (Hwy. 56), sells beads, jew-elry, gemstones, and crafts materials, along with a small selection of gifts and accessories. Across the street is the town's favorite fashion stop, **Island Hemp & Cotton,** where Hawaii's most stylish selection of this miracle fabric is sold: gor-geous silk-hemp dresses, linen-hemp sportswear, hemp aloha shirts, Tencel clothing, T-shirts, and wide-ranging, attractive, and comfortable clothing and accessories that have shed the hippie image. It's also a great store for gift items, from Balinese leather goods to handmade paper, jewelry, luxury soaps, and nat-ural-fiber clothing for men and women. A few doors to the north, **Orchid Alley** gets our vote for most adorable nursery on the island. A narrow alcove opens into a greenhouse of phalaenopsis, oncidiums, dendrobiums, and dozens of bril-liant orchid varieties for shipping or hand-carrying.

THE NORTH SHORE

Kauai's North Shore is the premier shopping destination on the island. Stylish, sophisticated galleries and shops, such as **Kong Lung,** in a 1942 Kilauea stone building (the last to be built on the Kilauea Plantation) off Highway 56 on Kilauea Road (© 808/828-1822), have launched these former hippie villages as top-drawer shopping spots. Save your time, energy, and most of all, discre-tionary funds for this end of the island. Kong Lung, through all its changes, including pricier merchandise in every category, remains a showcase of design, style, and quality, from top-of-the-line dinnerware and bath products to aloha shirts, jewelry, ceramics, women's wear, stationery, and personal and home acces-sories. The book selection is fabulous, and the home accessories—sake sets, tea sets, lacquer bowls, handblown glass, pottery—are unequaled in Hawaii. It's expensive, but browsing here is a joy.

Directly behind Kong Lung is newcomer **Lotus Gallery** (© 808/828-9898), a showstopper for lovers of antiques and designer jewelry. Good juju abounds here. The serenity and beauty will envelop you from the moment you remove your shoes to step in the door and onto the bamboo floor. There are gems, crystals, Tibetan art, antiques and sari clothing from India, 12th-century Indian bronzes, temple bells, Oriental rugs, pearl bracelets—items from $30 to $50,000. Owners Kamalia (jewelry designer) and Tsajon Von Lixfeld (gemologist) have a staggering sense of design and discovery that brings to the gallery such things as Brazilian amethyst crystal (immense and complex), emeralds, a fine, 100-strand lapis necklace ($4,000), and Kamalia's 18-karat pieces with clean, elegant lines and gemstones that soothe and elevate.

In Hanalei, at **Ola's,** by the Hanalei River on the Kuhio Highway (Hwy. 560) after the bridge and before the main part of Hanalei town (© 808/826-6937), Sharon and Doug Britt, an award-winning artist, have amassed a head-turning assortment of American and island crafts, including Doug's paintings and the one-of-a-kind furniture that he makes out of found objects, driftwood, and used materials. Britt's works—armoires, tables, lamps, bookshelves—often serve as the display surfaces for others' work, so look carefully. Lundberg Studio hand-blown glass, exquisite jewelry, intricately wrought pewter switch plates, sensational handblown goblets, and many other fine works fill this tasteful, seductive shop. Be on the lookout for the wonderful koa jewel boxes by local woodworker Tony Lydgate.

From health foods to groceries to Bakelite jewelry, the **Ching Young Village Shopping Center,** in the heart of Hanalei, covers a lot of bases. It's more funky than fashionable, but Hanalei, until recently, has never been about fashion. People take their time here, and there are always clusters of folks lingering at the few tables outdoors, where tables of Kauai papayas beckon from the entrance of **Hanalei Health and Natural Foods.** Next door, **Hot Rocket** is ablaze with aloha shirts, T-shirts, Reyn Spooner and Jams sportswear, flamingo china, backpacks and pareus, swimwear, and, for collectors, one of the finest collections of Bakelite accessories you're likely to see in the islands.

Next door to Ching Young Village is **On The Road to Hanalei** (© 808/826-7360), worth your time to wander around and check out the unusual T-shirts (great gifts to take home because they don't take up much suitcase space), scarves, pareos, jewelry, and other unique gifts.

Across the street in the **Hanalei Center,** the standout boutique is the **Yellowfish Trading Company** ✦ (© 808/826-1227), where owner Gritt Benton's impeccable eye and zeal for collecting are reflected in the 1920s to 1940s collectibles: menus, hula-girl nodders, hula lamps, rattan and koa furniture, vases, bark-cloth fabric, retro pottery and lamp bases, must-have vintage textiles, and wonderful finds in books and aloha shirts.

11 Kauai After Dark

Suffice it to say that you don't come to Kauai to trip the light fantastic. This is the island for winding down—from New York, Houston, or even the hiking trails of Kokee or the Na Pali Coast. But there are a few nightlife options.

Hanalei has some action, primarily at **Sushi & Blues,** in Ching Young Village (© 808/826-4105). Reggae, rhythm and blues, rock, and good music by local groups draw dancers and revelers Wednesday, Thursday, and Sunday from 8:30pm on. The format changes often there, so call ahead to see who's playing.

Hanalei Bay Resort (© 808/826-6522) is a also a music lover's gem, with a Sunday Jazz Jam in its Happy Talk Lounge from 3 to 7pm Sundays and contemporary Hawaiian music at the Happy Talk Lounge Monday through Saturday from 6:30 to 9:30pm. Al Jarreau and Quincy Jones are among those who have stopped by the Sunday Jazz Jam, and the evening crowd has had its share of well-known Hawaiian jammers. On Saturday evenings, Kenny Emerson, a fabulous guitar and steel guitar player, performs with Michelle Edwards; if they play "Hula Blues" or any other 1920s to 1940s hits, you'll never leave.

On the south shore, the Hyatt's **Stevenson's Library** is the place for an elegant after-dinner drink with live jazz nightly from 8 to 11pm. Also in Poipu, **Keoki's Paradise** (© 808/742-7534) offers live music Thursday and Friday evenings from 8:30 to 10pm, with the cafe menu available from 11am to 11:30pm. Hawaiian, reggae, and contemporary music draws the 21-and-over dancing crowd. No cover.

Down the street at **Sheraton Kauai Resort** (© 808/742-1661), **The Point,** on the water, is the Poipu hot spot. There's a DJ on Fridays from 9pm to 1:30am, spinning Top 40 hits for dancing. Saturday through Thursday from 8:30 to 11:30pm, local groups play contemporary Hawaiian music for a mellower mood. There's no cover charge.

Appendix: Hawaii in Depth

As the sun rises on the dawn of the 21st century, other tropical islands are closing in on the 50th state's position as the world's premier beach destination. But Hawaii isn't just another pretty place in the sun. There's an undeniable quality ingrained in the local culture and lifestyle—the quick smiles to strangers, the feeling of family, the automatic extension of courtesy and tolerance. It's the aloha spirit.

1 History 101

Paddling outrigger canoes, the first ancestors of today's Hawaiians followed the stars and birds across a trackless sea to Hawaii, which they called "the land of raging fire." Those first settlers were part of the great Polynesian migration that settled the vast triangle of islands stretching from New Zealand in the southwest to Easter Island in the east to Hawaii in the north. No one is sure exactly when they came to Hawaii from Tahiti and the Marquesas Islands, some 2,500 miles to the south, but a dog-bone fish hook found at the southernmost tip of the Big Island has been carbon-dated to A.D. 700.

An entire Hawaiian culture arose from these settlers. Each island became a separate kingdom. The inhabitants built temples, fish ponds, and aqueducts to irrigate taro plantations. Sailors became farmers and fishermen. The *alii* (high-ranking chiefs) created a caste system and established taboos. Ritual human sacrifices were common.

THE "FATAL CATASTROPHE"   No ancient Hawaiian ever imagined a *haole* (a white person; literally, one with "no breath") would ever appear on one of these "floating islands." But then one day in 1778, just such a person sailed into Waimea Bay on Kauai, where he was welcomed as the god Lono.

The man was 50-year-old Captain James Cook, already famous in Britain for "discovering" much of the South Pacific. Now on his third great voyage of exploration, Cook had set sail from Tahiti northward across uncharted waters to find the mythical Northwest Passage that was said to link the Pacific and Atlantic oceans. On his way, Cook stumbled upon the Hawaiian Islands quite by chance. He named them the Sandwich Islands, for the Earl of Sandwich, first lord of the admiralty, who had bankrolled the expedition.

Overnight, stone-age Hawaii entered the age of iron. Gifts were presented and objects traded: nails for fresh water, pigs, and the affections of Hawaiian women. The sailors brought syphilis, measles, and other diseases to which the Hawaiians had no natural immunity, thereby unwittingly wreaking havoc on the native population.

After his unsuccessful attempt to find the Northwest Passage, Cook returned to Kealakekua Bay on the Big Island, where a fight broke out over an alleged theft, and the great navigator was killed by a blow to the head. After this "fatal catastrophe," the British survivors sailed home. But Hawaii was now on the sea charts. French, Russian, American, and other traders on the fur route between

Canada's Hudson Bay Company and China anchored in Hawaii to get fresh water. More trade—and more disastrous liaisons—ensued.

Two more sea captains left indelible marks on the islands: The first was American John Kendrick, who in 1791 filled his ship with sandalwood and sailed to China. By 1825, Hawaii's sandalwood forests were gone, enabling invasive plants to take charge. The second captain was Englishman George Vancouver, who in 1793 left cows and sheep, which spread out to the high-tide lines. King Kamehameha I sent for cowboys from Mexico and Spain to round up the wild livestock, thus beginning the islands' *paniolo* tradition.

The tightly woven Hawaiian society, enforced by royalty and religious edicts, began to unravel after the death in 1819 of King Kamehameha I, who had used guns seized from a British ship to unite the islands under his rule. One of his successors, Queen Kaahumanu, abolished old taboos and opened the door for religion of another form.

STAYING TO DO WELL   In April 1820, God-fearing missionaries arrived from New England and were bent on converting the pagans. Intent on instilling their brand of rock-ribbed Christianity on the islands, the missionaries clothed the natives, banned them from dancing the hula, and nearly dismantled their ancient culture. They tried to keep the whalers and sailors out of the bawdy houses, where a flood of whiskey quenched fleet-size thirsts and the virtue of native women was never safe. They taught reading and writing, created the 12-letter Hawaiian alphabet, started a printing press, and began recording the islands' history, which until then was only an oral account in memorized chants.

Children of the missionaries became the islands' business leaders and politicians. They married Hawaiians and stayed on in the islands, causing one wag to remark that the missionaries "came to do good and stayed to do well." In 1848, King Kamehameha III proclaimed the Great Mahele (division), which enabled commoners and eventually foreigners to own crown land. In two generations, more than 80% of all private land was in haole hands. Sugar planters imported waves of immigrants to work the fields as contract laborers. The first Chinese came in 1852, followed by Japanese in 1885 and Portuguese in 1878.

King David Kalakaua was elected to the throne in 1874. This popular "Merrie Monarch" built Iolani Palace in 1882, threw extravagant parties, and lifted

Did You Know?

- The aloha shirt that Montgomery Clift wore in his final scene in *From Here to Eternity* is worth $3,500 today.
- Honolulu is second only to San Francisco in restaurant spending—but the locals' favorite meat is Spam.
- There haven't been any billboards in Hawaii since 1926.
- Although it's the capital of the 50th state, Honolulu is closer to Tokyo than to Washington, D.C.
- The Big Island's 13,796-foot Mauna Kea volcano often wears a crown of snow between December and March—which makes Hawaii one of the few places in the world where you can ski and snorkel on the same day. One year, a late snow allowed a ski meet to be held on the Fourth of July.

the prohibitions on the hula and other native arts. For this, he was much loved. He also gave Pearl Harbor to the United States; it became the westernmost bastion of the U.S. Navy. In 1891, King Kalakaua visited chilly San Francisco, caught a cold, and died in the royal suite of the Sheraton Palace. His sister, Queen Liliuokalani, assumed the throne.

A SAD FAREWELL   On January 17, 1893, a group of American sugar planters and missionary descendants, with the support of gun-toting U.S. Marines, imprisoned Queen Liliuokalani in her own palace, where she later penned the sorrowful lyric "Aloha Oe," Hawaii's song of farewell. The monarchy was dead.

A new republic was established, controlled by Sanford Dole, a powerful sugarcane planter. In 1898, through annexation, Hawaii became an American territory ruled by Dole. His fellow sugarcane planters, known as the Big Five, controlled banking, shipping, hardware, and every other facet of economic life on the islands.

Oahu's central Ewa Plain soon filled with row crops. The Dole family planted pineapple on its vast acreage. Planters imported more contract laborers from Puerto Rico (1900), Korea (1903), and the Philippines (1907–1931). Most of the new immigrants stayed on to establish families and become a part of the islands. Meanwhile, the native Hawaiians became a landless minority.

For nearly a century on Hawaii, sugar was king, generously subsidized by the U.S. government. The sugar planters dominated the territory's economy, shaped its social fabric, and kept the islands in a colonial plantation era with bosses and field hands. But the workers eventually struck for higher wages and improved working conditions, and the planters found themselves unable to compete with cheap third-world labor costs.

THE TOURISTS ARRIVE   Tourism proper began in the 1860s. Kilauea volcano was one of the world's prime attractions for adventure travelers, who rode on horseback 29 miles from Hilo to peer into the boiling hellfire. In 1865, a grass Volcano House was built on the Halemaumau Crater rim to shelter visitors; it was Hawaii's first tourist hotel. But tourism really got off the ground with the demise of the plantation era.

In 1901, W. C. Peacock built the elegant beaux arts Moana Hotel on Waikiki Beach, and W. C. Weedon convinced Honolulu businessmen to bankroll his plan to advertise Hawaii in San Francisco. Armed with a stereopticon and tinted photos of Waikiki, Weedon sailed off in 1902 for 6 months of lecture tours to introduce "those remarkable people and the beautiful lands of Hawaii." He drew packed houses. A tourism promotion bureau was formed in 1903, and about 2,000 visitors came to Hawaii that year.

The steamship was Hawaii's tourism lifeline. It took 4½ days to sail from San Francisco to Honolulu. Streamers, leis, and pomp welcomed each Matson liner at downtown's Aloha Tower. Well-heeled visitors brought trunks, servants, even their Rolls-Royces, and stayed for months. Hawaii amused the idle rich with personal tours, floral parades, and shows spotlighting that naughty dance, the hula.

Beginning in 1935 and running for the next 40 years, Webley Edwards's weekly live radio show, "Hawaii Calls," planted the sounds of Waikiki—surf, sliding steel guitar, sweet Hawaiian harmonies, drumbeats—in the hearts of millions of listeners in the United States, Australia, and Canada.

By 1936, visitors could fly to Honolulu from San Francisco on the *Hawaii Clipper,* a seven-passenger Pan American Martin M-130 flying boat, for $360 one-way. The flight took 21 hours, 33 minutes. Modern tourism was born, with five flying boats providing daily service. The 1941 visitor count was a brisk 31,846 through December 6.

WORLD WAR II & ITS AFTERMATH   On December 7, 1941, Japanese Zeros came out of the rising sun to bomb American warships based at Pearl Harbor. This was the "day of infamy" that plunged the United States into World War II.

The aftermath of the attack brought immediate changes to the islands. Martial law was declared, stripping the Big Five cartel of its absolute power in a single day. Feared to be spies, Japanese Americans and German Americans were interned in Hawaii as well as in California. Hawaii was "blacked out" at night, Waikiki Beach was strung with barbed wire, and Aloha Tower was painted in camouflage. Only young men bound for the Pacific came to Hawaii during the war years. Many came back to graves in a cemetery called Punchbowl.

The postwar years saw the beginnings of Hawaii's faux culture. Harry Yee invented the Blue Hawaii cocktail and dropped in a tiny Japanese parasol. Vic Bergeron created the mai tai, a rum and fresh lime-juice drink, and opened Trader Vic's, America's first theme restaurant that featured the art, decor, and food of Polynesia. Arthur Godfrey picked up a ukulele and began singing *hapahaole* tunes on early TV shows. Burt Lancaster and Deborah Kerr made love in the surf at Hanauma Bay in 1954's *From Here to Eternity*. In 1955, Henry J. Kaiser built the Hilton Hawaiian Village, and the 11-story high-rise Princess Kaiulani Hotel opened on a site where the real princess once played. Hawaii greeted 109,000 visitors that year.

STATEHOOD   In 1959, Hawaii became the 50th of the United States. That year also saw the arrival of the first jet airliners, which brought 250,000 tourists to the fledgling state. The personal touch that had defined aloha gave way to the sheer force of numbers. Waikiki's room count virtually doubled in 2 years, from 16,000 in 1969 to 31,000 units in 1971, and more followed before city fathers finally clamped a growth lid on the world's most famous resort. By 1980, annual arrivals had reached 4 million.

In the early 1980s, the Japanese began traveling overseas in record numbers, and they brought lots of yen to spend. Their effect on sales in Hawaii was phenomenal: European boutiques opened branches in Honolulu, and duty-free shopping became the main supporter of Honolulu International Airport. Japanese investors competed for the chance to own or build part of Hawaii. Hotels sold so fast and at such unbelievable prices that heads began to spin with dollar signs.

In 1986, Hawaii's visitor count passed 5 million. Two years later, it went over 6 million. Expensive fantasy megaresorts bloomed on the neighbor islands like giant artificial flowers, swelling the luxury market with ever-swankier accommodations.

The highest visitor count ever recorded was 6.9 million in 1990, but the bubble burst in early 1991 with the Gulf War and worldwide recessions. In 1992, Hurricane Iniki devastated Kauai, which is only now staggering back to its feet. Airfare wars sent Americans to Mexico and the Caribbean. Overbuilt with luxury hotels, Hawaii slashed its room rates, giving middle-class consumers access to high-end digs at affordable prices—a trend that continues as Hawaii struggles to stay atop the tourism heap.

September 11, 2001, also sent a blow to Hawaii; tourism dropped abruptly, sending Hawaii's economy into a tailspin. By 2002, Hawaii's economy was recovering, but hotel occupancy still lagged behind previous years' rates by about 20%.

2 Hawaii Today

A CULTURAL RENAISSANCE A conch shell sounds, a young man in a bright feather cape chants, torchlight flickers at sunset on Waikiki Beach, and hula dancers begin telling their graceful centuries-old stories. It's a cultural scene out of the past come to life once again—for Hawaii is enjoying a renaissance of hula, chant, and other aspects of its ancient culture.

The biggest, longest, and most elaborate celebrations of Hawaiian culture are the Aloha Festivals, which encompass more than 500 cultural events from August to October. "Our goal is to teach and share our culture," says Gloriann Akau, who manages the Big Island's Aloha Festivals. "In 1946, after the war, Hawaiians needed an identity. We were lost and needed to regroup. When we started to celebrate our culture, we began to feel proud. We have a wonderful culture that had been buried for a number of years. This brought it out again. Self-esteem is more important than making a lot of money."

In 1985, native Hawaiian educator, author, and *kupuna* George Kanahele started integrating Hawaiian values into hotels like the Big Island's Mauna Lani and Maui's Kaanapali Beach Hotel. (A *kupuna* is a respected elder with leadership qualities.) "You have the responsibility to preserve and enhance the Hawaiian culture, not because it's going to make money for you, but because it's the right thing to do," Kanahele told the Hawaii Hotel Association. "Ultimately, the only thing unique about Hawaii is its Hawaiianess. Hawaiianess is our competitive edge."

From general managers to maids, resort employees went through hours of Hawaiian cultural training. They held focus groups to discuss the meaning of *aloha*—the Hawaiian concept of unconditional love—and applied it to their work and their lives. Now many hotels have joined the movement and instituted Hawaiian programs. No longer content with teaching hula as a joke, resorts now employ a real *kumu hula* (hula teacher) to instruct visitors and have a *kupuna* take guests on treks to visit *heiau* (temples) and ancient petroglyph sites.

THE QUESTION OF SOVEREIGNTY The Hawaiian cultural renaissance has also made its way into politics. Under the banner of sovereignty, many *kanaka maoli* (native people) are demanding restoration of rights taken away more than a century ago when the U.S. overthrew the Hawaiian monarchy and claimed the islands. Their demands were not lost on President Bill Clinton, who was picketed at a Democratic political fund-raiser at Waikiki Beach in July 1993. Four months later, Clinton signed a document stating that the U.S. Congress "apologizes to Native Hawaiians on behalf of the people of the United States for the overthrow of the Kingdom of Hawaii on January 17, 1893, with the participation of agents and citizens of the United States, and deprivation of the rights of Native Hawaiians to self-determination."

But even neonationalists aren't convinced that complete self-determination is possible. First, the Hawaiians themselves must decide if they want sovereignty because each of the 30 identifiable sovereignty organizations (and more than 100 splinter groups) has a different stated goal, ranging from total independence to nation-within-a-nation status, similar to that of Native Indians. In 1993, the state legislature created a Hawaiian Sovereignty Advisory Commission to "determine the will of the native Hawaiian people." The commission plans to pose the sovereignty question in a referendum open to anyone over 18 with Hawaiian blood, no matter where they live.

Dancing the Hula

That naughty dance, the hula—once banned by missionaries and then almost forgotten in the rush to embrace America's consumer-based ideals—is today a movement of its own. It's also a major event: The **Merrie Monarch Festival** (see "Hawaii Calendar of Events," in chapter 2), in honor of King David Kalakaua, attracts an annual crowd of 20,000 to Hilo, on the Big Island, for a week of ancient and modern hula competition and celebration. In fact, it's rare to visit the islands these days and not see the real hula danced in traditional costumes.

3 Life & Language

Plantations brought so many different people to Hawaii that the state is now a rainbow of ethnic groups. Living here are Caucasians, African Americans, American Indians, Eskimos, Japanese, Chinese, Filipinos, Koreans, Tahitians, Vietnamese, Hawaiians, Samoans, Tongans, and other Asian and Pacific islanders. Add a few Canadians, Dutch, English, French, Germans, Irish, Italians, Portuguese, Scottish, Puerto Ricans, and Spaniards. Everyone's a minority here.

In combination, it's a remarkable potpourri. Nearly everyone, we've noticed, retains an element of the traditions of their homeland. Some Japanese Americans in Hawaii, even three and four generations removed from the homeland, are more traditional than the Japanese of Tokyo. And the same is true of many Chinese, Korean, Filipinos, and the rest of the 25 or so ethnic groups that make Hawaii a kind of living museum of various Asian and Pacific cultures.

THE HAWAIIAN LANGUAGE

Almost everyone here speaks English, so except for pronouncing the names of places, you should have no trouble communicating in Hawaii.

But many folks in Hawaii now speak Hawaiian as well, for the ancient language is making a comeback. All visitors will hear the words *aloha* and *mahalo* (thank you). If you've just arrived, you're a *malihini*. Someone who's been here a long time is a *kamaaina*. When you finish a job or your meal, you are *pau* (finished). On Friday, it's *pau hana,* work finished. You put *pupu* (Hawaii's version of hors d'oeuvres) in your mouth when you go *pau hana.*

The Hawaiian alphabet, created by the New England missionaries, has only 12 letters: the five regular vowels (a, e, i, o, and u) and seven consonants (h, k, l, m, n, p, and w). The vowels are pronounced in the Roman fashion, that is, *ah, ay, ee, oh,* and *oo* (as in "too")—not *ay, ee, eye, oh,* and *you,* as in English. For example, *huhu* is pronounced *who-who.* Most vowels are sounded separately, though some are pronounced together, as in Kalakaua: *Kah-lah-cow-ah.*

WHAT *HAOLE* MEANS   When Hawaiians first saw Western visitors, they called the pale-skinned, frail men *haole* because they looked so out of breath. In Hawaiian, *ha* means *breath,* and *ole* means an absence of what precedes it. In other words, *haole* literally means a lifeless-looking person. Today, the term *haole* is generally a synonym for Caucasian or foreigner and is used casually without any intended disrespect. However, if uttered by an angry stranger who adds certain adjectives (like "stupid"), the term can be construed as a mild racial slur.

SOME HAWAIIAN WORDS   Here are some basic Hawaiian words that you'll often hear in Hawaii and see throughout this book. For a more complete

list of Hawaiian words, point your Web browser to www.geocities.com/~olelo/
hltableofcontents.html or www.hisurf.com/hawaiian/dictionary.html.

akamai   smart

alii   Hawaiian royalty

aloha   greeting or farewell

halau   school

hale   house or building

heiau   Hawaiian temple or place of worship

hui   club, assembly

kahuna   priest or expert

kamaaina   old-timer

kapa   tapa, bark cloth

kapu   taboo, forbidden

keiki   child

lanai   porch or veranda

lomilomi   massage

mahalo   thank you

makai   a direction, toward the sea

malihini   stranger, newcomer

mana   spirit power

mauka   a direction, toward the mountains

muumuu   loose-fitting gown or dress

nene   official state bird, a goose

ono   delicious

pali   cliff

paniolo   Hawaiian cowboy(s)

wiki   quick

PIDGIN: 'EH FO'REAL, BRAH

If you venture beyond the tourist areas, you might hear another local tongue:
pidgin English. A conglomeration of slang and words from the Hawaiian language, pidgin developed as a method sugar planters used to communicate with
their Chinese laborers in the 1800s.

"Broke da mouth" (tastes really good) is the favorite pidgin phrase and one
you might hear; "'Eh fo'real, brah" means "It's true, brother." You could be
invited to hear an elder "talk story" (relating myths and memories) or to enjoy
local treats like "shave ice" (a tropical snow cone) and "crack seed" (highly seasoned preserved fruit). But because pidgin is really the province of the locals,
your visit to Hawaii is likely to pass without your hearing much pidgin at all.

4 A Taste of Hawaii

TRIED & TRUE: HAWAII REGIONAL CUISINE

It was only a matter of time before the humble plate lunch became a culinary
icon in Hawaii. These days, even the most chichi restaurant has a version of this
modest Island symbol (not at plate-lunch prices, of course), while the real-thing,
carbo-driven lunch wagons have queues that never end.

Peter Merriman, a founding member of Hawaii Regional Cuisine (HRC)and
a nominee for the James Beard Award for Best Chef/Northwest/Hawaii (along
with George Mavrothalassitis of Chef Mavro Restaurant), describes the current
trend in Hawaii as a refinement, a tweaking upward, of everything from fine
dining to down-home local cooking. "While fine dining is becoming finer, with

more sophisticated wine lists and better service, the trend at the other end is that local food is becoming more refined as well," he explains. "Even the local, Hawaii-style cooks are using techniques they've learned from fancy hotels." Translated on the plate, this means sesame- or nori-crusted fresh catch on plate-lunch menus, and huli huli chicken at five-diamond eateries, paired with Beaujolais and leeks and gourmet long rice.

At the same time, says Merriman, HRC, the style of cooking that put Hawaii on the international culinary map, has become watered down, a buzzword: "A lot of restaurants are paying lip service."

As it is with things au courant, it is easy to make the claim but another thing to live up to it. As Merriman points out, HRC was never solely about technique; it is equally about ingredients and the chef's creativity and integrity. "We continue to get local inspiration," says Merriman. "We've never restricted ourselves." If there is a fabulous French or Thai dish, chefs like Merriman will prepare it with local ingredients and add a creative edge that makes it distinctively theirs, distinctively Hawaii Regional.

Hawaii's tried-and-true baseline remains HRC, established in the mid-1980s in a culinary revolution that catapulted Hawaii into the global epicurean arena. The international training, creative vigor, fresh ingredients, and cross-cultural menus of the 12 original HRC chefs have made the islands a dining destination applauded and emulated nationwide. (In a tip of the toque to island tradition, *ahi*—a word ubiquitous in Hawaii—has replaced *tuna* on many chic New York menus.) And other options have proliferated at all levels of the local dining spectrum: Waves of new Asian residents have transplanted the traditions of their homelands to the fertile soil of Hawaii, resulting in unforgettable taste treats true to their Thai, Vietnamese, Japanese, Chinese, and Indo-Pacific roots. When combined with the bountiful, fresh harvests from sea and land for which Hawaii is known, these ethnic and culinary traditions take on renewed vigor and a cross-cultural, uniquely Hawaiian quality.

While in Hawaii, you'll encounter many labels that embrace the fundamentals of HRC and the sophistication, informality, and nostalgia it encompasses. Euro-Asian, Pacific Rim, Indo-Pacific, Pacific Edge, Euro-Pacific, Fusion cuisine, Hapa cuisine—by whatever name, Hawaii Regional Cuisine has evolved as Hawaii's singular cooking style, which some say is this country's current gastronomic, as well as geographic, frontier. It highlights the fresh seafood and produce of Hawaii's rich waters and volcanic soil, the cultural traditions of Hawaii's ethnic groups, and the skills of well-trained chefs—such as Merriman (Merriman's on the Big Island and Hula Grill on Maui), Roy Yamaguchi (Roy's on Oahu, Maui, the Big Island, and Kauai), Mavrothalassitis (Chef Mavro Restaurant on Oahu), Alan Wong (Alan Wong's Restaurant and his newly opened Pineapple Room, both on Oahu), Beverly Gannon (Haliimaile General Store on Maui), Philippe Padovani (Padovani's Restaurant & Wine Bar on Oahu), and Jean-Marie Josselin (A Pacific Cafe on Kauai)—who broke ranks with their European predecessors to forge new ground in the 50th state.

Fresh ingredients are foremost here. Farmers and fishermen work together to provide steady supplies of just-harvested seafood, seaweed, fern shoots, vine-ripened tomatoes, goat cheese, lamb, herbs, taro, gourmet lettuces, and countless harvests from land and sea. These ingredients wind up in myriad forms on ever-changing menus, prepared in Asian and Western culinary styles. Exotic fruits introduced by recent Southeast Asian emigrants—such as sapodilla, soursop, and rambutan—are beginning to appear regularly in Chinatown markets.

Aquacultured seafood, from seaweed to salmon to lobster, is a staple on many menus. Additionally, fresh-fruit sauces (mango, lychee, papaya, pineapple, guava), ginger-sesame-wasabi flavorings, corn cakes with sake sauces, tamarind and fish sauces, coconut-chile accents, tropical-fruit vinaigrettes, and other local and newly arrived seasonings from Southeast Asia and the Pacific impart unique qualities to the preparations.

Here's a sampling of what you can expect to find on a Hawaii Regional menu: seared Hawaiian fish with lilikoi shrimp butter; taro-crab cakes; Pahoa corn cakes; Molokai sweet-potato or breadfruit vichyssoise; Ka'u orange sauce and Kahua Ranch lamb; fern shoots from Waipio Valley; Maui onion soup and Hawaiian bouillabaisse, with fresh snapper, Kona crab, and fresh aquacultured shrimp; blackened ahi summer rolls; herb-crusted onaga; and gourmet Waimanalo greens, picked that day. You may also encounter locally made cheeses, squash and taro risottos, Polynesian imu-baked foods, and guava-smoked meats. If there's pasta or risotto or rack of lamb on the menu, it could be *nori* (red algae) linguine with *opihi* (limpet) sauce, or risotto with local seafood served in taro cups, or rack of lamb in cabernet and *hoisin* sauce (fermented soybean, garlic, and spices). Watch for ponzu sauce, too; it's lemony and zesty, much more flavorful than the soy sauce it resembles, and a welcome new staple on local menus.

PLATE LUNCHES & MORE: LOCAL FOOD

At the other end of the spectrum is the vast and endearing world of "local food." By that, we mean plate lunches and poke, shave ice and saimin, bento lunches and manapua—cultural hybrids all.

Reflecting a polyglot population of many styles and ethnicities, Hawaii's idiosyncratic dining scene is eminently inclusive. Consider Surfer Chic: Barefoot in the sand, in a swimsuit, you chow down on a **plate lunch** ordered from a lunch wagon, consisting of fried mahimahi, "two scoops rice," macaroni salad, and a few leaves of green, typically julienned cabbage. (Generally, teriyaki beef and shoyu chicken are options.) Heavy gravy is often the condiment of choice, accompanied by a soft drink in a paper cup. Like **saimin**—the local version of noodles in broth topped with scrambled eggs, green onions, and, sometimes, pork—the plate lunch is Hawaii's version of high camp.

Because this is Hawaii, at least a few licks of *poi*—cooked, pounded taro (the traditional Hawaiian staple crop)—are a must. Other **native foods** include those from before and after Western contact, such as *laulau* (pork, chicken, or fish steamed in ti leaves), *kalua* pork (pork cooked in a Polynesian underground oven known here as an *imu*), *lomi* salmon (salted salmon with tomatoes and green onions), squid *luau* (cooked in coconut milk and taro tops), *poke* (cubed raw fish seasoned with onions and seaweed and the occasional sprinkling of roasted *kukui* nuts), *haupia* (creamy coconut pudding), and *kulolo* (steamed pudding of coconut, brown sugar, and taro).

Bento, another popular quick meal available throughout Hawaii, is a compact, boxed assortment of picnic fare usually consisting of neatly arranged sections of rice, pickled vegetables, and fried chicken, beef, or pork. Increasingly, however, the bento is becoming more health-conscious, as in macrobiotic bento lunches or vegetarian brown-rice bentos. A derivative of the modest lunch box for Japanese immigrants who once labored in the sugar and pineapple fields, bentos are dispensed everywhere, from department stores to corner delis and supermarkets.

Also from the plantations come **manapua,** a bready, doughy sphere filled with tasty fillings of sweetened pork or sweet beans. In the old days, the Chinese "manapua man" would make his rounds with bamboo containers balanced on a rod over his shoulders. Today, you'll find white or whole-wheat manapua containing chicken, vegetables, curry, and other savory fillings.

The daintier Chinese delicacy **dim sum** is made of translucent wrappers filled with fresh seafood, pork hash, and vegetables, served for breakfast and lunch in Chinatown restaurants. The Hong Kong–style dumplings are ordered fresh and hot from bamboo steamers from invariably brusque servers who move their carts from table to table. Much like hailing a taxi in Manhattan, you have to be quick and loud for dim sum.

For dessert or a snack, particularly on Oahu's north shore, the prevailing choice is **shave ice,** the island version of a snow cone. Particularly on hot, humid days, long lines of shave-ice lovers gather for the rainbow-colored cones heaped with finely shaved ice and topped with sweet tropical syrups. (The sweet-sour *li hing mui* flavor is a current favorite.) The fast-melting mounds, which require prompt, efficient consumption, are quite the local summer ritual for sweet tooths. Aficionados order shave ice with ice cream and sweetened adzuki beans plopped in the middle.

AHI, ONO & OPAKAPAKA: A HAWAIIAN SEAFOOD PRIMER

The seafood in Hawaii has been described as the best in the world. In Janice Wald Henderson's pivotal book *The New Cuisine of Hawaii,* acclaimed chef Nobuyuki Matsuhisa (chef/owner of Matsuhisa in Beverly Hills and Nobu in Manhattan and London) writes, "As a chef who specializes in fresh seafood, I am in awe of the quality of Hawaii's fish; it is unparalleled anywhere else in the world." And why not? Without a doubt, the islands' surrounding waters, including the waters of the remote northwestern Hawaiian Islands, and a growing aquaculture industry contribute to the high quality of the seafood here.

The reputable restaurants in Hawaii buy fresh fish daily at predawn auctions or from local fishermen. Some chefs even catch their ingredients themselves. "Still wiggling" or "just off the hook" are the ultimate terms for freshness in Hawaii. The fish can then be grilled over *kiawe* (mesquite) or prepared in innumerable other ways.

Although most menus include the Western description for the fresh fish used, most often the local nomenclature is listed, turning dinner for the uninitiated into a confusing, quasi-foreign experience. To help familiarize you with the menu language of Hawaii, here's a basic glossary of island fish:

ahi   yellowfin or bigeye tuna, important for its use in sashimi and poke at sushi bars and in Hawaii Regional Cuisine

aku   skipjack tuna, heavily used by local families in home cooking and poke

ehu   red snapper, delicate and sumptuous, yet lesser known than opakapaka

hapuupuu   grouper, a sea bass whose use is expanding from ethnic to nonethnic restaurants

hebi   spearfish, mildly flavored, and frequently featured as the "catch of the day" in upscale restaurants

kajiki   Pacific blue marlin, also called *au,* with a firm flesh and high fat content that make it a plausible substitute for tuna in some raw fish dishes and as a grilled item on menus

kumu   goatfish, a luxury item on Chinese and upscale menus, served *en papillote* or steamed whole, Oriental style, with sesame oil, scallions, ginger, and garlic

mahimahi   dolphin fish (the game fish, not the mammal) or dorado, a classic sweet, white-fleshed fish requiring vigilance among purists, because it's often disguised as fresh when it's actually "fresh-frozen"—a big difference

monchong   bigscale or sickle pomfret, an exotic, tasty fish, scarce but gaining a higher profile on Hawaiian Island menus

nairagi   striped marlin, also called *au;* good as sashimi and in poke, and often substituted for ahi in raw-fish products

onaga   ruby snapper, a luxury fish, versatile, moist, and flaky

ono   wahoo, firmer and drier than the snappers, often served grilled and in sandwiches

opah   moonfish, rich and fatty, and versatile—cooked, raw, smoked, and broiled

opakapaka   pink snapper, light, flaky, and luxurious, suited for sashimi, poaching, sautéeing, and baking; the best-known upscale fish

papio   jack trevally, light, firm, and flavorful and favored in island cookery

shutome   broadbill swordfish, of beeflike texture and rich flavor

tombo   albacore tuna, with a high fat content, suitable for grilling and sautéing

uhu   parrot fish, most often encountered steamed, Chinese-style

uku   gray snapper of clear, pale-pink flesh, delicately flavored and moist

ulua   large jack trevally, firm-fleshed and versatile

5 The Natural World: An Environmental Guide to the Islands

The first Hawaiian islands were born of violent volcanic eruptions that took place deep beneath the ocean's surface about 70 million years ago—more than 200 million years after the major continental land masses had been formed. As soon as the islands emerged, Mother Nature's fury began to carve beauty from barren rock. Untiring volcanoes spewed forth rivers of fire that cooled into stone. Severe tropical storms, some with hurricane-force winds, battered and blasted the cooling lava rock into a series of shapes. Ferocious earthquakes flattened, shattered, and reshaped the islands into precipitous valleys, jagged cliffs, and recumbent flatlands. Monstrous surf and gigantic tidal waves rearranged and polished the lands above and below the reaches of the tide.

It took millions of years for nature to shape the familiar form of Diamond Head on Oahu, Maui's majestic peak of Haleakala, the waterfalls of Molokai's northern side, the reefs of Hulopoe Bay on Lanai, and the lush rain forests of the Big Island. The result is an island chain like no other—a tropical dream of a landscape, rich in unique flora and fauna, surrounded by a vibrant underwater world.

THE ISLAND LANDSCAPES

Each of the six main islands has its own particular climate and topography.

OAHU   Oahu is the third-largest island in Hawaii (behind the Big Island and Maui). As the home of Honolulu, it's also the most urban island, with a population of nearly 900,000. Oahu is defined by two mountain ranges: the Waianae Ridge in the west and the jagged Koolaus in the east, which form a backdrop for Honolulu. These ranges divide the island into three different environments. The windward (eastern) side is lush with greenery, ferns, tropical plants, and waterfalls. On the leeward (western) side, the area between the Waianae Range and the ocean is drier, with sparse vegetation, little rainfall, and an arid landscape. Between the two mountain ranges lies the central Ewa Valley; it's moderate in temperature and vibrant with tropical plants, agricultural fields, and trees.

HAWAII, THE BIG ISLAND   By far the largest island at some 4,034 square miles (and still growing), the Big Island is twice the size of all the other islands combined. Here you'll find every type of climate zone existing in Hawaii. It's not uncommon for there to be 12 feet of snow on the two largest mountain peaks, 13,796-foot Mauna Kea and 13,680-foot Mauna Loa. These mountains are the tallest in the state; what's more, when measured from their true base on the ocean floor, they reach 32,000 feet, making them the tallest mountains in the world. The 4,077-foot Kilauea volcano has been continuously erupting since January 3, 1983, and has added more than 560 acres of new land to the Big Island since then. Just a few miles from the barely cooled barren lava lies a pristine rain forest. On the southern end of the island is an arid desert. The rest of the island contains tropical terrain; white-, black-, and even green-sand beaches; windswept grasslands; and productive farming and ranching areas growing tropical fruits, macadamia nuts, coffee, and ornamental flowers.

MAUI   When two volcanoes—Mauna Kahalawai, a 5,277-foot ancient volcano in the West Maui Mountains, and 10,000-foot Haleakala—flowed together a million or so years ago, the event created a "Valley Isle" with a range of climates from arid desert to tropical rain forest. This 728-square-mile island is the only place in the world where you can drive from sea level to 10,000 feet in just 38 miles, passing from tropical beaches through sugar and pineapple plantations and rolling grassy hills up past the timber line to the lunarlike surface of the top of Haleakala. In addition to 33 miles of public beaches on the south and west shores, Maui is home to the arid lands of Kihei, the swampy bogs of the West Maui Mountains, the rain forest of Hana, and the desert of Kaupo.

MOLOKAI   Roughly the shape of Manhattan, Molokai is 37 miles long and 10 miles wide, with a "thumb" protruding out of the North Shore. The North Shore begins on the west, with miles of white-sand beaches that fringe a desertlike landscape. The thumb—the Kalaupapa Peninsula—is cut off by a fence of cliffs, some 2,000 feet tall, that line the remainder of the north side. Molokai can be divided into two areas: the dry west end and the rainy, tropical east and north ends. Its highest point is Mount Kamakou, at 4,970 feet.

LANAI   This small, kidney bean–shaped island—only 13 miles wide by 17 miles long—rises sharply out of the ocean, with cliffs on the west side that rise to a high point of 3,370 feet. Lanai slopes down to sea level on the east and south sides. The only town, Lanai City, sits in the clouds at 1,600 feet. The island's peak is covered with Norfolk pines and is usually shrouded in clouds, while the arid beaches survive on minimal rainfall. One area in particular stands out: the Garden of the Gods, just 7 miles from Lanai City, where oddly strewn boulders lie in the amber- and ocher-colored dirt and bizarre stone formations dot the landscape. The ancient Hawaiians formed romantic legends explaining this enigma, but modern-day scientists still debate its origins.

KAUAI   This compact island, 25 miles long by 33 miles wide, has Mount Waialeale, the island's highest point at nearly 5,000 feet and the earth's wettest spot, with more than 400 inches of rain annually. Just west of Mount Waialeale is the barren landscape of Waimea Canyon, dubbed "the Grand Canyon of the Pacific"—the result of the once 10,000-foot-tall Olokele shield volcano, which collapsed and formed a *caldera* (crater) some 3,600 feet deep and 14 miles across. Peaks and craters aren't Kauai's only distinctive landscape features, though: Miles of white-sand beaches rim most of the island, with majestic 2,700-foot cliffs—the spectacular Na Pali Coast—completing the circle. Lush tropical jungle inhabits the north side of the island, while balmy, palm tree–lined beaches are located in the south.

THE FLORA OF THE ISLANDS

Hawaii is filled with sweet-smelling flowers, lush vegetation, and exotic plant life.

AFRICAN TULIP TREES   Even from afar, you can see the flaming red flowers on these large trees, which can grow to be more than 50 feet tall. Children in Hawaii love them because the buds hold water—they use the flowers as water pistols.

ANGEL'S TRUMPETS   These small trees can grow up to 20 feet tall, with an abundance of large (up to 10 inches in diameter) pendants—white or pink flowers that resemble, well, trumpets. The Hawaiians call them *nana-honua,* which means "earth gazing." The flowers, which bloom continually from early spring to late fall, have a musky scent. *Warning:* All parts of the plant are poisonous and contain a strong narcotic.

ANTHURIUMS   One of Hawaii's most popular cut flowers, anthuriums originally came from the tropical Americas and the Caribbean islands. There are more than 550 species, but the most popular are the heart-shaped red, orange, pink, white, and even purple flowers with tail-like spathes. Look for the heart-shaped green leaves in shaded areas. These exotic plants have no scent but will last several weeks as cut flowers. Anthuriums are particularly prevalent on the Big Island.

BANYAN TREES   Among the world's largest trees, banyans have branches that grow out and away from the trunk, forming descending roots that grow down to the ground to feed and form additional trunks, making the tree very stable during tropical storms. The banyan in the courtyard next to the old Court House in Lahaina, Maui, is an excellent example of a spreading banyan—it covers two-thirds of an acre.

BIRDS OF PARADISE   These natives of Africa have become something of a trademark of Hawaii. They're easily recognizable by the orange and blue flowers nestled in gray-green bracts, looking somewhat like birds in flight.

BOUGAINVILLEA   Originally from Brazil, these vines feature colorful, tissue-thin bracts, ranging in color from majestic purple to fiery orange, that hide tiny white flowers. A good place to spot them is on the Big Island, along the Queen Kaahumanu Highway stretching from Kona Airport to Kailua-Kona.

BREADFRUIT TREES   A large tree—more than 60 feet tall—with broad, sculpted, dark-green leaves, the famous breadfruit produces a round, head-size green fruit that's a staple in the diets of all Polynesians. When roasted or baked, the whitish-yellow meat tastes somewhat like a sweet potato.

BROMELIADS   There are more than 1,400 species of bromeliads, of which the pineapple plant is the best known. "Bromes," as they're affectionately called,

Marijuana

This not-so-rare-and-unusual plant—called *pakalolo,* or "crazy weed," in Hawaiian—is grown throughout the islands, despite years of police efforts to eradicate the plant. You probably won't see it as you drive along the roads, but if you go hiking, you may glimpse the feathery green leaves with tight clusters of buds. Don't be tempted to pick a few buds; the captains of this nefarious industry don't take kindly to poaching.

are generally spiky plants ranging in size from a few inches to several feet in diameter. They're popular not only for their unusual foliage but also for their strange and wonderful flowers. Used widely in landscaping and interior decoration, especially in resort areas, bromeliads are found on every island.

COFFEE   Hawaii is the only state that produces coffee commercially. Coffee is an evergreen shrub with shiny, waxy, dark-green, pointed leaves. The flower is a small, fragrant white blossom that develops into half-inch berries that turn bright red when ripe. Look for coffee at elevations above 1,500 feet on the Kona side of the Big Island and on large coffee plantations on Kauai, Molokai, Oahu, and Maui.

GINGER   White and yellow ginger flowers are perhaps the most fragrant in Hawaii. Usually found in clumps growing 4 to 7 feet tall in areas blessed by rain, these sweet-smelling, 3-inch-wide flowers are composed of three dainty petal-like stamens and three long, thin petals. Ginger is so prevalent that many people assume it is native to Hawaii; actually, it was introduced in the 19th century from the Indonesia-Malaysia area. Look for white and yellow ginger from late spring to fall. If you see ginger on the side of the road, stop and pick a few blossoms—your car will be filled with a divine fragrance the rest of the day.

Other members of the ginger family frequently seen in Hawaii (there are some 700 species) include red, shell, and torch ginger. Red ginger consists of tall, green stalks with foot-long red "flower heads." The red "petals" are actually bracts, which protect the 1-inch-long white flowers; to see the flowers, look down into the red head. Red ginger, which does not share the heavenly smell of white ginger, lasts a week or longer when cut. Look for red ginger from spring through late fall. Shell ginger, which originated in India and Burma, thrives in cool, wet mountain forests. These plants, with their pearly-white, clam shell–like blossoms, bloom from spring to fall.

Perhaps the most exotic ginger is the red or pink torch ginger. Cultivated in Malaysia as seasoning (the young flower shoots are used in curries), torch ginger rises directly out of the ground. The flower stalks, which are about 5 to 8 inches in length, resemble the fire of a lighted torch. This is one of the few types of ginger that can bloom year-round.

HELICONIA   Some 80 species of the colorful heliconia family came to Hawaii from the Caribbean and Central and South America. The bright yellow, red, green, and orange bracts overlap and appear to unfold like origami birds. The most obvious heliconia to spot is the lobster claw, which resembles a string of boiled crustacean pincers. Another prolific heliconia is the parrot's beak; growing to about hip height, it's composed of bright-orange flower bracts with black tips. Look for parrot's beaks in spring and summer.

HIBISCUS   The 4- to 6-inch hibiscus flowers bloom year-round and come in a range of colors, from lily white to lipstick red. The flowers resemble crepe paper, with stamens and pistils protruding spire-like from the center. Hibiscus hedges can grow up to 15 feet tall. The yellow hibiscus is Hawaii's official state flower.

JACARANDA   Beginning around March and sometimes lasting until early May, these huge, lacy-leaved trees metamorphose into large clusters of spectacular lavender-blue sprays. The bell-shaped flowers drop quickly, leaving a majestic purple carpet beneath the tree.

MACADAMIA   A transplant from Australia, macadamia nuts have become a commercial crop in recent decades in Hawaii, especially on the Big Island and

Maui. The large trees—up to 60 feet tall—bear a hard-shelled nut encased in a leathery husk, which splits open and dries when ripe.

MONKEYPOD TREES The monkeypod is one of Hawaii's most majestic trees; it grows more than 80 feet tall and 100 feet across. Seen near older homes and in parks, the leaves of the monkeypod drop in February and March. Its wood is a favorite of woodworking artisans.

NIGHT-BLOOMING CEREUS Look along rock walls for this spectacular night-blooming flower. Originally from Central America, this vinelike member of the cactus family has green scalloped edges and produces foot-long white flowers that open as darkness falls and wither as the sun rises. The plant also bears an edible red fruit.

ORCHIDS To many minds, nothing says Hawaii more than orchids. The orchid family is the largest in the entire plant kingdom. The most widely grown variety—and the major source of flowers for leis and garnish for tropical libations—is the vanda orchid. The vandas used in Hawaii's commercial flower industry are generally lavender or white, but they grow in a rainbow of colors, shapes, and sizes. The orchids used for corsages are the large, delicate cattleya; the ones used in floral arrangements—you'll probably see them in your hotel lobby—are usually dendrobiums. On the Big Island, don't pass up a chance to wander through the numerous orchid farms around Hilo.

PANDANUS (HALA) Called *hala* by Hawaiians, pandanus is native to Polynesia. Thanks to its thick trunk, stiltlike supporting roots, and crown of long, swordlike leaves, the hala tree is easy to recognize. In what is quickly becoming a dying art, Hawaiians weave the *lau* (leaves) of the hala into hats, baskets, mats, bags, and the like.

PLUMERIA Also known as frangipani, this sweet-smelling, five-petal flower, found in clusters on trees, is the most popular choice of lei makers. The Singapore plumeria has five creamy-white petals, with a touch of yellow in the center. Another popular variety, ruba—with flowers from soft pink to flaming red—is also used in leis. When picking plumeria, be careful of the sap from the flower, as it's poisonous and can stain clothes.

PROTEA Originally from South Africa, this unusual oversize shrub comes in more than 40 different varieties. The flowers of one species resemble pincushions; those of another look like a bouquet of feathers. Once dried, proteas will last for years.

SILVERSWORD This very uncommon and unusual plant is seen only on the Big Island and in the Haleakala Crater on Maui. This rare relative of the sunflower family blooms between July and September. The silversword in bloom is a fountain of red-petaled, daisylike flowers that turn silver soon after blooming.

TARO Around pools, near streams, and in neatly planted fields, you'll see these green heart-shaped leaves, whose dense roots are a Polynesian staple. The ancient Hawaiians pounded the roots into *poi*. Originally from Sri Lanka, taro is not only a food crop but also grown for ornamental reasons.

THE FAUNA OF THE ISLANDS

When the first Polynesians arrived in Hawaii between A.D. 500 and 800, scientists say they found some 67 varieties of endemic Hawaiian birds, a third of which are now believed to be extinct. What's even more astonishing is what they didn't find—there were no reptiles, amphibians, mosquitoes, lice, fleas, or even a cockroach.

There were only two endemic mammals: the hoary bat and the monk seal. The **hoary bat** must have accidentally blown to Hawaii at some point, from either North or South America. It can still be seen during its early evening forays, especially around the Kilauea Crater on the Big Island.

The **Hawaiian monk seal,** a relative of warm-water seals found in the Caribbean and the Mediterranean, was nearly slaughtered into extinction for its skin and oil during the 19th century. These seals have recently experienced a minor population explosion; sometimes they even turn up at various beaches throughout the state. They're protected under federal law by the Marine Mammals Protection Act. If you're fortunate enough to see a monk seal, just look; don't disturb one of Hawaii's living treasures.

The first Polynesians brought a few animals from home: dogs, pigs, and chickens (all were for eating), as well as rats (stowaways). All four species are still found in the Hawaiian wild today.

BIRDS

More species of native birds have become extinct in Hawaii in the last 200 years than anywhere else on the planet. Of 67 native species, 23 are extinct and 30 are endangered. Even the Hawaiian crow, the **alala,** is threatened.

The **aeo,** or Hawaiian stilt—a 16-inch-long bird with a black head, black coat, white underside, and long pink legs—can be found in protected wetlands like the Kanaha Wildlife Sanctuary on Maui (where it shares its natural habitat with the Hawaiian coot), the Kealia Pond on Maui, and the Hanalei National Wildlife Refuge on Kauai, which is also home to the Hawaiian duck. Other areas in which you can see protected birds are the Kipuku Puaulu (Bird Park) and the Olaa Rain Forest, both in Hawaii Volcanoes National Park on the Big Island, and at Goat Island bird refuge off Oahu, where you can see wedge-tailed shearwaters nesting.

Another great birding venue is Kokee State Park on Kauai. Various native birds that have been spotted include some of the 22 species of the native honey creepers, whose songs fill the forest. Frequently seen are the **apapane** (a red bird with black wings and a curved black bill), **iiwi** (another red bird with black wings but with orange legs and a salmon-colored bill), **amakihi** (a plain olive-green bird with a long, straight bill), and **anianiau** (a tiny yellow bird with a thin, curved bill). Also in the forest is the **elepaio,** a small, gray flycatcher with an orange breast and an erect tail. A curious fellow, the elepaio comes out to investigate any unusual whistles. The most common native bird at Kokee—and the most easily seen—is the **moa,** or red jungle fowl, a chicken brought to Hawaii by the Polynesians.

To get a good glimpse of the seabirds that frequent Hawaii, drive to Kilauea Point on Kauai's North Shore. Here, you can easily spot **red- and white-footed boobies, wedge-tailed shearwaters, frigate birds, red-tailed tropic birds,** and the **Laysan albatross.**

The **nene** is Hawaii's state bird. It's being brought back from the brink of extinction through strenuous protection laws and captive breeding. A relative of the Canada goose, the nene stands about 2 feet high and has a black head and yellow cheek, a buff neck with deep furrows, a grayish-brown body, and clawed feet. It gets its name from its nasal, two-syllable call, "nay-nay." The approximately 500 nenes in existence can be seen in only three places: at Haleakala

Leapin' Lizards!

Geckos are harmless, soft-skinned, insect-eating lizards that come equipped with suction pads on their feet, enabling them to climb walls and windows to reach tasty insects such as mosquitoes and cockroaches. You'll see them on windows outside a lighted room at night or hear their cheerful chirp.

National Park on Maui, at Mauna Kea State Park bird sanctuary, and on the slopes of Mauna Kea on the Big Island.

The Hawaiian short-eared owl, the **pueo,** which grows to between 12 and 17 inches, can be seen at dawn and dusk on Kauai, Maui, and the Big Island, when the black-billed, brown-and-white bird goes hunting for rodents. Pueos are highly regarded by Hawaiians; according to legend, spotting a pueo is a good omen.

SEA LIFE

Approximately 680 species of fish are known to inhabit the waters around the Hawaiian Islands. Of those, approximately 450 species stay close to the reef and inshore areas.

CORAL   The reefs surrounding Hawaii are made up of various coral and algae. The living coral grows through sunlight that feeds a specialized algae, which in turn allows the development of the coral's calcareous skeleton. The reef, which takes thousands of years to develop, attracts and supports fish and crustaceans, which use it for food and habitat. Mother Nature can batter the reef with a strong storm or large waves, but humans—through seemingly innocuous acts such as touching the coral—have proven far more destructive.

The corals most frequently seen in Hawaii are hard, rocklike formations named for their familiar shapes: antler, cauliflower, finger, plate, and razor coral. Wire coral looks like a randomly bent wire growing straight out of the reef. Some coral appears soft, such as tube coral; it can be found in the ceilings of caves. Black coral, which resembles winter-bare trees or shrubs, is found at depths of more than 100 feet.

REEF FISH   Of the approximately 450 types of reef fish here, about 27% are native to Hawaii and are found nowhere else in the world. During the millions of years it took for the islands to sprout up from the sea, ocean currents—mainly from Southeast Asia—carried thousands of marine animals and plants to Hawaii's reef; of those, approximately 100 species adapted and thrived.

Some species are much bigger and more plentiful than their Pacific cousins, and many developed unique characteristics. Some, like the lemon or milletseed butterfly fish, developed specialized schooling and feeding behaviors. Hawaii's native fish are often surprisingly common: You can see the saddleback wrasse, for example, on virtually any snorkeling excursion or dive in Hawaiian waters. You're likely to spot one or more of the following fish while underwater:

Angel fish, often mistaken for butterfly fish, can be distinguished by the spine, located low on the gill plate. These fish are very shy; several species live in colonies close to coral for protection.

Blennies are small, elongated fish, ranging from 2 to 10 inches long, with the majority in the 3- to 4-inch range. Blennies are so small that they can live in tide pools; you might have a hard time spotting one.

Butterfly fish, among the most colorful of the reef fish, are usually seen in pairs (scientists believe they mate for life) and appear to spend most of their day feeding. There are 22 species of butterfly fish, of which three (bluestripe, lemon or milletseed, and multiband or pebbled butterfly fish) are endemic. Most butterfly fish have a dark band through the eye and a spot near the tail resembling an eye, meant to confuse their predators (moray eels love to lunch on them).

Moray and **conger eels** are the most common eels seen in Hawaii. Morays are usually docile except when provoked or when there's food or an injured fish around. Unfortunately, some morays have been fed by divers and—being intelligent creatures—associate divers with food; thus, they can become aggressive. But most morays like to keep to themselves, hidden in their hole or crevice. While morays may look menacing, conger eels look downright happy, with big lips and pectoral fins (situated so that they look like big ears) that give them the appearance of a perpetually smiling face. Conger eels have crushing teeth so they can feed on crustaceans; because they're sloppy eaters, they usually live with shrimp and crabs that feed off the crumbs they leave.

Parrot fish, one of the largest and most colorful of the reef fish, can grow up to 40 inches long. They're easy to spot—their front teeth are fused together, protruding like buck teeth and resembling a parrot's beak. These unique teeth allow them to feed by scraping algae from rocks and coral. The rocks and coral pass through the parrot fish's system, resulting in fine sand. In fact, most of the white sand found in Hawaii is parrot-fish waste; one large parrot fish can produce a ton of sand a year. Native parrot-fish species include yellowbar, regal, and spectacled.

Scorpion fish are what scientists call "ambush predators": They hide under camouflaged exteriors and ambush their prey. Several kinds sport a venomous dorsal spine. These fish don't have a gas bladder, so when they stop swimming, they sink—that's why you usually find them "resting" on ledges and on the ocean bottom. Although they're not aggressive, an inattentive snorkeler or diver could feel the effects of those venomous spines—so be very careful where you put your hands and feet in the water.

Surgeonfish, sometimes called *tang,* get their name from the scalpel-like spines located on each side of the body near the base of the tail. Some surgeonfish have a rigid spine, while others have the ability to fold the spines against the body until they're needed for defense purposes. Several surgeonfish, such as the brightly colored yellow tang, are boldly colored; others are adorned in more conservative shades of gray, brown, or black. The only endemic surgeonfish—and the most abundant in Hawaiian waters—is the convict tang, a pale white fish with vertical black stripes (like a convict's uniform).

Wrasses are a very diverse family of fish, ranging in length from 2 to 15 inches. Wrasses can change gender from female (when young) to male. Some have brilliant coloration that changes as they age. Several types of wrasse are endemic to Hawaii: Hawaiian cleaner, shortnose, belted, and gray (or old woman).

GAME FISH   Hawaii is known around the globe as *the* place for big-game fish—marlin, swordfish, and tuna—but its waters are also great for catching other offshore fish like mahimahi, rainbow runner, and wahoo; coastal fish like barracuda and scad; bottom fish like snappers, sea bass, and amberjack; and inshore fish like trevally and bonefish.

Six kinds of **billfish** are found in the offshore waters around the islands: Pacific blue marlin, black marlin, sailfish, broadbill swordfish, striped marlin, and shortbill spearfish. Hawaii billfish range in size from the 20-pound shortbill spearfish and striped marlin to the 1,805-pound Pacific blue marlin, the largest marlin ever caught with rod and reel in the world.

Tuna ranges in size from small (a pound or less) mackerel tuna used as bait (Hawaiians call them *oioi*) to 250-pound yellowfin ahi tuna. Other local species of tuna are bigeye, albacore, kawakawa, and skipjack.

Other types of fish, also excellent for eating, include **mahimahi** (also known as dolphin fish or dorado), in the 20- to 70-pound range; **rainbow runner,** from 15 to 30 pounds; and **wahoo** (*ono*), from 15 to 80 pounds. Shoreline fishermen are always on the lookout for **trevally** (the state record for a giant trevally is 191 pounds), **bonefish, ladyfish, threadfin, leatherfish,** and **goatfish.** Bottom fishermen pursue a range of **snapper**—red, pink, gray, and others—as well as **sea bass** (the state record is a whopping 563 pounds) and **amberjack** (which weigh up to 100 pounds).

WHALES   Humpback whales are popular visitors who come to Hawaii to mate and calve every year, beginning in November and staying until spring (Apr or so), when they return to their summer home in Alaska. On every island, you can take winter whale-watching cruises that will let you observe these magnificent leviathans close up. You can also spot their signature spouts from shore as they expel water in the distance. Humpbacks grow to up to 45 feet long, so when one breaches (propels its entire body out of the water) or even waves a fluke, you can see it for miles.

Humpbacks are among the biggest whales found in Hawaiian waters, but other whales—such as pilot, sperm, false killer, melon-headed, pygmy killer, and beaked—can be seen year-round, especially in the calm waters off the Big Island's Kona Coast. These whales usually travel in pods of 20 to 40 animals and are very social, interacting with one another on the surface.

SHARKS   Yes, there *are* sharks in Hawaii, but you more than likely won't see one unless you're specifically looking. About 40 different species of sharks inhabit the waters surrounding Hawaii, ranging from the totally harmless whale shark (at 60 ft., the world's largest fish), which has no teeth and is so docile that it frequently lets divers ride on its back, to the not-so-docile, infamous, and extremely uncommon great white shark. The most common sharks seen in Hawaii are white-tip or gray reef sharks (about 5 ft. long), and black-tip reef sharks (about 6 ft. long).

HAWAII'S ECOSYSTEM PROBLEMS

Officials at Hawaii Volcanoes National Park on the Big Island saw a potential problem a few decades ago with people taking a few rocks home with them as "souvenirs." To prevent this problem from escalating, the park rangers created a legend that the fiery volcano goddess, Pele, did not like people taking anything (rocks, chunks of lava) from her home, and bad luck would befall anyone disobeying her wishes. There used to be a display case in the park's visitor center filled with letters from people who had taken rocks from the volcano, relating stories of all the bad luck that followed. Most of the letters begged Pele's forgiveness and instructed the rangers to please return the rock to the exact location that was its original home.

Unfortunately, Hawaii's other ecosystem problems can't be handled as easily.

MARINE LIFE   Hawaii's beautiful and abundant marine life has attracted so many visitors that they threaten to overwhelm it. A great example of this overenthusiasm is Oahu's beautiful **Hanauma Bay.** Crowds flock to this marine preserve, which features calm, protected swimming and snorkeling areas loaded with tropical reef fish. Its popularity forced government officials to limit admissions and charge an entrance fee. Commercial tour operators have also been restricted in an effort to balance the people-to-fish ratio.

Another marine-life conservation area that suffers from overuse is **Molokini,** a small crater off the coast of Maui. In the 1970s, residents made the area a conservation district in order to protect the unique aquarium-like atmosphere of the waters inside the arms of the crater. Unfortunately, once it was protected, everyone wanted to come here just to see what was worth special protection. Twenty-five years ago, one or two small six-passenger boats made the trip once a day to Molokini; today, it's not uncommon to sight 20 or more boats, each carrying 20 to 49 passengers, moored inside the tiny crater. One tour operator has claimed that, on some days, it's so crowded that you can actually see a slick of suntan oil floating on the surface of the water.

Hawaii's **reefs** have faced increasing impact over the years as well. Runoff of soil and chemicals from construction, agriculture, erosion, and even heavy storms can blanket and choke a reef, which needs sunlight to survive. In addition, the intrusion of foreign elements—caused by such things as breaks in sewage lines—can cause problems; human contact with the reef can also upset the ecosystem. Coral, the basis of the reef system, is very fragile; snorkelers and divers grabbing onto it can break off pieces that took decades to form. Feeding the fish can also upset the balance of the ecosystem (not to mention upsetting the digestive systems of the fish). One glass-bottom boat operator reported that divers fed an eel for years, considering it their "pet" eel. One day, the eel decided that he wanted more than just the food being offered and bit the diver's fingers. In areas where they're fed, the normally shy reef fish become more aggressive, surrounding divers and demanding food.

FLORA   The rain forests are among Hawaii's most fragile environments. Any intrusion—from hikers carrying seeds on their shoes to the rooting of wild boars—can upset the delicate balance of these complete ecosystems. In recent years, development has moved closer and closer to the rain forests. On the Big Island, people have protested the invasion of bulldozers and the drilling of geothermal wells in the Wao Kele O Puna rain forest for years, claiming that the damage done is irreparable.

FAUNA   The biggest impact on the fauna in Hawaii is the decimation of native birds by feral animals, which have destroyed the bird's habitats, and by mongooses that have eaten the birds' eggs and young. Government officials are vigilant about snakes because of the potential damage they can do to the remaining bird life.

Index

See also Accommodations index, below.

ACCOMMODATIONS

Travel Around The World In Style – Without Breaking The Bank – With Frommer's Dollar-a-Day Guides!

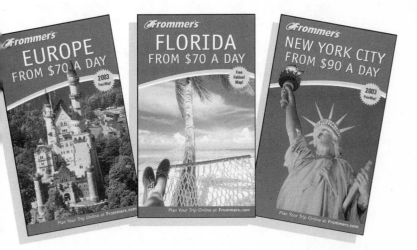

The ultimate guides to comfortable low-cost travel.

FROMMER'S® COMPLETE TRAVEL GUIDES

Alaska
Alaska Cruises & Ports of Call
Amsterdam
Argentina & Chile
Arizona
Atlanta
Australia
Austria
Bahamas
Barcelona, Madrid & Seville
Beijing
Belgium, Holland & Luxembourg
Bermuda
Boston
Brazil
British Columbia & the Canadian Rockies
Brussels & Bruges
Budapest & the Best of Hungary
California
Canada
Cancún, Cozumel & the Yucatán
Cape Cod, Nantucket & Martha's Vineyard
Caribbean
Caribbean Cruises & Ports of Call
Caribbean Ports of Call
Carolinas & Georgia
Chicago
China
Colorado
Costa Rica
Cuba
Denmark
Denver, Boulder & Colorado Springs
England
Europe
European Cruises & Ports of Call

Florida
France
Germany
Great Britain
Greece
Greek Islands
Hawaii
Hong Kong
Honolulu, Waikiki & Oahu
Ireland
Israel
Italy
Jamaica
Japan
Las Vegas
London
Los Angeles
Maryland & Delaware
Maui
Mexico
Montana & Wyoming
Montréal & Québec City
Munich & the Bavarian Alps
Nashville & Memphis
New England
New Mexico
New Orleans
New York City
New Zealand
Northern Italy
Norway
Nova Scotia, New Brunswick & Prince Edward Island
Oregon
Paris
Peru
Philadelphia & the Amish Country
Portugal

Prague & the Best of the Czech Republic
Provence & the Riviera
Puerto Rico
Rome
San Antonio & Austin
San Diego
San Francisco
Santa Fe, Taos & Albuquerque
Scandinavia
Scotland
Seattle & Portland
Shanghai
Sicily
Singapore & Malaysia
South Africa
South America
South Florida
South Pacific
Southeast Asia
Spain
Sweden
Switzerland
Texas
Thailand
Tokyo
Toronto
Tuscany & Umbria
USA
Utah
Vancouver & Victoria
Vermont, New Hampshire & Maine
Vienna & the Danube Valley
Virgin Islands
Virginia
Walt Disney World® & Orlando
Washington, D.C.
Washington State

FROMMER'S® DOLLAR-A-DAY GUIDES

Australia from $50 a Day
California from $70 a Day
England from $75 a Day
Europe from $70 a Day
Florida from $70 a Day
Hawaii from $80 a Day

Ireland from $60 a Day
Italy from $70 a Day
London from $85 a Day
New York from $90 a Day
Paris from $80 a Day

San Francisco from $70 a Day
Washington, D.C. from $80 a Day
Portable London from $85 a Day
Portable New York City from $90 a Day

FROMMER'S® PORTABLE GUIDES

Acapulco, Ixtapa & Zihuatanejo
Amsterdam
Aruba
Australia's Great Barrier Reef
Bahamas
Berlin
Big Island of Hawaii
Boston
California Wine Country
Cancún
Cayman Islands
Charleston
Chicago
Disneyland®
Dublin
Florence

Frankfurt
Hong Kong
Houston
Las Vegas
Las Vegas for Non-Gamblers
London
Los Angeles
Los Cabos & Baja
Maine Coast
Maui
Miami
Nantucket & Martha's Vineyard
New Orleans
New York City
Paris
Phoenix & Scottsdale

Portland
Puerto Rico
Puerto Vallarta, Manzanillo & Guadalajara
Rio de Janeiro
San Diego
San Francisco
Savannah
Seattle
Sydney
Tampa & St. Petersburg
Vancouver
Venice
Virgin Islands
Washington, D.C.

FROMMER'S® NATIONAL PARK GUIDES

Banff & Jasper
Family Vacations in the National Parks

Grand Canyon
National Parks of the American West
Rocky Mountain

Yellowstone & Grand Teton
Yosemite & Sequoia/Kings Canyon
Zion & Bryce Canyon

FROMMER'S® MEMORABLE WALKS

Chicago	New York	San Francisco
London	Paris	

FROMMER'S® WITH KIDS GUIDES

Chicago	Ottawa	Vancouver
Las Vegas	San Francisco	Washington, D.C.
New York City	Toronto	

SUZY GERSHMAN'S BORN TO SHOP GUIDES

Born to Shop: France	Born to Shop: Italy	Born to Shop: New York
Born to Shop: Hong Kong, Shanghai & Beijing	Born to Shop: London	Born to Shop: Paris

FROMMER'S® IRREVERENT GUIDES

Amsterdam	Los Angeles	San Francisco
Boston	Manhattan	Seattle & Portland
Chicago	New Orleans	Vancouver
Las Vegas	Paris	Walt Disney World®
London	Rome	Washington, D.C.

FROMMER'S® BEST-LOVED DRIVING TOURS

Britain	Germany	Northern Italy
California	Ireland	Scotland
Florida	Italy	Spain
France	New England	Tuscany & Umbria

HANGING OUT™ GUIDES

Hanging Out in England	Hanging Out in France	Hanging Out in Italy
Hanging Out in Europe	Hanging Out in Ireland	Hanging Out in Spain

THE UNOFFICIAL GUIDES®

Bed & Breakfasts and Country Inns in:
California
Great Lakes States
Mid-Atlantic
New England
Northwest
Rockies
Southeast
Southwest
Best RV & Tent Campgrounds in:
California & the West
Florida & the Southeast
Great Lakes States
Mid-Atlantic
Northeast
Northwest & Central Plains

Southwest & South Central Plains
U.S.A.
Beyond Disney
Branson, Missouri
California with Kids
Central Italy
Chicago
Cruises
Disneyland®
Florida with Kids
Golf Vacations in the Eastern U.S.
Great Smoky & Blue Ridge Region
Inside Disney
Hawaii
Las Vegas
London
Maui

Mexio's Best Beach Resorts
Mid-Atlantic with Kids
Mini Las Vegas
Mini-Mickey
New England & New York with Kids
New Orleans
New York City
Paris
San Francisco
Skiing & Snowboarding in the Wes
Southeast with Kids
Walt Disney World®
Walt Disney World® for Grown-ups
Walt Disney World® with Kids
Washington, D.C.
World's Best Diving Vacations

SPECIAL-INTEREST TITLES

Frommer's Adventure Guide to Australia & New Zealand
Frommer's Adventure Guide to Central America
Frommer's Adventure Guide to India & Pakistan
Frommer's Adventure Guide to South America
Frommer's Adventure Guide to Southeast Asia
Frommer's Adventure Guide to Southern Africa
Frommer's Britain's Best Bed & Breakfasts and Country Inns
Frommer's Caribbean Hideaways
Frommer's Exploring America by RV
Frommer's Fly Safe, Fly Smart

Frommer's France's Best Bed & Breakfasts and Country Inns
Frommer's Gay & Lesbian Europe
Frommer's Italy's Best Bed & Breakfasts and Country Inns
Frommer's Road Atlas Britain
Frommer's Road Atlas Europe
Frommer's Road Atlas France
The New York Times' Guide to Unforgettable Weekends
Places Rated Almanac
Retirement Places Rated
Rome Past & Present

Booked aisle seat.

Reserved room with a view.

With a queen – no, make that a king-size bed.

Fly.
Sleep.
Save.

Now you can book your flights and
hotels together, so you can get even better deals
than if you booked them separately.

Travelocity
Visit www.travelocity.com
or call 1-888-TRAVELOCITY